Chambers
Scottish
Biographical
Dictionary

Chambers
Scottish
Biographical
Dictionary

Editor

Rosemary Goring

EDINBURGH   NEW YORK

Published 1992 by W & R Chambers limited
43–45 Annandale Street, Edinburgh EH7 4AZ

British Library Cataloguing in Publication Data

A catalogue record for this book is
available from the British Library

ISBN 0-550-16043-4

The publisher acknowledges subsidy from the Scottish Arts
Council towards the publication of this volume.

Editorial Manager: Min Lee

Cover design by John Marshall

Typeset by Cambridge University Press

Printed in England by Clays Ltd, St Ives, plc

Contents

Acknowledgements

For a variety of contributions, advice and help I would like to thank the following: Nigel Billen; George Davidson; Owen Dudley Edwards; Tom Goring; Rear Admiral Edward Gueritz; Alastair Holmes; Alison Horsburgh; Allan Hunter; Professor Roland Ibbett; Archie P Lee; Alison Morrison-Low; Professor Robin Milner; Dr Paul O'Farrell; Dr Lindsay Paterson; Professor Stuart Pawley; Richard Perry; Dr David Rees; Alan Taylor; Sir Henry P Wood, and the Institution of Civil Engineers, London.

Contributors

Academia
Owen Dudley Edwards
Reader
Department of History
Edinburgh University

Aeronatics
Professor John E Allen
Consulting Engineer

Anthropology
Dr Timothy Ingold
Senior Lecturer
Department of Social Anthropology
Manchester University

Dr Jonathan Spencer
Lecturer
Department of Social Anthropology
Edinburgh University

Archaeology
Dr Peter Richards
Reference Editor
Cambridge University Press

Dr Anna Ritchie
Freelance Archaeologist

Architecture
Simon Green
Investigator
Royal Commission on the Ancient and
 Historical Monuments of Scotland

Dr Deborah Mays
Inspector
Historic Scotland

Harriet Richardson
Royal Commission on the Historical
 Monuments of England

Aristocracy
Dr Michael Lynch
Senior Lecturer
Department of Scottish History
Edinburgh University

Gerald Warner
Author, Broadcaster and Journalist

Army, Navy and Airforce
Rear Admiral Edward Gueritz
Defence Consultant and Research Adviser

Trevor Royle
Author and Journalist

Art
Denis Gifford
Writer

Ralph Hughes
Teacher of Art History
Fettes College
Edinburgh

Dr David Mannings
Lecturer
Department of the History of Art
Aberdeen University

Gillian Tait
Conservation Consultant

Astronomy
Dr Mary Brück
Former Senior Lecturer in Astronomy
Edinburgh University

Biology
Professor Ian Millar
Emeritus Professor of Chemistry
Keele University

Margaret Millar
Freelance Writer and Science Contributor

Professor Peter Walker
Honorary Professor
Edinburgh University

Botany
Professor Peter Walker
Honorary Professor
Edinburgh University

Chemistry
Dr Robert Anderson
Director
The British Museum
London

Jean Jones
Freelance Researcher and Editor

Business and Industry
Ian Hinton
Lecturer
Kingston Regional Management Centre
Kingston Polytechnic

Roger Oldcorn
Senior Tutor
Henley – The Management College

Philip Taylor
Research Fellow
Department of Economic History
Glasgow University

Crafts
Thomas Wilson
Managing Director
The Open Eye Gallery
Edinburgh

Crime
Dr J J McManus
Senior Lecturer
Department of Law
Dundee University

Kristina Woolnough
Freelance Journalist and Writer

Dance
Alice Bain
Arts Journalist

Design
Ian Cox
Acting Director
Christie's Decorative Arts Programme
Department of History of Art
Glasgow University

Earth Science
Norman Butcher
Consultant and former Staff Tutor in Earth
    Sciences, The Open University in
    Scotland

Eccentricity
J K Gillon
Town Planner
Edinburgh District Council

Andrew MacFarlane
Planner/Conservator
Edinburgh District Council

Economics
Donald Rutherford
Lecturer
Department of Economics
Edinburgh University

Education
Dr Ethel M Gray
Former Principal, Craigie College of
    Education

Professor H M Knox
Emeritus Professor of Education
Queen's University
Belfast

Professor Stanley Nisbet
Former Professor of Education
Glasgow University

Engineering
Ronald Birse
Historian of Science and Technology

Fashion
Cate Devine
Assistant Editor, *Scottish Field* magazine;
Editor, *Style* magazine

Film
Allan Hunter
Freelance Writer and Broadcaster
    specializing in cinema

Food and Drink
Min Lee
Reference Manager
W & R Chambers

Philip Taylor
Research Fellow
Department of Economic History
Glasgow University

Geography
Michael Wood
Senior Lecturer
Aberdeen University

History
Owen Dudley Edwards
Reader
Department of History
Edinburgh University

Invention
Ronald Birse
Historian of Science and Technology

Journalism
Kenneth Roy
Journalist

Law
Professor David M Walker
Regius Professor Emeritus of Law
Glasgow University

Literature and Poetry
Alan Taylor
Literary Editor, *Scotland on Sunday*

Jeffrey McCarthy
Research Student
Department of English
Edinburgh University

Kenny Mathieson
Freelance Writer

Mathematics
Christopher Shaddock
Senior Lecturer
Department of Mathematics
Edinburgh University

Media
Allan Hunter
Freelance Writer and Broadcaster
    specializing in cinema

Medical Sciences
Dr William F Bynum
Reader in the History of Medicine
University College London

Dr A R Mills
Former Consultant Physician and World
    Health Organization Representative

Miscellaneous
Gillian Ferguson
Poet and Journalist

Kenny Mathieson
Freelance Writer

Music: Classical
Derek Watson
Composer, Writer and Broadcaster

Music: Folk
Alastair Clark
Journalist

Music: Jazz
Anthony Troon
Journalist

Music: Pop/Rock
Trevor Pake
Freelance Journalist and Rock Critic

Natural History and the Environment
James McCarthy
Consultant/Lecturer (Heritage Presentation)

Philosophy
Robert R Calder
Freelance Writer and Editor

Jeremy Mynott
Editorial Director
Cambridge University Press

Photography
Dr Patricia Macdonald
Photographic Artist, Writer and Lecturer

Julie Lawson
Research Assistant
Scottish National Portrait Gallery

Sara Stevenson
Curator of Photography
National Galleries of Scotland

Physics
Professor Ian Millar
Emeritus Professor of Chemistry
Keele University

Margaret Millar
Freelance Writer and Science Contributor

Professor William Cochran
Former Professor of Natural Philosophy
Edinburgh University

Politics and Diplomacy
Dr Denis Derbyshire
Political Communications Consultant

Dr Ian Derbyshire
Specialist in Contemporary History
Cambridge University

Dr Ian Hutchison
Lecturer
Department of History
Stirling University

Psychology
Dr John Beloff
Senior Lecturer
Department of Psychology
Edinburgh University

Professor Robert Grieve
Department of Psychology
Edinburgh University

Professor Ian Hunter
Professor Emeritus of Psychology
Keele University

Religion
Dr James D Douglas
Lecturer
Singapore Bible College

Dr Philip Hillyer
Theological Author and Editor

Rev Lawrence Twaddle
Minister

Royalty and Rulers
Dr Michael Lynch
Senior Lecturer
Department of Scottish History
Edinburgh University

Gerald Warner
Author, Broadcaster and Journalist

Sociology
Dr David McCrone
Reader

Department of Sociology
Edinburgh University

Sport
Stuart Bathgate
Journalist

Bob Crampsey
Writer and Broadcaster

Theatre
Peter Whitebrook
Journalist and Writer

Denis Gifford
Writer

Travel and Exploration
Shane Winser
Information Officer
Royal Geographical Society

Zoology
Professor Peter Walker
Honorary Professor
Edinburgh University

BIOGRAPHIES BY SUBJECT

Academia and Scholarship
Anderson, James (1662–1728)
Anderson, John (1726–96)
Anderson, Robert (1750–1830)
Baikie, William Balfour (1825–64)
Balfour, Robert (c.1550–1625)
Bannatyne, George (1545–1608)
Blackie, John Stuart (1809–95)
Buchanan, George (c.1506–1582)
Burnet, John (1863–1928)
Campbell, Sir James MacNabb
  (1846–1903)
Campbell, John Francis, of Islay (1822–85)
Campbell, Lewis (1830–1908)
Carlyle, Thomas (1795–1881)
Chalmers, George (1742–1825)
Chapman, Robert (1881–1960)
Clerk, Sir John (1676–1755)
Craigie, Sir William Alexander
  (1867–1957)
Craik, George Lillie (1798–1866)
Crawfurd, John (1783–1868)
Crichton, James (1560–c.1585)
Dempster, Thomas (c.1579–1625)
Donaldson, Sir James (1831–1915)
Douglas, Gavin (c.1474–1522)
Dyce, Alexander (1798–1869)
Elliott, Kenneth (1929–)
Erskine, David Stewart (1742–1819)
Findlater, Andrew (1810–85)
Fulton, Robin (1937–)
Gairdner, William Henry Temple
  (1873–1928)
Grant, William (1863–1946)
Grierson, Sir Herbert John Clifford
  (1866–1960)
Halkett, Samuel (1814–71)
Hamilton, Terrick (1781–1876)
Hamilton, Sir William (1730–1803)
Hay, Malcolm Vivian (1881–1962)
Herd, David (1732–1810)
Hunter, Sir William Wilson (1840–1900)
Jamieson, John (1759–1838)
Jebb, Sir Richard Claverhouse (1841–1905)
Johnson, David Charles (1942–)
Johnston, Arthur (1587–1641)
Keith, Arthur Berriedale (1879–1944)

Ker, William Paton (1855–1923)
Laing, David (1793–1878)
Laing, Samuel (1780–1868)
Legge, James (1815–97)
Leyden, John (1775–1811)
Lorimer, William Laughton (1885–1967)
McArthur, Tom (1938–)
MacDonald, Robert David (1929–)
Mackail, John William (1859–1945)
Miln, James (1819–81)
Morgan, Edwin (1920–)
Morrison, Robert (1782–1834)
Muir, John (1810–82)
Muir, Willa (1890–1970)
Muir, Sir William (1819–1905)
Murray, Alexander (1775–1813)
Murray, Sir James Augustus Henry
  (1837–1915)
Napier, Macvey (1776–1847)
Nicolson, Alexander (1827–93)
Phillimore, John Swinnerton (1873–1926)
Picken, Ebenezer (1769–1816)
Pinkerton, John (1758–1826)
Reid, Alastair (1926–)
Rhind, Alexander Henry (1833–63)
Robertson, Joseph (1810–66)
Ross, Ian Anthony (1917–)
Roy, William (1726–90)
Ruddiman, Thomas (1674–1757)
Rutherford, Samuel (c.1600–1661)
Scott, Michael (c.1175–c.1230)
Scott-Moncrieff, Charles Kenneth Michael
  (1889–1930)
Sellar, William Young (1825–90)
Sharpe, Charles Kirkpatrick (1781–1851)
Simpson, William Douglas (1896–1968)
Skene, Sir John (c.1543–1617)
Smellie, William (1740–95)
Smith, Sir George Adam (1856–1942)
Smith, William Robertson (1846–94)
Spalding, John (c.1609–1670)
Tennant, William (1784–1848)
Thompson, Sir D'Arcy Wentworth
  (1860–1948)
Thomson, Thomas (1768–1852)
Veitch, John (1829–94)
Veitch, William (1794–1885)

Watt, Robert (1774–1819)
Wilson, John (Christopher North)
(1785–1854)
Young, Douglas (1913–73)
Young, John (?1750–1820)

Administration
Anderson, John (1882–1958)
Brotherston, Sir John Howie Flint
(1915–85)
Crawfurd, John (1783–1868)
Dalhousie, James Andrew Broun-Ramsay
(1812–60)
Dinwiddie, Robert (1693–1770)
Hetherington, Sir Hector James Wright
(1888–1965)
Macdonald, Malcolm (1901–81)
Paterson, William (1755–1810)
Turner, Sir William (1832–1916)
Walker, Ernie (1928–)

Aeronautics
Brown, Sir Arthur Whitten (1886–1948)
Dowding, Hugh Caswell Tremenheere
(1882–1970)
Fresson, Ernest Edmund (1891–1963)
Hamilton, Douglas (1903–73)
Hamilton, Sir James Arnot (1923–)
Hislop, George Steedman (1914–)
Lickley, Sir Robert Lang (1912–)
Mollison, James Allan (1905–59)
Pilcher, Percy Sinclair (1867–99)
Tedder, Arthur William (1890–1967)
Tytler, James 'Balloon' (1745–1804)
Thompson, Sir Adam (1926–)
Watson-Watt, Sir Robert Alexander
(1892–1973)

Agriculture and Horticulture
Anderson, James (1739–1808)
Fortune, Robert (1813–80)
Matthews, James Robert (1889–1978)
Shirreff, Patrick (1791–1876)
Sinclair, Sir John (1754–1835)
Smith, James (1789–1850)

Anthropology
Fenton, Alexander (1929–)
Frazer, Sir James George (1854–1941)
Keith, Sir Arthur (1866–1955)
Lewis, Ioan Myrddin (1930–)
Little, Kenneth Lindsey (1908–91)
Littlejohn, James (1921–88)
McLennan, John Ferguson (1827–81)
Monboddo, James Burnett (1714–99)
Spence, Lewis Thomas Chalmers
(1874–1955)
Turner, Victor Witter (1920–83)

Archaeology
Anderson, Joseph (1832–1916)
Childe, Vere Gordon (1892–1957)
Curle, Alexander Ormiston (1866–1955)
Graham, Angus (1892–1979)
Henshall, Audrey Shore (1927–)
Macdonald, Sir George (1862–1940)
MacKie, Euan Wallace (1936–)
Munro, Robert (1835–1920)
Piggott, Stuart (1910–)
Ramsay, Sir William Mitchell (1851–1939)
Rhind, Alexander Henry (1833–63)
Robertson, Anne Strachan (1910–)
Stevenson, Robert Barron Kerr (1913–)
Thom, Alexander (1894–1985)
Wilson, Sir Daniel (1816–92)

Architecture
Adam, James (1730–94)
Adam, Robert (1728–92)
Adam, William (1689–1748)
Anderson, Sir Robert Rowand (1834–1921)
Bruce, Sir William (1630–1710)
Bryce, David (1803–76)
Burnet, Sir John James (1857–1938)
Burn, William (1789–1870)
Campbell, Colen (1679–1726)
Campbell, John Archibald (1859–1909)
Chambers, Sir William (1723–96)
Clerk, Sir John (1676–1755)
Coia, Jack Anthony (1898–1981)
Cousin, David (1809–78)
Craig, James (1744–95)
Crichton-Stuart, John Patrick (1847–1900)
Cruft, Catherine Holway (1927–)
Dunbar-Nasmith, James Duncan (1927–)
Ednie, John (1876–1934)
Geddes, Sir Patrick (1854–1932)
Gibbs, James (1682–1754)
Gowans, Sir James (1821–90)
Graham, James Gillespie (1776–1835)
Hamilton, David (1768–1843)
Hamilton, Thomas (1784–1858)
Kininmonth, Sir William (1904–88)
Laird, Michael (1928–)
Lindsay, Ian Gordon (1906–66)
Lorimer, Sir Robert Stodart (1864–1929)
Loudon, John Claudius (1783–1843)
MacGibbon, David (1831–1902)
Mackintosh, Charles Rennie (1868–1928)
MacLaren, James Majoribanks (1853–90)
Macnair, Herbert (1868–1955)
McWilliam, Colin (1928–89)
Matthew, Sir Robert (1906–75)
Merrylees, Andrew (1933–)
Mylne, Robert (1734–1811)
Niven, David Barclay (1864–1942)
Peddie, John Dick (1824–91)

Pilkington, Frederick Thomas (1832–98)
Playfair, William Henry (1790–1857)
Reiach, Alan (1910–)
Rhind, David (1808–83)
Richards, John Deacon (1931–)
Ross, Thomas (1839–1930)
Shaw, Richard Norman (1831–1912)
Smith, James (c.1645–1731)
Spence, Sir Basil Urwin (1907–76)
Stark, William (1770–1813)
Stevenson, John James (1831–1908)
Tait, Thomas Smith (1882–1952)
Walker, David Morrison (1933–)
Wallace, William (d.1631)
Womersely, Peter (1923–)

Aristocracy
Albanie, Count d'
Albany, Duke of
Albany, Alexander, Duke (1454–85)
Albany, John, 2nd Duke (1481–1536)
Argyll
Argyll, Archibald, 1st Duke (d.1705)
Argyll, Archibald, 2nd Earl (d.1513)
Argyll, Archibald, 5th Earl (1530–73)
Argyll, Archibald, 7th Earl (c.1576–1638)
Argyll, Archibald, Marquis and 8th Earl
    (1598–1661)
Argyll, Archibald, 9th Earl (1629–85)
Argyll, John, 2nd Duke (1678–1743)
Argyll, John Douglas Sutherland, 9th Duke
    (1845–1914)
Asquith, Margot (1864–1945)
Atholl, John, 4th Earl of (d.1579)
Bothwell, James Hepburn, 4th Earl of
    (c.1537–1578)
Bruce, Robert (c.1078–1141)
Bruce, Robert (d.1245)
Bruce, Robert de, 5th Lord of Annandale
    (1210–95)
Bruce, Robert de (1253–1304)
Cameron, Archibald (1707–53)
Cameron of Lochiel, Donald (c.1695–1748)
Cameron of Lochiel, Sir Ewen (1629–1719)
Campbell
Carr, Robert, Earl of Somerset
    (c.1590–1645)
Comyn, Cumming, or Cumyn
Crawford and Balcarres, Alexander William
    Crawford Lindsay, 25th/8th Earl of
    (1812–90)
Douglas, Earls of Angus
Douglas, Earls of Douglas
Douglas, Earls of Morton
Drummond, Margaret (c.1472–1502)
Dunbar, Agnes (c.1312–1369)
Elgin, Earls of

Erskine of Cambo, Sir Alexander
    (1663–1727)
Gordon
Gordon, Alexander, 4th Duke of Gordon
    (c.1745–1827)
Gordon, George, 2nd Earl of Huntly
    (d.c.1502)
Gordon, George, 4th Earl of Huntly
    (1514–62)
Gordon, George, 6th Earl, and 1st Marquis
    of Huntly (1562–1636)
Hamilton
Hamilton, Sir James, 1st Lord (d.1479)
Hamilton, James, 2nd Earl of Arran, 3rd
    Baron (?1515–1575)
Hamilton, James, 3rd Earl of Arran, 4th
    Baron (1530–1609)
Hamilton, James, 3rd Marquis and 1st Duke
    of (1606–49)
Hamilton, James Douglas, 4th Duke of
    (1658–1712)
Hamilton, John, 1st Marquis of
    (?1532–1604)
Hope
Hope, Sir Charles, 1st Earl of Hopetoun
    (1681–1742)
Johnstone
Kerr, or Ker
Leslie, Lesly, or Lesley
Lockhart of Carnwath, George (1673–1731)
Lovat, Simon Fraser, Lord (c.1667–1747)
Magnus Erlendsson, (St Magnus) (d.1117)
Oliphant of Gask, Laurence (1691–1767)
Queensberry, Sir John Sholto Douglas, 8th
    Marquis of (1844–1900)
Roehenstart, Count, Charles Edward
    Augustus Maximilian Stuart, Baron
    Korff (c.1784–1854)
Ruthven, John, 3rd Earl of Gowrie
    (c.1578–1600)
Ruthven, William, 1st Earl of Gowrie
    (c.1541–1584)
Scott
Sinclair, or St Clair
Stewart, Alexander, Earl of Buchan
    (c.1343–c.1405)
Stewart, Frances Teresa, Duchess of
    Richmond and Lennox
    (1647–1702)
Stewart, Walter (d.1177)
Stuart, House of
Stuart, Arabella (1575–1615)

Army, Navy and Airforce
Abercromby, Sir Ralph (1734–1801)
Argyll, John (1678–1743)
Armstrong, William (16th century)
Baird, Sir David (1757–1829)

Ballantrae, Bernard Edward Fergusson
(1911–80)
Barton, Andrew (d.1511)
Braddock, Edward (1695–1755)
Brisbane, Sir Thomas Makdougall
(1773–1860)
Bryson, Admiral Sir Lindsay Sutherland
(1925–)
Cameron, Sir Alan (1750–1828)
Cameron, Neil (1920–85) Campbell, Sir
Colin (1792–1863)
Campbell, Sir Colin (1792–1863)
Cathcart, Charles Murray (1783–1859)
Cathcart, Sir George (1794–1854)
Cathcart, Sir William Schaw (1755–1843)
Christison, Sir Alexander Francis Philip
(1893–)
Cleland, William (c.1661–1689)
Cochrane, Sir Ralph Alexander
(1895–1977)
Cochrane, Thomas (1775–1860)
Colomb, Philip Howard (1831–99)
Cunningham, Sir Alan Gordon (1887–1983)
Cunningham, Andrew Brown (1883–1963)
Dalrymple-Hamilton, Sir Frederick Hew
George (1890–1974)
Dowding, Hugh Caswell Tremenheere
(1882–1970)
Dalyell, Thomas (c.1615–1685)
Duncan, Adam (1731–1804)
Dundas, Sir David (1735–1820)
Dundee, John Graham of Claverhouse
(c.1649–1689)
Elphinstone, George Keith (1746–1823)
Falconer, William (1732–69)
Ferguson, Patrick (1744–80)
Fergusson, Sir Bernard Edward (1911–80)
Fresson, Ernest Edmund (1891–1963)
Gleig, George Robert (1796–1888)
Gordon, James Alexander (1782–1869)
Gordon, Patrick (1635–99)
Gordon of Auchintoul, Alexander
(1669–1751)
Grant, James Augustus (1827–92)
Grant, Sir James Hope (1808–75)
Greig, Sir Samuel (1735–88)
Haig, Douglas (1861–1928)
Haldane, Richard Burdon (1856–1928)
Halkett, Hugh (1783–1863)
Hamilton, Sir Ian Standish Monteith
(1853–1947)
Hamilton, Sir James Arnot (1923–)
Hayes, Sir John Osler Chattock (1913–)
Heathfield, George Augustus Eliott
(1717–90)
Hepburn, Sir John (?1598–1636)
Hope, Sir John (1765–1823)
Hunter, John (1737–1821)

Ironside, William Edmund (1880–1959)
Johnstone, James, 'Chevalier de'
(1719–c.1800)
Jones, John Paul (1747–92)
Keith, James (1696–1758)
Leslie, Alexander (c.1580–1661)
Leslie, David (1601–82)
Lockhart, James (1727–90)
Lockhart, Philip (?1690–1715)
Lovat, Simon Christopher Joseph Fraser
(1911–)
Lynedoch, Thomas Graham (1748–1843)
MacCartney, Sir Samuel Halliday
(1833–1906)
Macdonald, Sir Hector (1857–1903)
MacDonell, Ranald (d.1847)
McGeoch, Sir Ian Lauchlan Mackay
(1914–)
Macgregor, Sir Charles (1840–87)
Mackenzie, Sir Hugh Stirling (1913–)
Mackintosh, William (1662–1743)
Maclean, Sir Fitzroy Hew (1911–)
Macmillan, Sir Gordon (1897–1986)
Macquarie, Lachlan (1761–1824)
Mar, John Erskine (1675–1732)
Melville, Robert (1723–1809)
Menteith, Sir John de (13th–14th century)
Mollison, James Allan (1905–59)
Montrose, James Graham (1612–50)
Moore, Sir John (1761–1809)
Murray, Lord George (c.1700–1760)
Murray, Sir John (1715–77)
Napier, Sir Charles (1786–1860)
Napier, Sir Charles James (1782–1853)
Nares, Sir George Strong (1831–1915)
Pasley, Sir Charles William (1780–1861)
Porteous, John (?1690–1736)
Ramsay, Sir Alexander (d.1342)
Randolph, Sir Thomas (d.1332)
Reid, John (1721–1807)
Reid, Sir William (1791–1858)
Rennie, Sir John (1794–1874)
Rennie, Thomas Gordon (1900–45)
Ritchie, Sir Neil Methuen (1897–1983)
Rob Roy (1671–1734)
Ross, Sir James Clark (1800–62)
Ross, Sir John (1777–1856)
Roy, William (1726–90)
Ruthven, Patrick (c.1573–1651)
Scott, Walter of Satchells (c.1614–c.1694)
Selkirk, Alexander (1676–1721)
Snell, John (1629–79)
Stair, John Dalrymple (1673–1747)
Stewart, Sir David (1772–1829)
Stewart, John (c.1381–1424)
Stewart, Walter (1293–1326)
Stirling, Sir Archibald David (1915–90)
Tedder, Arthur William (1890–1967)

Thompson, Sir Adam (1926–)
Wallace, Sir William (c.1274–1305)
Wauchope, Sir Arthur Grenfell
    (1874–1947)
Wood, Sir Andrew (c.1455–1539)

Art
Aikman, William (1682–1731)
Allan, David (1744–96)
Allan, Sir William (1782–1850)
Amour, Elizabeth Isabel (1885–1945)
Ballantine, James (1808–77)
Beaty, Stuart (1921–)
Bell, John Zephaniah (1794–1883)
Bellany, John (1942–)
Blackadder, Elizabeth (1931–)
Blair, Catherine (1872–1946)
Bone, Sir Muirhead (1876–1953)
Bone, Phyllis Mary (1896–1972)
Bough, Sam (1822–78)
Boyle, Mark (1934–)
Cadell, Francis Campbell Boileau
    (1883–1937)
Cameron, Sir David Young (1865–1945)
Campbell, Steven (1953–)
Chalmers, George Paul (1833–78)
Colquhoun, Robert (1914–62)
Conroy, Stephen (1964–)
Cowie, James (1886–1956)
Currie, Ken (1960–)
Davie, Alan (1920–)
Demarco, Richard (1930–)
Donaldson, David (1916–)
Douglas, Sir William Fettes (1822–91)
Duncan, Thomas (1807–45)
Dunnett, Dorothy (1923–)
Dyce, William (1806–64)
Eardley, Joan (1921–63)
Faed, John (1819–1902)
Faed, Thomas (1826–1900)
Fairweather, Ian (1891–1974)
Fergusson, John Duncan (1874–1961)
Finlay, Ian Hamilton (1925–)
Fleming, Ian (1906–)
Flint, Sir William Russell (1880–1969)
Gear, William (1915–)
Geddes, Andrew (1783–1844)
Geikie, Walter (1795–1837)
Gillies, Sir William George (1898–1973)
Gordon, Sir John Watson (1788–1864)
Graham, Alex (1915–)
Grant, Duncan James Corrowr (1885–1978)
Grant, Sir Francis (1803–78)
Gray, Alasdair James (1934–)
Guthrie, Sir James (1859–1930)
Hamilton, Gavin (1723–98)
Hardie, Gwen (1962–)
Harvey, Sir George (1806–76)

Henry, George (1858–1943)
Hornel, Edward Atkinson (1864–1933)
Houston, John (1930–)
Howson, Peter (1958–)
Hunter, Leslie (1877–1931)
Hutchison, Sir William Oliphant
    (1889–1970)
Jamesone, George (c.1588–1644)
Johnstone, William (1897–1981)
Kay, John (1742–1826)
King, Jessie Marion (1875–1949)
Knox, John (1778–1845)
Lauder, Robert Scott (1803–69)
Lorimer, John Henry (1856–1936)
Lumsden, Ernest Stephen (1883–1948)
McBey, James (1883–1959)
MacBryde, Robert (1913–66)
McCance, William (1894–1970)
MacColl, Dugald Sutherland (1859–1948)
McCulloch, Horatio (1805–67)
MacDonald, Frances (1873–1921)
MacDonald, Margaret (1865–1933)
MacGillivray, James Pittendrigh
    (1856–1938)
MacGregor, William York (1855–1923)
Mach, David (1956–)
Mackintosh, Charles Rennie (1868–1928)
McLaren, Norman (1914–87)
McLean, Bruce (1944–)
Macpherson, Robert (d.1872)
McTaggart, William (1835–1910)
McTaggart, Sir William (1903–81)
Marshall, William Calder (1813–94)
Maxwell, John (1905–62)
Melville, Arthur (1858–1904)
Moffat, Alexander (1943–)
More, Jacob (1740–93)
Morrocco, Alberto (1917–)
Nasmyth, Alexander (1758–1840)
Nasmyth, Patrick (1787–1831)
Newbery, Frances Henry (1853–1946)
Nicol, Erskine (1825–1904)
Orchardson, Sir William Quiller
    (1832–1910)
Paolozzi, Eduardo Luigi (1924–)
Paton, Sir Joseph Noel (1821–1901)
Patrick, James McIntosh (1907–)
Peploe, Samuel John (1871–1935)
Pettie, John (1839–93)
Philipson, Sir Robin (1916–)
Phillip, John (1817–67)
Raeburn, Sir Henry (1756–1823)
Ramsay, Allan (1713–84)
Redpath, Anne (1895–1965)
Roberts, David (1796–1864)
Royds, Mabel Alington (1874–1941)
Runciman, Alexander (1736–85)
Schotz, Benno (1891–1986)

Scott, David (1806–49)
Scott, William (1913–89)
Scott, William Bell (1811–90)
Scougall, David (fl.1654–77)
Smith, Ian McKenzie (1935–)
Smith, James Moyr (1839–1912)
Steell, Sir John (1804–91)
Stirling-Maxwell, Sir William (1818–78)
Strachan, Douglas (1875–1950)
Strang, William (1859–1921)
Thomson, John (1778–1840)
Thorburn, Archibald (1860–1935)
Turnbull, William (1922–)
Walker, Dame Ethel (1861–1951)
Walton, Edward Arthur (1860–1922)
Watkins, Dudley Dexter (1907–69)
Wilkie, Sir David (1785–1841)
Wilson, Scottie (1888–1972)
Wilson, William (1905–72)
Wiszniewski, Adrian (1958–)
Wylie, George (1921–)

Astronomy

Blair, Robert (1748–1828)
Brisbane, Sir Thomas Makdougall
    (1773–1860)
Brück, Hermann Alexander (1905–)
Copeland, Ralph (1837–1905)
Crawford, James Ludovic Lindsay
    (1847–1913)
Dick, Thomas (1774–1857)
Ferguson, James (1710–76)
Fleming, Williamina Paton (1857–1911)
Forbes, George (1849–1936)
Gill, David (1843–1914)
Grant, Robert (1814–92)
Gregory, James (1638–75)
Henderson, Thomas (1798–1844)
Jackson, John (1887–1958)
Lamont, Johann von (1805–79)
Longair, Malcolm Sim (1941–)
Macpherson, Hector Copland (1888–1956)
Matthew, Norman Graham (1908–82)
Nasmyth, James (1808–90)
Nichol, John Pringle (1804–59)
Roy, Archie (1924–)
Sadler, Flora Munro (1912–)
Scott, Michael (c.1175–c.1230)
Short, James (1710–68)
Smyth, Charles Piazzi (1819–1900)
Stewart, Balfour (1828–87)
Thom, Alexander (1894–1985)
Wilson, Alexander (1714–86)

Biology

Boyd Orr, John (1880–1971)
Gregory, William (1805–58)
Mitchison, John Murdoch (1922–)

Russell, Edward Stuart (1887–1954)
Subak-Sharpe, John Herbert (1924–)
Thomson, Sir Charles Wyville (1830–82)
Yonge, Sir Maurice (1899–1986)

Botany

Alston, Charles (1685–1760)
Balfour, Sir Andrew (1630–94)
Brown, Robert (1773–1858)
Dick, Robert (1811–66)
Don, David (1800–41)
Douglas, David (1798–1834)
Falconer, Hugh (1808–65)
Fletcher, Harold Roy (1907–78)
Forrest, George (1873–1972)
Fortune, Robert (1813–80)
Gardner, George (1812–49)
Geddes, Sir Patrick (1854–1932)
Grant, James Augustus (1827–92)
Hope, Sir John (1725–86)
Hutchison, Isobel Wylie (1889–1982)
Kirk, Sir John (1832–1932)
Loudon, John Claudius (1783–1843)
Matthews, James Robert (1889–1978)
Morison, Robert (1620–83)
Oudney, Walter (1790–1824)
Paterson, William (1755–1810)
Rutherford, Daniel (1749–1819)
Sibbald, Sir Robert (1641–1722)
Smith, Sir William Wright (1875–1956)
Taylor, Sir George (1904–)

Broadcasting

Barnett, Lady Isobel (1918–80)
Baxter, Stanley (1926–)
Boyle, Andrew (1919–)
Burnet, Sir Alastair (1928–)
Corbett, Ronnie (1930–)
Crampsey, Bob (1930–)
Cruickshank, Andrew John Maxton
    (1907–88)
Elrick, George (1910–)
Fleming, Tom (1927–)
Forman, Sir Denis (1917–)
Fulton, Rikki (1924–)
Garden, Neville (1936–)
Garscadden, Kathleen (1897–1991)
Gray, Muriel (1959–)
Hood, Stuart (1915–)
Isaacs, Jeremy Israel (1932–)
Kennedy, Ludovic Henry Coverley (1919–)
Lindsay, Maurice (1918–)
Macdonald, Gus (1940–)
MacDonald, Margo (1944–)
Macgregor, Jimmie (1932–)
McGregor, Oliver Ross (1921–)
Mackay, Fulton (1922–87)
McKellar, Kenneth (1927–)

McLaren, Bill (1923–)
McPherson, Archie (1935–)
Magnusson, Magnus (1929–)
Naughtie, James (1952–)
Purser, John (1942–)
Reith, John Charles Walsham (1889–1971)
Robertson, Fyfe (1902–87)
Somerville, Mary (1897–1963)
Stewart, Andrew (1907–)
Watt, Jim (1948–)
Weir, Tom (1914–)

Chemistry
Anderson, Thomas (1819–74)
Arnott, Struther (1934–)
Auerbach, Charlotte (1899–)
Beevers, Arnold (1908–)
Beilby, Sir George Thomas (1850–1924)
Bell, Ronald Percy (1907–)
Black, Joseph (1728–99)
Brown, Alexander Crum (1838–1922)
Burnett, George (1921–80)
Cottrell, Tom Leadbetter (1923–73)
Couper, Archibald Scott (1831–92)
Cullen, William (1710–90)
Cullen, William (1867–1948)
Dewar, Sir James (1842–1923)
Dobbie, Sir James Johnston (1852–1924)
Dunitz, Jack David (1923–)
Fleck, Sir Alexander (1889–1968)
Graham, Thomas (1805–69)
Gregory, William (1805–58)
Hirst, Sir Edward Langley (1898–1975)
Hope, Thomas Charles (1766–1844)
Irvine, Sir James Colquhoun (1877–1952)
Keir, James (1735–1820)
Kemball, Charles (1923–)
Kendall, James Pickering (1889–1979)
Knox, John Henderson (1927–)
Lapworth, Arthur (1872–1941)
Macintosh, Charles (1766–1843)
Melvill, Thomas (1726–53)
Ottaway, John Michael (1939–86)
Pauson, Peter Ludwig (1925–)
Playfair, Lyon (1819–98)
Purdie, Thomas (1843–1916)
Ramsay, Sir William (1852–1916)
Read, John (1884–1963)
Robertson, John Monteath (1909–89)
Robertson, Sir Robert (1869–1949)
Roebuck, John (1718–94)
Spence, Peter (1806–83)
Stevens, Thomas (1900–)
Tennant, Charles (1768–1838)
Thomson, Thomas (1773–1852)
Todd, Alexander Robertus (1907–)
Ure, Andrew (1778–1857)
Walker, Sir James (1863–1935)

Young, James (1811–83)

Colonial Service
Dinwiddie, Robert (1693–1770)
Elgin, James Bruce (1811–63)
Elphinstone, Mountstuart (1779–1859)
Fergusson, Sir James (1832–1907)
Hope, John Adrian Louis (1860–1908)
Hope, Victor Alexander John (1887–1952)
Hunter, John (1737–1821)
Macquarie, Lachlan (1761–1824)
Muir, Sir William (1819–1905)
Paterson, William (1755–1810)
Reid, Sir William (1791–1858)
Selkirk, Thomas Douglas (1771–1820)
Waverley, John Anderson (1882–1958)

Comedy and Humour
Anthony, Jack (1900–62)
Asquith, Margot (1864–1945)
Aytoun, William Edmonstoune (1818–65)
Baxter, Stanley (1926–)
Beattie, Johnny (1926–)
Brown, Janet (1924–)
Carr, Walter (1925–)
Coltrane, Robbie (1950–)
Connolly, Billy (1942–)
Corbett, Ronnie (1930–)
Fulton, Rikki (1924–)
Fyffe, Will (1885–1947)
Gordon, Harry (1893–1957)
Houston, Renée (1902–80)
Lauder, Sir Harry (1870–1950)
Logan, Jimmy (1928–)
McLean, Lex (c.1907–1975)
Milroy, Jack (1920–)
Munro, Alex (1911–86)
Murray, Chic (1919–85)
Naughton, Charles (1887–1976)
Sim, Alastair (1900–76)
Stewart, Andy (1933–)
Tate, Harry (1872–1940)
Willis, Dave (1894–1973)
Wilson, Robert (1909–)

Business and Industry
Abbott, Jack Sutherland (1900–79)
Allan, Sir Hugh (1810–82)
Auldjo, John (1710–86)
Baird, James (1802–76)
Barr Smith, Robert (1824–1915)
Baxter, Sir David (1793–1872)
Beardmore, William (jnr) (1856–1936)
Bell, Sir Thomas (1865–1952)
Broadwood, John (1732–1812)
Buchanan, James (1849–1935)
Buick, David Dunbar (1854–1929)
Burns, Sir George (1795–1890)

Burrell, Sir William (1861–1958)
Campbell, Sir Malcolm Brown
(1848–1935)
Carnegie, Andrew (1835–1918)
Coats, Sir Peter (1808–90)
Colquhoun, Patrick (1745–1820)
Colville, David (1813–98)
Connell, Charles (1822–84)
Cox, James (1809–85)
Cranston, Kate (1850–1934)
Dale, David (1739–1806)
Denny, Sir Maurice Edward (1886–1955)
Dewar, John Alexander (1856–1929)
Dick, James (1743–1828)
Dunlop, John Boyd (1840–1921)
Elder, Sir Thomas (1818–97)
Ewing, Sir Archibald Orr (1819–93)
Fettes, Sir William (1750–1836)
Fraser, Sir Hugh (1931–87)
Fraser, Hugh (1903–66)
Fresson, Ernest Edmund (1891–1963)
Gillespie, James (1726–97)
Grant, William (1839–1923)
Howden, James (1832–1913)
Keiller, John Mitchell (1851–99)
Kidd, William (c.1645–1701)
Laird, Macgregor (1808–61)
Lipton, Sir Thomas Johnstone (1850–1931)
Lithgow, Sir James (1883–1952)
McAlpine, Sir Robert (1847–1934)
MacBrayne, David (1818–1907)
McCance, Sir Andrew (1889–1983)
McColl, Robert Smyth (1876–1959)
McEwan, William (1827–1913)
McGowan, Lord Henry Duncan
(1874–1961)
McGregor, Ian Kinloch (1912–)
Mackie, Sir Peter Jeffrey (1855–1924)
MacTaggart, Sir John (1867–1956)
Mavor, Henry (1858–1915)
Menzies, John Ross (1852–1935)
Merry, James (1805–77)
Morton, Thomas (1781–1832)
Murray, David Edward (1951–)
Murray, Thomas Blackwood (1871–1929)
Mushet, David (1772–1847)
Pollock, Sir John Donald (1868–1962)
Pringle, Derek Hair (1926–)
Pringle, Robert William (1920–)
Reid, Robert Paul (1934–)
Rennie, George (1791–1866)
Smith, George (1792–1871)
Stephen, Sir Alexander Murray
(1892–1974)
Teacher, William (1811–76)
Tennant, Charles (1768–1838)
Tennent, Hugh (1863–90)
Thin, James (1823–1915)

Thomson, Sir William Johnston
(1881–1949)
Walker, Sir Alexander (1869–1950)
Watson, George (1654–1723)
Weir, William Douglas (1877–1959)
Wolfson, Sir Isaac (1897–1991)
Yarrow, Alfred Fernandez (1842–1932)
Yule, Sir David (1858–1928)

Crafts
Amour, Elizabeth Isabel (1885–1945)
Auchterlonie, Willie (1872–1963)
Ballantyne, James (1772–1833)
Chepman, Walter (c.1473–c.1538)
Davidson, Peter Wylie (1870–1963)
Fleming, Ian (1906–)
Forsyth, Gordon Mitchell (1879–1953)
Foulis, Robert (1707–76)
Gardner, Peter (1836–1902)
Ged, William (1690–1749)
Geikie, Walter (1795–1837)
Hardie, Matthew (1755–1826)
Heriot, George (1563–1624)
Kinnaird, Alison (1949–)
Lumsden, Ernest Stephen (1883–1948)
Macbeth, Ann (1875–1948)
Nekola, Karel (1857–1915)
Newbery, Jessie (1864–1948)
Paterson, Robert (1715–1801)
Phyfe, Duncan (1768–1854)
Royds, Mabel Alington (1874–1941)
Smellie, William (1740–95)
Stead, Tim (1952–)
Stirling, William Alexander (c.1567–1640)
Strange, Sir Robert (1721–92)
Tassie, James (1735–99)
Taylor, Ernest Archibald (1874–1951)
Traquair, Phoebe Anna (1852–1936)
Wilson, Alexander (1714–86)
Wilson, William (1905–72)
Wyse, Henry Taylor (1870–1951)

Crime
Armstrong, Johnnie (d.c.1530)
Boyle, Jimmy (1944–)
Brady, Ian (1938–)
Brodie, William (Deacon Brodie)
(1741–88)
Burke, William (1792–1829)
Burnett, Henry (1942–63)
Ellis, Walter Scott (c.1932–)
Ferguson, Robert (c.1637–1714)
Haggart, David (1801–21)
Kello, John (d.1570)
Kidd, William (c.1645–1701)
Lauder, William (c.1680–1771)
Laurie, John Watson (c.1864–1930)
McLachlan, Jess (1834–?1899)

Maitland, William (c.1528–1573)
Manuel, Peter (1931–58)
Meehan, Patrick Connolly (1927–)
Nelson, James Robert (1945–)
Nilsen, Dennis (1945–)
Porteous, John (?1690–1736)
Pritchard, Edward (1825–65)
Ramenski, Johnny (c.1905–1972)
Rob Roy (1671–1734)
Ruthven, William (c.1541–1584)
Sellar, Patrick (1780–1851)
Slater, Oscar (1873–1948)
Smith, Madeleine Hamilton (1835–1928)
Stuart, Arabella (1575–1615)
Winters, Larry (1943–77)

Dance
Clark, Michael (1962–)
Darrell, Peter (1929–87)
Kemp, Lindsay (1939–)
MacDonald, Elaine (1943–)
Macmillan, Sir Kenneth (1929–)
Morris, Margaret (1891–1980)

Design
Adam, Stephen (1848–1910)
Beaty, Stuart (1921–)
Brown, William Kellock (1856–1934)
Cottier, Daniel (1838–91)
Davidson, Peter Wylie (1870–1963)
Dresser, Christopher (1834–1904)
Ednie, John (1876–1934)
Forsyth, Gordon Mitchell (1879–1953)
King, Jessie Marion (1875–1949)
Kinnaird, Alison (1949–)
Logan, George (1866–1939)
Loudon, John Claudius (1783–1843)
Mackintosh, Charles Rennie (1868–1928)
Macnair, Herbert (1868–1955)
Morris, Talwin (1865–1911)
Pryde, James Ferrier (1866–1941)
Smith, James Moyr (1839–1912)
Talbert, Bruce James (1838–81)
Taylor, Ernest Archibald (1874–1951)
Walton, George (1867–1933)
Wilson, Scottie (1888–1972)

Drama
Archer, William (1856–1924)
Baillie, Joanna (1762–1851)
Boyd, Edward (1916–89)
Bridie, James (1888–1951)
Bryden, Bill (1942–)
Byrne, John (1940–)
Campbell, Donald (1940–)
Conn, Stewart (1936–)
Corrie, Joe (1894–1968)

Cruickshank, Andrew John Maxton (1907–88)
Heggie, Iain (1953–)
Home, John (1722–1808)
Kelman, James (1946–)
Kesson, Jessie (1915–)
Lochhead, Liz (1947–)
MacDonald, Robert David (1929–)
MacDonald, Sharman (1951–)
MacDonald, Stephen (1935–)
McGrath, John Peter (1935–)
McGrath, Tom (1940–)
Mackintosh, Elizabeth (1896–1952)
McLellan, Robert (1907–85)
MacMillan, Hector (1929–)
McMillan, Roddy (1923–79)
Purser, John (1942–)
Stewart, Ena Lamont (1912–)
Taylor, C P (1929–81)

Earth Sciences
Bailey, Sir Edward Battersby (1881–1965)
Bowie, Stanley Hay Umphray (1917–)
Broom, Robert (1866–1951)
Buchan, Alexander (1829–1907)
Cadell, Henry Moubray (1860–1934)
Clough, Charles Thomas (1852–1916)
Cullen, William (1867–1948)
Dick, Robert (1811–66)
Forbes, James David (1809–68)
Geikie, Sir Archibald (1835–1924)
Geikie, James (1839–1915)
Glennie, Kenneth William (1926–)
Hall, Sir James (1761–1832)
Harker, Alfred (1859–1939)
Heddle, Matthew Forster (1828–97)
Horne, John (1848–1928)
Horner, Leonard (1785–1864)
Hutton, James (1726–97)
Jameson, Robert (1774–1854)
Kennedy, William Quarrier (1903–79)
Kidston, Robert (1852–1924)
Lapworth, Charles (1842–1920)
Lyell, Sir Charles (1797–1875)
McCance, Sir Andrew (1889–1983)
MacCulloch, John (1773–1835)
MacGregor, Murray (1884–1966)
MacLaren, Charles (1782–1866)
Maclure, William (1763–1840)
Mellanby, Kenneth (1908–)
Miller, Hugh (1802–56)
Murchison, Sir Roderick Impey (1792–1871)
Mykura, Walter (1926–88)
Necker, Louis Albert (1786–1861)
Nicol, James (1810–79)
Nicol, William (1768–1851)
Peach, Benjamin Neeve (1842–1926)

Phemister, James (1893–1986)
Playfair, John (1748–1819)
Reid, Sir William (1791–1858)
Thomson, Sir Charles Wyville (1830–82)
Traquair, Ramsey Heatley (1840–1912)
Watson, Janet Vida (1923–85)
Wood, Stanley Purdie (1939–)

Eccentricity
Barry, James (1795–1865)
Cameron, Alan Barnard (1927–91)
Duff, 'Bailie' Jamie (d.1788)
Graham, James (1745–94)
Gunn, Willie (c.1755–c.1825)
Hamilton, Douglas Alexander (1767–1852)
Monboddo, James Burnett (1714–99)
Petrie, Alexander Wylie (1853–1937)
Stout, George Frederick (1860–1944)
Williamson, Peter (1730–99)

Economics
Alexander, Sir Kenneth John Wilson
  (1922–)
Cairncross, Sir Alexander Kirkland
  (1911–)
Cunningham, William (1849–1919)
Giffen, Sir Robert (1837–1910)
Gray, Sir Alexander (1882–1968)
Hodgson, William Ballantyne (1815–80)
Horner, Francis (1778–1817)
Hunter, Laurence Colvin (1934–)
McCrone, Robert Gavin Louden (1933–)
McCulloch, John Ramsay (1789–1864)
Maitland, James (1759–1839)
Nicholson, Joseph Shield (1850–1927)
Peacock, Sir Alan Turner (1922–)
Rae, John (1786–1873)
Ramsay, Sir George (1800–71)
Smith, Adam (1723–90)
Steuart, Sir James (1712–80)
Wilson, James (1805–60)
Young, John (1811–78)
Youngson, Alexander John (1918–)

Education
Adam, Alexander (1741–1809)
Adams, Sir John (1857–1934)
Alexander, Sir Kenneth John Wilson
  (1922–)
Almond, Hely Hutchinson (1832–1903)
Bell, Alexander Melville (1819–1905)
Boyd, William (1874–1962)
Braidwood, Thomas (1715–1806)
Brunton, John Stirling (1903–77)
Burnet, John (1863–1928)
Craik, Sir Henry (1846–1927)
Dalgarno, George (c.1626–1687)
Dickson, Alec (1914–)

Donaldson, Sir James (1831–1915)
Erskine, Mary (1629–1707)
Gordon, Robert (1580–1661)
Grant, Sir Alexander (1826–84)
Hetherington, Sir Hector James Wright
  (1888–1965)
Hodgson, William Ballantyne (1815–80)
Jardine, George (1742–1827)
Laurie, Simon Somerville (1829–1909)
Lindsay, Alexander Dunlop (1879–1952)
McAllister, Anne Hunter (1892–1983)
McClelland, William (1889–1968)
McMillan, Margaret (1860–1931)
McPherson, Andrew Francis (1942–)
Melville, Andrew (1545–c.1622)
Neill, Alexander Sutherland (1883–1973)
Nisbet, John Donald (1922–)
Robertson, Sir James Jackson (1893–1970)
Rusk, Robert Robertson (1879–1972)
Somerville, Mary (1897–1963)
Spens, Sir William (1882–1962)
Stephenson, Elsie (1916–67)
Stow, David (1793–1864)
Thomson, Sir Godfrey Hilton (1881–1955)
Wood, Sir Henry Peart (1908–)
Young, Sir Peter (1544–1628)

Engineering
Arrol, Sir William (1839–1913)
Atwell, Sir John William (1911–)
Baird, Hugh (1770–1827)
Baird, John Logie (1888–1946)
Bald, Robert (1776–1861)
Balfour, George (1872–1941)
Barr, Archibald (1855–1931)
Beare, Sir Thomas Hudson (1859–1940)
Bell, Henry (1767–1830)
Beveridge, Gordon Smith Grieve (1933–)
Bremner, James (1784–1856)
Brown, Sir Samuel (1776–1852)
Brunlees, Sir James (1816–92)
Brunton, Richard Henry (1841–1901)
Bryson, Admiral Sir Lindsay Sutherland
  (1925–)
Clerk, Sir Dugald (1854–1932)
Deas, James (1827–99)
Drummond, Dugald (1840–1912)
Drummond, Thomas (1797–1840)
Eckford, Harry (1775–1832)
Elder, John (1824–69)
Elphinstone, Sir Keith (1864–1944)
Ewing, Sir Alfred (1855–1935)
Fairbairn, Sir William (1789–1874)
Fleming, Sir Sandford (1827–1915)
Fulton, Angus Anderson (1900–83)
Geddes, William George Nicholson
  (1913–)
Gibb, Sir Alexander (1872–1958)

Grainger, Thomas (1794–1852)
Howden, James (1832–1913)
Inglis, Sir Robert John Mathison
  (1881–1962)
Jardine, James (1776–1858)
Kirk, Alexander Carnegie (1830–92)
Kirkaldy, David (1820–97)
McAdam, John Loudon (1756–1836)
McCallum, Sir Donald Murdo (1922–)
MacColl, Sir Edward (1882–1951)
McDonald, Sir Duncan (1921–)
MacDonald, Sir Murdoch (1866–1957)
MacFarlane, Alistair George James
  (1931–)
McNaught, William (1813–81)
Mavor, Henry (1858–1915)
Miller, Sir Donald John (1927–)
Mitchell, Joseph (1803–83)
Moncrieff, Colonel Sir Alexander
  (1829–1906)
Montrose, James Graham (1878–1954)
Muirhead, Alexander (1848–1920)
Murdock, William (1754–1839)
Napier, Robert (1791–1876)
Nasmyth, James (1808–90)
Neilson, James Beaumont (1792–1865)
Newall, Robert Stirling (1812–89)
Newbigging, Thomas (1833–1914)
Pasley, Sir Charles William (1780–1861)
Peebles, David Bruce (1826–99)
Rankine, William John Macquorn
  (1820–72)
Reid, Sir Robert Gillespie (1842–1908)
Rennie, George (1791–1866)
Rennie, John (1761–1821)
Rennie, Sir John (1794–1874)
Robertson, Henry (1816–88)
Roy, William (1726–90)
Russell, John Scott (1808–82)
Salter, Stephen Hugh (1938–)
Sinclair, George (c.1625–1696)
Smith, Charles Stuart (1936–91)
Stevenson, Robert (1772–1850)
Stewart, Allan Duncan (1831–94)
Stirling, Patrick (1820–95)
Stirling, Robert (1790–1878)
Swinburne, Sir James (1858–1958)
Swinton, Alan Archibald Campbell
  (1863–1930)
Symington, William (1763–1831)
Telford, Thomas (1757–1834)
Thom, Alexander (1894–1985)
Thom, Robert (1774–1847)
Thomson, James (1822–92)
Thomson, Robert William (1822–73)
Thomson, Sir William Johnston
  (1881–1949)
Wallace, Sir William (1881–1963)

Watt, James (1736–1819)
Weir, Robert Hendry (1912–)
Weir, William Douglas (1877–1959)
Wilson, Robert (1803–82)

Fashion
Blair, Alistair (1957–)
Clyne, Chris (1954–)
Davies, Betty (1935–)
Donaldson, Marion (1944–)
Freeman, Carol Wight (1953–)
Gibb, Bill (1943–88)
Hogg, Pam (1958–)
Robertson, Belinda (1959–)
Wilson, Simon (1945–)
Withers, Moira and Bill (both 1947–)

Film
Bannen, Ian (1928–)
Caton-Jones, Michael (1957–)
Coltrane, Robbie (1950–)
Connery, Sean Thomas (1930–)
Connolly, Billy (1942–)
Conti, Tom (1941–)
Currie, Finlay (1878–1968)
Cuthbertson, Iain (1930–)
Douglas, Bill (1934–91)
Forsyth, Bill (1946–)
Glen, Iain (1961–)
Grierson, John (1898–1972)
Hardy, Forsyth (1910–)
Hayman, David (1948–)
Higson, Paddy (1941–)
Jackson, Gordon Cameron (1923–90)
Kerr, Deborah (1921–)
Lawson, Denis (1947–)
Lloyd, Frank (1888–1960)
McCallum, David (1933–)
McDougall, Peter (1947–)
McGrath, John Peter (1935–)
Mackendrick, Alexander (1912–)
Mackenzie, John (1932–)
McLaren, Norman (1914–87)
McMillan, Roddy (1923–79)
Macrae, Duncan (1905–67)
Marzaroli, Oscar (1933–88)
Murray, Chic (1919–85)
Myles, Lynda (1947–)
Richardson, Ian William (1934–)
Robertson-Justice, James Norval Harald
  (1905–75)
Sharp, Alan (1934–)
Sim, Alastair (1900–76)
Watt, Harry (1906–87)
Young, Colin (1927–)

Finance
Coutts, Thomas (1735–1822)

Forbes, Sir William (1739–1806)
Gairdner, Charles (1824–99)
Law, John (1671–1729)
Norie-Miller, Sir Francis (1859–1947)
Paterson, William (1658–1719)
Smith, Donald Alexander (1820–1914)
Stenhouse, Alexander Rennie (1876–1952)
Stephen, George (1829–1921)
Thomson, William Thomas (1813–83)

Food and Drink
Allen, Betty (1936–)
Brown, David (1951–)
Buchanan, James (1849–1935)
Campbell, Sir Malcolm Brown
   (1848–1935)
Dewar, John Alexander (1856–1929)
Erikson, Gunn (1956–)
Grant, William (1839–1923)
Johnstone, Isobel (1781–1857)
Keiller, John Mitchell (1851–99)
McEwan, William (1827–1913)
Mackie, Sir Peter Jeffrey (1855–1924)
Smith, George (1792–1871)
Teacher, William (1811–76)
Tennant, Hugh (1863–90)
Walker, Sir Alexander (1869–1950)
Wilson, David (1938–)

Geography
Adair, John (c.1655–?1722)
Ainslie, John (1745–1828)
Bartholomew, John George (1860–1920)
Geddes, Sir Patrick (1854–1932)
Gordon, Robert (1580–1661)
Herbertson, Andrew John (1865–1915)
Holmes, James Macdonald (1896–1966)
Johnston, Alexander Keith (1804–71)
Keates, John Stanley (1925–)
Keltie, Sir John Scott (1840–1927)
McHarg, Ian Lennox (1920–)
Mackenzie, Murdoch (1712–97)
Mill, Hugh Robert (1861–1950)
Miller, Ronald (1910–90)
Murchison, Sir Roderick Impey
   (1792–1871)
O'Dell, Andrew Charles (1909–66)
Ogilby, John (1600–76)
Ogilvie, Alan Grant (1887–1954)
Pont, Timothy (c.1560–1630)
Sissons, John Brian (1926–)
Tivy, Joy (1924–)
Watson, James Wreford (1915–90)

History
Alison, Sir Archibald (1792–1867)
Balfour, Sir James (1600–57)
Barrow, Geoffrey Wallis Steuart (1924–)

Black, John Bennett (1883–1964)
Boece, Hector (c.1465–1536)
Bower, Walter (1385–1449)
Brogan, Sir Denis William (1900–74)
Brown, Peter Hume (1850–1918)
Browning, Andrew (1889–1972)
Burton, John Hill (1809–81)
Calder, Angus (1942–)
Carlyle, Thomas (1795–1881)
Crawfurd, George (d.1748)
Cruft, Catherine Holway (1927–)
Dalrymple, Sir John (1726–1810)
Dickinson, William Croft (1897–1963)
Donaldson, Gordon (1913–)
Ferguson, Adam (1723–1816)
Forbes, Eric Gray (1933–84)
Fordun, John of (d.c.1384)
Fraser, Sir William (1816–98)
Gairdner, James (1828–1912)
Gillies, John (1747–1836)
Grahame, James (1790–1842)
Guthrie, Douglas James (1885–1975)
Hailes, Sir David Dalrymple (1726–92)
Hargreaves, John Desmond (1924–)
Hay, Malcolm Vivian (1881–1962)
Hume, David (c.1560–c.1630)
Innes, Cosmo (1798–1874)
Innes, Thomas (1662–1744)
Laing, Malcolm (1762–1818)
Leslie, John (1527–96)
MacColl, Dugald Sutherland (1859–1948)
McCrie, Thomas (1772–1835)
Macfarlane, Leslie John (1913–)
Mackie, John Duncan (1887–1978)
McNeill, Florence Marian (1885–1973)
Mair, John (1469–1550)
Masson, David (1822–1907)
Mitchison, Rosalind Mary (1919–)
Moncreiff, James (1811–95)
Napier, Mark (1789–1879)
Nisbet, Alexander (1657–1725)
Pinkerton, John (1758–1826)
Pitscottie, Lindsay Robert of (c.1532–1580)
Rait, Sir Robert Sangster (1874–1936)
Ridpath, George (c.1717–1772)
Robertson, Joseph (1810–66)
Robertson, William (1721–93)
Row, John (1568–1646)
Scott, Walter of Satchells (c.1614–c.1694)
Shepperson, George Albert (1922–)
Simpson, William Douglas (1896–1968)
Sinclair, Sir John (1754–1835)
Skene, William Forbes (1809–92)
Skinner, John (1721–1807)
Smout, Thomas Christopher (1933–)
Spalding, John (c.1609–1670)
Stewart, Sir David (1772–1829)
Stirling-Maxwell, Sir William (1818–78)

Stone, Norman (1941–)
Stuart, Gilbert (1742–86)
Terry, Charles Sanford (1864–1936)
Tranter, Nigel (1909–)
Tytler, Alexander Fraser (1747–1813)
Tytler, Patrick Fraser (1791–1849)
Tytler, William (1711–92)
Walker, David Morrison (1933–)
Watson, Robert (?1730–1781)
Welwod, William (?1552–1622)
Wodrow, Robert (1679–1734)
Wyntoun, Andrew of (?1350–?1420)
Youngson, Alexander John (1918–)

Invention

Anderson, James (1739–1808)
Anderson, John (1726–96)
Bain, Alexander (1810–77)
Baird, John Logie (1888–1946)
Bell, Alexander Graham (1847–1922)
Bell, Patrick (1799–1869)
Blair, Robert (1748–1828)
Bremner, James (1784–1856)
Brewster, Sir David (1781–1868)
Brown, Sir Samuel (1776–1852)
Chalmers, James (1782–1853)
Cochrane, Archibald (1749–1831)
Colomb, Philip Howard (1831–99)
Creed, Frederick George (1871–1957)
Dewar, Sir James (1842–1923)
Donald, Ian (1910–87)
Dudgeon, Robert Ellis (1820–1904)
Dunlop, John Boyd (1840–1921)
Fairbairn, Sir William (1789–1874)
Fairlie, Robert Francis (1831–85)
Faulds, Henry (1843–1930)
Ferguson, Patrick (1744–80)
Forsyth, Alexander John (1769–1843)
Ged, William (1690–1749)
Holden, Sir Isaac (1807–97)
Howden, James (1832–1913)
Kelvin, William Thomson (1824–1907)
Kirkaldy, David (1820–97)
Lee, James Paris (1831–1904)
Leslie, Sir John (1766–1832)
Lindsay, James Bowman (1799–1862)
McAdam, John Loudon (1756–1836)
MacInnes, Hamish (1930–)
Macmillan, Kirkpatrick (1813–78)
McNaught, William (1813–81)
Meikle, Andrew (1719–1811)
Melville, Robert (1723–1809)
Miller, Patrick (1731–1815)
Moncrieff, Colonel Sir Alexander
    (1829–1906)
Montrose, James Graham (1878–1954)
Morton, Thomas (1781–1832)
Munro, Sir Hugh Thomas (1856–1919)

Mushet, David (1772–1847)
Napier, John (1550–1617)
Pauson, Peter Ludwig (1925–)
Peebles, David Bruce (1826–99)
Salter, Stephen Hugh (1938–)
Smith, James (1789–1850)
Stevenson, Robert (1772–1850)
Stirling, Robert (1790–1878)
Swinton, Alan Archibald Campbell
    (1863–1930)
Symington, William (1763–1831)
Thomson, Robert William (1822–73)
Watt, James (1736–1819)
Wilson, Charles Thomson Rees
    (1869–1959)
Young, James (1811–83)

Journalism

Archer, William (1856–1924)
Ascherson, Neal (1932–)
Barnetson, Baron William Denholm
    (1917–81)
Bennett, James Gordon (1795–1872)
Blake, George (1893–1961)
Bold, Alan (1943–)
Boyle, Andrew (1919–)
Brown, Ivor (1891–1974)
Bruce, Sir Robert (1871–1955)
Buchan, Alastair Francis (1918–76)
Burnet, Sir Alastair (1928–)
Cameron, James Mark (1911–85)
Carswell, Catherine Roxburgh (1879–1946)
Dent, Alan Holmes (1905–78)
Drawbell, James Wedgwood (1899–1979)
Dunnett, Alastair MacTavish (1908–)
Gordon, John Rutherford (1890–1974)
Grant, James Shaw (1910–)
Gray, Cecil (1895–1951)
Gray, Muriel (1959–)
Hardy, Forsyth (1910–)
Harkness, Jack (1907–85)
Hetherington, Alastair (1919–)
House, Jack (1906–91)
Hunter, Samuel (1769–1839)
Jack, Ian (1945–)
Jeffrey, Francis Jeffrey (1773–1850)
Johnstone, Isobel (1781–1857)
Junor, Sir John (1919–)
Kernohan, Bob (1931–)
Macdonald, Gus (1940–)
McIlvanney, Hugh (1933–)
Mackie, Albert David (1904–85)
MacLaren, Charles (1782–1866)
Magnusson, Magnus (1929–)
Massie, Allan (1938–)
Montgomery, James (1771–1854)
Munro, Neil (1864–1930)
Naughtie, James (1952–)

Neil, Andrew Ferguson (1949–)
Power, William (1874–1951)
Reid, Sir Thomas Wemyss (1842–1905)
Reston, James Barrett (1909–)
Riddell, George Allardice Riddell (1865–1934)
Ritchie, William (1781–1831)
Robertson, Fyfe (1902–87)
Robieson, Sir William (1890–1977)
Russel, Alexander (1814–76)
Sterling, John (1806–44)
Swinton, John (1829–1901)
Tytler, James 'Balloon' (1745–1804)
Waters, Sir George Alexander (1880–1967)
Wilson, Charles Martin (1935–)
Wilson, James (1805–60)
Wilson, John (Christopher North) (1785–1854)
Yates, Edmund (1831–94)

Law
Aberdeen, George Gordon (1637–1720)
Balfour, Sir James (c.1525–1583)
Balmerino, John Elphinstone (1682–1736)
Bankton, Andrew McDougall (?1685–1760)
Bayne, Alexander (d.1737)
Bell, George Joseph (1770–1843)
Bisset, Habakkuk (?1560–?1630)
Braxfield, Robert Macqueen (1722–99)
Brougham, Henry Peter (1778–1868)
Burnett, John (?1764–1810)
Cameron, Sir John (1900–)
Campbell, Sir Ilay (1734–1823)
Campbell, John (1779–1861)
Cockburn, Henry Thomas (1779–1854)
Cooper, Thomas Mackay (1892–1955)
Craig, Sir Thomas (1538–1608)
Dirleton, Sir John Nisbet (?1609–1687)
Dundas, of Arniston
Dundas, Henry (1742–1811)
Dundas, Robert (1685–1753)
Dundas, Robert (1713–87)
Dunedin, Andrew Graham Murray (1849–1942)
Durie, Sir Alexander Gibson (d.1644)
Edward, David Alexander Ogilvy (1934–)
Elchies, Patrick Grant (1690–1754)
Erskine, Henry (1746–1817)
Erskine, Thomas (1750–1823)
Erskine of Carnock, John (1695–1768)
Falconer, Sir David (1640–86)
Finlay, Robert Bannatyne (1842–1929)
Forbes, Duncan (1685–1747)
Forbes, William (?1675–1745)
Fountainhall, Sir John Lauder (1646–1722)
Fraser, Patrick (1817 or 1819–89)
Gibb, Andrew Dewar (1888–1974)

Gifford, Adam (1820–87)
Glendook, Sir Thomas Murray (?1630–1685)
Gloag, William Murray (1865–1934)
Grant, Sir William (1755–1832)
Grub, George (1812–92)
Haddington, Thomas Hamilton (1563–1637)
Haldane, Richard Burdon (1856–1928)
Henryson, Edward (?1510–?1590)
Hermand, George Fergusson (1743–1827)
Hope, David (1938–)
Hope, Sir Thomas (1580–1646)
Hume, David (1757–1838)
Inglis, John (1810–91)
Jeffrey, Francis Jeffrey (1773–1850)
Kames, Henry Home (1696–1782)
Kennedy, Helena (1950–)
Kidd, Dame Margaret Henderson (1900–88)
Kilmuir, David Patrick Maxwell Fyfe (1900–67)
Loreburn, Robert Threshie Reid (1846–1923)
Lorimer, James (1818–90)
Loughborough, Alexander Wedderburn (1733–1805)
Macdonald, Sir John Hay Athole (1836–1919)
Mackay, James (1927–)
Mackenzie of Rosehaugh, Sir George (1636–91)
Mackenzie Stuart, Alexander John (1924–)
McLennan, John Ferguson (1827–81)
Macmillan, Hugh Pattison (1873–1952)
Maidment, James (1794–1879)
Maitland, Sir John (?1545–1595)
Maitland of Lethington, Sir Richard (1496–1586)
Millar, John (1735–1801)
Monboddo, James Burnett (1714–99)
Moncreiff, James (1811–95)
Moncreiff, Sir James Wellwood (1776–1851)
Muir, Thomas (1765–99)
Murray, Andrew Graham (1849–1942)
Napier, Macvey (1776–1847)
Napier, Mark (1789–1879)
Paul, Sir James Balfour (1846–1931)
Pinkerton, Allan (1819–84)
Reid, James Scott Cumberland (1890–1975)
Riddell, George Allardice Riddell (1865–1934)
Roughead, William (1870–1952)
Seton, Sir Alexander (?1555–1622)
Seton, George (1822–1908)
Skene, Sir John (c.1543–1617)
Slater, Oscar (1873–1948)

Smith, Madeleine Hamilton (1835–1928)
Smith, Sir Thomas Broun (1915–88)
Spottiswood, Robert (1596–1646)
Spottiswood, John (1565–1639)
Stair, James Dalrymple (1619–95)
Stair, Sir John Dalrymple (1648–1707)
Steuart, Sir James (1635–1713)
Stuart, Gilbert (1742–86)
Tytler, Alexander Fraser (1747–1813)
Watson, William (1827–99)
Welwod, William (?1552–1622)
Wheatley, John (1908–89)
Wilson, James (1742–98)

Literature

Alexander, William (1826–94)
Anderson, Robert (1750–1830)
Annand, J K (1908–)
Arbuthnot, John (1667–1735)
Armstrong, John (c.1709–1779)
Baillie-Cochrane, Alexander Dundas Ross
    Wishart (1816–90)
Ballantyne, Robert Michael (1825–94)
Bannerman, Helen Brodie (1862–1946)
Barke, James (1905–58)
Barrie, Sir James Matthew (1860–1937)
Bell, John Jay (1871–1934)
Black, William (1841–98)
Blake, George (1893–1961)
Bold, Alan (1943–)
Boswell, James (1740–95)
Boyd, William Andrew Murray (1952–)
Brown, George Douglas (1869–1902)
Brown, George Mackay (1921–)
Brown, John (1810–82)
Bruce, George (1909–)
Brunton, Mary (1778–1818)
Buchan, John (1875–1940)
Bury, Lady Charlotte Susan Maria
    (1775–1861)
Calder, Angus (1942–)
Calder, Ritchie (1906–82)
Carlyle, Jane Baillie (1801–66)
Carswell, Catherine Roxburgh (1870–1946)
Chalmers, Alexander (1759–1834)
Crawford and Balcarres, Alexander William
    Crawford Lindsay
    (1812–80)
Crockett, Samuel Rutherford (1859–1914)
Cronin, A J (1896–1981)
Cunningham, Allan (1784–1842)
Cunninghame Graham, Robert (d.1797)
Cunninghame Graham, Robert Bontine
    (1852–1936)
Currie, James (1756–1805)
Daiches, David (1912–)
Darling, Sir Frank Fraser (1903–79)
Davidson, John (1857–1909)

Davie, Elspeth (1919–)
Dempster, Thomas (c.1579–1625)
Douglas, Norman (1868–1952)
Douglas, O (1877–1948)
Doyle, Sir Arthur Conan (1859–1930)
Duncan, Jane (pseudonym Janet Sandison)
    (1910–76)
Dunnett, Dorothy (1923–)
Ferrier, Susan Edmonstone (1782–1854)
Findlater, Jane (1866–1946)
Findlater, Mary (1865–1963)
Finlay, Ian Hamilton (1925–)
Fleming, Margaret (1803–11)
Frazer, Sir James George (1854–1941)
Friel, George (1910–75)
Gaitens, Edward (1897–1966)
Galt, John (1779–1839)
Gibbon, Lewis Grassic (1901–35)
Gleig, George Robert (1796–1888)
Grahame, Kenneth (1859–1932)
Grant, Anne (1755–1838)
Grant, Elizabeth (1797–1885)
Grant, James (1822–87)
Gray, Alasdair James (1934–)
Greig, Gavin (1856–1914)
Gunn, Neil Miller (1891–1973)
Haldane, Elizabeth Sanderson (1862–1937)
Hall, Basil (1788–1844)
Hamilton, Thomas (1789–1842)
Hanley, Clifford (1922–)
Hay, Ian (1876–1952)
Hay, John Macdougall (1881–1919)
Hogg, James (1770–1835)
Hood, Stuart (1915–)
House, Jack (1906–91)
Howison, John (d.1859)
Hunter, Mollie (1922–)
Jacob, Violet (1863–1946)
Japp, Alexander Hay (1837–1905)
Jeffrey, Francis Jeffrey (1773–1850)
Jenkins, Robin (1912–)
Johnstone, Isobel (1781–1857)
Kelman, James (1946–)
Kennaway, James (1928–68)
Kesson, Jessie (1915–)
Lang, Andrew (1844–1912)
Lauder, Sir Thomas Dick (1784–1848)
Lindsay, David (1878–1945)
Lindsay, Frederic (1933–)
Lindsay, Maurice (1918–)
Lingard, Joan (1932–)
Linklater, Eric (1899–1974)
Lockhart, John Gibson (1794–1854)
Loudon, John Claudius (1783–1843)
McCrone, Guy (1898–1977)
Macdonald, George (1824–1905)
MacDonald, Sharman (1951–)
McGonagall, William (1830–1902)

McGrath, John Peter (1935–)
McIlvanney, William Angus (1936–)
MacInnes, Hamish (1930–)
Mackenzie, Sir Compton (1883–1972)
Mackenzie, Henry (1745–1831)
Mackintosh, Elizabeth (1896–1952)
Mackintosh, Sir James (1765–1832)
Maclaren, Ian (1850–1907)
McLean, Alan Campbell (1922–89)
Maclean, Alistair (1922–87)
Maclehose, Agnes (1759–1841)
MacRae, David (1837–1907)
Maidment, James (1794–1879)
Marshall, Bruce (1899–1987)
Martin, Sir Theodore (1816–1909)
Massie, Allan (1938–)
Masson, David (1822–1907)
Miller, Hugh (1802–56)
Mitchell, Sir Peter Chalmers (1864–1945)
Mitchison, Naomi Margaret (1897–)
Moir, David Macbeth (1798–1851)
Molesworth, Mary Louisa (1839–1921)
Moon, Lorna (1886–1930)
Moore, John (1729–1802)
Motherwell, William (1797–1835)
Muir, Willa (pseudonym Agnes Neil Scott)
    (1890–1970)
Munro, Neil (1864–1930)
Nicoll, Sir William Robertson (pseudonym
    Claudius Clear)
(1851–1923)
Niven, Frederick John (1878–1944)
Oliphant, Margaret (1828–97)
Pitcairn, Robert (1793–1855)
Pitcairne, Archibald (1652–1713)
Pringle, Thomas (1789–1834)
Purser, John (1942–)
Reid, Alastair (1926–)
Reid, John MacNair (1895–1954)
Reid, Sir Thomas Wemyss (1842–1905)
Row, John (c.1525–1580)
Scott, Michael (1789–1835)
Scott, Sir Walter (1771–1832)
Sempill, Robert (?1530–1595)
Sharp, Alan (1934–)
Sharp, William, (pseudonym Fiona
    Macleod) (1855–1905)
Sharpe, Charles Kirkpatrick (1781–1851)
Shepherd, Nan (1893–1981)
Smiles, Samuel (1812–1904)
Smith, Alexander (1830–67)
Smith, Iain Crichton (1928–)
Smollett, Tobias George (1721–71)
Somerville, Mary (1780–1872)
Spark, Muriel Sarah (1918–)
Spence, Catherine Helen (1825–1910)
Steel, Flora Annie (1847–1929)
Sterling, John (1806–44)

Stevenson, Robert Louis Balfour (1850–94)
Stewart, James Stuart (1896–1990)
Stewart, J I M (pseudonym Michael Innes)
    (1906–)
Swan, Annie S (1859–1943)
Tranter, Nigel (1909–)
Urquhart, Fred (1912–)
Urquhart, Sir Thomas (c.1611–1660)
Weir, Molly (1920–)
White, Kenneth (1936–)
Whyte-Melville, George John (1821–78)
Williams, Gordon (1934–)
Wilson, Alexander (1766–1813)
Wilson, John (Christopher North)
    (1785–1854)
Yates, Edmund (1831–94)

Mathematics and Computer Science

Aitken, Alexander Craig (1895–1967)
Anderson, Alexander (c.1582–c.1619)
Chrystal, George (1851–1911)
Cochran, William Gemmell (1909–80)
Craig, John (d.1731)
Forsyth, Andrew Russell (1858–1942)
Gregory, David (1659–1708)
Gregory, Duncan Farqharson (1813–44)
Gregory, James (1638–75)
Ivory, Sir James (1765–1842)
Keill, John (1671–1721)
Kelvin, William Thomson (1824–1907)
Maclaurin, Colin (1698–1746)
Michaelson, Sidney (1925–91)
Michie, Donald (1923–)
Milner, Robin Gorell (1934–)
Napier, John (1550–1617)
Playfair, John (1748–1819)
Rankin, Robin Alexander (1915–)
Simson, Robert (1687–1768)
Sneddon, Ian Naismith (1919–)
Stewart, Matthew (1717–85)
Stirling, James (1692–1770)
Tait, Peter Guthrie (1831–1901)
Wallace, William (1786–1843)
Wedderburn, Joseph Henry Maclagan
    (1882–1948)
Whittaker, Sir Edmund Taylor (1873–1956)

Medical Sciences

Alison, William Pulteney (1790–1859)
Arbuthnot, John (1667–1735)
Armstrong, John (c.1709–1779)
Auerbach, Charlotte (1899–)
Baillie, Matthew (1761–1823)
Baird, Sir Dugald (1899–1986)
Balfour, Sir Andrew (1630–94)
Barclay, John (1758–1826)
Barry, James (1795–1865)
Bell, Benjamin (1749–1806)

Bell, Sir Charles (1774–1842)
Bell, John (1691–1780)
Black, Sir James Whyte (1924–)
Black, Joseph (1728–99)
Blane, Sir Gilbert (1749–1834)
Boyd, George Scott (1924–83)
Braid, James (?1795–1860)
Brotherston, Sir John Howie Flint (1915–85)
Brown, John (c.1735–1788)
Bruce, Sir David (1855–1931)
Buchan, William (1729–1805)
Burnett, Sir William (1799–1861)
Carswell, Sir Robert (1793–1857)
Cheyne, George (1671–1743)
Christison, Sir Robert (1797–1882)
Cochrane, Archibald Lenman (1909–88)
Cohen, Philip (1945–)
Combe, Andrew (1797–1847)
Combe, George (1788–1858)
Crofton, Sir John Wenman (1912–)
Cruickshank, Robert (1899–1974)
Cullen, William (1710–90)
Currie, James (1756–1805)
Davidson, James Norman (1911–72)
Davidson, Sir Leybourne Stanley Patrick (1894–1981)
Donald, Ian (1910–87)
Dott, Norman McOmish (1897–1973)
Dudgeon, Robert Ellis (1820–1904)
Duncan, Andrew (1744–1828)
Duncan, Archibald Sutherland (1914–)
Dunlop, Sir Derrick Melville (1902–80)
Faulds, Henry (1843–1930)
Ferrier, Sir David (1843–1928)
Fleming, Sir Alexander (1881–1955)
Forrest, Sir Patrick McEwen (1923–)
Goodsir, John (1814–67)
Graham, James (1745–94)
Gregory, James (1753–1821)
Gregory, John (1724–73)
Guthrie, Douglas James (1885–1975)
Haddow, Sir Alexander (1906–76)
Haldane, John Scott (1860–1936)
Hunter, John (1728–93)
Hunter, William (1718–83)
Inglis, Elsie Maud (1864–1917)
Isaacs, Alick (1921–67)
Jamieson, 'JK' (1873–1948)
Jennett, Bryan (1926–)
Knox, Robert (1791–1862)
Lane, Arbuthnot (1856–1943)
Leishman, Sir William Boog (1865–1926)
Lind, James (1716–94)
Liston, Robert (1794–1847)
Littlejohn, Sir Henry Duncan (1826–1914)
McCleod, James Walter (1887–1978)
MacEwen, Sir William (1848–1924)

Mackie, Thomas Jones (1888–1955)
Macleod, John James Rickard (1876–1935)
Macphail, Katherine Stewart (1888–1974)
Manson, Sir Patrick (1844–1922)
Moir, David Macbeth (1798–1851)
Monro, Alexander, 'Monro Primus' (1697–1767)
Monro, Alexander, 'Monro Secundus' (1733–1817)
Moore, John (1729–1802)
Murray, John (1809–98)
Oliver, Michael Francis (1925–)
Passmore, Reginald (1910–)
Philip, Sir Robert William (1857–1939)
Pickford, Mary (1902–)
Pitcairne, Archibald (1652–1713)
Pollock, Sir John Donald (1868–1962)
Pringle, Sir John (1707–82)
Rae, John (1786–1873)
Ritchie, Jean Atkinson Smail (1913–)
Rutherford, Daniel (1749–1819)
Sharpey-Schafer, Sir Edward Albert (1850–1953)
Sibbald, Sir Robert (1641–1722)
Simpson, Sir James Young (1811–70)
Smith, John (1825–1910)
Stephenson, Elsie (1916–67)
Stewart, Matthew John (1885–1956)
Stiles, Sir Harold Jalland (1863–1946)
Subak-Sharpe, John Herbert (1924–)
Syme, James (1799–1870)
Turner, Sir William (1832–1916)
Waddington, Conrad Hal (1906–75)
Watt, Robert (1774–1819)
Whitteridge, David (1912–)
Wilkie, Sir David (1882–1938)
Woodruff, Sir Michael Francis Addison (1911–)

Miscellaneous
Armstrong, Archy (d.1672)
Blacklock, Thomas (1721–91)
Blackwell, Alexander (c.1700–c.1747)
Brown, John (1826–83)
Burrell, Sir William (1861–1958)
Caskie, Donald (1902–83)
Dunbar, Agnes (c.1312–1369)
Elliott, Grace Dalrymple (c.1758–1823)
Geddes, Jenny (c.1600–c.1660)
Grange, Lady (d.1745)
Grierson, Sir Robert (c.1655–1733)
Macdonald, Flora (1722–90)
Montgomerie, William (1904–)
Nicol, William (c.1744–1797)
Sampson, Agnes (d.1592)
Thomson, George (1757–1851)

Music: Classical

Baillie, Dame Isobel (1895–1983)
Black, Andrew (1859–1920)
Brydon, Roderick (1939–)
Buchanan, Isobel Wilson (1954–)
Cairns, Christine (1959–)
Carver, Robert (c.1484–c.1568)
Chisholm, Erik (1904–65)
Crawford, Robert Caldwell (1925–)
Dalby, Martin (1942–)
Dickson, Joan (1921–)
Dillon, James (1950–)
Dorward, David Campbell (1933–)
Drysdale, Learmont (1866–1909)
Elliott, Kenneth (1929–)
Finnie, Linda (1952–)
Garden, Mary (1874–1967)
Garden, Neville (1936–)
Geddes, John Maxwell (1941–)
Gibson, Sir Alexander Drummond (1926–)
Glennie, Evelyn (1965–)
Gray, Cecil (1895–1951)
Hamilton, Iain Ellis (1922–)
Hislop, Joseph (1884–1977)
Horne, David (1970–)
Johnson, David Charles (1942–)
Johnson, Robert (c.1500–c.1560)
Lamond, Frederic (1868–1948)
Leighton, Kenneth (1929–88)
Loughran, James (1931–)
MacCunn, Hamish (1868–1916)
MacDonald, Malcolm (pseudonym Calum MacDonald) (1948–)
McEwen, Sir John Blackwood (1868–1948)
McGibbon, William (c.1690–1756)
McGuire, Edward (1948–)
Mackay, Neil (1947–)
Mackenzie, Sir Alexander Campbell (1847–1935)
Mackie, Neil (1946–)
McLachlan, Murray (1965–)
McLeod, John (1934–)
Macmillan, James Loy (1959–)
McPherson, Gordon (1965–)
McQueen, Ian (1954–)
Marshall, Margaret Anne (1949–)
Maxwell, Donald (1948–)
Maxwell Davies, Sir Peter (1934–)
Musgrave, Thea (1928–)
Orr, Robin (1909–)
Purser, John (1942–)
Reid, John (1721–1807)
Robertson, Sir Hugh S (1874–1952)
Runnicles, Donald Cameron (1954–)
Scott, Francis George (1880–1958)
Smith, Robert Archibald (1780–1829)
Stevenson, Savourna (1961–)
Stevenson, Ronald (1928–)
Sweeney, William (1950–)

Thomson, Bryden (1928–91)
Thorpe Davie, Cedric (1913–83)
Wallace, William (1860–1940)
Ward, David (1922–83)
Weir, Judith (1954–)
Welsh, Moray (1947–)
Whyte, Ian (1901–60)
Wilson, Thomas Brendan (1927–)

Music: Folk
Anderson, Tom (1910–91)
Bain, Aly (1945–)
Blythman, Morris (pseudonym Thurso Berwick) (1919–81)
Browne, Ronnie (1937–)
Burgess, John Davey (1934–)
Cunningham, Phil (1960–)
Fisher, Archie (1939–)
Fraser, Marjory Kennedy (1857–1930)
Fraser, Captain Simon (1773–1852)
Gaughan, Dick (1948–)
Gow, Nathaniel (1766–1831)
Gow, Niel (1727–1807)
Grant, Angus (1931–)
Greig, Gavin (1856–1914)
Hardie, Alastair (1946–)
Hardie, Bill (1916–)
Henderson, Hamish (1919–)
Henderson, John Murdoch (1902–72)
Jackson, William (1955–)
MacAndrew, Hector (1903–80)
McBeath, Jimmy (1894–1972)
MacColl, Ewan (1915–89)
MacCrimmon
McGinn, Matt (1928–77)
Macgregor, Jimmie (1932–)
McGuire, Edward (1948–)
Mackay, Charles (1814–89)
MacLean, Dougie (1954–)
MacLennan, George Stewart (1884–1929)
Marshall, William (1748–1833)
Nairne, Carolina (1766–1845)
Rafferty, Gerry (1947–)
Redpath, Jean (1937–)
Reid, Robert (1895–1965)
Robertson, Jeannie (1908–75)
Ross, William (1879–1966)
Scott, William (1897–1990)
Skinner, James Scott (1843–1927)
Stevenson, Savourna (1961–)
Stewart, Belle (1906–)
Thomson, George (1757–1851)
Williamson, Robin (1943–)
Williamson, Roy (1937–90)

Music: Jazz
Brown, Sandy (1929–75)
Chisholm, George (1915–)

Deuchar, Jimmy (1930–)
Fairweather, Al (1927–)
Galloway, Jim (1936–)
Kidd, Carol (1944–)
Lyall, Chick (1959–)
McQuater, Tommy (1914–)
Mullen, Jim (1945–)
Smith, Tommy (1967–)
Temperley, Joe (1929–)
Wellins, Bobby (1936–)
Welsh, Alex (1929–82)

Music: Pop/Rock
Adamson, Stuart (1958–)
Anderson, Ian (1947–)
Anderson, Moira (1938–)
Bell, Maggie (1945–)
Byrne, David (1952–)
Dickson, Barbara (1947–)
Donegan, Lonnie (1931–)
Donovan (1944–)
Easton, Sheena (1959–)
Elrick, George (1910–)
Fyffe, Will (1885–1947)
Gorrie, Alan (1946–)
Harvey, Alex (1935–82)
Kane, Pat (1964–)
Kerr, Jim (1959–)
Lennox, Annie (1954–)
Lipton, Celia (1923–)
Longmuir, Alan (1953–)
Lulu (1948–)
Macdonald, Rory (1949–)
McKellar, Kenneth (1927–)
Martyn, John (1948–)
Pellow, Marti (1965–)
Rafferty, Gerry (1947–)
Reid, Charlie and Craig (1962–)
Ross, Ricky (1957–)
Scott, Mike (1958–)
Somerville, Jimmy (1961–)
Stewart, Andy (1933–)
Ure, Midge (1953–)

Natural History and the Environment
Christison, Sir Alexander Francis Philip
 (1893–)
Cleghorn, Hugh (1820–95)
Darling, Sir Frank Fraser (1903–79)
Drummond, Henry (1851–97)
Falconer, Hugh (1808–65)
Gordon, Seton (1886–1977)
Hume, Allan Octavian (1829–1912)
Hunter, John (1737–1821)
Jardine, Sir William (1800–74)
Kerr, Sir John Graham (1869–1957)
Kirk, Sir John (1832–1932)
MacGillivray, William (1796–1852)

Mellanby, Kenneth (1908–)
Menzies, Archibald (1754–1842)
Muir, John (1838–1914)
Robertson-Justice, James Norval Harald
 (1905–75)
Stephen, David (1910–89)
Unna, Percy (1878–1950)
Waterston, George (1911–80)

**Philanthropy, Patronage and the
 Foundation of Institutions**
Baird, James (1802–76)
Barr, Archibald (1855–1931)
Barr Smith, Robert (1824–1915)
Baxter, Sir David (1793–1872)
Buchanan, James (1849–1935)
Carnegie, Andrew (1835–1918)
Coats, Sir Peter (1808–90)
Connery, Sean Thomas (1930–)
Cranston, Kate (1850–1934)
Crichton-Stuart, John Patrick (1847–1900)
Dale, David (1739–1806)
Dewar, John Alexander (1856–1929)
Dick, James (1743–1828)
Donaldson, James (1751–1830)
Drummond, George (1687–1766)
Duncan, Andrew (1744–1828)
Duncan, Henry (1774–1846)
Elphinstone, William (1431–1514)
Erskine, Mary (1629–1707)
Fettes, Sir William (1750–1836)
Fraser, Sir Alexander (c.1537–1623)
Fraser, Sir William (1816–98)
Gillespie, James (1726–97)
Gillespie, Thomas (1708–74)
Gordon, Robert (1580–1661)
Graham, John Anderson (1861–1942)
Grant, Sir Alexander (1826–84)
Guthrie, Thomas (1803–73)
Hepburn, Sir John (?1598–1636)
Heriot, George (1563–1624)
Hope, Sir John (1725–86)
Huchesone, George (c.1560–1639)
Lipton, Sir Thomas Johnstone (1850–1931)
McGill, James (1744–1813)
Macpherson, Annie (c.1824–1904)
Manson, Sir Patrick (1844–1922)
Paterson, William (1658–1719)
Pitcairne, Archibald (1652–1713)
Pollock, Sir John Donald (1868–1962)
Quarrier, William (1829–1903)
Reid, John (1721–1807)
Ritchie, William (1781–1831)
Smith, James (1789–1850)
Smith, Sir William Alexander (1854–1914)
Snell, John (1629–79)
Stephen, George (1829–1921)
Stewart, Daniel (1740/1–1814)

Unna, Percy (1878–1950)
Watson, George (1654–1723)
Wilson, James (1805–60)
Wolfson, Sir Isaac (1897–1991)
Yarrow, Alfred Fernandez (1842–1932)

Philosophy
Adamson, Robert (1852–1902)
Anderson, John (1893–1962)
Bain, Alexander (1818–1903)
Balfour, Arthur James (1848–1930)
Balfour, Robert (c.1550–1625)
Bowman, Archibald Allan (1883–1936)
Brown, Thomas (1778–1820)
Burnet, John (1863–1928)
Caird, Edward (1835–1908)
Campbell, Charles Arthur (1897–1974)
Carmichael, Gerrhom (1672–1729)
Combe, George (1788–1858)
Davie, George Elder (1912–)
Duns Scotus, John (c.1265–1308)
Ferguson, Adam (1723–1816)
Ferrier, James Frederick (1808–64)
Flint, Robert (1828–1910)
Hamilton, Sir William (1788–1856)
Hume, David (1711–76)
Ireland, John (1440–96)
Jack, Gilbert (?1578–1628)
Jones, Sir Henry (1852–1922)
Kames, Henry Home (1696–1782)
Lindsay, Alexander Dunlop (1879–1952)
Lokert, George (1485–1547)
McCosh, James (1811–94)
Macintyre, Alasdair Chalmers (1929–)
Mackinnon, Donald Mackenzie (1913–)
Macmurray, John (1891–1976)
Mill, James (1773–1836)
Mitchell, William (1861–1962)
Oswald, James (1703–93)
Ramsay, Sir George (1800–71)
Reid, Thomas (1710–96)
Ritchie, Arthur David (1891–1967)
Ritchie, David George (1855–1903)
Robertson, George Croom (1842–92)
Sinclair, George (c.1625–1696)
Smith, Adam (1723–90)
Smith, Norman Kemp (1873–1958)
Sorley, William Ritchie (1855–1936)
Stewart, Dugald (1753–1828)
Stirling, James Hutchison (1820–1909)
Turnbull, George (1698–1748)
Wallace, William (1844–97)
Watson, John (1847–1939)

Photography
Adamson, John (1809–70)
Adamson, Robert (1821–48)
Annan, James Craig (1864–1946)

Annan, Thomas (1829–87)
Bremner, Frederick (1863–1941)
Carrick, William (1827–78)
Charity, John (1946–)
Clark, William Donaldson (1816–73)
Colvin, Calum (1961–)
Cooper, Thomas Joshua (1946–)
Donaldson, Mary Ethel Muir (1876–1958)
Gardner, Alexander (1821–82)
Gillanders, Robin (1952–)
Gordon, Seton (1886–1977)
Graham, James (1806–69)
Henderson, Alexander (1831–1913)
Hill, David Octavius (1802–70)
Johnston, Murray (1949–90)
Keith, Thomas (1827–95)
Logan, Owen (1963–)
Macdonald, Patricia Clare (1945–)
McKenzie, Joseph (1929–)
Macpherson, Robert (d.1872)
Marzaroli, Oscar (1933–88)
Maude, Clementina (1822–65)
Murray, John (1809–98)
Notman, William (1826–91)
O'Donnell, Ron (1952–)
Ponton, Mungo (1801–80)
Ross, Horatio (1801–86)
Smyth, Charles Piazzi (1819–1900)
Stirling, Ruth (1957–)
Thomson, John (1837–1921)
Valentine, James (1815–80)
Williams, David (1952–)
Wilson, George Washington (1823–93)

Physics
Aitken, John (1839–1919)
Allen, John Frank (1908–)
Appleton, Sir Edward Victor (1892–1965)
Barkla, Charles Glover (1877–1944)
Born, Max (1882–1970)
Brewster, Sir David (1781–1868)
Clarke, Alexander Ross (1828–1914)
Cochran, William (1922–)
Croll, James (1821–90)
Curran, Sir Samuel Crowe (1912–)
Dee, Philip Ivor (1904–83)
Feather, Norman (1904–78)
Forbes, James David (1809–68)
Gunn, Sir John Currie (1916–)
Henderson, Richard (1945–)
Higgs, Peter Ware (1929–)
Howie, Archibald (1934–)
Jones, Reginald Victor (1911–)
Kelvin, William Thomson (1824–1907)
Kemmer, Nicholas (1911–)
Kerr, John (1824–1907)
Leslie, Sir John (1766–1832)

MacDonald, David Keith Chalmers
(1920–63)
Maxwell, James Clerk (1831–79)
Moffat, Henry Keith (1935–)
Nicol, William (1768–1851)
Playfair, John (1748–1819)
Pringle, Derek Hair (1926–)
Pringle, Robert William (1920–)
Rankine, William John Macquorn
(1820–72)
Robison, John (1739–1805)
Smith, Robert Allan (1909–80)
Smith, Stanley Desmond (1931–)
Spear, Walter Eric (1921–)
Stewart, Balfour (1828–87)
Swinton, Alan Archibald Campbell
(1863–1930)
Thomson, James (1822–92)
Wallace, David James (1945–)
Waterston, John James (1811–?1883)
Watson-Watt, Sir Robert Alexander
(1892–1973)
Wilson, Charles Thomson Rees
(1869–1959)

Poetry and Verse
Aneirin (f1.late 6th century)
Angus, Marion (1866–1946)
Annand, J K (1908–)
Ayton, Sir Robert (1570–1638)
Aytoun, William Edmonstoune (1818–65)
Baillie, Grizel (1665–1746)
Baillie, Joanna (1762–1851)
Ballantine, James (1808–77)
Barbour, John (c.1316–1396)
Barclay, Alexander (?1475–1552)
Beattie, James (1735–1803)
Black, David Macleod (1941–)
Blair, Robert (1699–1746)
Blythman, Morris (1919–81)
Bold, Alan (1943–)
Boswell, Alexander (1775–1822)
Bonar, Horatius (1808–89)
Brown, George Mackay (1921–)
Bruce, George (1909–)
Buchanan, Dugald (1716–68)
Burns, Robert (1759–96)
Campbell, Thomas (1777–1844)
Cockburn, Alison (1713–94)
Conn, Stewart (1936–)
Craig, Isa (1831–1903)
Cruickshank, Helen (1886–1975)
Cunninghame Graham, Robert (d.1797)
Dickson, Barbara (1947–)
Donovan (1944–)
Douglas, Gavin (c.1474–1522)
Drummond, William (1585–1649)
Dunbar, William (c.1460–c.1520)

Dunn, Douglas Eaglesham (1942–)
Elliot, Jean (1727–1805)
Falconer, William (1732–69)
Fergusson, Robert (1750–74)
Fleming, Tom (1927–)
Fulton, Robin (1937–)
Garioch, Robert (1909–81)
Gaughan, Dick (1948–)
Glen, William (1789–1826)
Gordon, Alexander (c.1745–1827)
Gow, Niel (1727–1807)
Graham, Dougal (c.1724–1779)
Grahame, James (1765–1811)
Gray, Sir Alexander (1882–1968)
Gray, David (1838–61)
Gray, John (1866–1934)
Haliburton, Hugh (1846–1922)
Hamilton, William (c.1665–1751)
Hamilton, William (1704–54)
Harry, Blind (f1.1470–92)
Hay, George Campbell (pseudonym Deórsa
Caimbeul Hay) (1915–84)
Henderson, Hamish (1919–)
Henryson, Robert (c.1425–c.1508)
Holland, Sir Richard (c.1415–c.1482)
Jackson, Alan (1938–)
Jacob, Violet (1863–1946)
Johnston, Arthur (1587–1641)
Laidlaw, William (1779–1845)
Leonard, Tom (1944–)
Leyden, John (1775–1811)
Lindsay, Maurice (1918–)
Lochhead, Liz (1947–)
Logan, John (1748–88)
Lyndsay, Sir David (c.1486–1555)
Lyte, Henry Francis (1793–1847)
MacCaig, Norman Alexander (1910–)
MacCodrum, Ian (1693–1779)
MacDiarmid, Hugh (1892–1978)
Macdonald, John (1624–1710)
McGinn, Matt (1928–77)
McGonagall, William (1830–1902)
McGrath, Tom (1940–)
McIlvanney, William Angus (1936–)
McIntyre, Duncan Ban (1724–1812)
Mackay, Charles (1814–89)
Mackay, Robert (1714–78)
Mackie, Albert David (1904–85)
MacLean, Dougie (1954–)
MacLean, Sorley (1911–)
MacLeod, Mary (c.1615–1705)
MacMhuirric, Niall (c.1637–1726)
Macpherson, James (1736–96)
Maitland of Lethington, Sir Richard
(1496–1586)
Mallet, David (c.1705–1765)
Martyn, John (1948–)
Mathieson, George (1842–1906)

Mickle, William Julius (1735–88)
Miller, William (1810–72)
Montgomerie, Alexander (c.1545–c.1611)
Montgomerie, William (1904–)
Montgomery, James (1771–1854)
Morgan, Edwin (1920–)
Muir, Edwin (1887–1959)
Mure, Sir William (1594–1657)
Murray, Charles (1864–1941)
Nairne, Carolina (1766–1845)
Ogilvie, John (1733–1813)
Picken, Ebenezer (1769–1816)
Rafferty, Gerry (1947–)
Ramsay, Allan (c.1685–1758)
Reid, Alastair (1926–)
Reid, John MacNair (1895–1954)
Ross, Ricky (1957–)
Scott, Alexander (c.1525–1584)
Scott, Mike (1958–)
Scott, Tom (1918–)
Scott, William Bell (1811–90)
Sempill, Francis (c.1616–1682)
Sempill, Robert (?1595–?1665)
Singer, James Hyman (pseudonym Burns
    Singer) (1928–64)
Skinner, John (1721–1807)
Smith, Alexander (1830–67)
Smith, Iain Crichton (1928–)
Smith, Sydney Goodsir (1915–75)
Sorley, Charles Hamilton (1895–1915)
Soutar, William (1898–1943)
Spence, Lewis Thomas Chalmers
    (1874–1955)
Spottiswoode, Alicia Ann (1810–1900)
Stewart, Belle (1906–)
Stirling, William Alexander (c.1567–1640)
Taliesin (late 6th century)
Tannahill, Robert (1774–1810)
Tennant, William (1784–1848)
Thomas the Rhymer (c.1220–c.1297)
Thompson, Derick (1921–)
Thomson, James (1700–48)
Thomson, James (1834–82)
Todd, Ruthven (1914–78)
Veitch, John (1829–94)
Watson, James Wreford (1915–90)
White, Kenneth (1936–)
Williamson, Robin (1943–)
Wilson, Alexander (1766–1813)
Young, Andrew John (1855–1971)
Young, Douglas (1913–73)

Politics and Diplomacy

Aberdeen, George Hamilton Gordon
    (1784–1860)
Aberdeen, James Campbell Hamilton
    Gordon (1847–1934)
Adamson, William (1863–1936)

Albany, John (1481–1536)
Alness, Robert Munro (1868–1955)
Anderson, John (1882–1958)
Argyll, Archibald (1530–73)
Argyll, Archibald (c.1576–1638)
Argyll, Archibald (1598–1661)
Argyll, Archibald (1629–85)
Argyll, George Douglas Campbell
    (1823–1900)
Argyll, John (1678–1743)
Argyll, John Douglas Sutherland
    (1845–1914)
Atholl, John (d.1579)
Atholl, Katharine Marjory (1874–1960)
Baillie-Cochrane, Alexander Dundas Ross
    Wishart (1816–90)
Balfour, Arthur James (1848–1930)
Balfour, Gerald William (1853–1945)
Balfour of Burleigh, Alexander Hugh Bruce
    (1848–1921)
Ballantrae, Bernard Edward Fergusson
    (1911–80)
Balmerino, Arthur Elphinstone
    (1688–1746)
Balmerino, John Elphinstone (1682–1736)
Barnes, George (1859–1940)
Beaton, David (1494–1546)
Beaton, James (1470–1539)
Bogle, George (1746–81)
Boothby, Sir Robert John Graham
    (1900–86)
Borthwick, Peter (1804–52)
Brougham, Henry Peter (1778–1868)
Brown, Gordon (1951–)
Buchan, Alastair Francis (1918–76)
Buchan, John (1875–1940)
Burnes, Sir Alexander (1805–41)
Bute, John Stuart (1713–92)
Cameron, Archibald (1707–53)
Campbell-Bannerman, Sir Henry
    (1836–1908)
Carnegie of Boysack, John (?1680–1750)
Clark, Gavin Brown (1846–1930)
Clerk, Sir John (1676–1755)
Collins, Sir Godfrey Pattison (1875–1936)
Connolly, James (1868–1916)
Cook, Robin Finlayson (1946–)
Cormack, John (1894–1978)
Craig, Isa (1831–1903)
Cunninghame Graham, Robert (d.1797)
Cunninghame Graham, Robert Bontine
    (1852–1936)
Dalyell, Tam (1932–)
Darnley, Henry (1545–67)
Dewar, Donald Campbell (1937–)
Douglas, Thomas Clement (1904–86)
Drummond, Flora (1869–1949)
Drummond, Thomas (1797–1840)

Duncan, Sir Patrick (1870–1943)
Dundas, of Arniston
Dundas, Henry (1742–1811)
Dunrossil, William Shepherd Morrison (1893–1961)
Elgin, James Bruce (1811–63)
Elgin, Victor Alexander Bruce (1849–1917)
Elliot, Walter (1888–1958)
Elphinstone, William (1431–1514)
Erskine of Cambo, Sir Alexander (1663–1727)
Ewing, Winnie (1929–)
Fergusson, Sir James (1832–1907)
Finlay, Robert Bannatyne (1842–1929)
Fisher, Andrew (1862–1928)
Fletcher, Andrew (1655–1716)
Forbes, Duncan (1685–1747)
Forsyth, Michael Bruce (1954–)
Fraser, Peter (1884–1950)
Gallacher, Willie (1881–1966)
Gibb, Andrew Dewar (1888–1974)
Gilmour, Sir John (1876–1940)
Glasgow, David Boyle (1833–1915)
Glasier, John Bruce (1859–1920)
Gordon, George (d.c.1502)
Gordon, George (1514–62)
Grimond, Jo (1913–)
Hardie, James Keir (1856–1915)
Henderson, Arthur (1863–1935)
Home of the Hirsel, Baron Alexander Frederick Douglas-Home (1903–)
Horne of Slamannan, Robert Stevenson Horne (1871–1940)
Hume, Joseph (1777–1855)
Hume, Sir Patrick (1641–1724)
Jameson, Sir Leander Starr (1853–1917)
Johnston, Tom (1881–1965)
Keith, Arthur Berriedale (1879–1944)
Kilmuir, David Patrick Maxwell Fyfe (1900–67)
Kirkcaldy, Sir William (c.1520–1573)
Lang, Ian (1940–)
Lauderdale, John Maitland (1616–82)
Law, Andrew Bonar (1858–1923)
Lee, Jennie (1904–88)
Lennox, Matthew (1516–71)
Lindsay, Robert Burns (1824–1902)
Lockhart of Carnwath, George (1673–1731)
Lothian, Henry Schomberg Kerr (1833–1900)
MacArthur, Mary Reid (1880–1921)
MacCormick, John MacDonald (1904–61)
McCulloch, Sir James (1819–93)
Macdonald, Sir John Alexander (1815–91)
Macdonald, Malcolm (1901–81)
MacDonald, Margo (1944–)
Macdonald, Ramsay (1866–1937)
Macdonnell, Alastair Ruadh (c.1724–1761)

MacIntyre, Robert Donald (1913–)
MacKenzie, Alexander (1822–92)
MacKenzie, Thomas (1854–1930)
Mackenzie, William Forbes (1801–62)
Mackenzie, William Lyon (1795–1861)
Mackintosh, John Pitcairn (1929–78)
Mackintosh, William (1662–1743)
Maclaren, Duncan (1800–86)
MacLean, Sir Donald (1864–1932)
Maclean, Sir Fitzroy Hew (1911–)
Maclean, John (1879–1923)
Maclennan, Robert Adam Ross (1936–)
Macleod, Iain Norman (1913–70)
Macmillan, Chrystal (1882–1937)
Maitland, James (1759–1839)
Maitland, William (c.1528–1573)
Maxton, James (1885–1946)
Melville, Sir James (1535–1617)
Millan, Bruce (1927–)
Minto, Gilbert John Murray Kynynmond-Elliot (1845–1914)
Moncreiff, James (1811–95)
Montrose, James Graham (1612–50)
Muirshiel, John Scott Maclay (1905–)
Napier, Francis (1819–98)
Nithsdale, William Maxwell (1676–1744)
Novar, Robert Crawford Munro Ferguson (1860–1934)
Pentland, John Sinclair (1860–1925)
Perth, James Eric Drummond (1876–1951)
Playfair, Lyon (1819–98)
Reid, Sir George Houstoun (1845–1918)
Rifkind, Malcolm (1946–)
Ritchie of Dundee, Charles Thomson Ritchie (1838–1906)
Rose, Sir John (1820–88)
Rosebery, Archibald Philip Primrose (1847–1929)
Ross, William (1911–88)
Ruthven, John (c.1578–1600)
Salmond, Alex (1955–)
Sharp, James (1613–79)
Shaw, Geoffrey Mackintosh (1927–78)
Shinwell, Emmanuel (1884–1986)
Sillars, Jim (1937–)
Sinclair, Sir Archibald Henry MacDonald (1890–1970)
Sinclair, Sir John (1754–1835)
Smillie, Robert (1857–1940)
Smith, John (1938–)
Spence, Catherine Helen (1825–1910)
Spence, Lewis Thomas Chalmers (1874–1955)
Spottiswood, John (1565–1639)
Stair, James Dalrymple (1619–95)
Stair, John Dalrymple (1673–1747)
Stair, Sir John Dalrymple (1648–1707)
Steel, Sir David (1938–)

Stirling, William Alexander (c.1567–1640)
Stonehaven, Sir John Lawrence Baird (1874–1941)
Stout, Sir Robert (1844–1930)
Stuart of Findhorn, James Gray Stuart (1897–1971)
Thomson of Monifeith, George Morgan Thomson (1921–)
Urquhart, David (1805–77)
Urquhart, Sir Thomas (c.1611–1660)
Wallace, Sir William (c.1274–1305)
Waverley, John Anderson (1882–1958)
Welsh, John (c.1568–1622)
Wheatley, John (1869–1930)
Whitelaw, Viscount William Stephen Ian (1918–)
Wilson, Gordon (1938–)
Wilson, James (1742–98)
Wilson, James (1805–60)
Wishart, George (c.1513–1546)
Witherspoon, John (1723–94)
Wolfe, Willie (1924–)
Wright, Frances (1795–1852)
Young, Douglas (1913–73)
Young, Sir Peter (1544–1628)
Younger, George Kenneth Hotson (1931–)
Younger of Leckie, Sir George Younger (1851–1929)

Psychology
Bain, Alexander (1818–1903)
Bower, Thomas Gillie Russell (1941–)
Craik, Kenneth (1914–45)
Donaldson, Margaret Caldwell (1926–)
Drever, James, 'Drever Primus' (1873–1951)
Drever, James, 'Drever Secundus' (1910–)
Fairbairn, Ronald Dodds (1889–1964)
Hunter, Ian Melville Logan (1927–)
Laing, Ronald David (1927–89)
Pickford, Ralph William (1903–86)
Rushforth, Winifred (1885–1983)
Semeonoff, Boris (1910–)
Stout, George Frederick (1860–1944)
Sutherland, John Derg (1905–91)
Thomson, Sir Godfrey Hilton (1881–1955)

Publishing and Bookselling
Black, Adam (1784–1874)
Blackie, John (1782–1874)
Blackwood, William (1776–1834)
Boswell, Alexander (1775–1822)
Cadell, Robert (1788–1849)
Chambers, Robert (1802–71)
Chambers, William (1800–83)
Collins, William (1789–1853)
Constable, Archibald (1774–1827)
Creech, William (1745–1815)

Cruden, Alexander (1701–70)
Foulis, Robert (1707–76)
Hardie, Alastair (1946–)
Hodge, Harry (1872–1947)
Japp, Alexander Hay (1837–1905)
MacDonald, Callum (1912–)
Macmillan, Daniel (1813–57)
Menzies, John Ross (1852–1935)
Murray, John (1745–93)
Nelson, Thomas (1780–1861)
Riddell, George Allardice Riddell (1865–1934)
Smith, John (1724–1814)
Tait, William (1792–1864)
Thomson, David Couper (1861–1954)
Thomson, George (1757–1851)

Reform
Alison, William Pulteney (1790–1859)
Balfour, Lady Francis (1858–1931)
Balnaves, Henry (?1512–1579)
Bell, Robert Fitzroy (?1858–1908)
Blair, Catherine (1872–1946)
Braidwood, James (1800–61)
Colquhoun, Patrick (1745–1820)
Craig, Isa (1831–1903)
Drummond, Flora (1869–1949)
Erskine, John (1509–91)
Inglis, Elsie Maud (1864–1917)
Kennedy, Helena (1950–)
Knox, John (c.1513–1572)
MacArthur, Mary Reid (1880–1921)
Machabeus, Johannes (d.1557)
Macmillan, Chrystal (1882–1937)
McMillan, Margaret (1860–1931)
Marjoribanks, Ishbel-Maria (1857–1939)
Melville, Andrew (1545–c.1622)
Muir, Thomas (1765–99)
Nicolson, Alexander (1827–93)
Ogg, Derek (1954–)
Owen, Robert (1771–1858)
Owen, Robert Dale (1801–77)
Ross, Ian Anthony (1917–)
Row, John (c.1525–1580)
Smiles, Samuel (1812–1904)
Spottiswood, John (1565–1639)
Steel, Flora Annie (1847–1929)
Stephens, Joseph Rayner (1805–79)
Swinton, John (1829–1901)
Wishart, George (c.1513–1546)
Wright, Frances (1795–1852)

Religion
Aidan, St (d.651)
Alesius, Alexander (1500–65)
Allan, Tom (1916–65)
Baillie, John (1886–1960)
Baillie, Robert (1599–1662)

Baldred, St (?d.608)
Barclay, John (1734–98)
Barclay, Robert (1648–90)
Barclay, William (1907–78)
Beaton, James (1517–1603)
Begg, James (1808–83)
Bellenden, John (d.1587)
Black, James (1879–1949)
Blackadder, John (1615–86)
Blair, Hugh (1718–1800)
Bogue, David (1750–1825)
Bonar, Horatius (1808–89)
Boston, Thomas (1676–1732)
Boyd, Zachary (c.1585–1653)
Brown, John (1722–87)
Bruce, Frederick Fyvie (1910–90)
Bruce, Robert (1554–1631)
Buchanan, Claudius (1766–1815)
Buchan, Elspeth (1738–91)
Burnet, Gilbert (1643–1715)
Caird, John (1820–98)
Cairns, David (1862–1946)
Calderwood, David (1575–1625)
Cameron, Alan Barnard (1927–91)
Cameron, John (c.1579–1625)
Cameron, Richard (1648–80)
Campbell, George (1719–96)
Campbell, John McLeod (1800–72)
Candlish, Robert Smith (1806–73)
Cant, Andrew (c.1590–1663)
Cargill, Donald (c.1619–1681)
Carlyle, Alexander (1722–1805)
Carstares, William (1649–1715)
Caskie, Donald (1902–83)
Chalmers, Thomas (1780–1847)
Charteris, Archibald (1835–1908)
Cleland, William (c.1661–1689)
Columba, St (521–97)
Cormack, John (1894–1978)
Craig, Archie (1888–1985)
Craig, John (1512–1600)
Cunningham, William (1805–61)
Currie, Jimmy (1921–87)
Dalrymple, Jock (1923–85)
Davidson, Randall Thomas (1848–1930)
Denney, James (1856–1917)
Dods, Marcus (1834–1909)
Douglas, Gavin (c.1474–1522)
Douglas, John (1721–1807)
Douglas, Robert (1594–1674)
Dowie, John Alexander (1847–1907)
Drummond, Henry (1851–97)
Duff, Alexander (1806–78)
Duncan, Henry (1774–1846)
Duns Scotus, John (c.1265–1308)
Eadie, John (1810–76)
Elphinstone, William (1431–1514)
Erskine, Ebenezer (1680–1754)

Erskine, John (1509–91)
Erskine, Ralph (1685–1752)
Erskine, Thomas (1788–1870)
Fairbairn, Andrew Martin (1838–1912)
Falconer, Ronnie (1911–)
Forbes, Alexander Penrose (1817–75)
Forbes, Robert (1708–75)
Forsyth, Peter Taylor (1848–1921)
Gairdner, William Henry Temple
    (1873–1928)
Geddes, Alexander (1737–1802)
Gillespie, George (1613–48)
Gillespie, Thomas (1708–74)
Glas, John (1695–1773)
Glass, Jack (c.1937–)
Gordon, George (1562–1636)
Graham, Henry Grey (1874–1959)
Graham, John Anderson (1861–1942)
Gray, Gordon Joseph (1910–)
Gray, John (1866–1934)
Grub, George (1812–92)
Guthrie, Thomas (1803–73)
Haldane, James Alexander (1768–1851)
Haldane, Robert (1764–1842)
Hamilton, Patrick (1503–28)
Hastings, James (1852–1922)
Hay, George (1729–1811)
Henderson, Alexander (c.1583–1646)
Home, Daniel Dunglas (1833–86)
Ireland, John (1440–96)
Irving, Edward (1792–1834)
Kello, John (d.1570)
Kennedy, James (c.1408–1465)
Kentigern, St (c.515–603)
Knox, John (c.1513–1572)
Lang, Cosmo Gordon (1864–1945)
Lang, John Dunmore (1799–1878)
Laws, Robert (1851–1934)
Lee, Robert (1804–68)
Leighton, Robert (1611–84)
Leslie, John (1527–96)
Levison, Mary (1923–)
Liddell, Eric Henry (1902–45)
Livingstone, David (1813–73)
Lorimer, William Laughton (1885–1967)
McDonald, Andrew Thomas Joseph
    (1871–1950)
Macdonald, Murdo Ewan (1914–)
McGregor, James (1832–1910)
Machabeus, Johannes (d.1557)
Mackay, John Alexander (1889–1983)
Mackinnon, Donald Mackenzie (1913–)
Mackintosh, Hugh Ross (1870–1936)
Maclaren, Ian (1850–1907)
McLeod, Donald (1940–91)
MacLeod, Baron George Fielden
    (1895–1991)
Macleod, Norman (1812–72)

Macmillan, John (1670–1753)
Macpherson, Hector Copland (1888–1956)
Macquarrie, John (1919–)
MacRae, David (1837–1907)
Mair, John (1469–1550)
Marshall, Peter (1902–49)
Mathieson, George (1842–1906)
Melville, Andrew (1545–c.1622)
Melville, James (1556–1614)
Moffatt, James (1870–1944)
Moffat, Robert (1795–1883)
Moncreiff, Sir James Wellwood
   (1776–1851)
Morison, James (1816–93)
Morrison, Robert (1782–1834)
Mylne, Walter (d.1558)
Neill, Stephen Charles (1900–84)
Nelson, James Robert (1945–)
Nicoll, Sir William Robertson (1851–1923)
Ninian, St (fl.390)
Ogilvie, St John (1579/80–1615)
Orr, James (1844–1913)
Oswald, James (1703–93)
Paterson, W P (1860–1939)
Paton, John (d.1684)
Paton, John Gibson (1824–1907)
Paton, William (1886–1943)
Peddie, James Cameron (1887–1968)
Peden, Alexander (c.1626–1686)
Pitcairne, Archibald (1652–1713)
Rainy, Robert (1826–1906)
Ramsay, Edward Bannerman Burnett
   (1793–1872)
Read, David Carswell (1910–)
Renwick, James (1662–88)
Robertson, William (1721–93)
Row, John (c.1525–1580)
Row, John (1568–1646)
Rutherford, Samuel (c.1600–1661)
Sampson, Agnes (d.1592)
Scott, Andrew (1772–1846)
Scott, Hew (1791–1872)
Serf, St (?7th century)
Sharp, James (1613–79)
Shaw, Geoffrey Mackintosh (1927–78)
Skinner, John (1721–1807)
Slessor, Mary (1848–1915)
Small, Leonard (1905–)
Smith, Sir George Adam (1856–1942)
Smith, Ronald Gregor (1913–68)
Smith, Sir William Alexander (1854–1914)
Smith, William Robertson (1846–94)
Spottiswood, John (1565–1639)
Stalker, James (1848–1927)
Stewart, James Stuart (1896–1990)
Still, William (1911–)
Tait, Archibald Campbell (1811–82)
Thomson, 'D P' (1896–1974)

Thomson, John (1778–1840)
Torrance, Thomas Forsyth (1913–)
Triduana, St (4th century)
Tulloch, John (1823–86)
Wardlaw, Henry (d.1440)
Welsh, John (c.1568–1622)
White, John (1867–1951)
Whitley, Harry (1906–76)
Wilson, John (1804–75)
Winzet, Ninian (1518–92)
Wishart, George (c.1513–1546)
Witherspoon, John (1723–94)
Wodrow, Robert (1679–1734)
Wright, Ronald Selby (1908–)
Young, Andrew John (1855–1971)
Young, Thomas (1587–1655)

Revolt
Baillie, Robert (c.1634–1684)
Baird, John (1787/8–1820)
Balfour, John (fl.1675)
Hardie, Andrew (1791/2–1820)
Smith, Joseph, 'General' (d.1780)

Royalty and Rulers
Alexander I (c.1077–1124)
Alexander II (1198–1249)
Alexander III (1241–86)
Balliol, Edward de (c.1283–1364)
Balliol, John de (c.1250–1315)
Bruce, Robert (1274–1329)
Darnley, Henry (1545–67)
David I (c.1080–1153)
David II (1324–71)
Drummond, Annabella (c.1350–1402)
Guise, Mary of Lorraine (1515–60)
James I (1394–1437)
James II (1430–60)
James III (1451–88)
James IV (1473–1513)
James V (1512–42)
James VI and I (1566–1625)
James VII and II (1633–1701)
Kenneth I (Macalpin) (9th century)
Lennox, Matthew (1516–71)
Lovat, Simon Fraser (c.1667–1747)
Macbeth (c.1005–1057)
Malcolm I (943–54)
Malcolm II (b.c.954)
Malcolm III (c.1031–1093)
Malcolm IV (1141–65)
Margaret, St (c.1046–1093)
Margaret, 'Maid of Norway' (1283–90)
Margaret Tudor (1489–1541)
Mary, Queen of Scots (1542–87)
Moray, James Stewart (1531–70)
Morton, James Douglas (c.1516–1581)
Robert II (1316–90)

Robert III (c.1340–1406)
Stewart, Alexander (1214–83)
Stewart, James (1243–1309)
Stewart, Murdoch (d.1425)
Stewart, Robert (?1340–1420)
Stewart, Walter (1293–1326)
Stuart, Prince Charles Edward Louis Philip
    Casimir (1720–88)
Stuart, Henry Benedict Maria Clement
    (1725–1807)
Stuart, Prince James Francis Edward
    (1688–1766)
William I (1143–1214)

Sociology
Burns, Tom (1913–)
Cochran, William Gemmell (1909–80)
Geddes, Sir Patrick (1854–1932)
McGregor, Oliver Ross (1921–)
McPherson, Andrew Francis (1942–)
MacRae, Donald (1921–)
Nairn, Tom (1932–)

Sport
Barclay-Allardice, Robert (1779–1854)
Baxter, Jim (1939–)
Braid, James (1870–1950)
Bremner, Billy (1942–)
Brown, Kenneth (1957–)
Buchanan, Ken (1945–)
Busby, Sir Matt (1909–)
Calder, Finlay (1957–)
Carson, Willie (1942–)
Clark, Jim (1936–68)
Crampsey, Bob (1930–)
Dalglish, Kenny (1951–)
Denness, Michael (1940–)
Docherty, Tommy (1928–)
Drysdale, Dan (1901–86)
Gallacher, Bernard (1949–)
Greig, John (1942–)
Harkness, Jack (1907–85)
Hastings, Gavin (1962–)
Haston, Dougal (1940–77)
Hendry, Stephen (1969–)
Irvine, Andy (1951–)
James, Alex (1901–53)
Jeffrey, John (1959–)
Johnston, Maurice (1963–)
Johnstone, Jimmy (1944–)
Keenan, Peter (1929–)
Kelly, Sir Robert (1902–71)
Laidlaw, Roy (1953–)
Law, Denis (1940–)
Liddell, Eric Henry (1902–45)
Lipton, Sir Thomas Johnstone (1850–1931)
Lyle, Sandy (1958–)
Lynch, Benny (1913–46)

McCoist, Ally (1962–)
McColgan, Liz (1964–)
McColl, Robert Smyth (1876–1959)
McGeechan, Ian (1946–)
McGowan, Walter (1942–)
McIlvanney, Hugh (1933–)
MacInnes, Hamish (1930–)
McKean, Tom (1963–)
McLaren, Bill (1923–)
McLauchlan, Ian (1942–)
MacLeod, Ally (1931–)
McNeill, Billy (1940–)
McPherson, Archie (1935–)
McStay, Paul Michael Lyons (1964–)
Millar, Robert (1959–)
Morris, Thomas ('Old Tom') (1821–1908)
Morris, Thomas ('Young Tom') (1851–75)
Morton, Alan Lauder (1893–1971)
Munro, Sir Hugh Thomas (1856–1919)
Murray, Yvonne (1964–)
Queensberry, Sir John Sholto Douglas
    (1844–1900)
Ross, Horatio (1801–86)
Rutherford, John (1955–)
Scotland, Ken (1936–)
Shankly, Bill (1913–81)
Sole, David Michael Barclay (1962–)
Souness, Graeme James (1953–)
Stein, Jock (1922–85)
Stewart, Jackie (1939–)
Struth, William (1875–1956)
Torrance, Sam (1953–)
Waddell, Willie (1921–)
Walker, Ernie (1928–)
Walker, Tommy (1915–)
Watt, Jim (1948–)
Weir, Tom (1914–)
Wells, Allan (1952–)
Whyte-Melville, George John (1821–78)
Wilson, Jocky (1951–)
Wood, Willie (1938–)
Young, George (1922–)

Theatre
Anderson, John Henry (1814–74)
Bannen, Ian (1928–)
Baxter, Stanley (1926–)
Beattie, Johnny (1926–)
Brown, Janet (1924–)
Bryden, Bill (1942–)
Carr, Walter (1925–)
Charleson, Ian (1949–90)
Coltrane, Robbie (1950–)
Conti, Tom (1941–)
Cox, Brian (1946–)
Cruickshank, Andrew John Maxton
    (1907–88)
Currie, Finlay (1878–1968)

Cuthbertson, Iain (1930–)
Dallmeyer, Andrew (1945–)
Fleming, Tom (1927–)
Fulton, Rikki (1924–)
Gordon, Hannah Cambell Grant (1941–)
Grieve, John (1924–)
Havergal, Giles (1938–)
Hayman, David (1948–)
Houston, Renée (1902–80)
Hunter, Russell (1925–)
Jackson, Gordon Cameron (1923–90)
Kemp, Lindsay (1939–)
Kerr, Deborah (1921–)
Lauder, Sir Harry (1870–1950)
Laurie, John (1897–1980)
Lawson, Denis (1947–)
Lipton, Celia (1923–)
Lochhead, Liz (1947–)
Logan, Jimmy (1928–)
MacDonald, Robert David (1929–)
MacDonald, Sharman (1951–)
MacDonald, Stephen (1935–)
McGrath, John Peter (1935–)
McGrath, Tom (1940–)
McGuire, Leonard (1924–)
Mackay, Fulton (1922–87)
McLean, Una (1930–)
McManus, Mark (1940–)
McMillan, Roddy (1923–79)
Macrae, Duncan (1905–67)
Murray, Chic (1919–85)
Paterson, Bill (1945–)
Prowse, Philip (1937–)
Richardson, Ian William (1934–)
Robertson-Justice, James Norval Harald
    (1905–75)
Sim, Alastair (1900–76)
Simpson, Bill (1931–86)
Stafford-Clark, Max (1941–)
Watson, Tom (1932–)
Weir, Molly (1920–)

Travel and Exploration
Baikie, William Balfour (1825–64)
Bell, John (1691–1780)
Bruce, James (1730–94)
Bruce, William Spiers (1867–1921)
Burnes, Sir Alexander (1805–41)
Clapperton, Hugh (1788–1827)
Gardner, George (1812–49)

Gordon Cumming, Eka (1837–1924)
Grant, James Augustus (1827–92)
Haston, Dougal (1940–77)
Howison, John (d.1859)
Hutchison, Isobel Wylie (1889–1982)
Kirk, Sir John (1832–1932)
Laing, Alexander Gordon (1793–1826)
Laird, Macgregor (1808–61)
Livingstone, David (1813–73)
MacInnes, Hamish (1930–)
Mackenzie, Sir Alexander (1764–1820)
Martin, Martin (d.1719)
Mitchell, Sir Thomas Livingstone
    (1792–1855)
Moir, John William (b.1851)
Nares, Sir George Strong (1831–1915)
Oudney, Walter (1790–1824)
Park, Mungo (1771–1806)
Paterson, William (1755–1810)
Rae, John (1813–93)
Richardson, Sir John (1787–1865)
Ross, Sir James Clark (1800–62)
Ross, Sir John (1777–1856)
Simpson, Sir George (1792–1860)
Simpson, Myrtle Lillias (1931–)
Stuart, John McDouall (1815–66)
Thomson, Sir Charles Wyville (1830–82)
Thomson, Joseph (1858–95)

Zoology
Balfour, Francis Maitland (1851–82)
Blaxter, Sir Kenneth (1919–91)
Calman, William Thomas (1871–1952)
Crew, Francis Albert Crew (1886–1973)
Ewart, James Cossar (1851–1933)
Gray, Robert (1825–87)
Jarrett, William Fleming Hoggan (1928–)
Kerr, Sir John Graham (1869–1957)
Mitchell, Sir Peter Chalmers (1864–1945)
Murray, Sir John (1841–1914)
Richardson, Sir John (1787–1865)
Robertson, Alan (1920–89)
Robertson, Sir Alexander (1908–90)
Sibbald, Sir Robert (1641–1722)
Thompson, Sir D'Arcy Wentworth
    (1860–1948)
Thorburn, Archibald (1860–1935)
Weipers, Sir William (1904–90)
Wilson, Alexander (1766–1813)
Yonge, Sir Maurice (1899–1986)

PREFACE

Described by Byron as 'a land of meanness, sophistry and mist', Scotland and its people have received a mixed and often clichéd press beyond – and even within – the border. Myth abounds about the uncanny Scots precocity of intellect and will-power, the deeply engrained image of the lad o' pairts colouring much of our memory of the past. Accounts of Scottish intransigence and ferocity are equally commonplace, excused in some eyes by what is seen as our rough deal at the hands of the 'auld enemy' (England), tolerated by others as the inevitable outcome of the natural savagery of our landscape and lifestyle.

One of the primary aims behind the compilation of a Scottish biographical dictionary is to lay out the facts of Scotland's heritage without sentiment or bias. If Emerson's dictum that 'there is properly no history, only biography' is accepted as true, then a pressing weight of responsibility is thrown not only onto the shoulders of those who attempt to encapsulate the lives of others, but equally on those who select which biographies should be put forward as representative of a nation's experience.

The aspiration of this dictionary has been to present a wide coverage of the most significant names from the annals of Scottish endeavour. Our aim has been twofold. First, to create a compendium of personal histories which, when viewed collectively, will reflect the changing situation and character of Scotland as it has evolved through each period. More importantly, however, each biography has been chosen according to its individual merits and is expected to stand alone rather than be viewed simply as part of the general weave.

Attempting to gather together without prejudice the great, good, bad and unusual of any country is a daunting undertaking. In the case of Scotland it is complicated by what appears to have been a conspiracy of professional snobbery. The fortresses of traditional Scottish excellence – law, religion, literature, education, medicine – are well documented, and names from these areas are scattered throughout reference books, from the *Dictionary of National Biography* to specialist works devoted to any one of these disciplines. Consequently there is no problem discovering the details of a relatively obscure 18th-century Church of Scotland cleric graced with a penchant for free verse, or the exact career moves, from preparatory school to Lincoln's Inn, of a run-of-the-mill High Court judge. More difficult to unearth, though, are the bare bones of lives spent in less prominent realms. Particularly if the achievers were women. The astronomer Williamina Fleming, for example, remains virtually unknown in scientific circles, despite the possibility that it was she and not Edward Pickering who discovered Beta Lyrae. David Buick, manufacturer of the legendary American car, has earned himself little recognition on his native side of the Atlantic, and closer to home, while the by-products of many a distiller linger on the lips, the details of the lives beyond the bottle are frequently less accessible than a cask of imported Japanese blend.

Despite the problems raised by poor sources and lack of information, we have attempted to give an even-handed spread of individuals from each subject area. Starting from the premise that the qualification for inclusion in this work ought not to be restricted only to those born in Scotland whose achievements have been made largely within the country, we have encompassed those non-Scots who have contributed markedly in some way to their field within Scotland, and those who, though born in Scotland, have moved away and made their name elsewhere. Hence, for example, the inclusion of Alexander Henderson who, after emigrating to Canada in 1855, earned a reputation as one of its most prestigious amateur photographers, or of T C Smout, an English-born historian who has greatly advanced the understanding of Scottish social history.

While some names have been included predominantly because they have become part of the national landscape, others, though almost unheard of, have been deemed essential as keystones in their area of expertise. Particular attention has been paid to the twentieth century, resulting in colourful juxtapositions indicating the complexity and variety of Scottish talent that have combined to create a society which, more than many, remains thirled to its past.

Although we have striven to avoid serious omissions, we accept that there will be some names looked for that have either slipped through the net, or who have, perhaps unwisely, been rejected. We would be grateful to have these brought to our attention.

Rosemary Goring

A

ABBOTT, Jack (John) Sutherland
(1900–79)

English-born shoe manufacturer, born in Northampton. For 40 years he was intimately associated with the Kilmarnock-based company of Saxone, which had been founded by his father. After education at Ayr Academy, Bedales School in Sussex and Cambridge University, he joined Saxone in 1920. Two years in the USA taught him marketing and promotional styles which he then put to good use in pushing Saxone to the fore through a series of stylish retail outlets in the post-1945 period. His hugely creative approach enabled the selling of both high fashion and traditional shoes to meet the burgeoning demand of the 1950s. He launched the famous Hush Puppie in 1962, before being taken over by Charles Clore's holding company.

ABERCROMBY, Sir Ralph
(1734–1801)

Soldier, and hero of the Napoleonic wars. Born in Menstrie, Clackmannanshire, he went to Rugby and studied law at Edinburgh and Leipzig. He joined the 3rd Dragoons in 1756 and served in Europe in the Seven Years' War (1756–63). He was MP for Clackmannanshire from 1774 to 1780. Rejoining the army in 1793 he distinguished himself as a major-general in Flanders under Frederick, Duke of York, and led successful operations against the French in St Lucia and Trinidad (1795–6). He held commands in Ireland and Scotland (1797–9), and in 1800 he was in command in the Mediterranean to deal with the French army left by Napoleon in Egypt; he led the successful amphibious operation of the Anglo-Turkish forces against the French at Aboukir Bay in 1801, but was mortally wounded in the action.

ABERDEEN, George Gordon, 1st Earl of
(1637–1720)

Lawyer and statesman. He was appointed a lord of session in 1680, and advanced to be Lord President in 1681, Lord Chancellor of Scotland in 1682–4, and was created earl in 1682. He was a strong supporter of the Act of Union with England in 1707.

ABERDEEN, George Hamilton Gordon, 4th Earl of
(1784–1860)

Statesman, and Prime Minister of Britain 1852–5, born in Edinburgh. Educated at Harrow, he became Lord Haddo at the age of seven when his father died; his joint guardians were William Pitt the Younger and **Henry Dundas**, 1st Viscount Melville. He succeeded his grandfather as earl in 1801, was elected a Scottish representative peer in 1806, and in 1813 was sent as special ambassador to Vienna to negotiate the Treaty of Töplitz that created the alliance of Great Powers against Napoleon. He was Foreign Secretary twice, under the Duke of Wellington (1828–30) and then under Sir Robert Peel (1841–6), during which time he saw to the conclusion of the Chinese War, established an *entente cordiale* with France, and cemented relations with the USA. A confirmed free-trader, he resigned with Peel over the repeal of the corn-laws in 1846. In 1852, on the resignation of Lord Derby, he was made Prime Minister of a coalition government that was immensely popular at first, until he reluctantly committed Britain to an alliance with France and Turkey in the Crimean War in 1854. The gross mismanagement of the war aroused popular discontent, and he was forced to resign in February 1855.

ABERDEEN, James Campbell Hamilton Gordon, 7th Earl of, and 1st Marquis
(1847–1934)

Statesman and Laird of Haddo House in Aberdeenshire for 64 years. He was appointed Viceroy of Ireland twice (1886 and 1905–15), Governor of Canada (1893–8), and was made a marquis in 1915. In 1877 he married the

1

dynamic **Ishbel-Maria Marjoribanks**, with whom he turned Haddo House into a model estate for the local community.

ADAIR, John
(c.1655 – ?1722)

Surveyor and cartographer, who did notable work in mapping Scotland and its coast and islands. Little is known of him until 1683 when he was commissioned 'to survey the shires'. He prepared maps of counties in the central belt of Scotland (1680–6), and in 1703 published *Description of the Sea-Coast and Islands of Scotland* (Part 1). He was elected FRS in 1688, and his work was paid for (inadequately) by a tonnage act of 1686. His maps and charts set new standards of quality and accuracy.

ADAM, Alexander
(1741–1809)

Teacher and writer, born near Forres, Aberdeenshire. The son of a small farmer, he went to Edinburgh University in 1757. In 1761 he obtained the headmastership of Watson's Hospital, and in 1768 the rectorship of the High School. He was the author of a textbook, *Latin Grammar* (1762), and a popular compendium of *Roman Antiquities* (1791).

ADAM, James
(1730–94)

Architect, brother and partner of **Robert Adam** and son of **William Adam** of Maryburgh (1689–1748), also an architect of renown. He studied in Rome and joined the family partnership in 1763. In 1769 he succeeded his brother as architect of the king's works, notably the Glasgow Royal Infirmary (1792). His fame lies under the shadow of his elder brother, though their names are linked inextricably in their work and cemented by their publication of *The Works in Architecture of Robert and James Adam* (3 vols: 1773, 1779, 1822).

ADAM, Robert
(1728–92)

Architect, born in Kirkcaldy, the son of **William Adam** and brother and partner of **James Adam**. He studied at Edinburgh and in Italy (1754–8). From 1761 to 1769 he was architect of the king's works, jointly with Sir **William Chambers**. He established a practice in London in 1758 and during the following decades he and his brother James succeeded in transforming the prevailing fashion in architecture by a series of romantically elegant variations on diverse classical originals. Their style of interior decoration was based on ancient Greek and Roman styles, characterized by the use of the oval and lines of decoration in hard plaster, enlivened by painted panels in low relief. One of their greatest projects was the Adelphi (1768–72, demolished 1936), off the Strand in London, a residential block built as a speculative venture, which brought the brothers' finances to a low ebb, and was eventually disposed of by a lottery. Good surviving examples of their work are Home House in Portland Square, London, Lansdowne House (1765), Derby House (1773–4, demolished), Charlotte Square (1791), Register House (1774) and the 'Old Quad' of the university (1789), all in Edinburgh, and Culzean Castle, Ayrshire (1777–90).

ADAM, Stephen
(1848–1910)

Stained-glass artist, born in Bonnington, near Edinburgh. Educated at Cannonmills School and apprenticed to the Edinburgh firm of Ballantine and Allan, he completed his training in 1866. In 1865 he won a silver medal whilst a part-time student at the Haldane Academy, for the best design for a stained-glass window. In 1870 he moved to Glasgow and set up his own studio at 168 Bath Street, in partnership with David Small. Over the next 40 years he received ecclesiastic and domestic commissions for work all over the west of Scotland, and developed a distinctly personal, modern style, influenced by **Daniel Cottier** and Burne Jones, and fiercely rejecting the current trend of imitating designs from earlier periods. His designs incorporated new types of glass and combined simplicity of composition with unusual mixtures of colour, a style which gained him a distinguished reputation. In 1877 he outlined his approach to stained-glass design in a pamphlet entitled *Stained Glass — its History and Development*; a further pamphlet, *The Truth in Decorative Art — Stained Glass Medieval and Modern*, was published in 1896. Fine examples of his work can be seen in Paisley Abbey and at New Kilpatrick Church, Bearsden, in Glasgow, where a superb four-light window depicts episodes from the life of

Christ. Other examples of domestic work, for example panels illustrating Glasgow trades and professions, can be seen in the People's Palace, Glasgow.

ADAM, William
(1689–1748)

Architect and entrepreneur, father of **Robert** and **James Adam**, and 'Elder Adam'. Born near Kirkcaldy, the son of a builder-architect, he inherited a legacy of classicism from Sir **William Bruce** and of Palladianism from **James Smith** (c.1645–1731), and he developed a Baroque style after Sir John Vanbrugh (1664–1726) and **James Gibbs**, which he disseminated through his large practice. He was popular and well-connected, patronized by a leading enlightenment figure, Sir **John Clerk**, for whom he built Mavisbank (1723). His entrepreneurial spirit saw the launch of a wide range of industrial projects, ranging from brickworks and salt pans to barley mills and marble works. In 1727 he began to collect engravings of contemporary architectural masterpieces for publication, resulting in the posthumous *Vitruvius Scoticus* (1812). He landscaped several gardens, for example at Newliston in West Lothian (1725). His practice was continued by his sons, John, Robert and James. Other major works include Arniston and The Drum (both 1726), House of Dun (1730), Chatelherault (1731), Duff House (1735) and additions to Hopetoun House (1721–46).

ADAMS, Sir John
(1857–1934)

Educationist, born in Glasgow, an outstanding figure in the field of educational theory and psychology. Educated at Glasgow University, he also studied under Tuiskon Ziller in Leipzig, and became a follower of the educational philosopher J F Herbart. Successively Rector of the Free Church Training Colleges in Aberdeen (1890) and then Glasgow (1898), he was concurrently lecturer in education at Glasgow from 1899. He was Principal of London Day Training College and Professor of Education at London University from 1902 to 1922. He was knighted in 1925. His numerous works include *The Herbartian Psychology Applied to Education* (1897), a lively work which brought him recognition, *Modern Developments in Educational Practice* (1922), and *Everyman's Psychology* (1929), all his books distinguished by

his wisdom and wit. His favourite slogan was that verbs of teaching take two accusatives, ie if a teacher wishes to teach John Latin successfully, he must have knowledge of pupil as well as subject matter. A young teacher, he held, should be both pupil and teacher, and the course of his or her career should be a gradual passage from one pole to the other. An inspirational lecturer, he had a huge influence on the development of teacher training.

ADAMSON, John
(1809–70)

Doctor and photographic pioneer, born in St Andrews. He was the eldest son of a farmer, and elder brother of the ultimately more famous **Robert Adamson**, who was **David Octavius Hill**'s partner during the 1840s. Trained in Edinburgh and Paris as a doctor, he was one of the first to take calotypes in Scotland, including the first portrait in 1842. He was a disciple of Sir **David Brewster**, who learned of William Talbot's process before its publication through his correspondence with the inventor. Brewster encouraged a group of St Andrews friends to follow Talbot's postal instructions, with some success. John Adamson taught his younger brother the new art, but became embroiled in local medical duties, although he continued to practise photography until the end of his life.

ADAMSON, Robert
(1821–48)

Pioneer of photography, born in St Andrews, the younger brother of Dr **John Adamson**. He apparently began to train as an engineer, but poor health forced him to give this up. In the summer of 1842 he returned to St Andrews, where Sir **David Brewster** had already begun encouraging a circle of friends to follow William Talbot's instructions for positive/negative photography. Taught the new art by his elder brother, he then left for Edinburgh in May 1843, where he set up a studio on Calton Hill. The Disruption of the Church of Scotland that month inspired the artist **David Octavius Hill**, who worried that the participants would soon be dispersed. Brewster introduced Hill to the calotype, and to Adamson, and thus began one of the great photographic partnerships. Their short period of collaboration resulted in over 3000 calotype images of quite remarkable quality.

ADAMSON, Robert
(1852–1902)

Philosopher, born in Edinburgh. One of six children and fatherless from a young age, he began at Edinburgh University at the age of 14. After work as teaching assistant, he became philosophy editor of *Encyclopaedia Britannica* in 1874, then, in 1876, Professor of Owen's College, later the University of Manchester. His *Philosophy of Kant* (1879), contrasting current German thought with that of Kant, was immediately translated into German. Other than a short book on Fichte he wrote only essays thereafter, and scarcely anything at all after 1893, the year he became Professor of Logic at Aberdeen. He filled the same post at Glasgow from 1896 till his sudden death. His mature views are known from student lecture-notes collated by his friend **W R Sorley**, and had widespread influence on subsequent Realist philosophy.

ADAMSON, Stuart
(1958 –)

Rock singer and guitarist, born in Dunfermline. He had his first success with the punk group The Skids, who recorded three albums between 1978 and 1980. Their hit singles included 'Into The Valley' and 'Working For The Yankee Dollar'. After they disbanded Adamson teamed up with guitarist Bruce Watson (1961 –) and bassist and drummer Tony Butler and Mark Brzezicki, to form Big Country. Adamson's distinctive guitar style was central to the success of the group, who had their first major hit single with 'Fields Of Fire' in 1983. Their début album, *The Crossing* (1983), helped to establish the band in the USA. Subsequent albums have included *Steeltown* (1984), *The Seer* (1986) and *No Place Like Home* (1991).

ADAMSON, William
(1863–1936)

Labour politician. Born in Halbeath, by Dunfermline, he left school at the age of 11 to work in coal mining. In 1908 he became leader of the Fife miners' union, and in 1910 he was elected MP for Fife West, the first miner to win a Scottish seat for Labour. Leader of the Labour Party in the House of Commons from 1917 to 1921, he became the first Labour Scottish Secretary in 1924 and was reappointed to the Scottish Office from 1929 to 1931. He lost his seat in 1931 and was

defeated again in 1935 by **Willie Gallacher**. A Baptist and a teetotaller, he had a dour and uncharismatic presence.

AIDAN, St
(d.651)

Celtic monk, known as the 'Apostle of Northumbria'. From the monastery on the island of Iona, he was summoned in 635 by King Oswald of Northumbria to evangelize the north. He established a church and monastery on the island of Lindisfarne, of which he was appointed the first bishop, and from there he travelled throughout Northumbria founding churches. He died in the church he had built at Bamburgh.

AIKMAN, William
(1682–1731)

Painter, born in Forfar, Angus. After graduating from Edinburgh University in 1701, he chose a career as a painter rather than that of a merchant, making him one of the first Scottish painters to emerge from a non-artisan background. He was painting portraits in Edinburgh professionally by 1703 but, in the following year, moved to London. In 1707 he travelled to Italy, where he probably studied with the portraitist Carlo Maratta. In 1709–10 he continued his travels as far as Constantinople and Smyrna. On his return to Edinburgh in 1711 he became the city's major portrait painter though, probably due to lack of patronage, he again moved to London where, in 1722, he took up permanent residence and where, apart from a visit to Edinburgh in 1730, he remained until his death. In a period more usually characterized by baroque flamboyance, Aikman's portraits are important for their more restrained and balanced design and their direct observation.

AINSLIE, John
(1745–1828)

Surveyor, born in Jedburgh. He started as a surveyor/engraver under Thomas Jeffreys, geographer to King George III, working on English County surveys. Most of his own cartographic work was done in Scotland, producing maps of Scottish counties and estate plans. He also produced important corrected maps of Scotland in 1782 and 1789, for which he carried out extensive new surveys. He has been referred to as the outstanding surveyor of his time, both for the quality and the quantity of his work. His later publications include the text *Comprehensive Treatise on Land Surveying Comprising the Theory and Practice of all its Branches* (1812).

AITKEN, Alexander Craig
(1895–1967)

New Zealand-born mathematician, born in Dunedin of Scottish descent. His studies at Otago University were interrupted by World War I, in which he was severely wounded, and he was sent home in 1917. In 1923 he went to Edinburgh to work under Professor **Edmund Whittaker**, and spent the rest of his life there, succeeding Whittaker as professor in 1946, and retiring in 1965. His main work was in mathematical statistics, numerical analysis and matrix algebra. He had remarkable powers of mental computation, and was an accomplished violinist. His account of his wartime experiences was published towards the end of his life as *Gallipoli to the Somme* (1963), which won the Hawthornden Prize.

AITKEN, John
(1839–1919)

Physicist, born in Falkirk, Stirlingshire. He is known for his researches on atmospheric dust, dew, cyclones, evaporation, etc, his more notable works being *Dust, Fogs and Clouds* (1881) and a paper entitled *Condensation*, both highly useful to meteorologists. His *Collected Scientific Papers* were edited posthumously in 1923.

ALBANIE, Count d'

The title assumed successively by two brothers, 'John Sobieski Stolberg Stuart' (1795–1872) and 'Charles Stolberg Stuart' (1799–1880), the sons of a Royal Navy lieutenant, Thomas Allen, who claimed to be the son of Prince **Charles Edward Stuart**. Handsome and plausible, they were lionized by Edinburgh society, and produced a Latin history of clan tartans called *Vestiarum Scoticum*, whose manuscript they claimed to have discovered in a monastery in Cadiz.

ALBANY, Duke of

The title conferred in 1398 upon Robert (?1340–1420), brother of **Robert III** of Scot-

land, who was succeeded by his son Murdoch (d.1425). Queen Victoria made her youngest son Leopold (1853–84) Duke of Albany in 1881. His son Leopold (1884–1918), Duke of Saxe-Coburg (1905–18), forfeited his British titles in 1917.

ALBANY, Alexander, Duke of
(1454–85)

Second son of **James II**. Created Duke of Albany in his infancy, in 1464 he was sent to France to complete his education, was captured on the way by the English, but released shortly afterwards. Since he and his brother John, Earl of Mar, were hated by their brother **James III**, they were imprisoned in Edinburgh Castle in 1479. Mar died there, but Albany escaped on board a French ship at Newhaven. In his absence his estates were forfeited. In 1482 Albany left France for England where he entered into an alliance with Edward IV to attack Scotland, ceding Berwick and part of the Borders to Edward in return for the Scottish crown. He joined the English invasion of Scotland but was restored to favour by his brother the king, whom he rescued from the power of his uncles, the Earls of Buchan and Atholl. In December 1482, Albany was appointed Lieutenant General of the Realm by Parliament, and received a grant of the earldoms of Mar and Garioch. He resumed his treasonable alliance with the English, however, surrendering his castle of Dunbar to them and retiring south of the border. Attainted by Parliament, in 1484 he invaded Scotland with the Earl of Douglas and an English force, but was defeated at Lochmaben and narrowly escaped to France, where he was killed at a tournament in Paris the following year.

ALBANY, John, 2nd Duke of
(1481–1536)

Son of Alexander, Duke of **Albany**. Invited to become regent during the minority of **James V**, he landed from France, his mother's country, at Dumbarton in 1515, where he was received with great pomp and was even crowned. He was also declared the sole legitimate son of his father (his elder brother by a previous marriage consenting to this). His regency was weak and lasted for eight years, during which he did not reside permanently in Scotland. Between June 1517 and September 1523 he lived in France, except for part of 1521. In 1524 he left Scotland and returned finally to France. The following year he accompanied Francis I of France on his expedition into Italy and in 1533 he escorted his niece Catherine de' Medici to France to marry Henri II. He was appointed Governor of Bourbonnais, Auvergne, Forez and Beaujolais.

ALESIUS, Alexander
(1500–65)

Lutheran reformer, born in Edinburgh. Educated at St Andrews, he became a canon there. Won over to the Reformation by **Patrick Hamilton**, he had to flee to the Continent (1532) and, settling at Wittenberg, signed the Augsburg Confession, and gained the friendship of Melanchthon. In 1535 he came over to England, was well received by Cranmer and Cromwell, and lectured for a time on theology at Cambridge; but the persecuting 'Six Articles' forced him to return to Germany. He was successively appointed Professor of Theology at the universities of Frankfurt-on-the-Oder and Leipzig.

ALEXANDER I
(c.1077–1124)

King of Scotland, the fifth son of **Malcolm Canmore** and Queen **Margaret**. In 1107 he succeeded his brother, Edgar, but only to that part of the kingdom north of the Forth (see **David I**). He married Sibilla, a natural daughter of Henry I of England, and initiated a shift towards a more diocesan-based episcopacy.

ALEXANDER II
(1198–1249)

King of Scotland, born in Haddington, East Lothian, succeeded as the only son of his father, **William I**, in 1214. By 1215 he had begun to show a much more independent stance toward England than his father; he allied with the disaffected English barons and made an incursion as far south as Dover. This brought temporary papal excommunication which was lifted in 1218. The accession of Henry III of England allowed a rapprochement, cemented by his marriage to Henry's sister, the princess Joan (1221), which brought about the settlement of the frontier question in 1237 by the Treaty of York. Relations with England were strained by Joan's death, without children, in 1238, and Alexander's marriage to the daughter of a Picardy nobleman, Marie de Coucy, who gave birth to a son, **Alexander**, in 1241. His reign is notable for the vigorous assertion of royal authority in the western Highlands and the south-west during the years of peace with England. His death, at Kerrara near Oban, came during an expedition attempting to extend his rule, at the expense of Norway, to the Western Isles.

ALEXANDER III
(1241–86)

King of Scotland, in 1249 succeeded his father, **Alexander II**, and in 1251 married the princess Margaret (1240–75), eldest daughter of **Henry III** of England. He completed the consolidation of the western part of the kingdom by annexing the Hebrides and the Isle of Man after his defeat of King Haakon IV of Norway at Largs in 1263 and the Treaty of Perth (1266). The emerging status of Scotland as a European kingdom of middling rank was confirmed by the pattern of royal marriages of Alexander and his children: his only daughter, Margaret (1261–83) married King Eric of Norway in 1281, further cementing the relationship begun in 1266; and his son, Alexander (1264–84), married Marguerite, daughter of the Count of Flanders, in 1282. The period between 1266 and the death of Queen Margaret in 1275 has often been seen as a golden age for Scotland: factional politics had almost disappeared, the kingdom had been consolidated, the king's authority was unquestioned, and there was a considerable, favourable balance of trade. The death of his only surviving son, without issue, in 1284 and of his daughter the previous year left only his infant daughter, **Margaret, 'Maid of Norway'**, as a successor and prompted Alexander's second marriage, to Yolande, daughter of the Count of Dreux, in 1285. While on his way to a reunion with her he died as he rode in the dark along the cliffs between Burntisland and Kinghorn. His death left the way open for a disputed succession and the renewed interference of England in Scottish affairs.

ALEXANDER, Sir Kenneth John Wilson
(1922 –)

Economist and educationist, born in Edinburgh. He was educated at George Heriot's

School, Edinburgh, and the School of Economics, Dundee. After holding university posts in Leeds, Sheffield and Aberdeen he became Professor of Economics at Strathclyde University (1963–80). His publications include *The Economist in Business* (1967) and *The Political Economy of Change* (1975). From 1981 to 1986 he was Principal and Vice-Chancellor of Stirling University, and since 1986 he has been Chancellor of Aberdeen University. His many public services include chairmanship of the Highlands and Islands Development Board (1976–80). He has been a governor of Newbattle Abbey College, and he chaired the committee on adult education which produced what is always referred to as 'the Alexander Report' (1975).

ALEXANDER, William

(1826–94)

Novelist, born in Chapel of Garioch, Aberdeenshire. He worked as a ploughman until losing a leg in an accident, after which he turned to journalism. He wrote a novel in racy dialect, *Johnny Gibb of Gushetneuk* (1871), a series of realistic sketches of the remote country folk and places of north-eastern Scotland, which was serialized in the *Aberdeen Free Press*, of which he later became editor.

ALISON, Sir Archibald

(1792–1867)

Historian and lawyer, born in Kenley, Shropshire, the son of a Scottish minister, and grandson of **John Gregory**. In 1800 his family moved to Edinburgh, where, on his father's advice, he studied law at the university. He was called to the Bar in 1814, quickly achieving success. A mildly liberal Tory, he travelled widely throughout Europe, and was appointed Advocate-Depute in 1822. He left office with the fall of the Wellington ministry in 1830, and refused the solicitor-generalship in 1834, although later he became Sheriff of Lanarkshire, living at Possil House near Glasgow. In 1832 he published *Principles of the Criminal Law of Scotland*, followed by its *Practice* (1833). A vigorous and controversial writer in *Blackwood's Magazine*, he wrote a *History of Europe during the French Revolution* in 10 volumes (1833–42), and its continuation to the accession of Louis Napoleon as Napoleon III in nine volumes (1852–9). He also published biographies of political figures and an autobiography. His history of Europe and himself were highly popular, less for their Tory principles than for

their charm and generosity of nature. He was elected Lord Rector of Marischal College, Aberdeen (1845) and of Glasgow (1851), and was created a baronet in 1852.

ALISON, William Pulteney

(1790–1859)

Physician and health reformer, born in Edinburgh, brother of **Archibald Alison**. A brilliant student of **Dugald Stewart** at Edinburgh University, he went on to study medicine and became physician to the New Town Dispensary in 1815. Here he came into close contact with the poorer classes, thus stimulating a life-long concern for their welfare. Interested in the cause of fevers and epidemics, he did much research into these areas, concentrating particularly on the problem of smallpox. Professor of Medical Jurisprudence at Edinburgh from 1820 to 1822, he went on to become Professor of 'Institutes Medicine', holding this post for two decades, and from this position impressing the medical fraternity with his theories on physiology and pathology. In 1840 he produced a report on the appalling living conditions in Scottish cities, a situation which he believed contributed directly to increased incidence of disease. Entitled 'Observations on the Management of the Poor in Scotland, and its Effects on the Health of the Great Towns', this report, which criticized the existing system of poor relief in the country, led to a Royal Commission of Inquiry (1844) and subsequently to an act (1845) which contained many of Alison's ideas. In 1842 he became Professor of the Practice of Medicine, but in 1856 he retired as a result of epilepsy. His work in improving public standards of health has been claimed as the forerunner of the National Health Service.

ALLAN, David

(1744–96)

Genre and portrait painter, known as the 'Scottish Hogarth', and forerunner of Sir **David Wilkie**. Born in Alloa, Clackmannanshire, he studied in Glasgow and in Rome, where he trained under **Gavin Hamilton** and won the gold medal. He went to London for a time (1777–80) to paint portraits, then moved to Edinburgh as a master at The Edinburgh Academy of Arts, of which he became Director in 1786. He illustrated **Allan Ramsay**'s *Gentle Shepherd* (1725) and some of **Robert Burns**'s poems. His better-known works include *Highland Dance* and *Repentance Stool*.

ALLAN, Sir Hugh
(1810–82)

Scottish-born Canadian shipowner, born in Saltcoats in Ayrshire. He settled in 1826 in Canada, where his firm became eminent as shipbuilders, and founded the Allan Line of steamers.

ALLAN, Tom
(1916–65)

Church of Scotland minister and evangelist, a significant leader in the Tell Scotland Movement. Educated at Glasgow University (1934–46), his studies were interrupted by war service in the RAF (1940–5). Ordained in 1946 to North Kelvinside, Glasgow, he found his ministry exposing the glaring inadequacies of the Church's outreach to the people of Scotland, and the hunger among many for a direct invitation to faith. His book describing his time in his first parish, *The Face of my Parish* (1954), is a classic for any student of parish ministry. Appointed Evangelist to the Home Board of the Church of Scotland in 1953, he pushed his evangelistic vision in co-operation with **D P Thomson** and others of an open-minded but aggressively evangelical persuasion, the result of which was the drive and effectiveness of the Tell Scotland Movement.

ALLAN, Sir William
(1782–1850)

Historical painter, born in Edinburgh. He was a fellow-pupil with Sir **David Wilkie** at the Trustees' Academy, and then studied at the Royal Academy schools in London. In 1805 he went to St Petersburg, and spent several years in Russia and Turkey, painting scenes of Russian life. In 1835 he was elected RA, in 1835 President of the Royal Scottish Academy. In 1841 he succeeded Wilkie as Queen's Limner (painter) in Scotland. His Scottish historical paintings include scenes from the novels of Sir **Walter Scott**.

ALLEN, Betty
(1936–)

Chef and restaurateur, born in Bathgate, West Lothian. Like many other successful Scottish chefs of her generation, she is self-taught. She developed her professional skills in her first hotel in Largo (1973–8), which she ran with her husband Eric, and in 1978 moved to Port Appin, Argyll, opening the Airds Hotel. There, with her son and fellow-chef Graeme (1966–), whom she taught, and her husband, she has won wide acclaim, her success being based on an imaginative but simple presentation of excellent local produce. National recognition by food writers and restaurant guides was followed by international appreciation. In 1990 she and **Hilary Brown** became the first women in Scotland to receive a Michelin star.

ALLEN, John Frank
(1908–)

British physicist. He attended school in Winnipeg and is a graduate of the University of Manitoba and of Toronto University. After some years with the National Research Council of Canada he went to Cambridge (1935), where he engaged in research on low-temperature physics, particularly liquid helium. He was appointed to a lectureship in Cambridge in 1944, and in 1947 became Professor of Natural Philosophy at St Andrews University, a post which he held until his retiral in 1978.

ALMOND, Hely Hutchinson
(1832–1903)

Educationist and author, born in Glasgow. Precociously clever as a child, he was educated at Glasgow and Balliol College, Oxford. He became a tutor at Loretto School, Musselburgh (then a preparatory school) in 1857, then Master at Merchiston School, Edinburgh, the following year. In 1862 he acquired Loretto School, making it a public school. He sought to rule by persuasion, not force, and believed passionately 'that the laws of physical well-being are the laws of God'. Insisting on open windows, shorts, shirt-sleeves, compulsory cold baths all year, and long runs in wet weather, he epitomized the late 19th-century cult of athleticism in public schools. He published *Health Lectures* (1884) and a number of volumes of sermons. In his later years he had to be dissuaded from watching house and school matches as it was bad for his heart.

ALNESS, Robert Munro, Baron
(1868–1955)

Liberal politician, born in Alness, Ross and Cromarty. Educated at Aberdeen Grammar School and Edinburgh University, he took silk in 1910. Liberal MP for Wick (1910–18) and Roxburgh and Selkirk (1918–22), he was appointed Lord Advocate in 1913, and was Scottish Secretary from 1916 to 1922 in Lloyd George's government. He had to handle the wartime unrest on Clydeside, and in 1919 called troops into Glasgow to deal with a threatened general strike. He carried through the Education Act of 1918, which promoted the expansion of secondary schooling. In 1922 he was appointed Lord Justice Clerk, and after his retiral in 1933 he remained active in public life, chairing several government committees on Scottish affairs.

ALSTON, Charles
(1685–1760)

Medical botanist. Born in Lanarkshire, he studied medicine in Glasgow and Leiden before taking over the Physic Garden in 1720 after **James Sutherland**'s death. Appointed Professor of Botany in 1735, his influence and teaching considerably enhanced the university's reputation. He published a *Materia Medica* which was said to have been the best in Europe. His interest in botany was less in the detailed description of the species and more in general principles, such as respiration and reproduction. He quarrelled with Linnaeus, who maintained that all plants required external fertilization, Alston being proved right for certain species. This disagreement may have coloured his judgement about the great classification system Linnaeus proposed, and, unlike his Edinburgh contemporary, Sir **John Hope**, Alston did not support it. Nevertheless his studies and interest in plant physiology were about two centuries in advance of their time.

AMOUR, Elizabeth Isabel
(1885–1945)

English-born ceramic artist, born in Manchester. She studied at Glasgow School of Art, where she gained a diploma in Design and Decorative Art in 1912. She founded the Bough Pottery in Edinburgh (c.1921–42) which specialized in decorative pottery, where she was assisted by her three brothers and her sister. Of these the youngest, Richard Amour (1899–1949) was also a talented ceramic decorator. The studio collaborated with the artist Robert Burns on tableware for Crawford's Hanover Street Tearooms. She was a professional member of the Scottish Society of Artists and a founder member of the Scottish Society of Women Artists, where she regularly exhibited ceramics and, latterly, paintings.

ANDERSON, Alexander
(c.1582 – c.1619)

Mathematician, born in Aberdeenshire. He taught in Paris at the beginning of the 17th century, from 1612 to 1619, where he published several mathematical tracts. He is best known for his posthumous edition of the works of François Viète, one of the founders of modern algebraic notation.

ANDERSON, Ian
(1947 –)

Rock singer and flautist, born in Dunfermline. Moving to Blackpool he formed the 'progressive' rock group Jethro Tull in 1968, the name taken from the 18th-century inventor of the seed drill. Their longwinded and ostentatious style of rock was offset by Anderson's sense of showmanship. While their greatest commercial success came in the early 1970s with the albums *Aqualung* (1971), *Thick As A Brick* (1972) and *A Passion Play* (1973), attracting a greater following in the USA than in Britain, they have retained a strong worldwide following for over 20 years. Anderson now divides his time between music and running a salmon farm on Skye.

ANDERSON, James
(1662–1728)

Antiquary and lawyer, born in Edinburgh. In 1705 he published a treatise vindicating the independence of Scotland and in 1727 a valuable collection of historical documents; he spent the rest of his unhappy life working on his *Selectus Diplomatum et Numismatum Scotiae Thesaurus* (1739).

ANDERSON, James
(1739–1808)

Agricultural economist, born in Hermiston, near Edinburgh. He had a farm in Aberdeenshire, where he invented the 'Scotch plough' (a two-horse plough without wheels). He edited *The Bee* in Edinburgh (1790–3), and settled in London in 1797. His *Observations on the Means of Exciting a Spirit of National Industry* (1777) proposed economic development of the Scottish Highlands through the promotion of manufacturing, government stabilization of prices and the building of roads. He set out clearly for the first time the differential theory of rent in his *An Inquiry into the Nature of the Corn Laws, with a View to the Corn Bill Proposed for Scotland* (1777), anticipating the ideas of Malthus and Ricardo.

ANDERSON, Sir John See
WAVERLEY, John Anderson

ANDERSON, John
(1726–96)

Scientist, born in Roseneath, Dunbartonshire, the son of a minister. He studied at Glasgow, where from 1756 to 1760 he was Professor of Oriental Languages, and then of Natural Philosophy. He also established a bi-weekly class for mechanics, allowing workmen to attend in their working clothes, and at his death left all he had to found Anderson's College in Glasgow. The author of several works, including *Institutes of Physics* (1786), he also invented the balloon post, and a gun which, in 1791, he presented to the French National Convention.

ANDERSON, John
(1882–1958)

Administrator and statesman, born in Edinburgh and educated at George Watson's College and Edinburgh University, graduating in both humanities and science. He joined the Colonial Office in 1905, and began a long and distinguished career in the civil service and in government. He was involved in a number of crucial developments, including the National Health Insurance Committee (1912), the new Ministry of Health (1919), and the preparations for air-raid precautions and evacuation. He served in Ireland at the difficult time of the Black and Tans (1920), and was responsible for measures to combat the General Strike (1925–6). Permanent Under-Secretary at the Home Office from 1922 to 1932, he was appointed Governor of Bengal in 1932, and was elected to the House of Commons as an independent nationalist representing the Scottish universities (1938–50). He remained without party affiliation, but served in wartime governments under Chamberlain and Churchill, as Home Secretary (1939–43) and as Chancellor of the Exchequer (1943–5). He was made Viscount Waverley in 1952. The Anderson Shelter, an air-raid shelter he commissioned, was named after him.

ANDERSON, John
(1893–1962)

Scottish-born Australian philosopher. He was Professor of Philosophy at Sydney from 1927, and can be regarded as the founder and main exponent of an Australian school of philosophy, espousing a distinctive blend of realism, empiricism and materialism.

ANDERSON, John Henry
(1814–74)

Magician. Under the title of 'Professor Anderson, Magician of the North' he began performing in 1831, travelling across Scotland and to London, then to the USA (1851–3). One of his favourite tricks was to appear to catch a bullet, fired from a gun, between his teeth.

ANDERSON, Joseph
(1832–1916)

Archaeologist, born in Arbroath, Angus. He was Keeper of the National Museum of Antiquities of Scotland (1869–1913) and a prolific writer both on archaeology and on the management of museums. He had a formative influence on the development of Scottish archaeology, particularly through his Rhind Lectures of 1879–82, published as *Scotland in Early Christian Times* (1881, 2 vols), *Scotland in Pagan Times: the Iron Age* (1883) and *Scotland in Pagan Times: the Bronze and Stone Ages* (1886). Another set of Rhind Lectures (1892), when published became part of an essential database still used today: *The Early Christian Monuments of Scotland* (1903, with J R Allen).

ANDERSON, Moira
(1938 –)

Singer, born in Kirkintilloch, Dunbartonshire, daughter of a deep-sea diver. Educated at Ayr Academy and the Royal Scottish Academy of Music, she joined the Kirkintilloch Junior Choir at the age of seven, making her first broadcast on BBC Radio Scotland the following year. Teaching music for two years, she made her television début on the BBC's *White Heather Club* in 1960. Her own TV series followed, first in Scotland, then nation-wide. In 1970 she appeared in the first of several Royal Variety Shows and starred at the London Palladium. She later introduced *Stars on Sunday* (ITV) and in 1982 was awarded the Gold Star of the British Academy of Song Writers.

ANDERSON, Robert
(1750–1830)

Editor and biographer, born in the parish of Carnwath, Lanarkshire. Originally intending to enter the Church he went to Edinburgh University, but studied medicine instead. Marrying shortly after taking his MD, he abandoned this career and turned to writing and editing, producing, among other works, *A Complete Edition of the Poets of Great Britain* (1792–5). His reluctant publisher eventually allowed him to include pre-Shakespearean poets in this, thus resurrecting several almost forgotten names. The book sold well, and had a great influence on the Romantic poets, such as Coleridge, who found in it important links with the Elizabethan period. Anderson published several other works, largely of a biographical nature, and was for a while Editor of the *Edinburgh Magazine*.

ANDERSON, Sir Robert Rowand
(1834–1921)

Architect and military engineer, born in Edinburgh, the son of a solicitor, and educated in Edinburgh. After rejecting a legal career, he trained at the Royal Institution and with John Lessels, and gained experience with Sir George Gilbert Scott (1811–78) in London. He studied on the continent, publishing *Examples of the Municipal, Commercial and Street Architecture* (1868). From 1860 he worked for the Royal Engineers, starting an independent practice in 1868. He had a passion for gothic styles and was an exponent of Ecclesiologist tenets. His versatility is seen in the Byzantine design for Santa Sophia, Galston (1882), and classical additions to Pollock House, Glasgow (1901). His design for the University Medical School in Edinburgh (1874) was a *pièce de resistance*. In domestic architecture he was among the pioneers of the 17th-century Scottish revival. He executed a series of conservative restorations, such as Dunblane Cathedral (1890–3). His contribution to architectural education and the profession in Scotland was considerable: he established the School of Applied Arts, initiated the National Art Survey, and instigated the revival of the professional Institute (now the RIAS). He was knighted in

1902 and received the RIBA Gold Medal in 1916. A man with deep convictions and powerful personality, he was widely respected and immeasurably influential.

ANDERSON, Thomas
(1819–74)

Pioneer organic and agricultural chemist. Born in Leith, Edinburgh, he was educated at the Royal High School and Edinburgh Academy, and graduated with an MD from Edinburgh University in 1841. He then studied with Berzelius in Stockholm and Liebig at Giessen before returning to Edinburgh. In 1852 he was appointed Regius Professor of Chemistry at Glasgow University, where he discovered picoline and the pyridine series of bases. He also investigated codeine and other opium derivatives, and discovered the structure of anthracene. He was appointed Chemist to the Highland and Agricultural Society of Scotland, and worked on the composition of wheat and the chemistry of soils and manures.

ANDERSON, Tom
(1910–91)

Fiddler and composer, born in Eshaness, Shetland. A fine player in his own right and a prolific composer, with over 500 tunes to his credit, he became best known for his work in nurturing the growth of the distinctive Shetland fiddling style, both as a teacher and as a collector. In 1980 his vast collection of tape-recorded tunes, compiled over a period of 30 years, was donated to Stirling University, where he taught at the Heritage of Scotland summer schools. For many years he led a group known as the Forty Fiddlers, and he also travelled extensively as a solo performer. In 1977 he was made an MBE for services to Shetland music.

ANEIRIN, or ANEURIN
(fl.late 6th century)

Poet, creator of the oldest surviving poetry composed in Scotland. He was Bard of Gododdin, the p-Celtic kingdom south of the Firth of Forth whose citadel was Din Eidyn (Edinburgh) until its capture by the Angles in 638, when the kingdom ended. Nennius speaks of him, together with **Taliesin**, as a poet in the Old North, while an earlier Triad speaks of him as 'Aneirin of flowing verse, prince of poets'. The great *Y Gododdin* ascribed to him describes the ill-fated expedition of a band of warriors defeated and destroyed after a march of about 150 miles to Catterick in Yorkshire under the leadership of Mynyddawg Mwynfawr in AD 600 or shortly before. In 1480 lines of sweetness, power and bitter lamentation it extols the martial virtues and generosity of the dead heroes. Its initial composition was evidently oral and it was apparently transferred down the generations in that form for some 300 years, survivors from the lost kingdom having made their way to Wales. As a poet Aneirin proves himself a loyal follower of exceptional devotion.

ANGUS, Earls of See DOUGLAS

ANGUS, Marion
(1866–1946)

Poet, born in Aberdeen, the daughter of a Church of Scotland minister. She grew up in Arbroath, and later lived in Aberdeen, Edinburgh and Helensburgh. Her volumes of verse, mostly in Scots, include *The Lilt and Other Verses* (1922), *Sun and Candlelight* (1927), *The Singin' Lass* (1929), and *Lost Country* (1937). Her best-known poem is a lament for **Mary, Queen of Scots**, 'Alas, Poor Queen'.

ANNAN, James Craig
(1864–1946)

Photographer, the son of **Thomas Annan**. After studying chemistry and natural philosophy, he joined the family firm of T and R Annan. In Vienna he studied the art of photogravure, a photographic etching process, with its inventor, Karl Klic, and was to become one of the masters of this medium. Annan belonged to the artistic community in Glasgow in the 1890s. Among his friends were **David Young Cameron**, **William Strang** and **Muirhead Bone**. He made several trips to the Continent with Cameron, notably to the Low Countries (1892) and Italy (1894), when the work they produced is complementary in character and subject. Annan gained an international reputation during his lifetime, participating in exhibitions in Europe and the USA. He exhibited with the pictorialist photographers of the 'Linked Ring Brotherhood', who promoted photography as Art. The American photographer, Alfred Stieglitz, admired Annan's work and published examples in his influential magazine *Camera Work* (1903–17). Annan continued to run the Annan studio in Glasgow until his death in 1946.

ANNAN, Thomas
(1829–87)

Photographer, born in Fife, the son of a farmer and flax-spinner. After apprenticeship and early work as a lithographer in Cupar and Glasgow, he joined with a medical student called Berwick and set up a photographic studio in 1855. He was much encouraged and influenced by **David Octavius Hill**. By 1857 he was independent and, in 1859, opened his own printing works. Annan was known in his own day for the accurate reproduction of paintings, including Hill's enormous *Signing of the Deed of Demission* .... He took a particular interest in the question of permanence and purchased the Scottish rights to the carbon process in 1866 and the British rights to Karl Klic's photogravure process in the 1880s. In the late 1850s and 1860s, he took a number of lyrical landscape photographs. These have been overshadowed by his series, *The Old Closes and Streets of Glasgow* (1868–71), a curiously moving group of photographs of the derelict areas condemned to destruction by the Glasgow Improvement Act of 1866. His son was the photographer **James Craig Annan**.

ANNAND, J K (James King)
(1908 –)

Poet, translator and editor, born in Edinburgh. He was educated at Broughton High School, where he edited the *Broughton Magazine* (which published some of the early work of **Hugh MacDairmid**), and at Edinburgh University. He taught in Whithorn and in Edinburgh, and was Principal Teacher of History at Firrhill Secondary School from 1962 until he retired in 1971. His poems, which are small in number but highly crafted, are written in a heightened strain of Scots, and share some of MacDairmid's preoccupation with arcane knowledge, but in more rigorously scholarly fashion. His writing, including translations from Latin and German, is collected in *Poems and Translations* (1975). He translated *Songs from Carmina Burana* (1978) from medieval Latin, and has written three volumes of verse for children. He was founder editor of *Lallans*, the magazine of the Scots Language Society, which he edited from 1973 to 1983.

ANTHONY, Jack, originally John Herbertson

(1900–62)

Comedian, born in Glasgow. He joined the RAF in 1916 and after the war became a scientific instrument maker. In 1926 he joined the Millport Entertainers as juvenile lead and graduated from light comedy to Scots comedy. From 1931 he starred in pantomime at the Pavilion Theatre, Glasgow, every year until his retirement, establishing as his catch-phrase 'Nae better at a'!' He retired to become the proprietor of a hotel in Dunbar, East Lothian.

APPLETON, Sir Edward Victor

(1892–1965)

English physicist, born in Bradford, York-shire. Trained at St John's College, Cam-bridge, he was appointed assistant demon-strator in experimental physics at the Caven-dish Laboratory in 1920. His researches on the propagation of wireless waves led to his appointment as Wheatstone Professor of Physics at London University (1924). In 1936 he returned to Cambridge as Jacksonian Professor of Natural Philosophy. In 1939 he became Secretary of the DSIR (Department of Scientific and Industrial Research), and in 1949 was appointed Principal and Vice-Chancellor of Edinburgh University. In 1947 he won the Nobel Prize for Physics for his contribution 'in exploring the ionosphere'. His work revealed the existence of a layer of electrically charged particles in the upper atmosphere (the Appleton layer) which plays an essential part in making wireless com-munication possible between distant stations, and is also fundamental to the development of radar.

ARBUTHNOT, John

(1667–1735)

Physician and writer, son of the Episcopalian manse at Arbuthnott, Kincardineshire. A close friend of Jonathan Swift and all the literary celebrities of the day, he was also a distinguished doctor and writer of medical works, and a physician-in-ordinary to Queen Anne (1705). He studied at Aberdeen and Oxford, and took his MD degree at St Andrews. In London he was much admired for his wit and erudition. In 1712 he published five satirical pamphlets against the Duke of Marlborough, called *The History of John Bull*, which was the origin of the popular image of John Bull as the typical Englishman. With Swift, Alexander Pope, John Gay and others he founded the Scriblerus Club, and was the chief contributor to the *Memoirs of Martin Scriblerus* (1741). As a physician he was ahead of his time, and wrote *An Essay Concerning the Nature of Ailments* (1731), which stressed the value of suitable diet in the treatment of disease.

ARCHER, William

(1856–1924)

Dramatic critic, playwright, and translator of Ibsen, born in Perth. Educated at Edinburgh University, he became a journalist with Edin-burgh *Evening News* in 1875. The following year he travelled through Australia (1876–7), then settled in London. Remaining a vigorously Scottish critic of the parochialism of London culture, he was dramatic critic of the London *Figaro* (1879–81) and the London *World* (1884–1905), where he became the most advanced prophet of the new theatre of his day until the advent of his friend and fellow-Ibsenite George Bernard Shaw. He was alone among the critics in welcoming Oscar Wilde's first two comedies (1892, 1893) and began collaboration with Shaw in *Wid-owers' Houses*, dropping out as Shaw realized his dramatic creativity. He collaborated with his brother and future biographer, Charles Archer, in a translation of Ibsen's *Peer Gynt* (1892) and produced editions of Ibsen's prose works, and plays (12 volumes, 1906–12). His books on the theatre include two major theoretical works, *Masks or Faces* (1888), and *Play-making* (1912). He published *About the Theatre* (1886), and five volumes covering his observations as a critic, *The Theatrical World* (1893–7), as well as *Study and Stage* (1899), a year-book of criticism. After visiting America he left two important volumes of impressions, *America To-day* (1900), and *Through Afro-America* (1910). Championing the cause of the executed Spanish liberal educationist, Francisco Ferrer, he wrote an impassioned account of his, *Life, Trial and Death* (1911). His later works included *The Old Drama and the New* (1923). An early advocate of a National Theatre, he collaborated with Harley Granville-Barker in a published scheme and estimates (1907). A vehement and hard-working opponent of theatrical censorship, he forced public attention and enquiry on the question. In later life he was dramatic critic for a number of journals, including the London *Nation*, the *Manchester Guardian*, the *Morning Leader*, and the London *Star*. A critic who played an outstanding part in the improvement of theatre standards, he also wrote several plays, of which *The Green Goddess* (1921) ran successfully in New York and London.

ARGYLL

Title of the chiefs of the Campbells, the powerful West Highland clan. They had achieved knighthood in the 13th century and obtained the barony of Lochow in 1315. From 1445 the chief was styled Lord Campbell until, in 1457, the earldom of Argyll was conferred upon Colin, Lord Campbell.

ARGYLL, Archibald, 1st Duke
(d.1705)

Son of Archibald, 9th Earl of **Argyll**. An active promoter of the Glorious Revolution (1688–9), he accompanied William of Orange to England in 1688. In 1689 he was restored to his father's earldom. With two others, John Campbell, Earl of Breadalbane, and Sir John Dalrymple, he was responsible for the Massacre of Glencoe (1692), in which the Jacobite Macdonalds were slaughtered, ostensibly for refusing to submit to the new king. He was created Duke of Argyll in 1701.

ARGYLL, Archibald, 2nd Earl
(d.1513)

Son of Colin, 1st Earl. He was Lord High Chancellor in 1483. He was killed at the Battle of Flodden.

ARGYLL, Archibald, 5th Earl
(1530–73)

A follower of **Mary, Queen of Scots**. He was involved in the assassination of **Darnley** (1567), and led Mary's forces at Langside (1568), but later (1571) supported **James VI and I** and became Lord High Chancellor (1572).

ARGYLL, Archibald, 7th Earl
(c.1576–1638)

He succeeded to the title in 1584, and as king's lieutenant he was defeated by Errol and Huntly at Glenlivet in 1594. In 1607 he was given a Charter of Crown lands in Kintyre, and suppressed risings by the Macdonalds in 1614 and 1615 in order to plant Lowland settlers in Inveraray. He also helped in the extermination of the MacGregor clan from 1610 onwards. He later became a convert to Catholicism and served the King of Spain.

ARGYLL, Archibald, Marquis and 8th Earl
(1598–1661)

Son of Archibald, 7th Earl of **Argyll**, and known as the 'covenanting marquis' and also 'cross-eyed Archibald'. He became a member of Charles I's Privy Council in 1626, but in 1638, just before succeeding his father to the title, he joined the Covenanters in support of Scottish presbyterianism. In 1641 he was reconciled with Charles and was created Marquis of Argyll. In the English Civil War he joined the parliamentary side, and after being defeated by **Montrose** at Inverlochy in 1645 took part in the defeat of Montrose and his Royalists at Philiphaugh in 1645. He formed a Scottish government under Cromwell's patronage, but after the execution of the king he repudiated Cromwell and accepted the proclamation of Charles II as king of Scotland (1649), and crowned him at Scone in 1651. After the defeat of the Scottish army at Worcester that autumn, however, he submitted to Cromwell again. At the Restoration of Charles II in 1660 he was arrested, found guilty of complying with the English occupation, and executed.

ARGYLL, Archibald, 9th Earl
(1629–85)

Son of Archibald, 8th Earl of **Argyll**. A Royalist, he was imprisoned by Cromwell for a suspected Royalist plot (1657–60), and after the Restoration in 1660 was eventually restored to the titles and lands forfeited at his father's execution in 1661. In 1681, however, he opposed the Test Act that forced all public office holders to declare their belief in Protestantism, and was sentenced to death for treason. He escaped to Holland. In 1685, after the accession of King **James VII and**

II, he conspired with James, Duke of Monmouth, to overthrow the king. Monmouth's invasion of England was delayed; Argyll landed in Scotland, but failed to rouse the Covenanters to his cause, and was captured and executed.

ARGYLL, George Douglas Campbell, 8th Duke of Argyll
(1823–1900)

Politician. Born in Ardencaple, Dunbartonshire, and educated privately, he succeeded to the title in 1847. A Cabinet minister by the age of 30, he held office virtually continuously from 1853 to 1874. An outstanding parliamentary debater, almost on Gladstone's level, he acted as spokesman in the Lords for the Liberals, to whom he moved across in the 1850s from a position of moderate conservatism. He was India Secretary 1868–74, initiating territorial expansion and introducing financial and administrative reforms. His commission of enquiry into Scottish education led to the Education Act of 1872. In the 1880s he left the Liberals as a result of their land and Irish policies. An eminent amateur scientist, he was a geologist and ardent anti-Darwinian. His daughter was Lady **Francis Balfour**.

ARGYLL, John, 2nd Duke
(1678–1743)

Son of Archibald, 1st Duke of **Argyll**, he succeeded to the title in 1703. A committed Unionist, he was a High Commissioner to the Scottish Parliament of 1704 and one of the strongest supporters of the Act of Union of 1707. An outstanding soldier, he took part in the War of the Spanish Succession (1701–14), and fought under Marlborough at Oudenarde (1708) and Malplaquet (1709). At the time of the Jacobite rising in Scotland (1715–16) he commanded the Hanoverian forces that dispersed the Jacobite troops without a battle. He was created Duke of Greenwich in 1719.

ARGYLL, John Douglas Sutherland, 9th Duke
(1845–1914)

Married Queen Victoria's fourth daughter Princess Louise. An MP (1868–71 and 1895–1900), he was Governor-General of Canada from 1878 to 1883.

ARMSTRONG, Archy
(d.1672)

Court-jester of **James VI and I** and Charles I. He gained much wealth and influence, but was dismissed in 1637 for insolence to Archbishop Laud, and withdrew in 1641 to Arthuret in Cumberland.

ARMSTRONG, John
(c.1709–1779)

Physician and poet, born in Liddesdale, Roxburghshire, the son of a minister. He took his MD at Edinburgh in 1732, and went into practice in London. In 1736 he published a sex manual in blank verse for newly weds called *The Oeconomy of Love*, and in 1744 another didactic medical work in blank verse. In 1746 he was appointed physician to the London Soldiers' Hospital, and from 1760 to 1763 he was physician to the forces in Germany.

ARMSTRONG, Johnnie
(d.c.1530)

Border freebooter and cattle-rustler ('reiver'), and hero of many Border ballads. He was either John Armstrong of Gilnockie, near Langholm, who was seized by King **James V** at a parley at Caerlanrig Chapel and summarily hanged with several of his followers in 1529, or John Armstrong ('Black Jock'), brother of Thomas Armstrong of Mangerton, executed in 1530.

ARMSTRONG, William
(16th century)

The 'Kinmont Willie' of the Border ballad, a Dumfriesshire moss-trooper. He was rescued from Carlisle Castle in 1596 by **Walter Scott**, 1st Lord Scott of Buccleuch (1565–1611).

ARNISTON, Lord Robert See DUNDAS, Robert

ARNOTT, Struther
(1934–)

Organic chemist, born in Larkhall, Lanarkshire, and educated at Glasgow University.

After some years in the Medical Research Council's biophysical unit at King's College, London, he moved to the Chair of Molecular Biology at Purdue University in Indiana (1970), and later became Dean of the Graduate School and Vice-President for Research. He was appointed Principal and Vice-Chancellor of St Andrews University in 1986. Arnott is known for his work on the structures of fibrous biopolymers, particularly nucleic acids and polysaccharides, and on the techniques necessary to visualize these complex molecules. His discovery of new conformations of DNA is proving to be significant for genetics.

ARRAN, Earl of See HAMILTON

ARROL, Sir William
(1839–1913)

Engineer, born of humble parentage in Houston, Renfrewshire. He got his first job in a thread mill as a cotton boy at the age of ten by lying about his age, became an apprentice blacksmith at the age of 14, studied mechanics and hydraulics at night school, and started his own engineering business at the age of 29. In 1865 he made a railway viaduct at Greenock, constructed the second Tay Railway Bridge (1882–7) to replace the ill-fated bridge that had collapsed in 1879, the Forth Railway Bridge (1883–90), and Tower Bridge in London (1886–94). He was an MP from 1892 to 1906.

ASCHERSON, (Charles) Neal
(1932–)

Journalist, born in Edinburgh. Educated at Eton College, Windsor, and King's College, Cambridge, he joined the *Manchester Guardian* as a reporter in 1956, and became the Commonwealth Correspondent for *The Scotsman* in 1959. In 1960 he was appointed as a Foreign Correspondent to *The Observer*, and covered events in Central Europe and Germany. Re-joining *The Scotsman* as Scottish Political Correspondent in 1975, he held this position for four years before going freelance (1979). A columnist on *The Observer* from 1985 to 1989, he then joined *The Independent On Sunday* as political columnist and Senior Assistant Editor. A highly-respected political commentator, he has made a special study of the problems inherent in the political and cultural development of small nations. His publications include *The King Incorporated* (1963), *The Polish August* (1981) and *Games Into Shadows* (1988).

ASQUITH, Margot, née Emma Alice Margaret Tennant
(1864–1945)

Society figure and wit, born in Peebleshire, the 11th child of Sir Charles Tennant. 'Unteachable and splendid', she received little formal education but possessed unusual literary, artistic and musical talents. She 'came out' into society in 1881 and, though far from a beauty ('I have no face, only two profiles clapped together'), was an immense success. A brilliantly witty hostess, she led a group of young intellectuals and aesthetes, known as 'The Souls', who advocated greater freedom for women. Her friends also included Gladstone and Virginia Woolf. In 1894 she married Liberal Herbert Asquith, prime minister from 1908 to 1916, and had seven children, of whom two survived. She was highly influential in society, though her devastating wit could be cruel. Seemingly impervious to the opinions of others, she neglected the war effort, continuing her extravagant lifestyle unabashed. When Asquith was forced to resign (1916) Margot wrote two infamously indiscreet autobiographies.

ATHOLL, John, 4th Earl of
(d.1579)

Statesman, the son of John Stewart, 3rd Earl of Atholl. A devoted Catholic, he opposed the Reformation in the Parliament of 1560, along with Lords Borthwick and Somerville, each saying he would believe as his father had done. Made a Privy Councillor in 1561, he helped to promote the marriage of **Mary, Queen of Scots**, and **Darnley**. In October 1562, with the Earls of **Moray** and **Morton**, he defeated the Earl of Huntly at Corrichie. Appointed Lieutenant in the North in 1565, he was present at the crowning of **James VI** in 1567 and was provisionally nominated regent. Voting for Mary's divorce from **Bothwell** in 1569, he became Chancellor of Scotland in 1578. He opposed the return to office of the Regent Morton, but was apparently reconciled to him and given a feast by the regent at Stirling in April 1579. Atholl died a few days later and poison was strongly suspected. The French ambassador described him as 'a very great Catholic, bold and valiant … but lacking in judgement and experience'.

ATHOLL, Katharine Marjory, Duchess of
(1874–1960)

Conservative politician, born in Banff, Perthshire, daughter of historian Sir James Ramsay. Educated at Wimbledon High School and the Royal College of Music, she was an accomplished pianist and composer. In 1899 she married the future 8th Duke of Atholl, becoming Duchess of Atholl in 1917. During the Boer War and World War I she organized concerts for the troops abroad and helped in hospital work. An early opponent of women's suffrage, she became MP for Kinross and Perthshire in 1923; from 1924 to 1929 she was the first Conservative woman minister as Parliamentary Secretary to the Board of Education. She successfully resisted changes in policy which would have adversely affected the education of poorer children, and from 1929 to 1939 campaigned against ill-treatment of women and children in the British Empire. She was responsible for translating an unexpurgated edition of *Mein Kampf* to warn of Hitler's intentions. On principle she opposed Britain's policy of imagining a collective European policy of 'non-intervention' in the Spanish Civil War, while not advocating British assistance to the Spanish Republic. She published the best-selling *Searchlight on Spain* in 1938. She opposed the Munich agreement, and was dropped as Tory candidate, resigned her seat in Parliament and was defeated in the resultant by-election where she was lampooned as the 'Red Duchess'. From 1939 to 1960 she worked to aid refugees from totalitarianism. Her other publications include *Women and Politics* (1931).

ATWELL, Sir John William
(1911 –)

Mechanical engineer, born in Glasgow, who began his career as an apprentice in **Yarrow**'s shipyard. He studied engineering and management at Glasgow and Cambridge, then joined Stewarts and Lloyds as a management trainee in 1939. He moved to G & J Weir in 1954 as works manager, being appointed works director in 1955 and managing director in 1961; he was a member of the Weir Group board from then until his retirement in 1974. He was involved in the management of many other Scottish companies, including Anderson Strathclyde and Govan Shipbuilders. He was a member of the University Grants Committee (1965–9), and President of the Institution of Mechanical Engineers (1973–4) and of the Royal Society of Edinburgh (1982–5). He was awarded the CBE (1970) and an honorary LLD from Strathclyde University (1973).

AUCHTERLONIE, Willie
(1872–1963)

Golf-club maker, born in St Andrews. He won the Open Golf Championship at the age of 21, using only seven home-made clubs. In 1935 he was appointed professional to the Royal and Ancient in St Andrews, where his workshop and store became a mecca for golfers.

AUERBACH, Charlotte
(1899 –)

German-born geneticist, born in Crefel. She was educated in Berlin, before attending university courses in Berlin, Würzburg and finally Freiburg, under the embryologist Hans Spemann, graduating in 1925. She then took up school teaching before starting her PhD course at the Kaiser Wilhelm Institute under Otto Mangold. In 1933 all Jewish students were forbidden to enter the university and she moved to Edinburgh, completing her thesis with Professor **Crew** at the Institute of Animal Genetics. In 1938 she worked with Hermann Müller, the American geneticist. She was the first to discover chemical mutagenesis, arising from her work on the effects of nitrogen mustard and mustard gas on *Drosophila*. Chemical mutagenesis thereafter became her main research, with particular emphasis on the biological side and the kinds of mutations induced. She was appointed Lecturer in Genetics at Edinburgh (1947), Reader (1957) and Professor (1967–9). She was one of the very first to work out how chemical compounds cause mutations and to compare the differences between the actions of chemical mutagens and X-rays, contributing many papers and books on the subject. These include *Genetics in the Atomic Age* (1956) and *The Science of Genetics* (1961). She was elected FRS in 1957 and was their Darwin Medallist in 1976.

AULDJO, John
(1710–86)

Founder of the Aberdeen Pottery. Originally manufacturing pan-tile and brick, his pottery introduced brown earthenware in 1749. Over a period of years he tried to introduce various

17

types of earthenware through the involvement of John Rose, an Aberdeen merchant. They also imported utilitarian wares and sold these through a shop in the Shiprow. In 1771 John Auldjo was voted Treasurer of Aberdeen and two years later chosen Dean of Guild. In the year before his death he was elected a Merchant Counsellor. His son George took over the works in 1784.

AVERAGE WHITE BAND See **GORRIE, Alan**

AYTON, Sir Robert
(1570–1638)

Poet and courtier, born in Kinaldie, near St Andrews. He was educated at St Andrews University, studied law in Paris, and became a courtier of **James VI and I** in London. He wrote lyrics in English and Latin, and is credited with the prototype of 'Auld Lang Syne'.

AYTOUN, William Edmonstoune
(1818–65)

Poet and humorist, born in Edinburgh, the son of a lawyer. Educated at The Edinburgh Academy and Edinburgh University, he was called to the Bar in 1840. He published a collection of romantic pastiches, *Poland, Homer and Other Poems* (1832), and in 1836 began a lifelong connection with *Blackwood's Magazine*, to which he contributed countless parodies and burlesque reviews. In 1845 he was appointed Professor of Rhetoric and Belles-Lettres at Edinburgh University, and in five years quintupled the number of his students. In 1849 he married a daughter of Professor **John Wilson** (1785–1854). In 1852 was made Sheriff of Orkney. His works include *Lays of the Scottish Cavaliers* (1848); *Firmilian, a Spasmodic Tragedy* (1854); *Bon Gaultier Ballads* (1855), and *Poems of Goethe* (1858), conjunctly with **Theodore Martin**; *Bothwell* (1856); and *Norman Sinclair* (1861), a semi-autobiographical novel.

B

BAIKIE, William Balfour
(1825–64)

Explorer, naturalist and linguist, born in Kirkwall, Orkney. He studied medicine at Edinburgh, and in 1848 became a naval surgeon. On the Niger expedition of 1854 he succeeded through the captain's death to the command of the *Pleiad*, and penetrated 250 miles further up river than any previous traveller. In a second expedition in 1857 the *Pleiad* was wrecked and he was left to continue his work single-handed from Lukoja. Within five years he had opened the navigation of the Niger, constructed roads, collected a native vocabulary, translated parts of the Bible and prayer book into Hausa and founded a city state.

BAILEY, Sir Edward Battersby
(1881–1965)

English geologist, born in Marden, Kent, and educated at Kendal School and Cambridge, where he was a Harkness Scholar. A great eccentric, he devoted his life to Scottish geology, particularly the Dalradian part of the Highlands and the Tertiary igneous rocks of the Western Isles. After an early period on the staff of the Geological Survey of Great Britain (1902–29), he was Professor of Geology at Glasgow University (1929–37). He then returned to the Survey as its Director until 1945. Having been wounded in active service during World War I, he is said to have patrolled the galleries of the Survey's Museum in London at night during World War II, armed with a revolver to ward off enemy aircraft. Knighted in 1945, he received many honours.

BAILLIE, Grizel, Lady, née Hume
(1665–1746)

Poet, daughter of the Covenanter Sir **Patrick Hume**. In 1684 she supplied him with food during his concealment in the vault beneath Polwarth Church, and helped shelter the Covenanting scholar, **Robert Baillie of Jerviswood** (1634–84), whose son, George, she married in 1692. She is remembered by her songs, particularly 'And werena my heart licht I wad dee'. In 1911 her domestic notebook was published as *The Household Book*, giving a fascinating, detailed insight into the trivia of daily household management.

BAILLIE, Dame Isobel
(1895–1983)

Soprano, born in Hawick, Roxburghshire, the daughter of a baker, on the estate of the Earl of Dalkeith. When her family moved to Manchester the quality of her voice was recognized and she had singing lessons from the age of nine. After leaving school she worked as an assistant in the piano-roll department of a music shop, then as a clerk in Manchester Town Hall, and made her début with the Hallé Orchestra under Sir Hamilton Harty in 1921. After studying in Milan, she won immediate success in her opening season in London in 1923. Regarded as one of this century's greatest oratorio singers, she regularly sang with such conductors as Sir Thomas Beecham, Arturo Toscanini and Bruno Walter, and gave over 1000 performances of Handel's *Messiah*.

BAILLIE, Joanna
(1762–1851)

Poet and playwright, born to an old Scottish family in the manse of Bothwell in Lanarkshire. She was educated in Glasgow and displayed literary talent from an early age. Her first collection of poems, *Fugitive Verses*, was published anonymously in 1790. Her plays, written mostly in verse, were praised by her peers. Sir **Walter Scott** spoke highly of her *Plays on the Passions* (1798–1812) and called her 'the immortal Joanna'. In these *Plays* she attempted to define the mind's passions and render each in a tragedy and a comedy. She wrote until the age of 80. Her plays are mainly forgotten but her lyrics in *Fugitive Verses* are recognized for their accurate representation of Lowland Scots folk song.

BAILLIE, John
(1886–1960)

Theologian, born in Gairloch, Ross-shire, son of the Free Church minister there. Educated at Inverness Academy, he studied philosophy at Edinburgh, and trained for the ministry at New College, Edinburgh, Marburg and Jena. During World War I he served with the YMCA in France. After the war he went to the USA, where he was Professor of Christian Theology at Auburn Theological Seminary, New York (1920–7), and Roosevelt Professor of Systematic Theology at Union Seminary, New York (1930–5). Back in Scotland he was Professor of Divinity at New College from 1935 to 1936. He published a number of theological works, including the modern devotional classic, *Diary of Private Prayer* (1937), and *Our Knowledge of God* (1939). A key contributor to mid-century religious, social and intellectual life in Scotland, he was chairman of the influential Church committee that produced the report *God's Will for Church and Nation* (1946), in favour of the Welfare State and state intervention in the economy.

BAILLIE, Matthew
(1761–1823)

Physician and anatomist, born in Shotts, Lanarkshire. After seven years at Glasgow and Oxford (1773–80) he studied anatomy under **William Hunter**, his mother's brother, and in 1783 succeeded to his uncle's famous anatomy school in Great Windmill Street in London. He was the author of the first treatise in English on morbid anatomy (1793).

BAILLIE, Robert
(1599–1662)

Presbyterian clergyman, born and educated in Glasgow. In 1622 he received episcopal ordination, and was shortly after presented to the parish of Kilwinning, Ayrshire. In 1637 he refused to preach in favour of Laud's service book, and in 1638 sat in the famous General Assembly which met in Glasgow to protest against episcopacy. In 1639 he served as chaplain in the Covenanting army at Duns Law, and in 1640 was selected to go to London with other commissioners and draw up charges against Archbishop Laud. On his return to Scotland in 1642 he was appointed joint Professor of Divinity at Glasgow. In 1643 he was a delegate to the Westminster Assembly, and in 1649 was chosen by the Church to go to Holland to invite Charles II to accept the covenant and crown of Scotland. He performed his mission skilfully and, after the Restoration, was made Principal of Glasgow University.

BAILLIE, Robert, of Jerviswood
(c.1634–1684)

Nationalist leader and conspirator, a native of Lanarkshire. Keen to see the Scottish Presbyterian Church freed from Anglican domination, in 1683 he entered into correspondence with, and subsequently joined, the Duke of Monmouth's supporters in London. On the discovery of the Rye-house Plot against Charles II (1683) he was arrested and sent to Scotland. He was tried at Edinburgh, condemned to death on insufficient evidence, and hanged. His son married Lady **Grizel Baillie**.

BAILLIE-COCHRANE, Alexander Dundas Ross Wishart, 1st Lord Lamington (name later rendered as Cochrane-Baillie)
(1816–90)

Politician and writer. Educated at Eton and Trinity College, Cambridge, he entered Parliament as Tory member for Bridport in 1841. He was one of the four members of Disraeli's Young England group, and the original of the character Buckhurst in his *Coningsby*. Defeated in a contest for Southampton in 1852, he returned to Parliament in 1857 as member for Lanarkshire until 1859, then for Honiton until 1868. The fall of Disraeli's government prevented him from taking up an appointment as Governor of Cape Colony. He represented the Isle of Wight from 1870 to 1880, when he was created Lord Lamington. Also a man of letters, he published 12 works of prose and poetry; from 1864 to 1868 he edited the satirical weekly *The Owl*. He was noted as an improving landlord on his estate at Lamington in Lanarkshire. His memoirs *In the Days of the Dandies*, containing reminiscences of fashionable life in Britain and Europe, were being serialized in *Blackwood's Magazine* when he died; they were subsequently published as a book.

BAIN, Alexander

(1810–77)

Clockmaker and inventor of telegraphic apparatus, born in the parish of Watten, Caithness. Apprenticed first to a clockmaker in Wick, he then went to London (1837) as a journeyman. His first patent in 1841 was for a clock with a pendulum actuated by electromagnetic impulses; he also foresaw the possibility of synchronizing many clocks from one central control. In a patent of 1843 he outlined a system for the electrical transmission of images, the forerunner of today's facsimile (fax) apparatus, and a device for the automatic chemical recording of telegraph messages. He returned to Edinburgh in 1844 and two years later patented the first practical method for the automatic transmission of telegraph messages, using strips of perforated paper, later developed by Wheatstone and **Creed**. Despite these and other inventions he died a poor man.

BAIN, Alexander

(1818–1903)

Empirical philosopher and psychologist, born in Aberdeen. Overcoming poverty he managed to study at Aberdeen University. He was Secretary to the London Board of Health (1848–50) and Examiner in Logic and Moral Philosophy at London University (1857–62). From 1860 to 1881 he was Professor of Logic at Aberdeen. He was one of a circle which included J S Mill and George Grote, and he wrote books on the two Mills. A tirelessly thorough writer of several painstaking books, his more important works include *The Senses and the Intellect* (1855), *The Emotions and the Will* (1859) and *Mental and Moral Science* (1868). He also founded the famous journal, *Mind*, in 1876 (from the proceeds of the American sale of his textbook *Rhetoric*), which he handed over in 1891, having spent £3000 on it since its inception. A valuable observer, his psychology was firmly based on physiology and he sought to explain the mind through a physical theory of the association of ideas, an association considered inadequate by some. He was also noted for his interest in improving standards of education in Scotland.

BAIN, Aly

(1945 –)

Fiddler, born in Lerwick, Shetland. An early pupil of **Tom Anderson**, he worked as a joiner before leaving Shetland for Glasgow in 1968 to play traditional music professionally. An extraordinarily gifted fiddler — arguably the best that Scotland has ever produced — he first showed his mastery of Shetland and other styles when he teamed up with singer/guitarist Mike Whellans. In 1972 the duo merged with Cathal McConnell and Robin Morton to form the Boys of the Lough, a group which has been touring, recording and broadcasting ever since, with a particularly strong following in the USA (in 1989 they played to a capacity audience in New York's Carnegie Hall). Bain, a vibrant and virtuosic soloist, has also made his mark on television as anchor-man for several network series, notably *Aly Bain and Friends*. Apart from numerous recordings with the Boys of the Lough and other groupings, he has produced a solo album, *Aly Bain* (1984).

BAIRD, Sir David

(1757–1829)

Soldier, born in Newbyth, East Lothian. He joined the army in 1772, and in 1779 sailed to India with the Highland Light Infantry (then 73rd Foot). In the 2nd Mysore war (1780–4) he was captured and imprisoned at Seringapatam (1780) for nearly four years. After active service elsewhere he returned to India, took part in several sieges and attacks and returned in 1799, a major-general, and led the victorious attack on Seringapatam. He commanded Indian troops against the French in Egypt in 1801. In 1805–6 he commanded an expedition which successfully wrested the Cape of Good Hope from the Dutch. He was at the siege of Copenhagen (1807), and in 1809 distinguished himself and lost an arm in the Battle of La Coruña (1809) in the Peninsular War, succeeding Sir **John Moore**. He was Commander-in-Chief in Ireland from 1820 to 1822.

BAIRD, Sir Dugald

(1899–1986)

Pioneer in community obstetrics and gynaecology, born in Greenock, Renfrewshire, and educated at Glasgow University. His experience as a medical student attending the wards and home confinements in the Glasgow slums was fundamental in shaping his career. On moving to become Regius Professor of Midwifery (1937–65) at Aberdeen he saw unrivalled opportunities for research into environmental causes for social discrepancies in maternal and infant mortality rates. Introducing and applying the concept of social obstetrics in the Grampian region, he greatly improved the morbidity and mortality rates. He brought dietitians, sociologists, and statisticians into his department and with the help of the Medical Research Council set up the obstetric medicine research unit of which he was the first director. The influence of his teaching and methods has been immense. His work did much to change the pattern of reproduction in Britain and abroad, and he will be remembered for his research on perinatal health and for his efforts to secure for women what he called the Fifth Freedom — freedom from the tyranny of excessive fertility. He was a driving force in the movement for abortion law reform in the 1960s. He was knighted in 1959.

BAIRD, Hugh

(1770–1827)

Surveyor and civil engineer, born in Kelvinhead, near Kilsyth, Stirlingshire. He was the son of Nicol Baird, surveyor to the Forth and Clyde Canal Company, and succeeded his father on his death in 1807. He became resident engineer to the Canal Company in 1812 and the following year surveyed a route for the Union Canal from Camelon to Edinburgh. His proposed route having been approved by **Thomas Telford**, he was appointed engineer in 1817 and from 1818 to 1822 supervised the construction of the canal, including the Falkirk tunnel and the aqueducts over the Avon, the Almond and the Water of Leith, on the design of which Telford was again consulted.

BAIRD, James

(1802–76)

Ironmaster, born in Old Monkland, near Glasgow, one of the seven brothers who founded the firm of William Baird and Company. Their father, Alexander, had been a farmer who realized that his sons would have a more prosperous future in the rapidly expanding coal and iron industries of Lanarkshire. They began to build their first blast furnace in 1828, incorporating the hot-blast process developed by **James Beaumont Neilson**, and over the next 25 years became the largest producers of pig iron in Britain. James Baird was strongly opposed to any trade union activity in his works, but provided schools, churches and recreation facilities for his workers and their families; a generous man, he gave much time and money to the Tory Party and the Church of Scotland.

BAIRD, John

(1787/8–1820)

Radical martyr. A weaver from Condorrat, Dunbartonshire, he served seven years in the 95th Regiment of Foot. In March 1820 he was elected captain of the Scottish Radicals in Condorrat, forming a Committee for Organising a Provisional Government. Induced to lead armed rebels on 5 April by John King, who was actually a government *agent provocateur*, he gathered 10 followers, and was joined by **Andrew Hardie**, who led 25 more. Scattered by yeomanry after an exchange of shots at the 'battle of Bonnymuir', they surrendered after an offer to negotiate had been refused. Baird was tried with Hardie and found guilty on two out of four charges of High Treason. Before his death he wrote to his brother Robert from Stirling Castle, 'My hopes are not in this world — I look for a better. The sentence of death had as little impression on me as if the Lord President had read an old ballad'. He was hanged with Hardie on 8 September, both showing a steadfast stoicism. On the scaffold he said 'I declare I never gave my consent to anything inconsistent with truth and justice'.

BAIRD, John Logie

(1888–1946)

Electrical engineer and television pioneer, born in Helensburgh, Dunbartonshire. He studied electrical engineering at Glasgow University. Poor health compelled him to give up the post of engineer to the Clyde Valley electric power company, and after a brief career as a sales rep he settled in Hastings (1922) and began research into the possibilities of television. In 1926 he gave the first demonstration of a television image. His 30-line mechanically-scanned system was adopted by the BBC in 1929, being superseded in 1936 by his 240-line system. In the following year the BBC chose a rival 405-line system with electronic scanning made by Marconi-EMIO. Other lines of research initiated by Baird in the 1920s included radar and infra-red television ('Noctovision'). He continued his research up to the time of his death, and succeeded in producing three-dimensional and coloured images (1944) as well as projection on to a screen and stereophonic sound.

BALD, Robert

(1776–1861)

Civil and mining engineer, born in Culross, Fife, son of the viewer or manager of the Erskine family's collieries near Alloa. He visited Sweden with **Thomas Telford** in 1808 to assist in surveying the route of the Gotha Canal, and in the same year published his *General View of the Coal Trade of Scotland*, in which he strongly condemned the employment of women and girls in 'bearing' baskets of coal on their backs from the face to the surface, a practice finally prohibited by an Act of 1843. He built up an extensive practice as a consulting engineer, but his evangelical reforming zeal sometimes brought him into conflict with both workers and colliery owners. He was elected a Fellow of the Geological Society in 1810, and of the Royal Society of Edinburgh in 1817.

BALDRED, St

(?d.608)

Saint. After a spell as suffragan of St **Kentigern**, his fame spread throughout Lothian. He chose the hermit's life, electing to live on deserted islands, including the Bass Rock off North Berwick, East Lothian. Practising meditation and fasting, he taught in the parish churches of Aldhame, Tyninghame and Prestonkirk, which had been granted to his care by Kentigern. Baldred died in old age at Aldhame.

BALFOUR, Sir Andrew

(1630–94)

Physician, born in Denmylne, Fife. He studied at St Andrews, Oxford, Blois and Paris, and with Sir **Robert Sibbald** helped to establish a 'physic garden' near Holyrood House in Edinburgh (1676–80), the second oldest botanic garden in Britain and the forerunner of the present Royal Botanic Garden in Edinburgh (1822–4). He was third president (1685) of the Royal College of Physicians of Edinburgh.

BALFOUR, Arthur James, 1st Earl of Balfour

(1848–1930)

Statesman and philosopher, the brother of **Francis** and **Gerald Balfour**. Born, on his father's side, into an ancient Scottish family,

he succeeded to the family estate in East Lothian in 1856. His mother was sister of Lord Robert Cecil (Lord Salisbury). Educated at Eton and Trinity College, Cambridge, he entered Parliament in 1874 as a Conservative member for Hertford, and from 1878 to 1880 was Private Secretary to his uncle, Lord Salisbury, whom he accompanied to the Berlin Congress. In 1879 he published *A Defence of Philosophic Doubt*, a critique of the encroaching dogmatism of science. He was President of the Society for Psychical Research for a time in the 1880s. He was returned for East Manchester (1885), was Secretary for Scotland (1886), Chief Secretary for Ireland (1887), and First Lord of the Treasury and Leader in the Commons (1892–3). His premiership (1902–6) saw the end of the South African war (1905), the Education Act (1905), and the establishment of the Committee of Imperial Defence. In 1911 he resigned the leadership of the House owing to the constitutional crisis, and delivered the Gifford Lectures in 1915 on *Theism and Humanism*. He followed Churchill to the Admiralty (1915) and served under Lloyd George as Foreign Secretary (1916–19). He was responsible for the famous Balfour Declaration (1917) which promised Zionists a national home in Palestine; he keenly supported the League of Nations, and as Lord President of the Council (1921) was responsible for the controversial note cancelling Allied war debts to America.

BALFOUR, Lady Francis

(1858–1931)

Suffragist, churchwoman and author, born in London. The daughter of George, 8th Duke of **Argyll**, she spent her early years at Rosneath Castle and Inverary Castle. Her political ambitions were stifled by the role of women at that time, but she had strong connections with both the Whig and Tory parties, the former through her own family, and the latter through her marriage to Eustace Balfour, the brother of **Arthur James Balfour**. She was a tireless worker for women's rights, and employed her eloquent and acerbic gift for oratory on behalf of the National Union of Woman's Suffrage Societies. She also spoke out on such issues as Irish Home Rule and free trade. Her crusading, but essentially conservative, spirit — she did not approve of suffragist militants like the Pankhursts — also characterized her work for the Church of Scotland, and she fought throughout her life for the re-union of

1929, just as her father had opposed the Disruption in 1843. She wrote a number of memoirs, including those of her sister, Lady Victoria Campbell (1911), and Dr **Elsie Inglis** (1918), and an autobiography, *Ne Obliviscaris* (1930).

BALFOUR, Francis Maitland
(1851–82)

Zoologist, born in Edinburgh, brother of **Arthur James Balfour**. Educated at Harrow and Trinity College, Cambridge, he worked at Naples zoological station (1873–6) before becoming a lecturer at Cambridge (1876–82), where he was appointed the first Professor of Animal Morphology in 1882 after publishing his *Treatise on Comparative Embryology* (1880), the first overview of the subject. He died in a climbing accident on Mont Blanc.

BALFOUR, George
(1872–1941)

English electrical engineer and pioneering contractor, born in Portsmouth, founder of the construction firm of Balfour Beatty Ltd. He served an apprenticeship in a foundry in Dundee and qualified as a journeyman engineer. After working for a New York company specializing in electric tramways and power plants, he founded his own company in 1909 with an accountant, Andrew Beatty. They built and operated the tramway systems for Dunfermline, Llanelly and many towns in the Midlands, and the first major hydro-electrical schemes in Scotland, as well as pioneering the National Grid in the 1930s. He also built the giant Kut Barrage on the Tigris for Iraq. He was Unionist MP for Hampstead (London) from 1918 until his death.

BALFOUR, Gerald William, 2nd Earl of Balfour
(1853–1945)

Statesman. The brother of **Arthur James Balfour**, he was educated at Eton and Trinity College, Cambridge, of which he became a fellow (1878). He was Chief Secretary for Ireland (1895–6), President of the Board of Trade (1900–5) and of the Local Government Board (1905–6), and succeeded his brother as earl in 1930. He had a keen interest in the supernatural, and spent much time on psychical research.

BALFOUR, Sir James, of Kinnaird and Denmilne
(1600–57)

Historian, probably born in Denmilne, Fife, son of the Comptroller of Charles II's household. He travelled widely but devoted himself to the study of Scottish history and antiquities and associated with many contemporary Scottish historians. He studied in London under William Dugdale and contributed an account of the Scottish religious houses to Dugdale's *Monasticon Anglicanum* (1655; 1661–73). He compiled *Annals of the History of Scotland from Malcolm III to Charles II* (1824), useful mainly for 17th-century events, and wrote numerous other work, mostly relating to heraldry and genealogy, all still unpublished. He held the office of Lord Lyon from 1630 till his death and was created a baronet of Nova Scotia in 1633. He did much to regularize the work of Lyon Office and got Sir **David Lyndsay**'s register of arms recognized as an official national record. This was the essential predecessor of the Public Register of All Arms and Bearings in Scotland, begun in 1672. His greatest work, however, was to collect many of the surviving cartularies and records of the (recently dissolved) Scottish monastic houses, many of which were later acquired (1696) by the Advocates' Library and are now in the National Library of Scotland.

BALFOUR, Sir James, of Pittendreich
(c.1525–1583)

Jurist and politician. After the murder of Cardinal **David Beaton** in 1547 he was taken prisoner with **John Knox** at St Andrews Castle and sent to France. Released in 1549, he returned to Scotland and 'served with all parties, deserted all, and yet profited by all'. He was involved in the murder of Lord **Darnley** in 1567, served as Lord President of the Court of Session from 1567 to 1571, and withdrew to France in 1579–80. He was commissioned to compile the *Practicks or a System of the More Ancient Law of Scotland* (1579; published 1754), an invaluable repertory of ancient statutes and decisions.

BALFOUR, John, of Kinloch
(fl.1675)

Conspirator, chiefly responsible for Archbishop **Sharp**'s assassination in 1679. He fought at Drumclog and Bothwell Brig and is said to have escaped to Holland. Sir **Walter Scott**, in his *Old Mortality*, confused him with John Balfour, 3rd Lord Balfour of Burleigh, who died in 1688.

BALFOUR, Robert
(c.1550–1625)

Philosopher and philologist, born in Angus. He studied at St Andrews and Paris, making a considerable impression with his skill in public disputation. Invited to the College of Guienne, Bordeaux, he was appointed Professor of Greek there, and in 1586 became Principal of the College. An outstanding linguist in Greek and Latin, as well as a mathematician, he was noted for his commentary on Aristotle. Of noted grace and accomplishment, he remained a committed Roman Catholic despite the Reformation.

BALFOUR OF BURLEIGH,
Alexander Hugh Bruce, 6th Baron
(1848–1921)

Politician, born in Kennet, Alloa, and educated at Loretto and Eton schools and Oxford University. Active in public life from an early age, he chaired commissions on educational endowments and rating reform in the 1880s and 1890s. As Scottish Secretary (1895–1903) in the Salisbury and Balfour Conservative governments, he legislated for higher public health standards and for the relief of congested districts in the Highlands. He resigned office over tariff reform. He chaired the enquiry into wartime unrest on Clydeside, which helped to restore good relations between employers and men. A prominent member of the Church of Scotland, he spent many of his later years promoting presbyterian reunion in Scotland.

BALFOUR PAUL, Sir James See
PAUL, Sir James Balfour

BALIOL See BALLIOL

BALLANTINE, James
(1808–77)

Artist and poet, born in Edinburgh. Originally a housepainter, he learned drawing under Sir **William Allan**, and was one of the first to revive the art of glass-painting. Two prose volumes, *The Gaberlunzie's Wallet* (1843) and *Miller of Deanhaugh* (1845), contain some of his best-known songs and ballads.

BALLANTRAE, Bernard Edward Fergusson, Baron
(1911–80)

Politician and soldier, born in London into an old Scottish landed family with a tradition of political and public service. After education at Eton and the Royal Military Academy at Sandhurst, he joined the Black Watch and in World War II was attached to Orde Wingate's Chindits, commanding the 16th brigade on an extremely dangerous march through central Burma. He left the army with the rank of brigadier and became Governor-General of New Zealand (1962–7). He was very successful there, despite New Zealand anxieties about British entry into the European Common Market. He was also Lord High Commissioner to the General Assembly of the Church of Scotland (1973–4). He published his autobiography, *The Trumpet on the Wall*, in 1970.

BALLANTYNE, James
(1772–1833) and **John** (1774–1821)

Printers, the sons of a merchant of Kelso. In 1783 they were both at Kelso Grammar School with Sir **Walter Scott**. James was trained for the law, but in 1797 started the Tory *Kelso Mail*, and in 1802, having already printed some ballads for Sir Walter Scott, he produced the first two volumes of the *Border Minstrelsy*. At Scott's suggestion he moved the firm to Edinburgh, and in 1805 Scott became a secret partner in the business, which in 1808 expanded into the printing, publishing, and bookselling firm of John Ballantyne & Co., Scott having a one-half share, and each of the brothers a quarter. As early as 1813 bankruptcy threatened the firm, and it was hopelessly involved in **Archibald Constable**'s ruin (1826). John had died bankrupt five years earlier, and James was employed by the creditors' trustees to edit the *Weekly Journal* and in the literary management of the printing office.

BALLANTYNE, John See
BELLENDEN, John

BALLANTYNE, Robert Michael
(1825–94)

Author of boys' books, born in Edinburgh, a nephew of **James** and **John Ballantyne**.

Educated at The Edinburgh Academy, he joined the Hudson's Bay Company in 1841, and worked as a clerk at the Red River Settlement in the backwoods of northern Canada until 1847, before returning to Edinburgh in 1848. He wrote his first stories about his experiences in Canada, with books such as *The Young Fur Traders* (1856). *Coral Island* (1858) is his most famous work.

BALLIOL, Edward de
(c.1283–1364)

King of Scotland (1332–56), elder son of **John de Balliol**. In 1332, accompanied by the 'disinherited barons' who were bent on recovering their forfeited Scottish estates, he landed with 3400 followers at Kinghorn in Fife, and at Dupplin Moor in Perthshire, on 12 August, surprised and routed the Scottish army under the new Regent, the Earl of Mar. On 24 September he was crowned King of Scotland at Scone. Less than three months later he was himself surprised at Annan and fled across the Border on an unsaddled horse. Two further incursions into Scotland, in 1334–5, were unsuccessful, and he resigned his claims to the Scottish throne to Edward III in 1356. He died without heirs.

BALLIOL, John de
(c.1250–1315)

King of Scotland (1292–6), latterly nicknamed 'Toom Tabard' or 'Empty Jacket'. The son of the founder of Balliol College, Oxford, he succeeded in his mother's right to the lordship of Galloway as well as to his father's vast possessions in England and Normandy. On the death of **Margaret, 'Maid of Norway'** in 1290 he became a claimant to the crown of Scotland; Edward I of England pronounced his claim superior to that of **Robert Bruce**, Lord of Annandale. Balliol swore fealty to Edward before and after his investiture at Scone (1292) and was forced to repudiate the Treaty of Bingham of 1290 with its guarantees of Scottish liberties. By 1295 a council of twelve of the magnates had taken control of government out of his hands and concluded an alliance with France, then at war with England; Edward invaded Scotland, took Balliol prisoner, and forced him to surrender his crown on 10 July 1296. Balliol was confined for three years at Hertford and in the Tower of London; in 1302 he was permitted to retire to his estates in Normandy, where he died.

BALMERINO, Arthur Elphinstone, 6th Baron
(1688–1746)

Jacobite. He fought with the Jacobites in the Rising of 1715, escaped to the Continent, and was pardoned in 1733. He was one of the first to join Prince **Charles Edward Stuart** in the 1745 Rising, was captured at Culloden in 1746 and beheaded on Tower Hill in London.

BALMERINO, John Elphinstone, 4th Lord
(1682–1736)

Lawyer and politician. Although his father John, 3rd Lord Balmerino, had been fined for conforming under the Commonwealth, his politics were Tory and Jacobite. A well-known and able lawyer, he was made a privy councillor by **James VII and II** in 1687. Under Queen Anne he was an opponent of the Act of Union and would have been the parliamentary leader of the Scottish Tories at Westminster if he had secured election in 1708 as a representative peer for Scotland; he failed in this, however, despite having been included in the Court list of 'approved' candidates as a sop to the Jacobites. Instead **George Lockhart of Carnwath** became the Scottish Tory parliamentary leader, but when Balmerino was returned to the Lords in 1710 the two collaborated, their most significant success being the passing of an Act in 1712 which restored lay patronage in the Scottish Church. He was again returned as a representative peer in 1713, but on the collapse of the Tories the following year he was expelled from all his offices. In his later years he was a member of the secret committee working to promote the Jacobite cause in Scotland.

BALNAVES, Henry
(?1512–1579)

Reformer, born in Kirkcaldy. In 1538 he was made a Lord of Session by **James V**. In 1543 he was appointed Secretary of State by the regent **James Hamilton**, Earl of Arran. Shortly after, however, he was imprisoned, with **John Knox**, in St Andrews Castle for his Protestantism. When the castle was captured by the French (1547), Balnaves, with Knox and others, was sent to Rouen. While in prison there he wrote a treatise on Justification which, with notes and a preface by Knox, was published in 1584 as *The Con-*

fession of Faith. In 1566 he was allowed to return to Scotland and took an active part on the side of the Lords of the Congregation.

BANKTON, Andrew McDougall, Lord
(?1685–1760)

Judge and jurist, educated at Edinburgh University. He is mainly remembered for his three-volume *Institute of the Laws of Scotland in Civil Rights* (1751–3), which follows the general order of Viscount **Stair**'s *Institutions of the Law of Scotland*. A notable feature of this work is the 'Observations upon the Agreement or Diversity between Scots Law and the Law of England', appended to most of the titles, and which draws valuable comparisons. It was a sound and useful book and is still quoted in Scotland, though not regarded as of the very highest authority.

BANNATYNE, George
(1545–1608)

Antiquary and collector of poems, born in Edinburgh but a native of Forfarshire. He became a wealthy merchant and burgess in Edinburgh, but his claim to fame was his 800-page manuscript of early Scottish poetry of the 15th and 16th centuries (the *Bannatyne Manuscript*), compiled during an outbreak of plague in Edinburgh when he withdrew to his father's estate at Kirktown or Newtyle in Forfarshire. The Bannatyne Club was founded in his honour in 1823 to encourage the study of Scottish history and literature.

BANNEN, Ian
(1928 –)

Actor, born in Airdrie, Lanarkshire. He first stepped on stage at the Gate Theatre, Dublin, in a production of *Armlet of Jade* (1947). Later joining the Shakespeare Memorial Theatre Company, he subsequently established himself as a distinguished classical and contemporary theatre actor in such productions as *A View from the Bridge* (1956), *Sergeant Musgrave's Dance* (1959) and a 1961 season with the Royal Shakespeare Company. He made his film début in *Private's Progress* (1956) and was seen in a succession of incisive supporting performances across a range of gently comic and abrasive dramatic roles, including *The Hill* (1965), *The Flight of the Phoenix* (1965), for which he received an Academy Award nomination, and *The Offence* (1972). He has maintained a successful international career in all media with such television work as *Jesus of Nazareth* (1977), *Tinker, Tailor, Soldier, Spy* (1979) and *Uncle Vanya* (1991); later stage appearances such as *Hedda Gabler* (1977) and *A Moon for the Misbegotten* (1983); and many film performances, notably *Bite the Bullet* (1975) and a much-praised role as the curmudgeonly grandfather in *Hope and Glory* (1987).

BANNERMAN, Helen Brodie, née Boog Watson
(1862–1946)

Children's writer and illustrator, born in Edinburgh, the daughter of a Free Church minister. Her husband was a doctor in the Indian Medical Service and she spent much of her life in India, where she produced the children's classic, *The Story of Little Black Sambo* (1899), the story of a black boy and his adventures with the tigers, based on illustrated letters she had written to her children. Phenomenally popular when it first appeared, it was judged by some after her death to be racist and demeaning to black people. She wrote several other illustrated books for children.

BARBOUR, John
(c.1316–1396)

Poet, prelate and scholar, known as the 'father of Scottish poetry and history'. He was probably born in Aberdeen, and was Archdeacon of Aberdeen from 1357, or earlier, till his death. He studied at Oxford and Paris, and in 1372 was appointed Clerk of Audit for King **Robert II**. His national epic, *The Brus*, written in the 1370s and first printed at Edinburgh in 1571, is a narrative poem on the life and deeds of King **Robert I, the Bruce**, having as its climax the Battle of Bannockburn, and preserving many oral traditions. He also wrote two lost epics, *The Brut* (a history of the Britons) and *The Stewart is Original* (a fictitious pedigree of the kings of Scotland).

BARCLAY, Alexander
(?1475–1552)

Poet and author. He was most probably born in Scotland, may have studied at universities in England, France and Italy, and in 1508 was

Chaplain of Ottery St Mary, Devon. Perhaps about 1511 he became a monk of the Benedictine monastery of Ely; he later became a Franciscan. His famous poem, *The Shyp of Folys of the Worlde* (1509), is partly a translation and partly an imitation of the German *Narrenschiff* by Sebastian Brant. He also published *Egloges* (Eclogues), a translation of Sallust's *Jugurthine War*.

BARCLAY, Captain See BARCLAY-ALLARDICE, Robert

BARCLAY, John
(1734–98)

Presbyterian minister. While assistant minister of Fettercairn he was suspected of heresy and went to England to be ordained. He returned to Edinburgh in 1773 and founded the sect of the Bereans (from Acts xvii), stressing the mystical element in Calvinism.

BARCLAY, John
(1758–1826)

Anatomist, born in Perthshire. He was instrumental in founding the Dick Veterinary College in Edinburgh. The Barcleian museum of the Edinburgh College of Surgeons was founded from his anatomical collection.

BARCLAY, Robert
(1648–90)

Quaker, born in Gordonstoun, Moray, the son of a distinguished soldier who had served under Gustav IV Adolf of Sweden and Charles I. Educated at the Scots College in Paris, where his uncle was rector, he refused to stay in France and embrace Roman Catholicism as heir to his uncle's estates. In 1664 he returned to Scotland, where his father joined the Society of Friends in 1666, and became a Quaker himself in 1667. He married a fellow Quaker in Aberdeen in 1670, the first Quaker wedding in Scotland, which caused a furore, and took over his father's estate at Ury. In 1672 he startled Aberdeen by walking through its streets in sackcloth and ashes. He published many scholarly and lucid tracts in defence of Quakerism, endeavouring to harmonize it with the great religious concepts of his day, especially in his classic *Apology for the True Christian Divinity* (1678). He was frequently imprisoned for attending illegal meetings, but at last found a protector in the Duke of York (the future **James VII and II**), because of distant family connections. He made several journeys to Holland and Germany, the latter with William Penn of Pennsylvania and George Fox. He became one of the proprietors of East New Jersey in 1682, and was appointed its nominal non-resident Governor.

BARCLAY, William
(1907–78)

Theologian and religious writer and broadcaster, born in Wick, Caithness. Educated in Motherwell, and at the universities of Glasgow and Marburg, he was ordained in the Church of Scotland in 1933. After 13 years as a parish minister in Renfrew he returned to academic work in 1946 as a lecturer at Trinity College in Glasgow, specializing in Hellenistic Greek, and in 1963 was appointed Professor of Divinity and Biblical Criticism, from which he retired in 1974. During his career he wrote many serious academic studies, particularly on Graeco-Roman thought, but it is for his popular writings and broadcasts, in which he spoke plainly to the ordinary person about Christian teaching and beliefs, that he is best remembered and greatly loved. His first popular book, *A New Testament Wordbook*, was published in 1955, and like many of his books grew from his contributions to the *British Weekly* journal. An immensely prolific writer, he produced well over 60 books as well as broadcasting on radio and television; his series of televised talks for Lent 1965 formed the basis of his *New People's Life of Jesus*. He was involved in the preparation of the New English Bible. His *Daily Study Bible* (New Testament) won international acclaim and was published in many languages. In 1968 he published his own translation of the New Testament.

BARCLAY-ALLARDICE, Robert, known as **Captain Barclay**
(1779–1854)

Soldier and sportsman, celebrated for walking 1000 miles in 1000 consecutive hours. He succeeded to the estate of Urie, near Stonehaven, in 1797, and joined the army in 1805, taking part in the Walcheren expedition of 1809 before retiring to take up management of his estates. His remarkable walking feat was performed at Newmarket from June to July 1809; he was also the sponsor and trainer of the prize-fighter Tom Cribb.

BARKE, James
(1905–58)

Novelist, born in Torwoodlee, Selkirk. He retired from his position as chief cost accountant with a ship-building company to devote himself to writing. His novels include *The World his Pillow* (1933), and *The Land of the Leal* (1939), but he is chiefly remarkable for his devoted research on the life of **Robert Burns**, resulting in a five-volume cycle of novels (1946–54), an edition of *Poems and Songs of Robert Burns* (1955) and the posthumous *Bonnie Jean*, about Burns and Jean Armour.

BARKLA, Charles Glover
(1877–1944)

English physicist, born in Widnes, Lancashire. He became Professor of Physics at London (1909–13) and of Natural Philosophy at Edinburgh (1913–44). He conducted notable researches into X-rays and other short-wave emissions and was awarded the 1917 Nobel Prize for Physics.

BARNES, George
(1859–1940)

Labour politician, born in Dundee. Originally an engineer, he was active in the engineers' union, becoming its general secretary from 1896 to 1908, when he was elected on a left-wing ticket. One of the first two Scottish Labour MPs, he won Glasgow Blackfriars and Hutchesontown in 1906, defeating **Andrew Bonar Law**. He supported British entry into World War I and organized recruiting campaigns. In 1916 he joined the war administration as Minister for Pensions, one of the first Labour politicians to hold office. In 1917, on **Arthur Henderson**'s resignation, he entered the War Cabinet. He was MP for Glasgow Gorbals (1918–22) as Coalition Labour Party candidate, and was then defeated in 1922.

BARNETSON, Baron William Denholm
(1917–81)

Journalist and newspaper executive, born in Edinburgh. In 1936 he interrupted his studies at Edinburgh University to become a freelance war correspondent in the Spanish Civil War. After World War II, in which he reached the rank of major, he worked on the re-organization of West German newspaper and book publishing, helping to launch *Die Welt*. He was successively Leader Writer, Editor and General Manager of the *Edinburgh Evening News* (1948–61) before joining the board of United Newspapers. Shrewd and dynamic, he was a successful chairman of Reuters news agency (1968–79) and briefly Chairman of Thames TV.

BARNETT, Lady Isobel
(1918–80)

Showbusiness personality, born in Aberdeen. Raised near Charing Cross in Glasgow, she attended Laurel Bank School and graduated from Glasgow University as a doctor. After practising as a GP for several years, she retired from medicine to rear her son. When her husband, Sir Geoffrey Barnett, was Lord Mayor of Leicester, she was spotted by a local member of the BBC and became one of the four original panellists on the long-running television quiz show, *What's My Line?* (1951–63), where her ladylike manner, wit, and chic dress sense endeared her to viewing millions. Soon a national celebrity, she made countless radio and television appearances and was energetically active in public service. Out of the limelight towards the end of her life, she committed suicide after being convicted of a minor shoplifting offence.

BARR, Archibald
(1855–1931)

Engineer, born near Paisley. As an engineering apprentice he graduated at Glasgow University. He was Professor of Civil and Mechanical Engineering at Leeds from 1884 to 1889, when he succeeded his teacher, **James Thomson** (1822–92), in the Regius Chair of Civil Engineering at Glasgow; he set up the **James Watt** research laboratories in 1900. With William Stroud he founded the firm of scientific instrument-makers who were pioneers of naval range-finding, and later invented height finders for anti-aircraft gunnery.

BARRIE, Sir James Matthew
(1860–1937)

Novelist and dramatist, born in Kirriemuir, Angus, the son of a weaver. He was educated there and at Dumfries Academy, graduating at Edinburgh University in 1882. After a year and a half as a journalist in Nottingham he settled in London, and became a regular contributor to the *St James's Gazette* and *British Weekly* (as 'Gavin Ogilvy'). He wrote a series of autobiographical prose works, including *A Window in Thrums* (1889) and *The Little Minister* (1891, dramatized 1897), set in his native village disguised as 'Thrums'. From 1890 onwards he wrote for the theatre, works including the successful *Walker, London* (1892), *Quality Street* (1902) and *The Admirable Crichton* (1902), a good-humoured social satire. These established his reputation, but it is as the creator of *Peter Pan* (1904) that he will be chiefly remembered. Aware of the popular demand for dramatic sentimentality on the London stage, Barrie provided surface romance within dramatic structures which used indirect poetic methods to suggest a bleaker vision of life. He continued his excursions into faeryland in such later plays as *Dear Brutus* (1917) and *Mary Rose* (1920), and in his last play, *The Boy David* (1936), tried a biblical theme which despite containing some of his finest writing won no laurels in the theatre.

BARROW, Geoffrey Wallis Steuart
(1924 –)

English-born historian born in Headingly, Leeds, and educated at St Andrews and Oxford universities. Following various appointments, he became Sir **William Fraser** Professor of Scottish History and Palaeography at Edinburgh University in 1979. His books began with *Feudal Britain* (1956) and *Acts of Malcolm IV, King of Scots* (1960, which he followed in 1971 with the successor volume *Acts of William I, King of Scots*). His great achievement was *Robert Bruce and the Community of the Realm of Scotland* (1965, heavily revised in later editions in the light of further research), in which he simultaneously offered the great major biography of Scotland's hero-king of the Wars of Independence and placed him firmly in the developing concepts of Scottish identity and popular sentiment in his time. Later books included *Kingdom of the Scots* (1973), *The Anglo-Norman Era in Scottish History* (1980), and *Kingship and Unity: Scotland 1000–1306* (1981). As a teacher he combined austerity with searing commitment to his subject, remaining perpetually watchful against efforts of an alien metropolitan culture to erode it. His inaugural address at Edinburgh, on the latter theme, was published in its entirety in the Scottish National Party newspaper, *Scots Independent*. His emphasis on encouraging historical consciousness was particularly

marked in his innumerable student expeditions across Scottish hills in quest of visible evidence of the past. He was made a Fellow of the British Academy in 1976, and the following year a Fellow of the Royal Society of Edinburgh. In 1988 he was made an honorary DLitt of Glasgow University.

BARR SMITH, Robert
(1824–1915)

Scottish-born Australian pastoralist and wool-broking pioneer, born in Renfrewshire and educated at Glasgow University. He settled in South Australia in 1854. There he joined the company established by a fellow Scot, **Thomas Elder** from Kirkcaldy, whose sister Joanna he later married. The two men went into partnership under the style of Elder, Smith & Co to become one of the world's largest wool-brokers with extensive pastoral holdings. Barr Smith built up considerable interests in mining, shipping and finance, and helped found the Bank of Adelaide. Closely involved for many years with Adelaide University, he established the library there which bears his name, and made philanthropic gifts to state and Church. The pastoral interests established by the company are still maintained, after many mergers, in the name of Elders IXL, the brewing giant.

BARRY, James
(1795–1865)

Surgeon and Inspector General of the Army Medical Department. The most astonishing fact about 'James Barry' is that she was a woman, a pretence she maintained throughout her professional life. It was only on her death that the secret was revealed. Her real name and birthplace are not recorded, although she was said (perhaps romantically) to be the granddaughter of a Scottish earl, and was described by Lord Albemarle in 1819 as having 'an unmistakably Scotch type of countenance', as well as a 'certain effeminacy in his manner'. She graduated in medicine from Edinburgh University in 1812 and entered the army as a hospital assistant in 1813. She rose to Assistant Surgeon in 1815, Surgeon Major in 1827, Deputy Inspector General in 1851, Inspector General in 1858, and retired on half-pay in 1859. She fought a duel in Capetown in 1819, and was reputed to be an excellent surgeon, but quarrelsome and prone to breaches of discipline. Her actions were said, again probably romantically, to have been inspired by her love for an army surgeon.

BARTHOLOMEW, John George
(1860–1920)

Cartographer, born in Edinburgh, son of John Bartholomew (1831–93), map engraver and publisher. After graduating at Edinburgh University he entered his father's firm. He published the *Survey Atlas of Scotland* (1895–1912), followed by a similar atlas of England and Wales, a *Physical Atlas of the World* (2 vols, 1889–1911), and *The Times Survey Atlas of the World* (1921), which appeared after his death. He is best known for his system of layer colouring of contours.

BARTON, Andrew
(d.1511)

Naval commander. He cleared the Scottish coast of pirates and in 1506 sent **James IV** three barrels full of Flemish pirates' heads. He was killed in an engagement with two English ships off the Suffolk Downs.

BAXTER, Sir David
(1793–1872)

Linen manufacturer and philanthropist, born in Dundee. After some experience as a manager of a sugar refinery, in 1826 he became a partner in the firm of Baxter Brothers with his father and two younger brothers. All three died within a few years, but with the firm's manager as a partner he successfully introduced power-loom weaving, and the firm rapidly became one of the largest linen manufacturers in the world. During his lifetime he presented to his native city the Baxter Park, the Albert Institute and other benefactions; and at Edinburgh University he endowed the Chair of Engineering in 1868. He left substantial sums of money to the Free Church of Scotland and to several educational institutions.

BAXTER, Jim (James Curran)
(1939 –)

Footballer, born in Fife. The last major footballer produced from the Fife coalfields, once a major nursery of the game, he was at his elegant peak with Glasgow Rangers between 1960 and 1964. For three years he was probably the best left-half in Europe, but did not repeat his Scottish success during spells with Sunderland and Nottingham Forest. Capped 34 times by Scotland, he was never dedicated to training, and left the game soon after the age of 30.

BAXTER, Stanley
(1926 –)

Comic actor, born in Glasgow. A starstruck youngster, be hegan his multifaceted show-business career in radio and gravitated towards the legitimate theatre after the war, making his professional début as Correction's Varlet at the Edinburgh Festival production of *The Thrie Estates* in 1948. A successful appearance in *The Tintock Cup* (1949) began his enduring association with the art of pantomime, and his many other stage appearances include *The Amorous Prawn* (1959), *Chase Me, Comrade* (1965) and *What The Butler Saw* (1969). He made his television début in *Shop Window* (1951) and his film début in *Geordie* (1956). A firm favourite on the small screen, his many television series include *Stanley Baxter On …* (1960–4) and *The Stanley Baxter Show* (1967–71). He subsequently created glittering comic extravaganzas such as *Stanley Baxter's Christmas Box* (1976), which gave full rein to his talent for rubber-faced mimicry, satire and lavish recreations of Hollywood musicals. An uncompromising performer, dedicated to the highest standards, he is also the voice behind myriad diverse television commercials.

BAY CITY ROLLERS See
LONGMUIR, Alan and Derek

BAYNE, Alexander, of Rires
(d.1737)

Jurist. He passed advocate in 1714 but, not securing any great practice, began lecturing privately in Edinburgh on Scots Law. In 1722 he was elected the first Professor of Scots Law in Edinburgh University, an office he held until his death. He published an edition of Sir **Thomas Hope**'s *Minor Practicks* in 1726, to which he appended a 'Discourse on the Rise and Progress of the Law of Scotland and the Method of Studying it', following this with a slim *Institutions of the Criminal Law of Scotland* (1730; 2nd ed 1748), *Notes for the Use of Students of the Municipal Law in the University of Edinburgh*, being a *Supplement to Sir George Mackenzie's Institutions* (1731) and *Notes on the Criminal Law* (1748). One of his daughters, Anne, married the artist **Allan Ramsay**.

BEARDMORE, William (jnr), Lord Invernairn
(1856–1936)

English-born shipbuilder, born in Greenwich, one of Scotland's great industrialists. Educated at Glasgow High School and Ayr Academy he was then apprenticed to his father's firm at the Parkhead Forge. Having completed his education in London, he became a junior partner after his father's death in 1877. He directed a wide-ranging expansion of the steel forging business, combined with the acquisition of a number of mills and iron works. A large modern shipyard and engineering works were added at Dalmuir by 1906. Managing all the businesses which he controlled in a style which has frequently been described as autocratic, he stood astride an integrated industrial empire which nevertheless had underlying financial problems. Partly as tribute to his contribution to the war effort he was created Lord Invernairn in 1921. However, by 1926 his company was bankrupt and effective control was wrested from him two years later while the company that he had created was reconstructed. The result was an enforced retirement.

BEARE, Sir Thomas Hudson
(1859–1940)

Australian-born civil engineer, born in Adelaide, where he attended the university. He moved to England on a scholarship in 1880 and undertook further studies at University College, London. From 1887 he held the Chair of Engineering successively at the following institutions: Heriot-Watt College, Edinburgh; University College, London (1889); and Edinburgh University (1901–40), where he became Dean of the Faculty of Science (1914–40). He translated Cremona's *Graphical Statics* (1872) in 1888, and published many other papers in scientific and engineering journals. For many years he held the rank of Captain in the Forth Volunteer Division of the Royal Engineers.

BEATON, or BETHUNE, David
(1494–1546)

Statesman and prelate, nephew of **James Beaton** (1470–1539), born in Balfour, Fife, and educated at the universities of St Andrews, Glasgow, and Paris. He was at the French court (1519) as Scottish 'resident' and twice later as ambassador to negotiate James V's marriages. He was given French rights of citizenship and appointed Bishop of Mirepoix by Francis I (1537). In 1525 he took his seat in the Scots Parliament as Abbot of Arbroath and was appointed Privy Seal. Made a cardinal in 1538, on the death of his uncle in 1539 he succeeded him as Archbishop of St Andrews. On James's death he produced a forged will, appointing himself and three other regents of the kingdom during the minority of the infant **Mary, Queen of Scots**. The nobility, however, elected the Protestant Earl of **Arran** as Regent. Beaton was arrested, but soon regained favour and was made Chancellor (1543). He was assassinated by a band of conspirators in his castle at St Andrews. His mistress, Marion Ogilvy, had borne him at least two sons and one daughter.

BEATON, or BETHUNE, James
(1470–1539)

Prelate and statesman, uncle of Cardinal **David Beaton**. He graduated from St Andrews in 1493, and rose rapidly to be Archbishop of Glasgow (1509), and of St Andrews (1522). One of the regents during **James V**'s minority, he upheld the **Hamilton** against the **Douglas** faction; and in 1526 he had 'to keep sheep in Balgrumo', while the Douglases plundered his castle. He was soon, however, reinstated in his see, and figured as a zealous supporter of France. An opponent of the Reformation, he initiated persecution of Protestants: as a result **Patrick Hamilton** and three other Protestants were burnt at the stake during his primacy.

BEATON, or BETHUNE, James
(1517–1603)

Prelate, nephew of Cardinal **David Beaton**. He was Archbishop of Glasgow during the Reformation, from 1552 until the death of the Queen-Regent, **Mary of Guise**, in 1560, when he withdrew to Paris as Scottish Ambassador.

BEATTIE, James
(1735–1803)

Poet and essayist, born in Laurencekirk, Kincardineshire, the son of a shopkeeper. He was educated at the village school and at Marischal College, Aberdeen, and after some years as a schoolmaster in Fordoun he became a master at Aberdeen Grammar School, and then in 1760 became Professor of Moral Philosophy at Aberdeen. His over-rated *Essay on Truth* (1770) attacked the philosopher **David Hume**, but he is chiefly remembered for his long poem, *The Minstrel* (1771–4), a forerunner of Romanticism.

BEATTIE, Johnny
(1926 –)

Comedian, entertainer and compère, born in Glasgow. He appeared in an amateur concert party in Glasgow in 1950, and two years later was invited by the tenor **Robert Wilson** to be the principal comic in his touring revue. Today, he is deemed one of Scotland's leading comedians, pantomime dames and all-round entertainers, and is particularly associated with the Gaiety Theatre, Ayr, where he has appeared in many summer seasons, including the 60th anniversary of *The Gaiety Whirl* in 1990.

BEATY, Stuart
(1921 –)

Sculptor/designer, born in Ayrshire. He studied sculpture at Glasgow School of Art and in Mexico. Working mainly in wood, he combines his interest in both the figurative and abstract with comparative ease. He has undertaken various public and private commissions, mainly of three-dimensional reliefs, for, among others, St Joseph's Church, Selkirk, the Scottish College of Textiles and the Scottish Development Agency. He has exhibited regularly since 1950, and is an associate of the Royal Society of British Sculptors.

BEEVERS, Arnold
(1908 –)

English crystallographer, born in Manchester. He studied and then taught at Liverpool University, where he and Henry Solomon Lipson used X-ray crystallography to determine the structures of the crystal hydrates of several sulphates. Together they developed a new arrangement of trigonometrical tables, known worldwide as Lipson-Beevers strips, to speed up calculations of electron densities from X-ray diffraction patterns. They continued their work with W L Bragg in Manchester, before Beevers' move to the Edinburgh University Chemistry De-

partment in 1938. Here he became a key worker, making crystallographic techniques available to his colleagues while himself solving the structures of many organic molecules, for example those of sucrose and strychnine. Subsequently he established a unit to make complex molecular models for teaching purposes.

BEGG, James
(1808–83)

Free Church minister, born in New Monkland, Lanarkshire, a leading exponent of the Anti-Establishment movement that led to the Disruption of 1843. After graduating from Glasgow University, he was ordained at Maxwellton, Dumfries, going on to serve at Middle Parish Church, Paisley, and at Liberton, in Edinburgh, from 1835 to 1843. The remaining 40 years of his ministry were pursued at Newington Free Church, Edinburgh. While his views might today be considered reactionary, anti-ecumenical and aggressively divisive (he was strongly anti-papist, and rejected any form of union with the United Presbyterian Churches), he was typical of many of his generation and the style and belligerence of the Free Church mentality of that era. Opposed to hymn singing and the use of musical instruments in church, he remained an influential and respected exponent of a narrow, rigid religiosity.

BEILBY, Sir George Thomas
(1850–1924)

Industrial chemist, born in Edinburgh. He improved the method of shale oil distillation and invented a manufacturing process for synthesizing alkaline cyanides. He founded the fuel research station at East Greenwich.

BEITH, Major-General John Hay
See **HAY, Ian**

BELL, 'A K' (Arthur Kinmond)
(1870–1942)

Distiller, born in Perth, the eldest son of a wine and spirit merchant. At the age of 19 he joined the small and conservative family business and proceeded, particularly in the decade after he acceded to the partnership in

1895, to expand the firm's activities. The pace of growth quickened after the death of his father as he utilized the advantages of agents and advertising to sell his blended product, particularly in the lucrative export market. He ensured the supply of plentiful whisky stocks by the acquisition of three distilleries between 1933 and 1936. In 1938, for his local philanthropic efforts, he was made a freeman of his native city. By the time of his death Bell's profits exceeded £100 000 per annum.

BELL, Alexander Graham

(1847–1922)

Scottish-born American inventor, born in Edinburgh, son of **Alexander Melville Bell**. Educated at Edinburgh and London, he worked as assistant to his father in teaching elocution (1868–70). In 1870 he went to Canada, and in 1871 moved to the USA, becoming Professor of Vocal Physiology at Boston in 1873 and devoting himself to the teaching of deaf-mutes and to spreading his father's system of 'visible speech'. After experimenting with various acoustical devices he produced the first intelligible telephonic transmission with a message to his assistant on 5 June 1875, and patented the telephone in 1876. He defended the patent against Elisha Gray, and formed the Bell Telephone Company in 1877. In 1880 he established the Volta Laboratory, and invented the photophone (1880) and the graphophone (1887). He also founded the journal *Science* (1883). After 1897 his principal interest was in aeronautics: he encouraged S P Langley, and invented the tetrahedral kite.

BELL, Alexander Melville

(1819–1905)

Scottish-born American educationist, father of **Alexander Graham Bell**, born in Edinburgh. A teacher of elocution at Edinburgh University (1843–65) and University College, London (1865–70), he moved to Canada in 1870 to Queen's College, Ontario (1870–81), thereafter settling in Washington. In 1882 he published his system of 'visible speech' (*Visible Speech: The Science of Universal Alphabets*), showing the position of the vocal chords for each sound.

BELL, Benjamin

(1749–1806)

Surgeon. The eldest of 15 children, he studied medicine at Edinburgh University and later

in London and Paris. He is credited with early research into anaesthesia, was known as the 'foremost operator of his day', and published a six-volume *System of Surgery*. In 1778 he was appointed surgeon to George Watson's Hospital in Lauriston, Edinburgh, and at the peak of his career was offered a Baronetcy, which he declined. He obtained the feu charter for Newington, a southern suburb of Edinburgh, in 1803, and was responsible for its layout. He also built Newington House, where he died. He was the great grandfather of Dr **Joseph Bell**.

BELL, Sir Charles

(1774–1842)

Anatomist and surgeon, famous for his neurological discoveries. Born in Edinburgh, he lectured in anatomy and surgery in London. In 1807 he distinguished between the sensory and motor nerves in the brain, and in 1812 was appointed surgeon to the Middlesex Hospital. To study gunshot wounds he went to Haslar Hospital after the Battle of La Coruña in 1809; after Waterloo he took charge of a hospital in Brussels. His work on the functions of the spinal nerves led to disputes with François Magendie. He was Professor of Surgery at Edinburgh from 1836. The type of facial paralysis known as 'Bell's Palsy' is named after him. He was distantly related to the Edinburgh surgeon Joseph Bell (1837–1911), said to have been the inspiration for **Conan Doyle**'s Sherlock Holmes.

BELL, George Joseph

(1770–1843)

Jurist, born in Edinburgh, the brother of the surgeon Sir **Charles Bell**. He became Professor of Scots Law at Edinburgh University in 1822. He published *Commentaries on The Laws of Scotland and on the Principles of Mercantile Jurisprudence* (1804) and *Principles of the Law of Scotland* (1829), both standard authorities and very influential. He also drafted the report of the Commission on Scottish Judicial Proceedings (1823) which resulted in the Scottish Judicature Act (1825).

BELL, Henry

(1767–1830)

Engineer and pioneer of steam navigation, born at Torphichen Mill, Linlithgow, West Lothian. After a time apprenticed as a wheelwright and as a shipbuilder he then worked with a civil engineer in London before returning to Scotland and becoming an engineer in Helensburgh. In 1812 he successfully launched the 30-ton *Comet* on the Clyde. Plying regularly between Greenock and Glasgow, it was the first passenger-carrying steamboat in European waters.

BELL, John
(1691–1780)

Physician and traveller, born in Stirlingshire. After graduating as a doctor he went to St Petersburg in 1714 . He was physician to Russian embassies to Persia (1715–18), went to China through Siberia (1719–22), and again to Persia (1722). In 1737 he settled at Constantinople as a merchant, but in about 1746 returned to Scotland. His *Travels* were published in 1763.

BELL, John Jay
(1871–1934)

Journalist and humorous writer. He is best known for his *Wee MacGreegor* (1902), an amusing, poignant evocation of boyhood in Glasgow in the days before World War I. Dramatized in 1911, it has been described as Scotland's equivalent of *Huckleberry Finn* and *Just William*. It is still in print.

BELL, John Zephaniah
(1794–1883)

Painter, born in Dundee, the second son among 16 children of William Bell, a substantial figure in the Dundee business community. Educated at the Royal High School in Edinburgh, he was originally trained for a career in law, but in 1817, with a letter of introduction to Sir **David Wilkie**, he travelled to London in order to enrol at the Royal Academy Schools. Dissatisfied with the teaching of drawing there, he went to Paris and attended the studio of Antoine Gros. In 1825 he travelled to Rome where he came into contact with the Nazarenes, a group of painters interested in early Italian art, especially religious fresco painting. Bell had ambitions to become a painter of large-scale narrative history paintings, although it is for portraiture that he is best known. His long and varied career brought him neither popular nor professional recognition, and his death went unnoticed even by the Royal

Scottish Academy, of which he was one of the earliest members.

BELL, Maggie
(1945 –)

Rock singer, born in Glasgow. She made her first live appearance with **Alex Harvey** for a bet, and later worked with Harvey's younger brother Les (1947–72) in the bands Kinning Park Rangers and Power. Power worked the European live circuit before being discovered by Led Zeppelin's manager, Peter Grant. Renamed Stone The Crows, the band signed a recording deal in 1970 and the same year released two blues-based LPs, *Stone The Crows* and *Ode To John Law*. *Ontinuous Performance* (1972) was the band's most successful LP, but they split the same year following Harvey's electrocution on stage in Swansea. Bell recorded the solo albums *Queen Of The Night* (1973) and *Suicide Sal* (1975), and had some success with the theme music for the television series Hazell (1978).

BELL, Patrick
(1799–1869)

Clergyman and inventor, born in Auchterhouse, near Dundee, the son of a farmer. He worked on the development of a mechanical reaper, the prototype of which earned a 50 premium from the Highland and Agricultural Society in 1827. Its adoption by British farmers was very slow, however, and when four of his reapers were sent to the USA they enabled Cyrus McCormick and others to realize their full potential. By 1843 he had abandoned his active interest in agricultural machinery and entered the Church as minister of Carmylie, Arbroath. Belatedly, in 1868, he was awarded £1000 in appreciation of his pre-eminent services as the inventor of the first efficient 'reaping machine'.

BELL, Robert Fitzroy
(?1858–1908)

Student leader, lawyer and editor. He was educated at Jena University. Impressed by the system of student self-policing there, he introduced this in 1883 at Edinburgh University (where he was studying law) as the Students' Representative Council. According to *The Scotsman* (1908) Bell's 'attractive personality and social gifts, combined as these were with genuine organizing ability, made him a centre of University life among the students in a sense in which perhaps no other undergraduate at the University of Edinburgh has ever stood'. He was also the prime mover in the creation of Edinburgh University Union, other Scottish and English universities thereafter following suit. Unions and SRCs were legalized in 1889, and Bell became Secretary of the Scottish Universities Commission under Lord Kinnear (1889–94). In 1884 he was called to the Scottish Bar. Staunchly Tory, he founded the *Scots Observer* (1889), and played a part in Kipling's rise to fame by publishing his hitherto rejected 'Cleared', a ferocious denunciation of the Parnell Commission.

BELL, Ronald Percy
(1907 –)

English physical chemist, who spent most of his working life in England, but towards the end of it contributed significantly to scientific progress and education in Scotland. He was born in Maidenhead, Berkshire, and after leaving Oxford University spent four years in Johannes Brönsted's laboratory in Copenhagen. In 1932 he returned to Oxford, where he later became Reader in Physical Chemistry and Vice-Master of Balliol College. He made valuable contributions to solution chemistry, especially acid-base catalysis, the theory of the tunnel effect, and the influence of isotopes on the speed of reactions. He moved to the new university at Stirling in 1967 where, under the aegis of Principal **Tom Cottrell**, he set up a chemistry department that was soon widely renowned.

BELL, Sir Thomas
(1865–1952)

Shipbuilder, born in Sirsawa, India, of Scottish parents. Educated in Germany and England, at 15 he entered the Royal Naval Engineering College but was prevented from following a naval career because of poor eyesight. Instead, in 1886 he joined the design staff at J & G Thomson's shipyard in Clydebank, which was taken over by John Brown of Sheffield in 1899, and by 1909 he was Managing Director of John Brown's, Clydebank. He was seconded to the Admiralty in 1917–18, where his technical and managerial abilities were severely tested in the depression after World War I. It was largely his determination that brought the contract for the *Queen Mary* to Clydebank in 1930.

BELLANY, John
(1942 –)

Painter and etcher, born in Port Seton, East Lothian. He studied at Edinburgh College of Art (1960–5) and at the Royal College of Art (1965–8). He is one of the generation of Scots who, in the 1970s, adopted an expressive form of realism inspired by Léger and by German art. A retrospective of his work was held at the Scottish National Gallery of Modern Art and at the Serpentine Gallery, London, in 1986.

BELLENDEN, or BALLANTYNE, John
(d.1587)

Ecclesiastic and writer, born towards the close of the 15th century. In 1508 he matriculated from St Andrews and completed his theological studies at the Sorbonne. His translations in 1533 of Boece's *Historia Gentis Scotorum*, and of the first five books of Livy, are interesting as vigorous specimens of early Scottish prose. The *Croniklis of Scotland* is a very free translation, and contains numerous passages not found in **Boece**, so that it is in some respects almost an original work. Bellenden enjoyed great favour at the court of **James V**, at whose request the translations were made. As a reward, he received considerable grants from the Treasury, and afterwards was made Archdeacon of Moray and Canon of Ross. Becoming involved, however, in ecclesiastical controversy, he went to Rome.

BENNETT, James Gordon
(1795–1872)

Scottish-born American journalist, father of James Gordon Bennett (1841–1918), born in Keith, Banffshire. He emigrated to Nova Scotia in 1819, and became a journalist for the *New York Enquirer* (1826–8) and the *Morning Courier and New York Enquirer* (1829–32). In 1835 he started the *New York Herald*, which he edited until 1867, pioneering many journalistic innovations, such as the use of European correspondents.

BETHUNE, David and James See BEATON, David and James

BEVERIDGE, Gordon Smith Grieve
(1933 –)

Chemical engineer and academic administrator, born in St Andrews. Educated in

Inverness, and at Glasgow, Strathclyde and Edinburgh universities, he was engaged in teaching and research in chemical and process engineering in Heriot-Watt College, Edinburgh, Minnesota and Texas universities from 1956 to 1971. At Strathclyde University he was Professor of Chemical Engineering (1971–86). He was President of the Institution of Chemical Engineers (1984–5), and has served on many academic and industrial bodies, such as the Council of Engineering Institutions, the Council for National Academic Awards, and the Science and Engineering Research Council, and as Chairman of the Cremer and Warner group of companies. In 1986 he was appointed President and Vice-Chancellor of the Queen's University of Belfast. He has published widely in scientific and professional journals.

BIG COUNTRY See ADAMSON, Stuart

BISSET, Habakkuk
(?1560 – ?1630)

Jurist, said to have been the son of **Mary, Queen of Scots**' caterer. Little is known about him. He was employed by Sir **James Balfour of Pittendreich** about 1582 as a research assistant and worked on the compilation of Balfour's *Practicks* (published 1754). He became a Writer to the Signet but was suspended for not wearing his gown. From 1609 to 1613 he was a clerk and assistant to Sir **John Skene** and made a collection of the forms of process in Civil actions. He compiled a *Rolment of Courtis* (printed 1920–6) comprising 'A Short Forme of Process', (which is a revised edition of 'Ane Short Forme of Process', printed in Skene's edition of *Regiam Majestatem* (1609) and 'Civil Process Used of Old'; an important record of old court procedure, its later parts also contain material interesting for legal history.

BLACK, Adam
(1784–1874)

Publisher, born in Edinburgh, the son of a master builder. Educated at the High School of Edinburgh, he was apprenticed at the age of 15 to an Edinburgh bookseller. He set up his own bookshop in 1807, and started publishing in 1817. In 1826 he bought the *Encyclopaedia Britannica* after **Archibald Constable**'s failure and in 1854 he bought the rights to **Scott**'s novels from **Robert Cadell**'s representatives. He was Lord Provost between 1843 and 1848, and Liberal MP for the burgh (1856–65).

BLACK, Andrew
(1859–1920)

Concert baritone, born in Glasgow. He was originally an organist before going to London to train his voice. After his début in 1887 he became renowned especially for oratorio, although he also sang in opera. He was the original Judas in Elgar's *The Apostles* (1903). He toured America, taught singing at the Manchester Royal College of Music from 1893, and made a number of records.

BLACK, David Macleod
(1941 –)

South African-born poet, born in Wynberg and living there and in Malawi and Tanzania until the age of eight, when he moved to Scotland. He left school at 17 and eventually returned to education, taking a degree in philosophy at Edinburgh University. He later did a postgraduate degree in religion at Lancaster University. He edited the magazine *Extra Verse* from 1963 to 1965 and has published several pamphlets and books of poetry, including *Rocklestakes* (1960), *With Decorum* (1967), *The Educators* (1969), *The Happy Crow* (1974), and *Gravitations* (1979). He was included in the 1968 edition of *Penguin Modern Poets*. His *Collected Poems 1964–1987* was published in 1991. The form of his first long dramatic poem 'Anna's Affairs' (published in *The Educators*) has become his trademark. His work is recognized for its innovative rhyming schemes and he describes it as 'concerned with inner reality rather than outer reality'. Described by **Alan Bold** as one of the most individual voices of the 1960s in Scotland, since the 1970s he has devoted much of his time and energy to his work as a psychotherapist and has written only a handful of short poems.

BLACK, James
(1879–1949)

Church of Scotland minister, lecturer and writer, a towering figure in the Church of his generation. Educated at Glasgow University, the United Free Church College and Marburg University, he was ordained at Forres in 1903, moving from there to Broughton Place Church, Edinburgh (1907–21). He became minister of the important city centre charge of St George's West, Edinburgh, in 1921, and stayed there until 1949, where his inspired ministry formed a landmark in Church life. He had also served as a chaplain to the Forces in France, with the Royal Scots and the Seaforths (1915–18), being mentioned in Despatches. Appointed Chaplain to the King in 1942, he combined successful ministry with high-profile lectureships in preaching. In 1938–9 his particular gifts and contribution to the life of the Church were recognized when he became Moderator of the General Assembly. A dazzling preacher and highly regarded minister, he was also a successful author, *The Pilgrim Ship* (1910), *The Mystery of Preaching* (1924) and *His Glorious Shame* (1932) being among his most popular works.

BLACK, Sir James Whyte

(1924 –)

Pharmacologist, winner of the Nobel Prize for physiology or medicine. He was educated at Beath High School, Cowdenbeath and St Andrews University, where he graduated in medicine, becoming assistant lecturer in physiology in 1946. After three years as lecturer in physiology at the University of Malaya he became senior lecturer at Glasgow Veterinary School (1950–8). He joined ICI Pharmaceuticals Ltd (1958–64) and then became Head of Biological Research and Development at Smith, Kline and French (1964–73). He was Professor and Head of the Department of Pharmacology at University College, London (1973–7), Director of Therapeutic Research at the Wellcome Research Laboratories (1978–84), taking up his present post at King's College Hospital Medical School from 1984. He became FRS in 1976 and was knighted in 1981. In 1988 he received the Nobel Prize, for his work at ICI, where, with his colleagues, he brought forward the first beta-blocking drug to have clinical application; from his later work (for Smith, Kline and French) on histamine-receptor antagonists, cimetidine emerged.

BLACK, John Bennett

(1883–1964)

Historian, born in Glasgow. After taking first-class honours degrees in English (Glas-

gow) and modern history (Oxford), he became lecturer in British History at Glasgow (1910–19), during which time he served in the army and was a prisoner of war (1918). He spent one year as Professor of Modern History at Queen's University, Kingston, in Ontario (1919–20). From 1920 to 1930 he was Professor of Modern History at Sheffield University, and from 1930 to 1953 Burnett-Fletcher Professor of History at Aberdeen University. His most remarkable work was *The Art of History* (1926), an invaluable study of the 18th-century historians Voltaire, **David Hume**, Edward Gibbon, and **William Robertson**. The status he won as a Scottish interpreter of English history was symbolized by George N Clark's commission for him to write *The Reign of Elizabeth* for the leading multi-volume *History of England* of his time, the Oxford series. Admirably lucid, this reflected his conviction of ideological background as the determinant for historical interpretation. Published in 1936, it was dominated by his interests in diplomacy and government, but, while old-fashioned, it remained a standard text for over half a century. A Fellow of the Royal Historical Society (1920–54), he was President of the Historical Association of Scotland (1937–40), and was made Honorary LLD of Glasgow (1949) and Aberdeen (1954). As a teacher and colleague he was loved for his courtesy, kindness, and devotion to learning.

BLACK, Joseph

(1728–99)

Physician and chemist, born in Bordeaux, the son of a wine merchant. Educated at Belfast, Glasgow and Edinburgh, he became an assistant to **William Cullen**. In an extension of his MD thesis (1756) he showed that the causticity of lime and the alkalis is due to the absence of the 'fixed air' (carbon dioxide) present in limestone and the carbonates of the alkalis. In 1756 he succeeded William Cullen as Professor of Anatomy and Chemistry at Glasgow, but soon after exchanged duties with the Professor of the Institutes of Medicine, practising also as a physician. Between 1756 and 1761 he evolved the theory of 'latent heat' on which his scientific fame chiefly rests. In 1766 he succeeded Cullen as Professor of Medicine and Chemistry at Edinburgh.

BLACK, William

(1841–98)

Novelist, born in Glasgow. Educated at the Glasgow School of Art, he moved to London as a journalist and was a war correspondent during the Austro-Prussian War (1866) and the Franco-Prussian War (1870–1). An early member of the 'Kailyard School', his first success was *A Daughter of Heth* (1871), followed by a succession of stereotypical novels, usually with Highland settings, such as *A Princess of Thule* (1874) and *White Heather* (1885).

BLACKADDER, Elizabeth
(1931 –)

Painter, born in Falkirk, Stirlingshire. She studied at Edinburgh University and Edinburgh College of Art, where she later taught. Her early work was mainly landscape, but from the 1970s she began to concentrate on still-life, for which she is now best known. In both oil and water colour she combines recognizable objects with apparently random associations (cats, fans, ribbons, etc) depicted on an abstract empty background. Her interest in calligraphic gesture and the space between motifs shows considerable Japanese influence. By the late 1970s the representational elements increasingly included flowers and plants, which have come to dominate her compositions. She has achieved considerable academic distinction by being the first Scottish woman painter to be elected to full membership of both the Royal Academy and the Royal Scottish Academy.

BLACKADDER, John
(1615–86)

Covenanting minister of Troqueer, near Dumfries. Deprived of his living after the Restoration, in 1662, he preached in conventicles in defiance of the law and was outlawed in 1674. He fled to Rotterdam, but returned to Scotland in 1679, and in 1681 was imprisoned on the Bass Rock, where he died. His fifth son, John (1664–1729), became colonel in command of the Cameronians in 1709.

BLACKIE, John
(1782–1874)

Publisher. In 1809 he founded the Glasgow firm of Blackie & Son, expanding this in 1829 with the addition of Duncans, the university printers, and opening a London branch in 1830. Among his notable publications were **James Hogg**'s complete poems, and an

edition of **Burns**, prefaced by an essay by Christopher North (**John Wilson**).

BLACKIE, John Stuart
(1809–95)

Scholar, born in Glasgow, the son of a banker. Educated at Aberdeen Grammar School and Edinburgh and Aberdeen universities, he contemplated going into the ministry but was persuaded by his father to study abroad until he was old enough to preach. Returning to Edinburgh he studied law, and in 1834 was called to the Bar, though he never practised; the same year he published a metrical translation of Goethe's *Faust*. His magazine articles on German subjects became widely known and he became Professor of Humanities at Aberdeen (1841–52) and of Greek at Edinburgh till 1882. He helped to reform the Scottish universities, was a keen advocate of Scottish nationalism, and raised funds for the endowment of a Celtic chair at Edinburgh. He published prolifically on philosophy, history, legal subjects, and on language teaching. His two lectures in Aberdeen in 1852 'On the Studying and Teaching of Languages' set out the first recorded account of what became known as the 'direct method'.

BLACKLOCK, Thomas
(1721–91)

Poet and clergyman, born in Annan, Dumfriesshire. Blind from smallpox in infancy, he was educated at Edinburgh University. He became a minister in Kirkcudbright in 1759 but returned to Edinburgh in 1764. He published a volume of poems in 1760, but he is remembered for a letter of encouragement to **Robert Burns** after the publication of the Kilmarnock edition, which helped persuade the latter to remain in Scotland.

BLACKWELL, Alexander
(c.1700 – c.1747)

Adventurer, born in Aberdeen, possibly a younger son of the Principal of Marischal College. In about 1730 he was a printer in London and, becoming bankrupt in 1734, was supported in prison by his wife, who published a *Herbal* (2 vols, 1737–9) with 500 cuts, drawn, engraved, and coloured by herself, her husband adding their Latin names and a brief description of each. In 1742 he turned up in Sweden where, having cured the king of an illness, he was appointed a royal physician and undertook the management of a model farm. In 1747 he was arrested on a trumped-up charge of conspiring against the Constitution, and was beheaded.

BLACKWOOD, William
(1776–1834)

Publisher, born in Edinburgh. Apprenticed to a bookseller at the age of 14, he established himself as a bookseller — principally of anti-quarian books — in Edinburgh in 1804. In 1817 he started *Blackwood's Magazine* as a Tory rival to the Whig *Edinburgh Review*, and from the seventh number assumed the edi-torship himself along with **John Wilson** ('Christopher North'), **Lockhart**, **Hogg** and others as contributors. His sons Alexan-der and Robert took over the firm (1834–52), followed by John (1818–79), who published all but one of George Eliot's novels.

BLAIR, Alistair
(1957 –)

Fashion designer, born in Freetown, Sierra Leone, of Scottish parents, and brought up in Helensburgh, Dunbartonshire. A graduate of the St Martin's School of Art, London, he assisted Marc Bohan on the Couture at Christian Dior in Paris, moving to Givenchy, Chloé and later to Karl Lagerfeld. In 1986 he launched his own label, his simple, classic and wearable designs winning clients such as HRH The Princess of Wales, Faye Dunaway, Whitney Houston and Catherine Bailey. He was Designer at Balmain in Paris until 1991, and is currently with the Italian label Cerruti, based in Paris. He designs for the Scottish label Ballantyne Cashmere, and has designed for Jaeger and Cecil Gee.

BLAIR, Catherine
(1872–1946)

Painter and reformer, born in Bathgate, Midlothian. From her late thirties she was at the forefront of the Women's Suffrage Move-ment and deeply involved in the Scottish Women's Rural Institute. A few years later, in 1920, she founded the Mak' Merry Pottery in Macmerry, East Lothian, which specialized in painting pottery blanks to an extremely high standard in a colourful and decorative manner. Throughout her life she was an outspoken champion of the ordinary Cottar woman and she happily passed on her skills, enabling this cottage industry to develop.

BLAIR, Hugh
(1718–1800)

Preacher, born and educated in Edinburgh. He was licensed as a preacher in 1741 and was appointed in 1758 to one of the charges of the High Kirk, Edinburgh. In 1762 he was appointed to a new Regius Chair of Rhetoric and Belles-Lettres at Edinburgh. His dis-courses, sermons and lectures enjoyed a reputation beyond their merit, and George III bestowed a pension on him in 1780.

BLAIR, Robert
(1699–1746)

Poet and preacher, born in Edinburgh. Edu-cated at Edinburgh University, in 1731 he was ordained minister of Athelstaneford, East Lothian. He is best known as the author of *The Grave* (1743), a blank-verse poem which heralded the 'churchyard school' of poetry. The 1808 edition was finely illustrated with rare imaginative power by William Blake.

BLAIR, Robert
(1748–1828)

Astronomer, born in Garvald, East Lothian, the son of a minister. Originally a surgeon, he was appointed to a specially created pro-fessorship at Edinburgh in 1785, becoming the first Regius Professor of Astronomy there. He became famous for his researches in the science of optics, and in particular for his efforts to improve the optical performance of refracting telescopes. The work of optician John Dollond in this field had required the use of compound lenses made of crown and flint glasses. The difficulty of obtaining flaw-less disks of flint suggested to Blair the use of hollow fluid-filled lenses with similar optical properties to flint. Using a fluid lens con-taining hydrochloric acid mixed with salt solutions interspaced between crown glass lenses, he succeeded in constructing tele-scopes several inches in size which won the praise of experts such as **David Brewster**.

BLAKE, George
(1893–1961)

Novelist and journalist, born in Greenock, Renfrewshire. He studied law at Glasgow University, but after being wounded at Gal-lipoli in World War I, turned to journalism, first in Glasgow and later in London. He became a director of the publishing firm Faber & Faber from 1930 to 1932, when he returned to Scotland, remaining there until his death, with the exception of a period at the Ministry of Information in London during World War II. His naturalistic novels offer a romantic and sentimental view of the urban working class, in direct opposition to the rural staples of the Kailyard, which he criticized in *Barrie and the Kailyard School* (1951). His most notable books are *The Shipbuilders* (1935), a powerful if schematic Clydeside epic, and his series of six novels about the Oliphant family, set in Garvel (a fictionalized Greenock) and Glasgow. He was an important forerunner of writers such as **Alan Sharp**, Archie Hind and **William McIlvanney**.

BLANE, Sir Gilbert
(1749–1834)

Physician, born in Blanefield, Ayrshire. In 1779 he sailed with Admiral George Rodney to the West Indies. As head of the Navy Medical Board, he was instrumental in introducing the compulsory use of lemon juice on board navy ships to prevent scurvy. He also pioneered the use of statistics in clinical medicine, and played an important part in formulating the rules which were the foundation for modern quarantine laws.

BLAXTER, Sir Kenneth
(1919–91)

English animal nutritionist. Educated at Norwich School and Reading University, where he graduated in agriculture, his first appointment was at the National Institute for Dairying in Essex. His main contributions to animal husbandry were made, however, after he became, first, Director of the Hannah Dairy Institute, near Ayr, and then of the Rowett Research Institute, Aberdeen. Initially concerned with calf nutrition, he was able to show that, with proper supplements, early weaning had no harmful effect, so that the practice is now adopted worldwide. In parallel he made careful study of trace elements and their effect on calf and lamb growth. He then went on to gather an immense amount of information on the way in which cows metabolize their food. This has led to meaningful ways of evaluating the energy available for foodstuffs, methods which are now widely used. Elected FRS in 1967, he was much honoured by the agricultural and scientific community.

BLIND HARRY See HARRY, Blind

BLYTHMAN, Morris, pseudonym Thurso Berwick
(1919–81)

Songwriter and poet, born in Inverkeithing, Fife. One of the most influential figures in the early folk-music revival movement in Glasgow in the 1950s, he wrote under the pseudonym of Thurso Berwick, a catch-all name which he devised in the hope (unfulfilled) that it would be used by other writers as well as himself. His fierce blend of Scottish nationalism and Marxism produced a host of biting, radical songs and poems, often laced with devastating wit, which did much to inspire a political consciousness in Scottish songwriting. He edited a number of crucial publications, including *Rebel Ceilidh Song Book*, *Homage to John Maclean* and *Sangs Against the Bomb*.

BOECE, BOYIS, or BOETHIUS, Hector
(c.1465–1536)

Historian, born in Dundee. He studied at Montaigu College, Paris, where from c.1492 to 1498 he was a Regent or Professor of Philosophy, and where he formed a friendship with Erasmus. Bishop **Elphinstone** then invited him to be Principal of his newly founded University of Aberdeen. Boece accepted the office, and he was at the same time made a Canon of the cathedral. In 1522 he published his Lives, in Latin, of the Bishops of Mortlach and Aberdeen, and in 1527 *Scotorum historiae a prima gentis origine*, a history of Scotland which, though proved to contain a large amount of fiction, was deemed distinctly critical at the time of its publication. The king awarded him a pension until he was promoted to a benefice in 1534.

BOETHIUS, Hector See BOECE, Hector

BOGLE, George
(1746–81)

Diplomat, born near Bothwell, Lanarkshire. He entered the service of the East India Company, and in 1774 was selected by

Warren Hastings to act as envoy to the Dalai Lama in Tibet. He was the first Briton to cross the Tsanpu in its upper range, and he established commercial links with Tibet, becoming a personal friend of the lama. He returned in 1775, and died in Calcutta.

BOGUE, David
(1750–1825)

Congregational minister and one of the founders of the London Missionary Society, born in Coldingham, Berwickshire. He became an Independent minister and tutor at a Gosport seminary, out of which grew the London Missionary Society. He was also a founder of the British and Foreign Bible Society and the Religious Tract Society and (with Dr James Bennet) wrote a *History of Dissenters* (1809).

BOLD, Alan
(1943 –)

Poet, biographer, critic and editor, born in Edinburgh. He was educated at Broughton High School, where he showed signs of the rebelliousness which was to mark his early poetry, and went on to Edinburgh University. After trying a variety of jobs, including journalism, he became a full-time writer in 1967 and settled in Markinch, Fife. Quickly establishing himself as one of the most prolific writers in the country, his contribution to Scottish literature is likely to rest at least as much on his prodigious critical writings and anthologies as on his poetry. He has been a particularly influential commentator on **Hugh MacDairmid**, his biography of the poet winning the McVitie Scottish Writer of the Year Award in 1989. He has published several volumes of poetry in both English and Scots, including *In this Corner: Selected Poems* 1963–83, which traces the development in his work from an initial angry humanism into a more cooly-observed scrutiny of the natural world and of the society which surrounds him. As a literary critic and book reviewer he is a trenchant and combative commentator.

BONAR, Horatius
(1808–89)

Hymn-writer, born in Edinburgh. He was minister at Kelso (1837–66), but joined the Free Church of Scotland and was minister of Chalmers Memorial Church in Edinburgh from 1866. He wrote well-known hymns such as 'Glory be to God the Father', 'Here, O my Lord, I see thee face to face', and 'I heard the voice of Jesus say', collected in the three-volume *Hymns of Faith and Hope* (1857–66).

BONE, Sir Muirhead
(1876–1953)

Artist, born in Glasgow. Although he studied architecture, he was self-taught as an artist. He married Gertrude Dodd, author of *Days in Old Spain* (1936) which, along with other books, he illustrated. He sacrificed the profession of architect for that of draughtsman and exhibited extensively from 1902. Generally accepted as one of the greatest etchers practising in the 20th century, he was trustee of both the National Gallery and the Imperial War Museum. His work, which has been likened, technically, to that of Piranesi, combines meticulous realism with a strong sense of composition, and his subject matter ranges from the architectural to portraiture and landscape. During his long career he made over 500 etchings, drypoints and lithographs besides many thousands of drawings and watercolours. He travelled to America, Spain, Italy, Holland, France, Turkey and Sweden. His son Stephen (1904–58) was an artist and critic.

BONE, Phyllis Mary
(1896–1972)

English-born animal sculptor, born in Hornby, Lancashire. She studied at Edinburgh College of Art, in Italy and in Paris under Édouard Navellier. She exhibited at the Royal Academy, Royal Scottish Academy, Paris Salon, British Empire Exhibition and the Royal Glasgow Institute, and undertook many commissions, including a Scottish National War Memorial granite sculpture on Inchcape Monument, a carving for St Winifred's Church, Welbeck, and works for St John's Church, Perth, and Edinburgh's Zoological Building. Her works are held in many public and private collections including Aberdeen Art Gallery and Glasgow Museum and Art Gallery. She was the first woman to be elected to the Royal Scottish Academy.

BOOTHBY, Sir Robert John Graham, 1st Baron Boothby of Buchan and Rattray Head
(1900–86)

Conservative politician, born in Edinburgh. He was educated at Eton and Oxford University, and in 1924 was elected MP for East Aberdeenshire, the seat he held until 1958. 'Discovered' in 1926 by Winston Churchill, he became his Parliamentary Private Secretary till 1929. In the 1930s he was highly critical of his party's appeasement policy, and advocated greater state activity to relieve unemployment and stimulate economic growth. From 1940 to 1941 he was Parliamentary Secretary to the Ministry of Food and later served in the RAF. He became in 1948 an original member of the Council of United Europe and was a British delegate to its Consultative Assembly (1949–54). He was raised to the peerage in 1958. An outstanding commentator on public affairs on radio and TV, he brought to political argument a refreshing candour, a robust independence and a talent for exposing the easy hypocrisies of public life. He wrote *The New Economy* (1943), *I Fight To Live* (1947) and *My Yesterday, Your Tomorrow* (1962).

BORN, Max
(1882–1970)

German physicist, born in Breslau (Wroclaw). Professor of theoretical physics at Göttingen (1921–33), lecturer at Cambridge (1933–6) and Professor of Natural Philosophy at Edinburgh (1936–53), he shared the 1954 Nobel Prize with Walther Bothe for work in the field of quantum physics.

BORTHWICK, Peter
(1804–52)

Politician, born in Cornbank, in the parish of Borthwick, Midlothian. Educated at Edinburgh University he was subsequently in residence at Jesus College, Cambridge, and later a fellow-commoner of Downing College. From 1832 he made his name as a speaker in the slavery debate on the side of the slave owners, favouring gradual rather than instant abolition. He contested Evesham unsuccessfully as Tory candidate in 1832, being successfully returned in 1835. His speeches in the Commons in support of the established Church and the Carlist cause in Spain made him the forerunner of Disraeli's Young England movement, which adopted many of his ideas. His principal achievement was the insertion of 'the Borthwick Clause' in the poor law, by which married couples over the age of 60 were no longer separated on entering a poor-house. Borthwick remained in the Commons until 1847, then was called to the

Bar at Gray's Inn. In 1850 he became Editor of the *Morning Post*, for which he wrote vigorous articles right up to his death. Lord George Bentinck observed of him: 'Borthwick is a very remarkable man. He can speak, and speak well, upon any subject at a moment's notice'.

BOSTON, Thomas
(1676–1732)

Theologian, the son of a Covenanting minister. Employed in 1689 by Alexander Cockburn, he studied at Edinburgh and in 1696 became a schoolteacher at Glencairn, Dumfriesshire. Ordained into the Church in 1699, from 1707 until his death he was minister of Ettrick. In 1720 he and 12 others opposed the act of assembly which condemned *The Marrow of Modern Divinity*, a 17th-century (1645) compilation of theological articles, which was considered to contain antinomian theories. This breakaway group came to be known variously as 'the twelve apostles' and the 'Marrow-men', and Boston attracted a considerable following. He is remembered chiefly for his *Fourfold State of Man* (1720), long recognized as a standard exposition of Calvinistic theology.

BOSWELL, Alexander, 1st Baronet
(1775–1822)

Songwriter and printer, son of **James Boswell**. Educated at Westminster and Oxford, he set up a private press at Auchinleck, at which he printed many rare books of early English and Scottish literature, besides a volume of vigorous poems in the Ayrshire dialect (1803); in 1817 he contributed 12 songs to **George Thomson**'s *Select Collection*, of which 'Good night, and joy be wi' ye a'', 'Jenny's Bawbee', and 'Jenny dang the Weaver' were very popular. He was created a baronet in 1821, and died of a wound received in a duel with James Stuart of Dunearn, who had challenged him as the author of anonymous political lampoons. His younger brother, James (1778–1822), edited the third *Variorum Shakespeare* (1821).

BOSWELL, James
(1740–95)

Man of letters and biographer of Dr Johnson, born in Edinburgh, the eldest son of a judge, Lord Auchinleck. He was educated privately in Edinburgh and at the University of Edinburgh. He then studied civil law at Glasgow, but his true goal was literary fame and the friendship of the famous. At the age of 18 he began to keep an astonishingly frank and self-probing journal. In spring 1760 he ran away to London and turned Catholic. To discourage such religious fervour, Lord Eglinton, a London-based friend of Boswell's father, saw to it that Boswell became more of a libertine than ever and he reverted to his original faith. Young Boswell hobnobbed with the young Duke of York, with Sheridan's father, made plans to join the army, and skilfully resisted all attempts to lure him into matrimony. He first met Dr Johnson on his second visit to London, on 16 May 1763, at Tom Davies's bookshop in Russell Street. By the following year they were on such cordial terms that Johnson accompanied him as far as Harwich. Boswell was on his way to Utrecht to continue his legal studies, but stayed only for the winter and then toured Germany, France, Switzerland, and Italy. By an astounding process of literary gatecrashing he introduced himself to Voltaire and Rousseau. From Rousseau he procured an introduction to Paoli, the hero of Corsica, whom he 'Boswellized' in *Account of Corsica* (1768), which had an immediate success and was translated into several languages. Boswell had many love affairs. There was the serious and high-minded affair with 'Zélide' of Utrecht, and liaisons with the Irish Mary Anne Montgomery, and with numerous others in London, Rome and elsewhere, including a disreputable episode with Rousseau's mistress, Thérèse Le Vasseur. He finally married in 1769 a cousin, Margaret Montgomerie, a prudent, amiable woman who put up with his shortcomings. He returned from the Continent in 1766, was admitted advocate, in 1773 was elected to Johnson's famous literary club, and took the great doctor on a memorable journey to the Hebrides. A major literary enterprise (1777–83) was a series of 70 monthly contributions to the *London Magazine* under the pseudonym 'The Hypochondriak'. After Johnson's death appeared *The Journal of the Tour of the Hebrides* (1785). Its great success made Boswell plan his masterpiece, the *Life of Samuel Johnson* (1791), of which *The Journal* served as a first instalment. Meanwhile Boswell had entered the Inner Temple and had been called to the English Bar in 1786. He hardly practised, however, except to publish anonymously *Dorando, a Spanish Tale* (1767), a thinly disguised summary of a topical case which, at the time of publication, was still *sub judice*. Boswell's

wife died in 1789, leaving him six children, and his drinking habits got the better of him. His work is that of a conscious artist, a born journalist, and a biographical researcher. The discoveries of Boswell's manuscripts, at Malahide Castle in Ireland in 1927 and at Fettercairn House in Scotland in 1930, which have been assembled by Yale University, are proof of his literary industry and integrity.

BOTHWELL, James Hepburn, 4th Earl of
(c.1537–1578)

Nobleman, and third husband of **Mary, Queen of Scots**. One of the greatest nobles in 16th-century Scotland, he succeeded his father as earl and hereditary Lord High Admiral in 1556. A professed Protestant, he nevertheless was a staunch supporter of **Mary of Guise**, Regent for Mary, Queen of Scots, and was appointed Warden of the Border Marches in 1558. In 1560 he was sent on a mission to France where he met, and was entranced by, the young Mary shortly before the death of her first husband, Francis II of France. When Mary returned to Scotland in 1561 she appointed him a Privy Councillor, but in the following year he was accused of plotting to kidnap the queen, and was imprisoned. He was recalled by Mary in 1565, shortly after her marriage to **Darnley**. In February 1566 he married, with Protestant rites at Holyrood, the Catholic sister of the Earl of Huntly. Shortly afterwards, in March 1566, the queen's secretary, Rizzio, was murdered by Darnley, and Bothwell became Mary's protector and chief adviser. The following year, 1567, was to be a year of high drama. On 9 February Darnley himself was murdered in an explosion in Edinburgh, doubtless at Bothwell's instigation; Bothwell was tried but acquitted in a rigged trial a few weeks later, on 12 April. On 23 April he pretended to abduct Mary, who was now pregnant (probably by him) and carried her off to Dunbar. On 3 and 7 May his divorce from his countess was finalized, on 12 May he was elevated to the Dukedom of Orkney, and on 15 May he and the queen were married at Holyrood with Protestant rites. The marriage did not last long. On 20 June Mary was forced to surrender to an army of rebellious Scottish noblemen at Carberry Hill, while Bothwell fled the country and was storm-driven to Norway, where he was arrested on a trumped-up charge and imprisoned in Bergen. On 24 July, Mary miscarried (twins), and on the same day was forced to abdicate in favour of her son, the infant **James VI**. The marriage was eventually annulled in 1570. By then, Bothwell was incarcerated at Malmö in Sweden; in 1573 he was transferred to a prison at Dragsholm in Zeeland, Denmark, where he died, apparently insane.

BOUGH, Sam
(1822–78)

English-born painter, born in Carlisle. He was self-taught although much influenced by **Horatio McCulloch**'s landscape painting. Between 1852 and 1854 he lived in Hamilton, and subsequently moved to Edinburgh. His considerable reputation rested mainly on his seascapes, which owed a great deal to Turner. **Robert Louis Stevenson** was an admirer of his work and wrote him an affectionate obituary.

BOWER, Thomas Gillie Russell
(1941 –)

Psychologist, born in Dunfermline. Graduating from Edinburgh in 1963, he completed doctoral studies at Cornell in 1965. Research associate and assistant professor at Harvard (1965–9), he then held various appointments at Edinburgh until his appointment as Professor of Experimental Child Psychology (1984–8). In 1988 he moved to the University of Texas at Dallas. His publications have proved provocative and influential: *Development in Infancy* (1974), *A Primer of Infant Development* (1977), *The Perceptual World of the Child* (1977), *Human Development* (1979) and *The Rational Infant* (1990). To the study of the abilities and development of human infants Bower brought to bear a highly imaginative mix of theoretical ideas from philosophy and empirical techniques from experimental psychology, provoking much discussion on the relative contributions to development of 'nature' (genetic endowment) and 'nurture' (environmental experience).

BOWER, or BOWMAKER, Walter
(1385–1449)

Chronicler, Abbot of Inchcolm in the Firth of Forth from 1417. Born in Haddington, he is believed to have been among the first Batchelors of Arts at St Andrews University, whose foundation he records in 1410. A severely nationalistic Scot, he was one of two commis-

sioners appointed to collect ransom money for King **James I** on his return to Scotland in 1424. He also undertook various other assignments in government service, including acting as diplomat at the negotiations at Perth in 1432 for peace with the English, when he vigorously defended the needs of the Franco-Scottish 'auld' alliance. From about 1440 he continued the Latin *Scotichronicon* of **John of Fordun** from 1153 down to 1437, the first connected history of Scotland. Less austere than Fordun's annals, Bower's are full of political and moral opinions. The *Scotichronicon* concludes 'Christ! he is not a Scot to whom this book is displeasing'.

BOWIE, Stanley Hay Umphray
(1917 –)

Geologist, born in Shetland. He graduated in geology at Aberdeen University in 1941 and started research on some iron ores in Skye. Briefly joining the Meteorological Office in 1942, he then served in the RAF until 1946. In that year he joined the staff of the Geological Survey of Great Britain in its Atomic Energy Division, and subsequently made the study of atomic energy raw materials his life's work. He became Chief Geologist of the Division and later Assistant Director Chief Geochemist (1968–77). He was not only responsible for worldwide surveys in the search for uranium and related deposits, but he also developed instrumental methods for such surveys. He was Chief Geological Consultant to the UK Atomic Energy Authority until 1972, and was appointed a Visiting Professor at Strathclyde University in 1968.

BOWMAKER, Walter See BOWER, Walter

BOWMAN, Archibald Allan
(1883–1936)

Philosopher, born in Beith, Ayrshire. He studied at Glasgow University, and in Germany. From 1906 he taught at Glasgow till appointed Professor of Logic at Princeton, New Jersey, in 1912. Taking war-time leave of absence, he served in the Highland Light Infantry (1914–19), and was latterly a prisoner of war. After the war he returned to Princeton. Appointed Professor of Logic at Glasgow in 1926, he switched to Moral Philosophy the following year. Deeply revered, his teaching led many students to religion. After his sudden death two large, uncompleted, works were published, *Studies in the Philosophy of Religion* (1938) and *A Sacramental Universe* (1939).

BOYD, Edward
(1916–89)

Dramatist, born in Stevenston, Ayrshire. Educated at Ardrossan Academy, he served in the Royal Air Force from 1939 to 1945. He worked mainly in radio and television. His early radio works such as *The Candle of Darkness* (1954) and *The Wolf Far Hence* (1971) won acclaim and influenced many contemporary Scottish prose writers. Geddes Thomson, writing on urban west of Scotland literature, identifies him as 'the great progenitor' in homage to this influence. His television credits include the series *The Odd Man* and *Good Morning Yesterday*. His film *Robbery* (1967) was a co-winner of the Screen Writers' Guild Award.

BOYD, George Scott
(1924–83)

Biochemist, born in Crieff, Perthshire. He studied chemistry at Heriot-Watt College, Edinburgh, and went on to research in biochemistry at Edinburgh University Medical School for his PhD. He became a lecturer in biochemistry, then reader and was appointed to a personal chair in 1970. His research interests were in cholesterol metabolism in man and other species, with studies on plasma lipid and lipoprotein metabolism. These researches were of importance because of their role in understanding heart disease; his work was carried out in collaboration with the clinical studies of Professor **Michael Oliver**. He was elected Fellow of the Royal Society of Edinburgh and served on many national scientific bodies, including the Biological Committee of the Scientific Research Council and the Medical Research Council.

BOYD, William
(1874–1962)

Educational pioneer, born in Riccarton, Ayrshire, and educated at Kilmarnock Academy and Glasgow University. In 1907 Glasgow University put him in charge of its embryonic Education Department, and for the next 39 years his influence was felt in most sections of the Scottish educational scene: the academic study of education (his *History of Western Education*, 1921, became a standard work); the 'progressive' movement, for freedom and activity in schools instead of authoritarian teaching and rote learning; 'experimental education', including the use of standardized tests of spelling, arithmetic and reading as prognostic instruments; and child guidance (he started an 'educational clinic' in 1926). In 1920–1, as President of the Educational Institute of Scotland he mobilized the support of teachers for educational research.

BOYD, William Andrew Murray
(1952 –)

Novelist, born in Ghana, West Africa. He was educated at Gordonstoun School, and at the universities of Nice, Glasgow and Oxford. He lectured in English at Oxford (1980–3) and wrote television criticism for the *New Statesman*, before concentrating on fiction. His first book was the novel *A Good Man in Africa* (1981), which drew on the experiences of his formative years, and introduced the character of Morgan Leafy, a minor diplomat in an insignificant West African state who keeps boredom at bay by resorting to sex and alcohol. For this Boyd was hailed for his comic touch and likened to Kingsley Amis. His next book was a collection of stories, *On the Yankee Station* (1981), in which Leafy reappeared; then came *An Ice-Cream War* (1982), set in East Africa during World War I. In *Stars and Bars* (1984) the tone is conspicuously lighter as Henderson Dores, an English art expert, grapples with the shock of the New World. In *The New Confessions* (1987) Boyd introduced another memorable character, John James Todd, a Scottish filmmaker. *Brazzaville Beach* marked a return to Africa and the theme of conflict — professional, personal and political — as Hope Clearwater, an idealist anthropologist, studies a colony of apes against a backdrop of civil unrest and academic backstabbing.

BOYD, Zachary
(c.1585–1653)

Clergyman. He studied at Glasgow and St Andrews and in 1607 became a regent of the Protestant college of Saumur in France. Returning to Scotland in 1621, he was appointed (1623) to the Barony parish, Glasgow, and was thrice elected Rector of the university. He wrote *The Last Battel of the Soule in Death* (1629), a prose work, and *Zion's Flowers* (1644), metrical versions of Scripture history, popularly known as 'Boyd's Bible'.

BOYD ORR, John, 1st Baron Boyd Orr

(1880–1971)

Biologist, born in Kilmaurs, Ayrshire. Educated at Glasgow University, he served with distinction in World War I, winning the DSO and MC. He was founder of the Imperial Bureau of Animal Nutrition (1929). He became Director of the Rowett Research Institute and Professor of Agriculture at Aberdeen (1942–5), and was the first Director of the United Nations Food and Agriculture Organization (1945–8). His pessimistic prognostications on the world food situation gained him a reputation as an apostle of gloom, but his great services in improving that situation brought him the Nobel Peace Prize in 1949, in which year he was made a peer. His works include *Minerals in Pastures and their Relation to Animal Nutrition* (1928), *Food and the People* (1944), *The White Man's Dilemma* (1952) and *As I Recall* (1966).

BOYIS, Hector See BOECE, Hector

BOYLE, Andrew

(1919 –)

Journalist and broadcaster, born in Dundee. He attended Paris University and escaped from France as a student in 1940. He served in the RAF (1941–3), then in Military Intelligence and as a military correspondent in the Far East until 1946. In 1947 he joined the BBC as a scriptwriter and producer on Radio Newsreel, becoming an assistant editor in 1954. He was founding editor of *World At One* in 1965, and became Head of News and Current Affairs for radio and television at BBC Scotland in 1976. He is the author of several books, including *Only The Wind Will Listen: Reith of the BBC* (1972), and *Poor Dear Brendan: The Quest for Brendan Bracken* (1974), which won the Whitbread Award for Biography. He later successfully resisted Inland Revenue attempts to tax the prize in a historic test case (1978). His book *The Climate of Treason* (1979) was influential in the unmasking of Anthony Blunt as a former Soviet spy, a subject he returned to in *The Fourth Man: A Study of Robert Parsons* (1986).

BOYLE, Jimmy

(1944 –)

Convicted murderer, now sculptor and author. Born in the Gorbals, then a notorious slum area of Glasgow, he was involved in shop-lifting, street-fighting and vandalism from a very early age. In his early teens he was sent to Larchgrove Remand Home for theft. This was followed by a spell in Borstal. Later charges of serious assault led to two years in prison. A member of a powerful gang in Glasgow, Boyle was subsequently twice charged with murder and cleared, and was eventually imprisoned for serious assault. His reputation as 'Scotland's Most Violent Man' appeared to be confirmed when he was convicted for the murder of Babs Rooney and was given a life-sentence. In 1973 he was one of the first offenders to participate in Barlinnie Prison Special Unit's rehabilitation programme. He went on to produce many sculptures, which were exhibited in several countries, and to write his autobiography, *A Sense of Freedom* (1977), later adapted for the screen by **Peter McDougall**. After his release, he worked with young offenders and has become Scotland's most celebrated reformed criminal.

BOYLE, Mark

(1934 –)

Artist, born in Glasgow. He began as a law student at Glasgow University, at the same time writing poems and making paintings, constructions and 'assemblages'. In 1964 he organized an event called 'Street', in which a group of people looked out through an ordinary shop window into an ordinary street. His recent project, *Journey to the Surface of the Earth*, began with 1000 darts thrown at a map of the world by blindfolded persons; Boyle visits each site in turn, selects a six-foot square and makes a cast of it.

BRADDOCK, Edward

(1695–1755)

Soldier, born in Perthshire. Commissioned in the Coldstream Guards in 1710, he saw service in France on Admiral Lestock's expedition to L'Orient (1746) and in the Netherlands under the Prince of Orange (1746–8). Rising to the rank of major-general in 1754, in 1755 he was appointed to command against the French in America. He was mortally wounded when ambushed on his way to attack Fort Duquesne (now Pittsburgh) on 9 July. His force was decimated and of his staff only George Washington escaped unhurt.

BRADY, Ian

(1938 –)

Convicted murderer, born in Glasgow. A clerk with a fascination for Nazi memorabilia, Brady was found guilty of the murder of two children, John Kilbride and Lesley Ann Downey, and a 17-year-old boy, Edward Evans, on 6 May 1966. In a case which horrified the public, it was revealed that Brady, with his lover Myra Hindley, lured young children into their home in Manchester and subjected them to torture before killing them. Brady and Hindley recorded their crimes with photographs and a tape. The tape of Lesley Ann Downey's last hours, as she was being tortured, was played in court. The lovers were described as the 'Moors Murderers' because they buried most of their victims on Saddleworth Moor in the Pennines. Hindley made a private confession to two other murders in 1986, and the body of Pauline Reade was found in August 1987, 24 years after her disappearance. The body of 12-year-old Keith Bennett has never been found.

BRAID, James

(?1795–1860)

Surgeon and hypnotist, born in Fife. Educated at Edinburgh University, he spent most of his life practising surgery in Manchester, where his operation for club-foot was famous. In 1841, however, he attended a popular demonstration of 'Mesmerism' and devoted much of the rest of his working life to investigating the phenomena associated with what he himself first called 'neurohypnotism', later shortened to 'hypnotism'. His papers and books on the subject helped keep serious concerns with hypnotism alive and Braid was looked upon as an important pioneer in the field by Charcot, Bernheim and others who, from the 1880s, systematically incorporated hypnotism in their treatment of nervous disorders.

BRAID, James

(1870–1950)

Golfer, born in Earlsferry, Fife. He trained as a joiner and went to work in St Andrews, the home of golf, where he became an outstanding player. In 1893 he moved to London as a club-maker at the Army & Navy Stores,

before becoming a professional at Romford later that year, and at Walton Heath from 1904 until his death. In a remarkable playing career he won the Open championship five times between 1901 and 1910 (when he became the first player to break 300 for 72 holes at St Andrews), four *News of the World* matchplay championships between 1903 and 1911, and the French Championship in 1910. With Harry Vardon and John Henry Taylor he formed what was known as the 'Great Triumvirate' of British golf in the Edwardian era. In addition to being a fine teacher, he became a celebrated designer of golf courses.

BRAIDWOOD, James

(1800–61)

Firemaster, born in Edinburgh and educated at the High School there. He worked as a builder and surveyor until, at the age of 24, was appointed superintendent of fire engines for the Edinburgh Police Fire Engine Establishment. Just three weeks later a huge fire broke out in the High Street and raged for three days before his men could extinguish it. Appalled at the loss of life and property, he realized that great improvements had to be made in organization, training and equipment if similar tragedies were to be avoided. As a result of his experience he published in 1830 a classic manual on fire-fighting, and three years later was appointed Master of the London Fire Engine Establishment, which under his direction became one of the most efficient in the world. He was killed by falling debris while fighting a fire alongside his men at a warehouse in Tooley Street near London Bridge; seven years previously, he had issued a warning that such a building, if erected on that site, would be an unacceptable fire hazard.

BRAIDWOOD, Thomas

(1715–1806)

Teacher. After studying at Edinburgh University he set up a mathematical school in Edinburgh, followed later (1760) by a school for the deaf and dumb, the first such in Britain. The school, which was visited by Dr Johnson in 1773, was moved in 1783 to Hackney, London.

BRAXFIELD, Robert Macqueen, Lord

(1722–99)

Judge, born near Lanark. Educated at Edinburgh, he was admitted advocate in 1744 and went on to achieve eminence at the Bar, particularly in feudal land law. He became a judge in 1776 and Lord Justice Clerk of Scotland in 1788. As a judge, he was noted for his harshness towards political prisoners. Hard-headed, hard-hearted and hard-drinking, he was the original of Lord Weir in **Robert Louis Stevenson**'s unfinished novel, *Weir of Hermiston* (1896).

BREMNER, Billy (William John)
(1942 –)

Football player and manager, born in Stirling. He joined Leeds United in 1958, turning professional the following year. From 1969, when they won the league championship, until the mid 1970s, Leeds were one of the top teams in Europe, and Bremner, as captain, was one of the main reasons for their success. He stayed with the club until 1976, and then played for Hull City. Retiring in 1978, he embarked on a career in management with Doncaster. Eventually returning to Leeds as manager in 1985, he was one of a succession of former players to be charged with attempting to rekindle the club's days of glory. An inspiring, hugely energetic midfielder, given at times to indiscipline, he won 54 caps for Scotland betwen 1965 and 1977, latterly as captain.

BREMNER, Frederick
(1863–1941)

Photographer, born in Aberchirder, Banffshire, and educated at Banff Academy. He was trained in his father's photographic studio before leaving for India, at the age of 19, to work for his brother-in-law, the photographer G W Lawrie, who was based in Lucknow. Bremner opened his own studio in Karachi in 1889 and soon afterwards opened a second branch in Quetta, Baluchistan. Enjoying a great commercial success, he eventually established branches in Lahore and Simla, which he ran with assistants and his wife, Emily (née Anton). His major photographic achievement of the 1890s was the publication *Types of the Indian Army*. In 1900 he published *Baluchistan Illustrated*, containing 50 collotypes. Bremner's most significant artistic work was produced on an expedition, which he undertook in about 1900, through the Himalayas to Kashmir. In 1922 he wrote that his 'reputation was second to none throughout India'. He left an autobiographical account in the privately-published *My Forty Years in India* (1940).

BREMNER, James
(1784–1856)

Engineer and inventor, born in Keiss near Wick, Caithness. He was apprenticed to a shipbuilder in Greenock and made two voyages to North America before settling in his native parish at Pulteney Town. He took over the local shipyard, where he built a large number of vessels up to 500 tons in weight, and he also raised or re-floated more than 200 sunken or stranded ships around the coasts of Scotland and beyond. As a civil engineer he designed and built many harbours and piers in the north of Scotland, including Keiss and Lossiemouth. To facilitate these works he devised an improved pile driver and a new type of crane.

BREWSTER, Sir David
(1781–1868)

Physicist, born in Jedburgh, Roxburghshire. Educated for the Church, he became Editor of the *Edinburgh Magazine* (1802), and in 1808 of the *Edinburgh Encyclopaedia*. He had previously been interested in the study of optics, and in 1816 he invented the kaleidoscope, and later improved Sir Charles Wheatstone's stereoscope by introducing refracting lenses. After much difficulty he succeeded in persuading the British authorities to adopt the use of dioptric lenses in their lighthouses. In 1819 the *Edinburgh Philosophical Journal* took the place of the *Magazine*; and in 1831 Brewster was one of the chief originators of the British Association for the Advancement of Science. In 1818 he was awarded the Rumford gold and silver medals for his discoveries on the polarization of light. In 1838 he was appointed Principal of St Salvator and St Leonard's, St Andrews. He was Principal of Edinburgh University from 1859.

BRIDIE, James, pseudonym of
Osborne Henry Mavor
(1888–1951)

Dramatist, born in Glasgow, the son of **Henry Mavor**. He qualified as a doctor at Glasgow University and became a successful general practitioner and consultant. Always interested in theatre, he seized his chance when the Scottish National Players produced his *Sunlight Sonata* in 1928 under the pseudonym of Mary Henderson. After that, he wrote a stream of plays, among them *The Anatomist* (1931), *A Sleeping Clergyman* (1933), *Mr*

Bolfry (1943) and *Dr Angelus* (1947). He served in both world wars in the Royal Army Medical Corps and after the second he became Head of the Scottish Committee of CEMA. He founded the Citizens' Theatre in Glasgow in 1943.

BRISBANE, Sir Thomas Makdougall
(1773–1860)

Soldier and astronomer, born in Largs, Ayrshire. Educated privately and at Edinburgh University, he entered the army in 1789, and served with distinction in Flanders, the West Indies, Spain, and North America, and was promoted major-general in 1813. From 1821 to 1825 he was Governor of New South Wales. In this post he had to fight against the indiscipline of his associates; despite this he managed to improve the disorganized system of land grants, reform the currency, and improve the efficiency of several government projects. In 1822 he set up an observatory at Paramatta, near Sydney. He catalogued in Australia 7385 stars, and received the Copley Medal from the Royal Society. Brisbane, the capital of Queensland, was named after him.

BROADWOOD, John
(1732–1812)

Piano manufacturer, born in Cockburnspath, Berwickshire. At the age of 29 he left home and reputedly walked to London to become a cabinet maker. There he married the daughter of the Swiss-born harpsichord-maker, Burkhardt Tschudi, and in 1770 founded with him the great London pianoforte house of Tschudi and Broadwood, later just Broadwood. Highly gifted, he made great advances in the design of the pianoforte, both upright and grand, such as adding pedals and increasing the range of the keyboard. By the 1790s he had abandoned harpsichord making altogether in favour of the increasingly successful pianoforte. His grandson, Henry Fowler Broadwood (1811–93), was also a great improver of the instrument.

BRODIE, William (Deacon Brodie)
(1741–88)

Carpenter and thief, born into a respectable Edinburgh family. Rising to become Deacon of the Guild of Wrights on Edinburgh City Council and a freeman of the city, his private life — including two mistresses with five children between them, and a predilection for gaming — put him under considerable financial pressure. This he relieved by carrying out a series of robberies on premises to which his official position had given him access, allowing him to make clay casts of the keys. One such venture, on the Excise Office, led to his eventual arrest when his co-conspirators informed on him. He escaped to Holland but was extradited to stand trial in Edinburgh. Two of his companions turned king's evidence against him, resulting in his conviction and hanging (on a new gallows designed earlier by himself). He is remembered by a public house named after him in Edinburgh's Royal Mile, close to the spot where he was hanged.

BROGAN, Sir Denis William
(1900–74)

Historian, born in Rutherglen, near Glasgow, of Irish descent. He was educated at Glasgow, Oxford and Harvard, became a fellow of Corpus Christi College, Oxford, in 1934, and Professor of Political Science at Cambridge in 1939. He is known for his books on historical and modern America, such as *The American Political System* (1933) and *Introduction to American Politics* (1954), as well as more general works, such as *The English People* (1943) and *The French Nation* (1957).

BROOM, Robert
(1866–1951)

Scottish-born South African palaeontologist, born in Paisley. He graduated in medicine from Glasgow and practised in Australia before moving to South Africa in 1897 as a general physician. He was appointed Professor of Zoology and Geology at Victoria College (1903–10), where in 1934 he became palaeontologist at the Transvaal Museum, Pretoria. In 1936 he began to study fossil hominids and concluded that Raymond Dart was correct in his view that *Australopithecus africanus* is an ancestor of man. In 1947 he found a partial skeleton of this hominid (*Australopithecus*), including the pelvis, which proved that he had walked upright, about 1–2 million years ago. His studies on human ancestry are given in his book *Finding the Missing Link* (1950). He also wrote *The Coming of Man* (1933).

BROTHERSTON, Sir John Howie Flint
(1915–85)

Public health academic and administrator, born in Edinburgh, his mother was a doctor of distinction. Educated at George Watson's College, he had a prize-winning academic career at Edinburgh University Medical School, followed by service with the RAMC in World War II. After studying in the USA with a Rockefeller Fellowship he held posts at Guy's Hospital Medical School, London, and the London School of Hygiene and Tropical Medicine. In 1955 he was appointed to the Chair of Public Health in Edinburgh. He became Chief Medical Officer for Scotland in 1964. In both these posts he was a great innovator and a pioneer of integration of health care. He also played an important part in the work of the World Health Organization. He was the originator of the integration of general practitioners, hospital staff and the public health service in Scotland, which formerly had functioned in separate spheres. He was knighted in 1972.

BROUGHAM, Henry Peter, 1st Baron Brougham and Vaux
(1778–1868)

Scottish-born judge and politician, born in Edinburgh; his father was of an old Westmorland family, and his mother a niece of the historian **William Robertson**. Educated at the Royal High School and Edinburgh University, he helped in 1802 to found the *Edinburgh Review*. His liberal views excluded him from hope of promotion in Scotland and in 1805 he settled in London; in 1806 he was secretary to a mission to Lisbon, and in 1808 was called to the English Bar. Entering Parliament in 1810, he carried an act making participation in the slave trade a felony. In 1812 he carried the repeal of the Orders in Council; but, contesting Liverpool against George Canning, was defeated, and remained without a seat till 1816, when he was returned for Winchelsea. He never acquired a very large practice at the Bar, but he repeatedly distinguished himself by speeches of great vigour and ability — his most famous appearance being in defence of Queen Caroline of Brunswick (1820). His eloquence and boldness made him a popular hero for some time (1820–30). In 1822 he tried to use his power in support of a scheme of national education, and he did much for the establishment of London University, of the first

Mechanics' Institute, and of the Society for the Diffusion of Useful Knowledge. In 1828 he delivered a masterly speech on the need for law reform. In 1830 he was returned for the county of York. The aristocratic Whigs found him indispensible for the Reform ministry; he was persuaded to accept a peerage and the chancellorship (1830), and assisted materially in carrying the Reform Bill, but his arrogance, self-confidence and eccentricities made him as unpopular with his colleagues as he was on the bench. He went out with the Whig government in 1834, and on its reconstruction was shelved, never to hold office again. He was founder of the Social Science Association (1857), but it is as a law reformer that he will be best remembered. In 1816 he introduced a bill amending the law of libel, and in 1827 made proposals for dealing with law reform on a large scale. He was responsible for the creation of the Judicial Committee of the Privy Council and the Central Criminal Court. After he left office he secured great changes in the law of evidence. As an orator and debater in Parliament he was inferior only to Canning, though he often carried fiery declamation and fierce invective too far. His miscellaneous writings cover an almost incredible variety of subjects, but have little permanent value. His own *Life and Times* (3 vols, 1871), written in extreme old age, is very untrustworthy. The brougham (carriage) is named after him.

BROWN, Alexander Crum
(1838–1922)

Organic chemist, born in Edinburgh, where he qualified as a doctor in 1861. He then studied chemistry in London and Leipzig, under Adolf Kolbe. He taught in Edinburgh from 1863 and held the Chair there from 1869 to 1922. Building on earlier attempts, he devised the first satisfactory system of representing chemical formulae graphically, using solid lines emanating from chemical symbols to illustrate the valency of an atom, and parallel lines to represent a double bond. His system forms the basis of that still in use today. He also did important work on the position of groups entering the benzene ring and, as a physiologist, on the connection between vertigo and the inner ear.

BROWN, Sir Arthur Whitten
(1886–1948)

Aviator, born in Glasgow of American parents. As navigator with Sir John William

Alcock he made the first non-stop crossing of the Atlantic in a Vickers-Vimy biplane on 14 June 1919, and shared a £10 000 prize given by the London *Daily Mail*. Both men were knighted after the flight.

BROWN, David

(1951 –) and **Hilary** (1952 –)

Husband and wife team of restaurateurs, born in Glasgow. David Brown attends to the front of house and the celebrated wine list, while Hilary Brown is the chef. She graduated in food and nutrition from Glasgow College of Domestic Science and taught home economics for two years before she and her husband decided to start their own restaurant. In 1975 they opened La Potinière in Gullane, East Lothian, attending to all branches of the business themselves, an aspect of the operation which they have preserved. The restaurant soon earned acclaim for the excellently chosen and executed no-choice menus and impressive wine list, resulting in tables for Friday and Saturday night dinners being booked up several months ahead. In 1990 Hilary Brown and **Betty Allen** became the first women in Scotland to receive a Michelin star.

BROWN, George Douglas

(1869–1902)

Writer, born in Ochiltree, Ayrshire, the illegitimate son of a farmer. Educated at the village school and Ayr Academy, he went to Glasgow University and Balliol College, Oxford, on a scholarship. He settled in London as a journalist, published a boys' adventure book, *Love and Sword* (1899), but made his name, under the pseudonym 'George Douglas', with *The House with the Green Shutters* (1901), a powerfully realistic novel and an antidote to the 'Kailyard School'. He died of pneumonia before he was able to complete two other novels.

BROWN, George Mackay

(1921 –)

Poet, novelist and short-story writer, born in Stromness, Orkney, the 'Hamnavoe' of his stories and poems. Suffering from tuberculosis, he was unable to work when he left school. In 1957 he went to Newbattle Abbey College, where **Edwin Muir** was warden. Encouraged in his poetry by his mentor and fellow Orcadian, Brown was introduced by Muir to a London publisher. His first collection was *The Storm* (1954), followed five years later by *Loaves and Fishes*. Though illness prevented him from completing the course at Newbattle, he went on to Edinburgh University where he did postgraduate work on Gerard Manley Hopkins. In 1964 he returned to Stormness, and he has since rarely left it. A prolific and easily identifiable writer, his best work is ruggedly elemental, drawing on old sea yarns, myths, Scandinavian sagas and the folklore of Orkney. His conversion to Catholicism in 1961 brought into relief his concern with religion. A lyrically intense, poetic writer, his popularity lies in his stories and novels. Published in 1967, *A Calendar of Love*, a collection of stories, was the first trickle in what has become a dam burst of fiction. *A Time to Keep* (1969), widely regarded as his best collection of stories, is the closest he comes to confronting contemporary life. His first novel was *Greenvoe* (1972), which describes the last days of an island community on 'Hellya' in the 1960s. *Magnus* (1973), its unconventional successor, is more a meditation on the eponymous saint than a novel, but is no less effective. His *Selected Poems* were published in 1991.

BROWN, (James) Gordon

(1951 –)

Labour politician. The son of a Church of Scotland minister, he won a first in history at Edinburgh University before he was 20, and went on to complete his doctorate. While still a student there he was elected Rector of the university (1972–5). After experience as a lecturer and television journalist, he entered the House of Commons in 1983, as Labour Member for Dunfermline East. Despite losing the sight of one eye in a sporting accident, he is an avid reader and meticulous researcher and this, combined with his formidable debating skills, made his rise within the Labour Party unusually swift. At the age of 38 he topped the Labour Party Shadow Cabinet poll.

BROWN, Ivor

(1891–1974)

Journalist and critic, born in Malaya of Scottish parents. Educated at Balliol College, Oxford, he entered the Civil Service, but resigned after two days to become a freelance journalist. One of the most influential figures in the British theatre, he was a perceptive dramatic critic of the *Observer* (1929–54), continuing in this post even when he was editor of the paper (1942–8). He was the first drama director of CEMA (the precursor of the Arts Council). Prolific and wide-ranging in his sympathies, he wrote 13 books about popular English usage.

BROWN, Janet

(1924 –)

Actress, comedienne and impressionist, born in Rutherglen, Glasgow. She made her first appearance at the Savoy Cinema, Glasgow, at the age of 13, followed by her broadcasting début on Radio Scotland the same year. After her first London stage appearance at His Majesty's (1945) she appeared in many radio variety series (*Music Hall, Variety Bandbox*), finally achieving her own series on Radio Scotland (1949). Early television appearances include *Rooftop Rendezvous* and a star role in the sitcom *Friends and Neighbours* (1954) with her husband Peter Butterworth. She made her film début in *Floodtide* (1949), followed by pantomime with Nervo and Knox at Adelphi. She made her stage début as actress in James Bridie's *Mr Gillie*, King's, Glasgow (1950), and attained national fame with her impression of Prime Minister Thatcher on television and radio during the 1980s.

BROWN, John

(1722–87)

Clergyman and theologian, born in Carpow, near Abernethy, Perthshire. A boy herdsman, he had little schooling, but taught himself Greek, Latin and Hebrew. His career was varied. For a time he was a pedlar; during 1745 he served in the Fife militia; he taught in several schools and, having studied theology in connection with the Associate Burgher Synod, in 1750 he was called to the congregation of Haddington. In 1768 he accepted the Burgher Chair of Divinity at Glasgow University and in 1778 published his immensely popular biblical commentary, *Self-Interpreting Bible*.

BROWN, John

(c.1735–1788)

Physician, founder of the Brunonian system of medicine, born of poor parents in Bunkle

parish, Berwickshire. He taught at Duns and Edinburgh, and after studying medicine became assistant to Professor **William Cullen**. Thinking himself slighted by Cullen, he began to give lectures himself on a new system of medicine, according to which all diseases are divided into the sthenic, depending on an excess of excitement, and the asthenic, the former to be removed by debilitating medicines, and the latter by stimulants. He also condemned the practice of bloodletting. His ideas attracted many followers, but he died in poverty.

BROWN, John

(1810–82)

Physician and essayist, born in Biggar, Lanarkshire. He attended the High School of Edinburgh and studied medicine at Edinburgh University. He wrote *Horae subsecivae* (Leisure Hours, 1858–61) and *John Leech and other Papers* (1882). Humour and pathos are the chief features of his style, as exemplified in his essay on the human nature of dogs in 'Rab and his Friends' and 'Pet Marjorie', an essay on the child writer **Margaret Fleming**.

BROWN, John

(1826–83)

Royal retainer, born in Craithenaird, Balmoral. For 34 years he was Queen Victoria's personal attendant at Balmoral. He died at Windsor.

BROWN, Kenneth

(1957 –)

Golfer, born in Harpenden, Hertfordshire. He turned professional in 1974, and made his first appearance in the Ryder Cup three years later. Since then he has been a regular in the Ryder Cup team, and in Scotland's World Cup team. His tournament wins include the Carrolls Irish Open (1978) and the KLM Dutch Open (1983). Renowned for his slow play and poker-faced wit, he has never reached the peak levels of world golf, but remains a consistent underrated performer.

BROWN, Peter Hume

(1850–1918)

Historian, born near Haddington, East Lothian. He studied at Edinburgh and was author of Lives of **George Buchanan** (1890), **John Knox** (1895), and Goethe (1920), and wrote a *History of Scotland* (1898–1909). In 1898 he became editor of the Privy Council Register of Scotland, in 1901 Professor of Ancient Scottish History at Edinburgh and in 1908 Historiographer Royal for Scotland.

BROWN, Robert
(1773–1858)

Botanist, born in Montrose, Angus, the son of an Episcopal clergyman. Educated at Aberdeen and Edinburgh, he served with a Scottish regiment in Ireland (1795). In 1798 he visited London, where his ability so impressed Sir Joseph Banks that he was appointed naturalist to Matthew Flinders's coastal survey of Australia in 1801–5. He brought back nearly 4000 species of plants for classification. Appointed librarian to the Linnaean Society, he published *Prodromus Florae Novae Hollandiae et insulae Van-diemen* (1810). He adopted, with modifications, the Jussieu natural system of plant classification, thus encouraging its general acceptance in place of Linnaeus's artificial 'sexual system'. In 1810 he received charge of Banks' library and splendid collections; when they were transferred to the British Museum in 1827 he became botanical keeper there. He is renowned for his investigation into the impregnation of plants. He was the first to note that, in general, living cells contain a nucleus, and to name it. In 1827 he first observed the 'Brownian movement' of fine particles in a liquid, significant in shaping physicists' later ideas on liquids and gases.

BROWN, Sir Samuel
(1776–1852)

Naval officer and structural engineer. Born in London of Scottish parents, he served with distinction in the Royal Navy from 1795 to 1812. He is best known, however, as the inventor of an improved type of wrought iron bar-link chain and other components of suspension bridges, described in his patents of 1816 and 1817. He used this construction for bridges at Aberdeen and Montrose, and chain piers at Newhaven, near Edinburgh, and Brighton. His greatest achievement was the Union Bridge over the River Tweed, about four miles above Berwick. Completed in 1820, this was the first suspension bridge in Britain to carry loaded carts and carriages. The span of the chains is 449 feet, and the bridge is still in use today for light road traffic.

BROWN, Sandy (Alexander)
(1929–75)

Jazz clarinettist, bandleader and composer. Born in Izatnagar, India, to a Scots father and Indian mother, he was brought up in Scotland from the age of six. After teaching himself to play the clarinet at the age of 12, he became the leading light in a group of pupils at the Royal High School, Edinburgh, with an interest in traditional jazz. He continued playing as a semi-professional after leaving school, and in 1954 went to London to form a band along with two Edinburgh colleagues, trumpeter **Al Fairweather** and pianist and drummer Stan Greig. Although this move was inspired by the traditional jazz revival in Britain in the 1950s (the 'trad boom'), the music of the Fairweather-Brown All-Stars developed along original lines. With his unconventional technique and intonation, stemming from deliberate avoidance of formal training, Brown was a distinctive jazz voice of this period and internationally recognized as an outstanding blues player. He continued to work with the band, also pursuing his career as an acoustic architect, until his health began to fail in his forties.

BROWN, Thomas
(1778–1820)

Philosopher, born in Kirkmabreck, Kirkcud-brightshire, the son of a minister. He studied first law and then medicine at Edinburgh, and in 1810 became a colleague of **Dugald Stewart**, succeeding him as Professor of Moral Philosophy in 1810. Relatively scornful of the philosophy of **Thomas Reid** and Stewart, he was influenced by the French sensationist philosophy of Destutt de Tracy. He had original contributions to make to both philosophy and psychology, but never developed these fully as a result of his early death. He had some disciples, but his enthusiasm for his own poetry was not shared.

BROWN, William Kellock
(1856–1934)

Art metalworker, teacher and sculptor, born in Glasgow. He trained under his father, who was also an art metalworker, and attended part-time sculpture classes at the Glasgow

School of Art. After winning a scholarship he moved to London to complete his education at the Royal College of Art and the Royal Academy Schools. In the 1890s he taught metalwork at the Glasgow Art School and worked in his own sculpture studio in the city. He was a member of the Century Guild, the Art Workers' Guild, the Scottish Guild of Handicrafts, the Scottish Society of Art Workers, and his work, especially his repoussé metalwork and portrait busts, was widely exhibited.

BROWNE, Ronnie
(1937 –)

Folk singer, musician, entertainer and portrait-painter, born in Edinburgh. In 1961 he formed the Corries Folk Trio with **Roy Williamson** and Bill Smith while all three were studying at Edinburgh College of Art. He later took a job as an art teacher, but in 1966 he and Williamson launched their careers as professional musicians, rapidly establishing the Corries on the popular front of Scottish folk music, their robust singing and cheerful performing style attracting huge audiences, especially within Scotland. Around 1980 the Corries cut down on their engagements and Browne devoted more time to his 'second string' career as a portrait painter. Since Williamson's death (1990), Browne has continued successfully as a solo performer.

BROWNING, Andrew
(1889–1972)

Historian, educated at Glasgow and Oxford universities. He was appointed Professor of Modern History at Glasgow in 1931. A notable teacher, with a firm grasp on historical sources, he elevated his department into an institution of distinguished repute. His most remarkable publication was a three-volume historical biography of Thomas Osborne, Earl of Danby and Duke of Leeds (1944–51), setting in his times one of the most controversial and elusive statesmen of the Restoration and Revolution. He also edited the Memoirs of Sir John Reresby (1936), a traveller and court politician of the reign of Charles II and James II, whose lively witness and remarkable observation had invited historical scepticism, so that the grounding of the work in sound judgement by an editor with no less lively a mind performed a considerable service. Browning's edition of

English Historical Documents 1660–1714 was the most distinguished work in the series, the introductory essay being a masterpiece in commentary.

BRUCE, Robert
(c.1078–1141)

Nobleman, son of **Robert de Bruis (Bruce)**, a companion in arms of Prince David of Scotland, afterwards **David I**, from whom he received the lordship of Annandale. Robert renounced his allegiance to David during the war in England between Stephen and Matilda, niece of the King of Scots.

BRUCE, Robert
(d.1245)

Nobleman, 4th Lord of Annandale. He married Isabel, second daughter of David, Earl of Huntingdon and Chester, brother of King **William I**, and thus founded the royal house of Bruce.

BRUCE, Robert, or ROBERT I
(1274–1329)

King of Scotland from 1306, hero of the Scottish War of Independence, born either at Turnberry or in Essex. In 1296, as Earl of Carrick, he swore fealty to Edward I at Berwick, and in 1297 renewed his oath of homage at Carlisle. Shortly after, with his Carrick vassals, he joined the Scottish revolt under **William Wallace**. He was appointed one of the four guardians of Scotland in 1298, but did not fight against Edward again until the final rising in 1306. His stabbing of John Comyn, the nephew of **Balliol** and a rival with a better claim to the throne, in the church of the Minorite Friars at Dumfries (10 February 1306), allowed him to assert his own rights and two months later he was crowned king at Scone. His career between 1306 and 1314 saw the emergence of a master of guerrilla warfare into a national leader, despite scepticism by some as to his legal status. Two defeats in 1306, one by an English army at Perth, the other by the Lord of Argyll, a kinsman of the **Comyn**s, at Dalry, forced him to flee, probably to Rathlin Island off the north coast of Ireland. The turnabout in his fortunes between 1307 and 1309 began, predictably, in his own territory of the south-west, with the defeat of an English force at Loudoun in May 1307. The death of Edward

I the following July brought to the English throne a king, Edward II, who lacked his father's iron will and drive. By 1309 Robert was able to hold his first parliament; this was, however, attended only by Bruce supporters. Spectacular military success between 1310 and 1314, when he won control of northern Scotland, resolved the doubts of many. A series of strongholds were recaptured, leaving only Lothian outside his control. In early 1314 the castles of Edinburgh and Roxburgh also fell to him, leaving Stirling as the only English stronghold north of the Forth. The victory at Bannockburn, near Stirling, over a larger English army of nearly 20 000 men on 24 June 1314 did not end the Anglo-Scottish war, which went on until 1328 or later, but it did virtually settle the Scottish civil war, leaving Robert I unchallenged. For ten years the north of England was raided and a second front was opened up by his brother, Edward, in Ireland in 1315. The Declaration of Arbroath, composed in 1320 by his chancellor, Bernard de Linton, and a mission to Avignon, finally persuaded Pope John XXII to recognize Robert as king in 1323. A truce with England brought hostilities to an end in 1323, but Robert took advantage of the accession of the young Edward III in 1327 to force the Treaty of Northampton (1328), which secured English acknowledgement of Scottish independence and his own right to the throne.

BRUCE, Robert de, 5th Lord of Annandale
(1210–95)

Nobleman. He did homage to **Henry III** in 1251, on the death of his mother, for her lands in England, and was made sheriff of Cumberland and constable of Carlisle. When the Scottish throne became vacant at the death in 1290 of **Margaret, 'Maid of Norway'**, granddaughter of **Alexander III**, **John de Balliol** and Bruce claimed the succession. Edward I of England as umpire decided in favour of Balliol in 1292. To avoid swearing fealty to his successful rival, Bruce resigned Annandale to his eldest son, **Robert de Bruce**.

BRUCE, Robert de
(1253–1304)

Nobleman, eldest son of **Robert de Bruce**. He is said to have accompanied **Edward I** of England to Palestine in 1269. In 1271 he

married Marjory, Countess of Carrick, and in her right became Earl of Carrick. In 1292 he resigned the earldom to his eldest son, **Robert Bruce**, the future King Robert I. On the death of his father in 1295 he did homage to Edward for his English lands, was made Constable of Carlisle, and fought for the English against **John de Balliol**. On Balliol's defeat he applied to Edward for the crown, but was refused it.

BRUCE, Sir David
(1855–1931)

Australian-born microbiologist and physician, after whom the cattle disease brucellosis is named. As an officer in the Royal Army Medical Corps (1883–1919), he identified in Malta the bacterium that causes undulant fever in humans, named *Brucella* (1887). In 1895 in South Africa he also discovered that the tsetse fly was the carrier of the protozoan parasite (*Trypanosoma brucei*) responsible for the cattle disease nagana, and sleeping sickness in humans. He was commandant of the Royal Army Medical College during World War I.

BRUCE, Frederick Fyvie
(1910–90)

Classicist and biblical scholar, born in Elgin, Morayshire, son of a Plymouth Brethren preacher. He was educated at Aberdeen, Cambridge and Vienna, and taught at Edinburgh, Leeds and Sheffield before moving to the historic Rylands Chair of Biblical Criticism and Exegesis at Manchester (1959–78). A welcome speaker and lecturer in evangelical circles, he edited the *Evangelical Quarterly* (1949–80) and *Palestine Exploration Quarterly* (1957–71). An indefatigable writer, he produced commentaries on nearly every New Testament book. Among his many other works are *The Books and the Parchments* (1950), *Second Thoughts on the Dead Sea Scrolls* (1956), *Israel and the Nations* (1963), *New Testament History* (1969), *Paul and Jesus* (1974), *History of the Bible in English* (1979), the autobiographical *In Retrospect* (1980), and *The Real Jesus* (1985).

BRUCE, George
(1909–)

Poet and critic, born in Fraserburgh, Aberdeenshire. He was educated at Fraserburgh

Academy and Aberdeen University. He worked as a teacher until he joined the BBC in 1946, where he worked as a producer of radio talks until 1970. He was visiting professor at various American universities during the 1970s, and Scottish-Australian Writing Fellow in 1982. His first book of poems, *Sea Talk* (1944), established the spare, rather austere language which he favours, partly under the acknowledged influence of Ezra Pound. Many of his poems have focused on the landscape and people of Buchan, and his childhood in Fraserburgh. His *Collected Poems* was published in 1970, followed by the more eclectic *Perspectives: Poems 1970–1986* (1987), which included a number of poems in Scots, although English is his preferred medium. His other writing includes studies of Scottish art and poetry, a history of the Edinburgh Festival, and anniversary volumes for the Cockburn Association (1975) and the Saltire Society (1986). He co-edited a series of annual anthologies of new Scottish poetry from 1966 to 1972, and compiled an anthology of writing about the Scottish countryside, *The Land Out There* (1991).

BRUCE, James
(1730–94)

Explorer, known as 'the Abyssinian', born in Stirlingshire. He became Consul-General in Algiers (1763–5), and in 1768 journeyed to Abyssinia by the Nile, Assouan, the Red Sea and Massowah. In 1770 he reached the source of the Abbai, or headstream of the Blue Nile, then considered to be the main stream of the Nile. His *Travels to Discover the Sources of the Nile* was published in 1790, but contained such curious accounts of the manners of the Abyssinians that many considered them fictitious at the time.

BRUCE, Robert
(1554–1631)

Churchman, born in Airth, near Falkirk, Stirlingshire, the son of the laird. He studied law and theology at Paris and St Andrews respectively, and became Laird of Kinnaird. From 1587 to 1600 he was a presbyterian minister in Edinburgh. He annointed Queen Anne of Denmark at her coronation in 1590 as wife of **James VI**, but he opposed James's attempts to introduce episcopacy into Scotland, and was twice banished to Inverness (1605–9 and 1620–4). He published *Sermons on the Sacraments*.

BRUCE, Sir Robert
(1871–1955)

Journalist, born in Alloa, Clackmannanshire. Leaving school at the age of 15, he joined the *Alloa Advertiser* as an office boy. After a taste of political reporting with the *Aberdeen Journal*, he worked in London for 20 years as the *Glasgow Herald*'s parliamentary correspondent (1898–1917), going on to become Editor of the *Glasgow Herald* (1917–36). Although he was essentially a political journalist with a sharp eye for a scoop, he made an effective editor and soon introduced the Herald's first regular feature for women. During the General Strike (1926) he edited an emergency press in Glasgow. He retired to become a director of the London Midland and Scottish Railway Company.

BRUCE, Sir William, of Kinross
(1630–1710)

Architect and diplomat, born in Blairhall, Fife. Together with **James Smith** (c.1645–1731) he is recognized as a founder of British Palladianism. He was probably self-educated during his travels in England, Holland and possibly France. Apparently involved in the negotiations leading to the Restoration, he was knighted thereafter, and became Surveyor to the king's works (1671–8), but his Jacobite sympathies caused him to be out of favour after the accession of **James II**. He introduced the classical tradition to Scotland as a complete design philosophy, not just a source of ornament to be applied to fortified dwellings as it had appeared a century before he was born. The restrained classicism demonstrated in his alterations to Balcaskie (1668), and his major designs such as Kinross House (1686), Holyroodhouse (1671–9) and Hopetoun House (1699–1703), was enhanced in several cases by a formal landscape after the French example.

BRUCE, William Spiers
(1867–1921)

Polar explorer, surgeon and oceanographer. Born in London, he read medicine at Edinburgh University before joining the Antarctic voyage of the *Balaena* (1892–3). In 1895 he ran the meteorological observatory on Ben Nevis, before joining expeditions to Franz Josef Land (1896), Novaya Zemalya and the Barents Sea (1898). With the Prince of Monaco he charted Red Bay, Spitzbergen, in

1899. He was leader of the Scottish National Antarctic Expedition (1902–4) which discovered Coats Land, a 150-mile stretch of the Antarctic coast, and explored the Weddell Sea. Between 1906 and 1920 he surveyed Prince Charles Foreland in Antarctica, and the coal-bearing regions of Svalbard. He founded the Scottish Oceanographical Laboratory in Edinburgh (1907–20). On his death his ashes were scattered in the Southern Ocean.

BRÜCK, Hermann Alexander
(1905–)

German-born astronomer, born in Berlin. Graduating in theoretical physics from Munich University, he held research positions in Rome, Cambridge and Dublin before being appointed Astronomer Royal for Scotland and Professor of Astronomy at Edinburgh (1957–75). There he embarked on a major programme of modernization, applying new technology to astronomical instrumentation and introducing automatic methods of measurement and data processing to astronomical tasks. He was a strong advocate of the policy of locating telescopes in the best possible climates; as a pilot scheme he set up an observing station in Italy, and was responsible for site-testing experiments which preceded the establishment of British observing facilities overseas.

BRUNLEES, Sir James
(1816–92)

Civil engineer, born in Kelso, Roxburghshire. He worked for some years as a landscape gardener, then turned to surveying and later, after studying at Edinburgh University, became a consulting civil engineer. Much of his work in the second half of the 19th century was concerned with the construction of railways in Britain and South America; he also built the rack railway over the Mont Cenis pass in the Alps which operated from 1868 until 1871; when the Mont Cenis tunnel was opened. He designed the first Avonmouth Dock, and the Whitehaven Dock works, as well as piers at Southend and several other seaside resorts. He was one of the engineers of the original Channel Tunnel Company from its inception in 1872 until its demise in 1886.

BRUNTON, John Stirling
(1903–77)

Reforming educationist, born in Glasgow. After teaching in Scottish schools, Brunton joined HM (Scottish) Inspectorate of Schools in 1932 and rose to occupy its top position as Senior Chief Inspector (1955–66). During these years he set about changing the role of school inspectors. He reduced their load of routine examining and visiting and channelled their energies into active leadership of 'Working Parties', whose membership included teachers and college lecturers. Such working parties produced influential reports on the Senior Secondary curriculum (1959) and on 'the vocational impulse' as motivation for non-academic learners (1963). Another working party produced the 'Primary Memorandum' (1965) which in due course transformed Scottish primary education.

BRUNTON, Mary, née Balfour
(1778–1818)

Novelist, born on the isolated island of Barra in the Orkneys, the daughter of an army officer. In 1798 she married the Reverend Alexander Brunton, whom she called 'my companion and instructor', and they settled in the parish of Bolton, East Lothian. Between 1803 and her death she lived in Edinburgh where her husband was minister of the Tron Kirk and Professor of Oriental Languages at Edinburgh University. She made her name with her first novel *Self Control* (1810), which she dedicated to her close friend **Joanna Baillie**, and which Jane Austen called an 'elegantly written work, without anything of nature or probability in it'. Her next novel was *Discipline* (1814). Both were so-called improving works, very popular in their day, and she was included in the school of 'improver-satirists' along with **Susan Ferrier** and Elizabeth Hamilton. After a visit to England in 1815 she planned a series of domestic sketches on middle-class manners, but only one, *Emmeline* (1819), was completed before her death in childbirth.

BRUNTON, Richard Henry
(1841–1901)

Civil engineer and the 'father of Japanese lighthouses', born in Fetteresso, Kincardineshire. After being educated at private schools in Scotland, his early engineering experience was gained on the construction of railways, docks and harbours, and water and drainage schemes in Scotland and south Wales. When the Tariff Convention of 1866 opened up Japan to trade with the rest of the world, modern lighthouses had to be built around her coasts, and the planning of this was entrusted to **David** and **Thomas Stevenson** of Edinburgh. In 1868, on their recommendation, Brunton was appointed chief engineer to the Japanese Government Lighthouse Department, and over the next eight years he supervised the construction of almost 50 lights, as well as playing a major part in the development of the city and harbour of Yokohama. On his return to Scotland he was appointed manager of **James Young**'s paraffin oil company, and from 1881 he was engaged in the building industry as manufacturer, architect and consulting engineer.

BRYCE, David
(1803–76)

Architect, born in Edinburgh, the son of a builder architect. Educated in Edinburgh, he became a pupil and assistant of **William Burn**, with whom he formed a partnership (1841–50). He was among the pre-eminent architects of Victorian Scotland. His work was distinguished by its boldness and powerful massing which became increasingly apparent in later years. His imaginative approach to design was complemented successfully by a practical sense of planning. He evolved the Scottish Baronial style, not least by adding elements reminiscent of French chateaux to his designs. Among the major works of his extensive practice are several classical banks in Edinburgh: the Edinburgh and Leith Bank (1841, now Clydesdale), the British Linen Bank (1846–51, now Bank of Scotland) and Baroque additions to the Bank of Scotland on The Mound (1864). Torosay (1856), Craigends (1857) and Castlemilk (1863) demonstrate his command of the Baronial style, perhaps known to most at **Fettes** School (1864–70).

BRYDEN, Bill (William)
(1942 –)

Stage director and dramatist, born in Greenock, Renfrewshire. He began his career as a documentary scriptwriter for Scottish Television (1963–4), before becoming Assistant Director at the Belgrade Theatre, Coventry (1965–7) and Associate Director of the Royal Lyceum Theatre, Edinburgh (1971–4). His productions at Edinburgh included two of his own plays, *Willie Rough* (1972) and *Benny Lynch* (1974), gritty dramas set in industrial urban Scotland. From 1975 to 1985 he was an associate of the National Theatre, where he was Director of the small Cottesloe Theatre from 1978 to 1980 and where he became particularly associated with the production of American plays. In 1985 he became head of drama for BBC Television Scotland. He has directed two films from his own screenplays: *Ill Fares the Land* (1982) and *The Holy City* (1985). In 1990 he directed *The Ship*, a large-scale epic play about the Glasgow shipbuilding industry, set at a Clydeside quay, in the course of which a ship was built and launched.

BRYDON, Roderick
(1939 –)

Orchestral and operatic conductor, born in Edinburgh. After early association with Sadler's Wells Opera and Scottish Opera he was Music Director at Lucerne and Bern opera houses, and has conducted in Germany, Denmark, France, Israel, Australia and Los Angeles. As their former artistic administrator, he has a close association with the Scottish Chamber Orchestra.

BRYSON, Admiral Sir Lindsay Sutherland
(1925 –)

Naval electrical engineer, born and educated in Glasgow. He entered the Royal Navy as an engineering cadet in 1942 and took an external degree at London University. Progressing through the ranks, he became a Controller of the Navy from 1981 to 1984, a period that included the Falklands campaign in 1982. He was involved in the early development of naval airborne radar and guided weapons, and promoted the concept of reliability as a quantitative property capable of specification and measurement. He was elected FRSE in 1984, and served as President of the Institution of Electrical Engineers (1985–6); he was awarded an honorary DSc by Strathclyde University in 1987. He has been Deputy Chairman of the Marconi Company and GEC Avionics since 1987.

BUCHAN, Earls of See under COMYN, ERSKINE, David and STEWART, Alexander

BUCHAN, Alastair Francis
(1918–76)

Journalist and writer, an authority on geopolitics, the third son of **John Buchan**

(Lord Tweedsmuir). Educated at Eton and Oxford University, in 1939, when his father was Governor-General of Canada, he was made junior fellow at Virginia University, but was commissioned in the Canadian Army on the outbreak of World War II, taking part in the Dieppe Raid and becoming a Major in the 14th Canadian Hussars. He graduated from *The Economist* (1948–51) to *The Observer* (1951–8), serving first as Washington and then as defence and diplomatic correspondent. He was Director of the Institute for Strategic Studies from 1958 to 1969. In 1973 he delivered the **Reith** Lectures, published as *Change without War*, and was the author of a number of works on international relations as well as a life of Walter Bagehot, titled *The Spare Chancellor* (1959).

BUCHAN, Alexander

(1829–1907)

Meteorologist, born in Kinnesswood, near Kinross, Fife. Starting out as a teacher, he developed an interest in meteorology, making his name with a paper entitled *The Mean Pressure of the Atmosphere and the Prevailing Winds of the Globe*. Among his discoveries was the fact that European weather is determined by pressure conditions over Iceland. He became Secretary of the Scottish Meteorological Society in 1860. He postulated the 'Buchan spells' theory, based on earlier statistics, that the British climate is subject to successive warm and cold spells falling approximately between certain dates each year. His publications include *The Handy Book of Meteorology* (1867) and *Report on Atmospheric Circulation* (1889).

BUCHAN, Elspeth, née Simpson

(1738–91)

Religious, the wife of a potter. In 1784 she founded at Irvine a fanatical sect, the Buchanites, announcing herself to her 46 followers as the Woman of Revelations xii.

BUCHAN, John, 1st Baron Tweedsmuir

(1875–1940)

Author and statesman, born in Perth, the son of a Free Church minister. He was educated at Hutcheson's Grammar School and Glasgow University and at Brasenose College,

Oxford, where he won the Newdigate Prize for Poetry in 1898. In 1901 he was called to the Bar and became Private Secretary to Lord Milner, High Commissioner for South Africa. He returned in 1903 to become a director of **Nelson**'s the publishers. During World War I he served on HQ staff until 1917, when he became Director of Information. He wrote *Nelson's History of the War* (1915–19), and became President of the Scottish History Society (1929–32). He was MP for the Scottish Universities (1927–35), and was raised to the peerage in 1935, when he became Governor-General of Canada. In 1937 he was made a Privy Councillor, and Chancellor of Edinburgh University. Despite his busy public life, Buchan wrote over 50 books, beginning with a series of essays, *Scholar Gipsies* (1896). His strength as a writer was for fast-moving adventure stories, which included *Prester John* (1910), *Huntingtower* (1922) and *Witch Wood* (1927). He became best known, however, for his spy thrillers featuring Richard Hannay: *The Thirty-Nine Steps* (1915), *Greenmantle* (1916), *The Three Hostages* (1924), and others. He also wrote biographies, including *Montrose* (1928) and *Sir Walter Scott* (1932). His sister, Anna, was the novelist **O Douglas**.

BUCHANAN, Claudius

(1766–1815)

Missionary, born in Cambuslang, near Glasgow. In 1797 he became chaplain to the East India Company at Barrackpur, translated the Gospels into Persian and Hindustani, and made two tours through southern and western India. Returning in 1808 to England, he excited so much interest in Indian missions that before his death the first English bishop had been appointed to Calcutta.

BUCHANAN, Dugald (D'ughall Bochanan)

(1716–68)

Gaelic poet, born in Ardoch, Strathyre. He received a rudimentary education at his parish school and left Strathyre at the age of 14 to live first in Stirling and then Edinburgh. He pursued the trade of carpentry as an apprentice, married, and eventually returned to his native parish. There, he found carpentry spiritually unsatisfying and he became obsessed with the morbid religious fears that had haunted the dreams of his youth — the diary he kept between 1741 and 1750 describes his frightening spiritual struggle. He became a travelling teacher, settled as a schoolmaster at Kinloch Rannoch, and was licensed as an evangelist in 1753. He assisted with the publication of the first Gaelic New Testament and his own poems, a collection called *Spiritual Songs*, was published in 1767. These poems, and his songs, reveal his preoccupation with moral and religious subjects. His 'L'a a Bhreitheanais' ('The Day of Judgement') is more than 500 lines long and treats the doom all sinners will have to endure when Christ descends on the last day. His didactic songs advocate attention to the Scriptures as a cure for the ills of avarice and ambition, but present a more contented view of the human condition.

BUCHANAN, George
(c.1506–1582)

Scholar and humanist, born near Killearn, Stirlingshire. Because of straitened family circumstances he attended the local grammar school, but at the age of 14 was sent by an uncle to study Latin at the University of Paris. He returned to Scotland in 1523, and did service in the army of the Duke of Albany (the future King **James V**). Thereafter he was enrolled at St Andrews as a poor student, before returning to Paris, where he taught at the College of Sainte Barbe (1528–37). In 1537 King James appointed him tutor to one of his illegitimate sons, the future Earl of **Moray**, but he was soon charged with heresy at St Andrews after writing *Franciscanus*, a satirical poem about friars, which offended Cardinal **Beaton**. He fled to France, where he taught at Bordeaux (1539–42), with Montaigne as one of his pupils, and wrote two tragedies in Latin, *Jeptha* and *Baptistes*. In 1547 he went to teach at Coimbra in Portugal, where he was arrested by the Inquisition as a suspected heretic. During his confinement (1547–53) he made a Latin paraphrase of the Psalms, which was published in 1566 with a dedication to **Mary, Queen of Scots**. He returned to Scotland in 1561 and was appointed classical tutor to the 19-year-old queen, despite his acknowledged leanings towards Protestantism. The queen awarded him a handsome pension, and in 1566 he was appointed Principal of St Leonard's College at St Andrews. He abandoned the queen's cause after the murder of Lord **Darnley** in 1567, and charged her with complicity in a scurrilous pamphlet, *Ane Detectioun of the Duings of Mary Quene* (1571). In 1567 he was

elected Moderator of the newly-formed General Assembly of the Church of Scotland, and was later appointed Keeper of the Privy Seal of Scotland, and tutor to the four-year-old King **James VI** of Scotland (1570–8). He proved a hard taskmaster, ensuring that the king learned his classics thoroughly. Buchanan's main works were *De juri regni apud Scotos* (1579), an attack on the divine right of monarchs and a justification for the deposition of Mary, and a monumental but unreliable history of Scotland, *Rerum scoticarum historia* (20 vols), which he completed shortly before his death.

BUCHANAN, Isobel Wilson
(1954 –)

Soprano, born in Glasgow. After studies at the Royal Scottish Academy of Music and Drama, she became a principal singer with Australian Opera (1975–8). In 1978 she made sensational débuts at both Glyndebourne and the Vienna Staatsoper, and the following year appeared at Santa Fé, Chicago, New York and Cologne. She has also sung with Scottish Opera, English National Opera, at Covent Garden and the Paris Opéra. In 1980 she married the actor Jonathan Hyde.

BUCHANAN, James, Lord Woolavington
(1849–1935)

Whisky merchant and distiller, born in Brockville, Ontario, the son of Scottish emigrants, who returned to Glasgow when James was one year old. As a late starter in the spirit trade his rise was meteoric. Within two decades of having set up in business (at the age of 35) he had established his brand of whisky throughout many of London's bars and hotels. Railway company and House of Commons' contracts proved lucrative, as did the export trade. Expansion continued as the distinctive brand name 'Black and White' was adopted from 1900. Through his own efforts Buchanan created a company which came to be ranked as one of the top firms, alongside the long-established family concerns of **Dewar** and **Walker**. In 1919 he was created a baron. In 1922 he was involved in the merger of the 'big three' which formed the Distillers Company. Noted for his philanthropy, he was also famous as a race-horse owner, activities which occupied an increasing amount of his time until his death.

BUCHANAN, Ken (Kenneth)
(1945 –)

Boxer, born in Edinburgh. For almost 10 years he was one of the world's leading lightweight boxers, being British Champion from 1968 to 1971 and again from 1973 to 1974. He was European Champion from 1974 to 1975 and World Boxing Association Lightweight Champion from 1970 to 1972. On retiring from the ring he entered the hotel business in Edinburgh, and was later associated with a boxing school for young fighters.

BUICK, David Dunbar
(1854–1929)

Scottish-born American automobile manufacturer, born in Arbroath, Angus, and taken to the USA when two years old, the family settling in Detroit, Michigan. Starting as a farm labourer, by 1882 he had bought a plumbing company, establishing this as a wholesale plumbing supply business. Selling this in 1899 he continued his interest in experimenting with gasoline motors and three years later established the Buick Manufacturing Company to make automobile engines. He built his first car in 1903 and formed the Buick Motor Company. He left the company after three years and in 1908 it was taken over by the General Motors Corporation, Buick becoming President of the Buick Oil Company and manager of a gold mining company. Afflicted by money problems, at the time of his death he was a clerk in a Detroit trade school.

BURGESS, John Davey
(1934 –)

Piper, born in Aberdeen. He took bagpipe lessons as a boy when his family moved to Edinburgh, and soon developed prodigious piping powers. At the age of eight he made a 'live' broadcast on BBC radio, and after dominating the junior competitions in Scotland he turned professional at the age of 16, going on to win all the major piping awards, including the gold medals at Oban and Inverness, some of them several times. He was justly hailed as 'The King of the Highland Pipers' in the title of a 1970 recording. During the 1970s he also recorded a set of three definitive albums, *The Art of the Highland Bagpipe*. He has been employed for many years as piping tutor in Easter Ross

schools, and became an MBE in 1989 for services to piping.

BURKE, William
(1792–1829)

Irish murderer, convicted of the murder of one woman and confessing to 15 others. With his partner William Hare (1790 – c.1860) he committed a series of murders in Edinburgh to supply dissection subjects for anatomical research in Edinburgh medical schools. All the victims were suffocated in such a way that the cause of death was never suspected, and they were only discovered because a fellow resident of the 16th victim saw them at work. Popular myth suggests that they also dug up recently buried bodies to sell them, but there is no evidence to support this. Hare, the more villainous of the two, was admitted king's evidence and, according to one report, died some time in the 1860s, a blind beggar in London, while Burke was hanged, to the general satisfaction of the crowd. The judge, Lord **Meadowbank**, described the affair as 'one of the most monstrous exhibitions of atrocity ever disclosed in the annals of criminal jurisprudence'. Burke himself ended up as an anatomical specimen, and his body is preserved in Edinburgh. **Bridie**'s play *The Anatomist* was based on the case.

BURN, William
(1789–1870)

Architect, born in Edinburgh, the son of Robert Burn (1752–1815), architect and builder. His prolific output is evident across Scotland in numerous country houses and their estates. He was educated in Edinburgh but trained as an architect with Sir Robert Smirke (1780–1867) in London. His early works display the classical influence of his teacher, as seen at John Watson's School, Edinburgh (1825, now the Gallery of Modern Art), and North Leith Church (1814). The Tudor gothic designs of Saltoun Hall (1818) and Blairquhan (1820), and the austere classicism of Camperdown House (1824) were clearly derived from precedents, but he led the field in reviving the Jacobean style, in its Scottish and English variants, for example Madras College, St Andrews (1832) and the House of Falkland (1839). His planning was ingenious, responsive to the social mores of 19th-century Britain. He was partnered by **David Bryce**, and from 1844 worked independently from London. He commissioned

R W Billings (1813–74) to write the influential *Baronial and Ecclesiastical Architecture of Scotland* (1848–52). His design of interiors was adventurous, from Baroque at Harlaxton to Louis Quinze at Stoke Rochford.

BURNES, Sir Alexander
(1805–41)

Traveller and diplomat, born in Montrose, Angus, and distantly related to **Robert Burns**. In 1821 he entered the Indian Army, where his knowledge of oriental languages gained him rapid promotion. In 1832, wearing Afghan dress, he travelled through Peshawar and Kabul, and crossed the Hindu Kush to Balkh. From there he passed on to Bukhara, Astrabad and Teheran and, journeying through Isfahan and Shiraz, embarked at Bushire for India. In 1834 he published *Travels into Bokhara*. Appointed political resident at Kabul in 1839, he was murdered there by a mob.

BURNET, Sir Alastair (James William Alexander)
(1928 –)

Journalist and broadcaster, born in Edinburgh and educated at Leys School, Cambridge, and Worcester College, Oxford. He joined the *Glasgow Herald* as a sub-editor and leader writer in 1951, and was a Commonwealth Fund Fellow in 1956–7. He was a leader writer for *The Economist* from 1958 to 1962, and Political Editor at *ITN News* from 1963 to 1964. The following year he returned to *The Economist* as Editor, a position he held until he assumed a similar post at the *Daily Express* in 1974. He returned to *ITN News* in 1976, and became Associate Editor on *News At Ten* in 1982. He worked on a number of political and current affairs programmes, including *This Week* and *TV Eye*, but is best known as a distinguished news-reader on *News At Ten*, a position he held until his retirement in 1991. He served on several public committees, won a number of broadcasting awards, and was knighted in 1984.

BURNET, Gilbert
(1643–1715)

Churchman and Anglican historian, born in Edinburgh. At the age of 10 he entered Marischal College, Aberdeen, and applied himself first to law and then to divinity with such diligence that in 1661 he was admitted a probationer of the Church of Scotland. In 1663 he visited Cambridge, Oxford and London, and the next year perfected his Hebrew under a rabbi from Amsterdam. In 1669 he was appointed Professor of Divinity at Glasgow, but in 1674, having brought on himself the enmity of his old patron the Duke of **Lauderdale**, he resigned his post, and settled in London, where he associated with the Whig broad-church opposition and was made Chaplain to the Rolls Chapel, and afterwards lecturer at St Clements. During this time he published several works, including in 1679–81 the first two volumes of his *History of the Reformation*. In 1680 he declined the bishopric of Chichester; in 1683 he attended the execution of his friend William, Lord Russell for complicity in the Ryehouse Plot. Charles II exhibited his spite by depriving him of his lectureship, and on James II's accession Burnet went to the continent, and travelled through Europe, eventually taking Dutch nationality. In 1684 he met the Prince of Orange, with whom he became a great favourite. When William III came over in the 'Glorious Revolution' of 1688, Burnet accompanied him as Royal Chaplain, and in 1689 was appointed Bishop of Salisbury. His first pastoral letter, founding William's right to the throne on conquest, gave so much offence to Parliament that it was burned by the hangman. In 1699 he published his *Exposition of the Thirty-nine Articles*, which was condemned as heterodox by the Lower House of Convocation. In 1714 he published the third volume of his *History of the Reformation*. He also wrote *History of My Own Time* (1724–34).

BURNET, John
(1863–1928)

Philosophical classicist and educationist, born in Edinburgh. Educated at the Royal High School and Edinburgh University, he won the first Open Classical Scholarship to Balliol College, Oxford. He served as private assistant to Professor **Lewis Campbell** at St Andrews University, where he developed a life-long fascination with the work of Plato. He was elected Professor of Greek at St Andrews on Campbell's retirement in 1891, and remained there until 1926, when he resigned through ill health. He is best known for his critical edition of the complete works of Plato for the Oxford Classical Texts series (1900–13), which became the standard edition of the period. Highly regarded as a teacher, he presented Plato, pre-Socratic Greek science and Greek culture as part of a humanistic education, and helped to build bridges between philosophy and science. The relationship between language and thought was one of his keenest interests, but he took an active interest in fostering the theory and methods of education. His *Higher Education and the War* (1915) has prophetic force. His final work, *Platonism* (1926), charts the influence of Plato on almost all major European institutions.

BURNET, Sir John James
(1857–1938)

Architect, born in Glasgow, the son of an architect. He trained in his father's office and at the Ecole des Beaux Arts, under Jean-Louis Pascal. In 1879 he became a partner in his father's firm, having already won the competition (1878) for the Glasgow Institute of Fine Arts, Sauchiehall Street (demolished). He maintained a varied practice in Scotland and also opened a London office. The King Edward VII Galleries, which he added to the British Museum (1905–14), demonstrate his mastery of Beaux Arts planning, and his Kodak House, Kingsway (1911) was a pioneering exposed steel-frame construction.

BURNETT, George
(1921–80)

Organic chemist, who transformed polymer chemistry from an empirical art into a quantitative science. Born in South Africa of Aberdeenshire parents, he attended Aberdeen University and after his degree joined the chemistry department there to work on synthetic high polymers with Harry Melville, moving to Birmingham with him in 1948. He is particularly remembered for his pioneering methods which achieved, for the first time, accurate determinations of the rates at which the various processes of polymerization take place. He returned to Aberdeen as professor in 1955 and continued his research until 1974, when he was appointed Principal and Vice-Chancellor of Heriot-Watt University, Edinburgh.

BURNETT, Henry
(1942–63)

Convicted murderer, the last person to be hanged in Scotland. He was convicted, on a majority verdict, of the murder by shotgun of an Aberdonian merchant seaman with whose wife Burnett was thought to be amorously involved. His hanging, in August 1963, was the first carried out in Aberdeen for 106 years and the only one, therefore, which was not carried out in public.

BURNETT, John
(?1764–1810)

Jurist, born in Aberdeen. He passed advocate and became an Advocate Depute in 1792, Sheriff of Haddingtonshire in 1803 and, shortly before his death, Judge Admiral of Scotland. He wrote a substantial *Treatise on Various Branches of the Criminal Law of Scotland* (1811), which deals thoroughly with all the major kinds of crimes and with criminal evidence. The Appendix contains notes of pleadings, arguments and opinions in a large number of important cases, made by himself, and the book is still a valuable authority.

BURNETT, Sir William
(1799–1861)

Physician, born in Montrose, Angus. Physician-General of the navy and Physician-in-Ordinary to the king (1835), he patented 'Burnett's fluid', a strong solution of zinc chloride used as a preservative for wood and textiles.

BURNS, Sir George
(1795–1890)

Shipowner, born in Glasgow. With his brother James (1789–1871) he pioneered steam navigation from Glasgow. In 1839, with Samuel Cunard, **Robert Napier** and others, he founded the British and North American Royal Mail Steam Packet (the future Cunard Line). He retired in 1858 and was succeeded by his son John (1829–1901), later Lord Inverclyde.

BURNS, Robert
(1759–96)

Poet, born in Alloway near Ayr, the son of a farmer. His education, begun at a school at Alloway Mill, and continued by a tutor called John Murdoch, was thoroughly literary. Among early influences were the popular tales, ballads and songs of Betty Davidson, an old woman who lived with the poet's family. He read **Allan Ramsay**, and began to write a little. Acquaintance with sailors and smugglers broadened his outlook, and his interest in women made him a kind of rural Don Juan. The death of Burns's father in 1784 left him to try to farm for himself. Burns's husbandry at Mossgiel near Mauchline went badly; the entanglement with Jean Armour (1767–1834) began; and out of his poverty, his passion, his despair and his desperate mirth, came the extraordinary poetic harvest of 1785. To this year belong the 'Epistle to Davie', 'Death and Dr Hornbook', 'The Twa Herds', 'The Jolly Beggars', 'Halloween', 'The Cotter's Saturday Night', 'Holy Willie's Prayer', 'The Holy Fair', and 'The Address to a Mouse'. The next year produced yet more excellent work, though much of the verse is satirical. 'The Twa Dogs' is a masterpiece of humour, and 'The Lament' and 'Despondency' are fine works. In this year there was abundant trouble with Jean Armour, and there was a love episode involving 'Highland Mary' (Mary Campbell) and her subsequent death. Looking about for money to emigrate to Jamaica, Burns published the famous Kilmarnock edition of his poems (1786). Their fame spread, and with the money he received he decided to leave Scotland for good. He was just about to sail when the praises and promises of admirers induced him to stay in Scotland. That winter he went to Edinburgh and was greeted with acclaim. On returning to the country, he 'fell to his old love again', Jean Armour; then, after a Highland tour, went back to Edinburgh, and began the epistolary flirtations with 'Clarinda' (**Agnes Maclehose**). By this time James Johnson had set about publishing his *Scots Musical Museum*, which contains all that is briefest and brightest of Burns. He contributed an astonishing number of the most beautiful, tender, passionate and vivacious songs in any language, chiefly adapted to old Scottish airs, and moulded now and then on old Scots words. In 1788 he married Jean Armour. He took a lease of Ellisland farm, on the Nith, above Dumfries, and next year became an excise officer. 'Tam o'Shanter' (1790) was written in one day; by this time Ellisland had proved a failure. Burns left his farm, withdrew to Dumfries, flirted with the French Revolution, drank, wrote songs, expressed opinions then thought radical, and made himself unpopular with the local lairds. However, in 1795 he turned patriot again. He died of endocarditis induced by rheumatism, and is buried in Dumfries. His humble origin and his identification with the Scottish folk tradition, which he rescued, refurbished and in part embellished, are factors that help to explain his unwaning popularity as the national poet of Scotland.

BURNS, Tom

(1913 –)

English-born sociologist, born in London, and educated there and at Bristol University. Serving with the Friends Ambulance Unit in World War II, he was a prisoner of war from 1941 to 1943. After the war he worked in research on reconstruction and planning in the English Midlands before going to Edinburgh University in 1949 to work in the Research Centre for the Social Sciences. He was Lecturer, Senior Lecturer and Reader in Sociology before being appointed Professor of Sociology in 1965, the first such appointment in Scotland, retiring in 1981. During his career he made an international contribution to the sociology of organizations and bureaucracy. His main publications include: *The Management of Innovation* (1961), *Industrial Man* (editor, 1969), *The Sociology of Literature and Drama* (editor, 1973), and *The BBC: Public Institution and Private World* (1977). He was elected a Fellow of the British Academy in 1981.

BURRELL, Sir William

(1861–1958)

Shipowner and art collector, born in Glasgow, the son of a shipping agent. He entered his father's business at the age of 15, and during his lifetime he accumulated a magnificent collection of 8000 works of art from all over the world, including modern French paintings, which he gave to the city of Glasgow in 1944, with provision for a gallery. In 1949 he donated an art gallery and a number of pictures to Berwick-on-Tweed. The Burrell Collection was finally opened to the public in 1983 in a new gallery specifically built for it on the south side of Glasgow.

BURTON, John Hill

(1809–81)

Historian and lawyer, born in Aberdeen. He studied law at Aberdeen and was called to the Bar in Edinburgh, but turned to writing to supplement his income. In 1839 he published

Manual of the Law of Scotland. He was a disciple of Jeremy Bentham, whose works he edited, and during the 1840s acted as Editor of *The Scotsman*, whose literary pages he guided for three decades. He wrote biographies of **David Hume** (1846), using much new material, and of Simon Fraser, Lord **Lovat** and **Duncan Forbes** (1847). He published manuals on p olitical and social economy and emigration, as well as *Narratives from Criminal Trials in Scotland* (1852) and *Treatise on the Law of Bankruptcy in Scotland* (1853). His major work was his *History of Scotland*, which he began in 1853 and finished in 1870, producing a much-improved new edition in 1873. He advised Macauley on the Scottish material in his *History of England*. In 1854 he was appointed Secretary to the Prison Board of Scotland, and later a Commissioner (1877). In 1860 he published a delightful work on bibliophily, *The Book Hunter*, testifying to his enthusiasm for book collecting (his library ultimately weighed 11 tons). He wrote *The Scot Abroad* (1862), opening up study of Scottish emigration. In 1867 he was appointed Historiographer Royal for Scotland. He edited the first two volumes of the *Register of the Privy Council of Scotland* (1877 –).

BURY, Lady Charlotte Susan Maria
(1775–1861)

Novelist, youngest child of the 5th Duke of Argyll. She married in 1796 Colonel John Campbell (d.1809), and in 1818 the Rev Edward John Bury (1790–1832). She briefly became lady-in-waiting to Princess Caroline of Wales (1809). Beautiful and accomplished, she published 16 novels, including *Flirtation* and *Separation*, and was reputedly the anonymous author of the spicy *Diary illustrative of the Times of George IV* (1838).

BUSBY, Sir Matt
(1909 –)

Footballer and football manager, born in Bellshill, Lanarkshire. After a comparatively undistinguished playing career with Manchester City and Liverpool, he became Manager of Manchester United in 1945. Almost immediately the club won the FA Cup in 1948 and the League shortly afterwards. Rebuilding the team in 1958, he seemed likely to bring the European Cup to Britain for the first time but his young side was largely wiped out in an air crash at Munich airport. He

himself was severely injured, but patiently reconstructed the side until European Cup success eventually came in 1968.

BUTE, 3rd Marquess See
CRICHTON-STUART, John Patrick

BUTE, John Stuart, 3rd Earl of
(1713–92)

Statesman. He succeeded his father in 1723, and about 1737 was made one of his lords of the bedchamber by Frederick, Prince of Wales. On the prince's death (1751) Bute became groom of the stole to his son, afterwards George III, whom he strongly influenced. He became the main instrument for breaking the power of the Whigs and establishing the personal rule of the monarch through Parliament. He was made Prime Minister in 1762, replacing the popular Pitt, thus making him the most disliked politician in the country. He resigned in 1763, after the Seven Years' War.

B V See **THOMSON, James**

BYRNE, David
(1952 –)

Pop singer and guitarist, born in Dumbarton. He moved to the USA as a child and after graduating from design school in Rhode Island formed the band Talking Heads with drummer Chris Frantz and bass guitarist Martina Weymouth. Originally a part of the New York 'punk' scene the group subsequently attained more mainstream success, in part by incorporating the rhythms of contemporary black music. By the mid 1980s they were one of the most critically acclaimed groups in the USA. Their albums include *Talking Heads 77* (1977), *Fear of Music* (1979), *Remain In Light* (1980) and *Naked* (1988). Byrne also collaborated with record producer and keyboardist Brian Eno on the album *My Life In The Bush Of Ghosts* (1981), and has himself produced records by the B-52s and Fun Boy Three. In 1986 he directed and starred in the film *True Stories*, which was accompanied by an album of the same name. Byrne's 1990 album *Rei Momo* was a collaboration with New York-based Latin American musicians. In 1992 he released the album *uh-oh*.

BYRNE, John
(1940 –)

Dramatist and stage designer, born in Paisley. He had designed plays for the 7:84 Theatre Company before writing his first play, *Writer's Cramp*, produced at the Edinburgh Festival Fringe (1977). *The Slab Boys* (1978), concerning the lives of the employees of a carpet factory, grew into a trilogy with *Cuttin' A Rug* (1980) and *Still Life* (1983). Other plays include *Normal Service* (1979) and *Cara Coco* (1982). He wrote the highly acclaimed *Tutti Frutti* (1987), a BBC Scotland television series about an ageing pop group, and followed this with *Your Cheatin' Heart*, using country and western music as a backdrop to a comedy of Glasgow life. He has designed stage sets for most of his own work and many other productions.

C

CADELL, Francis Campbell Boileau
(1883–1937)

Painter, born in Edinburgh. He studied in Paris from 1899 to 1903, where he was influenced by impressionism and Fauvism, and visited Munich in 1907, returning to Edinburgh in 1909. In 1912 he founded the Society of Eight, a group of artists with similar outlook to his own, among whom were John Lavery and, later, **Samuel John Peploe**. One of the 'Scottish Colourists', he painted landscapes, interiors and still-life in broad patches of brilliant, high-keyed colour. Following service in the army during World War I his style changed, growing more precise.

CADELL, Henry Moubray
(1860–1934)

Geologist, born in Bo'ness, West Lothian, into a family long associated with the coal-mining activity of the area. After studying at Edinburgh University, he joined the staff of the Geological Survey of Great Britain in its Scottish office in 1883, but resigned in 1888 on the death of his father in order to assume control of the family's mining interests. During those five years he made important contributions to knowledge of the West Lothian oil shale fields. He is also well known for his mountain building experiments which he conducted outside his home in Bo'ness. He later published two major books, *The Story of the Forth* (1913) and *The Rocks of West Lothian* (1925).

CADELL, Robert
(1788–1849)

Publisher. In 1809 he joined the Edinburgh publishing house of **Constable** & Co., becoming a partner in 1811, but dissolving the connection in 1826, following the company's failure. Soon after, having acquired the rights to Sir **Walter Scott**'s novels, he began business again, making a tidy fortune by his editions of Scott's works.

CAIRD, Edward
(1835–1908)

Philosopher and teacher, born in Greenock, Renfrewshire, brother of **John Caird**. He studied at Glasgow University. While contemplating entering the ministry he came under the influence of Benjamin Jowett and became a close friend of Thomas Green. Liberal in politics and religion, he became Professor of Moral Philosophy at Glasgow (1866) where, after Green's death, he maintained a stronghold of moral tradition and neo-Hegelian philosophy. He published important studies of Hegel and Kant, and works on the evolution of religion. His writings reflect a historical interest in the evolution of points of view, whether in Greek or modern philosophy. He taught perspective and intellectual moderation, but beyond the academic world he made a huge contribution to the culture of the west of Scotland, in the extension of education, the emancipation of women, and in broad social action. He returned to Oxford as Master of Balliol College (1893–1907). One of the school of British idealists, he was a diligent man rather than a major thinker, but an important figure nevertheless.

CAIRD, John
(1820–98)

Clergyman and philosopher, brother of **Edward Caird**. His *Religion in Common Life*, preached before Queen Victoria at Crathie in 1855, was said by Arthur Stanley, Dean of Westminster, to be the greatest single sermon of the century. He was appointed Professor of Divinity at Glasgow in 1862, and was Principal from 1873. He published *Sermons* (1858), *An Introduction to the Philosophy of Religion* (1880) and *Spinoza* (1888).

CAIRNCROSS, Sir Alexander Kirkland
(1911 –)

Economist, born in Lesmahagow, Lanarkshire, and educated at Hamilton Academy

68

and Glasgow and Cambridge universities. Beginning his career as lecturer in economics at Glasgow University (1935–9), he was a civil servant (1940–5), Economic Adviser to the Board of Trade (1946–9) and to the OEEC (now OECD) (1949–51). From 1951 to 1961, he was Professor of Applied Economics, Glasgow University, and subsequently Economic Adviser to HM Government (1961–4), Head of the Government Economic Service (1964–9), Master of St Peter's College, Oxford (1969–78) and Chancellor of Glasgow University from 1972. His *Introduction to Economics* (1944, 6th ed 1982), one of the first comprehensive textbooks in economics, sold over 100 000 copies in the postwar period. *Home and Foreign Investment* 1870–1913, *Studies in Capital Accumulation* (1953) established him as a talented economic historian. His experience as a policy adviser led to authoritative works including *Essays in Economic Management* (1971), *Control of Long-term International Capital Movements* (1973), *Inflation, Growth and International Finance* (1975), *The Managed Economy* (editor, 1970), *Britain's Economic Prospects Reconsidered* (editor, 1971), *The Price of War. British Policy on German Reparations 1941–49* (1986) and *The Economic Section 1939–61. A study in economic advising* (1989, with Nina Watts).

CAIRNS, Christine
(1959 –)

Mezzo-soprano, born in Ayrshire. She studied viola and singing at the Royal Scottish Academy of Music and Drama. Her international career began with André Previn and the Los Angeles Philharmonic (1985), leading to extensive tours of North and South America, Europe, the Far East, and frequent appearances in London with various orchestras. Her repertoire ranges from Monteverdi to Mahler and Prokofiev.

CAIRNS, David
(1862–1946)

Minister, born in Stitchel, Roxburghshire. After studying at Edinburgh University, the United Presbyterian College, Edinburgh, and Marburg University, he became minister of the United Presbyterian and United Free Church in Ayton, Berwickshire (1895–1907). His brilliant academic career began with his appointment as Professor of Dogmatics and Christian Apologetics at the United Free

College, Edinburgh, where he taught from 1907 to 1935, when he was granted the Chair of Christian Dogmatics at Aberdeen University. His ecclesiastical preoccupations were mission and Church unity, and he combined his interest in these matters with a distinguished programme of lecture tours to the USA. Elected Moderator of the General Assembly of the Free Church (1923–4), he was an outstanding and eloquent exemplar of the Free Church tradition, combining scholarship with a generous-spirited willingness to emphasize what is held in common in the Reformed tradition of thought and Church life.

CALDER, Angus
(1942 –)

English-born historian and literary critic, born in Surrey. He was educated at King's College, Cambridge and the University of Sussex, and taught at the University of Nairobi (1968–71), before settling in Edinburgh. In 1969 he published *The People's War: Britain 1939–45*, an exemplary social history which burrowed deep beneath the accepted myths and gained him widespread recognition. The equally rigorously researched *Revolutionary Empire: The Rise of the English Speaking Empires from the 15th Century to the 1780s* (1981) won him the Scottish Arts Council Book Award in 1982. He co-wrote a study of **Walter Scott** with his first wife, the writer Jenni Calder, in 1969, and published monographs on Byron and T S Eliot in 1987, but his major work of literary criticism is *Russia Discovered: 19th Century Fiction from Pushkin to Chekov* (1976). He co-edited *The Journal of Commonwealth Literature* (1981–7), and is Reader in Literature and Cultural Studies and Staff Tutor to the Open University in Scotland.

CALDER, Finlay
(1957 –)

Rugby union player, born in Haddington, East Lothian. Educated at **Daniel Stewart**'s and Melville College, Edinburgh, and a grain exporter by trade, he still plays for the Former Pupils. He was first capped for Scotland in 1986, captaining the side — and the touring British Lions — in 1989. Although he had passed on the captaincy to **David Sole**, he was still a highly influential member of the Scotland team which won the Grand Slam in 1990, forming part of the ferociously predatory back-row trio. He subsequently retired from the international scene for a year, but was recalled to the 1991 world cup squad.

CALDER, (Peter) Ritchie, Lord
(1906–82)

Journalist and educationist, born in Forfar, Angus. Specializing in the spread of scientific knowledge to lay readers, he wrote numerous books, including *Men Against the Desert* (1951), *Men Against the Jungle* (1954), *Living with the Atom* (1962) and *The Evolution of the Machine* (1968). He was made a life peer in 1966 and took the title Baron Ritchie-Calder of Balmashannar.

CALDERWOOD, David
(1575–1650)

Clergyman and ecclesiastical historian, minister of Crailing in Roxburghshire from 1604. In 1617 he joined in a protest against granting the power of framing new Church laws to an ecclesiastical council appointed by King **James VI and I**, and was imprisoned and banished to Holland in 1619. There he published *Altare Damascenum* (1625), a massive defence of presbyterianism against episcopacy. After the king's death (1625), he returned to Scotland to become minister of Pencaitland, and spent years collecting materials for his *History of the Church of Scotland*, published in 1678.

CALMAN, William Thomas
(1871–1952)

Zoologist and museum curator. He was born in Dundee in straightened circumstances, but in his youth he became an amateur microscopist, studying mainly pond life. A first career in insurance was cut short by his stammer, but **D'Arcy Thompson** gave him a job as laboratory assistant which also enabled him to take a degree without paying fees. After obtaining a BSc with distinction he became Assistant Lecturer and Demonstrator, often doing the department's teaching while D'Arcy Thompson was abroad. He specialized in Crustaceans and contributed a volume to Ray Lamkester's *A Treatise on Zoology* (1909). In 1904 he was put in charge of the crustacea at the British Museum (Natural History), eventually becoming Keeper of the Department of Natural History

in 1927. Elected FRS in 1921, he contributed many other books and learned articles before retiring to Tayport in 1936. Later he assisted as a part-time lecturer in zoology at St Andrews and Dundee during World War II.

CAMERON, Sir Alan, of Erracht
(1750–1828)

Soldier, and founder of the Cameron Highlanders, born at Erracht in Lochaber, Inverness-shire. After killing a neighbour in a duel, Cameron was forced to escape to North America where he found employment with the Loyalist forces in the war against the American revolutionaries. In 1778 he returned to Britain and while living in London he played a leading role in the repeal of the Unclothing Act which had banned the wearing of Highland dress in the aftermath of the 1745 Jacobite rebellion. Having won the support of Pitt and **Henry Dundas** he raised the 79th Regiment in 1793; and this was first mustered as the Cameron Highlanders in Stirling on 3 January 1794. For the next 20 years Cameron and his men saw service in the wars against France, fighting in Holland under the Duke of York and in the Peninsula under Sir Arthur Wellesley, later the Duke of Wellington. Cameron was appointed lieutenant-general in 1819.

CAMERON, Alan Barnard, originally Alan Hasson
(1927–91)

Minister, piper and eccentric, of Welsh descent. He spent most of his childhood in Inverness-shire and later lived in Edinburgh. He graduated from Glasgow University, was ordained into the Church of Scotland and served as a minister in Dunbartonshire. Resigning from the Church in 1963 over controversy with the Orange Lodge, he moved to Canada. In Toronto and Vancouver he worked as a radio chat-show host and was known as 'the Hot Scot'. On his return to Scotland in 1971, a three-year prison sentence for embezzlement was quashed on appeal. During the 1980s he was Edinburgh's best-known busker and was reputedly the first bag-pipe busker on Princes Street, until the idea became so popular that he was forced to relocate to Waverley Bridge. A flamboyant performer, dressed in kilt, dog-collar and a shirt emblazoned with the Scottish Saltire, he donated the proceeds of his busking to charity.

CAMERON, Archibald
(1707–53)

Jacobite, born in Lochaber, Inverness-shire, the fourth son of John Cameron, 18th of Lochiel. He studied medicine at Edinburgh and Paris and lived and practised as a physician among his clansmen until the rebellion of 1745, when he exercised his medical skills in Prince **Charles Edward Stuart**'s army. After Culloden he played an active part in assisting the prince's escape to France, he and his brother Lochiel accompanying him there. Thereafter he held a commission successively in Albany's and Ogilvie's regiments in the French service. In 1749 he paid a clandestine visit to England to collect Jacobite funds and in 1753 he returned secretly to Scotland, apparently to recover the 'Loch Arkaig treasure' — buried Jacobite gold. Captured at Glenbucket, he was tried in London and hanged there on 7 June, the last man in Britain to be executed for Jacobitism.

CAMERON, Sir David Young
(1865–1945)

Artist, born the son of a Glasgow minister. He studied at the Glasgow School of Art (1881–5) and was introduced to the collector George Stevenson who discovered his pen and ink drawings in 1887. As a result of this he gave up a career in business and concentrated on art. One of the finest and most romantic of British etchers, he followed the lead of Whistler and Haden. Turning to his native landscape for inspiration, he introduced drypoint to produce some of the most memorable images seen in British printmaking this century. He was appointed King's Limner in 1933.

CAMERON, James Mark
(1911–85)

Journalist, born of Scottish parents in Battersea, London. His career began as an office boy for the *Weekly News* (1935) and progressed, via Dundee and Glasgow, to Fleet Street in 1940. Rejected for military service, he worked as a sub-editor on the *Daily Express* (1940–5) and subsequently returned to reporting. Covering the atom-bomb experiments at Bikini (1946) formed his antiauthoritarian views and convinced him to become a member of CND. He resigned from the *Daily Express* in 1950 and *Picture Post* in 1951 over points of principle before settling

with the *New Chronicle* (1952–60) as a roving reporter on war, poverty and injustice. Renowned for his integrity, dry wit and concise summation of a situation, he painted literary pictures of some of the great events in world affairs, from the Vietnam War to ill-treatment of the under-privileged in India. A writer and presenter of many television programmes, including *Men of Our Time* (1963), the intermittent *Cameron Country* and the autobiographical *Once Upon a Time* (1984), his radio play *The Pump* (1973) won the Prix Italia and was dramatized for television in 1980. His books include *Witness in Vietnam* (1966) and the autobiography *Point of Departure* (1967).

CAMERON, John
(c.1579–1625)

Theologian, known as the 'walking library', born in Glasgow. He was educated at Glasgow University, and in 1600 went to the Continent, where his erudition secured him appointments at Bergerac, Sedan and Saumur. In 1622 he was appointed Principal of Glasgow University. In less than a year, however, he returned to Saumur, and from there went to Montauban, where he received a divinity professorship. Here, as at Glasgow, his moderate Calvinist doctrine of passive obedience made him many enemies, one of whom stabbed him mortally in the street. His eight theological works, in Latin and French (1616–42), are said to be the foundation of Amyraut's doctrine of universal grace (1634).

CAMERON, Sir John
(1900 –)

Judge, born in Edinburgh. Having served in World War I he passed advocate in 1924, became QC in 1936 and served in and won the DSC in World War II. He had a large practice and was part-time Sheriff Principal of Inverness (1945–8), Dean of the Faculty of Advocates (1948–55). Knighted in 1954, he became a judge in the Court of Session and the High Court of Justiciary (1955–85). He was President of the Royal Society of Edinburgh, (1973–6), and for many years was Chancellor's Assessor on the Court of Edinburgh University. He was created a Knight of the Thistle in 1978 and received many other honours for extensive public services. His son Kenneth John Cameron (1931 –) became Lord Advocate (1984–9), a life peer (Lord Cameron of Lochbroom), and a judge in 1989.

CAMERON, Neil
(1920–85)

Marshal of the Royal Air Force, born in Perth and educated at Perth Academy. After working in a bank he joined the Royal Air Force Volunteer Reserve in May 1939 and, on the outbreak of war, was commissioned as a pilot officer. He saw service in North Africa and Russia, and as a squadron leader flying Thunderbolts in Burma he was awarded the DSO and DFC. A serious illness put an end to his flying career, but after the war he directed his energies toward international strategy and built up a reputation as one of the RAF's leading thinkers on nuclear warfare. Several staff jobs followed and in 1977 he crowned his career as Chief of the Defence Staff. Ever cautious of growing Soviet air power, he opposed successive governments' attempts to cut back the RAF, and he was a firm believer in the nuclear deterrent. After his retirement in 1979 he was appointed Principal of King's College, London.

CAMERON, Richard
(1648–80)

Covenanter, born in Falkland, Fife. Having studied at St Andrews (1662–5), he became precentor and schoolmaster at Falkland under an Episcopal incumbent, but was subsequently 'converted by the field preachers'. In 1678 he went to Holland, and returned in 1680 in time to publish the Sanquhar Declaration, in which he and his followers ('Cameronians') renounced their allegiance to the king and declared war on him and his agents. Retiring with some 60 armed comrades to the hills between Nithsdale and Ayrshire, he succeeded in evading capture for a month. In 1680, however, the band was surprised by a body of dragoons on Airds Moss, near Auchinleck and, after a brave fight, Cameron fell. His hands and head were fixed on the Netherbow Port, Edinburgh.

CAMERON OF LOCHIEL, Donald, 'Gentle Lochiel'
(c.1695–1748)

Jacobite and chief of the Camerons, grandson of Sir **Ewan Cameron of Lochiel**. He succeeded to the title of chieftain in 1719. His reluctant support of the Young Pretender (**Charles Edward Stuart**) in 1745 encouraged other chieftains. Supporting Prince Charles at Edinburgh, Derby and Falkirk, he was badly wounded at Culloden (1746), and died in exile in France, where he had been commander of a regiment.

CAMERON OF LOCHIEL, Sir Ewen
(1629–1719)

Jacobite and chief of clan Cameron, grandfather of **Donald, Cameron of Lochiel**. Held hostage by Archibald, 8th Earl of **Argyll** from 1641 to 1647, he was a combative figure, who often waged battle against the Macdonalds. Famous for his prodigious feats of strength, he led his clan against the parliamentary forces of the English Commonwealth (1652), fought at Killiecrankie (1689), and in 1692 submitted to King William III. He supported the Earl of **Mar** in the 1715 Rising by sending his men to join him. He is said to have killed the last wolf in Scotland.

CAMPBELL

Ancient family, whose members have held the titles of **Argyll**, Breadalbane, and Cawdor. Sir Duncan Campbell of Lochow was created Lord Campbell in 1445, and his successor was created Earl of Argyll in 1457. From his younger son, Sir Colin Campbell of Glenorchy (c.1400–1478), are descended the Earls and Marquises of Breadalbane, and from the younger son of the second Earl of Argyll, who fell at Flodden in 1513, are descended the Earls of Cawdor.

CAMPBELL, Charles Arthur
(1897–1974)

Philosopher, born in Glasgow. A teacher of moral philosophy in Glasgow before becoming Professor of Philosophy at the University College of North Wales, Bangor, in 1932, he returned to Glasgow as Professor of Logic and Rhetoric (1938–61). His unfashionable yet indefatigable pursuit of the traditional concerns of philosophy against the trend to reduce the subject to questions of linguistic analysis is demonstrated in *Scepticism and Construction* (1931), his 1953–5 Gifford lectures expanded in *On Selfhood and Godhood* (1957), and selected essays written during the period 1935–62, published as *In Defence of Free Will* (1967).

CAMPBELL, Colen
(1679–1726)

Architect, born near Forres, Moray, the son of Donald Campbell, Laird of Boghole. He trained as a lawyer, moving to London in about 1710. He was a prime instigator of British Palladianism, along with Sir **William Bruce** and his childhood neighbour **James Smith** (c.1645–1731), who possibly trained him. His earliest recorded design was Shawfield Mansion, Glasgow (1712, demolished 1795). The three-volume publication *Vitruvius Britannicus* (1712, 1718, 1725) was a key text in disseminating the classical style; it was named after the Roman architect whom he greatly admired. In 1728 he published a revision of Palladio's *First Book of Architecture*. His major works include Rolls House (1717), Burlington House (1718–19) and Wanstead House (1714–20, demolished 1824), all in London, Mereworth Castle, Kent, after a Palladian villa (1722–5), and Houghton Hall, Norfolk (1722–6).

CAMPBELL, Sir Colin, Baron Clyde
(1792–1863)

Soldier, born in Glasgow. His father was a carpenter, named Macliver, but Colin assumed the name of Campbell from his mother's brother, Colonel John Campbell, who in 1802 sent him to school at Gosport. He was gazetted an ensign in 1808, and by 1813 had fought his way up to a captaincy, serving on the Walcheren expedition (1809), and throughout the Peninsular War, where he was twice badly wounded. He took part in the expedition to the USA (1814), and then spent almost 30 years in garrison duty at Gibraltar, Barbados, Demerara, and various places in England, becoming Lieutenant-Colonel of the 98th foot in 1837. For the brief Chinese campaign of 1842 he was made a CB, and for his brilliant services in the second Sikh war (1848–9) he received a KCB, thereafter commanding for three years at Peshawar against the frontier tribes. On the outbreak of the Crimean War in 1854 he was appointed to the command of the Highland Brigade; the victory of Alma was mainly his, as was the repulse of the Russians by the 'thin red line' in the Battle of Balaclava. He was rewarded with a KGCB, with a sword of honour from his native city, and several foreign orders, and in 1856 was appointed Inspector-General of Infantry. On the outbreak of the Mutiny (July 1857) Lord Palmerston offered him the command of the forces in India. He effected the final relief of Lucknow in November, was created Baron Clyde in July 1858, and had brought the rebellion to an end by December. Returning the following year to England, he was made a

field-marshal. He was buried in Westminster Abbey.

CAMPBELL, Donald
(1940 –)

Playwright, born in Caithness and educated in Edinburgh. His best-known works include *The Jesuit* (1973) and *The Windows of Clyth* (1979), about the aftermath of a Caithness fishing tragedy when five widows were left to bring up 25 children. He has also adapted **Stevenson**'s *Jekyll and Hyde*, and has become one of Scotland's most prolific and versatile writers for the stage and radio.

CAMPBELL, George
(1719–96)

Theologian, born in Aberdeen, and educated there at the grammar school and Marischal College. Abandoning law for divinity, he was ordained minister in 1748, taking on the parish of Banchory Ternan in Aberdeenshire. In 1759 he was appointed Principal of Marischal College, and in 1771 Professor of Divinity; he held this post until 1792 and was concurrently minister of Grey Friars, Aberdeen. His works include *Dissertation on Miracles* (1762) in answer to **David Hume**, *Philosophy of Rhetoric* (1776), and *Lectures on Ecclesiastical History* (1800).

CAMPBELL, Sir Ilay, Lord Succoth
(1734–1823)

Judge. He was admitted to the Bar in 1757 and acquired a large practice, being of counsel in the famous **Douglas** Cause, a succession dispute of 1762–9, which aroused violent feelings. He was also one of the reporters of *Faculty Decisions* Vol.II, 1756–9. He served as Solicitor-General in 1783 and Lord Advocate from 1784 and was also an MP from 1784. In 1785 he introduced a proposal to reduce the number of Scottish judges from 15 to 10 and to increase their salaries, but the proposal was violently opposed. In 1789 he was promoted Lord President of the Court of Session, an office he held until 1808 when the Court ceased to sit as a unitary court and was divided into the First and Second Divisions. As Lord President he was highly regarded as a great lawyer and a good judge. After retirement he presided over two commissions appointed to inquire into the structure of the Scottish courts. He published *Hints on the*

Question of Jury Trial as applicable to Proceedings in the Court of Session (1809) and a valuable collection of the *Acts of Sederunt of the Lords of Council and Session*, 1532–53 (1811), adding a long introduction.

CAMPBELL, Sir James MacNabb
(1846–1903)

Indian official, born in Glasgow. He was educated at Glasgow Academy and Glasgow University, and joined the Indian Civil Service as an assistant collector in Bombay in 1869. He held a number of senior posts, in which he served with distinction, notably during the great plague and famine of 1897, and was held in high esteem. His major achievement was the compilation of the *Gazeteer of Bombay*, which he began in 1873, and which had grown to 27 large volumes by 1884, when his official commission for the work ended. He carried on until its completion in 34 volumes in 1901, although it was added to by others after his death. Even though he collected a great deal of material on Indian customs and folklore, he published very little outside the formidable *Gazeteer*.

CAMPBELL, John, 1st Baron Campbell
(1779–1861)

Scottish-born judge, born in Cupar, Fife, and Lord Chancellor of England. He studied for the Church at St Andrews, turned to law and journalism, and was called to the English Bar in 1806. A Whig MP (1830–49), he was knighted and made Solicitor-General in 1832, and became Attorney-General in 1834. As such he sponsored some important reforming Acts. Created a baron in 1841, he was successively appointed Lord Chancellor of Ireland (1841), Chancellor of the Duchy of Lancaster (1846), Chief Justice of the Queen's Bench (1850), and Lord Chancellor of England (1859–61). His *Lives of the Chief Justices* (1849–57) and *Lives of the Lord Chancellors* (1845–7) are entertaining, but marred by prejudiced comments and, in later volumes, by inaccuracy.

CAMPBELL, John Archibald
(1859–1909)

Architect, regarded as an early pioneer of the vertical articulation of tall buildings. He studied at the École des Beaux Arts, Paris

(1880–3). From 1886 to 1897 he was in partnership with **John J Burnet** in Glasgow, with whom he produced the Athenaeum Theatre (1891) in a wilfully asymmetrical free style. One of his major independent works was the Northern Insurance Building in Glasgow (1908–9), where he contrasted a vertically proportioned Scots Renaissance façade with a functional rear elevation, and pioneered a steel frame which gave maximum daylighting from the cramped rear court. He also designed numerous houses, particularly around his own residence at Bridge of Weir.

CAMPBELL, John Francis, of Islay
(1822–85)

Folklorist, born on the Hebridean island of Islay and educated at Eton and Edinburgh University. He held offices at court, and was afterwards secretary to the lighthouse and coal commissions. An enthusiastic Highlander and profound Gaelic scholar, he collected folk traditions, which he translated in his *Popular Tales of the West Highlands* (4 vols, 1860–2).

CAMPBELL, John McLeod
(1800–72)

Theologian and preacher, born in Kilninver, Argyll. He entered Glasgow University at the age of 11, and was ordained minister of Rhu, near Helensburgh, in 1825. His views on the personal assurance of salvation and on the universality of the atonement led to his deposition for heresy in 1831. For two years he laboured in the Highlands as an evangelist, and then preached quietly without pay to a congregation that gathered around him in Glasgow (1833–59). From 1870 he lived in Rosneath, Dunbartonshire. He wrote *Christ the Bread of Life* (1851), *The Nature of the Atonement* (1856), and *Thoughts on Revelation* (1862).

CAMPBELL, Lewis
(1830–1908)

Classical scholar, born in Edinburgh. Educated at Glasgow and Balliol College, Oxford, where he took a first in Classics (1853) and became a Fellow of Queen's College (1855–8). Taking Anglican orders, he became vicar of Milford, Hampshire (1858–63) before accepting the post of Professor of Greek at St Andrews University (1863–92). He is particularly known for his editions and translations of Sophocles and Plato.

CAMPBELL, Sir Malcolm Brown
(1848–1935)

Wholesale and retail greengrocer, born in Kilwinning, Ayrshire, known as the man who introduced the banana to the Scottish palate. From very modest beginnings as a child labourer and errand boy for a Glasgow greengrocer, he rose to become both chairman and managing director of a chain of greengrocers' shops bearing his name. His climb was rapid. In 1878 he owned only three shops in Glasgow. Growth came through his exploitation of the swelling urban consumer demand for a greater variety of fresh fruit and vegetables. A particular feature of his enterprise was the siting of kiosks at railway stations across Scotland and northern England. In 1922 he was knighted for his services to the fruit trade and to the City of Glasgow. Both the Peoples' Palace and the Royal Infirmary benefited from his generosity.

CAMPBELL, Steven
(1953 –)

Painter, born in Glasgow. After a period of employment as a steel-works maintenance engineer, he enrolled at Glasgow School of Art in 1978. After graduation, he won a Fulbright Scholarship to New York where he was resident from 1982 to 1986, and where he had a one-man exhibition as early as 1983. This was followed by exhibitions in, among other cities, Chicago, Munich, Berlin, Edinburgh and London. His early and considerable success coincided with an international revival in figurative painting, coming after a period of abstraction. His approach is governed by improvisation — influenced by his study of performance art at college — in which the image may change several times as new developments are suggested. His painting technique is bold and the world depicted is an odd, illogical one in which mythology, philosophy, science and history all combine in a manner appropriate to paintings with such titles as *English Landscape with a Disruptive Gene* (1987).

CAMPBELL, Thomas
(1777–1844)

Poet and journalist, born and educated in Glasgow, the eleventh child of a tobacco merchant who was ruined by the American War of Independence. In 1797 he went to Edinburgh to study law, but was increasingly drawn to the reading and writing of poetry. *The Pleasures of Hope*, published in 1799, ran through four editions in a year. During a tour on the Continent (1800–1) he visited Hohenlinden, only just missing the battle there, fell in with the prototype of his 'Exile of Erin' at Hamburg, and sailed past the batteries of Copenhagen. In 1803 he married and settled in London, having refused the offer of a professorship at Wilna, and resolved to adopt a literary career. He contributed articles to *The Edinburgh Encyclopaedia*, and compiled *The Annals of Great Britain from George II to the Peace of Amiens*. In 1809 *Gertrude of Wyoming* appeared; in 1818 he visited Germany again, and on his return he published his *Specimens of the British Poets* (1819). In 1820 he delivered a course of lectures on poetry at the Surrey Institution, and from 1820 to 1830 he edited *The New Monthly Magazine*, contributing 'The Last Man' and other poems. He was buried in Westminster Abbey. 'Hohenlinden', 'Ye Mariners of England' and 'The Battle of the Baltic' are among his best-known poems.

CAMPBELL-BANNERMAN, Sir Henry
(1836–1908)

Liberal prime minister, the second son of Sir James Campbell, a Glasgow draper who became Lord Provost of Glasgow. He assumed the name Bannerman in 1872. Educated at Glasgow High School and Trinity College, Cambridge, he represented Stirling burghs as a Liberal from 1868 to 1908. Appointed Chief Secretary for Ireland in 1885, he supported Irish Home Rule and was Secretary for War (1886 and 1892–5). He became GCB in 1895, Liberal Party leader in 1899 and Prime Minister in 1905. He resigned on 4 April and died seven days later. A critic of aspects of British policy in the Boer War, he granted the ex-republics responsible government when he was premier; he also initiated the introduction of old age pensions and launched the campaign against the House of Lords.

CANDLISH, Robert Smith
(1806–73)

Free Church ecclesiastic, born in Edinburgh. Educated in Glasgow, he was minister of

St George's, Edinburgh, from 1834. After the Disruption (1843) he cooperated with **Thomas Chalmers** in organizing the Free Church, and from Chalmers' death he was its virtual leader. He was made Moderator of the Free Assembly in 1861, and Principal of the New College in 1862.

CANT, Andrew
(c.1590–1663)

Covenanting minister. Although invited to Edinburgh to hold a charge there, his appointment was blocked by **James VI and I**. He became minister of Pitsligo, Aberdeenshire, in 1633, and in 1638 was sent to Aberdeen to persuade the inhabitants to subscribe to the Covenant. In November of the same year he was a member of the Glasgow Assembly which abolished Episcopacy. He was nevertheless a zealous Royalist, and in 1641 preached before Charles I in Edinburgh. His son Andrew was Principal of Edinburgh University, 1675–85.

CARGILL, Donald
(c.1619–1681)

Covenanter, born in Rattray, near Blairgowrie, Perthshire. He studied at Aberdeen and St Andrews, and in 1655 was ordained minister of the Barony parish in Glasgow. Ejected for denouncing the Restoration, he became an indefatigable field preacher, fought and was wounded at Bothwell Brig (1679), and participated with **Richard Cameron** in the famous Sanquhar declaration (1680). Having excommunicated Charles II, the Duke of York, and others at Torwood, Stirlingshire, he was seized, and executed at the Mercat Cross in Edinburgh.

CARLYLE, Alexander, of Inveresk
(1722–1805)

Churchman, known as 'Jupiter' because of his imposing demeanour, born in Prestonpans, East Lothian. Educated at Edinburgh, Glasgow and Leiden universities, he was minister of Inveresk, Midlothian, from 1748 to 1805. He was the friend of **David Hume**, **Adam Smith**, **Tobias Smollett**, **John Home** and others. With **William Robertson** the historian he led the 'Broad Church' or moderate party in the Church of Scotland; in 1769 he went to London to request that the Scottish clergy be exempt from the window

tax. He was Moderator of the General Assembly in 1770, and was made Dean of the Chapel Royal in 1789. He wrote various political articles, and published an autobiography in 1860.

CARLYLE, Jane Baillie, née Welsh
(1801–66)

Literary figure, born in Haddington, East Lothian. The only daughter of Dr John Welsh, from whom she received a thorough classical education, she inherited from him a small family estate at Craigenputtock on the moors of Dumfriesshire. She was tutored by the revivalist minister **Edward Irving**, who in 1821 introduced her to his friend **Thomas Carlyle**, whom she married, despite her mother's reservations, in 1826. They lived at Craigenputtock from 1828 to 1834, and thereafter at 5 Cheyne Row, Chelsea. Forthright and quick-witted, she declined to become a writer despite Carlyle's promptings. The marriage was a difficult one, and they seem to have had considerable sexual problems; Carlyle was an unhappy, withdrawn, even tormented man, but she supported him loyally through his depressions and chronic ill-health. After her sudden death in 1866, Carlyle was grief-stricken and retired from public life. He wrote an anguished memoir of her in his *Reminiscences* (1881); he also edited her letters and diaries, which are full of vivid insights and writing of high quality, and were eventually published after his death in 1883.

CARLYLE, Thomas
(1795–1881)

Historian, essayist and sage, born in Ecclefechan, Dumfriesshire, the son of a stonemason (and later farmer). Brought up in a strictly Calvinist and Secessionist home, he was educated at Ecclefechan village school, Annan Academy and Edinburgh University, where he studied arts and mathematics under Sir **John Leslie**. He graduated in 1813 and spent a year studying for the Secessionist Church in Edinburgh, but turned to teaching instead, initally at Annan Academy and then in Kirkcaldy (1816–18), where he met the revivalist minister **Edward Irving**, who became a lifelong friend. He moved back to Edinburgh in 1818 to study law, but turned to private tutoring. He wrote several articles for Sir **David Brewster**, editor of the *Edinburgh Encyclopaedia*, and immersed himself in the study of German literature, publishing his first major essay, on Goethe's *Faust*, in the *New Edinburgh Review* (1922). He translated Legendre's *Elements of Geometry* from the French, and wrote an ambitious *Life of Schiller*, which was published in instalments in *The London Magazine* from October 1823 and in book form in 1825. His major work during this period was his translation of Goethe's *Wilhelm Meister*, which was published in 1824 and earned him the acquaintance of Coleridge, Hazlitt, **Thomas Campbell** and other literary figures in London. In 1825 he moved to the farm of Hoddam Hill, near his parents' farm of Mainhill in Dumfriesshire, where he prepared a four-volume collection of translations of various writers, *German Romance* (1827). In 1826 he married Jane Baillie Welsh (**Jane Carlyle**), and settled in Edinburgh, where he wrote articles for **Francis Jeffrey** in the *Edinburgh Review*. However, in 1828 he moved to the estate of Craigenputtoch, near Dumfries, which Jane had inherited, and where they lived for the next six years. There he began an unfinished novel, *Wotton Reinfred*, and wrote articles for the *Edinburgh Review*, and a *History of German Literature* (subsequently published in a series of essays). He also wrote his first major work on social philosophy, *Sartor Resartus*, which was published in instalments in *Fraser's Magazine* in 1833–4; it was produced in book form in the USA in 1836 with an introduction by Ralph Waldo Emerson, who had visited Carlyle at Craigenputtock. It was partly a satirical discourse on the value of clothes by 'Professor Teufelsdröckh', and partly a semi-autobiographical discussion of creeds and human values. In 1834 the couple moved to London, to 5 Cheyne Row in Chelsea, where Carlyle spent the rest of his life. Here he completed his romantic history of *The French Revolution* (1837), despite the accidental burning of the manuscript of most of the first volume by John Stuart Mill's maidservant. He was now established as a man of letters, and engaged in a series of lectures, collected as *On Heroes, Hero Worship and the Heroic in History* (1841), which foreshadowed his advocacy of the view that a strong hero-figure as a nation's leader was the best remedy for society's ills. On this theme of strong, benevolent autocracy as the best form of protection of freedom he also wrote an important essay on *Chartism* (1839), and a major political essay, *Past and Present* (1843). In 1845 he published *Oliver Cromwell's Letters and Speeches*, which revolutionized contemporary attitudes to the Protector and his dictatorship. Another collection of essays, *Latter Day Pamphlets*

(1850), highlighted his increasingly right-wing political attitudes, with their emphasis on duty, obedience and punishment. His most ambitious work was then published: a six-volume *History of ... Frederick the Great* (1858–65), a compelling portrait of the practical autocrat as a heroic idealist. In 1866 Carlyle was installed as Lord Rector of Edinburgh University with a rectorial address entitled *On the Choice of Books*. His wife died suddenly at this time, and he wrote little more except for a minor work, *The Early Kings of Norway* (1875). He refused an honour from Disraeli, and was buried at his own wish in Ecclefechan, not Westminster Abbey. The cottage where he was born is now in the care of the National Trust for Scotland.

CARMICHAEL, Gerrhom
(1672–1729)

Philosopher, described by Sir **William Hamilton** as 'the real founder of the Scottish School of philosophy'. The son of a Church of Scotland minister exiled to England, he was possibly born in London, and educated at Edinburgh University. He taught at St Andrews and Glasgow, and with the establishment of a professorate in 1727 became the first Professor of Moral Philosophy there. His reputation attracted students, while his temper led to disputes with college authorities. He wrote on philosophy and theology, and prepared an edition of Samuel von Puffendorf's *De Officiis Hominis et Civis*. Francis Hutcheson was his pupil.

CARNEGIE, Andrew
(1835–1918)

Scottish-born American industrialist and philanthropist, born in Dunfermline, the son of a weaver. His father emigrated to Pittsburgh in 1848. After several jobs, including factory hand, telegraphist, and railway clerk, Andrew invested his savings in oil lands and, after the Civil War (1861–5), in the business which grew into the largest iron and steel works in America. He retired in 1901, a multimillionaire, to Skibo Castle in Sutherland, Scotland, and died in Lenox, Massachusetts. His benefactions came to more than £70 000 000, including public libraries throughout the USA and Britain, Pittsburgh Carnegie Institute, Washington Carnegie Institution, Hero Funds, the Hague Peace Temple, Pan-American Union Building, and great gifts to Scottish and American universities, and to the city of Dunfermline. Among his works are *The Gospel of Wealth* (1900) and an autobiography, edited and published posthumously (1920).

CARNEGIE OF BOYSACK, John
(?1680–1750)

Lawyer, parliamentarian and Jacobite, born in Forfarshire. He was admitted to the Bar in 1703 and elected Tory member of Parliament for Forfarshire in 1708. Returned again in 1710, when the Scottish Tory group at Westminster became divided, he was one of the three members who attached themselves to Bolingbroke rather then to **George Lockhart of Carnwath**, the Scots Tory leader in the Commons. When Sir James Stuart, the Solicitor-General for Scotland, turned against the government and was dismissed in March, 1714, Boysack was appointed in his place, but was dismissed in September, on the fall of the Tories. Re-elected unopposed in 1715, he took part in the Jacobite rising and was expelled from the Commons on 30 July 1716 'for being in open rebellion'. He fled to France and remained abroad until 1726 when he returned home, finding his affairs 'in great confusion'. Fellow Jacobites suspected he was an agent of Lord **Mar**, who had been dismissed from his position as Jacobite Secretary of State, but Boysack assured the titular James VIII (**James Stuart**): 'I never wrote once to Lord Mar these three years past … I am attached to nobody but you and you only'. He evidently proved this by rebelling again in 1745 for, in the Act of Indemnity of 1747, his was one of 85 names specifically excepted from the general pardon.

CARR, Robert, Earl of Somerset
(c.1590–1645)

Courtier. Handsome and high-spirited, he became the favourite of **James VI and I**, who made him constitutional adviser, Viscount Rochester (1611), Earl of Somerset (1611) and Treasurer of Scotland (1613). He fell in love with Frances Howard (1592–1632), the wife of Robert Devereux, 3rd Earl of Essex. His plan to marry her was opposed by his friend, Thomas Overbury, who then died of poisoning in the Tower in 1613. By royal influence the divorce was granted and Carr married the countess. However, in 1614 he was displaced as royal favourite by George Villiers, 1st Duke of Buckingham, and in 1615 the couple were both arraigned for conspiring to murder Overbury. The countess pleaded guilty and was pardoned, but Carr, prosecuted by Roger Bacon, was imprisoned in the Tower until 1621, when he was pardoned.

CARR, Walter
(1925 –)

Comedian and actor. Born in Larkhall, Lanarkshire, he appeared at the age of seven as a ploughboy in an amateur musical revue at the Swinhill Miners' Welfare, near Larkhall. In 1940 he became a professional singer, dancer and comic, and during the war, attached to the naval base at Lyness, Orkney, he appeared in several variety concerts alongside stars such as Will Hay and Gracie Fields. In 1947 he joined the company at the Royal Lyceum Theatre, Edinburgh, and has since appeared as a straight actor in numerous seasons at the Perth Repertory Theatre, the Pitlochry Festival Theatre, and more recently in Edinburgh Festival productions of *Ane Satyre of the Thrie Estaits* and *Treasure Island*. He is renowned for his many comic roles and as a dame in pantomime.

CARRICK, William
(1827–78)

Photographer. Born in Edinburgh of Scottish parents, he was brought up in Russia. After studying architecture at the Academy of Arts in St Petersburg for nine years, he spent three years in Italy. He passed part of 1857 in Edinburgh, where he learned photography from James Good Tunny, and made the acquaintance of the Scottish photographer, John MacGregor. When Carrick established his photographic studio in St Petersburg in 1859, MacGregor joined him. Their partnership lasted for 13 years, until MacGregor's death. Together, they made a series of 'Russian Types', depicting the life of the capital through portraits of representatives of various trades and professions. Later, in the 1870s, Carrick made an important series of studies of rural life, depicting the peasants and workers on the land in the Simbirsk region.

CARSON, Willie (William Fisher Hunter)
(1942 –)

Jockey, born in Stirling. Late to develop his technique, he was 19 years old before he rode his first winner, and was further held back by a car accident in 1967. In 1972, however, he became the first Scotsman to be champion jockey, and he recorded his first Classic success, on High Top, in the 2000 Guineas. Fiery and combative on the track, good-humoured and outgoing off it, he recorded a notable royal double for the Queen in 1977 when winning the Oaks and the St Leger on Dunfermline. He had to wait until 1979 for his first Derby winner, Troy, but immediately won again on Henbit in 1980.

CARSTAIRS, George Morrison
(1916–91)

Psychiatrist, born in Mussoorie, India, where his father was a Church of Scotland missionary, and where he spent his first 10 years. Throughout his life he continued to be bilingual in Hindi and English. After graduating from Edinburgh he obtained postgraduate qualifications in psychiatry and anthropology, thus embracing individual psychopathology within a closely defined social context, which was to become the hallmark of his life's work. His first book, on the cultural structure of a community of caste Hindus and its psychological characteristics, *The Twice-Born* (1957), remains a classic in its field. He joined the Medical Research Council's Unit for Social Psychiatry at the Maudsley Hospital, London (1954–60) and in 1963 took up the Chair of Psychiatry at Edinburgh. There he built up the Department of Psychiatry to be the second largest in the country, where education and research were outstanding. In 1962 his **Reith** lectures 'This Island Now' aroused considerable controversy over his liberal views on sexuality. Vice Chancellor of York University (1973–8), he was a Fellow at the Smithsonian Institution in Washington DC, USA, before retiring. He ran for Britain in the Olympic Games in 1936.

CARSTARES, William
(1649–1715)

Clergyman, born in Cathcart, Glasgow, the son of a Presbyterian minister. He studied at Edinburgh and Utrecht, and became friend and adviser to the Prince of Orange (William III). He moved to London in 1672, was arrested as a spy in 1675, and imprisoned in Edinburgh until 1679. In 1683 he was again arrested, and tortured by the boot and thumbscrew. After imprisonment for a year and a half, he returned to Holland to be chaplain to the Prince of Orange, and afterwards secured good relations between the new king and the Church of Scotland. From 1693 until the death of the king in 1702 he could not have had more influence in Scottish affairs if he had been prime minister; he was popularly known as 'Cardinal Carstares' by the Jacobites. He was elected Principal of Edinburgh University in 1703, and between 1705 and 1714 was four times Moderator of the General Assembly. His influence helped to pass the Treaty of Union.

CARSWELL, Catherine Roxburgh, née **Macfarlane**
(1879–1946)

Novelist and critic, born in Glasgow, the daughter of a merchant. Educated at the Park School, Glasgow, and in Frankfurt-am-Main, she became a Socialist after reading Robert Blatchford at the age of 17, and went on to study English at Glasgow University. Her first marriage was annulled after her husband attempted to kill her. She married fellow journalist and critic Donald Carswell in 1917. She made her reputation as a dramatic and literary critic for the *Glasgow Herald* from 1907 to 1915 but lost this position when she wrote a review of D H Lawrence's banned novel *The Rainbow*. Lawrence encouraged her to complete her autobiographical novel of Glasgow life *Open the Door* (1920), a work depicting a young woman's escape from the confinement of a middle-class, Calvinistic Glasgow family. Lawrence also encouraged her to emphasize Burns's passionate nature in her *The Life of Burns* (1930). She hoped to bring **Robert Burns** out of the shroud of myth which surrounds him, but the work was unfavourably received by Burns scholars in Scotland. She also wrote biographies of Lawrence, *The Savage Pilgrim: A Narrative of D.H. Lawrence* (1932), and Boccaccio, *The Tranquil Heart* (1937), but is best remembered as a critic.

CARSWELL, Sir Robert
(1793–1857)

Pathologist and physician, born in Paisley. He studied medicine at Glasgow University, although his MD was from Marischal College, Aberdeen. He spent two extensive periods of study in Paris, where he put his considerable artistic talents to work in producing a fine series of pathological drawings that were eventually published as *Illustrations of the Elementary Forms of Disease* (1837). He was Professor of Pathology at University College, London, until 1840, when ill health led him to accept an appointment as physician to Leopold I, the King of the Belgians.

CARVER, Robert
(c.1484 – c.1568)

Composer, canon of Scone, and attached to the Chapel Royal of Scotland. Five of his Masses have survived, each displaying a florid style with free use of counterpoint; one is the only early 16th-century British example based on the *cantus firmus* 'L'Homme armé'. Of two surviving motets, *O bone Jesu* is for a remarkable 19 voice parts.

CASKIE, Donald
(1902–83)

Church of Scotland minister, born in Bowmore, Islay, the legendary 'Tartan Pimpernel', whose wartime exploits in Nazi-occupied France stirred the imagination of a generation. After graduating from Edinburgh University in 1931, he began a ministry at St Andrew Gretna, Dumfriesshire, before moving to Paris in 1935. His Doctorate in Divinity from Edinburgh University provides some clue as to the action in which he was involved during the war, when what are euphemistically described as 'church and patriotic duties in France, 1939–44' revealed his inspiring courage and faith during the tense and deadly experience of Occupied France and the heroic business of channelling escapees from Nazism to safety. For this he was imprisoned and sentenced to death, but was later reprieved and released. The tale is well told in his autobiography, *The Tartan Pimpernel* (1957). Donald Caskie returned to postwar ministry in Skelmorlie and Wemyss Bay (1961–8).

CATHCART, Charles Murray, 2nd Earl
(1783–1859)

Soldier, eldest son of Sir William, 1st Earl **Cathcart**, and styled as Lord Greenock from 1807 from one of his titles. He joined the army in 1800, serving with high distinction in Italy (1805–6), Walcheren (1809), in the Peninsular War from 1810 to 1812, and at

Waterloo (1815). From 1846 to 1849 he held the position of Commander-in-Chief in British North America. He was appointed general in 1854. A keen amateur geologist, in 1841 he discovered the mineral that subsequently became known as 'greenockite'.

CATHCART, Sir George
(1794–1854)

Soldier, son of Sir William, 1st Earl **Cathcart**. Joining the army in 1810, he served as aide-de-camp to his father when he was military commissioner with the Russian army (1813–15). He served with the Russians in the campaigns of 1812 and 1813, and with Wellington at Quatre Bras and Waterloo. After helping to suppress the Canadian rebellion of 1835, and being Deputy-Lieutenant of the Tower, in 1852 as Governor of Cape Colony he brought to a successful end the 8th Kaffir War (1850–3). He was killed in command of the 4th division at Inkermann in the Crimea. He wrote the valuable *Commentaries on the War in Russia and Germany in 1812–13* (1850).

CATHCART, Sir William Schaw, 1st Earl Cathcart
(1755–1843)

Soldier and diplomat, son of the 9th Baron Cathcart, father of Sir **George Cathcart**. Educated at Eton and Glasgow University, he abandoned law and entered the army, serving in the wars in America, Flanders and Germany. From 1803 to 1805 he was Commander-in-Chief in Ireland; in 1807 he commanded the land forces at the bombardment of Copenhagen. Appointed general in 1812, the following year he was sent as ambassador and military commissioner to the Russian Army at St Petersburg, and accompanied Tsar Alexander I on his campaigns. He was created Earl Cathcart in 1814.

CATON-JONES, Michael
(1957 –)

Film director, born in Broxburn, West Lothian. A dedicated cinemagoer as a child, who aspired to play for Celtic, he moved to London and worked as a theatre stagehand before a spell as a carpenter on *The Last Horror Film* (1982) convinced him that he could do no worse than the nominal director. He subsequently attended the National Film and Television School, winning high praise for his graduation film *The Riveter* (1986). He then directed the television mini-series *Brond* (1987) and swiftly progressed to feature-film success, where his love of the old Hollywood masters has served him well. He has directed *Scandal* (1989), a moving and stylish re-creation of the Profumo scandal, *Memphis Belle* (1990), a tribute to World War II heroism, and the bucolic Preston Sturges-like comedy '*Doc' Hollywood* (1991), which marked a promising American début.

CHALMERS, Alexander
(1759–1834)

Journalist and biographer, born in Aberdeen, the son of a printer. He studied medicine in Aberdeen, but in about 1777 became an active writer in London, working there until his death. He published editions of several major authors, a few biographies, and a glossary to Shakespeare (1797), but his reputation rests mainly on his monumental *The General Biographical Dictionary* (32 vols, 1812–17).

CHALMERS, George
(1742–1825)

Antiquarian, born in Fochabers, Moray. Educated at Aberdeen, he studied law at Edinburgh, and from 1763 practised as a lawyer in Baltimore, Maryland, until the outbreak of the American War of Independence (1775), whereupon he settled in London. He published biographies of Defoe, Paine, **Ruddiman** and **Mary, Queen of Scots**, and editions of the poetry of **Allan Ramsay** and Sir **David Lyndsay**. However, his most ambitious project, which remained unfinished at his death, was a monumental history of Scotland and its antiquities, *Caledonia: an Account, Historical and Topographical, of North Britain* (3 vols, 1807–24).

CHALMERS, George Paul
(1833–78)

Artist, born in Montrose, Angus. He worked as an errand boy to a surgeon, and apprentice to a shipchandler, but in 1853 moved to Edinburgh, and studied art under **Robert Scott Lauder**. Primarily a portrait painter, he also did some memorable landscapes, although his output was relatively small. He was murdered by thieves in Charlotte Square, Edinburgh. He is represented in the National Gallery of Scotland by *The Legend*.

CHALMERS, James
(1782–1853)

Bookseller and inventor, born in Arbroath, Angus. A bookseller and newspaper publisher in Dundee, he advocated faster mail services in 1825, and invented the adhesive postage stamp in 1834.

CHALMERS, Thomas
(1780–1847)

Theologian and preacher, born in Anstruther, Fife. Educated at St Andrews, he was ordained minister of Kilmany in 1803. He held mathematical and chemistry classes at St Andrews in 1803–4, and in 1808 published an *Inquiry into National Resources*. In 1815 he became minister to the Tron parish in Glasgow, where his magnificent oratory, partly published as *Astronomical Discourses* (1817) and *Commercial Discourses* (1820), took the city by storm. In 1823 he became Professor of Moral Philosophy at St Andrews University, where he wrote his *Use and Abuse of Literary and Ecclesiastical Endowments* (1827). In 1827 he moved to Edinburgh as Professor of Theology, and in 1832 published a work on political economy. In 1833 his Bridgewater treatise, *On the Adaptation of External Nature to the Moral and Intellectual Constitution of Man*, was published. Meanwhile, the struggles regarding church patronage became keener, until in 1843 Chalmers led the Disruption when he, followed by 470 ministers, seceded from the Church of Scotland, and founded the Free Church of Scotland, whose swift and successful organization was mainly due to his indefatigable activity. He was the first moderator of its assembly, and Principal of the Free Church College from 1843 to 1847, when he completed his *Institutes of Theology*. His works, in 34 volumes, deal in particular with natural theology, apologetics and social economy. As a religious orator he was unrivalled.

CHAMBERS, Robert
(1802–71)

Writer and publisher, younger brother of **William Chambers**, born in Peebles, the son of a cotton manufacturer. He began business as a bookseller with his brother in Edinburgh in 1819, and wrote in his spare time. In 1824 he produced *Traditions of Edinburgh*. The success of *Chambers's Edinburgh Journal*, started by his brother in 1832, was largely due to his essays and his literary insight. Later that year he and his brother united to form the publishing house of W & R Chambers. In 1844 he published anonymously the pre-Darwinian *Vestiges of Creation*. A prolific writer of reference books, he edited the *Chambers Encyclopaedia* (1859–68) and *The Cyclopaedia of English Literature* (1842), and himself wrote *A Biographical Dictionary of Eminent Scotsmen* (1832–4), *Domestic Annals of Scotland* (3 vols, 1858–61), extracts from Scottish historical sources, and *The Book of Days* (2 vols, 1863, an almanac of historical data), which broke his health. His other works include *Popular Rhymes of Scotland* (1826), *A History of the Rebellions in Scotland*, *Life of James I*, *Scottish Ballads and Songs* (1829), *Ancient Sea Margins* (1848), *The Life and Works of Robert Burns* (4 vols, 1851), and *Songs of Scotland prior to Burns* (1862). His son Robert (1832–88) became head of the firm in 1883, and ran the *Journal* until his death.

CHAMBERS, Sir William
(1723–96)

Architect, born in Gothenburg, Sweden, son of a Scottish merchant. He became the leading public architect of 18th-century Britain. Educated in Edinburgh and Ripon, he then joined the Swedish East India Company, studying architecture on his travels. He trained formally with J F Blondel in Paris from 1849. In 1755 he became architectural tutor to the future King George III. Although remembered in particular for his classical works, a fusion of restrained British classicism and French neo-classicism, such as Somerset House, London (1776–96), and for his essential publication, *Treatise on Civil Architecture* (1759), his designs for Chinese buildings were exemplary, the earliest being at Kew (from 1757, published in 1763). He provided additions and alterations to many country houses. In Edinburgh he designed Dundas House (1771, now the Royal Bank of Scotland) and Duddingston House, and in Dublin, Charlemont House (1763).

CHAMBERS, William
(1800–83)

Publisher and writer, brother of **Robert Chambers**, born in Peebles, the son of a cotton manufacturer. In 1814 he was apprenticed to a bookseller in Edinburgh, and in 1819 started his own business, first book-selling and later printing as well. Between 1825 and 1830 he wrote the *Book of Scotland* and, in conjunction with his brother Robert, a *Gazetteer of Scotland*. In 1832 he started *Chambers's Edinburgh Journal*, six weeks in advance of the *Penny Magazine*, and he later joined Robert in founding the business of W & R Chambers. In 1859 he founded and endowed a museum, library and art gallery in Peebles. Lord Provost of Edinburgh from 1865 to 1869, he promoted a successful scheme for improving the older part of the city. At his own cost he carried out a restoration of St Giles' Cathedral. Besides many contributions to the *Journal*, he wrote a *Youth's Companion*, a *History of Peeblesshire* (1864), *Ailie Gilroy*, *Stories of Remarkable Persons*, *Stories of Old Families*, and a *Historical Sketch of St Giles' Cathedral* (1879).

CHAPMAN, Robert
(1881–1960)

Scholar and publisher, born in Eskbank, Dalkeith. He was educated at St Andrews University and Oriel College, Oxford, and joined the Clarendon Press as assistant to Charles Cannan in 1906. He succeeded Cannan in 1920, and wrote an *Account of the Oxford University Press* 1468–1921 (1922). His principal scholarly interest lay in the work of Samuel Johnson and Jane Austen. In collaboration with his wife, Katherine Marion Metcalfe, he prepared an edition of Austen's novels (1923), followed later by volumes of juvenilia, minor works, letters and bibliography. His contribution to Johnson scholarship was even greater. He was responsible for publishing collated and annotated editions of the major works of Johnson and **Boswell**, but his most substantial achievement lay in his own edition of *The Letters of Samuel Johnson* (3 vols, 1952). An ardent and scrupulous editor and bibliographer, he was an eminent supporter of the Society of Pure English.

CHARITY, John
(1946 –)

English-born photographer, born in Nottingham. He studied photography at Nottingham College of Art and Design (1969–72), and since then has worked as a photographer and teacher of photography. From 1974 to 1981 he was Lecturer in Documentary Photography at Gwent College, Wales. He then moved to Ross and Cromarty to work as an independent photographer and was commissioned by the District Council to take photographs in the area. His work is based on a broad approach and is designed to be widely accessible. He is concerned to work as a part of the society he photographs, 'using the camera to associate himself with the world'. As a result of knowledge and understanding of that community, his photographs are both truthful and sympathetic.

CHARLESON, Ian
(1949–90)

Actor, born in Edinburgh. After two years at **Frank Dunlop**'s Young Vic Company, London, he appeared as Hamlet with the Cambridge Theatre Company before joining the Royal Shakespeare Company and playing a variety of leading roles in Shakespearian and other plays. At the National Theatre he appeared in several leading roles, including Brick in Tennessee Williams's *Cat on a Hot Tin Roof* (1988). He scored a notable film success in 1981 as the runner **Eric Liddell** in *Chariots of Fire*. Terminally ill, he gave a moving stage performance of *Hamlet* at the National Theatre in 1989, directed by Richard Eyre, and his decision to request the announcement of his death from AIDS was a courageous final act. A leading player of charm and power, he was one of the finest British actors of his generation.

CHARTERIS, Archibald
(1835–1908)

Church of Scotland minister and innovator, born in Dumfriesshire. After gaining degrees of MA and BD at Edinburgh University, he held ministries at St Qivox and Park Parish, Glasgow. He was subsequently granted the Chair of Biblical Criticism at Edinburgh University. Chaplain to Queen Victoria and Edward VII, he was also appointed Moderator of the General Assembly in 1892. In 1879 he founded *Life and Work*, the enduring and perennial magazine of the Church's life and, in 1887, the Woman's Guild. He was also responsible for the revival of the order of Deaconesses, the foundation of the Deaconess Hospital, and a wide-ranging commitment to social work, all the while with an eye to the missionary work of the church, such that the Mission Hospital at Kalimpong bears his name. A man of inexhaustable energy, vision and dedication, his writings include *The Church of Scotland and Spiritual Independence* (1874) and many volumes on biblical criticism.

CHEPMAN, Walter
(c.1473 – c.1538)

The first Scottish printer. A notary and merchant in Edinburgh, in 1507 he received a patent from **James IV** to set up the first Scottish printing press, with an Edinburgh bookseller, Andrew Myllar, who had learned printing in Rouen. Little remains of their output apart from the *Aberdeen Breviary* (1510) and fragments of *The Wallace* by **Blind Harry**. He founded a chantry in St Giles' Cathedral, Edinburgh.

CHEYNE, George
(1671–1743)

Physician, born in Methlick, Aberdeenshire. After studying at Edinburgh, he started a London practice in 1702. There rich living made him enormously overweight (32 stone), as well as asthmatic, but he derived so much benefit from a milk and vegetable diet that he recommended it in all the later volumes of his 12 medical treatises. His *Essay of Health and Long Life* was eulogized by Dr Johnson.

CHILDE, Vere Gordon
(1892–1957)

Australian archaeologist, born in Sydney. Educated at Sydney University and Oxford, he established a reputation with his first book, *The Dawn of European Civilisation* (1925), a brilliant and erudite work that charted the prehistoric development of Europe in terms of its various peoples and their archaeological cultures. With *The Most Ancient Near East* (1928) and *The Danube in Prehistory* (1929) it established him as the most influential archaeological theorist of his generation. A lifelong Marxist and prodigious traveller and linguist, he was Professor of Archaeology at Edinburgh University (1927–46) and Director of the University of London Institute of Archaeology (1946–56). A companionable, eccentric but essentially lonely man, he returned to Australia on retirement, falling to his death in the Blue Mountains near Sydney soon after.

CHISHOLM, Erik
(1904–65)

Composer, born in Glasgow. He studied under Tovey and from 1930, as conductor of the Glasgow Grand Opera Society, produced many rarely heard works, including *The*

Trojans by Berlioz. In 1945 he was appointed Professor of Music at Capetown. His works include two symphonies, concertos for piano and violin, other orchestral music, and operas.

CHISHOLM, George
(1915 –)

Jazz trombonist, born in Glasgow, who played the piano with pierrot troupes from the age of 11. Taking up the trombone at 16, he was working in the pit at Green's Playhouse when he was heard by the American bandleader Teddy Joyce and offered work in London. Moving there in 1936 and working with such major society bands as the Ambrose Orchestra, he developed an outstanding facility as a jazz soloist. He was one of the first British jazz musicians to impress such American stars as Benny Carter and Fats Waller, recording with both in the late 1930s. In 1941 he joined the Squadronaires, the RAF dance orchestra, as arranger and leader of the trombone section, and during the 1950s he was a member of the BBC Showband. He also joined in comedy routines, both in the Goon Show and, while working with his own small band, on the television *Black and White Minstrel Show*. Latterly he worked as a freelancer, performing in many parts of the world.

CHRISTISON, Sir Alexander Francis Philip
(1893 –)

Soldier and ornithologist, born in Edinburgh and educated at The Edinburgh Academy and Oxford University. During World War I he won the MC and bar while serving with the Cameron Highlanders, and he later occupied several staff posts in India. An inspired corps commander in Burma during World War II, he inflicted the first heavy defeat on the Japanese forces at Arakan in 1944, and as Commander-in-Chief Allied Land Forces South-East Asia he completed the rout of the Japanese a year later. For this achievement he was knighted in the field, a unique occurrence. In the aftermath of the war he commanded the allied forces in the Netherland East Indies, where his wise counsels ended the fighting between the Dutch and the Indonesians. After his retirement in 1949 he led a busy public life and was particularly interested in the promotion of Gaelic culture. A noted ornithologist, his publications include *Birds of Northern Baluchistan* (1940) and *Birds of Arakan* (1946).

CHRISTISON, Sir Robert
(1797–1882)

Toxicologist, born in Edinburgh, the son of the Professor of Humanity. After graduating MD from Edinburgh (1819), he became house-physician at Edinburgh Infirmary (1817–20), before going on to study in London, where he was taught by John Abernethy. He then studied toxicology in Paris under Mathieu Orfila. In 1822 he was appointed Professor of Medical Jurisprudence at Edinburgh, and from 1832 Professor of Materia Medica. He wrote a *Treatise on Poisons* (1829) and was medical adviser to the crown from 1829 to 1866, becoming physician to Queen Victoria in 1848.

CHRYSTAL, George
(1851–1911)

Mathematician, born near Old Meldrum, Aberdeenshire. Graduating from Aberdeen in 1871, he went to Cambridge, studied with **James Clerk Maxwell** and obtained a fellowship in 1875. In 1877 he became professor at St Andrews, and in 1879 he moved to the Chair of Mathematics at Edinburgh, which he held until his death. As Dean of the Faculty of Arts he implemented the many changes introduced by the Universities (Scotland) Act of 1889. His textbook *Algebra* (1886–9) was a standard work for many years, and he contributed the articles on electricity and magnetism to the 9th edition of *The Encyclopaedia Britannica*. His researches included the study of seiches on Scottish lochs.

CLAPPERTON, Hugh
(1788–1827)

Explorer, born in Annan, Dumfriesshire. At sea from the age of 13, in 1821 he was sent with Dixon Denham to discover the source of the Niger. They travelled south across the Sahara to Lake Chad in 1823; from there he journeyed on alone to Sokoto, returning to England in 1825. His travels had thrown light on Bornu and the Houssa country, but the great problem of the source of the Niger remained untouched. In a new attempt to resolve it he started again from the Bight of Benin in December 1825, travelling north in the company of Richard Lander and others. The others died early on the journey, but Clapperton and Lander reached Sokoto, where Clapperton was detained by the sultan and died.

CLARK, Gavin Brown
(1846–1930)

Politician, born in Kilmarnock, Dunbartonshire. He studied medicine at Glasgow and Edinburgh universities. A Radical, he worked with Gladstone in the campaign against the Bulgarian Atrocities in 1877–8. In the 1880s he was closely identified with Highland crofter unrest, and was Chairman of the Highland Land League. He won Caithness in 1885 as a Crofters' Party candidate, and did much to secure the passage of the Crofters Act of 1886. Vice-President of the Scottish Home Rule Association, he sponsored a Home Rule Bill in 1889. He was also Vice-President and a founder member of **James Keir Hardie**'s Scottish Labour Party, which was formed in 1888. His strong pro-Boer views cost him his Caithness seat in 1900.

CLARK, Jim (James)
(1936–68)

Racing driver and world champion, born in Kilmaddy, Fife. Educated at Loretto School in Musselburgh, he won his first motor race in 1956, and became Scottish Speed Champion in 1958 and 1959. In 1960 he joined the Lotus team as a Formula One driver, and thereafter won the world championship in 1963 and 1965. Also in 1965 he became the first non-American since 1916 to win the Indianapolis 500. In all, he won 25 Grand Prix events, breaking the record of 24 held by Juan Fangio. He was killed during practice for a Formula Two race at Hockenheim, in West Germany.

CLARK, Michael
(1962 –)

Dancer and choreographer, born in Aberdeen, where he took lessons in Scottish country dancing from the age of 4. Accepted by the Royal Ballet School at 13, he went on to dance with the Royal Ballet. A move to the Ballet Rambert led to roles in Richard Alston's *Dutiful Ducks* and *Soda Lake*. After studying with Merce Cunningham in New York for a short time, he began to choreograph. While developing his own style he worked as a dancer with Karole Armitage in Paris, starting his own company in 1984. His brilliantly original style incorporates punk, 1960s fantasy, nudity, video, platform shoes and giant hamburgers, but it is his keen, sculptural choreography which makes him one of the most inventive artists today. Major full-length productions include *Our caca phony H. our caca phony H* (1985), *No Fire Escape in Hell* (1986), *Because We Must* (1987) and *I Am Curious, Orange* (1988). Commissions include *Swamp* for the Ballet Rambert (1986).

CLARK, William Donaldson
(1816–73)

Photographer, born in Ayr, the son of a shipmaster. He became a successful calico printer, running his own printing works in the north of England. On his retiral he returned to Scotland, a wealthy man. A member of the artistic community in Edinburgh, numbering several Royal Scottish Academicians among his friends, he became, briefly, a picture-dealer. He joined the Photographic Society of Scotland in 1864 and subsequently became Secretary. From the late 1850s he exhibited regularly in Scotland and received critical acclaim. Praised by contemporaries as a landscape photographer, his major known surviving works are topographical: views of Edinburgh and a series of studies of Melrose Abbey, which were taken in 1866 with the photographer, John Smith, from Darnick. Clark's work is exceptional for its aesthetic and technical merit (he mainly employed the collodio-albumen or 'Taupenot' process). Although his background was scientific and technical, Clark championed the cause of photography as an artistic rather than a scientific activity.

CLARKE, Alexander Ross
(1828–1914)

Geodesist. He began his career as an army engineer and was later attached to the Ordnance Survey. He is remembered for his work on the principal triangulation of the British Isles, and for his book, *Geodesy* (1880).

CLEGHORN, Hugh
(1820–95)

Forester, born in Madras, and described as the father of scientific forestry in India. After graduating in medicine at Edinburgh, he joined the East India Company and for the rest of his life lived largely in India. He made important collections of plants and published *Forests and Plants of South India* in 1861. He succeeded in establishing laws to prevent destructive forms of cultivation and was one of the first to challenge the destruction of the rain forests.

CLELAND, William
(c.1661–1689)

Covenanter and poet. He studied at St Andrews, joined the Covenanters, fought at Drumclog and Bothwell Brig (1679), and fled to Holland, where he studied at Leiden. He took part in the abortive rebellion by Archibald, 9th Earl of **Argyll**, in 1685, and fled back to Holland. After the 'Glorious Revolution' of 1688 he returned to Scotland as Colonel of the Cameronians, and fell in the defence of Dunkeld against the Jacobite rebels. His poetry was published posthumously (1697).

CLERK, Sir Dugald
(1854–1932)

Engineer, born in Glasgow. He studied at Anderson's College, Glasgow, and at the Yorkshire College of Science in Leeds, intending to become a chemical engineer. Having studied the properties of petroleum oils, from 1877 he devoted himself to research on the theory and design of gas engines. In 1881 he patented a gas engine that worked on the two-stroke principle which became known as the Clerk cycle, and was extensively used for large gas engines and later for small petrol engines.

CLERK, Sir John, of Penicuik
(1676–1755)

Advocate, politician, antiquary, gentleman-architect, landscape gardener, man of letters, cultural virtuoso, scientific dilettante and arbiter of taste. Educated in Glasgow and Leyden, he completed his studies with a Grand Tour, and was admitted to the Bar in 1700. A Whig politician, he was part designer of the Treaty of Union. He was the author of various works, including the influential georgic, *The Country Seat* (1727). He was also a friend and patron of **Allan Ramsay**. He collaborated with **William Adam** to produce a key design, the villa of Mavisbank (c.1723), near Penicuik. His unparalleled influence among Scottish intelligentsia in the first half of the 18th century was furthered by his contacts with England which, together

with his élite patronage, earned him the soubriquet, the 'Scottish Burlington'.

CLERK-MAXWELL, James See
MAXWELL, James Clerk

CLOUGH, Charles Thomas
(1852–1916)

English-born geologist, born in Huddersfield, where he received his early education. Following Rugby School and St John's College, Cambridge, he joined the staff of the Geological Survey of Great Britain in 1875, transferring to Scotland in 1884. He was appointed District Geologist in 1902 and was killed in 1916 while engaged in field work at a railway cutting in West Lothian. He was renowned both within and beyond the Survey for the quality of his geological mapping, particularly in the Scottish Highlands. His powers of observation in the field extended to meticulous attention to the details of rock exposures. He received the **Murchison** medal of the Geological Society of London in 1906, and is himself commemorated in the annual Clough Medal of the Edinburgh Geological Society.

CLYNE, Chris
(1954 –)

Fashion designer, born in India. She studied at St Martin's School of Art, London. After working in Paris, she established her own fashion company in London, moving to Edinburgh in 1980 and forging links with Scottish Borders textile companies. Concentrating on special occasion and evening wear, she has created exclusive designs and tartans in wool, cashmere and silk, and has a dedicated and growing private clientele in Britain, as well as retail outlets in the USA and Europe. She also works on special commissions for the theatre and film industry. Her clients include members of the British royal family and celebrities such as Meryl Streep, Glenn Close and Diana Rigg.

COATS, Sir Peter
(1808–90) and **Thomas** (1809–83)

Industrialists, born in Paisley. Their father founded the thread factory at Ferguslie, Paisley, which they continued, later making many munificent gifts to Paisley, including a park, playgrounds, and an observatory. Thomas was also a coin collector.

COCHRAN, William

(1922 –)

Physicist, born in Newton Mearns, Renfrewshire. After studying at Edinburgh University he joined Sir Lawrence Bragg's team in Cambridge (1946), laying the foundations of modern crystallography and contributing to the elucidation of the double helix. He participated in the development of neutron scattering, a technique for probing the details of atomic and molecular motion in matter. The lattice dynamical 'soft mode' theory of the second-order solid-state phase transitions he propounded in 1960 is now well-established fundamental physics. In 1964 he took the newly established Chair of Physics at Edinburgh University and built a flourishing Condensed Matter group. After serving as Head of Department and Dean of the Faculty of Science he became a vice-principal of Edinburgh University (1984–7). While at Edinburgh he was awarded the Hughes Medal of the Royal Society of London (1978).

COCHRAN, William Gemmell

(1909–80)

Statistician, born in Rutherglen, Lanarkshire. Educated at Glasgow University, his studies for a PhD at Cambridge were broken when he moved to Rothamsted Experimental Station (1934). Following this he lectured at the universities of Iowa State (1939), Princeton (1944), North Carolina (1946), Johns Hopkins (1949, head of bio-statistics) and Harvard (1957–76, head of statistics). During this time he carried out fundamental work on the design of agricultural experiments, forecasting the effect of weather on crop yields, and the design of sample surveys. He wrote scientific papers on (inter alia) the effects of World War II bombing, smoking and health, and educational opportunity. He was author or joint author of standard texts on the design of experiments, sample surveys, and statistical methods. President of numerous professional statistical bodies, he was elected to the US National Academy of Sciences in 1974. He was awarded honorary degrees from Glasgow and Johns Hopkins.

COCHRANE, Archibald, 9th Earl of Dundonald

(1749–1831)

Naval officer and chemical manufacturer, born into a noble but impoverished family. In his youth he served in both the navy and the army. For most of his life he engaged in experimental pursuits which resulted in, for example, an improved method of making sailcloth, new methods of manufacturing alkali, British gum and white lead, and the construction on his estate at Culross of retorts for the distillation of tar from coal. Between 1781 and 1812 he took out 10 patents, several of them for processes from which others subsequently made their fortune, but he never managed to turn any of them to his own financial advantage. It is said that he had to borrow £100 from a friend in order to equip his son **Thomas Cochrane** for entry into the navy.

COCHRANE, Archibald Lenman

(1909–88)

Researcher in community medicine, born in Galashiels, Selkirkshire. Educated at Cambridge, because of personal problems he was attracted to psychiatry and underwent psychoanalysis in Berlin. Returning to London he studied medicine at University College Hospital Medical School but left to join a field ambulance in the Spanish Civil War. In 1937 he returned to University College Hospital. In 1939 he joined the RAMC, and in 1941 was captured in Crete, spending the rest of the war as a POW. In charge of prisoners with tuberculosis, his realization that treatment was given without a rational basis was the genesis of his interest in randomized controlled trials (RCT). In 1948 he joined the MRC Pneumoconiosis Research Unit in Cardiff. Comparing two mining valleys for the incidence of progressive massive fibrosis evaluated by RCT, he showed that measurements could be made in community research comparable in accuracy with those in laboratory experiments. In 1972 he published *Effectiveness and Efficiency: Random Reflections on Health Services*, which stressed the importance of RCTs applied to monitoring the effectiveness of medical and surgical treatments and to health service organizations. The book has become a classic.

COCHRANE, Sir Ralph Alexander

(1895–1977)

Air Chief Marshal, born in Springfield, Fife. Educated at the Royal Naval College at Osborne and Dartmouth, he entered the Royal Navy in 1912. During World War I he transferred to the Royal Flying Corps and was commissioned in the Royal Air Force in April 1918. During the 1920s he was one of the officers responsible for the evolution of 'Air Power', the policy used by the RAF to police remote and recalcitrant areas of the empire, such as the north-west frontier and Kurdistan. After occupying various staff posts he became Director of Flying Training and, on the outbreak of World War II, returned to Bomber Command. As the commander of 5 Group he was responsible for planning the British heavy bomber offensive against German industry, including the famous 'Dambuster' raid of October 1943. In the postwar years he commanded Flying Training Command and Transport Command before his retirement in 1952.

COCHRANE, Thomas, 10th Earl of Dundonald
(1775–1860)

Naval commander, born in Annsfield, Hamilton. He entered the navy in 1793, and in 1800 received the command of a sloop, the *Speedy*, with which he took over 50 prizes in 15 months, including a 32-gun frigate. He was captured shortly afterwards by the French, but was quickly exchanged, and promoted to post-captain. After protecting the Orkney fisheries, he returned to prize-taking off the Azores in 1805, and by April had made £75 000 of prize money for his own share. In 1805 he stood unsuccessfully for election to Parliament for Honiton, but by judicious bribery was elected the following year. In 1807 he was returned for Westminster, and campaigned against naval abuses, but was ordered to the Mediterranean. In 1809 he was selected to burn the French fleet then blockaded in Aix Roads by Lord Gambier; the operation was only partly successful. Discredited and on half-pay, Cochrane pursued his crusade against naval corruption, until in 1814 he was arrested on a charge of fraud. He was accused, with two others, of spreading a rumour of Napoleon's overthrow that sent up the funds, and then selling out upwards of a million sterling at a gross profit of £10 000. The others were guilty; Cochrane, who was by some held to be innocent, was sentenced to pay a fine of £1000, to suffer a year's imprisonment, and to stand for an hour in the pillory. Westminster re-elected him, and in March 1815 he broke out of jail and re-appeared in the House, to be forcibly removed and reimprisoned for the remaining three months of his sentence, and was fined a further £100. In 1818 he was in command of Chile's navy (1818–22) in the War for Freedom by Chile and Peru; he stormed the 15 strong forts of Valdivia (1819), and in two and a half years he restored to Chile control over her own waters. He took command of the Brazilian navy (1823–5), and later the Greek navy (1827–8). In 1831 he succeeded to the earldom of Dundonald, and in 1832 was granted a free pardon for past misdeeds. Restored to the navy as a rear-admiral, he was later Commander-in-Chief on the North American station (1848–51), and Rear Admiral of the UK (1854). He was buried in Westminster Abbey. Throughout his life he was a prolific inventor, with 14 patents to his name for the manufacture of coal-gas and its use in lighting, steam boilers and screw propulsion for ships, the use of compressed air and air-locks in excavations, and a rotary steam engine. For many years he sought to convince the Admiralty of the superiority of steam power, tubular boilers and screw propellers.

COCKBURN, Alison or Alicia, née Rutherford
(1713–94)

Poet, born in Selkirkshire. In 1731 she married Patrick Cockburn, an advocate, and for over 60 years she was a leading figure in Edinburgh society. Of her lyrics, the best known is the exquisite version of 'The Flowers of the Forest' ('I've seen the smiling of Fortune beguiling'), which commemorates a wave of calamity that swept over Ettrick Forest, and was first printed in 1765. In 1777 she discerned in **Walter Scott** 'the most extraordinary genius of a boy'; in 1786 she made **Robert Burns**'s acquaintance.

COCKBURN, Henry Thomas
(1779–1854)

Judge, born perhaps in Cockpen, Midlothian, but more probably in the Parliament Close of old Edinburgh. He entered the Royal High School in 1787, and Edinburgh University in 1793. Through a debating club he became the companion of **Francis Jeffrey, Francis Horner** and **Henry Brougham**. He was called to the Bar in 1800, and in 1807 his uncle, the all-powerful Lord Melville (**Henry Dundas**), gave him an advocate-deputeship a non-political post from which, on political grounds, he 'had the honour of being dismissed' in 1810. He rose, however, to share with Jeffrey the leadership of the Bar. A zealous supporter of parliamentary reform, he became Solicitor-General for Scotland in 1830, had the chief hand in drafting the Scottish Reform Bill, and was elected Lord Rector of Glasgow University (1831). In 1834 he was made a judge of the Court of Session, as Lord Cockburn, and three years later a Lord of Justiciary as well. He contributed to the *Edinburgh Review*, and was author of a *Life of Jeffrey* (1852), the delightful *Memorials of his Time* (1856), *Journal*, 1831–44 (2 vols, 1874) and *Circuit Journeys* (1888).

COHEN, Anthony Paul
(1946 –)

English social anthropologist, born in London. He was educated at the University of Southampton. After a series of teaching and research posts in Canada and a period at Manchester University, he took up the post of Professor of Social Anthropology at Edinburgh in 1989. He has conducted extensive fieldwork in Shetland, culminating in the publication of *Whalsay* (1987), his study of a Shetland fishing community. He has been at the forefront of a revival of interest in anthropological community studies of rural Britain, in which his two edited collections, *Belonging* (1982) and *Symbolising Boundaries* (1986), have been extremely influential. He has also published *The Management of Myth* (1975) and *The Symbolic Construction of Community* (1985).

COHEN, Philip
(1945 –)

Biochemist and enzymologist, born in London and educated at Hendon Grammer School and University College, London, where he took his PhD in 1969. He moved to Dundee as lecturer in biochemistry in 1971 and established a keen interest in glycogen metabolism. He became reader in 1978, Professor of Enzymology in 1981, and Royal Society Research Professor in 1984. He is also now the Honorary Director of the Medical Research Council's Protein Phosphorylation Unit. He has made many important contributions to our knowledge of how the activity of enzymes is controlled, in particular on the ideas that most intracellular processes are controlled by enzymes, called kinases, which are able to phosphorylate proteins at many different sites. He published *Control of Enzyme Activity* (1976, 2nd ed 1983) and edited the series of volumes *Molecular Aspects of Gene Activity* (1980 –), as well as over 250 publications elsewhere. He was elected FRS in 1984.

COIA, Jack Anthony, or Giacomo Antonio
(1898–1981)

Architect, born in Wolverhampton, the son of a retailer. Educated in Glasgow and apprenticed to J Gaff Gillespie (1870–1926) from 1915, his work was inspirational and imaginative. He lectured at Glasgow School of Architecture and was a governor of the Glasgow School of Art. He served as president of the RIAS and was an Associate of the RSA. He won the Queen's Royal Gold Medal for Architecture. He is best known for his Roman Catholic church designs of the 1930s, modern interpretations of Italian basilicas, notably St Anne's, Dennistoun (1933) and St Columbkille, Rutherglen (1939). The powerful composition and spatial drama of his later churches evolved from St Laurence's, Greenock (1951) and St Mary's, Bo'ness (1962), to St Benedict's, Drumchapel (1965, demolished). The thoughtful, practical design of the addition to Our Lady and St Francis School, Glasgow, demonstrated his instinctive design philosophy for architecture as an expressive whole.

COLLINS, Sir Godfrey Pattison
(1875–1936)

Liberal politician, born in Glasgow. Educated on *HMS Britannia*, he retired from a naval career in 1893 with the rank of captain. He then entered business, becoming a very successful managing director of the family publishing firm. From 1910 to 1936 he represented Greenock as a Liberal. He was Scottish Liberal whip, 1918–20, and Chief Liberal whip, 1924–6. In 1931 he joined the Coalition government, and was appointed Secretary of State for Scotland, 1932–6. His Housing Act (1935) aimed to attack directly slum housing for the first time; his Education Act proposed to raise the school leaving age to 15 in 1939, but this was postponed on the outbreak of war. He also established the Herring Industry Board (1935).

COLLINS, William
(1789–1853)

Publisher, born in Eastwood, Renfrewshire. A weaver by trade, he opened a private school for the poor in Glasgow in 1813. A friend of the evangelist **Thomas Chalmers**, in 1819 he set up business in Glasgow as a bookseller and publisher with Chalmers' brother. He specialized in Church history and pioneered school textbooks.

COLOMB, Philip Howard
(1831–99)

Naval officer and historian. He entered the navy in 1846 and served in the Burmese war (1852) and in China (1874–7). After reporting to the Admiralty on methods of signalling, he devised the system of night signalling known as 'Colomb's Flashing Signals' (1858). He wrote *Naval Warfare* (1891), on the importance of naval supremacy, and was promoted vice-admiral in 1892.

COLQUHOUN, Patrick
(1745–1820)

Merchant and reformer, born in Dumbarton. After visiting Virginia, he became a tobacco merchant in Glasgow (1766–89) and was Lord Provost in 1782. He founded the Glasgow Chamber of Commerce in 1783, the oldest of its kind in Britain. After moving to London in 1789 he became a police magistrate and wrote many reforming pamphlets on subjects such as poor relief, the most notable of which was his *Police of the Metropolis* (1795).

COLQUHOUN, Robert
(1914–62)

Artist, born in Kilmarnock, Ayrshire. He studied at the Glasgow School of Art (where he was a pupil of **Ian Fleming** and became a friend of **Robert MacBryde**), and in Italy, France, Holland and Belgium. Injured during ambulance service in World War II, he returned to Britain in 1941, setting up studio with MacBryde in London and later in Sussex. His enigmatic, dreamlike figures (eg *Girl with a circus goat*) are usually presented in a characteristic colour scheme of reds and browns.

COLTRANE, Robbie, originally Robin McMillan
(1950 –)

Actor, born in Rutherglen, near Glasgow. Educated at Glenalmond and Glasgow School of Art, he won the Scottish Council Film of the Year Award for his 50-minute documentary *Young Mental Health* (1973). His career progressed via theatre work and especially an involvement with writer **John Byrne** on *The Slab Boys* (1978) and its sequel *Cuttin' A Rug* (1980). A talented mimic and wit, his comic skills were seen on television in a succession of satirical sketch shows, beginning with 81 *Take* 2 (1981) and as a member of the *Comic Strip* team. He has also contributed invaluable supporting performances in scores of films, including *Mona Lisa* (1986), *The Fruit Machine* (1987) and *Henry V* (1989), in which he played Falstaff. His performance as rock'n'roller Danny McGlone in the television series *Tutti Frutti* (1987) earned him a BAFTA Best Actor nomination, and his reputation continued to grow through warmly received one-man shows in the theatre such as *Yr Obedient Servant* (1987), in which he played Dr Johnson, and *Mistero Buffo* (1990), which was also televised. Increasingly recognized internationally, he has starred in such comic films as *Nuns on the Run* (1990) and *The Pope Must Die* (1991).

COLUMBA, St, also known as Colmcille ('Colm of the Churches')
(521–97)

Irish apostle of Christianity in Scotland, born into the royal warrior aristocracy of Ireland at Gartan in County Donegal. According to his 7th-century biographer, Adomnán, he studied under St Finnian at Clonard with St Ciaran. In 546 he founded the monastery of Derry. In 561, however, he was accused of having been involved in the bloody Battle of Cuildreimhne, for which he was excommunicated and sentenced to exile; it was perhaps in this battle that he received the wound that left a livid scar on his side. In 563, at the advanced age of 42 and accompanied by 12 disciples, he set sail to do penance as a missionary, and found haven on the Hebridean island of Iona, where he founded a monastery that became the mother church of Celtic Christianity in Scotland. From Iona he travelled to other parts of Scotland, especially to the north to evangelize amongst the Picts, and won the respect of the pagan King Brude (Bridei) at his stronghold near Inverness (possibly the hill-fort at Craig Phadrig). He and his missionaries founded numerous churches in the islands of the Hebrides (hence his Gaelic name of Colmcille). A formidably energetic administrator, he organized his monastery on Iona as a school for missionaries, and played a vigorous role in the politics of the country. Although he spent the last 34 years of his life in Scotland, he visited Ireland on occasions, and towards the end of his life he founded the monastery of Durrow in

Ireland. He was renowned as a man of letters; he wrote hymns, and is credited with having transcribed 300 books with his own hand; but he was also revered as a warrior saint, and his supernatural aid was frequently invoked for victory in battle. He died on Iona and was buried in the abbey.

COLVILLE, David
(1813–98)

Industrialist, born in Campbeltown, Argyll. In 1871, employing 200 men, he began constructing malleable plates and angles for Scottish shipbuilders. In 1879 he built five of the largest Siemens furnaces for the production of steel, and in 1880 he obtained the contract to supply Siemans furnaces. In 1885 he took his three sons into partnership, but two of them died in 1916 and the third, John, became an MP. Thus the chairmanship passed to a former office boy, Sir John Craig (1874–1957), who made the firm the fourth largest steel concern in Great Britain.

COLVIN, Calum
(1961 –)

Photographer, born in Glasgow. He studied sculpture and photography at Duncan of Jordanstone College of Art, Dundee, and continued his studies in photography at the Royal College of Art in London. A highly inventive and original photographer, his method is to use a large format studio camera as the fixed 'eye' or viewpoint from which his spacially complex constructed images are seen. The final photograph — generally large in scale and always in colour — is a record of a set which Colvin has built and assembled and upon which he has painted an image which only falls into place, spacially and conceptually, from the camera's point of view. Colvin's most recent work combines photographic and computer imaging. His themes, whilst often making art-historical reference, generally concern Scottish culture and identity.

COMBE, Andrew
(1797–1847)

Physician and phrenologist, brother of **George Combe,** born in Edinburgh, the son of a brewer. After studying at Edinburgh and Paris he began to practise in Edinburgh in 1823. In 1836 he was appointed physician to the King of the Belgians, but his health failed and he returned to Scotland, where in 1838 he became physician to Queen Victoria. His *Principles of Physiology* (1834) was influential and went through 15 editions. He also wrote popular works on general health and, as a member of the Phrenological Society, contributed over several years to the *Phrenological Journal.*

COMBE, George
(1788–1858)

Phrenologist, moral philosopher and brother of **Andrew Combe,** born in Edinburgh, a brewer's son. He became a solicitor in 1812, retiring from law in 1837. Through the German phrenologist Johann Spurzheim he became, like his brother, a convert to phrenology, and wrote *Essays on Phrenology* (1819) and *The Constitution of Man* (1828), which was violently opposed as inimical to revealed religion. He travelled and lectured in Britain, Germany and the USA, and published *Notes on the United States* (1841). In 1833 he married Cecilia (1794–1868), the daughter of Sarah Siddons. His ideas on popular education were implemented for some years in a school which he founded in Edinburgh in 1848.

COMYN, CUMMING, or CUMYN

A family that took its name from the town of Comines near Lille, on the Franco-Belgian frontier. While one branch remained there, and gave birth to Philippe de Comines, another followed William of Normandy to England. In 1069 William the Conqueror made Robert of Comines, or Comyn, Earl of Northumberland; his younger son, William, became Chancellor of Scotland about 1133. By 1250 his descendants in Scotland included four earls (Buchan, Monteith, Angus and Athole) and 32 belted knights of the name of Comyn; but 70 years afterwards this great house was overthrown.

CONN, Stewart
(1936 –)

Poet and playwright, born in Glasgow and educated at Glasgow University. Following National Service, he entered the BBC, becoming Head of Drama at Radio Scotland in 1977. As a playwright he is best known for *The Burning,* produced at Edinburgh's Royal

Lyceum Theatre in 1971, and *Herman*, produced in 1981. Other plays include *The Aquarium* (1973), while his television work includes *The Kite* (1979) and *Bloodhunt* (1986). His collections of poetry include *An Ear to the Ground* (1972), *In the Kibble Palace* (1987), and *The Luncheon of The Boating Party* (1992), each distinguished by its unobtrusive lyricism and reflective introspection. His production of *Carver* by **John Purser** won the gold medal award at the 1991 International Radio Festival in New York.

CONNELL, Charles

(1822–84)

Shipbuilder, born in Ayrshire. Having completed a basic education he was apprenticed as a shipwright to a Greenock shipbuilder, Robert Steele. After becoming a foreman in a yard on the upper Clyde he joined Stephen and Sons and was appointed shipyard manager. In 1861 he established his own yard at Scotstoun, Glasgow. In doing so he founded one of the most notable of the Clyde's family shipbuilding firms, associated particularly with cargo ships. Charles Connell and Co. was to remain prominent until the merger with Upper Clyde Shipbuilders in 1968. A reserved man whose shareholding interests included public utilities and shipping, his estate totalled more than a quarter of a million pounds.

CONNERY, Sean Thomas

(1930 –)

Actor, born in Edinburgh. After a succession of jobs, including milkman, lifeguard and coffin-polisher, his powerful physique won him a position in the chorus line of the London stage production of *South Pacific* (1951–2). Sporadic film work followed, although there were more significant opportunities in television drama, particularly *Requiem for a Heavyweight* (1956) and *Anna Karenina* (1957). Chosen over more fancied contenders for the role of secret agent James Bond in *Dr. No* (1962) he became an international film star, imbuing the character with a rough-hewn masculinity and sardonic wit. He played the role on seven occasions until *Never Say Never Again* (1983). An adventurous actor, he struggled hard to avoid typecasting, giving notable performances in such films as *The Hill* (1965), *The Molly Maguires* (1969), *The Offence* (1972) and *The Man Who Would Be King* (1975). Maturity

and the loss of his hair have merely enhanced his charisma and refined his considerable skills, and he won the BAFTA Best Actor Award for *The Name of The Rose* (1986) and an Oscar for his portrayal of an ageing Irish cop in *The Untouchables* (1987). His many recent successes include *Indiana Jones and the Last Crusade* (1989) and *The Hunt for Red October* (1990). A highly competitive golfer and a stickler for fair play, his salary from *Diamonds are Forever* (1971) established the Scottish Education Trust and he has also offered financial support to many causes, including the National Youth Theatre. Created a freeman of Edinburgh in 1991, he has also controversially placed his support behind the political aspirations of the Scottish National Party.

CONNOLLY, Billy

(1942 –)

Comedian, born in Glasgow. A shipyard welder who entertained his workmates with caustic patter and tunes plucked out on a banjo, he performed as an amateur before turning professional in 1965. He later joined with **Gerry Rafferty** and Tam Harvey to form the folk group The Humblebums. Going solo, he appeared in the popular *The Great Northern Welly Boot Show* at the 1972 Edinburgh Festival and, affectionately known as 'The Big Yin', he gained a loyal following as a stand-up comic and singer whose acute observations of life, cheerful vulgarity and scatalogical humour could induce helpless laughter. In 1975 he enjoyed a number one hit with the single 'D.I.V.O.R.C.E.'. His subsequent move to London and involvement with actress Pamela Stephenson (who became his second wife in 1989) began an abrasive relationship with the Scottish media, but his popular appeal has remained undiminished. His stage act was captured in the documentary film *Big Banana Feet* (1975), and he has acted in such films as *Absolution* (1979), *Water* (1984) and *The Big Man* (1990). His other work includes a production of *Die Fledermaus* (1978) and such television dramas as *Just Another Saturday* (1975), *Androcles and the Lion* (1984) and *Dreaming* (1990). A committed supporter of Comic Relief, he has recently starred in the American television sit-com *Head of the Class* (1990 –).

CONNOLLY, James

(1868–1916)

Scottish-born Irish Labour leader and insurgent, born in Edinburgh of Irish immigrant parents. He joined the British army at the age of 14 and was stationed in the Curragh and Dublin, but deserted to marry an Irish girl in Scotland. Returning to Ireland in 1896, he organized the Irish Socialist Republican Party and founded *The Workers' Republic*, the first Irish Socialist paper. He toured the USA as a lecturer from 1902 to 1910 and helped found the Industrial Workers of the World ('Wobblies'). Back in Ireland, in 1913 with James Larkin he organized the great transport strike in Dublin. He organized Socialist 'citizen armies', and took part in the Easter Rebellion (1916) in command of the GPO. Severely wounded, he was arrested and executed on 12 May, tied to a chair because he was unable to stand. He wrote *Labour in Irish History* (1912).

CONROY, Stephen
(1964 –)

Painter, born in Helensburgh, Dunbartonshire. In 1987, while still completing his postgraduate year at Glasgow School of Art (where he had been an undergraduate from 1982–6), his work was included in the exhibition *The Vigorous Imagination* at the Scottish National Gallery of Modern Art. He is very concerned with the traditional qualities of figure drawing, light and shade, and very specific spatial organization. The paintings themselves appear to belong to the late Victorian or Edwardian age, in that they depict dark, crowded interiors populated by stiffly posed and dressed figures. Such images, recognizable yet still enigmatic in subject matter, received popular as well as critical attention. In 1989 he received a good deal of media coverage when he was the subject of a legal dispute concerning the ownership of many of his paintings.

CONSTABLE, Archibald
(1774–1827)

Publisher, born in Carnbee, Fife. He became a bookseller's apprentice in Edinburgh in 1788, and in 1795 started as a bookseller on his own account, quickly gathering round him the chief book-collectors of the time. He drifted into publishing, bought the *Scots Magazine* in 1801, and was chosen as publisher of the *Edinburgh Review* (1802). On account of his flair and respect for editorial independence he is regarded as the first modern publisher. He published for all the leading figures of the time, and his early appreciation of **Walter Scott** became the envy of the book trade. In 1812 he purchased the copyright of the *Encyclopaedia Britannica*. Although in 1826 he suffered a financial crash which ruined him and plunged Scott heavily into debt, he was nevertheless incorrigibly innovative and launched *Constable's Miscellany* (1827), a series of volumes on literature, art and science, moderately priced to encourage sales among the ordinary reader; sadly, he died before he could capitalize on its success.

CONTI, Tom
(1941 –)

Actor, born in Paisley, partly of Italian extraction. Studying acting at the Royal Scottish Academy of Music and Drama, he made his stage début in *The Roving Boy* (1959). A part-time tour guide and singing waiter, he struggled for many years before finding theatrical success in *The Black and White Minstrels* (1972) and *Savages* (1973). Dark-haired, with expressive brown eyes and a saturnine manner, he attained stardom in the television series *The Glittering Prizes* (1976) and *The Norman Conquests* (1978), and won universal praise for his performance on stage as the defiant paraplegic in *Whose Life Is It Anyway?* (1978), a role he later repeated on Broadway. He made his film début in *Galileo* (1973) and appeared mainly in supporting roles until he received an Academy Award nomination for his engagingly witty performance as the dissolute, womanizing poet in *Reuben, Reuben* (1983). His subsequent films include *Heavenly Pursuits* (1986) and *Shirley Valentine* (1989). Particularly adept at wry comedy and romantic farce, his many stage performances include *Jeffrey Bernard Is Unwell* (1990) and the world premiere of Arthur Miller's *The Ride Down Mount Morgan* (1991).

COOK, Robin (Robert Finlayson)
(1946–)

Politician, born in Bellshill, Lanarkshire. Educated at Aberdeen Grammar School, the Royal High in Edinburgh, and Edinburgh University, he was a teacher and an adult education organizer before embarking on a political career with the Labour Party. An Edinburgh town councillor from 1971 to 1974, he was elected MP for Edinburgh Central in the latter year. After retaining the seat in 1979, he moved to the Livingston constituency in the general election of 1983. He became an Opposition Spokesman on Health and Social Security in 1987, and two years later was promoted to Chief Opposition Health Spokesman. He is widely recognized as one of the most intellectually formidable parliamentarians of recent years.

COOPER, Thomas Joshua

(1946 –)

American photographic artist and teacher, born in San Francisco. He was educated at Humboldt State University (1965–9) and the University of New Mexico, Albuquerque (1970–2). After teaching at Trent Polytechnic, Nottingham, he became the founding Head of the Department of Photography in the School of Fine Art of the Glasgow School of Art (1982). A passionately committed and inspirational practitioner and teacher, his highly individual, profound and often disturbing landscape works are often conceptually orientated, dealing with themes of myth, ritual and transformation. They are best represented in the exquisite books *Between Dark and Dark* (1985) and *Dreaming the Gokstadt* (1988).

COOPER, Thomas Mackay, Lord, of Culross of Dunnet

(1892–1955)

Judge and legal scholar, born in Edinburgh. Educated at George Watson's College and Edinburgh University, he was successively Lord Advocate (1938), Lord Justice-Clerk (1941) and Lord Justice-General of Scotland and Lord President of the Court of Session (1947). An outstanding judge and leader of the court, in his judgements he stressed reliance on Scottish principles rather than incautious following of English precedents. Many of his judgements are of great and permanent value. He was also keenly interested in legal history and published *Select Scottish Cases of the Thirteenth Century* (1944) and edited *The Register of Brieves* (1946) and **Skene**'s *Regiam Majestatem* (1947).

COPELAND, Ralph

(1837–1905)

English astronomer, born in Woodplumpton, Lancashire. A graduate of Göttingen University, he took part in the second German Polar expedition of 1869–70 and in Lord **Lindsay**'s Transit of Venus expedition to Mauritius in 1874. He was appointed Director of Lord Lindsay's observatory in Dunecht, Aberdeenshire, in 1876 where he pursued an intense observational programme in modern astrophysics. Among his discoveries was the presence in the Orion Nebula of the element helium, formerly known only in the Sun. In 1888, on being appointed Astronomer Royal for Scotland and Regius Professor at Edinburgh University, he became responsible for re-establishing Scotland's Royal Observatory on its new site on Blackford Hill on the south side of Edinburgh.

CORBETT, Ronnie (Ronald Balfour)

(1930 –)

Comedian, born in Edinburgh. After national service in the RAF and 18 months as a civil servant, he branched out into showbusiness via amateur dramatics, seaside shows and stand-up comedy, making an early film appearance in *You're Only Young Once* (1952). Spotted in Danny La Rue's nightclub by David Frost, he appeared on television in *The Frost Report* (1966–7) and *Frost on Sunday* (1968–9). His diminutive stature, impish sense of fun and inimitably discursive delivery of comic monologues soon gained him national popularity and his own series have included *No, That's Me Over Here* (1970) and *Sorry!* (1981–8). A fruitful partnership with Ronnie Barker led to the long-running *The Two Ronnies* (1971–87) and numerous cabaret appearances. His stage work includes *Twang!* (1965) and many pantomimes, notably *Cinderella* (1971–2) at the London Palladium. Later film appearances comprise *Casino Royale* (1967) and *No Sex Please, We're British* (1972). A keen amateur golfer, he has written *Armchair Golf* (1986).

CORMACK, John

(1894–1978)

Sectarian demagogue, born in Edinburgh, son of a Baptist lay preacher. After a local education, he enlisted in the Argylls (1909–22). While on active service in western Ireland he became embittered by evidence of Roman Catholic clerical collaboration with Irish insurgent guerrilla fighters and apparently convinced himself that he saw proof of priests' obsession with pornography. Possibly demoted for exercising excessive repression in the line of duty, he was demobilized to a General Post Office job in Edinburgh in 1922, where he joined the Scottish Protestant League, becoming involved in controversies and brawls with Catholic public speakers. In 1933 he founded the Protestant Action Society, leading an attack on Canon **John Gray** for supposedly having a female mistress for a quarter-century. Cormack was suspended from the General Post Office job on a charge of theft. This was not followed up by criminal proceedings but neither was he reinstated. Leader of Portobello True Blue Lodge No. 188 Orange Order, in 1934 he was elected for North Leith to Edinburgh Corporation, where he demanded repeal of the 1918 Education Act, and removal of Roman Catholics from the armed forces. In 1935 he mobilized a 10 000-strong protest against Roman Catholic Eucharistic Congress in Edinburgh, an event which included the stoning of school buses carrying children. He also demanded the expulsion of Catholics from Scotland. He was tried, fined and briefly imprisoned for inciting a riot during the visit of Ronald Knox in 1936. The Protestant Action Society, under his leadership, elected nine members of the corporation (1936), winning over 30 per cent of the city vote. No other marginal party came remotely close to this at this time. Cormack's organization cracked in 1937. He lost his seat in the council, but won South Leith (1938), retaining this until his retirement in 1962. An inspirational speaker, capable of rousing audiences to ferocious action, he was distinguished by his absence of corruption, and by his frugality.

CORRIE, Joe
(1894–1968)

Miner and playwright, born in Bowhill, Fife. While working down the mines he began writing, becoming a full-time writer in 1923. His early pieces, *The Poacher* (1926) and *The Shillin' a Week Man* (1927), were produced by the Scottish National Players, and represent the working class's sense of community and their struggles against an often hostile social environment. His most famous play was his first, *In Time o' Strife* (1926), written after the General Strike and portraying its effects on the Fife mining community. Immediately recognized as a valuable and realistic account of the miners' situation, the play toured with great success to over 25 mining villages during 1928 and later to nearly every music-hall in Scotland. His plays appealed because of their frank expression of emotion and sentiment, balanced by a gentle humour, and because of the realistic use of local context and dialect. Regarded by contemporary critics as the Scottish Zola, or Sean O'Casey, Corrie himself has been quoted as saying he liked to give his audiences a good cry as well as making them laugh.

COTTIER, Daniel
(1838–91)

Stained-glass artist, designer, interior decorator and dealer in fine and decorative arts, born in Glasgow, the son of a seaman. Little is known of his early education, but in the 1850s he was apprenticed to David Kier, one of the foremost stained-glass firms in Glasgow, and by 1862 he was working as Chief Designer for the firm of Field and Allan in Leith. In 1864 he established a studio in George Street, Edinburgh, but in 1867 moved back to Glasgow, where he established a studio in Anderston and began working with the famous Glasgow architect, **Alexander 'Greek' Thompson**, producing decorative schemes and stained-glass designs for the interiors of at least two of Thompson's best-known commissions — painted panelling at the United Presbyterian Church, Queen's Park, Glasgow, and the interior decoration of the eastern section of Great Western Terrace, also Glasgow. Cottier's stained-glass designs reveal William Morris's influence, especially in his earlier work, but show the development of a distinctive personal 'aesthetic' style, combining unusual figurative compositions with dramatic use of colour. By the beginning of 1870 Cottier was in London, where he went into partnership with **Bruce Talbert**, William Wallace and J M Brydon. The business was called Cottier and Co., Art Furniture Makers, Glass and Tile Painters, and in 1873 branches were opened in America and Australia. While in America Cottier collaborated with the renowned stained-glass artist John Lafarge and produced designs for a window in Holy Trinity Parish Church, Copley Square, Boston. Examples of Cottier's stained glass can be seen in Paisley Abbey, St Machar's Cathedral, Aberdeen, Dowanhill Church, Glasgow, and at Greenock West Kirk. He was a major exponent of the 'aesthetic movement', and his fashionable decorative schemes received critical acclaim amongst contemporary arbiters of taste as, for example, in Mrs Haweis's *Art of Decoration* in 1878.

COTTRELL, Tom Leadbetter
(1923–73)

Physical chemist, born and educated in Edinburgh. After leaving Edinburgh University he worked for Imperial Chemical Industries at their Nobel division at Stevenson, and later directed their physical research section (1948–58). In 1959 he succeeded **James Pickering Kendall** as Professor of Chemistry at Edinburgh, where research and teaching flourished under his direction, and in 1965 he was appointed the first Principal and Vice-Chancellor of Stirling University. He made significant contributions to research on rates of energy transfer, calorimetry, gas kinetics, equations of state and quantum theory. He developed a number of sophisticated techniques for investigating the collisions of electrons with simple molecules, including the spectrophone, and wrote several widely used textbooks, such as *The Strength of Chemical Bonds* (1954).

COUPER, Archibald Scott
(1831–92)

Organic chemist, born in Kirkintilloch, the pioneer of structural organic chemistry. The son of a cotton-weaving mill owner, he studied classics at Glasgow and philosophy at Edinburgh, then turned to chemistry and travelled in Germany, and studied in Paris under Charles Adolphe Wurtz. In 1858 he asked Wurtz to present to the French Academy a paper he had written *On a New Chemical Theory* in which he argued that carbon had a valence of two or four and that its atoms could self-link to form chains. This is fundamentally important in assigning structural formulae to organic compounds. Unfortunately Wurtz procrastinated in his presentation and Friedrich Kekulé von Stradonitz published first. In many ways Couper's ideas were ahead of Kekulé's, but Kekulé forcefully pressed his superiority, Couper quarrelled with Wurtz, and returned to Edinburgh where he was ignored as a chemist, and suffered a permanent depressive illness. Kekulé's successor at Bonn discovered Couper's early work in which he had used the graphic formulae, and his paper on chemical theory, and Couper's work then received belated recognition.

COUSIN, David
(1809–78)

Architect, born in Edinburgh, the son of a joiner. He trained in the office of **William** Henry Playfair at the time when work was in progress on Donaldson's Hospital and the National Gallery. He began his career primarily as a church architect, publishing model plans for the newly formed Free Church of Scotland after the Disruption. Playfair's influence is apparent in many of his works, although he did digress into the Romanesque, notably at the former St Thomas's Church, Rutland Place (1842–3). Cousin was Edinburgh City Architect and worked on the City Improvement Trusts. He also laid out East Princes Street gardens.

COUTTS, Thomas
(1735–1822)

Banker, son of the Edinburgh merchant and banker John Coutts (1699–1751, Lord Provost 1742–4). He founded the London banking-house of Coutts & Co. with his brother James, on whose death in 1778 he became sole manager. Keen and exact in all matters of business, on his death he left £900 000. By his first wife, a servant of his brother's, he had three daughters, who married the Earl of Guilford, the Marquis of Bute and Sir Francis Burdett; in 1815 he married the actress Harriot Mellon. His grand-daughter was the philanthropist Angela Burdett-Coutts.

COWIE, James
(1886–1956)

Painter, born in the parish of Monquhitter, Aberdeenshire. After attending Monquhitter parish school, where from 1901 to 1905 he was a pupil teacher, he began — but failed to complete — an English course at Aberdeen University. Instead he took up drawing and, from 1912, he studied for two years at Glasgow School of Art. He spent the war years in the Pioneer Corps. From 1918 to 1935 he was Art Master at Bellshill Academy near Glasgow. Some of his best-known work — especially his paintings of schoolgirls — dates from this period, in which his classroom became his studio. In 1935 he was appointed Head of the Painting Department at Gray's School of Art, Aberdeen, and the following year he became an associate of the Royal Scottish Academy. In 1937 he became Warden of Hospitalfield near Arbroath, a summer school for the four Scottish Art Colleges. In 1948 he retired to Edinburgh, becoming Secretary of the Royal Scottish Academy, and was awarded an honorary doctorate from

Edinburgh University. As a painter he was much less interested in colour and painterly qualities than in line and tone and, while his work ranged from landscape to still life, all is solidly founded on drawing and linear design.

COX, Brian

(1946 –)

Actor, teacher and director, born in Dundee. He made his London début as Orlando in *As You Like It* in 1967; his subsequent West End appearances include Alan Bennett's *Getting On* (1971) and Eugene O'Neill's *Strange Interlude* (1984). At the Royal Court he won huge acclaim for his performance as a police inspector in *Rat in the Skull* (1984). At the National Theatre, he appeared in *Tamburlaine* (1976), *Julius Caesar* (1977) and *Danton's Death* (1982). At the Royal Shakespeare Company his performances have included the title role in *Titus Andronicus* (1987), directed by Deborah Warner, who also directed his *King Lear* at the National Theatre in 1990. He has made several television and film appearances, has taught drama extensively in London, and became the first British actor to teach at the Moscow Art Theatre, an experience he recorded in his book *From Salem to Moscow* (1990).

COX, James

(1809–85)

Linen and jute manufacturer, born in Lochee, Dundee. Educated at Dundee Academy, he took over the running of his father's linen manufacturing business in 1927 at the age of 18. In 1840 he and his brother Thomas formed a partnership with their other two brothers. Between 1850 and the 1880s the Cox Brothers developed the largest jute firm in the world. Although their fortunes varied, by 1885 they were employing as many as 5000 staff in their works. Cox developed wide investment interests in shipping, railways and in the USA. Wealth brought municipal status culminating in his appointment as Provost of Dundee (1872–5). He bequeathed that his son, Edward, was to continue his stewardship of the company, as the fifth generation to run the family business.

CRAIG, Archie

(1888–1985)

Church of Scotland minister, born in Kelso, Roxburghshire, whose long and distinguished career as an academic and spiritual leader won him a unique place in the folklore of the Church. War service, during which he won the Military Cross 'for gallantry in France' was followed by ministry at Gilmorehill in Glasgow, university chaplaincy, a spell with the BBC, and a key role in the Iona Community. He was Lecturer in Biblical Studies at Glasgow University from 1957, and Moderator of the General Assembly of the Church of Scotland in 1961, receiving in the same year honorary doctorates from Dublin and Glasgow universities. The international reputation he enjoyed is indicated by the unusual award of the Order of St Mark of Alexandria, First Class, in 1970. As the respected first Secretary of the British Council of Churches (from 1942), at a crucial period for its development, he helped set the agenda, the direction and the pace for ecumenical progress.

CRAIG, Isa

(1831–1903)

Feminist and poet, born in Edinburgh. The daughter of a hosier, she was orphaned as a child and brought up by her grandmother. Mainly self-educated, she contributed poems to *The Scotsman* and joined its editorial staff in 1853. In 1857, in a revolutionary and controversial move, she was appointed Secretary of The National Association for the Promotion of Social Science in London, where she remained until her marriage to her cousin John Knox, an iron merchant. She campaigned for the women's movement and, continuing to write, became a well-known author. She published several volumes of poetry, books for children and a novel, *Esther West* (1870), whose popularity only declined after her death.

CRAIG, James

(1744–95)

Architect, born in Edinburgh, nephew of the poet, **James Thomson**. His principal contribution to architectural history was his work on Edinburgh's New Town. In 1766 a competition was held for laying out new streets and squares for the city, which needed to expand beyond the Old Town limits. The entries were judged by the Lord Provost and **John Adam**. Craig's winning plan comprised a simple geometrical pattern of parallel principal streets, terminated by squares, and provided views north across the Forth and south towards the Castle and the Old Town. Craig was not responsible for the design of the buildings which graced his town plan, although he was later commissioned to design the plan and buildings of St James' Square.

CRAIG, John
(1512–1600)

Protestant preacher. He lost his father at the Battle of Flodden (1514), and was educated at St Andrews, where he joined the Dominicans. Falling under suspicion of heresy, he was briefly imprisoned (1536). Going to Rome, through Cardinal Reginald Pole he gained admission to the Dominican convent of Bologna; but Calvin's *Institutes* converted him to Protestantism. Sentenced to death in 1559 by the Inquisition in Rome, he was lying in the Inquisition's dungeon, condemned to go to the stake the next morning, when Pope Paul IV died, and the mob set the prisoners free. A bandit befriended him, a dog brought him a purse of gold and he escaped to Vienna, where he preached in his friar's habit, one of his listeners being Archduke Maximilian. Subsequently the new pope, learning his whereabouts, demanded his surrender, but Maximilian gave him a safe conduct, and in 1560 he returned to Scotland. In 1563 he was appointed coadjutor to **John Knox**. In 1567 he incurred some censure for proclaiming, under strong protest, the banns between **Mary, Queen of Scots** and **Bothwell**; in 1572 he was sent to 'illuminate the dark places' in Angus and Aberdeenshire. He returned to Edinburgh in 1579 as a royal chaplain, had a share with **Andrew Melville** in the Second Book of Discipline, and drew up the 'Confession of Faith'.

CRAIG, John
(d.1731)

Mathematician. A pupil of **David Gregory** in Edinburgh, he later settled in Cambridge and joined the circle around Sir Isaac Newton. Between 1685 and 1718 he published a number of books and papers on the theory of fluxions, which he helped to propagate in Scotland through his correspondence with Gregory and others. In 1699 he published *Christianae Theologiae Principia Mathematica*, a curious attempt to apply mathematics to theology, in which he claimed that the world would end by the year 3144. He was ordained in 1708 and became FRS in 1711.

CRAIG, Sir Thomas, of Riccarton
(1538–1608)

Writer on feudal law, born either in Craigfintray, Aberdeenshire, or in Edinburgh. From St Andrews University he moved to Paris in 1555, and in 1563 was admitted a Scottish advocate. The following year he was appointed a justice-depute of Scotland, and in 1573 Sheriff-Depute of Edinburgh. Besides an epithalamium on the marriage of **Mary, Queen of Scots** to Lord **Darnley**, several more Latin poems, and the masterly *Jus Feudale* (1608), which is a Scottish legal classic relating the development of Scots land law to that of European systems, he wrote *De Unione Regnorum* (Scottish History Society 1910), and Latin treatises on **James VI's** right to the English throne and on the homage controversy between Scotland and England.

CRAIGIE, Sir William Alexander
(1867–1957)

Philologist and lexicographer, born in Dundee. Educated in Dundee and at St Andrews, he went to Balliol College, Oxford, for a year before going to Copenhagen to study Old Icelandic. While he was assistant to the professsor of Latin at St Andrews (1893–7), he produced *Scandinavian Folk-Lore* (1897). In 1897 he joined Sir **James Murray** in the compilation of the *Oxford English Dictionary* (joint editor, 1901–33). In 1916 he was appointed Professor of Anglo-Saxon at Oxford, and from 1925 to 1936 was Professor of English at the University of Chicago, where he compiled the *Historical Dictionary of American English* (4 vols, 1936–44). From 1936 to 1955 he was Editor of the *Dictionary of the Older Scottish Tongue*. A scholar of encyclopedic knowledge, he also wrote *The Icelandic Sagas* (1913), *The Pronunciation of English* (1917), *Easy Readings in Anglo-Saxon* (1923), *The Poetry of Iceland* (1925), and a monumental study of Iceland *rímur* ('rhymes'), *Sýnisbók íslenkra rímna* (3 vols, 1952).

CRAIK, George Lillie
(1798–1866)

Scholar, born in Kennoway, Fife. He studied for the Church at St Andrews, and for a time was Editor of a newspaper called the *Star*, but went to London in 1826, and in 1849 became Professor of History and English Literature at Queen's College, Belfast. He wrote *The*

History of English Literature and the English Language (1861). His youngest daughter, Georgiana Marion (1831–95; Mrs May), was a popular novelist.

CRAIK, Sir Henry
(1846–1927)

Educational administrator, born in Glasgow, one of the most significant figures in 19th-century Scottish education. Educated at Glasgow University and Balliol College, Oxford, he entered the Scottish Education Department in 1878, making a special investigation into the condition of education in the Highlands and Islands (1884). On the transfer of the department from Privy Council to the Scottish Office (1885) he was appointed Permanent Secretary (1885–1904). A highly able, if remote and bureaucratic administrator, his reforms included the encouragement of Gaelic on the syllabus in Highland schools (1887), the establishment of a leaving certificate (1888), additional funding of secondary education (1892) and the total remission of fees in primary schools (1894), which allowed elementary education to be offered free to all aged 3 to 15. He brought in Higher Grade Schools for pupils aged up to 16 (1899) and achieved the virtual raising of the school leaving age to 14 by abolishing the system of exemption by examination (1901). He also initiated the policy of transferring the control of teacher training colleges from the Church to public committees (1905). He was created baronet in 1926.

CRAIK, Kenneth
(1914–45)

Experimental psychologist. Educated at Edinburgh and Cambridge, he spent much of World War II engaged in applied military research on topics that included servo-mechanisms and 'human factors' in design. In 1944 he was appointed Director of the new Unit for Research in Applied Psychology at Cambridge set up by the Medical Research Council. He pioneered that major modern psychological school of thought in which the mind is regarded as a complex example of an information-processing system. The development of this metaphor, with the help of digital computers, is known today as Cognitive Science. He died tragically early following a cycling accident in Cambridge on the eve of VE Day. His writings established him as an original thinker, whose ideas have been of lasting influence in postwar experimental and physiological psychology.

CRAMPSEY, Bob (Robert)
(1930 –)

Writer and broadcaster, born in Glasgow. Educated at Glasgow and London universities, he served in the RAF (1952–5) before turning to teaching, becoming Assistant Head of his old school, Holyrood in Glasgow, in 1971. Three years later he became Rector of St Ambrose High, Coatbridge, a post he held until 1986. Winning BBC Radio's *Brain of Britain* title in 1965 helped him to begin a concurrent career in sports broadcasting, where his genteel but authoritative analysis has proved a perfect foil to the more frenzied commentators, particularly in football. He has written extensively, chiefly on sport, his publications including histories of Queen's Park FC and the Scottish Football League, and a biography of **Jock Stein**.

CRANSTON, Kate (Catherine)
(1850–1934)

Tea-room proprietress and patron of designers from Glasgow School of Art, such as **George Walton** and **Charles Rennie Mackintosh**. She was born in Glasgow, the daughter of a hotelier and dealer in fine teas. Between 1884 and 1904 she opened a chain of highly successful tea rooms in Glasgow, which became known for their distinctive 'artistic' interiors. In 1896 Mackintosh was commissioned to redesign the furniture and fittings for the Argyle Street tea rooms, and he later did the interior decorative schemes for the Ingram Street branch (1900) and also the Willow tea rooms in Sauchiehall Street (1911). She commissioned George Walton to take charge of the decorative schemes for the Buchanan Street tea rooms, which opened in 1896, though Mackintosh also produced mural designs for these interiors. In 1901 and 1911 she organized and ran the tea rooms for the Glasgow International Exhibitions. After the death of her husband, John Cochrane, she sold the Argyle and Buchanan Street branches (1917) and finally retired in 1919. Widely known for her eccentric appearance (she wore crinoline dresses long after they had gone out of fashion) she was a highly respected and efficient business woman, who played an important role in drawing attention to the progressive nature of art and design in Glasgow at the turn of the century.

CRANSTOUN See DALRYMPLE, Sir John

CRAWFORD, James Ludovic Lindsay, 26th Earl of
(1847–1913)

Astronomer, son of the 25th Earl of **Crawford and Balcarres**. President of the Royal Astronomical Society from 1878 to 1880, in 1888 he presented to the nation the well-equipped observatory at Dunecht; the apparatus and library were later transferred to the Royal Observatory, Blackford Hill, in Edinburgh.

CRAWFORD, Robert Caldwell
(1925 –)

Composer, born in Edinburgh. A pupil of Hans Gal and Benjamin Frankel, he won success with two string quartets (1951 and 1957). He has also composed songs and piano music. He was Music Producer for the BBC from 1970 to 1985.

CRAWFORD AND BALCARRES, Alexander William Crawford Lindsay, 25th/8th Earl of
(1812–80)

Nobleman, born in Muncaster Castle, Cumberland, and educated at Eton and Trinity College, Cambridge. His researches enabled him in 1848 to establish his father's claim to the Crawford title (the premier earldom of Scotland; cr. 1398). A great book-collector, he wrote *Letters on the Holy Land* (1838), *Progression by Antagonism* (1846), *Sketches of the History of Christian Art* (1847), *Lives of the Lindsays* (1849) and *The Earldom of Mar* (1882). He died in Florence and his body, stolen from the mausoleum at Dunecht, near Aberdeen, was found in a nearby wood some months afterwards.

CRAWFURD, George
(d.1748)

Genealogist and historian, born in Greenock, Renfrewshire. He is chiefly remembered for a *Genealogical History of the Family of Stewart from 1034 to 1710* and, more importantly, the *Peerage of Scotland, containing an Historical and Genealogical Account of the Nobility of that Kingdom* (1710) and the *Lives and Characters of the Officers of the Crown and of the State in Scotland, from the reign of King David I to the Union of the Two Kingdoms* (1726). This last, of which he completed only one volume, deals with the chancellors, chamberlains and treasurers and was, for its time, a great achievement. While requiring revision, it has not yet been superseded.

CRAWFURD, John
(1783–1868)

Orientalist, born on Islay. He served as an East Indian army doctor (1803–27), serving in Java under Lord Minto from 1811, was envoy to Siam, and in 1823 succeeded Sir **Thomas Stamford Raffles** as administrator of Singapore. He published *History of the Indian Archipelago* (1820) and *A Grammar and Dictionary of the Malay Language* (1852).

CREECH, William
(1745–1815)

Publisher, born in Newbattle, Midlothian. He studied medicine at Edinburgh, but became a partner in a printing firm in 1771 and sole proprietor in 1773. His premises became a centre of literary and social activity in Edinburgh. He published the first Edinburgh edition of **Robert Burns**, the works of **James Beattie** and **Dugald Stewart**, and **Henry Mackenzie**'s periodicals, *The Mirror* and *The Lounger*. He was Lord Provost of Edinburgh from 1811 to 1813.

CREED, Frederick George
(1871–1957)

Inventor of the Creed teleprinter. Born in Nova Scotia of Scottish parents, he left school at 14 to qualify as a telegraph operator. After working in Canada, Chile and Peru he moved to Glasgow in 1897 where, after some initial setbacks, he successfully realized his idea of an automatic perforated tape teleprinter. In 1909 he opened a factory in Croydon to meet the demand for his invention from newspapers all over the world, but after being bought out by ITT in 1927, he lost most of his fortune through a series of impractical inventions.

CREW, Francis Albert Eley
(1886–1973)

Geneticist and animal breeder, born in Tipton, Staffordshire. First educated in Birmingham, he became a medical student in Edinburgh, qualifying in 1921. He served as a Medical Officer in France during World War I before returning to Edinburgh in 1919 as assistant in the Department of Natural History, working with **James Cossar Ewart** and with **Sharpey-Schafer** in Physiology, and becoming deeply interested in genetics and animal reproduction. In 1920 he was appointed the first Director of the Animal Breeding Research Department and then Buchanan Professor of Animal Genetics in the then new Institute of Animal Genetics at Edinburgh, which became noted for its development of the Ascheim-Zondek test and other investigations of pregnancy. He trained and inspired many who later became eminent in animal genetics. Leaving the Institute of Animal Genetics rather suddenly to become Professor of Social Medicine in 1939, he was appointed to lead medical research for the Army Medical Directorate. He also found time to set up the Polish Medical Faculty in Edinburgh. A man of great physical and mental energy, he not only built animal houses and equipped laboratories in his early days, but contributed five volumes to the *History of the Second World War: United Kingdom Medical Series*, each entitled *The Army Medical Services: Campaigns* (1956–66).

CRICHTON, James
(1560 – c.1585)

Prodigy and epitome of the Scottish Enlightenment, known as 'the Admirable'. The son of the Scottish Lord Advocate, he was born in Cluny, Perthshire, and educated at St Andrews University, where his tutor was **George Buchanan**. After graduating in 1575, he earned a tremendous reputation as a scholar, poet, linguist and swordsman on the Continent. He spent two years in France as a teenager, apparently in the French army, delivered a Latin oration before the Senate in Genoa in 1579, took part in a great scholastic disputation in Venice in 1580, and again in Padua in 1581. Later he went to Mantua in the service of the duke, and was killed in a nocturnal brawl by the duke's son. His popular reputation rests on the fantastic account of his exploits written by Sir **Thomas Urquhart** in his panegyric on the Scots nation, *The Discoveryie of a Most Exquisite Jewel* (1652). 'Admirable Crichton' became synonymous with all-round talents, the ideal man; the phrase was used by **J M**

Barrie for his play about a perfect butler, *The Admirable Crichton* (1902).

CRICHTON-STUART, John Patrick, 3rd Marquess of Bute
(1847–1900)

Scholar, dilettante, conservationist, enlightened paternalist and patron. Born at Mount Stuart, Bute, he was educated at Harrow and Oxford. He continued the family's patronage in Cardiff, and worked in conjunction with William Burges in a romantic restoration of Cardiff Castle (from 1865), continuing their collaboration at Castell Coch (1871–9) in a fantastic recreation. The larger part of his patronage was enjoyed in Scotland. He initiated several excavations and numerous scholarly, cautious restorations in the 1890s, such as those by John Kinross (1855–1931) at Falkland Palace, and Greyfriars in Elgin, and by Robert Weir Schultz (1861–1951) at Kames Castle. Universities were among the many recipients of his considerable generosity. He commissioned the rebuilding of Mount Stuart from **Robert Rowand Anderson**. A shy, sensitive man, and an ardent convert to Roman Catholicism, he was the model for Disraeli's *Lothair*. In addition to this, he is remembered as a linguist and historian, and was possibly one of Britain's most generous private patrons.

CROCKETT, Samuel Rutherford
(1859–1914)

Popular novelist, born in Little Duchrae, Kirkcudbright, of tenant-farming stock. Paying his way by journalism and travelling tutorships, he attended Edinburgh University and New College, Edinburgh. Becoming a Free Church minister in Penicuik, he wrote sardonic congregational sketches, of which 24, collected as *The Stickit Minister* (1893), brought immediate fame; this was consolidated in 1894 by *The Raiders, The Lilac Sunbonnet* (a seemingly innocent love story which ridiculed narrow religious sects) and two novellas. Resigning the ministry in favour of full-time writing in 1895, he wrote a variety of books, from tales of Covenanting and medieval Scotland, to European historical romances and (often sensational) stories of mining, industrialism and Edinburgh slums. His posthumous works include one detective and one theological science-fiction novel.

CROFTON, Sir John Wenman
(1912 –)

Pioneering tuberculosis specialist. As Professor of Respiratory Diseases and Tuberculosis at the University of Edinburgh from 1952 to 1977 his researches on the chemotherapy of tuberculosis and his demonstration that ambulatory treatment with chemotherapy was as effective as bed rest with chemotherapy was a fundamental step forward in the control of tuberculosis. Its repercussions on the concepts and practice of control have been particularly important in developing countries, and culminated in the closure of tuberculosis hospitals in Britain and elsewhere. Sir John and his team in Edinburgh showed that by attention to detail and adequate duration of chemotherapy a 100 per cent cure of pulmonary tuberculosis was achievable. Under these regimes the notifications of tuberculosis fell by 48 per cent in three years, a figure not attained by any other centre in the world. Through education and enlisting the support of the International Union Against Tuberculosis he was able to convince a sceptical world of the truth of his methods. A physician-epidemiologist, he has coordinated clinical and public health activities, thus dramatically influencing the epidemiology of disease. He is co-author of the influential *Respiratory Diseases* (1969, 3rd ed 1981) and of *Clinical Tuberculosis* (1991). He was knighted in 1977.

CROLL, James
(1821–90)

Physicist, born in Little Whitefield, near Coupar-Angus. He received an elementary school education, but in science was wholly self-trained. Successively millwright, insurance-agent, manager of a temperance hotel and keeper of the museum of Anderson's College, Glasgow, he was on the Scottish Geological Survey, 1867–81. Among his works were *Climate and Time* (1875) and *The Philosophic Basis of Evolution* (1890).

CRONIN, A J (Archibald Joseph)
(1896–1981)

Novelist, born in Cardross, Dunbartonshire. He graduated in medicine at Glasgow in 1919, but in 1930 abandoned his practice as a result of a breakdown in his health, and turned to literature. He had an immediate success with his brooding and melodramatic autobiographical novel *Hatter's Castle* (1931). Subsequent works include *The Citadel* (1937), *The Keys of the Kingdom* (1941), *Beyond this Place* (1953), *Crusader's Tomb* (1956) and *A Song of Sixpence* (1964). The medical stories in his Scottish novels formed the basis of the popular radio and television series *Dr Finlay's Casebook* in the 1960s. Towards the end of his life he lived largely in the USA and Switzerland.

CRUDEN, Alexander
(1701–70)

Bookseller and religious fanatic, born in Aberdeen. Educated there at Marischal College, he started to work as a secretary to the 10th Earl of Derby (1729), but was dismissed because he did not have French, and took to tutoring instead. In 1732 he started as a bookseller in the Royal Exchange, London, and in 1737 published his biblical *Concordance of the Holy Scriptures*. From then on he suffered frequent bouts of insanity. Working as a printer's proof-reader he assumed the title of 'Alexander the Corrector', believing that God had entrusted him with the mission of reforming the masses; in 1755 he began to travel the country reproving Sabbath-breaking and profanity.

CRUFT, Catherine Holway
(1927 –)

English-born architectural historian and curator, a leading figure in the conservation world. Born in London, she was educated at Edinburgh University, where she studied social studies. Subsequently, she worked with the Scottish National Building Record (SNBR, now the National Monuments Record of Scotland), working simultaneously for the Scots Ancestry Research Society. After two years producing lists of buildings of special interest for Edinburgh with **Ian Lindsay**, she became the curator of the SNBR (1958). With **Colin McWilliam**, she developed an integrated approach to the Monuments Record, with buildings, photographs, original architectural drawings, survey drawings and biographical material kept in one location. She has amassed an extensive knowledge of Scottish architectural history, and her careful representations have saved innumerable archives for the nation. She is active in the Architectural Heritage Society of Scotland and the Old Edinburgh Club, of which she has been secretary and vice-president. In 1990 she received an Honorary Fellowship of the RIAS.

CRUICKSHANK, Andrew John Maxton
(1907–88)

Actor, born in Aberdeen. Educated at Aberdeen Grammar School, he intended becoming a civil engineer before turning to acting and making his London début in the celebrated Paul Robeson production of *Othello* (1930). A fiery, authoritative classical actor, long associated with the works of Shakespeare and Ibsen and with such companies as the Old Vic and the National Theatre, his many stage performances include *Dial M for Murder* (1952), *Inherit the Wind* (1960), *The Master Builder* (1962 and 1972), *The Wild Duck* (1980) and his last in *Beyond Reasonable Doubt* (1988). He made his film début in *Auld Lang Syne* (1938) and worked extensively in television, gaining his greatest renown as the gruff but kindly Dr Cameron in *Dr Finlay's Casebook* (1962–71). A playwright whose works include *Unfinished Journey* (1961) and *Games* (1975), he also wrote *An Autobiography* (1988). A pillar of the theatrical establishment, he served for almost a decade as Chairman of the Edinburgh Festival Fringe Society.

CRUICKSHANK, Helen
(1886–1975)

Poet, born in Hillside, Angus. Educated at Montrose Academy, in 1903 she joined the Civil Service in London. After her return to Edinburgh in 1912 her home became a centre for Scottish writers. She contributed poems to **Hugh MacDiarmid**'s *Scottish Chapbook* and *Northern Numbers* and the two became friends. Cruickshank served as secretary to Scottish PEN between 1927 and 1934. In this function she was teacher and confidante to writers such as **Lewis Grassic Gibbon**. Her poems were first published in 1934 in *Up the Noran Water*. She published both in English and a dialect Scots that drew on her Angus heritage. Her work is marked by an economy of language and she uses a number of forms including prose-poetry and blank verse to express herself. In 1971 she was awarded an Honorary MA from Edinburgh University for her contributions to Scottish literature. **MacDiarmid** complimented her in a radio tribute as a 'catalyst' to the Scottish Renaissance.

CRUICKSHANK, Robert
(1899–1974)

Bacteriologist, born in Aberdeenshire. Graduating with honours from Aberdeen University in 1922, he was resident medical officer in the Royal Hospital for Sick Children in Glasgow and the Belvedere Hospital for Infectious Diseases (1924–7). He became lecturer in bacteriology at Glasgow University (1928–36) and bacteriologist to the Royal Infirmary where his main preoccupation was in the application of his subject to the diagnosis and treatment of disease. During the war years he was pathologist in charge of the North Western Group Laboratory of the London County Council, and in 1955 he succeeded Sir **Alexander Fleming** as Principal of the Wright-Fleming Institute. He became Professor of Bacteriology at Edinburgh in 1958 where he became increasingly involved in the epidemiological aspects of communicable diseases, especially in underdeveloped countries, in which he travelled widely, frequently under the aegis of the World Health Organization. He promoted the establishment of laboratory services as the basis of the control of communicable diseases. On retiring from Edinburgh he became Professor of Social and Preventive Medicine in the University of the West Indies. He was editor of *Modern Trends in Immunology* (1963) and of *Medical Microbiology*, which reached its 12th edition in 1973.

CULLEN, William
(1710–90)

Physician and chemist, born in Hamilton, Lanarkshire. After studying at Edinburgh he started a practice in Hamilton, where **William Hunter** became one of his pupils. In 1740 he set up as a physician in Glasgow, and lectured on medicine. Although primarily remembered as a doctor, he was also a talented chemist and teacher, providing his students with opportunities for experimental work and establishing chemistry as a discipline in its own right, when previously it had always been studied as an adjunct to medicine. In 1747 he was appointed lecturer in chemistry at Glasgow University, the first such post in Britain. Although he held chairs of medicine from 1751 onwards, first in Glasgow, then in Edinburgh (1755–90), he continued to stress the importance of chemistry and its usefulness to agriculture and industry, for example in brewing, bleaching, and the manufacture of alkali. His influence was considerable, although he only published one chemical paper, on the cooling effects of evaporation. In the field of medicine he is largely responsible for the recognition of the important part played by the nervous system in health and disease. He bitterly opposed the Brunonian system (see **John Brown,** c.1735–1788). His chief works were *Synopsis Nosologiae Methodicae* (1769), *Institutions of Medicine* (1772), *Practice of Physic* (1776–84), and *Treatise of Materia Medica* (1789).

CULLEN, William
(1867–1948)

Chemist and metallurgist, born in Shettleston, Glasgow. He was educated at Hutcheson's Grammar School and at the Andersonian College in Glasgow, and studied chemistry under William Ditmar in Saxony. He joined the Nobel's Explosives Company in 1890, and in 1900 was appointed manager of the Modderfontein factory in South Africa, then the largest explosives factory in the world. There he carried out important work on the development of smokeless powders for use in mining, and on the design of plant for handling the volatile constituent materials in the manufacture of explosive compounds. He worked to promote healthier conditions in South African mines, and supported a number of scientific societies. He was first Chairman of the South African Red Cross Society, and commanded two South African cavalry regiments.

CUNNINGHAM, Sir Alan Gordon
(1887–1983)

Soldier and administrator, born in Edinburgh, brother of **Andrew Cunningham of Hyndhope**, and educated at Cheltenham and the Royal Military Academy at Woolwich. Commissioned in the Royal Artillery, he won a DSO and an MC on the western front during World War I and in the postwar years he moved quickly up the promotion ladder to become a major-general in 1938. His greatest military moment came in January 1941 when the forces under his command recovered Abyssinia from the Italians in a daring campaign over difficult terrain. The success took him to North Africa to command the 8th Army in the rank of general, but he met his match in Rommel and after the loss of Tobruk he was replaced by General **Neil Ritchie**. Illness prevented him from playing any further operational role in the fighting, but after the war he was appointed

High Commissioner of Palestine during the last days of the British mandate.

CUNNINGHAM, Allan
(1784–1842)

Poet and man of letters, born in the parish of Dalswinton, Dumfriesshire. His father was neighbour of **Robert Burns** at Ellisland and Allan, as a boy, was present at the poet's funeral. At ten he was apprenticed to a stonemason, but he continued to pore over songs and stories. His first publications were his sham-antique verse and prose contributions to Cromek's *Remains of Nithsdale and Galloway Song* (1810). He already knew **James Hogg**, and through him he made the acquaintance of Sir **Walter Scott**, with whom 'Honest Allan' was always a great favourite. He moved to London, and became one of the best-known writers for the *London Magazine*, as well as manager of Francis Chantrey's sculpture studio (1815–41). Among his works were *Traditional Tales of the English and Scottish Peasantry* (1822), *Songs of Scotland, Ancient and Modern* (1825), *Lives of the most Eminent British Painters, Sculptors, and Architects* (6 vols, 1829–33), and *Life of Wilkie* (3 vols, 1843).

CUNNINGHAM, Andrew Brown, Viscount Cunningham of Hyndhope
(1883–1963)

Naval commander, born in Dublin of Scots parents, brother of **Alan Cunningham**. He was educated at The Edinburgh Academy and Dartmouth. During the Boer War he served as a gunner with the Naval Brigade, a move which won him an undeserved reputation for self-advancement. His career then took him to small boats and destroyers, and during World War I he caught the eye of his superiors for his professionalism and verve while commanding destroyers in the Dardanelles and the English Channel. In 1929 his career took a major step forward with command of the battleship HMS *Rodney*, but he returned to his first love of destroyers before the outbreak of World War II. As Commander-in-Chief of the Mediterranean he inflicted several defeats on the Italian navy, including the victory at Cape Matapan in March 1941. Two months later, during the evacuation of British forces from Crete, Cunningham's ships suffered heavy losses from German air attack, but these would have been worse if the Italian navy had still been in a position to intervene. Having secured a reputation as one of Britain's greatest sailors, Cunningham was promoted Admiral of the Fleet and First Sea Lord in 1943. In 1951 he published a volume of memoirs about his life at sea in *A Sailor's Odyssey*.

CUNNINGHAM, Phil
(1960 –)

Instrumentalist and composer, born in Edinburgh. He showed early prowess as an accordionist and in 1976 joined Silly Wizard, which rapidly became one of the most popular folk groups in Scotland. He travelled with the group throughout Europe and the USA and recorded many albums with them. When Silly Wizard disbanded in 1983, his accordion and piano playing became much in demand, and he performed with the Irish groups Relativity and Altan as well as with **Aly Bain** and others. He has written numerous tunes in the folk idiom, and in 1990 he composed the music for **Bill Bryden**'s theatrical production, *The Ship*, in Glasgow. Other activities have included working as a record producer and television musical director.

CUNNINGHAM, William
(1805–61)

Churchman and theologian, born in Hamilton, Lanarkshire, a chief leader of the Disruption. Educated at Edinburgh, he became minister at Greenock (1830) and Edinburgh (1834), then Professor (1843) and Principal (1847) at the Free Church College, writing on theology and Church history.

CUNNINGHAM, William
(1849–1919)

Leading founder of economic history as a separate discipline. Born in Edinburgh, he was educated at Edinburgh Institution, Edinburgh Academy, and the Universities of Edinburgh, Tubingen and Cambridge. Ordained to the Church of England ministry in 1872, he pursued parallel careers: as a clergyman he rose to be Vicar of Great St Mary's, Cambridge (1885–1908) and Archdeacon of Ely in 1907; as an economic historian he was Fellow of Trinity College, Cambridge, and Tooke Professor of Economics and Statistics, King's College, London (1891–7). Of his numerous works on economic history and the relationship between Christianity and economics, his most famous was *The Growth of English Industry and Commerce* (1882 and subsequent editions to 1910).

CUNNINGHAME GRAHAM, Robert, originally **Robert Graham**
(d.1797)

Laird and songwriter, born on the family estates at Gartmore, Stirlingshire. His mother was a daughter of the 12th Earl of Glencairn. He was educated at Glasgow University. He became a planter and receiver-general in Jamaica, was chosen Rector of Glasgow University on his return in 1785, and became an MP (1794–6). He warmly supported the French Revolution, moved an abortive bill of rights and composed 'If doughty deeds my lady please' and other lyrical poems. On the death of the last Earl of Glencairn in 1796, he succeeded to the latter's estates and changed his name to Cunninghame Graham.

CUNNINGHAME GRAHAM, Robert Bontine
(1852–1936)

Writer and politician, grandson of **Robert Cunninghame Graham**, born in London. He was educated at Harrow and from 1869 was chiefly engaged in ranching in the Argentine, until he succeeded to the family estates in 1883. In 1879 he married a Chilean poetess, Gabriela de la Belmondiere. He was Liberal MP for North-West Lanarkshire (1886–92) and was imprisoned with John Burns, the Socialist leader, for 'illegal assembly' in Trafalgar Square during a mass unemployment demonstration in 1887. He was the first President of the Scottish Labour Party in 1888. He travelled extensively in Spain and Morocco (1893–8), where an incident described in his *Mogreb-El-Acksa* (1898) inspired George Bernard Shaw's *Captain Brassbound's Conversion*. He wrote a large number of travel books, but is best known for his highly individual, flamboyant essays and short stories, collections of which are entitled *Success* (1902), *Faith* (1909), *Hope* (1910), *Charity* (1912) and *Scottish Stories* (1914). He was elected the first President of the National Party of Scotland in 1928, and of the Scottish National Party in 1934. Conrad and Hudson were among his close literary friends. He died in Argentina, where he was known as 'Don Roberto'.

CURLE, Alexander Ormiston
(1866–1955)

Archaeologist, born in Melrose, Roxburghshire. Educated at Cambridge, he was the first secretary to be appointed to the newly created Royal Commission on the Ancient and Historical Monuments of Scotland (1908–13), producing single-handed its early *Inventories*, and he remained a Commissioner for the next 40 years. He became Keeper of the National Museum of Antiquities of Scotland (1913–19) and Director of the Royal Scottish Museum (1916–31), the overlap being a consequence of the two museums' closure during World War I. His major excavations included Jarlshof in Shetland and Traprain Law in East Lothian, the discovery of a huge hoard of late Roman silver there being published as *The Treasure of Traprain* (1922).

CURRAN, Sir Samuel Crowe
(1912–)

Physicist, educated at the universities of Glasgow and Cambridge. After two years of research at the Cavendish Laboratory, Cambridge University, he served during World War II at the Royal Aircraft Establishment, and in the Ministries of Aircraft Production and of Supply, where he was involved in research on the development of nuclear weapons. After the war he was a lecturer in physics in Glasgow University until 1955, when he joined the UK Atomic Energy Authority, transferring as Chief Scientist to the Atomic Weapons Research Establishment in 1958. From 1959 to 1964 he was Principal of the Royal College of Science and Technology, Glasgow, and in 1964 became Principal of Strathclyde University. He has been active in both academic and industrial affairs, having been a member of committees concerned with, for example, medical research, electricity supply and oil development, and was Chief Scientific Adviser to the Secretary of State for Scotland (1967–77). He was a director of Scottish Television (1964–82), and of several companies. He was knighted in 1970.

CURRIE, Finlay
(1878–1968)

Actor, born in Edinburgh. A promising music student at Edinburgh University, he played the organ for a production of *Henry IV* and thereafter committed himself to the theatre.

Working first in repertory, he then utilized his ability to sing both soprano and baritone to develop a music-hall act as 'the boy with the double voice'. On tour in South Africa, he met his future wife, American musical comedy star Maude Courtney, and they formed the variety act of Currie and Courtney. After service in World War I, he spent 10 years in Australia before returning to Britain to appear in a succession of Edgar Wallace plays. He is alleged to have made his film début in *The War in the Air* (1908) and his craggy features and redoubtable manner made him an indispensable character actor in scores of British films, including *Rome Express* (1932) and *Great Expectations* (1946), in which he played the convict Magwitch. He was later seen in many international ventures, historical adventures and biblical epics, such as *Quo Vadis* (1951), *Ben-Hur* (1959) and *Bunny Lake Is Missing* (1965).

CURRIE, James
(1756–1805)

Physician and editor, born in Kirkpatrick-Flemish Manse, Dumfriesshire. In 1771 he became a merchant in Virginia, returning to Scotland in 1776 and going on to study medicine at Edinburgh and Glasgow. From 1780 he practised in Liverpool. His chief medical work was *Reports on the Effects of Water in Febrile Diseases* (1797), and he was a strong supporter of the anti-slavery movement. He is best remembered, however, as the first editor of **Robert Burns** (1800), with a life and criticism of the writings, undertaken solely for the benefit of Burns' family.

CURRIE, Jimmy (James)
(1921–87)

Church of Scotland minister, who came to be regarded as the archetypal down-to-earth, anecdotal minister, much in demand, nationally and internationally, as an after-dinner speaker and **Burns** expert. Degrees of MA and BD from Glasgow University were followed by ordination at Renton Millburn, Glasgow, a long and successful ministry at Pollock, Glasgow, followed by an equally long and high-profile ministry at Dunlop, Ayrshire. He was never afraid to court controversy, but the Scottish public warmed to his couthy, undemanding kind of religion. His fellow professionals were not always so enamoured, for his style of ministry came to represnt in the mind of the ordinary Scot the paradigm of parish ministry. Many ministers have since tried to emulate his style, in the hope of winning a similar place in the hearts of the Scottish public.

CURRIE, Ken

(1960 –)

English-born painter, born in North Shields. He studied social sciences at Paisley College (1977–8) and then, from 1978 to 1983, he took a degree and postgraduate diploma at Glasgow School of Art. Between 1983 and 1985 he worked on two community-based films about Glasgow and the shipbuilding industry on the Clyde; this stimulated an interest in painting about Glasgow and its social and industrial conditions. His art is overtly left-wing, a favourite subject being that of workers teaching themselves about politics. His inspiration comes from social realist painters of the 19th century and especially the 20th-century political realist art of Germany and Mexico. His most ambitious polemical work to date has been a series of murals for the People's Palace Museum in Glasgow, depicting the Socialist history of Glasgow. As in all his work, the paintings are openly polemical, packed with detail, and executed in a precise linear style.

CUTHBERTSON, Iain

(1930 –)

Actor, born in Glasgow. Educated at Glasgow Academy and Aberdeen University, he began his professional career in radio, and in 1955 made his stage début in *The Man Upstairs* in Leven. Part of the Citizens' Theatre Company in Glasgow (1958–60), his roles included Othello, Proctor in *The Crucible* and Big Daddy in *Cat On A Hot Tin Roof*. Later General Manager and Director of Productions at the Citizens (1962–5), his other theatre work has included *Gay Landscape* (1958), *The Wallace* (1960), *Sergeant Musgrave's Dance* (1965) and *Dr Angelus* (1977). A familiar figure on television in such series as *Budgie* (1971–3) and *Sutherland's Law* (1973–6), he has also appeared in films such as *The Railway Children* (1970), *The Assam Garden* (1985) and *Gorillas in the Mist* (1989), and has taken part in over a thousand radio broadcasts. Rector of Aberdeen University from 1975 to 1978, he has also written documentary films.

D

DAICHES, David
(1912 –)

Critic and scholar, born in Sunderland. The son of a rabbi, he was brought up in Edinburgh, and educated at George Watson's College and Edinburgh University. He did research on English translations of the Hebrew Bible at Balliol College, Oxford, before moving to Chicago University (1937). During World War II he served in the British Embassy in Washington, then returned to academic life at Cornell University (1947–51). He taught at Cambridge (1951–61), and was Professor of Literature at the University of Sussex from 1961 to 1977, when he retired to Edinburgh. He made many valuable contributions to literary criticism, and was especially influential in arguing for the inclusion of modern literature within the academic syllabus. His principal contributions to Scottish studies are his book on **Robert Burns** (1950, revised 1966), the first serious study of the relationship between the poet's work and the broader literary and intellectual movements of the period; his masterly and provocative study of the Scottish Enlightenment in *The Paradox of Scottish Culture* (1964); and an autobiographical account of his upbringing in Edinburgh, *Two Worlds* (1956).

DALBY, Martin
(1942 –)

Composer, born in Aberdeen. He studied composition at the Royal College of Music with Herbert Howells. He was chamber music producer at BBC Radio 3 (1965–71), Cramb Research Fellow in Composition, Glasgow University (1971–2), and Head of Music, BBC Scotland (from 1972). In 1990 he took the post of Executive Producer, to devote more time to composition. His work includes a large quantity of chamber music, various choral works, songs and orchestral music. Among them are a *Waltz Overture* (1965), a symphony (1970), *Concerto Martin Pescatore* for strings (1971), string quintet (1972), viola concerto (1974), *Man Walking* (octet for wind and strings, 1981), chamber symphony (1982), and *The Mary Bean* for orchestra (1991).

DALE, David
(1739–1806)

Industrialist and philanthropist, born in Stewarton, Ayrshire, the son of a grocer. He was apprenticed to a Paisley weaver, then travelled the country as an agent buying up homespun linen, and became a clerk to a Glasgow silk mercer. In 1763 he set up his own business in Glasgow, importing linen yarn from Holland and Flanders. In 1768 he was a founder member of an independent dissenting sect, the 'Old Scotch Independents', who were firm believers in practical Christianity, and became their best-known lay preacher. In 1777 he married the daughter of an Edinburgh director of the Royal Bank of Scotland, and was appointed the first Glasgow agent of the bank in 1783. In 1784 he met Richard Arkwright, who was being given the freedom of Glasgow, and set up a business partnership to build cotton mills at New Lanark, near the Falls of Clyde; but the partnership was dissolved in 1785 when Arkwright lost his legal battle over patents for his 'water-frame' machines. Spinning began at New Lanark in 1786, followed by a mill at Blantyre in 1787. From 1791 he was concerned with alleviating the plight of impoverished Highlanders tempted to emigrate; he gave work and housing at New Lanark to destitute would-be emigrants from the Western Isles shipwrecked off the west coast, and started industrial ventures to provide more work, with spinning mills at Spinningdale in Sutherland and at Oban. He also employed hundreds of pauper children from Edinburgh and Glasgow at New Lanark, providing a school as well as accommodation for them. He became one of the first directors of the Glasgow Royal Infirmary in 1795, which was opened that year to help the sick and diseased poor. In 1799 he sold the New Lanark mills, with their tradition of benevolent management, to his son-in-law, **Robert Owen**.

DALGARNO, George
(c.1626–1687)

Educationist, born in Old Aberdeen. He studied at Marischal College, Aberdeen, and ran a school for 30 years in Oxford. He published a book on philosophy using letters of the alphabet for ideas, *Ars Signorum, vulgo Character Universalis* (1661), to which Leibniz later made some reference, and a deaf-and-dumb sign language, *Didascalocophus, or the Deaf and Dumb Man's Tutor* (1680).

DALGLISH, Kenny (Kenneth Mathieson)
(1951 –)

Footballer and manager, born in Glasgow. One of Scotland's greatest internationals, he won 102 caps for his country. He joined Celtic in 1967 and in 10 years there won every honour in the Scottish game. Transferred to Liverpool in August 1977 for a then record fee between two British clubs of £440 000, he won every major English honour in addition to three European Cups. Unusually, Dalglish combined great skill with extreme durability and rarely missed a match. Unexpectedly invited to manage Liverpool while he was still a player, he confounded the pundits by being an instant success. In his first season (1985–6), Liverpool won both Cup and League. In 1991 he retired as manager of Liverpool, and, as he said at the time, from football, but later that year he became manager of Blackburn Rovers. He is the only player to have scored 100 goals in both English and Scottish football.

DALHOUSIE, James Andrew Broun-Ramsay, Marquis of
(1812–60)

'Greatest of Indian proconsuls', third son of the 9th Earl of Dalhousie, born at Dalhousie Castle, Midlothian. Educated at Harrow and Christ Church College, Oxford, he succeeded in 1832, on the death of his only remaining brother, to the courtesy title of Lord Ramsay. In 1835 he stood unsuccessfully for Edinburgh as a Conservative; in 1837 was elected MP for Haddingtonshire; in 1838, on the death of his father, he entered the House of Lords as Earl of Dalhousie. In 1843 Peel appointed him Vice-President of the Board of Trade, and in 1845 he succeeded Gladstone as President. When Peel resigned office in 1846, Lord John Russell asked Dalhousie to remain

at the Board of Trade in order to carry out the regulations he had framed for the railway system. In 1847 he was appointed Governor-General of India, the youngest viceroy ever sent there. His Indian administration was not less successful in the acquisition of territory than in developing Indian resources and improving the administration. Pegu and the Punjab were conquered; Nagpur, Oudh, Sattara, Jhansi and Berar were annexed. Railways on a colossal scale were planned and begun; 4000 miles of telegraph were spread over India; 2000 miles of road were bridged and metalled; the Ganges Canal was opened, and important irrigation works all over India were carried out. In addition to these developments, Dalhousie took energetic action against suttee, thuggee, female infanticide and the slave-trade; the organization of the Legislative Council; the improved training of the civil service, which was opened to all natural-born British subjects, black or white; the development of trade, agriculture, forestry, mining and the postal service. In 1848 he was made a KT; in 1849 he received the marquisate and the thanks of Parliament. With his health severely damaged, he left India in 1856.

DALLMEYER, Andrew
(1945 –)

Actor, writer and director, born in St Boswells, Roxburghshire. He studied at Webber Douglas Drama School, and subsequently appeared at the National Theatre, Royal Court and Bristol Old Vic. Since the 1970s, he has directed almost 50 productions at the Leeds Playhouse, Sheffield Crucible, Liverpool Playhouse and Edinburgh Traverse. He is the author of over 40 plays, many taking an offbeat look at a real figure, such as Salvador Dali, or Rudolf Hess. Among his finest works is the political satire, *The Boys in the Backroom* (1982); among his most idiosyncratic, a sharp parody of theatrical pretensions, *A Grand Scam* (1991). He is considered by many to be the finest and most individual Scottish playwright for many years.

DALRYMPLE, Jock
(1923–85)

Roman Catholic priest, born in North Berwick, an inspirational leader of devotional retreats, whose ministry had a profound impact upon a generation of Catholics and others within the life of the Church in

Scotland. Schooling at Ampleforth College, National Service with the Scots Guards and training at the Scots College in Rome brought a breadth to his understanding that was to be reflected in the realism and good sense of his spiritual guidance. Ordained in 1954, he served as a parish priest in Edinburgh, served 10 years as Spiritual Director at Drygrange Training College (1960–70), was University Chaplain at St Andrews, and spent the last 10 years of his ministry in a parish in Edinburgh. However, it is as a leader of spiritual retreats and a writer of minor spiritual classics that he is best remembered. He brought an authentic spiritual honesty and a deep love for God to his writings, and they have endured as devotional signposts to clergy and laity alike. His titles include *The Christian Affirmation* (1975) and *Costing Not Less than Everything* (1976).

DALRYMPLE, Sir John, later Dalrymple Hamilton Macgil, 4th Baronet of Cranstoun

(1726–1810)

Historian, descended from a distinguished Scottish legal and political family. Educated at Edinburgh and Cambridge, he was admitted to the Bar in 1748, and was for a time Solicitor to the Board of Excise. He published *An Essay Towards a General History of Feudal Property in Great Britain under Various Heads* (1757). Travelling on the Continent, he obtained vital copies from Jacobite archives which revealed for the first time that leading Whig politicians were drawing financial support from Louis XIV and, after his exile, James II of England, thus implicating among others Algernon Sidney and John Churchill, later Duke of Marlborough. These he published as appendices to his *Memoirs of Great Britain and Ireland from the Dissolution of the Last Parliament until the Sea Battle of La Hogue* (3 vols, 1771, 1790). He also discovered how to make soap from herrings and, as a lay member of the General Assembly of the Church of Scotland, defended the playwright **John Home** for having staged his play *Douglas* in 1756.

DALRYMPLE-HAMILTON, Sir Frederick Hew George

(1890–1974)

Naval commander, born in London, the son of Colonel the Hon. North de Coigny

Dalrymple of the Scots Guards. The name Hamilton was added after the family's acquisition of Bargany in Ayrshire in 1896. Following his cadetship in the Royal Navy, he served on the cruiser *Cumberland* during World War I and transferred to destroyers in 1917. Between the two world wars he served on the Royal Yacht, on the battleship HMS *Renown* and as Commander of the Royal Naval College at Dartmouth. He is best remembered for his part in the sinking of the German battleship *Bismark* in 1941 when he was in command of HMS *Rodney*. Promoted to admiral in 1948, he served with the British Joint Services Commission in Washington until his retirement in 1950.

DALYELL, Tam

(1932 –)

Labour politician, born into an ancient Scottish landed family. After education at Eton and Oxford University, he trained as a teacher at Moray House, Edinburgh, and taught at Bo'ness in West Lothian. A convert to the Labour Party, he was MP for West Lothian (1962–83), then for Linlithgow (1983 –). In Parliament he has established a reputation as the quintessential backbencher, ready to champion unpopular causes and to question ministers mercilessly. He opposed his own governments's Scottish devolution legislation in the mid 1970s, and in the 1980s he campaigned tirelessly on such issues as the sinking of the *Belgrano* during the Falklands War, the allegedly mysterious death of Hilda Murrell and, more recently, the environmental consequences of the Gulf War.

DALYELL, or DALZELL, Thomas

(c.1615–1685)

Royalist soldier, known as the 'Muscovy general', born at The Binns, West Lothian. The son of a laird, he served in the unsuccessful expedition against Rochelle led by the 1st Duke of Buckingham (1628), and fought for the Royalists in Ireland in the 1640s. In the attempted revolution he was taken prisoner at Worcester (1651), but escaped from the Tower of London in 1652 and joined Charles II in exile. In 1655 he entered the service of Russia and fought against the Tartars and Turks. In 1666, appointed Commander-in-Chief in Scotland, he defeated the Covenanters at Rullion Green in the Pentlands. He was Commander-in-Chief again from 1679 to 1685, charged with the bloody suppression of the Convenanters. He raised the Royal Scots Greys in 1681.

DALZELL, Thomas See DALYELL, Thomas

DARLING, Sir Frank Fraser
(1903–79)

Naturalist and author, born in Edinburgh and educated at Midland Agricultural College and at Edinburgh University's Institute of Animal Genetics. A member of the Buckinghamshire County Council from 1924 to 1928, he then returned to Edinburgh where international research fellowships allowed him to pursue his interests in ecology and agriculture. He was Director of the West Highland Survey from 1944 to 1950. His later work was carried out primarily in North America but his research took him all over the world and won him international acclaim. His books are mostly specialized studies and his many publications are illustrated with his own photographs and descriptions. *Natural History in the Highlands and Islands* (1947) remains unsurpassed in its field. His publishing career spans five decades, from *Biology of the Fleece of the Scottish Mountain Blackfaced Breed of Sheep* (1932) to *Wilderness and Plenty* (1970). He travelled widely and argued for the rights of natural species that were threatened by modern civilization. He received a knighthood in 1970.

DARNLEY, Henry, Lord
(1545–67)

King of Scots, born at Temple Newsome, England, the eldest son and heir of Matthew, 4th Earl of **Lennox**. He visited France in his youth, where he made a favourable impression so that, on the death of Francis II of France, he was proposed as a husband for **Mary, Queen of Scots**, his cousin. On 15 May 1565 he was created Lord Ardmannoch and Earl of Ross and, on 20 July, Duke of Albany. On 29 July 1565, he married Mary at Holyrood in the presence of just seven witnesses, having been proclaimed Henry, King of Scots, the previous day. Despite the birth of a son (the future **James VI and I**) the marriage was disastrous. Darnley's participation in the plot to murder David Rizzio, the queen's Italian secretary, finally estranged him from her. On 10 February 1567, while lying ill at Kirk o'Field, Edinburgh, he was himself murdered by being blown up by gunpowder at the instigation of his wife's new suitor, the Earl of **Bothwell**, who subsequently married the queen.

DARRELL, Peter
(1929–87)

English choreographer, director and dancer, born in Richmond, Surrey. After training at Sadler's Wells Ballet School, he remained as a dancer with the company, creating roles in pieces like Frederick Ashton's *Valses Nobles et Sentimentales* (1947). After developing a taste for choreography as dance-theatre, he became co-founder of Western Theatre Ballet in Bristol with Elizabeth West in 1957, becoming director after her death in 1962. While there he made the first ballet to Beatles music, *Mods and Rockers* (1963). Most of his dancers moved with him in 1969 to Scotland, where he created Scottish Ballet. As well as numerous short works, he made his own versions of the classics *Giselle* (1971), *Swanlake* (1977) and *The Nutcracker* (1973), and created the full-length ballets *Sun Into Darkness* (1966), *Beauty and the Beast* (1969), *Tales of Hoffman* (1972), *Mary Queen of Scots* (1976), *Chéri* (1980) and *Carmen* (1985). He staged several ballets abroad for companies in Australia, Yugoslavia, Japan and the USA. He was awarded the CBE in 1984 and remained with Scottish Ballet until his death.

DARUSMONT, Frances See WRIGHT, Frances

DAVID I
(c.1080–1153)

King of Scotland from 1124, the youngest of the six sons of **Malcolm Canmore** and St **Margaret**. In 1093 he was sent to England along with his sister Matilda (who in 1100 married Henry I of England), and remained at the English court for several years. In 1107, when his elder brother **Alexander I** succeeded to the throne, David became Prince of Cumbria, with a territory which, besides part of Cumberland, included all southern Scotland except Lothian. By his marriage in 1113 to Matilda, widow of the Norman Earl of Northampton and daughter of the Saxon Earl of Northumbria, he became Earl of Huntingdon. In 1124 he succeeded his brother on the Scottish throne. Although complicated by David's possession of large estates in England, which had entailed his swearing fealty to Henry I's daughter, Matilda, Empress Maud, in 1127, Anglo-Scots relations remained generally good until the death of Henry and the accession of Stephen in 1135.

David's invasion of northern England in support of Matilda's claims resulted in the Treaty of Durham (1136), by which he retained Cumbria and refused homage to Stephen, but allowed his son to do homage in respect of his estates at Huntingdon. An uneasy peace was followed by open warfare in 1138 and a further treaty made in 1139 at Durham, which brought the earldom of Northumberland to his son, Henry (d.1152). He was succeeded by his grandson, **Malcolm IV**. His reign was remarkable for enhancing the monarch's prestige, consolidating a feudal settlement of Scotland, and revitalizing and transforming the Scottish Church. The kingdom of the Scots, which was always how he termed his realm, began to be seen as a clearly defined entity; massive grants were made to Norman and English knights in southern Scotland by feudal tenure, but elsewhere there was considerable continuity, old custom and law being redefined and harmonized with feudal practice to produce a common law of Scotland. Sheriffdoms and justiciars were erected; a chain of castles was built in the south to act as centres of royal and baronial authority; burghs were founded, especially on the east coast, by royal charter and given specific privileges to encourage trade. David, like Alexander I, resisted English claims of jurisdiction over the Scottish Church. The claim that he founded a diocesan episcopate is exaggerated, for the organization of the Scottish Church, like that of the kingdom as a whole, became in his reign an amalgam of the new and the old. By 1154 there were 10 dioceses, but only three, Caithness, Moray and Ross, were wholly new creations. Royal patronage of the religious orders was more dramatic: during his reign more than 20 religious houses were founded, such as the Cistercians at Melrose and the Premonstratensians at Dryburgh. By 1154 the transformation of the Scottish Church that had begun with Malcolm Canmore and St Margaret was almost complete.

DAVID II
(1324–71)

King of Scotland from 1329, only surviving son of King **Robert I, the Bruce**, born in Dunfermline, and married in 1328 to Edward II's daughter, Joanna. In 1329 he succeeded his father, and in 1331 was crowned, with his child queen, at Scone. In 1334 the success of **Edward Balliol** and Edward III's victory at Halidon Hill forced David's guardians to send him and his consort to France, from where he returned in 1341. Five years later he invaded England, but at Neville's Cross, near Durham, was routed and captured (17 October 1346). He remained a prisoner for 11 years until 1357 when he was released on promise of a ransom of 100 000 marks. The treaty of 1357 brought 27 years of truce, but strains over payment of the ransom forced pursuit of more revenue, particularly through customs duties and direct taxation, and caused resentment when the hostages of 1357 were abandoned in 1363 as a result of defaulting on payments. However, until his sudden death, he maintained a firm grip on his kingdom, with little sign of the tensions between king and magnates which afflicted later reigns. He was succeeded by his sister's son, **Robert II**, for despite a second marriage to Margaret Drummond of Logie in 1363, a year after Queen Joanna died, he left no issue.

DAVIDSON, James Norman
(1911–72)

Biochemist, born in Edinburgh. He graduated in medicine from Edinburgh University in 1937, having already completed a first-class BSc in chemistry. The same year he was a fellow at the Otto Warburg Laboratory in Berlin and later became lecturer in biochemistry at University College, Dundee. An outstanding researcher, he received an MD from Edinburgh for a thesis on enzyme uricase and at Dundee investigated nucleic acids and techniques of tissue culture. In 1945 he received a DSc from Edinburgh for a thesis on cellular proliferation. From the Medical Research Council he was appointed Professor of Biochemistry at St Thomas's Hospital Medical School and in 1947 was appointed to the Gardiner Chair of Physiological Chemistry at Glasgow, where he developed the independent Department of Biochemistry, winning it an international reputation. Aware of the need for medical students to be trained in both medicine and science, he was an excellent teacher. His publications include *The Biochemistry of the Nucleic Acids* (with G H Bell and D Emslie-Smith, 7th ed 1972), and *Textbook of Physiology and Biochemistry* (with E Chargaff, 8th ed 1972).

DAVIDSON, John
(1857–1909)

Poet, novelist and dramatist, born in Barrhead, Renfrewshire, the son of an Evangelical minister. Educated at the Highlander's Academy, Greenock, where he became a pupil-teacher (1872–6), and Edinburgh University, he became an itinerant teacher in Scotland. He had started to write in 1885 (four verse dramas and a couple of novels), and in 1889 moved to London where, among other works, he wrote *Fleet Street Eclogues* (1893) and *Ballads and Songs* (1894). T S Eliot later acknowledged a debt to the urban imagery and colloquialism of 'Thirty Bob a Week'. He produced some further verse dramas, but eventually committed suicide by drowning himself at Penzance.

DAVIDSON, Sir Leybourne Stanley Patrick
(1894–1981)

Consultant physician, born in Ceylon. He went to Trinity College, Cambridge, to study medicine but in 1914 enlisted as a combatant in the Gordon Highlanders and was badly wounded. In 1917 he resumed his medical studies at Edinburgh and graduated with distinction. He did original work on the anaemias and was elected to the Regius Chair of Medicine at Aberdeen, becoming the first full-time Professor of Medicine in Scotland. He returned to Edinburgh in 1938 to become Professor of Medicine and Clinical Medicine, and established the Western, Northern and Eastern General Hospitals as highly rated centres of medical teaching. An outstanding figure in teaching and research, as a writer he became internationally known. His works include *Principles and Practice of Medicine* (1963) and *Human Nutrition and Dietetics* (with **Reginald Passmore**, 1963). He was knighted in 1955, and retired in 1959.

DAVIDSON, Mary See GARDEN, Mary

DAVIDSON, Peter Wylie
(1870–1963)

Metalwork craftsman, designer and teacher, born in Bridge of Allan, near Stirling, the son of a horse trainer and coachman. In the 1880s he served an apprenticeship in silversmithing with the Glasgow firm of Reid, and attended part-time classes at the Glasgow School of Art. In the 1890s he formed a partnership with his brother, set up a metalworking studio in Hope Street, and began part-time teaching of metalworking skills at the Art School. In 1897 he moved to teach full-time there, and over the next 35 years influenced generations of metalworking students. His technical skills and expertise are encompassed in *Educational Metalcraft* (1913) and *Applied Designs in the Precious Metals* (1929). He produced a variety of commissioned work, including some to the designs of **Charles Rennie Mackintosh**, and his work was exhibited in Glasgow, Edinburgh, Liverpool, Paris and Turin.

DAVIDSON, Randall Thomas, Baron Davidson of Lambeth
(1848–1930)

Anglican prelate and Archbishop of Canterbury, born in Edinburgh into a Presbyterian family. He studied at Harrow and Trinity College, Oxford, and was chaplain to Archbishop Tait (his father-in-law, whose Life he wrote in 1891) and to Queen Victoria, Dean of Windsor, Bishop of Rochester (1891) and of Winchester (1895), and Archbishop of Canterbury (1903–28). In his time as archbishop he worked hard to increase the role of the Church in society, and was not afraid to speak out on social and political issues.

DAVIE, Alan
(1920 –)

Painter, born in Grangemouth, the son of a painter and etcher. He studied at Edinburgh College of Art (1937–40). During wartime service with the Royal Artillery he concentrated on his other major pursuit, as a jazz saxophonist. His early work showed the influence of Klee and Picasso. In 1948, on a travelling scholarship tour of Europe, he was introduced, in Venice, to the work of Pollock and Rothko, and his paintings in the subsequent decade had much in common with contemporary American Abstract Expressionism. His imaginative use of pictographic images suggestive of myth and magic, increasingly bold and colourful since the early 1970s, reflects his preoccupation with Zen and oriental mysticism.

DAVIE, Elspeth
(1919 –)

Novelist, born in Kilmarnock, Ayrshire. She was educated at Edinburgh University and Edinburgh College of Art, and worked as an art teacher in Northern Ireland, the Borders of Scotland and Aberdeen before settling in Edinburgh, where she married the philosopher **George Elder Davie**. Her first novel, *Providings*, was published in 1965. Her work runs against the grain of mainstream Scottish fiction, in that they characteristically eschew high drama or lurid subject matter in favour of an exploration of the subtle emotional nuances and human vulnerability underlying ordinary, everyday behaviour. Edinburgh general provides the backdrop for her fiction. She won the Katherine Mansfield Award for her short stories in 1978, and they have been collected in several volumes, including *The Spark* (1968) and *The Night of the Funny Hats* (1980). Her novels, which include *Creating a Scene* (1971), *Climbers On A Stair* (1978), and *Coming to Light* (1989), are deeply perceptive and sympathetic accounts of middle-class life.

DAVIE, George Elder
(1912 –)

Philosopher, born in Dundee. While a student at Edinburgh University he met **Hugh MacDiarmid**, for whom he was a major intellectual contact, as well as others such as **Sorley MacLean**. Teaching at Edinburgh until 1939, he moved to Queen's University Belfast (1945–59), returning thereafter to Edinburgh. He was a pioneer in studies in the Scottish Enlightenment. *The Democratic Intellect* (1961) explores 18th to 20th-century cultural/educational continuity and attacks uncomprehending 'reforms'. *The Crisis of the Democratic Intellect* (1986) shows a concern with culture generally, and on its ideas on education is close to **John Burnet** and **John Anderson**. He is married to short-story writer **Elspeth Davie**.

DAVIES, Betty
(1935 –)

English fashion designer, born in Nottingham. After studying at the Guildhall School of Music in London, she went on to work in public relations before founding the Campus group in 1966. In 1987 she launched her award-winning designer label, The Academy Collection, in Glasgow and Paris, and in 1989 the Betty Davies Tartan, winning the Scottish Style Award the same year. She has based her current work on designing Harris tweed as a fashion fabric, specially woven and manufactured for her in the Western Isles. She also works in silk. She now operates on the Betty Davies label, and her clients include **Evelyn Glennie** and Elizabeth Harwood. Recent projects include designing new tartans for Japan. She was appointed Governor of the Edinburgh College of Art in 1989.

DEACON BLUE See ROSS, Ricky

DEAS, James
(1827–99)

Civil engineer, born in Edinburgh. He entered the workshops of the Edinburgh & Glasgow Railway and rose to become their chief engineer in 1864. Five years later he was appointed engineer to the Clyde Navigation Trust, for whom he built the Queen's and Prince's Docks, the Govan dry docks and Stobcross Quay. His outstanding ability led to his being much in demand as a consultant and expert witness, in which latter capacity it was apparently not unknown for him to appear for both parties at the same time. He contributed many papers and articles on the Clyde to engineering journals throughout the world.

DEE, Philip Ivor
(1904–83)

English physicist, born in Stroud, Gloucestershire, where he attended Marling School and proceeded with a scholarship to Cambridge University. As a research student he was supervised by **C T R Wilson**, and later used the cloud-chamber technique to obtain some of the first results on transmutations of elements, following the discovery of the neutron by his colleague James Chadwick. He played an important part in wartime research on nuclear fission in Cambridge and in the development of radar at the Telecommunications Research Establishment in Malvern. In 1945 he was appointed Professor of Natural Philosophy in Glasgow University, where he built up a large and active research group concerned with nuclear and particle physics. He was awarded a CBE in 1946, and the Hughes medal of the Royal Society in 1952.

DEMARCO, Richard
(1930 –)

Artist, broadcaster and teacher, born in Edinburgh, where he studied at the College of Art (1949–53). A vivid, outspoken personality, he has been a leading promoter of modern art in Scotland, including the work of such international figures as Joseph Beuys, as well as contemporary Scottish artists, especially at the Edinburgh Festival since 1967, and has presented annual programmes of theatre, music and dance. He was co-founder of the Traverse Theatre Club, and director (from 1966) of the Richard Demarco Gallery.

DEMPSTER, Thomas
(c.1579–1625)

Scholar and poet, born in Aberdeenshire. Educated at Turriff, Aberdeen, Cambridge, Paris, Louvain, Rome and Douai, he held several provincial professorships, and was a professor at Paris for seven years. He was a skilled swordsman, but had an unruly temper, and a brawl with his students drove him to England. There he married a beautiful woman and then, finding his Catholicism was an obstacle to his advancement, he returned to the continent, where he obtained a professorship at Pisa in 1616. His wife's infidelities ruined his peace of mind, and he left for Bologna where he became Professor of Humanities, and where he died. His less than honest autobiography forms part of his *Historia Ecclesiastica Gentis Scotorum* (1627) an erudite work in which, however, his desire to magnify his country often led him to forge the names of persons and books that never existed, and to claim as Scotsmen writers whose birthplace was doubtful.

DENHAM, Sir James See STEUART, Sir James Denham

DENNESS, Michael
(1940 –)

Cricketer, born in Bellshill, Lanarkshire. Having learned his cricket in Scotland, he went on to captain Kent and England. In his first-class career he made over 25 000 runs and hit four Test centuries. With K R Fletcher of Essex he holds the Test record for a fourth wicket partnership of 266 against New Zealand, at Auckland in 1974–5.

DENNEY, James
(1856–1917)

Free Church minister and academic, born in Paisley, whose support for the idea of the reunion of the churches in Scotland was crucial to the successful outcome of unity discussions. A degree in classics and philosophy from Glasgow University was followed by studies in theology at the Glasgow Free Church College. Ministry at Broughty Ferry (1886–97), during which his writing career was begun, was followed by his appointment as Professor of Systematic Theology at the Glasgow Free Church College in 1897. In 1900 he received the Chair of New Testament on the strength of his theological contribution. A key figure in Church life in Scotland, he was no ivory-tower theologian but was prepared to engage the issues facing the Church, and to involve himself in controversy. Coming from the Free Church tradition, he brought an openness and charity to the idea of reunion after the Disruption of 1843, attitudes that were creative and healing, and did much to set the tone of the ongoing debate. He ended his career as Principal of Glasgow United Free College.

DENNY, Sir Maurice Edward
(1886–1955)

Shipbuilder, born in Dumbarton into a well-known shipbuilding family. He was educated in Tonbridge and at universities in Europe as well as at the Massachusetts Institute of Technology, where he gained a first in naval architecture. In World War I he served in France and with the government, and was awarded the CBE in 1918. In 1922, four years after the merger of the shipbuilding and marine engine components of the company, he became Chairman, a position he was to hold for 30 years. During this period Denny's gained a reputation for technical innovation. The problems that beset the firm and the industry thrust him into an active role in shipbuilding politics as, for example, with the Shipbuilding Conference, the industry's trade organization. In 1936 he was created a baronet, in 1946 a KBE and in 1949 he was awarded an honorary LLD from Glasgow University. His company was to survive only a decade after his retiral in 1952.

DENT, Alan Holmes
(1905–78)

Critic and journalist, born in Ayrshire. Educated at Glasgow University, he began his career covering the London theatre for the *Manchester Guardian* (1935–43). He was dramatic critic of the *News Chronicle* (1945–60) and President of the Critics' Circle in 1962. A frequent lecturer on the art of criticism, he was a leading authority on Shakespeare and worked as text editor for Sir Laurence Olivier's films of *Henry V*, *Hamlet* and

Richard III. Among his books are biographies of Mrs Patrick Campbell and Vivien Leigh; he also wrote a study of his fellow Ayrshireman, **Robert Burns**.

DEÒRSA CAIMBEUL HAY See HAY, George Campbell

DEUCHAR, Jimmy (James)
(1930 –)

Jazz trumpeter, composer and arranger, born in Dundee into a musical family. He was taught locally and played in London around 1950 while serving with the RAF. He became a member of the modernist Johnny Dankworth Seven and was recognized as an important emerging talent as a soloist and arranger for medium-sized and big bands. He played under such leaders as Tubby Hayes, Ronnie Scott, Jack Parnell and in Lionel Hampton's touring orchestra. From 1957 to 1971 he worked mainly on the European continent, with Kurt Edelhagen's radio orchestra and with the Kenny Clarke-Francy Boland Big Band. Returning to Britain in 1971, and eventually settling again in Dundee, he has been active as an arranger for various BBC projects, a bandleader and a freelance player on both trumpet and flugelhorn.

DEWAR, Donald
(1937–)

Politician, born in Glasgow. Educated at Glasgow Academy and Glasgow University, he qualified as a solicitor, and is still a partner in Ross, Harper & Murphy. He won Aberdeen South for the Labour Party in 1966, having previously stood unsuccessfully there. He lost his seat in 1970, and spent eight years out of parliament before returning in the Glasgow Garscadden by-election of 1978. He retained the seat with ease in the general elections of 1979, 1983, 1987 and 1992. The Chief Opposition Spokesman on Scottish Affairs since 1983, he is extremely able intellectually, if a touch too cerebral ever to enjoy wide popularity.

DEWAR, Sir James
(1842–1923)

Chemist and physicist, born in Kincardine-on-Forth. Educated at Dollar Academy,

Edinburgh University and Ghent, he became Professor of Natural Experimental Philosophy at Cambridge in 1875. He liquified and froze many gases, invented the vacuum flask and (with Sir Frederick Abel) discovered cordite.

DEWAR, John Alexander, Lord Forteviot
(1856–1929)

Wine and spirit merchant and distiller, born in Perth and educated at Perth Academy. In association with his brother Thomas, he succeeded in transforming his father's modest family firm into one of the 'big three' of the whisky industry with a product which became a household name. John's contribution in financial matters was equalled by Tommy's outgoing marketing skills. The capital for expansion was provided from 1890 by Distillers Company. Merger with Buchanan's was followed by a tripartite union, which created Distiller's Company Ltd in 1925, the board of which both brothers joined. John served as Liberal MP for Inverness-shire from 1900 to 1916, in which year he acceded to the peerage. In so doing he became the first of the 'Whisky Barons'. His native city benefited from a range of philanthropic endeavours funded out of his huge personal fortune.

DICK, James
(1743–1828)

Merchant and philanthropist, born in Forres, Aberdeenshire. He made a fortune in American trading with the West Indies, and left the 'Dick Bequest' to promote higher learning in the parish schools of the counties of Moray, Banff and Aberdeen.

DICK, Robert
(1811–66)

Self-taught geologist and botanist, born in Tullibody, Clackmannanshire. Working as a baker in Thurso, he supplied **Hugh Miller** with fossils and scientific information.

DICK, Thomas
(1774–1857)

Popular writer on astronomy, born in Dundee and educated at Edinburgh University.

His scientific and philosophical writings were coloured by his strong religious convictions and by his desire to bring education to ordinary people. His books, such as *Celestial Scenery* (1837), were lucidly written and had wide appeal in Britain and in the USA.

DICKINSON, William Croft
(1897–1963)

Historian, educated at Millhill, Perthshire, and St Andrews and London universities. During World War I he served in France and Flanders, winning the Military Cross. As Librarian of the British Library of Political and Economic Science at the London School of Economics (1933–44), he published an edition of *The Sheriff Court Book of Fife* (1928) and of *The Court Book of the Barony of Carnwath* (1937), both for the Scottish History Society. He also collaborated on a facsimile edition of the *Chronicle of Melrose* (1936). In 1944 he was appointed Sir **William Fraser** Professor of Scottish History and Palaeography at Edinburgh University, holding the chair until his death. His term of office brought with it a determined revival of Scottish historical studies, symbolized by his own editorship of the *Scottish Historical Review* (from 1947 to his death). He produced a two-volume edition of **John Knox**'s *History of the Reformation in Scotland* (1949), and prepared an invaluable three-volume *Source Book of Scottish History* in collaboration with his colleague **Gordon Donaldson**, as well as resuming his work for the Scottish History Society with *Early Records of the Burgh of Aberdeen* (1957). He also wrote for a wider audience, with such works as *Robert Bruce* (1960) and *A History of Scotland from the Earliest Times to 1603* (1961), as well as some distinguished ghost stories.

DICKSON, Alec (Alexander Graeme)
(1914 –)

Educationist, born in London. A pioneer of community service involving young volunteers from the UK, he was educated at Rugby and New College, Oxford. He trained as a journalist on the *Yorkshire Post*, but after war service in Africa he set up Community Service Volunteers (CSV) to enable young people to give voluntary service to the community in Britain. Since 1984 he has been consultant to International Baccalaureate schools worldwide. His publications include *A Community Service Handbook* (with his wife Mora Dickson, 1967), *School in the Round* (1969), *A Chance to Serve* (1976), and *Volunteers* (1983).

DICKSON, Barbara
(1947 –)

Pop singer and songwriter, born in Dunfermline. While working as a civil servant she started her musical career singing in Scottish folk clubs where her talent was recognized by Bernie Theobald. Her first major break came in 1973 when she starred in Willy Russell's musical *John, Paul, George, Ringo and Bert*. She had her first chart success with the title track to the album *Answer Me* (1976). Although she did not appear in the West End production of the Tim Rice/Andrew Lloyd Webber musical *Evita*, the show did provide her with the hit single *Another Suitcase, Another Hall* (1977). She played the lead role in Willy Russell's *Blood Brothers* (1983) and recorded the album *Tell Me It's Not True*, featuring songs from the show. Other albums have included *You Know It's Me* (1981), *All For A Song* (1982), *The Barbara Dickson Songbook* (1985) and *The Right Moment* (1986).

DICKSON, Joan
(1921 –)

Cellist. Born in Edinburgh, she studied with Ivor James, Pierre Fournier in Paris, and Enrico Mainardi in Rome and Salzburg. In 1953 she gave her début recital in London and became a founder member of the Edinburgh Quartet. She was soon a leading concerto soloist with all the major UK orchestras, frequently appearing at the London Proms, and in duo perfomances with her pianist sister Hester Dickson (1924 –), with whom she premiered several works specially written for them. She taught at the Royal Scottish Academy of Music (1954–81) and the Royal College of Music (1967–81). Based in London since 1980, she is a distinguished teacher at various institutions and international masterclasses.

DILLON, James
(1950 –)

Self-taught composer, born in Glasgow. His music has been widely performed at European festivals and centres for contemporary music such as Darmstadt and IRCAM in Paris. He was guest lecturer at the State University of New York (1986) and taught composition at Goldsmiths' College, London University (1986–7). He was one of the main composers featured in Glasgow's 1987 'Musica Nova', when the Scottish National Orchestra played *helle Nacht*, his first large orchestral work. His output includes two string quartets, several works for small orchestra, percussion, and a large-scale electro-acoustical project *Nine Rivers* (1982 –).

DINWIDDIE, Robert
(1693–1770)

Colonial administrator, born near Glasgow. He was appointed Collector of Customs for Bermuda in 1727 and Surveyor-General for southern America in 1738. Appointed Lieutenant-Governor of Virginia in 1751, he tried to prevent French occupation of the Ohio district in 1753. He sent a young surveyor, George Washington, to demand a French withdrawal, followed by troops in 1754, but Washington was forced to surrender at Fort Necessity. In 1755 General **Edward Braddock** was defeated near Fort Duquesne in Ohio, thus precipitating the French and Indian War (1755–63). Dinwiddie was recalled in 1758.

DIRLETON, Sir John Nisbet, Lord
(?1609–1687)

Judge. Son of a judge (Lord Eastbank) and descended on his mother's side from Sir **Thomas Craig**, he passed advocate in 1633, defended **Montrose** in 1641 and in 1664 was appointed Lord Advocate and also promoted to the bench as Lord Dirleton, being the last person to combine the office of Lord Advocate and judge. He became notorious as a persecutor of the Covenanters, often stretching the law to secure conviction, as when in 1667 after the Pentland Rising he sought convictions in the absence of the accused. In 1670 he was a Commissioner to London to negotiate for the union of the Scottish and English parliaments but he opposed the abolition of the Scottish Parliament. In 1677 he was forced to resign the office of Lord Advocate under suspicion of having taken fees from both sides in a case. He is reputed to have been a good scholar and lawyer and published *Some Doubts and Questions in the Law, especially of Scotland, as also Some Decisions of the Lords of Council and Session* (1698), but his public career was discreditable.

DOBBIE, Sir James Johnston
(1852–1924)

Physical and organic chemist and scientific administrator. Born in Glasgow, he studied at the universities of Glasgow, Leipzig and Edinburgh. As a lecturer in Glasgow he worked with **William Ramsay** on quinine and other alkaloids and on the ultra-violet absorption spectra of organic compounds. Professor of Chemistry at Bangor from 1884 to 1903, he helped to establish there the first department of agriculture south of Scotland, and thereafter worked continually to advance agricultural education in other contexts. Appointed Director of the Royal Scottish Museum, Edinburgh, in 1903, he extended the Egyptian, engineering and natural history collections. In 1909 he became Principal of the Government Laboratory in London, and was knighted in 1915.

DOCHERTY, Tommy (Thomas Henderson)
(1928 –)

Footballer and manager, born in Glasgow. In a tempestuous career he played 25 times for Scotland and managed many clubs including Aston Villa, Manchester United, Derby County and Queen's Park Rangers. From September 1971 he managed the Scotland side for just over a year. A superb short-term motivator, he frequently fell out with his employers. On leaving football he built a successful career as an after-dinner speaker.

DODS, Marcus
(1834–1909)

Clergyman and scholar. He was minister of Renfrew Free Church, Glasgow (1864–89), and Professor of New Testament Exegesis at the (United) Free Church College in Edinburgh (1889), and Principal (1907). He published several theological works and commentaries on scripture, most notably *On the Incarnation of the Eternal Word*, in which he argued against **Edward Irving**'s theology.

DODS, Meg See JOHNSTONE, (Christian) Isobel

DON, David
(1800–41)

Botanist, born in Forfar, Angus, the son of George Don, sometime Keeper of the Edinburgh Botanic Gardens. Using his father's work as a basis, he published *Descriptions of Several New or Rare Native Plants Found in Scotland*, among 52 papers presented in the Royal Society Catalogue, which included the then unknown arctic-alpine flora of Scotland. He became a Fellow of the Linnean Society and, in 1822, its secretary. In 1836 he was appointed Professor of Botany at King's College, London.

DONALD, Ian
(1910–87)

Obstetrician and inventor of the first successful diagnostic ultrasound machine and originator of the pregnancy scan. The son of a Paisley doctor, he graduated in medicine at St Thomas's Hospital Medical School, London, where he was Reader in Obstetrics and Gynaecology. In 1954 he was appointed to the Regius Chair of Midwifery in Glasgow, a post he held for 22 years. His *Practical Obstetric Problems* (2nd ed 1959) was a best-seller. With the help of a brilliant engineer, Tom Brown, and the Scottish electronics company Kelvin Hughes, he developed echo-sounding with radar techniques to create the first contact compound scanner. His pioneering ultrasound diagnosis was reported in *The Lancet* in 1958. The first images were poor but he improved the apparatus and by the 1970s it was used routinely, Glasgow becoming a world centre in this field. A man of enthusiasm and strong opinions, his anti-abortion stance gained him more media publicity than his contributions to obstetrics.

DONALDSON, David
(1916 –)

Painter, born in Chryston, Glasgow. He studied at Glasgow School of Art (1931–8) and rose to become Head of Painting there in 1967. In that position he exerted a strong influence on painting, which reflected both the tradition of the Scottish colourists and the figurative tradition of artists such as **James Cowie**. His work covers a wide range of subject matter, but he is especially known for his portraits, which successfully combine the imitative requirements of the genre with a direct and bold handling of paint.

DONALDSON, Gordon
(1913 –)

Historian, born in Edinburgh, of Shetland origin, and educated at the Royal High School, Edinburgh, and Edinburgh and London universities. In 1947 he became Lecturer in Scottish History at Edinburgh, becoming Reader in 1955. He succeeded to the Sir **William Fraser** Chair in Scottish History and Palaeography in 1963, retiring in 1979. As professor and as his predecessor **Croft Dickinson**'s collaborator in *A Source-Book of Scottish History*, he quickly won a commanding place, inaugurating the four-volume *History of Scotland*. A life-long Scottish Episcopalian, his religious interests and understanding of theological conviction first showed themselves in *The Making of the Scottish Prayer Book of* 1637 (1954), and later in *The Faith of the Scots* (1990), a work weakened by his lack of sympathy with modern theological directions. A prolific and influential writer, with an invigorating style, he compiled *Scottish Historical Documents* (1970), and wrote engagingly, if conservatively, on Shetland history. He edited volumes 5–8 of the *Register of the Privy Seal of Scotland*, while in a more popular vein he produced *Who's Who in Scottish History* (1974), and a *Dictionary of Scottish History* (1977), which placed a wholly unrivalled knowledge at the disposal of readers of all ages. His *Scottish Kings* (1967) catered for a wide public, with hard-hitting judgements, and he greatly enriched the perennial topic of **Mary, Queen of Scots** with an authoritative account of her first trial (1969), a biography (1974), and a study of her entourage, *All the Queen's Men* (1983). The recipient of a host of awards, he was made Historiographer to the Queen in Scotland in 1979, and received honorary doctorates from Aberdeen (1976) and Stirling (1988).

DONALDSON, James
(1751–1830)

Newspaper proprietor and philanthropist, born in Edinburgh, the son of a bookseller. He inherited the *Edinburgh Advertiser*, and left about £240 000 to found a 'hospital' (school) for 300 poor children, an act that led his relatives to try to prove his insanity and thus overrule his will. It was built between 1842 and 1851 from designs by **William Playfair** at a cost of about £120 000; it subsequently became Donaldson's School for the Deaf.

DONALDSON, Sir James
(1831–1915)

Educational administrator and classical scholar, born in Aberdeen. Despite humble circumstances he was educated at Aberdeen Grammar School and University. He studied briefly at New College, London, with a view to joining the Congregationalist ministry, but left to further his classical and theological studies in Berlin, where he discovered the psychology of education and the work of Herbart and Beneke. From 1852 to 1854 he was assistant to the Professor of Greek at Edinburgh; from 1854 to 1856 he was rector of Stirling High School; and he was classical master, 1856–66, and then rector, 1866–81, at Edinburgh High School. He was Professor of Humanity, Aberdeen University, 1881–6, Principal of the United College at St Andrews, 1886–90, and Principal and Vice-Chancellor of St Andrews University from 1890 to his death. His most significant work of scholarship, *A Critical History of Christian Literature and Doctrine from the Death of the Apostles to the Nicene Council*, was published in three volumes, 1864–6. He was active in educational politics and promoted the Education Act of 1872, which established primary education in Scotland on a compulsory basis.

DONALDSON, Margaret Caldwell
(1926 –)

Psychologist, born in Paisley. Graduating in French and education at Edinburgh University, she subsequently completed doctoral studies in psychology at Edinburgh, and studied at Geneva and Harvard. Following appointments in the Departments of Education and Psychology at Edinburgh, she was appointed Professor of Developmental Psychology in 1980. Her publications on children's intellectual, linguistic and social skills, *A Study of Children's Thinking* (1963) and *Children's Minds* (1978), have been widely influential in developmental psychology and education.

DONALDSON, Marion
(1944 –)

Self-taught fashion designer, born in Glasgow. Originally trained as a primary school teacher, she founded her own fashion company in the mid 1960s with her husband David (1943 –), son of **David Donaldson**. She designs two ladies' collections each year on the Marion Donaldson and Le MiDi labels, producing mainly dresses and co-ordinates for day and evening wear. She supplies Liberty branches throughout Britain in addition to 300 independent UK outlets.

DONALDSON, Mary Ethel Muir
(1876–1958)

English-born photographer and writer, born and educated in England. She travelled extensively in the Western Highlands and Islands from c.1905 and settled in 1927 at Sanna in Ardnamurchan, Argyll, where she had a house built using largely traditional methods, so that it would be sympathetic to the Highland landscape. She lived there until 1947 when the house was destroyed by fire. Devastated by this she moved to Edinburgh. M.E.M.D., as she styled herself, was the author of numerous books, most of which are sympathetic studies of aspects of Highland life and history. The best-known of these are *Wanderings in the Western Highlands and Islands* (1921) and *Further Wanderings – Mainly in Argyll* (1926), both illustrated by her own sensitive photographs of landscapes and people and by the line drawings of her life-long friend Isabel Bonus.

DONEGAN, Lonnie, real name Anthony Donegan
(1931 –)

Singer and guitarist, born in Glasgow. He changed his name at the start of his career in tribute to American blues artist Lonnie Johnson. His rhythm-based versions of American folk songs (particularly those of Woody Guthrie and Leadbelly) were responsible for the emergence of the skiffle genre of British pop, and he had over 30 chart hits between 1958 and 1962, including 'Gambling Man', 'My Old Man's A Dustman' and 'Does Your Chewing Gum Lose Its Flavour (On The Bedpost Overnight)'. Although he helped inspire a generation of British musicians, including The Beatles, ironically he was consigned to the cabaret circuit as a novelty act following the British pop renaissance of the early 1960s.

DONOVAN, full name Donovan Leitch
(1944 –)

Singer and songwriter, born in Glasgow. He moved to London aged 10. Making his first records at the age of 18, he had his first hits with his own song 'Colours' and a version of Buffy Saint Marie's protest song 'Universal Soldier'. His folk-based pop was largely overshadowed by the success of Bob Dylan, although he found a new audience in the hippie era with hits which included 'Mellow Yellow' and 'Hurdy Gurdy Man'. He has also published a book of poems, *Dry Songs And Scribbles*. In 1972 he starred in and scored the film *The Pied Piper* and wrote the score for the Zeffirelli film *Brother Sun, Sister Moon* (1972). His career was revived in 1990 following an interest in his work from several contemporary groups including The Happy Mondays.

DORWARD, David Campbell
(1933 –)

Composer, born in Dundee. After reading English and philosophy at St Andrews University, he studied composition at the Royal Academy of Music with Manuel Frankell and John Gardiner. His works include a one-act opera *Tonight, Mrs Morrison* (1968), a symphony (1961), *Golden City* for orchestra (1988), four string quartets, concertos for violin, viola, cello and piano; songs, other chamber and orchestral music, and much incidental music. He was BBC Music Producer from 1962 to 1991.

DOTT, Norman McOmish
(1897–1973)

Pioneer in neurological surgery, born in Edinburgh. He left George Heriot's School to become an engineering apprentice, but a motor cycle accident put him in hospital where he became fascinated with medicine. He graduated in medicine at Edinburgh in 1919. As a student he was responsible for a number of advances in anaesthesia particularly the use of the endotracheal tube. He was resident at the Royal Infirmary and part-time lecturer in Sir Edward **Sharpey-Schafer**'s physiology department. His work was rewarded by a Rockefeller Fellowship to work with Harvey Cushing at Boston, USA; his inspiration led Dott to devote his life to neurosurgery. Returning to the Royal Hospital for Sick Children in Edinburgh he was able to practise paediatric surgery while developing neurosurgery. His operation for congenital dislocation of the hip was an important contribution to paediatric surgery. In 1937 a ward for surgical neurology was created at the Royal Infirmary and Dott, who was already lecturer in surgical neurology, was able to create an excellent department. During World War II he set up a Brain Injuries Unit at Bangour Hospital. In 1947 he was appointed professor, and in 1960 he

created a new department at the Western General Hospital which has won an international reputation. His contributions to neurological surgery have been considerable. He was a pioneer in demonstrating an aneurysm of the circle of Willis by angiography and successfully treating it operatively. He made important contributions to knowledge of the circulation of the cardiospinal fluid and to the management of facial pain, and he was one of the pioneers of rehabilitation. A remarkable teacher, he had an intense interest in the real needs of the patient. He was the recipient of many honours. With Sir Geoffrey Jefferson at Manchester, Sir **Hugh Cairns** at Oxford and Norman Dott at Edinburgh, British neurological surgery was established.

DOUGLAS

A family which includes William the Hardy, crusader, who harried the monks of Melrose, and was the first man of distinction to join **Wallace** in the rising against the English in 1297. His son, the Good Sir James Douglas (c.1286–1330), also called 'the Black Douglas' on account of his swarthy complexion, was **Robert Bruce**'s greatest captain in the War of Independence. The hero of 70 fights, he was slain in Andalusia, bearing the heart of Bruce. His son William fell at Halidon Hill, and the next Lord of Douglas, Hugh, brother of Sir James, and a canon of Glasgow, made over the now great domains of the family in 1342 to his nephew Sir William.

DOUGLAS, Earls of Angus

The first of these, William, 1st Earl of Douglas (?1327–1384), while securing the earldom of Mar, also secured the affections of the young widow of his wife's brother, Margaret, Countess of Angus and Mar. The issue of this affair was a son, George, 1st Earl of Angus, who in 1389 had a grant of his mother's earldom of Angus. George, 4th Earl (c.1412–1462), aided the king against the Douglases in 1454; his loyalty was rewarded by a grant of their old inheritance of Douglasdale and other lands; and so, in the phrase of the time, 'the Red Douglas put down the Black'. His son Archibald, 5th Earl (c.1449–1514), was nicknamed Bell-the-Cat from the lead he took against Lord Cochrane at Lauder; he filled the highest offices in the state and added largely to the family possessions. His grandson Archibald, 6th Earl (c.1489–1557), married **Margaret Tudor**, widow of **James IV** of Scotland, in 1514. This marriage produced a daughter, Margaret, who on marrying the 4th Earl of **Lennox**, became the mother of **Darnley**, **Mary, Queen of Scots**' husband and **James VI and I**'s father. The Earl of Angus had for a time supreme power in Scotland, but in 1528 **James V** escaped from his hands, and sentence of forfeiture was passed against him and his kinsmen. On James's death in 1542 Angus was restored to his estates and honours. He was succeeded by his nephew, David, whose son Archibald, the 'Good Earl' (1558–88), died without male issue, and the earldom passed to a kinsman, William Douglas of Glenbervie.

DOUGLAS, Earls of Douglas

Since the time of William the Hardy (see **Douglas**) the Douglases had held the title of Lords of Douglas; in 1358 Sir William (c.1327–1384) was made Earl of Douglas, and by marriage he became Earl of Mar about 1374. His son, James, 2nd Earl of Douglas (c.1358–1388), fell at Otterburn, leaving no legitimate issue. His aunt had married for her second husband one of her brother's esquires, James of Sandilands, and through her Lord Torphichen, whose barony was a creation of **Mary, Queen of Scots**, in 1564, is now the heir general of the House of Douglas. The Earldom of Douglas was meanwhile bestowed on an illegitimate son of the Good Sir James Archibald (c.1328–1400), Lord of Galloway, surnamed 'the Grim'. By his marriage with the heiress of Bothwell he added that barony to the Douglas domains; and he married his only daughter to the heir-apparent of the Scottish crown (David, Duke of Rothesay, son of **Robert III**, murdered in 1402) and his eldest son to Margaret, eldest daughter of Robert III. His son, Archibald, 4th Earl (c.1369–1424), called 'Tyneman' ('loser'), was wounded and taken prisoner by Hotspur (see Percy family) at Homildon Hill in 1402. The following year, fighting on Hotspur's side at Shrewsbury, he was again wounded and taken prisoner and ransomed. Going to France, he earned himself the title of Duke of Touraine by heading a troop of Scottish soldiers in aid of the regent, Charles VIII, in 1423. He was killed at Verneuil, after defeat by the Duke of Bedford. His son Archibald, 5th Earl (c.1391–1439), fought in the French wars. His son, William, 6th Earl (c.1423–1440), was decoyed into Edinburgh Castle by **James II** and beheaded, along with

his brother David. His Scottish earldom was bestowed on his grand-uncle (the second son of Archibald the Grim), James the 'Gross' (c.1371–1443), who in 1437 had been made Earl of Avondale. His son William, 8th Earl (c.1425–1452), was for a time all-powerful with James II, who made him Lieutenant-General of the realm; he afterwards entered into a confederacy against the king, by whom he was stabbed in Stirling Castle. His brother James, 9th and last Earl (1426–88), in 1454 made open war against James II. The issue seemed doubtful until the **Hamilton**s sided with the king, and Douglas fled to England. His brothers, who still maintained the struggle, were defeated at Arkinholm (Langholm) in May 1455 and the earldom of Douglas came to an end by forfeiture. The last earl lived for many years in England, leagued himself in 1484 with the exiled Duke of **Albany**, was defeated and taken prisoner at Lochmaben, and died in the abbey of Lindores.

DOUGLAS, Earls of Morton

Sir Andrew de Douglas, who appears in record in 1248, was apparently a younger son of Sir Archibald, the second chief of the house. His great-grandson, Sir William Douglas, the 'Knight of Liddesdale' (c.1300–1353), was assassinated by his kinsman, William, 1st Earl of Douglas. The grandson of his nephew, Sir James Douglas of Dalkeith, married a daughter of **James I**, and in 1458 was created 1st Earl of Morton. His grandson, the 3rd Earl, having died without male issue in 1553, the earldom devolved on his youngest daughter's husband, the regent **Morton**, and from him the present Earl of Morton is descended. James, 2nd Earl of Douglas and Mar, had an illegitimate son, Sir William Douglas of Drumlanrig, whose descendants were created Viscounts of Drumlanrig in 1628, Earls of Queensberry in 1633, Marquises of Queensberry in 1681, Dukes of Queensberry in 1683, Earls of March in 1697, and Earls of Solway in 1706. On the death of the 4th Duke of Queensberry in 1810, that title went to the Duke of Buccleuch; the title of Marquis of Queensberry went to Sir Charles Douglas of Kelhead, and that of Earl of March to the Earl of Wemyss. In 1646 the third son of the 1st Marquis of Douglas was created Earl of Selkirk; in 1651 the eldest son was created Earl of Ormond, and in 1661 Earl of Forfar; and in 1675 the fourth son was created Earl of Dumbarton. In 1641 the second son of the 10th Earl of Angus was created Lord Mordington. In 1633 Sir Robert Douglas (c.1574–1639) was created Viscount Belhaven.

DOUGLAS, Bill
(1934–91)

Film director, born in Newcraighall, near Edinburgh. The illegitimate son of a miner, his childhood of almost unrelenting misery and penury later formed the basis of his famed autobiographical trilogy. After National Service he pursued a career as an actor and writer for the theatre, working as an assistant to Joan Littlewood, and ultimately attending film school before making his directorial début with *My Childhood* (1972). Together with *My Ain Folk* (1973) and *My Way Home* (1977), it formed an intense, dramatic interpretation of his childhood and adolescence, bringing a bleak poetry to bear on the moving story of a human spirit confronted by a harsh and loveless world. A painstaking, uncompromising artist, he made only one further feature film, *Comrades* (1986), an ambitious, epic account of the Tolpuddle Martyrs, partly conveyed as a pre-history of the cinema by an itinerant lanternist.

DOUGLAS, David
(1798–1834)

Botanist, born in Scone, Perthshire. He travelled in North America as a collector for the Horticultural Society of London, and discovered many trees, shrubs and herbaceous plants which he introduced to Britain, including the Giant Fir (*Abies grandis*) in Western North America in 1825 and the Sitka Spruce (*Picea sithchensis*), now the most ubiquitous conifer in Britain. The Oregon Pine (*Pseudotsuga menziesii*) was renamed the Douglas fir after him, as was the Douglas squirrel. He was gored to death by a wild bull in the Sandwich Islands.

DOUGLAS, Gavin
(c.1474–1522)

Poet and prelate, born at Tantallon Castle, East Lothian, the third son of Archibald, 5th Earl of Angus (see **Douglas, Earls of Angus**). Educated at St Andrews and possibly Paris for the priesthood, from 1501 to 1514 he was Dean or Provost of the Collegiate Church of St Giles, Edinburgh. After the Battle of Flodden (1513), in which King **James IV** fell, Douglas's nephew, the 6th Earl of Angus, married the widowed queen, **Margaret Tudor**. Through her influence, he obtained the bishopric of Dunkeld (January 1515), but was imprisoned under an old statute for receiving bulls from the pope, and was not consecrated until more than a year after. On the fall of Angus in 1521, the bishop fled to England to obtain the aid of Henry VIII, but died suddenly of the plague in London. His works include *The Palice of Honour*, presumably written in 1501, an allegory of the life of the virtuous man, and a magnificent translation of Virgil's *Aeneid*, with prologues, finished about 1513, the first version of a Latin poet published in English. He may also have written *King Hart*, an allegory about the control exercised by the heart in human personality and behaviour.

DOUGLAS, John
(1721–1807)

Prelate, the son of a Pittenweem shopkeeper. He was educated at Dunbar and Oxford and, as an army chaplain, was present at Fontenoy (1745). He became Bishop of Carlisle (1787), Dean of Windsor (1788) and Bishop of Salisbury (1791). He wrote mucha defence of Milton from **William Lauder**'s charge of plagiarism (1750), the famous *Letter on the Criterion of Miracles* (1754) against **David Hume**, ironical attacks on the Hutchinsonians, and political pamphlets.

DOUGLAS, (George) Norman
(1868–1952)

Novelist and essayist, born in Tilquhillie, Deeside. His mother was part-German and he was educated at Uppingham School and at Karlsruhe, and joined the Foreign Office in 1894. He served in St Petersburg before settling in Capri in 1896, where his circle embraced **Compton Mackenzie**, Ouida and D H Lawrence. His first book, *Unprofessional Tales* (1901), was co-authored with his wife and published under the pseudonym 'Normyx'. *Siren Land* (1911) was, however, the book that first attracted critical attention. An account of his travels in southern Italy, it is an exotic collage of anecdote, philosophy and myth. *Old Calabria* (1915) garnished his reputation and is a minor classic. Other travel books are *Fountains in the Sun* (1912), *Alone* (1921) and *Together* (1923). Of his novels, *South Wind* (1917) is the most famous. Set in

Nepenthe (Capri) among a floating population of expatriates, it is an unapologetic celebration of hedonism to which its author was a happy convert. *Looking Back* (1933) is an unusual autobiography, in which he recalls his life and his friends by taking up their calling cards and describing them one by one, at length or tersely, depending on his mood.

DOUGLAS, O, pseudonym of Anna Buchan
(1877–1948)

Novelist, born in Perth, the daughter of a Free Church minister and sister of **John Buchan**. She and John grew up together in Fife, the Borders, and Glasgow, where she was educated at Hutcheson's Grammar School. She lived most of her life at her family's home in Peebles and this setting became the 'Priorsfield' of many of her works. Her fist novel, *Olivia in India* (1913), was written after a holiday in India. Her second, *The Setons* (1917), is set in Glasgow and describes a minister's daughter caring for her widowed father. It observes the middle-class parishioners and confronts the effects of World War I. *Ann and her Mother* (1922), another description of manse life, is roughly autobiographical and set in a slightly earlier time. She published a biography of the Buchan family in 1945 (*Unforgettable, Unforgotten*); her own memoir, *Farewell to Priorsford* (1950), appeared posthumously.

DOUGLAS, Robert
(1594–1674)

Presbyterian minister, chaplain to a Scottish regiment in Swedish service, and minister in Edinburgh from 1641. He was thought to be the grandson of **Mary, Queen of Scots**. He preached at the coronation of Charles II in Scotland in 1651, but after the Restoration, in which he played a significant part, he would not acknowledge episcopacy, he refused the bishopric of Edinburgh, and resigned his charge. He was admitted to a charge in Pencaitland by the Declaration of Indulgence of 1669.

DOUGLAS, Thomas Clement
(1904–86)

Scottish-born Canadian politician, born in Falkirk, Stirlingshire. His family emigrated to Canada in 1910. Educated at Brandon College, Manitoba, he was ordained a Baptist minister in 1930. His first church was in Saskatchewan, where the widespread poverty he witnessed turned him into a Socialist. A co-founder of the Co-operative Commonwealth Federation Party in 1932, he became Prime Minister of Saskatchewan in 1944, the first Socialist prime minister in a Canadian state. He remained in this post until 1961, introducing major social welfare reforms, notably universal hospital insurance. In 1961 he entered national politics as leader of the New Democratic Party, but he never attained office and stood down in 1971, retiring from Ottawa politics in 1979.

DOUGLAS, Sir William Fettes
(1822–91)

Landscape and figure painter, born in Edinburgh. Starting work as an assistant in the Commercial Bank in Edinburgh, after 10 years in this post he turned to painting (1847), becoming a regular exhibitor at the Royal Scottish Academy. His works include *Hudibras and Ralph Visiting the Astrologer*, *The Alchemist* and *David Laing in his Study*. Extremely knowledgeable about art, he was appointed Curator of the National Gallery of Scotland in 1771.

DOUGLAS-HOME, Sir Alexander Frederick See HOME OF THE HIRSEL

DOWDING, Hugh Caswell Tremenheere, 1st Baron
(1882–1970)

Air force chief, born in Moffat. Educated at Winchester and the Royal Military Academy, Woolwich, he joined the Royal Artillery in 1900. He transferred to the Royal Flying Corps in 1914 and was decorated for service in World War I. As Commander-in-Chief of Fighter Command (1936–40), he organized the air defence of Britain; despite the disasters to France in May–June 1940 he stood for the retention of his force at home, and in August – September the German air force was defeated in the momentous Battle of Britain. He was relieved of his post in November 1940 and made representative of the Minister for Aircraft Production in the USA (1940–2) before retiring. He was created a peer in 1943. He was interested in spiritualism, and his *Many Mansions* (1943) included communications attributed to men killed in the war.

DOWIE, John Alexander
(1847–1907)

Scottish-born American religious leader, born in Edinburgh. He emigrated to Australia in 1860 and became a Congregational pastor in Sydney. In 1888 he emigrated to the USA, where he organized the Christian Catholic Church in Zion (1896). Becoming a faith healer, he proclaimed himself 'Elijah the Restorer', and in 1901 he founded near Chicago the prosperous industrial and banking community called 'Zion City'. He was deposed from his autocratic rule there in 1906.

DOYLE, Sir Arthur Conan
(1859–1930)

Writer of detective stories and historical romances, nephew of the caricaturist Richard Doyle. Born of Irish parentage in Edinburgh, he was educated at Stonyhurst and in Germany, and studied medicine at Edinburgh. Initial poverty as a young practitioner in Southsea and as an oculist in London coaxed him into authorship. His début was a story in *Chambers's Journal* (1879), and his first book introduced that prototype of the modern detective in fiction, the super-observant, deductive Sherlock Holmes, his good-natured doctor friend Dr John Watson, and the whole apparatus of detection mythology associated with Baker Street. *The Adventures of Sherlock Holmes* were serialized in the *Strand Magazine* (1891–3). They were so popular that when Conan Doyle, tired of his popular creation, tried to kill off his hero on a cliff, he was compelled in 1903 to revive him. The serials were published as books with the titles *The Sign of Four* (1890), *The Hound of the Baskervilles* (1902), etc. Conan Doyle, however, set greater stock by his historical romances, *Micah Clarke* (1887), *The White Company* (1890), *Brigadier Gerard* (1896) and *Sir Nigel* (1906), which have greater literary merit but are underrated. A keen boxer himself, *Rodney Stone* (1896) is one of his best novels. *The Lost World* (1912) and *The Poison Belt* (1913) are essays into the pseudo-scientifically fantastic. He served as a physician in the 2nd Boer War (1899–1902), and his pamphlet, *The War in South Africa* (1902), correcting enemy propaganda and justifying Britain's action, earned him a knighthood (1902). He used his detective powers to some effect outside fiction in attempting to show that the criminal cases of the Parsee Birmingham lawyer, Edaljee (1903), and alleged murderer **Oscar Slater** (1909) were instances of mistaken identity. He also wrote on spiritualism, to which he became a convert in later life.

DRAWBELL, James Wedgwood
(1899–1979)

Journalist, one of the youngest Fleet Street editors. After a traumatic childhood with an alcoholic father, he left Scotland as a young man and worked as a newspaper reporter in Montreal and New York. When he returned to Britain, his progress was meteoric; he was appointed Editor of the *Sunday Chronicle* at the age of 24. Later, he pioneered the development of *Woman's Own* as a mass-circulation magazine, and achieved mild notoriety by publishing the memoirs of a royal governess ('Crawfie'). His autobiography, *The Sun Within Us*, includes a compelling account of his boyhood in a Falkirk tenement.

DREGHORN, Allan
(1706–64)

Wright, merchant and architect. He was one of the founders of the first Glasgow bank, and held the municipal offices of treasurer (1739) and baillie (1841). With John Craig he designed two major civic buildings, the Town's Hospital (1733, demolished) and the Town Hall, Trongate (c.1738, demolished). His greatest architectural achievement (and only surviving building) is St Andrew's Parish Church (1739–56), a handsome 18th-century hall church in the manner of **James Gibbs'** St Martin's-in-the-Fields, London.

DRESSER, Christopher
(1834–1904)

Scottish-born English designer and writer, born in Glasgow. His first area of study was botany, in which he excelled as a draughtsman, and from which he developed the stylized plant motifs which became the basis for his interest in decorative design. He contributed to Owen Jones's *Grammar of Ornament* (1856) and later wrote *The Art of Decorative Design* (1862) and *The Principles of Decorative Design* (1873). As something of a pioneer consultant designer, he designed glass, ceramics and cast-iron furniture for a number of manufacturers, but his outstanding works were well-researched items of functional metalwork such as teapots and soup tureens. These, in their unadorned, geometric forms, are some of the most strikingly 'modern' designs of the 19th century.

DREVER, James, known as 'Drever Primus'
(1873–1951)

Psychologist, the first holder of a Chair of Psychology in a Scottish university. Born in Orkney, he studied at Edinburgh University and became a schoolteacher. In 1906 he became assistant to the Edinburgh Professor of Education. He was appointed Combe Lecturer in Psychology (1919), and Professor of Psychology (1931–45). Under his leadership, the Department of Psychology at Edinburgh became a notable centre for the study of psychology in all its branches and practical applications. His *The Instinct in Man* (1917) was influential in its day, as were a number of books of a more popular or instructional nature, mostly written in collaboration with Mary Collins (1895–1989), for many years a mainstay of the Edinburgh Psychology Department. His contribution to the development and teaching of psychology was immense, and he is commemorated by the university in the Annual Drever Lecture. His son was **James Drever**, 'Drever Secundus'.

DREVER, James, known as 'Drever Secundus'
(1910 –)

Psychologist, educationist and administrator. Born in Edinburgh, the son of **James Drever**, 'Drever Primus', he studied at the universities of Edinburgh and Cambridge. In 1944 he was appointed to succeed his father as Professor of Psychology at Edinburgh, at which point the two were distinguished as 'Primus' and 'Secundus'. His principal contribution to psychology lay in the study of visual perception. Sought after as a member of committees, he served many organizations, for example, the British Psychological Society, the Social Science Research Council, the International Union for Scientific Psychology, and the influential Robbins Committee on the future of higher education in the UK (1961–3). From 1967 to 1978 he was the first Principal and Vice-Chancellor of the new University of Dundee.

DRUMMOND, Annabella
(c.1350–1402)

Queen of Scotland, born at Stobhill near Perth, the daughter of Sir John Drummond of Stobhill. Beautiful and kindly, in 1367 she married John Stewart, afterwards **Robert III** of Scotland, and was crowned queen in 1390. During Henry IV's invasion of England (1399) she assisted her eldest son David, Duke of Rothsay. He later became regent, but shortly after her death from the plague, he was murdered. Her second son, James, became **James I**.

DRUMMOND, Dugald
(1840–1912)

Locomotive engineer, born in Ardrossan, Ayrshire. The chief mechanical engineer of the London & South Western Railway from 1905, he made his reputation in Scotland in 1876–8 with the 4-4-0 'Abbotsford' class, examples of which were still running in the 1960s. His younger brother Peter (1850–1918), born in Polmont, Stirlingshire, was also a locomotive engineer with the Highland and Glasgow & South Western Railways.

DRUMMOND, Flora
(1869–1949)

Suffragette. Having spent most of her childhood in the Highlands, she trained as a telegraphist. Rotund and very short, she found the position of postmistress denied to her because of her small stature. Already involved in social affairs during her teenage years in Glasgow, she became a Socialist in Manchester, working in a factory and the Ancoats settlement to gain first-hand experience, and joining the Co-operative Movement. She was later a Women's Social and Political Union organizer, earning the sobriquet, 'General Drummond' for her habit of wearing a uniform and leading a Fife and Drum band on marches. A colourful character and an excellent speaker, she once harangued MPs in the House of Commons from a hired launch and was imprisoned nine times. Growing more conservative in later years, she was from 1928 the Commander-in-Chief of the Women's Guild of Empire, an organization which opposed strikes and Communism.

DRUMMOND, George

(1687–1766)

Entrepreneur and philanthropist, born in Perthshire, and known as the founder of the New Town in Edinburgh. An anti-Jacobite Whig, he fought at the Battle of Sheriffmuir (1715) and commanded a company in the 1745 Rising. A skilled accountant, he worked on the accounts for the Union of Parliaments in 1707, and was appointed Accountant-General of Excise. He became a member of Edinburgh town council in 1716, Treasurer in 1717, and was six times Lord Provost of Edinburgh between 1725 and 1764. He was the driving force behind the building of the Royal Infirmary (1738) and the Royal Exchange (1760, now the City Chambers), the expansion of Edinburgh University, and the proposal to create a New Town to the north of Princes Street. He drained the Nor' Loch (1759), and in 1763 laid the foundation stone of the North Bridge.

DRUMMOND, Henry

(1851–97)

Evangelical theologian and biologist, born in Stirling. He studied at Edinburgh, and in 1873 became an evangelical Christian. In 1877 he was appointed lecturer in natural science at the Free Church College, Glasgow (professor, 1884). He travelled in the Rocky Mountains, Central Africa, Japan and Australia, where he made various scientific studies. He attempted to reconcile Christianity and Darwinism in such works as *Natural Law of the Spiritual World* (1883), *The Ascent of Man* (1894) and *Tropical Africa* (1888).

DRUMMOND, Margaret

(c.1472–1502)

Gentlewoman, youngest daughter of Lord Drummond. One of the many mistresses of King **James IV** of Scotland, she enjoyed royal favour in 1496 and bore him a daughter. She and two of her sisters died suddenly after a suspect breakfast.

DRUMMOND, Thomas

(1797–1840)

Engineer and statesman, born in Edinburgh. Educated there and at Woolwich, he entered the Royal Engineers in 1815, and in 1820 joined the ordnance survey, whose work was immensely facilitated by his improved helio-stat and lime-light (the 'Drummond Light'); the latter was also developed at about the same time by Sir Goldsworthy Gurney. He became head of the Boundary Commission under the Reform Bill, and Under-Secretary for Ireland (practically its governor) in 1835. Here he gained the affection of the people; he coined the memorable phrase, 'Property has its duties as well as its rights' (1838).

DRUMMOND, William, of Hawthornden

(1585–1649)

Poet, born in Hawthornden, near Roslin, Midlothian, the son of a courtier to King **James VI and I**. He was educated at the High School of Edinburgh, graduated MA at Edinburgh in 1605, studied law at Bourges and Paris, and on his father's death in 1610 became laird of Hawthornden. Devoting his life to poetry and mechanical experiments, he was on the point of marrying Euphemia Cunningham of Barns when she died on the eve of their wedding (1615). He took a mistress, by whom he had three children, and married Elizabeth Logan of Restalrig in 1630. He had to subscribe to the National Covenant of 1638 but witnessed its triumph with a sinking heart that not even the most sarcastic verses could relieve. His death was hastened by grief for Charles I's execution. He enjoyed the friendship of Ben Jonson who paid him a memorable visit in 1618–19, and Drummond's *Notes* of their talk form a charming chapter of literary history. His chief works are the pastoral lament *Tears on the Death of Moeliades* (ie Prince Henry) (1613); *Poems, Amorous, Funereall, Divine, Pastorall in Sonnets, Songs, Sextains, Madrigals* (1614); *Forth Feasting* (1617); and *Flowers of Sion* (1623). In prose he wrote *A Cypress Grove* (1630) and a *History of the Five Jameses*. He also wrote a *History of Scotland 1423–1524*, posthumously published in 1655.

DRYSDALE, Dan

(1901–86)

Rugby player, a timber merchant by profession, born in Kippen, Stirlingshire. Educated at George Heriot's school, Edinburgh, then at Edinburgh and Oxford Universities, he was one in a long line of Heriot's full-backs to represent Scotland (**Ken Scotland** and **Andy Irvine** being notable others). He made his international début in 1923, and was capped a total of 26 times for his country, being team captain on 11 occasions between 1925 and 1929.

DRYSDALE, Learmont

(1866–1909)

Composer, born in Edinburgh. He abandoned studies in architecture for music. While a student at the Royal Adademy of Music (1888–92) he attracted attention with an overture *Tam O'Shanter* (1890). Subsequent works — a cantata *The Kelpie* (1894), a light opera *The Red Spider* (1898) and *A Border Romance* for orchestra (1904) — evince an energetic and original talent. Another opera, *Fionn and Tera*, remained unperformed. His early death was a particular loss to Scotland since, unlike Sir **Alexander Mackenzie**, **William Wallace** and **Hamish Mac-Cunn**, he had returned to his homeland to pursue his profession in 1904.

DUDGEON, Robert Ellis

(1820–1904)

Homoeopath and inventor, born in Leith, Edinburgh. He was educated privately and at Edinburgh University, and graduated in medicine in 1841. He studied abroad for a period before setting up a practice in Liverpool, where he became interested in homoeopathy. He co-edited the *British Journal of Homoeopathy* from 1846 to 1884, published *The Homoeopathic Treatment and Prevention of Asiatic Cholera* in 1847, and translated the works of Hahnemann, the founder of homoeopathy. He helped found the Homoeopathic Hospital in Bloomsbury, and held office in the British Homoeopathic Society on several occasions. He invented spectacles for underwater use in 1870–1, and in 1878 devised the pocket instrument for measuring pulse rate, which bears his name. His other writings include *The Prolongation of Life* (1890).

DUFF, Alexander

(1806–78)

Missionary, born near Pitlochry. In 1829 he became the first Scottish missionary to India, and in 1830 he opened a college in Calcutta that combined religious teaching with Western science. In 1843, at the time of the Disruption in Scotland, he joined the Free Church, and had to give up his college; but he built another one, and soon his work was on a larger scale than before. In 1844 he helped to start the *Calcutta Review*. He was Moderator of the Free Church Assembly in 1851, and again in 1873. He was one of the founders of the University of Calcutta, but because of persistent ill-health he had to leave India permanently in 1863. He endowed a missionary chair in New College, Edinburgh, of which he was the first occupant.

DUFF, 'Bailie' Jamie

(d.1788)

Eccentric, who achieved prominence in Edinburgh by taking part, without a mount, in a horse race at Leith. A popular character, he was given the title 'Bailie' from his habit of wearing a brass chain around his neck, although this was eventually confiscated following a complaint from a real Bailie about the mockery of his office. Duff's passion for following funerals resulted in the custom of paying for his services as a mourner, and he attended almost every funeral in Edinburgh for 40 years. He refused to accept silver money and his mother had to appoint a purse bearer to accept payment on his behalf. He was very fond of his mother and, when eating out, would invariably put portions of food, both solid and liquid, in his pockets to take home to her.

DUNBAR, Agnes

(c.1312–1369)

Heroine, the Countess of March and Dunbar. Known as Black Agnes due to her swarthy complexion, she was daughter of the Earl of Moray and grand-niece of **Robert Bruce**. In 1320 she married Patrick, Earl of March and Dunbar, who was initially a supporter of the English king, Edward II, but became loyal to the nationalist cause from 1334 after changing sides several times. While Patrick was absent, Dunbar Castle (one of the few important castles remaining in Scottish hands) was besieged by the Earls of Salisbury and Arundel. Agnes not only organized and sustained the defence, but jeered at the attackers during the 19-week siege. The castle nearly fell twice but the English finally withdrew, defeated by her immense courage.

DUNBAR, William

(c.1460 – c.1520)

Poet, probably born in East Lothian. He seems to have studied at St Andrews University from 1475 to 1479. He became a Franciscan novice, and diligently visited every significant town in England. He preached at Canterbury but later left the order. He appears next to have been secretary to some of **James IV**'s numerous embassies to foreign courts. In 1500 he obtained a pension from the king, and the following year visited England, probably with the ambassadors sent to arrange the king's marriage to **Margaret Tudor**, daughter of Henry VII. Early in 1503, before the queen's arrival, he composed in honour of the event his most famous poem, *The Thrissil and the Rois*, perhaps the happiest political allegory in English literature. It now seems that he lived chiefly about court, writing poems and sustaining himself with the vain hope of Church preferment. In 1508 **Walter Chepman** printed seven of his poemsthe earliest specimen of Scottish typography. He visited the north of Scotland in May 1511, in the train of Queen **Margaret**, and his name disappears altogether after the Battle of Flodden (1513). He was certainly dead by 1530. He reached his highest level in his satires, *The Twa Marriit Wemen and the Wedo*, and *The Dance of the Sevin Deadly Synnis*. His *Lament for the Makaris* is a masterpiece of pathos.

DUNBAR-NASMITH, James Duncan
(1927 –)

English-born architect and lecturer, born in Dartmouth, and educated at Cambridge and Edinburgh universities. A leading architect, in the vanguard of conservation movements, he has shared his knowledge and experience widely and held the presidencies of both the Edinburgh Architectural Association and the Royal Incorporation of Architects in Scotland. An associate of RIBA since 1954, in 1957 he was founding partner of the Law and Dunbar-Nasmith Partnership, with Graham Law. He designed the acclaimed Exbury, from offices in Edinburgh and Forres. He designed the discreet house in the walled garden at Leuchie (1962) and, for the Rothschilds, Upper Exbury, Hampshire (1964–5), subsequently subdividing Exbury House for them (1987). He produced the designs for Sunninghill, Berkshire (1987), for the Duke and Duchess of York. Restoration projects by the firm include work at St Machar's Cathedral, Aberdeen (1982) and the refurbishment of the Empire Theatre, Edinburgh (1991).

DUNCAN, Adam, Viscount
(1731–1804)

Naval commander, born in Dundee. He entered the navy in 1746, and commanded the *Valiant* in the sack of Havana (1762). He commanded the *Monarch* at Cape St Vincent (1780), and as admiral took command in 1795 of the North Sea Squadron to watch the Dutch fleet (Holland and France being at war with Britain). His blockade of the Texel was effective, and Dutch trade was almost ruined. In the spring of 1797 the mutiny of the Nore spread to Duncan's seamen, and his position was for some weeks critical. In the autumn he gained a brilliant victory over Ian De Winter, the Dutch admiral, at Camperdown.

DUNCAN, Andrew
(1744–1828)

Physician, born in Pinkerton, St Andrews. Educated at St Andrews and Edinburgh universities, he was admitted to the Royal College of Physicians in Edinburgh in 1770. He went on to become an eminent professor of medicine, but is particularly remembered for two important contributions to public health in the city. In 1776 he began to give public lectures on health, and set up a dispensary for medicines in Richmond Street, which later became the Royal Public Dispensary (1818). In 1782 he proposed the establishment of a public lunatic asylum in the city, an idea prompted by the squalid death of the poet **Robert Fergusson** in a pauper's asylum in 1774. The project was eventually granted a Royal Charter in 1807, and Craighouse Asylum was built in Morningside. He was granted the freedom of the city in 1808 in recognition of his services.

DUNCAN, Archibald Sutherland
(1914 –)

Obstetrician and gynaecologist, born in Darjeeling, India, and educated at Merchiston Castle School, Edinburgh and Edinburgh University, where he graduated in 1936. He served in World War II as a surgeon lieutenant-commander and received the Distinguished Service Cross. After appointments in Aberdeen and Edinburgh as a consultant obstetrician and gynaecologist he became Professor of Obstetrics and Gynaecology at the Welsh National School of Medicine in 1953. From 1966 to 1976 he was Professor of Medical Education at Edinburgh, the first such appointment in Europe. As Executive

Dean of the Faculty of Medicine at Edinburgh in the same period, he was involved in the relationship between the medical faculty, the university and the National Health Service and he introduced a more project- and elective-orientated curriculum. He also introduced quality assurance and medical audit to meet the growing demand for evaluation. Associate editor of the *British Journal of Medical Education* (1971–5), he was also an important contributor to the field of medical ethics. He became Vice President of the Institute of Medical Ethics in 1985 and was Consultant Editor of the *Journal of Medical Ethics* 1975–81.

DUNCAN, Henry

(1774–1846)

Clergyman and founder of savings banks, born in Lochrutton. From 1799 he was minister of Ruthwell, Dumfriesshire, where he restored the 7th-century runic cross now in Ruthwell Kirk. He imported grain from England during a shortage, and in 1810 he established at Ruthwell the first savings bank. A man of wide interests, he brought to general attention the footprints of quadrupeds preserved in sandstone at Corncockle Muir, near Dumfries, and in 1809 he founded the *Dumfries and Galloway Courier*. At the time of the Disruption in 1843 he joined the Free Church.

DUNCAN, Jane, pseudonym Janet Sandison, originally Elizabeth Jane Cameron

(1910–76)

Novelist, born in Renton, Dunbartonshire. She was educated at Lenzie Academy and Glasgow University, and during World War II served in Air Intelligence. She moved to Jamaica to join her husband in 1948, where she wrote seven novels and lived until his death (1958), when she returned to Scotland to live on the Cromarty Firth. Her books fall mainly into two distinct series. The first is the *Reachfar Series*, beginning with *My Friend Muriel* (1959) and continuing to the autobiographical *Letter from Reachfar* (1974), each known for its descriptions of life in the Black Isle. The other grouping, the *Jean Robertson Quartette*, was written between 1969 and 1975 under the pseudonym Janet Sandison and is the story of a Lowland girl's rise from poverty to wealth. The central character of the *Reachfar Series* is called Janet Sandison and her experiences, including a Caribbean background in the later novels, roughly follow Jane Duncan's own.

DUNCAN, Sir Patrick

(1870–1943)

Scottish-born South African statesman, born in Fortrie, Banffshire. The son of a tenant farmer, he excelled in the local school, won a scholarship to George Watson's College in Edinburgh, and went on to Edinburgh University and Balliol College, Oxford. He became the Colonial Treasurer of the Transvaal in 1901, and Colonial Secretary in 1903, and played a crucial part in the re-establishment of civil government in the wake of the South African War. He was elected to the South African Parliament as a pro-Unionist candidate for the Progressive Party in 1910, and served there for all but one year until 1926. While strongly in favour of the domination of European influence in South Africa, he argued against segregation of the races, which would deny the native population the benefits of European culture. Despite ideological differences, he served under Herzog after the amalgamation of Progressive and Nationalist parties into the Union Party in 1933. He was appointed Governor-General of South Africa in 1937, and supported participation in World War II. The newly completed Duncan Dock in Cape Town was named in his honour.

DUNCAN, Thomas

(1807–45)

Painter, born in Kinclaven, Perthshire. He is best known for historical and genre works, many with a Jacobite flavour, such as *Prince Charles's Entry into Edinburgh after Prestonpans*, and *Charles Edward Asleep after Culloden*. He taught at the Trustees' Academy for a time, becoming head the year before his death.

DUNDAS, of Arniston

A family distinguished for their legal and political talent. Sir James Dundas, the first of Arniston, was knighted by **James VI and I**, and was Governor of Berwick. His son, Sir James (d.1679), was a judge of the Court of Session under the title of Lord Arniston (1662), but was deprived of his office in 1663 for refusing to abjure the Covenant. His eldest son, Sir Robert, was also a judge of the Court of Session, 1689–1726. The latter's son, Robert, was Solicitor-General for Scotland (1717), Lord Advocate (1720), and Lord President of the Court of Session (1748–53). His son, also Robert, was Solicitor-General for Scotland (1742), Lord Advocate (1754), and Lord President of the Court of Session (1760–87).

DUNDAS, Sir David
(1735–1820)

Soldier, born in Edinburgh and educated at the Royal Military Academy, Woolwich. After serving with General **Roy** in the military survey of Scotland he joined the Royal Artillery in 1756 and saw service with Prince Frederick of Brunswick during the Seven Years' War. A noted tactician, he visited Prussia in 1764 to study Frederick the Great's military theories and to gather material for his study *The Principles of Military Movements* (1788). The publication of this book made Dundas's reputation: in 1789 he was promoted adjutant-general in Ireland and the following year he became a major-general. As quartermaster-general under the Duke of York he wrote the Rules and Regulations for infantry and cavalry which formed the basis for military discipline throughout the Napoleonic wars. Between 1809 and 1811 he served as Commander-in-Chief of the British army.

DUNDAS, Henry, 1st Viscount Melville and Baron Dunira
(1742–1811)

Lawyer and statesman, son of **Robert Dundas, Lord Arniston** (1685–1753). Admitted to the Bar in 1763, his assiduity, ability and family influence soon gained him promotion, and he was successively Advocate-Depute and Solicitor-General. In 1774 he became MP for Midlothian, in 1775 Lord Advocate, and in 1777 Keeper of the Signet for Scotland. His career in Parliament was highly successful, although it earned him a reputation for inconsistency. Elected in opposition to the ministry, he soon became a strenuous supporter of Lord North, and one of the most obstinate defenders of the war with America. When North resigned in 1781, Dundas continued as Lord Advocate under Lord Rockingham. On the formation of the coalition he passed over to William Pitt, and became his ablest coadjutor. When Pitt returned to power in 1784, Dundas was appointed President of the Board of Control, and he introduced a bill for restoring the Scottish estates forfeited after the 1745 Jacobite rebellion. Secretary of State for the Home Department (1791), he also held a number of other offices, and many of the most important public measures originated with or were

promoted by him. He resigned with Pitt in 1801, and in 1802, under the Addington administration, was made Viscount Melville and Baron Dunira. For 30 years he was the effective ruler of Scotland. In 1805 he was impeached for 'gross malversation and breach of duty' as Treasurer of the navy. There was a fortnight's trial before his peers acquitted him on all charges involving his honour. Thereafter he lived mostly at Dunira, his seat near Comrie, Perthshire.

DUNDAS, Robert, Lord Arniston
(1685–1753)

Son of a Scottish judge, Sir Robert Dundas (Lord Arniston, 1689–1720). In 1717 he became Solicitor-General, in 1720 Lord Advocate, and as MP for Midlothian from 1722 distinguished himself by his attention to Scottish affairs. After Sir Robert Walpole came into power in 1725, Dundas resigned his office, when he was elected Dean of the Faculty of Advocates. In 1737 he was raised to the bench, as Lord Arniston. He became Lord President of the Court of Session in 1748.

DUNDAS, Robert, Lord Arniston
(1713–87)

Judge, son of **Robert Dundas**. He was admitted to the Bar in 1738, and rose to be Lord Advocate (1754) and Lord President of the Court of Session (1760–87).

DUNDEE, John Graham of Claverhouse, 1st Viscount
(c.1649–1689)

Soldier, known as 'Bonny Dundee' or 'Bloody Claverse'. He studied at St Andrews University, and then served in both the French and Dutch armies as a professional soldier. In 1674 at the Battle of Seneff he is said to have saved the life of William of Orange. In 1677 he returned to Scotland, and became lieutenant in a troop of horse commanded by his kinsman, the Marquis of **Montrose**, against the Covenanters. At Drumclog (1679) he was routed by an armed body of Covenanters, but three weeks later he commanded the cavalry at Bothwell Brig, where the Covenanters were defeated. From 1682 to 1685 he was active in hunting down Covenanters in the south-west of Scotland. When William III landed in England in 1688 at the start of the 'Glorious Revolution', Dundee marched into England in support of **James VII and II**, and was created Viscount

Dundee. He was allowed to withdraw unscathed by William, and in Scotland, after leaving the Convention of 1689, he raised an army in the Highlands. He defeated the Loyalist forces in a fierce encounter at Killiecrankie (July 1689), but was mortally wounded in the hour of victory, and was buried in the church at Old Blair.

DUNDONALD, Earl of See
COCHRANE, Thomas

DUNEDIN, Andrew Graham Murray, Viscount, of Stenton
(1849–1942)

Statesman and judge, born in Edinburgh. Educated at Harrow and Trinity College, Cambridge, he became an MP and successively Solicitor-General for Scotland (1891–2 and 1895–6), Lord Advocate (1896–1903) and Secretary for Scotland (1903–5), before becoming Lord Justice-General of Scotland and Lord President of the Court of Session (1905–13) and then a Lord of Appeal in Ordinary (1913–32). A highly skilled lawyer with a great grasp of principle, particularly in feudal land law, he was an excellent expositor and a very distinguished judge.

DUNITZ, Jack David
(1923 –)

Organic chemist. Born in Glasgow, he went on from Glasgow University to research fellowships at Oxford and at the California Institute of Technology. From 1957 to 1990 he was Professor of Chemical Crystallography at the Swiss Federal Institute, Zürich, and he has also taught in many other parts of the world, including Israel and Japan. His detailed X-ray crystallographic and theoretical studies of molecular structures have revealed important aspects of their shape (stereochemistry), flexibility (conformation) and reactivity. He is the author of *X-Ray Analysis and the Structure of Chemical Bonds* (1979).

DUNLOP, Sir Derrick Melville
(1902–80)

Consultant physician, born in Edinburgh and educated at Oxford and Edinburgh universities. After a spell in general practice in London he returned to Edinburgh as a research worker under the guidance of Sir **Robert Philip**. In 1936 he became Professor of Therapeutics at Edinburgh and consultant at the Royal Infirmary, beginning his work in

this field just as the new chemotherapy was starting and his career covered the period of therapeutic revolution in medicine. Famous as a clinician and teacher, he had both style and erudition. He was Chairman of the British Pharmacopoeia Commission (1948–58), and a prime mover in the creation of the Committee on the Safety of Drugs (1964–9), known as the Dunlop Committee, which put in place a voluntary reporting system from the medical profession regarding the side effects of drugs. The author of articles and books on a wide range of subjects, he was an exceptional physician, and a great orator. He was knighted in 1960.

DUNLOP, John Boyd
(1840–1921)

Inventor, born in Dreghorn, Ayrshire, and generally credited with inventing the pneumatic tyre. He became a veterinary surgeon in Edinburgh and then Belfast from 1867; in 1887 he fitted the wheels of his child's tricycle with inflated rubber hoses instead of solid rubber tyres. The principle had already been patented, in 1845, by a Scottish engineer, **Robert William Thomson**, but in 1889 Dunlop formed a business that became the Dunlop Rubber Company Ltd, produced commercially practical pneumatic tyres for bicycles and, subsequently, for motor cars.

DUNN, Douglas Eaglesham
(1942 –)

Poet, born in Inchinnan, Renfrewshire. He was educated at Renfrew High and Camphill schools, Paisley, before attending the Scottish School of Librarianship and Hull University, where he was employed in the library simultaneously with Philip Larkin, who became a friend and mentor. His first collecton of poems, *Terry Street* (1969), articulates contempt and warmth in almost equal measure for the working-class suburb of Hull where he was then living. The two subsequent collections — *The Happier Life* (1972) and *Love or Nothing* (1974) — rather disappointed readers who had been drawn to *Terry Street* by its bleak humour and tacky glamour. In *Barbarians* (1979), however, he echoed and extended that first collection, and has subsequently demonstrated that he is one of Scotland's finest contemporary poets, technically accomplished and artistically ambitious. *Elegies* (1985), his sixth collection, is his best-known. Written on the death of his first wife, it is a moving valediction, emotionally raw but tightly controlled. It won the Whitbread Prize. *Secret Villages*, a collection of stories, was published in 1985, and his *Selected Poems: 1964–1983* in 1986.

DUNNETT, Alastair MacTavish
(1908–)

Journalist, born in Kilmacolm, Ayrshire. He was educated at Hillhead High School, Glasgow, and joined the head office of the Commercial Bank of Scotland at the age of 17. He gave up his secure job to publish a magazine for Scottish boys, and though short-lived, this venture launched him on his journalistic career. He was chief press officer to the Secretary of State for Scotland (1940–6) and Editor of the *Daily Record* (1946–55) before becoming editor of *The Scotsman* from 1956 to 1972, thereafter serving as Chairman of Thomson Scottish Petroleum. Intensely committed to his native country, he served with distinction on the boards of several national bodies. His wife is the novelist **Dorothy Dunnett**.

DUNNETT, Dorothy, née Halliday
(1923 –)

Novelist, born in Dunfermline and educated at James Gillespie's High School for Girls in Edinburgh. She began her career with the Civil Service as a Press Secretary in Edinburgh, and in 1946 married **Alastair Dunnett**. A recognized portrait painter since 1950, she has exhibited at the Royal Academy and is a member of Scottish Society of Women Artists. She has used her maiden name for a series of detective novels but her best-known works comprise a series of six historical novels. Featuring the fictional Scottish mercenary Francis Crawford of Lymond, these novels continue the Scottish tradition of historical romance. She became a director of the Edinburgh Book Festival in 1990.

DUNROSSIL, William Shepherd Morrison, 1st Viscount
(1893–1961)

Conservative politician, born at Torinturk, Argyll, and a fluent Gaelic speaker. Educated at George Watson's College, Edinburgh, and Edinburgh University, he became a barrister of the Inner Temple. He was MP for Cirencester and Tewkesbury (1924–59), and from 1932 to 1936 was Chairman of the 1922 backbenchers committee. He became successively Minister for Agriculture (1936–9), for Food (1939–40), Postmaster General (1940–43) and Minister for Town and Country Planning (1943–5). Despite his high prewar reputation as an able minister, he never held office again. He became Speaker of the Commons from 1951 to 1959, the first Scot in this position for 120 years. A great friend of Sir Robert Menzies, he took up the governor-generalship of Australia in 1959, and died in office.

DUNS SCOTUS, John
(c.1265–1308)

Scholastic philosopher who rivalled Aquinas as the greatest theologian of the middle ages but whose brief life is scantily documented. He was probably from Duns, Berwickshire. He became a Franciscan and was ordained priest in St Andrews Church, Northampton, in 1291. He studied and taught at Oxford and Paris, probably also in Cambridge, and finally at Cologne where he died and was buried. His writings were mainly commentaries on the Bible, Aristotle and the *Sentences* of Peter Lombard, and were left in various stages of completion at his death. His associates collected and edited them (not always very responsibly), and the main works in the canon are now taken to be the *Opus Pariense* (the Parisian Lectures, as recorded by a student), the *Opus Oxiense* (the Oxford lectures, also known as the *Ordinatio*, and probably revised by the author), the *Tractatus de Primo Principio* and the *Quaestiones Quodlibetales*. His philosophy represents a strong reaction against both Aristotle and Aquinas. He propounded the primacy of the individual (in the dispute about universals) and the freedom of the individual will. He saw faith as the necessary foundation of Christian theology, but faith was for him exercised through an act of will and was practical, not speculative or theoretical. The Franciscans followed Scotus as the Dominicans did Thomas Aquinas; he was known by his contemporaries as *Doctor Subtilis* on account of the refinement and penetration of his criticisms of Thomism, but in the Renaissance the Scotists were dubbed 'Dunses' (hence 'dunce') for their obstinacy and conservatism. More recently, however, he has been admired by figures as diverse as C S Peirce, Martin Heidegger and Gerard Manley Hopkins, who found him 'of realty the rarest veinèd unraveller'.

DURIE, Sir Alexander Gibson, Lord
(d.1644)

Judge. He began his career as a Clerk of Session but was appointed a judge in 1621 and was twice elected President of the College

133

of Justice (1642 and 1643). He married a daughter of Sir **Thomas Craig**. During his years as a judge he recorded the more important decisions of the court. These were published in 1690, forming the earliest published collection of decisions of the Court of Session. Described as a man of penetrating wit and clear judgement, polished and improved by a combination of scholarly application and exercise, he is reputed to have been constantly studying the civil law of Rome. He is said to have been kidnapped by a litigant, who considered that Durie was unfavourable to his cause, and was not released until the case had been decided. His son, of the same name, became Clerk Register and in 1646 a judge, again as Lord Durie.

DYCE, Alexander
(1798–1869)

Scholar, born in Edinburgh and educated there and at Oxford. He edited George Peele (1828–39), John Webster (1830), Robert Greene (1831), James Shirley (1833), Thomas Middleton (1840), Francis Beaumont and John Fletcher (1843–6), Marlowe (1850), Shakespeare (1857) and others, as well as writing *Recollections of the Table-Talk of Samuel Rogers* (1856). On his death his library was bequeathed to the Victoria and Albert Museum in London.

DYCE, William
(1806–64)

Historical and religious painter, born in Aberdeen. At first intending to enter the Church, he turned to art, going to study at the Royal Academy in London. In 1825 he went to Rome, where he developed sympathies with the Nazarenes, which he transmitted to the Pre-Raphaelites. From 1844 Professor of Fine Arts at King's College, London, he executed frescoes in the new House of Lords, Osborne House, Buckingham Palace, and All Saints', Margaret Street.

E

EADIE, John
(1810–76)

Theologian and scholar, born in Alva, Clackmannanshire. Educated at Glasgow University, he became Professor of Biblical Literature at the United Secession Divinity Hall, Glasgow (1843–76). A prolific scholar, his works include a *Biblical Cyclopaedia* (1848), *Ecclesiastical Encyclopaedia* (1861), a number of commentaries, and a critical history of *The English Bible* (1876).

EARDLEY, Joan
(1921–63)

English-born painter, born in Warnham, Sussex. She began her studies at Goldsmith's College of Art, London (1938), but moved to Glasgow where she enrolled at the School of Art in 1940. After the war she studied at Hospitalfield, Arbroath, and at Glasgow School of Art, winning various prizes and travelling to France and Italy on a Carnegie bursary. Greatly influenced by Van Gogh, both technically and in terms of her choice of subjects, in 1949 she took a studio in Cochrane Street, Glasgow, and began to paint poor children of the nearby tenements. In 1950 she first visited Catterline, the tiny fishing village on the north-east coast of Scotland which inspired her finest landscapes and seascapes. Here she lived and worked until her death.

EASTON, Sheena, real name Sheena Orr
(1959 –)

Pop singer, born in Glasgow. A former drama student, her pop career received a considerable boost when she was the subject of a BBC documentary, *Big Time*, which showed how record company EMI went about 'manufacturing' a pop star. The single '9 to 5', released after the programme was aired, gave Easton her first top-ten hit. She had several UK hits, including the theme to the James Bond movie *For Your Eyes Only* (1981),

before moving to the USA. Since then almost all of her success has been in America, where she has worked with artists ranging from Country and Western singer Kenny Rogers to Prince.

ECKFORD, Harry
(1775–1832)

Scottish-born American naval architect, born in Irvine, Dumfriesshire. He went out to Quebec in 1790 and New York in 1796, and from 1800 built up a reputation for strong and speedy sailing ships. He built the famous early steamship *Robert Fulton* (1822).

EDNIE, John
(1876–1934)

Architect/designer, amateur painter and exponent of the Glasgow Style of Art Nouveau, born in Glasgow, the son of a railway engineer. After attending Heriot-Watt College he was apprenticed to the Edinburgh interior-decorating firm of Scott Morton and the architect John Kinross. On returning to Glasgow he worked for the furnishing firm of Wylie and Lochhead and designed their pavilion for the 1901 Glasgow International Exhibition, which was also shown at Budapest the following year. In 1906 he became Director of the Industrial Art Section of the Glasgow and West of Scotland Technical College, later becoming Principal of the Decorative Arts Trades School. His freelance work included designs for furniture, stained glass and decorative schemes for houses and commercial premises all over Scotland. He became a member of the Scottish Guild of Handicrafts and the Edinburgh Architectural Association, and exhibited at the Royal Glasgow Institute and the Royal Academy. In 1928 he moved to Egypt to become Principal of the School of Art in Cairo.

EDWARD, David Alexander Ogilvy
(1934 –)

Judge, born in Perth. Educated at Oxford and Edinburgh, he passed advocate in 1692. He held offices in the Faculty of Advocates, became QC in 1974 and in 1979–80 President of the Consultative Committee of the Bars and Law Societies of the European Communities, being awarded the CMG in 1981. From 1985 to 1989 he was Salvesen Professor of European Institutions at Edinburgh University. He became British Judge of the Court of the First Instance of the European Communities in 1989, and in 1992 was promoted to British Judge of the Court of Justice of the European Communities. Throughout his career he has strengthened the international connections of Scots Law.

ELCHIES, Patrick Grant, Lord
(1690–1754)

Judge, son of the laird of Easter Elchies, born in Craigellachie, Banffshire. He passed advocate in 1712 and developed a good practice at the Bar. In 1732 he was promoted to the bench and in 1737 made a Lord of Justicary also, in which capacity he was said to be upright but harsh and overbearing. He is reputed to have had a strong grasp of legal principles, acute reasoning powers and an intuitive perception of the correct principle to apply. He made a large collection of the decisions of the Court of Session from 1733 to 1754 under alphabetical headings, which was printed by W M Morison as a branch of the Second Appendix of his *Dictionary of Decisions* (1804–15), together with Elchies' own notes, from which he had prepared the reports, and which are sometimes more valuable than the reports themselves. To him also is attributed a volume of notes on **James Stair**'s *Institutions*, published in 1824.

ELDER, John
(1824–69)

Marine engineer and shipbuilder, born in Glasgow, the third son of David Elder, a manager in the Napiers' shipbuilding firm. He was educated at the High School and university in Glasgow, served his apprenticeship with Napiers, and then after some experience in the south returned in about 1848 to take charge of Napiers' drawing office. In 1852 he formed with Charles Randolph (1809–78) the firm of Randolph, Elder and Company (later the Fairfield Shipbuilding and Engineering Company), and within a few years introduced the marine compound steam engine which achieved economies in fuel consumption of 30–40 per cent, and reigned supreme on the seas until it was superseded by the triple-expansion engines of **A C Kirk** in the 1880s.

ELDER, Sir Thomas
(1818–97)

Scottish-born Australian pastoralist and entrepreneur, born in Kirkcaldy. He emigrated to Adelaide, South Australia, in 1854, where he joined his brother, Alexander, in the firm of Elder and Co. They financed copper mines in South Australia. With the proceeds and in partnership with **Robert Barr Smith**, who later married Thomas's sister Joanna, Thomas founded the firm of Elder, Smith & Co in 1863. This grew into one of the world's largest wool-broking firms, which built up extensive pastoral holdings to source the supply of wool, stretching into Western Australia and Queensland. He brought in camels to provide efficient transport in the outback, and Afghans to manage them. His stud of camels was invaluable, especially for some of the early expeditions into the 'centre' made by Warburton, Ross, Giles and Lewis, all of whose expeditions were financed by Elder. He was appointed GCMG in 1887. The company which he helped establish is perpetuated in the international brewing and resources group Elders IXL.

ELGIN, Earls of Peers of the Bruce family.

ELGIN, James Bruce, 8th Earl of Elgin and 12th Earl of Kincardine
(1811–63)

Son of the 7th Earl of Elgin, born in London. As Governor of Jamaica (1842–6) and as Governor-General of Canada (1847–54) he displayed great administrative abilities. While on his way to China in 1857, as plenipotentiary, he heard at Singapore of the Indian mutiny, and diverted the Chinese expedition therethus delaying his own mission which, after some military operations and diplomacy, issued in the Treaty of Tientsin (1858). He also negotiated a treaty with Japan, and on his return home became Postmaster-General. In 1860 he was again in China to enforce the treaty, and in 1861 he became Governor-General of India.

ELGIN, Victor Alexander Bruce, 9th Earl of Elgin and 13th Earl of Kincardine
(1849–1917)

Politician. Born in Montreal (his father was Governor-General of Canada), he was educated at Eton and Oxford University. He was Chairman of the Scottish Liberal Association in the mid 1880s. As Viceroy of India (1894–7) he faced many difficulties, including unrest in the border areas and rising nationalist feeling against Imperial economic and commercial policies. The situation worsened in 1897 when a serious famine broke out, accompanied by the appearance of the bubonic plague in the Bombay region. On his return to Britain he chaired a committee on the lessons of the Boer War, which resulted in the formation of the Territorial Army. He was colonial secretary from 1905 to 1908.

ELLIOT, Jean or Jane
(1727–1805)

Lyricist, the author of 'The Flowers of the Forest', and daughter of Sir Gilbert Elliot of Minto House, Teviotdale. She lived in Edinburgh (1756–1804), but died at the family seat, or at Monteviot. Her eldest brother, Sir Gilbert Elliot (1722–77), was himself a songwriter, whilst John (d.1808), the third brother, was a distinguished admiral.

ELLIOT, Walter
(1888–1958)

Conservative politician. He was MP for Lanark (1918–23), Kelvingrove (1924–45) and Scottish Universities (1946–9), and Secretary of State for Scotland (1936–8) and Minister of Health (1938–40). Also known as a writer and broadcaster, he published *Toryism and the Twentieth Century* (1927). His wife, Baroness Katharine Elliot of Harwood (1903 –), was created Scotland's first life peeress in October 1958.

ELLIOTT, Grace Dalrymple
(c.1758–1823)

Courtesan, the daughter of an Edinburgh advocate, Hew Dalrymple. In 1771 she married Sir John Elliott, MD (1736–86), who divorced her in 1774. She was the mistress successively or simultaneously of Lord Valentia, Lord Cholmondley, the Prince of Wales (the future George IV), Charles Windham, George Selwyn, Philippe Égalité (Duke of Orléans), and many others. She died at Ville d'Avray near Sèvres, leaving an interesting but untrustworthy *Journal of My Life During the Revolution*, published in 1859 by her granddaughter.

ELLIOTT, Kenneth
(1929 –)

Musical scholar, editor and musician, born in Dundee. He studied music at St Andrews University with **Cedric Thorpe Davie**, and at Cambridge with **Robin Orr** and Thurston Dart. A notable authority on early Scottish music, his works include *Music of Scotland 1500–1700* (Musica Britannica Vol XV), collections and anthologies of keyboard music, Renaissance airs, dances and songs from the 16th to 18th centuries. As a harpsichordist and continuo player he has performed and recorded much of this repertoire.

ELLIS, Walter Scott
(c.1932 –)

Convicted thief. He first came to public attention when he was tried, and acquitted, in October 1961 for the murder of John Walkenshaw, a Glasgow taxi-driver. The evidence against Ellis included glass splinters in his shoe, which were thought to have been planted there. Ellis had taken a taxi home that night, but via a route that did not include the location of the murder. Fingerprints were discovered in the taxi which were not Ellis's. He was found not guilty. Taxi-drivers jeered outside the courtroom. In the mid 1960s he was charged with and convicted of housebreaking. A subsequent charge in 1965 of writing threatening letters to the procurator fiscal who was in attendance at the housebreaking trial led to a verdict of not guilty. In July 1966 Ellis was charged with armed bank robbery. After a long trial, he was found guilty and was sentenced to 21 years' imprisonment. In total, 19 convictions preceded this last one.

ELPHINSTONE, George Keith, Viscount Keith
(1746–1823)

Naval officer, born in Elphinstone Tower, Stirling. He entered the navy in 1761 and fought in the American War of Indpendence (1775–83). In the French revolutionary wars (1792–1800) he helped to capture Toulon. Promoted rear admiral, he commanded the expedition that captured Cape Town (1795) and Ceylon (1796). He helped to quell the Nore mutiny in 1797, and took Malta and Genoa (1800). He landed **Abercromby**'s army at Aboukir Bay (1801). As Commander of the Channel fleet (1812–15) he arranged Napoleon's transfer to St Helena.

ELPHINSTONE, Sir Keith
(1864–1944)

Electrical engineer, born in Musselburgh, East Lothian. He was educated at Charterhouse, after which he entered the firm of M Theiler & Sons, for whom he installed some of the earliest private electric light and telephone systems in London. In 1893 he left to become a partner in Elliott Brothers, electrical and mechanical engineers of Lewisham in south London, eventually becoming Chairman of the Board. They were the first British firm to make micrometers, and for them he designed the first continuous-roll strip chart recorder. He designed and installed the original speed recording system at the Brooklands motor racing track which opened in 1907, and he also devised a speedometer for the ordinary motorist. During and after World War I he worked on the development of fire-control equipment for ships of the Royal Navy.

ELPHINSTONE, Mountstuart
(1779–1859)

Colonial administrator and historian, 11th Lord Elphinstone. He entered the Bengal civil service in 1795, served with distinction on Wellesley's staff (1803) at the Battle of Assaye, and was appointed resident at Nagpur. In 1808 he was sent as the first British envoy to Kabul; and as resident from 1810 at Poona he both ended the Mahratta war of 1817 and organized the newly acquired territory. He was Governor-General of Bombay (1819–27), where he founded the system of administration, and did much to advance state education in India. He returned to Britain in 1829 and, declining the governor-generalship of India, lived in comparative retirement until his death. He wrote a *History of India* (1841) and an incomplete *Rise of British Power in the East* (published in 1887).

ELPHINSTONE, William
(1431–1514)

Churchman and statesman, born in Glasgow, the illegitimate son of a canon. Ordained a priest, he spent five years in France, and lectured on law at Paris and Orléans. Returning to Scotland, he was appointed Bishop of Ross (1481) and of Aberdeen (1488). For four months before the death of **James III** (1488) he was Chancellor of Scotland. Under **James IV** he was Am-

bassador to France (1491), and Keeper of the Privy Seal from 1492. It was chiefly through his influence that the first printing pressthat of **Walter Chepman** and Andrew Myllarwas established in Scotland. In 1494, after applying to Pope Alexander VI for the requisite bull, he founded the University of Aberdeen (King's College), described by the historian James Scotland as 'the most efficient University foundation in Scotland before the Reformation'. Unlike St Andrews and Glasgow it comprised four faculties — arts, theology, medicine and law, and as an additional benefit provided tuition in Latin for all arts students (since lectures were given in that language). Elphinstone's influence on education in Scotland was considerable, and he is thought to have been the driving force behind the Education Act of 1494. He was also responsible for additions to the cathedral in Aberdeen and a stone bridge over the Dee. The disastrous Battle of Flodden (1513) is said to have broken his heart and, shortly after his appointment as Archbishop of St Andrews the following year, he died. His *Breviarium Aberdonense* was printed by Chepman and Myllar in 1509–10.

ELRICK, George
(1910 –)

Popular singer, band leader and disc-jockey, born in Aberdeen. He began broadcasting with Henry Hall and his BBC Dance Orchestra (1935), first as a drummer, then adding vocals, achieving national fame with his rendition of 'The Music Goes Round and Around'. On the basis of this success he formed his own band, George Elrick and his Goofy Swing (1937), and toured variety halls with great success. Becoming a recording star (with, for example, 'I'm Just Nuts About Goofy Music') and songwriter, he toured with his own show, *When You're Smiling*. He started a second career as a disc-jockey compèring the BBC's *Housewife's Choice* series, his trademark being to sing along with the signature tune. He was elected King Rat by the Grand Order of Water Rats in 1954 and 1973.

ERIKSON, Gunn
(1956 –)

Norwegian-born chef and restaurateur, born in Grimstad. An artist by training, she went to Ullapool to pursue her craft and there met Fred Brown, owner of the Altnaharrie Inn across Loch Broom from Ullapool. She joined him there in 1980 and began to develop the distinctive cooking style which has brought her renown. With no formal culinary training, she combines unusual hedgerow ingredients (nettles, sorrel, hawthorn sprouts) with local seafood and imported ingredients to make memorable meals which reveal her Scandinavian origins. Given the hotel's somewhat isolated location (practical access only by boat), the willingness of visitors to seek out its cooking makes its own point.

ERSKINE, David Stewart, 11th Earl of Buchan
(1742–1819)

Nobleman, brother of **Henry Erskine** and **Thomas Erskine**. A noted antiquarian, if considered somewhat eccentric and vain, he founded the Society of Antiquaries of Scotland and brought about a reform in the election of Scottish peers. He published various essays and literary biographies. In 1792 he presented George Washington with a snuff box made from the tree under which **Robert Wallace** had reputedly sheltered.

ERSKINE, Ebenezer
(1680–1754)

Clergyman, born in Chirnside, Berwickshire, the son of the minister there, and brother of **Ralph Erskine**. The founder of the Secession Church in Scotland in 1733, he was minister of Portmoak in Kinross-shire from 1703 to 1711, and then of Stirling. He took the Evangelical side in the rise of the Marrow Controversy in 1718 (over the place of Grace as opposed to Works). In the patronage dispute of 1733 he advocated the right of the people to choose their own pastors, and together with three other ministers he was suspended and then deposed. The sentence was revoked in the following year, but Erskine declined to return unless the evils he had contended against were removed. The invitation remained open until 1740, when he was finally deposed. Meanwhile, in 1733 he and the other three ministers formed an Associate Presbytery, setting up the Secession Church of Marrowkirk. In the divisions of 1747 (Seceders into Burghers and Antiburgers), Erskine headed the Burghers.

ERSKINE, Henry
(1746–1817)

Jurist and writer, born in Edinburgh, brother of **David Stewart Erskine** and **Thomas Erskine**. He joined the Bar in 1768, became Lord Advocate (1783), and Dean of the Faculty of Advocates (1785), but was deposed in 1796 for supporting a resolution against the government's Seditious Writings Bill at a public meeting. Returned by the Haddington burghs in March 1806, and in November by the Dumfries burghs, he was again Lord Advocate (1806–7). He published metrical translations from the classics, *The Emigrant* (1773), etc. The recorded fragments of his speeches justify his strong reputation as an orator and a wit.

ERSKINE, John, of Dun
(1509–91)

Reformer. He took an active share in public affairs, steadfastly supporting the reformed preachers, particularly **Wishart** and **Knox**, while his moderate and conciliatory temper gave him influence even with the Catholics and the Court, his tact managing to assuage the anger of **Mary, Queen of Scots** at Knox. From 1560 to about 1589 he was a superintendent of the reformed district of Angus and Mearns. Although a layman, he was five times Moderator of the General Assembly, and was one of the compilers of the *Second Book of Discipline* (1578). Early in his career he set up a French teacher of Greek in Montrose, something of a first in Scotland.

ERSKINE, Mary
(1629–1707)

Pioneer of girls' education in Scotland, born in Garlet, Clackmannanshire. Relatively little is known about her private life. She was married twice: first in 1661 to an Edinburgh writer called Robert Kennedy (d.1671), then in 1671 to an Edinburgh druggist and apothecary, James Hair (d.1683). After his death she reverted to her maiden name and set up business as a private banker. In 1694 she contributed to a scheme by Edinburgh Merchant Company for founding Merchant Maiden Hospital, for the education of the daughters of burgesses. For this purpose she left a benefaction of 10 000 merks Scots. **Deacon Brodie** is reputed to have been a governor of the school. (In 1869 it was transformed into a day school for girls, known as Edinburgh Ladies' College, and in 1944 changed its name to Mary Erskine School.) In 1704 she was instrumental in the establishment of the more vocationally oriented Trades Maiden Hospital which, unlike other similar foundations, did not run its own school but provided boarding and clothing.

ERSKINE, Ralph
(1685–1752)

Clergyman, brother of **Ebenezer Erskine**. Minister of Dunfermline from 1711, he joined his brother in the Secession (Associate Presbytery) in 1737, and also participated with the Burghers in the splits of 1747. His sermons were highly prized, and many of them were translated into Dutch. His *Gospel Sonnets* and *Scripture Songs* are well known. His *Practical Works* were published in 1764.

ERSKINE, Thomas, 1st Baron
(1750–1823)

Scottish-born judge, born in Edinburgh, brother of **David Erskine** (11th Earl of Buchan) and **Henry Erskine**. In 1764 he was sent to sea, in 1768 he bought a commission in the 1st Royals, and at Minorca (1770–2) he studied English literature. On leaving the army, he entered Lincoln's Inn (1775) and Trinity College, Cambridge (1776), where he took an honorary MA in 1778, just before being called to the Bar. His success was immediate and unprecedented. His brilliant defence (1778) of Captain Baillie, Lieutenant-Governor of Greenwich Hospital, who was threatened with a criminal prosecution for libel, overwhelmed him with briefs. The next year saw an equally successful defence of Admiral Lord Keppel, and in 1781 he secured the acquittal of Lord George Gordon. In 1783 he became a king's counsel, and MP for Portsmouth. His first appearance in the House of Commons was a failure and he never became a parliamentary orator. His sympathy with the French Revolution led him to join the 'Friends of the People', and to undertake the defence in many political prosecutions of 1793–4. His acceptance of a retainer from Thomas Paine cost him the attorney-generalship to the Prince of Wales (held since 1786). His speeches for Paine, the Scottish radical, Thomas Hardy (1794) and John Horne Tooke (1794) are among the finest specimens of forensic skill. That for Hadfield (1800), indicted for shooting at George III, was a destructive analysis of the current theory of criminal responsibility in mental disease. In 1802 he was appointed Chancellor to the Prince of Wales, an ancient office revived in his favour. In 1806 he was appointed Lord Chancellor, but he resigned the following year and gradually retired into private life. He published a pamphlet on army abuses in 1772, a discussion of the war with France in 1797, a political romance, *Armata*, a pamphlet in favour of the Greeks, and several poems. His decisions as Lord Chancellor were styled the 'Apocrypha', and have contributed nothing to his fame. His reputation was solely forensic, and in this respect is unrivalled in the history of the English Bar.

ERSKINE, Thomas
(1788–1870)

Religious writer, born in Linlathen, near Dundee. He was admitted advocate in 1810, but ceased to practise when his elder brother's death left him the estate of Linlathen. He published several religious works, his cardinal belief being ultimate universal salvation. His Letters were published in 1878. He was described by the diplomat Prévost-Paradol, on his visit to Britain in 1868, as a 'kind of old prophet'.

ERSKINE OF CAMBO, Sir Alexander
(1663–1727)

Lord Lyon King of Arms and parliamentarian. In 1677 he succeeded his father as Lord Lyon. In this office he took an especial interest in the regulation of state ceremonial. He was elected Tory Member of Parliament for Fife in 1710 and acted as lieutenant to **Lockhart of Carnwath**, the Scots Tory leader. In 1711 he was appointed joint keeper of the Signet and, in 1713, Steward of the Earldom of Menteith. When the Scottish Tory party split into rival factions after the general election of 1713, he was one of those MPs who supported Lockhart of Carnwath in remaining aloof from Bolingbroke, the English Tory leader. In 1715 he lost his Fife seat to his Whig opponent Sir John Anstruther. During the 1715 Jacobite rebellion he was unable to join his kinsman the Earl of **Mar**, as the government held him in preventative custody. Thus, he was able to retain the office of Lord Lyon, of which he was a distinguished incumbent until his death.

ERSKINE OF CARNOCK, John
(1695–1768)

Jurist. Called to the Bar in 1719, he became in 1737 Professor of Scots Law at Edinburgh University. His two works, *Principles of the Law of Scotland* (1754) and the more important *Institutes of the Law of Scotland* (1773), which is one of the classics of Scots law, are still held in deserved repute.

EWART, James Cossar
(1851–1933)

Zoologist, born in Penicuik, Midlothian. Professor of Natural History at Aberdeen (1879–82) and Edinburgh (1882–1927), he carried out notable experiments on animal breeding and hybridization, and disproved the theory of telegony.

EWING, Sir (James) Alfred
(1855–1935)

Engineer and physicist, born in Dundee and educated at Edinburgh University. He was Professor of Engineering at Tokyo (1878–83) and Dundee (1883–90), of Mechanism at Cambridge (1890–1903), Director of Naval Education (1903–16), and Principal of Edinburgh University (1916–29). During World War I he worked on the deciphering of intercepted messages. His works include *Magnetic Induction in Iron and Other Metals* (1891) and *Thermodynamics for Engineers* (1920).

EWING, Sir Archibald Orr
(1819–93)

Dyer, merchant and landed proprietor, born in Glasgow. Educated at Glasgow University, he received practical training in the works of his brother John, where he learnt Turkey-red dyeing, printing and colour making. In partnership he built a factory in the Vale of Leven to print and dye cloth. By 1857 he had acquired all the firms in the partnership and continued the policy of acquiring neighbouring lands. Although profits were hit as a consequence of the American Civil War, which damaged the British cotton trade, he continued to make money through his extensive land holdings and stock in railways and shipping. His huge wealth and the fact that he was the county's largest employer provided a sound base for political activities, and he became MP for Dunbartonshire from 1868 to 1892. He was created a baronet in 1886.

EWING, Winnie (Winifred Margaret)
(1929 –)

Nationalist politician. Born in Glasgow, she was educated at Queen's Park School, Glasgow, and Glasgow University. A lawyer and President of the Glasgow Bar Association, her victory at the Hamilton by-election of 1967 established the Scottish National Party as a major political force. Although ousted there in 1970, she won the Moray and Nairn seat in 1974, defeating the Conservative Secretary of State for Scotland. After losing this position in 1979 she was elected to the European Parliament in the same year, representing the Highlands and Islands. Her work on behalf of her constituents won her the title 'Madame Ecosse', and her flamboyant electioneering style and combative debating techniques have made her one of the best-known figures in the SNP. She became president of the party in 1988.

F

FAED, John
(1819–1902)

Painter, born in Burley Mill, Kirkcudbright-shire, brother of **Thomas Faed**. He studied at the Edinburgh School of Design from 1841, and became a noted painter of minia-tures in London. He also painted figure subjects such as *The Cottar's Saturday Night* (1854).

FAED, Thomas
(1826–1900)

Painter, born in Burley Mill, Kirkcudbright-shire, brother of **John Faed**. He studied at the Edinburgh School of Design, and was elected an associate of the Royal Scottish Academy in 1849 when he produced *Scott and his Friends at Abbotsford*, engraved by his brother. He went to London in 1852 and made his name with paintings of humble incidents in Scottish life. Elected RA in 1864, he resigned in 1893.

FAIRBAIRN, Andrew Martin
(1838–1912)

Congregational theologian, born in Inver-keithing, Fife. He is known for his brilliant essays in the *Contemporary Review*, and his *Studies in the Philosophy of Religion and History* (1876), and *Christ in Modern Theo-logy* (1894). From 1888 to 1909 he was Principal of Mansfield College (Congregation-al), Oxford.

FAIRBAIRN, (William) Ronald Dodds
(1889–1964)

Co-founder of the 'Object Relations' ap-proach to psychoanalysis, born in Edinburgh. He studied there, at Kiel, Strasbourg, Man-chester and London, before gaining an MD at Edinburgh University in 1929. He taught in the departments of psychology and psy-chiatry, Edinburgh University, between 1927

and 1935. As a practising psychoanalyst (1930–65) he was critical of Freud's instinct theory. For him the divorce between energy and structure and the dominant position given to impulse and the satisfaction of desires were not adequate explanations for the tragic failures in human relationships that he encountered. He therefore fashioned a radically new theory of personality in terms of dynamic structures developed from ex-perience within the first personal relationship between the infant and the mother. Some of his scientific papers were published in his *Psychoanalytic Studies of the Personality* (1952).

FAIRBAIRN, Sir William
(1789–1874)

Engineer, born in Kelso, Roxburghshire. In 1804 he was apprenticed to an engine-wright at North Shields, where he studied math-ematics, and made the acquaintance of George Stephenson. After moving to Man-chester in 1817 he began to make machinery for cotton-mills, etc, and in 1830 he took a lead in making iron boats; his works at Millwall, London (1835–49), turned out hun-dreds of vessels. For Stephenson's bridge over the Menai Strait he invented the rec-tangular tube that was ultimately adopted, and he erected a thousand bridges upon this principle. He aided Joule and Lord **Kelvin** in their investigations in 1851, and he directed the experiments of the government committee (1861–5) on the use of iron for defensive purposes.

FAIRLIE, Robert Francis
(1831–85)

Inventor of the Fairlie articulated loco-motive, born in Scotland and trained as a locomotive engineer at Crewe and Swindon. After some years as general manager of railways in Ireland and India he established himself as a consulting engineer in London, and in 1863–4 patented his double-bogie engine, which was intended for heavy freight traffic on winding, narrow-gauge lines. After a few initial difficulties, and despite continuing problems, by the time of his death 20 years later Fairlie locomotives were in service on 52 railways on gauges from 1'-10" upwards. Three examples, built in 1879, 1886 and 1979, can be seen at work on the Ffestiniog Railway in North Wales.

FAIRWEATHER, Al (Alastair)
(1927 –)

Jazz trumpeter, composer and bandleader, born in Edinburgh, a contemporary and associate of **Sandy Brown**. Their partnership began at the Royal High School, Edinburgh, in about 1941 and continued when both went to London in 1954 with the Fairweather-Brown All-Stars. Fairweather was responsible for writing and arranging many of the band's distinctive tunes — from outside the standard traditional repertoire, showing African and West Indian influences — which were their hallmark. After several years Fairweather took over the leadership because of Brown's commitment to his architectural practice. But although the All-Stars worked outside the 'trad jazz' style, the band broke up in the mid-1960s when the end of the British trad boom caused many clubs to close. In 1966 Fairweather joined the Acker Bilk Band, contributing compositions which helped the band's change from a trad to a mainstream style. He went back to teaching but continued to play and arrange jazz in his spare time, notably with the London Jazz Big Band in the 1970s. After recovering from a heart attack in 1983, he returned to Edinburgh, where he continues to work as a bandleader and jazz soloist.

FAIRWEATHER, Ian
(1891–1974)

Scottish-born Australian painter, born in Bridge of Allan, Stirlingshire. After serving in the army in World War I, he attended the Slade School of Art in London from 1920, where he developed an interest in Oriental art. He eventually became a student of Chinese and his painting was very much influenced by the art of non-European cultures. From 1924 he travelled extensively, living and working in, amongst other places, Germany, Canada, China, Japan and India, as well as Australia. In 1940 he served as a captain in the British army in India until, invalided out in 1943, he returned to Australia. In 1952 he attempted to sail from Darwin to Indonesia in a home-made raft. Although he eventually landed, he had been presumed lost at sea and an obituary had already appeared in the Australian press. After several more adventures, he returned to Australia in 1953 and, from that time until his death, he lived and worked in a hut he had built on Bribie Island, off the Queensland coast.

FALCONER, Sir David
(1640–86)

Judge. He studied law under his father, who was a Commissary of Edinburgh, passed advocate in 1661 and was appointed a Judge of the Court of Session in 1676, a Lord of Justiciary in 1678, and was promoted Lord President of the Court of Session in 1682. He also sat in Parliament. He made a collection of the decisions of the Court of Session covering 1681 to 1686 which were published, along with Sir John Gilmour's *Decisions* (as Lord President) in 1701. His third daughter became mother of **David Hume**.

FALCONER, Hugh
(1808–65)

Botanist and palaeontologist, born in Forres, Aberdeenshire. He studied medicine at Edinburgh, joined the Bengal medical service, became Keeper of the botanic garden at Saháranpur (1832), and discovered many fossils in the Siwálik hills. He performed the first experiments on growing tea in India. Back in England for health reasons (1842), he wrote on Indian botany and palaeontology, arranged Indian fossils in the British Museum and East India House, and prepared his great illustrated folio, *Fauna Antiqua Sivalensis* (1846–9). He returned to India in 1847 as superintendent of the botanic garden and Professor of Botany at Calcutta. His *Palaeontological Memoirs and Notes* were published in 1868.

FALCONER, Ronnie
(1911 –)

Church of Scotland minister and broadcaster, who played a pioneering role in establishing the principles and norms for religious broadcasting. Degrees from Aberdeen University (1931–7) were followed by ministry at Coatbridge Trinity, Lanarkshire. In 1945 he was appointed Religious Broadcasting Assistant, from which position he rose to become Religious Broadcasting Organiser for BBC Scotland, a post he held until his retirement in 1974. During this time he successfully maintained a balance between the twin requirements of Church and broadcasting, being respected as a practitioner of the broadcasting art, while retaining his particular theological vision. In 1960 Aberdeen University awarded him a DD. His book *Message, Media and Mission* (1977) set the agenda for the would-be religious broadcaster.

FALCONER, William
(1732–69)

Poet and seaman, born in Edinburgh. A barber's son, he went to sea, and was soon shipwrecked off Greece, this voyage forming the subject of his long poem, *The Shipwreck* (1762). He then entered the royal navy, being appointed purser on the frigate *Aurora* in 1769, which foundered with all hands near Capetown. His *Demagogue* (1764) is a satire on Wilkes and Marlborough, and he was also author of the *Universal Marine Dictionary* (1769).

FAULDS, Henry
(1843–1930)

Physician, born in Beith, Ayrshire. He trained as a doctor, and spent most of his working life in Japan, where he rose to a position of considerable importance in his profession. While employed as a physician at the Tsukiji Hospital in Tokyo, he began to work on the science of finger-printing, and recorded some of his discoveries in a letter to *Nature* in 1880. This sparked a vitriolic dispute over the rightful claim to having discovered the significance of finger-print identification, the other contender being a civil servant in India, William Herschel, who advocated their use as a means of detecting impersonation. Faulds is credited with discovering the applicability of finger-print techniques to criminal investigation, but could not persuade the authorities to act on his findings. It was not until 1891 that finger-printing was first employed, by police in Buenos Aires, using a different system to that suggested by Faulds. He is largely forgotten in the West, but is commemorated by a statue in Japan.

FEATHER, Norman
(1904–78)

English physicist, born in Yorkshire and educated at Bridlington Grammar School and Cambridge University. In 1929 he became a Fellow of Trinity College, and later a university lecturer. He played a part in the discovery of the neutron by his colleague, James Chadwick. During the war years he was the senior member of the group working in Cambridge towards the development of nuclear weapons. In 1945 he was appointed Professor of Natural Philosophy at Edinburgh University. His research there was mainly on β-ray spectroscopy and nuclear ternary fission, and he was the author of several textbooks and many articles on topics in physics and the history of physics. He was President of the Royal Society of Edinburgh from 1967 to 1970.

FENTON, Alexander
(1929 –)

Ethnologist, born in Shotts, Lanarkshire. After studying at Aberdeen and Cambridge universities he worked on the Scottish National Dictionary before joining the staff of the National Museum of Antiquities of Scotland in 1959. In 1978 he became Director and later, after the creation of the amalgamated National Museums of Scotland in 1985, Research Director. He was awarded the CBE in 1986. Since 1989 he has held a personal chair at Edinburgh as Head of the European Ethnological Research Centre. He has stimulated the development of regional ethnology not only in Scotland but also in Scandinavia and Central Europe. Among his many publications *The Northern Isles: Orkney and Shetland* (1978) is typical for its detailed and meticulous research.

FERGUSON, Adam
(1723–1816)

Philosopher and historian, born in Logierait, Perthshire. He served as a Black Watch chaplain before settling in Edinburgh, where he became Professor of Natural Philosophy (1759) and then of Moral Philosophy (1764). He travelled to Philadelphia as Secretary to the 1878–9 commission sent by Lord North to negotiate with the American colonists. A member of the Scottish 'common sense' school of philosophy, together with **Thomas Reid** and **Dugald Stewart**, his works include *The History of the Progress and Termination of the Roman Republic* (1783) and *Principles of Moral and Political Science* (1792). His *Essay on the History of Civil Society* (1767) was a major contribution to political thought. Underlining the necessity and fact of conflict in society, it influenced Hegel, Schiller and Marx. It has been credited with an influence on the Greek revival, with planting the seed of sociology, and with articulating decisively the problem called 'alienation'.

FERGUSON, James
(1710–76)

Astronomer, born in Rothiemay, Banffshire, the son of a farm labourer. While keeping sheep he was constantly occupied in making mechanical models and mapping the stars, at which he developed considerable skill. From the age of 10 he spent many years in service (including a time as a butler). During this period he continued star watching, and constructed a variety of ingenious machines. Following a spell in Edinburgh as an untrained but popular portrait painter, he moved to Inverness, where he pursued his interest in astronomy, writing papers such as 'A Dissertation upon the phenomena of the Harvest Moon' (1747), and embarking (1748) on a career as a lecturer on astronomy and mechanics. His inventions from this period include a tide-dial, an 'eclipsarion' for showing the main features of a solar eclipse, and a wide range of astronomical clocks. An assiduous writer, his principal works are *Astronomy Explained upon Newton's Principles* (1756) and *Lectures on Mechanics, Hydrostatics, Pneumatics, and Optics* (1760). Renowned for his abilities as a teacher, he gained great respect among the scientific establishment, and was described by **Hutton** as possessing 'very uncommon genius'.

FERGUSON, Patrick
(1744–80)

Soldier and inventor, born in Pitfour, Aberdeenshire. He served in the army in Germany and Tobago. In 1776 he invented a breech-loading rifle, that fired seven shots a minute, and sighted for ranges of 100 to 500 yards. With it he armed a corps of Loyalists, who at the Battle of Brandywine (1777) helped to defeat the Americans. He was killed at the Battle of King's Mountain, South Carolina.

FERGUSON, Robert
(c.1637–1714)

Conspirator, known as the 'Plotter', born near Alford, Aberdeenshire. In 1662 he was ousted as a Presbyterian from the vicarage of Godmersham in Kent. For 10 years he played a leading role in every treasonable scheme against the last two Stuart kings, and twice had to flee the kingdom. However, after the 'Glorious Revolution' of 1688, of which he published a history in 1706, he conspired as earnestly for the Jacobite cause. He was arrested for treason in 1704, but was not tried. His younger brother, James (d.1705), commanded a brigade at Blenheim, and died at Bois-le-Duc.

FERGUSSON, Sir Bernard Edward
(1911–80)

Soldier and military historian, born in London, the third son of General Sir Charles Fergusson of Kilkerran in Ayrshire. Commissioned in the Black Watch in 1931 he remained a loyal servant of his regiment and expressed some of the affection he felt for it by writing its wartime history, *The Black Watch and the King's Enemies* (1950). During the early part of World War II he held various staff positions, but he will be best remembered for his service with the Chindit forces in Burma. Raised by Orde Wingate to fight behind enemy lines, these special forces had to operate under difficult conditions, but their successes were a great boost to British morale in the war against Japan. After the war Fergusson was appointed Assistant Inspector-General of the Palestine Police and took part in anti-terrorist operations during the last days of the British mandate and the civil war between Arabs and Zionists. He was promoted to brigadier in 1956 and during his retirement he held several important positions, including Governor-General of New Zealand (1962–7) and Chairman of the British Council (1972–6). He wrote engagingly about his wartime experiences in *Beyond the Chindwin* (1945) and *The Trumpet in the Hall* (1970).

FERGUSSON, George, Lord Hermand See HERMAND, George Fergusson

FERGUSSON, Sir James
(1832–1907)

Statesman, born in Edinburgh. He was Conservative MP for Ayrshire (1854–7; 1859–68), Under-Secretary of State (1867–8), Governor of South Australia (1868–73), Governor of New Zealand (1873–4) and Governor of Bombay (1880–5). In 1885 he was elected for Manchester, and he was Foreign Under-Secretary (1886–91), and Postmaster-General (1891–2). He was killed in the earthquake of 1907 in Kingston, Jamaica.

FERGUSSON, John Duncan
(1874–1961)

Painter, born in Perthshire. He took up painting after a medical training. One of the group of Scottish Colourists, together with **Samuel John Peploe** and **Francis Cadell**, he acknowledged a debt to the Glasgow School of painting which emphasized colour rather than line. Trips to North Africa, Spain (1897) and Paris (which he made his home before and after World War I) brought him into contact with Mediterranean light and landscape, and with the painting of the Post-Impressionists and Fauves. He is best known for his series of World War I paintings of naval dockyards and his portraits of the female nude, which reveal an understanding of Cézanne, Cubism and Fauve colour, as well as an interest in new ideas about dance, movement and rhythm. He was married to the dancer **Margaret Morris**.

FERGUSSON, Robert
(1750–74)

Poet, born in Edinburgh, the son of a solicitor's clerk. He was educated at the High School of Edinburgh and of Dundee, and at St Andrews University, where he excelled. He was employed in the commissary office in Edinburgh, contributing poems to **Ruddiman**'s *Weekly Magazine* from 1771, which gained him local fame. His company was much sought and convivial excesses permanently injured his health. Following an awakening of religious interest, inspired by a meeting with the minister **John Brown**, he fell into deep depression, and was reduced to insanity by a fall downstairs. He died in a public asylum. He was a major influence on and inspiration to **Robert Burns**, who placed a headstone on his grave in 1789. He left 33 poems in Scots, and 50 poems in English. Essentially an Edinburgh poet, his most famous poem is *Auld Reekie* (1773), tracing a day in the life of the city. Other major and well-known poems are *Elegy on the Death of Scots Music*, *The Daft Days* (his first published poem), *Hallow Fair*, *To the Tron Kirk Bell*, *Leith Races* and the satirical *The Rising of the Session*.

FERRIER, Sir David
(1843–1928)

Neurologist, who provided the theoretical and experimental basis for brain surgery. Born in Aberdeen, he took a first in classics and philosophy at Aberdeen University, where he was taught by **Alexander Bain**. He took his MD at Edinburgh in 1868. In 1871 he joined the staff of King's College, London, where he was appointed to the specially created Chair of Neuropathology in 1889. Through his research on a variety of vertebrates, notably monkeys, he gained considerable renown for his work on the localization of brain functions. From this work came the realization that some types of brain tumour and brain injury could be effectively treated by surgery.

FERRIER, James Frederick
(1808–64)

Philosopher, born in Edinburgh. He became Professor of History at Edinburgh University in 1842 and Professor of Moral Philosophy at St Andrews University in 1845. His book *The Institutes of Metaphysic* (1854) was the first important work of the British Idealist (neo-Hegelian) movement. He introduced the term 'epistemology' into English and also propounded an 'agnoiology', or theory of ignorance.

FERRIER, Susan Edmonstone
(1782–1854)

Novelist, born in Edinburgh, the tenth child of a lawyer who became principal clerk to the Court of Session with Sir **Walter Scott**. With the death of her mother in 1797 she took over the running of the house, and looked after her father until his death in 1829. Her first work, *Marriage* (1818), a novel of provincial social manners, was followed by *The Inheritance* (1824) and *Destiny* (1831), a Highland romance. She enjoyed a close friendship with Scott, who was for a time credited by some with the authorship of her books. Following the publication of these works she was converted to evangelical Christianity, and became a member of the Free Church, concentrating on charitable works rather than on writing. Towards the end of her life she lived in relative seclusion, her eyesight failing badly.

FETTES, Sir William
(1750–1836)

Merchant and philanthropist. He made a fortune from tea and wine, was twice lord provost of Edinburgh, and left £166 000 to found **Fettes** College (1870), designed by **David Bryce**, and intended for the education of poor or orphaned children.

FINDLATER, Andrew
(1810–85)

Editor, born near New Aberdour, Aberdeenshire. He graduated from Aberdeen, and from 1842 to 1849 was headmaster of Gordon's Hospital there. He came to Edinburgh (1853) to supervise for Messrs **Chambers** a new edition of the *Information for the People* (1857). He also edited the first edition of *Chambers's Encyclopaedia* (1860–8), and wrote manuals on astronomy, philology and physical geography.

FINDLATER, Jane
(1866–1946)

Novelist, born in Lochearnhead, Perthshire, daughter of a Free Church minister, and sister of **Mary Findlater**. She had a great success with her first novel, *The Green Graves of Balgowrie* (1896), an 18th-century fiction based on family papers. It was followed by *A Daughter of Strife* (1897), *Rachel* (1899), *The Story of a Mother* (1902) and *The Ladder to the Stars* (1906). In collaboration with her sister she wrote the novel *Crossriggs* (1908) and other works.

FINDLATER, Mary
(1865–1963)

Novelist, born in Lochearnhead, Perthshire, daughter of a Free Church minister, and sister of **Jane Findlater**. She wrote several novels of her own, and collaborated with her sister on the novel *Crossriggs* (1908) and other works.

FINLAY, Ian Hamilton
(1925 –)

Artist, poet and writer, born in the Bahamas to Scottish parents who returned to their native country when he was a child. He spent a brief period at Glasgow School of Art before World War II. In the 1950s he began

his career as a writer, and became increasingly concerned with the formal qualities of individual words; his writings of the early 1960s played a leading part in the foundation of the 'concrete poetry' movement. Since then the major theme of his art has been the relationship between words and images. In 1966 he moved, with his wife Sue, to a farmhouse near Dunsyre in the Pentland Hills, later named 'Little Sparta', and began to transform the grounds into an original modern conception of a classical garden, with sculptures and stone inscriptions carefully placed within the landscape. Like his prints, posters and other works, these are produced in collaboration with a number of skilled craftsmen.

FINLAY, Robert Bannatyne, Viscount
(1842–1929)

Judge and statesman, born in Edinburgh. He studied medicine there, and was called to the English Bar in 1867. He was MP (Liberal 1885–6, thereafter Liberal Unionist) for Inverness burghs (1885–92, 1895–1906) and for Edinburgh and St Andrews universities (1910–16). Solicitor General (1895–1900) and Attorney General (1900–5), he was Lord Chancellor from 1916 to 1919, the year in which he was created viscount. In 1920 he became a member of the Hague Permanent Court of Arbitration, and in 1921 a judge of the Permanent Court of International Justice.

FINNIE, Linda
(1952 –)

Mezzo-soprano concert and opera singer, born in Paisley. She studied at the Royal Scottish Academy of Music and Drama with Winifred Busfield, and made her début with Scottish Opera in 1976. After winning the Kathleen Ferrier Prize at 's-Hertogenbosch in the Netherlands (1977) she began to sing widely throughout Europe, also with Welsh National and English National Operas (from 1979), and as guest at Covent Garden. As a concert singer her touring engagements have included Chicago and San Francisco. Her Wagner roles include Brangaene (Cardiff), Waltraute (Nice) and Fricka (Bayreuth début, 1988).

FISHER, Andrew
(1862–1928)

Scottish-born Australian politician, born in Crosshouse, Ayrshire. A coal-miner from the age of 12, he emigrated to Queensland in 1885. From mining he gradually moved into trade union activity and politics, entering the Queensland State Assembly in 1893 and the first Federal Parliament in 1901. He became Australian Labor Party (ALP) Leader in 1907 and then Prime Minister (1908–9, 1910–13 and 1914–15). At the start of World War I he made the dramatic promise to support the war effort 'to the last man and the last shilling'. He was Australian High Commissioner in London (1916–21).

FISHER, Archie

(1939 –)

Folk singer, guitarist, composer, broadcaster and administrator, born in Glasgow. An outstanding acoustic guitarist, he pioneered in his teens a folk-singing style that was gentler than the norm, and he has remained a sensitive interpreter of both traditional and contemporary songs, some of them his own. He has made suprisingly few solo recordings since his first album, *Archie Fisher* (1966). In *Orfeo* (1970) he broke new ground by setting the poet Pete Morgan's work to music, and he played a prominent role in **Barbara Dickson**'s first recordings. *Sunsets I've Galloped Into* (1988) is a much-praised later album. He has presented the BBC radio programme *Travelling Folk* for many years, and from 1988 to 1992 he was Artistic Director of the Edinburgh International Folk Festival.

FLECK, Sir Alexander, Baron Fleck

(1889–1968)

Industrial chemist, born in Glasgow. Educated at Glasgow University, he lectured there for two years, before working as a physical chemist on radium and later on the manufacture of sodium. He became Chairman of ICI in 1953 and was chairman of the committee that investigated the nationalized coal industry.

FLEMING, Sir Alexander

(1881–1955)

Bacteriologist, and the discoverer in 1928 of penicillin, born in Loudoun, Ayrshire. He was educated at Kilmarnock, and became a shipping clerk in London for five years before matriculating (1902) and embarking on a brilliant medical studentship, qualifying as a surgeon at St Mary's Hospital, Paddington,

where he spent the rest of his career. It was only by his expert marksmanship in the college rifle team, however, that he managed to gain a place in Sir Almroth Wright's bacteriological laboratory there. As a researcher he became the first to use antityphoid vaccines on human beings, and pioneered the use of salvarsan against syphilis, and while a medical officer in France during World War I, he discovered the antiseptic powers of lysozyme, present in tears and mucus. In 1928, by chance exposure of a culture of *staphylococci*, he noticed a curious mould, penicillin, which he found to have unsurpassed antibiotic powers. Unheeded by colleagues and without sufficient chemical knowledge, he had to wait 11 years before two brilliant experimentalists, Howard Florey and Sir Ernst Chain, with whom he shared the 1945 Nobel Prize for Physiology or Medicine, perfected a method of producing the volatile drug. Fleming was appointed Professor of Bacteriology at London University in 1938.

FLEMING, Ian

(1906 –)

Painter and printmaker, born in Glasgow. He studied at Glasgow School of Art, where he later taught printmaking. As a leading member of the Society of Artist Printmakers he played an important part in a revival of printmaking in Scotland in the 1930s and had a central role in the formation of Peacock Printmakers in Aberdeen in the 1970s. His work has been particularly concerned with the urban environment, and many of his images have focused on the changing face of Glasgow, from the effects of the wartime blitz to the changes wrought through modern urban development.

FLEMING, Margaret

(1803–11)

Child author, born in Kirkcaldy. She was distantly related to Sir **Walter Scott**, who referred to her as 'Pet Marjorie', and she was the theme of an exquisite essay by Dr **John Brown** (1810–82). She wrote poems and a three-volume diary.

FLEMING, Sir Sandford

(1827–1915)

Scottish-born Canadian railway engineer, born in Kirkcaldy. He went to Canada in

1845, and became chief engineer of the Inter-colonial Railway (1867–76) and of the Canadian Pacific Railway (1872–80). He surveyed several famous routes, including Yellowhead and Kicking Horse passes. In 1884 he came up with a system of standard time which was internationally recognized.

FLEMING, Tom
(1927 –)

Actor, director and poet, born in Edinburgh. His first speaking role was as Bruce McRae in Emlyn Williams' *The Late Christopher Bean* during a tour of India in 1945. In 1953 he co-founded the Gateway Theatre, Edinburgh, appearing in and directing many productions there until 1962. That year he joined the Royal Shakespeare Company, appearing in the title role in *Cymbeline*, and the following year he returned to Stratford to play Prospero in *The Tempest*. In 1965 he was appointed the first director of the Edinburgh Civic Theatre Trust, and founded a new company at the Royal Lyceum Theatre in the city. He has subsequently appeared as an actor and director in many Scottish theatres. He revived David Lyndsay's 16th-century political pageant for the Edinburgh Festival in 1984 and 1991. His books of poetry include *So That Was Spring* (1954) and *Sax Roses for a Luve Frae Hame* (1961). Since 1952 he has also been a radio and television commentator on state and royal events.

FLEMING, Williamina Paton, née Stevens
(1857–1911)

Scottish-born astronomer, born in Dundee. She emigrated to Boston at the age of 20, after marrying James Orr Fleming. The marriage failing, to support herself and her child, she took up domestic work for the Director of the Harvard College Observatory, Edward Pickering. By 1906 she had been made an honorary member of the Royal Astronomical Society. After beginning work at the Observatory she frequently collaborated with Pickering and some feel the discovery of the duplicity of Beta Lyrae has been wrongly accredited to Pickering rather than to Fleming. She also discovered new stars and variables, investigated stellar spectra, including 10 of the 24 novae recorded up until 1911, and categorized 10 351 stars in the Draper Catalogue of Stellar Spectra (1890).

FLETCHER, Andrew, of Saltoun
(1655–1716)

Patriot. He sat in the Scots Parliament in 1681, and so consistently opposed Stuart policy latterly that he twice had to escape to Holland. Joining William of Orange, he returned to Scotland during the revolution of 1688. He was the first patron of **William Paterson**, the projector of the Darien expedition, and the bitterness caused in Scotland by the treatment of the Darien colonists empowered Fletcher and the Nationalist Party in the struggle against the union with England. The proponent of the famous idea that a country's songs are more influential than its laws, his 'limitations' aimed to construct a federative instead of an incorporating union. Briefly imprisoned (1708) for supposed conspiracy in the French invasion, after the Union he retired from public life in disgust, devoting himself to the promotion of agriculture; he introduced fanners and the mill for pot-barley from Holland. His writings were reprinted in London in 1732.

FLETCHER, Harold Roy
(1907–78)

Botanist. Educated at the grammar school in Glossop and Victoria University, Manchester, he became Assistant Lecturer in Botany at Aberdeen University (1929), botanist at the Royal Botanic Gardens, Edinburgh (1934), and Director of the Royal Horticultural Society's Gardens at Wisley, before becoming Assistant Regius Keeper at the Royal Botanic Gardens to **Wright Smith** (1954), eventually succeeding him in 1958 after this appointment had been split from the Chair of Botany. Once installed as Regius Keeper he did much to modernize and develop the gardens, putting particular emphasis on making them more accessible to the public. He contributed many papers, both to learned journals and for those with wider interests in gardening and horticulture. His books include *The Royal Botanic Garden* (1970) and *A Quest for Flowers, the plant explorations of Ludlow and Sherriff* (1975).

FLINT, Robert
(1828–1910)

Philosopher, deemed by **Alastair MacIntyre** the most unjustly forgotten philosopher of his day. He studied for 10 years at Glasgow University before entering the ministry. Professor of Moral Philosophy at St Andrews (1864–76), he began a never-finished *magnum opus* on *The History of the Philosophy of History*. Awarded a Theology chair at Edinburgh in 1876, he began another vast work on Natural Theology. Two earlier volumes discuss much dated minor work, but *Agnosticism* (1903) – like his *Socialism* (1894), a long critique of collectivism, and his book on the great Italian thinker *Vico* (1884) – remain outstanding. He did not live to give his Gifford Lectures.

FLINT, Sir William Russell
(1880–1969)

Artist and illustrator, born in Edinburgh. Originally a lithographic draughtsman, he studied art in his spare time and settled in London in 1900, where he painted many watercolours to illustrate books (eg Chaucer, Matthew Arnold) and paintings of Scottish and foreign subjects. He wrote *Models of Propriety* (1951). A highly successful artist, his style was much imitated.

FORBES, Alexander Penrose
(1817–75)

Prelate, born in Edinburgh, the son of a law lord. In 1848 he was consecrated Bishop of Brechin. He laboured to further Tractarian principles, but his charge (1857) on the manner of the Eucharistic Presence led to his trial before the other Scottish bishops in 1860, and a censure and admonition. He was a close friend of Pusey and Dollinger. He edited the *Arbuthnot Missal* (1864), and published *Kalendars of Scottish Saints* (1872).

FORBES, Duncan, of Culloden
(1685–1747)

Statesman and judge, born in Bunchrew near Inverness. After studying at Edinburgh and Leiden, he was called to the Bar, and appointed Sheriff of Midlothian. He rose rapidly in practice and political influence through the 2nd Duke of **Argyll**. In 1715 he was in the north of Scotland, actively opposing the followers of the 'Old Pretender' (**James Francis Edward Stuart**); afterwards he protested against trying the prisoners in England, and resisted the forfeitures. In 1725 he became Lord Advocate, and in 1737 Lord President of the Court of Session; in 1734 he succeeded his brother to the family estates.

For a long time he largely ruled the destinies of Scotland and contributed to her dawning prosperity by developing her internal resources, by winning over the Jacobites, and by forming Highland regiments under loyal colonels. The 1745 rebellion rather took him by surprise. He hurried to the north, and did much to check the Jacobites, fending off the attack on Culloden House. However, he had to take refuge in Skye, and after his return was regarded with disfavour by the government because he advocated treating the rebels with mercy.

FORBES, Eric Gray
(1933–84)

Historian of science, born in St Andrews. He started his academic life as a solar physicist at the universities of St Andrews, Arcetri in Italy and Göttingen in Germany. Joining the staff of the University of Edinburgh in 1965 he was Professor of the History of Science there from 1978 until his death. In Göttingen he discovered important unpublished papers of the 18th-century astronomer Tobias Mayer, which he edited and published as *Tobias Mayer's Opera Inedita* (1971). These kindled in him an interest in the history of nautical astronomy, in which he became a master. He took a prominent part in the commemoration of the tercentenary of the Royal Observatory at Greenwich with the publication of Volume 1 of the history of the Observatory, *Greenwich Observatory*, *Origins and Early History* 1675–1825 (1975) and of *The Gresham Lectures of John Flamsteed* (1975).

FORBES, George
(1849–1936)

Physicist and engineer, born in Edinburgh, where his father, **James David Forbes**, was Professor of Natural Philosophy. He was educated at St Andrews and Cambridge universities and had a varied and colourful life as an astronomer, inventor, traveller and war correspondent. He was for some years Professor of Experimental Philosophy at Anderson's College, Glasgow, and while there took charge of one of the British Transit of Venus expeditions of 1874, to Hawaii. In his later life as an electrical engineer he worked on dynamos and invented the carbon brush. He made improvements in the method of measuring the velocity of light (with **James Young**), and in the field of rangefinding. In 1880 he forecast the existence of Pluto.

FORBES, James David

(1809–68)

Physicist, born in Edinburgh, grandson of Sir **William Forbes of Pitsligo**. Professor at Edinburgh (1833–60) and Principal of St Andrews College (1860–8), he is known for his work on glaciers, being one of the first to study them scientifically. He wrote *Travelling Through the Alps* (1843) and *Theory of Glaciers* (1859).

FORBES, Robert

(1708–75)

Episcopalian churchman. A minister in Leith from 1735, in 1745 he was imprisoned as a Jacobite. In 1762, despite his Jacobitism, he was appointed Bishop of Ross and Cromarty. He collected the Jacobite material for *The Lyon in Mourning* (1747–75).

FORBES, William

(?1675–1745)

Jurist. Called to the Bar in 1696 he became the first reporter of decisions appointed by the Faculty of Advocates and published in 1714 *A Journal of the Session*, containing decisions from 1705 to 1713. In 1713 he was appointed the first holder of the Regius Chair of Law at Glasgow University. Holding this post until 1745, he was active in the affairs of the university. He published extensively, on *Elections* (1700), *Bills of Exchange* (1703), *Justices of the Peace* (1703), *Church Lands and Tithes* (1705), but his magnum opus, *Great Body of the Law of Scotland*, still lies in seven volumes of manuscript in Glasgow University library. He published also *The Institutes of the Law of Scotland* (1722 and 1730), based on his *Great Body*. Highly regarded as a scholar in his time, his lesser works have merit, though they were overshadowed by those of **John Erskine**; it is unfortunate that *Great Body* was never published.

FORBES, Sir William, of Pitsligo

(1739–1806)

Banker, born in Edinburgh, grandfather of **James David Forbes**. He worked with, and in 1761 became a partner in, the Edinburgh bank of Coutts & Co., which changed its name to Forbes, Hunter & Co. in 1763 (later the Union Bank, 1830). He was a

founder member of the Society of Antiquaries of Scotland (1780) and the Royal Society of Edinburgh (1783). His second son, John Hay (1776–1854), was the judge, Lord Medwyn.

FORDUN, John of

(d.c.1384)

Chronicler, probably born in Fordoun, Kincardineshire. He may have been a chantry priest in Aberdeen. He was the compiler of *Chronica Gentis Scotorum*, the chief authority for the history of Scotland prior to the 15th century. He brought his history down to 1153, but he left collections extending to 1383. **Walter Bower** in 1441 resumed and enlarged the unfinished work as the *Scotichronicon*, but many of his alterations corrupted Fordun's narrative.

FORMAN, Sir Denis

(1917–)

Television executive, born near Dumfries. Educated at Loretto School and Pembroke College, Cambridge, he served with the Argyll and Sutherland Highlanders (1940–5), losing a leg in action at Monte Cassino in 1944. In the postwar years he pursued a career in the film industry, serving as Chief Production Officer of the Central Office of Information (1947) and as a director of the British Film Institute (1948–55) before becoming involved in the running of Granada Television (1955–90). A skilled administrator and respected leader who has strongly defended broadcasting independence from outside interference, he was Joint Managing Director (1965–81) and Chairman (1974–87) of the company, encouraging, among many others, television coverage of parliamentary affairs and elections, *Coronation Street* (1960–), *The World in Action* (1963–), *Brideshead Revisited* (1981) and *The Jewel in the Crown* (1984). He has served on numerous industry committees and public bodies, ranging from the Royal Opera House (1983–) to the Booker Prize Committee (1990), and is the current Chairman of the Scottish Film Production Fund (1989–). His autobiographical books include *Son Of Adam* (1990) and *To Reason Why* (1991).

FORREST, George

(1873–1972)

Botanist, born in Falkirk, Stirlingshire. He became Keeper of the Herbarium of the

Royal Botanic Garden in Edinburgh in 1902, but distinguished himself as a plant collector in China over a period of 28 years, specializing in Yunnan Province, where he made seven expeditions between 1904 and 1932. He was responsible for the introduction of many new species of rhodedendron and primula to Europe. He was also a notable zoologist, and by 1925 had added more than 100 species to the known bird list of Yunnan, as well as making substantial contributions to knowledge of mammals in South-East Asia.

FORREST, Sir (Andrew) Patrick McEwen

(1923 –)

Surgeon, born in Mount Vernon, Lanarkshire, and educated at Dundee High School. He read medicine at St Andrews University, graduating in 1945. He was a Surgeon-Lieutenant in the RNVR from 1946 to 1948 and took up his first academic post as Lecturer in Surgery in Glasgow (1955), working with Professor Tom Symington with a research interest in studying the effects of endocrine surgery in breast cancer. He was Professor of Surgery at the Welsh National School of Medicine from 1962, doing both gastro-intestinal research and later setting up a special clinic for breast cancer patients. He was then appointed Regius Professor of Clinical Surgery in Edinburgh (1970). From 1981 to 1987 he held the part-time post of Chief Scientist at the Scottish Home and Health Department, doing much to guide and support the application of scientific research to medicine. His interests continued in the treatment of gastro-intestinal disease and breast cancer. In the latter field he was Chairman of the British Breast Group (1974–7) and of the important Working Group on Breast Cancer Screening, which reported in 1986 and has stimulated a number of initiatives and long-term investigations on the prevention and treatment of this widespread disease. Knighted in 1986 and awarded many other honours, in his work he was humane and modest.

FORSYTH, Alexander John

(1769–1843)

Inventor and clergyman. Minister from 1791 of Belhelvie, Aberdeenshire, in 1807 he patented his improved detonating mechanism for firearms, which resulted in the adoption of the percussion-cap by the British forces.

Napoleon offered him £20 000 for the secret of his invention, but he patriotically refused. The first instalment of the pension tardily awarded to him by the British government arrived on the day of his death.

FORSYTH, Andrew Russell

(1858–1942)

Mathematician, born in Glasgow. Educated at Liverpool and Cambridge, he became professor at Liverpool in 1882, but returned to Cambridge in 1884, becoming FRS in 1886 and Sadleirian Professor in 1895. He worked in function theory and was instrumental in introducing the work of continental analysts to Britain. His book *Theory of Functions* (1893) was said by Sir **Edmund Whittaker** to have had 'a greater influence on British mathematics than any work since Newton's *Principia*'. His *Theory of differential equations* in six volumes (1890–1906) was a standard work in its time. From 1913 to his retirement in 1923 he held a chair at Imperial College, London.

FORSYTH, Bill

(1946 –)

Filmmaker, born in Glasgow. He entered the film industry in 1963 and started making his own documentaries after the death of his employer. He was a first-year drop-out from the National Film School in 1971, but his *That Sinking Feeling* ('a fairytale for the workless') was warmly received at the 1979 Edinburgh Film Festival. Particularly interested in exploring the lives of characters on the edge of society, he enjoyed considerable commercial success with the adolescent romance *Gregory's Girl* (1980) and *Local Hero* (1983), which focused on the impact of the oil business on a remote Scottish community. He has since explored the more fragile melancholy of dislocated individuals: a love-struck radio DJ in *Comfort and Joy* (1984), and an eccentric hobo in *Housekeeping* (1987), his first American film.

FORSYTH, Gordon Mitchell

(1879–1953)

Ceramic designer and teacher, born in Fraserburgh, Aberdeenshire. He trained in Aberdeen and at the Royal College of Art, winning a travelling scholarship to Italy in 1902. From 1902 to 1905 he was art director to Minton,

Hollins & Co. and moved to Pilkington Tile & Pottery Co. in 1906, where he specialized in lustre ware. He frequently made use of lettering and mottoes as a title to his work. He encouraged throwers to produce individual decorative designs and to sign and date their own work. He served as a designer to the Royal Air Force (1916–19) before his appointment as superintendent of art instruction at the Stoke-on-Trent School of Art. His influence on the period was enormous, and among his many pupils were Clarice Cliff and Susie Cooper. He was art adviser to the British Pottery Manufacturers Federation and was noted for the breadth of his knowledge in artistic education, aspects of design and his awareness of the demands of industry. His publications include *The Art and Craft of the Potter* (1934) and *20th Century Ceramics* (1936).

FORSYTH, Michael Bruce
(1954–)

Politician, born in Montrose. Educated at Arbroath High School and St Andrews University, he was a company director before embarking on a political career. He was a Westminster City Councillor from 1978 to 1983, then became Conservative MP for Stirling. Chairman of the Scottish party from 1989 to 1990, then Minister of State at the Scottish Office, he came to be regarded as the conscience of Thatcherism at St Andrews House, in contrast to the more liberal **Malcolm Rifkind**, then his immediate superior. More ideologically motivated than most Scots Tories, he appears to thrive on adversity. Following the 1992 general election he was moved to the Department of Employment.

FORSYTH, Peter Taylor
(1848–1921)

Congregational theologian and preacher, born in Aberdeen. As Principal of Hackney Theological College, Hampstead (1901–21), he championed a high doctrine of Church, ministry, sacrament and preaching in the Congregational Church. Influenced in his student days by Albrecht Ritschl at Göttingen, he rejected theological liberalism in the early 1880s, and came to a deep belief in God's holiness and the realities of sin and grace. His *The Cruciality of the Cross* (1909), *The Person and the Place of Jesus Christ* (1909), and *The Work of Christ* (1910), which

in some ways anticipated the neo-orthodoxy of Barth and Brunner, have enjoyed renewed popularity since World War II.

FORTUNE, Robert
(1813–80)

Horticulturist, born in Edrom, Berwickshire. He was at first employed as a gardener in the Royal Botanic Garden, Edinburgh, and at the Horticultural Society, Chiswick. From 1843 he travelled extensively in the East for the London Botanical Society, introducing many oriental plants into Britain (including the double yellow rose, the Japanese anemone, and the fan-palm *Chamaerops Fortuneii*), and he planted tea successfully in India's North-West Provinces. He published accounts of his travels, including *Yeddo and Peking* (1863).

FOULIS, Robert
(1707–76)

Bookseller and printer. He set up shop in Glasgow in 1741, and in 1743 became printer to the university and produced famous editions of the classics, including the 'immaculate' *Horace* (with only six misprints). In 1744 he took his brother Andrew (1712–75) into partnership, and in 1753 he established an academy of art in Glasgow which produced many prints, oil-paintings, etc. However, the printing business declined with Andrew's death, and Robert was compelled to sell off the pictures in London.

FOUNTAINHALL, Sir John Lauder, Lord
(1646–1722)

Judge. Having studied at Edinburgh, Poitiers and Leiden, he passed advocate in 1668 and at once began to record the decisions of the Court of Session. He sat in Parliament between 1685 and 1707 and supported the revolution of 1688–9. In 1689 he became a Judge of the Court of Session and in 1690 of the High Court of Justiciary also, but resigned the latter office in 1708. He is reputed to have had wide knowledge of the law and to have been conscientious and careful as a judge. He left two readable and interesting volumes of *Decisions of the Court of Session, 1678–1712* containing also transactions of the Privy Council, Criminal Court and Court of Exchequer. His *Historical Observes of Mem-*

orable Occurrents 1680–1701 (published 1840) and Historical Notices of Scottish Affairs (1848) are both important historical sources.

FRASER, Sir Alexander
(c.1537–1623)

Land-owner and entrepreneur, the 7th laird of Philorth in Aberdeenshire. He founded the harbour-town of Fraserburgh on his estates in 1576. In 1592 he founded a short-lived University of Fraserburgh, which closed down in 1597 from lack of funds.

FRASER, Sir Hugh
(1931–87)

Businessman, son of **Hugh Fraser**. He was educated at St Mary's School, Melrose and Kelvinside Academy, Glasgow. At the age of 17 he started work in one of his father's shops and in an early imaginative career he brought some life to the rather staid House of Fraser. He became Chairman of the firm in 1966, and in 1973 won the Guardian's Young Business-man of the Year Award. His career then declined, his sale of the House of Fraser being blocked by the Monopolies and Mergers Commission. Three years later he was found guilty of improper share and loans dealings through his financial conglomerate, Scottish and Universal Investments. Many of his holdings then passed into the hands of the Lonrho Group and a battle ensued for the control of his prestigious department store Harrod's. He was never again to be a com-pany chairman, despite later setting up Allan-der Holdings. A colourful character, dogged by the legacy of a successful father and the vast wealth inherited from him, he was frequently in the headlines. Much was made of his gambling and his support for the Scottish National Party; less well known was his purchase of the Isle of Iona for the National Trust.

FRASER, Hugh, Lord of Allander
(1903–66)

Retailer, perhaps the most dominant figure of his generation in the retail and distributive industries. After education at Warriston School, Moffat, in Dumfriesshire, and at Glasgow Academy, he entered the famous Fraser family stores in Buchanan Street in Glasgow. He became Managing Director in 1925 and then Chairman in 1941 of the parent company, Fraser Sons and Co, during which time he personally directed the expansion of a retail empire which came to include Harrod's and prestigious department stores in many provincial towns. His business interests were diverse. Chairmanship of George Outram and Co, publishers of the Glasgow Herald, was accompanied by his control of Scottish Universal Investment Trusts and many other concerns. He was awarded an Honorary LLD from St Andrews University in 1962 and two years later was raised to the peerage. He was both Honorary Treasurer of the Automobile Association and Treasurer of the Scottish Conservative Party. His son **Hugh Fraser** assumed control of his interests after his death.

FRASER, Marjory Kennedy
(1857–1930)

Singer and folk-song collector, born in Perth. One of a large musical family, she trained in Paris as a concert singer. In 1882 she started studying Gaelic music, took lessons in Gaelic, and started to collect Hebridean folk-songs, for which she composed modern harmonic settings. In 1909 she published Songs of the Hebrides. She also wrote the libretto of Granville Bantock's opera The Seal Woman.

FRASER, Patrick, Lord
(1817 or 1819–89)

Judge. Educated at St Andrews, he was called to the Bar in 1843 and made rapid progress, becoming part-time Sheriff of Renfrewshire in 1862 and Dean of the Faculty of Advocates in 1878. He was engaged in busy practice and appeared in many of the notable cases from about 1860 to 1881, when he was appointed to the bench. His judicial career was, however, unfortunately short and he did not make the mark he might have. As a young man he wrote Treatise on the Personal and Domestic Relations, later split into three substantially rewritten works: Parent and Child and Guard-ian and Ward (1866), Master and Servant (1872) and Husband and Wife (1876). All three were notable for careful statement and the wide range of authorities cited; all were still recently being cited in court and all were standard authorities until well into the 20th century.

FRASER, Peter
(1884–1950)

Scottish-born New Zealand politician. Born in Fearn, Ross-shire, and educated locally, his trade was carpentry. He became politically involved in the Liberal Party, then the Independent Labour Party (ILP), but emigrated to New Zealand in 1910, where he became a dock labourer and was elected leader of the general labourers' union. In 1919 he entered Parliament, becoming Secretary of the Parliamentary Labour Party (1919–35), and Deputy Leader (1933–40). As Minister for Education (1935) he introduced sweeping reforms; at the Health Ministry from 1938 he improved social security provision. Prime Minister from 1940 to 1949, he presided over radical welfare-state legislation. As premier he strongly championed Maori interests, promoted Commonwealth involvement in the war, and after 1945 helped develop ties with India and Ireland.

FRASER, Captain Simon
(1773–1852)

Fiddler, composer and collector, born in Ardachie, Inverness-shire. He is best known as the compiler of one of the major collections of early Gaelic and Scots music, *The Airs and Melodies Peculiar to the Highlands of Scotland and the Isles*, a work full of nostalgia for the Jacobite period. Published in 1816, this consists of 230 tunes and remains a vital source-book for musicologists. Fraser acquired most of the material from his grandfather and father, both of whom were leading musicians of their day. Other tunes he claimed as his own compositions. After army service he farmed for many years at Knockie, Inverness-shire. It was said that none could make the Gaelic fiddle sound sweeter.

FRASER, Sir William
(1816–98)

Archivist and genealogist, born of farming and craftsman stock in Kincardineshire. Educated in Edinburgh, where he worked for a law firm and took classes in law at the university, he became a solicitor in 1851. The following year he gave this up to take the far more poorly remunerated post of Assistant Keeper of the Register of Sasines. Appointed Deputy Keeper of Records of Scotland (1880–92), he issued a series of sumptuous family histories with original charters, valuable as sources for Scottish history. By his will he endowed the Edinburgh Chair of Scottish History, financed the *Scottish Peerage*, and allocated £25 000 for 'the endowment of homes for the poor in the city or

county of Edinburgh', especially for writers or artists 'who either from non-success in the profession or work of literature or art or from whatever cause are in necessitous circumstances'. These became known as the Fraser Homes.

FRAZER, Sir James George
(1854–1941)

Anthropologist and folklorist, born in Glasgow. Educated at Larchfield Academy in Helensburgh, Dunbartonshire, Glasgow University and Trinity College, Cambridge, he became a classics fellow there. He studied law and was called to the English Bar in 1879, but never practised, and turned his attention instead to anthropology which, in combination with his classical studies, resulted in the production of his monumental work, *The Golden Bough: A Study in Comparative Religion* (12 vols, 1890–1915), named after the golden bough in the sacred grove at Nemi, near Rome. His other anthropological works included *Totemism* (1884), *Totemism and Exogamy* (1911), *The Belief in Immortality and the Worship of the Dead* (1913–22), and *Magic and Religion* (1944). He also published an edition of Sallust (1884), and a translation of Pausanias's *Description of Greece* (1898). He was Professor of Social Anthropology at Liverpool (1907–8) and Cambridge (from 1908).

FREEMAN, Carol Wight
(1953 –)

Fashion designer, born in Edinburgh, now living and working in New York. Trained at Edinburgh College of Art and at the Royal College of Art, London, she has designed for Valentino in Rome, for Wallis in London, and for Dodwell in Hong Kong, moving in 1982 to Liz Claiborne in New York. In 1987 she joined Episode in New York, where she is now Vice-President, Design, designing the entire Episode collection of ladies' separates in all-natural fibres (silk, linen, cotton and wool) in classic styles for branches in the USA, the UK and the Far East.

FRESSON, Ernest Edmund
(1891–1963)

English aviator, born in Essex. He returned home from engineering training in Shanghai to join the Royal Flying Corps in World

War I. In China again after the war he set up the beginnings of an aircraft industry, but was squeezed out by more powerful French and German interests, and returned to Britain in 1927. While touring the north of Scotland with an 'aerial circus' he saw the potential for regular air services in the highlands and islands, and began scheduled services between Inverness and Kirkwall in 1933. Over the next four years Highland Airways flew 98 per cent of its advertised services, carrying passengers, mail and newspapers in all weathers. Captain Fresson himself flew regularly throughout World War II, but within two years of nationalization in 1946 he was made redundant by BEA (British European Airways), and spent his last years in East Africa.

FRIEL, George
(1910–75)

Novelist, born in Glasgow, where he lived and worked throughout his life. Educated at St Mungo's Academy and Glasgow University (the only one of seven children to go to university), he trained as a teacher at Jordanhill College, Glasgow. When war broke out he served in the RAOC and then returned to teaching, a profession he grew to loathe and distrust, although he always retained his concern for children. His experiences at the chalkface are at the heart of *Mr Alfred M.A.* (1972), which has been described as 'one of the great Scottish novels'. The story of the eponymous teacher's disillusionment and downfall, betrayed by one of his wretched girl pupils, it eloquently and ironically depicts a society and an education system in a state of disintegration, the result of a breakdown in communication. Other novels include *The Bank of Time* (1959), *The Boy Who Wanted Peace* (1964), *Grace and Miss Partridge* (1969) and *An Empty House* (1975).

FULTON, Angus Anderson
(1900–83)

Civil engineer. Born in Dundee, he was educated there at the High School and the University College. After three years with Dundee Water Department he joined the hydro-electric engineers Boving and Company, surveying and designing hydro schemes in India, Australasia and many other countries. He returned to Dundee Water Department in 1934 as chief assistant engineer, becoming engineer and manager four years later. In 1943 he was invited to join the newly

created North of Scotland Hydro-Electric Board, five years later becoming their first chief hydraulic and civil engineer, and from 1955 to his retirement in 1966, general manager. In all these capacities his experience and enthusiasm were invaluable assets to **Tom Johnston** and Sir **Edward MacColl**, with whom he shares the credit for the successful development of Scotland's hydro-electric potential in the postwar years. In 1969 he was elected President of the Institution of Civil Engineers, and in 1970 was awarded an honorary LLD by Dundee University.

FULTON, Rikki
(1924 –)

Actor, writer and comedian, born in Glasgow. He began his career as a broadcaster at the BBC in Glasgow, appearing in drama, features, children's and religious programmes, and at several Scottish repertory theatres, before moving to London. From 1951 to 1955 he presented various weekly programmes, and on returning to Scotland he starred in the *Five Past Eight* variety shows in Edinburgh and Glasgow. Since the 1950s he has regularly appeared in pantomime in both cities, and is acknowledged as one of the great pantomime dames. Francie and Josie, his stage double act with **Jack Milroy**, in which Fulton plays Josie, one of two 1950s Glaswegian wideboys, has become one of the legends of Scottish variety theatre. On television his series of sketches *Scotch and Wry*, begun in 1978, remains hugely popular. In 1985 he co-adapted and appeared in *A Wee Touch of Class*, a successful transposition of Molière's *Le Bourgeois Gentilhomme* from 17th-century France to 19th-century Edinburgh. He has recently starred in the summer variety shows, *Kings High*, at the King's Theatre, Glasgow, which have confirmed him as the finest contemporary Scottish comic.

FULTON, Robin
(1937 –)

Poet and translater, born on the Isle of Arran and educated at Edinburgh University. A schoolteacher for some years, he held a Writer's Fellowship at Edinburgh University (1967–71), and was Editor of the poetry magazine *Lines Review* (1967–77). Since 1973 he has worked and lived in Norway. His own poetry, first published in *Instances* (1967), is composed largely of incisive, detached observations of human life. *Tree Lines* (1974) is his best-known poetical work. He has gained international prominence for his translations of contemporary Scandinavian poets and has published essays on the art of translation.

FYFFE, Will (William)

(1885–1947)

Comedian, singer and actor, born in Dundee. He made his stage début as a child, playing 'Little Willie' in his father's repertory version of *East Lynne*, and by the age of 15 was playing Polonius in *Hamlet*. He wrote several character sketches for **Harry Lauder**, but when they were rejected decided to perform them himself. Making his London début at the Middlesex Theatre in 1916, by 1921 he was topping the bill at the Palladium. He appeared in the Royal Variety Performance (1922), the first of four, and made his film début in *Elstree Calling* (1930), in which he sang his popular serenade to Scotch, 'Twelve and a Tanner a Bottle'. His character studies included a ship's engineer 'Sailing Up the Clyde', and his most popular song was 'I Belong to Glasgow'. He was King Rat of the Water Rats for six years, and acted engagingly in over 20 films, both British and American.

G

GAIRDNER, Charles
(1824–99)

Banker, born in Ayr. He began his career in accountancy and soon gained experience in stockbroking and insurance. Peter White, a founder member of the Glasgow Stock Exchange, offered him a partnership in 1845. Gairdners's main interest was as an accountant, leading him, with others, to found the Institute of Accountants and Actuaries. Having gained experience as a liquidator he was appointed by the directors of the Union Bank of Scotland to be their General Manager. The bank was heavily involved in financing both the decline of the cotton industry and the rise of the metal working industries, to which developments he brought a highly personalized and strict control. However, although he was a good lender, some of the bank's subsequent relative decline must be attributed to him. He was awarded an LLD from Glasgow University and founded the **Adam Smith** Club in the city.

GAIRDNER, James
(1828–1912)

Historian, born in Edinburgh. He entered the Public Record Office in London, where he became assistant-keeper in 1859. He showed erudition, accuracy, and good judgement in editing historical documents, as also in his own works *The Houses of Lancaster and York* (1874), *Life of Richard III* (1878), *Lollardy and the Reformation in England* (1908–13), and others.

GAIRDNER, William Henry Temple
(1873–1928)

Missionary and Islamic scholar, born in Ardrossan, Ayrshire. He graduated from Cambridge, and in 1898 went to work with the Church Missionary Society in Cairo. A master of colloquial Arabic and Islamic literature, and a writer of hymns and poems, he sought to train indigenous Christian leaders, and was convinced that Muslims could be won to Christianity by personal testimony and by seeing how Christians lived their faith. He wrote *The Reproach of Islam* (1909) and (with W A Eddy) *The Values of Christianity and Islam* (1927).

GAITENS, Edward
(1897–1966)

Novelist, born in Glasgow. He grew up in the Gorbals, then a notorious slum area, and left school at 14, the end of his formal education. He was imprisoned as a conscientious objector during World War I. Encouraged by O H Mavor (**James Bridie**), he submitted stories to the *Scots Magazine*, many of which were collected in *Growing up and Other stories* (1942). Never a prolific writer, he re-used material from six of these stories in his only novel, *Dance of the Apprentices* (1948). His reputation largely rests on this work, one of the least sentimental and most clear-headed of the fictional representations of working-class life in Glasgow's slums. He subsequently lived in Dublin and London, and on his death left a number of unpublished sketches and stories.

GALLACHER, Bernard
(1949 –)

Golfer, born in Bathgate, Midlothian. He turned professional in 1967, and the following year was voted Rookie of the Year. He has been Scottish professional champion on four occasions; his other significant tournament wins include the Spanish Open (1977), and the French Open (1979). First selected for the Ryder Cup team in 1969, when he was regarded as something of a child prodigy, he was a regular member of the team until 1983. In 1991 he was the non-playing captain of the side which came close to retaining the cup at Kiawah Island, South Carolina.

GALLACHER, Willie (William)
(1881–1966)

Communist politician. Born in Paisley, he attended Camphill School and went on to work as a brassfounder. Involved with the revolutionary Socialist Labour Party before 1914, he was a leader of the militant shop-stewards' movement during the wartime unrest on Clydeside. Arrested and deported in 1916, he met Lenin in Moscow after the Russian revolution, and helped found the Communist Party of Great Britain. He was MP for Fife West (1935–51), making him the longest-serving Communist MP in British history. He steadfastly advocated the Communist line, although in private he disapproved of the Nazi-Soviet pact. After losing his seat, he wrote several volumes of autobiography.

GALLOWAY, Jim (James Braidie)
(1936 –)

Jazz saxophonist, bandleader and broadcaster, born in Kilwinning, Ayrshire, and based in Toronto, Canada, since 1964. He taught himself to play the clarinet while in his teens and started to play with local bands. After studying at Glasgow College of Art be became an art teacher; but turning to alto, baritone and, principally, soprano saxophone, he began to concentrate on a musical career. On emigrating to Canada he played in the company of such international stars as pianists Ray Bryant and Dick Wellstood and singer Jimmy Rushing, also presenting the coast-to-coast radio programme *Toronto Alive!*. After appearing at the Montreux Jazz Festival in 1976 with the veteran American musicians Buddy Tate, Jay McShann and Buck Clayton, he became a regular performer on the international jazz circuit, frequently touring, recording and making many appearances at the Edinburgh International Jazz Festival.

GALT, John
(1779–1839)

Novelist and Canadian pioneer, born in Irvine, Ayrshire, the son of a sea-captain. Educated at Greenock Grammar School, he became a junior clerk in a local merchant's firm in 1796. After contributing to local journals, he moved to London in 1804 and set up in business as a merchant. The venture was not a success, and from 1809 to 1811 he travelled for his health's sake in the Levant, where he met Byron. On his return he published *Letters from the Levant* and other accounts of his travels. He busied himself in various business posts, and wrote a number of school textbooks under the pseudonym 'Rev T Clark'. He then started to write novels for *Blackwood's Magazine*. The *Ayrshire Legatees* appeared in 1820, followed by *The Steam-Boat* in 1821. Its successor, *The Annals of the Parish* (1821), is his masterpiece, in which the description of events in the life of a parish minister throws interesting light on contemporary social history. He produced in quick succession *Sir Andrew Wylie* (1822), *The Provost* (1822) and *The Entail* (1823). His historical romances were less successful. He went to Canada in 1826, founded the town of Guelph, and played a prominent part in organizing immigration, but returned ruined in 1829, and produced a new novel, *Lawrie Todd* (1830), and *The Member* (1832), on corruption in politics. He also wrote a *Life of Byron* (1830) and an autobiography (1834). In his depiction of life in small towns and villages Galt has few rivals. He possesses rich humour, genuine pathos and a rare mastery of Scottish dialect.

GAMBLE, Josias Christopher
(1776–1848)

Industrialist, born in Enniskillen. He was a founder with James Muspratt of the British chemical industry based in the St Helens area near Liverpool. A graduate in theology from Glasgow, he spent a period as a cleric before manufacturing chemicals in Dublin and then in Glasgow, and most profitably in partnership with Muspratt in St Helens, making bleaching powder, soda ash and sulphuric acid.

GARDEN, Mary, originally Mary Davidson
(1874–1967)

Soprano, born in Aberdeen. Taken to America as a child, she studied singing in Chicago and then in Paris. Her career began sensationally when she took over in mid-performance the title role in Charpentier's new *Louise* at the Opéra-Comique in 1900, when the singer was taken ill. In 1902 she created the role of Mélisande in Debussy's *Pelléas et Mélisande* at the composer's request, and in 1903 she recorded songs with Debussy. Massenet and Erlanger also wrote leading roles for her. She sang at Covent Garden (1902–3), and she was a legendary Manon, Thaïs, Violetta, Salomé, Carmen, and Juliet (Gounod). Her American début was in 1907, and in 1910 she began a 20-year association with Chicago Grand Opera, which she also briefly directed (1921–2). She returned to Scotland in 1939.

GARDEN, Neville

(1936 –)

Broadcaster and conductor, born in Edinburgh. Educated at George Watson's College, Edinburgh, he made his radio début as the Little Star of Bethlehem for a *Children's Hour* broadcast in 1948. Following his father into journalism, he began as a tea-boy on the *Evening Dispatch* and steadily worked his way through the ranks to the *Scottish Daily Express* before becoming an anchorman on BBC Radio Scotland's *Good Morning Scotland* (1978–90), where his dulcet tones and unflappable good humour eased thousands of listeners through the breakfast hours. He subsequently hosted the daily arts magazine *Queen Street Garden* (1990 –). A music afficionado with a record collection in excess of 6000 albums, he wrote and compiled *The Good Music Guide* (1989), and writes a regular musical column for *Scotland on Sunday*.

GARDNER, Alexander

(1821–82)

Scottish-born American photographer and journalist, born in Paisley. He emigrated to America in 1856. Employed by Matthew Brady, he became manager of Brady's Washington studio in 1858, but left, following a dispute over copyright, to open his own gallery in Washington in 1863. He specialized in documentary projects, the best-known of which are his work on the American Civil War (some of it produced while he and his son James were employed in making maps at the headquarters of the army of the Potomac); on the Lincoln Conspiracy (he had earlier made several portraits of Abraham Lincoln); on the building of the Union Pacific Railroad; and on several Indian Peace Conferences. His most significant published work is his *Sketch Book of the War* (1866) which contains, in addition to his own original prints, fully-attributed photographs by other photographers, including Timothy O'Sullivan.

GARDNER, Peter

(1836–1902)

Potter, generally regarded as one of the principal makers of Art Pottery in the second half of the 19th century. At the age of 30 he took over the family business of Dunmore Pottery. Animals feature a great deal in his work and his pioneering style in applied design and glaze techniques ranged from tiles and teapots to garden seats and umbrella stands. He was encouraged by the Earl and Countess of Dunmore and received royal recognition in 1871 when he was visited by the Prince of Wales.

GARIOCH, Robert, pen-name of Robert Garioch Sutherland

(1909–81)

Poet, born in Edinburgh. Educated at the Royal High School, Edinburgh, and Edinburgh University, he spent most of his professional career as a teacher in Scotland and England. He made his literary début in 1933 with the surrealistic verse play *The Masque of Edinburgh* (published in expanded form in 1954). His first publications, *Seventeen Poems for Sixpence* (1940), in which he collaborated with **Sorley MacLean**, and *Chuckies on the Cairn* (1949), were hand-printed. His later work included *Selected Poems* (1966), *The Big Music* (1971), *Dr Faust in Rose Street* (1973) and *Collected Poems* (1977). He favoured the Scots language, in which he wrote in various styles and moods, from the colloquial to the literary. He translated into Scots works as diverse as Pindar, Hesiod, **George Buchanan**'s Latin plays *Jeptha* and *Baptistes*, Anglo-Saxon elegies, and the poems of the 19th-century Italian dialect poet Giuseppe Giacchino Belli. His prose works include *Two Men and a Blanket* (1975), an account of his experience in prisoner-of-war camps during World War II. He particularly acknowledged the influence on his poetry of **Robert Fergusson**, perhaps most clearly seen in his sonnet on Fergusson's grave, his *To Robert Fergusson* and *The Muir*. He was writer-in-residence at Edinburgh University from 1971 to 1973.

GARSCADDEN, Kathleen

(1897–1991)

Broadcaster, born in Glasgow. Educated at Hutchesons' Girls Grammar School, she trained in London as a singer, but abandoned her original intention to sing in opera. Her career in broadcasting began when she acted as an all-round announcer, pianist and singer on her father's private broadcasting station. When this was bought by Lord **Reith** (his first Scottish station) she joined the British Broadcasting Company (later Corporation) as a programme assistant (1923), working mainly on vocal concerts and the *Woman's*

Hour series. Involved in the world's earliest experiments in broadcasting to schools, she started to run the early *Children's Hour*, discovering that this was a full-time occupation. Known as 'Auntie Cyclone' in her early days, since she sometimes read the weather, she was later dubbed 'Aunt Kathleen'. She worked as a presenter, broadcaster, programme organizer and producer throughout the 42-year life of *Children's Hour*, and during World War II was responsible for organizing the broadcasting link between Scottish families and their evacuated children. During her career she strove to put across to her young audience inspiring ideals, religious teaching and the history and tradition of Scotland. She also introduced many notable performers to broadcasting, including **Gordon Jackson**, **Stanley Baxter**, **Jimmy Logan**, and **Moira Anderson**.

GAUGHAN, Dick
(1948 –)

Folk singer and songwriter, born in Glasgow. Widely recognized as the finest Scots interpreter of both contemporary and traditional folk-song, he has a repertoire that ranges from classic ballads to powerful broadsides on modern political and sociological issues, some self-composed. Brought up in Leith, he began singing in Edinburgh pubs as a teenager. In 1972–3 he was a member of the Boys of the Lough, and in 1975 he helped to form Five Hand Reel, which whom he appeared for more than three years. Since then he has been a solo performer with a particularly strong Scottish following, although he has also toured the Soviet Union and the USA. His first album, *No More Forever*, was issued in 1972, and he has recorded regularly since then.

GEAR, William
(1915 –)

Painter, born in Methil, Fife. He was one of the first Scottish artists to win international recognition in the postwar period. In 1937–8, after studying at Edinburgh University and Edinburgh College of Art, he studied in Paris with Fernand Léger and, after extensive travel throughout Europe, lived there from 1947 to 1950, where he was associated with the 'Cobra' group of artists (so-called because its principal members came from Copenhagen, Brussels and Amsterdam). In his painting, characteristically of interlocking diagonal areas of colour, he drew together current aesthetic ideas on abstraction from Europe and America. In 1949 he shared an exhibition with the American Abstract Expressionist Jackson Pollock in New York. He moved to England in 1950, and in 1964 was appointed Head of Fine Art at Birmingham College of Art.

GED, William
(1690–1749)

Printer and inventor. He began as a goldsmith in Edinburgh, and in 1725 he patented a process of stereotyping. He was commissioned by Cambridge University to stereotype prayer books and bibles, but his partner's unfairness and workmen's opposition compelled him to return to Edinburgh (1733). He died very poor.

GEDDES, Alexander
(1737–1802)

Biblical scholar, born in Rathven parish, Banff. Educated for the priesthood at Paris (1758–64), in 1769 he took a charge at Auchinhalrig, Banff, where his sympathy with local Protestants and his fondness for hunting led to his dismissal (1780). The previous year he had published a verse translation of Horace's *Satires*, which brought him recognition. Going to London following his dismissal, he made a new translation of the Bible for English Catholics (1792–1800).

GEDDES, Andrew
(1783–1844)

Portrait and landscape painter, and etcher, born in Edinburgh. He worked with his father in the Excise office, but in 1806 he moved to London to study painting as a fellow pupil of Sir **David Wilkie** at the Royal Academy Schools. Although he travelled widely, he worked in London for most of his life. One of his best-known works is *Sir David Wilkie*.

GEDDES, Jenny
(c.1600 – c.1660)

Vegetable-seller, traditionally reputed to have started the riots in St Giles' Cathedral, Edinburgh, when Laud's prayer book was introduced on Sunday 23 July, 1637. According to popular legend she threw her folding-stool at Bishop Lindsay, shouting: 'Thou false thief, dost thou say mass at my lug?'. There is no historical evidence of her exploit. Sydserf in 1661 mentions 'the immortal Jenet Geddes' as having burned 'her leather chair of state' in a Restoration bonfire, and the story appears in full detail in Phillips's continuation of Sir Richard Baker's *Chronicle* (1660).

GEDDES, John Maxwell
(1941 –)

Composer and lecturer in music, born in Glasgow. He studied at the Royal Scottish Academy of Music and with Niels Bentzon in Copenhagen. Associate Professor of Music at Oregon State University (1979–80), he has taught at various conservatories in Germany, the USA and the USSR, and at St Andrew's College, Glasgow. His orchestral work includes film scores, 3 *Orchestral Pieces* (1965), *Portrait of a City* (1971), *First Symphony* (1974), *Lacuna* (1977), *Ombre* and *Voyager* (1985). A second symphony was commissioned by **Bryden Thomson** in 1991. His oboe sonata (for Evelyn Barbirolli, 1973) was followed by a substantial series of virtuoso works for solo instruments, including *Coronach* and *Callanish* I–V; also a cello sonata (1991). His vocal works include settings of **Burns**, and the choral *In Tempore Belli* (1991).

GEDDES, Sir Patrick
(1854–1932)

Biologist, sociologist and pioneer of town planning, born in Perth. Educated at Perth Academy and University College, London (under T H Huxley), he was a demonstrator in botany at Edinburgh before becoming Professor of Botany at Dundee (1889–1914). Taking the theory of evolution as a basis for ethics, history and sociology, he wrote *The Evolution of Sex* (1889). In 1892 he established the 'world's first sociological laboratory' in the Outlook Tower on Castlehill, Edinburgh, to demonstrate regional differentiation. Increasingly involved in town and regional renovation, he wrote *City Development* (1904) and *Cities in Evolution* (1915), in which he coined the terms 'megalopolis' and 'kakatopia'. He had some original concepts of urban ecology, linking people, work and a sense of place. After World War I he was Professor of Civics and Sociology at Bombay University (1920–3), and in 1924 he

moved to France and established an unofficial 'Scots College' at Montpellier.

GEDDES, William George Nicholson
(1913 –)

Civil engineer, born in Oldhamstocks, East Lothian. After graduating from Edinburgh University he entered the design office of Sir **William Arrol** and Company in 1935. He gained further experience with F A Macdonald & Partners, ICI, and the Shell and Royal Dutch Oil companies, before he joined the Glasgow firm of consulting civil engineers, Babtie, Shaw and Morton, in 1974. He was made a partner in 1950 and senior partner from 1976 until his retirement in 1979. He specialized in heavy civil engineering works such as the Kielder Water Dam and the large dry dock at Harland and Wolff's shipyard in Belfast. He was President of the Institution of Structural Engineers (1971–2) and the Institution of Civil Engineers (1979–80), and was awarded an honorary DSc by Edinburgh University in 1980.

GEIKIE, Sir Archibald
(1835–1924)

Geologist, brother of **James Geikie**, born in Edinburgh. Educated at the Royal High School and Edinburgh University, in 1855 he was appointed to the Geological Survey. In 1867 he became Director of the Geological Survey in Scotland; from 1870 to 1881 he was Professor of Geology at Edinburgh; and he was Director-General of the survey of the UK (1882–1901), and head of the Geological Museum, London. He did much to encourage microscopic petrography and volcanic geology, and he wrote several notable textbooks as well as biographical works.

GEIKIE, James
(1839–1915)

Geologist, brother of Sir **Archibald Geikie**, born in Edinburgh. He served on the Geological Survey of Scotland from 1861, and was Professor of Geology at Edinburgh (1882–1914). As well as verse translations from **Heinrich Heine**, a large number of geological maps, sections and memoirs published by the Geological Survey, he wrote a standard work on the glacial period (1874) and several other geological books.

GEIKIE, Walter
(1795–1837)

Printmaker and painter, born in Edinburgh. Deaf and dumb, he was taught to read and write by **Thomas Braidwood**. Best known for his scenes of everyday life, he was much influenced by his great contemporary **David Wilkie**. Unlike Wilkie, he remained in Edinburgh, and his topographical drawings of the city and its environs provide the most vivid contemporary image of Edinburgh. Although a painter, his best work comprises drawings and etchings, and his most notable work is a collection of etchings published posthumously under the title *Sketches of Scottish Life and Character*.

GIBB, Sir Alexander
(1872–1958)

Civil engineer, born near Dundee. He was fifth generation in a line of civil engineers that started with his great-great-grandfather William (1736–91), who was a master mason and what would now be known as a civil engineering contractor. His son John (1776–1850) became **Thomas Telford**'s trusted deputy on bridges and harbour works in Scotland, then turned to contracting like his father before him. His son Alexander (1804–67) was apprenticed to Telford, worked with **Robert Stevenson**, and built railways in Scotland and England, and his son Easton (1841–1916) built reservoirs, railways, and the bridge over the Thames at Kew. His son Alexander joined the firm of Easton Gibb & Son in 1900, and from 1909 to 1916 worked on the construction of Rosyth naval dockyard, and then after five years in government posts set up in practice as a consulting engineer. His firm became one of the world's largest companies, their work at home and abroad including hydro-electric schemes, bridges, docks and harbours, and many other kinds of civil engineering project.

GIBB, Andrew Dewar
(1888–1974)

Jurist, born in Paisley. He studied at Glasgow, was called to the Scottish (1914) and English (1917) Bar, and after lecturing at Edinburgh and Cambridge became Regius Professor of Law at Glasgow (1934–58). He wrote several works on Scots Law and on the case for Scottish home rule, and he was Chairman of the Scottish National Party

(1936–40) and of the Saltire Society (1955–7), and President of the Covenant Association from 1957.

GIBB, Bill
(1943–88)

Fashion designer, born in Fraserburgh, Aberdeenshire. After studying in London at St Martin's School of Art and the Royal College of Art, he launched his first collection in 1970 with Kaffé Fassett, for which he was voted Designer of the Year by British *Vogue* magazine. He then worked for Baccarat before opening a retail business in London in 1975. His work with appliqué and embroidery was much acclaimed, and he became internationally famous for his glamorous sequinned and beaded ladies' evening wear and special occasion wear, which reflected his passion for Renaissance art.

GIBBON, Lewis Grassic, pseudonym of James Leslie Mitchell
(1901–35)

Novelist, born on the farm of Hillhead of Seggat, Auchterless, Aberdeenshire. His father was a farmer and he was educated at the local school before attending Mackie Academy, Stonehaven, which he left after a year to become a newspaper reporter. Stirred by the promise of the Russian Revolution he became a member of the Communist Party. In 1919 he moved to Glasgow where he was employed on the *Scottish Farmer*, but his career in journalism was curtailed when he was dismissed for fiddling expenses. He attempted suicide, returned home and decided to enlist. He spent three and a half years with the Royal Army Service Corps in Persia, India and Egypt. In 1923 he left the army but poverty drove him to join up again, this time in the Royal Air Force, where he served as a clerk until 1929. His first published book was *Hanno, or the Future of Exploration* (1928) and others followed rapidly: *Stained Radiance* (1930), *The Thirteenth Disciple* (1931), *Three Go Back* (1932) and *The Lost Trumpet* (1932). *Sunset Song*, his greatest achievement, was published in 1932, the first of his books to appear under his pseudonym. Written in less than two months it was published under his mother's name as the first in a projected trilogy of novels, *A Scots Quair*, on the life of a young girl called Chris Guthrie. The second volume, *Cloud Howe*, appeared in 1933 and the third part, *Grey Granite*, in 1934. An unfinished novel, *The Speak of the Mearns*, was published in 1982. He also wrote a life of the Scottish explorer, **Mungo Park** (1934), and published *The Conquest of the Maya* (1934).

GIBBS, James
(1682–1754)

Architect, born in Aberdeen. He studied in Holland as a protégé of the exiled Earl of **Mar** and then, under Carlo Fontana, in Italy. A friend and disciple of Sir Christopher Wren, in 1713 he became one of the commissioners for the building of new churches in London, but was dismissed in 1715 for his Roman Catholicism. He designed St Mary-le-Strand (1717), the steeple of St Clement Danes (1719), St Peter's, Vere Street (1724), and St Martin-in-the-Fields (1726), the latter being perhaps his most influential and attractive work. He was also responsible for St Bartholomew's Hospital (1730), the circular Radcliffe Camera at Oxford (1737–47) and the Senate House at Cambridge (1730). His *Book of Architecture* (1728) helped to spread the Palladian style, and influenced the design of many churches of the colonial period in America.

GIBSON, Sir Alexander See DURIE, Sir Alexander Gibson

GIBSON, Sir Alexander Drummond
(1926 –)

Conductor, born in Motherwell, Lanarkshire. He studied the piano at the Royal Scottish Academy of Music and read music at Glasgow University. In 1948, after military service, he won a scholarship to the Royal College of Music in London, where he studied the piano and conducting, and formed and conducted a student orchestra. After studying in Salzburg with Markevich and in Siena with Van Kempen, he joined Sadler's Wells Opera as a répétiteur. From 1952 to 1954 he was Associate Conductor of the BBC Scottish Symphony Orchestra, then returned to Sadler's Wells becoming, in 1957, the company's youngest musical director. In 1959 he moved to Scotland as the first native-born Principal Conductor and Artistic Director of the Scottish National Orchestra, bringing many new works to Scotland, often well in advance of their London performances. In 1962 he

helped to form Scottish Opera and as its artistic director was responsible for many notable successes, such as the first complete performance of Berlioz's *Les Troyens* in 1969, and in 1971 the first production in Scotland of Wagner's *Ring* cycle in German. He retired from the Scottish National Orchestra in 1984.

GIFFEN, Sir Robert
(1837–1910)

Statistician, born in Strathaven, Lanarkshire, the son of a village grocer. Apprenticed to a solicitor and briefly at Glasgow University, he started a career as a journalist in 1860 at the *Stirling Journal*. He then moved into financial journalism with *The Economist* and the *Daily News* in London. In 1876 he became Chief of the Statistical Department at the Board of Trade. He was famous for his 'Giffen paradox', attributed to him by the economist Alfred Marshall. This asserted that a rise in the price of necessities can lead to an increase in the demand for them.

GIFFORD, Adam
(1820–87)

Judge, born in Edinburgh. He was called to the Bar in 1849, and was raised to the bench as Lord Gifford in 1870. In his will he left endowments to Edinburgh, Glasgow, Aberdeen and St Andrews universities for regular series of undogmatic lectures on natural theology, which have enabled many leading thinkers to expound their views on society and morals.

GILL, David
(1843–1914)

Astronomer, born in Aberdeen. He started life as a watchmaker and amateur astronomer before being put in charge of Lord **Lindsay**'s private observatory at Dunecht, Aberdeenshire, in 1872. He achieved recognition for his high-precision determinations of the solar distance made on expeditions to Mauritius and Ascension Islands. As HM Astronomer at the Royal Observatory, Cape of Good Hope (1876–1907), he initiated a photographic survey of the southern sky and, as President of an international Astrographic Congress convened in Paris, became responsible for enormous photographic projects of the *Carte du Ciel* and *Astrographic Catalogue*; some 22 000 photographs were taken in the Cape's allotted part in this undertaking. Among Gill's other important contributions was the geodetic survey of South Africa.

GILLANDERS, Robin
(1952 –)

Photographer, born in Edinburgh. Taking an arts degree at Edinburgh University, he began his career as a history teacher before turning full-time to photography in 1983. His first work in photography was in advertising and fashion; he also became a lecturer at Napier Polytechnic (1983 –). His particular interest in portraiture came to the fore in his one-man exhibition, *Significant Others* (1989), which showed work of characteristic quiet sensitivity 'amplified into a universal statement about the significance and importance of relationships between those we admire and love' (in the words of **Murray Johnston**).

GILLESPIE, George
(1613–48)

Clergyman, born in Kirkcaldy. He studied at St Andrews University and in 1638 was ordained minister of Wemyss. A leader of Scottish Church opposition to Charles I's innovations in worship, he published *English Popish Ceremonies* in 1637. He became minister of Greyfriars, Edinburgh, in 1642, and in 1643 was sent to the Westminster Assembly where, as the youngest member, he played a prominent role in the debates on discipline and dogma. His *Aaron's Rod Blossoming* (1646) is a masterly statement of the high presbyterian claim to spiritual independence. In 1648 he became minister at the High Church, Edinburgh, and was Moderator of the General Assembly. In 1661 his tombstone in Kirkcaldy was smashed at the command of the Committee of Estates.

GILLESPIE, James
(1726–97)

Snuff and tobacco merchant in Edinburgh. He bought the estate of Spylaw, and left money to found a hospital (1801–3), which subsequently became a school run by the Merchant Taylors' Company.

GILLESPIE, Thomas
(1708–74)

Clergyman, born in Duddingston, Edinburgh. From 1741 he was minister of Carnock near Dunfermline, where in 1749 he opposed the ordination of a minister, was deposed by the General Assembly in 1752 and founded in 1761 the Relief Church, which was later absorbed into the United Presbyterian Church.

GILLIES, John
(1747–1836)

Historian, born near Brechin, Angus. Educated at Glasgow University, he worked as a tutor in Europe before moving to London (from 1784). He published a translation (1778) of Isocrates and Lysias, *History of Ancient Greece* (1786), *Frederick II of Prussia* (1789), and *History of the World from Alexander to Augustus* (1807–10). In 1793 he was appointed Historiographer Royal for Scotland.

GILLIES, Sir William George
(1898–1973)

Artist, born in Haddington, East Lothian. He studied at the Edinburgh College of Art, in Italy, and under André Lhote in France. His finely organized interpretations of Scottish landscape (many in watercolour) are well known, and his work is represented in the Tate Gallery. He was Principal of Edinburgh College of Art from 1961 to 1966.

GILMOUR, Sir John, 2nd Baronet
(1876–1940)

Politician. Born in Montrave, Fife, he was educated at Glenalmond and at Edinburgh and Cambridge universities. He served in the Boer War (winning the DSO) and World War I. Unionist MP for East Renfrewshire (1910–18) and Pollok (1918–40), he was Scottish Unionist Whip (1919–24), then Scottish Secretary (1924–9). He passed the Local Government Act 1929, which set up burgh and county councils and established a new grant system. As Minister of Agriculture (1931–2) he introduced protective quotas on wheat. He was Home Secretary (1932–5), and Minister of Shipping (1939–40). An able administrator and forceful debater, he chaired the committee in 1937 which advocated the reorganization of the Scottish Office Administration.

GLAS, John
(1695–1773)

Sectarian, born in Auchtermuchty, Fife, the founder in about 1730 of the small religious sect of Glassites or Sandemanians. From 1719 he was minister of Tealing near Dundee. Deposed in 1728, he formed a congregation based on simple apostolic practice. The name Sandemanians was derived from his son-in-law Robert Sandeman (1718–71). They held that Church establishments were unscriptural and that congregations should be self-governing.

GLASGOW, David Boyle, 7th Earl of
(1833–1915)

Politician. Born in Edinburgh, he joined the Royal Navy at the age of 13. Rising to the rank of captain, he saw action in the Crimean War and the China war of 1857. He succeeded to the title in 1890. Appointed Governor-General of New Zealand (1892–7), he replaced his cousin, Sir **James Fergusson**. In this post he created a constitutional crisis by refusing to accede to the request of the colony's premier that new members of the Upper House be appointed in order to give the ruling party a majority. He was overruled by the Colonial Office in London, and retired from the governor-generalship in 1897.

GLASIER, John Bruce
(1859–1920)

Socialist politician, born in Glasgow and brought up in Ayrshire. He trained as an architectural draughtsman in Glasgow, where he was influenced by William Morris, the poet and Socialist, becoming a pioneer Socialist in Glasgow in the 1880s. In the early 1890s he joined the Independent Labour Party and was its chairman from 1900 to 1903. For many years editor of the *Labour Leader*, a Socialist propaganda journal, he was one of the foremost speakers and organizers on behalf of the ILP in the pre-1914 era, travelling all over Britain. He opposed World War I from the outset, and was a champion of women's suffrage.

GLASS, Jack
(c.1937 –)

Evangelical Baptist minister, born in Glasgow. He grew up connected with a variety of Baptist churches, and studied at Glasgow University for a short spell before gaining a Diploma in Theology at the Free Church College, Glasgow. In 1967 he founded his own church, Zion Sovereign Grace Evangelical Baptist Church in Glasgow, which served as a base for his particular theological stance. Extreme Calvinism and a firm commitment to believers' baptism are the marks of his individualistic approach, and lie behind his strong anti-ecumenical position. Increasingly isolated from other extreme Protestant groups, he persists in a high-profile style, with an enthusiasm for protest, publicity and political engagement, going so far as to stand on several occasions as a Parliamentary Candidate. Although increasingly marginalized, he remains a familiar figure of protest, fiercely out of tune with the ecumenical and tolerant spirit of the age, but nonetheless a feature on the church landscape of Scotland since the 1960s.

GLEIG, George Robert
(1796–1888)

Novelist and historian, born in Stirling, the son of the Bishop of Brechin. He studied at Glasgow and Balliol College, Oxford, joined the army, and served in the Peninsular War (1813) and in North America (1814). He took orders (1820), and became Chaplain-General of the army (1844) and Inspector-General of military schools (1846). He wrote *The Subaltern* (1825) and other novels, and books on military history and biographies of Wellington and Warren Hastings.

GLEN, Iain
(1961 –)

Actor, born in Edinburgh. A graduate of Aberdeen University, he won the Bancroft Gold Medal at RADA and came to wide public prominence as the cold-blooded gangster in the television series *The Fear* (1988). The impact of the series and his handsome, aquiline features soon found him gainfully employed, but the television play *The Picnic* (1989) and minor supporting roles in films such as *Paris By Night* (1989) and *Gorillas in the Mist* (1989) left audiences unprepared for the passion and conviction he brought to the role of tormented Barlinnie prisoner **Larry Winters** in *Silent Scream* (1990). This performance won him many awards, including Best Actor at the Berlin Film Festival. Other film appearances include *Mountains of the Moon* (1990), *Fools of Fortune* (1990) and *Rosencrantz and Guildenstern are Dead* (1990). Among his extensive stage credits are *Hapgood* (1988), *The Man Who Had All The Luck* (1990) and *Hamlet* (1991).

GLEN, William

(1789–1826)

Poet, born in Glasgow. He spent most of his life in the West Indies. His only volume of poems and songs, *Poems Chiefly Lyrical*, published posthumously in 1815, contains the popular Jacobite lament, 'Wae's me for Prince Charlie'.

GLENCORSE, Baron See INGLIS, John

GLENDOOK, or GLENDOICK, Sir Thomas Murray, Lord

(?1630–1685)

Clerk Register and judge. Having passed advocate in 1661 he was soon appointed Lord Clerk Register and in 1674 a judge of the Court of Session. In 1679 he was given a royal licence to reprint the Acts of the Parliaments of Scotland, old and new, but the work was carelessly done and copied almost completely from Sir **John Skene**'s edition of the *Lawes and Actis of Parliament* of 1597, with the later Acts added from sessional publications to 1681. There are two editions, a handsome folio and two volumes duodecimo. The second edition is distinctly less accurate, re-peating Skene's typographical errors, yet this is the text of the statutes usually used and cited from its time onwards. Glendook lost his offices in 1681.

GLENNIE, Evelyn

(1965 –)

Percussion player, born in Aberdeen. She studied timpani and percussion from the age of 12, and from 1982 at the Royal Academy of Music, gaining an honours degree. She also studied marimba with Keiko Abe in Japan. Judged by the highest critical inter-national standards to be a percussionist of outstanding abilities, her achievement is ad-ditionally remarkable as she experienced a gradual but total loss of hearing in her early teens. The recipient of innumerable prizes and awards, she is a Fellow of the Royal College of Music, and an honorary Doctor of Music (Aberdeen, 1991). Many leading com-posers have written specially for her. She has recorded and appeared widely throughout Europe, the USA, Australia and the Far East, and has been the subject of many television and radio documentaries. She published an autobiography, *Good Vibrations*, in 1990.

GLENNIE, Kenneth William

(1926 –)

English-born geologist, born in Somerset of Scottish parents. Educated at school in Lon-don, he then studied geology at Edinburgh University, where he became the first MSc in a Scottish university. Joining Shell Oil in 1954 he embarked on a career in petroleum geology in which he is an acknowledged world figure. He is the editor and a principal author of the *Petroleum Geology of the North Sea*, now in its 3rd edition (1990). He has made a par-ticular study of ancient and modern deserts, and on land in Scotland he is known for his work on the intriguing Permian desert sands which fringe the southern edge of the Moray Firth Basin. Although now retired from the post he held in Shell Expro as senior geologist, he is based in Ballater as a consultant.

GLOAG, William Murray

(1865–1934)

The outstanding Scottish jurist of the 20th century. Son of William Ellis Gloag, Lord Kincairney, he was called to the Bar in 1889. He worked as a part-time assistant to Sir John Rankine, Professor of Scots Law at Edinburgh University, 1899–1905, and also lectured on evidence and procedure from 1902 to 1905. In 1905 he was appointed Regius Professor of Law at Glasgow Uni-versity, where he built a reputation as a brilliant teacher. He published in 1897 (with J M Irvine, later professor at Aberdeen) *Rights in Security and Cautionary Obligatons*, which is still a respected authority. In 1914 he published a treatise on the *Law of Contract* (2nd ed 1929), a major work which secured high professional regard, little short of that accorded to **Stair, John Erskine** and **George Bell**. In 1927 along with Candlish Henderson, he produced a new *Introduction to the Law of Scotland*, which, much modified by later editors, is still in use.

GOLD, Jimmy See NAUGHTON, Charles

GOODSIR, John

(1814–67)

Anatomist, born in Anstruther, Fife. He studied at St Andrews and Edinburgh univer-sities, where he became Professor of Anatomy in 1846. A prolific writer, who damaged his health by neglect, he is best known for his work on cellular theory.

GORDON

Name of a family which takes its origin and name from the lands of Gordon in Berwickshire and whose members became Lords of Strathbogie from 1357, Earls of Huntly from 1445, Marquesses of Huntly from 1599 and Dukes of Gordon from 1684 until 1836, when the title became extinct. Its 157 branches include the Lochinvar line (Viscounts of Kenmure from 1633, extinct in 1847), the Earlston branch, a cadet branch of the latter, and according to tradition the Earls of **Aberdeen** are descended from an illegitimate brother of Sir Adam of Gordon, who was killed at Homildon in 1402.

GORDON, Alexander, 4th Duke of Gordon

(c.1745–1827)

Nobleman and song-writer, the author of the well-known song, 'Cauld Kail in Aberdeen'. Lord Keeper of Scotland, he was a loyal patriot, who raised regiments for several wars. His wife, Jane Maxwell (c.1749–1812), was known as the 'beautiful Duchess of Gordon'.

GORDON, George, 2nd Earl of Huntly

(d.c.1502)

Nobleman, and high chancellor of Scotland (1498–1501). He married Princess Annabella, daughter of **James I** of Scotland. Their second son married the Countess of Sutherland and was progenitor of the Earls of Sutherland. Their third son was progenitor of the turbulent Gordons of Gight, from whom Byron's maternal ancestors were descended.

GORDON, George, 4th Earl of Huntly

(1514–62)

Nobleman and high chancellor of Scotland. He supported Cardinal **Beaton** against Arran (1543, see **James Hamilton, 2nd Earl of Arran**), but when stripped by the crown of his new earldom of Moray he rushed into revolt and was killed at Corrichie.

GORDON, George, 6th Earl, and 1st Marquis of Huntly

(1562–1636)

Nobleman, and head of the Roman Catholics in Scotland. He defeated a royal force under the Earl of **Argyll** in 1594 at Glenlivet but, after submitting to the king, was pardoned and made marquis in 1599.

GORDON, Hannah Cambell Grant

(1941 –)

Actress, born in Edinburgh. Winner of the **James Bridie** Gold Medal at the Royal College of Dramatic Art in Glasgow (1962), she subsequently worked at Dundee Rep and the Glasgow Citizens' Theatre, and made her television début in *Johnson Over Jordan* (1965). A perceptive portrayer of the humorous and serious aspects of middle-class life, her vast array of television credits includes the situation comedies *My Wife Next Door* (1972) and *Joint Account* (1989 –), as well as such popular drama series as *Upstairs, Downstairs* (1974) and *Telford's Change* (1979). Rare film appearances include *Spring and Port Wine* (1969), *Alfie Darling* (1974) and *The Elephant Man* (1980). Theatre work has provided more opportunities to display her versatility, and her credits include *Can You Hear Me At The Back?* (1979), *The Jeweller's Shop* (1982), *The Country Girl* (1983) and *Shirley Valentine* (1989). She has also worked extensively in radio drama.

GORDON, Harry

(1893–1957)

Comedian, born in Aberdeen. In 1912 he made his stage début with the local concert party Monty's Pierrots in Stonehaven. His first London appearance was at the Palladium (1929). He established the first touring 'tab show', *Winners* (1922), and *Harry Gordon's Entertainers* at the Pavilion, Aberdeen (1924). From 1929 he worked in pantomime, including an 11-year run at the Alhambra, Glasgow, from 1937, and made over 100 radio broadcasts from Aberdeen, including his own series, such as *Harry's Half Hour* and *Gordon Gaieties*. Of his repertoire of over 200 character sketches, the most famous was 'The Laird of Invernsecky'.

GORDON, James Alexander

(1782–1869)

Naval commander, born in Wardhouse, Aberdeenshire. He entered the Royal Navy as a midshipman in 1793. After serving in a succession of warships, in which he saw service at the battle of Cape St Vincent and the Nile, he joined the sloop *Racoon* in the West Indies station. Between 1805 and 1808 he scored several notable successes against French and Spanish privateers. Transferred to the Adriatic, he lost a leg during the naval action at Lissa in 1811. He returned to the service a year later as senior naval officer in the expedition which forced its way up the Potomac to destroy Fort Washington during the war against America. His peacetime appointments included command in North America and Madagascar and the position of Superintendent of the Chatham dockyard. He was made Admiral of the Fleet in 1868.

GORDON, John Rutherford
(1890–1974)

Journalist, one of the most notable products of Dundee journalism. Born and educated there, he left school at the age of 14 to join a local newspaper, and worked as a sub-editor in London. Appointed Editor of the *Sunday Express* in 1928, he turned a failing title into one of the most profitable newspapers in the world, increasing its circulation from 450 000 to 3 200 000 by the end of his reign. He introduced the first crossword puzzle and the first astrology column in a British newspaper. When he retired as editor (1952), he began an acerbic weekly column for the paper, called Current Events, which he continued until his death.

GORDON, Sir John Watson
(1788–1864)

Painter, born in Edinburgh. Originally intending to become an engineer, he turned to art, becoming a pupil of **Raeburn**, and succeeding him in 1823 as the leading portrait painter of Scotland. His portraits of **Macaulay**, the Prince of Wales and many others are in the Scottish National Gallery, and his portrait of De Quincey is in the National Portrait Gallery, London.

GORDON, Patrick
(1635–99)

Soldier of fortune, born in Easter Auchleuchries, Aberdeenshire. A Catholic, at 16 he entered the Jesuit College of Braunsberg, but absconded in 1653, eventually joining the Swedish army during the war with Poland in 1655. During the next six years he was repeatedly captured, and each time fought for his captors until he was retaken. In 1661 he joined the Russian army and rose to high rank, being so valued that he was not allowed to retire. Although he was sent on missions to Britain in 1665 and 1685, he did not fulfil his desire to return to Scotland permanently. Under Tsar Peter the Great he was made general in 1688, crushed a conspiracy in 1689 and a serious revolt in 1698. He was buried in Moscow.

GORDON, Robert
(1580–1661)

Cartographer, of Straloch, Aberdeenshire. Together with his son, James (c.1615–1686), who was minister of Rothiemay, Banffshire, he revised and edited **Timothy Pont**'s Scottish maps for Willem Blaeu's *Atlas*. The son also wrote *Scots Affairs* 1624–51 (Spalding Club, 1841). A grandson, Robert Gordon (1665–1732), founded a boys' school, Robert Gordon's College, in Aberdeen.

GORDON, Seton
(1886–1977)

Naturalist, writer and wildlife photographer, born in Aboyne, Aberdeenshire. His reputation was established by his first publication, *Birds of the Loch and Mountain* (1904), and he subsequently became a prolific writer on the natural history of Scotland, which he publicized in lectures throughout Britain. Specializing in the golden eagle, his photographs of this and other wild birds in the Scottish Highlands are among the very earliest.

GORDON CUMMING, Eka
(Constance Fredereka)
(1837–1924)

Traveller and author. The twelfth child of Sir William Gordon-Cumming, Baronet of Altyre and Gordonstown, she began her travels with a visit to her married sister in India in 1867. Over the next 12 years she journeyed through the Pacific to Fiji and Hawaii, California and the Sierrra Nevada, Egypt, China and Ceylon (Sri Lanka), and wrote eight widely popular books, which she illustrated with her own paintings.

GORDON OF AUCHINTOUL, Alexander
(1669–1751)

Soldier of fortune, born in Aberdeenshire, the son of Lewis Gordon of Auchintoul, a lord of session. In 1688 he became a cadet in a Scottish company raised to help the French in Catalonia. He went to Russia in 1693, where his kinsman **Patrick Gordon** was high in the military command, and in 1696 relieved the siege of Azoff. He married Patrick Gordon's daughter the following year, but in 1700 was captured by Charles XII at Narva, until exchanged for another officer. Promoted brigadier-general, he routed the Swedes at Kysmark. He helped defeat the Poles at Podkamian, sending several captured Polish standards to Scotland. On his father's death in 1711 he returned home, fought with the Jacobites at Sheriffmuir, and escaped abroad. He later refused the rank of lieutenant general in the Spanish army. Gordon wrote a life of Peter the Great and a memoir of himself, published in Aberdeen in 1755.

GORRIE, Alan
(1946 –)

Rock singer and bass guitarist, born in Perth. Together with Onnie McIntyre (1945 –), Robbie McIntosh (1950–74), Roger Ball (1944 –), Malcolm Duncan (1945 –) and Mike Rosen he formed the group Average White Band in 1972. Rosen was soon replaced by Hamish Stuart (1949 –). The group's name referred to the fact that almost uniquely at the time they were a white band playing a style of music influenced by black soul and funk. The band's début album, *Show Your Hand* (1973), went largely unnoticed, but *AWB* (1974) brought success both in Britain and the USA. It remains their best-known work, although subsequent albums include *Shine* (1980) and *Cupid's In Fashion* (1982). Gorrie released the solo album *Sleepless Nights* in 1985 and Ball, Duncan and Rosen undertook session work as The Dundee Horns. Gorrie, McIntyre and Ball reformed the group with a new line-up in 1989.

GOW, Nathaniel
(1766–1831)

Musician, teacher and music publisher, described as 'the greatest preserver and improver of the Age'. He was born in Inver, near Dunkeld, Perthshire, the son of **Niel Gow**, who taught him, like his brothers, on the kit. He later studied in Edinburgh, playing the violin, cello and trumpet. In 1782 he was appointed one of His Majesty's Herald Trumpeters of Scotland. In 1791 he succeeded his brother William as leader of the orchestra that played at the fashionable concerts in Edinburgh, and became the leading musical figure of the capital. In 1796, with William Shepherd, he set up a music publishing business (which later failed), popularizing Scottish melodies, airs and dance tunes. He was also a fine composer in his own right, demonstrated by the Strathspey *Lady Charlotte Campbell*, the spirited reel *Largo's Fairy Dance* and the heart-rending *Nathaniel Gow's Lament for the Death of his Brother*.

GOW, Niel
(1727–1807)

Scotland's most famous fiddler and songwriter, known as 'the father of Strathspey and Reel players'. Born in Inver, near Dunkeld, Perthshire, the son of a plaid weaver, he started playing the fiddle at the age of five and was largely self-taught. Patronized by the Dukes of Atholl, he was much in demand as a player at important balls and parties. His compositions include Strathspeys, jigs and reels, and the exceptional elegiac pieces *Niel Gow's Lamentation for James Moray Esq. of Abercarney* and *Niel Gow's Lament for the Death of his Second Wife*. His open, honest character, unique style of playing, long career and fine compositions combined to make him a household name during his lifetime and a legend after it. His influence on Scottish music continued through the work of his sons Andrew, John and **Nathaniel**, all of whom were practising musicians.

GOWANS, Sir James
(1821–90)

Architect, born in Blackness, West Lothian, the son of a mason. Educated in Edinburgh, he was apprenticed to **David Bryce** until 1846. Before starting his architectural career, he turned to railway engineering and became master of several quarries. He is recognized particularly for his imaginative approach to masonry construction, employing an original, modular grid system and cyclopean stonework. His romantic outlook was founded on rationalist theories and motivated by financial and social concerns. He collaborated briefly with like-minded romanticist, **Fred-**

erick **Thomas Pilkington**. He was at his peak in the 1850s and 1860s when he designed the colourful Edinburgh villas of Rockville (1858, demolished), Lammerburn (1860) and Gowanbank (1859). Concern for the condition of workers' housing and pollution stand out among his far-sighted philosophies. A popular figure throughout his career, he was made Dean of Guild in 1885 and was a prime mover in 1886 of the Edinburgh International Exhibition. Rosebank Cottages (1855) and tenements on Castle Terrace, Edinburgh (1866) may be compared with railway stations at Creetown (1859) and Lochee, Dundee (1861), as examples of his inventive capacity.

GRAHAM, Alex (Alexander)

(1915 –)

Cartoonist, creator of 'Fred Basset', born in Glasgow. He attended the Glasgow School of Art where he won several prizes for portrait painting. His cartooning career began when he submitted gag drawings to various Scottish papers. He then developed his first comic strip, 'Wee Hughie' for the *Weekly News*. This was followed by 'Our Bill' for the same paper (1946), which led to his first national success, 'Willy Nilly', in *Sunday Graphic* (1947). He then raised his sights to the glossy society weekly *Tatler*, introducing 'Briggs the Butler' (1949), a character who was to run for 17 years. Then came 'Graham's Golf Club' in *Punch*, a series built around his favourite hobby, and finally his greatest success, 'Fred Basset', the famous 'thinking dog'. This strip first appeared in the *Daily Mail* in 1963, where it has been running ever since. The strip is syndicated world-wide, and is especially popular in the USA.

GRAHAM, Angus

(1892–1979)

Archaeologist, born in Skipness, Argyll. After studying at Oxford University, he began his career in forestry in Britain and Canada, but an early interest in archaeology led to his appointment as Secretary to the Royal Commission on the Ancient and Historical Monuments of Scotland (1935–57) and latterly as a Commissioner (1960–74). He also served as Secretary to the Society of Antiquaries of Scotland (1938–66) and was made an Honorary Fellow in 1977. Improving standards of recording and interpretation in RCAHMS, he expanded the scope of its work, and published many papers on diverse aspects of Scottish archaeology, from surgery with flint to harbours and graveyard monuments.

GRAHAM, Dougal

(c.1724–1779)

Ballad and chap-book writer, born in Raploch near Stirling. He followed Prince **Charles Edward Stuart**'s army in 1745–6 and wrote a metrical (doggerel) eyewitness account of the campaign. He was appointed bellman of Glasgow about 1770. Of his rambling ballads, the best known are *John Hielandman's Remarks on Glasgow* and *Turnimspike*.

GRAHAM, Henry Grey

(1874–1959)

Roman Catholic priest, born, the son of a minister, in Moxton, Roxburghshire. Educated at Kelso High School and St Andrews University, he became a Church of Scotland minister in Avondale, Lanarkshire (1901–3). In 1903 he was received into the Roman Catholic Church at Fort Augustus, thus causing a sensation as the first major convert from the Church of Scotland. Ordained a priest in 1906, he became curate at Motherwell (1907) and parish priest at Logriggend (1916). From 1917 to 1929 he was auxiliary to the Archbishop of St Andrews and Edinburgh as Titular bishop of Tipasa, becoming effective administrator of the Archdiocese. His outspoken manner and combustible effect on his former coreligionists probably militated against his expected appointment to the archbishopric, which went instead to **Andrew Joseph McDonald**, while Graham became Rector of Holy Cross, Glasgow. He published a variety of brief works, and was famous as a preacher, his most famous sermon being to a gathering of 10 000 on 24 June, 1935 at Waverley Market, Edinburgh, during a Eucharistic Congress, preceding though not of itself necessarily inducing the riots led by **John Cormack**. Graham is caricatured as 'Archbishop Gillespie, of Midlothian' in **Bruce Marshall**'s *Father Malachy's Miracle*.

GRAHAM, James

(1745–94)

Quack-doctor, born in Edinburgh. He studied medicine there but did not graduate, although he styled himself 'Dr Graham'. After several years abroad he set up practice, first in Bristol (1774), then in Bath (1775), and finally also in London, where he established 'temples of Health and hymen', prescribed remedies and lectured. He put his patients on a 'magnetic throne', into electrically charged baths or into 'celestial beds'. Although denounced as a quack and frequently imprisoned, he became fashionable, his clientele including the Prince of Wales and the Duchess of Devonshire. In 1781, it is alleged, he exhibited Emma Lyon, later Lady Hamilton, as the 'Goddess of Health'. In 1783 he was arrested in Edinburgh after writing articles in support of his lectures (which had been prohibited), under a forged eminent name. In 1790 he indulged in 'earth bathing', turned religious and styled himself 'the servant of the Lord O.W.L.' (Oh wonderful love). His pamphlets and extravagant advertisements show that he was an admass man born two centuries before his time.

GRAHAM, James
(1806–69)

Photographer, the youngest son of Alexander Graham of Lymekilns and Fereneze, whose family estate was in Renfrewshire. As Honorary Secretary of the Anglican Mission in Jerusalem, described as 'The London Society for Promoting Christianity Amongst the Jews', he visited Jerusalem in 1853, remaining until 1857. While there, he met the artists William Holman Hunt and Thomas Seddon. Graham was a highly accomplished amateur photographer, and these artists used the photographs he took in the Holy Land as the basis of several of their religious paintings. His photographs, albumen prints from paper negatives, are extremely rare, as he did not produce them commercially. An album of photographs taken in Italy between 1858 and 1864 is now in the Alinari Collection in Florence.

GRAHAM, James Gillespie,
originally **James Gillespie**
(1776–1835)

Architect and town planner, born in Dunblane, Perthshire. His churches, St Mary's Roman Catholic Cathedral, Edinburgh (1813–14), St Andrew's Cathedral, Glasgow (1814–17), and the Tolbooth Church (with A W N Pugin), Edinburgh (1839–44), introduced into Scotland a purer gothic style based on authentic architectural detailing. In 1815 he married the heiress Margaret Graham of Ochill, and took her surname. Gillespie Graham also specialized in picturesque country houses and castles, such as Dunninald, Angus (c.1820–4), and Murthley House, Perthshire (1829–30, demolished), and was a town planner of some genius: his Moray Estate (designed 1822) is the most imaginative and successful of the Edinburgh New Town schemes.

GRAHAM, John Anderson
(1861–1942)

Missionary and philanthropist, born in London. He was educated at Cardross School and Glasgow High School, and worked in a law office and as a civil servant before studying divinity at Edinburgh. He was ordained by the Church of Scotland in 1889, and became the first missionary of the Church's Young Men's Guild when he and his wife, Catherine Graham (who is credited with a joint role in their philanthropic work) were posted to Kalimpong in northern Bengal. Their mission became the focal point of religious life in the region, and they made great progress in medical and educational provision, leading to the establishment of an indigenous church. They became joint founders and builders of the St Andrews Colonial Homes in 1900 (later known as Dr Graham's Homes) for needy children. John Graham was the first missionary to be elected Moderator of the General Assembly (1931), and received honorary degrees from Edinburgh (1904) and Aberdeen (1932) universities.

GRAHAM, Robert See
CUNNINGHAME GRAHAM,
Robert

GRAHAM, Thomas
(1805–69)

Chemist and physicist, one of the founders of physical chemistry, born in Glasgow. In 1830 he became Professor of Chemistry at Glasgow, and in 1837 at University College, London. In 1855 he was appointed Master of the Mint. His researches on the molecular diffusion of gases led him to formulate the law 'that the diffusion rate of gases is inversely as the square root of their density'. He discovered the properties of colloids and their separation by dialysis.

GRAHAME, James
(1765–1811)

Poet, born in Glasgow. He studied law at Glasgow University and was called to the Bar, but was forced to give up his career because of ill-health. He took Anglican orders in 1809 and became a curate in Shipton, Gloucestershire and later Sedgefield, Durham. He wrote a dramatic poem, *Mary, Queen of Scots* (1801), but most of his poetry was evocative of the quiet Scottish countryside, particularly *The Sabbath* (1804) and *The Birds of Scotland* (1806), with an introduction that made it 'popular ornithology'. Christopher North (**John Wilson**) thought highly of him, but he was not rated by Byron.

GRAHAME, James
(1790–1842)

Historian, born in Glasgow. Educated by a French emigrant priest, and then at Glasgow Grammar School, Glasgow University, and St John's College, Cambridge, he was called to the Scottish Bar in 1812. Influenced by the theories of Malthus, he contributed to various literary reviews, and in 1827 he published his two-volume *The History of the Rise and Progress of the United States of North America 'till the British Revolution in 1688*. He followed this with *The History of the United States of North America, from the plantation of the British Colonies, 'till their revolt and Declaration of Independence* (4 vols, 1836). His work, which was highly important as British narrative sympathetic to the colonies, was nevertheless attacked by the Jacksonian historian George Bancroft but defended by Josiah Quincy. His final work was *Who is to blame? or, a cursory review of 'American Apology for American accession to Negro Slavery'* (1842).

GRAHAME, Kenneth
(1859–1932)

Children's writer, born in Edinburgh, the son of an advocate. He was brought up in Inverary, Argyll, until 1864, and then by his grandmother in Cookham Dene, Berkshire. He was educated at St Edward's School, Oxford, and in 1876 entered the Bank of England as a gentleman clerk. He became its secretary in 1898 and retired for health reasons in 1908. His early work consisted of collected essays and country tales, *Pagan Papers* (1893), *The Golden Age* (1895) and *Dream Days* (1898), which revealed a re-markably subtle, delicate and humorous sympathy with the child mind. In 1908 he published his best-known work, *The Wind in the Willows* (1908), with its quaint and unforgettable riverside characters, Rat, Mole, Badger and Toad, which has become a children's classic.

GRAINGER, Thomas
(1794–1852)

Civil engineer, born in Ratho, near Edinburgh. After training he set up business as a land surveyor in 1816. From 1823, with John Miller (1805–83) as assistant, he surveyed, designed and built the Monkland & Kirkintilloch Railway, one of the earliest lines in Scotland, which opened in 1825. Over the next 20 years, with Miller as his partner, he was responsible for many railways in Scotland and the north of England. For the Edinburgh, Perth and Dundee Railway he proposed the idea of ferrying rail wagons across the Forth and Tay estuaries on specially designed steamships; when the Granton and Burntisland service started in 1849 it was the world's first open-water train ferry.

GRANGE, Lady, née **Rachel Chiesley**
(d.1745)

Wife of the Lord Justice Clerk of Scotland, James Erskine, Lord Grange (1679–1754), who kept her a prisoner on St Kilda for seven years. She was a bad-tempered woman, opposed to her husband's Jacobite views (he was the brother of the 6th Earl of **Mar**, who had been the leader of the 1715 Jacobite rising). On threatening to expose her husband's conspiratorial views one night in 1731, she was spirited away to the Hebrides, while her death was announced in Edinburgh and a mock funeral held. After three years of captivity on a lonely island off North Uist, she was sent to the remote island group of St Kilda, where she was held incommunicado on the island of Hirta for eight years (1734–42). She was then taken back to the Western Isles, where she managed to smuggle a letter to her cousin, the Lord Advocate, who sent a gunboat to look for her, but failed to trace her whereabouts. She died on the Vaternish peninsula.

GRANT, Sir Alexander
(1826–84)

British educationist, born in New York, the son of Sir Robert Innes Grant, seventh

Baronet of Dalvey, and of Judith Tower Battelle of Santa Cruz. Educated at Harrow and Balliol College, Oxford, he was elected a Fellow of Oriel in 1849. Impoverished by slave emancipation in Santa Cruz, he was forced to work and as result edited Aristotle's *Ethics* (1857), which became the standard edition for the century. He was Examiner for the Indian Civil Service (1855) and Oxford Examiner in Classics (1856), succeeding his father as baronet in 1856 and becoming Inspector of Schools in Madras (1859), Professor of History at Elphinstone College, Bombay (1860) and Vice-Chancellor of the University of Bombay (1863–8). In 1868 he defeated Sir **James Simpson** for the principalship of Edinburgh University. A natural diplomat, as was evident from his biographies of Aristotle and Xenophon (which took the middle road in any scholarly controversy, whether it existed or not), he ended some of the worst feuding with the town and obtained the needed funding for new medical buildings. Among his publications was *Happiness and Utility as Promoted by the Higher Education of Women* (1872). He was awarded honorary doctorates from Oxford, Cambridge, Edinburgh and Glasgow universities.

GRANT, Angus

(1931 –)

Traditional fiddler, born in Fort Augustus. As a teenager he worked as a shepherd before taking a job in forestry, and although fiddling has never been his full-time occupation, he has performed in the USA and Europe as well as at folk festivals throughout Scotland. He is recognized as the outstanding exponent of the West Highland fiddling style, distinguished by its heavy traces of bagpipe phrasing and intonation. Among his recorded work is a solo album, *Highland Fiddle* (1978). A largely self-taught player, his execution is as rare as his musical style: he bows the fiddle with his left hand.

GRANT, Anne, née MacVicar

(1755–1838)

Poet and essayist, born in Glasgow, the daughter of an army officer. She lived in North America as a child (1758–68). In 1779 she married the Rev James Grant, minister of nearby Laggan. Left a widow in 1801, she turned to writing and published *Poems* (1803), *Letters from the Mountains* (1806), *Memoirs of an American Lady* (1808), and *Superstitions of the Highlanders* (1811). In

1810 she moved to Edinburgh, where she mixed in the best literary circles, and in 1825 received a pension of 50 through the influence of Sir **Walter Scott**.

GRANT, Duncan James Corrowr

(1885–1978)

Painter, born in Rothiemurchus, Invernessshire. He studied at the Westminster and Slade Schools, in Italy and Paris, and was associated with Roger Fry's Omega Workshops, and later with the London Group. His works, mainly landscapes, portraits and still-life, owe something to the influence of Roger Fry and Cézanne, but he also designed textiles, pottery, etc. His *Girl at the Piano* is in the Tate Gallery, London.

GRANT, Elizabeth, of Rothiemurcus

(1797–1885)

Diarist of Scottish and Irish social history, known for her posthumous work *Memoirs of a Highland Lady* (1898), which details her family's many misfortunes. She was born in Edinburgh, the daughter of Sir John Peter Grant, a lawyer, Whig MP and Highland landowner, who moved his family from Edinburgh to London and back in search of a profitable legal practice. His final Edinburgh venture failed and the family moved under the shadow of debt to the family house at The Doune, near Aviemore. Elizabeth and her sisters were obliged to write stories and articles to raise money. Her brother was imprisoned by his creditors in 1826 and the next year her father fled to India to escape a similar fate. There he became Judge of Bombay and Chief Justice of Calcutta, and Elizabeth married Colonel Henry Smith of Baltiboys, County Wicklow, Ireland (1829), who had ten days previously inherited the 1200-acre estate from his brother. She raised a family, Smith dying in 1867, managed the estate with awe-inspiring maternalism through the Irish great famine and beyond, and wrote memoirs and diaries for the amusement of her children. These memoirs, written under her maiden name, are famous for their account of Edinburgh society and customs. Her diaries were published in part in *The Irish Journals of Elizabeth Smith* 1840–1850 (1980), in part as *The Highland Lady in Ireland* (1991). A strikingly forceful, if self-righteous witness, she makes the reader a confidant while describing her difficult life in an interesting period of personal and national change.

GRANT, Sir Francis
(1803–78)

Painter, born in Kilgraston, Perthshire, the brother of Sir **James Hope Grant**. He painted sporting scenes, and his portrait groups were in great demand. Among the best known of these are the *Meet of HM Staghounds* and the *Melton Hunt*, executed for the Duke of Wellington. He was President of the Royal Academy in 1866.

GRANT, James
(1822–87)

Prolific novelist and historical author, born in Edinburgh. After a childhood in Newfoundland and military service, he published a long series of novels and histories, that were illustrative mainly of the achievements of Scottish arms abroad. Among his works are *The Romance of War* (1845) and *British Battles on Land and Sea* (1873).

GRANT, James Augustus
(1827–92)

Soldier and explorer, born in Nairn. Educated at Marischal College, Aberdeen, he joined the Indian army, eventually reaching the rank of colonel, and seeing service in the Battle of Gujerat, the Indian Mutiny, and in the Abyssinian campaign of 1868. With John Hanning Speke he explored the sources of the Nile (1860–3) and made important botanical collections. On Speke's death he became the main spokesman for the expedition, becoming a leading African specialist. In 1864 he published *A Walk Across Africa*, and in the same year was awarded the Gold medal of the Royal Geographical Society.

GRANT, Sir James Hope
(1808–75)

Soldier, born in Kilgraston, Perthshire, the brother of Sir **Francis Grant**. He distinguished himself in the two Sikh wars (1845–9), the Indian Mutiny (1857) and the 1860 expedition against China. He commanded the army of Madras (1861–5).

GRANT, James Shaw
(1910 –)

Journalist and newspaper proprietor, born in Stornoway, where his father ran the main newspaper of the Hebrides. Educated at the Nicolson Institute and Glasgow University, he inherited the *Stornoway Gazette* in 1932 and continued as proprietor/editor for 31 years. Chairman of the Crofters Commission (1963–78), he combined his professional life with an active involvement in the promotion of the Highlands and Islands. Keenly interested in the theatre, he wrote several stage plays and was Chairman of Pitlochry Festival Theatre (1971–83).

GRANT, Robert
(1814–92)

Astronomer, born in Grantown-on-Spey, Morayshire. Professor of Astronomy at Glasgow University, he is principally remembered for his historical researches. These culminated in his *History of Physical Astronomy from the Earliest Ages to the Middle of the 19th Century* (1852), which earned for him the Gold Medal of the Royal Astronomical Society. As an observing astronomer he published two catalogues of the positions of 8000 stars, which he compiled with very little assistance. He observed from Spain the total solar eclipse of July 1860, and was one of the first to assert the true nature of solar prominences and the solar chromosphere.

GRANT, Sir William
(1755–1832)

Scottish-born English judge, born near Elgin, Moray. Educated at Elgin Grammar School, King's College, Aberdeen, and Leiden, he was called to the English Bar, served as Attorney-General of Quebec (1776), as MP for Shrewsbury (1790) and then Banff (1796). A Welsh judge in 1793, and Chief Justice of Chester (1798), he was appointed Master of the Rolls (1801–17). In this office he achieved a very high reputation as an equity judge, while in the Privy Council he contributed substantially to the development of prize law during the Napoleonic wars.

GRANT, William
(1839–1923)

Distiller, born in Dufftown, Banffshire. He began his career in quarrying and lime-burning. Following this, he worked as bookkeeper and manager at the Mortlach distillery for almost two decades. His personal history at this time borders on the romantic. Having bought second-hand equipment from a neighbouring distiller he proceeded, along with his six sons, to build the Glenfiddich distillery.

This accomplished, production began in 1887. From the outset most of the whisky was sold for blending. Such was its success that a second distillery was opened at Balvenie in 1893. Grant then sent both his son and his son-in-law to Glasgow to set up the family's own blending business. From this time Glenfiddich became established as a popular five-year old, and William's eldest son, John, withdrew from schoolteaching to run the company.

GRANT, William
(1863–1946)

Lexicographer, born in Elgin, Moray. He studied in France, Belgium and Germany, and became a lecturer in English, modern languages and phonetics at Aberdeen University. He was until his death Editor of the *Scottish National Dictionary*, and published various works on Scottish dialects.

GRAY, Alasdair James
(1934 –)

Novelist, painter and playwright, born in Glasgow. He was educated at Whitehill Secondary School and Glasgow School of Art. Painting was his first vocation and he came late to novel writing; *Lanark*, his first novel, was published in 1981. A gargantuan effort, it is a phantasmagoric exploration of modern city life related by Duncan Thaw, in which science fiction is counterbalanced by stark realism, the setting being a place called Unthank, palpably Glasgow. In *1982 Janine* (1984), the hero — if he can be called that — is a divorced, alcoholic, insomniac supervisor of security installations who is telling his story to the mirror in a dismal Borders' hotel. Like others of Gray's works it is erotically charged and very funny. *Unlikely Stories, Mostly* (1983), a collection of stories, demonstrated his versatility, and with *The Fall of Kelvin Walker* (1985), Gray showed that he was adept at social satire, the story being that of a Scotsman on the make in the media who gets his comeuppance. Wickedly inventive and typographically unconventional, his hallmark is a debunking of Received Pronunciation, a hilarious example of which is to be found in *Something Leather* (1990), typically described by the puckish author as 'the first British fiction since the *Canterbury Tales* to show such a wide social range in such embarrassing sexual detail'. Other books include *Old Negatives* (1989), a collection of poems, and *McGrotty and Ludmilla* (1990), 'the Aladdin story set in modern Whitehall'.

GRAY, Sir Alexander
(1882–1968)

Economist and poet, born in Dundee and educated at Dundee High School and the universities of Edinburgh (double first in mathematics and economics), Göttingen and the Sorbonne in Paris. His first work was the completion of **John Davidson**'s *The Scottish Staple at Veere* (1909). His work as a civil servant (1905–21) included administration of national insurance and intelligence work. During World War I he translated *J'accuse, von einem Deutschen* (1915) and wrote pamphlets on German attitudes to the war. He was Professor of Political Economy at Aberdeen University (1921–34), and at Edinburgh University (1935–56). His leading, and still respected, economic works were *The Development of Economic Doctrine* (1931) and *The Socialist Tradition* (1946). He also translated German and Danish ballads into Scots and published many of his own poems.

GRAY, Cecil
(1895–1951)

Writer on music and composer, born in Edinburgh. He was closely associated with the composer Philip Heseltine (Peter Warlock, of whom he wrote a study in 1934), with whom he edited *The Sackbut* magazine (from 1920), and wrote in collaboration *Carlo Gesualdo, Prince of Venosa, Musician and Murderer* (1926). Gray was an important champion of Sibelius (in two books, 1931 and 1935) and served as music critic for the *Daily Telegraph* and the *Manchester Guardian*. He published his memoirs, *Musical Chairs or Between Two Stools* in 1948; his *Notebooks* were published posthumously (1989). He composed three operas on a grand scale, to his own texts, and other music.

GRAY, David
(1838–61)

Poet, born in Merkland, near Kirkintilloch, Dunbartonshire, the son of a handloom weaver. He studied divinity at Glasgow University, but took to poetry and in 1860 moved to London with **Robert Buchanan**, although he died of consumption the following year. His only collection of poetry, *The Luggie and Other Poems*, a lyrical poem in praise of the stream near his birthplace, was published posthumously in 1874. It also contained *In the Shadows*.

GRAY, Gordon Joseph
(1910–)

Roman Catholic Archbishop and Cardinal, born in Edinburgh. Educated at Holy Cross Academy, Edinburgh, St Joseph's Seminary, Sussex, and St John's, Surrey, he was ordained a priest in 1935. Following various appointments, in 1951 he was appointed Archbishop of St Andrews and Edinburgh. In 1969 he was named Cardinal by Pope Paul VI, the first such appointment in Scottish history (apart from exiled clerics in Rome). In 1982 he played a major part in bringing Pope John Paul II to Scotland. A traditionalist in manner, his pacific temperament and kindly nature made him a valuable force in furthering, if not inaugurating, ecumenical advances, and made possible the great improvement in the acceptability of Catholics in Scottish life.

GRAY, John
(1866–1934)

English-born priest and poet, born in London, the son of a Scottish wheelwright and carpenter. Educated for one year at a grammar school, he became a metal turner at Woolwich Arsenal. Studying privately, he passed the Civil Service examinations and became Librarian at the Foreign Office (1890). He was incorrectly identified as the original of Oscar Wilde's *Dorian Gray*, but Wilde did pay for the publication of his poems, *Silverpoints* (1893). Their friendship was broken by Mark André Raffalovich (1864–1934), a wealthy Polish Jew with whom Gray wrote *The Blackmailers*, a play produced in 1893. Gray's striking verse translations of Verlaine and Rimbaud were followed by translations from more religious and devotional authors, published as *Spiritual Poems* (1896). Gray entered the Scots College in Rome in 1898, was ordained priest and served as Curate in St Patrick's Church, Edinburgh, a slum parish in the Cowgate from which he was rescued by Raffalovich's gift to the Archdiocese of St Andrews and Edinburgh of the site and construction costs of St Peter's Church in Morningside. The archdiocese readily accepted Raffalovich's proposal of Gray as St Peter's priest. Gray, ultimately made Canon, remained its incumbent until his death. He continued to produce occasional poetry, notably *The Long Road* (1926), as well as singular prose, including his fantastical novel *Park* (1932). Raffalovich left his fortune to Gray, from whom it was invested as The John Gray Trust, funding the Roman Catholic Chaplaincy of Edinburgh University under the Dominican fathers. Gray continues to excite interest, not only as a decadent poet and experimental fiction writer, but also as the object of a gay romantic cult.

GRAY, Muriel
(1959–)

Journalist and broadcaster, born in East Kilbride, Lanarkshire. A graduate of the Glasgow School of Art, she became Assistant Head of Design at the National Museum of Antiquities in Edinburgh and a member of the rock group The Family Von Trapp. An audition for the television pop series *The Tube* led to her début as a presenter on the show in 1982. A career as a seemingly ubiquitous presenter followed on such programmes as *Bliss* (1985), *Frocks on the Box* (1987) and *The Media Show* (1987–9), where her unimpressionable manner, incisiveness and sharp wit marked her out from the crowd. An outspoken columnist for *Time Out*, *The Sunday Mail* and *Scotland on Sunday*, she served as the first female rector of Edinburgh University (1988–91) and, in 1989, formed her own production company, Gallus Besom, which has been responsible for such series as the chat-show *Walkie Talkie* (1989), *Art Is Dead, Long Live TV* (1991), which mercilessly debunked the élitism surrounding modern art, and the hugely popular *The Munro Show* (1991), which resulted in the book *The First Fifty: Munro Bagging Without A Beard* (1991).

GRAY, Robert
(1825–87)

Ornithologist, and founder of the Glasgow Natural History Society (1851). A cashier with the Bank of Scotland, he was co-author of *Birds of Ayrshire and Wigtownshire* (1869) and wrote *Birds of the West of Scotland* (1871).

GREGORY, David
(1659–1708)

Mathematician, nephew of **James Gregory**, born in Aberdeen. He became Professor of Mathematics at Edinburgh in 1683, and Savilian Professor of Astronomy at Oxford in 1692. He lacked the originality of his uncle, but published textbooks on geometry, astronomy (promoting Newton's gravitational theories) and optics, in which he suggested the possibility of an achromatic lens.

GREGORY, Duncan Farqharson

(1813–44)

Mathematician, born in Edinburgh of a long line of academics. His father, grandfather and great-grandfather were professors of medicine at Edinburgh, and his great-great-grandfather was **James Gregory** the mathematician (1638–75). He studied in Geneva and Edinburgh, went to Cambridge in 1833 and became a Fellow of Trinity in 1840. He founded the *Cambridge Mathematical Journal*, published textbooks on calculus and geometry, and introduced operational methods which were ahead of his time and not then widely accepted.

GREGORY, James

(1638–75)

Mathematician, born in Drumoak, Aberdeenshire. He graduated from Aberdeen University and went to London in 1662, and the following year published *Optica promota*, which contains a description of the Gregorian reflecting telescope that he had invented in 1661. From 1664 to 1667 he was in Padua, where he published a book on the quadrature of the circle and hyperbola, giving convergent infinite sequences for the areas of these curves. In 1668 he became Professor of Mathematics at St Andrews University. Considering himself badly treated there, he moved to the same post at Edinburgh in 1674 at double the salary, but died a year later. Much of his later work was concerned with infinite series, a term which he introduced into the language.

GREGORY, James

(1753–1821)

Physician, born in Aberdeen, the great-grandson of **James Gregory**. Educated at Aberdeen, Edinburgh and Leiden, he became Professor of Physic at Edinburgh (1776). Known as the 'starving doctor', he gave his name to 'Gregory's Mixture', a revolting laxative powder made from magnesia, rhubarb and ginger.

GREGORY, John

(1724–73)

Physician and professor of medicine, born in Aberdeen, the grandson of **James Gregory** the mathematician. He studied metaphysics under his cousin **Thomas Reid** and medicine at Edinburgh (1741) under **Alexander Munro** ('Primus'), and subsequently at Leyden 1745–6, an MD being conferred on him by Aberdeen *in absentia*. He was Professor of Philosophy at Aberdeen (1746–9) and worked concurrently in medical practice (1749–54). After a period in London, he succeeded his brother in the Aberdeen professorship until 1864. Moving to Edinburgh in 1766 to win a more lucrative position, he competed successfully against **William Cullen** for the Chair of Medicine. A straightforward and clear lecturer and expositor, he was an important link in the Scottish Enlightenment due to his friendships with **David Hume**, Lord **Monboddo** and others. His works included *A Comparative View of the State and Faculties of Man with those of the Animal World* (1766) and the influential *Observations on the Duties and Offices of a Physician* (1770) as well as *A Father's Legacy to his Daughters* (1774), which commanded a readership for a hundred years and still requires serious consideration in any estimate of the status of women in Britain at that time.

GREGORY, John Walter

(1864–1932)

Geologist, born in London. Educated at Stepney Grammar School, he then pursued science part-time at the University of London whilst working in business. In 1887 he obtained an assistantship in the Geology Department of the British Museum of Natural History. In 1891 he went to the Rockies and thus began the worldwide expeditions for which he became famous, especially his recognition of the Great East African Rift Valley. He was the first Professor of Geology at Melbourne in 1900 and also in Glasgow (1904–29). He was particularly known for the wide range of his studies and his popularization of geology, for example in his last books, *Dalradian Geology* and *The Story of the Road*, both published in 1931. He was killed in the gorge of the river Urubamba in the Peruvian Andes.

GREGORY, William

(1805–58)

Organic chemist and biologist, born in Edinburgh into a distinguished scientific family, he studied medicine there before working as an assistant to Liebig and other distinguished chemists on the Continent. In 1839 he was appointed Professor of Chemistry at King's College, Aberdeen, moving in 1844 to the chair at Edinburgh University, which he held until his death. Gregory isolated and studied natural substances, for example he investigated the preparation of morphine and codeine from opium, and was the first person to prepare isoprene from crude rubber. His work as a translator was important, bringing advances by Liebig and others to English-speaking scientists. He also wrote on animal magnetism and diatoms.

GREIG, Gavin
(1856–1914)

Folklorist and writer, born in Parkhill, Newmachar, Aberdeenshire. After graduating from Aberdeen University he became a schoolmaster at Whitehill, New Deer, and there, for the rest of his life, he carried out the task of compiling one of the largest written collections of folk-song in existence. An Aberdeenshire minister, James Bruce Duncan, joined forces with Greig. The entire Greig-Duncan manuscript collection consists of 3500 texts and 3300 tunes, mostly taken from sources in the north-east of Scotland. Sections of this monumental work first appeared in the 1920s, but it was not until 1981 that publication of the complete collection began with the first volume of *The Greig-Duncan Folk Song Collection*. Gavin Greig wrote a weekly folk-song column in the *Buchan Observer* from 1907 to 1911. He also had four novels to his credit, and one of his plays in the Buchan dialect, *Mains's Wooin'*, is still performed.

GREIG, John
(1942 –)

Footballer and manager, born in Edinburgh. All his senior career, from 1960 to 1978, was spent with Rangers, much of it as club captain. He won five league championships and six Scottish Cups while with the club, as well as the European Winners' Cup in 1972. Winning 44 caps for Scotland, he was voted Scottish player of the year in 1966 and 1976. Retiring as a player in May 1978, he became Rangers' manager later that month, holding the post until 1983. He then became a radio football commentator, before returning to his old club in 1990 to take up a position in Rangers' publicity department. Not an outstanding success as a manager, he is remembered as a player for his inspirational captaincy, his fierce shot, and commanding defensive qualities.

GREIG, Sir Samuel
(1735–88)

Naval commander in the Russian navy, born in Inverkeithing, Fife. He transferred to the Russian navy in 1763, just after the assumption of power by the empress Catherine II, the Great, and fought in the war with the Turks (1768–72) and the victory at Česme (1770). Promoted rear admiral (1770) and vice admiral (1773), he reformed the fleet and led it in the Baltic war against Sweden (1788–90). His son, Alexis Samuelovich (1775–1845), also became an admiral in the Russian navy and fought in the Russo-Turkish wars of 1807 and 1828–9.

GRIERSON, Sir Herbert John Clifford
(1866–1960)

Critic and scholar, born in Lerwick, Shetland. He was educated at King's College, Aberdeen, where he became professor (1894–1915), and Christ Church, Oxford. He was appointed Regius Professor of Rhetoric and English Literature at Edinburgh (1915–35), and was elected rector (1936–9). He edited the poems of Donne (1912), and his studies include *Metaphysical Poets* (1921), *Cross Currents in the Literature of the 17th Century* (1929), *Milton and Wordsworth* (1937), and *Essays and Addresses* (1940).

GRIERSON, John
(1898–1972)

Documentary film producer, born in Kilmadock, Stirlingshire, the 'father of British documentary'. After studying communications in the USA he joined the Empire Marketing Board in 1928, with whom he made his reputation with *Drifters* (1929), a film about herring fishermen. He headed the British GPO unit from 1933, inspiring hundreds of short films (including *Night Mail*, with a verse commentary by W H Auden). During World War II he set up the National Film Board of Canada, and was then appointed Director of Mass Communications for UNESCO (1946–8) and film controller at the Central Office of Information in London (1948–50). From 1957 to 1965 he presented an anthology of international documentary films on television.

GRIERSON, Sir Robert, of Lag
(c.1655–1733)

Jacobite laird. He succeeded his cousin to the Dumfriesshire estates in 1669. For some years steward of Kirkcudbright, he so harried the Covenanters that his name became a byword for cruelty; he was one of the judges of the Wigtown martyrs, and witnessed their execution. In 1685 he received a Nova Scotia baronetcy, with a pension of £200. After the revolution (1688) he was fined and imprisoned as a Jacobite, and in 1696 he was arraigned on a false charge of coining.

GRIEVE, Christopher Murray See MacDIARMID, Hugh

GRIEVE, John
(1924 –)

Actor, born in Glasgow. He trained at the Glasgow Citizens' Theatre, and has since become established as one of Scotland's best-known actors, equally at home in comic and serious work, and appearing in many Scottish theatres over the years. He has also appeared several times at the Edinburgh Festival, notably in productions of *Ane Satyre of the Thrie Estaits* in 1984 and 1985.

GRIMOND, Jo (Joseph), Baron Grimond
(1913 –)

Liberal politician, born in Dundee. Educated at Eton and Balliol College, Oxford, he was called to the English Bar in 1937, and served during World War II with the Fife and Forfar Yeomanry. In 1945 he contested the Orkney and Shetland seat, which he ultimately won in 1950. He was Secretary of the National Trust for Scotland (1947–9) and Rector of Edinburgh University (1960–4). From 1956 to 1967 he was Leader of the Liberal Party, during which time Liberal representation in Parliament was doubled. His aim of making the Liberal Party the real radical alternative to Conservatism was only partially realized in the creation of the Social Democratic Party, and later the (Social and) Liberal Democrats. He retired from Parliament in 1983. He

published *A Personal Manifesto* in 1983, and in the same year was made a life peer.

GRUB, George
(1812–92)

Church historian, born in Aberdeen. He was librarian to the Society of Advocates in Aberdeen (1841), lecturer in Scots Law at Marischal College, Aberdeen (1842), and professor from 1881. He was the author of an *Ecclesiastical History of Scotland* (1861), written from the Episcopalian viewpoint.

GUISE, Mary of Lorraine
(1515–60)

French noblewoman, daughter of Claude of Lorraine, 1st Duke of Guise. In 1534 she married Louis of Orléans, Duke of Longueville, and in 1538 **James V** of Scotland, at whose death (1542) she was left with one child, **Mary, Queen of Scots**. During the troubled years that followed, the queen mother acted with wisdom and moderation, but after her accession to the regency in 1554 she allowed the Guises so much influence that the Protestant nobles raised a rebellion (1559), which continued to her death in Edinburgh Castle.

GUNN, Sir John Currie
(1916 –)

Physicist, educated at Glasgow Academy and the universities of Glasgow and Cambridge. During the war he served in the Admiralty Scientific Service; later he was a lecturer in applied mathematics at Manchester University and at University College, London. Appointed Cargill Professor of Natural Philosophy at Glasgow University in 1949, he influenced the development of physics nationally through his chairmanship of Science Research Council committees, and as a member of the University Grants Committee. He was awarded a CBE in 1976 and knighted in 1982.

GUNN, Neil Miller
(1891–1973)

Novelist, born in Dunbeath, Caithness, the son of a fisherman. Educated at the village school, and privately in Galloway, he passed the Civil Service examination in 1907, and moved to London. He was in the Civil Service until 1937, from 1911 as an officer of customs and excise in Inverness and elsewhere in Scotland. After writing a number of short stories, his first novel, *Grey Coast* (1926), was immediately acclaimed, and was followed by *The Lost Glen* (serialized in 1928) and a historical novel on the Viking Age, the even more successful *Morning Tide* (1931). Other works include *Sun Circle* (1933), *Butcher's Broom* (1934), *Highland River* (1937, Tait Black Memorial Prize), *Wild Geese Overhead* (1939) and *The Silver Darlings* (1941). Gunn was at his best when describing the ordinary life and background of a Highland fishing or crofting community, and when interpreting in simple prose the complex character of the Celt. His last novels were *The Well at the World's End* (1951), *Bloodhunt* (1952) and *The Other Landscape* (1954).

GUNN, Willie
(c.1755 – c.1825)

Golf caddy and eccentric, born in the Highlands. After moving to Edinburgh around 1780, he took up employment as a golf caddy at Bruntsfield Links and became famed for his knowledge of the game of golf and for his eccentric habits. He ate only bread and milk, and the money saved by living on this Spartan diet was set aside to ensure that he had sufficient funds to avoid a pauper's grave. The hallmark of his eccentricity was his all-weather clothing, which comprised all the clothes he owned worn one on top of the other, with the red uniform jacket of the Bruntsfield caddies as the outermost garment. After over 40 years as a caddy at Bruntsfield, he re-visited his Highland home and was not heard of again.

GUTHRIE, Douglas James
(1885–1975)

Medical historian, born in Dysart, Fife, a minister's son. Graduating in medicine form Edinburgh in 1907, he studied abroad and spent a period in general practice in Lanark before serving with the RAMC and the RAF in World War I. After war service he specialized in otolaryngology and was on the staff of the Royal Hospital for Sick Children in Edinburgh. During this period (1919–45) he became particularly concerned with speech disorders in childhood and with George Seth wrote a pioneering book *Speech in Childhood* (1935). He also initiated a training scheme for speech therapists. After retirement he devoted himself to the study of the history of medicine and he succeeded John Comrie as lecturer on the history of medicine at Edinburgh, a post he held from 1945 to 1956. His widely acclaimed *History of Medicine* (1945) was translated into several languages. Travelling widely, he became internationally known as a medical historian. In 1948 he founded the Scottish Society of the History of Medicine, and in 1965 founded a history of medicine lectureship under the aegis of the Edinburgh Royal College.

GUTHRIE, Sir James
(1859–1930)

Painter, born in Greenock, Renfrewshire, the son of a minister. He began to study law at Glasgow, but abandoned this in 1877 to become an artist. Almost entirely self-taught, he was a follower of the Glasgow School, and attracted some attention in Paris with his early works. He later turned from genre to portraiture, of which he became a notable exponent. As President of the Royal Scottish Academy he was instrumental in improving the conditions and facilities of the National Galleries of Scotland.

GUTHRIE, Thomas
(1803–73)

Clergyman and social reformer, born in Brechin, Angus. He studied at Edinburgh, and was minister at Arbirlot (1830), Old Greyfriar's, Edinburgh (1837), and St John's, Edinburgh (1840). At the Disruption of 1843 he helped to found the Free Church, and until 1864 was minister of Free St John's, Castle-hill, Edinburgh. Over a period of 11 months (1845–6) he raised £116 000 for the provision of Free Church manses. In 1847 he published his first *Plea for Ragged Schools*, and became an authority on the case of juvenile delinquents. He also used his gifts of oratory in the cause of temperance and other social reforms, and in favour of compulsory education. He was the first editor of the *Sunday Magazine* from 1864. He also wrote *The City: Its Sins and Sorrows* (1857).

H

HADDINGTON, Thomas Hamilton, 1st Earl of
(1563–1637)

Public servant, judge and jurist. Son of Thomas Hamilton, Lord Priestfield, a judge, he was educated by his uncle in Paris, and passed advocate in 1587, becoming a Lord of Session in 1592, as Lord Drumcairn. He was a commissioner for revision of the law, along with Sir **John Skene**, in 1592. He was on good terms with **James VI**, who called him Tam o' the Cowgate, from the place of his residence, and he may have suggested to the king the appointment of the Commission of Eight, the Octavians, to put the royal finances on a sound footing. Hamilton gradually acquired a position of great influence with the king, and became King's Advocate in 1596. In 1604 he was, with Sir **Thomas Craig** and others, a Commissioner to London to discuss fuller union with England. In 1612 he became Lord Clerk Register and Secretary of State. In 1613 he was ennobled as Lord Binning, in 1616 appointed President of the Court of Session, in 1619 Earl of Melrose and in 1626 exchanged the earldom of Melrose for that of Haddington. He resigned the office of Lord President in 1626 and that of Secretary of State shortly thereafter, becoming Lord Privy Seal. A shrewd lawyer and a capable administrator, he was also a man of varied culture. He left a large collection of *Decisions of the Court of Session* of the years 1592–1624, still unpublished, a collection of state papers, published in 1837, and various transcripts of records now lost.

HADDOW, Sir Alexander
(1906–76)

Pioneer in the development of the chemical treatment of cancer. He was educated at Broxburn High School and Edinburgh University, where he graduated MB in 1929. He did research in the Department of Bacteriology, Edinburgh, before moving in 1935 to the Royal Cancer Hospital in London and in 1946 becoming Director of the Chester Beatty Research Institute, where he remained until his retirement in 1972. Perhaps his greatest contribution was the realization of the close similarity between the substances which can induce cancer and those which kill both normal and cancer cells, and which therefore can sometimes be used in their treatment. Elected FRS in 1972, he took a leading part in the international organizations co-ordinating the study and treatment of cancer. He also gave much of his time to organizations concerned with the misuse of science and the prevention of war.

HAGGART, David
(1801–21)

Criminal. A fairground pickpocket and thief, he frequented race-courses and was imprisoned for theft six times, but usually escaped from jail. On the last occasion he killed a warder at Dumfries in 1820 and fled to Ireland, where he was captured, sent back to Edinburgh for trial, and hanged. He compiled an autobiography in Scottish thieves' slang, which was published by the phrenologist **George Combe**.

HAIG, Douglas, 1st Earl Haig of Bemersyde
(1861–1928)

Soldier and field-marshal, born in Edinburgh. Educated at Clifton, Oxford University and the Royal Military College, Sandhurst, he was commissioned in the 7th Hussars. Active service in Egypt and South Africa, followed by staff and command assignments in India, led to his appointment in 1911 as GOC Aldershot. In August 1914 he took the 1st Corps of the British Expeditionary Force to France, and succeeded Sir John French as Commander-in-Chief in December 1915. With the flanks of the battle zone sealed by the sea and the Swiss Border and the Germans operating on interior lines, Haig was forced to forgo war of movement and wage a costly and exhausting war of attrition, a difficult task that was appreciably aggravated by the progressive deterioration of the French after the failure of the Nivelle offensive of 1917, and Lloyd George's hampering distrust and irresponsible attempts to control strategy.

Under the overall command of Foch, Haig's reward came with his army's successful offensive of August 1918, leading to the German plea for an armistice. After the war, he organized the Royal British Legion for the care of ex-servicemen.

HAILES, Sir David Dalrymple, Lord
(1726–92)

Jurist and historian, born in Edinburgh, a great grandson of the 1st Viscount Stair. He became a judge of the Court of Session in 1766 and also a judge of the High Court of Justiciary in 1776, but is best known for his historical writings, the chronological *Annals of Scotland* (1776–9), still regarded as a valuable work.

HALDANE, Elizabeth Sanderson
(1862–1937)

Author, sister of **John Scott Haldane** and **Richard Burdon Haldane**. She studied nursing, for a while managed the Royal Infirmary, Edinburgh, and became the first woman justice of the peace in Scotland (1920). She wrote a Life of Descartes (1905) and edited his philosophical works, translated Hegel and wrote commentaries on George Eliot (1927) and Mrs Gaskell (1930).

HALDANE, James Alexander
(1768–1851)

Minister, born in Dundee, brother of **Robert Haldane**. Educated there and at Edinburgh, he served with the East India Company (1785–94). With Charles Simeon of Cambridge he made an evangelistic tour of Scotland in 1797, from which Congregational Churches developed. With his brother Robert he opened a tabernacle in Edinburgh in 1801, where he preached gratuitously for 50 years, and which in 1808 he led into the Baptist fold. His pamphlets were widely read.

HALDANE, John Scott
(1860–1936)

Physiologist, brother of **Richard Burdon Haldane** and **Elizabeth Haldane**, grand-nephew of **Robert Haldane**, father of **J B S Haldane** and **Naomi Mitchison**. Born in Edinburgh, he became Demonstrator and Reader in medicine at Oxford (1887–1913), and was elected Fellow of New College, Oxford. He became an authority on the effects of industrial occupations upon respiration, and served as a director of a mining research laboratory at Birmingham from 1912.

HALDANE, Richard Burdon, Viscount Haldane of Cloan
(1856–1928)

Politician, jurist and Liberal Secretary of State for War, brother of **John Scott Haldane** and **Elizabeth Haldane**, grandson of **James Alexander Haldane**. Born in Edinburgh, he was educated there and at the University of Göttingen, where he studied philosophy. Called to the Bar in 1879 he became Liberal MP for East Lothian in 1885, and was associated with the party's imperialist wing. Although it was expected that he would be appointed Lord Chancellor, in 1905 he became Secretary of State for War under **Campbell-Bannerman** and was responsible for the introduction of far-reaching military reforms. Principal amongst these were the creation of the Territorial Force as a second line of defence and the establishment of an expeditionary force. These innovations allowed Britain to engage in continental warfare, but during World War I Haldane was accused of pro-German sympathies and was forced to resign. He twice held the office of Lord Chancellor, under the Liberals between 1912 and 1915 and as a Labour MP in 1924. He also ranked high as a judge. His other interests were philosophy and education and he was a supporter of the Workers Educational Association.

HALDANE, Robert
(1764–1842)

Evangelist and writer, born in London, brother of **James Haldane**. He was in the navy during the relief of Gibralta, but settled on his estates at Airthrey, near Stirling, in 1783. The French Revolution brought about a spiritual revolution within him, and with his brother James he founded the Society for Propagating the Gospel at Home (1797), built tabernacles for itinerant preachers (the first Congregational Churches) and lectured to theological students in Geneva and Montauban (1817).

HALIBURTON, Hugh, pseudonym of James Logie Robertson
(1846–1922)

Poet, born in Milnathort, Kinross. He became a student-teacher in Haddington, East Lothian, and later he studied at Edinburgh. He became the first English master at Edinburgh Ladies' College, later Mary Erskine's

School (1876–1913). In the guise of a shepherd in the Ochil Hills, 'Hugh Haliburton', he published *Horace in Homespun: A Series of Scottish Pastorals* (1886) and *Ochil Idylls* (1891). He also wrote essays, and edited the poet **James Thomson**.

HALKETT, Hugh, Baron von

(1783–1863)

Hanoverian soldier, born in Musselburgh, East Lothian. He served with distinction in the British Army in the Napoleonic wars, fought in the Peninsula and commanded the Hanoverian militia at Waterloo (1815).

HALKETT, Samuel

(1814–71)

Scholar. He was librarian to the Advocates' Library in Edinburgh (from 1848), and compiled the *Dictionary of Anonymous Literature* (4 vols, 1882–8), completed by the Rev John Laing (1809–80). From 1850 he was librarian of New College, Edinburgh.

HALL, Basil

(1788–1844)

Travel writer, born in Edinburgh. A naval officer (1802–23), he wrote popular works on Korea (1818), Chile, Peru and Mexico (1824) and *Travels in North America* (1829). He also wrote novels and short stories. He died insane.

HALL, Sir James,

(1761–1832)

Geologist, of Dunglass, East Lothian, a Haddingtonshire baronet. He sought to prove in the laboratory the geological theories of his friend and mentor **James Hutton**, and thus founded experimental geology.

HAMILTON

Name of a noble family, believed to be of English origin, which can be traced back to Walter FitzGilbert, called Hamilton, who in 1296 held lands in Lanarkshire, swore fealty to Edward I, and in 1314 held Bothwell Castle for the English. His surrender of it, with the English knights who had fled there

from Bannockburn, was rewarded by **Robert Bruce** with a knighthood and grants of lands in Clydesdale, West Lothian and elsewhere. His grandson, Sir David of Hamilton of Cadzow, was the first to assume the surname of Hamilton. The Earls of Haddington are descended from a younger son of Sir David. Other titles apart from those appearing below that were conferred on members of the house were those of Lord Belhaven, Viscount Boyne, Baron Brancepeth, Viscount Clanboy and Earl of Clanbrassil.

HAMILTON, Douglas, Duke of Hamilton and Brandon

(1903–73)

Aviator, educated at Eton and Balliol College, Oxford. The holder of many distinguished royal positions, such as Hereditary Keeper of Holyroodhouse and Lord Steward of HM Household (1940–64), his aviation interests developed in the 1920s and 30s, first as pilot and aircraft owner, then as Commander of the 602 Squadron of the Auxiliary Air Force (1927–36). In 1932 he was the chief pilot in the Houston Mount Everest Expedition, about which he wrote in *The Pilot's Book of Everest* (1936). He played a large part in the formation of Scottish Aviation Ltd at Prestwick Airport (now part of British Aerospace). During World War II he held various senior positions in the RAF, and commanded the Air Training Corps in Scotland. In 1941 Rudolf Hess flew to Scotland seeking the duke's help as an intermediary in possible peace negotiations. The duke flew in his Hurricane to report to Churchill, who was unimpressed, and Hess remained a prisoner for the rest of his life. In 1964 Hamilton chaired a committee on pilot training and was President of the British Air Line Pilots' Association. He was an active elder of the Church of Scotland and Lord High Commissioner to the General Assembly (1953–5, 1958). In 1964 he received the Royal Victorian Chain from the queen.

HAMILTON, Douglas Alexander, 10th Duke of

(1767–1852)

Aristocrat and eccentric, who believed himself to be the true heir to the throne of Scotland and was described as the proudest man in Britain. In recognition of his own importance he commissioned a mausoleum which he intended to be the the the eighth wonder of the world. As a finishing touch, he paid £11 000 for a sarcophagus which reputedly belonged to an Egyptian princess. Such was the discrepancy between the Duke's height and the length of the sarcophagus, however, that when he was finally laid to rest his feet had to be cut off. In 1927 the tomb was demolished and a re-examination of the sarcophagus revealed that it belonged to a court jester and not a princess.

HAMILTON, Sir James, 1st Lord
(d.1479)

Great-grandson of Sir David of Hamilton of Cadzow, created Lord of Parliament in 1445. Allied by marriage and descent to the **Doug-las**es, he followed them in the beginning of their struggle with the crown, but forsook them in 1454, and was rewarded with large grants of their forfeited lands. After the death of his first wife, he married Princess Mary Stewart in 1469, eldest daughter of **James II** of Scotland, formerly the wife of the attainted Earl of Arran. His son James (c.1477–1529) was created Earl of Arran in 1503.

HAMILTON, James, 2nd Earl of Arran, 3rd Baron
(?1515–1575)

Nobleman, grandson of Sir James, 1st Lord **Hamilton** by the niece of Cardinal **Beaton**, and still a young man when the death of **James V** in 1542 left only an infant, the future **Mary, Queen of Scots**, between him and the throne. He was chosen to be regent and tutor to the young queen, and held these offices until 1554. He received a grant of the duchy of Châtelherault from Henri II of France in 1548.

HAMILTON, James, 3rd Earl of Arran, 4th Baron
(1530–1609)

Nobleman, eldest son of **James Hamilton**, the 2nd Earl. He was proposed as the husband both of **Mary, Queen of Scots** and of Queen Elizabeth of England. With a distinguished military career behind him, he became a Protestant and supported his father's religious policy. Becoming increasingly mentally unstable, he unwisely disclosed to **John Knox** Lord **Bothwell**'s suggestion

that Hamilton abduct Mary and murder Moray and Maitland. For this slip he was imprisoned (1562), and thereafter became completely insane.

HAMILTON, James, 3rd Marquis and 1st Duke of
(1606–49)

Nobleman. He led an army of 6000 men to the support of King Gustav II Adolf of Sweden in 1631–2, and later played a conspicuous role in the contest between Charles I and the Covenanters. Created duke in 1643, he led a Scottish army into England (1643), but was defeated by Cromwell at Preston, and beheaded.

HAMILTON, James Douglas, 4th Duke of
(1658–1712)

Nobleman. He was created 1st Duke of Brandon in 1771, a title that was challenged by the House of Lords. He fought against Monmouth, led Scottish opposition to the Union, but discouraged bloodshed. He helped to negotiate the Treaty of Utrecht (1713) and was killed, as described in Thackeray's *Henry Esmond*, in a duel with Lord Mohun.

HAMILTON, John, 1st Marquis of
(?1532–1604)

Nobleman, brother of the insane **James Hamilton**, 3rd Earl of Arran. A devoted adherent of **Mary, Queen of Scots**, he helped to rescue her from captivity on Loch Leven and reinstate her on the throne (1568). He fled to France in 1579, but was reconciled with King **James VI** in 1585. In 1588 he was sent to negotiate the king's marriage to Anne of Denmark, and he was created Marquis in 1599.

HAMILTON, David
(1768–1843)

Architect, born in Glasgow, the son of a mason. Educated first as a mason, he later turned to architecture. Little is known about his life, but he became the dominant architect in Glasgow in the first decades of the 19th century, and was a popular, paternalistic and influential figure. The influences of **Adam**, Wyatt and Soane can be detected in his work. Known predominantly for neo-classical public designs, such as Hutcheson's Hospital (1802) and the Royal Exchange (1829) in Glasgow, his versatility is shown in a number of fine Gothic churches, notably Campsie Parish Church, Lennoxtown (1828) and the Gothick masterpieces of Kincaid House (1812) and Crawford Priory, Fife (addition, 1813). He turned his hand to Scottish Jacobean designs with academic correctness and sensitivity, as at Dunlop House (1833), and to the Norman style on a large scale at Lennox Castle, in late partnership with his son, James.

HAMILTON, Gavin

(1723–98)

Painter and picture-dealer, born in Lanarkshire. He studied at Glasgow University before going to Italy in the mid 1740s. On his return in 1751 he worked, for a time, as a portrait painter but, by 1756, he was back in Rome where he remained for the rest of his life. There, he became a leading member of a circle of artists and scholars concerned with the archaeology of Rome, and he made many archaeological excavations which resulted in important additions to collections of antique art. It was in this role of art dealer that he was best-known in Britain, but his paintings, mostly of Homeric subjects, became well-known throughout Europe through engravings and were an important influence on the development of the Neo-classical movement.

HAMILTON, Iain Ellis

(1922–)

Composer, born in Glasgow. Originally trained as an engineer, in 1947 he entered the Royal College of Music, first attracting attention when his clarinet quintet was played at a concert of the Society for the Promotion of New Music. In 1951 he won the Royal Philharmonic Society's prize for his clarinet concerto, and an award from the Koussevitsky Foundation for his second symphony, which was followed by the symphonic variations (1953). He taught in the USA from 1961 to 1981, and produced many orchestral, choral and chamber works as well as operas, including *The Royal Hunt of the Sun* (1967–9) and *The Cataline Conspiracy* (1972–3). Since his return to London he has completed several large-scale choral works, the operas *Lancelot* and *Raleigh's Dream* (1983).

HAMILTON, Sir Ian Standish Monteith

(1853–1947)

Soldier, born in Corfu, and on his mother's death brought up by his grandparents at Hafton, Argyllshire. He entered the army (1873), and served with distinction with the Gordon Highlanders in Afghanistan (1878) and the Boer wars (1881, 1899–1901). He was a general in World War I and led the disastrous Gallipoli expedition (1915). Relieved of his command, he later became lieutenant of the Tower (1918–20).

HAMILTON, Sir James Arnot

(1923–)

Aeronautical engineer, born in Edinburgh. Graduating in civil engineering from Edinburgh University, he joined the Marine Aircraft Experimental Establishment at Helensburgh (1943), working initially on the design and development of airborne anti-submarine weapons and, later, full-scale flight research associated with the design of seaplanes and flying boats. In 1948 he became head of Flight Research. He joined the Royal Aircraft Establishment at Farnborough in 1951 to work on the aerodynamics of supersonic flight. Knighted in 1952, he became head of the Project Assessment Group in 1963. Transferred to the Ministry of Aviation in 1964 as Director of Anglo-French Military Aircraft, he was Project Director of Jaguar and Tornado aircraft, and became the first Director-General of the Concorde project (1966), taking the aircraft from early concepts to the first flights of the two prototypes. In 1971 he was appointed to the Department of Trade and Industry as Deputy Secretary with responsibility for government policy for the aircraft industry. Two years later he was transferred to the Cabinet Office as Deputy Secretary to the Cabinet on economic and industrial affairs. In 1976 he became Permanent Under-Secretary of State at the Department of Education and Science, the first engineer to become permanent head of a Government department. He retired from the Civil Service in 1983.

HAMILTON, Patrick

(1503–28)

'The protomartyr of the Scottish Reformation', son of Sir Patrick Hamilton and Catherine Stewart, the illegitimate daughter of the Duke of **Albany**, second son of **James II**. Born in the diocese of Glasgow, he took his MA at Paris in 1520, then proceeded to Louvain, and in 1523 was at St Andrews. He returned to the Continent in 1527 to escape troubles on account of his Lutheranism. After a brief stay in Wittenberg, where he met Luther and Melanchthon, he settled for some months in Marburg, where he wrote (in Latin) a series of theological propositions known as 'Patrick's Places', which propounded the doctrines of the Lutherans. One of his converts was **Alexander Alesius**. He returned that autumn to Scotland, and married. The following year he was summoned to St Andrews by Archbishop **James Beaton** (1470–1539), and on a renewed charge of heresy he was burned before St Salvator's College. His death did more to extend the Reformation in Scotland than his life could ever have done.

HAMILTON, Terrick
(1781–1876)

Linguist and orientalist. He was the translator (1820) of the first four volumes of *Sirat Antarah*, narrative of the poet Antar. After service with the East India Company he became Secretary of the British Embassy at Constantinople.

HAMILTON, Sir Thomas See
HADDINGTON, Sir Thomas

HAMILTON, Thomas
(1784–1858)

Architect, born in Glasgow. He studied as a mason with his father, beginning independent practice in Edinburgh before 1817. He was a leading figure in the international Greek Revival, together with his contemporary in Edinburgh, **William Henry Playfair**. In 1826 he was among the founders of the Royal Scottish Academy. His Grecian designs include the Burns Monument, Galloway (1820), the Royal High School, Edinburgh (1825–9), and the Royal College of Physicians Hall (1844–5) in Edinburgh. Cumston (Compstone) House, Kirkcudbright (1828), built in a Tudor style, and a handful of gothic church designs, demonstrate his versatility. As a prime mover of the Edinburgh Improvement Act (1827) he was concerned with the link between the Old and New Towns of

Edinburgh, and designed the George IV and King's bridges.

HAMILTON, Thomas
(1789–1842)

Novelist and travel-writer, born in Glasgow, brother of the metaphysician Professor Sir **William Hamilton**. He went, unsuccessfully, into business before entering the army (1810) and serving in the Peninsular War. He also served in Nova Scotia and New Brunswick during the war of 1812 against the USA. He retired to Edinburgh in 1818, becoming a writer on *Blackwood's Magazine*, and befriending **John Gibson Lockhart** and **John Wilson** ('Christopher North'). His autobiographical novel, *The Youth and Manhood of Cyril Thornton* (1827), was a valuable account of student life and society in Glasgow, notable for its shrewd observation. In 1829 he published *Annals of the Peninsular Campaign* and following a visit to the USA, published *Men and Manners in America* (1833). His observations were hostile, malicious and highly anti-democratic, but nevertheless showed vigorous powers of description and analysis (from a strongly Tory standpoint unconvincingly masked by assertions of objectivity).

HAMILTON, William
(c.1665–1751)

Poet, of Gilbertfield, near Glasgow, born in Ladyford, Ayrshire. An army officer like his father, he turned to writing and collecting verse. He was the friend and correspondent of **Allan Ramsay**, with whom he exchanged a series of *Familiar Epistles*. His most notable poem is the mock heroic *Last Dying Words of Bonny Heck*, about a greyhound. In 1772 he published an English translation of **Blind Harry**'s *Wallace*.

HAMILTON, William
(1704–54)

Poet, born in Bangour, West Lothian. Educated at the High School of Edinburgh, and Edinburgh University, he contributed romantic songs and ballads to **Allan Ramsay**'s *Tea-table Miscellany* (1724). He joined in the Jacobite Rising of 1745, and on its collapse escaped to Rouen, but was permitted to return in 1749 and to succeed to the family estate of Bangour. The first collection of his poems was edited by **Adam Smith** in 1748. He is best known for his ballad, 'The Braes of Yarrow'

HAMILTON, Sir William
(1730–1803)

Diplomat and antiquary, husband of Lady Emma Hamilton. He was British Ambassador at Naples (1764–1800), and in 1791 married Emma there. He took an active part in the excavation of Herculaneum and Pompeii, and formed rare collections of antiquities, one of which was purchased in 1772 for the British Museum. He wrote several works on Greek and Roman antiquities. He may have condoned his wife's intimacy with Nelson, as the latter was present at his death.

HAMILTON, Sir William
(1788–1856)

Philosopher and scholar, born in Glasgow. Educated at Glasgow and Balliol College, Oxford, he first made his name with papers in the *Edinburgh Review* where, among other subjects, he deplored the decayed state of Oxford and the high degree of illiteracy that was tolerated in England. These papers had a great influence on subsequent educational reform. His essays on philosophy contained many fruitful suggestions, and he ventured into religion, psychology and logic, a subject that he did much to revive. As Professor of Civil History at Edinburgh (1821–38) and of Logic and Metaphysics (1838–56), he also revived philosophical scholarship. His main work was published posthumously as *Lectures on Metaphysics and Logic* (1859–60), presenting views on perception and knowledge that were later (unjustly) criticized in J S Mill's *An Examination of Sir William Hamilton's Philosophy* (1865). Many of his articles were collected in 1852 under the title *Discussions on Philosophy and Literature, Education and University Reform*, and he edited a major edition of the works of **Thomas Reid** (1846), in itself a considerable achievement. He was in his day a figure of great importance in the revival of philosophy in Britain.

HANLEY, Clifford
(1922 –)

Novelist, dramatist and journalist, born in Glasgow. He began working as a journalist in Glasgow in 1940 and enjoyed a literary success with his first — considered by some best — book, *Dancing in the Streets* (1958), an acutely observed and mordantly funny autobiographical account of a Glasgow childhood. His early novels, *Love From Everybody* (1959) and *A Taste Too Much* (1960), drew on a similar background, and are characterized by a ready wit and a combative irreverence. His accounts of a Glaswegian family decamping on a Highland holiday in *The Hot Month* (1967), and the world of Glasgow theatre in *The Redhaired Bitch* (1969), further established his ability to mine a rich comic mode, while at the same time embracing a sometimes grim reality. He has also written crime fiction under the name 'Henry Calvin', and a number of plays, but these have lacked the sureness of touch evident in his fiction. Professor of Literature at York University, Toronto (1979–80), he published a further volume of autobiographical reminiscences, *Another Street, Another Dance*, in 1983.

HARDIE, Alastair
(1946 –)

Violin player and teacher, born in Aberdeen, the son of **Bill Hardie**. With his father he set up the Hardie Press, a Scottish Music publisher. He has written the influential fiddle tutor *The Caledonian Companion* (1981) and was co-founder, in 1978, of Kist o'Musick, a group dedicated to playing traditional and classical music of 18th-century Scotland.

HARDIE, Andrew
(1791/2–1820)

Radical martyr. A Glasgow weaver, he served in the armed forces, probably in the war against Napoleon. A member of Castle Street Radical Union Society, in 1820 he supported a call to arms which urged insurrection, mutiny and strike action. At the instigation of John King, a government agent, he acted as second-in-command of the Radical forces at the 'Battle of Bonnymuir' (5 April, 1820) when about 35 men exchanged shots with yeomanry. Hardie surrendered, was tried with his commander **John Baird**, found guilty on two out of four counts of High Treason, and was sentenced to death. Hardie's prison letters from Edinburgh and Stirling Castles give dignified and honourable witness to his beliefs and experience leading to his trial. (They are the basis of a play by **James Kelman**.) Hardie was hanged at Stirling on 8 September. In his last letter he wrote 'I am not afraid to die; I shall hail the scaffold as the harbinger of my salvation'.

HARDIE, Bill (William)
(1916–)

Fiddler, teacher and conductor, born in Aberdeen into a family which can trace its fiddling roots back to the 18th-century violin maker, **Matthew Hardie**. Trained by Theodore Crozier and Alex Milne Smith, he was influenced in his early years by J F Dickie and **James Scott Skinner**. A highly distinctive stylist and celebrated exponent of the Scott Skinner style, particularly in the playing of slow strathspeys, he made his first BBC broadcast at the age of 16 and won the first of many challenge cups in Aberdeen a few years later. His son is **Alastair Hardie**.

HARDIE, Gwen
(1962 –)

Painter, born in Newport, Fife. After studying at Edinburgh College of Art (1979–84), she moved to West Berlin where she studied under Georg Baselitz. She first received critical notice in her postgraduate diploma show at Edinburgh, in which she exhibited a number of paintings of close-ups of female heads and torsos on a monumental scale. She has continued to explore the theme of the female form from a feminist viewpoint, sometimes schematizing the figure by opening it up to reveal internal organs. The importance of these works lies particularly in the intention to re-invent the female form in pictorial art.

HARDIE, James Keir
(1856–1915)

Labour leader, one of the founders of the Labour Party, born near Holytown, Lanarkshire. He worked in a coalpit from childhood. Victimized as champion of the miners (whom he organized), he moved to Cumnock and became a journalist. The first of all Labour candidates, he was defeated (1888) in Mid-Lanark, sat for West Ham South (1892–5) and Merthyr Tydfil (1900–15), and in and out of Parliament worked strenuously for Socialism and the unemployed. He started and edited the *Labour Leader*, and handed it over in 1903 to the Independent Labour Party, founded in 1893, of which he was Chairman until 1900 and again in 1913–14. He strenuously opposed Liberal influence on the trade unions and strongly advocated the formation of a separate political party, as distinct from the existing Labour Representation League. A strong pacifist, he lost his seat through his opposition to the Boer War.

HARDIE, Matthew
(1755–1826)

Violin maker, known as the 'Scottish Stradivari'. Born in Edinburgh, he probably trained as a cabinet maker or pattern maker, later studying the art of violin making with John Blair. He established a flourishing business, making and repairing instruments in the Low Calton area of the city, and passing on his skills to a number of excellent violin makers, including his son Thomas, and Peter Hardie his cousin. He followed the Stradivarian model in all his work, and his violins are highly esteemed for their good wood, graceful lines and full, rich tones. His latter years, however, were clouded with debt because of competition from cheap, mass-produced instruments, and he died in St Cuthbert's poorhouse.

HARDY, (Henry) Forsyth
(1910 –)

Journalist and filmmaker, born in Bathgate, West Lothian. A tireless activist on behalf of the Scottish film community, he was the first film critic of *The Scotsman* (1932–41) and served as an office-bearer of the Edinburgh Film Guild (1930), the Federation of Scottish Film Societies (1933) and the Scottish Film Council (1933). Instrumental in rendering assistance to such international figures as **John Grierson** and Michael Powell, he was one of the founders of the Edinburgh International Film Festival in 1947 and the first Director of the Films of Scotland Committee (1955–75), encouraging generations of filmmakers in the documentary field and winning Scotland an Academy Award for *Seawards the Great Ships* (1961). Co-editor of *Cinema Quarterly* (1933–6) and Chairman of BBC Scotland's *Arts Review* (1941–55), his many books include *Grierson on Documentary* (1946 and 1961), *Grierson On The Movies* (1981) and *Scotland in Film* (1990).

HARE, William See BURKE, William

HARGREAVES, John Desmond
(1924 –)

English-born historian, born in Lancashire. Educated at Manchester University, he served in World War II and became Assistant Principal at the War Office in 1948. He was Lecturer in History at Manchester (1948–52), where he was influenced by Sir Lewis Namier, lecturer in Farah College, Sierra Leone (1952–4), and lecturer at Aberdeen University (1954–62). He was Visiting Professor at Union College, Schenectady, New York (1960–1). Burnett-Fletcher Professor of History at Aberdeen (1962–85), on his appointment he gave an inaugural lecture on the teaching of history in Scottish universities, which proved a shrewd stock-taking on the development of Scottish history as an academic subject in relation to the non-Scottish surroundings, and was influential in promoting the remote but growing consciousness of Scottishness in universities. Thus, while he built up an impressive teaching department and a list of publications such as *Prelude to the Partition of West Africa* (1963), *West Africa: the former French States* (1967), *West Africa Partitioned* (2 vols, 1974, 1985), *The End of Colonial Rule in West Africa* (1979), and *Decolonization in Africa* (1988), he also furthered the development of Aberdeen educational and imperial history, works in this area including *Aberdeenshire to Africa* (1981) and *Aberdeen University* 1945–81 (1989).

HARKER, Alfred
(1859–1939)

English geologist, born in Kingston-upon-Hull. After schooling in Hull and Windsor he entered St John's College, Cambridge (1878), and thus began a life-long connection with that college. Renowned in the field of petrology, the study of the mineralogical structure and origin of rocks, he developed a special fascination with the Inner Hebrides. In Cambridge he was University Demonstrator, Fellow of St John's and later Reader in Petrology. In 1895 Sir **Archibald Geikie** invited him to become a part-time officer of the Geological Survey, which post he held until 1905. This bore fruit in the classic Survey Memoir *The Tertiary Igneous Rocks of Skye* (1904), testimony to his prowess as a geologist and mountaineer. He also published works on Rhum, Eigg and the other volcanic centres of the Small Isles. A Fellow of the Royal Society of London, receiving a Royal Medal, he was awarded both the **Murchison** and Wollaston medals of the Geological Society of London.

HARKNESS, Jack (John Diamond)
(1907–85)

Footballer and journalist, born in Glasgow. A goalkeeper, he joined Queen's Park in 1925, turning professional on moving to Hearts three years later. He was capped 11 times for Scotland, twice while still a teenager. The highlight of his international career was the famous 'Wembley Wizards' match of 1928, in which Scotland beat England 5–1. Upon retiring from the game he became a sales representative for a firm of brewers. Later taking up sports journalism with the *Sunday Post*, he was one of the few football commentators to enjoy the unalloyed affection of the reading public.

HARRY, Blind
(fl.1470–92)

Poet, blind from birth. He lived by telling tales, and from 1490 to 1492 was at the court of **James IV**, where he received occasional small gratuities. His major known work is the *Wallace*, on the life of the Scottish patriot **William Wallace**, written in rhyming couplets. The language is frequently obscure, but the work is written with vigour, and sometimes breaks into poetry. The author appears to have been familiar with the metrical romances, and represents himself as being indebted to the Latin Life of Wallace by Master John Blair, Wallace's chaplain, and to another by Sir Thomas Gray, parson of Liberton. The poem attributes to its hero some of the achievements of **Robert Bruce**, and contains many mistakes or misrepresentations, but much of the narrative can bear the test of historical criticism.

HARVEY, Alex
(1935–82)

Rock singer, born in Glasgow. Acclaimed as 'the Tommy Steele of Scotland' after winning a talent contest in 1956, he subsequently played in the Alex Harvey Big Soul Band, the Blues Council, and as a solo artist. He then had a minor role in the musical *Hair* for five years before joining the rock group Tear Gas in 1972. Renaming it the Sensational Alex Harvey Band, he turned the group's fortunes around. Their most successful albums included *Tomorrow Belongs To Me* (1975), *Live* (1975), *Penthouse Tapes* (1976) and *SAHB Stories* (1976). The band split in 1977, and Harvey's New Band released only one album, *The Mafia Stole My Guitar* (1979), before his death from a heart attack while on tour in Belgium.

HARVEY, Sir George
(1806–76)

Painter, born in St Ninians near Stirling. He settled in Edinburgh in 1823, and studied at the Trustees' Academy. Interested in historical subjects as well as genre and landscape, his acclaimed works include *The Covenanters' Covenant*, *The Curlers*, *Battle of Drumclog*, *A Highland Funeral*, and *Bunyan in Bedford Gaol*.

HASTINGS, (Andrew) Gavin
(1962 –)

Rugby player, an agency surveyor by profession, born in Edinburgh. Educated at George Watson's College, Edinburgh, and Cambridge University, he made his début for Scotland in 1986, in the same match as his younger brother Scott. A fearsomely powerful attacking full-back, he played in both the 1987 and 1991 World Cups, as well as being an indispensable member of the Scotland team which won the Grand Slam in 1990. The holder of the record for the number of points scored by a Scot in international matches, he has played three times for the British Lions. He plays his club rugby for his old school team, Watsonians.

HASTINGS, James
(1852–1922)

Clergyman and editor, born in Huntly, Aberdeenshire. Educated at the University and Free Church College, Aberdeen, he became minister at Kinneff (1884), Dundee (1897) and St Cyrus (1901–11). He founded the *Expository Times* (1889), and compiled Bible dictionaries and the notable *Encyclopaedia of Religion and Ethics* (12 vols, 1908–21).

HASTON, Dougal (Duncan MacSporran)
(1940–77)

Mountaineer, born in Currie, Midlothian, the son of a master baker, he studied philosophy at Edinburgh University and climbed extensively in Scotland before going on to climb in the Dolomites and western Alps. In 1966 he made a winter ascent of the Eiger direct by a new route where his friend John Harlin had been killed, and in 1967 he climbed the north face of the Matterhorn in winter. Moving further afield he took part in the Cerro Torre Expedition to Patagonia in 1969, made the first ascent of Annapurna via the south face (with Don Whillans) in 1970 and was a member of the ill-fated 1971 International Everest expedition. In 1974 he took

part in the first ascent of Changabang and climbed Everest by the south-west face, with Doug Scott, as a member of Chris Bonington's 1975 expedition. Director of the International School of Mountaineering in Leysin, Switzerland, from 1967, it was here that he was overwhelmed and killed by an avalanche while skiing, mimicking an incident described in his semi-autobiographical novel *Calculated Risk* (published posthumously in 1979).

HAVERGAL, Giles
(1938 –)

Artistic director, born in Edinburgh and educated at Harrow and Christ Church, Oxford. He became assistant stage manager of Carlisle Repertory Theatre in 1961, before joining the Old Vic as an actor. In 1969 he became a director of the Citizens' Theatre, Glasgow and, with **Robert David MacDonald** and **Philip Prowse**, transformed a local repertory theatre into one of the foremost theatres in the UK, producing a strong mix of English and European classical and modern work.

HAY, George
(1729–1811)

Roman Catholic Vicar-Apostolic, born in Edinburgh into a nonjuror and Jacobite family. He was apprenticed to the surgeon George Lauder at the age of 16 but followed Lauder into the Jacobite army after Prestonpans (1745), where he was attendant on the wounded. He accompanied **Charles Edward Stuart**'s troops southward and back to Ardoch. Detained in Edinburgh Castle, he was sent to London, where he received instruction on Roman Catholicism from a lay Catholic publisher who visited him in prison. Liberated under the Act of Indemnity (1747), he went into hiding to avoid citation as a witness against former comrades. In 1748 he was received into the Roman Catholic Church. Ordained a priest in Rome (1758), he returned to Scotland on a Scottish mission with **John Geddes** and William Guthrie, and resided with Bishop James Grant at the strongly Catholic Enzie of Banff. In 1769 he became coadjutor to Grant, with the title Bishop of Daulis, and on Grant's death (1768) was appointed Vicar-Apostolic of the lowland district of Scotland. Endangered by Protestant mob action following the government's proposal for Catholic emancipation, he unsuccessfully sought the government's protection in London with the aid of Edmund Burke. After a brief return to the Scots College in Rome (1781), and some years as head of an ecclesiastical seminary at Scalat, Glenlivet, in 1781 he started a new seminary near Inverurie, Aberdeenshire, which was completed in 1799. In 1802 he resigned his vicariate. Credited with a major part in the survival of Roman Catholicism in his time, his integrity won him the fidelity of fellow believers, and the respect of others. His writings, covering subjects such as miracles and the scriptural basis for Catholic doctrine, later influenced cardinals Wiseman and Newman.

HAY, George Campbell, pseudonym Deòrsa Caimbeul Hay
(1915–84)

Poet, born in Argyll, the son of **John MacDougall Hay**, and wrote poetry in English, Scots, and in Gaelic under the name Deòrsa Caimbeul Hay. Educated at Oxford, he served in North Africa and the Middle East during World War II, an experience which left him a semi-invalid. The immediate postwar years were productive in poetic terms, however. Writing under the name Deòrsa Caimbeul Hay he published his first Gaelic collection, *Fuaran Slibh* in 1947. This was followed by *Wind on Loch Fyne* (1948), a volume of his English and Scots poems (the latter are rather fewer in number), and a second, more assured Gaelic collection, *O na Ceither Airdean* (1952). While his poetry is concerned with the landscape and people of Scotland, it is informed by a poetic and linguistic sensibility which lifts it beyond the parochial. His later work appeared alongside poets like **Sorley MacLean** in *Four Points of a Saltire* (1970) and **Derick Thompson** in *Nuabhàrdachd Ghàidlig* (1976). His incomplete long poem *Mochtàr is Dùghall*, written during the war, was published in 1982, and explores the poet's experiences of the Arab world.

HAY, Ian, pseudonym of Major-General John Hay Beith
(1876–1952)

Novelist and dramatist, born in Manchester, the son of a cotton merchant. He was educated at **Fettes** College, Edinburgh and St John's College, Cambridge, and became a language master at his old school. He served in World War I, and was awarded the Military Cross. His light popular novels, *Pip* (1907), *A Safety Match* (1911) and *A Knight on Wheels* (1914), were followed by the war books *The First Hundred Thousand* (1915), *Carrying On* (1917) and *The Last Million* (1918). Many novels and comedies followed, the best known of the latter being *Tilly of Bloomsbury* (1919) and *Housemaster* (1936). He was director of public relations at the War Office (1938–41).

HAY, John Macdougall
(1881–1919)

Novelist, born in Tarbert, Loch Fyne, in Argyll. He took an arts degree at Glasgow University and proceeded to teaching posts at Stornoway and then Ullapool. There he was crippled by rheumatic fever and left teaching to become a minister in the Church of Scotland. He returned to university in 1905 and graduated five years later, helping to support himself in the meantime with reviews for Glasgow and London magazines. At his second parish, Elderslie, near Paisley, he wrote and published his first and most successful novel, *Gillespie* (1914). A realistic novel in the tradition of **George Brown**'s *House with the Green Shutters*, its protagonist is characterized by cunning and ambition with which he nearly ruins his town (based on Tarbert). The novel was highly praised by Thomas Hardy and by American critics. Hay's second novel, *Barnacles* (1916), and his poetry, *Their Dead Sons* (1918), were not as successful. His son is the poet **George Campbell Hay**.

HAY, Malcolm Vivian
(1881–1962)

English-born cryptologist and Catholic historian, born in Willesden, London. Brought up as a Roman Catholic by his father's sister, he served in World War I, in which he was severely wounded and was taken as a prisoner of war. On his release he became Head of the Military Intelligence cryptology unit, with great success. A Scottish Nationalist in sympathy, he was admitted to carry out research on Jacobite and Scots College Papers preserved at Blairs College, Aberdeen, subsequently publishing several works which controverted common assumptions about Celtic Church hostility to the Roman See, such as *A Chain of Error in Scottish History* (1927), *The Blairs Papers* 1603–1660 (1929), *The Jesuits and the Popish Plot* (1934), *Winston Churchill and James II* (1934), and *The Enigma of James II* (1938). As Editor of *Prisoner of War News* for the Scottish Red Cross (1940–5) he was overwhelmed with horror at the Nazi mass murder of Jewish prisoners, and went on to investigate Christian, especially Catholic, intellectual guilt in the rise of anti-Semitism. His situation as Catholic historical apologist now arraigning fellow-Catholics was unique for its time, and he was unable to find a British publisher for his invaluable study, *The Foot of Pride* (1950), whose American edition was reissued in 1960 as *Europe and the Jews*. In his advancement of scholarly historical apologetics to self-critical ecumenics, he was a quarter-century ahead of his time and showed outstanding courage and insight. His work greatly influenced Cardinal Bea in the work of Christian-Jewish reconciliation inaugurated at the Second Vatican Council.

HAYES, Sir John Osler Chattock
(1913 –)

Naval commander, educated at the Royal Naval College Dartmouth and commissioned in the Royal Navy in 1927. During World War II he was one of the survivors when the battleship HMS *Repulse* was sunk by Japanese aircraft off the coast of Malaya in December 1941. Before the fall of Singapore he served for a time as a liaison officer with the Argyll and Sutherland Highlanders, but returned to Britain to take part in the Russian convoys which were so vital for supplying the Soviet war effort. In 1944 he took part in the operations to liberate Greece. Promoted vice-admiral in 1965 he was Flag Officer Scotland and Northern Ireland from 1966 to 1968. On his retirement he settled at Nigg in Ross-shire and served as Lord Lieutenant of Ross and Cromarty, Skye and Lochalsh between 1977 and 1988.

HAYMAN, David
(1948 –)

Actor and director, born in Bridgeton, Glasgow. He went straight from school to the Possil steel works before studying at the Royal Scottish Academy of Music and Drama. With his performance as Hamlet (1969) he immediately began a decade-long association with the Citizen's Theatre in Glasgow that encompassed a régime of ensemble acting, ranging from pantomime to a

celebrated Lady Macbeth. Experienced in all media, he gave a mesmerizing performance as **Jimmy Boyle** in the television film *A Sense of Freedom* (1981) and his many subsequent acting appearances include *Paisley Patterns* (1983) on stage, *The Holy City* (1986) on television, and such feature films as *Ill Fares the Land* (1982), *Hope and Glory* (1987) and *Venus Peter* (1989). Committed to theatre with a strong social and political content, he has served as an associate director of the Royal Court Theatre in London, and succeeded **John McGrath** as Artistic Director of the 7:84 Theatre Company in Scotland (1988–92). He has directed such works as *The Slab Boys* (1978), *Robert Burns* (1986), *The Normal Heart* (1986) and *Nae Problem* (1990). He has also directed television pieces, including *You Never Slept in Mine* (1984) and the series *Firm Friends* (1992), as well as the internationally acclaimed cinema feature *Silent Scream* (1990).

HEATHFIELD, George Augustus Eliott, 1st Baron
(1717–90)

Soldier, born in Stobs, Roxburghshire. Educated at Leiden, the French military college of La Fère, and Woolwich, he served in the War of the Austrian Succession, the Seven Years' War and in Cuba (1762), returning as Lieutenant-General. When Britain became involved in hostilities with Spain in 1775, Eliott was sent out to Gibraltar. His heroic defence, from June 1779 to February 1783, ranks as one of the most memorable achievements of British military forces.

HEDDLE, Matthew Forster
(1828–97)

Mineralogist and chemist, born on Hoy, Orkney. Educated at school in Edinburgh and as a medical student at Edinburgh University, he then furthered an interest in minerals at Clausthal and Freiburg. On returning to Edinburgh in 1851, he subsequently became, as a born collector, pre-eminent in the field of mineralogy of Scotland. Appointed assistant to the Professor of Chemistry at St Andrews in 1856, he succeeded to the chair in 1862, holding the post for 23 years. Foremost in the chemical analysis of minerals, he is known particularly for his grand collection of Scottish minerals (now housed in the National Museums of Scotland), and for his major posthumous publication, the *Mineralogy of Scotland* (1901).

HEGGIE, Iain

(1953 –)

Playwright, born in Glasgow. A former physical-training instructor, he came to prominence with his first full-length play, *A Wholly Healthy Glasgow* (1987), an effervescent comedy set in a dubious Glasgow Health Club, which was first produced at the Manchester Royal Exchange Theatre, and subsequently at the Edinburgh Festival and Royal Court Theatre, London. His recent plays include *American Bagpipes* (1988), a suburban black comedy.

HENDERSON, Alexander

(c.1583–1646)

Covenanter, born in Creich, Fife, and educated at St Andrews University. In 1610, as an Episcopalian, he was made a Professor of Rhetoric and Philosophy there, and in 1611 or 1612 he was appointed to the parish of Leuchars. He was one of the authors of the National Covenant, and was Moderator of the General Assembly at Glasgow in 1638 which restored all its liberties to the Church of Scotland. Moderator again in 1641 and in 1643, he drafted the Solemn League and Covenant, and was a commissioner to the Westminster Assembly for three years. He was the author of *Bishop's Doom* (1638).

HENDERSON, Alexander

(1831–1913)

Scottish-born photographer, who emigrated to Canada in 1855. His earliest dated photograph belongs to the spring of 1858. Described as 'by far the outstanding Canadian amateur' of his time, he published *Canadian Views and Studies by an Amateur* in 1865 and, soon after, took up photography professionally in Montreal. In the 1890s he was Manager of the Canadian Pacific Railway Photography Department. Henderson's success in photographing in the snow — considered technically difficult with the collodion process — made his speciality of snow scenes and storms all the more remarkable. His photographs are characterized by a freshness of vision.

HENDERSON, Arthur

(1863–1935)

Labour politician, born in Glasgow. He was brought up in Newcastle, where he worked as an iron-moulder and became a lay preacher. He helped to build up the Labour Party, of which he was Chairman (1908–10, 1914–17, 1931–2), and he served in the Coalition cabinets (1915–17) and was Home Secretary (1924) and Foreign Secretary (1929–31), when he refused, with the majority of the Labour Party, to enter **Ramsay Mac-Donald**'s National Government (1931). A crusader for disarmament, he was President of the World Disarmament Conference (1932).

HENDERSON, Hamish

(1919 –)

Folklorist, composer and poet, born in Blairgowrie, Perthshire. One of his early poetic works, 'Ninth Elegy for the Dead in Cyrenaica' (1948), won him the Somerset Maugham Award, but his considerable literary output has been overshadowed by his outstanding contributions to folk-song. Through his researches in this area for the School of Scottish Studies he was largely responsible for bringing great but unknown traditional singers, such as **Jeannie Robertson**, to the fore, thereby ensuring the survival of the Scots ballad tradition. Many of his own compositions, notably 'Freedom Come All Ye', 'Farewell to Sicily' and 'The John Maclean March', have themselves become part of the traditional singer's repertoire.

HENDERSON, John Murdoch

(1902–72)

Composer and compiler of Scottish music, born in Oldwhat, New Deer, Aberdeenshire. A maths teacher by profession, he published two collections of fiddle music: *The Flowers of Scottish Melody* (1935), which contained some of his own compositions, and *The Scottish Music Maker* (1957), a compilation of **Scott Skinner** tunes.

HENDERSON, Richard

(1945 –)

Physicist and molecular biologist, educated at Hawick High School and Boroughmuir School, Edinburgh, and the universities of Edinburgh and Cambridge. He joined the staff of the Laboratory of Molecular Biology in Cambridge in 1973 and has been a Fellow of Darwin College since 1981. He is distinguished for his use of electron microscopy to study macromolecules.

HENDERSON, Thomas
(1798–1844)

Astronomer, born in Dundee. Although intended for a law career, he devoted his leisure hours to astronomical calculations, and in 1831 was appointed Director of the Royal Observatory at the Cape of Good Hope. In 1832 he measured the parallax of the star, alpha Centauri. In 1834 he became the first Astronomer Royal for Scotland.

HENDRY, Stephen
(1969 –)

Snooker player, born in Edinburgh. He started playing at the age of 12, and three years later was Scottish amateur champion. Turning professional at 16, he quickly gave notice of his exceptional talent, becoming the youngest-ever winner of a professional title with his 1987 victory in the Rothmans Grand Prix. In 1989 he won a host of titles, among them the British Open and, with Mike Hallett, the Fosters World Doubles. The following year he won the Embassy World Championship — again, the youngest ever to do so — beating his boyhood hero, Jimmy White, in the final. Laconic, self-deprecating and apparently nerveless, he has improved his discipline with maturity, and now has a virtually flawless all-round game.

HENRY, George
(1858–1943)

Painter, born in Irvine, Ayrshire. He studied at Glasgow School of Art, though just as important was his attendance at life classes at the Glasgow studio of **William McGregor**. In 1855 he met **Edward Hornel**, with whom he shared a studio. The two painters sometimes collaborated on paintings, most notably the impressively decorative *The Druids Bringing Home the Mistletoe* (1890), and they made a trip to Japan together in 1893. In his *A Galloway Landscape* (1889), Henry produced one of the most remarkable Scottish landscapes of the time.

HENRYSON, Edward
(?1510 – ?1590)

Judge and jurist. He studied at Bourges and later became Professor of Roman Law there (1554), being among the great legal scholars of his time. He was also a client of the wealthy German Fugger family, collecting and translating classical texts for them. About 1552 he returned to Scotland and in 1563 was made one of the first judges of the new Commissary Court of Edinburgh and in 1566 a Lord of Session. He was later a member of the commission set up by Parliament to revise and print the statutes. This produced the *Black Acts* of 1566, of which he was nominal editor, securing an exclusive privilege to print and sell the work for 10 years. His son Thomas became a judge as Lord Chesters in 1622.

HENRYSON, Robert
(c.1425 – c.1508)

Poet. He is usually designated 'schoolmaster of Dunfermline', and was certainly a notary in 1478. His best-known work was the *Testament of Cresseid*, a kind of supplement to Chaucer's poem on the same subject. Of his 14 extant poems, *Robene and Makyne* is the earliest Scottish specimen of pastoral poetry. His other works include a metrical version of 13 *Morall Fabels of Esope the Phrygian*, possibly his masterpiece.

HENSHALL, Audrey Shore
(1927 –)

English-born archaeologist, born in Oldham, Lancashire. Educated at Edinburgh University, she was Assistant Keeper of Archaeology in the National Museum of Antiquities of Scotland and latterly Assistant Secretary to the Society of Antiquaries of Scotland, as well as being a founder member of the Scottish Archaeological Forum. She has been a leading authority on early textiles, prehistoric pottery and neolithic chambered tombs, and her corpus *The Chambered Tombs of Scotland* (2 vols, 1963, 1972), currently being updated, has been the essential database for all subsequent work on chambered tombs.

HEPBURN, Sir John
(?1598–1636)

Soldier of fortune and effective founder of the Royal Scots regiment, born in Athelstaneford, East Lothian, and educated at St Leonard's College, St Andrews. Despite being a Catholic, he joined the Scottish contingent fighting for the Elector Palatine in Bohemia and campaigned from 1620 to 1623. When the army was disbanded, he led the Scottish companies into the Swedish service where, in 1625, Gustavus Adolfus gave him command of a Scottish regiment. He fought in Prussia, Hungary and Poland during the following six years and in 1631 the four Scots regiments were formed into the Green Brigade, with Hepburn as commander. Over the next year he enjoyed a series of successes at Landsberg, Leipzig, Mentz and other engagements. In June 1632, while encamped at Nuremberg, Gustavus Adolfus insulted Hepburn's Catholic faith. Sheathing his sword, the affronted Scot said: 'Now sire, I shall never draw it more on your behalf'. In 1633 he entered the French service, having raised a large number of volunteers in Scotland. These amalgamated with the Scots Archer Guard to form the *Régiment d'Hebron*. During the next three years he enjoyed similar successes, being promoted *maréchal de camp*. In 1635 Duke Bernard of Weimar brought the remnant of the Scots Brigade into the French service, where it was incorporated with the Régiment d'Hebron; from this unit descended the Royal Scots regiment in the British Army. Hepburn was killed while besieging Saverne.

HERBERTSON, Andrew John
(1865–1915)

Geographer, born in Galashiels, Selkirkshire, and educated at Edinburgh University. After a period at the Ben Nevis and Fort William observatories (1892–3) and an assistantship with **Patrick Geddes** at Dundee (1892), he taught at Manchester (1894–6), Heriot-Watt College, Edinburgh (1896–9), and finally at Oxford (1899–1915), where he became Head of the Department of Geography after Halford John Mackinder (1905). There he introduced what was to become a distinctive interest in human and regional geography, and developed his scheme of world natural regions, based on the association of physical features, vegetation and climate.

HERD, David
(1732–1810)

Anthologist, born in Marykirk, Kincardine, the son of a farmer. He worked for most of his life as an accountant in Edinburgh, collecting songs and ballads in his spare time. He was the editor of *Ancient Scottish Ballads* (2 vols, 1776), and acted as literary adviser to **Archibald Constable.**

HERIOT, George
(1563–1624)

Goldsmith and philanthropist, born in Edinburgh. He started business in 1586, and in 1597 was appointed goldsmith to Anne of Denmark, and then to her husband King **James VI and I** in 1603. Heriot followed the king to London where, as court jeweller and banker, he amassed considerable wealth. He bequeathed £23 625 to found a hospital or school in Edinburgh for sons of poor burgesses. As 'Jingling Geordie' he figures in Sir **Walter Scott**'s *Fortunes of Nigel*.

HERMAND, George Fergusson, Lord
(1743–1827)

Judge, born in Kilkerran, Ayrshire, son of Sir James Fergusson, Lord Kilkerran, a judge. Admitted an advocate in 1765 he was appointed a Commissary of Edinburgh in 1775. Raised to the bench in 1790 he was appointed a Lord of Justiciary in 1808. He resigned both offices in 1826. A colourful character and eccentric, he had, according to Lord **Cockburn**, 'a sincere respect for drinking, indeed a high moral approbation, and a serious compassion for the poor wretches who could not indulge in it; with due contempt for those who could, but did not'. But drinking did not interfere with business. He left a dictionary of consistorial decisions covering 1684–1777 (edited and published in 1940), which was a principal authority used in James Fergusson's *Reports of some Recent Decisions of the Consistorial Courts of Scotland* (1817) and is an important record of matrimonial law in the 18th century.

HETHERINGTON, (Hector) Alastair
(1919 –)

Journalist and broadcaster, born in Llanishen, Glamorgan. The son of a former Principal of Glasgow University, he was educated at Corpus Christi College, Oxford, and launched his journalistic career with the *Glasgow Herald* (1946–50). His long association with the *Guardian* began in 1950. He was Foreign Editor (1953–6) and Editor (1956–75) of Britain's only liberal-left daily newspaper during an important period of transition in which the paper dropped Manchester from its title and moved its head office to London. He returned to Glasgow in 1975 as controller of BBC Scotland, before being appointed Professor of Media Studies at Stirling University in 1987.

HETHERINGTON, Sir Hector James Wright

(1888–1965)

University statesman, born in Cowdenbeath, Fife, and educated at Dollar Academy and the universities of Glasgow and Oxford. Between 1910 and 1927 he taught philosophy in the universities of Glasgow, Sheffield and Cardiff and was for some years Principal of University College, Exeter. Then, after nine years as Vice-Chancellor of Liverpool University, he returned to Glasgow University in 1936 to embark on a quarter century as Principal and Vice-Chancellor, as doyen of the cultural life of its surrounding community, and finally as the elder statesman of British and Commonwealth universities.

HIGGS, Peter Ware

(1929 –)

English physicist, educated at Cotham Grammar School, Bristol and King's College, London. He was a Research Fellow at London and Edinburgh universities, and in 1960 was appointed to a lectureship in mathematical physics in Edinburgh University, where he became Professor of Theoretical Physics in 1980. He is distinguished for his work on theories of elementary particles, and was awarded the Hughes medal of the Royal Society in 1981. His work has been extended by others and currently forms the basis of the 'Standard Theory' of elementary particles.

HIGSON, Paddy, née Frew

(1941 –)

Irish-born film producer, born in Belfast. She began her career in radio and television as a production secretary and assisted her first husband, editor/director Patrick Higson (1931–83), in his endeavours on documentary and promotional productions as well as the cinéma vérité documentary *Big Banana Feet* (1975), an account of **Billy Connolly** on tour. Gaining experience, she was associate producer of the **Bill Forsyth** films *That Sinking Feeling* (1979), *Gregory's Girl* (1980) and *Comfort and Joy* (1984). Following her husband's death, she became a full-time producer and the doyenne of the Scottish film industry, instrumental in instigating the careers of many first-time directors. Her films include *The Girl in the Picture* (1986) and the award-winning *Silent Scream* (1990). In 1985 she purchased Black Cat Studios in Glasgow to provide facilities for the burgeoning Scottish independent production scene, but was forced into liquidation (1990). Recently at work in the drama department of BBC Scotland, she subsequently returned to independent production with her revived company Antonine Films.

HILL, David Octavius

(1802–70)

Painter and photographer, a pioneer in the use of the calotype process in photographic portraiture. Born in Perth, he was educated at Perth Academy and the School of Design in Edinburgh. In 1821 he issued probably the first set of lithographs published in Scotland, *Sketches of Scenery in Perthshire*. He maintained an interest in book illustration throughout his life, culminating in his two-volume work, *The Land of Burns*, with text by Professor **John Wilson**, published in 1840. Hill was a landscape and genre painter, poetic in character and influenced by J M W Turner. His successful paintings include *Edinburgh, Old and New* (1848), *The Viaduct at Ballochmyle* (1851) and *Ruins of the Palace of Dunfermline* (1854). As one of the founders of the Scottish Academy in 1829, he became its secretary the following year. In this post he was extremely active in securing the loans of major paintings for the annual exhibitions and, in the 1840s, in working to secure the Academy's independence from the constricting control of the Board of Trustees. He was also one of the originators of the Association for the Promotion of the Fine Arts, which raised money for the purchase of Scottish works, and he was generally involved in promoting art education. He became interested in photography in 1843, when he undertook to paint a large historical picture celebrating the founding of the Free Church of Scotland (The Signing of the Deed of Demission, which was only completed 20 years later). Sir **David Brewster** introduced him to the newly-established photographer, **Robert Adamson**, and in July 1843 they entered into partnership. This collaboration lasted effectively only three and a half years, but in that time they took over 3000 photographs by the calotype process, which explored a surprising range of ideas and possibilities within the medium. Most of the photographs were portraits, giving a commanding and vivid overview of Edinburgh society. They proposed (in 1844), but never completed, a project to publish six books of photographs. The most impressive of these, *The Fishermen and Women of the Firth of Forth*, was to give a structure to the photographs, principally of life in the village of Newhaven, which challenges the 20th-century idea of the documentary series. Together they produced photographs of considerable skill — chemical, physical, aesthetic and social — and their work is a landmark and a model in the history of photography.

HIRST, Sir Edward Langley
(1898–1975)

Organic chemist, born in Preston, Lancashire, and educated at St Andrews University. Originally a classics student, he turned to chemistry after working as a volunteer in Sir **James Irvine**'s laboratory making chemicals for the war effort. On returning to St Andrews from active service he became assistant to Irvine, beginning the work on polysaccharides that was to bring him such distinction. He moved to Bristol in 1927 to work with Walter Haworth. Their most spectacular success was the synthesis of vitamin C, the first time a vitamin had been made artificially. Hirst became professor at Bristol in 1936, and during the war he ran an explosives manufactury in his laboratory. In 1945 he moved to Manchester and in 1947 was appointed to the first Chair of Organic Chemistry at Edinburgh University. Under his direction substantial progress was made in many branches of carbohydrate chemistry and in the study of plant gums and mucilages, while links were forged between his department and industry and agriculture. He was knighted in 1964.

HISLOP, George Steedman
(1914 –)

Aeronautical engineer, born in Edinburgh. Educated at Clydebank High School, he went on to apprenticeship with **William Beardmore** & Co, the shipbuilders, at Clydebank. He graduated from the (then) Royal Technical College at Glasgow in mechanical engineering, subsequently becoming the Sir James Caird Scholar in Aeronautics at Cambridge University (1937–9). He was at the Aircraft and Armament Experimental Establishment (A & AEE) at Boscombe Down (1939–45) leading the High Altitude Flight; and at the Royal Aircraft Establishment (RAE), Farnborough (1945–7), working in the Wind Tunnel and on helicopter research.

After a time with British European Airways, working on Research and Helicopter Development, he devoted his career to rotorcraft. He became Chief Designer, Helicopters, then Chief Engineer and Director at Fairey Aviation and, following the merger with Westlands, Chief Engineer and Special Director Westland Aircraft until 1962. He was Executive Vice-Chairman Westland Aircraft (1972–6), where he carried major responsibility for the development of virtually all the helicopter types now in the British Services. He was involved with the early stages of the Anglo-French helicopter programme, and won distinguished awards for his many technical contributions to aeronautics. He was President of the Royal Aeronautical Society (1973–4) and Chairman of the Airworthiness Requirements Board (1982–3).

HISLOP, Joseph
(1884–1977)

Operatic tenor, born in Edinburgh but closely associated with Scandinavia. He trained as a photoprocessor engraver and went to work in Gothenburg, Sweden, where his fine tenor voice was noticed in a male voice choir. After tuition in Stockholm he made his début at the Royal Swedish Opera in 1914 as Faust in Gounod's opera. He subsequently performed in many countries, and in 1927 and 1931 he made an Empire concert tour of Australia, New Zealand and South Africa. In 1928 he sang Faust in a controversial production at Covent Garden opposite Chaliapin. In the 1930s he appeared in a film, *The Loves of Robert Burns* (directed by Herbert Wilcox), created the role of Goethe in the British première of Franz Lehar's musical play *Frederica*, and sang Sir Walter Raleigh in a revival of Edward German's *Merrie England*. From 1937 to 1947 he taught at the Royal Academy and the Opera School in Stockholm, where his pupils included Birgit Nilsson and Jussi Björling, and later coached singers in London. From 1947 he was an adviser at the Royal Opera House, Covent Garden, and at Sadler's Wells, and later became a professor at the Guildhall School of Music.

HODGE, Harry
(1872–1947)

Legal publisher, born in Edinburgh. Educated at Leipzig and Glasgow universities, he inherited the family business of legal publishers, William Hodge & Co, in Glasgow. Expanding this to Edinburgh, he sought to give the firm a more popular commercial base, notably with his foundation of the *Notable Scottish Trials* series 1905, to which he later added *Notable English Trials* and combined to *Notable British Trials*. The system in these was to make as full as possible a report of the trial in question, supplemented by a scholarly but readable introduction. Eighty volumes followed, and the hallmark of commercial success was asserted when collections of four or five introductions were assembled for Penguin books in the 1940s, reaching a readership of six figures. Although general editor, Hodge left it to individual editors to do all the work, getting excellent results and driving hard commercial bargains. For all of his rapacity, he deserves credit for putting criminological records on a popular footing.

HODGSON, William Ballantyne
(1815–80)

Economist and educationist, born in Edinburgh and educated at Edinburgh High School and University. In his early years he was a lecturer on literature, education and phrenology in Fife before becoming Secretary then Principal of the Liverpool Mechanics' Institute (1839–47) where he added a girls' school, part of his lifelong crusade to promote female education. He was Principal of Chorlton High School, Manchester (1847–51). After years of travelling and lecturing, he was Examiner in Political Economy, University of London (1863–8) before becoming first Professor of Commercial and Political Economy and Mercantile Law, Edinburgh University (1871–80). He published many of his lectures; his extensive library of books and pamphlets on classical economics enhances the collections of Edinburgh University.

HOGG, James
(1770–1835)

Poet and novelist, known as the 'Ettrick Shepherd', born on Ettrickhall Farm in the Ettrick Forest, Selkirkshire. As a boy he tended sheep and had only a spasmodic education. However, he inherited a rich store of ballads from his mother. In 1790 he became shepherd to **William Laidlaw** at Blackhouse in Selkirkshire, who encouraged him to write. On a visit to Edinburgh in 1801 to sell his employer's sheep, he had his *Scottish Pastorals, Poems, Songs, etc.* printed, but without success. He was fortunate, however, in making the acquaintance of Sir **Walter Scott**, then Sheriff of Selkirkshire, who published several of Hogg's mother's ballads

in the second volume of his *Border Minstrelsy* (1803). With the proceeds of *The Mountain Bard* (1803) Hogg dabbled unsuccessfully in farming, but eventually settled in Edinburgh. Another volume of poems, *The Forest Minstrel* (1810), was unsuccessful, but *The Queen's Wake* (1813) at once gained him cordial recognition. A bequest of a farm at Altrive Lake (now Edinhope) from the Duchess of Buccleuch enabled him to marry in 1820 and to produce in rapid succession a number of works in both verse and prose. He ended his days a well-known figure in Edinburgh society, a regular contributor to *Blackwood's Magazine*, and was the 'Ettrick Shepherd' of **John Wilson**'s *Noctes Ambrosianae*. He described himself as 'the King of the Mountain and Fairy School'. His poems of the supernatural are at their best when he avoids gothic elaboration and relies on the suggestive understatement of the ballad style, as in his 'Kilmeny' and 'The Witch of Fife'. 'The Aged Widow's Lament' shows the influence of the Scottish vernacular tradition. His debt to **Burns** is apparent in 'The Author's Address to his Auld Dog Hector' and in the riotous 'Village of Balmaquhapple'. Of his prose works, the most remarkable is *Private Memoirs and Confessions of a Justified Sinner* (1824), a macabre novel which anticipates **Stevenson**'s *Dr Jekyll and Mr Hyde* with its haunting 'split personality' theme. In 1834 he published his *Domestic Manners and Private Life of Sir Walter Scott*, against the wishes of Scott's family.

HOGG, Pam
(1958 –)

Fashion designer, born in Paisley and brought up in Glasgow, regarded as one of Britain's most innovative contemporary independent designers. She studied Fine Art and Printed Textiles at Glasgow School of Art, winning the Newbery Medal of Distinction, the Frank Warner Memorial Medal, the Leverhulme Scholarship, and the Royal Society of Arts bursary, before pursuing Printed Textiles at the Royal College of Art in London. Launching her first collection in 1984, her use of psychedelic colours on figure-hugging bodysuits has since become her trademark. With outlets in Glasgow, Manchester, Belfast, New York and Los Angeles, as well as Harrods, she has her own shop in London, where she is based. Three of her outfits are now part of the permanent collection of Kelvingrove Art Gallery in Glasgow.

HOLDEN, Sir Isaac
(1807–97)

Inventor, born in Hurlet, Renfrewshire. He worked in a Paisley cotton mill, studied chemistry in his spare time, and became an assistant teacher in Reading in 1829. He invented the Lucifer match, but was anticipated by John Walker of Stockton-on-Tees. In 1846 he joined with Lister, who had done much to improve woolcombing, in starting a mill near Paris. Lister retired, the firm became Isaac Holden & Sons in 1859, and the Alston works near Bradford were founded. After he had spent some £50 000 on experiments, Holden's woolcombing machinery brought him fame and fortune. He was a Liberal MP from 1865 to 1895.

HOLLAND, Sir Richard
(c.1415 – c.1482)

Poet and member of the **Douglas** faction at the court of **James II** and member of the Earl of Moray's household in the north of Scotland. The facts of his life are largely unknown, though it is suggested that he moved to Shetland following the fall of the Douglas family in 1455. His only extant work is *The Buke of the Howlat* (c.1448) which exists in manuscript form and was first published by the Bannatyne Club in 1823. An alliterative poem, it allegorically recounts the behaviour and unkind fate of an owl who dresses up in the feathers of other birds to improve his appearance, but becomes so obnoxiously vain that Nature restores him to his original ugliness with the lesson that owls are always owls and doves always doves. The story of the Douglas family fall is interpolated into the plot.

HOLMES, James Macdonald
(1896–1966)

Geographer, born in Greenock and educated at Glasgow University, where he taught for a period before going to Durham University in 1927. He then became Associate Professor at Sydney University (1929). There he initiated a research programme on soil conservation and regional planning in Australia, and was consultant and adviser to federal and state governments on soil erosion and on new legislation for regional planning. In 1945 he became Australia's first Professor of Geography (at Sydney). His most significant publications include *The Geographical Basis of*

Government (1944) and *Soil Erosion in Australia and New Zealand* (1946).

HOME, Daniel Dunglas
(1833–86)

Spiritualist, born near Edinburgh. He went to the USA in the 1840s to live with an aunt, who became so alarmed at the unexplained noises and other phenomena associated with his presence that she turned him out of her house. He soon won fame as a medium and as an exponent of table-turning and levitation, and went to London in 1855 where his séances were attended by high society there, as they were also on the Continent. He published an autobiography, *Incidents of My Life* (2 vols, 1863 and 1872). He was the subject of Browning's sceptical poem, *Mr Sludge, the Medium* (1864), but persuaded scientists such as Sir William Crookes, in the full glare of electricity, that he was genuine.

HOME, John
(1722–1808)

Clergyman and dramatist, born in Leith, Edinburgh. He graduated at Edinburgh in 1742. Fighting on the government side in the 1745 Jacobite Rising, he was taken prisoner at Falkirk (1746), but made a daring escape from Doune Castle. The next year he became minister of Athelstaneford, where he wrote the tragedy *Agis* and, in 1754, *Douglas*, founded on a Scottish ballad. Each of these was rejected in London by David Garrick, but *Douglas*, produced in the Canongate Theatre, Edinburgh (1756), met with brilliant success, and evoked the often quoted and possibly apocryphal 'whaur's yer Wullie Shakespeare noo?' from an over-enthusiastic member of the audience. It also won great popularity in London, but it gave such offence to the Edinburgh Presbytery that Home resigned his ministry (1757), and became Private Secretary to the Earl of **Bute** and tutor to the Prince of Wales, who on his accession as George III gave him a pension of £300 a year, to which a sinecure of equal value was added in 1763. The success of *Douglas* induced Garrick to bring out *Agis*, and to accept Home's next play, *The Siege of Aquileia* (1760). His other works are *The Fatal Discovery* (1769), *Alonzo* (1773), *Alfred* (1778), occasional poems and, in prose, *A History of the Rebellion of* 1745 (1802). He married in 1770, and in 1779 settled in Edinburgh.

HOME OF THE HIRSEL, Baron Alexander Frederick Douglas-Home

(1903 –)

Conservative politician, born in London, heir to the Scottish earldom of Home. He was educated at Eton and Christchurch, Oxford, entered Parliament in 1931, and was Chamberlain's secretary during the latter's abortive negotiations with Hitler and Mussolini (1937–9). Out of Parliament (1945–51) he became Minister of State, Scottish Office (1951–5), succeeded to the peerage as 14th Earl (1951), was Commonwealth-Relations Secretary (1955–60), Leader of the House of Lords and Lord President of the Council (1957–60), and Foreign Secretary (1960–3). After Macmillan's resignation, he astonished everyone by emerging as premier (November 1963). He made history by renouncing his peerage and fighting a by-election at Kinross during which, although premier, he was technically a member of neither House. A similar situation was depicted in the play, *The Reluctant Peer* (1963), by his brother, William Douglas-Home. After defeat by the Labour Party in the general election of 1964, he was Leader of the opposition until he was replaced the following year by Edward Heath, in whose 1970–4 government he was Foreign Secretary. In 1974 he was made a life peer.

HOOD, Stuart

(1915 –)

Novelist and critic, born in Edzell, Angus, and educated at Edinburgh University. He was interned by the Italians in 1942, and fought with the Partisans on his release in 1943. Joining the BBC in 1946, he rose to executive level before joining the television company Rediffusion in 1964. Working as a freelance writer and programme-maker since 1965, he has written several books on television and the media, and was television critic of *The Spectator* from 1965 to 1968. He has taught at the Royal College of Art and Goldsmiths' College in London, and at the University of Sussex. His novels include *The Circle of the Minotaur* (1950), *The Upper Hand* (1987), *The Brutal Heart* (1989) and *A Den of Foxes* (1991). Deeply rooted in personal experience, they are unusual in the degree to which they confront radical political ideals. *A Storm From Paradise* (1985), about the tribulations of a schoolmaster who rebels against the mores of a small Scottish town, won the Saltire Prize. He has translated the work of numerous writers, including Pier Paulo Pasolini, Dario Fo and Ernst Junger. He published a volume of autobiography, *Pebbles From My Skull*, in 1964.

HOPE

Name of a noble family descended from John de Hope, 1500–60, who probably came to Scotland from France in 1537 with Magdalen de Valois, Queen of **James V**, and set up as a merchant in Edinburgh.

HOPE, Sir Charles, 1st Earl of Hopetoun

(1681–1742)

Nobleman. He was elected Privy Councillor and a peer in 1702. A supporter of the Union (1707) with England, he became Lord-Lieutenant of Linlithgow in 1715, and in 1723 was Lord High Commissioner to the General Assembly of the Church of Scotland. He commissioned **William Bruce** in 1699 to build Hopetoun House on his estates near Queensferry, and the building was considerably altered and completed in 1753 by the famous Scottish architects, **William** and **Robert Adam**.

HOPE, Sir John, 4th Earl of Hopetoun

(1765–1823)

Soldier. He served at the Battle of Alexandria (1801), under Sir **John Moore** in Spain where he distinguished himself in the retreat to La Coruña (1808), and finally under Wellington throughout the Peninsular War.

HOPE, John Adrian Louis, 7th Earl and 1st Marquis of Linlithgow

(1860–1908)

Politician, born in South Queensferry, Edinburgh, and educated at Eton. He held junior office in the Conservative administrations of 1885 and 1886, and was Governor-General of Victoria (1889–95) during a period of financial and economic instability. Paymaster General in Salisbury's administration (1895–8), he was appointed first Governor-General of Australia in 1900 in recognition of his success in Victoria, and organized the highly successful visit that year of the Prince of Wales.

Very reluctant to ratify the whites-only immigration measure of 1901, he then resigned (1902), claiming that his salary was inadequate to meet the burdens of office. He was created marquis in 1902. Secretary for Scotland in 1905, he was High Commissioner to the General Assembly of the Church of Scotland from 1887 to 1889.

HOPE, Victor Alexander John, 8th Earl and 2nd Marquis
(1887–1952)

Conservative politician, born in South Queensferry, Edinburgh, and educated at Eton. He succeeded to the title in 1908. He was First Lord of the Admiralty (1922–4) and Deputy Chairman of the Conservative Party (1924–6). He was Viceroy of India from 1936 to 1943, the longest term of this office since 1856. In this post he showed concern for the problems of rural India. He sought to encourage Gandhi and the Congress Party to take power in provincial administrations, and developed good relations with Jinnah, the leader of the Muslim community. During World War II he organized the defence of India. He was Chairman of the Medical Research Council (1934–6) and High Commissioner to the General Assembly of the Church of Scotland (1944–5).

HOPE, (James Arthur) David
(1938 –)

Judge, born in Edinburgh. Educated at Cambridge and Edinburgh universities, he passed advocate in 1965. He became QC in 1978, served as an advocate-depute 1978–82 and was Dean of the Faculty of Advocates 1986–9 before being promoted direct to the offices of Lord Justice-General and Lord President of the Court of Session in 1989, when he was sworn of the Privy Council. He shared in the editing of several editions of **Gloag** and Henderson's *Introduction to the Law of Scotland* and of some other textbooks.

HOPE, Sir John
(1725–86)

Founder of the Edinburgh Botanic Gardens. Born in Edinburgh, the grandson of Alexander Hope, Lord Rankeillor, he was a man of means, devoting his wealth largely to the advancement of science. First taking over the Old Physic Garden at Holyrood, he was then able to obtain a large grant from the Treasury to buy land and lay out the new Botanic Gardens between the city and the Firth of Forth. He also received a grant for running expenses. He personally supervised the planning of the new gardens and the transfer of the plants from Holyrood. He had a considerable influence on a generation of self-taught amateurs who investigated and published their findings in plant physiology. A firm supporter of Linnaeus, he was the first to apply the Linnaean System of classification in the UK.

HOPE, Sir Thomas, of Craighall
(1580–1646)

Judge and jurist, Lord Advocate (1626–46). He wrote *Minor Practicks* (1726), a short treatise on Scots Law, and *Major Practicks* (1937–8), a substantial collection of notes on statutes, cases and practical points distributed under eight major and many subsidiary headings. It is a valuable source for understanding early 17th-century law.

HOPE, Thomas Charles
(1766–1844)

Chemist, born in Edinburgh. He studied medicine there, and afterwards taught chemistry in Glasgow and from 1795 in Edinburgh where he taught with, and then succeeded, **Joseph Black**. Hope confirmed the earlier but neglected observations that water has a maximum density close to 4°C, an important result in biology, climatology and physics. In 1793 he recognized and described a new mineral from Strontian in Argyll; he even described the characteristic red flame colour of the new element that it contained (strontium), which was isolated by Sir Humphrey Davy in 1808. Hope was a highly successful teacher (his lectures were attended by 575 students in 1825) and was probably the first in Britain to teach the new ideas propounded by Lavoisier, the 'father of modern chemistry'.

HOPETOUN See HOPE

HORNE, David
(1970 –)

Composer and pianist, born in Stirling. At St Mary's Music School, Edinburgh, he studied composition with Geoffrey King. As a pianist he made his BBC Proms début with Prokofiev's third concerto (1990). He has composed several works for varied chamber groupings as well as *light, emerging...* for orchestra (1989) and *Nocturnes and Nightingales* for piano (1991).

HORNE, John
(1848–1928)

Geologist, born in Campsie, Stirlingshire. He attended Glasgow University, but joined the staff of the Geological Survey of Scotland in 1867 as a young assistant geologist, rising to become Assistant Director (Scotland) (1901–11). As the younger man in the extraordinary partnership with **Benjamin Neeve Peach**, he did most of the writing of the great Survey Memoirs on the Southern Uplands (1899) and the North-West Highlands (1907). In 1912 they led the famous British Association excursion to Assynt. Horne received many honours, including the **Murchison** and Wollaston medals of the Geological Society of London with Peach. Their final work, *Chapters on the Geology of Scotland*, was published posthumously in 1930.

HORNE OF SLAMANNAN, Robert Stevenson Horne, 1st Viscount
(1871–1940)

Conservative politician, born in Slamannan, Stirlingshire. Educated at George Watson's College, Edinburgh, and Glasgow University, he became an advocate in 1896, and in World War I was administrator of national service, railway organization and admiralty departments. MP for Glasgow Hillhead (1918–37), he went straight on to the front bench upon election as Minister of Labour in 1918. There he dealt successfully with mine and rail strikes, and also extended prewar insurance legislation. As President of the Board of Trade (1920–1), he became Chancellor of the Exchequer (1921–2), where he implemented massive cuts in public spending levels. Refusing to serve in **Andrew Bonar Law**'s Conservative administration of 1922, he remained thereafter on the back benches until he was elevated to a peerage in 1937. He became director of many railway, insurance, banking and shipping companies. A very sociable man and a brilliant mimic, his political career never fulfilled its early promise.

HORNEL, Edward Atkinson
(1864–1933)

Painter, born in Bacchus Marsh, Australia, of Scottish parents. He grew up in Kirkcudbright, where he was eventually to settle, and studied painting at the Trustees Academy, Edinburgh, and subsequently at the Antwerp studio of M. Verlot. In 1885 he met **George Henry**, with whom he was to share a studio and collaborate on a number of paintings. In 1893, the two painters made a trip to Japan which was influential, particularly in the case of Hornel, who subsequently produced a number of striking images of Japanese women. Most of Hornel's work depicts rural life, painted in rich, heavily worked pigment.

HORNER, Francis
(1778–1817)

Politician and economist, born in Edinburgh. He was educated at Edinburgh High School and University, where he was a contemporary of **Henry Brougham** and a close friend of **William Playfair**. With **Francis Jeffrey** and others he founded the *Edinburgh Review*. His lifelong interest in economics began with a study of the French Physiocrats and attendance at **Dugald Stewart**'s lectures on political economy. He was called to the Scottish Bar in 1800 and to the English Bar in 1802, where he practised for several years. In 1806 he was elected MP for St Ives, Cornwall, and subsequently for St Mawes in 1813. In 1810 he chaired the Bullion Committee for the House of Commons, which recommended that the pound return to convertibility, and he shared with classical economists a fervent opposition to the corn laws. He died in Pisa of a rare chest illness.

HORNER, Leonard
(1785–1864)

Geologist and educationist, born in Edinburgh and educated at Edinburgh High School and Edinburgh University. In 1804 he moved to London, and four years later was elected a Fellow of the Geological Society. Even after his return to Edinburgh in 1817 he maintained an active association with the society, and in 1846 became its president. In 1821 he founded the Edinburgh School of Arts for the Instruction of Mechanics; this was an immediate success and led to the establishment of many other mechanics' institutes throughout Great Britain. He was invited to assist in setting up the London Institution, and in 1828 became Warden of London University on its opening, but had to resign in 1831 because of ill health.

HOUSE, Jack

(1906–91)

Journalist, born in Glasgow. Leaving school at 15 he began an accounting apprenticeship but 'saw the light' and decided to pursue journalism instead. During World War II he served as a captain in the Army Kinematograph Service along with Peter Ustinov. An acknowledged authority on Glasgow life, he worked for all three Glasgow evening newspapers, was half of the Scottish Round Britain Quiz Team for 22 years, and published over 60 books, the first appearing in 1925. Most notable are *Glasgow the Smiling City* (1989) and his autobiography, *Pavement in the Sun* (1967). Fondly known as 'Mr Glasgow', he was awarded the St Mungo Prize in 1988, an honour given every three years to the person adjudged to have most benefited the city of Glasgow.

HOUSTON, John

(1930 –)

Painter, born in Buckhaven, Fife. He studied at Edinburgh College of Art (1948–54) where, after being awarded a scholarship in 1953, he became a teacher. He is best known for large landscapes painted in a semi-abstract manner, in rich and boldly handled pigment. He is married to the painter **Elizabeth Blackadder.**

HOUSTON, Renée, originally Katerina Gribbin

(1902–80)

Comedienne and actress, born in Johnstone, Renfrewshire. She made her stage début as a double-act with her sister, Billie (1920), in which they dressed as a precocious girl and boy. A booking in Tommy Lorne's revue *Froth* (1924) at the Glasgow Pavilion led to their London début in 1925. Their swift rise to popularity is shown by their appearance in the Royal Variety Performance (1926). For a while the act was a threesome, including their younger sister Shirley, but when Billie retired in 1936, Renée formed a new type of double-act with her husband, Donald Stewart. This too led to a Royal Variety Performance (1938). In her later years she became a notable character actress, appearing in over 40 films, and was a popular, if opinionated, panellist on the radio series, *Petticoat Line*.

HOWDEN, James

(1832–1913)

Engineer, born in Prestonpans, East Lothian. He was educated in Prestonpans and Tranent and in 1847 moved to Glasgow to be apprenticed as an engineer. Before completion of his apprenticeship he was made chief draughtsman with the firm of James Gray. By 1854 he had set up his own business, mainly as a marine engineer, manufacturing engines and boilers, and in 1857 he was a founder member of the Institute of Engineers and Shipbuilders in Scotland. In 1862 he established James Howden and Co., whose enduring success lay in his remarkable inventive ability. His most noteworthy innovation was the forced draught system, which enabled a more efficient combustion process in marine engines. His career paralleled and contributed to Glasgow's emergence through the 'second industrial revolution' as a city of prosperity and expansion. A mark of this is the fact that his estate was worth almost £400 000.

HOWIE, Archibald

(1934 –)

Physicist, educated at Kirkcaldy High School and Edinburgh University. After a few years as a research student and research fellow at Cambridge he was successively Demonstrator, Lecturer and Reader in Physics at the Cavendish Laboratory, Cambridge University. He became Professor of Physics there in 1986 and Head of Department in 1989. He is distinguished for his studies of the defect structures of metals by electron microscopy and was awarded the Hughes medal of the Royal Society in 1988.

HOWISON, John

(d.1859)

Literary traveller. His origins are unknown, save that he was evidently born in or near Edinburgh into a Quaker family with a strong literary bent, his brother William being a frequent contributor to the early numbers of *Blackwood's Magazine*. John Howison seems to have travelled in North America with extensive experience of survival in the wilderness, and also became a keen and hostile observer of slavery in the Caribbean. On his return to Edinburgh he published the successful *Sketches of Upper Canada* (1821), whose vivid prose and little-known terrain won reprints and translation into German. His most influential work, 'Vanderdecken's Message Home', the first use of the Flying Dutchman legend in modern fiction, appeared in 1821, and its theme of fidelity to loved ones from the eternally sea-trapped crew inspired the later melodrama of Edward Fitzball (1792–1873), performed 1827, and thence Heine's satire and Wagner's opera. Howison followed his story with further haunting sea-narratives in subsequent numbers of *Blackwood's*. Among these 'The Floating Beacon' was also staged and 'The Florida Pirate' is an outstanding early ex-slave fictional autobiography showing exceptionally imaginative sympathy. He travelled in 1822 to India for the East India Company, reaching Bombay that year. Out of this experience he published *Foreign Scenes and Travelling Recreations* (1825), *Tales of the Colonies* (1830), and *European Colonies* (1834). He was active in the Anti Corn-Law League in Edinburgh in the early 1840s, and elected to keep his authorship of 'Vanderdecken' unknown despite its occasional reappearance. His extensive influence has passed largely unnoticed.

HOWSON, Peter
(1958 –)

Painter, born in London. He moved to Scotland in 1962 and attended Glasgow School of Art (1975–7), to which he returned from 1979 to 1981 after employment in various jobs, including a period in the army. In 1985 he was artist-in-residence at St Andrews University and became part-time tutor at Glasgow School of Art. Through his paintings, drawings and prints, he tends towards a critique of class structure, focusing on working-class characters, especially soldiers, mercenaries, boxers and 'dossers', whom he portrays as physically powerful, yet uncertain of purpose.

HUCHESONE, George
(c.1560–1639) and **Thomas** (c.1585–1641)

Philanthropists, the eldest and youngest sons of Thomas Huchesone (c.1520–1590), a successful landowner. When their father died, George was over 30 and Thomas four years old, so George and his wife, Elspeth Craig, brought up Thomas as a son (they were to make him their heir). George became a notary, acting as an agent for the clergy, noblemen, and the city council. For a while he held the commission of Judge-Depute in the Commissary Courts of Glasgow and Hamilton. He acquired his wealth through money-lending, mainly to merchants. Thomas went to college in Glasgow, where he studied arts and theology. He then became a notary and was appointed Registrar of Sasines for Glasgow and the County of Renfrew. He instigated the building of the Hospital (originally envisaged as a semi-monastic home for destitute pensioners and orphans) but died the year the building was begun. He left a donation of 20 000 marks towards the building of the Hospital in his will. After his death his wife, Marion Stewart, proposed the introduction of women to the hospital, but they were not formally admitted until 1757. The buildings and ground of the hospital were disposed of by the patrons around 1800 and the pensioners received charitable grants instead. A boys' school was built in Crown Street in 1841, and a girls' school was later founded in Elgin Street (1876).

HUE AND CRY See KANE, Pat

HUME, Allan Octavian
(1829–1912)

Colonialist and naturalist, son of **Joseph Hume**. Educated at Haileybury Training College, Hertfordshire, he studied medicine at University College Hospital in London and joined the Bengal Civil Service in 1849. He became Commissioner of Customs for the North-West Provinces, and Director-General of Agriculture. He built a huge library and museum for his vast collection of Asiatic birds at Simla, and in 1872 he founded a quarterly journal on Indian ornithology. He retired in 1882, but in 1883 the manuscript of his projected book on Indian birds was stolen and sold as waste paper. In despair he presented his whole collection to the British Museum. In 1885 he was founder and first secretary (until 1908) of the first National Congress in Bombay. Hume's Tawny Owl, Lesser Whitethroat and Wheatear are named after him.

HUME, David
(1711–76)

Philosopher and historian, born in Edinburgh. His early years were unsettled. He studied but did not graduate at Edinburgh University; he then took up law, but suffered from bouts of depression, and tried his hand instead at commerce as a counting-house clerk in Bristol. In 1734 he went to La Flèche in Anjou where he stayed for three years, studying and working on his first and most important work, *A Treatise of Human Nature*, which he had published anonymously in London (1739–40) when he had returned to Scotland to stay on the family estate at Ninewells in Berwickshire (1739–45). The subtitle, 'an attempt to introduce the experimental method of reasoning into moral subjects' states Hume's intention to apply the scientific method of Robert Boyle and Sir Isaac Newton and to establish a new 'Science of man'. The discussions of causation, personal identity and ethics have often been interpreted one-sidedly as mere workings out of John Locke's theory, but they mark an advance in understanding that is still not fully understood. In political theory he argued for the 'artificiality' of the principles of justice and political obligation, and challenged the rationalistic 'natural law' and 'social contract' theories of Thomas Hobbes, Richard Hooker, Locke and Rousseau. Hume was bitterly disappointed at the initial reception of the *Treatise* ('it fell dead-born from the press') and put out the more popular *Essays Moral and Political* (1741, 1742), which were immediately successful and helped gratify his literary ambitions. These essays heralded the new school of classical economics, of which his friend **Adam Smith** was to be the leader, advocating free trade and clearly stating the relationship between international specie flows, domestic prices and the balance of payments. His efforts to secure an independent income still proceeded by fits and starts. His views doomed his applications for the professorships of moral philosophy at Edinburgh (1744) and logic at Glasgow (1751); he became tutor for a year in 1745 to an insane nobleman, the Marquis of Annandale, and then became secretary to General St Clair on an expedition to France in 1746 and secret missions to Vienna and Turin in 1748. In 1748 he published a revised and abridged version of the *Treatise* entitled *An Enquiry Concerning Human Understanding*. **James Beattie**'s unsound, unwisely circulated attack on this book 'woke' Immanuel Kant from his 'dogmatic slumbers' by revealing that Hume had refuted earlier views, and led to the major development of Kant's 'Critical Philosophy'. The brilliant *Dialogues Concerning Natural Religion* were written in 1750 but were prudently left unpublished until after Hume's death (1779). He became Keeper of the Advocates' Library in Edinburgh in 1752 and achieved real fame and recognition with his *Political Discourses* (1752) and his monumental *History of England* in five volumes (1754–62). From 1763 to 1765 he acted as secretary to the ambassador in Paris, and was received with great enthusiasm by the French court and literary society ('Here I feed on ambrosia, drink nothing but nectar, breathe incense only, and walk on flowers'). He returned to London in 1766 with Rousseau, whom he had befriended but who was to provoke a bitter and famous quarrel with him, and he became Under-Secretary of State for the Northern Department in 1767, returning finally to Scotland in 1768 to settle in Edinburgh, where he died and was much mourned.

HUME, David
(1757–1838)

Jurist and judge, nephew of **David Hume** the philosopher, born in Ninewells, Berwickshire. Educated at Edinburgh High School, and Edinburgh and Glasgow universities, he was Professor of Scots Law at Edinburgh (1786–1822), and then Baron of the Scottish Court of Exchequer (1822–34). He wrote the classic text on Scottish criminal law, *Commentaries on the Law of Scotland Respecting the Description and Punishment of Crimes* (2 vols, 1797), and *Commentaries on the Law of Scotland Respecting the Trial for Crimes* (2 vols, 1800), later combined into one work. These were based on exhaustive investigation of court records. His *Lectures on Scots Law*, published posthumously, are also highly regarded.

HUME, David, of Godscroft
(c.1560 – c.1630)

Genealogist, born in Dunbar, East Lothian, the historian of the **Douglas** family. He probably studied at St Andrews, Paris and Geneva, before returning to Scotland to become secretary to the Douglases. At the time of the union of crowns between England and Scotland (1603) he wrote *De Unione Insulae Britanniae* (1605), but his main work, the eulogistic *Origin and Descent of the Family* *of Douglas*, was published posthumously in 1633, and extended as *History of the House and Race of Douglas and Angus* in 1644. During rural retirement at Godscroft in Berwickshire, he turned to writing Latin verse in the style of Ovid.

HUME, Joseph
(1777–1855)

Radical politician, born in Montrose, Angus. He studied medicine at Edinburgh, and in 1797 became assistant surgeon under the East India Company. He acquired several native languages, and in the Mahratta war (1802–7) he filled important offices. On the conclusion of peace he returned to England (1808), his fortune made. A political and economic philosopher of the school of **James Mill** and Jeremy Bentham, he sat in Parliament (1812, 1818–55), representing at different times Border burghs, Aberdeen and Montrose burghs. One of the most frequent and lengthiest speakers in Parliament, he advocated strict economy in public spending and minimum government regulation of social and economic affairs, Catholic emancipation, the establishment of savings banks, franchise extensions, free trade (especially with India), the abolition of flogging in the army, of impressment in the navy, and of imprisonment for debt.

HUME, Sir Patrick
(1641–1724)

Statesman and Covenanter, Lord Chancellor of Scotland. In 1690 he was created Lord Polwarth, and in 1679 Earl of Marchmont. He was the father of Lady **Grizel Baillie**.

HUNTER, Ian Melville Logan
(1927 –)

Psychologist, born in Largs, Ayrshire. A graduate of Edinburgh and Oxford, he was a lecturer in psychology at Edinburgh from 1953 to 1962. He was first Professor of Psychology at Keele University (1962–82), where he established the Department of Psychology. His book *Memory* (1957) was widely influential for a quarter of a century. His study in 1961 of the Edinburgh mathematician and mental calculator, **Alexander Craig Aitken**, helped inaugurate scientific studies of cognitive expertise. He later used case studies to clarify the biographical, moti-vational and social conditions that encourage exceptional human achievements in the use of knowledge and skill.

HUNTER, John
(1728–93)

Physiologist and surgeon, born in Long Calderwood, East Kilbride, the 'founder of scientific surgery,' and brother of **William Hunter**. His father was a younger son of the ancient house of Hunterston, in Ayrshire. He worked as assistant to his brother in the dissecting room (1748–59), studied surgery at Chelsea Hospital and St Bartholomew's, and in 1754 entered St George's Hospital, becoming house-surgeon in 1756 and lecturer for his brother in the anatomical school. In 1760 he entered the army as staff-surgeon, and served in the expedition to Belleisle and Portugal. At the commencement of peace in 1763 he started the practice of surgery in London, and devoted much time and money to comparative anatomy. One of his pupils was Edward Jenner. In 1768 he was appointed surgeon at St George's Hospital, in 1776 Surgeon-Extraordinary to King George III, and in 1790 Surgeon-General to the army. In 1785 he built his museum, with lecture-rooms, and performed his first artery ligature for the cure of aneurysm. His collection, which contained 10 563 specimens, was bought by the government in 1795 and presented to the Royal College of Surgeons, but was destroyed during an air raid in World War II. His *Natural History of Human Teeth* (1771–8) revolutionized dentistry. He investigated a large number of subjects, from venereal disease and embryology to blood, inflammation and gunshot wounds. In 1771 he married Anne Home (1742–1821), author of 'My mother bids me bind my hair' and other songs set to music by Haydn. He was buried in the church of St Martin-in-the-Fields, and transferred to Westminster Abbey in 1859.

HUNTER, John
(1737–1821)

Naval captain and administrator, born in Leith, Edinburgh. He studied for the ministry at Aberdeen University, but left at the age of 17 to join the navy. In 1786 he was appointed second captain on the *Sirius*, flagship of the first fleet, which was to sail for Australia under the command of Captain Arthur Phillip. Hunter arrived in New South Wales in 1788, and then sailed round the Horn to

Cape Town for desperately needed supplies. He continued eastward, eventually circumnavigating the globe, and on his return to Sydney set off for Norfolk Island, where the ship was wrecked and the crew were marooned for 11 months. In 1792 he returned to England, but went back to New South Wales as its second governor in 1795. Here he found the military had effectively taken over the running of the colony, and Hunter had great difficulty in restoring civil government, making such powerful enemies that he was recalled to London in 1800. During his governorship he greatly encouraged the exploratory voyages of George Bass and Matthew Flinders, and as a keen natural scientist he promoted many valuable expeditions in search of botanical and zoological specimens.

HUNTER, Laurence Colvin

(1934 –)

Leading Scottish authority on labour economics and industrial relations, who was educated at Hillhead High School, Glasgow and at Glasgow and Oxford universities. After appointments at Manchester and Chicago universities, he joined the Department of Applied Economics, Glasgow University in 1962, rising from a lectureship to a chair by 1969. His books include *Urban Worker Mobility* (1968, with G L Reid), *Economics of Wages and Labour* (1969, with D J Robertson, and 1981, with C Mulvey) and *Pay, Productivity and Collective Bargaining* (1973, with R B McKersie). He was on the council of ACAS (1974–86) and has been Editor of the *Scottish Journal of Political Economy* since 1966 and Chairman of the Police Negotiating Board from 1987.

HUNTER, Leslie

(1877–1931)

Painter, born in Rothesay, Isle of Bute. In 1892 his family emigrated to California where, in San Francisco, he became a magazine illustrator. He visited Paris and returned to Glasgow for a time around 1903. Although he intended to become a professional artist in San Francisco, he lost all his work in an earthquake in 1906, which prompted a return to Scotland. After a period working as an illustrator in Glasgow and London, and occasional visits to France, he attracted the attention of the art collector Alexander Reid, who became an important patron. One of the Scottish colourists, his painting was much

influenced by the work of artists he saw in France, such as Van Gogh and Matisse, and his landscapes and still-lifes typically display vibrant colour and broken brushwork.

HUNTER, Mollie

(1922 –)

Writer, born in Longniddry, East Lothian. Until 1960 she worked as a freelance journalist, but she is best known for her work in children's fiction, and has published 25 books of various types in this field, including fantasy and historical fiction. Her works include *Hi Johnny* (1963), *Haunted Mountain* (1972) and *A Stranger Came Ashore* (1975). She has been Writer-in-Residence at Dalhousie University in Halifax, Canada, and has lectured and written on writing for children. She has been the recipient of many major awards, including the Scottish Arts Council Literary Award (1972), the Carnegie Medal (1975), and the Arbuthnot Lectureship (1975).

HUNTER, Russell

(1925 –)

Actor, born in Glasgow. After serving an apprenticeship as a loftsman scriever at the John Brown Shipyard in Clydebank, he began his career as an amateur with the Glasgow Unity Theatre, turning professional in 1946. A gaunt, versatile character actor, he has worked with many of Britain's most respected repertory companies, including the Royal Shakespeare Company and the Old Vic, and his many theatrical credits include *The Servant O' Twa Maisters* (1965), *A Midsummer Night's Dream* (1966), *Hamlet* (1968), *Cocky* (1969) and *The Merchant of Venice* (1981). Long active in pantomime, he has also become a regular fixture of the Edinburgh Fringe with tour de force appearances in one-man shows and revues by W Gordon Smith, including *Jock* and *Knox*. A useful supporting performer in numerous television shows, he achieved his greatest popularity as Lonely, the malodorous, downtrodden petty crook in the espionage series *Callan* (1967–73), and received warm praise for his portrayal of a veteren Clydeside rebel in *Dunroamin' Rising* (1988). Actress **Una McLean** became his third wife in 1991.

HUNTER, Samuel

(1769–1839)

Journalist, soldier, physician and wit, born, a minister's son, in Wigtownshire. He graduated from Glasgow University in 1785, qualified as a surgeon, and served as a captain in the North Lowland Fencibles. After a disastrous interlude as a businessman, in 1803 he was appointed Editor of the *Glasgow Herald*, which was then only 20 years old, and he held this post until 1836. Although he lacked any journalistic experience, he had a natural talent for robust epigrammatic prose. One of the most extrovert characters in the history of Glasgow, in 1818 he raised 1000 men to form the Glasgow Volunteer Sharpshooters with the aim of putting down radical weavers.

HUNTER, William
(1718–83)

Anatomist and obstetrician, brother of **John Hunter**, born in Long Calderwood, East Kilbride. He studied divinity for five years at Glasgow University, but in 1737 took up medicine with **William Cullen**, and was trained in anatomy at St George's Hospital in London. From about 1748 he confined his practice to midwifery, in 1764 he was appointed physician-extraordinary to Queen Charlotte Sophia, and in 1768 he became the first Professor of Anatomy to the Royal Academy. His most important work was on the uterus. In 1770 he built a house with an amphitheatre for lectures, a dissecting-room, a museum, and a cabinet of medals and coins. His Hunterian museum was finally bequeathed, with an endowment of £8000, to Glasgow University.

HUNTER, Sir William Wilson
(1840–1900)

Statistician, born in Glasgow. He studied there, at Paris and in Bonn, and in 1862 entered the civil service of India. His post as Superintendent of Public Instruction in Orissa (1866–9) gave him the opportunity to write the *Annals of Rural Bengal* (1868) and *A Comparative Dictionary of the Non-Aryan Languages of India* (1868). Then, after being secretary to the Bengal government and the

government of India, in 1871 he became Director-General of the Statistical Department of India; the Indian census of 1872 was his first work. In 1887 he retired and returned home to write books, mostly on Indian subjects.

HUNTLY, Earls of See GORDON

HUTCHISON, Dr Isobel Wylie
(1889–1982)

Plant hunter in Arctic regions. She started her explorations in East Greenland in 1927, followed in 1928 by a year in North Greenland living in an Eskimo village. In 1934 she travelled by coastal steamer and dog sledge through Alaska, and returned in 1936 to visit the Aleutian Islands. In addition to accounts of her travels she published many scientific papers, a novel and four volumes of verse. For many years she was Honorary Editor of the *Scottish Geographical Magazine*, of which she was a vice-president and recipient of the **Mungo Park** Medal. She was awarded the honorary degree of LLD from St Andrews University for her contributions to horticulture.

HUTCHISON, Sir William Oliphant
(1889–1970)

Artist, born in Collessie, Fife. He studied at Edinburgh and in Paris, and is known for his portraits and landscapes. He was Director of the Glasgow School of Art from 1933 to 1943.

HUTTON, James
(1726–97)

Geologist, born in Edinburgh. He studied medicine there, in Paris and in Leiden. In 1754 he devoted himself in Berwickshire to agriculture and chemistry, which led him to mineralogy and geology, and in 1768 he moved to Edinburgh. The Huttonian theory, emphasizing the igneous origin of many rocks and deprecating the assumption of causes other than those we see still at work, was expounded before the Royal Society of Edinburgh in *A Theory of the Earth* (1785; expanded, vols i, ii 1795; iii 1899), and formed the basis of modern geology.

I

INGLIS, Elsie Maud
(1864–1917)

Surgeon and reformer, born in Naini Tal, India. One of the first women medical students at Edinburgh and Glasgow, she inaugurated the second medical school for women at Edinburgh (1892). In 1901, appalled at the lack of maternity facilities and the prejudice held against women doctors by their male colleagues, she founded a maternity hospital in Edinburgh that was completely staffed by women. In 1906 she founded the Scottish Women's Suffragette Federation, which sent two women ambulance units to France and Serbia in 1915. She set up three military hospitals in Serbia (1916), fell into Austrian hands, was repatriated, but in 1917 returned to Russia with a voluntary corps, which was withdrawn after the revolution.

INGLIS, John, Baron Glencorse
(1810–91)

Judge, born in Edinburgh. He established himself as a leading advocate by his brilliant defence of **Madeleine Smith** in 1857, and rose to be successively Lord Justice-Clerk (1858) and Lord President of the Court of Session (1867–91). As such he ranks very highly as a judge, and many of his judgements are classics. He also played a major role in the reform of the Scottish universities.

INGLIS, Sir Robert John Mathison
(1881–1962)

Civil engineer. He graduated in engineering at Edinburgh University and in 1900 joined the North British Railway, for whom he supervised a variety of track improvement schemes until 1919, when he joined the Ministry of Transport, becoming Chief Engineer, Railways, in 1921. Returning later in the same year to the NBR in Glasgow as district engineer, he became Chief Engineer for the southern area of the LNER in 1937, and Divisional General Manager for Scotland in 1941. In 1949 he was appointed Chairman of the Glasgow and District Transport Committee, which in its 1951 report recommended electrification of railways in Glasgow and the Clyde valley.

INNES, Cosmo
(1798–1874)

Jurist and historian, born in Durris, Moray. Educated at Glasgow and Oxford, he was called to the Bar in 1822. He became Sheriff of Moray in 1840, then an official of the Court of Session, and in 1846 Professor of Constitutional Law and History in the University of Edinburgh. He is best known as the author of *Scotland in the Middle Ages* (1860), *Sketches of Early Scotch History* (1861) and *Lectures on Scotch Legal Antiquities* (1872). He prepared volume one of *Acts of the Parliament of Scotland*, was a member of the Bannatyne, Maitland and Spalding Clubs, and edited for them several cartularies of the old religious houses of Scotland. He also published several memoirs, including one of **Edward Ramsay**.

INNES, Thomas
(1662–1744)

Catholic historian, born in Drumgask in the parish of Aboyne, Aberdeenshire, the son of a wadsetter. His brother was Lewis Innes (1651–1738), Principal of the Scots College in Paris (1682–1713) and archivist to the Jacobite court. Thomas followed him to Paris. Ordained a priest in 1691, he was a resident of the Scots College in Paris from 1681 (with intermissions), assisting his brother from 1692 in arranging the papers of the Archdiocese of Glasgow which had been deposited there by the exiled Archbishop James Beaton, priest of the Scots mission at Inveravon, Banffshire from 1698 to 1701. Graduating from Paris University in 1694, Innes was suspected of Jansenism, but was vindicated, partly by support from his brother. Vice-Principal of the Scots College in Paris from 1727, he published *A Critical Essay on the Ancient Inhabitants of the Northern Parts of*

Britain or Scotland (1729), a work of the foremost importance in the demythologization of early Scottish history, placing historians of every and no religious persuasion in his widely-acknowledged debt. His *The Civil and Ecclesiastical History of Scotland* was published posthumously (1853), again with great value for future historians. Innes also left letters on liturgical, and Jacobite-related matters. He is commemorated by the journal of modern professional Scottish Catholic history, the *Innes Review*.

IRELAND, John
(1440–96)

Theologian and philosopher, born in the diocese of St Andrews, author of the first original work in the Scots tongue to be published, the *Meroure of Wyssedome* (Mirror of Wisdom). He attended university at St Andrews (1455–8), and at Paris, where he graduated and began teaching in 1460. Rector at Paris in 1469, he was involved in the early-1470s ecclesiastical-political disputes over the curriculum. In 1480 he returned to Scotland on embassy from the French king. He served as a Scots judge in July 1480, sat in Parliament, and entered **James III**'s service. Little that he wrote survives, apart from the *Mirror of Wisdom*, presented to **James IV** in 1490. A fascinating compendium of literary and philosophical material, its clear exposition is still much admired by scholars.

IRONSIDE, William Edmund, 1st Baron Ironside
(1880–1959)

Soldier, born in Ironside, Aberdeenshire. He served as a secret agent disguised as a railwayman in the 2nd Boer War (1899–1902), and held several staff-appointments during World War I. He commanded the Archangel expedition against the Bolsheviks (1918) and the allied contingent in North Persia (1920). At the outbreak of World War II he was chief of the Imperial Staff, was promoted Field Marshal (1940) and placed in command of the Home Defence forces (1940). The 'Ironsides', fast, light-armoured vehicles, were named after him.

IRVINE, Andy (Andrew)
(1951–)

Rugby player, born in Edinburgh. He played soccer until the age of 12, then attended Heriot's School and took up rugby, eventually following in the tradition whereby George Heriot's School supplied the Scottish international team with full-backs (previous holders of the position being **Dan Drysdale** and **Ken Scotland**). He won 51 caps for Scotland, scored more points in South Africa than any touring Lion had previously done, and was the first player in the world to score more than 300 points in international rugby.

IRVINE, Sir James Colquhoun
(1877–1952)

Organic chemist, born and educated in Glasgow. In 1895 he was appointed assistant to Professor **Thomas Purdie** at St Andrews, subsequently studying briefly in Leipzig under Johannes Wislicenus and Friedrich Ostwald. Irvine's major work was all on carbohydrate chemistry. Early on he realized that the silver oxide reaction discovered in Purdie's laboratory could be used to investigate the structure of glucose and its derivatives, and by the early 1900s he had isolated methylated sugars. After be became professor in 1909, he and his colleagues consolidated the international reputation they had won under Purdie. During World War I his laboratory succeeded in synthesizing the sugars needed for vaccines and other medical supplies. Appointed Principal and Vice-Chancellor of St Andrews in 1920, he set about expanding the university and building student accommodation to recapture its traditional residential character.

IRVING, Edward
(1792–1834)

Clergyman and mystic, born in Annan, Dumfriesshire. He studied at Edinburgh University, became a schoolmaster, and in 1819 was appointed assistant to **Thomas Chalmers** in Glasgow. In 1822 he was asked to the Caledonian Church, Hatton Garden, London, where he enjoyed a phenomenal success as a preacher. In 1825 he began to announce the imminent second advent of Jesus Christ; this was followed up by the translation of *The Coming of the Messiah* (1827), supposedly written by a Christian Jew, but in fact by a Spanish Jesuit. By 1828, when his *Homilies on the Sacraments* appeared, he had begun to elaborate his views of the Incarnation, asserting Christ's oneness with humankind in all the attributes of humanity, and he was charged with heresy for maintaining the sinfulness of Christ's nature. He was convicted of heresy by the London presbytery in 1830, ejected from his new church in Regent's Square in 1832, and finally deposed in 1833. The majority of his congregation adhered to him, and a new communion, the Catholic Apostolic Church, was developed, commonly known as Irvingite, although Irving had little to do with its development.

ISAACS, Alick
(1921–67)

Virologist, born in Glasgow, the discoverer of interferon. He studied medicine at Glasgow, did research at Sheffield and Melbourne, and joined the virology division of the National Institute for Research in 1950 (chief, 1961). His research into the way in which influenza viruses interact and impede each other's growth led to his isolation of a substance he called interferon, which can inhibit viral infection.

ISAACS, Jeremy Israel
(1932 –)

Television executive, born in Glasgow. Educated at Merton College, Oxford, he became a producer with Granada Television in 1958 on such current affairs series as *What the Papers Say* and *All Our Yesterdays* (1960–3). He later worked on the BBC's *Panorama* (1965) and at Thames Television (1968–78), where he produced the comprehensive, clear-sighted documentary epic *The World at War* (1975). His later programmes include *Ireland: A Television History* (1981) and the brutal drama *A Sense of Freedom* (1981). He served as the first chief executive of Channel 4 (1981–7), vigorously defending its right to offer alternative programming and to service minority interests. In 1988 he became General Director of the Royal Opera House in Covent Garden, London.

IVORY, Sir James
(1765–1842)

Mathematician, born in Dundee. The son of a watchmaker, he studied mathematics and theology at St Andrews and Edinburgh intending to enter the Church of Scotland. Abandoning this intention in 1786, he returned to Dundee to teach mathematics, and in 1789 became manager of a flax mill near Forfar. He devoted all his spare time to mathematics and in 1804 became Professor of Mathematics at the Royal Military College, Marlow, shortly after **William Wallace**'s arrival there, and became FRS in 1815. He retired in 1819 because of ill health but continued his mathematical research. He was knighted in 1831. His principal work was on the gravitational attraction of ellipsoids (such as the earth), the orbits of comets, and atmospheric refraction, in which he continued the work of the French mathematicians Laplace, Legendre and Lagrange.

J

JACK, Gilbert
(?1578–1628)

Teacher of metaphysic and physic (philosophy and medicine). He was educated at the Grammar School and Marischal College, Aberdeen, and on the continent. Settling in Leyden, Holland, he became Professor of Philosophy there in 1604, and was a friend of Hugo Grotius. Increasingly famous as a teacher, in 1621 he declined an invitation to become Whyte's Professor of Philosophy at Oxford. He spent the rest of his life in Leyden, and was survived by ten children.

JACK, Ian
(1945 –)

Journalist. Educated at Dunfermline High School, he entered journalism in 1965 as a trainee with the *Glasgow Herald*. From 1970 to 1986 he worked for *The Sunday Times* as a feature writer and foreign correspondent, specializing in Indian affairs and winning wide admiration for his perceptive and penetrating writing. He was UK Journalist of the Year in 1986. His first book, *Before The Oil Ran Out* (1987), was notable for its vivid portrait of a Scottish childhood. He was appointed Executive Editor of the *Independent on Sunday* in 1991.

JACKSON, Alan
(1938 –)

Poet, known for his mocking and sardonic verse. A prominent spokesman for Scottish alternative culture in the 1960s, he used his aphoristic verse to criticize what he felt to be Scotland's hypocritical morality and argued for the replacement of conservative Presbyterian values with a more permissive liberalism. His first book of poetry was *Underwater Wedding* (1961). He was included in *Penguin Modern Poets* (1968) and his prose essay 'The Kilted Claymore. An Essay on Culture and Nationalism' was the *Lines Review* (number 37) in 1971; this combined a declaration of his personal philosophy with an attack upon aspects of Scottish life and letters. His *Salutations: Collected Poems* was published in 1990.

JACKSON, Gordon Cameron
(1923–90)

Actor, born in Glasgow. He performed in BBC radio plays as a child before leaving school at 15 to become an engineering draughtsman with Rolls Royce. Cast as a young Scottish soldier in the film *The Foreman Went To France* (1941), he began his professional career as callow servicemen in such films as *Millions Like Us* (1943) and *San Demetrio London* (1943). Following his stage début in *George and Margaret* (1943) at Rutherglen, his distinguished theatrical career included performances as Ishmael in Orson Welles's production *Moby Dick* (1955), Banquo to Alec Guinness's *Macbeth* (1966) and Horatio in *Hamlet* (1969), a New York début for which he received the Clarence Derwent Award. A reliable character actor whose self-effacing dedication to his craft was respected throughout the acting profession, his many film appearances include *Whisky Galore* (1948), *The Great Escape* (1963), *The Prime of Miss Jean Brodie* (1969) and *The Shooting Party* (1984). Television brought him lasting popularity as the imperturbable butler Hudson in *Upstairs, Downstairs* (1970–5), for which he received an Emmy, and as the tough-talking CI5 boss in the action series *The Professionals* (1977–81).

JACKSON, John
(1887–1958)

Astronomer, born in Paisley. Educated at Glasgow and Cambridge universities, he began his astronomical career at the Royal Observatory, Greenwich, where he remained until his appointment as HM Astronomer at the Cape, South Africa. His work there was in the field of classical astronomy, determining parallaxes and magnitudes of stars in the southern hemisphere. He was awarded the Gold Medal of the Royal Astronomical

Society and served as the society's President between 1953 and 1955.

JACKSON, William

(1955 –)

Instrumentalist and composer, born in Cambuslang, Lanarkshire. He began life as a professional musician, playing double-bass with Contraband while still at school. After a period in London with the band, he returned to Scotland in 1976 as one of the founder members of Ossian, a group which went on to set new standards in the interpretation of traditional folk music from both Scotland and Ireland. By the beginning of the 1980s he had mastered many instruments, including the traditional Scots harp (clarsach), on which he excelled, and bagpipes and flute. His first extended composition was the titlepiece of Ossian's 1982 album 'Dove Across the Water'. His full-length 'Wellpark Suite' followed in 1985. Later works included the 'St Mungo Suite' (1989) and the music for TAG Theatre's production of *Sunset Song* (1990).

JACOB, Violet, née Kennedy-Erskine

(1863–1946)

Poet and novelist, born in Montrose, Angus, the daughter of the laird of Dun. She married Major Arthur Otway Jacob and lived for some years in India. Although she began her writing career as a novelist, she is best known for poems in the Angus dialect, such as *Songs of Angus* (1915), *More Songs of Angus* (1918), *Bonnie Joann* (1922) and *The Northern Lights* (1927). Her *Lairds of Dun* (1931) is a standard history of her native district.

JAMES I

(1394–1437)

King of Scotland from 1424, second son of **Robert III**, born in Dunfermline. After his elder brother David, Duke of Rothesay, was murdered at Falkland (1402), allegedly by his uncle, the Duke of Albany, James was sent to France for safety, but was captured by the English. He remained a prisoner for 18 years, but also received a good education, exposure to the Lancastrian court of Henry IV, and military experience in Henry V's French campaigns. Albany meanwhile ruled Scotland as governor until his death in 1420, when his son, Murdoch, assumed the regency and

the country rapidly fell into disorder. Negotiations for the return of James were completed with the Treaty of London in 1423 and a ransom of £33 000 sterling (or £66 000 Scots) was agreed. In 1424 James married Joan Beaufort (d.1445), a daughter of the Earl of Somerset, niece of Richard II, and soon afterwards they moved to Scotland. James dealt ruthlessly with potential rivals to his authority. Within eight months Murdoch, his two sons and the 80-year-old Earl of Lennox were all beheaded at Stirling, the first state executions since 1320. Descendants of **Robert II** by his second marriage were treated with suspicion: the Earl of March was deprived of some of his estates, and the vast earldom of Mar was annexed to the crown on the death of the earl in 1435. Finance and law and order were the two other main domestic themes of his reign. The series of parliaments called after 1424, while encouraging attendance by lesser landowners, was dominated by the king's need for increased taxation, partly to pay off the ransom, and partly to meet increased expenditure on his court, artillery and building work at Linlithgow. In 1424 Parliament agreed to an increase in customs dues and a five per cent tax on lands and goods, which in itself realized £25 000, but by 1431 it was already showing reluctance to grant further taxes. James, described by the chronicler **Boece** as 'our lawgiver king', for the most part only refined, repeated or extended judicial enactments of previous kings and many of his activities, here as elsewhere, had a fiscal motive. In foreign affairs, he attempted to increase trade by renewing a commercial treaty with the Netherlands, and also concluded treaties with Denmark, Norway and Sweden. His relations with the Church were abrasive and his criticisms of monastic orders pointed. His treatment of his nobility caused much resentment, but his murder in the Dominican friary at Perth, the first assassination of a Scottish king for 400 years, was the work of a small, isolated group of dissidents led by Sir Robert Stewart and Sir Robert Graham, both of whom were descendants of Robert II's second marriage. The murderers failed to find support, and were brutally tortured to death. James left one surviving son (James, later **James II**), and six daughters; the eldest, Margaret (1424–45), who married the Dauphin, later Louis XI, of France, was a gifted poet. James was the first of many Stuart kings to act as a patron of the arts, and almost certainly wrote the tender, passionate collection of poems, *Kingis Quair* ('king's quire' or book), about 1423–4.

JAMES II
(1430–60)

King of Scotland from 1437, son of **James I** and known as 'James of the fiery face' because of a birth mark. He was six years old at the time of his father's murder. Thereupon the queen mother took shelter in Edinburgh Castle with her son, who was put under her charge and that of Sir Alexander Livingston. However, Sir William Crichton, the Chancellor, who was governor of the castle, contested custody of the boy; a closer liaison with Livingston lasted until 1444, when the Livingstons began to monopolize offices, power and access to the king. In 1449, shortly after James's marriage to Mary, daughter of the Duke of Gueldres, the Livingstons were dismissed from office but the king also had to contend with the accumulating power of the **Douglas** family. Opinions vary as to who was aggressor and who was victim in the sharp tussle between them, which came to a climax in 1452 when James stabbed to death William, the eighth earl, at Stirling Castle. The king was allowed to get away with the murder, and the royal campaign against the Douglases was completed by their wholesale forfeiture in 1455, which also smoothed the way for a series of grants of earldoms and lands to families such as the **Campbell**s, **Gordon**s and **Hamilton**s. A growing stability in domestic politics was vitiated by the king's reckless involvement in the English struggles between the houses of York and Lancaster. In 1460 he marched for England with a powerful army. He laid siege to Roxburgh Castle, which had been held by the English for over a hundred years, but was killed by the bursting of a cannon.

JAMES III
(1451–88)

King of Scotland from 1460, son of **James II**. He was brought up under the guardianship of Bishop **Kennedy** of St Andrews, while the Earl of Angus was made Lieutenant-General. His tutor was the leading humanist scholar, Archibald Whitelaw, who held the office of royal secretary for much of the reign and inspired James with a love of culture and a sincere piety. The beginnings of the flowering of vernacular literature that marked **James IV**'s court first became evident during this reign. His minority, although marked by the rise of the Boyds at the expense of others after 1466, did not see the degree of disturbance that had marked previous reigns. By 1469, when Parliament condemned the Boyds and

James married Margaret, daughter of Kristian I of Denmark, bringing Orkney and Shetland in pledge as part of her dowry, the king was firmly in control. Various aspects of his rule created resentment: short of finance, and with successive parliaments reluctant to grant taxes, by the 1480s James had resorted to debasement of the coinage, stigmatized as 'black money'; his efforts between 1471 and 1473 to engage in campaigns in Brittany and Gueldres fell on deaf ears, and his attempts between 1474 and 1479 to bring about a reconciliation with England were premature and almost as unpopular. The breakdown of relations with England brought war in 1480, and the threat of English invasion resulted in a calculated political demonstration by his nobles, who hanged Robert Cochrane and other unpopular royal favourites at Lauder Bridge in 1482. The rebellion which brought about his downfall and death at Sauchieburn resulted from a further crisis of confidence in the king, but ironically was less widespread. The eldest of his sons, James, who had appeared with the rebels in the field, succeeded him as **James IV**. Much of the unpopularity of James III, however, may be due to the garnishing of later royal apologists.

JAMES IV
(1473–1513)

King of Scotland from 1488 following the murder of his father **James III**, after Sauchieburn. His confederates in the rebellion took possession of the offices of state, the royal Treasury and the late king's jewels, and even accused the loyal barons of treason and deprived them of their estates. After 1489 moderation and conciliation replaced such opportunism. Much of the early 1490s was taken up with securing recognition for the new régime at home and abroad. As a result his council was composed of a far broader, and more stable, coalition of the great magnates than was the case under his three predecessors, and a vindication of Sauchieburn, sent around the courts of Europe, helped to win wide recognition for his rule. Athletic, warlike and pious, James has been called an ideal medieval king, for he did not resort to either the brutality or the outrageous venality of some of his predecessors. His provision of two successive royal bastards to the archbishopric of St Andrews began the treatment of the Church as a mere department of state, a policy which was to reach new heights in the next reign. Yet in other respects his reign was probably the epitome and climax of Scottish medieval kingship rather than of new monarchy (he was the last Scottish king to speak Gaelic). His rising status, as a king popular at home and respected abroad, was confirmed by his marriage in August 1503 to **Margaret Tudor**, eldest daughter of Henry VIIan alliance which ultimately led to the union of the crowns in 1603. The real beginnings of a Renaissance court belong to his reign, with vast sums being spent on building work, as at Stirling Castle, and on military and naval ventures. James's castles were the venues for a brilliant Renaissance court, inhabited by musicians such as **Robert Carver** and poets such as **William Dunbar**. The king's popularity ironically increased the scale of the disaster which ended his life, at Flodden on 9 September 1513. An army of no fewer than 20 000, probably the largest ever to be assembled in Scotland, which embarked on a Border raid to fulfil Scotland's obligations to its recently renewed alliance with France, was crushed. Although English claims that 10 000 Scots died on the battlefield are probably exaggerated, no fewer than a dozen nobles, two bishops and two abbots died beside their king.

JAMES V

(1512–42)

King of Scotland from 1513, son of **James IV**, born in Linlithgow. He was only an infant when his father's death left him the crown. The queen-dowager, **Margaret Tudor**, was appointed regent, but on her marriage (1514) with the Earl of Angus, the Duke of **Albany**, son of the younger brother of **James III** and heir presumptive, was made regent in her stead. Amid the contentions of the rival French and English factions, and the private quarrels of the nobles, the country was reduced to a state of anarchy. Albany, who was hampered by the changing priorities as much as by Scottish factional politics, retired to France in 1524. James's education was entrusted to Gavin Dunbar, who became Archbishop of Glasgow in 1524. In 1525 he fell into the hands of Angus, who kept him a close prisoner until in 1528 he made his escape from Falkland to Stirling, and as an independent sovereign began to carry out a judicious policy which was largely framed by the need to increase the delapidated crown revenues. He continued and greatly extended his father's policy of making the Church a virtual department of state. The Church granted him six separate taxes during the

1530s; only a fraction of the tax of 1532 went towards its ostensible purpose, the financing of a College of Justice, but this marked the final and important step in the emergence of a central civil law court. The Church, forced to raise cash to pay these taxes, resorted to feuing and permanent alienation of its lands, which fatally undermined its position as an institution on the eve of the Reformation. The pope, anxious to prevent a Henrician-style revolt against Rome in Scotland, acceded to the claims of the crown to make ecclesiastical appointments 'in commendam' and, as a result, some of the greatest religious houses, such as the Charterhouse at Perth, the abbeys of Coldingham and Holyrood, and St Andrews Priory, were given to five of the six young bastard sons of the king. In 1537 James married Madelaine, daughter of Francis I of France, but within a year of her death he married **Mary of Guise**-Lorraine; each brought a substantial dowry and confirmed the Franco-Scottish alliance. He developed a certain reputation as the 'poor man's king', but his increasingly brusque treatment of the nobility revealed the unacceptable face of Stuart monarchy, seen at its worst in 1537 in the unusual burning of a noblewoman, Lady Janet Glamis, allegedly for treason. Anglo-Scottish relations, which had been deteriorating from 1536, burst into open war after he failed to attend a conference with Henry VIII at York in 1541. There was great reluctance to join his army to repulse an English invasion, which made the subsequent rout at Solway Moss, in November 1542, a humiliating defeat for the king rather than a national disaster like Flodden (1513). He died, less due to illness than to a lack of will to live, leaving a week-old infant, **Mary, Queen of Scots**, to succeed him. Sometimes seen as the most unpleasant of all Stuart kings, who overstepped many unwritten conventions, he was also a highly talented Renaissance monarch. The monuments to his reign are the literary works produced at his glittering court, such as the poems and plays of Sir **David Lyndsay**, and the ambitious, costly architectural transformation of Stirling Castle and the palaces of Holyrood, Falkland and Linlithgow.

JAMES VI of Scotland, James I of England

(1566–1625)

King of Scotland from 1567, King of England from 1603, the son of **Mary, Queen of Scots**, and Henry, Lord **Darnley**. Born in Edinburgh Castle, he was baptized Charles James at Stirling Castle. On his mother's forced abdication in 1567 he was proclaimed king, as James VI. He was placed in the keeping of the Earl of Mar, and taught by **George Buchanan**. A civil war between his supporters, the 'king's men', and those of his mother, the 'queen's men', lasted until 1573 and saw three successive, short-lived regencies, of **Moray, Lennox** and Mar. A measure of stability emerged after 1572 during the regency of **James Morton**, who laid down some of the foundations for James's later personal reign. Morton fell briefly from power in 1578, recovered, but was arrested and executed in 1581, largely at the instigation of Captain James Stuart, created Earl of Arran, and James's cousin, Esme Stuart, made Duke of Lennox. Suspicion of these two royal favourites combined with ultra-Protestantism to induce a coup, the Ruthven Raid (1582), when the king was seized. Although presbyterian ministers were not involved, the General Assembly, by approving 'this late work of reformation', stamped a lifelong suspicion of the aims of the Church in the young king's mind. Within 10 months James had escaped and a counter-coup orchestrated by Arran was instituted. In 1584 a parliament reiterated the primacy of the crown over all estates, including the Church, and within days more than a score of radical ministers had fled into exile in England along with some of the Ruthven lords. The exiles returned by the end of 1585 and Arran was displaced from power, but the assertion of royal power, now under the guiding hand of the chancellor, **John Maitland** of Thirlestane, continued. The execution of Mary, Queen of Scots in 1587 drew a token protest from her son, but it was not allowed to disturb the league recently concluded with England (the Treaty of Berwick, 1586) or James's English pension. In 1589 he went to Denmark, where he married the Princess Anne of Denmark (1574–1619), and she was crowned queen in May 1590. The early 1590s saw a careful playing-off of Roman Catholic and ultra-Protestant factions against each other, and by 1596 a new stability had resulted. A mysterious presbyterian riot in Edinburgh in December 1596 heralded the beginning of a long campaign by the crown, first to influence the General Assembly and latterly to introduce bishops into the Church. This was completed by 1610 despite bitter opposition, particularly from **Andrew Melville**, who was imprisoned in the Tower of London for five years. On the death of Elizabeth of England (1603), James ascended

to the throne of England as great-grandson of **James IV**'s English wife, **Margaret Tudor**. Although he promised to visit Scotland once every three years, he did not return until 1617. A joint monarchy thus became absentee monarchy, although the king's political skill and knowledge allowed him to govern Scotland 'by his pen'. James, who went to England as an acknowledged, successful and learned king, was at first well received by his English subjects. However, the dislike of this scheme for a 'perfect union' of his two kingdoms, distrust of some of the crown's financial devices, and resentment of royal favourites accelerated and made more acrimonious the recasting of the relationship between Crown and Parliament that inevitably followed the end of a long reign such as that of Elizabeth. The death of the king's eldest son, Henry, Prince of Wales (1612), devolved the succession on his second son, the future Charles I, who became closely attached to the king's new favourite, Buckingham. It was James's vision of bringing peace to a war-torn Europe as much as their escapades in Spain which brought renewed friction with the House of Commons after 1621. James died at Theobalds. His achievements as King of England are still a matter of intense debate, but he is widely recognized as one of the most successful kings of Scotland, politics and society having been transformed during his long reign. A calculating, tough-minded and talented scholar-king, he does not deserve the derogatory half-truth so often ascribed to him as 'the wisest fool in Christendom'.

JAMES VII of Scotland, James II of England (both 1685–8)
(1633–1701)

Second son of Charles I, and brother of Charles II. He was born at St James's Palace, London, and was created Duke of York. Nine months before his father's execution in 1649 he escaped to Holland, served under Turenne (1652–5), and in 1657 took Spanish service in Flanders. At the Restoration (1660) James was made Lord High Admiral of England, twice commanding the English fleet in the ensuing wars with the Dutch. In 1659 he had entered into a private marriage contract with Anne Hyde, daughter of the Earl of Clarendon, and the year after her death in 1671 as a professed Catholic, he himself became a convert to Catholicism. In 1673 Parliament passed the Test Act, and James was obliged to resign the office of Lord High

Admiral. Shortly after, he married Mary of Modena, daughter of the Duke of Modena. The national ferment occasioned by the Popish Plot became so formidable that he had to retire to the continent, and during his absence an attempt was made to exclude him from the succession. He returned in late 1679, and was sent to Scotland to undertake the management of its affairs; this period saw the beginnings of a remarkable cultural renaissance under his patronage. Meanwhile the Exclusion Bill was twice passed by the Commons, but in the first instance it was rejected by the Lords, and on the second was lost by the dissolution of Parliament. During this period James spent much of his time in exile, but after defeat of the bill he returned to England, and in direct violation of the law took his seat in the council, and resumed the direction of naval affairs. At the death of Charles II in 1685 James ascended the throne, and immediately proceeded to levy, on his own warrant, the customs and excise duties which had been granted to Charles only for life. He sent a mission to Rome, heard mass in public and became, like his brother, the pensioner of the French king. In Scotland, Parliament remained loyal, despite renewed persecution of the Covenanters; in England the futile rebellion of Monmouth was followed by the 'Bloody Assize'. The suspension of the Test Act by the king's authority, his prosecution of the seven bishops on a charge of seditious libel, his conferring ecclesiastical benefices on Roman Catholics, his violation of the rights of the universities of Oxford and Cambridge, his plan for packing Parliament, and numerous other arbitrary acts showed his fixed determination to overthrow the constitution and the Church. The indignation of the people was at length aroused, and the interposition of William, Prince of Orange, James's son-in-law and nephew and the future William III, was formally solicited by seven leading politicians. William landed at Torbay on 4 November 1688 with a powerful army, and marched towards London. He was everywhere hailed as a deliverer, while James was deserted not only by his ministers and troops, but even by his daughter the Princess Anne (later Queen Anne). The unfortunate king, on the first appearance of danger, had sent his wife and infant son to France and, after one futile start and his arrest at Faversham, James also escaped and joined them at St Germain. He was hospitably received by Louis XIV, who settled a pension on him. In 1689, aided by a small body of French troops, he invaded Ireland and made an ineffectual attempt to regain his throne. He was defeated at the Battle of the Boyne (1690), and returned to St Germain, where he resided until his death. He left two daughters – Mary, married to the Prince of Orange, and Anne, afterwards queen – and one son, **James Francis Edward Stuart**, the 'Old Pretender', by his second wife. He had several illegitimate children, one of whom was Marshal Berwick.

JAMES, Alex

(1901–53)

Footballer, born in Mossend, Bellshill, Lanarkshire. Signed by Raith Rovers from junior club Ashfield in 1922, he moved on three years later to Preston North End. Capped eight times for Scotland, he scored twice in the celebrated 'Wembley Wizards' match. Transferred to Arsenal for £9000 in 1929, he became an essential element of the team which dominated the following decade, winning four league titles and two FA Cups before retiring in 1937. He later briefly coached in Poland. A small, slippery inside-left, utterly unpredictable, he was one of the great individualists of the game between the wars.

JAMESON, Sir Leander Starr, 1st Baronet

(1853–1917)

South African statesman, born in Edinburgh, studied medicine there and at London, and began practice at Kimberley in 1878. Through Cecil Rhodes, 'Dr Jim' (as he became known) engaged in pioneer work, was in 1891 made administrator for the South Africa Company at Fort Salisbury, and won enormous popularity. During the troubles at Johannesburg between the Uitlanders and the Boer government Jameson who, by order of Rhodes, had concentrated the military forces of Rhodesia at Mafeking on the Transvaal frontier, started with 500 troopers to support the Uitlanders (29 December 1895). At Krugersdorp they were overpowered by an overwhelming force of Boers, and, sleepless and famishing, were after a sharp fight compelled to surrender (2 January 1896). Handed over to the British authorities, Dr Jameson was in July condemned in London to 15 months' imprisonment, but was released in December. In 1900 he was elected to the Cape Legislative Assembly, and from 1904 to 1908 was (Progressive) Premier of Cape Colony. A baronet from 1911, he retired from politics in 1912, and became President of the BSA Company in 1913.

JAMESON, Robert
(1774–1854)

Naturalist and geologist, born in Leith, Edinburgh. After studying under A G Werner in Freiburg, he was appointed Professor of Natural History at Edinburgh University in 1804, which post he occupied for 50 years until his death. In this position he held great power and influence far beyond Edinburgh, establishing the Wernerian Natural History Society (1808) and acting as Keeper of the University Museum (noted for its live puma). Although Charles Darwin was completely put off science by Jameson, it seems that, especially at home, he was a very agreeable member of Edinburgh society. He published several descriptive mineralogical accounts of parts of Scotland. In time, his geognosy and his promotion of the Wernerian school withered away.

JAMESONE, George
(c.1588–1644)

Portrait painter, born in Aberdeen. In 1612 he was bound apprentice for eight years to John Anderson, a painter in Edinburgh. The earliest of the Scottish portraitists, he was painting in Aberdeen by 1620, but moved to Edinburgh in the 1630s.

JAMIESON, 'JK' (John Kay)
(1873–1948)

Anatomist, born in Sandness, Shetland. He attended the Sandness Madras School, which his father had established, and proceeded to Edinburgh University, where he graduated in medicine in 1894. He became a demonstrator of anatomy in the School of Medicine of the Royal Colleges at Surgeons' Hall, Edinburgh, and in 1895 went to Leeds Medical School as demonstrator in anatomy. In 1910 he became the first full-time Professor of Anatomy at Leeds and did much to develop the teaching of anatomy as the sound basis of medicine. He was a superb teacher and his research on the surgical anatomy of the lymphatic system, particularly of the tongue, stomach and large intestine, is now part of the corpus of medical knowledge. During World War I, he became acting dean of the medical school. In 1915 he was commissioned, becoming Lieutenant-Colonel O C at the Northern General Hospital at Leeds. In 1918 he was elected Dean of the Faculty of Medicine and was a driving force in expanding the School of Medicine. In 1936 he accepted the Chair of Anatomy and Embryology at Trinity College, Dublin, holding this post until 1947.

JAMIESON, John
(1759–1838)

Lexicographer and philologist, born in Glasgow. He studied theology at Glasgow University, and was an Anti-Burgher secessionist minister in Forfar (1781–97) and Nicholson Street, Edinburgh (1797–1830). He wrote several scriptural treatises, but his chief work was his monumental *Etymological Dictionary of the Scottish Language* (2 vols 1808–9, supplement 1825). He was a friend of Sir **Walter Scott**. He was awarded a DD from Princeton University for his reply (1795) to Joseph Priestley's *History of the Early Opinions Concerning Jesus Christ*. He also edited **Barbour**'s *The Brus* (1820) and **Blind Harry**'s *Wallace* (1820).

JAPP, Alexander Hay
(1837–1905)

Author and publisher, born in Dun, near Montrose, Angus. Educated at Milne's School in Montrose, he became a bookkeeper in Edinburgh in 1854. After studying philosophy at Edinburgh University (1860–1) he turned to journalism, editing the *Inverness Courier* and *Montrose Review* before settling in London in 1864. He worked as writer, editor, and literary adviser to publishers, including co-editing *The Contemporary Review* (1866–72). He assisted Robert Carruthers in preparing the 3rd edition of *Chambers's Cyclopedia of English Literature*. A publishing venture of his own in 1880 lasted only two years, but he continued to write on a wide variety of topics. He helped **Robert Louis Stevenson** to publish *Treasure Island* in *Young Folks* magazine, and later (1905) wrote a book on him. His many pseudonyms included H A Page, A F Scott, E Condor Gray, and A N Mount Rose.

JARDINE, George
(1742–1827)

Educationist, born in Wandel, Lanarkshire. Educated at Glasgow College, he travelled France as a tutor, and acted unofficially as Professor of Logic and Rhetoric at Glasgow (1774–87), thereafter holding the post officially until 1824. A dedicated teacher, he took over a routine drilling in logic, and devised the course of study described in his *An Outline of a Philosophical Education* (2nd ed 1825). A brilliant work, it considered the needs and problems of his early teenage pupils, and gave an excellent grounding in textual study, which proved important to **John McLeod Campbell**, one of his students. Jardine taught his course privately during summer-time, at Portobello, where he spent the vacation.

JARDINE, James
(1776–1858)

Civil engineer, born in Applegarth, Dumfriesshire. He was a teacher of mathematics at Edinburgh University until 1806 when, on the advice of **John Playfair**, he began to practise as a surveyor and civil engineer. While working on the shore of the Tay estuary in 1809 he is said to have been the first to determine, from observations of the tides along a great length of coast, the mean level of the sea. For almost 30 years he was engineer to the Edinburgh Water Company, and during this time he brought the water from the Crawley springs near Glencorse into Edinburgh. From 1825 he surveyed and engineered the line of the Edinburgh & Dalkeith railway which, when it opened in 1831, incorporated near the terminus at St Leonard's in Edinburgh the first railway tunnel in Scotland. The Edinburgh & Dalkeith afterwards became known as the 'Innocent Railway', supposedly because no accidents ever occurred on it.

JARDINE, Sir William
(1800–74)

Naturalist and physician, born in Dumfriesshire. He studied medicine at Edinburgh and Paris, but devoted himself to ornithology after inheriting the estate of Jardine Hall in Dumfries. With Prideaux John Selby he produced *Illustrations of Ornithology* (1825–43), and founded the *Magazine of Zoology and Botany* (1837). He also compiled the *Naturalist's Library* (1838–43) and *Contributions to Ornithology* (1848–52).

JARRETT, William Fleming Hoggan
(1928 –)

Veterinary pathologist and expert on the immune diseases of animals. Educated at Lenzie Academy, Glasgow Veterinary College and Glasgow University, his first post (1952) was as a lecturer in the Glasgow Veterinary College, then as Head of Hospital Pathology (1953) and Reader in Pathology (1962). He went to the University of East Africa in 1963–4 and was appointed Professor of Veterinary Pathology in Glasgow in 1968. His main work has been on tumour viruses, leucaemia and immunology, particularly in the cat. Latterly he has been much concerned with developing models of Human Immune Deficiency disease (AIDS) in animals. Such models have been very difficult to find and would be immensely important in finding effective treatments for the human condition. He was elected FRS in 1980, and his work has attracted considerable attention all over the world.

JEBB, Sir Richard Claverhouse
(1841–1905)

Scholar, born in Dundee. He graduated from Trinity College, Cambridge, was elected fellow, and in 1875 was appointed Professor of Greek at Glasgow, and in 1889 Regius Professor of Greek at Cambridge. In 1891 he was elected MP (Unionist) for Cambridge University. His greatest works are his editions of **Sophocles** (with translations, 9 vols, 1883–1917).

JEFFREY, Francis Jeffrey, Lord
(1773–1850)

Judge and critic, born in Edinburgh. He studied at Glasgow and Oxford, and in 1794 was called to the Bar, but as a Whig made little progress for many years. In the trials for sedition (1817–22) he acquired a great reputation; in 1820 and again in 1823 he was elected Lord Rector of Glasgow University, and in 1829 Dean of the Faculty of Advocates. In 1830 he was returned as MP for Perth, and on the formation of Earl Grey's ministry he became Lord Advocate. After the passing of the Reform Bill he was returned for Edinburgh, which he represented until 1834, when he was made a judge of the Court of Session. From 1815 he lived at Craigcrook. Along with Sydney Smith, **Francis Horner** and a few others, he established the *Edinburgh Review*, of which he was editor until 1829. He was a prolific and brilliant, if biased, contributor, as in his strictures on Wordsworth, Keats and Byron. While in the USA to marry his second wife, he dined with President Madison during the British-American War of 1812. A selection of his articles was published in 1844.

JEFFREY, John
(1959 –)

Rugby player, a farmer by profession, born in Kelso, Roxburghshire. Educated at Merchiston Castle School, Edinburgh, and Newcastle University, he first played for Scotland in 1984 and, once established as a first-choice backrow forward, he began to establish a reputation as one of the leading players in this position in the world. He played in Scotland's World Cup teams of 1987 and 1991, announcing his retirement from international rugby after the latter campaign. Loyal to his home-town club, Kelso, he was one of the most important members of the Scotland team that won the Grand Slam in 1990.

JENKINS, Robin
(1912 –)

Novelist, born in Cambuslang, Lanarkshire, and educated at Hamilton Academy and Glasgow University. At various times an English teacher in Scotland, Afghanistan, Spain and Borneo, he has set many of his stories in these countries. A prolific writer, his works begin with *So Gaily Sings the Lark* (1950), carry on to *Just Duffy* (1988), and fall into three main groups: those set in Scotland; those set in 'Norania', his fictional Afghanistan; and those dealing with 'Kalewentan', a far eastern sultanate. Interested in exploring human beings' moral possibilities, in those of his works set outside Scotland, such as *Dust on the Paw* (1961), he looks at the paradoxes of society's values. In his Scottish novels he concentrates on Calvinism, often dealing with characters, as in *A Wouldbe Saint* (1978), who are so holy that the concept of 'good' must be re-examined.

JENNETT, (William) Bryan
(1926 –)

English neurosurgeon, educated at King George V School, Southport, and received his medical education at Liverpool University, where he graduated in 1949, proceeding to MD in 1960. He was house surgeon to Sir **Hugh Cairns** in 1950, and served in the RAMC from 1951 to 1953. After registrarships in neurosurgery at Oxford and Cardiff he became lecturer in neurosurgery at Manchester University (1957–62). From 1958 to 1959 he held a Rockefeller Travelling Fellowship at the University of California. In 1963 he became consultant neurosurgeon at Glasgow University and succeeded to the chair in 1968. He was Dean of the Faculty of Medicine at Glasgow (1981–6). His publications include *Introduction to Neurosurgery* (1964), *Epilepsy After Non-Missile Head Injuries* (1962), and *High Technology Medicine, Benefits and Burdens* (1986). His major contributions have been establishing databases for predicting outcome after head injury, and devising the Glasgow Coma Scale and Glasgow Outcome Scale, which have been widely adopted. He has analysed economic and ethical aspects of decision-making in surgery and intensive care.

JOHNSON, David Charles
(1942 –)

Composer, cellist and music historian, born in Edinburgh and educated at Aberdeen and Cambridge universities. A tutor at Edinburgh University (1988 –), his works include four operas, a piano concerto, an orchestral suite, chamber music, songs and church music. He has made important contributions to the understanding of 18th-century Scottish music in various books, articles and scholarly performing editions, including *Music and Society in Lowland Scotland* (1972) and *Scottish Fiddle Music in the 18th Century* (1984).

JOHNSON, Robert
(c.1500 – c.1560)

Composer, born in Duns, Berwickshire. His importance is as a writer of both pre- and post-Reformation music, set to Latin and English texts, both sacred and secular. His range is from the imitative grandeur of the high Renaissance to a simpler chordal style that was developed in later 16th-century English music. Little is known of his life except that he was ordained a priest, was in York c.1530, and returned to Scotland, only to flee to England by c.1535. He is said to have been a chaplain to Anne Boleyn and was a 'peticanon' at Windsor. His surviving music includes a number of four- and five-part motets, anthems, madrigals, keyboard pieces, and other instrumental pieces and arrangements for lute, organ or viols.

JOHNSTON, Alexander Keith
(1804–71)

Cartographer, born near Penicuik, Midlothian. With his brother he founded the

Edinburgh map-making firm of W and A K Johnston (1826). His *National Atlas* (1843) procured him the appointment of Geographer Royal for Scotland. Other works are a *Physical Atlas* (1848) and the famous *Royal Atlas* (1861), as well as atlases of astronomy, etc, a physical globe, and a gazetteer.

JOHNSTON, or JONSTON, Arthur
(1587–1641)

Physician, poet and humanist, born in Caskieben, Aberdeenshire. He graduated MD at Padua in 1610, and visited many academic institutions. He practised medicine in France, and his fame as a Latin poet spread across Europe. In about 1625 he was appointed physician to King Charles I. His famous translation of the Psalms of David into Latin verse was published in Aberdeen in 1637. He edited the *Deliciae Poetarum Scotorum Hujus Aevi* (1637), an anthology of Latin poetry from Scotland, to which he also contributed notable poems. In 1637 he became Rector of King's College, Aberdeen.

JOHNSTON, Maurice
(1963 –)

Footballer, born in Glasgow. He joined Partick Thistle in 1980, then moved to Watford in 1983 for a year, before returning to Scotland and joining Celtic for £400 000, which was at the time a Scottish record. After a spell in France with Nantes, he appeared set to return to Celtic but, in an astonishing move, signed for Rangers instead, becoming that club's first major Roman Catholic player of recent times. Regarded as a traitor by most of the Celtic support, he also had to contend with the anti-Catholic bigotry of some of the followers of his new club. First capped for his country while still at Watford, he 'retired' from international football after the 1990 World Cup, but changed his mind a year later. One of the very few Scottish strikers of recent years to be truly international class, his move to Rangers was one of the most socially significant sporting events since the war. In 1991 he was transferred to Everton.

JOHNSTON, Murray
(1949–90)

Photographer, born in Fife and educated at Napier College, Edinburgh, and Duncan of

Jordanstone College, Dundee. He was the first photographer in residence at Kielder Forest in 1980 and worked for a time in the USA (1981–2). In 1982 he became Director of the Stills Gallery, where he organized an impressive exhibition programme and turned the gallery into a centre for the encouragement of contemporary Scottish photographers. In 1986 he established a new department of photography at Edinburgh College of Art and in 1987 he founded Scottish Photographic Works, a small gallery intended to promote Scottish work. His major exhibition, *Scottish Camera Art Now*, showing the work of 16 Scottish photographers (co-curated with David Brittain) was shown at the Houston Fotofest in 1990 and, subsequently, under the title *New Scottish Photography*, at the National Galleries of Scotland. Johnston's innate modesty concealed his own excellence as a photographer, whilst his generosity, intelligence and humour made him a focus and catalyst for the work of others. Pre-eminently an enthusiast who pursued and encouraged excellence, much contemporary Scottish work has been influenced by him.

JOHNSTON, Tom (Thomas)
(1881–1965)

Labour politician, born in Kirkintilloch, Dunbartonshire, and educated at Lenzie Academy and Glasgow University. He entered journalism and joined the Independent Labour Party. In 1906 he founded *Forward*, a Socialist weekly of considerable influence in the west of Scotland. He served as Labour MP for West Stirling (1922–4, 1929–31, 1935–45), and for Dundee (1924–9). Appointed Secretary of State for Scotland (1941–5), he did much to plan for postwar developments, and proved himself one of the most able Scottish secretaries. In 1942 he set up the Scottish Council (Development and Industry) to attract new industries, and in 1945 he became Chairman of the North of Scotland Hydro-Electric Board; he also sat on the Scottish Forestry Commission.

JOHNSTONE

Name of a noble family taken from the lordship of Johnstone in Annandale, Dumfriesshire. In former days it was one of the most powerful and turbulent clans of the west Border, and was constantly feuding with its neighbours, especially the Maxwells. Of three branches, Johnstone of Annandale, Johnstone of Westerhall, and Johnston of Hilton and Caskieben in Aberdeenshire, the first, which retained the ancient patrimony, was ennobled by Charles I, and became successively Lords Johnstone of Lochwood, Earls of Hartfell, and Earls and Marquises of Annandale.

JOHNSTONE, (Christian) Isobel
(1781–1857)

Cookery writer, novelist and journalist, born in Fife. She married her second husband, John Johnstone, in 1812, writing for the *Inverness Courier* when he was its owner and editor. Whilst in Inverness she wrote *Clan Albyn, A National Tale* (1815) and followed this with *Elizabeth de Bruce* (1827), both historical novels which enjoyed considerable popularity. She made her name, however, with *The Cook and Housewife's Manual* (1826), popularly known as *Meg Dod's Cookery*. A source of advice on kitchen practice, with recipes for national specialities and a lively commentary on food, using characters from Sir **Walter Scott**'s St Ronan's Well, it was purportedly written by a Margaret Dods of the Cleikum Inn, St Ronan's. It remains an invaluable source-book for modern cooks. Isobel Johnstone also maintained a successful career as a literary journalist, writing for the *Schoolmaster*, *Johnstone's Magazine*, and *Tait's Magazine*.

JOHNSTONE, James, 'Chevalier de'
(1719 – c.1800)

Jacobite soldier, born in Edinburgh, the son of a merchant. As Prince **Charles Edward Stuart**'s aide-de-camp he fought at Culloden in 1746 and then, taking service with the French, he was present at the capture of Louisbourg and the capitulation of Quebec (1759). He wrote his *Memoirs* (of the 1745 Rising).

JOHNSTONE, Jimmy (James)
(1944 –)

Footballer, born in Viewpark, Lanarkshire. Tiny and speedy, he was a member of the Glasgow Celtic side which won the European Cup in 1967, and he played a leading part in Celtic's virtual monopoly of domestic competition in the five years from 1965. He epitomized the classic Scots tradition of the

small, gifted individualist, but was not always amenable to discipline and he merited many more caps than the 23 he received. Unable to settle away from Scotland, his spells of playing in England, Ireland and the USA were not particularly productive.

JOHNSTONE, William
(1897–1981)

Painter, born in Denholm, Roxburghshire. He studied at Edinburgh College of Art and subsequently in Paris. His work in the late 1920s and 1930s shows the influence of Surrealism, in its use of rounded semi-abstract images suggestive of dream-like landscapes and human forms. He held a series of teaching posts in London, latterly as Principal of the Central School of Arts and Crafts (1947–60). It was during the last decade of his life that he produced what is arguably his best work: large, free abstract paintings and ink drawings which have something of the feeling of Eastern calligraphy, but are still evocative of the natural world.

JONES, Sir Henry
(1852–1922)

Welsh-born philosopher, born in Llangernyw, Denbighshire. First a shoemaker in Wales, he became a methodist preacher and went on to study at Glasgow University in 1875. Directed into an academic career by **Edward Caird**, he taught at Bangor and Dundee before succeeding Caird as Professor of Moral Philosophy at Glasgow in 1894, where he delivered resounding lectures. An adviser to Lloyd George, who was a personal friend, he dined with the rich to raise sponsorship and campaigned for science teaching and social studies. His works include *Idealism as a Practical Creed* (1909) and *The Working Faith of a Social Reformer* (1910). Suffering from intensely painful cancer, he refused the offer of drugs but managed to complete his Gifford Lectures just before he died.

JONES, John Paul, originally John Paul
(1747–92)

Scottish-born American naval officer, born in Kirkbean, Galloway, the son of a gardener, John Paul. Apprenticed as sailor, he made several voyages to America, and in 1773 inherited a property in Fredericksburg, Virginia, having been mate on a slaver for five years; about the same date he assumed the name of Jones. At the outbreak of the American War of Independence in 1775 he was commissioned as a Senior Lieutenant. In 1778 he cruised into British waters in the *Ranger* and made a daring descent on the Solway Firth in Scotland. In 1779, as commodore of a small French squadron displaying American colours, he threatened Leith, and off Flamborough Head won a hard-fought engagement on the *Bon Homme Richard* against the British Frigate *Serapis*. In 1788 he entered the Russian service, and as Rear Admiral of the Black Sea fleet fought in the Russo-Turkish war of 1788–9. He died in Paris, and his remains were taken to the USA in 1905.

JONES, Reginald Victor
(1911 –)

English physicist, educated at Alleyn's School and Oxford University. Joining the Air Ministry as a Scientific Officer in 1936, he became Assistant Director of Intelligence and later Director, describing his experiences as scientific adviser to Sir Winston Churchill in *Most Secret War* (1978). In 1946 he was appointed Professor of Natural Philosophy at Aberdeen University, a post he held until his retiral in 1981. He is distinguished for his research on instrumentation and on the history of physics, and has been active in defence and educational affairs. His numerous awards range from the US Medal for Merit to being an Honorary Member of the US Air Force. He was awarded a CBE in 1942.

JONSTON, Arthur See JOHNSTON, Arthur

JUNOR, Sir John
(1919 –)

Journalist, known as the 'Sage of Auchtermuchty', but born in Glasgow. Educated at Glasgow University, he was a pilot during World War II. He stood three times as a Liberal Parliamentary candidate for Scottish seats, but gave up his political ambitions when Lord Beaverbook offered him 'the golden crown' of journalism, editorship of the *Sunday Express* (1954–86). A successful editor, he is better known as a sardonic, sometimes savage columnist. Much parodied in the satirical magazine *Private Eye*, he is celebrated for the catch-phrases 'Pass the sick bag, Alice' and 'I think we should be told', though he claimed to have used each only once.

K

KAMES, Henry Home, Lord
(1696–1782)

Judge, jurist, legal historian and philosopher, born in Kames, Berwickshire. Called to the Bar in 1723, he was raised to the bench as Lord Kames in 1752. A leading figure in the Scottish Enlightenment, beside notable works on Scots Law and philosophy, his best-known book, *Elements of Criticism* (1762) was a major work of its time on aesthetics. His other works include *Historical Law Tracts* (1759), *Principles of Equity* (1760), *Essays on Morality and Natural Religion* (1751) and *An Introduction to the Art of Thinking* (1761). Having married into land he took a great interest in agricultural improvement. He has often been cited as representative of his times on account of his all-round interests, which extended to his *Sketches of the History of Man* (1774).

KANE, Pat (Patrick)
(1964 –)

Pop singer, born in Glasgow. In 1985, after graduating in English from Glasgow University he formed the group Hue And Cry with his brother Gregory (1966 –). He worked as a music journalist in London for a year before the pair signed a recording deal in 1986 and released their first single 'I Refuse'. Their first major success came the following year with 'Labour Of Love' (1987), a single inspired by the 1987 general election. The band's albums have included *Seduced And Abandoned* (1987), *Remote* (1988) and *Stars Crash Down* (1991). In 1990 he was elected Rector of Glasgow University.

KAY, John
(1742–1826)

Artist, born near Dalkeith, Midlothian. He was a prosperous Edinburgh barber, acquainted with Edinburgh society, and in 1785 he opened a print shop for caricatures of local celebrities etched by himself. During his career he executed nearly 900 works, including such notables as **Adam Smith**. His *Original Portraits, with Biographical Sketches* is an invaluable record of Edinburgh.

KEATES, John Stanley
(1925 –)

English-born geographer, born in Wallasey, Merseyside, and educated at Oxford University, he spent his early years in map publishing in Britain and Sweden. He was appointed to Glasgow University Department of Geography in 1960, later to become a Reader, and he played a key role in the establishment of pioneering courses in topographic science. A co-founder of the British Cartographic Society, he initiated and edited its journal for seven years. He was President of that society and has held key posts on numerous national and international cartographic bodies. He has published widely, with special interests in cartographic education, technology and communication. His book *Cartographic Design and Production* (1973, 2nd ed 1989) is an established student text. His awards include the British Cartographic Society Medal (1988).

KEENAN, Peter
(1929 –)

Boxer, born in Glasgow. A wiry, hugely energetic fighter, he made his mark while still an amateur, winning the Scottish flyweight title in 1948. Having turned professional, he won the British title in 1951, lost it two years later, but then regained it again in 1954, this time remaining champion until 1959; he won two Lonsdale belts outright for successful defences of the championship. The European champion in 1951–2 and again in 1953, he was also Empire champion from 1955 to 1959. In 1952 he fought Vic Toweel for the championship of the world, but was defeated. After retiring from the ring, he promoted bouts in his home town for a number of years.

KEILL, John
(1671–1721)

Mathematician, born and educated in Edinburgh. A pupil of **David Gregory**, Keill followed him to Oxford when he became Professor of Astronomy there in 1691. He became a disciple of Newton and from 1694 was one of the first to lecture on Newtonian natural philosophy. He became FRS in 1700, and in 1701 published *Introductio ad veram physicam* (an introduction to Newtonian physics), and *Introductio ad veram astronomicam* (1718), both later translated into English and French. In 1712 he became Savilian Professor of Astronomy at Oxford. He played a major part in fomenting the dispute between Newton and Leibniz over who had first invented the calculus, in which he championed Newton.

KEILLER, John Mitchell
(1851–99)

Confectionery and preserve manufacturer, born in Dundee and educated at the city's High School and at Edinburgh University. He entered the long-established family firm of James Keiller and Company. (It was John's great-aunt Margaret who first produced the marmalade for which the firm became famous.) John, an astute businessman with a wide portfolio of investments, guided the expansion of the company, ensuring that 'Keiller's Dundee Orange Marmalade' became one of the first trade marks registered after the registry was established in 1876. A year later he assumed control of the firm and reconstructed the Dundee factory to produce a wide range of sweets. In 1893 Keiller's became a limited liability company and thereafter, although John remained Chairman, his direct involvement declined due to ill health. Although he was a Justice of the Peace in the city his public profile remained modest, notwithstanding his varied local philanthropic activities.

KEIR, James
(1735–1820)

Chemist and industrialist, born in Edinburgh, the youngest of 18 children of a prosperous family. He was educated at the Edinburgh High School and University, where he studied medicine, and met Erasmus Darwin, who was to become a lifelong friend. He then joined the army, and served in the West Indies, resigning in 1768. He married and settled in West Bromwich and remained there. He joined Darwin's circle of friends and became a member of the Lunar Society of Birmingham, an organization founded to promote interest in science and technology. He assisted Joseph Priestley in Birmingham, and was a friend of Josiah Wedgwood (both fellow-members). Becoming interested in chemistry and geology, he set up a glass-making business at Stourbridge, but gave it up in 1778 to manage Boulton and **Watt**'s engineering works, and then in 1780 he began to make alkalis (soda and potash) and soap. He wrote widely on science, his most valuable contribution probably being a translation of Macquer's *Dictionary of Chemistry* (1776) with additions.

KEITH, Sir Arthur
(1866–1955)

Physical anthropologist, born in Aberdeen. Intending to enter medicine, he went to Aberdeen University (1884), coming under the influence of James Trail and John Struthers. In 1889 he took the post of medical officer to an industrial firm in Siam, where he began to study monkeys, and thus developed an interest in evolution and physical anthropology. In 1895 he moved to the London Hospital Medical School, later becoming a lecturer there. In 1908 he became Conservator of the Hunterian Museum of the Royal College of Surgeons; under his direction the museum earned an exceptionally high reputation. He wrote *Introduction to the Study of Anthropoid Apes* (1896), *Human Embryology and Morphology* (1901) and works on ancient man, including *Concerning Man's Origin* (1927) and *New Theory of Human Evolution* (1948). A talented lecturer and a modest man, he received many awards.

KEITH, Arthur Berriedale
(1879–1944)

Constitutional thinker and orientalist. Educated at the Royal High School, Edinburgh, and Edinburgh, Glasgow and Oxford universities, he took first place in the Civil Service competition (1901), and was appointed to the Colonial Office. Following various further government colonial posts, he became Lecturer in Ancient History at Edinburgh in 1907, and Deputy Boden Professor of Sanskrit at Oxford (1907–8), publishing editions of the Aranyakas of the Rigveda in 1908 and 1909. In 1912 he was Private Secretary to the Permanent Under-Secretary of State for the Colonies, and from 1914 to 1944 was Regius Professor of Sanskrit and Comparative Philology at Edinburgh. Among his works were *Imperial Unity and the Dominions* (1916) and *The Samkhya System* (1918). His initially divergent careers as Colonial Office civil servant and Indian scholar drew closer as he was made Member of the Committee on Home Administration of Indian Affairs (1919) and published the command paper on the question. He followed this with *The Belgian Congo and the Berlin Act* (1919). His *Selected Speeches and Documents on British Colonial Policy* 1763–1917 (2 vols, 1918) became standard in its field, but also consolidated his reputation as a constitutionalist thinker. He was of significance in a variety of evolving states after the war, from Palestine to Australia, and was also vital in the development of imperial political thought as an academic subject. He continued to publish extensively both on Indian philosophy, religion and literature and on developments in international law and policy, *Speeches and Documents on the British Dominions* 1918–1931 *from Self-Government to National Sovereignty* (1932) also becoming a seminal work. Exceptionally influential in the transformation of the British Commonwealth, both in its nature and self-awareness, in 1927 he became Lecturer at Edinburgh on the Constitution of the British Empire, retaining this post until his death.

KEITH, James
(1696–1758)

Soldier and field marshal in the Prussian army, born in the castle of Inverugie near Peterhead, Buchan. He came from an ancient family (represented now by the Earl of Kintore), which had for centuries held the hereditary office of Great Marischal of Scotland. He was destined for the law, but in 1715 he engaged with his brother in the Jacobite Rising, and in 1719 in Alberoni's futile expedition to the West Highlands, which ended in the 'battle' of Glenshiel. On both occasions the brothers escaped to the Continent. For nine years James held a Spanish colonelcy and took part in the siege of Gibraltar (1726–7), but his Episcopal beliefs were against him and in 1728 he entered the Russian service as a major-general. He distinguished himself in the wars with Turkey and Sweden, particularly at the siege of Otchakoff (1737) and the reduction of the Aøland Islands (1743). After this he visited Paris and London, where he made his peace with the Hanoverian government. In 1747, finding the Russian service disagreeable, he exchanged it for that of Prussia, and Frederick II, the Great, immediately bestowed on him the rank of field marshal. From this time his name has been associated with that of Frederick, who relied as much on Keith's

military genius as he did on the diplomatic ability of his brother, the Earl Marischal. His military talents became even more conspicuous on the outbreak of the Seven Years' War (1756). He shared Frederick's doubtful fortunes before Prague, was present at the victories of Lobositz and Rossbach, and conducted the masterly retreat from Olmütz. At Hochkirch he was shot dead while charging the enemy for the third time. He died poor and unmarried, but he left children by his Swedish mistress, Eve Merthens (d.1811).

KEITH, Thomas
(1827–95)

Doctor, surgeon and amateur photographer, born in Kincardineshire. His photographs were mostly taken in Edinburgh, where he spent most of his life, and on Iona, and he was most active as a photographer during the period 1852–7, after which his professional duties may have left him insufficient time to continue. His photographs are salted paper prints, made using the method invented by Gustave le Gray. He may have worked closely with his friend and brother-in-law, John Forbes White, and possibly with another Edinburgh doctor and amateur photographer, William Walker. Keith's work, superior to that of either of these associates, is notable for its technical and compositional authority. His subject matter, for the most part, was architectural. His work was 'discovered' by the American photographer, Alvin Langdon Coburn, who exhibited examples of his work at the Royal Photographic Society in London in 1914. Since then, Keith has been recognized as one of the masters of early British photography.

KEITH, Viscount See
ELPHINSTONE, George Keith

KELLO, John
(d.1570)

Minister and murderer. Described as 'a man of lowly origin and high ambition', he was minister of Spott Parish in East Lothian. Keen to advance his position, he planned to murder his wife and marry the daughter of the local laird. Spreading the unfounded rumour of his wife's suicidal tendencies, he strangled her on Sunday, 24 September 1570, then strung her from a hook in the ceiling to make it appear that she had hanged herself. He then went on to church where he preached, to all accounts, a fine sermon, returning afterwards with several church members and pretending to be horrified at the discovery of his dead wife. He would have escaped detection had it not been for the Reverend Andrew Simpson, minister at Dunbar, who, with sensitive antennae for deception, was made suspicious by Kello's admission of a troubled dream, and challenged him. Kello confessed and was hanged in Edinburgh soon after, delivering a final sermon from the scaffold in which he cautioned 'Measure not the truth of God's word altogether by the lives of such as are appointed pastors over you'.

KELLY, Sir Robert

(1902–71)

Football administrator, born in Glasgow, into one of the families which have traditionally run Celtic Football Club. His father was James Kelly, a Celtic player, club director from the board's inception in 1897, and chairman 1909–14. Robert Kelly joined the board in 1931 and became chairman in 1947, holding this post until his death. Not averse to influencing the team manager in his early years, he took a back seat with the appointment of **Jock Stein** in 1965, and thereafter witnessed the club's greatest years, including the European Cup success of 1967.

KELMAN, James

(1946 –)

Novelist, short-story writer and playwright, born in Glasgow, one of five brothers. His father was a frame maker and picture restorer. He left school at 15 to become an apprentice compositor, abandoning this two years later when his family decided to emigrate to America. However, he returned soon after and worked at various short-term jobs whose nature is clear to readers of his fiction: labouring, bus-conducting and stocking shelves in stores. For long periods he was unemployed, but he was a voracious reader and when his unemployment benefit was about to be cut he enrolled expediently at Strathclyde University. He left, nonetheless, in his third year, dissatisfied with the irrelevance of the philosophy course. In any case he was now determined to be a writer, and since 1983, with the publication of *Not Not While the Giro*, a collection of laconic stories, he has carved a niche as the spokesman for the disaffected, downtrodden and inarticulate. Invariably, he is associated with the west of Scotland and the working class. He writes in the demotic voice and uses swear words liberally, but few deny his potency or

authenticity. *The Busconductor Hines* (1984), a triumph of the mundane, confirmed his promise. *A Chancer*, the story of a small-time gambler, followed a year later. *Greyhound for Breakfast* (1987) evoked comparisons with Chekhov and Beckett, though the clipped style was quintessential Kelman. *A Disaffection*, his second novel, the story of a secondary-school teacher at odds with the system and society, found a wide audience through its shortlisting for the Booker Prize in 1989. Further stories were collected in *The Burn* (1991), and three plays are included in *Hardie and Baird & Other Plays* (1991).

KELTIE, Sir John Scott

(1840–1927)

Geographer, born in Dundee. He studied at the universities of St Andrews and Edinburgh. His early working life was spent in various aspects of publishing, but his geographical contributions were recognized in 1883 with his election to Fellowship of the Royal Geographical Society, and he edited the first volume of the *Geographical Journal*. He was also President of the Geographical Section of the British Association and of the Geographical Association. His work was widely acclaimed both at home and overseas, winning, for example, the Gold Medals of the Royal Scottish Geographical Society and the American Geographical Society. He was made Commander of the Swedish Order of North Star (1898), and was awarded the Orders of St Olaf, Norway (1907), and of the White Rose, Finland (1921). He was knighted for his services to geography and education in 1918.

KELVIN, William Thomson, 1st Baron

(1824–1907)

Irish-born physicist and mathematician, born in Belfast. He was brought to Glasgow in 1832 when his father was appointed Professor of Mathematics there. He entered Glasgow University at the age of 10, went to Cambridge at 16, graduated second wrangler and was elected a fellow of Peterhouse. After studying in Paris under Henri Victor Regnault, at the age of 22 he was appointed Professor of Mathematics and Natural Philosophy (1846–99), and turned his mind to physics. In a career of astonishing versatility, he brilliantly combined pure and applied science. In an early paper (1842) he solved important problems in electrostatics. He proposed the absolute, or Kelvin, temperature scale (1848), and simultaneously with Rudolf Clausius he established the second law of thermodynamics. He investigated geomagnetism and hydrodynamics (particularly wave-motion and vortex-motion). He was chief consultant on the laying of the first submarine Atlantic cable (1857–8), and grew wealthy by patenting a mirror galvanometer for speeding telegraphic transmission. He improved ships' compasses, and invented innumerable electrical instruments (his house in Glasgow was the first to be lit by electric light); these instruments were manufactured by his own company, Kelvin & White. He invented a tide predictor, a harmonic analyser, a siphon recorder and numerous other devices. He was created 1st Baron Kelvin of Largs in 1892. He is buried in Westminster Abbey, beside Sir Isaac Newton.

KEMBALL, Charles
(1923 –)

Physical chemist, born in Edinburgh and educated at Cambridge University. He held a number of college and university posts at Cambridge before moving to the Chair of Chemistry at Belfast in 1954. He became professor at Edinburgh in 1966, retiring in 1984. From 1988 to 1991 he was President of the Royal Society of Edinburgh. He is noted for his researches on surface chemistry and heterogeneous catalysis, especially the use of deuterium exchange to investigate the mechanism of catalytic reactions of hydrocarbons by determining the nature and reactivity of adsorbed intermediates. These studies provided fundamental new evidence about the behaviour of catalysts, and are also of interest to the chemical industry.

KEMMER, Nicholas
(1911 –)

Russian-born British physicist, born in St Petersburg, his parents being both from German families long settled in Russia. He attended a London preparatory school, and after his parents settled in Germany, the Bismarckschule in Hanover and the universities of Göttingen and Zurich. He returned to London as a research fellow at Imperial College, and from there joined the research team working on nuclear fission in Cambridge and later in Montreal. After the war he became a Fellow of Trinity College and a lecturer in mathematics. In 1953 he was appointed to the Tait Professorship of Mathematical Physics at Edinburgh University, where he built up a flourishing research group. His most important contributions to physics were in the field theory of nuclear forces and extensions of Hideki Yukawa's meson theory. The continuing influence of this and other work was marked by the award of the Max Planck medal of the German Physical Society in 1983.

KEMP, Lindsay
(1939 –)

Mime artist, actor, dancer, teacher and director, born on the Isle of Lewis. After studying at Bradford Art College, he began his dance training with Ballet Rambert. His teachers included Marie Rambert, Charles Weidman and mime artist Marcel Marceau. His colourful career was launched at the 1964 Edinburgh Festival. He has had his own company in various forms since the early 1960s and has created his own work in camp, extravagant style since then, including *The Parade's Gone By* (1975) and *Cruel Garden* (1977, in collaboration with Christopher Bruce), both for Ballet Rambert, and *Flowers* (based on the writings of Jean Genet, 1973), *Midsummer Night's Dream* (1979) and *The Big Parade* for his own company. He taught rock star David Bowie mime (which he used memorably in his Ziggy Stardust concerts in the early 1970s), and appeared in Ken Russell's films *Savage Messiah* and *Valentino* (1977) and Derek Jarman's *Sebastiane* (1975) and *Jubilee* (1977).

KENDALL, James Pickering
(1889–1979)

English physical chemist, who made notable contributions to solution chemistry. Born in Surrey, he took his degree at Edinburgh University. Subsequently he studied in Stockholm with Svante August Arrhenius, who had revolutionized chemistry by showing that many substances split into electrically charged particles or 'ions' when they dissolve. From 1913 to 1928 Kendall taught in the USA. He studied ionic equilibria in solution, using their conductivity as a measurement, and detected the formation of addition compounds by measuring changes in freezing point. He also pioneered the separation of isotopes by electrolysis, an unsuccessful technique which was later adapted to other uses. Kendall succeeded Sir **James Walker** in the Edinburgh chair in 1928, which he held until his retiral in 1959. He revised Alexander Smith's textbooks on chemistry, used worldwide, and wrote scientific biographies and chemistry books for children.

KENNAWAY, James
(1928–68)

Novelist, born in Auchterarder, Perthshire, into a quiet middle-class background, the son of a solicitor and a doctor. He went to public school at Glenalmond. He did national service before going to Trinity College, Oxford, after which he worked for a London publisher and began to write in earnest. He married in 1951, and *The Kennaway Papers* (1981), edited by his wife Susan, gives an insight into his mercurial character and their turbulent relationship. *Tunes of Glory* (1956) was his first novel and remains his best known. The author himself wrote the screenplay to what was a successful film starring **Alec Guinness** and John Mills in a classic class confrontation set in a military barracks in Scotland. *Household Ghosts* (1961) was equally powerful, and was made into a stage-play (1967) and a film (1969) under the title *Country Dance*. Later books of note are *The Bells of Shoreditch* (1967), *Some Gorgeous Accident* (1967) and *The Cost of Living Like This* (1969). *Silence*, a novel, was published posthumously in 1972.

KENNEDY, Helena
(1950 –)

Barrister, broadcaster and writer. Born in Glasgow into a working-class, Labour-voting family, she studied law in London and set up practice with several like-minded colleagues, taking on a variety of radical cases. Renowned for her persuasive charm in court, she has represented clients as diverse as anarchists, a member of the Guildford Four and Myra Hindley. She achieved public recognition with her appearance on the BBC documentary series *The Heart of the Matter* and with *Blind Justice*, a television drama loosely based on her own legal experiences. Overtly left-wing and feminist, she has hastened changes in attitudes within the English legal profession. In 1991 she was made a QC and was appointed to the Bar Council.

KENNEDY, James
(c.1408–1465)

Prelate, son of James Kennedy of Dunure, grandson of King **Robert III** of Scotland and nephew of King **James I**. A graduate of St Andrews University and Louvain, he became Bishop of Dunkeld in 1437, then Bishop of St Andrews in 1440. As advisor to **James II**, he opposed the growing dominance of the **Douglas**es in Scotland. During the minority of **James III**, he led the 'old lords' party in support of the Lancastrians. He founded St Salvator's College at St Andrews.

KENNEDY, Ludovic Henry Coverley
(1919 –)

Broadcaster and writer, born in Edinburgh. Educated at Christ Church, Oxford, he served in the Royal Navy (1939–46) before becoming a librarian, lecturer and later editor of the BBC's *First Reading* (1953–4). In 1950 he married the ballerina Moira Shearer. On television, he introduced *Profile* (1955–6), was an ITN newscaster (1956–8), hosted *This Week* (1958–60) and contributed to the BBC's *Panorama* (1960–3). He contested the Rochdale by-election as a Liberal in 1958 and general election of 1959. He has devoted himself to defending victims of alleged injustice, helping to set the record straight on the falsely accused and wrongly convicted. His many notable series include *Your Verdict* (1962), *Your Witness* (1967–70) and *A Life With Crime* (1979). He has also acted as host on, among many other programmes, *Face the Press* (1968–72), *Tonight* (1976–8) and *Did You See?* (1980–8). His books include *Ten Rillington Place* (1961), *The Trial of Stephen Ward* (1964) and *A Presumption of Innocence: The Amazing Case of Patrick Meehan* (1975). He published an autobiography, *On My Way To The Club*, in 1989.

KENNEDY, William Quarrier
(1903–79)

Geologist, the first baby to be born in the **Quarrier** Homes, Bridge of Weir, Renfrewshire. He was educated at Glasgow High School and Glasgow University, where he took degrees in agriculture and geology. Thereafter, his career was divided into two parts. From 1928 to 1945 he made immense contributions to the geology of Scotland, for instance, he was the first to recognize the large-scale horizontal movements on the Great Glen Fault. Then, as Professor of Geology at Leeds University (1945–67) he founded and directed the Research Institute of African Geology from 1955. Throughout, he acted as mentor to many others who themselves achieved eminence. For his far-seeing and fundamental contributions to geology he was elected a Fellow of both the Royal Society of Edinburgh (1948) and the Royal Society of London (1949), as well as receiving many other awards.

KENNETH I, called Macalpin
(9th century)

King of the Scots. He seems to have succeeded his father Alpin as king in 841, and to have won acceptance by the Picts by 843. His reign marked a decisive step in the establishment of a united kingdom, and also saw the shift of the centre of the Church from Iona to the court at Dunkeld.

KENTIGERN, St, also called Mungo
(c.518–603)

Celtic churchman, the apostle of Cumbria. According to legend he was the son of a Princess Thenew, who was cast from Traprain Law, then exposed on the Firth of Forth in a coracle. This carried her to Culross, where she bore a son (about 518). Mother and child were baptized (an anachronism) by St **Serf**, who reared the boy in his monastery, where he was so beloved that his name Kentigern ('chief lord') was often exchanged for Mungo ('dear friend'). He founded a monastery at Cathures (now Glasgow), and in 543 was consecrated Bishop of Cumbria. In 553 he was driven to seek refuge in Wales, where he visited St David, and where he founded another monastery and a bishopric, which still bears the name of his disciple, St Asaph. In 573 he was recalled by a new king, Rederech Hael, and about 584 was visited by **Columba**. He was buried in Glasgow Cathedral, which is named after him as St Mungo's. There remain a fragment of a biography, and the *Vita Kentigerni* by Joceline of Furness, both dating from the 12th century.

KER family See KERR

KER, William Paton
(1855–1923)

Scholar, born in Glasgow. Educated at Glasgow and Balliol College, Oxford, he was Professor of English at Cardiff (1883) and at University College, London (1889), and of Poetry at Oxford (1920). A talker, lecturer and writer of prodigious learning and vitality, he wrote *Epic and Romance* (1897), *The Dark Ages* (1904), *Essays on Medieval Literature* (1905) and *The Art of Poetry* (1923).

KERNOHAN, Bob (Robert Deans)
(1931 –)

Journalist and editor, born in Mount Vernon, Lanarkshire. Educated in Glasgow and then at Balliol College, Oxford, he served as a journalist at the *Glasgow Herald* as Associate Editor (1965–6) and London Editor (1966–7), before working as Director of the Scottish Conservative Central Office (1967–71). His appointment in 1972 as Editor of *Life and Work* (the official magazine of the Church of Scotland) was the first non-ministerial appointment for 40 years. His confrontational, highly independent and unmistakable editorial stance did little to disguise his political and theological preferences. At a time when the wider church in Scotland was sounding increasingly radicalized and anti-establishment, this made for a degree of conflict in which he was happy to engage. He retired to freelance journalism in 1991.

KERR, or KER

An Anglo-Norman family, first recorded in Scotland at the end of the 12th century. Sir Andrew Kerr of Cessford (d.1526), whose younger brother, George, was ancestor of the Kerrs of Faudonside, had two sons: Sir Walter, whose grandson, Robert Kerr, was created Earl of Roxburghe in 1616, and Mark, commendator of Newbattle, whose son, Mark Kerr, was created Earl of Lothian in 1606. The second Earl of Roxburghe was only a Kerr by his mother. His grandson, the 5th Earl, was created duke in 1707. John, 3rd Duke (1740–1804), was a renowned bookcollector, whose library was sold in 1812 for 23 341.

KERR, Deborah, originally Deborah Jane Kerr-Trimmer
(1921 –)

Actress, born in Helensburgh, Dunbartonshire. Trained as a dancer, she made her stage début in the corps-de-ballet of a Sadler's Wells production of *Prometheus* (1938). Choosing instead to act, she appeared in repertory in Oxford before making her film début in *Contraband* (1940). British successes in *The Life and Death of Colonel Blimp* (1943) and *Black Narcissus* (1947) brought her a Hollywood contract. Invariably cast in well-bred, ladylike roles, she played numerous governesses and nuns, sensationally departing from her established image to play a nymphomaniac in *From Here to Eternity* (1953). Nominated six times for an Academy Award, she retired from the screen in 1969, returning to the theatre in works such as *Seascape* (1975), *Long Day's Journey Into Night* (1977) and *Overheard* (1981). Active on stage and television, she returned to the cinema in *The Assam Garden* (1985).

KERR, Jim
(1959 –)

Rock singer, who formed the punk group Johnny And The Self Abusers in Glasgow in 1977. They split up after releasing one single but Kerr, together with guitarist Charlie Burchill and drummer Brian McGee, re-formed in 1978 as Simple Minds, adding bassist Derek Forbes and keyboard player Mick McNeill. Their first album, *Life In A Day* (1979), was recorded for the local Zoom record label, but brought national success. Their subsequent albums have included *Empires And Dance* (1980), *Sons And Fascination* (1981), *New Gold Dream* (1982), *Once Upon A Time* (1985) and *Real Life* (1991). The band established a strong following in Europe early in their career. Their first US success came with the single 'Don't You (Forget About Me)' (1985), recorded for the soundtrack to the film *The Breakfast Club*. Various line-up changes meant that by 1990 Kerr and Burchill were the only remaining members from the original band.

KERR, John
(1824–1907)

Physicist, born in Ardrossan, Ayrshire. Educated at Glasgow University in theology, from 1857 to 1901 he was a lecturer in mathematics at Glasgow Free Church teacher-training college. In 1876 he discovered the magneto-optic effect which was then named after him. He was the author of *An Elementary Treatise on Rational Mechanics* (1867).

KERR, Sir John Graham
(1869–1957)

Naturalist, zoologist and the last Member of Parliament for the Scottish Universities. Born in Hertfordshire, he was educated at the Royal High School, Edinburgh and Edinburgh University. As a young man he went on two long expeditions to the Gran Chaco in Argentina, where he made important discoveries, particularly concerning an evolutionarily interesting and rare species of fish. Papers published at the time and his *A Naturalist in the Gran Chaco* (1950) describe much of this work. In 1902 he was appointed to the Regius Chair of Natural History at Glasgow, where he reorganized the department, obtaining a new building and an innovative museum in 1923. He was particularly concerned with the teaching of basic biological knowledge to medical students, and his research interests encompassed in particular the natural history and marine biology of Scotland. After retiring from the Chair in 1935, he was elected Member of Parliament for the Scottish Universities, serving until university members were abolished in 1950. He was elected FRS in 1909 and knighted in 1939.

KESSON, Jessie, originally **Jessie Grant McDonald**
(1915 –)

Novelist, short-story writer and playwright, born in Inverness. Not knowing who her father was, she soon moved to Elgin with her mother. Estranged from many of the family, mother and daughter lived meagerly on their own resources, becoming adept at evading the Cruelty Inspector and the rent man. In her teens, however, Jessie was sent to an orphanage in Skene, Aberdeenshire. Later she entered service, settling in 1934 on a farm with her husband Johnnie, a cottar. Although she managed eventually to devote herself to writing, she worked for many years as a cinema cleaner, artists' model and a social worker in London and Glasgow. *The White Bird Passes* (1958), *Glitter of Mica* (1963), *Another Time, Another Place* (1983) and *Where the Apple Ripens* (1985) recreate faithfully, and without sentimentality, her hard early years in a farming community.

KIDD, Captain See KIDD, William

KIDD, Carol
(1944 –)

Jazz singer, born in Glasgow. While still at school she began to sing with traditional jazz bands, later joining the Glasgow-based band of Jimmy Feighan, whose style allowed her to develop her talent for interpreting ballads.

She began to work with her own permanent trio, developing a loyal following in Scotland but little-known outside until, in the late 1970s, she was featured in London at Ronnie Scott's and the Pizza Express jazz clubs. Then followed occasional work in Scotland on radio and television, as a singer and presenter, and the start of her recording career. During the late 1980s she began to give performances with specially assembled larger orchestras, including string sections, notably at the Glasgow and Edinburgh jazz festivals, winning various awards which gave her overdue recognition as one of Britain's finest jazz singers. By 1990 she had moved to England to develop her career, working and recording with a regular trio of London-based musicians, and was chosen to support Frank Sinatra at his Ibrox Stadium concert (1990).

KIDD, Dame Margaret Henderson
(1900–88)

Pioneering lawyer. The daughter of a Linlithgow solicitor she determined to go to the Bar and achieved an impressive list of 'firsts', as the first lady member of the Scottish Bar (1923), the first lady QC (1948) and the first lady (part-time) sheriff of a county (Dumfries 1960–6, Perth 1966–74), served as Keeper of the Advocates' Library, 1956–69, and was Vice-President of the British Federation of University Women. She was made DBE in 1975 and LLD (Dundee, 1982; Edinburgh, 1984). On her death she was described by a colleague as having 'paved the way for women in the legal profession and in the Scottish Bar in a way no-one else could have done'.

KIDD, William, known as Captain Kidd
(c.1645–1701)

Merchant and privateer, born in Greenock, Renfrewshire. His early life is unknown, but in the 1680s he was operating as a successful sea-captain with a small fleet of trading vessels, based in New York. During the War of the League of Augsburg against France (1688–97) he fought as a privateer to protect Anglo-American trade routes in the West Indies, and in 1691 he was rewarded by New York City for his exploits. In 1695 he went to London and was given command of an expedition against pirates in the Indian Ocean. He reached Madagascar early in 1697, but instead of attacking pirates he began to sanction attacks on merchant ships as well, including the *Quedagh Maiden*, an Armenian merchantman. After a two-year cruise he returned to the West Indies to find that he had been proclaimed a pirate. He sailed to Boston, where he surrendered on promise of a pardon in 1699. Instead he was sent as a prisoner to London, where he was convicted of piracy and hanged.

KIDSTON, Robert
(1852–1924)

Palaeobotanist, born at Bishopton House, Renfrewshire. He spent most of his life in Stirling, attending Stirling High School, and joining the Glasgow Savings Bank, which failed in 1878. Devoting his life thereafter to palaeobotany, he became one of the great amateur scientists. He had particularly cordial relations with the Geological Survey of Great Britain and studied the specimens of Carboniferous plants supplied by them, becoming the foremost authority on Carboniferous floras. His many publications extend from 1881 unti 1924. Volume One of his memoir on the *Fossil Plants of the Carboniferous Rocks of Great Britain* was published at the time of his death. He received many honours, being elected a Fellow of the Royal Society of Edinburgh in 1886 and a Fellow of the Royal Society of London in 1902.

KILMUIR, David Patrick Maxwell Fyfe, 1st Earl of
(1900–67)

Scottish-born judge and statesman, born in Aberdeen. Educated at George Watson's College, Edinburgh, and Balliol College, Oxford, he was called to the English Bar, and took silk in 1934, the youngest KC since the time of Charles II. Conservative MP for West Derby (Liverpool) (1935–54), he was Solicitor General (1942–5) and Attorney General (1945). He was Deputy Chief Prosecutor at the Nuremberg trial of the principal Nazi war criminals. His 1949 report on party organization transformed the Conservatives into a more democratic and efficient movement. Home Secretary and Minister for Welsh Affairs (1951–4), he advised on a heavy programme of controversial legislation. Lord Chancellor (1954–62), he was knighted in 1942, created Viscount in 1954 and made Earl and Baron Fyfe of Dornoch in 1962. He wrote *Monopoly* (1948) and *Political Adventure* (1964).

KING, Jessie Marion
(1875–1949)

Designer and illustrator, born in New Kilpatrick (now Bearsden), Glasgow, the daughter of a minister. She studied at Glasgow School of Art (1895–9), and won a travelling scholarship to Italy and Germany. She was an internationally renowned and much sought-after book illustrator who also designed jewellery, wallpaper and was greatly involved with batik and pottery. In 1908 she married the designer **Ernest Archibald Taylor**. She participated in the decoration of **Mackintosh**'s Scottish Pavilion at the Exposizione Nazionale in Turin, and won a gold medal for the design of a book cover. She also worked with Liberty's, designing fabrics and part of the Cymric silver range. With her husband, she moved to Paris in 1911 and returned to Scotland at the outbreak of World War I. She lived in Kirkcudbright and exhibited up to the time of her death.

KININMONTH, Sir William
(1904–88)

Architect, born in Edinburgh and educated at George Watson's College, Edinburgh College of Art and London University. He was first apprenticed in and then acted as an assistant in the office of Sir Edwin Lutyens. In 1933 he joined John Balfour Paul in partnership with **Basil Spence** in the practice begun by Sir **Robert Rowand Anderson**. An important modernist, comparable to Spence, he retained a sympathy for the Scottish vernacular, notably in the Victoria Street cottages, Dunbar (1935). He designed his own house in Dick Place, Edinburgh. He was President of the Royal Scottish Academy (1969–73) and a member of the Royal Fine Arts Commission for Scotland (1952–65).

KINNAIRD, Alison
(1949 –)

Studio glass artist/engraver, born in Edinburgh. She was educated at George Watson's Ladies College, Edinburgh, and went on to study Celtic history and archaeology at Edinburgh University, graduating in 1970. In her final year at university she took a one-year course in glass engraving at Edinburgh College of Art run by Helen Munro Turner. Since 1971 she has worked as a glass artist on a freelance basis. Her work exploits the qualities of her medium and she specializes in copper-wheel engraving as a decorative technique. Her pieces are inspired by myths and legends, music, naturalism and personal experiences. She was awarded the Worshipful Company of Glass Sellers of London prize for artistic achievement in glass in 1987 and has exhibited widely in Britain and abroad. Examples of her work can be seen in the National Museum of Scotland, Glasgow Museum and Art Gallery, Kelvingrove, Huntly House Museum in Edinburgh, and in the Corning Museum of Glass in New York.

KIRK, Alexander Carnegie
(1830–92)

Mechanical engineer, born in Barry, Forfarshire, and educated at Arbroath and Edinburgh University. He was first apprenticed to **Robert Napier** at the Vulcan Foundry in Glasgow, and then worked with Maudslay, Sons and Field in London and **James Young** in Bathgate, for whom he made many improvements in the shale-oil extraction process. He developed the compound steam engine of **John Elder** into the triple-expansion engine, which could make more effective use of the higher steam pressures that became possible following the change from iron to steel for ships' boilers. The success of his engines in Napier's steamship *Aberdeen* in 1881 led to a period of supremacy for multiple-expansion steam engines that lasted for a quarter of a century or more, until they were superseded by the steam turbine.

KIRK, Sir John
(1832–1932)

Naturalist, doctor and traveller, born in Arbroath, Angus. He is best known as **David Livingstone**'s second-in-command during the latter's five-year (1858–63) exploration of East Africa. However, he was also a notable plant collector in that region, sending specimens to Kew over a 30-year period. He became Consul-General for Zanzibar (1867) and received a number of government and scientific honours.

KIRKALDY, David
(1820–97)

Materials testing engineer, born in Mayfield, near Dundee, and educated there and in Edinburgh. He began work in his father's mercantile office but found it did not suit him, and at the age of 23 he became an apprentice in Robert Napier's Vulcan Foundry in Glasgow where, after a few years, he was appointed chief draughtsman. He carried out comparative tests on the strength of wrought iron and steel for Napiers (1858–61) and in 1865 he opened in London the first independent materials testing laboratory, equipped with a 300-ton hydraulic universal testing machine of his own design. His engineering drawings were of such high quality that examples were exhibited in the Louvre and the Royal Academy.

KIRKCALDY, Sir William, of Grange

(c.1520–1573)

Politician. As one of Cardinal **Beaton**'s murderers (1546) he was imprisoned at Mont St Michel (1547–50). He took service with France, but in 1559 he opposed the French cause in Scotland. He figured at Carberry Hill, was made governor of Edinburgh Castle, and did much to win the conflict at Langside in which **Mary, Queen of Scots**' army was defeated. However, going over to Mary's side, he held Edinburgh Castle for her until May 1573, when he was forced to surrender. Three months later he was hanged.

KNOX, John

(c.1513–1572)

Protestant reformer, born in or near Haddington, East Lothian. He was educated there and most probably at the University of St Andrews. From 1540 to 1543 he acted as notary in Haddington, and must till the latter year have been in Catholic orders. In 1544 he was acting as tutor to the sons of two families, by whom he was brought into contact with **George Wishart**, now full of zeal for the Lutheran reformation, and from then on Knox identified with him. Wishart was burned by Cardinal **David Beaton** in March 1546, and Beaton was murdered in May. The cardinal's murderers held the castle of St Andrews and Knox joined them there with his pupils (1547). While there he was formally called to the ministry. A few months later the castle surrendered to the French and for 18 months Knox remained a prisoner on the French galleys. In February 1549, on the intercession of Edward VI, Knox regained his liberty, and for four years lived in England. In 1551 he was appointed one of six chaplains to Edward VI, and in 1552 was offered, but refused, the bishopric of Rochester. Knox, with five others, was consulted by Cranmer about his forty-two articles, and largely on Knox's representation the thirty-eighth

article was so couched as to commit the Church of England to the Genevan doctrine of the eucharist. On Mary I's accession Knox fled to the continent, then ministered briefly to the English congregation at Frankfurt-am-Main. In Geneva he found a congregation in line with his own way of thinking, but in September 1555 he ventured back to Scotland, making preaching journeys to Kyle and Castle Campbell, among others, before returning to Geneva in July 1556. Remaining there for the next two years, he was considerably influenced by Calvin. In 1558 he published his *First Blast of the Trumpet against the Monstrous Regiment of Women*. In 1557 the advocates of reform in Scotland bound themselves to religious revolution by the *First Covenant*; and by 1558 they felt themselves strong enough to summon Knox to their aid. From May 1559 Knox, once again in Scotland, preached at Perth and St Andrews, gaining these important towns to his cause. He also won a strong party in Edinburgh. But the Reformers could not hold their ground against the regent, **Mary of Guise**, who was subsidized by French money and soldiers. Mainly through Knox's efforts, England's assistance was obtained against the French invasion; and by the Treaty of Leith and the death of the regent (1560) the French were expelled and the insurgent party became masters of the country. Parliament ordered the ministers to draw up a *Confession of Faith* and Protestantism was established (1560). The ministers then drew up the *First Book of Discipline* (1561), with its comprehensive and forward-thinking suggestions for the religious and educational organization of the country. The return of **Mary, Queen of Scots** (August 1561) introduced new elements into the strife of parties, and during the six years of her reign Knox's attitude towards her was that of uncompromising antagonism. The celebration of Mass in Holyrood Chapel was the first act to anger him, and a sermon delivered by him in St Giles' High Kirk led to the first of his famous interviews with Mary. He went so far as to alienate the most powerful noble of his own party — Lord James Stuart, afterwards the Regent **Moray**. The marriage of Mary with Lord **Darnley** (1565), however, brought them together again. After the murder of David Rizzio he withdrew to Ayrshire, where he wrote part of his *History of the Reformation in Scotland*. The murder of Darnley, Mary's marriage with **Bothwell**, and her flight into England again threw the management of affairs into the hands of the Protestant party; and under Moray as regent the acts of 1560 in favour of the Reformed religion were duly ratified by the Estates. The assassination of Moray in 1570, and the formation of a strong party in favour of Mary, once more endangered the cause, and Knox moved to St Andrews for safety. He made his last public appearance at St Giles in November 1572, at the induction of his successor. He was buried in the churchyard then attached to St Giles. His first wife, Marjory Bowes, died in 1560, leaving him two sons. By his second wife, Margaret Stewart, daughter of Lord Ochiltree, whom (then not older than 16) he married in 1564, he had three daughters. Knox is the preeminent type of the religious Reformer — singleminded and indifferent or hostile to anything that did not advance his cause. But although he has been described as a fanatic, the term is hardly applicable to one who combined in such degree the shrewdest worldly sense with ever-ready wit and humour. His immense personality, stamped on every page of his *History of the Reformation in Scotland*, makes his work unique.

KNOX, John

(1778–1845)

Painter, born in Glasgow. In many respects, he was a follower — though not a pupil — of **Alexander Nasmyth**, his paintings of Glasgow being in the manner of Nasmyth's views of Edinburgh. However, his best-known work, of historical as well as artistic importance, is the very fine landscape *The First Steamboat on the Clyde* (c.1820).

KNOX, John Henderson

(1927 –)

Physical chemist, born in Edinburgh. After studying at Edinburgh and Cambridge universities, he joined the Edinburgh Chemistry Department in 1953, was appointed Director of the Wolfson Liquid Chromatography Unit there in 1972, and Professor in 1974. Distinguished for his research into kinetics and dispersion processes, his work has revolutionized high performance liquid chromatography. This is an important technique for separating chemical substances, and is widely used in the pharmaceutical industry to assess the purity of drugs, and in clinical research to investigate the mechanisms of biological processes. He is consultant to a number of instrument manufacturers, and author of *Molecular Thermodynamics* (1971) and *High Performance Liquid Chromatography* (editor, 1978).

KNOX, Robert

(1791–1862)

Anatomist, born in Edinburgh. He became conservator of the newly established museum of Edinburgh's Royal College of Surgeons in 1824, and from 1826 to 1840 he ran an anatomy school. He won fame as a teacher but aroused considerable dislike through having obtained subjects for dissection from **William Burke** and **William Hare**. He wrote extensively on anatomy and anthropology. He is the subject of **James Bridie**'s play *The Anatomist*.

L

LAIDLAW, Roy
(1953 –)

Rugby player, born in Jedburgh, Roxburgh-shire. A scrum-half of considerable strength, and often at his best in adversity, he set a world record (since beaten) with **John Rutherford** for the highest number of international caps of any half-back partner-ship, playing alongside Rutherford 35 times out of his 47 internationals for Scotland. He also played in all four of the British Lions' 1983 Test matches in New Zealand. First capped in 1980, he played 31 consecutive matches for Scotland — including their Grand Slam win of 1984 — before injury forced him out of the squad in 1985. He played in the inaugural World Cup of 1987, retiring the folowing year. All his club rugby was played for his hometown team, Jed-Forest.

LAIDLAW, William
(1779–1845)

Poet, born in Blackhouse, Selkirkshire, in 1779, contrary to the date (1780) given on his gravestone. He wrote lyrics, but is best known as the friend and copying secretary of Sir **Walter Scott. James Hogg** was his shep-herd for 10 years, and together they helped Scott prepare his *Minstrelsy of the Scottish Border*. Laidlaw became factor at Abbots-ford, 1817–26.

LAING, Alexander Gordon
(1793–1826)

Explorer, born in Edinburgh. Having served for seven years as an officer in the West Indies, in 1825 he was sent to explore the Niger's source, which he found. He was murdered by Arabs after leaving Timbuktu.

LAING, David
(1793–1878)

Antiquary, born in Edinburgh, the son of a bookseller. He curtailed his studies at Edin-burgh University to join his father as a partner. In 1837 he was appointed librarian of the Signet Library. He was Honorary Secretary of the Bannatyne Club, and edited many of its issues. He left behind him a private library of unusual value, and be-queathed many rare manuscripts to Edin-burgh University. His more important works were his editions of **Robert Baillie**'s *Letters and Journals* (1841–2), of **John Knox** (4 vols, 1846–64), Sir **David Lyndsay, Dun-bar** and **Henryson**.

LAING, Malcolm
(1762–1818)

Historian, born in Orkney, brother of **Samuel Laing**. Educated in Kirkwall and at Edinburgh University, he graduated in law and was called to the Bar, but hardly practised as an advocate, turning to historical studies instead. He completed the last volume of Robert Henry's *History of Great Britain* (1783), and in 1802 published his own *History of Scotland* 1604–1707. This contained an onslaught on the authenticity of the Ossian poems translated by **James Macpherson**. He also published *The Life and Histories of James VI* (1804). He returned to Orkney in 1808 and was MP until 1812.

LAING, Ronald David
(1927–89)

Psychiatrist, born in Glasgow of working-class parents. A medical graduate of Glasgow University (1951), he practised as a psychia-trist in Glasgow (1953–6). He joined the Tavistock Clinic in London in 1957 and the Tavistock Institute for Human Relations in 1960, and was Chairman of the Philadelphia Association (1964–82). He sprang to promi-nence with his revolutionary ideas about mental disorder with the publication of *The Divided Self* (1960). His principal thesis was that psychiatrists should not attempt to cure or ameliorate the symptoms of mental illness (itself a term which he repudiated), but rather should encourage patients to view themselves as going through an enriching experience. In expounding this doctrine of 'anti-psychiatry', he implied in his writings that the primary responsibility for psychiatric breakdown lies with society and/or with the patient's immediate family. His writings extended from psychiatry into existential philosophy, and later into poetry. His other books included *The Politics of Experience* (1967), *Knots* (1970), *The Politics of the Family* (1976), *Sonnets* (1980) and *The Voice of Experience* (1982).

LAING, Samuel
(1780–1868)

Writer, born in Orkney, brother of **Malcolm Laing**. Educated at Edinburgh, he saw service in the Peninsular War. He travelled and wrote on Norway, Sweden, Russia and France. His major achievement was his monumental translation of *Heimskringla* by the Icelandic historian Snorri Sturluson (*History of the Kings of Norway*, 1844).

LAIRD, Macgregor
(1808–61)

Explorer and merchant, born in Greenock, Renfrewshire. He first travelled to the lower Niger with Richard Lander's last expedition (1832–4), and was the first European to ascend the Benue River. In 1837 he started a transatlantic steamship company, for which the *Sirius* became the first ship to cross entirely under steam in 1838. In 1854 he financed a second expedition to the Niger, led by **William Balfour Baikie**.

LAIRD, Michael
(1928 –)

Architect, born in Glasgow. He trained at Edinburgh University and Edinburgh College of Art. Simplicity and sensitivity to context are central to his design philosophy, achieving adventure within discreet parameters, and resulting in functional, expressive works such as the Music School at George Watson's College, Edinburgh (1962), with its acoustically appropriate and elegant paraboloid roof, and the powerful yet non-assertive Royal Bank Computer Centre (1978), Edinburgh. In addition to such distinctive landmarks as the chimney at King's Buildings, Edinburgh (1970), he has concurrently focused on restoration projects, notably Max-

welton (1968) and Inveresk Manor House (1976), showing himself to be respectful of history but uninhibited by its confines. In his responsiveness to indigenous tradition he has shown how successfully modern designs can complement historic fabric as, for example, in the extensions to the Standard Life Head Office, Edinburgh (1968 and 1975), and their administrative offices at Tanfield, Edinburgh.

LAMOND, Frederic
(1868–1948)

Pianist and composer, born in Glasgow. A pupil of Bülow and Liszt, he made his début at Berlin in 1885 and followed this by touring in Europe and America. He excelled in playing Beethoven. Among his compositions are an overture *Aus dem Schottischem Hochlande*, a symphony, and several piano works.

LAMONT, Johann von
(1805–79)

Scottish-born German astronomer, born in Braemar, Aberdeenshire. He went in 1817 to the Scottish seminary at Ratisbon, and became in 1835 Director of Bogenhausen Observatory. In 1852 he became Professor of Astronomy at Munich where his work included cataloguing over 34 000 stars. His best work, however, was on terrestrial magnetism. In 1840 he set up a magnetic observatory at Bogenhausen, and in 1849 published *Handbuch des Erdmagnetismus*.

LANE, (William) Arbuthnot
(1856–1943)

Surgeon, born in Fort George, Invernessshire. He was the first to join fractures with metal plates instead of wires. Other important contributions to medicine were his treatment of the cleft palate and of 'chronic intestinal stasis'. In 1925 he founded the New Health Society.

LANG, Andrew
(1844–1912)

Man of letters, born in Selkirk, nephew of **William Young Sellar**. Educated at The Edinburgh Academy, St Andrews and Glasgow universities and Balliol College, Oxford, he was a fellow of Merton College, Oxford (1868–74), studying myth, ritual and totemism. He moved to London in 1875 to take up journalism, and became one of the most versatile and famous writers of his day. He specialized in mythology, and took part in a celebrated controversy with Friedrich Max Müller over the interpretation of folk tales, arguing that folklore was the foundation of literary mythology. He wrote *Custom and Myth* (1884), *Myth, Ritual and Religion* (1887), *Modern Mythology* (1897) and *The Making of Religion* (1898). He wrote a *History of Scotland* (3 vols, 1899–1904) and a *History of English Literature* (1912), and published a number of popular fairy books. He also produced studies of many literary figures, including *Books and Bookmen* (1886) and *Letters to Dead Authors* (1886), a translation of Homer, and several volumes of verse.

LANG, (William) Cosmo Gordon, Baron Lang of Lambeth
(1864–1945)

Anglican prelate, and Archbishop of Canterbury, born in Fyvie, Aberdeenshire. He was the third son of John Marshall Lang (1834–1909), Principal of Aberdeen University. He was educated at Glasgow and Oxford universities. Entering the Church of England in 1890, he was a curate at Leeds, became Dean of Divinity at Magdalen College, Oxford, Bishop of Stepney (1901–8) and Canon of St Paul's. In 1908 he was appointed Archbishop of York and in 1928 Archbishop of Canterbury until he retired in 1942. A man of wide interests, he occasionally aroused controversy, as with his speech on Edward VIII's abdication. However, the implication that he had conspired to bring about the abdication is completely unfounded. A man of great talent and personality, he inspired genuine affection in a wide circle of acquaintances. Accepted by all parties in the Church of England, he was both counsellor and friend to the royal family.

LANG, Ian
(1940–)

Politician, born in Glasgow. Educated at Rugby School and Sidney Sussex College, Cambridge, he was an insurance broker and Lloyds' underwriter before entering parliament at the third attempt, becoming Conservative MP for Galloway in 1979. He retained his seat, by then called Galloway and Upper Nithsdale, in 1983, 1987 and 1992. Minister of State for Scotland from 1987, he was promoted to Secretary of State in 1990, faced with the task of administering a country in which only one in eight Members of Parliament belonged to the party of government.

LANG, John Dunmore
(1799–1878)

Scottish-born Australian clergyman and politician, born in Greenock, Renfrewshire. Educated at Glasgow University, he arrived in New South Wales in 1823 with a mission to establish Presbyterianism in the new colony. The foundation stone of Scots Church, Sydney, was laid in the following year. With the support of Lord Bathurst, Secretary of State for the Colonies, a grant was made from the Treasury, Lang was paid a salary, and the church opened in 1826. He started a weekly newspaper in 1835 and was soon involved in lawsuits as a result of his outspoken comments, being imprisoned on four occasions either for debt or libel. He was concerned about education, and energetic in assisting the emigration of skilled workers. He was elected member of the legislative council for three periods and of the legislative assembly from 1859 to 1869.

LAPWORTH, Arthur
(1872–1941)

Chemist, born in Galashiels, Selkirkshire, the son of **Charles Lapworth**. He was educated at Birmingham University and the City and Guilds College, London. After holding a number of senior academic posts, he was appointed Professor of Organic Chemistry at Manchester in 1913, becoming Professor of Physical and Inorganic Chemistry in 1922. He had early ideas on an electronic theory of organic chemical reactions. He classified reagents by charge type, and suggested the existence of alternating electrical polarity along a chain of atoms, and alternating positive and negative centres at which reactions occurred. These ideas, which were developed in discussion with his friend Robert Robinson, were expanded by the latter in the 1930s to dominate organic chemical theory, with notable success.

LAPWORTH, Charles
(1842–1920)

English-born teacher and geologist, born in Faringdon, Berkshire. He became a schoolteacher, first in Galashiels, then at Madras College in St Andrews. Finding fossils in the strata near Galashiels, he had begun an intensive study of the geology of the Southern Uplands of Scotland by 1869. He became an authority on the graptolites, the planktonic fossil organisms found at localities like Dobb's Linn near Moffat, which he made famous. In 1879 he proposed the Ordovician System. In 1881 he was appointed Professor of Geology at Birmingham University, retiring in 1913. He played an important role in the unravelling both of the Southern Uplands and the north-west Highlands in relation to the professional work of the officers of the Geological Survey. His honours included a Royal Medal of the Royal Society of London. His son was the chemist **Arthur Lapworth**.

LAUDER, Sir Harry
(1870–1950)

Comic singer, born in Portobello, East Lothian. He started his career on the music-hall stage as an Irish comedian, but made his name as a singer of Scots songs, many of which were of his own composition, such as 'Roamin' in the Gloamin''. He was knighted in 1919 for his work in organizing entertainments for the troops during World War I. His appeal was by no means confined to Scottish audiences; some of his biggest successes were on the stages of London's famous music halls, and his popularity abroad was immense, especially in the USA and the Commonwealth countries, which he toured almost annually after 1907. He wrote volumes of memoirs, the best known of which is *Roamin' in the Gloamin'* (1928).

LAUDER, Robert Scott
(1803–69)

Painter, born in Edinburgh. He studied at the Trustees' Academy, Edinburgh, later becoming a teacher there and inspiring many pupils. From 1833 to 1838 he lived in Italy and Munich, then in London until 1849, when he returned to Edinburgh. Sir **Walter Scott**'s novels provided him with subjects for his most successful historical paintings.

LAUDER, Sir Thomas Dick
(1784–1848)

Writer, born in Fountainhall, Midlothian. He served in the Cameron Highlanders and in 1808 married the heiress of Relugas in Morayshire. He succeeded to the baronetcy in 1820, and lived at the Grange, Edinburgh, from 1832 until his death. He was Secretary to the Board of Scottish Manufacturers (1839–48), and was a proponent of the establishment of technical and art schools. He wrote two romances, *Lochindhu* (1825) and *The Wolf of Badenoch* (1827), but his best

works are *An Account of the Great Morayshire Floods* (1830) and the unfinished *Scottish Rivers*, which appeared in *Tait's Magazine* (1847–9). He also compiled *Highland Rambles and Legends to Shorten the Way* (1837) and *Legends and Tales of the Highlands* (1841).

LAUDER, William
(c.1680–1771)

Literary forger, educated at Edinburgh University, where he was a good student. In 1747–50 he sought to prove, by blatant forgeries, that Milton's *Paradise Lost* had plagiarized various 17th-century poets who wrote in Latin. He was exposed by Bishop **John Douglas**, and published an apology in 1751 entitled 'A Letter to the Reverend Mr Douglas'. He died poor in Barbados.

LAUDERDALE, James, 8th Earl of
See **MAITLAND, James**

LAUDERDALE, John Maitland, Duke of
(1616–82)

Statesman, born at Lethington (now Lennox-love) near Haddington, East Lothian. He succeeded his father as second Earl of Lauderdale in 1645, was taken prisoner at Worcester in 1651, and spent nine years in the Tower, at Windsor and at Portland. At the Restoration he became Scottish Secretary of State and then made it his main object to bring about the absolute power of the Crown in Church and State. A member of the Privy Council, he had a seat in the so-called Cabal ministry and was created a duke in 1672. He made numerous enemies and in 1678 a vote was carried in the Commons praying for his removal from the royal presence forever, but it was thrown out, in dubious circumstances, by a single vote. It seems probable that many of Lauderdale's harsher measures, particularly against the Episcopal Church in Scotland, were the result not so much of personal ambition but of an inability to tolerate the follies of less astute contemporaries. His dukedom died with him in 1682, while his earldom passed to his brother.

LAURIE, John
(1897–1980)

Actor, born in Dumfries. Educated at Dumfries Academy, he studied at the Central School of Speech Training at the Royal Albert Hall. His stage début came in **J M Barrie**'s *What Every Woman Knows* (1921), and for the remainder of the decade he made valuable contributions to some of Britain's most prestigious classical theatre companies, including the Old Vic and the Shakespeare Memorial Theatre, where he played *Hamlet* (1927). He made his film début in *Juno and the Paycock* (1930), and his many supporting performances in the medium include *The 39 Steps* (1935), *The Edge of the World* (1937), *Henry V* (1944) and *I Know Where I'm Going* (1945). An idiosyncratic figure who loved his profession with a stirring passion, his range extended from the heroic to the eccentric, and he was much praised for his verse speaking, particularly his interpretations of **Burns** and Shakespeare. His best-remembered stage roles include *John Knox* (1947), *MacAdam and Eve* (1951), and a performance as **McGonagall** in *The Hero of a Hundred Fights* (1968). His greatest popularity, however, was achieved on television as Private Frazer, the prophet of doom in the comedy series *Dad's Army* (1968–77).

LAURIE, John Watson
(c.1864–1930)

Convicted murderer, born in Coatbridge, Lanarkshire. A pattern-maker by trade, while on holiday in Rothesay (1889) he befriended an Englishman, Edwin Robert Rose, with whom he later set out to climb Goat Fell in Arran. Laurie returned alone, and was later seen wearing Rose's hat, Some time later Rose's body was found on Goat Fell. Convicted of murder, Laurie was reprieved from sentence of death because of doubts about his sanity. Instead he was admitted to the criminal lunatic department of Perth prison where he spent 40 years and 11 months, making him the longest serving prisoner in the UK.

LAURIE, Simon Somerville,
pseudonym '**Scotus Novanticus**'
(1829–1909)

Philosopher and educationist, born in Edinburgh. Graduating from Edinburgh University, he worked variously as a teacher, examiner, and Secretary to the Church of Scotland Education Committee (1855–1905). From 1876 to 1903 he was Bell Professor of Education at Edinburgh, the first to hold such a post in an English-speaking university. His theory of education was extraordinarily thorough, and he wrote prolifically on philosophy, sometimes under his 'Novanticus' nom-de-plume. His Gifford Lectures, *Synthetica* (published 1906) on the development of the mind are outstanding.

LAW, Andrew Bonar
(1858–1923)

Canadian-born Scottish statesman, born in Kingston, New Brunswick, and brought up from the age of 11 in Glasgow. Starting work in merchant banking, in 1885 he became partner in an iron merchant firm in Glasgow, and from 1900 to 1906 was Unionist MP for Blackfriars and Hutchesontown, Glasgow. In 1906, and 1910, he was returned as MP for Dulwich. In 1911 he succeeded **Balfour** as Unionist leader in the House of Commons. He was Colonial Secretary (1915–16) then a member of the War Cabinet, Chancellor of the Exchequer (1916–18), Lord Privy Seal (1919), and from 1916 leader of the House of Commons. He retired in March 1921, but despite ill-health was premier from October 1922 to May 1923.

LAW, Denis
(1940 –)

Footballer, born in Aberdeen. One of the greatest of Scottish footballers, he never played at senior level in his own country, all his career being spent in England, with the exception of a brief and unsuccessful period in Italy. He made his international début when only 18 years old, and shortly afterwards moved to Manchester City. After the Italian failure with Turin, he returned to Manchester United, the club with which he is indelibly associated. With them he won every major domestic honour, although injury excluded him from the European Cup success of 1968. Needle-sharp in the penalty area and very powerful in the air, Law shares with **Kenny Dalglish** the record of 30 goals scored for Scotland.

LAW, John, of Lauriston
(1671–1729)

Financier, born in Edinburgh, son of a goldsmith and banker. Educated at the Royal High School, he became a successful gambler and speculator. He went to London to make his fortune, but in 1694 was imprisoned for killing a man in a duel over a lady. In 1695 he escaped from prison and fled to the Continent. In Amsterdam he made a study of the credit operations of the bank, and later settled in Genoa after eloping with the wife of a Frenchman. He made a fortune there and in Venice. In 1703 he returned to Edinburgh, a zealous advocate of a paper currency but his proposals to the Scottish Parliament on this subject, outlined in his *Money and Trade Considered* (1705), were unfavourably received. Back on the Continent, he won and lost vast sums in gambling and speculation, but finally settling in Paris, he and his brother William (1675–1752) set up a private bank in 1716. This was so successful that the regent, Philippe, Duc d'Orléans, adopted Law's plan of a national bank in 1718. In 1719 he originated a joint-stock company for reclaiming and settling lands in the Mississippi valley, called the *Mississippi Scheme*, which made him a paper millionaire. He became a French citizen and a Roman Catholic, and in 1720 was made Comptroller-General of Finance for France. When the bubble burst he became an object of popular hatred, left France, and spent four years in England. He finally settled in Venice, where he died.

LAWS, Robert
(1851–1934)

Pioneer missionary, born in Aberdeen. Educated at Aberdeen, Edinburgh and Glasgow universities, he was ordained by the United Presbyterian Church of Scotland in 1875. Inspired by the example of **David Livingstone**, he went as medical officer to Nyasaland in 1875. After an epic steamship voyage along African rivers, part of which required the dismantling of the ship for overland portage, he took part in setting up the settlement of Livingstonia on Lake Nyasa. His intention was to establish a network of schools for the dissemination of Christianity, which would eventually be run by African converts. He baptized his first convert in 1881, a figure which had grown to 60 000 by 1927, when he left Africa. He was Moderator of the General Assembly of the United Free Church in 1908, and served in an unofficial legislative capacity in Nyasaland from 1912 to 1916. Mount Nyamkawa was renamed Mount Laws in his honour.

LAWSON, Denis
(1947 –)

Actor, born in Govan, Glasgow, and raised in Crieff, Perthshire. A devotee of Hollywood cinema who saw four films a week as a child, he sold carpets in Dundee and immersed himself in amateur dramatics before gaining entrance to the Royal Scottish Academy of Music and Drama in Glasgow. He accumulated a variety of theatrical experience, from

Hair to Shakespeare, mime to Andrew Lloyd Webber, before making his film début in *Dinosaur* (1976) and the *Star Wars* trilogy. A versatile performer, he scored a great personal success on stage in *Pal Joey* (1981–2) and was subsequently cast in the film *Local Hero* (1983), which highlighted his dry comic talent. The cinema stardom he aspired to has so far failed to materialize, but he has become a versatile television star of such work as *The Kit Curran Radio Show* (1984–6), *That Uncertain Feeling* (1986) and two series of *The Justice Game* (1989 –), in which he plays Glasgow legal eagle Dominic Rossi. His many stage appearances include *Mr Cinders* (1983) and *Volpone* (1990).

LEE, James Paris
(1831–1904)

Scottish-born American inventor, born in Hawick, Roxburghshire. He emigrated with his parents to Canada, later going from Ontario to Hartford, Connecticut. The Lee-Enfield and Lee-Metford rifles are based in part on his designs.

LEE, Jennie, Baroness Lee of Ashridge
(1904–88)

Labour politician, born in Lochgelly, Fife, the daughter of a miner. She graduated from Edinburgh University with degrees in education and law and at the age of 24, as a Labour MP for North Lanark, became the youngest member of the House of Commons. A dedicated Socialist, she campaigned with great wit and intelligence. In 1934 she married Aneurin Bevan and, despite her feminist principles, consciously stepped to one side as he rose within the Labour Party. Appointed Britain's first arts minister in 1964, she doubled government funding for the arts and was instrumental in setting up the Open University. She published two autobiographies, *Tomorrow is a New Day* (1939) and *My Life with Nye* (1980).

LEE, Robert
(1804–68)

English theologian, born in Tweedmouth, Berwickshire. He was educated at Berwick (where he was also for a time a boat-builder) and St Andrews University. He was minister of Inverbrothock in 1833, and Campsie in

1836. In 1843 he became minister at Old Greyfriars, Edinburgh, and in 1846 he was appointed Professor of Biblical Criticism at Edinburgh University and a Queen's chaplain. In 1857 he began his reform of the Presbyterian church service. He restored the reading of prayers, kneeling at prayer and standing during the singing, and in 1863 he introduced a harmonium, in 1865 an organ, into his church. These 'innovations' brought bitter attacks. His works include a *Handbook of Devotion* (1845) and *Prayers for Public Worship* (1857).

LEGGE, James
(1815–97)

Missionary and sinologist, born in Huntly, Aberdeenshire. After graduating at Aberdeen (1835), he ran the Anglo-Chinese missionary college in Malacca, followed by 30 years in Hong Kong. In 1876 he became the first Professor of Chinese at Oxford. His greatest work was a monumental edition of *Chinese Classics* (28 vols, 1861–86).

LEIGHTON, Kenneth
(1929–88)

English composer and pianist, born in Wakefield, Yorkshire. After graduating from Oxford, he studied composition with Goffredo Petrassi in Rome. He in turn taught composition at Edinburgh University from 1956, and from 1970 was Reid Professor of Music there. His compositions showed vigorous and individual mastery of traditional forms and contrapuntal disciplines. A skilful and rewarding composer of choral music, he also wrote extensively for his own instrument (including three concertos) as well as three symphonies, other concertos, an opera *Columba* (1981), organ and chamber music.

LEIGHTON, Robert
(1611–84)

Prelate, probably born in London. His father was Alexander Leighton (c.1568 – c.1649), Presbyterian minister in London and Utrecht, author of *Sion's Plea Against the Prelacie* (1628), which earned him from Laud scourging, the pillory, branding and mutilation, a heavy fine and imprisonment. Robert studied at Edinburgh University and spent some years in France. He was ordained minister of Newbattle, Midlothian, in 1641, signed the Covenant two years later (but with reservations about its possible excesses), and took part in all the Presbyterian policy of the time; most of the *Sermons* and the *Commentary on the First Epistle of Peter* were the work of the Newbattle period. In 1653 he was appointed Principal of Edinburgh University. Soon after the Restoration he was induced by Charles II himself to become one of the new bishops, and chose Dunblane, the poorest of all the dioceses. For the next 10 years he worked strenuously to build up the shattered fabric of the Church. His aim was to preserve what was best in Episcopacy and Presbytery as a basis for comprehensive union, but he succeeded only in being misunderstood by both sides. The continued persecution of the Covenanters drove him to London in 1665 to resign his see, but Charles persuaded him to return. Again in 1669 he went to London to advocate his scheme of 'accommodation', and he became Archbishop of Glasgow in the same year. After this came fruitless conferences in Edinburgh (1670–1) with leading Presbyterians. Despairing of success, he was allowed to retire in 1674. He spent his last 10 years at Broadhurst Manor, Sussex, often preaching in the church of Horsted Keynes, where he is buried.

LEISHMAN, Sir William Boog
(1865–1926)

Bacteriologist, born in Glasgow. He became Professor of Pathology in the Army Medical College, and Director-General, Army Medical Service (1923). He discovered an effective vaccine for inoculation against typhoid, and was first to discover the parasite of the disease kala-azar.

LENNOX, Annie
(1954 –)

Pop singer, born in Aberdeen. She was waitressing in Hampstead in 1977 when she met musician and composer Dave Stewart. The pair formed The Tourists, a band which recorded three albums before splitting up in 1980. Lennox and Stewart stayed together as The Eurythmics, and continued the group even after their personal relationship ended the following year. The band's albums have included *Sweet Dreams* (1982), *Touch* (1983), *Be Yourself Tonight* (1985) and *Savage* (1987). Although she had become one of Scotland's best-known pop singers she took a break from music in 1990, but returned in 1992 to launch a solo career with the album *Diva*.

LENNOX, Matthew, 4th Earl of
(1516–71)

Regent of Scotland, born at Dumbarton Castle, son of John, 3rd Earl. In 1532 he entered the service of France and remained there until 1543. During the confused politics of Queen Mary's minority he sided firstly with the French interest, then the English. In 1544, in London, he married Margaret Douglas, heiress of Archibald, 6th Earl of Angus and **Margaret Tudor**, Queen Dowager of **James IV**. Remaining in England, he was proclaimed a traitor in Scotland and his estates confiscated. He participated in the Protector Somerset's invasion of Scotland. In 1564, however, he and his son were permitted to return home and their dignities and estates were restored the following year. His son Henry, Lord **Darnley**, then married **Mary, Queen of Scots**, but was subsequently murdered. Lennox attempted to bring **Bothwell** to book for his son's murder, but failed and retired into England until the imprisonment of Queen Mary in Lochleven. He returned once more to Scotland where he was elected Regent of the kingdom during the minority of his grandson **James VI**. He was killed the following year when the Earl of Huntly and Lord Claud Hamilton led an attack on the parliament sitting at Stirling.

LEONARD, Tom
(1944 –)

Poet, born in Glasgow. He was educated at Lourdes Secondary School and later Glasgow University. His first book, *Six Glasgow Poems* (1969), was written in an uncompromising and unpunctuated Glasgow dialect, a form which he has developed throughout his subsequent work. (The opening line of 'Good Style', which runs 'helluva hard tay read theez init' is his anticipation of the reviews.) Shot through with mordant humour, his poems deal in an unsentimental fashion with the everyday realities and occasional baroque fantasies of working-class culture, capturing the authentic speech rhythms of Glasgow in his transliteration. *Intimate Voices: Writing 1965–83*, a selection of dialect and English poems drawn from his earlier books, appeared in 1984. He has written a radio play, *If Only Buntie Was Here* (1979), and polemical essays and articles on working-class culture and education. He was writer-in-residence in Renfrew District Libraries from 1985 to 1987, where he devoted time to collecting the work of Renfrewshire poets.

LESLIE, LESLY, or LESLEY

Family, probably of Flemish origin, first found between 1171 and 1199, in possession of the pastoral parish of Lesslyn or Leslie in Aberdeenshire, and ennobled in 1457 when George Leslie of Rothes was made Earl of Rothes and Lord Leslie. The 4th Earl was father of Norman Leslie, Master of Rothes, chief participant in the murder of Cardinal **David Beaton**. John, 6th Earl (1600–41), was one of the ablest of the Covenanting leaders. His son John (1630–81) became Lord Chancellor of Scotland in 1667, and in 1680 was created Duke of Rothes. These honours became extinct upon his death without male issue in 1681. The earldom of Rothes went to his elder daughter, in whose family the title has continued. The Balquhain branch gave birth to several notable men, such as the learned **John Leslie**, Bishop of Ross, and champion of **Mary, Queen of Scots**; Sir Alexander Leslie of Auchintoul, a General in the Muscovite service (d.1663); and Charles Leslie, the Irish non-juror.

LESLIE, Alexander, 1st Earl of Leven
(c.1580–1661)

Soldier, the illegitimate son of the Captain of Blair Atholl Castle. He became a field marshal of Sweden under Gustav II Adolf. Recalled to Scotland in 1638, he took command of the Covenanting army and commanded it against Charles I. In 1641 he was made Earl of Leven and Lord Balgony, but from 1644 he led the Covenanting army into England on behalf of the Parliamentarians. He fought at Marston Moor (1644) and the storming of Newcastle. He accepted the surrender of Charles I at Newark in 1646, and handed him over to Parliament in 1647. He joined the Royalists in 1649, fought Cromwell in Scotland in 1650–1, was captured and imprisoned, but released on parole in 1654.

LESLIE, David
(1601–82)

Soldier. He served under Gustav II Adolf and, returning to Scotland in 1640, acted as Lieutenant-General to **Alexander Leslie**, the Earl of Leven. He fought at Marston Moor (1644), and defeated Montrose at Philiphaugh (1645). Routed by Cromwell at Dunbar in 1650, and taken prisoner by him at Worcester in 1651, he was imprisoned in the Tower until the Restoration (1660). He was made Lord Newark the following year.

LESLIE, John
(1527–96)

Historian and prelate, born in Kingussie, Inverness-shire, the son of a priest. Educated at King's College, Aberdeen, and Toulouse, Poitiers and Paris, he returned to Scotland and was named by the Lords of the Congregation as one of the Catholics to debate points of belief with **John Knox**. A zealous partisan of **Mary, Queen of Scots**, he was appointed a Lord of Session in 1564 and Bishop of Ross in 1566. After her downfall he published a popular *Defence of the Honour of the Right Highe, Mightye and Nobel Princesse Marie, Queen of Scotland and Dowager of France* (1569). He joined her during her imprisonment at Tutbury, but later gave evidence against her under torture. He went into exile on the continent, and in 1579 became suffragan Bishop of Rouen and Bishop of Coustances. His chief work was a Latin history of Scotland, *De origine, moribus, et rebus gestis Scotorum* (1578), which was later translated into Scots, and contains a vivid account of the Reformation from a Catholic point of view.

LESLIE, Sir John
(1766–1832)

Natural philosopher and physicist, born in Largo, Fife. He studied at St Andrews and Edinburgh, and travelled as tutor in America and on the Continent, meanwhile engaging in experimental research. He invented a differential thermometer, a hygrometer and a photometer, and wrote *An Experimental Inquiry into Heat* (1804). In 1805 he became Professor of Mathematics at Edinburgh University. In 1810 he succeeded in creating artificial ice by freezing water under the air pump. Transferred to the Chair of Natural Philosophy (1819), he also invented the pyroscope, atmometer and aethrioscope.

LESLY family See LESLIE

LEVEN, Earl of See LESLIE, Alexander

LEVISON, Mary
(1923 –)

English-born Church of Scotland reformer and minister, born in Oxford. She studied philosophy at Oxford University, and theology at Edinburgh, Heidelberg and Basel, eventually beginning work as a deaconess of the Church of Scotland in 1954. After a period as Assistant Chaplain to Edinburgh University, she petitioned the General Assembly in 1963 to be ordained to the Ministry of Word and Sacrament, setting in motion a process of debate that was to culminate in the historic decision of the General Assembly (1968) to permit the ordination of women. Although Levison was not, in the end, the first woman minister of the Church of Scotland (Catherine McConachie of Aberdeen enjoyed that honour in 1968), she inspired and engendered the momentum that made such a possibility a reality, and the integrity, intelligence and dignity with which she so effectively made her case did much to hasten the process. Levison was herself ordained to serve as the Assistant Minister at St Andrew's and St George's Parish Church in Edinburgh in 1978, and was later appointed the first female Chaplain to the Queen (1991).

LEWIS, Ioan Myrddin
(1930 –)

Social anthropologist, born in Glasgow. After a first degree in chemistry at Glasgow University he studied social anthropology at Oxford, carrying out field research among tribal nomads in what is now the Somali Democratic Republic. He has spent most of his career at London University, where he was appointed Professor of Anthropology at the London School of Economics in 1969. He has published extensively on the history and sociology of the Horn of Africa, and more generally on the anthropological study of religion. His best-known works are *Ecstatic Religion* (1971), a comparative study of spirit possession, and *Social Anthropology in Perspective* (1976).

LEYDEN, John
(1775–1811)

Poet and orientalist, born in Denholm, Roxburghshire, the son of a farmer. He studied medicine at Edinburgh University, and was licensed as a preacher in 1798. He wrote a book on European settlements in Africa (1799), helped Sir **Walter Scott** to gather materials for his *Border Minstrelsy*, and his translations and poems in the *Edinburgh Magazine* attracted attention. In 1803 he sailed for India as assistant surgeon at Madras, travelled widely in the East, acquired 34 languages, and translated the gospels into five of them. He accompanied Lord Minto as interpreter to Java, and died of fever at Batavia. His ballads have taken a higher place than his longer poems, especially *Scenes of Infancy* (1803). His dissertation on Indo-Chinese languages is also well known.

LICKLEY, Sir Robert Lang

(1912 –)

Aeronautical engineer, born in Dundee. Graduating in civil engineering at Edinburgh University in 1932, he took the DIC (Diploma of the Imperial College) in 1933. In the same year he joined Hawker Aircraft Ltd, Kingston, becoming Chief Project Engineer (1941–6). He was the first professor of aircraft design at the College of Aeronautics, Cranfield (1946–51), becoming Deputy Principal and Governer of the College (1960–70). He returned to industry as Chief Engineer Fairey Aviation Co Ltd (1951–60), introducing the Gannet Mark I to service, and, among other projects, was responsible for the design and development of the Fairey Delta 2 which in 1956 gained the world speed record of 1132 miles per hour. In 1960 he returned to Hawker Aircraft Ltd, becoming Director and Chief Executive of the Hawker-Blackburn Division of Hawker Siddeley Aviation. There he concentrated on the successful development of the Harrier V/STOL military aircraft for both the RAF and the US Marines. He was Assistant Managing Director of Hawker Siddeley Aviation from 1965 to 1976. Leaving industry, he became Head of Rolls-Royce Support Staff at the National Enterprise Board (1976–9).

LIDDELL, Eric Henry

(1902–45)

Athlete and missionary, known as 'The Flying Scotsman', born in Tientsin, China, of Scottish missionary parents. He was educated at Eltham College, London, and Edinburgh University, where his outstanding speed earned him seven caps in the Scotland rugby team as a wing threequarter. At the 1924 Olympics in Paris he would have been favourite to win the 100 metres had he not refused to take part on religious grounds because the heats were to be run on a Sunday (the gold medal was eventually won by Harold Abrahams). Instead, he won the bronze medal in the 200 metres, and then caused a sensation by winning the gold medal in the 400 metres (at which he was comparatively inexperienced) in a world record time of 47.6 seconds. In 1925, having completed his degree in science and a degree in divinity, he went to China to work as a Scottish Congregational Church missionary. During World War II he was interned by the Japanese at Weihsien camp and there, not long before the war ended, he died of a brain tumour. The story of his athletic triumphs was told in the film *Chariots of Fire* (1981).

LIND, James

(1716–94)

Physician, the 'father of naval hygiene', born in Edinburgh. He first served in the navy as a surgeon's mate and then, after qualifying in medicine at Edinburgh, became physician at the Haslar naval hospital at Gosport, where he encountered an alarming rate of scorbutic disease (scurvy). His work towards the cure and prevention of scurvy finally induced the Admiralty in 1795 to issue the order that the navy should be supplied with lemon juice. His *A Treatise of the Scurvy* (1753) is a medical classic. He was also interested in eliminating typhus, and stressed cleanliness in the prevention of fevers.

LINDSAY, Alexander Dunlop

(1879–1952)

Philosopher and educationist, born in Glasgow, son of the Free Kirk College principal and historian, T M Lindsay. Educated at Glasgow and Oxford, he taught at Glasgow, Manchester and Oxford, holding an army administration post in World War I. As Professor of Moral Philosophy at Glasgow (1922–4), he fostered the Workers' Educational Association. As Master of Balliol College (1924–49) and Vice Chancellor of Oxford University (1938) he promoted reforms in the teaching of science and attempted to make links between academia and society. As an associate of Mahatma Gandhi, he visited India in 1930. In the 1938 Oxford by-election he stood as anti-Appeasement candidate against the Conservative Quintin Hogg (Lord **Hailsham**). During the late 1930s he made regular pro-democracy radio broadcasts, and later served on a postwar commission on German universities. He was created Lord Lindsay of Birker in 1945. After retiring from Oxford he became founder and first Principal of Keele University (1949–52). A prodigious writer, his works include *Essentials of Democracy* (1929) and *The Modern*

Democratic State (1943). An outstanding philosopher, who was never unnecessarily formal, he is one of the 20th century's great figures.

LINDSAY, Sir David See **LYNDSAY, David**

LINDSAY, David
(1878–1945)

Novelist, born in Blackheath, London, where he spent his formative years. Much of his childhood, however, was spent in Jedburgh with his father's relations. Intent on taking up a university scholarship, he had to abandon this avenue when his father deserted the family. Instead, he became an insurance broker, a career he pursued successfully for 20 years. After World War I he left the City and moved to Cornwall to fulfil his ambitions to be a full-time novelist. Over the next two decades he published five books. *A Voyage to Arcturus* (1920) is his most notable work. Often ghettoized as science fiction, it has been more accurately described by the critic Roderick Watson as 'an allegory of spiritual and philosophical search'. It was a powerful and original work, and C S Lewis was not alone in declaring it an influence. Subsequent books, including *The Haunted Woman* (1922) and *The Violet Apple*, published posthumously in 1976, demonstrate that there was depth to Lindsay's talent, though the reading public remained largely impervious to it.

LINDSAY, Frederic
(1933 –)

Novelist and screen-writer, born in Glasgow. He was educated at Glasgow University, Jordanhill College, and Edinburgh University. He worked at the Mitchell Library, Glasgow (1950–4), then as a teacher (1961–6) and lecturer (1966–78), before becoming a full-time writer in 1979. His first book was a volume of poetry published in 1975, but he is best known as a novelist and screen writer. His first novel, *Brond* (1984), is a complex and multi-layered examination of the mysterious workings of the state intelligence machine; he later adapted this for television. *Jill Rips* (1987) also burrows into the world of political and business intrigue and corruption, through a powerful inversion of the Jack the Ripper story, in which male victims fall to a female killer in a fictionalized Glasgow. He published a third novel, *A Charm Against Drowning*, in 1988, and has also written for theatre and radio.

LINDSAY, Ian Gordon
(1906–66)

Architect. Born in Edinburgh, he was educated at the architecture school at Cambridge under Theodore Fyfe, and continued in apprenticeship with Reginald Fairlie (1883–1952) in Edinburgh. He travelled widely and became an authority on Scotland's architectural heritage. In independent practice, first with B N H Orphoot and F E Whiting, and then as Ian Lindsay and Partners, he produced functional, aesthetically excellent designs, ranging from Eventyr, Longniddry (1936) to Loch Gair power station. His scholarly restoration projects were of the highest order, for example, Canongate Church, Edinburgh (from 1946), Iona Abbey (1940s) and particularly Aldie (1950s), a pioneer example of conservative tower-house restoration. A leading conservationist, he carried out exemplary schemes at Culross, Inveraray and Cramond. He compiled lists of buildings of special interest for Lord Bute in the 1930s, the forerunners of the present statutory lists. The author of many books, such as *Cathedrals of Scotland* (1926) and *Inveraray and the Dukes of Argyll* (1973, with Mary Cosh), he disseminated his knowledge and expertise widely with considerable influence, commanding great respect. He was a particular inspiration to **Colin McWilliam, Catherine Cruft** and **David Walker**.

LINDSAY, James Bowman
(1799–1862)

Philologist and inventor, born in Carmyllie, Forfarshire. He was originally apprenticed as a weaver, but evinced such an aptitude for study that he attended St Andrews University and in 1829 became a lecturer in the Watt Institution in Dundee. He was a remarkable prophet and a pioneering experimenter in many applications of electricity: he devised an electric telegraph in 1832; in 1835 he pointed out the possibility of electric welding, and produced a continuous electric light; he proposed a transatlantic submarine telegraph in 1843; and in 1853 he demonstrated wireless telegraphy through water. He dissipated much time and energy, however, on his efforts to compile a massive *Pentecontaglossal Dictionary*, which he did not live to complete.

LINDSAY, Maurice
(1918 –)

Poet, critic and editor, born in Glasgow. Educated at Glasgow Academy, he trained as a musician at the Scottish National Academy of Music. Between 1946 and 1960 he worked as drama and music critic for the *Bulletin*, Glasgow. After working with Border Television (1961–7), first as Programme Controller and latterly as Chief Interviewer, he became (1967) Director of the Scottish Civic Trust, and in 1983 Honorary Secretary General of Europa Nostra. His poems reflect his concern for worldly affairs: they are short, more statements than meditations. His major works are his critical treatments of **Robert Burns** and his *History of Scottish Literature* (1977). His own poetry was first published in *The Advancing Day* (1940) and the best of his work is brought together in *Collected Poems* (1979).

LINDSAY, Robert Burns
(1824–1902)

Scottish-born statesman, born in Dumfriesshire. After studying at St Andrews University he emigrated to the USA (1844), becoming headmaster of a boys' academy in North Carolina, where he privately studied law. In 1849 he moved to Tuscumbia, Alabama, where he worked as a schoolteacher (1849). Called to the Alabama Bar in 1852, he was elected to the Alabama House of Representatives in 1853, and to the Alabama Senate in 1857, 1865, and 1870. He was presidential elector in 1860. He opposed secession but supported Confederacy, and served in the cavalry. Under the Reconstruction Constitution of Alabama (enacted 1867), those of foreign birth were not excluded from state office and Lindsay became Democratic candidate for governorship in 1870, beating the Republican incumbent William Smith, and thereby ending Reconstruction in Alabama. Under Lindsay the city of Birmingham, Alabama, obtained its charter and the Alabama Polytechnic Institute was founded. He refused to run for office again after serving for his statutory two years, and suffered partial paralysis shortly after leaving office; despite this he continued to practice law.

LINGARD, Joan
(1932 –)

Novelist, born in Edinburgh. She was educated in Belfast, where she was brought up from the age of two until eighteen, and at Moray House Training College in Edinburgh. She has been a prolific writer of novels for both adults and children since the publication of *Liam's Daughter* in 1963, most of which have drawn on either Belfast or Edinburgh for their setting. *The Prevailing Wind* (1964) exposes the veneer of respectability behind which the staunch Edinburgh bourgeoisie shelter from emotional engagement, a theme to which she has returned with some frequency. She began writing for children and teenagers in 1970, and has established a considerable reputation in the field. Her persistent themes are the complexities of family relationships, and the problems and fluctuations facing characters caught up in the whirlpool of social change.

LINKLATER, Eric
(1899–1974)

Novelist, born in Penarth, the son of a shipmaster. His paternal ancestors were Orcadian and he spent much of his childhood on the islands, returning there in later life. He was educated at the grammar school and university in Aberdeen, and served in World War I as a private in the Black Watch. In the mid 1920s he worked as a journalist on the *Times of India*, returning to Aberdeen as assistant to the Professor of English (1927–8). A commonwealth fellowship took him to the USA from 1928 to 1930, after which he had a varied career as a broadcaster and a prolific writer of novels, popular histories, books for children (*The Wind on the Moon* was awarded the Carnegie Medal in 1944), plays and memoirs. *Juan in America* (1931), a picaresque classic, is his most enduring novel. His other novels include *White Maa's Saga* (1929), *Poet's Pub* (1929), *Laxdale Hall* (1933), *Magnus Merriman* (1934), *Juan in China* (1937), *Private Angelo* (1946), *The House of Gair* (1953), *The Ultimate Viking* (1955) and *The Voyage of the Challenger* (1972). *The Man on My Back* (1941), *A Year of Space* (1953) and *Fanfare for a Tin Hat* (1970) are autobiographical.

LINLITHGOW, Marquis of See HOPE

LIPTON, Celia
(1923 –)

Popular singer and actress, born in Edinburgh. The daughter of the popular dance band leader Sidney Lipton, she began singing with his orchestra on radio and records at the age of 16. After making her stage début at the London Palladium (1939), in 1941 she went solo as a singing act in variety. The following year she was rated highly enough to take over Vera Lynn's role in *Apple Sauce* at the Palladium, which led to her playing the leading role of a night-club singer in the James Hadley Chase musical play, *Get A Load of This*, at the Hippodrome (1942). She played Jack in the pantomime *Jack and Jill* (1943) and the title role in *Peter Pan* (1944). Her longest run was as Prudence in a revival of the musical comedy *The Quaker Girl* (670 performances). Her films include *Calling Paul Temple* (1948). After long retirement she made a comeback as a recording star (1980).

LIPTON, Sir Thomas Johnstone
(1850–1931)

Businessman, yachtsman and philanthropist, born in a Glasgow tenement of Irish parents. When nine years old he began work as an errand-boy, and in 1865 went to the USA, where he worked successively on a tobacco plantation, in the rice-fields and in a grocer's shop. Returning to Glasgow, in 1870 he opened his first grocer's shop (in Finnieston), which was rapidly followed by many others, all selling a wide range of products at reasonable prices. With the help of advertising they prospered, making him a millionaire at the age of 30. He bought tea plantations and rubber estates, factories and packing houses, and made generous donations to various charities. A keen yachtsman, in 1899 he made his first challenge for the America's Cup with his yacht *Shamrock I*, followed at intervals by four other attempts between 1901 and 1930, all of them unsuccessful.

LISTON, Robert
(1794–1847)

Surgeon, born in Ecclesmachan Manse, Linlithgow. He studied at Edinburgh and London, and settled in Edinburgh in 1818 as lecturer in surgery and anatomy. His surgical skill soon won him a European reputation, and the 'Liston splint' is named after him. In 1835 he became Professor of Clinical Surgery at University College, London. It was he who first used a general anaesthetic in a public operation at University College Hospital on 21 December 1846. His chief works are *Elements of Surgery* (1831) and *Practical Surgery* (1837).

LITHGOW, Sir James
(1883–1952)

Shipbuilder, born in Port Glasgow. He was educated locally, at Glasgow Academy and in

Paris. Both he and his brother Henry chose to enter the family business in Port Glasgow which was already established as a notable engineering firm. They became partners in 1907 and a year later, on their father's death, assumed full joint ownership and control. There followed a remarkable collaboration between the brothers which led to the creation of the greatest industrial and financial power ever seen in Scotland. By 1920, after a period of acquisitions, they had forged a diversified and integrated empire with interests in coal, iron and steel, marine engineering and ship-owning, as well as shipbuilding. Their ship-yards on the lower Clyde remained, however, the fulcrum. Lithgow was also to play a wider political role in the industry and in relation to government. He was central to the rationalization of the shipbuilding industry in the late 1920s and 1930s and played an influential role in the steel industry. During a term as President of the Federation of British Industries (1930–2) he formed the Scottish National Economic Development Council (1931–9), acting as Chairman. Motivated by a deep sense of moral and religious duty, he was continuously involved on the national and international scene, and may be regarded as not only Scotland's greatest industrialist but also her greatest industrial statesman.

LITTLE, Kenneth Lindsey
(1908–91)

English social anthropologist, born in Liverpool. He began his career in repertory theatre but went on to study physical anthropology at Cambridge. One of the first anthropologists to take an interest in race relations in Britain in the 1940s, he subsequently conducted pioneering research on social change and urbanization in West Africa. In his later years he was particularly concerned with the position of women. He taught at Edinburgh University from 1950 and was made Professor of Social Anthropology there in 1965. The best known of his many publications are *The Negro in Britain* (1948) and *The Mende of Sierra Leone* (1967).

LITTLEJOHN, Sir Henry Duncan
(1826–1914)

Pioneer in public health, born in Edinburgh, and educated at Perth Academy and the Royal High School, Edinburgh. Trained at Edinburgh University and the Royal College of Surgeons of Edinburgh, he also studied for a year at the Sorbonne, graduating in 1854. A year later he joined the School of Medicine of the Royal College of Surgeons and for 42 years gave lectures on medical jurisprudence and public health. As part of his courses he took his students on field trips to slaughter houses and sewage farms. In 1897 he became Professor of Medical Jurisprudence in the University of Edinburgh. His work, however, was more than academic. In 1854 he had been appointed Surgeon of Police for Edinburgh and in 1862 he was made the first Medical Officer of Health for the city. In this post he set about remedying glaring defects in sanitation and health, making an epoch-making report on the sanitary conditions of the city for the Town Council; its publication made his reputation as a scientific sanitarian and led to a steady decrease in the death rate. This brought him international recognition. In 1879 he urged the Town Council to get an Act of Parliament compelling the notification of every case of infectious disease. Edinburgh was the first city to obtain such an Act. A founder of the Royal Hospital for Sick Children, he was Medical Adviser to the Crown, and was knighted in 1895.

LITTLEJOHN, James
(1921–88)

Social anthropologist, born in Hamilton, Lanarkshire. In 1941, after two years studying history at Glasgow University, he joined the Indian army. He resumed his education after the war at the London School of Economics where he completed a PhD in social anthropology under Raymond Firth. He joined Edinburgh University in 1948, becoming Professor of Social Anthropology in 1971. His field research in Scotland and West Africa resulted in the publication of *Westrigg: the Sociology of A Cheviot Parish* (1964) and a series of influential articles on the Temne people of Sierra Leone. He was also the author of a well-known textbook, *Social Stratification* (1972).

LIVINGSTONE, David
(1813–73)

Missionary and traveller, born in Low Blantyre, Lanarkshire, where from the age of 10 to 24 he worked in a cotton factory. A pamphlet by Karl Gutzlaff kindled in him a desire to become a missionary, and after studying medicine in London he was attracted to Africa by **Robert Moffat**, whose daughter Mary he married in 1844. He was ordained under the London Missionary Society in

1840, and for several years worked in Bechuanaland. Repulsed by the Boers in an effort to place native missionaries in the Transvaal, he travelled northward, discovered Lake Ngami, and determined to open trade routes east and west. The journey (1852–6) was accomplished with a handful of followers, amid great difficulties, but a vast amount of valuable information was gathered on the country, its products and native tribes. He also discovered the Victoria Falls of the Zambezi. He was welcomed home with extraordinary enthusiasm, and soon afterwards published his *Missionary Travels* (1857). In 1858 he was appointed chief of a government expedition for exploring the Zambezi, and explored the Zambezi, Shiré and Rovuma. He discovered Lakes Shirwa and Nyasa, and came to the conclusion that Lake Nyasa and its neighbourhood represented the best site for commercial and missionary operations, although he was hampered by the Portuguese authorities, and by the discovery that the slave trade was extending in the district. His wife died in 1862 and was buried at Shupanga, and the expedition was recalled in July 1863. At his own cost he then travelled 100 miles west from Lake Nyasa; then navigated a small steamer to Bombay, returning to England in 1864. His second book, *The Zambesi and its Tributaries* (1865), was designed to expose the Portuguese slave traders, and to find means of establishing a settlement for missions and commerce near the head of the Rovuma. The Royal Geographical Society asked him to return to Africa and settle a disputed question regarding the watershed of central Africa and the sources of the Nile. In March 1866 he started from Zanzibar, travelled westward, encountering considerable hardships, and in 1867–8 discovered Lakes Mweru and Bangweulu. Obliged to return for rest to Ujiji, he struck westward again as far as the river Lualaba, thinking it might be the Nile, which afterwards proved to be the Congo. On his return after severe illness to Ujiji, Livingstone was found there by Henry Morton Stanley, sent to look for him by the *New York Herald*. Determined to solve the problem, he returned to Bangweulu, but died in Old Chitambo (now in Zambia). His faithful followers embalmed his body and carried it to the coast. It was conveyed to England, and buried in Westminster Abbey.

LLOYD, Frank
(1888–1960)

Scottish-born film director, born in Glasgow. Starting out as an actor on the English stage, he emigrated to Canada in 1910 and worked with touring theatre companies for three years prior to arriving in Hollywood. Often cast as western villains, he quickly turned to direction and developed a reputation for his sensitive adaptations of such literary classics as *A Tale of Two Cities* (1917), *Les Misérables* (1918) and *Oliver Twist* (1922). A charter member of the American Academy of Motion Picture Arts and Sciences, he received Best Director Oscars for *The Divine Lady* (1929) and *Cavalcade* (1933), and was nominated again for *Mutiny on the Bounty* (1935). His career inexplicably declined thereafter as he worked at increasingly less prestigious studios on such historical dramas as *The Howards of Virginia* (1940) and his final film, *The Last Command* (1955).

LOCHHEAD, Liz

(1947 –)

Poet and dramatist, born in Motherwell, Lanarkshire. After studying at Glasgow School of Art (1965–70), she worked as an art teacher at Bishopbriggs High School, Glasgow, before becoming a full-time writer in 1979. A frank and witty poet, with a nice line in irony, she has published several collections, including *Dreaming Frankenstein and Collected Poems* (1984), and *True Confessions and New Clichés* (1985), a collection of songs, monologues and performance pieces. Her most powerful work has been written for the stage, where she has profitably re-worked the staples of Scottish history in *Mary Queen of Scots Got Her Head Chopped Off* (1987), literary biography (Mary Shelley in *Blood and Ice*, 1982), popular culture in *The Big Picture* (1988), and horror fiction in a version of Bram Stoker's *Dracula* (1985), which restored the serious intent of the original, all from a thoroughly modern perspective. She translated Molière's *Tartuffe* (1985) into demotic Glaswegian, and has written for radio and television. She wrote the text for the epic music theatre production *Jock Tamson's Bairns* in Glasgow in 1990.

LOCKHART, James, Count Lockhart-Wischeart of Lee and Carnwath

(1727–90)

Soldier of fortune, grandson of **George Lockhart**, the Scottish Tory leader in Queen Anne's reign. In about 1747 Lockhart served Shah Nadir of Persia, and later joined the

Austrian army as a private soldier. In 1752 he was commissioned in the 33rd (Waldeck) Regiment and was promoted captain in 1754. He distinguished himself at the Battle of Prague in 1757, and for his gallantry at Kunersdorf in 1759, Baron von Louden promoted him on the field to be Senior Sergeant Major of Cavalry. He further distinguished himself at the battles of Landshutt and Siegneiss and received the Military Order of Maria Theresa. In 1764 he became 4th Laird of Carnwath and in 1778 he also inherited the Lee estate, of which he was the 19th laird. He rose to be a general in the Austrian service and in 1783 was created a Count of the Holy Roman Empire. Although he resided abroad, he took a keen interest in the management of his Scottish estates. In his later years he was in the service of the Grand Duke of Tuscany.

LOCKHART, John Gibson

(1794–1854)

Biographer, novelist and critic, born in Cambusnethan, Lanarkshire, the son of a Church of Scotland minister. He spent his boyhood in Glasgow, where at 11 he went from the high school to the college. At the age of 13, with a Snell exhibition to Balliol College, he went up to Oxford. In 1813 he took a first in classics. Then, after a visit to the Continent to see Goethe in Weimar, he studied law at Edinburgh, and in 1816 was called to the Bar. While still at Oxford he had written the article 'Heraldry' for the *Edinburgh Encyclopaedia*, and translated Schlegel's *Lectures on the History of Literature*. From 1817 he turned increasingly to writing, and with **John Wilson** ('Christopher North') became the chief mainstay of *Blackwood's Magazine*. There he exhibited the cruelty with which he savaged other writers and the caustic wit that made him the terror of his Whig opponents. In 1819 he published *Peter's Letters to His Kinsfolk* in three volumes, a clever skit on Edinburgh intellectual society. In 1820 he married Sophia, eldest daughter of Sir **Walter Scott**, and wrote four novels *Valerius* (1821), *Adam Blair* (1822), *Reginald Dalton* (1823) and *Matthew Wald* (1824). *Ancient Spanish Ballads* appeared in 1823, Lives of **Burns** and Napoleon in 1828 and 1829, and the Memoirs of the Life of Scott, his masterpiece, in 1837–8 (7 vols). In 1825 he moved to London to become editor until 1853 of the *Quarterly Review*. In 1843 he also became auditor of the Duchy of Cornwall. His closing years were clouded by illness and deep depression; by his only daughter and her husband, J R Hope-Scott, becoming Catholic; and by the loss of his wife in 1837, and of his two sons in 1831 and 1853. The elder was the 'Hugh Littlejohn' of Scott's *Tales of a Grandfather*; the younger, Walter, was in the army. Like Scott, Lockhart visited Italy in search of health, and he too came back to Abbotsford to die. He is buried in Dryburgh Abbey beside Scott.

LOCKHART, Philip
(?1690–1715)

Soldier and Jacobite, younger brother of **George Lockhart of Carnwath**, the Scottish Tory leader. Having served as an officer in Lord Mark Kerr's regiment, he retired on half pay until the rebellion of 1715. Although his brother had been placed in preventative custody by the government, he succeeded in joining the Jacobite forces under the Viscount of Kenmure at Biggar. He accompanied them into England, was taken prisoner at Preston on 13 November and was court martialled for desertion. He was shot on 2 December, displaying great resolution at the end. As his brother recorded in his memoirs, he refused a blindfold, 'recommended himself to God … cocked his hat and, calling on them to do their last, he looked death and his murderers in the face, and received the shots that put an end to his days'.

LOCKHART OF CARNWATH, George
(1673–1731)

Jacobite and parliamentarian, eldest son of Sir George Lockhart, Lord President of the Court of Session, and brother of **Philip Lockhart**. He opposed the Act of Union in the Scots Parliament, but was the only anti-Unionist appointed among the commissioners to negotiate the treaty because he was nephew of Lord Wharton, the Whig leader. In 1708 he was elected to Westminster as Tory MP for the county of Edinburgh, and became leader of the Scottish Tories in the House of Commons. In 1710 he was returned for Wigtown Burghs and in 1712 he was instrumental in having acts passed for the toleration of Episcopacy and the restoration of lay patronage in the Church of Scotland. Re-elected for Wigtown in 1713, when the Scottish Tories split, he was one of those who stood aloof from Bolingbroke, the English Tory leader. He did not join in the 1715 rising

(in which his brother, **Philip Lockhart**, was executed) because the government placed him in preventative custody. From 1718 to 1727 he was confidential adviser to the exiled titular James VIII (**James Francis Edward Stuart**) and in 1722 he formed a committee to promote the Stuart interest. His activities were discovered in 1727 and he fled abroad, but was coldly received at the Stuart court. The following year he negotiated a pardon and went to London where he was dismayed to discover that the condition attached to this was that he should present himself before George II. However, as he wrote, 'I was under a necessity of bowing my knee to Baal now that I was in the house of Rim'. A quarrelsome man, he was killed in a duel.

LOGAN, George
(1866–1939)

Furniture designer, born in Beith, Ayrshire, where he served a traditional cabinetmaker's apprenticeship. Employed by Wyllie and Lochhead, the established firm of Glasgow cabinetmakers, until 1937, he worked with **Ernest Archibald Taylor** and **John Ednie** and successfully established a house-style that won critical acclaim at home and abroad. He exhibited at the International Exhibition, Turin, and was greatly influenced by the work of **Jessie King**, **Herbert Macnair** and **Charles Rennie Mackintosh**. He exhibited his watercolours regularly at the Royal Glasgow Institute.

LOGAN, Jimmy, originally James Short
(1928 –)

Entertainer, born in Glasgow. The son of music-hall act Short and Dalziel, he later joined them and his brothers and sisters to form The Logan Family. An all-round trouper, comic, dancer and singer, he made his pantomime début as the cat in *Dick Whittington* (1944) and has rarely missed a Christmas season since. He made his film début in *Floodtide* (1949) and was soon established as a stalwart of the Scottish showbusiness scene with panto in the winter and the *Five Past Eight Show* at the Alhambra, Glasgow, in the summer. Active in radio and television, he bought and ran the Metropole Theatre (1964–72). He subsequently appeared in the film *Carry On Abroad* (1972), made his London stage début in *The Mating Game*

(1973) and created the show *Lauder* (1976) in honour of **Harry Lauder**, one of his idols. Recently he has concentrated more on straight drama, appearing all over Britain in such productions as *The Entertainer* (1984), *Brighton Beach Memoirs* (1989) and *The Comedians* (1991).

LOGAN, John

(1748–88)

Poet and clergyman, born in Soutra, Midlothian. He was educated at Musselburgh Grammar School and Edinburgh University, and was appointed minister of South Leith in 1773. He wrote a successful play, *Runnemede*, in 1784, and moved to London. He is mainly remembered for his plagiarism of several poems of his friend Michael Bruce, including 'Ode to the Cuckoo', which he included in his own volume of poetry (1781).

LOGAN, Owen

(1963 –)

Photographer, born in Edinburgh to a Scottish father and Italian mother. Self-taught in photography, he began working independently in 1979. He is best known for his sensitive and beautiful photographic essays dealing with cultural ambiguities and conflicts, especially his work on the Sikh community in Scotland (begun 1982) and on Morocco (1983–8); the latter body of work is collected in the accompanying publication to the exhibition of the same title: *Al Maghrib: Photographs from Morocco* (1989). In 1990–1 he lived in Naples, where he began a major project on the people of the Mezzogiorno, in Italy and Scotland.

LOKERT, George

(1485–1547)

Logician and theologian, brought up in Ayr. In 1500 he went to Paris, taking his MA there in 1505. Prior of the College of the Sorbonne in 1519 he took his doctorate in 1520. He returned to Scotland as Provost of the Collegiate Church of Crichton, Lothian, in 1521. By the time of his appointment as Rector of St Andrews University in 1522 he had published numerous treatises on logic. He worked with **John Mair** to bring the St Andrews University system more into line with Paris. Back in Paris by 1526 he became overseer of the Scots College there. Escaping the controversies which anticipated the Reformation, he was back in Scotland by 1533. He was Dean of Glasgow from 1534.

LONGAIR, Malcolm Sim

(1941 –)

Astronomer, born in Dundee. Graduating in electronic physics from Queen's College, Dundee, he joined the Cambridge Radio Astronomy Group of Sir Martin Ryle, where his work on the origin and evolution of radio sources drew him into the fields of astrophysical cosmology and high energy physics. Having held various fellowships and visiting professorships in the USA and the USSR, from 1980 to 1990 he was Astronomer Royal for Scotland and Professor of Astronomy at Edinburgh University. During this period he directed at the Royal Observatory Edinburgh a wide range of projects in infra-red, millimetre wave and optical astronomy. His works include academic texts such as *High Energy Astrophysics* (1981), and semipopular books and lectures, such as his 1990 Royal Institution Christmas Lectures, *The Origins of our Universe* (1990). He became Jacksonian Professor of Natural Philosophy at Cambridge in 1991.

LONGMUIR, Alan

(1953 –) and **Derek** (1955 –)

Bass guitarist and pop drummer respectively, born in Edinburgh. In the late 1960s they formed the pop band The Saxons, later renaming it The Bay City Rollers. Under the management of dance-band leader Tam Paton — who completely overhauled the group's image — the band enjoyed a brief spell as Britain's most successful teenage idols. They had nine UK top-ten hits between 1974 and 1976, including 'Remember (Sha La La)', 'Bye Bye Baby' and 'Give A Little Love'. The band went through several changes of line-up, but during its most successful period it consisted of the Longmuirs, Stuart Wood (1957 –), Eric Faulkner (1955 –) and Les McKeown (1955 –), all from Edinburgh. The band sacked Paton in 1979, but despite several comeback attempts they never recaptured their earlier success.

LOREBURN, Robert Threshie Reid, 1st Earl of

(1846–1923)

Lawyer, born in Corfu. He studied at Balliol College, Oxford, was called to the English Bar in 1871, and became MP in 1880, Solicitor-General and then Attorney-General in 1894, Lord Chancellor and a baron in

1905, and in 1911 an earl. He resigned in 1912. As Lord Chancellor he delivered many important judgements.

LORIMER, James
(1818–90)

Jurist, born in Aberdalgie, Perthshire. An eminent authority on international law, he was Professor of Public Law at Edinburgh from 1862. In *The Institutes of Law* (1872) he combated positivism and utilitarianism. He wrote also on international law, notably *The Institutes of the Law of Nations* (1883–4).

LORIMER, John Henry
(1856–1936)

Painter, born in Edinburgh, brother of Sir **Robert Lorimer**. He trained at the Royal Scottish Academy under **William McTaggart** and **George Chalmers**. He continued his studies by repeatedly visiting the continent and in 1884 he entered the Paris studio of Carolus Duran. Some of his finest works are early flower pieces, but he is best known for genre painting, which follows very closely in the tradition of **David Wilkie**. Perhaps best remembered is his *Ordination of Elders in a Scottish Kirk*.

LORIMER, Sir Robert Stodart
(1864–1929)

Architect, born in Edinburgh, son of **James Lorimer**. Educated at The Edinburgh Academy and Edinburgh University, he left without a degree and was articled to an architect's office in Edinburgh (Wardrop, Anderson and Browne), receiving further experience subsequently in the London offices of George Frederic Bodley (1827–1907) and Watson and Dunn. He began independent practice in 1892 in Edinburgh, working on Scottish country houses such as Hill of Tarvit in Fife (1904), and creating a distinctive Scottish form of the Arts and Crafts tradition of his English contemporary Edwin Lutyens. He built or totally remodelled some 50 country houses in Britain, like Rowallan in Ayrshire (1902), Ardkinglas in Argyll (1906), and the classical Marchmont in Berwickshire (1914). His most notable public works were the Thistle Chapel in St Giles, Edinburgh (1909–11), and the Scottish National War Memorial in Edinburgh Castle (1923–8). He also restored many castles, mansions and churches, including Balmanno House in Perthshire, Dunrobin Castle, Sutherland, Paisley Abbey and Dunblane Cathedral. He took an interest in historic gardens and laid out some of his own, for example at Earlshall, Fife (1892). His elder brother was the painter **John Henry Lorimer**.

LORIMER, William Laughton
(1885–1967)

Classicist, born in Strathmartine, near Dundee, into a long tradition of Free Church of Scotland ministers. Educated at Dundee High School, **Fettes** College, Edinburgh and Trinity College, Oxford, he began studying spoken Scots privately at the age of nine. Assistant Lecturer and subsequently Lecturer in Greek (1910–29), Reader in Humanity (1929–53) and Professor of Greek (1953–5) at University College Dundee, St Andrews University, he was Chairman of the Executive Council and a member of the editorial committee of the *Scottish National Dictionary*. His *magnum opus* was his translation of the New Testament from Greek into Scots, necessarily recreating much of Scots prose in the process. His work dominated the last years of his teaching life and all of his retirement, involving the study of 180 translations in more than 20 languages, as well as the study of all known linguistic sources, and all significant commentaries. His manuscripts were revised after his death by his son, R L C Lorimer, and published in 1983 and 1985. Lorimer's achievement is as great in devotion as in language, and has an engaging immediacy in character and content.

LOTHIAN, Henry Schomberg Kerr, 9th Marquess of
(1833–1900)

Politician, born in Newbattle, Midlothian. Educated at Eton and Oxford University, he succeeded to the title in 1870, and pursued a diplomatic-service career until he became a peer. As Scottish Secretary in the Unionist government (1886–92) he introduced an important act which led to the modernization of the Scottish universities, notably by admitting women and introducing Honours degrees. He also legislated for the reform of local government structure, introducing county councils and laying a framework that lasted over 80 years. In addition, he also dealt with many economic and social problems in the Highlands and Islands.

LOUDON, John Claudius
(1783–1843)

Horticultural writer, dendrologist and designer, born in Cambuslang, Lanarkshire. He worked in England and travelled in Europe, and founded and edited *The Gardener's Magazine* (1826–43). He compiled an *Encyclopaedia of Gardening* (1822), in which he illustrated a wrought-iron sash bar he had invented in 1816, which could be bent in any direction but still maintained its strength. It was this which paved the way for spectacular edifices such as the Palm House in Kew Gardens and the Crystal Palace. In Porchester Terrace, London, he designed the prototype semi-detached house. He founded and edited the *Architectural Magazine* (1834), and published an influential *Encyclopaedia of Cottage, Farm and Villa Architecture and Furniture* (1834). His major work was *Arboretum et Fruticetum Britannicum* (8 vols, 1838), devoted to trees and shrubs.

LOUGHBOROUGH, Alexander Wedderburn, 1st Baron, later (1801) 1st Earl of Rosslyn
(1733–1805)

Scottish-born judge, born in Edinburgh, son of a Scottish judge (Lord Chesterhall). In 1757 he abruptly left the Scottish Bar for the English one. He entered Parliament in 1762, and became Chief Justice of the Common Pleas (1780) and Lord Chancellor (1793–1801).

LOUGHRAN, James
(1931 –)

Orchestral conductor, born in Glasgow. He studied music in Glasgow, Bonn, Amsterdam and Milan. After winning first prize in the Philharmonia Orchestra's Conducting Competition (1961), he was successively Associate Conductor of Bournemouth Symphony Orchestra (1962–5), Principal Conductor of the BBC Scottish Symphony Orchestra (until 1971), then of the Hallé Orchestra (until 1983) and has subsequently become the Hallé's conductor laureate. He has also directed the English Opera Group (1966) and Bamberg Symphony Orchestra (1979–83). He has appeared as guest conductor with most of the principal orchestras of Europe, America, Australia and Japan, and has made many recordings, including the complete symphonies of Beethoven and Brahms.

LOVAT, Simon Christopher Joseph Fraser, 15th Baron Lovat
(1911 –)

Soldier, commando leader, and 24th Chief of the Clan Fraser, born at Beaufort Castle in Inverness-shire and educated at Ampleforth College, Yorkshire, and Oxford. Between 1932 and 1937 he served with the Scots Guards, but on the outbreak of war he returned to the army as a captain in the Lovat Scouts, the regiment founded by his father for service in the Boer War. He will be best remembered as one of the founders of the commando forces and for his skill and determination in leading them during the early raids on Lofoten (1941) and Dieppe (1943). For his gallantry he received several decorations, including the MC, DSO and Croix de Guerre, and he was promoted to brigadier in 1943. The commando forces played a key role in the D-Day landings, but Lovat was badly wounded during the break-out battle in Normandy. Forced to retire from the army, he was appointed Under-Secretary of State for Foreign Affairs in the House of Lords but resigned in 1945. After the war he concentrated on the management of his Highland estates and was a member of Inverness-shire County Council for 42 years. His wartime memoirs were published in 1978 under the title *March Past*.

LOVAT, Simon Fraser, Lord
(c.1667–1747)

Clan chief, born in Tomich in Ross-shire. He graduated from Aberdeen in 1695. In 1696 his father, on the death of his great-nephew, Lord Lovat, assumed that title, and next year Simon, after failing to abduct the late lord's daughter and heiress, a nine-year-old child, forcibly married her mother, a lady of the Atholl familya crime for which he was found guilty of high treason and outlawed. In 1699 he succeeded his father as twelfth Lord Lovat, in 1702 he fled to France, but a year later returned to Scotland as a Jacobite agent and became involved in the abortive 'Queensberry plot', which forced him once again to escape to France. In 1715 he took the government side; his clan left the Jacobite rebels and he obtained a full pardon, with possession of the Lovat title and estates. In the 1745 Jacobite Rising Lovat sent his son and clan to fight for the Young Pretender (**Charles Edward Stuart**) while he protested his loyalty to the government. After Culloden he fled, but was captured and taken to London for trial. He defended himself with ability and dignity, and he met death (by beheading) with the same combination of gallantry and cynicism he had shown throughout his life.

LULU, real name Marie McDonald Mclaughlin Lawrie
(1948 –)

Pop singer and entertainer, born in Glasgow. With her band The Luvvers she had the first Scottish hit of the Beat era with a cover of the Isley Brothers' 'Shout' in 1964. Opting for a solo career in 1966, she had her greatest American success the following year with the title song from the film *To Sir With Love*, in which she had also acted. During the 1970s she became better known as an entertainer and TV personality than as a pop singer, and she had her own BBC series *It's Lulu*. She was married to Maurice Gibb of The Bee Gees from 1969 to 1973. Her albums have included *New Routes* (1969) and *Lulu* (1981). 'Shout' was re-released and brought fresh chart success in 1986.

LUMSDEN, Ernest Stephen
(1883–1948)

English artist printmaker, born in Edmonton, London. He studied art under Morley Fletcher at Reading School of Art, and travelled extensively throughout his career, joining the staff at Edinburgh College of Art in 1908, thus beginning his life-long association with Scotland. He married fellow artist **Mabel Royds** in 1914 and together they worked abroad, mainly in India and Spain. An extremely accomplished artist, his output consisted mainly of etchings and a number of landscapes and portraits. He was elected a member of the Royal Society of Painters, Etchers and Engravers in 1914 and RSA in 1933. In 1925 he published *The Art of Etching*, which remains a standard international work. His work is held in many public collections throughout the world.

LYALL, Chick (Charles)
(1959 –)

Jazz composer and musician, playing piano and synthesizers, born in Glasgow. He began to specialize in electronic music while studying piano and composition at Glasgow University. His early interest was in *avant-garde*

rock music, but he developed a style of electro-acoustic jazz performance, with improvisation set against pre-recorded tapes. In 1987 he was commissioned by the Scottish National Orchestra to write and perform a suite for the *Musica Nova Festival*. This was later recorded by the BBC. In 1989 he was given a Scottish Arts Council award to allow him to continue his piano studies under the Greek teacher George Hadjinikos. He has appeared at many British jazz festivals, working with more conventional modern groups as well as developing his electro-acoustic performances.

LYELL, Sir Charles
(1797–1875)

Geologist, born in Kinnordy, Forfarshire, the eldest son of the mycologist and Dante student, Charles Lyell (1767–1849). Educated at Ringwood, Salisbury and Midhurst, he studied law at Exeter College, Oxford, but discovered a taste for geology. His *Principles of Geology* (1830–3) exercised a strong influence on contemporary scientific thought. It denied the necessity of stupendous convulsions, and taught that the greatest geological changes might have been produced by forces still at work. *The Elements of Geology* (1838) was a supplement. *The Geological Evidences of the Antiquity of Man* (1863) startled the public by its unbiased attitude towards Charles Darwin. He also published *Travels in North America* (1845) and *A Second Visit to the United States* (1849). In 1832–3 he was Professor of Geology at King's College, London.

LYLE, Sandy (Alexander Walter Barr)
(1958 –)

Golfer, born in Shrewsbury of Scottish parents. He started his golfing career by representing England at Boys, Youth and full international levels, but has since represented Scotland. In 1980 and 1982 he was a narrowly beaten finalist in the World Match-Play Championship. His major championship successes have been the European Open in 1979, the French Open in 1981, the British Open in 1985 and the US Masters Championship in 1988. An extremely long hitter with an admirably phlegmatic temperament, together with Nick Faldo he was largely responsible for the revival of British professional golf at world level.

LYNCH, Benny
(1913–46)

Boxer, born in Glasgow. In 1935 he became the first Scot to hold a world title, taking the National Boxing Association/International Boxing Union version of the world flyweight title. From 1937 to 1938 he was undisputed world champion, but lax training routines led to weight problems and he forfeited the title in 1938 when he failed to make the weight for a title bout against Jacky Jurich of the USA. During his career he won 82 out of 110 bouts.

LYNDSAY, or LINDSAY, Sir David of the Mount
(c.1486–1555)

Poet, born probably at the Mount near Cupar, Fife, or at Garmylton (now Garleton), near Haddington, East Lothian. In 1512 he was appointed 'usher' of the newborn prince who became **James V**. In 1522 or earlier he married Janet Douglas, the king's seamstress. In 1524 (probably), during the regency of the Douglases, he lost or changed his place, but was restored to favour in 1529 when James V became king in his own right. In 1538 he appears to have been Lyon King-of-Arms. He went on embassies to the Netherlands, France, England and Denmark, and he (or another David Lyndsay) represented Cupar in the parliaments of 1540–6. For two centuries he was the poet of the Scottish people. His poems, often coarse, are full of humour, good sense and knowledge of the world, and were said to have done more for the Reformation in Scotland than all the sermons of **Knox**. The earliest and most poetic of his writings is the allegorical *The Dreme* (1528), followed by *The Complaynt of the King* (1529) and *The Testament and Complaynt of Our Soverane Lordis Papyngo* (1530). He wrote a satire on court life in *Ane Publict Confession of the Kingis Auld Hound Callit Bagsche* (1536). His most remarkable work was *Ane Satyre of the Thrie Estaitis*, a dramatic work first performed at Linlithgow in 1540, and revived with great success at the Edinburgh Festival; the most amusing was *The Historie of Squyer Meldrum*.

LYNEDOCH, Thomas Graham, 1st Baron
(1748–1843)

Soldier, son of the laird of Balgowan in Perthshire. In 1794 he raised the 90th Regiment of foot (the Perthshire Regiment), and served with it in Minorca (1798). He besieged Valetta in 1800. In the Peninsular War (1808–14) he was aide-de-camp to Sir **John Moore** at La Coruña (1809) and fought at Walcheren (1809), defeated the French at Barrosa (1811), fought at Ciudad Rodrigo (1812), Badajoz and Salamanca, commanded the left wing at Vitoria (1813), and captured Tolosa and San Sebastián. In Holland he won victory at Merxem, but failed to storm Bergen-op-Zoom (1814). He was created Baron Lynedoch of Balgowan (1814), and founded the Senior United Service Club (1817).

LYTE, Henry Francis
(1793–1847)

Hymnwriter, born in Ednam, near Kelso, Roxburghshire. After entering Trinity College, Dublin, he took orders in 1815, and was for 25 years incumbent of Lower Brixham. His *Poems, Chiefly Religious* (1833; reprinted as *Miscellaneous Poems*, 1868), are not as well known as his hymns, among which the most memorable are 'Abide with me' and 'Pleasant are thy courts'.

M

McADAM, John Loudon
(1756–1836)

Inventor and engineer, born in Ayr. He went to New York in 1770, where he made a fortune in his uncle's counting-house. On his return to Scotland in 1783 he bought the estate of Sauchrie, Ayrshire, and started experimenting with a revolutionary method of road construction. In 1816 he was appointed surveyor to the Bristol Turnpike Trust, and re-made the roads there with crushed stone bound with gravel, which was raised to improve drainage — the 'macadamized' system. His advice was sought from all directions. Eventually impoverished by his work, he petitioned Parliament in 1820, and in 1825 was voted £2000. In 1827 he was made Surveyor-General of metropolitan roads.

McALLISTER, Anne Hunter
(1892–1983)

Pioneer in speech training and therapy, born in Biggar, Lanarkshire. She taught in city schools in Glasgow before, in 1919, joining the staff of the college which later became Jordanhill College of Education. There, for 30 years, she blazed the trail for speech training in the education of teachers — personally training the teachers, writing their text-books, broadcasting, and conducting research (which won her a DSc from Glasgow University). Concurrently she studied for the new degree of EdB at Glasgow University and, from 1926, assisted in **William Boyd**'s educational clinic. She established the Glasgow School of Speech Therapy in 1935 and was a founder of the College of Speech Therapists, the British headquarters of the profession she had helped to create.

McALPINE, Sir Robert
(1847–1934)

Building contractor, born in Newarthill, Lanarkshire. At the age of 10 he left school to work in the pits, after which he was apprenticed as a bricklayer. Having set up as a jobbing builder in 1868 he built up business in the Hamilton area before winning contracts nationally. From a position of bankruptcy in 1877 he rebuilt his operations, winning the crucial contact to build the Singer's factory at Kilbowie, Dunbartonshire. This laid the basis for a rapid expansion as a contractor in which he made use of new building techniques, especially concrete and labour saving machinery. In the postwar period he won large contracts from local authorities, especially for roads, and it was his company that built Wembley Stadium. He was created a baronet in 1918.

MacANDREW, Hector
(1903–80)

Fiddler, born in Fyvie, Aberdeenshire, and a gardener by profession. Coming from a musical family, he learned the bagpipes as a child, but soon took up the fiddle. Formal training in light classical music gave him a good technical grounding, but unlike many of his contemporaries, he refused to play within the strict confines of Scottish dance bands, with the result that he evolved a highly idiosyncratic and appealing way of interpreting airs, strathspeys and reels. In 1972 he was seen on television coaching Sir Yehudi Menuhin in the art of Scots fiddling, but generally he did not receive the public exposure his playing deserved.

MACAN T-SAOIR, Donnachadh Ban See McINTYRE, Duncan Ban

MacAOIDH, Rob Donn See MACKAY, Robert

MacARTHUR, Mary Reid
(1880–1921)

Trade unionist, born in Glasgow. She was educated at Glasgow High School before working in her father's draper's shop. Joining the Shop Assistants' Union (1901), she later became President of the Scottish National District and, moving to London, Secretary of the Women's Trade Union League (1903). Maintaining an 'exuberant and contagious joy of life', she organized strikes and fought for better conditions and minimum wages. Her most famous campaigns concerned sweated labour (1906), outworkers (1907) and chain-makers (1910). She was delegate to the International Congress of Women in Berlin and the USA (1904, 1908), founded the National Federation of Women Workers (1906), the journal *Woman Worker* (1907), and was on the National Council of the Independent Labour Party (1909–12). During World War I she campaigned for women workers in munitions factories, becoming well known throughout Britain and the USA, and an unlikely friend of Queen Mary.

McARTHUR, Tom (Thomas Burns)
(1938 –)

Teacher, writer, linguist and lexicographer, born in Glasgow. A graduate in English Language and Literature of Glasgow University, he has carried out postgraduate studies in linguistics and lexicography at Edinburgh University. After serving as an officer-instructor in the British army and as a schoolteacher in England and in India, he taught English as a Foreign Language at Edinburgh University (1972–9) and was Associate Professor of English as a Second Language at the University of Quebec at Trois-Rivières from 1979 to 1983. He is currently editor of the journal *English Today*. Among his publications are the *Collins Dictionary of English Phrasal Verbs* (with Beryl Atkins, 1974), *Languages of Scotland* (co-editor with A J Aitken; 1979), the *Longman Lexicon of Contemporary English* (1981), *A Foundation Course for Language Teachers* (1983), *Worlds of Reference* (1986) and *The Oxford Companion to English Language* (1992). He has also written on Indian religious philosophy and related matters, including *Yoga and the Bhagavad-Gita* and *Understanding Yoga* (1986), and *Unitive Thinking* (1988), and was Chairman of the Scottish Yoga Association (1977–9).

McBEATH, Jimmy
(1894–1972)

Traditional singer, born in Portsoy, Banff-shire. He became a farm worker at the age of 13, but after service in World War I with the Gordon Highlanders he earned his living by doing odd jobs and singing for coins in streets, pubs and at markets in the north-east of Scotland. His talent was recognized by **Hamish Henderson** at Elgin in 1951, and McBeath played an important role in introducing old bothy ballads and other songs to the early devotees of the folk-music revival. A singer with a rich, gravelly voice and a wide-ranging, entertaining repertoire, he recorded two solo albums, *Wild Rover No More* (1973) and *Bound to be a Row* (1978).

MACBETH
(c.1005–1057)

King of Scotland from 1040, Mormaer of Moray and a grandson of **Malcolm II**. He married Gruoch, granddaughter of Kenneth II. In 1040 he defeated and killed King Duncan and drove Duncan's sons, Malcolm and Donald Bán, into exile. He seems to have represented a Celtic reaction against English influence and he ruled for over a decade. **Malcolm III, Canmore**, Duncan's son, ultimately defeated and killed him at Lumphanan, on 15 August 1057. Shakespeare got his story from Holinshed, who drew on **Boece**.

MACBETH, Ann
(1875–1948)

English embroideress, born in Little Bolton. She studied at Glasgow School of Art (1897–1900) and was a member of its staff from 1901 to 1920, latterly as Head of the Embroidery Department. She was influential in advocating new methods of teaching embroidery through lecturing, teaching and through several books, including an instruction manual called *Educational Needlecraft* (1911). She executed a number of ecclesiastical commissions and her embroidered panels decorate many Glasgow interiors. A member of the famous 'Glasgow School', she received the Lauder Award in 1930.

McBEY, James
(1883–1959)

Artist and etcher, born in Newburgh, Aberdeenshire. Entirely self-taught, he became particularly well known as a master of British etching. After working in a bank he left to become an artist, producing his first etching in 1902. He travelled extensively in the British Isles, Spain, Holland, North Africa, Central and North America and as a war artist in France and with the Australian Camel Patrol in Egypt and Palestine during World War I. His etched work has a spontaneity and strength almost unequalled in the history of British printmaking.

MacBRAYNE, David
(1818–1907)

Shipowner, born in Glasgow; he was related through his mother to the founders of the shipping firms of J & G Burns and D & A Hutcheson. By the age of 30 he was a partner in the Hutchesons' firm and worked with them for the next 30 years to develop the shipping routes of the Highlands and Islands in the Clyde estuary and the west of Scotland. In 1876 and 1878 the two Hutcheson brothers retired and the firm became David Mac-Brayne & Company which, by the end of the 1880s, ran their ferry and excursion services with a fleet of 28 vessels. His two sons took over the firm in 1905, but in 1928 the first of a series of financial rescues became necessary, leading eventually in 1973 to amalgamation with the Caledonian Steam Packet Company as Caledonian MacBrayne, part of the Scottish Transport Group.

MacBRYDE, Robert
(1913–66)

Artist, born in Maybole, Ayrshire. He worked in industry for five years before studying at the Glasgow School of Art, and later worked closely with **Robert Colquhoun**, painting brilliantly-coloured Cubist lifes and, later, brooding Expressionist figures.

MacCAIG, Norman Alexander
(1910 –)

Poet, born in Edinburgh, the son of a chemist. His mother was born in Scalpay, Harris, and, as he wrote in 'Return to Scalpay', 'Half my thought and half my blood is Scalpay'. A poet of town and country, his formative years were spent in Edinburgh; he was educated at the Royal High School and the university, where he read classics. He became a primary school teacher, for which his friend **Hugh MacDiarmid** pronounced he had 'a real vocation' and for nearly 40 years it engaged

his daylight hours. His first two collections *Far Cry* (1943) and *The Inward Eye* (1946) tarred him as a member of the New Apocalypse school and the label stuck 'long after it was contravening the Trades Description Act'. He disowned these poems when the *Collected Poems* were published in 1985. *Riding Lights* (1955) is the first evidence of the real MacCaig, lucid, direct and richly descriptive. His distinctive voice, witty and philosophical, is heard in numerous subsequent collections including *The Sinai Sort* (1957), *A Round of Applause* (1962), *Measures* (1965), *A Man In My Position* (1969), *The White Bird* (1973), *The Equal Skies* (1980), *A World of Difference* (1963), *Voice-Over* (1988) and *Collected Poems* (new ed, 1990). He was the first fellow in creative writing at Edinburgh University (1967–9), and on retiring from schoolteaching he lectured in English studies at Stirling University (1970–9). The finest Scottish poet of his generation writing in English, he was awarded the Queen's Gold Medal for Poetry in 1986.

McCALLUM, David
(1933 –)

Actor, born in Glasgow. The son of a noted musical family, he expressed an interest in acting from an early age and studied at the Royal Academy of Dramatic Art (1949–51) before completing his National Service as an officer of the British Army in Ghana. A slight, perennially youthful figure, he made his film début in *The Secret Place* (1957). Later resident in America, he was seen in films like *The Great Escape* (1963) and *The Greatest Story Ever Told* (1965), but achieved his greatest renown as ice-cool agent Illyia Kuryakin in the television series *The Man from U.N.C.L.E.* (1964–7), receiving 32 000 fan letters a month at the height of its popularity. Later attempts to establish him as a film star were unsuccessful, but he has remained in demand as a leading man for television in numerous series, including *Colditz* (1972–3), *The Invisible Man* (1975), and *Trainer* (1991 –). He has continued to appear in minor films and reprised the role of Kuryakin in the television film *The Return of the Man from U.N.C.L.E.* (1983). Recently he appeared in London's West End in the musical *The Hunting of the Snark* (1991).

McCALLUM, Sir Donald Murdo
(1922 –)

Electrical engineer. Born and educated in Edinburgh, he served in the Admiralty Signal Establishment from 1942 to 1946. He joined Ferranti in Edinburgh in 1947, led the design team that developed the first of Ferranti's successful airborne radar systems, and became general manager of the Scottish group in 1968. He was awarded the British Gold Medal of the Royal Aeronautical Society in 1985. A keen supporter of the individuality of the Scottish educational system, he chaired the Scottish Tertiary Education Advisory Council which reported in 1985. He was awarded the CBE in 1976, and is currently Chairman of the Scottish Council (Development and Industry).

McCANCE, Sir Andrew
(1889–1983)

Metallurgist, born in Cadder, near Glasgow. He was educated at Morrison's Academy, Crieff, Allan Glen's School, Glasgow and at the Royal School of Mines in London. Later, in 1916, he gained a BSc from London University. At **William Beardmore**'s Parkhead Forge he became an assistant manager, leaving in 1918 to set up as a manufacturer of alloy and special steels in the Clyde Alloy Steel Company. When Colville's Ltd, the steel firm, was formed he took a place on the board and was instrumental, as General Manager and Director, in implementing the rationalization which led to the formation of the Colville Group in 1936. After receiving a knighthood in 1947 his postwar plan was accepted, which led to the creation of a new iron and steel complex at Ravenscraig. He retired in 1965, having established a reputation as a metallurgist of distinction and having forged a steel-making complex from diverse parts. While Chairman of the Royal Technical College he supervised the establishment of the Royal College of Science and Technology in Glasgow. In 1964 this became Strathclyde University, where the McCance Building is named after him.

McCANCE, William
(1894–1970)

Artist, born in Cambuslang, Lanarkshire. In 1916, after training at Glasgow School of Art, he completed teacher training but, as a conscientious objector, was unable to obtain a teaching post and eventually, in 1919, moved to London where he stayed until 1930. There he developed a modernist style, especially in printmaking, based on a machine aesthetic of bold geometric forms, and he was associated with members of the Vorticist movement, such as Percy Wyndham Lewis and David Bomberg. An art critic as well as an artist, he expressed in his writings a nationalist view of culture which he shared with his close friend **Hugh MacDiarmid**.

MacCARTNEY, Sir Samuel Halliday
(1833–1906)

Official in the Chinese Service, born near Castle Douglas, Dumfriesshire. Educated at Edinburgh University, he served with the army medical staff in the Crimea in 1855. Graduating in 1858, he joined the 99th Regiment as 3rd Assistant Surgeon. He served in India (1859) and then China, where he took part in the advance on Peking. Joining the Chinese Service in 1863, he became friendly with the Chinese leader Li Hung Chang. He acted as a mediator between the Chinese and the British commander General Gordon, and commanded troops on behalf of the Chinese. After establishing an arsenal at Nanking in 1865, he commanded it for 10 years. He was appointed Secretary to the new Chinese Embassy in London in 1877, and although thereafter he never returned to China, he did much to organize diplomatic relations in Europe. He served in the Chinese legation until 1906, and was honoured by both the Chinese and British governments.

McCLELLAND, William
(1889–1968)

Educationist, born in Newton-Stewart, Wigtownshire and educated at Edinburgh University. From 1921 he held various lecturing posts at Edinburgh and Aberdeen before becoming concurrently Professor of Education at St Andrews and Director of Studies at Dundee Training College in 1925. He spent 1930–1 in New York as Visiting Professor of Education at Columbia University, later using this experience when he held a series of highly successful summer schools for teachers, run on American lines. Deeply interested in improving methods of teacher training, he was Executive Officer for the National Committee for Training Teachers in Scotland (1941–59) and Chairman of the Advisory Council on Education in Scotland (SACE) (1947–51), being generally credited with the 1946 SACE Report on Training of Teachers, which exercised a decisive influence within the training system. A specialist on statistical methods and educational psychology, his works include *Selection for Secondary*

Education (1942), a pioneering study of the 11-plus examination which became the basis for allocating pupils to courses in secondary education.

McCLEOD James Walter

(1887–1978)

Bacteriologist, born in Dumbarton, and received his schooling in Scotland and Switzerland. After graduating in medicine from Glasgow University (1908) he joined the Department of Pathology there, working on streptococcal haemolysins. He became assistant lecturer in pathology at the Charing Cross Hospital Medical School in 1912 and in 1914 joined the RAMC. He was mentioned four times in despatches. During this period he published papers on trench fever, trench nephritis and bacillary dysentery. After demobilization he joined the Department of Pathology at the School of Medicine in Leeds, where he was lecturer in bacteriology. His interest in Gram-positive anaerobic bacilli led to studies on bacterial respiration and the use of the oxidase reaction for the isolation of gonococcus strains in mixed cultures from clinical gonorrhoea resulted, some time later, in McLeod receiving international recognition. He later described three bio-types of diphtheria bacilli. Professor of Bacteriology from 1922 to 1952, he was Dean of the Faculty of Medicine (1948–52) and after retirement returned to Edinburgh, where he continued his researches.

MacCODRUM, Ian (John)

(1693–1779)

Gaelic poet, born in North Uist, the son of a tacksman to the **Macdonald**s. Living all his life on North Uist, he was known for his innovative and entertaining songs. He was a devout Jacobite and clansman and was appointed bard to James Macdonald in 1763. One of his works, *Oran do na fogarraich* ('Song to the Fugitives'), reflects unhappiness with the high rents imposed on the people of North Uist, which drove the Macdonalds and their tacksmen to emigrate. Most of his songs and poems are humorous observations of his fellow men, and the style of his work reflects a movement away from the bardic tradition embodied by **Niall MacMhuirrich**.

McCOIST, Ally (Alistair)

(1962 –)

Footballer, born in Bellshill, Lanarkshire. Blessed with the predatory instinct of all successful strikers, he made his début for St Johnstone at the age of 16, and soon attracted the attention of bigger clubs, among them Rangers, before signing for Sunderland in 1981. After two relatively unsuccessful seasons in the south, he joined Rangers in 1983, going on to play a significant role in the club's revival under **Graeme Souness**, becoming Ibrox's top postwar league goal-scorer. First capped for Scotland in April 1986, he has since been a regular internationalist. An ebullient, articulate character in a largely taciturn world, he is a particular favourite among younger supporters.

McCOLGAN, Liz (Elizabeth)

(1964 –)

Middle- and long-distance runner, born in Dundee. Committed to athletics from an early age, she studied at the University of Alabama before returning to Scotland, the scene of her first major success, winning the 10 000 m gold medal in the 1986 Commonwealth Games, held in Edinburgh. She won the silver medal at the Seoul Olympics of 1988, then retained her Commonwealth title in Auckland in 1990, as well as winning a bronze in the 3000 m behind her great rival, **Yvonne Murray**. Already possessed of great mental resolve and physical stamina, she returned to the sport after the birth of her daughter, seemingly stronger than ever. In a remarkable performance of front-running, she won the 10 000m at the World Championship in Tokyo in 1991. An enthusiastic worker with young athletes, she has been the Athletics Development Officer of Dundee District Council since 1987.

MacCOLL, Dugald Sutherland

(1859–1948)

Painter and art historian, born in Glasgow. He studied at London and Oxford, and after travelling Europe studying works of art, he established a reputation as a critic and brought out his *Nineteenth-Century Art* in 1902. As Keeper of both the Tate Gallery (1906–11) and of the Wallace Collection (1911–24) he instituted many reforms and improvements. He wrote *Confessions of a Keeper* (1931).

MacCOLL, Sir Edward

(1882–1951)

Electrical engineer, born in Dumbarton. He was apprenticed in John Brown's shipyard at

Clydebank, and then in 1901 joined Glasgow Corporation Tramways Department at Pinkston power station. In 1919 he was appointed Chief Technical Engineer of the Clyde Valley Electric Power Company and played a leading part in the development of the Falls of Clyde hydro-electric scheme. On its completion in 1927 he moved to the Central Electricity Board, for whom he created in central Scotland the first regional electricity supply grid in Britain, standardized on a frequency of 50 cycles and a voltage of 132k. In 1936 he proposed a large-scale pumped storage hydro-electric scheme linking Loch Sloy and Loch Lomond, but it was too far ahead of its time and the Central Electricity Board told him to abandon the idea. He was delighted, therefore, to accept the post of Deputy Chairman and Chief Executive of the newly formed North of Scotland Hydro-Electric Board in 1943. His enthusiasm and expertise, together with the political wisdom of **Thomas Johnston**, contributed much to the success of the Board's early schemes, including Loch Sloy, Tummel-Garry and Affric, at a time when there was strong opposition from Highland landowners and some sections of the public.

MacCOLL, Ewan, originally James Miller
(1915–89)

Folk-singer, composer, collector, author, playwright and Socialist, born in Salford, Lancashire. As a playwright he collaborated with Joan Littlewood in forming the experimental Theatre Workshop in the 1940s, and played an important role in reviving street theatre, but later became one of the most influential pioneers of the British folk-music revival. His series of 'Radio Ballads', begun in 1957, which combined contemporary social comment with traditional musical forms, had a powerful influence on songwriting and performing in subsequent decades. As a collector of traditional folk-songs, he has published several anthologies. Among his own compositions are 'The Shoals of Herring', 'Dirty Old Town', 'Freeborn Man' and 'The First Time Ever I Saw Your Face'.

McCOLL, Robert Smyth
(1876–1959)

Footballer and businessman, born in Glasgow. In 1894 he began playing for Queen's Park which was then, as now, an amateur club, and he moved to Newcastle seven years later, eventually turning professional. Returning to Scotland on signing for Rangers in 1904, he went back to Queen's Park in 1907, thus becoming the only professional to rejoin the club. A centre-forward, he won 13 caps for Scotland between 1896 and 1908, the high point being a hat-trick against England in 1900. After retiring from football he established a successful chain of confectioners, R S McColl's.

MacCORMICK, John MacDonald
(1904–61)

Nationalist politician, born in Glasgow. A graduate of Glasgow University, he became active in the Scottish movement for self-government initially through the Independent Labour Party and, from its inception, in the National Party of Scotland (1928). He was Chairman of the Scottish National Party from its foundation in 1934 until 1942, when the party refused his request that it seek all-party support for independence and cease fighting elections. He thereupon founded and became Chairman of the Scottish Convention, and Chairman of the National Assembly, organizing the Scottish Covenant in 1949, which attracted two million signatures but achieved nothing. He wrote *The Flag in the Wind* (1955).

McCOSH, James
(1811–94)

Philosopher, born in Carskeoch, Ayrshire. Educated at Glasgow and Edinburgh, he became a minister of the Church of Scotland at Arbroath and Brechin, and later of the Free Church. He went on to become Professor of Logic at Queen's College, Belfast (1851), and President of Princeton in 1868 (where he gave his name to the building which now houses the English Department). His main publication was *Intuitions of the Mind* (1860), which defended the 'Common Sense' philosophy of the Scottish school of **Thomas Reid** and **Dugald Stewart**, but his neo-Calvinist views had some unhappy spin-offs in American 'Social Darwinism'. His abiding achievement is the historical classic *The Scottish Philosophy* (1875), a thorough study extending from precursors of Francis Hutcheson and **George Turnbull** to Sir **William Hamilton** and his own day.

McCRIE, Thomas
(1772–1835)

Historian and divine, born in Duns, Berwick-shire. He studied for the ministry at Edinburgh, and became a minister there until 1809, when he was removed from office. He was the author of Lives of **John Knox** (1812) and **Andrew Melville** (1819) and of a *History of the Reformation in Spain* (1829). His son, Thomas (1798–1875), professor in the Presbyterian college at London, was the author of *Sketches of Scottish Church History* (1841) and *Annals of English Presbytery* (1872).

MacCRIMMON

A Skye family, hereditary pipers to Macleod of Dunvegan, the greatest of whom was Patrick Mor (fl.1650).

McCRONE, Guy
(1898–1977)

Novelist, born in Birkenhead, Cheshire. He was educated at Glasgow Academy and Pembroke College, Cambridge, before studying singing in Vienna. Music remained a central interest on his return to Glasgow, and he organized the first British performance of Berlioz's opera *Les Troyens* in the Theatre Royal in 1935. Involved in founding the Citizens' Theatre with his cousin O H Mavor (**James Bridie**), he enjoyed literary success with his trilogy of novels about the middle class Moorhouse family, known as the *Wax Fruit Trilogy* (1947), comprising the novels *Antimacassar City*, *The Philistines* and *The Puritans*. Despite a fondness for stereotypical characters and images, and an excess of sentimentality, the books proved popular, but his subsequent efforts, while in a similar vein, were unable to repeat that success.

McCRONE, Robert Gavin Louden
(1933 –)

Economist and leading authority on the Scottish economy. He was educated at St Catherine's College, Cambridge, University College of Wales at Aberystwyth and Glasgow University. He was lecturer in Applied Economics, Glasgow University (1960–5), Fellow of Brasenose College, Oxford (1965–72), Chief Economic Adviser, Scottish Office from 1972 and Secretary of the Scottish Development Department from 1987. He has written leading works on agricultural and regional policy and the state of the Scottish economy: *Economics of Subsidising Agriculture* (1962), *Scotland's Economic Progress 1951–60* (1962), *Agricultural Integration in Western Europe* (1963), *Regional Policy in Britain* (1969) and *Scotland's Future, The Economics of Nationalism* (1969).

McCULLOCH, Horatio
(1805–67)

Painter, born in Glasgow. As a landscape painter he was influenced, if not actually taught, by **John Knox** (1778–1845). In the mid 1820s he left Glasgow for Edinburgh, where he came into contact with **John Thomson of Duddingston**. He returned to Glasgow around 1827 and a period spent in Hamilton was the source of some fine paintings of Cadzow Forest. Back in Edinburgh in 1838, he was elected to the Royal Scottish Academy. He is best known for his dramatic and romantic landscapes of the Highlands.

McCULLOCH, Sir James
(1819–93)

Scottish-born Australian politician. Born in Glasgow and educated locally, he emigrated to Melbourne in 1853 to pursue a mercantile career. He entered local Victoria politics in 1856 as a member of the liberal-business party, which advocated free trade. He was almost continuously premier of the state between 1863 and 1871, holding that office three times, and thereby giving Victoria its first stable administration. As premier he opposed further penal stations in Australia, and introduced important land and education reforms. Knighted in 1870, he briefly withdrew from politics (1872–4), but returned for a fourth term as premier (1874–7). He finally retired from politics in 1878, and returned to Britain in 1886.

MacCULLOCH, John
(1773–1835)

English-born geologist, born in Guernsey. Schooled in Cornwall, he studied medicine in Edinburgh. His interest in mineralogy led him to be appointed by the Government as early as 1811 to conduct a mineralogical survey of Scotland. A rugged individualist, he is particularly notable for his descriptive account of the Western Isles of Scotland, including the Isle of Man, which was published in 1819. This work contains a fine series of hand-coloured geological maps of nearly all the islands, a remarkable achievement for that time. His life's work in Scotland saw the posthumous publication (1836) of his great Geological Map of Scotland in four sheets, with an accompanying Memoir presented to the Treasury.

McCULLOCH, John Ramsay
(1789–1864)

Economist, born in Whithorn, Wigtownshire, the son of a small landowner. He was a student, but did not graduate, at Edinburgh University (1807–11). From 1817 to 1821 he was editor of *The Scotsman* and gave public lectures on economics in Edinburgh (1820–7). As Edinburgh University refused to establish a chair of political economy for him, he took up a similar appointment at London University (1828–37). From 1838 to his death he was Comptroller of the Stationary Office, successfully reducing much waste. He wrote 43 books and pamphlets in the tradition of **Adam Smith**. His highly successful books, *Principles of Political Economy With a Sketch of the Rise and Progress of the Science* (1825), *Dictionary of Commerce* (1832) and *Dictionary of Geography* (1841–2), were published in several editions.

MacCUNN, Hamish
(1868–1916)

Composer, born in Greenock, Renfrewshire. He studied at the Royal College of Music, and from 1888 to 1894 was Professor of Harmony at the Royal Academy of Music. His works, largely Scottish in character and subject, include the overtures *Cior Mhor* (1887), *Land of the Mountain and the Flood*, and *The Dowie Dens of Yarrow*, choral works, such as *The Lay of the Last Minstrel*, the operas *Jeanie Deans* (1894) and *Diarmid* (1897), and songs.

MacDIARMID, Hugh, pen-name of Christopher Murray Grieve
(1892–1978)

Poet, pioneer of the Scottish literary renaissance, born in Langholm, Dumfriesshire. Educated at Langholm Academy, he became a pupil-teacher at Broughton Higher Grade School in Edinburgh before turning to journalism. He served with the Royal Army Medical Corps in Greece and France during World War I, and was a munitions worker in World War II. After World War I he married Peggy Skinner and settled as a journalist in Montrose, where he also became a town councillor (1922), and edited anthologies of contemporary Scottish writing, such as *Northern Numbers* (1920–2) and *The Scottish Chapbook* (1922–3), in which he published his own early poetry. Beginning with such outstanding early lyrical verse as *Sangschaw* (1925) and *Penny Wheep* (1926), he established himself as the leader of a vigorous Scottish Renaissance by *A Drunk Man Looks at the Thistle* (1926), full of political, metaphysical and nationalistic reflections on the Scottish predicament. In his later works, however, this master of polemic, or 'flyting', increasingly allowed his poetical genius to be overburdened by philosophical gleanings in the service of a customized form of Communism. Nevertheless, items such as 'The Seamless Garment', 'Cattle Shaw' and 'At Lenin's Tomb' raise these later works to a very high level. Other works include *To Circumjack Cencrastus* (1930), the two *Hymns to Lenin* (1930; 1935), *Scots Unbound* (1932), *Stony Limits* (1934), *A Kist o' Whistles* (1947) and *In Memoriam James Joyce* (1955). His numerous essays such as *Albyn* (1927) and *The Islands of Scotland* (1939) suffer from the same intellectual scrapbook tendency. Founder-member of the Scottish National Party, and intermittently an active Communist, he stood as a Communist candidate in 1963. He dedicated his life to the regeneration of the Scottish literary language, repudiated by his fellow Scottish poet, **Edwin Muir**, in 1936. He succeeded brilliantly by employing a vocabulary drawn from all regions and periods, intellectualizing a previously parochial tradition. In 1931 he met his second wife, Valda Trevelin, and in 1933 he went into self-imposed exile on the island of Whalsay, in Shetland. After World War II he lived in a cottage at Brownsbank, near Biggar, Lanarkshire. His autobiography was published in *Lucky Poet* (1943) and *The Company I've Kept* (1966).

McDONALD, Andrew Thomas Joseph
(1871–1950)

Roman Catholic Archbishop of St Andrews and Edinburgh, born near Fort William,

Inverness-shire, son of the landowner of Invernevis. Educated at Fort Augustus Abbey School and the Royal High School, Edinburgh, in 1889 he entered the Benedictine monastery at Fort Augustus as a novice, receiving the name 'Joseph'. He studied at Bonn University, and became a priest in 1896. His work in various parishes in Scotland and Liverpool culminated in service as parish priest of Benedictine parish (1911–19). As Abbot of Fort Augustus Abbey (1919–29) he refounded the school, and established three other religious houses, including two in the USA, which were subsequently elevated to abbey status. A strong and vigorous administrator, he was chosen as archbishop in preference to the controversial convert **Henry Grey Graham**. McDonald's appointment coincided with the rise of the anti-Catholic popular movement in Edinburgh. This had been growing since World War I, but was greatly inflamed by the demagogic town counsellor **John Cormack**. McDonald's judicious restraint in facing but refusing to inflame hostility to the Catholic Eucharistic Congress in 1935 was marked by principled insistence on the right to express religious faith, while at the same time eschewing provocation. A severe disciplinarian, he alienated Catholic workers by his intransigent hostility to Communism and refusal to discuss its origin in social deprivation. His faults were the legacy of a highland aristocracy surviving beyond its time; his virtues were the benefits of its having done so.

MacDONALD, Callum

(1912 –)

Printer and publisher, born in Braeclete, Isle of Bernera. He was educated at the Nicholson Institute in Stornoway and at Edinburgh University, but left before graduating. He served in the RAF, and after the war set up as a newsagent and stationer in Edinburgh. He quickly diversified into printing (a trade he learned by trial and error) and publishing. In 1953 he took over the publication of *Lines*, a newly founded poetry magazine. He convened an editorial board with his friends **Sidney Goodsir Smith** and **Robert Garioch** as well as **Hugh McDairmid** and **Sorley MacLean**, and the magazine was renamed *Lines Review*. It has published most of the important Scottish poets, often before anyone else, while MacDonald Publishing has collected their work in book form. As well as contemporary poetry, he issued *The Unpublished Poems* of **Robert Fergusson**

(1955), and the first definitive edition of **Robert Burns**'s *The Merry Muses of Caledonia* (1959).

MacDONALD, David Keith Chalmers

(1920–63)

Physicist, born in Glasgow and educated at The Edinburgh Academy and Edinburgh University. After the war, when he served in REME (Royal Electrical and Mechanical Engineers), he began research on the properties of metals at low temperatures in the Clarendon Laboratory, Oxford. In 1951 he was invited to set up a low-temperature physics laboratory in Ottawa, supported by the National Research Council. This laboratory achieved international recognition under MacDonald's leadership, despite his development of a crippling illness. He was awarded the Gold Medal of the Canadian Association of Physicists.

McDONALD, Sir Duncan

(1921 –)

Electrical engineer, born in Inverkeithing, Fife. He graduated from Edinburgh University in 1942 and joined British Thomson Houston at Rugby, where he became head of a research group. In 1954 he moved to Bruce Peebles in Edinburgh where he became chief engineer and, in 1962, managing director. After several amalgamations he was appointed Chairman and Chief Executive of Northern Engineering Industries in 1980. He was responsible for many patents relating to electromagnetic apparatus, and developed the application of analogue and digital computers in design. His pioneering work in this field was recognized by the award of honorary degrees from Heriot-Watt and Newcastle universities.

MacDONALD, Elaine

(1943 –)

Dancer, born in Tadcaster, Yorkshire. She trained at the Royal Ballet School, joining Western Ballet Theatre in 1964 and moving with the company to Glasgow when it became Scottish Ballet in the late 1960s. Although her career was limited by total loyalty to this company, she became a dancer of international calibre and created many roles for the choreographer/director **Peter Darrell**, including *Sun Into Darkness* (1966), *Beauty and Beast* (1969), *Tales of Hoffman* (1972), *Mary Queen of Scots* (1976) and *Five Ruckert Songs* (1978). She was made artistic controller of the company in 1988, but left in 1990, going on to become Associate Director of Northern Ballet Theatre, Halifax, in 1991.

MACDONALD, Flora
(1722–90)

Jacobite heroine, born in South Uist in the Hebrides. She lost her father, a tacksman, at the age of two, and at 13 was adopted by Lady Clanranald, wife of the chief of the clan. After the Battle of Culloden (1746) which finally broke the 1745 Jacobite Rising, she conducted the Young Pretender, **Prince Charles Edward Stuart**, disguised as her maid 'Betty Burke', from Benbecula to Portree. For this perilous feat she was much fêted during her year's captivity on the troopship in Leith Roads and in the Tower of London. In 1750 she married Allan Macdonald, the son of Macdonald of Kingsburgh in Skye, where in 1773 she entertained Dr Johnson. In 1774 she emigrated with her husband to North Carolina. In 1776 Allan became a brigadier-general in the War of Independence. He was made prisoner and Flora returned to Scotland in 1779. After two years she was rejoined by him, and they settled again at Kingsburgh.

MacDONALD, Frances
(1873–1921)

Painter and designer, born in Glasgow. The sister of **Margaret MacDonald**, she became the wife of **Herbert MacNair**; these three, together with **Charles Rennie Mackintosh**, comprised the Glasgow 'Group of Four', the prime exponents of Art Nouveau in Scotland, whose influence was international. Francis MacDonald's paintings and decorations are generally strongly poetic, incorporating insubstantial figures in symbolic settings.

MACDONALD, George
(1824–1905)

Novelist, lecturer and poet, born in Huntly, Aberdeenshire, the son of a farmer. He was educated at King's College, Aberdeen, and Highbury Theological College. He became a Congregationalist pastor at Arundel, but his unorthodox views — primarily his belief in purgatory, and in a place in heaven for everyone, even animals — caused conflict with his parishioners, and finally brought about his resignation. After the success of his first publication, the poem 'Within and Without' (1856), he turned to writing and lecturing, publishing the allegorical novel *Phantastes* (1858), which met with a cold reception. He followed this with a series of novels, including *David Elginbrod* (1863), *Robert Falconer* (1868) and *Lilith* (1895), confessing that he used his books as his pulpit. He is now best known for his children's books, among them *At the Back of the North Wind* (1871), *The Princess and the Goblin* (1872) and *The Princess and Curdie* (1888), but his adult works have enjoyed a revival, especially among evangelical Christians.

MACDONALD, Sir George
(1862–1940)

Archaeologist, born in Elgin, Moray. The son of an eminent antiquary, he was educated at Edinburgh and Oxford universities and became Honorary Curator of the Hunter Coin Cabinet in Glasgow University (1893–1940) after joining the staff of the Greek department. He left the university for the Scotch Education Department in 1902 but remained Honorary Curator and a foremost numismatist. Among many honours, he was made KCB for his work in public service and President of the Society of Antiquaries of Scotland. His Dalrymple Lectures resulted in the first detailed historical and archaeological study of *The Roman Wall in Scotland* (1911), and he influenced the development of frontier studies both in Britain and Germany.

MACDONALD, Gus (Angus John)
(1940 –)

Journalist and broadcasting executive, born in Larkhall, Lanarkshire. Educated at Allan Glen's School in Glasgow, he became a marine engineer at Stephens Shipyard before turning to journalism and working with *The Scotsman*. At Granada Television from 1969 to 1985, he was an editor on the highly respected current affairs series *World in Action* (1969–75), and subsequently Head of Current Affairs and Documentaries. A doughty presenter and political interviewer, he also hosted *Camera* (1979), a history of photography and cinema, and was a combative viewers' ombudsman in *Right to Reply* (1982–8). He became Director of Programmes at Scottish Television in 1986 and Managing Director in 1990, making great efforts to improve the quality and scope of material broadcast and to ensure the company's survival in a competitive multi-media age. A Fellow of the Royal Society of Arts, Governor of the National Film and Television School and founder Chairman of the Edinburgh International Television Festival, he has represented Scottish and national interests on a multitude of industry bodies. His publications include *The Documentary Idea and Television Today* (1977) and *Camera: Victorian Eyewitness* (1979).

MACDONALD, Sir Hector
(1857–1903)

Soldier, born on the Black Isle, Easter Ross, After serving an apprenticeship as a draper in Inverness, he joined the Gordon Highlanders and saw service in India and Afghanistan. Promoted from the ranks in 1880, an unusual occurrence in the Victorian army, he transferred to the Egyptian army and served with Kitchener in the Sudan campaign which ended in 1898. At the Battle of Omdurman his tactical awareness prevented a dervish counter-attack on the Anglo-Egyptian army in its moment of victory. He was promoted major-general and in 1901 he was knighted by King Edward VII. During the Boer War he commanded the Highland Brigade and in 1902 he became commander of the British forces in Ceylon. His career ended in disgrace when he committed suicide rather than face charges of paederasty.

MACDONALD, John (Iain Lom)
(1624–1710)

Gaelic poet, descended from the MacDonald chiefs of Keppoch. He was involved in the clan feuds as a staunch Catholic and bitter enemy to the Covenanters of the clan Campbell. His verse was often political, as in works such as 'L'a Inbhir L'ochaidh', in which he glories in the Royalist victory over the Marquis of Argyll, Archibald Campbell. He composed elegies and public poems in honour of the MacDonald chiefs and also wrote in support of the Jacobite cause. His poetry is in the traditional form of classical poets and is remarkable for its consistent loyalty to clan and to king. Charles II appointed him poet laureate in Scotland at the time of the Restoration. A poet of public affairs to the end of his long life, he denounced William of Orange as a 'borrowed king' and wrote a satire of the 1707 Act of Union.

MACDONALD, Sir John Alexander
(1815–91)

Scottish-born Canadian statesman, born in Glasgow. He emigrated with his parents in 1820. He was called to the Bar in 1836 and appointed QC. Entering politics, he became leader of the Conservatives and premier in 1856, and in 1867 formed the first government for the new Dominion. Minister of Justice and Attorney-General of Canada until 1873, he was again in power from 1878 until his death in Ottawa. He was instrumental in bringing about the confederation of Canada and in securing the construction of the Intercolonial and Canadian Pacific railways.

MACDONALD, Sir John Hay Athole, Lord Kingsburgh
(1836–1919)

Judge, born in Edinburgh, son of a Writer to the Signet. Having passed advocate in 1859 he realized the inadequate teaching of criminal law in the universities and sought to supply the deficiency by *A Practical Treatise on the Criminal Law of Scotland* (1867) which, for lack of anything better, was extensively used for about a century. It was a shapeless book and very weak on analysis of general concepts and principles. He was successively part-time Sheriff of Ross (1874–6), Solicitor-General for Scotland (1876–80), Sheriff of Perthshire (1880–5) and Dean of the Faculty of Advocates (1882–5) and Lord Advocate (1885–6 and 1886–8). He was an MP from 1885 to 1888 and carried the great Criminal Procedure Act, 1887. He then became Lord Justice-Clerk until his retirement in 1915. He was made KCB in 1900 and GCB in 1916. He was at his best at the Bar in jury trials and as a judge his judgements proceed on common sense rather then on legal subtleties. An ardent volunteer, he attained the rank of brigadier and wrote many manuals on training and tactics. He was a founder of the Scottish Rifle Association and the Royal Scottish Automobile Club.

MACDONALD, Malcolm
(1901–81)

Administrator, son of **James Ramsay Macdonald**, born in Lossiemouth, Moray. He studied at Oxford, was National Government MP (1936–45), and held several ministerial appointments, including those of Colonial Secretary (1935; 1938–40) and Minister of Health (1940–1). He was Commissioner in Canada (1941–6), Governor-General of Malaya and Borneo (1946–8), Commissioner-General in South-East Asia (1948–55), High Commissioner in India (1955–60), Governor-General (1963–4) and High Commissioner (1964–5) in Kenya, and special representative in East and Central Africa (1965–70). His books include *Borneo People* (1956), *Angkor* (1958), and several works on ornithology.

MacDONALD, Malcolm, pseudonym Calum MacDonald
(1948 –)

Writer on music and composer, born in Nairn, Angus and educated in Edinburgh and at Cambridge University. He has published major studies of Brahms, Havergal Brian, John Foulds, Schoenberg, **Ronald Stevenson** and Varèse. His compositions include works for piano and vocal music. As 'Calum MacDonald' he is a frequent broadcaster, and is editor of the periodical *Tempo*.

MacDONALD, Margaret
(1865–1933)

English artist, born in Staffordshire, sister of **Francis MacDonald**. She studied at the Glasgow College of Art, and in 1900 married **Charles Rennie Mackintosh**. Best known for her work in watercolours and stained glass, she exhibited widely on the Continent, winning the Diploma of Honour at the Turin International Exhibition of 1902. She collaborated with her husband in much of his work.

MacDONALD, Margo
(1944–)

Nationalist politician and broadcaster, born in Hamilton, Lanarkshire. Gaining a place at Hamilton Academy she went on to qualify as a PE teacher but increasingly devoted her attention to politics, becoming a bullish advocate for Scottish nationalism. In 1973 she won a momentous by-election victory for the Scottish National Party in the traditionally Labour seat of Govan. Although failing to secure a seat in Parliament in the two general elections of 1974, she remained in the vanguard of nationalistic feeling until 1982, when she was ousted from the party as a result of ideological differences. Retreating from the political arena, she built a second career in the media as the incisive presenter of various radio and television programmes. She is married to **Jim Sillars**.

MacDONALD, Sir Murdoch
(1866–1957)

Civil engineer, born in Inverness. He was articled as a clerk with the Highland Railway and was then apprenticed to the chief engineer, for whom he worked on railway extension schemes until 1898. Soon afterwards he became an assistant engineer on the construction of the Aswan Dam, beginning an association with Egypt that lasted for more than half a century. He designed several major works of irrigation and flood control, and in 1920 published *Nile Control*. He resigned as adviser to the Egyptian Ministry of Public Works in 1921 and established himself as a consulting engineer in London, continuing to design major hydraulic works in Egypt and many other countries. He was elected President of the Institution of Civil Engineers in 1932 and sat as MP for Inverness from 1922 to 1950.

MACDONALD, Murdo Ewan
(1914 –)

Church of Scotland minister and academic, born on Harris into a Gaelic-speaking community. Educated at St Andrews and **McGill** universities, he was appointed to the parish of Portree on Skye (1939–40) before serving in World War II as a combat officer in the 2nd Paratroopers. Wounded and taken prisoner, he acted as chaplain to the American Air Force in Stalag Luft III, for which he later earned the American Bronze Star. Following the war he was minister of Old Patrick, Glasgow (1946–9) and St George's West, Edinburgh (1949–63). As Professor of Practical Theology at Glasgow University from 1964 to 1984, he inspired a generation of future ministers with his deeply practical approach to the challenges of parish ministry. His publications include *The Vitality of Faith* (1952), *The Need to Believe* (1959) and *The Call to Communicate* (1975).

MACDONALD, Patricia Clare
(1945 –)

Photographer, born in Edinburgh. She was educated at Edinburgh University, and since 1972 has worked at the National Museums of Scotland. She is best known for her aerial photography, made working as a team with her husband, Angus Macdonald, as pilot. Her work has concentrated on aspects of the environment — geology, natural history, architecture and landscape. Her photographs are characterized by an intellectual and philosophical approach, seeing the world from different mental and physical angles, combined with a seductively beautiful visual interpretation, which gives her work considerable force. The publications which are most representative of her work are *Shadow of Heaven* (1989) and *Order and Chaos: Views of Gaia* (1990).

MACDONALD, (James) Ramsay
(1866–1937)

Labour politician, and first British Labour prime minister, born illegitimately in Lossiemouth, Moray, and educated at a board school, where he became a pupil-teacher. Over several difficult, penurious years in London, he wrote about Socialism and other problems. A member of the Social Democratic Federation (1885) and the Fabian Society (1886), he worked for a time as a journalist. He was a leading member of the Independent Labour Party (1893–1930), becoming Secretary (1900–11) and Leader (1911–14, 1922–31) of the Labour Party. A member of the London County Council (1901–4) and of Parliament from 1906, he became leader of the opposition in 1922, and from January to November 1924 was Prime Minister and Foreign Secretary of the first Labour government in Britaina minority government at the mercy of the Liberals. The election of 1924 put him out of office, while that of 1929 brought him in again. However, he met the financial crisis of 1931 by forming a predominantly Conservative 'National' government, the bulk of his party opposing, and in 1931 he reconstructed it after a general election. From 1935 to 1937 he was Lord President.

MacDONALD, Robert David
(1929 –)

Actor, translator and playwright, born in Elgin, Moray, and educated at Wellington College, Somerset, Oxford University and the Royal College of Music. He spent two years at the Munich Conservatoire, studying conducting, before working as a translator for UNESCO. Fluent in at least eight languages, he joined the Glasgow Citizens' Theatre in 1972, since when he has appeared as an actor and directed many productions, as well as providing new translations for plays by, among others, Goldoni, Lermontov, Sartre and Goethe, as well as writing his own, such as *Chinchilla* (1977) and *Summit Conference* (1978).

MACDONALD, Rory
(1949 –) and **Calum** (1953 –)

Rock bass guitarist and percussionist, born in Dornoch and Uist respectively. They formed the group Runrig on Skye in 1973. Singer Donnie Munro (1953 –) was an early addition to the line-up, later completed by Malcolm Jones (1959 –), Iain Bayne (1960 –) and Peter Wishart (1962 –). Originally a student dance band, their career only took off after they moved to Glasgow and then to Edinburgh in the early 1980s. Their first albums, including *Play Gaelic* (1978) and *Recovery* (1982), were folk-based, but they gradually moved towards a more rock-oriented sound. All of their records prior to 1988, when they signed a recording deal with Chrysalis Records, were released on the band's own independent Ridge Records label. By the time of *The Cutter And The Clan* (1987) they had established an almost unrivalled following in Scotland. Subsequent albums, including *Searchlight* (1989) and *The Big Wheel* (1991), have brought success throughout the UK.

MacDONALD, Sharman
(1951 –)

Playwright and novelist, born in Glasgow and educated at Edinburgh University. Her first play, *When I Was a Girl I Used to Scream and Shout*, a bitter and wry study of Scottish childhood and adolescence, produced at the Bush Theatre, London (1984), was an immediate success and won the *Evening Standard* Most Promising Playwright award for that year. She has since written *The Brave* (1988) for the Bush, and *When We Were Women* (1989) for the National Theatre Studio, plays that confirm hers to be a perceptive and individual voice. Her novels *The Beast* (1986) and *Night Night* (1988) have had less success.

MacDONALD, Stephen
(1935 –)

English-born actor, playwright and director, born in Birmingham. He has appeared in many regional repertory theatres — mainly in Edinburgh, Glasgow and Dundee — and in television plays and series. He was associate and then artistic director of the Leicester Phoenix Theatre (1969–71), and artistic director of Dundee Theatre (1972–6) and Edinburgh Lyceum (1976–9). As a playwright he is best known for *Not About Heroes* (1981), a two-character play about the relationship between Siegfried Sassoon and Wilfred Owen.

MACDONELL, Alastair Ruadh
(c.1724–1761)

Jacobite and clan chief, from Glengarry, Inverness-shire. He joined the French Scots brigade in 1743 and was sent to Scotland to support the 1745 Jacobite Rebellion, but was captured and imprisoned in the Tower of London (1745–7). He succeeded his father in 1754 as 13th Chief of Glengarry, and became known as 'one of the best men in the Highlands', but **Andrew Lang** proved that he had become a government spy on his fellow Jacobites, in *Pickle the Spy* (1897).

MacDONELL, Ranald
(d.1847)

Legitimist general in Spanish and Portuguese service. He fought for Spain in the Peninsular War. In 1823 he was captured by the Portuguese and imprisoned in Lisbon. There he befriended his future liberal opponent, Joao Carlos Saldanha, who gave him money for new clothes and passage home. In 1832 they met again in Paris, when MacDonell had lost his money at cards, and again Saldanha provided his fare to Scotland. In September 1833, MacDonell landed at S. Martinho with a party of Scottish and French officers, to fight for Dom Miguel, the Legitimist claimant to the Portuguese throne. On 18 September, after the failure of Marshal Bourmont to capture Lisbon, MacDonell succeeded him as Commander-in-Chief of the Miguelite army. Saldanha was the opposing Pedroite general. MacDonell's ordered withdrawal to Loures and Santarem after being attacked by Saldanha on 10 October was regarded, even by his opponents, as an operation of military genius. Dom Miguel, however, rejected MacDonell's advice to accept British and Spanish mediation, and MacDonell resigned his command. For most of the rest of his life he acted intermittently as a Miguelite agent in Portugal. In 1846, on the occasion of the revolt of Patuleia, MacDonell raised an army of 3000 in the Miguelite cause. Defeated in December at Braga by the liberal general Baron do Casal, MacDonell fled. The following year he was attacked and cut to pieces at Vila Pouca on 28 January.

McDOUGALL, Peter
(1947 –)

Screenwriter, born in Greenock. Apprenticed as a brass finisher in the shipyards, he moved to London at the age of 18 before completing his apprenticeship. There he began writing television screenplays, and scored a significant success with *Just Another Saturday*, which won the prestigious Prix Italia in 1974. Its powerful mixture of brutal reality and acerbic wit focused with typical frankness on religious division in the West of Scotland. *Elephant's Graveyard* (1976), a wryly observed two-hander for **Billy Connelly** and Jon Morrison, revealed a gentler side to his work, but he returned to more violent territory in *Just a Boy's Game* (1979). His only adaptation, **Jimmy Boyle**'s *A Sense of Freedom* (1981), was widely acclaimed, and he has continued to mine a narrow but deep vein of working-class experience in screenplays such as *Shoot for the Sun* (1985), which delved into Edinburgh's drug underworld, and *Down Where The Buffalo Go* (1988), starring American actor Harvey Keitel. He returned to live in Glasgow in 1987. Work-in-progress includes a new film, *Down Among The Big Boys*.

McEWAN, William
(1827–1913)

Brewer, born in Alloa, Clackmannanshire. Having learnt the industry at his uncle's Heriot Brewery in Edinburgh he set up his own Fountain Brewery in Edinburgh in 1856. Trade burgeoned with the west of Scotland and then with the British Empire, growth accelerating vastly in the 1880s and rivalling more established companies. From this sound industrial base he entered politics in 1886 as a Liberal, representing an Edinburgh constituency until 1900, and leaving much of the direction of the company in the hands of his nephew, **William Younger**. His outstanding success brought him great wealth, and he made many donations to Edinburgh, including the hall at the university which bears his name.

McEWEN, Sir John Blackwood
(1868–1948)

Composer, born in Hawick, Roxburghshire. He taught music in Glasgow, and was Professor of Composition and Harmony at the Royal College of Music in London (1898–

1924), and Principal from 1924 to 1936. His particular interest was to promote a revival of composition for chamber orchestras.

MacEWEN, Sir William
(1848–1924)

Neurosurgeon, who pioneered brain surgery, born and educated in Glasgow, where he worked throughout his life. His interest in surgery was stimulated by Joseph Lister, then Regius Professor of Surgery at Glasgow University. He adopted and then extended Lister's antiseptic surgical techniques and pioneered operations on the brain for tumours, abscesses and trauma. In addition, he operated on bones, introducing methods of implanting small grafts to replace missing portions of bones in the limbs. In 1892 he was appointed to the chair that Lister had held when MacEwen was a student.

MacFARLANE, Alistair George James
(1931 –)

Electrical engineer, born in Edinburgh. He graduated from Glasgow University and joined Metropolitan-Vickers in Manchester, 1953. He left to take up a lectureship at London University in 1959, and subsequently held chairs in engineering at UMIST and Cambridge University. His principal research field was the development of a general theory for complex feedback control systems, on which he has written and edited a number of influential publications. He was elected a Fellow of the Royal Society in 1984, and of the Royal Society of Edinburgh in 1990. Since 1989 he has been Principal and Vice-Chancellor of Heriot-Watt University, Edinburgh.

MACFARLANE, Leslie John
(1913 –)

Historian, born in Portsmouth. Educated at the Royal Military Academy, Sandhurst (after entry by open examination in which he was placed first in the British Empire), he was commissioned in the Black Watch Royal Highland Regiment. Invalided from service during World War II, he was converted to Roman Catholicism. He studied at London and Oxford universities, and went on to become the leading British authority on Vatican archives. Appointed Assistant Lec-

turer in History at Aberdeen University in 1953, he rose to Reader, retiring as Honorary Reader in 1983. Chairman of the committee for the *Calendar of Papal Registers Relating to Great Britain and Ireland*, he inaugurated and supervised its multi-volume publication. His *William Elphinstone and the Kingdom of Scotland* (1985) was a landmark in Scottish medieval historiography, winning for him honorary doctorates from the universities of Edinburgh (1988) and Aberdeen (1990). Un-rivalled as a teacher, he inspired his students with his love of Scottish and European medieval history. He mounted the exhibition 'Scotland and the Holy See' in the City Art Gallery, Edinburgh, for the visit of Pope John Paul II in 1982, which attracted 27 000 visitors. In 1983 he became a member of the Scottish Catholic Heritage Commission. Secretary of the Catholic Historical Association (1966–87), he has established himself as one of the foremost scholars of his time.

McGEECHAN, Ian
(1946 –)

Rugby player and coach. Having moved to Yorkshire as a teenager, he played his club rugby for Headingley, and made his international début in 1972 in the same match as **Andy Irvine**. He played 32 times for Scotland between then and 1979, 12 at fly-half and 20 as a centre. He also played eight times for the British Lions, on the 1974 tour of South Africa and the 1977 series in New Zealand. Scotland's assistant coach in the inaugural World Cup of 1987, he took over as head coach the following year, and was also coach of the British Lions in 1989. In 1990, his crucial role in Scotland's Grand Slam win heightened his reputation as one of the greatest coaches in world rugby.

McGEOCH, Sir Ian Lauchlan Mackay
(1914 –)

Naval commander, born in Helensburgh, Dunbartonshire, and educated at Pang-bourne College, Berkshire, and the Royal Naval College at Dartmouth. Although his early naval service was in destroyers, he transferred to the submarine service in 1937 and served in the Mediterranean during World War II. In 1943 his submarine HMS *Splendid* was sunk by a German destroyer and he became a prisoner of war in Italy. Following a daring escape through occupied

France and Spain he made his way back to Britain and ended the war with the 4th Cruiser Squadron in the Pacific. Promoted to flag rank in 1964 he held a number of executive posts including Flag Officer Submarines and Flag officer Scotland before his retirement in 1970. His wartime adventures are recounted in a volume of autobiography, *An Affair of Chances: A Submariner's Odyssey* (1991).

MacGIBBON, David
(1831–1902)

Architect, born in Edinburgh. He worked for a time in the London office of **William Burn** and, after extensive travelling and sketching on the continent, he began practice in Edinburgh in 1856. His early work was mainly of a commercial nature, often in a baronial style. In 1862 **Thomas Ross** joined MacGibbon's office, becoming a partner in 1872. MacGibbon & Ross continued with commercial commissions, also specializing in speculative housing, hotels and country houses, but are best remembered for their five-volume magnum opus, *Castellated and Domestic Architecture of Scotland* (1887–92), which firmly established them as the foremost architectural scholars in the country.

McGIBBON, William
(c.1690–1756)

Composer and violinist, born in Edinburgh. His father, Malcolm McGibbon, was an eminent oboist, and the young William was sent to London to study both violin and composition. He returned to Edinburgh, where he became principal violinist in the orchestra of the Edinburgh Musical Society, a position he held for two decades. He was highly regarded as a violinist, and was commemorated as such in **Robert Fergusson**'s poem 'Elegy on the Death of Scots Music' (1772). He published a number of sets of fiddle music based on the Scottish traditional style, and was considered to be one of the foremost Scottish composers of the late Baroque period. Modern musicologists, however, have been less impressed by the quality of his surviving works, most of which are composed in solo, duo or trio forms.

McGILL, James
(1744–1813)

Scottish-born Canadian entrepreneur and philanthropist, born in Glasgow. He emi-

grated to Canada in the 1770s, and made a fortune in the north-west fur trade and in Montreal. He bequeathed land and money (£10 000) to found McGill College, Montreal, which became McGill University in 1821.

MACGILL-EAIN, Somhairle See MacLean, Sorley

MacGILLIVRAY, James Pittendrigh
(1856–1938)

Sculptor and poet, born in Inverurie, Aberdeenshire, the son of a sculptor. He studied under William Brodie and John Mossman. His major sculptures included the huge statue of **Robert Burns** in Irvine, the Scottish National Memorial to Gladstone in St Andrew's Square, Edinburgh, the great statue to the third Marquis of Bute in Cardiff, the Byron statue in Aberdeen, and the **John Knox** statue in St Giles's Cathedral, Edinburgh. His most notable publications were verse (*Pro Patria*, 1915, and *Bog Myrtle and Peat Reek*, 1922) and various papers of professional significance. He was appointed the King's Sculptor in Ordinary for Scotland in 1921.

MacGILLIVRAY, William
(1796–1852)

Pioneer ornithologist. Born in Aberdeen, he studied medicine at King's College, Aberdeen. In 1823 he was appointed assistant to the Professor of Natural History at Edinburgh and Keeper of the Museum of Edinburgh University, and in 1831 became Conservator of the museum of the Royal College of Surgeons. He took great pride in his work in these museums, but in 1841 he was appointed to the Regius Chair of Natural History at Aberdeen University. He wrote a plethora of papers describing his own observations of plants and animals from all over Scotland, but his greatest work was the five volumes of *A History of British Birds*, published between 1837 and the year of his death. With this he can truly be said to have laid the foundations of British ornithology with a classification depending on precise anatomical descriptions of different species. Nevertheless, despite the precise descriptions, his accounts of the habits of the animals and plants which he observed read as freshly and clearly today as any modern writing and are well worth the effort of their discovery.

McGINN, Matt

(1928–77)

Singer and songwriter, born in Glasgow. After numerous jobs he gained a diploma in economics and political science at Ruskin College, Oxford, and then worked for periods as a schoolteacher, although he preferred to make his living as a songwriter and performer. An astonishingly prolific composer, he produced several hundred songs, many of which — like 'Rob Roy MacGreegor-O', 'Red Yo-Yo' and 'Coorie Doon' — became widely known in folk-music circles and beyond.

McGONAGALL, William

(1830–1902)

Poet and novelist, son of an immigrant Irish weaver. He spent some of his childhood on the island of South Ronaldsay in the Orkneys, settled with his family in Dundee at the age of 11, and became a handloom weaver with his father. In 1846 he married Jean King. He did some acting at Dundee's Royal Theatre, and in 1878 published his first collection of poems, including 'Railway Bridge of the Silvery Tay'. From then on he travelled in central Scotland, giving readings and selling his poetry in broadsheets. In Edinburgh he was lionized by the legal and student fraternity. He visited London in 1880 and New York in 1887. His poems are uniformly bad, but possess a disarming naïveté and a calypso-like disregard for metre which remain entertaining. His *Poetic Gems* were published in 1890, and *More Poetic Gems* in 1962), followed by others.

McGOWAN, Lord Henry (Harry) Duncan

(1874–1961)

Chemical manufacturer, born in Glasgow. He joined Nobel's Explosives Company as an office boy in 1889. Twenty years later he had risen to assistant manager, and was sent to Canada where Nobel, Du Pont and others were in competition for a share of the market. He recommended a merger of all the manufacturers into one company and, when that proved successful, he pursued a policy of mergers and marketing agreements for the rest of his life. In 1918, by which time he was Managing Director of Nobel's, he combined all the British explosives manufacturers into one group of companies, and began to di-

versify into other industries, becoming a director in 1919 of the British Dyestuffs Corporation. In 1926 he persuaded Alfred Mond and others to join him in forming Imperial Chemical Industries, of which he was Chairman and sole Managing Director from 1930 to 1950.

McGOWAN, Walter

(1942 –)

Boxer, born in Burnbank, Lanarkshire. He won the world flyweight championship in 1966, beating Italy's Salvatore Burruni on points in London. Later that year, however, he lost the title to Thailand's Chartchai Chionoi when the referee stopped the fight. Towards the end of 1967 he again tried to regain his title from Chionoi, but the result was the same. A courageous, indomitable fighter, he was among the last of a long line of small, seemingly malnourished, Scots boxers who made it to the top of the lower weight divisions.

McGRATH, John Peter

(1935 –)

English-born writer, director and filmmaker, born in Birkenhead, Cheshire. Following National Service, he studied at St John's College, Oxford (1955–9), where his earliest plays were performed. Subsequently moving into television, he was one of the creators of the innovative police drama series *Z Cars* in 1962, and wrote such programmes as *Diary of A Nobody* (1966) before writing the film scripts *Billion Dollar Brain* (1967) and *The Bofors Gun* (1968). In 1971 he founded the 7:84 Theatre Company, which dedicated itself to the production of radical populist drama and took its name from the fact that 7 per cent of the population owned 84 per cent of the country's wealth. Artistic Director of 7:84 Scotland from 1973 to 1988, with his plays he attempted to illuminate Scottish historical struggles and explore issues vital to the current political agenda in the country. Notable works include *The Cheviot, The Stag and The Black, Black Oil* (1973), *The Game's A Bogey* (1974) and *Women in Power* (1983). As founder of Freeway Films in 1983 he has made such television drama as *Blood Red Roses* (1986) and *Border Warfare* (1988) and the film *The Dressmaker* (1988). His passionate and critical commitment to Scottish theatre is reflected in books like *The Bone Won't Break: On Theatre and Hope in Hard*

Times (1990). Recent work, such as *Waiting for the Dolphins* (1991), has seen him question the changing validity of Socialism in contemporary Europe.

McGRATH, Tom
(1940 –)

Poet and dramatist, born in Rutherglen, Lanarkshire. He began to publish his poems in 1962, and read with Ginsberg, Ferlinghetti and Corso at the Albert Hall in 1965. He was founder editor of the underground magazine *International Times* (1966–7). He attended Glasgow University (1969–71), and became involved in the theatre, as well as editing *Nuspeak* (Scottish Arts Council magazine), promoting concerts, and acting as musical director for **Billy Connelly**'s *Great Northern Welly Boot Show*, an indication of the breadth of his interests. He was Director of the Third Eye Centre, Glasgow, from 1974 to 1977, and completed two of his best-known plays, *Laurel and Hardy* (1976) and *The Hardman* (1977), written with and about **Jimmy Boyle**. Plays with a radical and often experimental edge for both stage and television have followed at regular intervals, including the massive Glaswegian community drama *City* (1989). He has held a number of dramatist-in-residence positions, and is the Associate Literary Director of the Scottish Arts Council. He is also a jazz musician.

MACGREGOR, Sir Charles
(1840–87)

Soldier, born in Agra, India, and brought up in Perthshire before attending Marlborough College in Wiltshire. Commissioned into the 57th Bengal Native Infantry, he saw service with Sir **Colin Campbell** during the Indian Mutiny and was present at the raising of the siege of Lucknow. During the campaign against China of 1860 and later in the Assyrian war of 1867, Macgregor distinguished himself several times and was commended for his conduct in hand-to-hand combat. During the Afghanistan war he served as Chief of Staff to Sir Frederick Sleigh Roberts and commanded his 3rd Infantry Brigade during the march from Kabul to Kandahar. In 1885 he was given command of the Punjab Frontier Force, but his health broke and he was forced to return to Scotland. A noted traveller, he wrote two colourful accounts of his adventures: *Narrative of a*

Journey through the Province of Khorassan (1879) and *Wanderings in Baluchistan* (1882).

McGREGOR, Ian Kinloch
(1912 –)

Scottish-born American business executive, born in Kinlochleven, Argyll. Educated at Glasgow University and the Royal College of Science and Technology (now Strathclyde University), he went to the USA in 1941, when he was seconded to work with the US army. He developed his career in business in the USA, but in 1977 he returned to the UK as Deputy Chairman of British Leyland, working with Sir Michael Edwardes. In 1980 he was appointed Chairman of the British Steel Corporation, and then became Chairman of the National Coal Board from 1983 to 1986. Both industries required drastic cutbacks to survive, and he faced strong trade union opposition, particularly from the miners in 1984–5.

McGREGOR, James
(1832–1910)

Church of Scotland minister, born in Scone, Perthshire, one of the foremost preachers of his time. Educated at St Andrews University, he held ministries at Monimail in Fife, Tron in Glasgow, and finally at St Cuthbert's, Edinburgh, from 1873. In 1891 his particular gifts were acknowledged when he was appointed Moderator of the General Assembly. Chaplaincies to Queen Victoria and Edward VII were also features of his ministry. Noted for his short stature (he was commonly known as 'Wee McGregor'), he still managed to cut a dash in the salons of Edinburgh society, and he became something of a cult figure, the magnetism of his powers of communication holding large congregations spellbound.

MACGREGOR, Jimmie (James)
(1932 –)

Folksinger and broadcaster, born in Glasgow. After receiving a diploma in pottery from Glasgow College of Art, he worked as a schoolteacher before joining with Robin Hall (1937 –) to form a folksinging partnership that endured for 21 years and saw them established as resident singers on the *Tonight* (1961–5) television series. They released over 20 albums and reached number 17 in the 1959 pop charts with the single 'Fitba' Crazy'. As a broadcaster Macgregor has presented a daily magazine-format radio show, *Macgregor's Gathering* (1982 –), a mix of music and informal interviews that reflect the breadth and character of the Scottish nation. He has also traversed the Scottish landscape in a succession of television series, from *The West Highland Walk* (1986) to *Macgregor Across Scotland* (1991).

MacGREGOR, Murray
(1884–1966)

Geologist, born in Glasgow. Educated at Glasgow High School and Glasgow University, he remained a committed Glaswegian throughout his long life. He served on the staff of the Geological Survey of Great Britain in Scotland from 1909 until 1945, from 1925 as Assistant Director (Scotland). A prolific author of both official and unofficial publications, he was Scotland's most eminent coalfield geologist, serving as geological adviser to the National Coal Board in Scotland from 1948 until 1964. His *Scottish Carboniferous Stratigraphy* (1931) is a classic, and he contributed several wartime reports on mineral resources. A Fellow of the Royal Society of Edinburgh from 1922, he received the **Clough** Medal of the Edinburgh Geological Society in 1944.

McGREGOR, Oliver Ross, Lord McGregor of Durris
(1921 –)

Sociologist, educated at Aberdeen University and the London School of Economics, he worked as a civil servant in the War Office until being appointed to a lectureship in economic history at the University of Hull. He lectured at Bedford College, London, became a reader in 1960, and was appointed Professor of Social Institutions in 1964. He has been Chairman of the Advertising Standards Authority since 1980, a member of the Independent Television Authority's advisory committee, Chairman of the Royal Commission on the Press (1975–7), and was appointed to chair the Press Complaints Commission in 1990. A major figure in the making of public policy on the media in the UK, his publications include *Divorce in England* (1957), and *Separated Spouses* (1970). He was made a life peer in 1978, and took the Labour Whip, and then that of the Social Democratic Party.

MacGREGOR, Robert See ROB ROY

MacGREGOR, William York
(1855–1923)

Painter, born in Glasgow, a leading figure, along with Sir **James Guthrie**, among the so-called 'Glasgow Boys', whose paintings were based on a realistic approach to subject matter. He studied at the Slade School of Art in London. Like other painters of the Glasgow school, the bulk of his work includes human figures, although his masterpiece, *The Vegetable Stall* (1884) is an unusually large still-life. Painted in rich, solid chunks of colour, and remarkably modern in style, it is one of the great Scottish paintings of the late 19th century.

McGUIRE, Edward
(1948 –)

Musician and composer, born in Glasgow. He studied flute at the RSAM from 1966 to 1970 and then composition in London and Stockholm. When he joined the Whistlebinkies folk group in Glasgow in 1973 he was still essentially a classical instrumentalist, but folk music soon made its mark on his playing, and his first major composition, 'Trilogy', in the late 1970s, showed the influence of folk themes. His 'Rant' was the test piece for the 1978 Carl Flesch International Violin Competition in 1978, and his string quartet was performed in 1983 at an anniversary concert of the Society for the Promotion of New Music at the Barbican in London. Later compositions include the music for Scottish Ballet's *Peter Pan* (1989), 'A Glasgow Symphony' for the National Youth Orchestra of Scotland (1990) and a three-act opera, *The Loving of Etain*, for Paragon Opera's production in Glasgow (1990). The Paragon Ensemble also recorded his *Songs of New Beginnings* (1991).

McGUIRE, Leonard
(1924 –)

Actor, born in Manchester and trained at the Traverse Theatre, Edinburgh, one of the most familiar faces in Scottish theatre and British repertory. He has had a notable London career, from appearing with Vivien Leigh in Laurence Olivier's production of Thornton

Wilder's *The Skin of Our Teeth* (1945), and with John Gielgud in Anthony Quayle's production of his own adaptation of *Crime and Punishment* (1946), to appearing with the Royal Shakespeare Company in *Coriolanus* (1989). He has made several films and regularly appears on television.

MACH, David
(1956 –)

Sculptor, born in Methil, Fife. He studied at Duncan of Jordanstone College of Art, Dundee (1974–9), and the Royal College of Art, London (1979–82). He has attracted much critical as well as popular attention, through both his choice of materials and his working methods. Working to a time limit, often in public view, he has created monumental 'structures' from society's surplus materials. These have included a military tank constructed from car tyres and enormous classical columns built from magazines.

MACHABEUS, Johannes
(d.1557)

Religious reformer, one of the clan Macalpine. He was Dominican prior in Perth 1532–4 and then, converted to Protestantism by the Reformation, he fled as a heretic to England. There he married, went on to Germany, and from 1542 until his death was Professor of Theology at Copenhagen, where he helped to translate Luther's bible into Danish.

McHARG, Ian Lennox
(1920 –)

Geographer, born in Clydebank, Dunbartonshire, but after service in the British army (1939–46) he moved to the USA. He took degrees in landscape architecture and city planning at Harvard University, after which he returned to work in Scotland as a planner (1950–4). He returned to the USA as Professor of Landscape Architecture and Regional Planning at the University of Pennsylvania (1954 –). Since that time a distinguished career, mainly in the field of planning, has led to numerous prestigious posts and awards, medals and honorary degrees. His book *Design with Nature* (1969) is a respected work of reference; more recently, he has been associated with the development of computerized Geographic Information Systems.

McILVANNEY, Hugh
(1933 –)

Sports journalist and broadcaster, brother of **William McIlvanney**, born in Kilmarnock, Ayrshire. The doyen of Scottish sports journalists, he has long been chief sports writer of *The Observer*, applying his acerbic wit and lucid intelligence to a broad spectrum of sports. Boxing and football are his main interests. He covered the great years of Muhammad Ali's career, and has been a long-suffering commentator — on TV as well as in print — of the Scottish football team.

McILVANNEY, William Angus
(1936 –)

Novelist and poet, born in Kilmarnock, Ayrshire, brother of **Hugh McIlvanney**. He was educated at Kilmarnock Academy and Glasgow University and taught from 1960 to 1975, when he took up writing fulltime. His first novel was *Remedy is None* (1966), a paean to working-class values, in which a student avenges what he surmises is his mother's betrayal of his father. *A Gift from Nessus*, published two years later, developed the same theme as a travelling salesman chooses self-assertion over self-destruction. With *Docherty* (1975) McIlvanney extended his range without abandoning his roots, in the convincing story of the eponymous 'hard man', an Ayrshire miner, whose uncompromising life is seen through the eyes of his son. This won the Whitbread Prize. *The Big Man* (1985) is set in similar territory and pitches Dan Scoular, a hero in his own locality, into a bare-knuckle fight where there is more at stake than money. Though he has been described by **Alan Bold** as 'a rhetorician occasionally overcome by his own verbosity', he has an enviable way with metaphor and simile and in the thrillers featuring the Glasgow detective Jack Laidlaw — *Laidlaw* (1977), *The Papers of Tony Veitch* (1983) and *Strange Loyalties* (1991) — comparisons with Chandler are not inappropriate. Volumes of poetry include *The Longships in Harbour* (1970) and *These Words* (1984). His short stories are collected in *Walking Wounded* (1989), and his essays and journalism in *Surviving the Shipwreck* (1991).

MacINNES, Hamish
(1930 –)

Mountaineer, writer and broadcaster, born in Gatehouse of Fleet, Kirkcudbrightshire. He has climbed in Scotland, the European Alps, New Zealand, Caucasus and the Himalayas, and has been a member of two expeditions to Everest (spring and autumn 1972) and Deputy Leader of the successful south-west face of Everest expedition in 1975. He made the first ascent of the Great Prow on Mount Roraima, Guyana, in 1973. A leading authority on mountain rescue, he has been leader of the Glencoe Mountain Rescue Team, Honorary Secretary of the Mountain Rescue Committee of Scotland, founder of the Search and Rescue Dog Association and an honorary member of the Scottish Mountaineering Club. He also invents and designs specialized mountaineering equipment and advanced rescue equipment, and has written numerous travel books.

MACINTOSH, Charles

(1766–1843)

Manufacturing chemist, born in Glasgow. He patented (1823) and developed **James Syme**'s method of waterproofing, the resulting garments becoming known as 'mac(k)intoshes'.

MACINTYRE, Alasdair Chalmers

(1929 –)

Philosopher, born in Glasgow, the son of two medical practitioners. His family moved to Ireland while he was a young child. Educated at Epsom College and privately, he studied classics at Oxford and philosophy at London. Unusually broad in his intellectual sympathies, he wrote on and taught a wide range of subjects, variously holding posts in sociology and in philosophy of religion during a teaching career at, among others, the universities of Sussex, Manchester, Boston and Nashville. His time in the USA helped him shed English habits and he subsequently addressed a more general audience with some revision of his earlier views in his trilogy *After Virtue* (1981), *Whose Justice? Which Rationality?* (1986), and *Three Versions of Moral Inquiry*, the last of these being the 1989 Gifford Lectures at Edinburgh. He values 18th/19th-century Scottish philosophy, and places some importance on studies in Greek thought and language. A figure of considerable international reputation, he is considered by some to be the most famous living philosopher in the English language.

McINTYRE, Duncan Ban, English name of Donnchadh Ban Macan t-Saoir

(1724–1812)

Gaelic poet, and gamekeeper of Beinnodòrain, born in Glenorchy, Argyll. He worked as a forester, fought as a Hanoverian at Falkirk in 1746, and from 1799 to 1806 was one of the City Guard of Edinburgh. He composed a great deal of nature poetry which, since he was illiterate, was written down by the minister's son at Killin. Some of it has been translated into English by **Hugh MacDiarmid**.

MacINTYRE, Robert Donald

(1913 –)

Nationalist politician, born in Lanarkshire and educated at Hamilton Academy and Edinburgh University. One of the most influential figures in shaping the modern Scottish National Party, he did much to improve the party's organizational efficacy in the late 1930s and early 1940s. He helped to draft the party's revised policy declaration of 1948, a document which moved the SNP to a middle-of-the-road position. He was the first Scottish Nationalist MP, winning Motherwell at a by-election in 1945, but he lost the seat six months later. He was Chairman (1948–56) and President (1956–80) of the party, and Provost of Stirling (1967–75).

MACKAIL, John William

(1859–1945)

Classical scholar, born in Kingarth, Bute. After a career in the civil service he resigned in 1919 to give himself entirely to scholarship and criticism. He wrote *Latin Literature* (1895), and a biography of William Morris (1899). In 1906 he was elected Professor of Poetry at Oxford. He was the son-in-law of Edward Burne-Jones, and father of the novelist Angela Thirkell.

MACKAY, (Adam) Neil

(1947 –)

Composer, critic and teacher, born in Glasgow. He studied at Edinburgh University and privately with Hans Gal. Since 1976 he has taught at the Rudolf Steiner School, Edinburgh; he also lectures in adult education and writes regularly for the *Guardian* about music in Scotland. His works include a violin concerto (1980), *Variations on a Theme of*

Gustav Holst (string orchestra, 1984), *Veni Creator Spiritus* (soprano, choir, organ, 1984), *Missa Vexilla Regis* (1985), *The Trumpet* (two poems of Edward Thomas for female voices, 1988), and *Sequence Light Divided* (cello and chamber orchestra, 1991).

MACKAY, Charles
(1814–89)

Songwriter, born in Perth. He was editor of the Glasgow *Argus* (1844–7), and the *Illustrated London News* (1848–59), and New York correspondent of *The Times* during the civil war (1862–5). Two of his songs, 'There's a Good Time Coming' and 'Cheer, Boys, Cheer', had an extraordinary success. His prose works included *Popular Delusions* (1841) and *Forty Years' Recollections* (1877). His daughter was Marie Corelli, and his son Eric (1851–98) achieved a reputation as a poet.

MACKAY, Fulton
(1922–87)

Actor, born in Paisley. A quantity surveyor, he trained at RADA before making his professional stage début in *Angel* (1947). A member of the Citizens' Theatre in Glasgow (1949–51, 1953–8) and the Old Vic (1962–3) in London, his many stage performances in classical and contemporary roles include *Any Satyre of the Thrie Estaites* (1950), *Peer Gynt* (1962), *In Celebration* (1969), *Willie Rough* (1972) and *Old Movies* (1977). A gentle, self-effacing craftsman, he brought a sharp sense of observation and warm humanity to his most memorable creations. He also directed for the theatre, most notably on a production of *The Wild Duck* for the Scottish Actors Company in 1969. He made his film début in *I'm A Stranger* (1952) and was subsequently seen in the likes of *Gumshoe* (1971) and *Local Hero* (1983). Active on television in such series as *Special Branch* (1969–73) and plays like *Going Gently* (1981) and *The Holy City* (1986), he is fondly recalled as the officious prison warden in the popular comedy *Porridge* (1974–7). He also painted, wrote plays under the pseudonym of Aeneas MacBride and was a dedicated supporter of the Glasgow children's charity, Child and Family Trust.

MACKAY, James, Baron Mackay of Clashfern
(1927 –)

Judge, born in the village of Scourie, Sutherland, the son of a railway signalman. He won a bursary to George Heriot's School and from there went to Edinburgh University, where he was awarded a first in mathematics and physics. After teaching mathematics at St Andrews University and beginning a research degree at Cambridge he switched to law, being called to the Bar in 1955. Ten years later he was made a QC, specializing in tax law. He was successively Dean of the Faculty of Advocates (1976–9), Lord Advocate, and a life peer (1979–84), a judge of the Court of Session (1984–5), a Lord of Appeal in Ordinary (1985–7), and Lord Chancellor in 1987. He took the title of his peerage from the name of the shepherd's cottage he knew as a boy. As Lord Chancellor he forced through radical reforms of the legal profession. In 1989 he clashed with the Calvinist elders of his church, the Free Presbyterians, because of his attendance at the funeral of a Roman Catholic colleague.

MACKAY, John Alexander
(1889–1983)

Scottish-born American scholar and ecumenist, born into a Free Presbyterian family in Inverness. He was educated at Aberdeen, Princeton, and in Spain where he developed a lifelong love of Hispanic culture. He became the first Protestant to become Professor of Philosophy at Peru's National University (1915–25), served the Young Men's Christian Association in Uruguay and Mexico (1925–32), and later was appointed President of Princeton Theological Seminary (1936–59). A leader in the ecumenical movement, he was President of the World Alliance of Reformed Churches (1954–9). His works in English include *The Other Spanish Christ* (1932), *The Presbyterian Way of Life* (1960), and *Ecumenics: The Science of the Church Universal* (1964).

MACKAY, Robert, English name of Rob Donn MacAoidh
(1714–78)

Gaelic poet, born in Strathmore, Sutherland. He became a herdsman for the MacKay chief, Lord Reay. As an oral bard he became known as 'Rob Donn', describing rural life in his area and the disintegration of clan society on Strathnaver and Strathmore after the 1745 Jacobite Rising. His poetry was later collected and written down by local ministers, and a first edition appeared in 1828.

McKEAN, Tom

(1963 –)

Middle-distance runner, born in Bellshill, Lanarkshire. He won the European Cup 800m in 1985, his début international season, having come to the selectors' notice after compiling a run of 34 consecutive victories at this distance. He retained his European Cup title in 1987 and 1989, also winning the World Cup 800m in the latter year. In 1990 he won the European Championship. A robust runner, his main asset is his physical strength, his chief weakness a lack of tactical acumen, which has led to his losing races for which he was favourite. A large part of his success is due to his coach, Tommy Boyle, with whom he has been associated since his early teenage years.

McKELLAR, Kenneth

(1927 –)

Singer and composer, born in Paisley. He sang in his first concert in a local hall at the age of 13. Educated at Aberdeen University, he worked in forestry for two years before turning professional. Touring Australasia, he made numerous records, topped the bill at London Palladium, and provided the soundtrack singing for the film *The Great Waltz* (1972). His many TV appearances include *The Rolf Harris Show* and *The Good Old Days*. He had his own radio series, *A Song for Everyone*, in 1973–4. He is currently a director of Radio Clyde.

MACKENDRICK, Alexander

(1912 –)

American film director of Scottish origin, born in Boston. Educated at the Glasgow School of Art, he worked as an animator and commercial artist before joining the script department at Pinewood Studios. During the war he made documentaries, newsreels and propaganda films for the Ministry of Information, and subsequently joined Ealing Studios, making his directorial début on *Whisky Galore* (1948). A master of the Ealing comedy and a gifted director of children, his many successes include *The Man In The White Suit* (1951), *Mandy* (1952) and *The Maggie* (1954). Later, embarking on international projects, he created a memorable portrait of greed and venality in *Sweet Smell of Success* (1957), which illustrates his cynical view of human nature. He retired as an active film-maker after *Don't Make Waves* (1967) and lectured at the California Institute of Arts, where he was Dean of the Film Department from 1969 to 1978.

MACKENZIE, Sir Alexander

(1764–1820)

Explorer and fur-trader, born in Stornoway, Isle of Lewis. In 1779 he joined the Northwest Fur Company, and in 1788 established Fort Chipewayan on Lake Athabasca. From there he discovered the Mackenzie River (1789), followed it to the sea, and in 1792–3 became the first European to cross the Rockies to the Pacific, making the descent by canoe. He was knighted in 1802.

MacKENZIE, Alexander

(1822–92)

Scottish-born Canadian politician, born in Logierait, Perthshire, and trained as a stonemason. Emigrating in 1842 to Sarnia, Ontario, he prospered there as a builder. Entering the Canadian Parliament in 1861, he became leader of the Liberal Party in 1875 and one month later became premier. He legislated against electoral corruption, and set up the Supreme Court of Canada, thereby reducing the judicial role of Britain in Canada. A fervent Baptist, he also promoted temperance legislation. He built up the Liberal Party by incorporating various regional groupings, notably the French in Quebec. Incorruptible and highly efficient, he followed a stringent fiscal policy which delayed the completion of the trans-Canada rail and telegraph links. Defeated in 1878, he retired from politics. He thrice declined knighthood.

MACKENZIE, Sir Alexander Campbell

(1847–1935)

Composer, born in Edinburgh. He studied music at Sondershausen, and from 1862 at the Royal Academy, London. From 1865 to 1879 he was teacher, violinist, and conductor in Edinburgh, and from 1887 to 1924 he was Principal of the Royal Academy of Music. *The Rose of Sharon* (1884), an oratorio, contains some of his best work. He wrote operas, cantatas, Scottish rhapsodies, a concerto and a *pibroch* for violin, chamber music and songs. He also wrote *A Musician's Narrative* (1927).

MACKENZIE, Sir (Edward Montague) Compton
(1883–1972)

English-born writer, born in West Hartlepool, Cleveland. Educated at St Paul's School and Magdalen College, Oxford, he studied for the English Bar but gave up his law studies in 1907 to work on his first play, *The Gentleman in Grey*. His first novel, *The Passionate Elopement*, was published in 1911. There followed his story of theatre life, *Carnival* (1912), which was a huge success, succeeded by the autobiographical *Sinister Street* (2 vols, 1913–14) and *Guy and Pauline* (1915). In World War I he served in the Dardanelles, and in 1917 he became Director of the Aegean Intelligence Service in Syria, a time he described in his book on the Secret Service, *Extremes Meet* (1928). Settling on the island of Barra in the Outer Hebrides, he was one of the founders of the Scottish National Party (1928). His considerable output included *Sylvia Scarlett* (1918), *Poor Relations* (1919), *Rich Relatives* (1921), *Vestal Fire* (1927), *The Four Winds of Love* (4 vols, 1937–45), *Aegean Memories* (1940), *Whisky Galore* (1947), *Eastern Epic*, Vol I (1951), and *Rockets Galore* (1957). A theatrical, flamboyant character, he published a monumental autobiography, *My Life and Times* (1963–71), which came out in 10 *Octaves*.

MACKENZIE, Henry
(1745–1831)

Writer, known as the 'Man of Feeling', born in Edinburgh, the son of a doctor. He was educated at the High School and Edinburgh University. He became a crown attorney in the Scottish Court of Exchequer (1765), and in 1804 Comptroller of Taxes. For more than half a century he was 'one of the most illustrious names connected with polite literature in Edinburgh', and a regular contributor to the *Scots Magazine and General Intelligencer*. His sentimental novel, *The Man of Feeling*, was published in 1771, followed by *The Man of the World* in 1773, and *Julia de Roubigné* in 1777. He also wrote two tragedies, *The Spanish Father* (1773, but never performed), and *The Prince of Tunis* (1773). He was one of the founders of the Royal Society of Edinburgh (1783). He is also remembered for his recognition of **Burns**, and as an early admirer of Lessing and of Schiller. His memoirs were published as *Anecdotes and Egotisms* (1927).

MACKENZIE, Sir Hugh Stirling
(1913 –)

Naval commander, born in Inverness and educated at Cargilfield School, Edinburgh, and the Royal Naval College at Dartmouth. Commissioned in the Royal Navy in 1927, he joined the submarine service and during World War II he commanded HMS *Thrasher* and, between 1943 and 1945, HMS *Tantalus*, one of the recently introduced 'T' class general-purpose patrol submarines. He remained with the submarine service in the postwar years and, after reaching flag rank, he was appointed chief executive of the navy's Polaris nuclear deterrent in the rank of vice-admiral. In 1968 he retired and was appointed Director of the Atlantic Salmon Research Trust.

MACKENZIE, John
(1932 –)

Film and television director, born in Edinburgh. A history graduate from Edinburgh University, he initially worked as an actor and stage manager in the theatre before moving to London and becoming an assistant to director Ken Loach on such groundbreaking socially aware television dramas as *Cathy Come Home* (1966) and *Up the Junction* (1966). Graduating to direction, he has made a wide range of significant works, including *Bagelstein Boys* (1968) by Colin Welland, *The Cheviot, The Stag and The Black, Black Oil* (1974) by **John McGrath**, *Double Dare* (1976) by Dennis Potter and a number of plays by **Peter McDougall**, including *Just Another Saturday* (1975) and *A Sense of Freedom* (1981), based on the early life of **Jimmy Boyle**. He made his cinema début with *One Brief Summer* (1969) and attracted considerable attention with his muscular handling of the gangland saga *The Long Good Friday* (1980). His subsequent films include *The Honorary Consul* (1983), *The Fourth Protocol* (1987) and *The Last of the Finest* (1990).

McKENZIE, Joseph
(1929 –)

English-born photographic artist and teacher, born in London. After conscription and regular service in the RAF as a photographer (1947–52), he studied at the London College of Printing. He taught photography at St Martin's School of Art in London and then at

281

the Duncan of Jordanstone College of Art in Dundee until 1986. From 1974 to 1980 he operated the Victoria House Gallery of Photography from his home in Tayport, Fife. His masterly photographs are wide-ranging in subject matter, as seen in his *Pages of Experience: Photography 1947–87* (1987), and relate more closely to the American than to the European tradition of photography, combining aesthetic interests with strongly-felt ethical and political concerns. He is probably best known for his concerned, thoughtful and sometimes controversial photographic essays of people, often children, and their environments in mainly urban contexts in Scotland and Ireland.

MACKENZIE, Murdoch (the Elder)
(1712–97)

Marine cartographer, born in Orkney. He was recommended to the Admiralty in 1742 by **Colin Maclaurin** to make a geographic and hydrographic survey of the Orkney Islands, which he published in 1750. In the aftermath of the 1745 Jacobite rebellion he was commissioned by the Admiralty to survey the then relatively uncharted waters of the Hebrides and the sea lochs on the west coast of Scotland, a task which occupied him for the next 20 years. He was assisted by his nephew Murdoch Mackenzie (the Younger, 1743–1829) who, on Murdoch the Elder's retirement in 1771, succeeded him as surveyor to the Admiralty. In 1774 he published *A Treatise on Marine Surveying*, and in the same year was elected a Fellow of the Royal Society.

MacKENZIE, Thomas
(1854–1930)

Scottish-born New Zealand politician. Born in Edinburgh, he emigrated with his family at the age of four, and settled in New Zealand. There he became a surveyor and undertook several explorations of uncharted territory. He entered Parliament in 1887. Although widely regarded as politically independent, he joined the Liberal administration, holding the portfolios of industry and commerce and agriculture between 1908 and 1912. In 1912 he was elected Liberal Party leader (and therefore premier) as a compromise candidate, but lost office one month later at the general election. High Commissioner to Great Britain (1912–20), he had an important role in New Zealand's war effort, and

attended the Versailles Peace Conference in 1919.

MACKENZIE, William Forbes
(1801–62)

Politician, born in Portmore, Peeblesshire. MP for Peeblesshire (1837–52), he introduced a liquor Act for Scotland, passed in 1853, that provided for Sunday closing and other controls.

MACKENZIE, William Lyon
(1795–1861)

Scottish-born Canadian insurgent and politician, born in Dundee. He emigrated to Canada in 1820, and published the *Colonial Advocate* in Toronto from 1824 to 1834, in which he attacked the government ceaselessly. In 1828 he was elected to the provincial parliament for York, but was expelled in 1830 for libel on the assembly. He was Mayor of Toronto in 1834. In 1837 he published in his paper a declaration of independence for Toronto, headed a band of 800 insurgents, and attacked the city (5 December). Driven off by a superior force, he fled across the border, and on 13 December seized Navy Island in the Niagara River, where he declared a provisional government. A Canadian force promptly crossed the river (29 December) and burned the American steamer, *Caroline*, which had been supplying the rebels, thus precipitating an international incident. Mackenzie fled to New York (January 1638), where he was sentenced by the US authorities to 12 months' imprisonment. He returned to Canada in 1849, was an MP from 1850 to 1858, and died in Toronto. He was the grandfather of Canadian Prime Minister W L Mackenzie King.

MACKENZIE OF ROSEHAUGH, Sir George
(1636–91)

Jurist, born in Dundee. After studying at St Andrews, Aberdeen and Bourges, he was called to the Bar at Edinburgh in 1656, and in 1661 he unsuccessfully defended Archibald, Marquis of **Argyll**. He entered Parliament for Ross-shire in 1669, and in 1677 was named King's Advocate. In the popular mind he is regarded only as 'Bluidy Mackenzie', the criminal prosecutor in the days of the persecution of the Covenanters. He cultivated

Scottish literature, was a friend of Dryden, and was one of the first Scots to write English with purity. In 1682 he founded the Advocates Library in Edinburgh (now the National Library of Scotland). He retired to Oxford at the 'Glorious Revolution' of 1688, died in London, and was buried in Edinburgh in Greyfriars Churchyard. A good scholar and a prolific author, he wrote works of fiction, politics, history and law. His legal writings include *Laws and Customs of Scotland in Matters Criminal* (1674), *Institutions of the Law of Scotland* (1684) and *Observations on the Acts of Parliament* (1686), all of which are still important. His *Works* appeared between 1716 and 1722, and his *Memoirs of the Affairs of Scotland* were published in 1821.

MACKENZIE STUART, Alexander John, Lord, of Dean

(1924 –)

Scottish and European judge, born in Aberdeen. Educated at **Fettes** College, Sidney Sussex College, Cambridge, and Edinburgh University, he practised at the Scottish Bar. He became a judge of the Court of Session in 1972, and then the first British judge appointed to the Court of Justice of the European Communities (1973–88), being President of that court, 1984–8. He published *The European Communities and the Rule of Law* (1977).

MACKIE, Albert David

(1904–85)

Journalist and poet, born in Edinburgh, who began selling articles to newspapers at the age of 16. After graduating from Edinburgh University, where he was light-weight boxing champion in 1927, he worked briefly in Jamaica as news editor of the *Daily Gleaner*. He was editor of the *Edinburgh Evening Dispatch* for eight years. An accomplished vernacular poet, he adopted the pseudonym MacNib for a topical verse feature, usually humorous, which he contributed to the Scottish press for more than 30 years. Five of his plays were professionally produced in Edinburgh, and he wrote scripts for several Scottish comedians.

MacKIE, Euan Wallace

(1936 –)

English-born archaeologist, born in London. After studying at Cambridge University, he became Assistant Keeper and later Deputy Director of the Hunterian Museum in Glasgow University. His work on the development of brochs and their material culture has been highly influential, and he led the field in archaeoastronomy in attempting to test by excavation whether megalithic sites could have been used as solar observatories. In 1977 he published two controversial books on the wider implications of archaeoastronomy: *Science and Society in Prehistoric Britain* and *The Megalith Builders*. He has also written *Scotland: an archaeological guide* (1975).

MACKIE, John Duncan

(1887–1978)

Historian, educated at Middlesborough High School and Jesus College, Oxford. He was appointed Lecturer in Modern History and Head of the Department of Modern History at St Andrews University in 1908, remaining until 1926. Appointed Professor of Modern History at London University (Bedford College), in his publications he alternated between high Scottish historical scholarship and readable British historical narrative, aimed at a large public, as for instance with *Negotiations between James VI and I and Ferdinand I of Tuscany* (1927), and *Cavalier and Puritan* (1930). In 1930 he was made Professor of Scottish History and Literature at Glasgow University, and added a touch of the literary and controversial to his output with *Andrew Lang and the House of Stuart* (1935) while maintaining scholarly austerity with his edition of Thomas Thomson's *Memorial on an Old Extent* (1946) for the Stair Society. His *The Earlier Tudors* (1952) for the Oxford *History of England* series was disappointingly old-fashioned. He returned more to his own in his lively *The University of Glasgow 1451–1951* (1954), *A History of the Scottish Reformation* (1960, but rapidly outmoded by modern scholarship), and his Pelican *History of Scotland* (1964), which won a mass audience. In 1969 he produced his edition of the Calendar of State Papers relating to Scotland and **Mary, Queen of Scots** (vol XIII, 1597–1603). Although his work may seem somewhat thin today, and unduly reflective of the prejudices and conventions of the interwar period, he had an ability for prompting reflection in his audience.

MACKIE, Neil

(1946 –)

Concert and oratorio tenor singer, born in Aberdeen. He studied at the Royal Scottish

Academy of Music and Drama. He has appeared as soloist with several orchestras throughout Europe and the UK, toured Mexico for the British Council and America with the Scottish Chamber Orchestra. He made his New York début (at the Lincoln Centre) in 1986. He has close associations with the music of Britten — making a première recording of unpublished songs — and **Maxwell Davies** — performing premières of *The Martyrdom of St Magnus* (title role), the opera *The Lighthouse* and *Into the Labyrinth* (written specially for him).

MACKIE, Sir Peter Jeffrey
(1855–1924)

Whisky distiller and blender, born in Stirling, and educated at the local high school. On joining his uncle's firm, J L Mackie and Company, he went to Islay to study the distilling process. Shortly afterwards he established his own firm to manufacture blends. In 1890 his own and his uncle's firms merged. In the subsequent whisky trade boom he launched the famous White Horse blended brand. Despite opposition from malt distillers Mackie's business prospered. He achieved prominence as a vocal opponent of government duty policies, becoming Vice-President of the Whisky Association in 1917. He was made a baronet in 1920. Following several mergers and with his health failing he guided his company to public status, becoming White Horse Distillers Limited. Later that year he died, leaving a fortune of three-quarters of a million pounds.

MACKIE, Thomas Jones
(1888–1955)

Bacteriologist, born in Hamilton, Lanarkshire, and educated at Glasgow University where he graduated in 1910. He proceeded to a Carnegie Scholarship in the Department of Pathology in Glasgow. He became an assistant in bacteriology at the Middlesex Hospital but was almost immediately mobilized in the RAMC where he served at Gallipoli and was later in charge of the base bacteriology laboratory at Alexandria, Egypt. In 1918 he was appointed to the Chair of Bacteriology in Capetown University and in 1923 he became Professor of Bacteriology at Edinburgh, where he remained for 32 years. His early work included a study of surgical wound infections, which led to research on serological reactions of the coliform group of organisms. He also investigated the properties of complement, and advanced the diagnosis of the enteric organisms. He did a great deal of work on the serological typing of streptococci and he studied tetanus and *Brucella abortus*. He produced two standard and popular textbooks of world-wide renown: *A Textbook of Bacteriology* (1949, with C H Browning) and *A Handbook of Practical Bacteriology* (9th ed 1953, with J E McCartney).

MACKINNON, Donald Mackenzie
(1913–)

Philosopher of religion, born in Oban, Argyll. Professor of Moral Philosophy at Aberdeen (1947–60) and of philosophy of religion at Cambridge (1960–78), he explored the relations between theology, metaphysics and moral philosophy, championing realism over idealism. His wide concerns, ranging from the theory of knowledge to moral freedom and political action, and from Marxist-Leninism to a theological basis for unilateral disarmament, are evinced in numerous essays, some of which are collected in *Borderlands of Theology* (1968), *Explorations in Theology* 5 (1979), and *Themes in Theology* (1988). His 1965–6 Gifford lectures were published as *The Problem of Metaphysics* (1974).

MACKINTOSH, Charles Rennie
(1868–1928)

Architect, designer, water colourist and outstanding exponent of the Art Nouveau style in Scotland. Born in Glasgow, the son of a police superintendent, he was educated at Allan Glen's School. He was apprenticed to the architect John Hutcheson in Glasgow, simultaneously attending evening classes at Glasgow School of Art, before joining the established firm of Honeyman and Keppie in 1889. In 1900 he married **Margaret MacDonald**. His architectural output, although not large and mostly within the Glasgow region, exercised very considerable influence on European design. It included the outstanding Glasgow School of Art (1897–1909), the famous **Cranston** tearooms, and houses such as Hill House in Helensburgh (1903–4). His style contrasted strong rectilinear structures and elements with subtle curved motifs; in his houses there are deliberate references to traditional Scottish architecture, yet the modern style he evolved was distinct from those of his contemporaries. He was the leading exponent of Art Nouveau in Scotland and prime designer of what became known as the Glasgow Style. His schemes of interior decoration, his furniture and textile designs and metalwork, were all conceived and designed along a theme. His work was exhibited at the Vienna Secession Exhibition in 1900, where it was much admired. In 1914 he left Scotland and did no further major architectural work, but in his latter years he turned to painting, and produced a series of exquisite watercolours, chiefly in France (1923–7).

MACKINTOSH, Elizabeth
(1896–1952)

Novelist and playwright, born in Inverness. Under the pseudonym of Gordon Daviot she wrote serious works, including the historical drama *Richard of Bordeaux* (1932), the work for which she is most remembered, and a biography of **John Dundee** (1937). *The Franchise Affair*, a detective story, was one of several which she wrote under the pseudonym Josephine Tey.

MACKINTOSH, Hugh Ross
(1870–1936)

Theologian, born in Paisley. Professor of Systematic Theology at New College, Edinburgh (1904–36), and Moderator of the General Assembly of the Church of Scotland (1932), he sought to spread understanding of developments in continental theology, which he had studied at Marburg. He helped to produce translations of Ritschl's *Justification and Reconciliation* and Schleiermacher's *The Christian Faith*. His 1933 Croall lectures on trends from Schleiermacher to Barth, described by **John Baillie** as 'a fine mingling of generous appreciation with stern rebuke', were published posthumously as *Types of Modern Theology* (1937). His earlier books of note included *The Doctrine of the Person of Jesus Christ* (1912) and *The Christian Experience of Forgiveness* (1927).

MACKINTOSH, Sir James
(1765–1832)

Writer, born in Aldourie, Inverness-shire. He studied medicine at Aberdeen, but settled in London as a journalist. His *Vindiciae Gallicae* (1791) was written as a defence of the French Revolution in reply to Burke's *Reflections on the French Revolution*, and he became secretary of the 'Friends of the People' (he later recanted his views in *On the State of France*, 1815). He was called to the Bar in 1795. In 1799 he delivered a brilliant series of lectures on the law of nature and of nations at Lincoln's Inn. In 1804 he was appointed recorder of Bombay, and in 1806 judge of its

Admiralty Court. He spent seven years in Bombay, entering Parliament after his return as Whig member for Nairn (1813). He published a number of works on history and philosophy.

MACKINTOSH, John Pitcairn
(1929–78)

Politician and educator, born in Simla, India. Educated at Edinburgh, Oxford and Princeton, he taught history at Glasgow and Edinburgh until 1961, when he became senior lecturer in government at the University of Ibadan, Nigeria, for two years, after which he taught politics at Glasgow and in 1965 became Professor of Politics at Strathclyde University. He published major studies of *The British Cabinet* (1962) and *Nigerian Politics and Government* (1966). In 1966, as Labour Party candidate, he took the Conservative seat of Berwick and East Lothian and resigned his professorship. As an MP he was impressed by the rising tide of Scottish and Welsh nationalism, but in any case considered that measures of devolution were vitally necessary to the health of the British constitution, a theme he outlined in *The Devolution of Power* (1968). Labour premier Harold Wilson was hostile to these views, and it became increasingly evident that Mackintosh had no hope of office in a Wilson administration. He lost his seat in the election of February 1974, but regained it in October. He maintained strong links with his subject, bringing out *British Government and Politics* (1970), and his acceptance of a part-time professorship of politics at Edinburgh University in 1977 made it clear he intended to be an inspiration in the growing struggle for devolution. His premature death removed a major force in the Labour attempt to bridge the counterpulls of unionism and nationalism.

MACKINTOSH, Margaret See MacDONALD, Margaret

MACKINTOSH, William
(1662–1743)

Jacobite, of Borlum, Inverness-shire. He held a command in the 1715 Rising and led his force south to join the English rebels. He was captured and imprisoned, but escaped from Newgate in 1716. Back in Scotland he took part in the abortive 1719 rising, but was captured again and died after long captivity in Edinburgh Castle. He was an early arboriculturist.

McLACHLAN, Jessie
(1834 – ?1899)

Convicted murderer, the centre of a hugely controversial crime. The victim, a servant in a Glasgow house where McLachlan had once been a servant, was murdered while the family was absent, with the exception of the house-owner's father, a Mr Fleming. When the body was discovered Fleming was arrested on suspicion of having committed the murder. He was released after a week and McLachlan, who was friendly with both Fleming and the victim, was then charged, convicted (1862) and sentenced to death. Fleming denied any involvement in the offence. McLachlan likewise denied all knowledge of the deed and entered a special defence, naming the old man as the murderer. He appeared as the chief prosecution witness. After the conviction and sentence a petition was raised which attracted over 50 000 signatures protesting McLachlan's innocence and seeking justice. In the absence of a court of criminal appeal, Parliament set up a private enquiry which resulted in McLachlan being granted a conditional royal pardon, the condition being that she be detained in prison for the rest of her life. She spent 15 years in prison and subsequently emigrated to the USA. Fleming spent the rest of his life under a cloud of suspicion.

McLACHLAN, Murray
(1965 –)

Pianist, born in Dundee. He studied at Cambridge University, and his teachers included Ryszard Balest, Peter Katin and Norma Fischer. He has performed widely as a concerto player (Royal Festival Hall début, 1989) and has specialized as a soloist in concerts and recordings of Myaskovsky, Prokofiev and piano music of Scotland.

McLAREN, Bill
(1923 –)

Rugby broadcaster and writer, born in Hawick, Roxburghshire. A wing-forward for Hawick, he was selected for a Scottish trial, but injury prevented him from playing. After retiring from the game he combined a career as a PE teacher with journalism, starting off with a local paper before making his first broadcast in 1953. As the BBC's chief rugby union commentator, his love and knowledge of the game have given him an unrivalled reputation as a sports broadcaster of warmth, intelligence and integrity, a reputation enhanced by his loyalty to the BBC despite a lucrative offer to move to the independent network for the 1991 World Cup.

MacLAREN, Charles
(1782–1866)

Amateur geologist, born in Ormiston, East Lothian, and essentially self-taught. With others, such as **William Ritchie**, he established *The Scotsman* newspaper in 1817, which he edited from 1820 until 1845. During this period he was responsible for some of the earliest accounts of the geology of Arthur's Seat, Edinburgh's famous volcano, published in *The Scotsman* around 1830 and accompanied by some of the earliest newspaper illustrations. Elected a Fellow of the Royal Society of Edinburgh in 1837, he served as President of the Edinburgh Geological Society for the last two years of his life. His descriptive account, *A Sketch of the Geology of Fife and the Lothians*, first published in 1838, appeared posthumously in 1866.

MACLAREN, Duncan
(1800–86)

The most influential Scottish radical politician in the Victorian era, known as 'the MP for Scotland'. Born in Renton, Dunbartonshire, he became a draper in Edinburgh. As treasurer of the council in the 1830s he saved the city from bankruptcy. Liberal MP for Edinburgh from 1865 to 1881, he retired to make room for his son John, the Lord Advocate. As MP he espoused the causes of disestablishment, temperance, educational reform, free trade, a wider franchise system and crofter land rights. A lifelong Liberal, he broke with his party on the issue of Irish Home Rule in 1886. He was a leading lay figure in the United Presbyterian Church.

MACLAREN, Ian, pen-name of John Watson
(1850–1907)

Minister and writer, born in Manningtree, Essex. He was a Presbyterian minister in Liverpool from 1880 to 1895. His amazing success with his *Beside the Bonnie Brier Bush* (1894) gave rise to the name 'Kailyard School', and was followed by *Days of Auld Lang Syne* (1895) and others. He also wrote religious works, such as *Children of the Resurrection* (1912).

MacLAREN, James Marjoribanks
(1853–90)

Architect, born in Stirlingshire. Educated in Stirling, he served his apprenticeship in Glasgow, thereafter working in London in the office of **John James Stevenson**. An accomplished draughtsman, he ghosted for other architects in the early years. He formed an association with Richard Coad in London, working in south-west England. In 1886 he won a competition for the extension to Stirling High School, producing an influential watershed in his powerful design, relieving the massing with carved ornament in a bold and distinctively original combination. Commissions from Sir Donald Currie for work at Fortingall and the Glenlyon estate after 1887 gave him the opportunity to develop a Scottish Arts and Crafts style as a modern tradition, a trend that was perceptibly influenced by the work of the American, Henry Hobson Richardson. His contribution in this area in turn influenced **Charles Rennie Mackintosh** and Sir **Robert Lorimer**. His other major works include the extension to Ledbury Park, Herefordshire (1886), and 10–12 Palace Court, Bayswater, London (1889).

McLAREN, Norman
(1914–87)

Scottish-born animator, born in Stirling. A student of interior design at the Glasgow School of Art, he became an avid cineaste and his exposure to Russian cinema and German abstract art led to his own initial endeavours such as *Seven Till Five* (1934) and *Hell Unlimited* (1934), a mixture of live-action and drawn and object animation. His work soon brought him to the attention of **John Grierson**, who employed him at the GPO Film Unit on a number of documentaries and *Love on the Wing* (1939), which was drawn directly with pen and ink frame-by-frame on to raw film stock. He subsequently moved to New York and then emigrated to Canada to work at the National Film Board. His further experiments with form, content and the use of music include *Le Haut Sur Les Montagnes* (1945) and *Around Is Around* (1952), which featured his 'pixillation' technique of animating human actors. His diverse and innovative body of work includes paper cut-out films, abstract pieces and a trio of live-action dance studies that culminated in *Narcissus* (1981–3), his last work.

McLAUCHLAN, Ian
(1942 –)

Rugby player, born in Tarbolton, Ayrshire. Known as 'Mighty Mouse', he was short for a prop forward, but compensated with superior technique. He played 43 internationals for Scotland between 1969 and 1979, 19 of them as captain. The decline of the team after his retiral from international rugby was an indication of his importance, both as a player and as a leader. He also played eight matches for the British Lions, in the 1971 tour of New Zealand, and the 1974 trip to South Africa.

MACLAURIN, Colin
(1698–1746)

Mathematician, born in Kilmodan, Argyll. He graduated at Glasgow (1713), and became professor at Aberdeen (1717). In 1725 he was appointed Professor of Mathematics at Edinburgh on Newton's recommendation. He published *Geometria Organica* in 1720, and his best-known work, *Treatise on Fluxions*, in 1742, which gave a systematic account of Newton's approach to the calculus, taking a geometric point of view rather than the analytical one used on the continent. This is often thought to have contributed to the neglect of analysis in 18th-century Britain. In 1745 he organized the defences of Edinburgh against the Jacobite army, but his efforts impaired his health and he died early in the following year.

McLEAN, Alan Campbell
(1922–89)

Novelist, born on Walney Island, Barrow-in-Furness, Cumbria, the fourth son of a foreman in the Vickers shipbuilding yards. At the age of 14 he lasted two months as an apprentice motor mechanic before becoming an office boy, an unpromising career that was happily cut short by World War II, when he joined the RAF and saw service in the Mediterranean and North Africa. During this time he was sentenced to solitary confinement in the 'glasshouse' which provided the experience and title of the novel of the same name, published in 1968. After demobilization McLean set about earning his living by writing. Though he was an interesting and committed writer for adults — *The Islander* (1982) compares favourably with **Neil Gunn**'s *Highland River* — his claim to posterity lies in his work for children. His most popular book is undoubtedly *The Hill of the Red Fox*. First published in 1955, it owes an obvious debt to **Stevenson**'s *Kidnapped* and **Buchan**'s *Thirty-Nine Steps*, but McLean's concerns are modern; set on Skye, the author's adopted home, the plot involves MI5, atomic scientists and the KGB. Later books — *Ribbon of Fire* (1962) and *The Year of the Stranger* (1971) — were likewise located in the Highlands, an area that the author, a lifelong Socialist, held dear. Among his other books are a series of well-scripted detective novels.

MACLEAN, Alistair

(1922–87)

Author, born in Glasgow. He was educated at Inverness Royal Academy, Hillhead High School and Glasgow University. He served in the Royal Navy from 1941 to 1946. In 1954, while a school-teacher, he won a short-story competition held by the *Glasgow Herald*, contributing a tale of adventure at sea. At the suggestion of **Collins**, the publishers, he produced a full-length novel, *HMS Ulysses*, the next year, and this epic story of wartime bravery became an immediate best-seller. He followed it with *The Guns of Navarone* in 1957, and turned to full-time writing. He preferred the term 'adventure story' to 'novel' in describing his work. His settings are worldwide, including the China Seas (*South by Java Head*, 1958), Greenland (*Night Without End*, 1960), Florida (*Fear is the Key*, 1961), the Scottish islands (*When Eight Bells Toll*, 1966), a polar scientific station (*Ice Station Zebra*, 1963) and the Camargue (*Caravan to Vaccares*, 1970). As well as two secret service thrillers (written as Ian Stuart), *The Dark Crusader* (1961) and *The Satan Bug* (1962), he wrote a Western (*Breakheart Pass*, 1974) and biographies of T E Lawrence and Captain Cook. Other titles include *Where Eagles Dare* (1967), *Force Ten From Navarone* (1968) and *Athabasca* (1980). Most of his stories were made into highly successful films.

McLEAN, Bruce

(1944 –)

Artist, born in Glasgow. He attended Glasgow School of Art (1961–3) and St Martin's School of Art, London (1963–6). In 1971 he became a lecturer at Maidstone College of Art and, in the same year, formed The Pose Band, Nice Style, a group of performance artists. The aim of his performance art was to parody the self-regard of the art establishment. Not unusually, however, his art has itself become part of the establishment it originally set out to lampoon. Although continuing to produce performances, he has also turned to painting and other forms of visual art, including ceramics.

MacLEAN, Sir Donald

(1864–1932)

English Liberal politician, born in Farnworth, Lancashire, of Scottish parents. Educated at Haverfordwest and Carmarthen Grammar Schools, he practised as a solicitor. MP for Peeblesshire (1910–22), he was Deputy Speaker from 1911 to 1922. He was Chairman of several important wartime commissions, such as Poor Law administration, the health ministry, and labour relations in the docks. He was also Chairman of the independent Liberal Parliamentary Party (1919–22), leading it while Asquith was out of the House of Commons. He lost his seat in 1922 and did not return to Parliament until 1929, when he won the North Cornwall seat. In the National Coalition government he was Minister for Education (1931–2). His son Donald was at the centre of a notorious spy scandal after World War II.

MacLEAN, Dougie

(1954 –)

Singer, songwriter and instrumentalist, born in Glendevon, Perthshire. He gained his musical spurs as fiddler and guitarist with the Tannahill Weavers folk group in the late 1970s, and then began a solo career, performing mainly his own compositions and appearing in many parts of the world, including Australia and the USA. His gentle, uncluttered songs have won him a large following in Scotland, and he has recorded a string of highly successful albums, including *Craigie Dhu* (1983), *Singing Land* (1985), *Real Estate* (1988) and *Whitewash* (1990). His song 'Caledonia' achieved household fame in 1991 when sung by Frankie Millar in a television lager commercial.

MACLEAN, Sir Fitzroy Hew

(1911 –)

Diplomat and soldier. He was educated at Eton and Cambridge University, served with the Foreign Office from 1933, and in World War II distinguished himself as commander of the British military mission to the Yugoslav partisans (1943–5). MP for Lancaster from 1941, and for Bute and North Ayrshire from 1959, he was Under-Secretary for War from 1954 to 1957. His *Eastern Approaches* (1949), *Disputed Barricade* (1957), *A Person from England* (1958) and *Back from Bokhara* (1959) gained him a considerable reputation.

MACLEAN, John
(1879–1923)

Socialist politician, born in Pollokshaws, Glasgow, and educated at Pollokshaws Academy and Queen's Park School. Sacked from his post as a schoolteacher in Govan in 1915, he became a full-time Marxist educator and organizer. His Marxist classes recruited many working men, and in 1916 he formed the Scottish Labour College. A member of the British Socialist Party before the war, he became Soviet Consul on the Clyde after the Russian Revolution. When the Communist Party was formed he refused to join, instead setting up the Scottish Workers' Party, which promoted a more nationalistic message. He was arrested six times between 1916 and 1923 on various charges of sedition and incitement to strike. His health was badly broken by these prison sentences and he died young.

McLEAN, Lex (Alexander McLean Cameron)
(c.1907–1975)

Comedian, born in Clydebank, Dunbartonshire. An apprentice at John Brown's shipyard, his first brush with showbusiness came when he played the piano in the orchestra pit of his local cinema. Later, while a member of The Meltonians concert party, he became a straight-man and foil for Doris Droye, 'Scotland's Queen of Comedy'. When he began to earn more laughs than the nominal star, he made the transition to comic entertainer. Whether in the character of 'bunnet'-wearing 'Daft Jimmy' or elegantly attired in top hat and tails, he proved a natural funny man with his boisterous manner, mastery of innuendo and love of performing. Scotland's highest-paid comedian for many years, his record-breaking summer seasons from the mid 1950s at the Pavilion Theatre in Glasgow became an institution. Subsequent variety and television appearances, exclusively in Scotland, confirmed the affection and esteem in which he was held by the public.

MacLEAN, Sorley, or MacGill-Eain, Somhairle
(1911 –)

Gaelic poet, born on the island of Raasay, off Skye. He attended Raasay school and Portree High School on Skye before reading English at Edinburgh University (1929–33). He began to write while a student, and by the end of the 1930s was already an established figure on the Scottish literary scene. In 1940 he published *Seventeen Poems for Sixpence*, which he produced with **Robert Garioch**, and in 1943, after his recovery from wounds sustained during active service at El Alamein, came *Dàin do Eimhir* (*Poems to Eimhir*) which contained, among other shorter poems, many of his love lyrics addressed to the legendary Eimhir of the early Irish sagas. Influenced by the metaphysical poets as well as the ancient and later Celtic literature and traditional Gaelic song, he reinvigorated the Gaelic literary language and tradition, creating a medium capable of expressing contemporary intellectual challenge, much as his friend **Hugh MacDiarmid** was reinstating Scots as a serious literary language. A teacher and headmaster until his retirement in 1972, his major collection of poems, *Reothairt is Contraigh* (*Spring Tide and Neap Tide*), appeared in 1977. His work has been translated and issued in bilingual editions, and has reached a wide and appreciative public all over the world.

McLEAN, Una
(1930 –)

Actress, born in Strathaven, Lanarkshire. Educated at Larkhall, she trained at the Royal Scottish Academy of Music and Drama, making her professional début at the Byre Theatre, St Andrews, in 1955. She joined the Citizens' Theatre, Glasgow, in 1959, appearing as Emilia in *Othello*, and has consistently asserted her dramatic prowess in such productions as *The Wild Duck* (1969), *Woman in Mind* (1988), *The Guid Sisters* (1989), *Ines De Castro* (1989) and *Sky Woman Falling* (1991). A versatile comedienne with a rasping cackle of a laugh, she served as a foil to some of Scotland's top entertainers in the fondly recalled *Five Past Eight Shows* of the 1960s, and has proved herself a stalwart of pantomime since her début in *Mother Goose* (1958). Her musical talents have been displayed in the likes of *The Boyfriend* (1970) and *The Beggar's Opera* (1981) and she is a veteran of countless television shows, including the award-winning *Dreaming* (1990). In 1991 she married her frequent co-star **Russell Hunter**.

MACLEHOSE, Agnes, née Craig
(1759–1841)

Literary figure, daughter of an Edinburgh surgeon. In 1776 she married a Glasgow lawyer, from whom she separated in 1780. She met **Burns** at a party in Edinburgh in 1787, and subsequently carried on with him the well-known correspondence under the name 'Clarinda'. A number of Burns's poems and songs were dedicated to her.

McLELLAN, Robert
(1907–85)

Dramatist, born in Kirkfieldband, Lanarkshire, where his childhood on his grandparents' farm inspired his *Linmill* stories (collected 1977) and exerted a strong influence on all his work. McLellan's *Linmill* stories are told from a child's perspective in a rich Scots dialect. From 1938 until his death he lived on the Isle of Arran, which provided the setting for *Sweet Largie Bay* (1956) and *Arran Burn* (1965). His reputation, however, is based upon his plays. Wishing to create totally Scottish plays he achieved this by mixing Scottish folklore and spoken Scots on stage. *Jamie the Saxt* (1937) centres on **James VI** of Scotland and tells the story of the king's carefully calculated politics in the 1590s. Other of his plays, such as *The Flowers o' Edinburgh* (1947), likewise deal with Scottish history. His later play, *The Hypocrite* (1967), is a satire of Church standards.

MacLENNAN, George Stewart
(1884–1929)

Piper, composer and bagpipe-maker, born in Edinburgh. He was taught the Highland pipes by his father and his uncle, whom he commemorated in the pibroch 'Pipe Major John Stewart'. A prodigious talent, he was amateur champion of Great Britain by the time he was 10 years old. He enlisted in the Gordon Highlanders in 1899, and six years later, at the age of 21 became the Regimental Pipe Major. He served in the regiment until 1922, when he retired from the service and set up as a bagpipe-maker in Aberdeen. A brilliant composer of pibrochs, he was said to be the finest interpreter ever of marches, strathspeys and reels. He published a book of his pipe music shortly before his death.

McLENNAN, John Ferguson
(1827–81)

Lawyer and theorist of social evolution, born in Inverness. Educated at King's College, Aberdeen, he then studied at Cambridge before being called to the Bar in 1857. He became parliamentary draughtsman for Scotland in 1871. He is chiefly remembered for his theories of totemism and the evolution of familial organization. In *Primitive Marriage* (1865) he proposed an evolution from primitive promiscuity, through a stage of matriarchy, to patrilineal descent. He coined the terms 'exogamy' and 'endogamy', which are still in use today. He also wrote *The Patriarchal Theory*, published posthumously in 1885.

MACLENNAN, Robert Adam Ross
(1936 –)

Politician, born in Glasgow, the son of an eminent gynaecologist. He attended the Glasgow Academy, Balliol College, Oxford, Trinity College, Cambridge and Columbia University, New York, before being called to the Bar in 1962. He entered Parliament as Labour Member for Caithness and Sutherland in 1966 and has represented it ever since. He held junior posts in the governments of Harold Wilson and James Callaghan and was a founder member of the Social Democratic Party (SDP) in 1981. He came to prominence in 1987 when, after David Owen had resigned the SDP leadership because of his opposition to a merger with the Liberals, Maclennan offered himself as 'caretaker' leader until the terms of the merger had been agreed. He then became a leading member of the new party, the Social and Liberal Democrats (SLD), under Paddy Ashdown.

MacLEOD, Ally (Alistair)
(1931 –)

Football player and manager, born in Glasgow. He played for Third Lanark, St Mirren, Blackburn, Hibernian and Ayr United before turning to club management. He has been manager of Ayr United, Aberdeen, Motherwell, Airdrie and Queen of the South. His talent at club level to convince players of their abilities, and to inspire them to perform above themselves, led to his appointment as manager of the Scottish national side. He took his team to the World Cup in Argentina in 1978, having stated publicly that they could finish in the top three: they lost to Peru, and drew with the mighty Iran, thus failing to qualify for the second round. MacLeod was for a while the most vilified man in the country. He returned to club management with Ayr United, remaining there until 1990. After a brief spell out of the game, he took up management again at Queen of the South. His reign as Scotland boss is remembered by football supporters with a sarcastic sort of fondness.

McLEOD, Donald
(1940–91)

Minister, born in Lewis, a giant of the modern Free Church in Scotland. After taking an arts degree at Glasgow University, he studied theology at the Free Church College in Edinburgh. He was ordained in 1964, and his two ministries, at Kilmaddie Free Church (1964–70) and Partick Highland Free Church, Glasgow (1970–8), were followed by his appointment as Professor of Systematic Theology at the Free Church College in Edinburgh (1978). Through his writing and lecturing he made a significant contribution to intellectual debate about religion, and used his role as Editor of the *Monthly Record* of the Free Church (from 1977) to probe, challenge and stimulate. His early death robbed the Church in Scotland of a fine apologist and a very likeable champion.

MACLEOD, Fiona See SHARP, William

MacLEOD, Baron George Fielden, of Fuinary
(1895–1991)

Presbyterian clergyman, second son of Sir John MacLeod, 1st Baronet, a Glasgow MP. Educated at Winchester and Oriel College, Oxford, he won the MC and Croix de Guerre in World War I, and studied theology at Edinburgh, becoming minister of St Cuthbert's there (1926–30) and at Govan in Glasgow (1930–8). He founded the Iona Community, which set about restoring the ruined abbey on that historic island. The original dozen ministers and helpers soon grew in number and, working there every summer, renovated most of the monastic buildings. As Moderator of the General Assembly (1957–8) he created controversy by supporting the unpopular scheme to introduce bishops into the Church in the interests of Church unity. Well known as a writer and broadcaster, he was strongly left-wing, as his *Only One Way Left* (1956) testifies. He succeeded to the baronetcy in 1924, but preferred not to use the title. In 1967 he was created a life peer, as Baron MacLeod of Fuinary. One of the most satisfying moments of his career was the General Assembly of 1986. Hitherto the Church of Scotland had repeatedly resisted his pleadings for the rejection of the use by the British Government of nuclear weapons under any circumstances. In 1986, however, the Assembly completed a U-turn and accepted as official Church of Scotland policy the position argued for so long by MacLeod, that nuclear weapons were so immoral that under no circumstances might their use by countenanced by the Church.

MACLEOD, Iain Norman
(1913–70)

Politician. Regarded as one of the most gifted members of the postwar generation of Conservative politicians, he served as colonial secretary (1959–61) under Harold Macmillan and, in that capacity, oversaw the independence of many British territories in Africa. He became Chancellor of the Exchequer and seemed destined for the highest political office, but died prematurely at the age of 57.

McLEOD, John
(1934 –)

Composer, conductor and lecturer, born in Aberdeen. In London he studied composition with Lennox Berkeley and conducting with Sir Adrian Boult. He taught music at Merchiston Castle School, Edinburgh (1974–85) and was visiting lecturer in composition at Napier Polytechnic, Edinburgh. As a conductor he has won renown, particularly for 20th-century music. His orchestral works include *The Shostakovich Connection* (1974), symphonic song-cycles *Lieder der Jugend* (1979), *The Seasons of Dr Zhivago* (1982) and *The Whispered Name* (1986); a symphonic poem *The Gokstad Ship* (1982), two symphonies (1980, 1982), concertos for percussion (1987), piano (1988), and film music. Among his chamber works are a string quartet (1986) and piano music, including two sonatas and 12 preludes.

MACLEOD, John James Rickard

(1876–1935)

Physiologist, educated at Aberdeen, Leipzig and Cambridge. He became Professor of Physiology at Western Reserve University, Cleveland (1903), Toronto (1918) and Aberdeen (1928). In 1921, along with Sir Frederick Grant Banting and Charles Best, he discovered insulin, and in 1923 he shared the Nobel Prize for Physiology or Medicine with Banting. He was an outstanding teacher.

MacLEOD, Mary (Mairi nighean Alasdair Ruaidh)

(c.1615–1705)

Gaelic poet, born in Rodel on Harris. She first came to the MacLeod court at Dunvegan, on Skye, as a nurse and looked after several members of the family during her long life there. She depended upon the MacLeod court for favour and the leisure to write her songs, of which only 16 survive. One of these tells how she was sent away in disfavour and then later restored to Dunvegan by the new heir. Her songs and verses were composed in honour of the MacLeods and in honour of other great families such as the Mackenzies of Applecross. Her poetry, which praised the chiefs and their great generosity, is notable for its break from classical syllabic metres, being composed in the form of a freer, more spontaneous stress pattern.

MACLEOD, Norman

(1812–72)

Theologian and writer, a minister's son, born in Campbeltown, Argyll. He attended Glasgow University, and was minister of Loudon (1838–43), Dalkeith (1843–5) and the Barony Church, Glasgow, from 1851. He was a founder of the Evangelical Alliance (1847). From 1860 to 1872 he edited and contributed to *Good Words*. He wrote a host of books, including *The Golden Thread* (1861) and *Reminiscences of a Highland Parish* (1867).

MACLURE, William

(1763–1840)

Scottish-born American geologist, born in Ayr, known as the 'father of American geology'. Educated privately, he soon made a substantial fortune as a merchant and entrepreneur. He travelled widely in Europe, Russia and the USA, and lived at times in London, Spain and Mexico, settling in the USA around 1800. On his travels he always studied the geology of the area and met leading geologists. He employed a personal cartographer-naturalist (Charles Lesueur, 1778–1846) and organized expeditions by others. His work as an observer and writer in geology made him influential, and he helped to found the Academy of Natural Sciences in Philadelphia, of which he was President from 1817 to 1840. His *Observations on the Geology of the United States* (1817) gives the first full account of its subject, and he went on to study the West Indies and Mexico. His later writing supported the ideas on evolution offered by Jean Lamarck. He believed that primitive rocks have diverse origins and opposed Abraham Werner's theory of their exclusively sedimentary origin.

McMANUS, Mark

(1940 –)

Actor, born in Hamilton, Lanarkshire. A restless youth, employed as an unskilled worker, he emigrated to Australia and was briefly a professional boxer before finding employment at the docks in Sydney. Performances with the Dockers' Amateur Theatre Group gave him a taste for acting and he turned professional in 1964, touring in Shakespeare, co-starring in the film *Ned Kelly* (1970) and appearing in such television series as *Skippy* before returning to London in 1971. He then worked with the Royal Court and National Theatre companies and achieved television fame in *Sam* (1973). His many theatre appearances include *No Man's Land* (1975), *Julius Caesar* (1977) and *Macbeth* (1983). More recently, he has become best known as the dour, craggy television detective Taggart, a character first seen in *Killer* (1983), whose popularity remains unabated after eight years and countless murder investigations. His strong sense of social responsibility has also resulted in charity work with the teenage homeless, prisoners and incest victims.

MacMHUIRRIC, Niall

(c.1637–1726)

Last of the Gaelic professional poets, whose livelihood it was to write elegies and encomiums for their patrons. He is known primarily for his two elegies composed for Allan MacDonald of Clanranaland, who died in 1715, one elegy classical and the other vernacular. His political or Jacobite poetry was written in the old style of formal bardic verse. In this he stands in contrast to the innovations of **John MacDonald** and **Mary MacLeod**. The family of MacMhuirric was the chief bardic family of Scotland. They were powerful landowners and flourished in the Highlands and Western Isles from the 13th to the 18th centuries. Niall and his predecessor Cathal MacMhuirric are two of the greatest members of the family and a selection of their work may be found in the *Red Book of Clanranaland*.

MACMILLAN, Chrystal
(1882–1937)

Feminist, pacifist and lawyer, born in Edinburgh. She was educated at St Leonard's School, St Andrews, and Edinburgh University where, as one of its first women graduates, she obtained a first class degree before further study in Berlin. Called to the Bar in 1924, she never practised, but immersed herself in feminist causes. As the first woman to address the House of Lords (1908), she appealed for the right of women graduates to vote and served on a plethora of committees, as well as being a leader of the National Union of Suffrage Societies, Secretary of the International Women's Suffrage Alliance and founder of the Open Door Council (1929) which opposed legal restraints on women. As a pacifist, she was an instigator of the International Women's Congress at the Hague (1915) and Secretary of the International Alliance of Women (1913–23). She stood unsuccessfully as a Liberal candidate in the 1935 election.

MACMILLAN, Daniel
(1813–57)

Bookseller and publisher, born in Upper Corrie, Arran. Apprenticed to booksellers in Scotland and Cambridge, in 1843 he and his brother Alexander opened a bookshop in London, and in the same year moved to Cambridge. By 1844 he had branched out into publishing, first educational and religious works, and by 1855 English classics such as **Charles Kingsley**'s *Westward Ho!* and **Thomas Hughes**' *Tom Brown's Schooldays* (1857). In the year after his death (1858) the firm opened a branch in London and by 1893 had become a limited liability company with Daniel's son, Frederick (1851–1936), as

chairman. His other son, Maurice, father of Harold MacMillan, was also a partner.

MACMILLAN, Sir Gordon, of Macmillan
(1897–1986)

Soldier, born in Bangalore, Madras, and educated at St Edmund's School, Canterbury and Sandhurst. He gained his commission in the Argyll and Sutherland Highlanders, and during World War I he was one of the very few British officers to win the MC and two bars. A number of staff appointments followed and at the outbreak of World War II he served as a brigadier with 9 Corps in North Africa during the action in Tunis. As Commander of the 15th Scottish Division he was wounded in Normandy in 1944 and later took over command of the 51st (Highland) Division following the death of General **Thomas Rennie** during the Rhine crossings. In 1947 he was appointed General Officer Commanding Palestine and was responsible for the final withdrawal of British troops at the end of the mandate. After his retirement in 1955 he was Chairman of Cumbernauld New Town Corporation and held several other public positions. He was a prominent member of the 'Save the Argylls' campaign which prevented the disbandment of his old regiment in 1968.

MacMILLAN, Hector
(1929–)

Playwright, born in Glasgow. Having left school at the age of 14, he later ran his own electronics business. It was only after he had sold a play, *To Stand Alone*, to Scottish Television in 1966, that he decided to concentrate upon drama. His best-known plays are *The Rising* (1970), concerning the Scottish Insurrection of 1820, and *The Sash* (1973), which deals with religious bigotry on the day of an Orange Lodge March through Glasgow. He has written a sequel, *The Funeral* (1989).

MACMILLAN, Hugh Pattison, Lord, of Aberfeldy
(1873–1952)

Judge and statesman, born in Glasgow. Educated at Collegiate School, Greenock, and Edinburgh and Glasgow universities, he practised at the Scottish Bar, became non-political Lord Advocate in the first Labour government of 1924, then moved to London and developed a large practice at the parliamentary Bar and in the House of Lords. He served as a Lord of Appeal in Ordinary (1930–9, 1941–7), in the interim serving unsuccessfully as Minister of Information. He served on many governmental, educational, cultural and other commissions and committees, and his judicial speeches are highly regarded.

MACMILLAN, James Loy
(1959–)

Composer and lecturer in music, born in Kilwinning, Ayrshire. He has been a lecturer at Edinburgh and Manchester universities and at the Royal Scottish Academy of Music, Glasgow. He has composed several substantial orchestral works, including *The Keening* (1986), *Into the Ferment* (1988), *Tryst* (1989), *... as others see us ...* (1990) and *The Confession of Isobel Gowdie* (1990). For smaller instrumental forces he has written over a dozen works, including a string quartet *Visions of a November Spring* (1988); *Songs of a Just War* (1986); *Sowetan Spring* for wind ensemble (1990); *Tuireadh* (clarinet and strings, 1991); a piano sonata (1985) and several choral works.

MACMILLAN, John
(1670–1753)

Churchman, born in Minnigaff, Kirkcudbrightshire. Ordained in 1701, he joined the 'Cameronians' of **Richard Cameron**, and in 1743 founded with them the Reformed Presbyterian Church ('MacMillanites'), becoming the first minister of the sect.

MACMILLAN, Sir Kenneth
(1929–)

Choreographer, born in Dunfermline. He trained in the School of Sadler's Wells Ballet, with whom he subsequently performed. In 1953 he began to choreograph with the Royal Ballet. After three years as Director of Ballet at the Deutsche Oper, Berlin (1966–9), he returned to the Royal Ballet in 1970 as resident choreographer and director, and in 1977 became the company's principal choreographer. His ballets include *Romeo and Juliet* (1965), *The Seven Deadly Sins* (1973), *Élite Syncopations* (1974), *Mayerling* (1978) and *Isadora* (1981). As well as creating ballets for many of the world's foremost companies he has worked for theatre, television, and musical shows.

MACMILLAN, Kirkpatrick
(1813–78)

Inventor, born near Thornhill in Dumfriesshire, the son of the village blacksmith. He was a farm labourer and a coachman before taking up the same trade as his father, at Keir, Dumfriesshire. Having caught sight of a hobby-horse being ridden in the neighbourhood he resolved to make one himself, and did so. After a while he began to experiment with pedals and cranks as a means of propulsion. He applied pedals to a tricycle in 1834, and in 1840 succeeded in building the world's first primitive bicycle, riding it as far afield as Dumfries and, in two days, to Glasgow, some 70 miles away. He never patented his invention and it was widely copied, to such an extent that for many years afterwards it was usually credited to one of his imitators, Gavin Dalzell of Lesmahagow.

McMILLAN, Margaret
(1860–1931)

American-born British educational reformer, born in New York and brought up near Inverness. Educated in Frankfurt, Geneva and Lausanne, she joined the suffrage movement in London, becoming an active member, and in 1893 joined the newly-formed Independent Labour Party. A member of Bradford School Board, she agitated ceaselessly in the industrial north of England for medical inspection and school clinics. In 1902 she joined her sister Rachel (1859–1917) in London, where they opened the first school clinic (1908), and the first open-air nursery school (1914). After Rachel's death, the Rachel McMillan Training College for nursery and infant teachers was established as a memorial.

McMILLAN, Roddy
(1923–79)

Actor and playwright, born in Glasgow. Casting aside a boyhood ambition to become an aero-engineer, he first trod the boards at the age of 12 and became a full-time professional in 1946 with the Glasgow Unity Theatre, appearing in such plays as *The Gorbals Story* and *Men Should Weep* before joining the Glasgow Citizens' Theatre. Following his film début in *Morning Departure* (1950) he appeared in films such as *Laxdale Hall* (1952) and *Ring of Bright Water* (1969), but remained strongly committed to the theatre where, in the words of his friend

Fulton Mackay, he 'made the working man epic'. His many performances include *The Thrie Estates* (1959) and *Willie Rough* (1972), and he also wrote the plays *All In Good Faith* (1954) and *The Bevellers* (1973). His extensive list of television credits include *The Vital Spark* (1966–7, 1973–4), in which he played Para Handy, and a starring role as a seedy private detective in *The View From Daniel Pike*, which earned him the TV Personality of the Year Award in 1972 from the Radio Industries Club of Scotland. After his death friends commissioned a new variety of rose bearing his name.

MACMURRAY, John
(1891–1976)

Philosopher, born in Maxwellton, Kirkcudbrightshire. He was educated at Robert Gordon's College, Aberdeen, and Glasgow and Oxford universities. His Oxford studies interrupted by World War I, he served in the Queen's Own Cameron Highlanders, winning the MC. Returning to Oxford, he taught there (1919) and at Manchester (1919) and Johannesburg (1921), returning to Oxford in 1922. His reputation grew during his professorships at London (1928–44) and Edinburgh (1944–57). Much of his writing stemmed from broadcasts and public lectures. *Freedom in the Modern World* (1932) depicts Western decline dominated by a fearful craving for security. Key themes in his work are understanding science and the necessity of uncertainty in it, as well as the need for an experimental Christianity. His 1952–3 Gifford Lectures *The Self as Agent* and *Persons in Relation* have been very influential in psychology.

MACNAIR, Herbert
(1868–1955)

Architect and designer, born in Glasgow. Articled to the architect John Honeyman in Glasgow in 1888, he studied with **Charles Rennie Mackintosh** at evening classes at Glasgow School of Art, and opened up his own business specializing in the design of furniture, book illustration and posters. In 1897 he took up the post of Instructor in Design at Liverpool University. He also undertook a number of decorating commissions, including the design of the Writing Room for the Scottish Pavilion at the Exposizione Internazionale in Turin. He returned to Glasgow in 1909.

McNAUGHT, William
(1813–81)

Mechanical engineer and inventor, born in Paisley. He was apprenticed to **Robert Napier** at the age of 14 and attended classes at the Andersonian Institution in Glasgow. Eight years later he joined his father in the manufacture of steam-engine components, and became aware of the need felt by many industrialists for an increase in the power of the single-cylinder low-pressure beam engines they had already installed in their factories. In about 1845 he conceived the idea of adding a second smaller cylinder operating at a higher pressure and exhausting its spent steam into the original cylinder where its remaining energy could be utilized. For many years the process of adding an extra cylinder to an existing engine was called 'McNaughting'.

McNEILL, Billy (William)
(1940 –)

Footballer and manager, born in Bellshill, Lanarkshire. An inspirational captain, who was known as 'Caesar', he was the backbone of the highly successful Glasgow Celtic side in the 10 years which followed 1965. He received the European Cup after Celtic's victory at Lisbon in 1967, and had nine championship and seven Scottish Cup medals. Surprisingly he was capped only 29 times. Appointed to succeed **Jock Stein** as manager of his old club in 1978, he left after a quarrel with the board, but following comparatively unsuccessful spells with Manchester City and Aston Villa he returned in 1987, and in his first season guided Celtic to League and Cup victory in the club's centenary year. He was dismissed in 1991 following two poor seasons.

McNEILL, Florence Marian
(1885–1973)

Folklorist, born in Saint Mary's Holm, Orkney. Educated there and at the universities of Glasgow and Edinburgh, she spent two years travelling before returning to take up a position as Secretary to the Association for Moral and Social Hygiene. She was busy in these years as a suffragette and, after the breakdown of her health, as a tutor in Athens and a freelance journalist in London. Returning to Scotland in 1926 she worked for the Scottish National Dictionary. Best known for her work as a folklorist, her reputation is based upon *The Scots Kitchen* (1929), which examines Scottish culinary history, its links to France, and includes many traditional recipes. Her comprehensive *The Silver Bough* (1957–68) is a four-volume study of the folklore, festivals and traditions of Scotland. In a similar vein, her work *Hallowe'en* (1970) uses photographs and illustrations to explore the origins of the rites and ceremonies associated with this occasion in Scotland. Her only novel is *The Road Home* (1932), a romance based upon her life in Glasgow and London.

MACPHAIL, Katherine Stewart
(1888–1974)

Paediatrician, born in Coatbridge, Lanarkshire, graduating in medicine from Glasgow in 1911. During World War I she went to Salonika with the Scottish Women's Hospital Unit and later worked at the headquarters of the Serbian Army and its military medical unit. From the autumn of 1917 she worked behind the enemy lines for the civilian population in Macedonia. In 1918 she returned to Belgrade and the following year founded a hospital for children which later became the Anglo-Yugoslav Children's Hospital. Superintendent there until 1933, she organized the building of a hospital for surgical tuberculosis at Kamenica on the Danube, which she felt was much needed for children. Staying in Yugoslavia until the Germans arrived in 1941, she was interned by the Italians but later released and worked for two years in Lanarkshire. In 1944, at the request of Save the Children Fund, she returned to Yugoslavia and headed the Fund's first medical relief unit there. In 1945 she returned to her hospital which she re-organized and remained as its head until 1947, when she retired to Scotland. She received many Yugoslav decorations and in 1932 was awarded the Russian Red Cross insignia for her work among white Russian refugees and children.

McPHERSON, Andrew Francis
(1942 –)

English-born educational sociologist, born in Louth, Lincolnshire. Educated at Queen's College, Oxford, he became a lecturer in Sociology at Glasgow (1965–8). Since then he has worked at Edinburgh University, latterly (1989 –) as professor, establishing the Centre for Educational Sociology as a major centre of educational research. His research concentrates on the Scottish educational system, using large-scale surveys to build up extensive data banks about learners and teachers in educational institutions. From such data has issued an impressive succession of influential studies of Scottish facts (and myths) on such matters as comprehensive schooling, equality of opportunity and curricular 'breadth'. An excellent example is *Reconstructions of Secondary Education* (1983). Other publications include *Tell Them From Me* (1980) and *Governing Education* (1988). His contribution to the sociology of education in Scotland and in Britain generally has been outstanding.

MACPHERSON, Annie
(c.1824–1904)

Teacher and missionary. Born in Campsie, Stirlingshire, she trained as a teacher under Dr Friedrich Froebel and established her first orphanage in Spitalfields, London, in 1864, followed by a Farm Home which provided agricultural training for disadvantaged youngsters before she arranged for them to be re-settled in Canada. With the help of her sisters, over 14 000 child emigrants settled with families in the backwoods of Ontario and Quebec.

McPHERSON, Archie
(1935 –)

Sports broadcaster and writer, born in Glasgow. While headmaster of a Lanarkshire school, he began his career in broadcasting. With first Radio Scotland and then BBC Scotland, reporting and commentating on football matches, he developed a reputation as an intelligent broadcaster with a penchant for polysyllables. In the 1980s his career broadened and he reported on the 1984 and 1988 Olympic Games for the BBC network. When, in 1990, his contract with the BBC was not renewed, he moved effortlessly into independent broadcasting. Many of his professional experiences are recalled in his book *Action Replays* (1991).

McPHERSON, Gordon
(1965 –)

Composer, born in Dundee. His interest in composition and contemporary music stems from playing the accordion, and he studied composition at York University with John Paynter and David Blake. His works include concertos for viola (*Haar*, 1987), flute (*Ebb*, 1988) and violin (*Effective Mythologies*, 1989), as well as music for dance.

MACPHERSON, Hector Copland
(1888–1956)

Church of Scotland minister and writer on astronomy, born in Edinburgh. As a boy he took up astronomy as a hobby, and had his first popular article published at the age of 14. His first book, *Astronomers of Today*, appeared before he was 17, and for the rest of his life he continued to write and lecture on his favourite subject, dwelling especially on recent advances in the field. Among his contributions were obituary notices of astronomers in the American journal *Popular Astronomy*. His lecturing posts included a time as Thomson Lecturer in Natural Science at Church College, Aberdeen (1925–6), and Elder Lecturer in Astronomy at Glasgow's Royal Technical College (variously between 1929 and 1946). As minister at the Guthrie Memorial Church in Edinburgh, where he served for the greater part of his life, Macpherson was a forceful preacher and leader. An ardent patriot and historian, he made a special study of the Covenanters, published in his *The Covenanters under Persecution* (1922).

MACPHERSON, James
(1736–96)

Poet, renowned as the 'translator' of the legendary Gaelic bard Ossian, born in Ruthven, Inverness-shire, a farmer's son. He was educated at King's College and Marischal College, Aberdeen, and studied for the ministry, but in 1756 became a village schoolmaster in Ruthven. In 1758 he published an epic poem, *The Highlander*, and two years later, encouraged by **Carlyle**, **Adam Ferguson**, **Hugh Blair** and **John Home**, he published some fragments of Gaelic oral poetry, which he had collected and translated, as *Fragments of Ancient Poetry Collected in the Highlands of Scotland* (1870). In the introduction (by Hugh Blair) it was suggested that a great poetic epic relating to the legendary hero Fingal, as told by his son Ossian was still extant. In 1760, Macpherson was commissioned by the Faculty of Advocates in Edinburgh to tour the Highlands in search of this material, which he published in 1762 as *Fingal: an Ancient Epic Poem in Six Books*, followed by *Temora, an Epic Poem, in Eight Books* (1763). They were received with

huge acclaim, but a storm of controversy soon arose about their authenticity. Macpherson could not or would not produce any originals, and it appears that he used only about 15 genuine pieces of original verse which he altered and amended, and invented the rest to create an epic form for them. In 1763 he was appointed Surveyor-General of the Floridas, but soon returned to London and became a wealthy merchant with interests in the East India Company as agent to the Nabob of Arcot. He sat in Parliament as MP for Camelford from 1780. He was buried, at his own request and expense, in Westminster Abbey.

MACPHERSON, Robert
(d.1872)

Artist and pioneering photographer, born in Forfarshire. He studied medicine in Edinburgh (1831–5), but abandoned this calling in order to pursue an artistic career. He went to Italy in 1840 and lived in Rome for the rest of his life. In 1851, after making a living as a painter and picture-dealer for some years, he took up photography. He was to become one of the most prolific and successful photographers in Italy, and is acknowledged as one of the greatest architectural photographers. Using the wet collodion process and, from about 1857, the dry collodion process, he produced large-scale albumen prints, mostly of the buildings and antiquities of Rome. He was also the inventor of a photo-lithographic process. Macpherson exhibited his work internationally and his reputation was established during his lifetime.

MACQUARIE, Lachlan
(1761–1824)

Soldier and colonial administrator, born on the Isle of Ulva, off Mull. He joined the Black Watch in 1777, and after service in North America, India and Egypt, was appointed Governor of New South Wales following the deposition of Captain Bligh. The colony, depressed and demoralized, populated largely by convicts, and exploited by influential land-grabbers and monopolists, was raised by his energetic administration and firm rule to a state of prosperity; its population trebled, extensive surveys were carried out, and many miles of road were built. In 1821 political chicanery by the monopolists and his own ill health compelled him to return to Britain. Known as the 'Father of Australia' he has given his name to the Lachlan and Macquarie rivers, and to Macquarie Island.

MACQUARRIE, John

(1919 –)

Theologian and philosopher of religion, born in Renfrew. A lecturer at Glasgow (1953–62), and professor at Union Theological Seminary, New York (1962–70), and at Oxford (1970–86), he has written extensively across the whole field of theology. While the influence of Bultmann and Tillich may be traced in *An Existentialist Theology* (1955) and *Principles of Christian Theology* (1966), his catholic interests may be discerned in *Paths in Spirituality* (1972), *In Search of Humanity* (1982), Gifford lectures *In Search of Deity* (1984), and *Theology, Church and Ministry* (1986). Students have also appreciated successive revisions of *Twentieth Century Religious Thought* (1963–88), and his editing of *A Dictionary of Christian Ethics* (1967), revised, with J F Childress, as *A New Dictionary of Christian Ethics* (1986).

McQUATER, Tommy (Thomas Mossie)

(1914 –)

Jazz trumpeter, born in Maybole, Ayrshire. He moved to London in the 1930s to work with a succession of major dance orchestras. These included the bands of Lew Stone and Bert Ambrose where McQuater, recognized as one of Britain's finest jazz soloists of the period, worked in tandem with trombonist **George Chisholm**. He recorded in various small jazz groups and was also among the British players chosen to record with the American saxophonist and bandleader Benny Carter. During World War II he worked as lead trumpeter with the RAF band the Squadronaires, later joining the BBC showband and doing studio and freelance work. He continued to play into the 1980s, while encouraging a new generation of jazz musicians by teaching.

McQUEEN, Ian

(1954 –)

Composer, born in London to Scottish parents. He spent his childhood near Glasgow and studied with John Lambert at the Royal College of Music and with Per Nrgaørd in Denmark. His musical stage works include *Insight into Night* (1979), *Mirrors of the Truth* (1982), both involving soprano, jazz singer and visual projections; and *Line of Terror* (a chamber opera, 1987). Much of his work involves children (*Timeflight*, 'a space-age/stone-age parable', 1979, and *Beggarman – Thief!*, 1984), and other community projects; he has also written several orchestral and chamber works.

MacRAE, David

(1837–1907)

Independent divine and writer, born in Lathones, Fife, the son of a minister in the Secession Church. He studied at Glasgow and Edinburgh universities. As a student he became involved with the work of a theological society to send 10 000 bibles to the American freedmen, and is said to have been responsible for the success of the fundraising for this. He travelled in the USA after the Civil War, particularly among the black ex-slaves and published *The Americans at Home* (1870), an outstanding work of progressive sentiments and sympathetic observation, followed later by *Among the Darkies* (1876) and, after a further journey (1898–99) *America Revisited* (1908). Appointed United Presbyterian Minister at Gourock in 1872, he was deposed in 1879 for denying Scriptural warrant for the doctrine of infernal damnation. He then accepted the invitation of the congregation of the late Rev George Gilfillan in Dundee to succeed in the non-denominational ministry (1879–97). A vigorous Scottish nationalist, MacRae campaigned for revival of the teaching of Scottish history and protested, among many subjects, against its erosion by anglicization, and against inaccurate monarchical numeration. A prolific writer, his works include the temperance novel *George Harrington* (1863), and a collection of blunders and epitaphs. His *Works* were published in seven volumes in 1908. A dauntless fighter for his convictions, he was never dismayed by opinions which proved unpopular, but his chivalrous, sweet-tempered character bore out his lifelong struggle in the causes of peace and fraternity.

MacRAE, Donald

(1921 –)

Sociologist, born in Glasgow and educated at the High School and at Glasgow University as well as at Balliol College, Oxford. He became a lecturer at Oxford in 1949, a reader at London University in 1954, and Professor of Sociology there in 1961. He has been a visiting professor at the University of the Gold Coast (1956), University of California at Berkeley

(1959), and a fellow of Stanford University in 1967. He was review and productions editor of the *British Journal of Sociology* from 1950 until 1957 when he was appointed Managing Editor, a post he held until 1964. He has played a major part in establishing sociology as a mainstream social science in Britain. His main publications include: *Ideology and Society: papers in sociology and politics* (1960), *Ages and Stages* (1973), and *Max Weber* (1974).

MACRAE, (John) Duncan
(1905–67)

Actor, born in Glasgow. Educated at Allan Glen's School, Glasgow, and Glasgow University, he became a teacher and amateur actor before turning professional in 1940. He made his London début in *The Forrigan Reel* (1945), and his performances ranged from Ibsen, Chekhov, Shaw and Shakespeare to broad comedy and pantomime. His long association with the Citizens' Theatre in Glasgow dated from its opening production in 1943 and, in partnership with the Scottish playwright T M Watson, he ran a company to present plays on tour in Scotland (1952–5). His many performances include *Ane Satyre of the Thrie Estaitis* (1948), *The Tintock Cup* (1949), *Jamie The Saxt* (1955), *Let Wives Tak' Tent* (1956), *Rhinoceros* (1960) and *The Burdies* (1966). His craggy, lantern-jawed features and loose-limbed gait were also seen in films like *Whisky Galore* (1948), *The Kidnappers* (1953) and Casino Royale (1967) and in numerous television productions, including the series *Para Handy — Master Mariner* (1959), and he is well remembered for his many renditions of 'Wee Cock Sparra'. Dedicated to the cause of Scottish theatre, he served as Chairman of Scottish Equity until 1967.

McSTAY, Paul Michael Lyons
(1964 –)

Footballer, born in Hamilton, Lanarkshire. He turned professional with Celtic, his only senior club to date, in 1981. First capped for Scotland three years later, he has since been an automatic choice for the national side. His early successes at club level included being a part of the Celtic side which won the league and cup double in 1988, their centenary year. Latterly, with Celtic languishing in the shadow of their rivals Rangers, as club captain he has faced the often arduous task of maintaining on-field morale. Self-effacing despite his talent, he is a forward-going midfielder with a fierce shot.

MacTAGGART, Sir John
(1867–1956)

Builder and contractor, born in Glasgow. Educated in Glasgow, his first industrial experience was with Robert Mickel, timber merchants of Govan. In 1898 he set up in partnership, building tenements in Springburn, Glasgow. Founding his own firm he established a reputation with the construction of over 2000 tenements in the south and west of the city for middle-class dwellers. During and after World War I he was vocal in airing opinions on a resolution to the housing crisis. Winning the local authority contracts at Riddrie and Mosspark in Glasgow pushed him to the front rank of house builders in Scotland. In the process he was innovative with materials, and also experimented with the organization of the industry and with labour relations. In the 1930s he exploited the Western Heritable Investment Company (which he had taken over) in order to construct over 6000 houses under the terms of the 1924 Housing Act. The most influential figure the Scottish construction industry had produced, he was responsible for building over 20 000 flats and houses in Glasgow, Edinburgh and London.

McTAGGART, William
(1835–1910)

Painter, born on a croft in Kintyre, Argyll. Educated at school in Campbeltown, he was apprenticed, aged 13, to a doctor, who encouraged his artistic inclination. In 1852 he entered the Trustees' Academy, where he studied under **Robert Scott Lauder**. He lived in and near Edinburgh for most of his life. He became the outstanding landscape painter of his time, bringing a unique and highly sensitive perception of nature to his work. His grandson was Sir **William McTaggart**.

McTAGGART, Sir William
(1903–81)

Painter, born in Loanhead, near Edinburgh, the grandson of **William McTaggart**. He attended Edinburgh College of Art from 1918 to 1921, where he later taught, and was the recipient of many honours. His main subject matter was landscape and seascape, painted in an impasted, richly coloured expressionistic manner.

MACTHOMAIS, Ruaraidh See THOMPSON, Derick

McWILLIAM, Colin
(1928–89)

English-born architect, historian, teacher and conservationist. Born in London, he studied architecture at Cambridge, and went to Edinburgh from the British School, Rome, in 1951. He served as Curator of the Scottish National Buildings Record, where with **Catherine Cruft** he opted for an integrated collection. Subsequently he worked for the National Trust for Scotland as Assistant Secretary (Architecture). Thereafter, as senior lecturer at Edinburgh College of Art, he taught architectural history and the principles and techniques of conservation. A leading light in the Scottish conservation world, he represented many amenity bodies. His best-known works are *Scottish Townscape* (1975), and the Buildings of Scotland volumes, which Nikolaus Pevsner asked him to edit, and the first of which, *Lothian* (1978), was written by himself. His positive approach and informed judgement influenced contemporary conservationists as well as his many students.

MAGNUS ERLENDSSON, (St Magnus)
(d.1117)

Earl of Orkney. Early in the 12th century the Norse earldom of Orkney was shared by Magnus and his cousin, Earl Hakon. After years of feuding, they agreed to hold a peace-meeting on the island of Egilsay just after Easter, 1117. Hakon treacherously broke the terms of the truce, took Magnus prisoner, and had him executed. The manner of Magnus's death suggested martyrdom, and miracles were soon reported. His nephew, Earl Rognvald Kali, built St Magnus Cathedral in Kirkwall in his honour.

MAGNUSSON, Magnus
(1929 –)

Icelandic-born journalist and broadcaster, born in Reykjavík. Raised in Edinburgh and

educated at The Edinburgh Academy and Oxford University, he entered journalism in 1953 with the *Scottish Daily Express*, later becoming Assistant Editor of *The Scotsman* (1961–7). As a broadcaster his wide historical and cultural interests have informed such television series as *Chronicle* (1966–80), *BC:The Archaeology of the Bible Lands* (1977) and *Vikings!* (1980), although he remains best-known in this medium for acting as quizmaster of the long-running *Mastermind* (1972 –). A dedicated public servant, he has been Rector of Edinburgh University (1975–8), Chairman of the Ancient Monuments Board for Scotland (1981–9), and in 1989 was awarded the KBE. He was appointed Chairman of Scottish Natural Heritage from 1992 to 1996. His numerous publications and translations include *Introducing Archaeology* (1972) and *Treasures of Scotland* (1981). He was Editor of the fifth edition of *Chambers Biographical Dictionary* (1990), and of *The Nature of Scotland* (1991).

MAIDMENT, James
(1794–1879)

Lawyer and editor, born in London. Called to the Scottish Bar in 1817, he became a great authority on genealogical law cases. His most ambitious work was *The Dramatists of the Restoration* (14 vols, 1872–9), edited with W H Logan. His *Court of Session Garland* (1839 and later editions) is a collection of light verse.

MAIR, or MAJOR, John
(1469–1550)

Scholastic theologian, philosopher and historian, born in Gleghornie, near North Berwick, East Lothian, two miles from Tantallon Castle, whose owner's son, **Gavin Douglas**, was his future friend and patron. Educated at Haddington Grammar School, he studied at Oxford, Cambridge and Paris, and became MA in 1496, going on to publish books on logic (1503, 1508), and his great theological work, *A Commentary on the Four Books of Peter the Lombard's 'Sentences'* (1509–17). As Professor of Philosophy and Divinity at Glasgow University (1518), his pupils included **John Knox** and **Patrick Hamilton**. In 1521 he published his *History of Greater Britain, both England and Scotland* (1521), which examined the history of the two countries in counterpart. A work unprecedented in its critical approach, it discussed the character of the countries' rulers, making a valuable contribution to social history and supporting the union of the crowns. Mair moved to St Andrews University in 1522 to teach theology and logic, and in 1525 went to Paris University, where he published his *Physics* and *Aristotelian Ethics*. He returned to St Andrews in 1531 and became provost of St Salvator's College in 1533, holding this office until his death. Holding that the people were the true source of civil power, he advocated reform of ecclesiastical abuses, and was firm in adhering to Roman theological doctrines. He was outstanding in his insistence on truth as the means of destroying mythology.

MAITLAND, James, 8th Earl of Lauderdale
(1759–1839)

Politician and economist who was born at Ratho, Midlothian, educated at the universities of Oxford, Edinburgh, Glasgow and Paris and called to the Scottish Bar in 1780. MP for Newport (1780–4) and for Malmesbury (1784–9), he succeeded his father in 1789 and was granted a UK peerage as Baron Lauderdale of Thirlestane in 1806. At the beginning of his political career he was a Whig supporting Charles James Fox; after 1821 he was a fervent Tory, opposing parliamentary reform. In his first economic writings he strenuously opposed the fiscal and monetary policies used during the Napoleonic Wars. His major work, *An Inquiry into the nature and origin of Public Wealth and into the means and causes of its increase* (1804), presented a value theory using utility analysis to defy contemporary labour theories of value, distinguished individual wealth from national wealth, analysed capital as a supplanter of labour and provided one of the first macroeconomic models of the effects of aggregate demand in an open economy. In *Hints to the Manufacturers of Great Britain on the Consequences of the Irish Union* (1805) he examined the effects of absentee landlords remitting income to England. Later pamphlets ingeniously defended the Corn Laws and opposed the continuance of the Sinking Fund.

MAITLAND, Sir John, Lord Maitland of Thirlestane
(?1545–1595)

Jurist, second son of Sir **Richard Maitland of Lethington** and younger brother of

William Maitland. He studied in France and in 1567 became Lord Privy Seal and in 1568 a Lord of Session. He supported **Mary, Queen of Scots** and was imprisoned when Edinburgh Castle fell in 1573. He was ultimately restored to the bench in 1581 and appointed to the Privy Council in 1583. Thereafter he had great influence on **James VI**, becoming Secretary of State in 1584. In 1586 he became Vice-Chancellor and Lord Chancellor in 1587; in 1590 he was promoted Lord Maitland of Thirlestane. His influence on the king was beneficent and he contributed largely to the peace of Scotland in the last years of the century.

MAITLAND, William
(c.1528–1573)

Eldest son of Sir **Richard Maitland of Lethington** and brother of Sir **John Maitland of Thirlestane**, and known as 'Secretary Lethington'. Educated at St Andrews and abroad, in 1558 he became Secretary of State to **Mary of Guise**, the queen-regent, but in 1559 he turned against the French connection, supported alliance with England, and arranged the Treaty of Berwick, 1559–60, by which Queen Elizabeth sent a force to assist the Protestant side in Scotland. When **Mary, Queen of Scots** returned from France in 1561 Maitland became Secretary of State and sought to guide and advise her. He was privy to the murder of **Darnley** and was one of the commissioners who presented an indictment of Mary to Elizabeth in 1568. After Mary's abdication in 1567 he headed the queen's party and took refuge in Edinburgh Castle, but surrendered the castle to the English in 1573 and later died in prison in Leith.

MAITLAND OF LETHINGTON, Sir Richard
(1496–1586)

Lawyer and poet. Employed by **James V** and **Mary, Queen of Scots**, he became a Lord of Session in 1551, and (after losing his sight in 1561), Lord Privy Seal in 1562. He was conspicuous for his moderation and integrity. His poemsmostly lamentations for the distracted state of his countrywere published in 1830 by the Maitland Club. He made a collection of early Scottish poetry, which now forms two manuscript volumes, which are in the Pepysian collection at Cambridge. He also made a collection of the Decisions of the Court of Session 1550–65, and wrote a *Historie of the Hous of Seytoun*.

MAJOR, John See MAIR, John

MALCOLM I
(943–54)

King of Scotland, son of Donald II.

MALCOLM II
(b.c.954)

King of Scotland, son of Kenneth II.

MALCOLM III, called Canmore,
(Gaelic *Ceann-mor*, 'great head')
(c.1031–1093)

King of Scotland from 1057, he was a child when his father, King Duncan, was slain by **Macbeth** (1040). He spent his youth in Northumbria with his uncle, Earl Siward, who in 1054 established him in Cumbria and Lothian. In 1057, after Macbeth was killed, he became King of all Scotland. His first wife, Ingibjorg, widow of Thorfinn, Earl of Orkney, had died, and in 1069 Malcolm married **Margaret**, sister of Edgar the Ætheling. He invaded England five times between 1061 and 1093, when he was killed at Alnwick. He left five sons, of whom four succeeded him, Duncan, Edgar, **Alexander** and **David**.

MALCOLM IV
(1141–65)

Malcolm the Maiden, King of Scotland from 1153, when he succeeded his grandfather, **David I**. In 1157 he surrendered Northumberland and Cumberland to Henry II. He spent much of his time after 1160 suppressing rebellions at home.

MALLET, David, originally Malloch
(c.1705–1765)

Poet, born near Crieff, Perthshire, the son of a schoolmaster. After a period working as the janitor at Edinburgh High School (1717–18), he studied at the university. In 1720 he became a tutor, working from 1723 to 1731 in the family of the Duke of Montrose. Living mostly in London, he changed his name 'from Scots Malloch to English Mallet'. *William and Margaret* (1723), developed from the fragment of an old ballad, gained him a reputation as a poet, which he enhanced by *The Excursion* (1728). He also tried his hand at play-writing. *Mustapha* had a brief success in 1739; *Eurydice* (1731) and *Elvira* (1763), both tragedies, were failures. *Alfred, a Masque* (1740), was written in conjunction with **James Thomson**, and one of its songs, 'Rule Britannia', was claimed by both.

MANSON, Sir Patrick
(1844–1922)

Doctor, born in Aberdeenshire, known as 'Mosquito Manson' from his pioneer work with Sir Ronald Ross in malaria research. He practised medicine in China (1871) and Hong Kong (1883), where he started a school of medicine that became the University of Hong Kong. He became medical adviser to the Colonial Office, and in 1899 helped to found the London School of Tropical Medicine. He was the first to argue that the mosquito was host to the malaria parasite (1877).

MANUEL, Peter
(1931–58)

Criminal, perpetrator of at least eight of the most callous murders in Scottish criminal annals. Between September 1956 and January 1958, in addition to committing a number of other house breakings, he broke into the home of a Mr William Watt in Rutherglen and shot the three occupants dead, strangled and robbed a girl at Mount Vernon, robbed a house in Uddingston, killing all three of the family who lived there, and shot dead a Newcastle taxi driver. He was also accused of battering to death Ann Kneilands of East Kilbride, but was acquitted through lack of evidence. His trial at Glasgow High Court was one of the most sensational in legal history. Having already successfully defended himself against a former charge, he clearly considered himself more than a match for the conventional forces of law and order, and dismissed the counsel appearing on his behalf. Conducting his case with considerable skill, he brought in a special defence plea giving alibis and attributing the Rutherglen murders to William Watt himself, who had already suffered 67 days of imprisonment as a suspect. But he overreached himself, was found guilty of seven of the murders, and was hanged. The Newcastle shooting was later officially attributed to him by an inquest jury.

MAR, John Erskine, 6th or 11th Earl of
(1675–1732)

Jacobite, born in Alloa, Clackmannanshire. He began life as a Whig, but earned himself the nickname 'Bobbing Joan' by his frequent change of sides. He headed the Jacobite rebellion of 1715, was defeated at Sheriffmuir, and died in exile at Aix-la-Chapelle. His *Legacy* was published by the Scottish History Society in 1896.

MARGARET, St
(c.1046–1093)

Scottish queen, born in Hungary. She later came to England, but after the Norman Conquest, she fled from Northumberland to Scotland with her mother, sister and boy brother, Edgar the Ætheling. Young, lovely, learned and pious, she won the heart of the Scottish king, **Malcolm Canmore**, who married her at Dunfermline in 1069. Much of her reputation derives from her confessor and biographer, Turgot. She brought Benedictine monks to Dunfermline, stimulated a certain amount of change in usages in the Celtic Church, but institutional change and the real influx of new orders belong to the reigns of her sons. Canonized by Innocent IV in 1251, she remains the only Scottish royal saint.

MARGARET, 'Maid of Norway'
(1283–90)

Infant Queen of Scotland from 1286. The grand-daughter of **Alexander III** of Scotland, she was the only child of Alexander's daughter, Margaret (who died in childbirth), and King Erik II of Norway. When Alexander III died in 1286, Margaret was the only direct survivor of the Scottish royal line. In 1289 she was betrothed to the infant Prince Edward (the future Edward II of England), son of Edward I, but she died at sea the following year on her way from Norway to the Orkneys. In 1301 a woman claiming to be Margaret was burned to death in Bergen. Many believed her to be the real Margaret, and thereafter revered her as a saint.

MARGARET TUDOR
(1489–1541)

Queen of Scotland, the eldest daughter of Henry VII. In 1503 she married **James IV** of Scotland, in 1514 Archibald **Douglas**, Earl of Angus, and, having divorced him, in 1527 Henry Stewart, later Lord Methven. She was a significant, but shifting, enigma in the politics of the minority of **James V**.

MARJORIBANKS, Ishbel-Maria
(1857–1939)

Reformer, the youngest daughter of the 1st Lord Tweedmouth. In 1877 she married James Gordon, 7th Earl of **Aberdeen**. Concerned over a number of different issues, she was particularly interested in the position of women and the Irish peasantry. Her works include books on Canada (1894) and tuberculosis (1908). She and her husband turned Haddo House into a model estate for the local community, and published a book of reminiscences, *We twa'* (1925).

MARSHALL, Bruce
(1899–1987)

Novelist, born in Edinburgh and educated at The Edinburgh Academy, and St Andrews and Edinburgh universities. He served in the Royal Irish Fusiliers in World War I, when he was wounded and taken prisoner (subsequently losing a leg because of poor treatment). In World War II he worked in Intelligence and later served on the Allied Control Commission in Austria, dealing with displaced persons. He began writing in Paris between the wars, publishing *This Sorry Scheme* in 1924. Better known is *Father Malachy's Miracle* (1931), set in Presbyterian Scotland. Marshall's *George Brown's Schooldays* (1946) is an update of the 19th-century classic and confronts homosexuality and privilege in a British public school. His most successful novel, *The White Rabbit* (1952), tells the experiences of a British agent in France who is captured by the Gestapo.

MARSHALL, Margaret Anne
(1949–)

Soprano, born in Stirling. She studied at the Royal Scottish Academy of Music and Drama, and with Hans Hotter. She won first prize in the Munich International Competition in 1975, and has since performed in opera and concerts at most of the principal European festivals and music capitals. She made her London début in 1975; her operatic début at Florence, as Euridice in Gluck's

Orfeo in 1978; her American concert début in 1980, and she was first heard at Covent Garden that year (as the Countess in *Figaro*). In 1982 she made débuts at La Scala, Milan and in Salzburg (Fiordiligi). For Scottish Opera her roles have included Pamina and the Countess (*Figaro*).

MARSHALL, Peter
(1902–49)

Scottish-born American Presbyterian clergyman, born in Coatbridge, Lanarkshire. Educated at the technical school and mining college there, he served in the navy before finding himself called to the ministry. Entry to a regular course of training in Scotland seemed barred because of his inadequate qualifications, so he went to the USA, graduated from Columbia Theological Seminary, Decatur, Georgia, and served pastorates in the South before his appointment in 1937 to the historic New York Avenue Presbyterian Church in Washington, DC. In 1948 he became Chaplain to the US Senate, where his brief prayers were especially memorable. Much in demand as a speaker, he also wrote *Mr Jones, Meet the Master* (1949), and after his premature death was himself the subject of a film, *A Man Called Peter* (1955), based on his wife's biography of him.

MARSHALL, William
(1748–1833)

Fiddler and composer, born in Fochabers, Moray, who possibly worked under the patronage of the **Gordon** family. Hailed by **Robert Burns** as 'the first composer of strathspeys of the age', he set new standards of technical accomplishment in fiddle music and proudly claimed that he did not write for 'bunglers'. His two principal collections of compositions were published in 1781 and 1822, and among the many Marshall tunes that are still played are 'The Marquis of Huntly's Farewell' and 'Craigellachie Brig'.

MARSHALL, William Calder
(1813–94)

Sculptor, born in Edinburgh, and trained under Sir Francis Chantrey. As well as memorial statues, busts, etc, he did the group *Agriculture* on the Albert Memorial in Hyde Park, London.

MARTIN, Martin
(d.1719)

Author and traveller. He was a factor on Skye, who took his MD at Leiden. He wrote *Voyage to St Kilda* (1698) and *A Description of the Western Isles of Scotland* (1703), which aroused Dr Johnson's interest in the country.

MARTIN, Sir Theodore
(1816–1909)

Writer and biographer, born in Edinburgh. The well-known *Bon Gaultier Ballads* (1855), written in conjunction with **Aytoun**, were followed by verse translations from Goethe, Horace, Catullus, Dante and Heine. He was requested by Queen Victoria to write the life of Prince Albert (5 vols, 1874–80), and he also wrote biographies of Aytoun (1867), Lord Lyndhurst (1883) and the Princess Alice (1885). His wife, Helen Faucit (1820–98), was a well-known actress, noted for her interpretations of Shakespeare's heroines. The couple were frequent visitors to the royal household.

MARTYN, John
(1948 –)

Singer, songwriter and guitarist, born in Glasgow. Taught the guitar by folksinger Hamish Imlach, he worked the UK folk circuit as a teenager before releasing the albums *London Conversation* and *The Tumbler* in 1968. Although he has never enjoyed major commercial success, he has always commanded the respect of fellow performers in both folk and rock music. In 1970 he recorded the album *Stormbringer* with The Band in New York. Subsequent collaborations have included work with bassist Danny Thomson on *Bless The Weather* (1971), with Phil Collins and Eric Clapton on *Glorious Fool* (1981), and with Robert Palmer on *Piece By Piece* (1986).

MARY, QUEEN OF SCOTS
(1542–87)

The daughter of **James V** of Scotland by his second wife, **Mary of Guise**, born at Linlithgow, while her father lay on his deathbed at Falkland. A queen when she was a week old, she was promised in marriage by the regent Arran to Prince Edward of England, but the Scottish Parliament declared the promise null. War with England followed, and the disastrous defeat of Pinkie (1547). However, Mary was offered in marriage to the eldest son of Henri II of France and Catherine de' Medici. The offer was accepted, and in 1548 Mary sailed from Dumbarton to Roscoff, and was affianced to the Dauphin at St Germain. Her next 10 years were spent at the glittering French court, where she was carefully educated. She was brought up as a member of the large, young family of Henri II, and her special friend was Elizabeth of Valois, later wife of Philip II of Spain. In 1558 she was married to the Dauphin, who was a year younger than her. The marriage treaty contained a secret clause by which, if she died childless, both her Scottish realm and her right of succession to the English crown (she was the great-granddaughter of Henry VII) would be conveyed to France, for Henry II had laid claim to the English throne since the French victories of 1550. The death of Henri II (1559) brought the Dauphin to the throne as Francis II, and government passed into the hands of the Guises. When Francis died (1560), power shifted towards Catherine de' Medici, who acted as regent for her next son Charles IX. Mary, like Catherine, became a Dowager Queen of France, with her own estates and income amounting to some £30 000 Scots, but her presence was increasingly needed in Scotland. The death of her mother in 1560 had left the country in a highly fluid and dangerous state, with effective power in the hands of the Protestant Lords of the Congregation, who had held an illegal parliament in 1560 to implement a Reformation, and to ban the Catholic mass and the authority of the pope. Mary sailed from Calais on 14 August 1561, and arrived at Leith on 19th August. A Protestant riot threatened the first mass held in her private chapel at Holyrood, and within days a proclamation issued by her Privy Council imposed a religious standstill, which in effect banned the mass to all but the queen and her household. Her chief advisers were Protestant, the talented diplomat, **William Maitland** of Lethington, and her illegitimate brother, James Stewart, Earl of **Moray**. The first of her many progresses around her realm was made in the autumn of 1562; it saw the defeat and death of the Earl of Huntly, the greatest Catholic magnate in Scotland. A series of candidates were proposed (1562–5) for Mary's hand, including the archduke Charles of Austria (the pope's choice), and Don Carlos of Spain (Mary's own preference for a time). Elizabeth of England's proposal of the newly ennobled Earl of Leicester produced

negotiations which dragged on for 18 months but were brought to a sudden end by Mary's unexpected bethrothal and marriage in 1565 to her cousin, Henry Stewart, Lord **Darnley**, son of the Earl of **Lennox** and Lady Margaret Douglas, a granddaughter of Henry VII of England. One of the most enigmatic figures in Scottish history, he was three years younger than Mary, had been born and brought up in England, and inherited a family tradition of flexibility in religion and dynastic ambition. The immediate effect of the marriage was to end the 'amity' with England of 1560–5, to undermine the position of Moray and the **Hamilton** family, and to put an end to the dangerous isolation of the young queen, who had no legitimate kin in Scotland. By the end of 1565 both Darnley and his father attended the mass and were in the process of rebuilding the Lennox-Stewart power base. Darnley was too young to be granted the crown matrimonial and, unsatisfied with the title of king or the award of the French Order of St Michael, became involved with **William Ruthven**, **James Morton** and other Protestant lords in a conspiracy against the queen's Italian private secretary, David Rizzio. The Rizzio murder (1566) in the queen's antechamber at Holyrood Palace had almost as many motives as conspirators, for it helped to forestall a parliament and acted as a Protestant demonstration against the Catholic drift of Mary's policy. Within weeks Mary had succeeded in detaching Darnley from the conspirators, and escaped with him to Dunbar; Ruthven and Morton fled to England. Moray was later reinstated by the queen, but Darnley, who had betrayed both sides, became an object of mingled abhorrence and contempt. Shortly before the birth of their son, the future **James VI and I** (June 1566), the queen's affection for her husband seemed to revive briefly. In October 1566, while on progress through the Borders, she fell ill at Jedburgh, her condition being serious enough for her to make her last will and testament. During her recovery their estrangement continued and Darnley refused to attend either the elaborate baptism of their son, christened Charles James by Catholic rites at Stirling Castle, or the three days of festivities, culminating in a full-scale Renaissance 'triumph', which followed. Their divorce was openly discussed, and Darnley spoke of leaving the country, but fell ill of the smallpox at Glasgow in January 1567. Mary went to see him, and brought him to Edinburgh. He was lodged in a small mansion beside the Kirk o' Field, just outside the southern walls. There Mary visited him daily, slept for two nights in a room below his bedchamber, and passed the evening of Sunday 9 February by his bedside in kindly conversation. She left him between 10 and 11 o'clock to take part in a masque at Holyrood, at the marriage of Bastien Pagez, organizer of the Stirling fête, and about two hours after midnight the house in which Darnley slept was blown up by gunpowder, and his lifeless body was found in the garden. The chief actor in this tragedy was undoubtedly the Earl of **Bothwell**, who had recently enjoyed the queen's favour, but there were suspicions that the queen herself was not wholly ignorant of the plot. On 12 April Bothwell was brought to a mock-trial, and acquitted. On 24 April he intercepted the queen on her way from Linlithgow to Edinburgh, and carried her, with scarcely a show of resistance, to Dunbar. On 7 May he was divorced from his newly married wife, and on 12 May Mary publicly pardoned his seizure of her person, and created him Duke of Orkney; on 15 May, three months after her husband's murder, she married the man regarded by most as his murderer. This fatal step united her nobles in arms against her. Her army melted away without striking a blow on the field of Carberry (15 June), when nothing was left but to surrender to the confederate lords. They led her to Edinburgh, and the insults of the mob. Hurried next to Lochleven, she was constrained by a minority of the most radical of the nobles to sign an act of abdication in favour of her son who, five days afterwards, was crowned James VI at Stirling. Escaping from her island-prison, she found herself in a few days at the head of an army of 6000 men, which was defeated (13 May) by the regent Moray at Langside near Glasgow. Three days afterwards Mary crossed the Solway, and threw herself on the protection of Queen Elizabeth, only to find herself a prisoner for lifefirst at Carlisle, then at Bolton, Tutbury, Wingfield, Coventry, Chatsworth, Sheffield, Buxton, Chartley and Fotheringay. The presence of Mary in England was a constant source of uneasiness to Elizabeth and her advisers. A large Catholic minority naturally looked to Mary as the likely restorer of the old faith. Yet her position, as guest or prisoner, was always ambiguous. The so-called first trial, at York and Westminster in 1568, did not resolve the complex dilemma in which English policy found itself. Plot followed plot in England, but after that of Ridolfi (1571), few if any posed any real threat. The last, of Anthony Babington in 1586, was known to Walsingham's agents from the onset, and letters from Mary seem-

ingly approving Elizabeth's death passed along a postal route opened by Walsingham himself. Mainly on the evidence of copies of these letters, Mary was brought to trial in September 1586. Sentence of death was pronounced against her in October, but it was not until 1 February 1587 that Elizabeth signed the warrant of execution. It was carried into effect on 8th February, and she was buried at Peterborough; in 1612 her body was moved to Henry VII's chapel at Westminster where it still lies. Her beauty and personal accomplishments have never been disputed, though often undervalued. She spoke or read in six languages, including Greek; she sang well, played various musical instruments, and had by 1567 a library of over 300 books, which included the largest collection of Italian and French poetry in Scotland. Her own poetry is less important than the revival of vernacular poetry which has now been traced to the court during her personal reign, including the important collection, *The Bannatyne Manuscript*. The portraits and defences of her after 1571 largely fall into one of two moulds: Catholic martyr or papist plotter, making an accurate assessment of her all the more difficult.

MARZAROLI, Oscar

(1933–88)

Italian-born filmmaker and photographer, born in La Spezia. His family moved to Glasgow in c.1935; his education, in Italy and Scotland, was disrupted by illness. He worked as a freelance journalist in Europe from 1955, returning in 1959 to Glasgow, where in 1967 he co-founded Ogam Films, which developed a reputation for high-quality shorts on Scottish artists, and on life in the Highlands and Islands and in the city of Glasgow during a period of great change (1950s–80s). While filming, he also made many sympathetic still photographs of the same subjects as seen, for example, in *One Man's World: Photographs 1955–84* (1984), *Shades of Grey: Glasgow 1956–1987* (1987) and *Shades of Scotland 1956–88* (1989).

MASSIE, Allan

(1938 –)

Novelist, critic and journalist, born in Singapore and brought up in Aberdeenshire. Educated at Glenalmond and Cambridge, he taught in a private school before going to Italy, where he taught English as a foreign language. His first two novels — *Change and Decay In All Around I See* (1978) and *The Last Peacock* (1980) — placed him firmly in the camp of Ronald Firbank and Evelyn Waugh, but those who saw him as other than Scottish were off the mark. Although inclined to think in terms that transcend place, his sensibility is native and the concerns of **Scott** and **Stevenson**, as well as **Eric Linklater** and others unparochial in the location of their fictions, may be discerned. *The Death of Men* (1981) was widely regarded as his most accomplished work to date, a stylish thriller drawing on the kidnapping in Italy of Aldo Moro. In 1986 he turned again to Italy, with *Augustus*, a historical novel purporting to be the long-lost memoirs of the maligned emperor. *Tiberius* (1990) brilliantly perpetuated the conceit with Massie drawing on his knowledge of the ancient world while convincingly filling in gaps with his imagination. Although set in the 20th century, *A Question of Loyalties* (1989) and *The Sins of the Father* (1991) similarly demonstrate his unwillingness to allow history to remain the preserve solely of historians. In the former novel Vichy France is the location, while in the latter its *mise en scène* is peripatetic as the children of war criminals and victims attempt to cope with their parents' legacies; in both there are no pat answers, only sympathy and a quest to interpret the past from an unconventional point of view. *A Question of Loyalties* won the Saltire Society award. As well as being a prolific novelist, Massie has written books on **Muriel Spark**, the Caesars and Lord Byron. He is also a respected reviewer and a journalist, with trenchant political views.

MASSON, David
(1822–1907)

Historian and literary critic, born in Aberdeen, the son of a stonemason, and best known for his epic biography of John Milton. Educated at Aberdeen Grammar School and Marischal College, he studied divinity at Edinburgh, but moved to London in 1847 to take up a career in writing. He was appointed Professor of English at University College, London (1853–65), and was editor of *Macmillan's Magazine* (1859–68). He returned to Scotland as Professor of Rhetoric at Edinburgh (1865–95). His six-volume biography of Milton was published between 1859 and 1880; his many other works include editions of Goldsmith (1869) and De Quincey (1889–90), and critical studies of **Drummond of Hawthornden** (1873) and

Thomas Carlyle (1885). He also wrote *Modern Essays, Biographical and Critical* (1856), and two lively autobiographical works, *Memories of London in the Forties* (1908) and *Memories of Two Cities* (1911).

MATHIESON, George
(1842–1906)

Hymn-writer and minister, born in Glasgow, who wrote some the greatest hymns to grace Scottish church worship. Although almost blind from the age of 18, he still pursued a brilliant academic career at Glasgow University. While minister at Innellan, Argyleshire, he produced many works of great devotional power, which were much appreciated by his contemporaries. In 1886 he became minister of St Bernard's Church, Edinburgh. A prolific writer despite his disability, he pursued a much admired and highly successful ministry, gaining an international reputation for two particularly popular hymns: 'O love that wilt not let me go' and 'Make me a captive Lord, and then I shall be free'.

MATTHEW, Norman Graham
(1908–82)

Astronomer, born in Edinburgh. He was for 20 years a cartographer in the Edinburgh firm of John Bartholomew and Son. Appointed Director of Edinburgh City Observatory in 1938, he worked tirelessly to popularize astronomy in Scotland, transforming the observatory into a public centre for astronomical education. With the help of grants he delivered well over 1000 lectures on astronomy all over Scotland, organized hundreds of visits to the observatory and established firm contacts with amateur astronomers worldwide.

MATTHEW, Sir Robert
(1906–75)

Architect, son of J F Matthew, longstanding assistant to and partner of Sir **Robert Lorimer**. He was educated at Edinburgh College of Art and in 1936 joined the Department of Health for Scotland, becoming their chief architect in 1945. In the following year he became architect to the London County Council. In 1953 he was appointed Professor of Architecture at Edinburgh University and set up the firm of Robert

Matthew, Johnson-Marshall and Partners. Matthew's architectural work is predominantly represented by public buildings. He made significant contributions to hospital and educational buildings, notably at Ninewells Hospital, Dundee (designed 1960) and Stirling University, as well as to the development of town planning.

MATTHEWS, James Robert

(1889–1978)

Botanist and horticulturalist. Born in Dunning, Perthshire, and educated at Perth Academy, he first took up school teaching while making his early studies of horticulture and wild plants. He then worked in London at Birkbeck College and later at the Liverpool School of Tropical Medicine. He returned to Edinburgh in 1919 as Lecturer in Botany under **Wright Smith**. After a period as Professor of Botany at Reading, he became Regius Professor of Botany at Aberdeen in 1834. There he built up a centre of learning and research while, at the same time, becoming actively interested in agricultural and horticultural matters. He chaired the Macaulay Institute of Soil Research and in 1949 became Chairman of the Scottish Committee of the Nature Conservancy and of the Scottish Horticultural Research Committee. In all these posts he did much to improve the standard of land-use in Scottish agriculture. He became a CBE in 1956.

MAUDE, Clementina, Lady Hawarden

(1822–65)

Amateur photographer, born at Cumbernauld House, daughter of the Hon Charles Elphinstone-Fleming (MP for Stirlingshire). Married in 1845 to Cornwallis Maude, 4th Viscount Hawarden, she spent the rest of her life in England, much of it in London. In 1864 she met and became a close friend of Charles Dodgson (Lewis Carroll). Her photographs, apparently made over relatively few years, in the late 1850s and early 1860s, are mainly of women in country-house interiors. Romantic and sensuous, they are often conspiratorial in feeling, and are unusually light in comparison with the ponderous seriousness of much contemporary work.

MAVOR, Henry

(1858–1915)

Electrical engineer, born in Stranraer, Wigtownshire, one of the pioneers of the electrical engineering industry in Scotland. Inspired to study in this field after attending Lord Kelvin's classes at Glasgow, he attended classes at the College of Science and Arts in Glasgow and then worked part-time with Crompton and Co., an English firm, acting as their local agent. In 1883 he founded the firm of Muir and Mavor which undertook any electrical task, from lighting to the manufacture of dynamos. The firm was strengthened by the addition of Arthur Coulson and Mavor's brother Sam, so that by the early 20th century it had emerged as the country's leading maker of dynamos and motors. Sam gradually assumed a dominant role, moving the firm towards the construction of switchgear and coal cutting equipment, whilst Henry innovated in the field of electrical propulsion for ships. A cultured man, with an interest in the arts, he was the father of **James Bridie**.

MAVOR, Osborne Henry See BRIDIE, James

MAXTON, James

(1885–1946)

Socialist politician, born in Glasgow. He was educated at the university there and became a teacher in the east end of the city, where the poverty converted him from undergraduate conservatism to socialism. He was imprisoned during World War I for his opposition to the war. Elected as Labour MP for Glasgow Bridgeton in 1922 (a seat he held until his death), he established a reputation as a brilliant debater and one of the most turbulent 'Red Clydesiders', being expelled from the Commons in 1923 for calling a minister a murderer. Chairman of the Independent Labour Party from 1926 to 1940, he led its secession from the Labour Party in 1932, and became increasingly isolated from mainstream labour politics. Although his extreme views won few recruits, his sincerity won the respect of all.

MAXWELL, Donald

(1948 –)

Operatic and concert baritone, born in Perth. He studied singing with **Joseph Hislop**, and has sung with all the major British opera companies; among his many roles are Gunther (Covent Garden, 1991), Wozzeck (English National Opera, 1990), Figaro (*Il Barbiere di Siviglia*, Scottish Opera, 1980), Falstaff (Welsh National Opera, 1988, also in

Milan and Japan), Scarpia and the Flying Dutchman (Opera North, 1989), and he has made several international festival appearances. In addition to radio and television broadcasts, he has appeared in Vancouver, Buenos Aires, Nancy, Paris, Brussels, and in 1991 as Falstaff in Paris and Vienna (Staatsoper).

MAXWELL, James Clerk
(1831–79)

Physicist, born in Edinburgh, the son of a lawyer. One of the greatest theoretical physicists the world has known, he was nicknamed 'Dafty' at school (The Edinburgh Academy) because of his gangling appearance, but at the age of 15 he devised a method for drawing certain oval curves, which was published by the Royal Society of Edinburgh. He studied mathematics, physics and moral philosophy at Edinburgh University, where he published another paper, on rolling curves, and later graduated from Cambridge University as second wrangler. He was appointed Professor of Natural Philosophy at Marischal College, Aberdeen (1856) and King's College, London (1860), but resigned in 1865 to pursue his researches at home in Scotland. In 1871 he was appointed the first Cavendish Professor of Experimental Physics at Cambridge, where he organized the Cavendish Laboratory. During his brilliant career he published papers on the kinetic theory of gases, established theoretically the nature of Saturn's rings (1857), later to be confirmed by James Edward Keeler, investigated colour perception and demonstrated colour photography with a picture of tartan ribbon (1861). But his most important work was on the theory of electromagnetic radiation, with the publication of his great *Treatise on Electricity and Magnetism* in 1873, which treated mathematically Michael Faraday's theory of electrical and magnetic forces considered as action in a medium rather than action at a distance. He suggested that electromagnetic waves could be generated in a laboratory, as Heinrich Hertz was to demonstrate in 1887. His work is considered to have paved the way for Albert Einstein and Max Planck.

MAXWELL, John
(1905–62)

Painter, born in Dalbeattie, Kirkcudbrightshire. After training at Edinburgh College of Art (1921–6), he travelled to France and attended the Académie Moderne under Amédée Ozenfant and Fernand Léger. Con-trary to the strict order evident in these artists' work, Maxwell developed a style characterized by a more loosely painted dream-like imagery, composed of freely associated figures and objects. He taught alongside Sir **William Gillies** at Edinburgh College of Art for most of the period 1929–61.

MAXWELL DAVIES, Sir Peter
(1934 –)

English-born composer, born in Manchester. He studied at the Royal Manchester College of Music, at Manchester University and in Rome. After three years as Director of Music at Cirencester Grammar School he went to Princeton University in 1962 for further study. He has lectured in Europe, Australia and New Zealand, and was composer in residence at the University of Adelaide in 1966. Most of his music is written for chamber ensembles, often including a large percussion section. The Fires of London, a group founded by him, is particularly associated with his work. He has a keen interest in early English music, in particular the 16th-century composer John Taverner, the subject of his opera *Taverner* (1962–70), and has always experimented with different orchestral combinations; in later works he introduced stereo tape and electronic sounds. The scoring of one of the parts in *Vesalii Icones* (1970) for a dancer-pianist exemplifies his idea of 'music theatre', with no artificial division between the forms of expression. His works include *Prolation* (1959), *Revelation and Fall* (1965), two *Fantasies on an In Nomine of John Taverner* (1962, 1964), *Eight Songs for a Mad King* (1969), *Le Jongleur de Notre Dame* (1978), four symphonies, and an opera, *The Lighthouse* (1979). Since 1970 Maxwell Davies has done most of his work in Orkney, frequently using Orcadian or Scottish subject matter or music. He directed the St Magnus Festival from 1977 to 1986.

MEEHAN, Patrick Connolly
(1927 –)

Convicted thief who was also found guilty of murder, but later received a royal pardon. Born in the Gorbals, Glasgow, he spent most of his teenage life in approved schools and in Borstal for theft. In December 1947 he was arrested and charged with blowing up a safe. He was convicted and sentenced to three years' imprisonment in 1948. Other prison sentences followed. On 14 July 1969, after a routine interview with police on 12 July in which Meehan admitted that he had passed through Ayr on 6 July, two men, who called each other 'Jim' and 'Pat', broke into the Ayr home of Abraham and Rachel Ross. They assaulted the Rosses, and Rachel Ross died of her injuries shortly afterwards. Ross claimed to identify Meehan's voice and Meehan was charged. Suspicions arose about some of the police's evidence, but Meehan was nonetheless found guilty on 24 October. The next seven years were filled with appeals which failed, new evidence and confessions from the real killer. In May 1976, after the publication of **Ludovic Kennedy**'s book *A Presumption of Innocence* (1976), Meehan was pardoned.

MEIKLE, Andrew
(1719–1811)

Millwright and inventor, born at Houston Mill near Dunbar, East Lothian. He was the son of James Meikle (c.1690–1717), who invented fanners for winnowing grain in 1710 and a barley mill. Andrew inherited his father's mill and showed a keen interest and considerable talent in devising improvements to the machinery of the mill. He also turned his attention to the design of windmills, and in 1750 invented the fantail which kept the sails rotating at right angles to the direction of the wind. In 1768 he patented a machine for dressing grain, in 1772 he invented the 'spring' sail which counteracted the effect of sudden gusts of wind. His most significant invention was a drum threshing machine which could be worked by wind, water, horse or (some years later) steam power. He obtained a patent in 1788 and built a factory to produce these machines, but as with all his other inventions he derived very little financial return, and in his old age the sum of £1500 was raised by his friends to alleviate his distress.

MELLANBY, Kenneth
(1908 –)

Entomologist and environmentalist, born in Barrhead, Renfrewshire. Educated at King's College, Cambridge, and London University, his early career was in medical entomology at the London School of Hygiene and Tropical Medicine. In 1955 he was appointed Head of the Entomology Department at Rothamsted Experimental Station, and in 1961 he founded and directed the Nature Conservancy's experimental station at Monks Wood, Huntingdon. Here he led research into the deleterious affects of pesticides on the environment and advocated the advantages of biological con-

trol of insect pests. He wrote several books on entomology, ecology and pollution, notably *Pesticides and Pollution* (1967), and founded the leading journal, *Environmental Pollution*, in 1970.

MELVILL, Thomas
(1726–53)

Scientist. Educated at Glasgow University for the Church, he was the first (1752) to study the spectra of luminous gases. His early death in Geneva obscured the importance of his experiments.

MELVILLE, Andrew
(1545 – c.1622)

Religious and educational reformer, born in Baldowie, Angus. One of nine sons, and described as a puny youngster, he was educated at Montrose Grammar School and at St Andrews and Paris. In 1568 he became Professor of Humanity at Geneva. On his return to Scotland he was appointed Principal of Glasgow University (1574–80). Nicknamed 'the Blast' for his religious fervour, he did much to reorganize university education, introducing Greek for the first time in a Scottish university and raising the standard of teaching at Glasgow to such a level that it matched or surpassed most universities in Europe. In the words of his nephew **James Melville**, 'ther was na place in Europe comparable to Glasgow for guid letters during these yeirs'. He also had an important share in drawing up the *Second Book of Discipline* (1579). On the king's request he was chosen Principal of St Mary's College, St Andrews (1579) where, from 1580, he taught Hebrew, Chaldee and Syriac besides lecturing on theology. During his time there he likewise improved educational standards. In 1582 he preached boldly against absolute authority before the General Assembly and advocated a presbyterial system of Church government; in 1584, to escape imprisonment, he went to London. He was repeatedly Moderator of the General Assembly of the Church of Scotland. In 1596 he headed a deputation to 'remonstrate' with King **James VI**; and in 1606, with seven other ministers, he was called to England to confer with him. Having ridiculed the service in the Chapel Royal in a Latin epigram, he was summoned before the English Privy Council, and sent to the Tower. In 1611 he was released through the intercession of the Duke of Bouillon, who required his services as a professor of theology in his university at Sedan.

MELVILLE, Arthur
(1858–1904)

Painter, born in East Linton, East Lothian. He began his studies in Edinburgh and in 1878 went to Paris to the Académie Julian. There he began to work in watercolour, the medium for which he is still principally known. In 1880 he began an adventurous two-year journey in the Middle East, which provided source material for an exhibition of watercolours in London in 1883. In his direct observation and fresh handling of colour, not unlike the French Impressionists, he was one of the most important Scottish artists of his day and exerted considerable influence over his fellow Scots, especially the Glasgow school, until his untimely death from typhoid.

MELVILLE, Henry Dundas, 1st Viscount See DUNDAS, Henry

MELVILLE, James
(1556–1614)

Reformer and diarist, born near Montrose, Angus, nephew of **Andrew Melville**. He was Professor of Oriental Languages at St Andrews University and minister in 1586 of Kilrenny, Fife, despite having previously been banned from preaching. He took a leading part with his uncle in ecclesiastical politics, and went to London in 1606. In 1607 he was ordered to remain within a 10-mile radius of Newcastle. He was Moderator of the General Assembly in 1589. He is best known for his *Diary* (1556–1601), written in racy, vigorous and idiomatic Scots.

MELVILLE, Sir James, of Halhill
(1535–1617)

Soldier and diplomat. He went to France in 1550 as page to the young **Mary, Queen of Scots**, and subsequently undertook missions abroad and to the court of England, trying to reconcile Queen Elizabeth to Mary's marriage to **Darnley**, and later undertaking many diplomatic missions during **James VI**'s minority. He wrote *Memoirs of his Own Time* (Bannatyne Club, 1827).

MELVILLE, Robert
(1723–1809)

General, antiquary and inventor, born in Monimail, Fife. He studied at the universities of Glasgow and Edinburgh. From 1744 he served with the 'Edinburgh Regiment' in Flanders, then as a major in 1756 he was posted to the West Indies, where from 1760 to 1770 he acted as colonial governor. On his return he spent some time examining the sites of great military events, and was elected FRS, FRSE and FSA. He was consulted by the Carron Company in their efforts to manufacture an improved piece of ordnance, the result being a shorter, lighter gun, successfully introduced in 1778, which became known as the carronade.

MENTEITH, Sir John de
(13th – 14th century)

Knight. He was captured by the English in 1296 but released in 1297 and made Governor of Dumbarton. In 1305 he captured the Scottish patriot **William Wallace** in Glasgow and delivered him to his fate in London. Created Earl of Lennox he joined **Robert Bruce** in 1307, and was one of the signatories to the Declaration of Arbroath in 1320.

MENZIES, Archibald
(1754–1842)

Naturalist/surgeon during the round-the-world voyage of the *Discovery* under Captain George Vancouver (1790–5). He was born in Weims, Perthshire. He made original collections of plants in all the countries he visited, especially British Columbia and Chile, from where he brought back the Auracaria or monkey puzzle tree. In 1790 he became President of the Linnean Society.

MENZIES, John Ross
(1852–1935)

Wholesale publisher and distributor, born in Edinburgh. He joined the business which his father had established in a modest way in Princes Street, Edinburgh, and with his brother pushed the firm westwards, opening a branch in Glasgow in 1868. This was followed by establishing bookstalls in almost all towns of significance. He directed the creation of a huge network of railway station bookstalls, a lucrative development that raised the firm to a position second only to W H Smith in size. By the time of his death he had built Scotland's leading organization in the book, periodical and newspaper retailing and wholesale trade, becoming, in the process, a household name.

MERRY, James
(1805–77)

Coal and iron master, born in New Monkland, Lanarkshire. His family were amongst the earliest coalmasters of the Monkland fields. After attending Glasgow High School and University he joined the family business. A partner by 1830 he took control five years later on his father's retiral. Having formed a partnership with Alexander Cunninghame and Alexander Allison he proceeded to construct an industrial empire comprising, by the mid 1850s, 12 collieries, two iron works and many iron mines. His business style was autocratic and he treated his workforce harshly. On his retiral the empire consisted of 23 collieries, 26 iron mines and three iron works. Marriage brought him admission into the Glasgow social scene and, combined with his wealth, formed the basis for a political career. In 1857 he was elected MP for Falkirk and, though unseated a year later, was re-elected in 1859, holding the seat until 1874.

MERRYLEES, Andrew
(1933 –)

Architect, educated in Wishaw and at Strathclyde University. He joined **Basil Spence**, Glover and Ferguson in 1957, becoming associate in 1968 and partner in 1972. He began his own practice, Andrew Merrylees Associates, in Edinburgh in 1985. He specializes in the design of new buildings which are notable for the high quality of their finishing materials and the consistent use of well-considered detailing. His earlier work, such as the Edinburgh University Library (with J Hardie Glover, 1967), has an understated elegance. More recent work is characterized by the use of modern materials and frequent use of colour to make a bold statement, for example the Post Office Sorting Office, Leith Walk (1982) and the National Library Building, Causewayside (1986), both in Edinburgh. He has won many awards, including the RSA Gold Medal and the RIBA Bronze Medal.

MICHAELSON, Sidney
(1925–91)

English computer scientist, born in London and educated at Imperial College, London. From 1949 to 1963 he lectured there, pioneering the design of digital computers incorporating the principle of microprogramming. In 1963 he moved to Edinburgh University, where he founded the Department and held the Chair of Computer Science (1966–91). There, he initiated work in the UK on system software to provide shared interactive multiple access to computers and led a diverse range of research activities, from computational theory to VLSI design. He was a leader in the field of stylometry, the science of computer-based analysis of literary texts for authorship and chronology, and fought to promote the professional recognition of computer scientists. He was elected FRSE (1969), FRSA (1979) and FBCS (1980).

MICHIE, Donald
(1923 –)

British specialist in artificial intelligence, born in Rangoon, Burma. Educated at Rugby and Balliol College, Oxford, he served in World War II with the foreign office at Bletchley Park (1942–5), where work on the Colossus code-breaking project acquainted him with computer pioneers, such as Alan Turing, M H A Newman and T H Flowers. After a biological career in experimental genetics he developed the study of machine intelligence at Edinburgh University as Director of Experimental Programming (1963–6) and Professor of Machine Intelligence (1967–84). He is Editor-in-Chief of the *Machine Intelligence* series, of which the first 12 volumes span the period 1967–90. Since 1986 he has been Chief Scientist at the Turing Institute which he founded in Glasgow in 1984. In publications such as *On Machine Intelligence* (1982) and *The Creative Computer* (1984) he has argued that computer systems are able to generate new knowledge. His research contributions have primarily been to the study of machine learning.

MICKLE, William Julius
(1735–88)

Poet, the son of a minister, born in Langholm, Dumfriesshire. Educated at Edinburgh High School, he failed as a brewer, and turned author in London. In 1765 he published a poem, *The Concubine* (or *Syr Martyn*), and in 1771–5 his version rather than translation of the *Lusiad* of Camoens. In 1779 he went to Lisbon as secretary to Commodore Johnstone, but his last years were spent in London. His ballad of *Cumnor Hall* (which suggested *Kenilworth* to Sir **Walter Scott**) is poor poetry, but 'There's nae luck aboot the hoose' ensured his immortality.

MILL, Hugh Robert
(1861–1950)

Geographer and meteorologist, born in Thurso, Caithness. His formal education was limited by tubercular illness as a child, but he had read his way through the 8th edition of the *Encyclopaedia Britannica* by the age of 17. He studied at the Watt Institution (later Heriot-Watt University) and Edinburgh University. On graduation he was awarded a scholarship to the new Scottish Marine Station at Granton. He lectured in geography at Heriot-Watt College (1885–90), and was librarian to the Royal Geographical Society (1892–1900). He was joint director of the British Rainfall Organisation from 1901, and insisted on greater scientific rigour in meteorological studies. He published a number of textbooks and contributed the geographical entries to the 11th edition of the *Encyclopaedia Britannica* (1910–11). A widely-consulted authority on polar exploration, he wrote *The Siege of the South Pole* (1905). He received a number of honours, including an honorary degree from St Andrews University in 1900.

MILL, James
(1773–1836)

Philosopher, historian and economist, father and tutor of John Stuart Mill, whose education he began at the age of three, when he started teaching him Greek. Born in Logie-pert, near Montrose, Angus, a shoemaker's son, he studied for the ministry at Edinburgh. He was ordained in 1798, but moved to London in 1802 and supported himself through journalism and editorial work for periodicals such as the *Edinburgh Review* and *St James's Chronicle*. He became a disciple and friend of Jeremy Bentham, an enthusiastic proponent of utilitarianism, and a prominent member of the circle of 'Philosophical Radicals' which included George Grote, David Ricardo, John Austin and in due course his son John Stuart Mill. The group was active in social and educational causes and James Mill took a leading part in the founding of University College, London, in 1825. His first major publication was the *History of British India* (1817–18) on which he had worked for 11 years and which secured him a permanent position with the East India Company, where he rose to become Head of the Examiner's Office in 1830. His other works include *Commerce Defended* (1807), in which he discussed commerce as a cause of wealth and opposed the continuation of the Napoleonic wars. His *Elements of Political Economy* (1821), written mainly for his son, was based on Ricardo's *Principles*, but was a much clearer exposition, and was an important influence on Marx. *Analysis of the Phenomenon of the Human Mind* (1829), his main philosophical work, provides a psychological basis for utilitarianism, and *A Fragment on MacKintosh* (1835) argues that morality is based on utility.

MILLAN, Bruce
(1927 –)

Labour politician, born in Dundee. Educated at Harris Academy, he qualified as a chartered accountant. MP for Glasgow Craigton (1959–83), and for Govan (1983–8), he held junior ministerial appointments (1964–70, 1974–6), mainly in the Scottish Office. Appointed Secretary of State for Scotland (1976–9), he proved a competent administrator in a period dominated by devolution legislation, sharply rising unemployment, and a weakening Scottish economy. He left parliament to become European Community Commissioner in 1989, with responsibility for regional development.

MILLAR, John
(1735–1801)

Jurist, born in Shotts, Lanarkshire. Educated at Hamilton Grammar School and Glasgow University, he was Professor of Law at Glasgow. A friend of **Adam Smith** and Lord **Kames**, he had a great reputation as a law teacher and a leading liberal. His main works are the *Origin of the Distinction of Ranks* (1771), a pioneering work on sociology, and *An Historical View of the English Government* (1787), the first constitutional history of Britain or England, and a groundbreaking work offering many new and original insights. Both books were widely influential. An ardent Whig, he was regarded at the time as a radical, even a near-revolutionary.

MILLAR, Robert
(1959 –)

Cyclist, born in Glasgow. He turned professional in 1979, having already been British champion twice. He quickly made an impact at the sport's highest level, becoming (1983) the first Scot to win a stage of the Tour de France. The following year he won the King of the Mountains competition in the Tour de France, and finished fourth overall — the best-ever performance by a Briton in the world's toughest cycle race. Coming tenth in the world championship of 1985, he consolidated his reputation the following year with second places in the Tours of Spain and Switzerland. His success has come despite the lack of support in Britain for cycling, and he has lived for some years in Belgium.

MILLER, Sir Donald John
(1927 –)

Electrical engineer, born in London and educated at Banchory and Aberdeen University. After experience in power plant manufacture and in the electricity supply industry, he joined Preece, Cardew and Rider in 1955 and worked on major electricity supply projects overseas. He was appointed Chief Engineer of the North of Scotland Hydro-Electric Board in 1966, and Director of Engineering and General Manager of the South of Scotland Electricity Board in 1974; he has been Chairman of Scottish Power since 1982. He played a leading part in planning the modernization of electricity generating plant and distribution systems in Scotland, including the AGR nuclear power stations at Hunterston and Torness. He was elected to the Fellowship of Engineering in 1981 and became a Fellow of the Royal Society of Edinburgh in 1987.

MILLER, Hugh
(1802–56)

Geologist and man of letters, born in Cromarty. Having lost his father at sea at the age of 5, he had a rebellious school career in various schools, and was apprenticed as a stonemason at the age of 16. Working with stone for the next 17 years, he developed an interest in fossils, and he devoted the winter months to reading, writing and natural history. In 1829 he published *Poems Written in the Leisure Hours of a Journeyman Mason*, followed by *Scenes and Legends of the North of Scotland* (1835). He contributed to **John Mackay Wilson**'s *Tales of the Borders* (1834–40), and to *Chambers's Journal*. He married the daughter of an Inverness businessman and became a bank acountant for a time (1834–9), but when he became involved in the controversy over Church appointments that led to the Disruption of the Church of Scotland (1843) with a ferocious open *Letter to Lord Brougham* (1839), he was invited to Edinburgh to start *The Witness*, the newspaper of the anti-patronage 'Evangelicals' within the Church of Scotland, and became the outstanding journalist of the Disruption. At the same time he wrote a series of geological articles in *The Witness*, later collected as *The Old Red Sandstone* (1841). In 1845 he visited England for the first time and wrote *First Impressions of England* (1847). His *My Schools and Schoolmasters* (1854) is the story of his youth. A pioneer of popular science books, he combated the Darwinian evolution theory with *Footprints of the Creator* (1850), *The Testimony of the Rocks* (1857), and *Sketchbook of Popular Geology* (published posthumously, 1859). Worn out by illness and overwork, he shot himself. The old thatched cottage at Cromarty in which he was born is now a museum run by the National Trust for Scotland.

MILLER, James See MacCOLL, Ewan

MILLER, Patrick
(1731–1815)

Inventor, a pioneer of early experimental steamboats, who patented the paddle wheel. A merchant by trade, in 1767 he became a director of the Bank of Scotland, becoming Deputy Governor in 1790. After buying an estate, with a loch, at Dalswinton in Dumfriesshire in 1785, he concentrated on his experiments. In 1788 he launched a steamboat, with an engine by **William Symington**, his enthusiasm tempered by **James Watt**'s negative response to the invention. Also interested in agriculture, he introduced the fiorin grass to Scotland.

MILLER, Ronald
(1910–90)

Geographer, born in Stromness, Orkney. He studied geography at Edinburgh University and was the first Scottish geography graduate to continue directly into a full-time PhD. He taught at Manchester University and later joined the colonial service, pursuing his studies in Nigeria. He returned as lecturer at Edinburgh University (1946) and was appointed Professor of Geography at Glasgow University in 1953. He was the first geographer in Scotland to offer courses which allowed staff to specialize, thus helping to establish a degree in topographic science. He published widely but had special interests in Africa and Scottish studies. He edited the *Scottish Geographical Magazine* (1954–74) and was President of the Royal Scottish Geographical Society from 1974 to 1978.

MILLER, William
(1810–72)

Poet, born in Glasgow, known as the 'Laureate of the nursery'. He was a woodturner by profession, having relinquished a medical career through ill-health. In 1863, urged on by his friends, he published a collection of poems which brought him some fame. Today, however, he is remembered only as the author of 'Wee Willie Winkie', one of his numerous dialect poems about children and childhood.

MILN, James
(1819–81)

Antiquary. A former naval officer and merchant in China and India, he made excavations on a Roman site at Carnac, Brittany, and published the results in *Excavations at Carnac* (1877 and 1881). Miln Museum, Carnac, contains his collection.

MILN, Walter See MYLNE, Walter

MILNER, (Arthur John) Robin Gorell
(1934 –)

English computer scientist, born in Yealmpton, Devon. Educated at Eton and Cambridge, he worked for a few years in Ferranti Ltd, then re-entered academic life. He joined Edinburgh University in 1973, becoming Professor of Computational Theory in 1984. He worked on computer-assisted reasoning, and his system LCF (Logic for Computable Functions) was a model for several later systems. He led a team which designed and defined Standard ML, a widely-used programming language. His main contribution has been to the theory of concurrent computation, and this work is widely accessible through his book *Communication and Con-*

currency (1989). Elected FRS in 1988, he gained the A M Turing Award in 1990.

MILROY, Jack
(1920 –)

Comedian, born in Glasgow. He made his name in summer seasons at the Tivoli, Aberdeen, as a solo comic in *Whirl of Laughter* (1950–2). The following year he and his wife, the singer Mary Lee, starred in a 22-week *Whirl* season, and have appeared together ever since. In 1960 he created his most famous stage role, that of Francie to **Rikki Fulton**'s Josie. Glasgow wideboys of the 1950s, Francie and Josie have become one of the finest and most enduring Scottish comic double-acts.

MINTO, Gilbert John Murray Kynynmond-Elliot, 4th Earl of
(1845–1914)

Politician, born in London and educated at Eton and Cambridge University. Appointed Governor-General of Canada (1898–1904), he helped raise Canadian troops for the Boer War and settled a dispute over Alaska with the USA. From 1905 to 1910, as Viceroy of India he dealt with border friction with Russia over Persia, Tibet and Afghanistan. Within India he sternly repressed extremist nationalist elements after an attempt on his life in 1909. Simultaneously he initiated the Minto-Morley reforms, which admitted Indians in greater numbers to central and provincial government bodies, while at the same time protecting the position of the minority Muslim community.

MITCHELL, James Leslie See GIBBON, Lewis Grassic

MITCHELL, Joseph
(1803–83)

Civil engineer, born in Forres, Morayshire, and educated at Inverness and Aberdeen. In 1820 he was apprenticed as a stonemason on the construction of the Caledonian Canal at Fort Augustus, and so impressed **Thomas Telford** that he spent the next three years in London as one of his assistants. When his father died (1824) Joseph was appointed to succeed him as general inspector and superintendent of the Highland roads and bridges, a post he held for almost 40 years. During much of this time he was also the engineer to the Scottish Fisheries Board, building and improving many harbours round the Scottish coasts. As a consulting engineer he was employed on surveys for some of the principal Scottish railway lines, including Edinburgh to Glasgow (1837) and Perth to Inverness (1845, but not constructed until 1863). Between 1853 and 1874 he surveyed and superintended the railways from Inverness to Keith, Wick and Thurso, and Kyle of Lochalsh. He was elected FGS in 1825 and FRSE in 1843. He recounted the story of his life (and much else besides) in his rambling *Reminiscences*, the second volume of which was not published at the time in order to avoid threatened lawsuits.

MITCHELL, Sir Peter Chalmers
(1864–1945)

Zoologist and journalist, born in Dunfermline. He started his career as a lecturer at Oxford and London, and in 1903 was elected Secretary of the Zoological Society. He inaugurated a period of prosperity at the London Zoo and was responsible for the Mappin terraces, Whipsnade, the Aquarium and other improvements. He wrote a number of books on zoological subjects including *The Nature of Man* (1904) and *Materialism and Vitalism in Biology* (1930).

MITCHELL, Sir Thomas Livingstone
(1792–1855)

Explorer, born in Craigend, Stirlingshire. After service in the Peninsular War, from 1828 he was Surveyor-General of New South Wales. In four expeditions (1831, 1835, 1836, 1845–7) he did much to explore Eastern Australia ('Australia Felix') and Tropical Australia, in particular the Murray, Glenelg and Barcoo rivers.

MITCHELL, William
(1861–1962)

Philosopher, born in Inveravon, Banffshire. He attended Edinburgh University, going on to lecture there and then in London. Moving to Australia he was Professor of English Language, Literature, Philosophy and Economics at Adelaide University from 1894, gradually reducing his scope as more staff were appointed. He retired as Professor of Philosophy in 1923. Vice Chancellor of the university from 1916 to 1942, then Principal, he was known as 'The Philosopher King of Adelaide'. Part I of his *The Place of Minds in the World* appeared in 1933. Part II was lost, his copy in a fire, the other at a London publisher's in the 1941 blitz.

MITCHISON, John Murdoch
(1922 –)

English-born cell biologist. Educated at Winchester and Cambridge, he has spent almost his entire career in the Department of Natural History in Edinburgh, where he became Professor of Natural History in 1963. His main interests have been in the detailed study of the cycle of events by which all living cells grow and divide. Early on he chose for study a then obscure yeast, used in the brewing of native beer in Africa, which is one of the simplest organisms which yet have a nucleus and chromosomes like those of more complex animals and plants. He has lived to see the choice vindicated and the yeast become one of the main organisms for cellular and molecular studies. Very active in university and national affairs, serving on the Royal Commission on Environmental Pollution (1974–9), he also found time, initially with Michael Swann, to foster a flourishing group of cellular and molecular biologists in Edinburgh. He was elected FRS in 1966. He is married to the historian **Rosalind Mitchison**.

MITCHISON, Naomi Margaret, née Haldane
(1897 –)

British writer, born in Edinburgh, the daughter of **J S Haldane**, and sister of **J B S Haldane**. Educated at the Dragon School, Oxford, she won instant attention with her brilliant and personal evocations of Greece and Sparta in a series of novels such as *The Conquered* (1923), *When the Bough Breaks* (1924), *Cloud Cuckoo Land* (1925) and *Black Sparta* (1928). In 1931 came the erudite *Corn King and Spring Queen*, which brought to life the civilizations of Ancient Egypt, Scythia and the Middle East. She has travelled widely, and in 1963 was made Tribal Adviser and Mother to the Bakgatla of Botswana. She has written more than 70 books, including her memoirs in *Small Talk* (1973), *All Change Here* (1975) and *You May Well Ask* (1979). In 1916 she married Gilbert Richard Mitchison (1890–1970), who was a Labour MP (1945–64), and Joint Parliamentary Secretary, Ministry of Land (1964–6).

MITCHISON, Rosalind Mary, née **Wrong**
(1919 –)

English-born historian, born in Manchester, grand-daughter of George Mackinnon Wrong, a leading Canadian historian. Educated at Channing School, Highgate, London, and Lady Margaret Hall, Oxford, she became Assistant Lecturer in History first at Manchester University (1943–6), and then at Edinburgh (1954–7). Moving to Glasgow as Assistant Lecturer (1962–3), then Lecturer (1966–7), she returned to Edinburgh as Lecturer in Social and Economic History (1967–76). In 1970 she published *A History of Scotland*, a work conspicuous for its forthright language and integration of economic and social history with political history, and became a standard text for the next 20 years. Professor of Social History at Edinburgh from 1981 to 1986, her many works include *British Population Change since* 1869 (1977), *Lordship and Patronage: Scotland* 1603–1745 (1983) and *People and Society in Scotland, 1760–1830* (1988). A vigorous and inspirational lecturer and teacher, she was the foremost authority on the Scottish poor law. A trenchant analyst of class and property interests in the Scottish past, she has in recent years become the judicious but firm leader of Scottish feminist historians. She is married to the cell biologist **John Mitchison**.

MOFFAT, Alexander
(1943 –)

Painter, born in Dunfermline. He studied at the Edinburgh College of Art (1960–4), followed by a period (1964–6) working in an engineering factory in Edinburgh. In 1967, along with **Alan Bold** and **John Bellany**, he was invited to visit East German cities by the Republic's Ministry of Culture. This visit helped confirm his interest in German Expressionism and it was with this type of realism that he, along with Bellany, challenged the orthodox French-inspired decorative colourist tradition of the Edinburgh school. He went on to teach at the Glasgow School of Art from the late 1970s, where he

had a great influence on younger artists such as **Ken Currie** and **Peter Howson**.

MOFFAT, Henry Keith
(1935 –)

Physicist, educated at George Watson's College, Edinburgh, and Edinburgh and Cambridge universities. He was lecturer in mathematics at Cambridge from 1961 to 1976, when he became Professor of Applied Mathematics at Bristol University. He returned to Cambridge in 1980 as Professor of Mathematical Physics. He is distinguished for his research in fluid mechanics.

MOFFAT, Robert
(1795–1883)

Missionary, born in Ormiston, East Lothian. He turned from gardening to the mission field in 1815, and began his work in Great Namaqualand (1818). He finally settled at Kuruman in Bechuanaland (1826–70) which, through his efforts, soon became a centre of Christianity and civilization. He printed both New (1840) and Old (1857) Testaments in Sechwana and published *Labours and Scenes in South Africa* (1842). **David Livingstone**, whom he influenced, married his daughter, Mary.

MOFFATT, James
(1870–1944)

Scottish-born American theologian, born in Glasgow. Ordained a minister of the Free Church of Scotland in 1896, he was Professor at Mansfield College, Oxford (1911–14), and at the United Free Church College, Glasgow (1914–27). In 1927 he went to the USA and became Professor of Church History at Union Theological Seminary, New York (1927–39). His most famous work is the translation of the Bible into modern English, which combined academic rigour with courageous freshness. His New Testament was published in 1913 and his Old Testament in 1924. He also wrote theological works, including *Presbyterianism* (1928).

MOIR, David Macbeth
(1798–1851)

Physician and writer, born in Musselburgh, East Lothian, where he practised as a physician from 1817 until his death. Under his pen-name of *Delta* (δ) he contributed verses to *Blackwood's Magazine* (coll. 1852), and is remembered for his humorous *The Life of Mansie Wauch, Tailor in Dalkeith* (1828).

MOIR, John William
(b.1851) and Frederick Lewis Maitland (b.1852)

Explorers and traders. Both brothers were born in Edinburgh, and studied botany and natural history at the university before training as chartered accountants. In 1878 they founded the African Lakes Company which pioneered the trade route from the east coast to the Lakes Nyasa and Tanganyika. To exploit natural waterways, they had steamers built in sections to be carried overland. The *Lady Nyasa* was the first to ply the Zambezi and Shire rivers. Establishing an anti-slaving mission and trading post near Balantyre, they waged a two-year private war against Arab slave traders, which ended in 1889. This victory opened up an area which subsequently came under British rule as the Nyasaland Protectorate and Northern Rhodesia.

MOLESWORTH, Mary Louisa, née Stewart
(1839–1921)

Novelist and writer of children's stories, born in Rotterdam. She spent her childhood in Manchester, Scotland and Switzerland. She began writing as a novelist under the pseudonym 'Ennis Graham', but she is best known as a writer of stories for children, such as *Carrots: Just a Little Boy* (1876) and *Cuckoo Clock* (1877).

MOLLISON, James Allan
(1905–59)

Aviator, born in Glasgow. A consultant engineer by profession, he was commissioned into the RAF in 1923, and won fame for his record flight, Australia–England in 1931 in 8 days, 19 hours and 28 minutes. In 1932 he married Amy Johnson. He made the first solo east-west crossing of the north Atlantic in 1932, and in February 1933 the first England –South America flight. With his wife he made the first flight across the Atlantic to the USA in 1933, and to India in 1934. He was awarded the Britannia Trophy (1933). The marriage was dissolved in 1938.

MONBODDO, James Burnett, Lord
(1714–99)

Judge, pioneer anthropologist and eccentric, born at Monboddo House, Kincardineshire. Educated at Aberdeen, Edinburgh and Gröningen, he was called to the Bar, and in 1767 was raised to the bench as Lord Monboddo. Highly repected as a judge, he nevertheless held a variety of bizarre views, eg that babies are born with tails which mid-wives cut off before anyone has a chance to see them. He had a strong aversion to anything modern, such as sedan-chairs, and an ardent devotion to the ways of the Ancient Greeks, whose simple lifestyle he tried to emulate. His *Origin and Progress of Language* (6 vols, 1773–92) is a learned but idiosyncratic production, but his theory of human affinity with monkeys anticipated Charles Darwin and the modern science of anthropology. He also published, anonymously, *Ancient Metaphysics* (6 vols, 1779–99).

MONCREIFF, James, 1st Baron Moncreiff of Tullibole
(1811–95)

Advocate, historian and judge, born in Edinburgh, the son of Sir **James Wellwood Moncreiff**. He was educated at Edinburgh High School and Edinburgh University. Called to the Bar in 1833, he led several major cases leading up to the Disruption, and was one of the first contributors to the Disruption journal, the *North British Review* (1844). He was variously MP for the Leith Burghs (1851–9), for Edinburgh (1859–68), and for Glasgow and Aberdeen universities (1868–9). He was Solicitor-General for Scotland (1850), and Lord Advocate (1851–2, 1852–8, 1859–66, 1868–9). He introduced a successful bill to abolish religious tests in Scottish universities, but was defeated in measures to establish a uniform system of valuation and rating for Scotland, and education reform. He guided over 100 acts through Parliament, reforming legal procedure and mercantile law. He was public prosecutor in *Regina* versus *Madeleine Smith* (1857). Dean of the Faculty of Advocates (1858–69), he was Lord Justice-Clerk (1869–88). He presided over the trials of Eugene Marie Chantrelle for murder (1878), the City of Glasgow Bank directors for fraud (1878), the dynamite assassins in Scotland (1883), and the crofters during the land war (1886). A frequent speaker by request on literary, scientific and political questions, he published an anonymous novel, *A Visit to My Discontented Cousin* (1871). He was a contributor to the *Edinburgh Review*, in which his anonymous review-essays of Macaulay's *History of England* broke new ground, including what recent historians now regard as the correct solution of the Massacre of Glencoe. He received honorary doctorates from Edinburgh (1858) and Glasgow (1879), and was Rector of Glasgow University (1868–71). An outstanding writer, speaker and statesman, he possessed in all categories an admirable mixture of towering knowledge and persuasive deployment of it.

MONCREIFF, Sir James Wellwood, Lord Moncreiff
(1776–1851)

Advocate, judge and lay religious leader. He studied at Glasgow University and Balliol College, Oxford, and became famous as a passionate Whig during the Long Tory government (1807–32), presiding at the Pantheon meeting to petition the Crown for dismissal of Lord Liverpool's ministry (1820). As an advocate at the Bar, he was a model of clarity and conviction, reasoning with great force and energy. A close friend of **Francis Jeffrey** he was elected Dean of the Faculty of Advocates in 1826 when Jeffrey stood down in his favour. In 1828 he defended **William Burke** free of charge for having murdered persons to supply cadavers to anatomists, and co-ordinated with his friend **Henry Cockburn**, almost certainly at Burke's insistence, to ensure the not-proven verdict on Burke's probably innocent paramour Helen MacDougal when Burke was found guilty. They made the trial an indictment of the police state and its system of informers by demonstrating its protection for the mass-murderer William Hare. In 1829 Moncreiff was one of the major speakers at a great Catholic Emancipation meeting. The Tory government of Wellington subsequently offered him a judgeship of the Court of Session, presumably as a sop to increasing Whig power in Scotland. Moncreiff accepted, but maintained his status as member of the General Assembly where in 1834 he carried a motion demanding a popular veto on the presentation of ministers to livings by wealthy patrons. This issue brought about the Disruption of the Church of Scotland following the rejection of the Claim of Right (1842), and Moncreiff pointedly supported the 1843 secession. As a judge he was acknowledged to be one of the finest of his time.

MONCRIEFF, Colonel Sir Alexander
(1829–1906)

Soldier and engineer, born in Edinburgh. He invented the Moncrieff Pits and disappearing carriages for siege and fortress guns.

MONRO, Alexander, known as 'Monro Primus'
(1697–1767)

Anatomist, born in London. He studied at London, Paris, and in Leiden under Hermann Boerhaave. From 1719 he lectured at Edinburgh on anatomy and surgery (professor, 1725–59). He helped to found the Edinburgh Royal Infirmary, and made Edinburgh a major centre for medical training. He wrote *Osteology* (1726), *Essay on Comparative Anatomy* (1744), *Observations Anatomical and Physiological* (1758) and *Account of the Success of Inoculation of Smallpox in Scotland* (1764).

MONRO, Alexander, known as 'Monro Secundus'
(1733–1817)

Anatomist, son of **Alexander Monro**, 'Monro Primus'. He succeeded his father as Professor of Anatomy at Edinburgh University. He wrote on the nervous system (1783), the physiology of fishes (1785), and the brain, eye and ear (1797).

MONTGOMERIE, Alexander
(c.1545 – c.1611)

Poet, probably born at Hessilhead Castle near Beith in Ayrshire. He was 'maister poet' to **James VI and I**. He was detained in a continental prison, and embittered by the failure of a lawsuit involving loss of a pension. Implicated in Barclay of Ladyland's Catholic plot, he was denounced as a traitor in 1597, and went into exile. His fame rests on the *Cherrie and the Slae*, published twice in 1597, and his love lyrics, especially 'To his Mistress'.

MONTGOMERIE, William
(1904 –)

Poet, born in Glasgow and educated at Glasgow University. He has lived much of his life abroad, in Berlin, Provence and Andalusia. With his wife **Norah Montgomerie** he collected and edited Scottish nursery rhymes. Together they edited four collections of folklore, verse and rhyme for children between 1946 and 1964. They published *Scottish Nursery Rhymes* (1985), a collection of rhymes, songs and riddles, with the aim of gratifying **Robert Chambers**' early wish to 'complete ... the collection of the traditionary verse of Scotland'. These collections are intended as an introduction to the Scottish oral tradition and spring from rhymes noted down from recitation or singing. William Montgomerie edited the *Lines Review* from 1978 to 1982.

MONTGOMERY, James

(1771–1854)

Poet, born in Irvine, Ayrshire. The son of a Moravian pastor, he settled down, after various occupations, as a journalist in Sheffield, where in 1794 he started the *Sheffield Iris*, which he edited until 1825. In 1795 he was fined £20, and spent three months in York Castle for printing a 'seditious' ballad; in 1796 he was fined £30 and served six months for describing a riot. However, by 1832 he had become a moderate Conservative, and in 1835 he accepted a pension of £150 from Peel. He died in Sheffield. His poems (4 vols, 1849) have been described as 'bland and deeply religious'.

MONTROSE, James Graham, Marquis of

(1612–50)

Soldier and Royalist. He was educated at St Andrews and travelled in Italy, France and the Low Countries. He returned in the year (1637) of the 'Service-book tumults' in Edinburgh (see **Jenny Geddes**), and he was one of the four noblemen who drew up the National Covenant. In 1638 he was dispatched to Aberdeen, which he occupied for the Covenanters. When Charles I invited several Covenanting nobles to meet him in Berwick, Montrose was one of those who went. The Presbyterians dated his 'apostasy' from that occasion. In the General Assembly of 1639 he expressed misgivings about the Covenant. In the second Bishops' War, Montrose was the first of the Scottish army to ford the Tweed (20 August 1640), but the same month he had entered into a secret engagement against Archibald, 8th Earl of **Argyll**. It transpired that he had been communicating with the king. He was cited before a committee of the Scottish Parliament, and the next year was confined for five months in Edinburgh Castle. In 1644 he escaped from his forced inaction at Oxford and, disguised, made his way into Perthshire as Lieutenant-General and Marquis of Montrose. At Blair Atholl he met 1200 Scoto-Irish auxiliaries under Alastair MacDonald of Colonsay (d.1647), and the clans quickly rallied round him. He routed the Covenanters under Lord Elcho at Tippermuir near Perth. He then gained a victory at Aberdeen and took the city, which was this time abandoned to the horrors of war for four days. The approach of Argyll with 4000 men forced Montrose to retreat, but he suddenly appeared in Angus, where he laid waste the estates of the Covenanting nobles. Later, receiving large accessions from the clans, he marched into the Campbell country, devastated it, drove Argyll himself from his castle at Inveraray, and then wheeled north towards Inverness. The 'Estates' placed a fresh army under William Baillie of Letham, who was to take Montrose in front, while Argyll should fall on his rear, but Montrose instead surprised and utterly routed Argyll at Inverlochy (1645). He then passed ferociously through Moray and Aberdeenshire, eluded Baillie at Brechin, captured and pillaged Dundee and escaped into the Grampians. He defeated Baillie's lieutenant at Auldearn near Nairn, routed Baillie himself at Alford, and in July 1645 he marched southward with over 5000 men. Baillie, following, was defeated with a loss of 6000 at Kilsyth. This, the most notable of Montrose's six victories, seemed to lay Scotland at his feet, but the clansmen slipped away home to secure their booty. Still, with 500 horse and 1000 infantry, he had entered the Border country, when on 13 September he was surprised and routed by 6000 troopers under **David Leslie** at Philiphaugh near Selkirk. Escaping to Athole, he endeavoured in vain to raise the Highlands. On 3 September 1646 he sailed for Norway, and from there he went to Paris, Germany and the Low Countries. When news of Charles's execution reached him, he swore to avenge his death and, undertaking a fresh invasion of Scotland, lost most of his small army by shipwreck in the passage from Orkney to Caithness. Despite this he made for the borders of Ross-shire where, at Invercharron, his dispirited remnant was cut to pieces on 27 April 1650. He was almost starved to death in the wilds of Sutherland, when he fell into the hands of

Macleod of Assynt, who delivered him to Leslie, and having been taken to Edinburgh as quickly as possible, he was hanged in the High Street on 21 May 1650. Eleven years afterwards his mangled remains were collected and buried in St Giles's, where a stately monument was erected to him in 1888. Montrose's few but passionately loyal poems are little known, except for the stanza beginning, 'He either fears his fate too much'; even its ascription to Montrose (first made in 1711) is doubtful.

MONTROSE, James Graham, 6th Duke
(1878–1954)

Marine engineer and naval architect, born in London. Educated at Eton, he joined the merchant navy and subsequently served in the Auxiliary Naval Service and the RNVR. He was a director of **William Beardmore** and Company in Glasgow, and with them he designed and built the motor yacht *Mairi* in 1911, one of the first sea-going vessels propelled by a heavy oil engine. He is also credited with one of the earliest plans for an aircraft-carrying ship, drawn up in 1912. He was elected President of the Institution of Marine Engineers in 1911, and in the same year was awarded an honorary LLD by Glasgow University.

MOON, Lorna, pseudonym of (Helen) Nora Wilson Low
(1886–1930)

Short-story writer and novelist, born in Strichen, Aberdeenshire. Her father was a plasterer who worked mostly abroad. After an itinerant life he acquired the Temperance Hotel in Strichen, a haunt of commercial travellers. One, an American called Hebditch, who dealt in jewellery, persuaded Lorna to elope, and they left for America, where they married and had a child. Eventually she reached Hollywood, where she wrote scripts for Metro-Goldwyn-Mayer, who employed her on the screenplay for *Mr. Wu*, starring Lon Chaney, which was a huge success. In her spare time she wrote for magazines, contributing stories about Strichen, barely disguised as 'Pitouie'. Her first book, *Doorways in Drumorty* (1925), was a collection of stories; when it was published in Britain her parents had it banned from the local library, as they did her novel *Dark Star* (1929).

Wickedly and deftly puncturing her parents' social pretensions and the Nosey Parker proclivities of village life, she combined gothic tragedy with black humour, sharpened no doubt by distance from her targets. When she died of consumption in Albuquerque, New Mexico, it made front-page news in America.

MOORE, John
(1729–1802)

Physician and writer, father of Sir **John Moore**. After studying medicine and practising in Glasgow, he travelled with the young Duke of Hamilton (1772–8), and then settled in London. His *View of Society in France, Switzerland, Germany and Italy* (1779–81) was well received, but it is for the novel *Zeluco* (1789), which suggested Byron's *Childe Harold*, that he is best remembered today.

MOORE, Sir John
(1761–1809)

Soldier, born in Glasgow, son of the physician **John Moore**. He served in the American War of Independence from 1779 to 1783, and during the Revolutionary War in France he distinguished himself in the attack on Corsica (1794) and served in the West Indies (1796), Ireland (1798) and Holland (1799). He was in Egypt in 1801, and in 1802 he served in Sicily and Sweden. In 1808 he was sent with a corps of 10 000 men to strengthen the English army in the Peninsula, and in August he assumed the chief command. In October he received instructions to co-operate with the Spanish forces in the expulsion of the French, and moved his army from Lisbon towards Valladolid. However, Spanish apathy, French successes elsewhere, and the intrigues of his own countrymen soon placed him in a critical position. When the news reached him that Madrid had fallen, and that Napoleon was marching to crush him with 70 000 men, Moore, with only 25 000, was forced to retreat. In December he began a disastrous march from Astorga to La Coruña, almost 250 miles, through a mountainous country, made almost impassable by snow and rain, and harassed by the enemy. They reached La Coruña in a lamentable state, and Soult was waiting to attack as soon as the embarkation should begin. In a desperate battle on 19 January 1809, the French were defeated with the loss of 2000 men. Moore himself was mortally wounded by grape-shot in the moment of victory, and was buried early next morning (as described in Charles Wolfe's poem, *The Burial of Sir John Moore*).

MORAY, James Stewart, Earl of
(1531–70)

Regent of Scotland, the second eldest of the many illegitimate sons of **James V** of Scotland, by a daughter of Lord Erskine. In 1538 he was made Prior *in commendam* of St Andrews. He emerged as one of the leaders of the Protestant Lords of the Congregation whose revolt produced the Scottish Reformation of 1560. In 1561 he visited his half-sister, **Mary, Queen of Scots**, in France and after her return his robust defence of her right to attend mass in her private chapel resulted in his disaffection from **John Knox**. He was granted the earldoms of Mar and Moray in 1562, which resulted in the revolt and death of the Earl of **Huntly**, the greatest Catholic magnate in Scotland. He remained the queen's chief adviser until her marriage to **Darnley** in 1565, which triggered an abortive coup by him and the **Hamilton**s and his flight to England. He returned to Edinburgh on the day after Rizzio's murder in 1566 and was rehabilitated. His fore-knowledge of the plot to murder Darnley in 1567 induced another diplomatic absence, and he was also in France when Mary was overthrown and imprisoned at Lochleven. He returned in August to accept the regency during the minority of Mary's infant son, **James VI**. His regency was chequered : it saw for the first time a Prostestant government, but little was done by it to advance the fortunes of the reformed Church; the civil war continued, despite attempts to blacken the queen's reputation, and the majority of the major nobles ranged against him. He was assassinated at Linlithgow by James Hamilton of Bothwellhaugh. One of the few Protestant nobles who acted consistently from religious motives, it was he as much as any of the ministers, including Knox, who helped to give a Calvinist tone to the Scottish Reformation. His reputation has ironically been obscured by the brilliance of the case put in his defence in the writings of **George Buchanan**.

MORE, Jacob
(1740–93)

Painter, born in Edinburgh. A pupil of **Alexander Runciman**, he was, along with **Alexander Nasmyth**, the best Scottish landscape painter of his generation. In his use of a strong formal structure and diffused lighting he belonged to a tradition of classical landscape painters which looked back to Claude Lorraine. In 1771 he travelled to Rome where he was to remain for the rest of his life. His most successful and best-known works are a series of paintings, *The Falls of Clyde* (1771). Despite his considerable success and celebrity, he was all but forgotten after his death.

MORGAN, Edwin
(1920 –)

Poet and critic, born in Glasgow. His education at Glasgow University was split by service in the Royal Army Medical Corps during World War II, an option he chose as a conscientious objector. He was appointed Assistant Lecturer in English at Glasgow University in 1947, and remained there until 1980, rising to titular Professor of English in 1975. He published his first volume of poems, *The Vision of Cathkin Braes*, and a translation of *Beowulf*, in 1952. His verse from the 1950s is introspective and rather gloomy, unlike his later work, which is marked by an apparently irrepressible (although never simply naïve) optimism and a readiness to embrace change. By the time of *A Second Life* (1968), he had embraced his homosexuality, and given free rein to his willingness to be influenced by developments in American (both North and South) and European arts. His wide-ranging and often formally experimental work finds room for science fiction alongside a minute observation of reality. His work is defiantly non-parochial, but has remained rooted in Glasgow, where he has continued to live, playing a maverick role in the city's cultural life. An incomplete *Collected Poems* was published in 1990, followed by a collection of his influential essays and critical writings, *Crossing The Border* (1990). A skilled translator, he collected his translations of various writers, such as Pasternak and Lorca, in *Rites of Passage* (1976).

MORISON, James
(1816–93)

Clergyman, born in Bathgate, West Lothian. Educated at Edinburgh University, he became minister of Kilmarnock in 1840, but the following year was suspended by the United Secession Church for preaching universal atonement, and in 1843, with three other ministers, he founded the Evangelical Union of Congregational Churches, its system being a modified Independency.

MORISON, Robert
(1620–83)

Botanist, born in Aberdeen, where he graduated PhD in 1638. A Royalist, he escaped to France, took his MD at Angers (1648), and had charge of the garden of the Duke of Orléans. Charles II made him one of his physicians, 'botanist royal', and the first professor of botany at Oxford. His chief work is *Plantarum Historia Universalis Oxoniensis* (1680–99).

MORRIS, Margaret
(1891–1980)

English dancer, choreographer, designer, director, author and teacher, born in London. As a child she appeared in pantomime and plays and in 1907 joined the Frank Benson Shakespearian Company as principal dancer. In 1910 she designed the decor and costumes for Marie Brema's production of Gluck's *Orpheus* and in the same year founded the MMM School of Dancing in London, basing classes around her own dance technique, Margaret Morris Movement. In the interwar period she founded a summer school in Devon (which was to run throughout her life), lectured to doctors on the remedial possibilities of her dance and, after 1931, opened training schools in Paris, Cannes, Edinburgh, Glasgow, Aberdeen and Manchester. In 1939 she and her husband **J D Fergusson** settled in Glasgow, where she formed the Celtic Ballet Club, touring to the USA in 1954 and to Russia, Austria and Czechoslovakia in 1958, the same year that she founded a studio theatre in the centre of Glasgow. The school closed in 1961, but her teaching, writing and courses continued until her death.

MORRIS, Talwin
(1865–1911)

One of the best-known exponents of the Glasgow Style, who produced a wide range of designs for an equally wide variety of media, including book bindings, furniture, stained glass, metalwork and jewellery. Born in Winchester, the son of an auctioneer, he was educated at Lancing College and later became apprenticed to his uncle, Joseph Morris of

Reading, an architect. Graphics was his main area of interest, and after a short spell as sub art editor for the journal *Black and White* (1891) he moved to Scotland with his wife Alice, to take up an appointment as Art Director for the publishing firm **Blackie** and Sons. There he was responsible for the graphics for Blackie's wide range of titles, and he produced, with a small staff, a large number of designs for bindings and text plates, many of them in the avant-garde Glasgow Style. He was a personal friend of **Francis** and **Jessie Newbery** of the Glasgow School of Art, and was closely associated with **Charles Rennie Mackintosh** and his immediate circle. Indeed, it was Morris who introduced Mackintosh to Walter Blackie, who later commissioned him to build the Hill House at Helensburgh. Morris's work was regularly commented on in the artistic press, and the work he executed for his own home at Bowling was illustrated in *The Studio* in 1897. His work was exhibited in Britain and abroad, and in 1902 his designs were shown at Budapest and Turin.

MORRIS, Thomas ('Old Tom')
(1821–1908)

Golfer, born in St Andrews, and known as the 'Nestor of Golfe'. After serving an apprenticeship as a golfball-maker in St Andrews he went to Prestwick as a greenkeeper in 1851, returning to St Andrews as a professional in 1861. He won the British championship belt four times (1861, 1862, 1864 and 1866). His son, **'Young Tom' Morris**, became champion after him.

MORRIS, Thomas ('Young Tom')
(1851–75)

Golfer, the son of **'Old Tom' Morris**. Precociously brilliant, he won the British championship three times in succession (1868, 1869, 1870), thereby winning the championship belt outright; there was no contest in 1871, but he won it again in 1872. His early death was said to have been caused by grief at the loss of his young wife.

MORRISON, Robert
(1782–1834)

Scholar and missionary, born near Jedburgh, Roxburghshire. After studying theology in his spare time, in 1807 he was sent to Canton by the London Missionary Society as the first Protestant missionary to China. Between 1809 and 1814 he translated and printed the New Testament (1819); with some help, he translated the Old Testament into Chinese; and in 1823 he completed his great *Chinese Dictionary*. In 1818 he established an Anglo-Chinese College at Malacca.

MORROCCO, Alberto

(1917 –)

Painter, born in Aberdeen. He studied at Gray's School of Art, Aberdeen (1932–8) where, after war service in the army, he returned to teach. In 1950 he became Head of the School of Painting at Duncan of Jordan-stone College of Art, Dundee. He was a founder member of the 47 Group who exhibited together annually at the Aberdeen Art Gallery from 1947 to 1950. His paintings vary in subject matter, but he is best-known as a portraitist.

MORTON, Earls of See DOUGLAS

MORTON, Alan Lauder

(1893–1971)

Footballer, born in Glasgow. Possibly the best left-winger ever produced by Scotland, he won 31 international caps in a period when such matches occurred infrequently. Known as the 'Wee Blue Devil', he was a member of the famous 'Wembley Wizards' side which defeated England 5–1 in 1928. On his re-tirement from playing in 1934 he became a director of Glasgow Rangers, the club with which he had spent his entire playing career.

MORTON, James Douglas, 4th Earl

(c.1516–1581)

Regent of Scotland, the younger son of Sir George Douglas of Pittendriech near Edin-burgh. He became Earl of Morton in right of his wife in 1550, and in 1563 was made Chancellor. Conspicuous in Rizzio's assassi-nation (1566), he fled to England, but obtained his pardon from the queen. He was privy to the plan for **Darnley**'s murder, though absent from Edinburgh (1567). He joined the confederate nobles who defeated **Bothwell** and **Mary, Queen of Scots** at Carberry Hill, he 'discovered' the 'Casket

Letters', he led the van at Langside (1568) and, after the brief regencies of **Moray**, **Lennox** and Mar, in November 1572 was himself elected regent. After the end of the civil war in 1573 he bound Scotland more tightly to the 'amity' with England, but his attempts to control ecclesiastical appoint-ments and to bring the Church into episcopal conformity with England brought him into sharp conflict with the radical ministers, led by **Andrew Melville**, whose 'overseas dreams' of a Genevan polity Morton derided. His regency brought a welcome restoration of law and order, especially to the Borders, but it was achieved at the cost of an unwonted **Douglas** monopoly of many offices, which caused intense resentment. He fell briefly from power in 1578, but the arrival of the young king's cousin, Esme Stuart, in 1579 recast political expectations. His fall was engineered by Captain James Stewart, nomi-nally for his part in Darnley's murder, and he was beheaded by means of the 'Maiden', a guillotine which he had himself introduced to Scotland, in Edinburgh's Grassmarket. His regency, though brief, was in many respects a turning-point, not least in the beginning of the restoration of royal power which was to be continued in **James VI**'s personal reign.

MORTON, Thomas

(1781–1832)

Shipbuilder. In 1819 he invented the patent slip for docking vessels, which provides a cheap substitute for a dry dock.

MOTHERWELL, William

(1797–1835)

Collector of ballads, born in Glasgow. From 1819 to 1829 he was Sheriff-Clerk Depute of Renfrewshire, and editor of the *Paisley Ad-vertiser* from 1828 to 1830. He published *Minstrelsy, Ancient and Modern* (1819) and other verse collections, including *Poetical Remains* (1848). With **James Hogg** he published a new edition of **Burns** (1835).

MUIR, Edwin

(1887–1959)

Poet, born in Deerness on the Mainland of Orkney. The son of a crofter, he left the Orkneys at 14 when his family migrated to Glasgow, where he suffered the period of drab existence described in his *The Story and the Fable* (1940), revised as *An Autobiography* in 1954. He moved from job to job, but spent much time reading Nietzsche, Shaw, Ibsen, Heine and Blatchford, and became interested in left-wing politics. In 1919 he married the novelist Willa Anderson (1890–1970), with whom he settled in London, and travelled on the Continent from 1921 to 1924, where the couple collaborated in translations of Kafka and Feuchtwanger. Back in Scotland in 1925 he published his first volume of verse (*First Poems*), and then returned to France where he wrote novels, notably *The Marionette* (1927). He spent most of the 1930s in Sussex and St Andrews. On the outbreak of World War II he joined the staff of the British Council, and in 1945 returned to Prague as first director of the British Institute there, which was closed after the Communist coup of 1948. He then took over the British Institute in Rome until 1950, when he was appointed warden of the adult education college at Newbattle Abbey, Midlothian. After a year as Eliot Norton Professor of Poetry at Harvard (1955–6), he retired to Swaffham Prior near Cambridge. His verses appeared in eight slim volumes *First Poems* (1925), *Chorus of the Newly Dead* (1926, omitted from *Collected Poems*), *Variations on a Time Theme* (1934), *Journeys and Places* (1937), *The Narrow Place* (1943), *The Voyage* (1946), *The Labyrinth* (1949), *New Poems* (1949–51) and finally *Collected Poems* (1952). Further poems appeared in *The Listener* and other periodicals later. Muir's critical work includes a controversial study of **John Knox**, *Scott and Scotland* (1936), *Essays on Literature and Society* (1949) and *Structure of the Novel* (1928).

MUIR, John
(1810–82)

Sanskrit scholar, born in Glasgow, brother of Sir **William Muir**. After spending 25 years in the East India Company's Civil Service in Bengal, he settled in Edinburgh, where he founded a chair of Sanskrit. His great work was his *Original Sanskrit Texts* (5 vols, 1858–70). Also notable is *Metrical Translations from Sanskrit Writers* (1878).

MUIR, John
(1838–1914)

Scottish-born American naturalist, born in Dunbar, East Lothian, and considered the father of the modern environment movement.

He emigrated with his family to the USA in 1849, and after a difficult childhood, with a harsh father, studied at Wisconsin University. He was an ingenious inventor and constructor of devices until he lost an eye in 1867 in an industrial accident, and thereafter concentrated his interest on natural history, exploring the American West and especially the Yosemite area. After marriage to Louie Wanda Strentzel, the daughter of an Austrian who established the Californian fruit and wine industry in 1880, he farmed very successfully in California, and also campaigned with his friend Robert U Johnson (1853–1937), Editor of *Century Magazine*, for a national park there. In 1890 came apparent success; Congress approved a bill creating the Yosemite National Park. However, active opposition to the park's ideals did not cease, and it needed a decade of Muir's vigorous oratory and article-writing, and President Roosevelt's support, before the idea of wildlife conservation became widely accepted. Muir wrote a number of books, covering his own life and explorations, including *The Mountains of California* (1894), *Our National Parks* (1901), *My First Summer in the Sierra* (1911) and *The Yosemite* (1912). The John Muir Trust to acquire wild land in Britain was established in 1984.

MUIR, Thomas
(1765–99)

Advocate and radical reformer, born in Glasgow. He advocated parliamentary reform and in 1793 was transported for sedition to Botany Bay, where he was sentenced to 14 years' exile. He escaped in 1796, but died in France (1796) of a wound received on a Spanish frigate in a fight with British vessels at Cadiz.

MUIR, Willa, née Anderson, pseudonym Agnes Neill Scott
(1890–1970)

Novelist and translator, born in Montrose, Angus. She showed an early aptitude for languages as a child, speaking both her parents' Shetland dialect and English. Educated at St Andrews University, she taught classics and educational psychology in London until forced to resign when marrying the 'atheist' **Edwin Muir** in 1919. Despite her ill-health, brought on by poor medical treatment after the birth of their son Gavin in 1927, the Muirs punctuated their lives in

Scotland with much travelling, and lived for short periods in Prague, Rome and the USA. They translated jointly (although often only Edwin was credited), and were influential in spreading the work of Kafka in the 1930s. Her essay *Women: An Enquiry* (1925) dealt with the demoralizing effects of Scottish small-town life, a subject she returned to in her novel *Imagined Corners* (1931). *Mrs Grundy in Scotland* (1936) examined the role of women in Scottish culture. She wrote a moving account of her long and creative partnership with Edwin Muir, *Belonging* (1968), and finished his project *Living With Ballads* (1965) after his death.

MUIR, Sir William
(1819–1905)

Anglo-Indian administrator and scholar, born in Glasgow, brother of the Sanskrit scholar **John Muir**. He joined the Bengal Civil Service, and became Foreign Secretary to the Indian government in 1865. He held other high offices in India and from 1885 to 1902 was principal of Edinburgh University. His works include a *Life of Mahomet* (4 vols, 1858–61), *The Caliphate* (new ed 1915), and *The Corân* (1878).

MUIRHEAD, Alexander
(1848–1920)

Electrical engineer, born in Saltoun, East Lothian. He moved with his parents to London at an early age, but his broad Scots accent was not understood there, and he was educated privately until he was 15. Later he graduated with honours from University College, London. He worked with his elder brother John in his father's firm of telegraph engineers, and in 1875 he patented a method of duplexing, ie sending and receiving signals simultaneously in both directions. He had a genius for accurate measurement, and perfected the standard of electrical capacity which was subsequently adopted by the National Physical Laboratory. Around the turn of the century he collaborated with Sir Oliver Lodge on some early experiments in wireless telegraphy.

MUIRSHIEL, John Scott Maclay, 1st Viscount
(1905 –)

Liberal politician, born in Glasgow and educated at Winchester and Cambridge University. He was a member of a prominent Glasgow shipping family, and his father had been a minister in the Lloyd George wartime administration of 1916–18. National Liberal MP for Montrose (1945–50), and for West Renfrewshire (1950–64), he was Minister for Transport (1951–2), but resigned through ill-health. He returned to the Cabinet as Secretary of State for Scotland (1956–62). During his period of office much progress was made in the attempt to regenerate Scottish industry, notably the Ravenscraig steel works and car factories at Bathgate and Linwood. The provision of health and educational services also improved under his secretaryship.

MULLEN, Jim (James)
(1945 –)

Jazz guitarist and bandleader, born in Glasgow. He started to play the guitar at the age of 10 and became active as a local bandleader before moving to London in 1969. After playing with several bands, including Brian Auger's Oblivion Express, he lived in the USA from 1975 to 1977, where he worked in a succession of groups, including the Average White Band, and with flute player Herbie Mann. He began a musical association with the British saxophonist Dick Morrisey; on their return to Britain, the Morrisey-Mullen Band became one of the leading jazz-rock groups until it disbanded in 1985.

MUNGO, St See KENTIGERN, St

MUNRO, Alex, originally Alexander Horsbrugh
(1911–86)

Comedian, born in Glasgow. He made his stage début at the Star Cinema, Partick, in 1917, and his first London appearance at Shoreditch (1925) as the Star Trio. This was a comedy acrobatic act with his brother Archie and sister June, later known as the Horsbrugh Brothers and Agnes. On the advice of Flanagan and Allen, he introduced comedy into the act whilst touring with Florrie Forde's roadshow, and became a crazy comedy double-act as the Horsbrugh Brothers in the show *Good Night, Good Night*. He made his broadcasting début in 1932, establishing his catchprase 'The size of it!'. After war service in the RAF, he won his own half-hour radio series named after his catchphrase. His daughter, Janet Munro, became a film star via several Walt Disney productions.

MUNRO, Sir Hugh Thomas
(1856–1919)

Mountaineer, born in London. The eldest son of Sir Campbell Munro of Lindertis, he inherited the family estate near Kirriemuir. Although a fanatically keen traveller, he is remembered for his contribution to mountaineering. A founding member of the Scottish Mountaineering Club in 1889, he served as its president from 1894 to 1897. He compiled the first authoritative list of what have come to be known as 'Munros' when he published his *Tables of Heights over* 3000 *Feet* in the first issue of the *SMC Journal* in 1891. While 'Munro-bagging' has become a commonplace pastime, Munro himself never achieved the distinction of climbing all the peaks he listed, remaining two short at his death.

MUNRO, Neil
(1864–1930)

Novelist and journalist, born in Inveraray, Argyll, the son of a farmer. He worked in a law office before taking up journalism in Glasgow, where he became editor of the *Glasgow Evening News* (1918–27). He wrote romantic Celtic tales in *The Lost Pibroch* (1896) and *Gilian the Dreamer* (1899), and historical Highland novels in *John Splendid* (1898), *Doom Castle* (1901) and *The New Road* (1914). However, he is best known for his humorous tales about a Clyde puffer, published as *The Vital Spark* (1906) and collected as *Para Handy and Other Tales* (1931). His autobiography, *Brave Days*, was published posthumously in 1931.

MUNRO, Robert
(1835–1920)

Archaeologist, born in Assynt, Ross and Cromarty. His early intention to enter the Church was abandoned in favour of medicine as a result of his adoption of Darwin's theory of evolution. Poor health prompted an early retirement, after which he devoted himself to archaeology, becoming Britain's leading authority on lake-dwellings. He published extensively on medical, political and social topics as well as archaeology, but he is best known for *Ancient Scottish Lake Dwellings* (1882) and *The Lake Dwellings of Europe* (1890), and for the lectureship he founded in anthropology and prehistoric archaeology at Edinburgh University in 1910.

MURCHISON, Sir Roderick Impey
(1792–1871)

Geologist and geographer, born in Tarradale, Ross and Cromarty, and educated in Edinburgh and at Military College in London. After leaving the army in 1823, he turned to geography and geology. In 1835 he established the Silurian system and, with Adam Sedgwick, the Devonian system. From 1840 to 1845, with others, he carried out a geological survey of the Russian empire. Struck with the resemblance between the Ural mountains and Australian chains, he foreshadowed the discovery of gold in Australia (1844). Murchison Falls (Uganda) and Murchison River (Western Australia) are named after him. Co-founder of the Royal Geographical Society, he was its president for 16 years, while as President of the British Association (1850) he established Section E as the 'Geographical and Ethnological Society'. He was closely associated with many prominent explorers, **David Livingstone** in particular. In 1855 he was made Director-General of the Geological Survey and Director of the Royal School of Mines. His principal works were *The Silurian System* (1839) and *The Geology of Russia in Europe and the Urals* (1845). He was knighted in 1839 for services to science, and became a baronet in 1866.

MURDOCK, William
(1754–1839)

Engineer, and pioneer of coal gas for lighting, born near Auchinleck, Ayrshire. He worked with his father, a millwright, and then with Boulton and **James Watt** of Birmingham, by whom he was sent to Cornwall to erect mining engines. At Redruth he constructed in 1784 the model of a high-pressure engine to run on wheels, introduced labour-saving machinery, a new method of wheel rotation, an oscillating engine (1785), and a steam-gun, and he also improved Watt's engine. His distillation of coal gas began at Redruth in 1792, when he illuminated his own home with it. Successful experiments were conducted at Neath Abbey in 1796, but it was not until 1803 that Boulton's engineering works at Soho were lighted with gas.

MURE, Sir William
(1594–1657)

Poet, born in Rowallan, Ayrshire. A staunch Protestant and Royalist, he was wounded at Marston Moor (1644), but later led his regiment at Newcastle (1644). He wrote a long religious poem, *The True Crucifixe for True Catholikes* (1629), a fine version of the Psalms (1639), and some love and courtly poems. He also translated parts of Virgil's *Aeneid*.

MURRAY, Alexander
(1775–1813)

Philologist, born in Minnigaff parish, Kirkcudbright, the son of a shepherd. While he became a shepherd himself, he also acquired a mastery of the classics, the major European languages and Hebrew, and after 1794 he studied at Edinburgh. In 1806 he became minister in the parish of Urr, and in 1812 Professor of Oriental Languages at Edinburgh. He left the manuscript of a *History of the European Languages* (published in 1823).

MURRAY, Andrew Graham, Viscount Dunedin
(1849–1942)

Judge, born in Edinburgh. Educated at Harrow, and Cambridge and Edinburgh universities, he was admitted to the Faculty of Advocates in 1874. Both his father and his mother belonged to families with great influence in legal circles, and he made rapid progress. He was successively Senior Advocate Depute in the Crown Office (1888), Sheriff of Perthshire (1890), Solicitor-General for Scotland (1895–6), and Lord Advocate (1896–1903). From 1891 to 1905 he served as Conservative MP for Buteshire, and was Secretary for Scotland in 1903. He was Lord Justice General of Scotland in 1905, and became Baron (later Viscount) Dunedin. Deemed a careful and influential judge, his judgements were widely cited, particularly in matters of Patent Law and Feudal Law. He was appointed Lord of Appeal in Ordinary in London in 1913, and served in that capacity until his retirement in 1932.

MURRAY, Charles
(1864–1941)

Poet, born in Alford, Aberdeenshire. He trained as an engineer and had a successful career in South Africa, where in 1917 he became Director of Defence. His poems were written in the Aberdeenshire dialect and admirably portrayed country life and character at the turn of the century. His first major collection, *Hamewith* (1900), was his best and most characteristic.

MURRAY, Chic, originally Charles Thomas McKinnon Murray
(1919–85)

Comedian, born in Greenock, Renfrewshire. He began an apprenticeship in marine engineering at Kincaid's in 1934 whilst deploying his musical talents in such amateur groups as The Whinhillbillies and Chic and His Chicks. Rejected for military service, he met soubrette Maidi Dickson (1922 –), his wife from 1945 to 1972, and they formed a double-act. Billed as 'The Tall Droll with the Small Doll', their combination of jokes and songs made them a popular attraction on television and in theatres throughout the country. Later, working as a solo act, with a forbidding expression and omnipresent 'bunnet', Murray offered a comic vision of the world that was absurd, surreal and absolutely unique. Much mimicked and much loved by his fellow professionals, he acted in such films as *Casino Royale* (1967) and *Gregory's Girl* (1980), the television film *Saigon* (1983), and played football manager **Bill Shankly** in the musical play *You'll Never Walk Alone* (1984). His life was the subject of a bestselling biography, *The Best Way to Walk* (1989), by Andrew Yule.

MURRAY, David Edward
(1951 –)

Company director and property developer, born in Ayr. Educated at **Fettes** College and Broughton High School, Edinburgh, he built a prosperous and diversified business on the basis initially of steel stockholding. As Chairman and Chief Executive of Murray International Holdings his interests developed in the 1980s to encompass not just metal distribution but also electronic sub-assembly, property development and office equipment distribution. In recognition of his rapid rise he won the Young Scottish Businessman of the Year title in 1984 and was awarded an Honorary Doctorate from Heriot-Watt University in 1986. It is estimated that his holdings by 1991 provided an annual turnover of £150 million. As Chairman of Glasgow Rangers Football Club he established a relationship with manager **Graeme Souness** which, although ending with Souness' departure in 1991, has been said to have revolutionized the sport in Scotland.

MURRAY, Lord George
(c.1700–1760)

Jacobite soldier, son of the Duke of Atholl. He took part in the Jacobite risings of 1715 and 1719, fled to France but was pardoned in 1726. In 1745 he joined the Young Pretender (Prince **Charles Edward Stuart**), and was one of his generals. He won a victory at Prestonpans (September 1745) and conducted a masterly retreat from Derby. He had a decisive victory at Falkirk (January 1746), when he thoroughly routed the enemy. He opposed the decision to fight at Culloden, but nevertheless commanded the right wing. The next day he resigned and escaped abroad, having unsuccessfully tried to make Prince Charles stay in Scotland. He died in Holland.

MURRAY, Sir James Augustus Henry
(1837–1915)

Philologist and lexicographer, born in Denholm, Roxburghshire. He was for many years a schoolmaster at Mill Hill school. His *Dialects of the Southern Counties of Scotland* (1873) established his reputation. The great work of his life, the editing of the Philological Society's *New English Dictionary* (later called the *Oxford English Dictionary*), was begun at Mill Hill (1879) and completed (1928) at Oxford. Murray himself edited about half the work, but he created the organization and the inspiration for completing it.

MURRAY, John, originally McMurray
(1745–93)

Publisher, born in Edinburgh. He became an officer in the Royal Marines in 1762, but in 1768 bought Sandy's book-selling business in London, and published the *English Review*, Disraeli's *Curiosities of Literature*, and other works. His son, John (1778–1843), who carried the business from Fleet Street to Albemarle Street, launched the *Quarterly Review*, of which the first issue appeared in 1809. Byron received £20 000 for his works, George Crabbe, Thomas Moore and **Thomas Campbell** also being treated generously. His 'Family Library' was begun in 1829, and he issued the travels of **Mungo Park**, Belzoni, Parry, Franklin and others. His son, John Murray the third (1808–92), issued the works of **David Livingstone**, George Borrow, Darwin, **Samuel Smiles**, George Smith's

dictionaries, and *Handbooks for Travellers* (begun 1836). His son and successor, Sir John Murray (1851–1928), absorbed Smith, Elder & Co. in 1917, edited Gibbon's *Autobiography* and Byron's letters, and began publication of the *Letters of Queen Victoria*. Sir John (1884–1967), his son, completed their publication.

MURRAY, John
(1809–98)

Doctor and photographer, born in Blackhouse, Aberdeenshire, the son of a farmer. After studying medicine he joined the medical service of the East India Company. He was in charge of the medical school at Agra from 1849 until 1867 when he became Inspector General of Hospitals in the northwest provinces. Throughout the 1850s and 1860s he was active as a photographer. His photographs — large-scale salt and albumen prints from waxed paper negatives, generally of architectural subjects — were exhibited in Britain, and examples were published in London by J Hogarth. After retiring in 1871, Murray became President of the Epidemiological Society of London.

MURRAY, Sir John
(1841–1914)

Canadian-born marine zoologist, born in Cobourg, Ontario, of parents who had left Scotland in 1834. He studied in Canada and at Edinburgh University, and after a voyage on a whaler, was appointed one of the naturalists to the Challenger Expedition (1872–6). He was successively Assistant Editor and, in the wake of Sir **Charles Thomson**, Editor-in-Chief (1882–95) of the *Reports* of the scientific results. In 1897 he conducted a bathymetrical survey of Scotland's freshwater lochs. He wrote a *Narrative* of the expedition and a report on deep-sea deposits, and published many papers on oceanography and biology. In 1910 he went on an exploration of the North Atlantic.

MURRAY, Sir John, of Broughton
(1715–77)

Jacobite soldier, born in Peeblesshire. Educated at Edinburgh and Leyden, he visited Rome and made contact with the Jacobite court. He was Prince **Charles Edward Stuart**'s secretary during the 1745 Rising but, having been captured after Culloden, saved his life by betraying his fellow Jacobites. He succeeded as baronet in 1770.

MURRAY, Thomas Blackwood
(1871–1929)

Motor manufacturer, born in Biggar, Lanark-shire, Scotland's greatest pioneer and inventor of the early automobile industry. Educated at Biggar Board School, George Watson's College, Edinburgh, and at Edinburgh University, he then moved to Glasgow where he worked with, amongst others, **Henry Mavor** and Arthur Coulson, the electrical engineers. He then joined Scotland's first motor car project under George Johnstone but, frustrated at the lack of progress, in 1899 he set up, in partnership, the Albion Motor Company. In 1902 the factory moved to Scotstoun, Glasgow, where quality cars and, later, lorries were produced. By 1913 the firm was specializing in lorries alone and a year later the company's fortunes were boosted by the onset of war and the demand for vehicles and shells. In the postwar period Murray soundly directed the company's development.

MURRAY, Yvonne
(1964–)

Middle-distance runner, born in Edinburgh. She first came to prominence in 1982, breaking the UK junior record for 3000 m when she won the Scottish championships. Although also a 1500-m runner, her main successes have all come at 3000 m. In 1986 she was a bronze medallist at the Commonwealth Games, and a silver medallist at the European championships. She won bronze at the 1988 Olympics, and Commonwealth silver again in 1990 before, also in 1990, winning the European Championship in Split, Yugoslavia. An ebullient but modest figure, she was awarded the MBE in 1990 for services to sport.

MUSGRAVE, Thea
(1928–)

Composer, born in Edinburgh. She studied at Edinburgh University, the Paris Conservatoire, and with Nadia Boulanger. Her early work was largely Scottish in inspiration her *Suite o'Bairnsangs* (1953) and the ballet, *A Tale for Thieves* (1953), were followed by *Cantata For a Summer's Day* (1954), a chamber opera, *The Abbot of Drimock* (1955), and her *Scottish Dance Suite* (1959). In the late 1950s her work became more abstract, and she has used serial and aleatory devices. Her music includes two choral and orchestral works, *The Phoenix and the Turtle* (1962),

and *The Five Ages of Man* (1963), an opera *The Decision* (1964–5), a full-length ballet, *Beauty and the Beast* (1968), works for instruments and prerecorded tapes, the chamber opera *The Voice of Ariadne* (commissioned for the Aldeburgh Festival of 1974), the operas *Mary, Queen of Scots* (1977) and *A Christmas Carol* (1979), and a radio opera, *An Occurrence at Owl Creek Bridge* (1981).

MUSHET, David
(1772–1847)

Iron-master, born in Dalkeith, Midlothian. Like many of his contemporaries he was continually experimenting with new materials and processes in the search for better and cheaper iron and steel. He discovered black band ironstone at Calder Ironworks near Glasgow in 1801 and maintained against strong opposition that it was suitable for smelting. After the invention of the hot blast process by **James Beaumont Neilson** in 1828 it became widely used in the Scottish iron industry. He showed that non-phosphoric oxides of iron could be used to make better quality wrought iron, he patented a process for making cast steel from wrought iron, and discovered the beneficial effects of adding manganese to iron and steel. He moved from Scotland in 1805 to Derbyshire and later to the Forest of Dean.

MYKURA, Walter
(1926–88)

Czechoslovakian-born geologist, born in Sokolov. He moved as a refugee to Britain in 1938 and, after service in the RAF, graduated in geology at Birmingham University (1950). In that year he joined the staff of the Geological Survey of Great Britain in its Edinburgh office, where he remained until a stroke forced his retirement in 1985. An outstanding field geologist, known for his work throughout Scotland, he gained Special Merit Promotion to Senior Principal Scientific Officer in 1979. The recipient of several awards, he was elected a Fellow of the Royal Society of Edinburgh in 1970. He was the author of several Survey publications, the best-known being the first ever *Regional Handbook to the Geology of Orkney and Shetland* (1976).

MYLES, Lynda
(1947–)

Film and television producer, born in Arbroath, Angus. Whilst studying philosophy at Edinburgh University, she became involved in the running of the Edinburgh International Film Festival. Serving as Director from 1973 to 1980, she raised the event's international reputation through her informed championing of the New German Cinema, underappreciated Hollywood veterans, and the new generation of American directors, an enthusiasm that led her to co-author the book *The Movie Brats* (1979). Curator of the Pacific Film Archive in California between 1980 and 1982, she then returned to Britain and worked for Channel 4 and Enigma Films, where she produced the political thriller *Defence of the Realm* (1985). Senior Vice-President of European Production for Columbia Pictures during David Puttnam's brief reign as studio head, she subsequently worked for the BBC before returning to independent film production with the highly successful *The Commitments* (1991). In 1981 she received a BFI Special Award for services to the film industry.

MYLNE, Robert
(1734–1811)

Architect, born in Edinburgh of a notable family of stonemasons, architects and engineers. He studied on the Continent and designed Blackfriars' Bridge (erected in 1769 and pulled down in 1868) and planned the Gloucester and Berkeley Ship Canal and the Eau Brink Cut for fen drainage at King's Lynn. His buildings, for example St Cecilia's Hall, Edinburgh (1763–5), show an elegance typical of the best late 18th-century work. His brother, William, designed the North Bridge in Edinburgh.

MYLNE, or MILN, Walter
(d.1558)

Protestant martyr. While on a visit to Germany he grew interested in the doctrines of the Reformation, and later as priest of Lunan in Angus was denounced for heresy. Condemned by Cardinal **Beaton** to be burnt wherever he might be found, he fled the country, but after the cardinal's death he mistakenly thought it safe to return. Taken prisoner at Dysart, he was tried at St Andrews and although by this time over 80 years old was condemned to the stake, the last Scottish Protestant martyr.

N

NAIRN, Tom
(1932 –)

Sociologist, born in Freuchie, Fife, and educated at Edinburgh University where he graduated in philosophy in 1956. He was also educated at Oxford, Dijon and Scuola Normale in Pisa. He taught social philosophy at Birmingham University from 1962 to 1964, and sociology at Hornsey College of Art. A fellow of the Transnational Institute in Amsterdam, he was a longstanding member of the editorial board of *New Left Review*. He edited the *Bulletin of Scottish Politics* from 1981 to 1982, and writes a fortnightly column for *The Scotsman*. His work combines trenchant political comment with acute social analysis of Scotland and Europe. His publications include *The Left Against Europe* (1973), *The Break-Up of Britain?* (1977, revised ed 1981), and *The Enchanted Glass: Britain and its Monarchy* (1988).

NAIRNE, Carolina, née Oliphant, Lady
(1766–1845)

Song writer, born in Gask, Perthshire, the daughter of a Jacobite laird. In 1806 she married her second cousin, Major Nairne (1757–1830), who became Lord Nairne in 1824. She lived in Edinburgh, but travelled widely in Ireland and Europe after her husband's death. Collecting traditional airs, she wrote songs to them under the pseudonym 'Mrs Bogan of Bogan', which were published in *The Scottish Minstrel* (1821–4), and posthumously as *Lays from Strathearn*. They include the lament for Prince **Charles Edward Stuart**, 'Will ye no' come back again', 'The Land o' the Leal', 'Caller Herrin'', 'The Laird o' Cockpen', 'The Rowan Tree', and 'The Auld Hoose', as well as the martial setting for 'The Hundred Pipers'.

NAPIER, Sir Charles
(1786–1860)

Naval commander, born at Merchiston Hall near Falkirk, a cousin of Sir **Charles James Napier**. He went to sea at 13, received his first command in 1808, and later served as a volunteer in the Peninsular army. Commanding the *Thames* in 1811, he inflicted great damage on the French in the Mediterranean. In the American War of 1812–14 he led the way in the ascent of the Potomac, and took part in the operations against Baltimore. From 1831 to 1833, in command of the Loyalist Portuguese fleet, he defeated the fleet of the pretender, Maria Evaristo Miguel, and restored Queen Maria II to the throne. Returning to the British navy in 1839, in the war between the Porte and Mehemet Ali he stormed Sidon, defeated Ibrahim Pasha in Lebanon, attacked Acre, blockaded Alexandria, and concluded a convention with Ali. He commanded the Baltic fleet in the Crimean War (1854–5), but the capture of Bomarsund failed to realize expectations, and he was superseded. He twice sat in Parliament, and until his death he worked to reform naval administration.

NAPIER, Sir Charles James
(1782–1853)

Soldier, the conqueror of Sind, born in London, the brother of Sir **William Napier**. He was a descendant of the mathematician **John Napier** of Merchiston. He served in Ireland during the rebellion, in Portugal (1810), against the USA (1813), and in the storming of Cambrai (1815). In 1841 he was ordered to India to command in the war with Sind, and at the Battle of Meeanee (1843) he broke the power of the emirs. As Governor of Sind, he was soon engaged in an acrimonious war of dispatches with the home authorities, and allegedly sent the classically punny telegram 'Peccavi' ('I have sinned'). In 1847 he returned to England, but was back in India before the close of the Sikh War. As Commander-in-Chief of the army in India, he quarrelled with Lord **Dalhousie** about military reform, and finally left the East in 1851.

NAPIER, Francis, 10th Baron and 1st Baron Ettrick
(1819–98)

Politician, born at Thirlstane, Selkirkshire, and educated in Saxe-Meiningen, Germany, and Cambridge University. He succeeded his father in 1834, and was made Baron Ettrick in 1874. He held several diplomatic posts, including Ambassador to Russia (1861–4) and to Prussia (1864–6). As Governor of Madras (1866–72) he dealt with a serious famine, made major improvements in public health facilities, and began a huge public irrigation scheme. He was briefly Viceroy of India (1872). He took a general interest in questions of urban and rural poverty in Britain, and chaired the 1884 commission into Highland unrest, which substantially upheld the case of the crofters, although its conclusions were only partially enacted in 1886.

NAPIER, John
(1550–1617)

Mathematician, the inventor of logarithms, born at Merchiston Castle, Edinburgh. He matriculated at St Andrews University in 1563, travelled on the Continent, and settled down to a life of literary and scientific study. In 1593 he published his *Plaine Discouery of the whole Reuelation of Saint John.* He made a contract with Logan of Restalrig for the discovery of treasure in Fast Castle (1594), devised warlike machines (including primitive tanks) for defence against Philip II of Spain, and recommended salt as a fertilizer. A strict Presbyterian, he was also a believer in astrology and divination. He described his famous invention of logarithms in *Mirifici Logarithmorum Canonis Descriptio* (1614), and the calculating apparatus known as 'Napier's Bones' in *Rabdologiae* (1617).

NAPIER, Macvey
(1776–1847)

Lawyer and editor, born in Glasgow. In 1799 he became a Writer to the Signet in Edinburgh, in 1805 librarian of the Signet Library (until 1837), and in 1824 first Professor of Conveyancing at Edinburgh. He edited the supplement to the fifth edition of the *Encyclopaedia Britannica* (1816–24), the seventh edition (1830–42), and from 1829 the *Edinburgh Review*.

NAPIER, Mark
(1789–1879)

Advocate and romantic biographer. Educated at Edinburgh High School and Edinburgh University, he was called to the Scottish Bar in 1820. He proved a competent criminal lawyer, but took up family history, including *Memoirs of John Napier of Merchiston* (1834), throwing significant light on the inventor of logarithms (1580–1617), whose manuscripts he edited (1839), and *History of the Partition of Lennox* (1835). He then entered upon a literary, learned and almost theological Jacobitism, supporting this by a wealth of primary sources and a greater wealth of italics and block capitals. Among his many publications were *Montrose and the Covenanters* (1838), *Memoirs of the Marquis of Montrose* (2 vols, 1856), and *Memorials of Graham of Claverhouse, Viscount Dundee* (1859–62). The faint aura of flickering playfulness in contemporary neo-Jacobites is absent from Napier's sacramental prose, which drew him into bitter controversies with neo-Covenanters and romantic Whigs as to whether the Wigtown martyrs, Margaret Maclachlan and Margaret Wilson, had actually been executed. Napier's arrangement of material was clumsy and his fierce faith made concessions to persuasion almost undesirable, but his critique of Whig and neo-Covenanter apologetics was founded on strong fact as well as faith. For all of his historiographical labours, he retained his legal interests, becoming Sheriff-Depute of Dumfriesshire and Galloway, and publishing *The Law of Prescription in Scotland* (1839, 1854) and a controversial *Letter* on sheriff courts (1852). Despite his rich archaism, he was much loved.

NAPIER, Robert
(1791–1876)

Shipbuilder and engineer, born in Dumbarton. He built the engines for the first four Cunard steamships and, turning to shipbuilding in 1841, he also built some of the earliest ironclad warships, including the *Black Prince* in 1860. He built ships for many different countries, including France, Turkey and Denmark, his achievements helping to make the Clyde a great shipbuilding centre.

NARES, Sir George Strong
(1831–1915)

Naval commander and explorer, born in Aberdeen. Educated at the Royal Naval

College, New Cross, he entered the navy in 1846. He served as mate on the *Resolute* during its Arctic expedition of 1852, in the Crimea, and as Commander of the cadet sail-training ship *Britannia*, and worked on surveys of north-east Australia and the Mediterranean (1872–4). He commanded the *Challenger* (1872–4) on its oceanographic voyage around the world which resulted in a 50-volume report for its sponsors, the Admiralty and the Royal Society. In 1875 he was transferred to command the *Alert* and *Discovery* in the Arctic, and later, on the *Alert*, he surveyed the Magellan Straits.

NASMYTH, Alexander

(1758–1840)

Painter, born in Edinburgh. A pupil of **Allan Ramsay**, he returned to Edinburgh from London in 1778. At this time he participated in **Patrick Miller**'s paddle-steamer projects. Miller subsequently partly financed his visit to Italy (1782–4), which had a considerable influence on his work. Back in Edinburgh he established a reputation as a portrait painter. His portrait of **Burns** in the Scottish National Gallery is particularly famous. He later confined himself to landscape painting, and set up a school where his children also taught.

NASMYTH, James

(1808–90)

Engineer, son of **Alexander Nasmyth**, born in Edinburgh. From boyhood he showed a talent for mechanics; in 1834 he started in business at Manchester, and in 1836 he established at Patricroft the Bridgewater Foundry. His steam hammer was devised in 1839 for forging an enormous wrought-iron paddle-shaft, and in 1842 he found an identical steam hammer at work at Le Creusot in France; it had been adapted from his own scheme-book. Nasmyth patented his invention, and it was adopted by the Admiralty in 1843. He was also an amateur astronomer and telescope maker who cast his own speculum mirrors and designed an optical arrangement (the 'Nasmyth focus'), which was revived more than a century later. Among his other inventions was a steam pile-driver, a planing machine and a hydraulic punching machine. He published *Remarks on Tools and Machinery* (1858) and *The Moon* (1874).

NASMYTH, Patrick

(1787–1831)

Landscape painter, born in Edinburgh, son of **Alexander Nasmyth**. He settled in England, painted many English scenes and became known as the 'English Hobbema'.

NAUGHTIE, James

(1952 –)

Journalist and broadcaster, born in Rothiemay, Banffshire. A graduate of Aberdeen and Syracuse (New York) universities, he entered journalism with the *Aberdeen Press and Journal* in 1974 and subsequently moved to *The Scotsman* (1977–84), where he rose to become Chief Political Correspondent, winning numerous awards, including the Laurence Stern Fellowship (1981), Writer of the Year (1983) and Scottish Journalist of the Year (1984), for the precision and calibre of his writing. Subsequently Political Correspondent for the *Guardian* (1984–8), he has contributed extensively on political issues to radio and television programmes and, in 1988, his informed and penetrating analysis of current affairs, his ebullient personality and ready wit found him chosen to succeed Sir Robin Day as presenter of Radio 4's daily news and current affairs programme *The World at One*. A columnist for *Scotland on Sunday*, he wrote *Playing the Palace: A Westminster Collection* in 1984.

NAUGHTON, Charles

(1887–1976) and
GOLD, Jimmy, originally James McGonigal
(1886–1967)

Comedians, born in Glasgow. They first appeared as a double act, 'Naughton and Gold', at the Hippodrome, Glasgow, in 1908, and the same year made their London début at the Brixton Empress. In the early 1930s they joined several other double acts to form the London Palladium Crazy Gang, which raised their prestige from routine comedy to star billing. Their burlesque on British builders gave them the immortal catchphrase, 'Turn it round the other way'. They appeared in many Royal Variety Performances, and from 1947 staged Crazy Gang revival shows at the Victoria Palace, London. Their films included *Okay for Sound* (1937) and *Gasbags* (1940).

NECKER, Louis Albert

(1786–1861)

Geologist, born in Geneva, the grandson of

the geologist and mountaineer Horace Benedict de Saussure. He received his early education in Geneva, and in 1806, at the age of 20, he moved to Edinburgh to continue his studies at the university. There he was exposed immediately to the controversy then raging between the Huttonians and the Wernerians concerning the formation of rocks. In a series of journeys between 1806 and 1808 to the Western Isles and through the Scottish Highlands, he gathered enough information to compile the earliest known geological map of the whole of Scotland. This he presented on 4 November 1808 as a manuscript coloured map to the Geological Society of London. It was not published until 1939, by the Edinburgh Geological Society.

NEIL, Andrew Ferguson
(1949 –)

Journalist, born in Paisley and educated at Glasgow University. He was appointed Editor of *The Sunday Times* in 1983 without any previous experience of national newspapers. After working briefly in the Conservative Party's research department, he joined *The Economist* magazine (1973–83), becoming UK editor. In his position at *The Sunday Times*, with the encouragement of its proprietor, Rupert Murdoch, he changed the paper's soft-left bias and strongly supported most of the key policies of the Thatcher government. He identified himself publicly with Murdoch's coup against the unions at Wapping in 1986, which led to the introduction of new labour practices in the newspaper industry.

NEILL, Alexander Sutherland
(1883–1973)

Educationist and author, born in Kingsmuir, Angus, son of a village schoolmaster. He became a pupil-teacher at Kingsmuir (1899–1903), then assistant master at Kingskettle School, Fife (1903–6) and Newport Public School, Fife (1906–8), before studying English at Edinburgh University. After a period in publishing he became headmaster of Gretna Public School (1914–17). After World War I he taught at King Alfred School, Hampstead (1918–20). He was editor of *New Era* (1920–1). He started a community school at Hellerau, near Salzburg, which eventually settled at Leiston, Suffolk, in 1927, as Summerhill School, a co-educational progressive school which 'began as an experiment and became a demonstration'. It was an attempt to provide an education free even

of the authoritarian overtones of other progressive schools. He held with Freud that 'emotions are more important than intellect'. Like many progressive schools, Summerhill became a school for children, especially American children, from higher income groups. Many pupils were 'difficult' and Neill spent a lot of time giving psychotherapy, at first called 'Private Lessons'. He was the most extreme and radical of British progressive schoolmasters and a great publicist, publishing over 20 books from *A Dominie's Log* (1916) to *Neill! Neill! Orange Peel!* (1973). Summerhill is of more importance as an idea than as an institution. Neill believed in love and was generally loved, despite being a cantankerous character. He ran an independent school, but his philosophy influenced many teachers in the maintained sector, and he was revered abroad as well as in Britain.

NEILL, Stephen Charles
(1900–84)

Missionary and theologian of mission, born in Edinburgh. From 1924 he worked in south India as an evangelist, theological teacher, and latterly as Anglican Bishop of Tinnevelly (Tirunelveli). He became deeply concerned with producing Tamil Christian literature and promoting Church union. Returning to Europe in 1944 he maintained his ecumenical interests through working with the World Council of Churches and lecturing in Hamburg, Nairobi, and elsewhere. Author of many books, his *Anglicanism* (1958), *Interpretation of the New Testament* (1962), and *History of Christian Missions* (1964) remain classics in their fields, as does the *History of the Ecumenical Movement* (1954, edited with Ruth Rouse).

NEILSON, James Beaumont
(1792–1865)

Engineer, born in Shettleston, Glasgow. He invented the hot-blast which revolutionized iron manufacture in 1828, and he also improved the system of gas production. He was chief engineer and manager of Glasgow Gasworks from 1817 to 1847, where he worked to improve the technical abilities of his workforce.

NEKOLA, Karel
(1857–1915)

Pottery decorator, originally a carpenter with his father in Bohemia. In 1882 he was appointed decorator at the Fife Pottery of Robert Heron & Son, in Gallatown (now part of Kirkcaldy). Wemyss Ware was one of the products of the pottery and Karel Nekola was responsible for exerting a great deal of influence throughout its most popular period (1888–1915). Highly decorative and extremely colourful flowers, fruit, animals and birds were his main subject matter, which contrasted strikingly against the white body of each pot. He stayed with the firm for 30 years, painting and teaching others, including his sons Carl and Joseph.

NELSON, James Robert

(1945 –)

Church of Scotland minister and convicted murderer, whose appeal to the General Assembly to be accepted as a candidate for the ministry led to a heated and far-reaching debate. Born in Bellshill, Lanarkshire, he was convicted in 1970 for the murder of his mother, and served a sentence of nine years in prison. Converted to Christianity by the prison chaplain during his imprisonment, in 1984 he aroused great Church and public controversy by requesting admittance to the Church of Scotland as a trainee minister. His appeal challenged the Church on a crucial point of principle; as it was put at the time, 'do we really believe what we preach?'. Nelson's case was a hinge of the Church of Scotland's philosophy and convictions. The General Assembly voted 622 to 425 to allow him to proceed as a ministerial candidate. Following his training, he went on to become minister of Calderbank and Chapelhall in Lanarkshire (1986 –).

NELSON, Thomas

(1780–1861)

Publisher, born in Edinburgh. The company of the same name was established in 1798. His son William (1816–87) entered the business in 1835, and did much to improve the city of Edinburgh, including the restoration of Parliament House. Another son, Thomas (1822–92), is credited with the invention of a rotary press (1850), and established an office in London (1844). Specializing in tracts, educational books and affordable reprints, the company's authors included **John Buchan**.

NEWALL, Robert Stirling

(1812–89)

Engineer and astronomer, born in Dundee, where he spent a short time in a mercantile office before moving to London. After visiting the USA, in 1840 he took out the first of his patents for a new type of wire rope, and established a factory at Gateshead for its manufacture. He then turned his inventive genius to the submarine cable and devised such substantial improvements to both the cable and the means of laying it that his firm subsequently laid cables in many parts of the world. His interest in astronomy was combined with his engineering talents in the construction of a very large telescope with an aperture of 25 inches, which he presented shortly before his death to Cambridge University. His son Hugh Frank Newall (1857–1944) worked at the Cavendish Laboratory in Cambridge and in 1909 became the first professor of astrophysics. In 1913 he was appointed the first director of the Solar Physics Observatory, where he carried out important research into solar phenomena.

NEWBERY, Frances Henry

(1853–1946)

Director of the Glasgow School of Art, born in Membury, Devon, the son of a shoemaker. He studied at Bridport School of Art and in 1875 moved to London to continue his education at South Kensington, supplementing his income by taking part-time employment as an art teacher at two London schools. Between 1875 and 1885 he was employed by the Art Training Schools at South Kensington as a teacher of drawing and painting, and in 1885 he was appointed Headmaster of the Glasgow School of Art. During his period of charismatic leadership the Art School became internationally known for its progressive, modern curriculum. Newbery fostered links between design and industry and ensured that teaching in the school stressed the practical and commercial aspects of the applied arts. He also actively supported the avant-garde and sometimes controversial work of students and staff which contributed to the emergence of the Glasgow Style of decorative arts, and ensured that their work was exhibited on the continent at prestigious venues in Turin, Vienna and Liège. As part of an ambitious programme of expansion he helped raise funds for a new school building and almost certainly encouraged the young **Charles Rennie Mackintosh** to enter the ensuing competition, and he also played a key role in influencing the governor's choice of Honeyman and Keppie (Mackintosh's employers) as winners of the competition. An artist himself, Newbery was elected a member of the Glasgow Art Club in 1889 and became a member of the Institute of Fine Arts and 'Gravers. He exhibited at the Royal Glasgow Institute of Fine Arts, at the RSA, RA and Royal Society of Portrait Painters. In 1902 he was awarded the Crown of Italy for his contribution to the designs for the Scotland section of the Turin International Exhibition. He retired from the Art School in 1917 on grounds of ill health and moved to Corfe Castle in Dorset with his wife **Jessie Newbery**, whom he had married in 1889.

NEWBERY, Jessie, née Rowat
(1864–1948)

Art embroideress and teacher, born in Paisley, the daughter of a shawl manufacturer. She was educated in Paisley, Edinburgh, and at the Glasgow School of Art, and married the Director of the school, **Francis Newbery**, in 1889. In 1894 she was appointed to the staff of the Art School and introduced embroidery into the curriculum, but also taught enamelling and mosaic work. It is for her needlework and embroidery and her approach to the teaching of these subjects that she is best known. Her work was exhibited in Britain, Germany, France and America, and was often illustrated in journals such as *The Studio*, *Das Elgenkleid der Frau* and *Modern Stickerian*. In collaboration with the **Macdonald** sisters and **Ann Macbeth** she played an important role in the development of the Glasgow Style of Art Nouveau. In terms of design and technique her work was original, underpinned by a belief that embroidery should be conceived as an art form, a philosophy which had a major influence on her students. She retired from the Art School in 1908 and moved to Corfe Castle in Dorset with her husband in 1918.

NEWBIGGING, Thomas
(1833–1914)

Gas engineer, born in Glasgow. He entered the gas industry at the age of 18, and six years later was appointed Secretary and Manager of the Rossendale Union Gas Company in Lancashire. In 1863 he was one of the founders of the British Association of Gas Managers, and from 1870 to 1875 he was manager of the gas undertaking in Pernambuco in Brazil. On his return to England he became a consulting civil and gas engineer with a high reputation at home and abroad. His *Handbook for Gas Engineers and Managers*, first published in 1870, appeared subsequently in several enlarged editions.

NICHOL, John Pringle
(1804–59)

Astronomer. After several years of teaching he became Professor of Astronomy at Glasgow, and was well known for his public lectures.

NICHOLSON, Joseph Shield
(1850–1927)

Economist, born the son of an Independent minister at Wrawby, Lincolnshire, and educated at the universities of London, Edinburgh and Cambridge. He was Professor of Political Economy at Edinburgh University (1880–1925), establishing economics there as a separate academic discipline, and in 1885 he married the daughter of his academic predecessor **William Hodgson**. He vigorously entered into contemporary debates on bimetallism, tariff reform and the financing of World War I. His major works were *A Treatise Money* (1888), *The Principles of Political Economy* (1893–1901), and *A Project of Empire* (1909); he also wrote two novels and works on the Italian poet Ariosto.

NICOL, Erskine
(1825–1904)

Painter, born in Leith, Edinburgh. He studied art in Edinburgh and taught in Dublin before moving to London in 1862. He painted homely incidents in Irish and Scottish life, such as *Donnybrook Fair*.

NICOL, James
(1810–79)

Geologist, born at Traquair Manse, Innerleithen, Peeblesshire. After studying under **Robert Jameson** in Edinburgh he attended the universities of Berlin and Bonn. Thus attracted to geology, he began a survey of Scotland and by 1844 had published his *Guide to the Geology of Scotland*. In 1847 he was appointed Secretary to the Geological Society of London, and his contacts with leading geologists of the time, notably Sir **Roderick Murchison** and Sir **Charles Lyell**, helped him to secure the Chair of Geology at Queen's College, Cork (1849). In 1853, again with

Murchison's help, he was appointed Professor of Natural History at Aberdeen University. Increasing general disagreement with Murchison, particularly concerning the interpretation of the North-West Highlands, resulted in the overthrow of Murchison's ideas and the confirmation by **Benjamin Peach** and **John Horne** of Nicol's work.

NICOL, William
(c.1744–1797)

Schoolmaster, a classics master in the High School of Edinburgh. He was a convivial friend of **Robert Burns** who immortalized him in the poem 'Willie Brewed a Peck O' Maut'.

NICOL, William
(1768–1851)

Geologist and physicist, born in Edinburgh, where he lectured in natural philosophy at the university. In 1828 he invented the Nicol prism which utilizes the doubly refracting property of Iceland Spar, and which proved invaluable in the investigation of polarized light. He also devised a new method of preparing thin sections of rocks for the microscope, by cementing the specimen to the glass slide and then grinding until it was possible to view by transmitted light, thus revealing the mineral's internal structure. His reluctance to publish delayed the use of thin sections for some 40 years, until H C Sorby and others introduced them into petrology.

NICOLL, Sir William Robertson,
pseudonym **Claudius Clear**
(1851–1923)

Churchman and man of letters, born in Lumsden, Aberdeenshire. Educated at Aberdeen, he was Free Church minister at Dufftown (1874–7) and Kelso (1877–85). He moved to London for health reasons, turned to literary work, and became editor of *The Expositor* and *The British Weekly*. In 1891 he founded *The Bookman*, and in 1893 *The Woman at Home*, whose main contributor was **Annie S Swan**. He wrote books on theology, and edited *The Bookman's Illustrated History of English Literature* (1897) and the complete works of Emily Brontë (1910). His collected articles were published as *The Daybook of Claudius Clear* (1905) and *A Bookman's Letters* (1915).

NICOLSON, Alexander
(1827–93)

Gaelic scholar, born in Usabost in Skye. Educated for the Free Church at Edinburgh, he worked as assistant to the philosopher Sir **William Hamilton**, and became an advocate. A prolific writer in both English and Gaelic, he was a member of the Napier Commission that reported on crofting conditions in the Highlands and Islands (1884) and established the Crofters' Commission. He helped to revise the Gaelic Bible, and published *A Collection of Gaelic Proverbs and Familiar Phrases* (1881).

NILSEN, Dennis
(1945 –)

Convicted murderer, born in Fraserburgh, Aberdeenshire. After a period in the army and a year as a probationary policeman he became a civil servant in 1974. While living in two rented flats in London, he invited a series of young men home, strangling or attempting to strangle several of them. The dead victims he dissected, disposing of some of the remains by flushing them down the toilet. When, in 1983, the drains became blocked he was discovered and arrested. He has admitted to 15 murders. Throughout the four years of his offending, he had sustained his employment, gained promotion and was an active trade unionist.

NINIAN, St, also known as Nynia or Ringan
(fl.390)

Bishop and missionary, associated with Whithorn in Wigtownshire, and the earliest-known Christian leader in Scotland. According to Bede, writing about 730, he was a bishop of the Old Welsh British, and was instructed in Rome; he built a stone church for his see, called Candida Casa. According to his 12th-century biographer, Ailred of Reivaulx, he was the son of a Christian king and born near the Solway Firth. He was consecrated bishop by the pope (394) and sent as an apostle to the western parts of Britain. On his way home from Rome he visited St Martin of Tours, who supplied him with masons and to whom he later dedicated his church. He selected Wigtownshire for the site of a monastery and church, which was built around 400. Successful in converting the southern Picts, he died at Whithorn and was buried there, although other sources suggest he may have withdrawn to Ireland.

NISBET, Alexander
(1657–1725)

Heraldic writer. Educated for the law, he practised for a time but devoted himself chiefly to antiquities and heraldry. His major work was a *System of Heraldy, speculative and practical, with the True Art of Blazon* (1722). It is a systematic and valuable exposition based on enormous labour. A second volume (1742) contained only fragments from his notes. He left also in manuscript *Part of the Science of Heraldrie and the Exterior Ornaments of the Shield*. His *Genealogical Collections with some Heraldric Plates* were later found and published in 1892. His *System* is a standard authority on Scottish heraldry and a new edition of both volumes appeared in 1984.

NISBET, John Donald
(1922 –)

Educationist, born in Dunfermline, Fife. Educated at Dunfermline High School and Edinburgh and Aberdeen universities, he served in the RAF during the war and later went briefly into school-teaching (1946–9). Thereafter he spent 39 years in Aberdeen University's Department of Education, first as lecturer and from 1963 as professor. A founder member and first president of the Scottish Educational Research Association, he is a central figure in Scottish postwar educational research — in its conduct, promotion, organization and management, practical application, and links with public policy. He has chaired the (British) Educational Research Board, the Scottish Council for Research in Education and the (Scottish) Committee on Primary Education. He has edited the *British Journal of Educational Psychology* and *Studies in Higher Education*. His publications include books on primary-secondary transition, research methods, community education and 'learning to learn' (metacognition).

NITHSDALE, William Maxwell, 5th Earl of
(1676–1744)

Jacobite. He succeeded his father at the age of seven, and in 1699 he married Lady Winifred Herbert (1679–1749), youngest daughter of the Marquis of Powis, and lived at his Kirkcudbrightshire seat, Terregles. A Catholic, he joined the English Jacobites in the 1715 Rising and was taken prisoner at Preston. He was tried for high treason in London and sentenced to death, but on the night before the day fixed for his execution he escaped from the Tower in woman's clothing, through the heroism of his countess who had exchanged clothes with him. They settled in Rome, where the earl died.

NIVEN, David Barclay
(1864–1942)

Architect. Born and educated in Dundee, he trained there with C and L Ower from 1880, then worked as assistant to J Murray Robertson before moving to the London office of Aston Webb, where he became chief assistant. He spent a year in Italy working largely in Genoa on the reconstruction of an Institution for the British and Foreign Sailors' Society. On his return to London he began independent practice, joining Herbert Wigglesworth in partnership in 1893. Commanding a versatile range of styles, they designed several smaller country houses in Surrey and Kent, such as the neo-Georgian Ottershaw Park, Surrey (1910). Niven was renowned for his zealous enthusiasm for architecture and also for garden and town planning. Although he worked predominantly as an expatriate, he designed offices in Dundee for the *Dundee Courier* (1905) and Kincardine Castle in Kincardine O'Neil (1896).

NIVEN, Frederick John
(1878–1944)

Novelist, born in Chile of Scots parentage. Educated at Hutcheson's Grammar School, Glasgow, and Glasgow School of Art, he travelled widely in South America and worked as a journalist (1898–1914). After World War I he emigrated to Canada. He wrote more than 30 novels, mostly set in Glasgow or Canada, including *The Lost Cabin Mine* (1908), *The Justice of the Peace* (1914) and *The Staff at Simsons* (1937). His major work was a trilogy on Canadian settlement, comprising *The Flying Years*, *Mine Inheritance*, and *The Transplanted* (1935–44). He also published an autobiography, *Coloured Spectacles* (1938).

NORIE-MILLER, Sir Francis
(1859–1947)

English-born insurance company director, born in Cheshunt, Hertfordshire. He was educated privately and began his business career in fire insurance. In 1887 he became chief officer of the recently formed General Accident and Employers' Liability Assurance Association of Perth. In an astonishing career he transformed this parochial organization into one of the leading British insurance companies, maintaining its headquarters in Perth. He pioneered the integration of the various forms of insurance, and was knighted in 1936. After World War I motor insurance became big business and contributed to General Accident's rise to the position of third largest British insurance company by 1938. Throughout the growth of General Accident he maintained close personal control over its affairs. A magistrate in Perth for nearly five decades he was briefly elected MP there.

NORTH, Christopher See WILSON, John

NOTMAN, William
(1826–91)

Scottish-born photographer, born in Paisley. He emigrated to Canada in 1856 after failing to save the family business from bankruptcy. By the 1860s he had built up a photographic business with branches in Montreal, Ottawa, Toronto and Halifax and in the 1870s he moved also into the USA. Establishing a considerable studio practice in portraiture, he made a reputation for hunting and snow scenes, staged in the studio, and composite groups organized and painted by his studio assistants. Work outside the studio included landscape photography and the documenting of great engineering projects, such as the laying of the railways. In later years, Notman's studios effectively dominated North American photography.

NOVAR, Robert Crawford Munro Ferguson, 1st Viscount
(1860–1934)

Liberal politician. Born in Kirkcaldy, and educated at home and at the Royal Military Academy at Sandhurst, he was one of the largest Scottish landowners. He was MP for Ross and Cromarty (1884–5), for Leith (1886–1914), and private secretary to Lord **Rosebery** when the latter was Foreign Secretary (1892–4). From 1914 to 1920 he was Governor-General of Australia, where he did much to ensure Australian involvement in World War I, promoting recruitment campaigns and enjoying good relations with Prime Minister Hughes. He was created Viscount Novar in 1920. A Coalition Liberal after the war, he nevertheless served in the Conservative administrations of **Bonar Law** and Baldwin as Scottish Secretary (1922–4). He resigned in protest against protectionism.

O

O'DELL, Andrew Charles
(1909–66)

Geographer, born in Luipaardsvlei, Transvaal, and educated at London University. He was the first recipient of the Newbigin Medal for his study of Scottish railways. After a period at Birkbeck College, London, he took charge of the Department of Geography at Aberdeen University, where he became professor in 1951. His special research interests included Shetland, Scandinavia and transport studies, and he led the team that discovered the St Ninian's Isle Treasure. His books, *Railways and Geography* (1956) and *The Scandinavian World* (1957) became established texts. He was Vice-President of the Institute of British Geographers in 1965.

O'DONNELL, Ron
(1952 –)

Photographer, born in Stirling. He trained as a photographer at Stirling University and at Napier College, Edinburgh. His working method is similar to that of **Calum Colvin** and he produces large constructed colour photographs. The photograph is a record of an installation, which O'Donnell builds or assembles like a stage set. His materials are very diverse, and the set, once photographed, is destroyed. His photographs have a message that is often political and is usually tempered with humour.

OGG, Derek
(1954 –)

Advocate and social reformer, born in Dunfermline. Educated at Edinburgh University, he set up his own legal firm in 1980, and was called to the Bar in 1989. A prominent and fearless spokesman for People With AIDS and gay rights, who has striven to bring the problem of AIDS before the wider public, he was the founder in 1983 of Scottish Aids Monitor (SAM), a voluntary group aimed at providing information and assistance for those concerned about the disease. In 1987 he founded the Milestone Venture Trust, which led to the establishment of Scotland's first AIDS hospice in 1990. In 1991 he received the Whitbread Volunteer Action award.

OGILBY, John
(1600–76)

Topographer, printer and map-maker, born in Edinburgh. He became a dancing teacher in London and a tutor in the household of the Earl of Strafford, lost everything in the Civil War, but after the Restoration obtained court recognition and became a London publisher. The great fire of 1666 destroyed his stock but got him the job of surveying the gutted sites in the city. With the proceeds he established a thriving printing house and was appointed 'king's cosmographer and geographic printer'. His early productions include his own translations of Virgil and Homer (sneered at by Alexander Pope in the *Dunciad*), but his most important publications were the maps and atlases engraved in the last decade of his life, including Africa (1670), America (1671), Asia (1673), and a road atlas of Britain (1675), unfinished at his death.

OGILVIE, St John
(1579/80–1615)

Jesuit priest and martyr, born in Banff and ordained in Paris. He worked in Edinburgh, Glasgow and Renfrew, but was arrested, interrogated and hanged at Glasgow Cross for his defence of the spiritual supremacy of the pope. Beatified in 1927 and finally canonized in 1976, he is the only officially recognized martyr in post-Reformation Scotland.

OGILVIE, Alan Grant
(1887–1954)

Geographer, born in Edinburgh, the son of Sir Francis Grant Ogilvie, and educated at Oxford University. After a distinguished military career, he was appointed Reader in

Geography at Manchester University. He was later established at Edinburgh in the first Chair of Geography in Scotland (1931). Other posts included Head of the Hispanic American Division of the American Geographical Society of New York, President of the Royal Scottish Geographical Society (1946–50) and President of the Institute of British Geographers (1951–2). His awards included The Royal Scottish Geographical Society Research Medal and The Livingstone Gold Medal. Although known for establishing the fundamental importance of physical geography to the life of humankind, he has also been referred to as 'the' British regional geographer.

OGILVIE, John
(1733–1813)

Minister and poet, born in Aberdeen and educated at Aberdeen University. He was minister at Midmar, Aberdeenshire, from 1759 until his death. In 1753 he published *The Day of Judgment* (enlarged 1759), a richly profuse baroque apocalypse which **Boswell** felt had 'no inconsiderable share of merit', following this with *Poems on Various Subjects to which is prefix'd an Essay on the Lyric Poetry of the Ancients* (1762), in which Johnson could find 'no thinking', adding to Boswell's plea for their having imagination: 'Why, Sir, there is in them what *was* imagination, but it is no more imagination in *him*, than sound is sound in the echo'. He also published poems on *Providence* (1764), *Solitude* (1765), *Paradise* (1769), *Rona* (1777) and *The Fane of the Druids* (1787), his 'Ode to Evening' and 'Ode to the genius of Shakespeare' winning favour. His last poem was a 20-book epic *Britannia* (1801), prefixed by 'a critical dissertation on epic machinery'. He is famous for having praised Scotland's 'many noble wild prospects' to Johnson, thus eliciting the reply 'But, Sir, let me tell you, the noblest prospect a Scotchman ever sees, is the high road … to England'.

OLIPHANT, Margaret, née **Wilson**
(1828–97)

Novelist, born in Wallyford, Midlothian. When she was 10 years old her family moved to England. She took her name from her mother; little is known about her father, Francis Wilson, except that he once 'took affadavits' in a Liverpool customs house. Precocious, she wrote a novel when she was 16 but her first published work was *Passages in the Life of Mrs Margaret Maitland* (1849), and two years later she began her lifelong connection with the Edinburgh publishers **Blackwood** and *Blackwood's Magazine*, culminating in a history of the firm, which was published posthumously (1897). In 1852 she married her cousin, Frances Oliphant, an artist, but she was widowed in 1859 and found herself £1000 in debt with an extended family to support and educate. Her output was astonishing and uneven, hardly surprising in an author who wrote almost 100 novels, the best known of which are in the group known as *The Chronicles of Carlingford*, consisting of *The Rector and the Doctor's Family* (1863), *Salem Chapel* (1863), *The Perpetual Curate*, (1864), *Miss Majoribanks* (1866), and *Pheobe Junior* (1876), which earned her the sobriquet, a 'feminist Trollope'. She wrote novels of Scottish life, including *The Minster's Wife* (1869), *Effie Ogilvie* (1886) and *Kirsteen* (1890). Other notable works include *Hester* (1883), *Lady Car* (1889), *The Railway Man and His Children* (1891) and *Sir Robert's Fortune* (1895). She was awarded a Civil List pension in 1868, but her industry was unabated and she produced a spate of biographies, literary histories, translations, travel books and tales of the supernatural.

OLIPHANT OF GASK, Laurence
(1691–1767)

Jacobite laird. He fought at Sheriffmuir in 1715 and was in attendance on **James Francis Edward Stuart**, titular James VIII, at Scone. After the failure of the rising he went into hiding, but eventually returned home. In 1732 he inherited the estate of Gask and in 1745 he was again 'out' for Prince **Charles Edward Stuart**, who appointed him to look after his financial administration in the north of Scotland during the Jacobite advance into England. He fought at Falkirk and Culloden, after which he and his son went into hiding in Aberdeenshire until October 1746, when they sailed to Sweden, and from there travelled to France. The Gask estate was confiscated by the government, but bought by Oliphant's friends and handed back to him. When the 7th Lord Oliphant died in 1748, the Laird of Gask claimed the peerage, but it was taken up by Oliphant of Langton. He died in 1751, recognizing Gask as his heir. In 1760 the exiled James VIII also conferred a peerage upon the Laird of Gask, though it is possible it was a confirmation of the existing title; if not, this was the last Jacobite peerage conferred by the exiled Stuarts. Oliphant returned to Scotland in 1763 and later died, still attainted. His son Laurence (1724–92) continued intransigently Jacobite until his own death.

OLIVER, Michael Francis
(1925 –)

Cardiologist, educated at Marlborough College and Edinburgh University, where he graduated in medicine in 1947, receiving the MD with Gold Medal in 1957. He became consultant physician and senior lecturer in medicine at the Royal Infirmary of Edinburgh in 1961, and in 1977 received a personal chair in cardiology and was subsequently appointed to the Duke of Edinburgh Chair of Cardiology at the university. He has been on many committees on food policy and cardiovascular disease and has participated in many international clinical trials, notably one with the World Health Organization on the prevention of ischaemic heart disease. His publications include *Acute Myocardial Infarction* (1966), *Intensive Coronary Care* (1970), *Modern Trends in Cardiology* (1975) and *High Density Lipoproteins and Atherosclerosis* (1978). He has made fundamental contributions to, among other subjects, the understanding of the causes of coronary heart disease and population studies of vascular diseases.

ORCHARDSON, Sir William Quiller
(1832–1910)

Painter, born in Edinburgh. He studied at the Trustees' Academy with **John Pettie** and went to London in 1862. He painted portraits, but is best known for historical and social subject paintings. His most famous painting is the scene of Napoleon on board the *Bellerophon* (1880) in the Tate Gallery; among other well-known subjects are *Queen of the Swords* (1877), *Mariage de Convenance* (1884) and *Her Mother's Voice* (1888).

ORR, James
(1844–1913)

Theologian, born in Glasgow. As a long-time parish minister, Professor of Church History at the United Presbyterian Divinity Hall from 1891, and Professor of Apologetics and Theology at the new Trinity College, Glasgow (1900–13), he defended and promoted conservative evangelical views against contemporary challenges. His books, including *The Christian View of God and the World* (1893), *The Ritschlian Theology and the Evangelical Faith* (1897), *The Virgin Birth of Christ* (1907), and *Revelation and Inspiration* (1910), gave him considerable influence in North America as well as in Britain. His standing as a major representative of evangelical orthodoxy in the early 20th century was consolidated by his editorship of the *International Standard Bible Encyclopaedia* (1915).

ORR, Robin
(1909 –)

Composer, born in Brechin, Angus. He studied at the Royal College of Music, Cambridge University, and with E J Dent, Alfredo Casella and Nadia Boulanger. Organist at St John's College, Cambridge from 1938, he was Professor of Music at Glasgow University from 1956, and at Cambridge University (1965–76). He was co-founder of Scottish Opera (1962). His works include the operas *Full Circle* (one-act, 1968), *Hermiston* (1975), and *On the Razzle* (1988); three symphonies (the first a *Symphony in One Movement*, 1963); songs, sacred choral works and chamber music.

OSWALD, James
(1703–93)

Philosopher, born in Dunnet, Caithness. After university he succeeded his father as minister in Dunnet, moving to Methven, Perthshire in 1750. Moderator of the General Assembly in 1765, he was awarded a DD by Glasgow University. His ill-organized *Appeal to Common Sense on Behalf of Religion* (1766–72) sees 'Common Sense' as the process which brings about knowledge, in effect a form of natural revelation.

OTTAWAY, John Michael
(1939–86)

English physical chemist, born in Surrey. He took his first degree and his doctorate at Exeter University. He began teaching at Strathclyde University, Glasgow, in 1966, and was later appointed to the Chair. He made major contributions to our understanding of the mechanisms of oxidizing agents and to atomic spectroscopy, particularly flame chemistry. He also used catalysis to measure trace elements, employing as a catalyst the substance which contained the trace elements, and then monitoring the way in which their presence changed the catalyst's performance. While at Strathclyde he founded an internationally renowned course in analytical chemistry and established close contacts with industry, particularly the steel industry, both as an adviser and in training specialists for laboratory work.

OUDNEY, Walter

(1790–1824)

Explorer. Born in Edinburgh, he entered the Royal Navy as a surgeon's assistant and later qualified from Edinburgh University. Appointed British Consul at Bornu, he accompanied **Hugh Clapperton** as biologist on his expeditions to Bornu and Kano in Central Africa to explore Lake Chad and the sources of the Niger, proving particularly skilful in communicating with the Africans. He died of pneumonia at Murmur, near Katugum in the Sudan.

OWEN, Robert

(1771–1858)

Welsh social and educational reformer, born in Newtown, Montgomeryshire, a saddler's son. At the age of ten he was put into a draper's shop at Stamford, and by 19 had risen to be manager of a cotton mill. In 1799 he married Anne Caroline, eldest daughter of **David Dale**, and bought from him his cotton-mills and manufacturing village at New Lanark in Scotland. Here he established a model community with improved housing and working conditions, and built an Institute for the Formation of Character, a school (including the world's first day-nursery and playground, and also evening classes) and a village store, the cradle of the co-operative movement. In 1813 he formed New Lanark into a new company with Jeremy Bentham and others. In *A New View of Society* (1813) he contended that character was formed by the social environment, and went on to found several co-operative 'Owenite' communities, including one at New Harmony in Indiana (1825–8), but all were unsuccessful. In 1825 he ceased to be manager at New Lanark after disagreements with his partners, and in 1828 sold all his shares. He organized the Grand National Consolidated Trades Union in 1833, and spent the rest of his life campaigning for various causes, including (later) spiritualism. He also wrote *Revolution in Mind and Practice* (1849). He died in his home town of Newtown. Vigorous conservation and restoration work at New Lanark Village since the 1970s has made it a living community again; it was awarded a Europa Nostra Medal of Honour in 1988.

OWEN, Robert Dale

(1801–77)

Scottish-born American social reformer, born in Glasgow, the son of **Robert Owen**. In 1825 he accompanied his father to America to help set up the New Harmony colony in Indiana. He taught in the school there and edited the *New Harmony Gazette*. In 1829 he moved to New York, where he edited the *Free Inquirer*. He returned to Indiana in 1832 and became a member of the Indiana legislature, and entered Congress in 1843. He was US Ambassador to India (1855–8). An advocate of emancipation of slaves, he became a spiritualist. He wrote *The Policy of Emancipation* (1863), *The Wrong Slavery* (1864), and an autobiography, *Threading My Way* (1874).

P

PAOLOZZI, Eduardo Luigi
(1924 –)

Sculptor and printmaker, born in Leith, Edinburgh. He studied at Edinburgh College of Art and at the Slade School in London. He has held many teaching posts (eg London, Hamburg, California). His first one-man show was at the Mayor Gallery in 1947, and he has held many since, also at the Museum of Modern Art, New York (1964) and the Tate Gallery, London (1971). His early collages were inspired by Surrealism, and his use of magazine cuttings made him a pioneer of Pop Art. In the 1960s he made large, brightly painted metal sculptures. It has been said, half seriously, that were 20th-century civilization to become extinct, it could be partly reconstructed from the details of his work.

PARK, Mungo
(1771–1806)

Explorer of Africa, born in Foulshiels on the Yarrow, Selkirkshire. He studied medicine at Edinburgh (1789–91), through Sir Joseph Banks he was named assistant surgeon on the *Worcester* bound for Sumatra (1792), and in 1795 his services were accepted by the African Association. He learnt Mandingo at an English factory on the Gambia, started inland in December, was imprisoned by a chief, but escaped and reached the Niger at Sego in July 1796. He made his way westward along its banks to Bammaku, but fell ill while crossing mountainous country, and was eventually brought back to the factory by a slave trader after an absence of 19 months. He told his adventures in *Travels in the Interior of Africa* (1799), which at last determined the direction of flow of the Niger. After marrying in 1799, he settled as a surgeon in Peebles but, unhappy in this, in 1805 he undertook another journey to Africa at government expense. Again he started from Pisania on the Gambia, with a company of 45, but by the time he reached the Niger he had only seven followers. From Sansanding he sent back his journals and letters in November 1805 and embarked in a canoe with four European companions. Battling against great dangers and difficulties they reached Boussa, where they were attacked by the natives, and drowned in the fight.

PASLEY, Sir Charles William
(1780–1861)

Military engineer, born in Eskdalemuir, Dumfriesshire. A precocious pupil at the local school, in 1796 he was sent to the Royal Military Academy, where he soon obtained a commission, first in the Royal Artillery and then in the Royal Engineers. He saw service in the Mediterranean, at the siege of Copenhagen, and in Spain under Sir **John Moore**, but in 1809 was severely wounded at the siege of Flushing and was invalided for a year, being rendered unfit for further service in the field. He soon perceived the need for more systematic training of military engineers, and in 1811 he devised courses in his command at Plymouth which, in the following year, were adopted on a larger scale at Chatham. He was appointed the first Director of Field Instruction in the Royal Engineers establishment which eventually became the Royal School of Military Engineering at Chatham. In 1841 he was appointed Inspector-General of Railways with the rank of major-general, a post he held for five years. He was elected a Fellow of the Royal Society in 1816, and received the degree of DCL from Oxford in 1844.

PASSMORE, Reginald
(1910 –)

English-born physiologist and nutritionist, educated at Oxford and St Mary's Hospital Medical School, London. In 1937 he was appointed to the Nutrition Research Laboratory at Coonoor in India, and after service in the Indian Army in World War II he was appointed to the Usher Institute of Public Health at Edinburgh University (1947), where he studied the physiology of exercise and made a notable study of energy expenditure in Fife miners (1952). He was co-author of *Human Nutrition and Dietetics*

(1959, with Sir **Stanley Davidson**), which has gone through eight editions and is used throughout the English-speaking world. A consultant to the Food and Agriculture Organization and the World Health Organization, in 1960 he was Professor of Physiology at the University of Khartoum, Sudan. His contribution to the science of nutrition and its teaching has been to clarify many areas of confusion. An important influence in the international field of nutrition, he has helped to make Edinburgh an international centre for its study.

PATERSON, Bill

(1945 –)

Actor, born in Glasgow. Equally at home in theatre, television and film, he has become established as a remarkable actor in a wide variety of work. From his early days with the 7:84 Scotland Company during the early 1970s, he has since appeared at the National Theatre in Frank Loesser's *Guys and Dolls* (1982), the title role in Brecht's *Schweyk in the Second World War* (1982), which won him a *Plays and Players* best actor award, and Brecht's *The Good Person of Schezuan* (1990). At the Lyric, Hammersmith, he appeared in *Crime and Punishment* (1983), directed by Yuri Lyubimov. His television work includes *Licking Hitler* (1977), written and directed by David Hare.

PATERSON, Robert

(1715–1801)

Stonecutter, the original model for Sir **Walter Scott**'s *Old Mortality*, born, a farmer's son, near Hawick, Roxburghshire. In 1758 he deserted his wife and five children, and for over 40 years devoted himself to the task of repairing or erecting headstones to Covenanting martyrs.

PATERSON, William

(1658–1719)

Financier and founder of the Bank of England, born at Skipnayre farm in Tinwald parish, Dumfriesshire. He spent some years trading in the West Indies. Returning to Europe, he consolidated his fortune in London, and in 1691 proposed the establishment of the Bank of England. When it was founded in 1694 he became a director, but resigned in 1695. Instead he went to Edinburgh, where he promoted a scheme for establishing a new colony at Darien, on the Panama Isthmus. The Scottish Parliament created the Company of Scotland to finance the enterprise, and the whole nation backed it. He sailed with the first expedition in a private capacity, shared all its troubles, and returned with its survivors a broken man in December 1699. However, his energy remained unabated. He had a considerable share in promoting the Union of the parliaments of Scotland and England in 1707, and was elected to the first united parliament by the Dumfries burghs. He prepared the scheme for Walpole's Sinking Fund, and the conversion and consolidation of the National Debt (1717). In 1715 he was awarded £18 000 as indemnity for his Darien losses.

PATERSON, William

(1755–1810)

Lieutenant-Governor of New South Wales, botanist and explorer, born in Montrose, Angus. Inspired by Sir Joseph Banks, for whom he later collected, he became a keen botanist and was elected to the Royal Society in 1799. He made four major journeys of exploration between 1777 and 1779 in South Africa. From 1781 to 1788 he served in India and then in 1789 he travelled to Australia as a captain in the New South Wales Corps, which had been created to protect the new convict settlement at Botany Bay, becoming senior administrator (1794–5) and Lieutenant-Governor (1801). He founded a settlement at Port Dalrymple (Launceston) in Tasmania in 1807. In 1809 he took over as Lieutenant-Governor in Sydney after the arrest of Governor William Bligh. His excessive drinking led to gout and illness, and he retired in 1810, dying on his return voyage to Britain.

PATERSON, W P (William Paterson)

(1860–1939)

Minister and theologian, born at Skirling Mains, Peebleshire. Educated at Edinburgh University (1873–83), with spells of study at Leipzig, Erlangen and Berlin (1883–5), he became parish minister at Crieff, Perthshire (1887–94). Turning to the academic life, he became Professor of Systematic Theology at Aberdeen University (1894–1903), before being appointed Professor of Divinity at Edinburgh (1903–34). A series of key lectureships

(Baird, 1905–6; Gifford, 1923–4), and a shower of international academic honours gave recognition to his stature (honorary doctorates from Edinburgh, St Andrews, Glasgow and Dublin, LLDs from Glasgow, Edinburgh and Pennsylvania). He was appointed chaplain to the king in 1916, and Moderator of the General Assembly of the Church of Scotland in 1919. Some of his many publications, notably *The Apostle's Teaching* (1903), *The Rule of Faith* (1912) and *The Power of Prayer* (1920), became classics of academic writing and theological insight.

PATON, John
(d.1684)

Covenanter, the son of a farmer at Fenwick in Ayrshire. He became a captain in the army of Gustav II Adolf of Sweden, fought at Rullion Green and Bothwell Brig (1679) and, after being apprehended in 1684, was hanged.

PATON, John Gibson
(1824–1907)

Missionary, the son of a stocking-maker, born in Kirkmahoe, Dumfriesshire. In 1858 he went as a missionary of the Reformed Presbyterian Church to the cannibals of the New Hebrides. His brother published and edited his missionary narratives (1889).

PATON, Sir Joseph Noel
(1821–1901)

Painter, born in Dunfermline. He studied at the Royal Academy, London, and became a painter of historical, fairy, allegorical and religious subjects, in a style close to that of the Pre-Raphaelites. He was appointed Queen's Limner for Scotland from 1865. He also published two volumes of poems.

PATON, William
(1886–1943)

Missionary statesman and writer, born in England of Scottish parents. He was educated at Oxford and Cambridge, and served the Student Christian Movement (1911–21). Although a pacifist, he worked as an evangelist among British troops in India, and returned there to minister under ecumenical auspices (1922–7). He organized the international conferences in Jerusalem (1928) and Madras

(1938), and edited the prestigious *International Review of Missions*. Among his numerous writings are *Jesus Christ and the World's Religions* (1916), *The Church and the New Order* (1941) and *The Ecumenical Church and World Order* (1942).

PATRICK, James McIntosh
(1907–)

Painter and printmaker, born in Angus. He studied at Glasgow School of Art from 1925 and was part of a general revival of print-making during the 1920s and 30s. His subject matter is generally the cultivated or, sometimes, urban landscape, seen from a high viewpoint, and his style, in both painting and prints, is characterized by a high degree of finish and intense detail. His work had a huge audience in the 1950s due to commissions from the then British Railways for prints to decorate railway stations.

PAUL, Sir James Balfour
(1846–1931)

Jurist, born in Edinburgh. He passed advocate in 1870 and was appointed Lord Lyon in 1890 and Secretary of the Order of the Thistle in 1926. He was made KCVO in 1926. He was general editor of *The Scots Peerage* (9 vols, 1904–14) based on John Wood's edition (1814) of Sir Robert Douglas's *Peerage of Scotland* (1764), which is a goldmine of information about the great families. He wrote several other useful works on heraldry, notably *An Ordinary of Arms in the Public Register of all Arms and Bearings in Scotland* (1893).

PAUSON, Peter Ludwig
(1925–)

German-born British organic chemist, the first to synthesize ferrocenes. Born in Bamberg, he studied at Glasgow and Sheffield universities. After working in the USA for some years, he lectured at Sheffield from 1953 to 1959. He was then appointed professor at the Royal College of Science and Technology, Glasgow (now Strathclyde University). Ferrocenes, the new substances that he synthesized, are organometallic compounds that do not occur in nature. They consist of parallel five-membered carbon rings with an iron atom sandwiched between each parallel pair. Pauson's revolutionary discovery paved the way for the synthesis of a new class of similar compounds based on other metals. They have applications in the chemical industry, usually as intermediates in a chain of chemical reactions, and in medicine as sensors to monitor glucose levels, for example in diabetics.

PEACH, Benjamin Neeve
(1842–1926)

English-born geologist, born in Gorran Haven, Cornwall. After an early introduction to geology and to Scotland through his father, he was educated at the Royal School of Mines, London. Appointed by Sir **Roderick Murchison** to the newly formed Geological Survey of Scotland, he spent 43 years with the Survey, retiring in 1905, during which time his name became inseparably linked with that of **John Horne**. Their detailed work on the Southern Uplands of Scotland and the North-West Highlands culminated in the massive Memoirs of the Survey, published in 1899 and 1907 respectively. Peach had great artistic ability and was essentially the creative side of the extraordinary partnership. He also served as Acting Palaeontologist for the Survey. He received many honours, including both the **Murchison** and Wollaston medals of the Geological Society of London with John Horne.

PEACOCK, Sir Alan Turner
(1922 –)

Economist and economic adviser, educated at Dundee High School and St Andrews University. His distinguished academic career began with a lectureship in economics at St Andrews University (1947–8) and proceeded with a lectureship then readership in public finance, London University (1948–56); he succeeded **Alexander Gray** as Professor of Economic Science at Edinburgh University (1957–62) and was Professor of Economics at York (1962–78) and Buckingham (1978–80) where he succeeded Lord Beloff as Principal, then Vice Chancellor (1980–4). From 1973 to 1976 he was also Chief Economic Adviser to the Department of Industry and Trade. He was Chairman of the Arts Council Enquiry on Orchestral Resources (1969–70) and of the Committee on Financing the BBC (1985–6). His principal concern, economic policy, was obvious in his first work, *The Economics of National Insurance* (1952); later works expressing his devotion to market principles

included *The Economic Theory of Fiscal Policy* (1976, with G K Shaw) and *The Economic Analysis of Government and Related Themes* (1979).

PEDDIE, James Cameron
(1887–1968)

Pioneering Church of Scotland minister, born in Couland, Forgue, in Aberdeenshire. Educated at Aberdeen University, he had a series of ministries in Fife, Aberdeen and Glasgow, and finally in the united charge of Cunninghame, in Glasgow. His epoch-making publication *The Forgotten Talent* (1961) challenged mainstream Church thinking to a reassessment of the concept of the ministry of healing, a ministry hitherto regarded with some suspicion and scepticism, and considered better left to the lunatic fringes of Church practice. However, as a result of Peddie's influence this has been brought back as a legitimate concern of even the most conventional traditionalist or liturgical purist.

PEDDIE, John Dick
(1824–91)

Architect, who trained with **David Rhind**. Displaying a marked preference for classical styles, he continued in partnership with Charles George Hood Kinnear (1830–94), signing their works with the monogram, PK. He became a member of the RSA in 1856. Among his Italianate works is the Royal Bank, Stirling (1863), and among his Grecian designs, Trinity Duke Street Church, Glasgow (1857). The imposing classical monument to Grandfather Peddie in Warriston Cemetery, Edinburgh (1845), lies close to his design of a neo-Tudor burial tunnel. Working as a hotel specialist, his designs included Dunblane Hydro and the Blythswoodholme Hotel, Glasgow (1877). He was particularly adept at fine classical interiors, such as the Royal Bank head office, Edinburgh (1857). He stood as MP for the Kilmarnock Burghs from 1880 to 1885.

PEDEN, Alexander
(c.1626–1686)

Covenanter, born in Ayrshire. He studied at Glasgow, became a schoolmaster in Tarbolton, and minister at New Luce, Galloway (1660). In 1662 he was ejected from his charge, and subsequently wandered about preaching at conventicles and hiding in caves. Declared a rebel in 1665, he went to Ireland, but returned in 1673 and from then until 1678 was imprisoned on the Bass Rock. Many of his utterances were regarded as prophecies.

PEEBLES, David Bruce
(1826–99)

Gas engineer, born in Dundee. He served a general engineering apprenticeship before moving to Swindon, where he found employment in the workshops of the Great Western Railway Company. After further engineering experience he went to Edinburgh as a partner in a firm that made gas meters, but in 1866, having seen the potential in what was then a rapidly expanding industry, he left in order to set up his own business, Peebles and Company. He invented a number of devices which found a ready market in the gas industry, and before the turn of the century he had the foresight to diversify into heavy electrical engineering, in which sphere the firm of Bruce Peebles and Company became world-famous as manufacturers of some of the largest types of transformer and rectifier. Sir **Duncan McDonald** was managing director when they were merged with Reyrolle Parsons in 1969.

PELLOW, Marti, real name Mark McLachlan
(1965 –)

Pop singer, born in Clydebank. With schoolfriends Graeme Clarke (1965 –), Neil Mitchell (1965 –) and Tommy Cunningham (1964 –) he formed the group Wet Wet Wet. They had been together for over three years before they signed a recording deal, and it was a further two years before they released their first record, but that single, 'Wishing I Was Lucky' (1987), brought instant chart success. This was consolidated by their début album, *Popped In, Souled Out* (1987). Having initially attracted a primarily teenage audience, they attempted to broaden their appeal with the soul- and blues-influenced album, *Holding Back The River* (1989). In 1992 they released the highly successful album *High on the Happy Side*.

PENTLAND, John Sinclair, 1st Baron
(1860–1925)

Politician, born in Edinburgh, and educated at Edinburgh Academy, Wellington College,

Somerset, and the Royal Military College at Sandhurst. After a military career, he entered politics as Liberal MP for Dunbartonshire (1892–5) and then Forfarshire (1897–1909). As Scottish Liberal Whip (1900–5) he won the trust of Sir **Henry Campbell-Bannerman**, who appointed him Scottish Secretary in 1905. In this post his main legislative measures were the National Galleries Act, an Education Act of 1908 which developed secondary schools, and a Land Act, passed in 1911, which encouraged the setting up of smallholdings. Created a peer in 1909, he continued at the Scottish Office until 1912. He was appointed Governor of Madras (1912–19), where he stimulated the economic development of the region.

PEPLOE, Samuel John
(1871–1935)

Artist, born in Edinburgh. He studied at the Trustees' Academy in Edinburgh, and at the Académies Julian and Colarossi. As a mature and established painter he went to Paris (1911) and returned to Edinburgh to remodel his style in accordance with Fauve colouring and Cézannesque analysis of form. His later still-life paintings brought him fame as a colourist.

PERTH, James Eric Drummond, 16th Earl of
(1876–1951)

Liberal politician. Born in York and educated at Eton, he succeeded to the title in 1937. Until 1919 he worked in the Foreign Office as Private Secretary to Sir Edward Grey and Earl **Balfour**. He attended the Versailles Peace Conference, where he was appointed first Secretary-General (1919–33) of the League of Nations. In this role he built up the secretariat into an efficient machine and in the 1920s had several successes in resolving European and colonial disputes. From 1933 to 1939 he was British Ambassador to Italy, establishing good relations with Mussolini and his foreign secretary, Ciano. In 1946 he became Liberal Whip in the Lords.

PETRIE, Alexander Wylie
(1853–1937)

Eccentric, known as the 'Glasgow Clincher' from the title of the campaigning newspaper, which he wrote, edited and sold. A hairdresser by trade, he was flamboyant and unusually sharp-witted, which facility he claimed was due to a silver cell in his brain. He published the first edition of *The Glasgow Clincher* in 1897 and sold it in the streets of Glasgow, where he was a popular character. From the pages of *The Clincher* he waged a series of attacks on the Glasgow Establishment, particularly the City Council. This resulted in frequent charges of disorderly conduct until, in 1897, he was arrested and committed to Woodilee Asylum. A public outcry, and a certificate from an independent doctor testifying to his soundness of mind, secured his release. Thereafter, he claimed to be the only certified sane man in Glasgow.

PETTIE, John
(1839–93)

Painter, born in Edinburgh. He trained at the Trustees' Academy under **Robert Scott Lauder**, and joined Sir **William Quiller Orchardson** in London in 1862. His works, apart from his portraits, were mainly of historical and literary subjects and were highly popular. They include *Juliet and Friar Lawrence* (1874) and *The Vigil* (1884).

PHEMISTER, James
(1893–1986)

Geologist, born in Govan, Glasgow, and educated at Glasgow University. After war service in the army he taught science and mathematics for a short time in a Glasgow school before joining the staff of the Geological Survey of Great Britain in 1921. In an active and long career extending well beyond normal retirement, he contributed meticulous, detailed work on Scotland, particularly the Shetlands, and beyond. In the 1920s he carried out pioneering geophysical work in Persia as well as in Britain, and in 1936 was appointed Petrographer to the Survey. He received many honours and was elected a Fellow of the Royal Society of Edinburgh in 1931.

PHILIP, Sir Robert William
(1857–1939)

Pioneer in tuberculosis control, born in Glasgow. Educated at Edinburgh University, he graduated in medicine in 1882, the year in which Robert Koch discovered the tubercle bacillus. After postgraduate work at Leipzig,

Vienna and Berlin, he was appointed to the medical staff of the Royal Infirmary at Edinburgh. As a result of Koch's discovery he realized that infection could be prevented, and in 1887 he founded the Victoria Dispensary for Consumption in a small flat in Bank Street, Edinburgh, the first of its kind in the world. The Dispensary system, staffed by doctors and health visitors, was to become the keystone in the campaign against tuberculosis in the UK and, eventually, throughout the world. The Royal Victoria Hospital for Consumption was opened at Craigleith, where Philip was able to carry out the fresh-air treatment he advocated, and a farm colony for training men for suitable occupations was added at Liberton. A trust was formed which endowed a Chair of Tuberculosis at Edinburgh University and he was appointed the first professor (1917). Voluntary notification of tuberculosis was started in 1892, became compulsory in 1909, and in 1921 all county and borough councils in the UK were compelled to establish a tuberculosis scheme based on the pattern of the Dispensary. By 1937 there were 680 dispensaries and 35 000 beds for the treatment of tuberculosis. Philip was knighted in 1913.

PHILIPSON, Sir Robin (Robert James)
(1916–92)

English-born painter, born in Broughton-in-Furness, Lancashire. He studied at Edinburgh College of Art from 1936 to 1940, where he was Head of Drawing and Painting (1960–82). During World War II he served in India and Burma. His first one-man show was at the Scottish Gallery, Edinburgh, 1954. He was President of the Royal Scottish Academy from 1973 to 1983. Like many Scottish artists of his generation, he handled paint freely and colours boldly, yet always retained a precise figurative element in his work.

PHILLIMORE, John Swinnerton
(1873–1926)

Classicist, poet and Chestertonian. After a distinguished academic career at Christ Church, Oxford, his honours including the Chancellor's Prize for Latin verse (1895), he contributed to the famous credo from future dissidents and luminaries, *Essays in Liberalism by 6 Oxford Men* (1897). Professor of Greek at Glasgow University (1899–1906) and of Humanity (1906–26), he translated

Sophocles's Theban Plays into rhymed verse, with a major introduction placing Sophocles in context of his time and of Western literature (1902) and published the text of Propertius (1901) and *Index Verborum Propertius* (1902). In 1902 he published his own *Poems*, and in 1912 translated Philostratus's *Apollonius of Tyana*. He played a significant part in the team writing for Hilaire Belloc's paper *The Eye-Witness*, including authorship in the ballade series, the greatest ever achieved in that form. He followed the Chestertons' distributism philosophy and became its leading intellectual in Scotland. Writing for Chesterton's paper *The New Witness*, he adopted its anti-party philosophy, and continued to write for its successor under G K Chesterton, *G. K.'s Weekly*. In 1906 he became a Roman Catholic. His later publications include *Ille Ego*, *Virgil and Professor Richmond* (1920), defending the newly-propounded first four lines of the *Aeneid* against the Inaugural Lecture of his opposite number in Edinburgh, and an authoritative choice of *The Hundred Best Latin Hymns* (1925). Described by Gilbert Chesterton as a 'supreme example of unadvertised greatness, and the thing which is larger inside than outside', he informed his classical scholarship by a subversive consciousness and medievalism.

PHILLIP, John
(1817–67)

Painter, born in Aberdeen, a soldier's son. While apprenticed to a decorator and glazier he began to paint portraits and was sent by a patron to London to study art (1838). Most of his early subjects were Scottish, but after a visit to Spain (1851) for health reasons, he was influenced by Velasquez, and his main triumphs were in Spanish themes, earning him the nickname of Phillip of Spain.

PHYFE, Duncan
(1768–1854)

American cabinet-maker, born in Scotland. He emigrated to Albany in the USA in 1784, where he was originally known as Duncan Fife. After serving an apprenticeship to a local cabinet-maker he moved to New York City in the early 1790s, started up his own business, opened a shop in Partition Street, and changed his name to Phyfe. His early work was particularly influenced by the American Federal style and the designs of Thomas Sheraton. By the beginning of the

19th century he had become a major exponent of the Directory style which, in turn, was influenced by the British Regency. His work was characterized by designs that made use of figured mahogany, combined with restrained ornamentation in the form of reeding on legs and uprights, carved foliate details and paw feet. From c.1815 onwards Phyfe incorporated elements of the French Empire Style and became the most important name associated with the American interpretation of this new fashion. He went on to develop idiosyncratic and distinctively personal forms of revived Neoclassical prototypes. The Roman curule chair, for example, which normally had an X arrangement of legs at the front and back of the chair, was adapted by Phyfe by transposing this structural and decorative form to the sides, thus producing a unique design form. His influence on the development of the American Directory style gave rise to the term 'Phyfe Style' and to his recognition as New York's most important cabinet-maker in the early 19th century. He supplied furniture to a wide variety of wealthy patrons; when the shop closed in 1847 it marked the end of over 50 years of continuous production of superb quality furniture with a highly personal style. Examples of his work can be found in the Winterthur Museum, Delaware.

PICKEN, Ebenezer
(1769–1816)

Poet, born in Paisley, the son of a weaver. Educated at Glasgow University, he set up a school in Falkirk (1791), later moving to Edinburgh, where he continued to teach. He published several volumes of Scots poems and a *Pocket Dictionary of the Scottish Dialect* (1818).

PICKFORD, (Lillian) Mary
(1902–)

Physiologist, born in Jabbalpore, India. She was educated at Wycombe Abbey School and after taking a BSc at Bedford College, London (1925), she graduated in medicine from University College Hospital Medical School, London, in 1934. After holding a Beit Memorial Research Fellowship at Cambridge (1936–9) she became a lecturer in physiology at the University of Edinburgh Medical School (1939) where she remained throughout her career apart from visiting professorships in Nottingham and Brisbane. She was awarded the DSc of London in 1957 and was elected FRS in 1966 as well as being appointed to a personal chair in physiology in Edinburgh. She contributed to the knowledge of the regulation of the kidney function and the regulation of blood pressure through the interaction of drugs, and of hormones, with the nervous system. Her book *The Central Role of Hormones* (1968) was an important contribution to the field. In 1991 she received an honorary DSc from Heriot-Watt University. An outstanding teacher, she was greatly respected by her colleagues and students.

PICKFORD, Ralph William
(1903–86)

British psychologist and psychoanalyst. Born in Bournemouth, he studied at Cambridge University and, from 1930 until retirement in 1973, taught at the Department of Psychology at Glasgow University, as assistant lecturer, lecturer, senior lecturer and, from 1955, professor. He published in the fields of experimental, social and clinical psychology, and in the psychology of art and visual aesthetics. Actively involved in psychotherapy, he was from 1947 to 1980 Honorary Psychotherapist at the Notre Dame Child Guidance Clinic in Glasgow.

PIGGOTT, Stuart
(1910 –)

English-born archaeologist, born in Petersfield, Hampshire. After working in Wales, Wiltshire and India, he became Abercromby Professor of Prehistoric Archaeology at Edinburgh (1946–75), a Trustee of the British Museum (1968–74) and CBE in 1972. His wide archaeological interests have resulted in books as diverse as *The Earliest Wheeled Transport from the Atlantic Coast to the Caspian Sea* (1983) and *Ancient Britons and the Antiquarian Imagination: ideas from the Renaissance to the Regency* (1989). A special gift for synthesis over a broad canvas can be seen in *Prehistoric India* (1950), *Scotland before History* (1958) and *Ancient Europe* (1965). By example he has discouraged insularity of thought, and his contribution to archaeology was recognized in 1983 by the award of the Gold Medal of the Society of Antiquaries of London.

PILCHER, Percy Sinclair
(1867–99)

English-born aeronautical pioneer, born in Bath to an English father who died in 1874, and a Scottish mother, who died three years later. In 1880 he entered the Royal Navy as a cadet, but resigned in 1887 to take up an apprenticeship with Randolph, Elder and Company, shipbuilders at Govan in Glasgow. He had already become interested in gliding when he was appointed an assistant lecturer at Glasgow University in 1891, and after visiting Otto Lilienthal in Germany he completed his first glider, the *Bat*, and made some trial flights on a hill overlooking the Clyde at Cardross. By 1896 he had built his fourth machine, the *Hawk*, in which he made many successful flights, including his record of some 250 metres in the summer of 1897. Over the next two years he is known to have built a lightweight engine with the intention of fitting it to one of his machines, but on 30 September 1899 the *Hawk* disintegrated in the air, and Pilcher died from his injuries two days later.

PILKINGTON, Frederick Thomas
(1832–98)

English-born architect, born in Lincolnshire, the son of an architect, with whom he later trained. Educated at Edinburgh University, he began practice in 1960. Considered by some as a 'rogue' architect on account of his failure to conform to any stylistic genre, he has been acclaimed for such masterpieces as the Barclay Church in Edinburgh (1862) and his Asylum for Idiot Children at Larbert (1861). His buildings are rich in detail and movement. He managed to combine a lightness in his elaborately carved capitals with immense solidity in the massing of his buildings, broad chimney stacks and squat heavy porches.

PINKERTON, Allan
(1819–84)

Scottish-born American detective, born in Glasgow. A cooper by trade and a Chartist, he emigrated to the USA in 1842 and settled in West Dundee, Illinois. Becoming a detective and deputy-sheriff in Chicago (1850), in 1852 he formed a detective agency which solved a series of train robberies. In 1861 he guarded Abraham Lincoln on his way to his inauguration in Washington and foiled a plot to assassinate him when his train stopped at Baltimore. He became head of the American secret service during the Civil War (1861–2). His Chicago detective agency, the first in the USA, was carried on after his death by his sons Robert and William.

PINKERTON, John
(1758–1826)

Historian and antiquary, born in Edinburgh. Apprenticed to a writer to the signet (1775–80), he published the poem 'Craigmillar Castle: an Elegy' in 1776. Moving to London he wrote *Rimes* (1781), *Two Dithyrambic Odes* (1782), and *Tales in Verse* (1782). His *Select Scottish Ballads* (1783), involved forgeries of supposedly ancient ballads, later exposed and admitted. *Ancient Scottish Poems* (1786) was a valuable and authentic collection based on the Maitland manuscripts, although it was attacked as forgery. In 1787 he published *The Treasury of Wit*, an anthology of about 1200 jokes. His *Dissertation on the Origin and Progress of the Scythians or Goths* (1787) was an attempt to buttress his conviction as to the irredeemable intellectual inferiority of the Celts with scholarly support. He brought greater weight to the same thesis in *An Inquiry into the History of Scotland preceding the Reign of Malcolm III* (1790), and brought out his *magnum opus*, also reflecting extensive original research, *The History of Scotland from the Accession of the House of Stuart to that of Mary* (2 vols, 1797). He then quarrelled bitterly with his researcher, the Edinburgh lawyer William Anderson, involving (very) frank published exchanges. His later works included geographical works, travel recollections, and a discourse on petrology. Apart from his forgeries, his extensive publication of documents was very significant despite the tendentious theses to which he linked them.

PITCAIRN, Robert
(1793–1855)

Writer and antiquary, born in Edinburgh. He was editor of *Criminal Trials in Scotland, 1484–1624* (1830–3). He held a post in the Register House in Edinburgh.

PITCAIRNE, Archibald
(1652–1713)

Physician and satirist, born in Edinburgh. He practised medicine there before being appointed professor at Leiden (1692). Returning to Edinburgh in 1693, he was notorious as a Jacobite, an Episcopalian and satirist of Presbyterianism, his works including *The Assembly, or Scotch Reformation: a Comedy* (1692). He founded the medical faculty at Edinburgh, and his medical writings appeared in 1701 under the title *Dissertationes Medicae*.

PITSCOTTIE, Lindsay Robert of
(c.1532–1580)

Historian, born in Pitscottie near Cupar, Fife. He was the author of *The Historie and Cronicles of Scotland*, extending from 1436 to 1575. His style is quaint and graphic, but his facts trustworthy, except where he deals in marvels.

PLAYFAIR, John
(1748–1819)

Mathematician, physicist and geologist, born in Benvie near Dundee. He studied at St Andrews University and in 1785 became joint Professor of Mathematics at Edinburgh, but in 1805 he exchanged his professorship for that of natural philosophy. He was a strenuous supporter of the Huttonian theory in geology, and travelled widely to make geological observations. His *Illustrations of the Huttonian Theory* (1802) was a landmark in British geological writing.

PLAYFAIR, Lyon, 1st Baron Playfair
(1819–98)

Scientist, born in India at Meerut. He studied at St Andrews, Glasgow, London and Giessen universities, was manager of textile-printing works at Clitheroe (1840–3), Professor of Chemistry at Edinburgh (1858–68), and Liberal MP from 1868. He wrote on chemistry and political economy and education.

PLAYFAIR, William Henry
(1790–1857)

Architect, born in London, the son of the architect James Playfair (1755–94). Educated in Edinburgh, he trained with **William Stark** in Glasgow and then in the London office of Sir Robert Smirke (1780–1867) and James Wyatt (1747–1813). A key figure in the Greek revival (along with **Thomas Hamilton**), he was a leading exponent of the Picturesque, a scholarly perfectionist with a sad personal life. His early success in the completion of Edinburgh University quadrangle (1817–26), and the award in 1818 of the planning of the eastern extension of the Edinburgh New Town, saw him established at a young age. The influence of Stark is particularly apparent in the field of town planning and the terraces on Calton Hill, Edinburgh. Quality, not quantity, was essential to Playfair, who designed several major public buildings in the capital, notably the Royal Scottish Academy (previously the Royal Institution, 1822), the Surgeon's Hall (1830–2), and the National Gallery (1850), all in the classical style. Although associated primarily with classical architecture, he was versatile, designing Donaldson's Hospital (1842) in Jacobethan garb, and the Free Church College (1846) in Tudor gothic. Outside Edinburgh he designed Dollar Academy (1881–2) and remodelled Floors Castle (1837–45) in Jacobethan style.

POLLOCK, Sir John Donald

(1868–1962)

Surgeon, speculator and philanthropist, born in Galashiels, Selkirkshire. He was educated at Glasgow and Edinburgh universities, where the absence of collegiate life left him with a lifelong memory of isolation. After a time in medical practice in London (1895–1908) he obtained one of the most lucrative medical charges of those times, private attendant on a wealthy lunatic, in this instance the Duke of Leinster (1907–26), in which service he moved to Edinburgh while maintaining the duke at Morningside (Royal Edinburgh) Asylum and attending him as 'Personal Physician and General Adviser'. He held a captaincy in the Glasgow and Lanarkshire Yeomanry until 1911, and was in the Navy Medical Service from 1914. On the Duke's death he realised his savings, and became Chairman and President of the British Oxygen Co Ltd and Honorary President of Metal Industries Ltd, successfully bidding to the British government for the salvage rights to the German Navy sunk under Allied orders at Scapa Flow on the conclusion of World War I. Raising the former Imperial Fleet, he sold it to enormous profit. He made further investments of excellent returns, became a member of the Scottish Milk Marketing Board, and of the Economic Committee of the Scottish National Development Council. He was President of the XIIth International Congress of Acetylene, Oxy-Acetylene Welding and Allied Industries at London (1936), Chairman of the Edinburgh Motor Engineering Co Ltd (1939)

and Director of the Edinburgh and Dumfriesshire Dairy Co Ltd from 1929. His desire to cultivate collegiality among youths (he was President of the Leith Boys' Brigade 1937) encouraged him in a scheme for residential facilities for Edinburgh University, which responded by bestowing on him an honorary doctorate, and electing him to rectorship (1939–45). He responded in turn with a huge bequest intended to refurbish George Square for dormitory purposes. Towards the end of his life he was persuaded to accede to the alteration of this proposal into the demolition of the university's buildings on two sides of the Square, and their replacement by functional teaching blocks and the creation of the similarly functional Pollock Halls of Residence on Dalkeith Road. Despite this, he was a convinced believer in urban conservation, Convener of the Cockburn Society, and a member of the Advisory Committee of Three appointed by the City of Edinburgh to report upon its future development.

PONT, Timothy

(c.1560–1630)

Cartographer. He graduated at St Andrews in 1584, became minister of Dunnet (1601), and in 1609 subscribed for 2000 acres of forfeited land in Ulster. He first projected a Scottish atlas, and surveyed all the counties and isles of the kingdom. His collections were rescued from destruction by Sir John Scot of Scotstarvet, and his maps, revised by **Robert Gordon** of Straloch, appeared in Blaeu's *Theatrum Orbis Terrarum* (1654).

PONTON, Mungo

(1801–80)

Pioneer of photography, born in Edinburgh. He trained as a lawyer, and was one of the founders of the National Bank of Scotland. However, ill-health forced him to abandon his career, and he turned to science and literature. He gave a paper before the Society of Arts (later the Royal Scottish Society of Arts) on 29 May 1839 which was the first discussion of a photographic process which used no silver salts in its process. The discovery that sunlight renders potassium bichromate insoluble forms the basis of nearly all photo-mechanical processes. He became a Fellow of the Royal Society of Edinburgh, whose obituary of him credited him as 'the first who employed the photographic method for registering automatically the fluctuations in thermometers and other instruments', which he described in 1845 to the Royal Scottish Society of Arts, and for which he was awarded their silver medal.

PORTEOUS, John
(?1690–1736)

Soldier, born in the Canongate, Edinburgh, the son of a tailor. Trained as a tailor, he was disowned by his father because of his violent temper. He enlisted in the army and served in Holland, and soon after 1715 he returned home and was appointed drill-master of the Edinburgh town guard, which was being trained as a civil militia against the 1715 Jacobite Rising. He became Captain-Lieutenant of the guard in 1726. On 14 April 1736 he was in charge at the execution of Andrew Wilson, a smuggler who had robbed the Pittenweem custom-house. Expecting trouble at the execution, Porteous had armed his men and surrounded the Grassmarket, where the hanging was to take place. Evidence shows that stones were thrown by the crowd as Wilson's body was cut down, and it was claimed that Porteous then fired at and ordered his men to fire at the mob. Twelve people were wounded and three were killed. This became known as the 'Porteous Riot'. Porteous was tried and condemned to death (20 July), but was reprieved by Royal Warrant. Incensed by this, a mob broke him out of prison on the eve of the day originally set for his hanging and lynched him. Much warning had been given of the mob's intention to see Porteous hanged, but the Lord Provost had done nothing about it. The provost was subsequently taken into the custody of Parliament under a Bill of Pains and Penalties, which was finally passed in 1737. Under this Bill the city magistrates had to pay Porteous' widow £2000. These events formed the basis of Sir **Walter Scott**'s *The Heart of Midlothian*.

POWER, William
(1874–1951)

Journalist, son of an Angus schoolmaster. He was brought up in Glasgow and left school at the age of 13 to be apprenticed to a bank. Unusually, he succeeded in moving from bank-clerking to full-time journalism, as a leader writer and book reviewer with the *Glasgow Herald*, when he was well over 30 years old. In 1926 he founded and edited the *Scots Observer*, which was devoted to the revival of a distinctive Scottish culture. Three years later he joined the *Daily Record* as an influential columnist. Nationalist in his political outlook, he campaigned successfully for the establishment of a Scottish Development Board.

PRINGLE, Derek Hair
(1926 –)

Physicist and industrialist, educated at George Heriot's School, Edinburgh, and Edinburgh University. After some years as a Research Physicist at Ferranti he became a director of Nuclear Enterprises Ltd in 1960 and was later chairman. He has been a director of other companies, and active in business and academic life in Scotland, being a member of the Court of Heriot-Watt University, Edinburgh, from 1968 to 1977, and President of the Edinburgh Chamber of Commerce (1979–81). He was awarded a CBE in 1980.

PRINGLE, Sir John
(1707–82)

Physician and reformer, born in Roxburgh. He studied philosophy and classics at St Andrews University and medicine at Leiden. After a period teaching philosophy in Edinburgh, he moved to London, where he rose to become Head of the Army Medical Service and physician to various members of the Royal Family, including King George III. His *Observations on Diseases of the Army* (1752) is a classic of humane common sense, emphasizing cleanliness and hygiene in the prevention and treatment of many camp diseases. He participated fully in 18th-century intellectual life, corresponded with many European savants, and was President of the Royal Society from 1772 to 1778.

PRINGLE, Robert William
(1920 –)

Physicist and industrialist, educated at George Heriot's School, Edinburgh, and Edinburgh University. After a few years as a lecturer at Edinburgh, he was appointed to a professorship in the University of Manitoba, where he developed an interest in applied nuclear physics and geophysics. On his return to Edinburgh he founded Nuclear Enterprises Ltd and was Chairman and Managing Director until 1976. He was active in business and academic affairs and served on a number of Science Research Council committees. His company gained the Queen's Award for Industry on two occasions. He is a Fellow of the Royal Societies of Canada and of Edinburgh.

PRINGLE, Thomas
(1789–1834)

Writer, born in Blakelaw, Roxburghshire, the son of a farmer. He was educated at Kelso Grammar School and Edinburgh University, and in 1811 became an archivist in the Register Office. In 1817 he started the *Edinburgh Monthly Magazine*, later *Blackwood's Magazine*. In 1820 he emigrated to Cape Colony, and for three years was government librarian at Cape Town. He started a Whig paper, but it was suppressed by the governor. Returning to London in 1826 he became Secretary of the Anti-Slavery Society. He wrote *African Sketches* (1834), and published two collections of poems and lyrics, *The Autumnal Collection* (1817), and *Ephemerides* (1828).

PRITCHARD, Edward
(1825–65)

English convicted murderer, the last person to be publicly executed in Glasgow. Whether because of mounting debts or his affair with a former servant, Pritchard poisoned his wife over a period of some months. Her mother came from Edinburgh to nurse her as she grew more ill, and may have suspected what was happening. The mother-in-law died within two weeks and was buried without any suspicion having been aroused. On the death of Mrs Pritchard, however, an anonymous letter was sent to the Fiscal suggesting an enquiry into both deaths. Pritchard was immediately arrested and, despite his confident and endearing manner, was convicted of poisoning both.

PROCLAIMERS, THE See REID, Charlie and Craig

PROWSE, Philip
(1937 –)

English-born stage designer and director. Brought up in Worcestershire, he studied at the Slade School of Art. He worked for a year in the model rooms at Covent Garden, after which he began designing ballet. In 1969 he moved to Glasgow at the request of **Giles Havergal**, Artistic Director of the Glasgow Citizens' Theatre, and has been based there ever since, designing and directing numerous productions. His designs are recognizable by a painterly, architectural style of either severe austerity or extravagant luxury. He also designs and directs for the National Theatre, the Royal Shakespeare Company, and opera.

PRYDE, James Ferrier
(1866–1941)

Artist, lithographer and poster designer, born in Edinburgh. He studied at the Royal Scottish Academy Schools and in Paris at the Académie Julian. With his brother-in-law William Nicholson he set up the Beggarstaff Brothers in c.1894, which had a profound influence on poster design in the 1890s. He is best known for his large street scenes which have a foreboding theatrical quality. He also had some experience as an actor, touring Scotland in 1895 with Gordon Craig, a woodcarver and son of actress Ellen Terry. He had a wide circle of artistic friends, among them Whistler, **Carlyle** and Augustus John, and exhibited internationally.

PURDIE, Thomas
(1843–1916)

Organic chemist, the founder of the internationally famous reseach school of chemistry at St Andrews University. He was born in Biggar, Lanarkshire, and as a young man spent seven years as a rancher in Argentina before becoming a student at the Royal School of Mines, London. Thereafter he worked as a demonstrator at the Chemical Laboratories, South Kensington, London, and afterwards studied in Würzburg with Johannes Wislicenus. In 1884 he was appointed to the Chair of Chemistry at St Andrews and instantly set about gathering a team of talented young chemists round him, funding part of the expansion with his own resources. He is particularly remembered for his accurate measurements of the optical rotary power of organic compounds and, above all, for the discovery of the silver oxide reaction by his assistant W Pitkeathly. This reaction, in which hydroxyl groups are alkalized by treating the hydroxy-compound with dry silver iodide and an alkyl iodide, proved a powerful technique for determining molecular structures and formed the basis of much of the success at St Andrews. Working in conjunction with **James Irvine** and other colleagues, Purdie laid the foundation of our understanding of carbohydrates.

PURSER, John
(1942 –)

Composer, poet, playwright, lecturer and broadcaster, born in Glasgow of Irish parents. He studied at the Royal Scottish Academy of Music with Frank Spedding, and subsequently with Hans Gal and Michael Tippett. He was Manager of the Scottish Music Information Centre (1985–7). His compositions include two short operas: *The Undertaker* (1969) and *The Bell* (1971); numerous works for orchestra, choral music and songs, chamber music, including a string quartet (1981), and sonatas for clavier, clarinet, cello and violin. He is the author of *The Literary Works of Jack B. Yeats*, three books of poetry, several radio plays (notably *Carver*, 1991), and *Scotland's Music*, the companion to his major radio series of that name (1992).

Q

QUARRIER, William
(1829–1903)

Philanthropist. Born in Greenock, and father-less from the age of five, he worked in the Glasgow and Paisley shoemaking industry from the age of seven, encountering much poverty. However, the craftmanship he learned, his enterprising character and the Christianity he espoused from 17, were chan-nelled into a successful boot- and shoe-making business and into his efforts to address the needs of the poor and destitute. In 1877 he founded a village of family-style homes near Bridge of Weir, Renfrewshire, creating a model of residential care for orphans ahead of its time. He also joined with others in founding Industrial Brigades in Glasgow for shoe-blacks and news vendors, and set up shelters for homeless children, women and discharged prisoners.

QUEENSBERRY, Sir John Sholto Douglas, 8th Marquis of
(1844–1900)

Representative peer, and patron of boxing. In 1867 he supervised the formulation by John Graham Chambers of new rules to govern the sport, since known as the 'Queensberry rules'. In 1895 he was unsuccessfully sued for criminal libel by Oscar Wilde, of whose friendship with his son, Lord Alfred Douglas, he disapproved. It was his allegations of homosexuality that led in turn to Wilde's trial and imprisonment.

R

RAE, John
(1786–1873)

Political economist, physician and school-master, born at Footdee, Aberdeen, and educated at Marischal College, Aberdeen (1809–15). He did two years of the medical degree course at Edinburgh (1815–7) before studying physiology in Paris. In 1822 he emigrated to Canada where he was a school-master, defender of Presbyterianism and medical practitioner. From 1848 to 1851 he was a teacher and journalist in the USA before settling in Hawaii where he was a headmaster, medical attendant and district judge until 1871, dying at Staten Island, New York. His highly original *Statement of Some New Principles on the Subject of Political Economy* (1834) discussed capital accumulation, anticipating the Austrian School, and the economic significance of invention and luxuries. He also published works on education, the origin of languages and geology.

RAE, John
(1813–93)

Arctic traveller, born near Stromness in Orkney. After studying medicine at Edinburgh, in 1833 he became doctor to the Hudson Bay Company. In 1846–7 he made two exploratory expeditions, and in 1848 he accompanied Sir **John Richardson** on a search voyage for Sir John Franklin. In 1853–4 he commanded an expedition to King William's Land, and it was on this journey that he met the Eskimos who gave him definite news of Franklin's expedition and its probable fate. In 1860 he surveyed a telegraph line to America via the Faroes and Iceland, he visited Greenland, and in 1864 made a telegraph survey from Winnipeg over the Rockies.

RAEBURN, Sir Henry
(1756–1823)

Portrait painter, born in Edinburgh. Apprenticed to a goldsmith, he took to art, producing first watercolour miniatures and then oils. At 22 he married the widow of Count Leslie, a lady of means, studied for two years in Rome (1785–7), and then settled in Edinburgh, and soon attained pre-eminence among Scottish artists. He was knighted by George IV in 1822, and appointed king's limner for Scotland a few days before his death. His style was to some extent founded on that of Sir Joshua Reynolds, to which a positiveness was added by his bold brushwork and use of contrasting colours. Among his sitters were Sir **Walter Scott, Hume, Boswell, John Wilson** ('Christopher North'), **Henry Dundas**, Sir **David Baird, Henry Mackenzie, William Robertson**, Lord **Jeffrey** and Lord **Cockburn**.

RAFFERTY, Gerry
(1947 –)

Folk-rock singer and songwriter, born in Paisley. He launched his career with co-median **Billy Connolly** in the folk group the Humblebums, which released two albums in 1969–70. After the group split up he recorded the solo album *Can I Have My Money Back* (1971) before forming Stealer's Wheel with Rab Noakes. Noakes left before the band's best-known single 'Stuck In The Middle With You' was released in 1973. The group released three albums together and broke up in 1975. Rafferty's first solo album, *City To City*, topped the US charts in 1978 and included his best-known single 'Baker Street'. Subsequent solo albums have included *Night Owl* (1979) and *North & South* (1988).

RAINY, Robert
(1826–1906)

Theologian, born in Glasgow. He studied at Glasgow University and at New College in Edinburgh, and, after being minister of the Free Church in Huntly (1851) and the Free High Church in Edinburgh (1854), was from 1862 to 1900 Professor of Church History in the New (Free Church) College in Edinburgh, becoming its principal in 1874. In 1900 he organized the union of the Free and United Presbyterian Churches as the United Free Church of Scotland, of whose General Assembly he became the first Moderator. His works include *The Bible and Criticism* (1878).

RAIT, Sir Robert Sangster
(1874–1936)

Historian, educated at Aberdeen and Oxford. He was appointed Professor of Scottish History at Glasgow in 1913. Apart from numerous contributions to books and journals on various topics of Scottish history he published in 1924 *The Parliaments of Scotland*, still not superseded as a study of the origins, organization and working of that institution. In 1929 he became Principal of Glasgow University and was knighted in 1933.

RAMENSKI, Johnny, also known as Johnny Ramsay
(c.1905–1972)

Convicted safe-breaker and jail-breaker of Polish extraction. He spent much of his life in Scotland compulsively breaking into banks and safes or breaking out of prisons. He escaped five times from Peterhead Prison and several times from Barlinnie. Police dubbed him 'Gentle Johnny' because he was never violent. Indeed, his genial nature endeared him to many. One of his last coups, after which he planned to retire, was a bank break-in at Rutherglen. He eventually died in Perth Prison.

RAMSAY, Sir Alexander
(d.1342)

Patriot of Dalhousie, famed for his deeds of bravery. He relieved Dunbar Castle (1338), and captured Roxburgh Castle from English occupation (1342). He was captured and starved to death at Hermitage Castle in 1342 by William Douglas of Liddesdale.

RAMSAY, Allan
(c.1685–1758)

Poet, born in Leadhills, Lanarkshire. His father was manager of Lord Hopetoun's mines there, and his mother, Alice Bower, was the daughter of a Derbyshire mining expert. In 1704 he was apprenticed for five years to a wigmaker in Edinburgh. By 1718 he had become known as a poet, having issued several short humorous satires printed as broadsides. He had also written (1716–18) two additional cantos to the old Scots poem of *Christ's Kirk on the Green*, cheerful pictures of rustic life and broad humour. Ramsay then started business as bookseller, later adding a circulating library (1725), apparently the first in Britain. 'Honest Allan's' career was eminently prosperous, although the theatre he built in Edinburgh at his own expense (1736) was soon closed down by the magistrates. In 1740 he built himself a quaint house (the 'goose-pie') on the Castle Hill, where he spent his last years in retirement. He was buried in Greyfriars' Churchyard. Among his works are *Tartana, or the Plaid* (1718), *Poems* (collected edition published by subscription in 1721, by which it is said he realized 400 guineas; other editions, 1720, 1727, 1728), *Fables and Tales* (1722), *Fair Assembly* (1723), *Health, a Poem* (1724), *The Monk and the Miller's Wife* (1724), *The Tea-table Miscellany*, a collection of songs (4 vols, 1724–37), *The Evergreen* (1724), *The Gentle Shepherd, a Pastoral Comedy* (1725) — his best and most popular work, and *Thirty Fables* (1730).

RAMSAY, Allan
(1713–84)

Portrait painter, eldest son of the poet **Allan Ramsay**. He was a distinguished portrait painter, and after training in Italy, he worked first in Edinburgh, but in 1762 settled in London, and in 1767 was appointed portrait painter to George III. In his best works his painting is simple and delicate, and he excels in portraits of women, notably that of his wife. He delighted in conversation and was acquainted with many of the writers of his day, including Samuel Johnson. He also corresponded with such men as Rousseau and Voltaire.

RAMSAY, Edward Bannerman Burnett
(1793–1872)

Theologian, born in Aberdeen, the son of Alexander Burnett, Sheriff of Kincardineshire. In 1806 his father succeeded to his uncle Sir Alexander Ramsay's estates, took the surname Ramsay, and was created a baronet. Young Ramsay was educated at Durham and

St John's College, Cambridge, held two Somerset curacies (1816–24), and then moved to Edinburgh. In 1830 he became incumbent of St John's, and in 1846 also Dean of the diocese. He wrote various religious works, as well as the delightful *Reminiscences of Scottish Life and Character* (1857).

RAMSAY, Sir George
(1800–71)

Philosopher and political economist, educated at Harrow and Cambridge University; in 1859 he succeeded his elder brother as ninth baronet. His voluminous writings included works on philosophy, economics and politics. In his *An Essay on the Distribution of Wealth* (1836) he dissented from mainstream contemporary economic thinking by supporting the Corn Laws. His other works included *Political Discourses* (1838) and *An Introduction to Mental Philosophy* (1853).

RAMSAY, Johnny See RAMENSKI, Johnny

RAMSAY, Sir William
(1852–1916)

Chemist, discoverer of the noble gases, born in Glasgow. Professor of Chemistry at Bristol (1880–7) and at University College, London (1887–1912), in conjunction with Lord John Rayleigh he discovered argon in 1894. He later obtained helium, neon, krypton and xenon, and won the Nobel Prize for Chemistry in 1904. His writings include *The Gases of the Atmosphere* and *Elements and Electrons*.

RAMSAY, Sir William Mitchell
(1851–1939)

Archaeologist, born in Glasgow. He was Professor of Humanities at Aberdeen (1886–1911). An authority on Asia Minor, he wrote a *Historical Geography of Asia Minor* (1890), and he published several works on the history of the early Christian period, the best known being *The Church in the Roman Empire Before AD 170* (1893).

RANDOLPH, Sir Thomas
(d.1332)

Soldier and statesman, nephew of **Robert I, the Bruce**, who created him Earl of Moray.

He recaptured Edinburgh Castle from the English (1314), commanded a division at Bannockburn, took Berwick (1318), won the victory of Mitton (1319), reinvaded England (1320, 1327), and was Guardian of the kingdom from Bruce's death (1329) until his own death at Musselburgh.

RANKIN, Robert Alexander
(1915 –)

Mathematician, born in Garlieston, Wigtownshire. Educated at **Fettes** College, Edinburgh, and Cambridge University, he worked on rocket research during World War II, returned to Cambridge in 1945 and became professor at Birmingham in 1951. From 1954 to his retirement in 1982 he was Professor of Mathematics at Glasgow and Clerk of the Senate from 1971 to 1978. His work is in number theory, function theory, and the theory of modular forms. A musician and student of Gaelic culture, he is probably the only person to have published a mathematical paper in Scottish Gaelic.

RANKINE, William John Macquorn
(1820–72)

Engineer and scientist, born in Edinburgh. In 1855 he was appointed Professor of Engineering at Glasgow University. Elected a fellow of the Royal Society in 1853, his works on the steam engine, machinery, shipbuilding and applied mechanics became standard textbooks, and he also did much for the new science of thermodynamics and the theories of elasticity and of waves. He wrote humorous and patriotic *Songs and Fables* (1874).

READ, David Carswell
(1910 –)

Church of Scotland minister and writer, one of the most successful exiled Scottish churchmen. Degrees from Edinburgh University (1928–32) were followed by ministry at Coldstream, Greenbank, Edinburgh, and chaplaincy to the Forces, which was in turn followed by university chaplaincy at Edinburgh. However, the call in 1956 to Madison Avenue Presbyterian Church in New York signalled the beginning of an internationally respected ministry, and a series of published books of sermons that were recognized as classic examples of the preaching craft. Works such as *The Spirit of Life* (1939), *The*

Church to Come (1939) and *The Communication of the Gospel* (1952) became important resources for those keen to develop skills in communicating Christianity to an informed and critical modern world.

READ, John
(1884–1963)

English organic chemist, born in Maiden Newton, Dorset. After attending Finsbury Technical College he won scholarships which took him on to further study in London and then to research in Zürich under Alfred Werner. He then worked on stereochemistry in Manchester and Cambridge, before moving to professorships in Sydney (1915) and St Andrews (1923), a post he held until his death. He isolated and elucidated the structure of the isomers of menthol and other substances derived from essential oils. Like **Thomas Purdie** and Sir **James Irvine** before him, he inspired his younger colleagues in his research team, as well as his students. His *Textbook of Organic Chemistry* (1926) became a classic which served two generations of students. He also wrote books on early chemistry and alchemy.

REDPATH, Anne
(1895–1965)

Painter, born in Galashiels, Selkirkshire, the daughter of a tweed designer. She studied at Edinburgh College of Art (1913–18), and lived in France from 1920 to 1934 with her architect husband, during which time she did little work. Returning to Scotland, she began to paint, revealing the influence of her travels abroad. One of the most important modern Scottish artists, her paintings in oil and watercolour show great richness of colour and vigorous technique. She was elected a member of the RSA in 1952.

REDPATH, Jean
(1937 –)

Singer, born in Edinburgh. She became involved in folk music while studying at Edinburgh University. In 1961 she emigrated to the USA, where her outstanding ability, particularly as an interpreter of traditional Scots ballads and the songs of **Robert Burns**, was quickly recognized. She made her mark at an academic level, too, and for several years lectured in music at Wesleyan University. In the mid 1970s she returned to live and perform in Scotland, but she continued to pay frequent visits to the USA, where she had already embarked on a project to record all of the songs of Robert Burns (numbering more than 300) to musical arrangements written by the American composer, Serge Hovey.

REIACH, Alan
(1910 –)

English-born architect, born in London. He was educated in Edinburgh and trained in the office of Sir **Robert Lorimer** and at Edinburgh College of Art from 1928. After a travelling scholarship to America, Russia and Europe, he spent a year in the office of Robert Atkinson in London. He made a considerable contribution to housing and town planning before and during World War II, and with Robert Hurd he wrote a cautionary guide, *Building Scotland* (1940). He began independent practice in 1949, and is renowned for the Appleton Tower (1963), and the New Club (1964), both in Edinburgh, Kildrum Church, Cumbernauld (1962) and housing in East Kilbride (1960s). In 1964 he merged with Eric Hall and Partners, and now works as Reiach and Hall. His work shows an admiration for Scandinavian design, seen, for example, in his own house in Winton Loan, Edinburgh (1964).

REID, Alastair
(1926 –)

Scottish-born poet, essayist and translator, born in Whithorn, Wigtownshire. A son of the manse, he first left to serve in the Royal Navy during World War II, after which he became a professional itinerant, living variously in the USA, France, Spain (where he was befriended by the poet Robert Graves), Greece, Switzerland and Central and South America. Since 1955 he has made his living as a writer, four years after his first poems were published in the *New Yorker*. He later joined that magazine as a staff writer and the association has continued for over three decades. The *New Yorker* remains his only permanent address, though he has property in the Dominican Republic not far from the beach where, as legend has it, Columbus first landed in America. His poetry has been published in several volumes, including *Passwords*: *Places*: *Poems*; *Preoccupations* (1963) and *Weathering* (1978), both distinguished by a mischievous wit, an ambivalent view of Scotland and a pungent sense of place. As a translator, he has done much to introduce Spanish and Latin American writers to the English-speaking world, and he was particularly close to Jorge Luis Borges and Pablo Neruda. As an essayist he is eclectic and international, urbane and informative.

REID, Charlie and Craig
(1962 –)

Twins, pop singers and performers, born in Edinburgh. They moved to Auchtermuchty, Fife, when they were 10. After playing in three rock groups together they formed an acoustic duo, The Proclaimers, in 1983. Confined to the pub circuit for three years, they produced their first album, *This Is The Story* (1986, recorded in nine days), gaining considerable critical acclaim, although their marked Scottish accents saw them dismissed by many as a novelty act. Their second album, *Sunshine On Leith*, released in 1988, added a full backing band to their harmonized vocals and brought international success.

REID, Sir George Houstoun
(1845–1918)

Scottish-born Australian politician and statesman, born in Johnstone, Renfrewshire. He arrived in Melbourne with his parents in 1852, and in 1858 moved to Sydney, where he obtained a post with the Colonial Treasury. He studied law, and in 1878 became Secretary to the Attorney-General of New South Wales. In 1880 he was elected to the Legislative Assembly of New South Wales, and in 1891 succeeded Sir Henry Parkes as Leader of the New South Wales opposition, becoming Premier of the state from 1894 to 1899. He moved to the first Federal Parliament in 1901, still representing his old constituency, and became Leader of the Opposition in the House of Representatives. He became Prime Minister of Australia for a short time in 1904, but was defeated in 1905 and retired from politics in 1908. In 1909 he was appointed Australia's first High Commissioner to London, a post which he held with distinction until the end of his term in 1916. He then took up the seat for Hanover Square in the British House of Commons, which he held until his death.

REID, James Scott Cumberland, Lord, of Drem
(1890–1975)

Judge, born in Drem, East Lothian. Educated at The Edinburgh Academy, Jesus College, Cambridge, and Edinburgh University, he served in World War I, and practised at the Bar. He became Dean of the Faculty of Advocates (1945–8). An MP (1931–5, 1937–48), he was Solicitor-General for Scotland (1936–41) and Lord Advocate (1941–8). He then sat as a Lord of Appeal in Ordinary (1948–75), and by his judgements won a high reputation for accurate thought, precise reasoning and careful application of principle.

REID, or ROBERTSON, John
(1721–1807)

Soldier and musician, born into a Perthshire family. He entered the army in 1745 and rose to be General. A flute-player and composer, he left £50 000 to found a chair of music at Edinburgh University.

REID, John MacNair
(1895–1954)

Poet and novelist, born in Glasgow. He spent most of his working life as a journalist, writing for the *Glasgow Herald*. He began writing short stories in 1929 but little of his work was published in his lifetime. His novel *Homeward Journey* (1934) is the story of an unsuccessful love affair motivated by a young woman's efforts to move into the middle-class. His posthumously published *Judy from Crown Street* (1970) also dramatizes the division between middle-class and near-slum life and addresses the problems caused by social barriers. As a reviewer he helped to publicize the aims and efforts of the writers associated with the Scottish Renaissance.

REID, Robert
(1774–1856)

Architect, born in Edinburgh, the son of a mason. Nothing is known about his education or training. He flourished as government architect to Scotland, becoming Master of Works and Architect to the King in 1824. His known career began with the design for new Law Courts, Parliament Square, Edinburgh (1803). Working with fellow architect William Sibbald, he masterminded the fine northern extension to the Edinburgh New Town. Other major works include the Customs House, Leith (1811), the east wing to Paxton House, Berwickshire (1812) and the United College, St Andrews (1829). His public architecture was appropriately momentous, influenced by the **Adam** brothers, but received mixed acclaim from contemporaries.

REID, Robert
(1895–1965)

Piper, born in Slamannan, Stirlingshire. He was taught by his father, and then by the eminent piping teacher John MacDougall Gillies. He worked as a miner in Scotland and in Canada before enlisting in the Highland Light Infantry. He served in Palestine and France (1915–18), and was given the rank of Pipe Major in 1920, a position he held until 1940. He continued to work as a miner until 1933, when he set up a bagpipe-making business in Glasgow, which, except for his time in the forces during World War II, he and his wife ran until 1957. A prominent teacher as well as a famous player, he won all the available piping awards in the years between 1921 and 1949, including an unprecedented succession of unbroken wins in the Piobaireachd at the Cowal Games (1929–38).

REID, Sir Robert Gillespie
(1842–1908)

Scottish-born financier and bridge builder, born in Coupar Angus, Perthshire. He trained as a bridge builder with an uncle before setting up his own business, and in 1865 emigrated to Australia on the proceeds. He settled in Montreal in 1871, and made his name with the International Bridge across the Niagara River, the first of several major projects in Canada. In the USA he bridged the Rio Grande, Colorado and Delaware rivers. He turned to building railways in 1889, and in 1890 began a series of railroad projects in Newfoundland. The financial crisis in Newfoundland led to a remarkable deal in which Reid was granted exclusive tax-free rights to operate all railways on the island for 50 years from 1898, which he vested in the Reid-Newfoundland Company. His influence, wealth and power earned him the nickname 'Czar Reid'.

REID, Robert Paul
(1934 –)

Industrial executive. He joined Shell when he left St Andrews University in 1956, and worked in overseas subsidiaries until 1983,

when he returned to the UK. He was appointed Chairman and Chief Executive of Shell UK in 1985. In 1988, as Chairman of the British Institute of Management, he took a leading role in the reshaping of management education in the UK. In 1990 he was appointed chairman of British Rail.

REID, Thomas
(1710–96)

Philosopher, born in Strachan, Kincardineshire, the son of a minister and descended, on his mother's side, from the Gregory family of mathematicians. Educated at Marischal College, Aberdeen, where he was a student of **George Turnbull**, he became librarian there in 1733, and in 1737 he was appointed minister of Newmachar in Aberdeenshire. He became Professor of Philosophy at Aberdeen (1751–64), and succeeded **Adam Smith** as Professor of Moral Philosophy at Glasgow from 1764 to 1781; he then retired to write. A member of the Aberdeen Philosophical Society with **George Campbell** and others, initial misunderstanding of **Hume** led him to write his *Inquiry into the Human Mind on the Principles of Common Sense* (1764). In opposition to Hume — who proposed that the immediate objects of knowledge are ideas in the mind, and concluded that we cannot prove the existence of anything outside the mind, or even the existence of mind itself — his *Inquiry* described operations within the mind which give real objective knowledge of real things outwith the mind, and of true general principles. In retirement he published *Essays on the Intellectual Powers of Man* (1785) and *Essays on the Active Powers of Man* (1788), also leaving many unfinished manuscripts. A laborious writer, he owes some of his fame as the founder of the 'common sense' or 'Scottish' school of philosophy to his disciple **Dugald Stewart**. Attracting interest today, his name is revived whenever philosophy realizes it might have got carried away with itself.

REID, Sir Thomas Wemyss
(1842–1905)

Journalist and biographer, born in Newcastle. He edited the *Leeds Mercury* (1870–87), was then manager at the publishing firm Cassell, and from 1890 to 1899 was editor of the *Speaker*. He wrote lives of Charlotte Brontë and Lord Houghton, a book about Tunis, and several novels.

REID, Sir William
(1791–1858)

Meteorologist, soldier and administrator, a writer on winds and storms, born in Kinglassie, Fife. He served with high distinction in the Peninsular War, and was governor of Bermuda, the Windward Islands and Malta.

REITH, John Charles Walsham, 1st Baron Reith of Stonehaven
(1889–1971)

Engineer and pioneer of broadcasting, born in Stonehaven, Kincardineshire. Educated at Glasgow Academy and Gresham's School, Holt, he served an engineering apprenticeship in Glasgow. Later entering the field of radio communication, he became the first general manager of the British Broadcasting Corporation in 1922, and was its Director-General from 1927 to 1938. He was MP for Southampton in 1940, and Minister of Works and Buildings from 1940 to 1942. He was Chairman of the Commonwealth Telecommunications Board from 1946 to 1950. He wrote the autobiographical works *Into the Wind* (1949) and *Wearing Spurs* (1966). The BBC Reith Lectures on radio were instituted in 1948 in honour of his influence on broadcasting.

RENNIE, George
(1791–1866)

Engineer, born in London, the eldest son of Sir **John Rennie**. He was superintendent of the machinery of the Mint, and aided his father. With his brother Sir **John Rennie** he carried on an immense business — shipbuilding, railways, bridges, harbours, docks, machinery and marine engines. He built the first screw vessel for the Royal Navy, the *Dwarf*.

RENNIE, John
(1761–1821)

Civil engineer, born at Phantassie Farm, East Linton, East Lothian, father of **George** and **John Rennie**. After working as a millwright with **Andrew Meikle** he studied at Edinburgh University (1780–3). In 1784 he entered the employment of Boulton & **Watt**, and in 1791 he established a career in London as an engineer, soon becoming famous as a bridge-builder; he built Kelso, Leeds, Musselburgh, Newton Stewart, Boston, New Galloway, and the old Southwark and Waterloo Bridges, and planned London Bridge. He made many important canals, drained fens, designed the London Docks, and others at Blackwall, Hull, Liverpool, Dublin, Greenock and Leith, and improved harbours and dockyards at Portsmouth, Chatham, Sheerness and Plymouth, where he constructed the celebrated breakwater (1811–41).

RENNIE, Sir John
(1794–1874)

Engineer, born in London, the second son of Sir **John Rennie**. He completed London Bridge to his father's design (1831). He was engineer to the Admiralty and wrote on harbours.

RENNIE, Thomas Gordon
(1900–45)

Soldier, born in Foochow, China, the son of a Scottish doctor. He was educated at Loretto School and Sandhurst. He was commissioned in the Black Watch in 1919 and after attending staff college he returned to the 2nd battalion as adjutant. While serving with the 51st (Highland) Division in France at the outbreak of World War II he made a dramatic escape from enemy captivity when the formation was forced to surrender at St Valery in 1940. He commanded the 5th Black Watch in the North African campaign and was awarded the DSO after the Battle of Alamein in 1942. As a major-general he commanded the 3rd Division during the D-Day landings and was given command of the 51st (Highland) Division for the breakout battles in Normandy in July 1944. An inspired leader, he was killed by a German mortar bomb during the division's triumphant Rhine crossing in March 1945.

RENWICK, James
(1662–88)

Covenanter, born in Moniaive, Dumfriesshire. He studied at Edinburgh University, joined the 'Cameronians' as a field preacher, proclaimed the Lanark Declaration (1682), and was sent to complete his studies in Holland. In 1683 he preached his first sermon at Darmead Moss near Cambusnethan, Lanarkshire, and in 1684 he was outlawed for his *Apologetic Declaration*. On the accession of **James VII and II** he published at Sanquhar a declaration rejecting him. A reward was offered for his capture, and he was eventually taken in Edinburgh, and executed.

RESTON, James Barrett

(1909 –)

Scottish-born American journalist, popularly known as 'Scotty', born in Clydebank, he settled permanently in the USA (1929). A graduate of the University of Illinois, he began his career as a sports-writer for Associated Press in New York (1934–7) before joining the London bureau of the *New York Times*. He returned to America after World War II and became head of the paper's Washington Bureau (1953–64). His authoritative commentaries on American politics and diplomacy twice earned him the Pulitzer Prize (1945, 1957). He retired as Vice-President of the *New York Times* in 1974, but continues to write for the paper.

RHIND, Alexander Henry

(1833–63)

Antiquary, born in Wick, Caithness. He studied at Edinburgh University, but was forced to travel for the sake of his health, and published a book on Egyptian antiquities, *Thebes, Its Tombs and Their Tenants* (1862). The Rhind Lectures in archaeology, delivered at Edinburgh, were founded in his memory.

RHIND, David

(1808–83)

Architect, born in Edinburgh, the son of a cashier. He received his architectural training in the office of A C Pugin in London, followed by a year in Rome. His friendship with the well-connected English architect Sir Charles Barry was significant in advancing his career. Although best known for his Roman palazzo-like Commercial Bank designs, such as that in Gordon Street, Glasgow (1855), and his Graeco-Roman masterpiece in George Street, Edinburgh (1843), his unsuccessful design for the Houses of Parliament, Westminster (1835) and successful **Daniel Stewart**'s Hospital, Edinburgh (1848) show a mastery of the Jacobean. Similarly, the Venetian Renaissance Life Association offices, Edinburgh (1855, demolished) further demonstrated his capacity to diversify within his main field, public architecture. His imposing classical mausoleum to W H Miller at Craigentinny, Edinburgh (1848) and his capriccio of the monuments of Edinburgh (1862) demonstrate his spirited approach to architecture, an attitude passed on to his pupils, who included such notables as Robert

Morham, Hippolyte Jean Blanc and **John Dick Peddie**.

RICHARDS, John Deacon

(1931 –)

Architect. He was educated in Geelong, Australia, and Surrey, and trained at the Architectural Association in London. His work is respectful of setting and distinguished by a prevailing horizontal emphasis, embodied in the Royal Commonwealth Pool, Edinburgh (1967) and the award-winning campus for Stirling University (1967). Latterly Chairman of **Robert Matthew** Johnson-Marshall and Partners, he has recently begun an independent architectural consultancy, John Richards Associates. His initiatives with Scottish Homes have earned him a reputation for excellence in strategic planning. He is a past president of the RIAS and an RSA Gold Medallist.

RICHARDSON, Ian William

(1934 –)

Actor, born in Edinburgh. Winner of the **James Bridie** Gold Medal from the Royal College of Dramatic Art in Glasgow (1957), he subsequently joined Birmingham Repertory Theatre Company (1958–60) before becoming a member of the Royal Shakespeare Company. His work with the company includes *A Midsummer Night's Dream* (1962), *The Tempest* (1970) and *Richard III* (1975). His other theatre work includes Broadway appearances in *My Fair Lady* (1976) and *Lolita* (1981). An actor of steely intelligence, he made his television début in *As You Like It* (1962) and has worked extensively in the medium, graduating from supporting roles to a dazzling array of leading performances in the likes of *Tinker, Tailor, Soldier, Spy* (1979), *Porterhouse Blue* (1987), *The Winslow Boy* (1989) and the prescient thriller *House of Cards* (1990), for which his performance as a Machiavellian politician earned him a BAFTA Best Actor Award. His film appearances include *The Darwin Adventure* (1971), *Brazil* (1985) and *The Year of the Comet* (1991).

RICHARDSON, Sir John

(1787–1865)

Naturalist and Arctic explorer, born in Dumfries. He was a surgeon in the Royal Navy

(1807–55), and served in the Arctic expeditions of Parry and Franklin (1819–22, 1825–7). Leaving Franklin, he pursued his own journey to the Great Slave Lake. He was also part of the search expedition of 1848–9 for Franklin. He wrote *Fauna Boreali-Americana* (1829–37), and *Ichthyology of the Voyage of HMS Erebus and Terror* (1844–8), and made great contributions to our knowledge of ichthyology, particularly of the Indo-Pacific region.

RIDDELL, George Allardice
Riddell, 1st Baron
(1865–1934)

Scottish-born lawyer and newspaper proprietor, born in Duns, Berwickshire. Educated in London, he rose from boy clerk to solicitor, and through one of his clients, the Cardiff *Western Mail*, became further involved in the newspaper world, at first as legal adviser to the *News of the World*, and later as its chairman; he also became Chairman of George Newnes Ltd. Knighted in 1909, he represented the British press at the Paris Peace Conference in 1919, and the following year was raised to the peerage.

RIDPATH, George
(c.1717–1772)

Historian, born in Ladykirk Manse in Berwickshire. Minister of Stitchell from 1742, he wrote *The Border History of England and Scotland* (1776).

RIFKIND, Malcolm
(1946 –)

Conservative politician. Born in Edinburgh, he was educated at George Watson's College and Edinburgh University, and became a barrister. Elected Conservative MP for Edinburgh Pentlands in 1974, he enjoyed a meteoric career at Westminster. Despite resigning from the Opposition front bench in protest against the anti-devolution policy of his party, he was appointed Scottish Office minister (1979–82), and Foreign Office minister (1982–6). From 1986 to 1990 he was the youngest ever Secretary of State for Scotland, and the first Conservative in the post from a non-élite background. In this role he introduced the community charge and education reforms, and succeeded in enticing high-technology firms to settle in Scotland, to redress the economic balance as traditional

industries decayed. A most formidable debater, he was appointed Transport Minister in 1990 and Defence Secretary in 1992.

RITCHIE, Arthur David
(1891–1967)

English-born philosopher, born in Oxford, the son of **D G Ritchie**. Educated at St Andrews and Cambridge, he first taught biochemistry, but became Professor of Philosophy at Manchester (1937–44) and at Edinburgh (1944–57). Similar in stance to A N Whitehead, he had a keen interest in modern Scottish philosophy. His works include *Studies in History* and *Methods of the Sciences* (1958), both written with an endearing wit and informality.

RITCHIE, David George
(1855–1903)

Philosopher, born in Edinburgh. Educated at Edinburgh and Oxford, he was converted to Hegelianism, and began to publish prolifically, revealing Radical and Fabian sympathies. Optimistic for humankind's future, he made outstanding critical expositions of various key doctrines in various textbooks and essays. *Natural Rights* (1895) is his major work.

RITCHIE, Jean Atkinson Smail
(1913 –)

Nutritionist, born in Edinburgh and educated at Edinburgh College of Domestic Science. In 1939 she received the MSc in Nutrition from the University of Chicago. Following war service as an ambulance driver she joined the Rowett Institute in Aberdeen and worked with Lord **Boyd Orr**. After a period with the Ministry of Food and the United Nations Relief and Rehabilitation Administration (1944–6) she joined the Food and Agriculture Organization (FAO) (1946–78) as Regional Nutrition Officer for Africa and Regional Adviser to the Economic Commission for Africa. She taught at the London School of Hygiene and Tropical Medicine and University of Ibadan (1963–9). She has published *Teaching Better Nutrition* (1950), *Learning Better Nutrition* (1967) and *Nutrition and Families* (1983). Active in improving nutritional standards through education in Africa and South-East Asia, through workshops and seminars she has improved the situation of women, including their health and nutrition. In 1977 she received the Sen Award (FAO) for field work.

RITCHIE, Sir Neil Methuen
(1897–1983)

Soldier, born in Essequibo British Guiana, the son of a Scottish sugar planter. Educated at Lancing College, Sussex, and Sandhurst, he was commissioned in the Black Watch in 1915. During World War I he saw service in Flanders and Mesopotamia and was awarded the DSO and MC for his bravery under fire. An outstanding postwar staff officer, he commanded the King's Own Royal Regiment in Palestine in 1938, and after the British withdrawal from Dunkirk he was promoted major-general with the responsibility of re-building the 51st (Highland) Division. While commanding them in North Africa he caught the eye of Sir Claude Auchinleck and was given command of the 8th Army. It was an unhappy appointment for, although he raised the siege of Tobruk, he failed to counter Rommel's offensive in May 1942 and was sacked. Although he was later promoted general and was given postwar command of the Far East Land Forces, his career never recovered from this setback.

RITCHIE, William
(1781–1831)

Chief founder of *The Scotsman* (1817). Born in Fife, he practised as a solicitor before the Supreme Courts. Dismayed by the timid nature of newspapers in the city, he co-operated with his friend **Charles Maclaren** to establish an independent journal devoted to the cause of political and economic change. Ritchie suggested the title, drew up the prospectus and wrote most of the paper's articles on law and literature. Under his vigorous leadership the paper established a reputation for reforming zeal, intellectual distinction and liberal spirit. It was written of him that 'the benefit of his exertions was felt in every part of Scotland'.

RITCHIE OF DUNDEE, Charles Thomson Ritchie, 1st Baron
(1838–1906)

Conservative politician, born in Dundee. Educated at the City of London School, he then entered the family jute-making business. He was MP for Tower Hamlets (1874–85), St George's-in-the-East (1885–92), and Croydon (1895–1906). He was a keen social reformer, and as President of the Local Government Board (1886–92) reformed the local government system of London and of the rest of England and Wales, also improving public health standards. President of the Board of Trade (1895–1900), then Home Secretary (1900–2), he was responsible for a major Licensing Bill. Chancellor of the Exchequer from 1902 to 1903, he resigned after a dispute with protectionists over his Budget of 1903, in which he proposed the abolition of the corn duty. He was created a peer in 1906.

ROBERT I See BRUCE, Robert

ROBERT II
(1316–90)

King of Scotland from 1371, the son of **Walter Stewart** and of Marjory, only daughter of **Robert I, the Bruce**. He twice acted as guardian during the imprisonment in England of **David II**. On David's death (1371) he obtained the crown, founding the **Stuart** dynasty. His reign, although usually characterized as that of a king lacking in prestige and unsuited to rule, did not see serious factional disputes over either the succession or Anglo-Scottish politics, despite English invasions in 1384 and 1385. It saw, vitally, the extension of Stuart lands and patronage by grants made to his many legitimate sons and the beginnings of a transformation of the greater nobility. His complicated matrimonial history, however, was to bring problems for later Stuart kings. His first marriage, to Elizabeth, daughter of Sir Adam Mure of Rowallan, was within the prohibited degrees; his second, in 1355, was to Euphemia, Countess of Moray, daughter of Hugh, Earl of Ross. A papal dispensation for the children of the first marriage was obtained in 1347, and they were further recognized by an Act of Succession passed by Parliament in 1373.

ROBERT III
(c.1340–1406)

King of Scotland from 1390, the eldest son of **Robert II** by his first marriage. He was originally called John. He was created Earl of Carrick in 1368 and took the name Robert on his accession in 1390. The issue of guardianship dominated politics, since he was a permanent invalid as a result of a kick from a horse. The main contenders were his brother,

Robert, Duke of **Albany** (?1340–1420), and his elder son, David, Duke of Rothesay (?1378–1402), who was appointed Lieutenant of the Kingdom by a general council in 1398. Rothesay's fall in 1402, and his imprisonment and subsequent death at Falkland, brought Albany to an unrivalled position of power, made more secure by the imprisonment in England of many magnates captured at the Battle of Homildon Hill (1402). Robert, anxious for the safety of his younger son, James (the future **James I**), sent him to France; he died shortly after news arrived of James's capture by the English. He was perhaps the least impressive of Scotland's medieval kings, his reign being dominated by a family quarrel rather than by civil war.

ROBERTS, David
(1796–1864)

Painter, born in Edinburgh. Originally apprenticed to a housepainter, he became a theatre scene-painter, moving from the Theatre Royal in Glasgow, then Edinburgh, to Drury Lane in London. There he attracted attention with pictures of Rouen and Amiens cathedrals while he exhibited at the Royal Academy. From 1830 he devoted himself entirely to serious painting. His pictures, inspired by his wide travels, included *Departure of the Israelites from Egypt* (1829), *Jerusalem* (1845), *Rome* (1855) and *Grand Canal at Venice* (1856).

ROBERTSON, Alan
(1920–89)

Founder of quantitative genetics and of scientific animal breeding. Educated at Liverpool and Cambridge, he was originally a chemist and became involved in operational research in World War II. **Conrad Hal Waddington** persuaded him to join the Animal Breeding and Research Organisation, which moved to Edinburgh in 1947. Here he used his great mathematical abilities to apply genetics to the improvement of dairy cattle. Many genetic factors influence milk yield and the handling of the complex data collected is mathematically complex, but the advent of artificial insemination during this early period gave an impetus to the research, leading to results which have been hugely influential in improving dairy herds throughout the world. Later, Robertson turned to more general problems in quantitative genetics, including the long-term effects of breeding program-

mes. He was a Deputy Chief Scientific Officer for the Agricultural and Food Research Council and an Honorary Professor at Edinburgh University. Elected FRS in 1964, his published work has affected millions throughout the world.

ROBERTSON, Sir Alexander
(1908–90)

Expert in tropical veterinary medicine. He was educated at Stonehaven Mackie Academy and Aberdeen University, graduating MA in 1929, followed by a BSc in 1930. He was a Demonstrator in Anatomy at the Royal (Dick) Veterinary College and then a veterinary inspector for the Ministry of Agriculture and Senior Lecturer in Physiology, before being appointed Professor of Veterinary Hygiene (1944), William Dick Professor of Animal Health (1953), Director of the Royal Veterinary College (1964) and finally Professor of Tropical Animal Health in 1971. His greatest achievement, perhaps, was the setting up in 1970 of the Centre of Tropical Veterinary Medicine at the Veterinary Field Station outside Edinburgh at a time when the government was steadily withdrawing from commitments to the Commonwealth. He saw this as an important bridge between expertise in Scotland and the many countries which were by then setting up new veterinary training programmes. He has served on numerous advisory committees, both in the UK and, particularly, Africa, editing *The Journal of Tropical Animal Health and Production* and the five-volume *International Encyclopaedia of Veterinary Medicine*. Made CBE in 1963 and knighted in 1970, he has been particularly influential in the training of veterinarians in third world countries, and has done much to improve the quality of livestock there.

ROBERTSON, Anne Strachan
(1910 –)

Archaeologist, born in Glasgow. Educated at Glasgow and London universities, she became Reader and later Keeper of the Roman Collections and Hunter Coin Cabinet in Glasgow University, and in 1974 was made Professor of Roman Archaeology. Her excavations and research on the Antonine Wall elucidated many aspects of its history, and in 1960 she published a classic handbook, *The Antonine Wall*. She is a leading authority on Roman coins, publishing many papers as well as catalogues of the Anglo-Saxon and Roman

Imperial coins in the Hunter Coin Cabinet, and her work on Roman artefacts found on native settlements helped to clarify the relationship between the Roman army and the native population.

ROBERTSON, Belinda
(1959 –)

Fashion designer, born in Glasgow, who had a varied career in modelling, teaching and marketing before settling for fashion design. Self-taught, she designs Scottish cashmere, fine merino wool and merino silk from yarn supplied mostly by Todd and Duncan in Kinross. Operating from her workshop and showroom in Edinburgh, with her main factory in Hawick, Roxburghshire, she is recognized as one of the world's leading cashmere designers, creating what she describes as 'classics with an innovative twist'. Special commissions include 'own-label' collections for several international couture houses. She trades mostly with the Far East, the USA, France and Germany, but is developing outlets in Italy and Scandinavia.

ROBERTSON, Fyfe
(1902–87)

Journalist and broadcaster, born in Edinburgh. A vastly experienced reporter with the *Glasgow Herald*, *Sunday Express* and *Daily Express*, he worked for many years as a feature writer with *Picture Post* (1943–57), earning a reputation as a champion of the underdog, campaigner for social justice and sceptical inquisitor of the great and the good. He retained these qualities when he moved into television current affairs, where he made more than 750 documentary reports for series such as *Tonight* and 24 *Hours*. An inimitable figure with bony features, goatee beard and insistent nasal tones, he travelled the world to satisfy the curiosity of his viewers and himself, and was active throughout his seventies on such programmes as his own series *Robbie* (1978), the documentary *The Peat Programme* (1981) and a 40 *Minutes* special on *Picture Post* (1985).

ROBERTSON, George Croom
(1842–92)

Philosopher, born in Aberdeen. He studied philosophy at Aberdeen University under **Alexander Bain**, who had a formative influence on his thought. Winning the first Ferguson scholarship, he went on to study at London and various German universities. In 1866 he became Professor of Mental Philosophy and Logic at University College, London. Thereafter his life was dedicated to reform of education and scholarship, with particular attention to the contribution of philosophy. He travelled and lectured, campaigned for social causes with his friend **J S Mill**, and attempted to professionalize and organize the study of philosophy in Britain with a historical work on Hobbes, of which only a short preliminary version appeared in 1886, following the onset of a debilitating illness in 1880. His work as founding editor of Britain's first philosophy and psychology journal, *Mind* (from 1876), achieved part of his purpose, keeping readers abreast with continental work, coaching young writers, and commissioning reports and historical studies. Volume One contained contributions from Helmholtz, Sidgwick, Herbert Spencer, Henry Venn and Wundt. He resigned in 1892 as both editor and professor. Bain collected his writings with a detailed biographical preface. A need for textbooks led to the publication of his lectures: *Elements of General Philosophy*, a liberal-minded history, and *Elements of Psychology* (1896).

ROBERTSON, Henry
(1816–88)

Civil engineer, born in Banff. He graduated at Aberdeen University before he was 20 years old. He began as a mining engineer, but became a pupil of Robert Stephenson and worked on railway lines in Scotland and elsewhere. He then moved to Shropshire, where he formed a company to restore the Brymbo ironworks. He built many of the railway lines on both sides of the Welsh border, a number of fine masonry viaducts, and the Kingsland Bridge over the River Severn. In the 1880s he developed the Brymbo ironworks into the largest steelworks in north Wales, and acquired an interest in many other industrial concerns. He represented Shrewsbury as a Liberal in three parliaments, and later Merionethshire, of which county he was a Deputy Lieutenant.

ROBERTSON, Sir Hugh S
(1874–1952)

Choral conductor and composer, born in Glasgow. A self-taught chorus master, he founded the Toynbee Musical Association in 1901, which in 1906 became the Glasgow Orpheus Choir, an organization that enjoyed huge worldwide fame through its tours and recordings until it was disbanded a year before Robertson's death. He had a way with singers, not unlike that of Beecham with orchestral players, and was devoted to the minutiae of choral ensemble and technique. His breadth of repertory ranged from the sentimental to the challenging, and he composed much for the choir. He edited a monthly magazine, *The Lute*. He was knighted in 1931.

ROBERTSON, Sir James Jackson
(1893–1970)

Educationist, educated at Kilmarnock Academy and Hutchesons' Grammar School and graduating in Classics from Glasgow University. His teaching career culminated in the headship of Aberdeen Grammar School (1942–59). An influential member of the Advisory Council on Education in Scotland, he was author of its enlightened and forward-looking report *Secondary Education* (1947), which set a target for educational reform for the next 20 years and is still quoted. He chaired many national bodies, including the Schools Broadcasting Council for Scotland. His honours include LLD of Aberdeen University, fellowships of the Royal Society of Edinburgh and the Educational Institute of Scotland, and presidency of the Scottish Secondary Teachers' Association. Personally, he is remembered as a magnanimous character and a masterly user of the English language.

ROBERTSON, James Logie See HALIBURTON, Hugh

ROBERTSON, Jeannie
(1908–75)

Folk singer, born in Aberdeen, described by the American folklorist, Alan Lomax, as 'a monumental figure of world folk-song'. She was virtually unknown beyond the north-east of Scotland, until her talent was recognized in 1953 by **Hamish Henderson**. Her huge repertoire of classic traditional ballads and other songs, together with her powerful and magnetic singing style, exerted a profound influence on the folk-music revival. Although she spent most of her life in Aberdeen, she belonged to the 'travelling folk', whose music was passed down orally from generation to generation, and she represented an important link with this ancient culture.

ROBERTSON, John See REID, John

ROBERTSON, John Monteath
(1909–89)

Crystallographer, born on a farm near Auchterarder, Perthshire. After study at Glasgow University he joined W H Bragg's research team at the Royal Institution. Robertson turned to organic compounds and pioneered the investigation of the structures of organic molecules by passing X-rays through them and examining the resulting diffraction patterns. He soon solved many structures, including those of naphthalene and oxalic acid. Later he studied larger molecules by replacing key atoms in their structure with heavy metallic atoms whose effect on diffraction patterns enabled the postion of other atoms to be derived. This revolutionary technique changed the course of crystallography. Robertson moved to Sheffield University in 1939. He was chemical adviser to Bomber Command in 1941 and 1942, and from 1942 to 1970 held the Chair at Glasgow University, where he built up a world-famous school of crystallography.

ROBERTSON, Joseph
(1810–66)

Antiquary and historian, born in Aberdeen. Educated at Aberdeen Grammar School and Marischal College, he turned from law to literature. He was Editor of the Edinburgh *Evening Courant* (1848–53), and in 1853 became historical curator at the Edinburgh Register House. He was a founder-member of the Aberdeen Spalding Club (1839–70), which published works of Scottish historical interest, and contributed much to Chambers's *Encyclopaedia*. Among his works are *The Book of Bon-Accord* (1839) and *Concilia Scotiae: Ecclesiae Scoticanae Statuta 1225–1559* (1866).

ROBERTSON, Sir Robert
(1869–1949)

Industrial chemist, born in Cupar, Fife. He graduated in both arts and science at St

Andrews University. In 1892 he joined the staff of the Royal Gunpowder Factory at Waltham Abbey and, as chemist in charge of the laboratory from 1900, he made a particular study of the stability of explosives. In 1907 he was transferred to the research department at Woolwich Arsenal, and in World War I he was responsible for some important advances in the science of explosives. In 1921 he was appointed government chemist and subsequently served on numerous government committees, as well as undertaking fundamental research involving infrared spectroscopy. He retired from government service in 1936, but on the outbreak of World War II he again gave his country the benefit of his wide experience of explosives, as a result of which he received many honours and distinctions.

ROBERTSON, William

(1721–93)

Historian, born in Borthwick Manse in Midlothian. He studied at Edinburgh, and at the age of 22 was ordained minister of Gladsmuir, and of Lady Yester's in Edinburgh (1756). He volunteered for the defence of Edinburgh against the Jacobite rebels in 1745, from 1751 he took a prominent part in the General Assembly, and he soon became leader of the 'Moderates'. From 1761 he was joint minister of Greyfriars, Edinburgh. In 1761 he became a royal chaplain, in 1762 Principal of Edinburgh University, and in 1764 King's Historiographer. His *History of Scotland* 1542–1603 (1759) was a great success. Next followed a *History of Charles V* (1769), his most valuable work, which was highly praised by Voltaire and Gibbon. He made the first major published attempt to write the history of the Americas, but was prevented from concluding it by the outbreak of the American Revolution in 1776, which he believed must alter previous history of the British colonies. He therefore published only the completed portions on Spanish America (1777), whose dispassionate tone won him a membership of the Royal Academy in Madrid, while inspiring future romantic historians such as W H Prescott and poets such as Keats. The North American fragments were published by his son William (1796) but seem to be little more than worked-up notes on **Adam Smith** and others; Robertson had certainly contemplated a very different work. Turning from American history, he published *An Historical Disquisition concerning the Knowledge which the Ancients had of India* (1791).

Although he was a popular figure, his house was wrecked following his defence of the Roman Catholic Vicar General **Hay** during the anti-Catholic riots of 1779. Deeply opposed to racism, as can be seen in his quiet but deadly indictments of white treatment of Native Americans, he was amongst those who laid the foundations of modern European perceptions of the Americas.

ROBERTSON-JUSTICE, James Norval Harald

(1905–75)

Actor and naturalist, born in Wigtownshire. Educated at Marlborough College and Bonn University, he became a journalist with Reuters and also worked for the British United Press in Canada. He served in the International Brigade in the Spanish Civil War and was an officer in the Royal Navy during World War II before belatedly turning to acting. He made his film début in *Fiddlers Three* (1944) and was seen in a variety of features, including *Whisky Galore* (1948), before finding popularity as the irascible Sir Lancelot Sprat in the series of 'Doctor' comedies that began with *Doctor in the House* (1953). His bearded, ebullient presence was felt in many other films, such as *Moby Dick* (1956) and *Mayerling* (1968). He retired from the profession after *Doctor in Trouble* (1970). An unsuccessful Labour candidate in the 1950 general election, Rector of Edinburgh University (1957–60, 1963–6) and a Fellow of the Zoological Society, his many other interests included falcon-training and ornithology, and he invented a rocket-propelled net method of catching wildfowl for marking.

ROBIESON, Sir William

(1890–1977)

Journalist, twin son of the schoolmaster at Fossoway in Kinross-shire. Educated at Glasgow University, where he took a first in history and was briefly assistant to the Professor of History, he joined the editorial staff of the *Glasgow Herald* just before World War I, and rose to become editor (1937–55). Although he did not relish writing, he was regarded as an outstanding editor, scholarly, well-informed and balanced in his judgements. In 1938 he was responsible for a courageous editorial denouncing the Munich agreement and the policy of appeasement, for which he was summoned to London and reprimanded by a member of the Cabinet.

ROBISON, John
(1739–1805)

Physicist, born in Boghall, Stirlingshire, and educated at Glasgow Grammar School and Glasgow University. He spent some 10 or so years in various naval employments, then became a lecturer in chemistry at Glasgow University. In 1770 he was appointed Professor of Mathematics at Cronstadt, where he advised on the reorganization of the navy of Catherine the Great. He returned to Scotland in 1775 when he was appointed Professor of Natural Philosophy at Edinburgh, a post that he held until his death. Gifted as a practical physicist and engineer, he was also talented as a draughtsman, writer, editor, musician and linguist. **James Watt** described him as 'a man of the clearest head and the most science of anybody I have known'.

ROB ROY (Gaelic for '**Red Robert**'), properly **Robert Macgregor**
(1671–1734)

Freebooter, the second son of Lieutenant-Colonel Donald Macgregor of Glengyle. Until 1661 the 'wicked Clan Gregor' had for a century been pursued by fire and sword; even their name was proscribed. But from that year until the Glorious Revolution of 1688 the severe laws against them were somewhat relaxed, and Rob Roy lived quietly enough as a grazier at Balquhidder. However, his herds were so often plundered by the outlaws from the north that he had to maintain a band of armed followers to defend both himself and such of his neighbours as paid him protection money. And so with those followers espousing the Jacobite cause, in 1691 he did a little plundering for himself and, two or three years after having purchased the lands of Craigroyston and Inversnaid from his nephew, he claimed to be Chief of the clan. Suffering losses in cattle speculations (1712), for which he had borrowed money from the Duke of Montrose, his lands were seized, his houses plundered, and his wife turned adrift with her children in midwinter. Rob Roy gathered his clansmen and declared open war on the duke in 1716, the year after the Jacobite rebellion, in which, at Sheriffmuir, Rob Roy had stood watch for the booty. Marvellous stories were told around Loch Katrine and Loch Lomond of his hairbreadth escapes, of his evasions when captured, and of his generosity to the poor, whose wants he supplied at the expense of the rich. They in return warned him of the designs of his arch-foes, the Dukes of Montrose and Atholl, and of the redcoats. In addition, he enjoyed the protection of John, 2nd Duke of **Argyll**, having assumed his mother's name Campbell. In 1727 he was arrested and sentenced to transportation, but pardoned. His life was romanticized in Sir **Walter Scott**'s *Rob Roy* (1818). He left five sons, two of whom died in 1754, James, the notorious outlaw James Mohr, in Paris, and Robin, the youngest, on the gallows in Edinburgh for abduction.

ROEBUCK, John
(1718–94)

Industrial chemist, born in Sheffield. He studied chemistry at Edinburgh under **Joseph Black**, and in 1742 he graduated MD at Leiden. He gave up his practice in Birmingham to return to chemistry in partnership with Samuel Garbett, with whom he became interested in the production of sulphuric acid. The two men set up a large 'vitriol manufactory' at Prestonpans near Edinburgh in 1749, and in 1760 they joined forces with William Cadell to establish the Carron ironworks near Falkirk. By this time Roebuck had settled in Bo'ness, and he came to the assistance of **James Watt** in his development of the separate condenser for his steam engine. However, when he in turn became embroiled in financial difficulties it was left to Matthew Boulton to form the famous and successful partnership with Watt at the Soho manufactory in Birmingham.

ROEHENSTART, Count, Charles Edward Augustus Maximilian Stuart, Baron Korff
(c.1784–1854)

Doubly illegitimate grandson of Prince **Charles Edward Stuart**. Born in Paris, he was the son of Charlotte, Duchess of Albany and Prince Ferdinand de Rohan-Guémené, Archbishop of Cambrai. His early years were obscure because of the scandal surrounding his birth. He saw military service, probably with the Russians, but gave up soldiering in 1806. From 1807 to 1811 he was Chamberlain to the Duke of Wurttemberg at his court in Russia. In 1812 he travelled to America where he was involved in an unsuccessful business venture. Returning to Europe in 1814 he led a wandering life. In October 1816 he was in London where he presented a melodramatic and inaccurate memorial to the Prince Regent, setting out his Stuart origins in an attempt to receive a pension. After studying medicine in Edinburgh for just two months, he resumed his peripatetic existence abroad. About 1818 he married Maria Antoinetta Sophia Barbuonei (d.1821), and in 1826 he married Louisa Constance Smith, probably a cousin of Mrs Fitzherbert, wife of the Prince Regent (later George IV). Roehenstart was a high officer in the Order of Ancient Nobility and of the Four Emperors of Germany on whose affairs he travelled much between 1822 and 1825. He travelled for much of the remainder of his life, but he gained little recognition of his royal claims, although their validity is now evident. He was killed in a stage-coach accident at Dunkeld, and was buried in the cathedral there.

ROSE, Sir John

(1820–88)

Scottish-born Canadian diplomat, born in Turriff, Aberdeenshire. Educated at Udny Academy and King's College, Aberdeen, he emigrated with his parents to Huntingdon, Lower Canada, in 1836, and was called to the Montreal Bar in 1842. He was identified with the Hudson's Bay Company operations, acquired numerous directorates, and became a close friend and political associate of **John A Macdonald**. He was drawn into Anglo-American arbitration initially in deciding Oregon-related questions directly arising from his Hudson's Bay brief (1863–9), while at the same time entering into partnership in London with the American financier and future vice-president, Levi P Morton. He played a critical part in adjusting British-American hostilities after the Civil War. He later settled in England, but died in Scotland during a stag shoot.

ROSEBERY, Archibald Philip Primrose, 5th Earl of

(1847–1929)

Statesman, born in London. Educated at Eton and Christ Church College, Oxford, he succeeded his grandfather in 1868. In 1874 he was President of the Social Science Congress, he was Lord Rector of Aberdeen University in 1878, of Edinburgh in 1880, of Glasgow in 1899, and from 1881 to 1883 he was Under-Secretary for the Home Department, and in 1884 became First Commissioner of Works. In July 1886, and again from 1892 to 1894, he was Secretary for Foreign Affairs in the Gladstone administration. In 1889–90 and 1892 he was Chairman of the London County Council. On the retirement of Gladstone he became Liberal premier (March 1894), and after his government had been defeated at the general election (1895), he remained Leader of the Liberal opposition until 1896, when he resigned the leadership. A spokesman for imperial federation, he was an imperialist during the Boer War, and as head of the Liberal League from 1902 he represented a policy, first set forth in a famous speech at Chesterfield, but not accepted by official Liberals. His attitude in 1909–10 was Independent or Conservative. In 1911 he was created Earl of Midlothian. Lord Rosebery published books on Pitt (1891), Peel (1899), the 'last phase' of Napoleon's career (1900), Chatham (1910), and *Miscellanies* (2 vols, 1921). In 1878 he married Hannah (1851–90), the only daughter of Baron Meyer de Rothschild. A devoted race-goer, he won the Derby three times (1894, 1895 and 1905).

ROSS, Horatio

(1801–86)

Sportsman and pioneer of photography, the son of Hercules Ross of Rossie Castle and godson of Lord Nelson. He had a considerable reputation as a horseman, athlete and yachtsman, but his greatest skill lay in shooting. His photography ran parallel to his other enthusiasms and his photographs centred on the Highland landscape and animals. He was taught by a professional photographer, James Ross, in 1849, when he practised the calotype and also, apparently, the daguerreotype process, followed by the collodion and waxed paper processes in the 1850s. He was Vice President of the Photographic Society of Scotland from 1856.

ROSS, Ian Anthony

(1917 –)

Roman Catholic scholar and social reformer, born into a Highland family of Gaelic-speaking origin in Beauly, Inverness-shire. He was educated at Edinburgh University, where he became Scottish Nationalist student leader. Converted to Roman Catholicism in 1937, he entered the Order of Preachers (Dominican) (1939) and was ordained priest in 1945. He was founder and for many years Chairman of *Innes Review* (the journal of Scottish Catholic history), to which he contributed major articles on various subjects. A major force in the professionalization of Scottish Roman Catholic history, he was profoundly involved with the care and support of nomads, homeless, convicts, and friendless and frightened people at all levels. A member and for many years superior in the Dominican Chaplaincy in Edinburgh (1959–77), he was a charismatic figure, attracting an enthusiastic following among scholars, students, social workers, penologists, and writers. He carried out extensive work on comparative penology in Scandinavia and elsewhere with influential consequences on Scottish prison reform and rehabilitation. He was Chairman and founder of the *Scottish International Review* (1968–74), a journal of the arts and social analysis. A prominent force in the vanguard of ecumenical reappraisal of Scottish Catholicism, he was a well-known broadcaster. He was elected Rector of Edinburgh University (1979–82) and Provincial of the British Dominicans, during which terms he was columnist for the *Tablet*. He edited St Thomas Aquinas' *De Fortitudine* (with P G Walsh) for the definitive edition of the works of Aquinas, as *Courage*. He wrote brief stories of the lives of saints, *The Golden Man* (1955) and prepared *The Gude and Godlie Ballads* for the Saltire Classics. His autobiography, *The Root of the Matter*, (1989) was hailed as an outstanding witness to the social history of Scotland in the 1920s and 1930s.

ROSS, Sir James Clark

(1800–62)

Polar explorer and naval officer, born in London, son of a rich merchant and nephew of Sir **John Ross**. He first went to sea with his uncle at the age of 12, conducting surveys of the White Sea and the Arctic, and accompanied Parry on four Arctic expeditions (1819–27). From 1829 to 1833 he was joint leader with his uncle of a private Arctic expedition financed by the distiller, Sir Felix Booth, and in 1831 he located the magnetic north pole. After conducting a magnetic survey of the British Isles, he led an expedition to the Antarctic (1839–43) on the *Erebus* and the *Terror*, during which he discovered Victoria Land and the volcano Mount Erebus, and wrote an account of it in *Voyage of Discovery* (1847). He made a final expedition in 1848–9, searching for the ill-fated Franklin expedition in Baffin Bay. Ross Island, the Ross Sea and Ross's Gull are named after him.

ROSS, Sir John

(1777–1856)

Arctic explorer and naval officer, born at Inch Manse in Wigtownshire. He joined the navy at the age of nine and served with distinction in the Napoleonic wars. From 1812 he conducted surveys in the White Sea and the Arctic, and in 1818 he led an expedition, including his nephew Sir **James Clark Ross** and Sir Edward Sabine, in search of the northwest passage. He led another such expedition with his nephew, financed by the distilling magnate Sir Felix Booth, in 1829–33, during which he discovered and named Boothia Peninsula, King William Land and the Gulf of Boothia. In 1850 he made an unsuccessful attempt to discover the fate of Sir John Franklin.

ROSS, Ricky

(1957 –)

Rock singer and songwriter, born in Dundee. He worked as an English teacher and social worker before forming the group Deacon Blue in Glasgow in 1985. The band's other members are keyboard-player James Prime (1960 –), guitarist Graeme Kelling (1957 –), drummer Douglas Vipond (1966 –), bass guitarist Ewan Vernal (1964 –) and singer Lorraine McIntosh (1964 – , who later married Ross). Their début album *Raintown* (1987), which included the singles 'Dignity' and 'Chocolate Girl', established Ross's songwriting preoccupation with his adopted city, and brought their first UK chart success. Their second album, *When The World Knows Your Name* (1989) consolidated that success and included one of their best-known singles, 'Real Gone Kid'. Subsequent albums have included *Fellow Hoodlums* (1991). They also had a major UK hit in 1990 with an EP featuring four songs written by Burt Bacharach and Hal David.

ROSS, Thomas

(1839–1930)

Architect, born in Errol, Perthshire, the son of a tenant farmer. He was apprenticed for a time in the Glasgow offices of Alexander Kirkland and **Charles Wilson**. He joined the office of **David MacGibbon** in Edinburgh in 1862, and became a partner in the firm 10 years later. After MacGibbon's death (1902) the firm began to concentrate on restoration work, and Ross was a founder member of the Royal Commission on the Ancient and Historical Monuments of Scotland (RCAHMS). During the later years of his life Ross largely gave up his architectural practice, concentrating instead on his work for RCAHMS.

ROSS, William
(1879–1966)

Piper and composer, born in Glen Strathfarrer, Ross-shire, and taught to play the Highland pipes by his parents. In 1896 he enlisted in the Scots Guards, serving with distinction in the South African war, and was twice decorated. Pipe Major of the 2nd Scots Guards from 1905 to 1918, he served in World War I. Invalided out of active service in 1918, he was appointed to the position of Instructor at the Army School of Piping at Edinburgh Castle, where he remained for the rest of his professional career, earning a reputation as a fine teacher and distinguished piper and composer. He was Champion All-Round Piper of Scotland on several occasions, and published five books of pipe music.

ROSS, William, Lord Ross of Marnock
(1911–88)

Labour politician, the longest-serving Secretary of State for Scotland (1964–70, 1974–6). Born in Ayr, the son of a train driver, he was educated at Ayr Academy and Glasgow University, and became a schoolteacher before World War II. He entered Parliament as MP for Kilmarnock in a by-election in 1946, and represented that constituency until 1979, when he was created a life peer. As Secretary of State for Scotland, he was responsible for the creation of the Highlands and Islands Development Board and also the Scottish Development Agency.

ROUGHEAD, William
(1870–1952)

Criminologist and writer, son of a wealthy Edinburgh family of drapers. He was led to a lifelong fascination with murder when, as legal apprentice in 1889, he covered the trial of the baby-farmer Jessie King, and then that of John Watson Laurie for murder on Arran. Admitted Writer to the Signet in 1893, he married Janey More, daughter of an Edinburgh accountant, in 1900. In 1906, with the *Trial of Dr Pritchard*, he began his great partnership with publisher **Harry Hodge**; this resulted in 10 volumes in the Hodge 83-volume 'Notable British Trials' series. In addition to **Pritchard**, Roughead edited Deacon **William Brodie**, Captain **Porteous**, **Burke** and Hare, **Oscar Slater**, and many others. Harshly moralistic towards the guilty, he proved a formidable critic where he believed justice had erred, and his edition of the Slater trial (1909) was of major value in obtaining Slater's ultimate if vastly delayed pardon (1928), duly chronicled by Roughead in his next edition. He also published 119 essays on criminal cases in 14 individual books. He was an industrious pioneer, and was probably unrivalled in his influence on popular criminology.

ROW, John
(c.1525–1580)

Religious reformer and ecclesiastical lawyer, born near Stirling. Educated at Stirling and St Andrews, in 1550 he was sent by the archbishop to Rome as Scottish agent. In 1558 he returned to Scotland on the pope's request to investigate the reasons for the increasing spread of heresy, and the next year he turned Protestant. He helped to compile the *Confession of Faith* (1560) and *First Book of Discipline* (1561), and he became minister of Perth and sat in the first General Assembly. He was four times Moderator, and took a share in preparing the *Second Book of Discipline*.

ROW, John
(1568–1646)

Clergyman, son of **John Row**. He was minister from 1592 of Carnock near Dunfermline, and wrote a long-winded but reliable *History of the Kirk of Scotland from 1558 to 1637*. He was strongly opposed to the introduction of episcopacy into Scotland.

ROY, Archie (Archibald Edmiston)
(1924 –)

Astronomer, born in Yoker near Glasgow. He was educated at the University of Glasgow, which he has made his academic home, first as Lecturer in Astronomy (appointed in 1958), and progressing to the post of titular Professor of Astronomy in 1977. His special branch of research has been celestial mechanics, ie the study of motions in the solar system, a field which involves problems of modern space research. His text-books include *The Foundations of Astrodynamics* (1965) and *Long-term Dynamical Behaviour of Natural and Artificial N-body Dynamical Systems* (1988). Among his other interests are ancient astronomy, interplanetary exploration, parapsychology and science fiction, on which he has lectured and written extensively.

ROY, William
(1726–90)

Military surveyor, born in Miltonhead, Carluke, Lanarkshire. In 1747 he was engaged on the survey of Scotland, he held an army commission in 1755, he was elected FRS in 1767, and rose to be Major-General in 1781. In 1784, in connection with the triangulation of the south-eastern counties, he measured with great accuracy a base line of $5\frac{1}{5}$ miles of Hounslow heath, for which he received the Royal Society's Copley Medal. In 1764 he studied the Roman remains in Scotland, and his *Military Antiquities of the Romans in Britain* was published in 1793 by the Society of Antiquaries.

ROYDS, Mabel Alington
(1874–1941)

English artist printmaker, born in Little Barford, Bedfordshire, the fifth of eleven children. She won a scholarship to the Royal Academy Schools which she turned down in favour of the Slade, where she studied under Henry Tonks. Influenced by Walter Richard Sickert, whom she met in Paris at the turn of the century, she was an accomplished printmaker, using the medium of woodcuts which combined her interest in colour and line to great effect. From 1911 she taught at Edinburgh College of Art and in 1914 married **Ernest Stephen Lumsden**. She travelled extensively, particularly in India and Tibet. Her works are in many public collections including the Victoria and Albert and British Museums.

RUDDIMAN, Thomas
(1674–1757)

Classical grammarian and philologist, born in the parish of Boyndie, Banffshire. He studied classics at Aberdeen, and in 1700 obtained a post in the Advocates' Library in Edinburgh, being appointed Assistant Keeper in 1702 and Principal Keeper in 1730. In the meantime he also set up business as a book auctioneer (1707) and printer (1715). He edited Latin works of **Arthur Johnston**, and in 1715 published his great edition of the works of **George Buchanan**, with its controversial introduction in which he is severely critical of Buchanan's character and political views (Ruddiman was an ardent Jacobite). He also produced his own *Rudiments of the Latin Tongue* (1714), and the *Grammaticae Latinae Institutiones* (1725–32), on which his philological reputation mainly rests.

RUNCIMAN, Alexander
(1736–85) and **John** (1744–68)

Painters, brothers, born in Edinburgh. By 1767 Alexander was one of the major decorative painters in Scotland. The brothers worked closely together but the more inventive one seems to have been John who, in 1767, produced a remarkable painting, *King Lear in the Storm* which, in its colour, handling of paint, and dramatic interpretation, anticipates the Romantic movement of the early 19th century. In the same year the brothers travelled to Italy, where John died from consumption. Alexander's major work was the decoration of Penicuik House (1772) with scenes from Ossian and the history of Scotland. This work no longer survives, but parts are known from etchings made by the artist.

RUNNICLES, Donald Cameron
(1954 –)

Opera conductor, born in Edinburgh. He studied music at Edinburgh and Cambridge universities and the London Opera Centre. His career began as répétiteur at Mannheim Nationaltheater, where he made his conducting début with *Les Contes d'Hoffmann* (1980). During seven years as conductor there his repertoire included *Die Walküre* and *Parsifal*. Principal conductor at Hannover (1987) and general music director at Freiburg (1989), he has also been guest conductor at Hamburg, Frankfurt, Düsseldorf, Zürich and Amsterdam. His New York Metropolitan début (replacing James Levine at short notice) was *Lulu* (1988), but his 'official' début there was with *Der fliegende Holländer* (1990). After his *Ring* at San Francisco Opera (1990) he was appointed Music Director there (from

1992). He has had a long association with Bayreuth as musical assistant, making his Bayreuth conducting début with *Tannhäuser* (1992). Other débuts were Glyndebourne (*Don Giovanni*, 1991) and the Vienna Staatsoper (four operas in 1991–2, and the *Ring*, 1993).

RUNRIG See MACDONALD, Rory and Calum

RUSHFORTH, (Margaret) Winifred, née Bartholomew
(1885–1983)

Pioneer of psychotherapy in Scotland, born in Winchburgh, West Lothian. Educated at Edinburgh Medical School and University, in 1909 she sailed to India, where she spent 20 years as a medical missionary. Influenced by the works of William McDougall and Freud, she decided to become a psychoanalyst. After a period of personal analysis at the Tavistock Institute in London she moved to Edinburgh and set up practice as a private analyst. In 1939 she founded the Davidson Clinic there, with the aim of bringing analysis within the reach of anyone, regardless of income. In time the clinic expanded to include children's play therapy and family therapy. After the clinic's closure in 1973 she practised from home, concentrating particularly on dream therapy, which she conducted until the day before her death. Her publications include *Something is Happening* (1981), her autobiography *Ten Decades of Happenings* (1984) and *Life's Currency: Time, Money and Energy* (1985). Maintaining always a remarkable breadth and openness of mind, she exemplified in her life one of her favourite sayings: 'They will know we are old not by the frailty of the body but by the strength and creativity of the psyche'.

RUSK, Robert Robertson
(1879–1972)

Educationist, born in Ayr. With university degrees from Glasgow, Jena and Cambridge and experience in schools, he became professionally involved in teacher training and remained in that field for almost half a century, most of the time as Principal Lecturer in Education at Jordanhill College of Education, Glasgow. From 1946 to 1951 he was in charge of the Department of Edu-

cation in Glasgow University. His *Doctrines of the Great Educators* (1918) and *The Philosophical Bases of Education* (1928) have been extensively used in Britain and abroad. As Director (voluntary and part-time) of the Scottish Council for Research in Education (1928–58) he influenced planning for educational research throughout the British Commonwealth.

RUSSEL, Alexander
(1814–76)

Journalist, editor of *The Scotsman* from 1848, born in Edinburgh. A Liberal and an opponent of the corn-laws, he was a caustic wit and a great angler.

RUSSELL, Edward Stuart
(1887–1954)

Fisheries expert and philosopher of science, born in Port Glasgow the son of a Free Church minister. He was educated at Greenock and at Glasgow University before working in Aberdeen with J Arthur Balfour and **Patrick Geddes** on the biology of snails and sea anemonies. He then turned to animal behaviour and published a major work in 1916 called *Form and Function* in which he discussed theories of the development of form in relation to their function. He was a vitalist who believed that animals should be studied as a whole and he supported the views of Lamarck, publishing many books on these themes. In almost complete contrast to his philosophical and behavioural work, he was appointed in 1909 to the Board of Agriculture and Fisheries, becoming Director of Fisheries Investigations from 1921 to 1945. During this period he was instrumental in developing methods for investigating fish stocks and the factories which affect fishing yield. He advocated conservation methods which are still the basis for many current programmes worldwide, publishing his influential *The Overfishing Problem* in 1942.

RUSSELL, John Scott
(1808–82)

Engineer and naval architect. He was born near Glasgow and graduated from the university there at the age of 17. He moved to Edinburgh, where he taught mathematics and natural philosophy, built six steam carriages which plied regularly for a few months in

1834 between Glasgow and Paisley, and began his studies of wave motion and the resistance of ships' hulls. He carried out a large number of tests with ships of many different sizes and shapes on the Union Canal near Edinburgh, and used the results to develop his wave-line principle of ship construction, but it was subsequently shown to have been unduly influenced by the narrowness of the waterway. He was, however, one of the first to advocate and adopt a scientific approach to the design of ships, and he took a leading part in the building of I K Brunel's *Great Eastern*, launched in 1858 from his shipyard on the Thames. He was a prime mover both in the preparations for the Great Exhibition of 1851 and in the foundation of the Institution of Naval Architects (1860), of which he was for many years a vice-president.

RUTHERFORD, Alison See
COCKBURN, Alison

RUTHERFORD, Daniel
(1749–1819)

Physician and botanist, born in Edinburgh, where he became Professor of Botany in 1786. In 1772 he published his discovery of the distinction between 'noxious air' (nitrogen) and carbon dioxide.

RUTHERFORD, John
(1955 –)

Rugby player, now a building society executive, born in Selkirk. Along with scrum-half **Roy Laidlaw**, he set a record (since overtaken) for the highest number of international caps of any half-back partnership, playing alongside Laidlaw 35 times out of his total of 42 caps for Scotland. First capped in 1979, he proved a shrewd tactician, and played an important role in Scotland's Grand Slam win of 1984. He played one game in the 1987 World Cup before injury ended his involvement in the competition. He was also picked once for the British Lions, at centre. He played his club rugby for Selkirk.

RUTHERFORD, Samuel
(c.1600–1661)

Theologian and preacher, born in Nisbet near Jedburgh, Roxburghshire. He graduated from Edinburgh in 1621. In 1623 he was appointed Professor of Humanity there, but was dismissed in 1626, having 'fallen in fornication'. In 1627 he was settled as minister of Anwoth, Kirkudbright. Here he began a correspondence with his religious friends which formed 'the most seraphic book in our literature'. *Exercitationes Pro Divina Gratio* (1636) was against the Arminians, and brought him both an invitation to a divinity chair in Holland and a summons before the High Commission Court in July 1636, when he was forbidden to preach, and banished to Aberdeen (until 1638). He became Professor of Divinity at St Andrews University in 1639, and in 1648 Principal of St Mary's College, St Andrews. In 1643 he was sent to the Westminster Assembly, his *Due Right of Presbyteries* (1644) belonging to this period. At the Restoration he was deposed, having written *Lex Rex* (1661), a work of biblical and scholarly erudition which refuted the divine right of kings and argued for the limited powers of the ruler subject to the role of law and popular sovereignty. It was burned by the hangman in Edinburgh in 1661, and its author was deposed and summoned for high treason. However, he received the citation when on his deathbed.

RUTHVEN, John, 3rd Earl of Gowrie
(c.1578–1600)

Nobleman, second son of **William Ruthven**, 1st Earl of Gowrie. He succeeded a brother as 3rd Earl in 1588, and travelled in Italy, Switzerland and France. Soon after his return to Scotland he was killed with his brother Alexander in his house in Perth in what became known as the 'Gowrie Conspiracy', an alleged attempt, by Ruthven and Sir Robert Logan (d.1606), to murder or kidnap **James VI**.

RUTHVEN, Patrick
(c.1573–1651)

Mercenary soldier, the son of **William Ruthven** of Ballendean in Perthshire. His name first appeared in the list of Scottish captains in Swedish service in 1606, and he quickly established himself as one of Gustavus Adolphus's most capable military commanders. In 1638 he left Swedish service with the rank of major-general and returned to Scotland to take up the post of Muster Master-General of Edinburgh Castle. During the English Civil War he fought on the side of the Royalist forces of King Charles I, and was badly wounded during the Battle of Newbury in 1644. Exiled to Sweden, he eventually returned to Scotland at the time of the Restoration and made good a lifelong promise to die in his native land.

RUTHVEN, William, 1st Earl of Gowrie

(c.1541–1584)

Nobleman, created Earl of Gowrie in 1581, father of **John Ruthven**. He was involved in the murder of David Rizzio (1566), and was later the custodian of **Mary, Queen of Scots** during her captivity at Loch Leven (1567–8). In 1582 he kidnapped the boy king, **James VI**, to Castle Ruthven near Perth, for which he was first pardoned and then ordered to leave the country. However, he was beheaded at Stirling for his part in a conspiracy to take Stirling Castle.

S

SADLER, Flora Munro, née McBain
(1912 –)

Astronomer, born in Aberdeen and educated at Aberdeen University, where she graduated in mathematics and natural philosophy. She was a member of the British Expedition which successfully observed the total eclipse of the Sun in Omsk, Siberia, in June 1936. In the following year she was appointed to the scientific staff of the Royal Observatory, Greenwich, the first woman scientist ever to be employed there. Her work in the Observatory's Nautical Almanac Office, where she was Principal Scientific Officer until 1973, involved the production of astronomical and navigational tables and almanacs for the use of astronomers. She represented Great Britain on the International Astronomical Union's Commissions on the Moon and Astronomical Ephemerides from 1948 to 1970, and played an active part in the affairs of the Royal Astronomical Society, becoming its first woman secretary from 1949 to 1954.

SALMOND, Alex
(1955 –)

Nationalist politician, born in Linlithgow, West Lothian. Joining the Scottish National Party at the age of 19, while a student at St Andrews University, he graduated in economics, and worked for the Scottish agricultural ministry and the Royal Bank of Scotland before winning Banff and Buchan for the SNP in the 1987 general election. He soon endeared himself to the left-wingers in his own party, and his potential appeal to disaffected Scottish Labour voters helped him to achieve a clear victory in the party's 1990 election of a successor to party leader **Gordon Wilson**. His hopes for significant parliamentary advances were dashed in the 1992 general election.

SALTER, Stephen Hugh
(1938 –)

South African-born engineer and inventor, born in Johannesburg. He moved to Britain and was educated at Framlingham College, then joined Saunders-Roe as an apprentice fitter, tool-maker and instrument engineer. After reading natural sciences at Sidney Sussex College, Cambridge, he joined a research group in experimental psychology, for whom he designed instruments of many kinds. His wave energy research began at Edinburgh University in 1973, and by 1982 he had developed the celebrated 'Salter duck', thoroughly testing it in model form by using a special hydraulic test tank, largely of his own design, with multi-directional mixed-spectrum wave-making facilities. He estimated that full-scale ducks could generate electricity at a significantly lower cost than any other wave-power source, and less than that of nuclear power. Shortly afterwards, however, government funding for wave-power research was withdrawn, following the publication of an unfavourable report, which was later shown to contain misleading cost figures. There are now signs that Salter's ducks, and other 'clean' renewable energy sources, are again being considered as serious alternatives for Britain in the 21st century.

SAMPSON, Agnes
(d.1592)

Witch, born in Haddington, East Lothian. A lay-healer, she appears to have been an active witch rather than a victim of suspicion. She was put on trial after being named by a fellow and accused as the 'eldest witch of them all'. Severely tortured, she ultimately confessed to celebrating black Mass, where the devil himself appeared and gave instructions to plot the death of the king and queen. She also said she had organized meetings in North Berwick at Hallowe'en, when 200 people had danced in a circle by the sea. Sampson was finally interrogated by **James VI** himself, and was subsequently executed.

SCHOTZ, Benno
(1891–1986)

Estonian-born sculptor. In 1911 he went to Darmstadt, Germany, to study engineering, though by 1912 he was in Glasgow working in John Brown's shipyard, where he remained for nine years. At the same time he took evening classes in sculpture, becoming a professional sculptor in 1923, and he eventually (1981) received the title of Queen's Sculptor in Scotland and the freedom of the city of Glasgow. A prolific artist, he was best known for his portrait busts, though he also produced important religious works, most notably the *Stations of the Cross* for St Charles Chapel, Glasgow.

SCOTLAND, Ken
(1936 –)

Rugby player, born in Edinburgh. Educated at George Heriot's in Edinburgh, he is one of a series of full-backs (including **Dan Drysdale** and **Andy Irvine**) from the school to have represented his country. First capped in 1957, he played 27 times for Scotland between then and 1965, including two games at fly-half, in which he captained the side. He also played five times for the British Lions. Tactically astute, he did much to introduce the idea of the counter-attacking full-back, as well as being innovative in his goal-kicking methods. He also played for Scotland at cricket.

SCOTT

Name of a great Border family originating in Peeblesshire, possessors of Buccleuch in Selkirkshire in 1415, and of Branxholm near Hawick from 1420 onward. Sir Walter Scott fought for **James II** at Arkinholm against the Douglases (1455), and received a large share of the forfeited **Douglas** estates. His descendants acquired Liddesdale, Eskdale, Dalkeith, etc, with the titles Lord Scott of Buccleuch (1606) and Earl of Buccleuch (1619). Among them were two Sir Walters, one of whom (c.1490–1552) fought at Flodden (1513), Melrose (1526), Ancrum (1544) and Pinkie (1547), and was killed in a street fray in Edinburgh by Kerr of Cessford, while the other, 1st Lord Scott of Buccleuch (1565–1611), was the rescuer of **William Armstrong** ('Kinmont Willie') from Carlisle Castle (1596). Francis, 2nd Earl (1626–51), left two daughters — Mary (1647–61), who married the future Earl of Tarras, and Anna (1651–1732), who married James, Duke of **Monmouth**, who took the surname Scott and was created Duke of Buccleuch. After his

execution (1685) his duchess, who had borne him four sons and two daughters, retained her title and estates, and in 1688 married Lord Cornwallis. Her grandson Francis succeeded her as 2nd Duke, and through his marriage in 1720 with a daughter of the Duke of Queensberry, that title and estates in Dumfriesshire devolved in 1810 on Henry, 3rd Duke of Buccleuch (1746–1812), a great agriculturist. Walter Francis, 5th Duke (1806–84), was the builder of the pier and breakwater at Granton. The Harden branch (represented by Lord Polwarth) separated from the main stem in 1346, and from this sprang the Scotts of Raeburn, ancestors of the novelist Sir **Walter Scott**.

SCOTT, Alexander
(c.1525–1584)

Lyrical poet of the school of **Dunbar**. Little is known of his early life, except that he became musician and organist at the Augustinian priory of Inchmahome, in the Firth of Forth, in 1548. He had associations with the court of **Mary, Queen of Scots**, and in 1565 was a canon of Inchaffray in Perthshire. He bought an estate in Fife in 1567 and became a wealthy landowner. He wrote 36 short poems, either courtly love lyrics or poems offering moral advice. He is considered to be the last of the Scottish 'Makars' (15th/16th-century poets).

SCOTT, Andrew
(1772–1846)

Roman Catholic Vicar-General, born in the strongly recusant Roman Catholic Enzie of Banffshire, at Chapelford Farm. He is said to have decided on entering the priesthood at the age of five. Trained at the seminary at Scanlan (1784), he then went to Douai, returning to Aberdeen at the closure of the college during the French Revolution. He was ordained at Dee Castle, the poorest parish in Scotland, and worked there, and at Huntly, transferring to Glasgow, where his congregation rose from 450 on his arrival in 1805 to 3000 in 1814. There he attracted criticism of his elaborate if efficient system of collecting money for church-building. Accused of having refused baptism to a non-dues-paying mother, Scott sued for libel, with **Francis Jeffrey** and **Henry Cockburn** as counsel, and won, releasing £4000 raised for his costs and damages for the church building fund and thus ending the financial crisis. As a result of Glasgow's Catholic population rising to 15000 in 1822, further administrative reorganization was necessary and Scott became coadjutor bishop for the Western District, with responsibility for Clyde Valley (1828), effectively becoming its ruler (Rome having split Scotland into three vicariates in 1827). Friction with rising Irish Catholic immigrants may have played a part in his decision to tranfer Glasgow to his own coadjutor when he succeeded to the Western Vicariate in 1832. Thereafter his terrain became chiefly the western Highlands, in which he extended church-building, won admiration for courage in the midst of cholera, won hostility for his high-handed methods and lack of Gaelic, and laid the foundations of modern Scottish Catholicism in Argyll, Ayr, Bute, Dumbarton, southern Inverness, Lanark, Renfrew, Wigtown and the Western Isles. For all of his bitter disputes with the Irish immigrants over their nationalism and supposed squalor, he was a vital influence in enabling the Roman Catholic Church in Scotland to accommodate their huge post-famine incursion.

SCOTT, David
(1806–49)

Historical painter, brother of **William Bell Scott**, born in Edinburgh. Apprenticed to his father as a line-engraver, he studied at the Trustees' Academy, and in 1831 he designed his 25 'Illustrations to the *Ancient Mariner*' (1837). From 1832 to 1833 he visited Italy, and painted *The Vintager*, now in the National Gallery. Many imaginative and historical paintings followed, such as *The Traitor's Gate* and *Ariel and Caliban*.

SCOTT, Francis George
(1880–1958)

Composer, born in Hawick, Roxburghshire. He studied at the universities of Edinburgh and Durham, and in Paris under Roger-Ducasse. From 1925 to 1946 he was lecturer in music at Jordanhill Training College for Teachers, Glasgow. His *Scottish Lyrics* (five volumes, 1921–39) comprise original settings of songs by **Dunbar**, **Burns** and other poets, most notably of **Hugh MacDiarmid**, and exemplify Scott's aim of embodying in music the true spirit of Scotland. Primarily a song composer, he also wrote the orchestral suite *The Seven Deadly Sins* (after Dunbar's poem) and other orchestral works.

SCOTT, Hew
(1791–1872)

Minister, born in Haddington, East Lothian, and educated in Aberdeen. From 1839 he was minister of Wester Anstruther, Fife, and compiled *Fasti Ecclesiae Scoticanae* (1866–71), still regularly revised as a record of Church of Scotland ministers.

SCOTT, Michael
(c.1175 – c.1230)

Scholar and astrologer, the 'wondrous wizard', probably born in Durham, of Border ancestry. He studied at Oxford, Paris and Padua, was tutor and astrologer at Palermo to Frederick II, the Great, settled at Toledo from 1209 to 1220 and translated Arabic versions of Aristotle's works and Averroës' commentaries. Returning to the Imperial court at Palermo, he refused the proffered archbishopric of Cashel (1223). He wrote a learned work on astrology, *Quaestio Curiosa de Natura Solis et Lunae* (1622), and his translations of Aristotle were apparently used by Albertus Magnus, and represented one of the two translations familiar to Dante. The latter alludes to him in the *Inferno* in a way which confirms that his fame as a magician had already spread across Europe, and he is also referred to by Albertus Magnus and Vincent de Beauvais. In Border folklore he is credited with having, in the words of Sir **Walter Scott**, 'cleft the Eildon Hills in three and bridled the Tweed with a curb of stone'. His alleged grave is shown in Melrose Abbey.

SCOTT, Michael
(1789–1835)

Author, born in Cowlairs, Glasgow, the son of a merchant. Educated at Glasgow High School and Glasgow University (1801–5), he went to seek his fortune in Jamaica. He spent a few years in the West Indies, but in 1822 settled in Glasgow. His vivid, amusing stories, *Tom Cringle's Log* (1829–33) and *The Cruise of the Midge* (1834–5), first appeared serially in *Blackwood's Magazine*.

SCOTT, Mike
(1958 –)

Rock singer and songwriter, born in Ayr. After working with local band Another Pretty

Face while studying at Edinburgh University, he moved to London, where he formed the group The Waterboys in 1981. Since then he has been the group's only constant member. Their début eponymous album, in 1983, went largely unnoticed, but they attracted a growing following with *A Pagan Place* (1984) and *This Is The Sea* (1985). Their first entry into the UK singles chart was with 'The Whole Of The Moon' (1985), but Scott refused to appear on *Top Of The Pops* to promote the record and its success was limited. Shortly afterwards he moved to Dublin where folk influences have played an increasing role in his music, as typified by the albums *Fisherman's Blues* (1988) and *Room To Roam* (1990). In 1991 'Whole Of The Moon' was reissued, bringing fresh chart success.

SCOTT, Tom

(1918 –)

Poet, born in Glasgow and educated at St Andrews University, and later as a mature student at Edinburgh University. He was first published in *Poetry London* in 1940, but his first success was *Seeven Poems o' Maister Francis Villon* (1953), a Scots rendering of the French. His *The Ship and Ither Poems* (1963) takes the sinking of the *Titanic* as an allegory for the evils of the class structure and also examines the experiences of Ahab, Ulysses and others as examples of individuals gaining freedom through the difficulties of experience. He is best known for his poem 'Brand the Builder' (1975) which meditates upon Scottish working-class values and contrasts the real builders with the anti-Scottish academics and parochial Church stalwarts of St Andrews. He has published a critical study of **William Dunbar**'s poems and his work in English includes *The Tree* (1977), which examines universal themes of existence.

SCOTT, Sir Walter

(1771–1832)

Novelist and poet, born in Edinburgh, son of a Writer to the Signet and of Anne Rutherford, a daughter of the Professor of Medicine at the university. When young he contracted polio in his right leg, which lamed him for life, and was sent to his grandfather's farm at Sandyknowe to recuperate, thus coming to know the Border country which figures often in his work. Neither at the High School,

Edinburgh, nor at the university did he show much promise. His real education came from people and from books — Fielding and **Smollett**, Walpole's *Castle of Otranto*, Spenser and Ariosto and, above all, Percy's *Reliques* and German ballad poetry. He did better in his father's office as a law clerk, and became an advocate in 1792. His first publication consisted of rhymed versions of ballads by Bürger in 1796. The following year he was an ardent volunteer in the yeomanry, and on one of his 'raids' he met at Gilsland spa Charlotte Charpentier, daughter of a French émigré, whom he married in Carlisle on Christmas Eve, 1797. Two years later he was appointed Sheriff-Depute of Selkirkshire. The ballad meanwhile absorbed all his literary interest. *Glenfinlas* and *The Eve of St John* were followed by a translation of Goethe's *Göetz von Berlichingen*. His skill as a writer of ballads led to the publication by **James Ballantyne**, a printer in Kelso, of Scott's first major work, *The Border Minstrelsy* (vols 1 and 2, 1802; vol 3, 1803). The *Lay of the Last Minstrel* (1805) made him the most popular author of the day. The other romances which followed — *Marmion* (1808), and *The Lady of the Lake* (1810) — enhanced his fame, but the lukewarm reception of *Rokeby* (1811), *Lord of the Isles* (1815) and *Harold the Dauntless* (1817) warned him that he should turn his attention away from the ballad form and concentrate on writing novels. In 1811 he built his country seat, Abbotsford, near Galashiels, in the Borders. The business troubles that overshadowed his later career began when he set up a publishing firm with James Ballantyne and his brother John in the Canongate in Edinburgh. All went well at first, but with expanding business came expanding ambitions, and when **Archibald Constable** with his London connections entered the scene, Scott lost all control over the financial side of the vast programme of publication, much of it hack work, on which he now embarked; hence the bankruptcy in the middle of his great career as a novelist (1826). The Waverley novels fall into three groupsfirst, from *Waverley* (1814) to *The Bride of Lammermoor* (1819) and *A Legend of Montrose* (1819); next, from *Ivanhoe* (1820) to *The Talisman* (1825), the year before his bankruptcy; *Woodstock* (1826) opens the last period, which closes with *Castle Dangerous* and *Count Robert of Paris* (1832), in the year of his death. The first period established the historical novel based, in Scott's case, on religious dissension and the clash of races English and Scottish, Highland and Lowland, his aim being to illustrate manners but also to soften animosities. In *Guy Mannering* (1815) his great humorous characters first appear, and are found in *Old Mortality* (1816) and *The Heart of Midlothian* (1818). His Scottish vein exhausted, he turned to England in the middle ages in *Ivanhoe*. With *The Monastery* and *The Abbot* (1820) he moved to Reformation times, where he showed a respect for what was venerable in the ancient Church, a mood which might have been predicted from his harshness to the Covenanters in *Old Mortality*. This group of works is distinguished by its portrait gallery of queens and princes. The highlights in his last period are the not entirely successful *Woodstock* (1826), and *The Fair Maid of Perth* (1828), where again the ballad motif appears. He worked best on a traditional or ballad theme, as in *Proud Maisie*, but Highland themes, as in *Pibroch of Donuil Dhu* (1816), equally proved his lyric powers. He was also writing other works for the publishers, much of which was simply hack work — the editions of Dryden (1808), of Swift (1814), and the *Life of Napoleon* (9 vols, 1827). However, the *Tales of a Grandfather* (1828–30) keeps its charm, and his three letters 'from Malachi Malagrowther' (1826) are remembered for their patriotic assertion of Scottish interests. A national figure, he helped to supervise the celebration for George IV's visit to Edinburgh in 1822. His last years were plagued by illness, and in 1831–2 he toured the Mediterranean in a government frigate. He died at Abbotsford soon after his return, and was buried in the ruins of Dryburgh Abbey.

SCOTT, Walter of Satchells

(c.1614 – c.1694)

Soldier and genealogist. He served in Holland and at home from 1629 to 1686, and dictated (because he could not write) a metrical *History of the Scotts* (1688).

SCOTT, William

(1913–89)

Scottish-Irish painter, born in Greenock, Renfrewshire. He studied at Belfast College of Art (1928–31) and at the Royal Academy Schools (1931–5). After World War II he taught at Bath Academy of Art, Corsham (1946–56). He visited Canada and New York in 1953, meeting Jackson Pollock, de Kooning, and other leading Abstract Expressionists. His preferred subject was still-life, painted in a simplified, nearly-abstract way. He won first prize in the John Moores Liverpool Exhibition in 1959.

SCOTT, William Bell

(1811–90)

Painter and poet, born in Edinburgh, brother of **David Scott** and son of an engraver. While training as an engraver he also began to write poetry and had verses published for the first time in 1831. He exhibited paintings at the Royal Scottish Academy from 1834. He moved to London in 1837 and in the following year his first volume of poetry was published. He married in 1839, began exhibiting at the Royal Academy from 1842 and, in 1843, became Master of the Government School of Design in Newcastle. His major paintings were of scenes of Northumberland history which were exhibited in London and Newcastle prior to their installation (1861) at Wallington Hall, Northumberland. He moved back to London in 1864 and, in 1875, published *Poems* dedicated to his friends D G Rossetti, William Morris and A C Swinburne. His *Autobiographical Notes* were published posthumously in 1892.

SCOTT, Willie

(1897–1990)

Traditional singer, born in Canonbie, Dumfriesshire. He left school at the age of 11 to work on a Borders farm and later became a hill shepherd, spending the last 17 years of his working life at a farm near Duns, Berwickshire. Scott was renowned as one of the great traditional ballad-singers of his day, his pure vocal tone and rich, rolling dialect forming the perfect instrument for his large repertoire of little-known Border songs. While the School of Scottish Studies has a large collection of his work, his only solo commercial recording is *The Shepherd's Song* (1968).

SCOTT-MONCRIEFF, Charles Kenneth Michael

(1889–1930)

Man of letters, celebrated as the translator into English of Proust, Stendhal, Pirandello, *Beowulf* and the *Song of Roland*. He was educated at Winchester and Edinburgh University, and was on the staff of *The Times* from 1921 to 1923.

SCOUGALL, or SCOUGAL, David
(fl.1654–77)

Painter. Although little is known about him, he was the most important portrait painter in Scotland after the generation of **George Jamesone**. Many Scottish houses contain portraits attributed to him, although many might be by John Scougall, possibly a nephew, while others may simply be attributed to him on the grounds of age.

SELCRAIG, Alexander See
SELKIRK, Alexander

SELKIRK, or SELCRAIG, Alexander
(1676–1721)

Sailor, born in Largo, Fife, the son of a shoemaker. He was the original of Defoe's Robinson Crusoe. He ran away to sea in 1695, and in 1704 joined the South Sea buccaneers. In 1704 he quarrelled with his captain, William Dampier, and at his own request was put ashore on the uninhabited island of Juan Fernández. Having lived alone there for four years and four months, he was at last taken off by the London physician Thomas Dover, who was second captain onboard a privateer. He returned to Largo in 1712, and at his death was a lieutenant on a man-of-war.

SELKIRK, Thomas Douglas, 5th Earl of
(1771–1820)

Colonizer. He settled 800 emigrants from the Scottish Highlands in Canada in Prince Edward Island (1803), and in the Red River Valley, Manitoba, although twice evicted by soldiers from the Fort William post of the Northwest Fur Company (1815–16).

SELLAR, Patrick
(1780–1851)

Lawyer and estate factor, born in Moray. He became notorious during the Highland Clearances as factor to the 1st Duke of Sutherland for the brutality with which he evicted the crofting tenant families of Strathnaver in 1814 to make room for sheep. He was brought to trial by Robert MacKid, the Sheriff-Substitute of Sutherland, but was acquitted, and later became a sheep farmer in Morvern.

SELLAR, William Young
(1825–90)

Classical scholar, born near Golspie, Sutherland, son of the notorious **Patrick Sellar**. Educated at The Edinburgh Academy, he studied classics at Glasgow University and Balliol College, Oxford. He was Professor of Greek at St Andrews University (1859–63), and thereafter Professor of Latin at Edinburgh University. He made his name by his brilliant *Roman Poets of the Republic* (1863), which was followed by *The Roman Poets of the Augustan Age Virgil* (1877) and *Horace and the Elegiac Poets* (1892), the latter edited by his nephew, **Andrew Lang**.

SEMEONOFF, Boris
(1910 –)

Russian-born psychologist, born in St Petersburg. A graduate of Edinburgh University (MA, MEd, PhD), he joined the staff of its Department of Psychology in 1933 under **James Drever** 'Primus'. After World War II, during which he worked for the War Office Selection Boards, he returned to the department, now under **James Drever** 'Secundus', until his retirement in 1980. He was President of the British Psychological Society 1968–89. He was the author of *Diagnostic Performance Tests* (1958, with E Trist) and *Projective Techniques* (1976), and was editor of *Personality Assessment: Selected Readings* (1966). Highly influential in the study of projective testing for personality assessment, he was a salient figure for generations of psychology students at Edinburgh.

SEMPILL, Francis
(c.1616–1682)

Poet, born at the ancestral home of Beltrees in Renfrewshire. Little is known of his life. He studied law, probably in Europe, and was appointed Sheriff-Depute of Renfrewshire in 1677. He was the son of **Robert Sempill** (?1595 – ?1665) who is well known for his poem 'The life and death of Habbie Simpson, the Piper of Kilbarchan'. Francis shared his father's gift for vernacular poetry and wrote 'The Banishment of Poverty by James Duke of Albany', in which he recounts being pursued by merciless poverty until he takes refuge in the debtor's sanctuary at the Abbey of Holyrood. His authorship is tentatively ascribed to numerous other pieces, including the poems 'Blythesome Wedding' and

'Maggie Lauder', though it is suggested that he may only have re-worked them from earlier sources. He worked in the traditional form of the *Christis Kirk* stanza which was used largely to create comic caricatures of peasant customs and rites.

SEMPILL, Robert
(?1530–1595)

Ballad writer, a supporter of the Reformers. He spent some time in Paris, but left after the St Bartholomew's Day Massacre, and spent most of the rest of his life in Edinburgh. He was probably employed in some military capacity (he was present at the sieges of Leith and of Edinburgh), and there is evidence that he was at one point employed at court. He wrote witty ballads full of coarse vigour, such as *The Legend of a Lymaris Life* and *Sege of the Castel of Edinburgh*. He was an enemy of **Mary, Queen of Scots** and wrote satirical Reformation pieces, such as the *Life of the Tulchene Bishop of St Andrews*.

SEMPILL, Robert
(?1595 – ?1665)

Poet, from the hamlet of Beltrees, Renfrewshire. He revived the methods of the Scottish 'Makars', started a trend for poetry in the vernacular, and invented a 'Standard Habbie' six-line stanza. He wrote *Habbie Simson*, *The Blythesome Bridal* and, possibly, *Maggie Lauder*.

SERF, St
(? 7th century)

Saint who founded the Church of Culross between 697 and 706, but who nevertheless figures in the legend of St **Kentigern** as his teacher. He is associated with an island on Loch Leven.

SETON, Sir Alexander, first Earl of Dunfermline
(?1555–1622)

Jurist. He was intended for the Church but after the Reformation turned to the law and passed advocate. Admitted to the Privy Council in 1585, he became a Lord of Session in 1586 as Lord Urquhart. In 1593 he was advanced to be Lord President of the Court of Session and thereafter became one of the king's principal advisers and, in 1596, one of the Commission of Eight (the Octavians), charged with putting the royal finances in order. He was also Lord Provost of Edinburgh for nine years. In 1597/8 Fyvie was erected into a barony for him. Thereafter he was called Lord Fyvie, and was entrusted with the guardianship of Prince Charles, later Charles I. In 1604 he became Vice-Chancellor and one of the commission appointed to discuss closer union with England. Appointed Lord Chancellor, he resigned the office of Lord President. In 1605 he was created Earl of Dunfermline. Though inclined to Catholicism he was regarded as having acted with moderation towards religious disputants, and has been called the greatest lawyer that had to that date presided in the Court of Session.

SETON, George
(1822–1908)

Herald, genealogist and legal writer. He was called to the Scottish Bar in 1846 but did not achieve a practice. In 1854 he became secretary to the Registrar-General for Scotland and in 1862 also superintendent of civil service examinations in Scotland, offices which he held until 1889. He wrote *The Law and Practice of Heraldry in Scotland* (1863) which became accepted as a standard authority, *Memoirs of An Ancient House: A History of the Family of Seton during Eight Centuries* (2 vols, 1896), *The Life of Alexander Seton, Earl of Dunfermline, Lord Chancellor of Scotland* (1882) and numerous lesser works.

SHANKLY, Bill (William)
(1913–81)

Footballer and manager. With **Jock Stein** and Sir **Matt Busby** he was one of the greatest football managers in recent times. A tireless, biting wing-half, he won an FA Cup Medal with Preston North End and five Scotland caps. As a postwar manager he found success with Liverpool after unremarkable spells with Carlisle, Grimsby, Workington and Huddersfield. He created a team which was not only highly successful in Britain and Europe but one which encouraged individual expression and communicated great exhilaration to the spectators. Although he was fanatically committed to the game, there was nothing grim in the football which his team produced.

SHARP, Alan
(1934 –)

Novelist and filmmaker, born near Dundee and raised in Greenock. He left school at 14 and worked in the shipyards as an apprentice joiner. Following National Service in the army, his occupations ranged from labourer to assisting a private detective, before he began to write for BBC radio and television and completed a widely praised auto-biographical novel, *A Green Tree in Gedde* (1964), which evoked his working-class background. He followed this with *The Wind Shifts* (1967) and then embarked upon a career as a screenwriter in Hollywood. Able to invest traditional genres such as the western and the thriller with trenchant resonances of issues in contemporary American life, his filmed screenplays include *The Hired Hand* (1971), *Ulzana's Raid* (1972), *Night Moves* (1975) and *The Osterman Weekend* (1983). More recently he has turned to direction with the film *Little Treasure* (1985).

SHARP, James
(1613–79)

Prelate, born at Banff Castle. He studied for the Church at King's College, Aberdeen (1633–7). He signed the National Covenant against Charles I in 1638, and became minister at Crail in 1647. In 1651 he was taken prisoner to London by Cromwell's men, along with some other ministers, but was allowed back to Scotland the following year. In 1657 he was chosen by the more moderate party in the Church to plead their cause before Cromwell. In this he was unsuccessful, but his intelligence made a favourable impression on Cromwell. Sent by Monk to Breda, as part of Monk's plan to effect a Restoration, he had several interviews with Charles II in exile there (1660). His correspondence for some months after his return from Holland is full of apprehensions of Prelacy; but its perfidy stands revealed in a letter to the Earl of Middleton, which proves that he was then in hearty co-operation with Clarendon and the English bishops for the re-establishment of Episcopacy in Scotland. His bribe was a great one, for in December he was consecrated Archbishop of St Andrews. The wily tool of **Lauderdale**, an oppressor of those he had betrayed, he soon became an object of popular detestation and of contempt to his employers. On 3 May 1679, 12 Covenanters, led by **John Balfour of Kinloch** and David Hackston, dragged him from his coach on Magus Muir and brutally murdered him.

SHARP, William, pseudonym **Fiona Macleod**
(1855–1905)

Writer, born in Paisley, and educated at Glasgow University. After some time in Australia he settled in London (1879), working as a journalist and editor. Throughout his life he travelled widely. He published a collection of poetry, *Earth's Voices*, in 1884. He wrote books on contemporary English, French and German poets, but is chiefly remembered as the author of the remarkable series of Celtic — or neo-Celtic — tales and romances by 'Fiona Macleod' — a pseudonym he systematically refused to acknowledge. They include *Pharais* (1894), *The Mountain Lovers* (1895), *The Sin-Eater* (1895) and *The Immortal Hour* (1900).

SHARPE, Charles Kirkpatrick
(1781–1851)

Antiquary, born in Hoddam Castle, Dumfries. Educated in Edinburgh and at Christ Church College, Oxford, he was a lifelong friend of Sir **Walter Scott** and contributed two original ballads to Scott's *Minstrelsy of the Scottish Border* (3 vols, 1802–3). He edited editions for the Bannatyne Club and the Abbotsford Club, but is chiefly remembered for his lively correspondence (2 vols, 1888).

SHARPEY-SCHAFER, Sir Edward Albert
(1850–1953)

Pioneer physiologist. Born in London and educated at University College, London, he took his MRCS in 1874, before starting physiological research, first at Oxford, and then as Jodrell Professor of Physiology at University College. He went to Edinburgh as Professor of Physiology in 1899. His major research interests were in the ductless glands and their secretions, and he published *The Endocrine Organs* in 1916. But he was perhaps most widely known for the method of resuscitation after apparent death by drowning, known as the Schäfer method, and practised worldwide. He experimented on himself and studied the pulmonary circulation and the sensory changes resulting from nerve damage. He made many other contributions to physiological research and wrote or edited many important textbooks. Elected FRS in 1878, he received many other honours. He lived most of his later life in North Berwick, where he created a famous garden.

SHAW, Geoffrey Mackintosh
(1927–78)

Minister and politician, born in Edinburgh, and educated at Edinburgh Academy and Edinburgh University. Ordained a Church of Scotland minister, he was actively involved with the Gorbals Group in Glasgow, going on to work as a minister with the socially deprived in Harlem, New York, and Bridgeton, Glasgow. Elected as a Labour member of Glasgow City Council in 1968, and of Strathclyde Regional Council in 1974, in the same year he was appointed the first Convenor of Strathclyde Council, the largest local government unit in western Europe. Here he strove to integrate the diverse areas represented by the authority into a harmonious whole. He was keenly interested in inner-city problems, especially the Glasgow Eastern Area Renewal project. He died in office.

SHAW, Richard Norman
(1831–1912)

Scottish-born architect, born in Edinburgh, the son of a lace merchant. Educated in Edinburgh and Newcastle, he worked briefly for an unknown firm of architects in London before being articled to the office of **William Burn**, and then moving, after a period of foreign travel, to act as chief assistant to George Edmund Street. He published *Architectural Sketches from the Continent* (1858), an exemplary and influential folio. From 1862 he shared an office with William Eden Nesfield, forming a brief partnership. Together they developed the 'Old English' style which was adopted widely, notably at Glen Andred (1866), Groombridge, Sussex and Cragside, Northumberland (from 1870). He popularized the Queen Anne revival, introduced by **John James Stevenson**, in such designs as the enlightened garden suburb, Bedford Park (1877–80), leading the move away from Victorian style back to traditional Georgian. By the 1890s he was England's premier architect. A founder member of the Art Workers' Guild, he was co-editor of the controversial essays, *Architecture a Profession or an Art* (1892).

SHEPHERD, Nan
(1893–1981)

Novelist and critic, raised in Aberdeen, where she graduated from university in 1915. She worked until 1956 as a lecturer at Aberdeen College of Education and was a friend and correspondent of **Neil Gunn**. Her three novels—*The Quarry Wood* (1928), *The Weatherhouse* (1930), and *A Pass in the Grampians* (1933)—all deal with aspects of a young woman's development in north-east Scotland. In these works she is concerned to show the way women are societized to make compromises which do not allow them to fulfil their potential. Her creative work has been largely ignored by critics. As well as writing novels she was also involved in academic research. Her last book was a non-fiction study of the mountains, *The Living Mountain* (1977).

SHEPPERSON, George Albert
(1922 –)

English-born historian, born in Peterborough. Educated at King's School, Peterborough, he won a scholarship to St John's College, Cambridge, where he studied English and history. During World War II he was seconded to the King's African Rifles, (1942–6), notably in the Burma campaign. From his work with African soldiers stemmed his lifelong devotion to racial equality and the furtherance of Black studies in the history and literature of Africa and the USA. In 1948 he was appointed Lecturer in Imperial and American History at Edinburgh University, being promoted to Senior Lecturer (1960), Reader (1961), and **William Robertson** Professor of Commonwealth and American History (1963–86). There he sought to further the Scottish implications of his subjects. Unrivalled in his voracious reading and collection of evidence, oral and written, on Black history and its Scottish links, he was an outstanding pioneer in the professionalization of his several fields in the UK and beyond. He was a founder-member (and subsequent Chairman) of the British Association for American Studies, and a founder-member of the British Association for Canadian Studies. Largely due to his work, Edinburgh University embarked on its North American Studies Programme, Centre for Canadian Studies, and Centre for African Studies. Dean of Arts at Edinburgh (1974–7), he held various visiting professorships, particularly in the USA. His *magnum opus*, written jointly with John Price, was *Independent African: John Chilembwe* (1958), a study of the Nyasaland Rising of 1915, which opened up the intellectual origins of African nationalism. His *David Livingstone and the*

Rovuma (1964) was the most substantial of his many works on the Scottish-African connection. He received honorary doctorates from York (1987) and Edinburgh (1991) universities.

SHINWELL, Emmanuel, Baron
(1884–1986)

Labour politician, born in Spitalfields, London. He began work as an errand boy in Glasgow at the age of 12. An early student of public library and street-corner Socialism, he was elected to Glasgow Trades Council in 1911 and, one of the 'wild men of Clydeside', served a five-month prison sentence for incitement to riot in 1921. MP in 1931 and Secretary to the Department of Mines (1924, 1930–1), in 1935 he defeated **Ramsay MacDonald** at Seaham Harbour, Durham, in one of the most bitterly contested election battles of modern times. From 1942 he was Chairman of the Labour Party Committee, which drafted the manifesto 'Let us face the future' on which Labour won the 1945 election. As Minister of Fuel and Power he nationalized the mines (1946), and the following year, when he was said to be a scapegoat for the February fuel crisis, he became Secretary of State for War. From 1950 to 1951 he was Minister of Defence. In these last two offices, Manny's considerable administrative ability outshone his prickly party political belligerence and earned him the respect of such discerning critics in defence matters as Churchill and Montgomery. In his later years he mellowed into a backbench 'elder statesman'. He was parliamentary Labour Party Chairman 1964–7, was created CH in 1965 and awarded a life peerage in 1970. He wrote several autobiographical works, including *Conflict without Malice* (1955), *I've Lived through it All* (1973), and *Lead with the Left* (1981).

SHIRREFF, Patrick
(1791–1876)

Farmer, born near Haddington, East Lothian. The pioneer of cereal hybridizing, he produced many varieties of wheat and oats.

SHORT, James
(1710–68)

Astronomer and pioneering telescope maker, born in Edinburgh. Orphaned at the age of ten, he was educated in Edinburgh at George Heriot's Hospital, the High School and the university, where he became interested in science and mathematics. Encouraged by his professor, **Colin Maclaurin**, he learnt the difficult technique of making telescope mirrors, first of glass, then of speculum metal and spent the rest of his life perfecting the art. Establishing himself as a scientific instrument maker in London from 1738, he earned a high reputation in Britain and abroad. He was the first to parabolize a telescope speculum successfully, and the first to make high quality reflecting observatory telescopes in any number, the largest having a nominal focal length of 12 feet. In 1757 he was one of the few British scientists to be honoured with membership of the Royal Swedish Academy of Science, and in 1760 he was elected a member of council of the Royal Society. In his working life of about 38 years he is known to have made 1370 telescopes.

SIBBALD, Sir Robert
(1641–1722)

Naturalist and physician, born in Edinburgh. He became a physician there, but gave much time to botany and zoology. He helped to establish a botanic garden near Holyrood House with Sir **Andrew Balfour** (1676–80), and was the virtual founder of the Royal College of Physicians of Edinburgh. He was appointed Professor of Medicine and Scottish Geographer Royal. He wrote *History of Fife* (1710), and pamphlets on medical subjects, natural history and antiquities.

SILLARS, Jim (James)
(1937–)

Nationalist politician, born in Ayrshire and educated at Ayr Academy. A fireman by profession, he soon rose to prominence in his union, going on to enter Parliament as Labour MP for South Ayrshire in 1970, where he won a reputation as a vigorous and clever debater. In 1976 he left the Labour Party to form the Scottish Labour Party, which advocated greater self-government, but lost his seat in 1979. After winding up his new party, he joined the Scottish National Party, and in the early 1980s was the leader of the left-wing element in the SNP's internal struggles. He returned to Parliament as SNP candidate for Govan in 1988, which some saw as a turning point in the party's fortunes, but lost his seat in the 1992 general election. He is married to **Margo MacDonald**.

SIM, Alastair
(1900–76)

Actor, born in Edinburgh. Destined to follow in the family tailoring business, he was pulled in a different direction by his theatrical interests. He was a lecturer in elocution at Edinburgh University from 1925 to 1930 and made his professional stage début in a London production of *Othello* (1930). Further stage work, including a season with the Old Vic, led to his film début in *Riverside Murder* (1935). His lugubrious manner, distinctive physiognomy and inimitable vocal range made him a cherished comic performer, equally adept at mirthful or menacing characterizations. His numerous films include *Green for Danger* (1946), *The Happiest Days of Your Life* (1950), *Scrooge* (1951), *Laughter in Paradise* (1951) and *The Belles of St. Trinians* (1954). On stage he enjoyed a long association with playwright **James Bridie** and also appeared in *The Tempest* (1962), *Too True To Be Good* (1965), *The Magistrate* (1969) and *Dandy Dick* (1973) among many others.

SIMPLE MINDS See KERR, Jim

SIMPSON, Bill
(1931–86)

Actor, born in Dunure, Ayrshire. After spells of employment in a shoe shop, as an insurance clerk and in the Royal Air Force, he won a place at drama college in Glasgow and then spent two years as a newscaster with Scottish Television before securing a role as a thief in the long-running television series *Z Cars*. Fame arrived with the title role as **A J Cronin**'s family doctor in *Dr Finlay's Casebook* in 1962, and over the next nine years he played the character in 206 episodes. His close association with the part may have limited his subsequent career and, despite appearances on stage, in pantomime and in such television productions as *Scotch On The Rocks* (1972) and *The Good Companions* (1980), it was his alcohol-related health problems and private life that kept his name in the news, rather than fresh acting triumphs.

SIMPSON, Sir George
(1792–1860)

Scottish-born Canadian explorer. He was administrator of the Hudson's Bay Company's territory (1821–56). In 1828 he made an overland journey round the world. Simpson's Falls and Cape George Simpson are named after him.

SIMPSON, Sir James Young
(1811–70)

Obstetrician, born in Bathgate, West Lothian, the son of a baker. With the financial support of the rest of his large family he went to Edinburgh University at the age of 14, studying arts, then medicine, and becoming Professor of Midwifery in 1840. He originated the use of ether as anaesthetic in childbirth (January 1847), and experimenting on himself and his assistants in the search for a better anaesthetic, discovered the required properties in chloroform (November 1847). He championed its use against medical and religious opposition until its employment by Queen Victoria at the birth of Prince Leopold (1853) signalled general acceptance. He founded gynaecology by his sound tests, championed hospital reform, and in 1847 became Physician to the Queen in Scotland.

SIMPSON, Myrtle Lillias, née Emslie
(1931 –)

Arctic explorer, travel writer, mountaineer and long-distance skier. Born and educated in India, the daughter of a Scottish Army Officer, she spent her early twenties climbing in New Zealand and Peru. In 1957 she married the medical researcher and explorer Dr Hugh Simpson, with whom she travelled Surinam and the Arctic. In 1965, as a member of the Scottish Trans-Greenland Expedition, she became the first woman to ski across the Greenland ice cap. In 1969 she attempted to walk to the North Pole unsupported, man-hauling a sledge for 45 days and covering a distance of 90 miles from Ward Hunt Island, reaching the farthest north for a woman at that time.

SIMPSON, William Douglas
(1896–1968)

Librarian, born in Aberdeen, and educated at Aberdeen Grammar School and Aberdeen University, where he took a first in history and was Caithness Prizeman and Forbes Gold Medallist (1919). He was in charge of Boy Scouts in the Admiralty Coastwatching

Service in Scotland (1917–18) and served on the Secretariat of the Ministry of National Service (1918). In 1919–20 he was Assistant to the Professor of History, **Charles Sanford Terry**, going on to become Lecturer in British History (1920–6). Meanwhile he became an archaeologist of distinction, concentrating chiefly on castles and conducting extensive excavations. In 1926 he became Librarian of the university and Registrar and Clerk of the General Council, retiring 1966. During this time he accumulated an astonishing collection of publications on the history and antiquities of the north-east and built up the University Library's collections. He wrote several volumes on castles, including *The Scottish Castle* (1924), *Castles from the Air* (1949), *The Castle of Bergen* (1960) (which contributed to his being made Commander of the Royal Order of St Olaf, Norway) and *Castles in Britain* (2nd ed 1967), and published various works on Scottish saints and many papers on historical, ecclesiastical and archaeological subjects, including *The Ancient Stones of Scotland* (2nd ed 1968).

SIMSON, Robert

(1687–1768)

Mathematician, born in West Kilbride, Ayrshire. Educated at Glasgow University, where he originally intended to study for the Church, he concentrated instead on mathematics, and in 1711 became Professor of Mathematics there, holding the post until his retiral in 1761. His life-work was the editing and restoration of the work of the ancient Greek geometers; his edition of Euclid's *Elements* (1758) was the basis of nearly all editions for over a century.

SINCLAIR, or ST CLAIR

The name of the Earls of Orkney and afterwards of Caithness. They were hereditary grandmaster masons of Scotland 1455–1736. Roslin Castle near Edinburgh was the seat of the St Clairs.

SINCLAIR, Sir Archibald Henry MacDonald, 1st Viscount Thurso

(1890–1970)

Liberal politician, descendant of Sir **John Sinclair**. Educated at Eton and the Royal Military Academy at Sandhurst, he served in the army (1910–21), entered Parliament in 1922, became Chief Whip (1930–1) and leader of the Liberals (1935–45), and was Secretary of State for Air in the Churchill administration (1940–5).

SINCLAIR, George

(c.1625–1696)

Philosopher, civil engineer, mining consultant and inventor. He was probably born in East Lothian, as it is known that he possessed property in Haddington. In 1654 he was appointed to the Chair of Philosophy at Glasgow University, and in the following year he was involved in attempts to explore a sunken Spanish galleon with a primitive form of diving bell. In 1666 he was forced to resign the Glasgow chair on religious grounds, and he moved to Edinburgh, where he appears to have taught mathematics at the university for a time. It is known that he was frequently consulted by Lothian mine-owners regarding problems of geology and drainage in their pits. He was also asked by the Edinburgh magistrates in 1672 to design and superintend the work of bringing a new water supply into the city from the springs at Comiston, which he accomplished in 1676. He was at last able to return in 1689 to Glasgow, where he occupied successively the chairs of philosophy and mathematics until his death.

SINCLAIR, Sir John, 1st Baronet

(1754–1835)

Politician and agricultural improver, born in Thurso Castle, Caithness. He studied at Edinburgh, Glasgow and Oxford, was admitted to both the Scottish and English Bars (1775–82), and sat in Parliament (1780–1811). In 1784 he published a *History of the Revenue of the British Empire*; and in 1786 was created a baronet. He established the Board of Agriculture in 1793 and supervised the compilation of the first *Statistical Account of Scotland* (1791–9), comprising a description of every parish in Scotland, mainly with the help of parish ministers. He developed the town of Thurso, and gave it its present layout; his statue (by Sir Francis Chantrey) stands in the main square. His daughter, Catherine (1800–64), wrote children's books, including *Holiday House* (1839).

SINGER, James Hyman, pseudonym Burns Singer

(1928–64)

American-born poet, born to a Scottish mother in New York City. He moved in 1932 to Glasgow, where he lived until 1945, with a brief evacuation to Aberdeenshire during the war. He began a degree in English at Glasgow University, but fearing that the university 'would kill my interest in English Literature and cripple whatever talent might then have been mine' he left for London and began a period of emotional and physical searching. He taught mathematics in London, left this to stay for a time in Cornwall where he was befriended by the poet W S Graham, spent three years in Europe and then returned to Glasgow to study zoology because 'I wanted to write poems about animals'. He worked in marine biology until his early death, with an interruption as a London journalist between 1955 and 1960. In 1956 he married Marie Battle, an American psychologist and painter. A recognized reviewer and essayist, he contributed to *Encounter* and the *Times Literary Supplement*. *Still and All* (1957) is the one book of his poetry published in his lifetime; he published a book about fishing, *Living Silver*, in the same year. His *Collected Poems* were published in 1970 and are prefaced by **Hugh MacDiarmid**, a poet he deeply admired and wrote upon.

SISSONS, John Brian

(1926 –)

English geographer, born in Batley, Yorkshire. Educated at Cambridge University, he was then appointed to Edinburgh University (1953), where he later became a Reader (1967). He has served on the Councils of the Edinburgh Geological Society, the Quaternary Research Association and the Institute of British Geographers. He is believed to have made the greatest contribution to Quaternary geomorphology in Britain, and revolutionized the interpretation of glacial and related raised marine features. A key text is *Geomorphology of the British Isles* (1976). His awards include the Royal Scottish Geographical Society Research Medal (1969) and the Back Award of the Royal Geographical Society.

SKENE, Sir John, Lord Curriehill

(c.1543–1617)

Advocate, Regent of St Mary's College, St Andrews. He was Ambassador, Lord Advocate (1589–94), Lord Clerk-Register (1594–1612) and Lord of Session (1594). In his capacity as a royal advocate he was a fervent witch prosecutor. He published a collection of the old Scots Acts (1597), compiled a Scottish legal dictionary, *De Verborum Significatione* (1597) and edited and translated a collection of old Scots laws, *Regiam Majestatem* (1609). He was the first Scottish legal antiquary, but most of his work is inaccurate.

SKENE, William Forbes

(1809–92)

Historian, born in Inverie, Knoydart, Inverness-shire. Educated at the Royal High School, Edinburgh, Frankfurt, and Aberdeen, he was also privately tutored in Gaelic. He graduated in law and practised as a lawyer in Edinburgh. He wrote *The Highlanders of Scotland* (1837), but his chief work was *Celtic Scotland; a History of Ancient Alba* (3 vols, 1876–80), based on research into original documents. In 1881 he succeeded **John Hill Burton** as Historiographer Royal for Scotland.

SKINNER, James Scott

(1843–1927)

Fiddler and composer, known as the 'Strathspey King', born in Banchory, Kincardineshire. As a child he learned the rudiments of Scots music but also received classical tuition. At the age of 19 he was able to outplay many leading Scots fiddlers in a national competition, moving the judge to say: 'Gentlemen, we have never before heard the like of this from a beardless boy'. His virtuoso playing continued to dazzle audiences during his long career as a concert performer both in Britain and the USA. Several recordings, made when he was probably past his peak, are available. Of his many compositions — over 600 — some of the most popular are 'The Bonnie Lass o' Bon-Accord', 'The Laird o' Drumblair' and 'The Miller o' Hirn'.

SKINNER, John

(1721–1807)

Historian and songwriter, born in Birse, Aberdeenshire, the son of a teacher. Educated at Aberdeen University, he went on to work as a schoolmaster and tutor, before becoming an Episcopalian minister at Longside near Peterhead (1742). Although he was not a staunch Jacobite, his house was pillaged and his chapel burnt in 1746, and in 1753 he spent a few months in prison for preaching to a group larger than four. A dedicated minister, he also devoted much time to his own studies. He wrote *The Ecclesiastical History of Scotland* (1788) and *A Preservative against Presbytery*, as well as several songs, of which 'The Ewie wi' the crookit horn' and 'Tullochgorum' are the best known, the latter earning Burns's encomium of being 'the best Scotch song ever Scotland saw'. His son, John (1744–1816), was a Bishop of Aberdeen.

SLATER, Oscar
(1873–1948)

German Jew resident in Glasgow, Scotland, wrongly convicted of the murder of Marion Gilchrist in 1909. Three witnesses identified him as the man seen leaving the scene of the crime, although their descriptions varied considerably and at least one of them was thought to have seen Slater's photograph before identifying him. After the trial, at which he was not called to give evidence, he was sentenced to death but this was commuted to life imprisonment. Because of protests of injustice by **Conan Doyle** and others, he was released after 19 years and received £6000 in compensation.

SLESSOR, Mary
(1848–1915)

Missionary, born in Aberdeen. She worked as a mill girl in Dundee from childhood but, conceiving a burning ambition to become a missionary, got herself accepted by the United Presbyterian Church for teaching in Calabar, Nigeria (1876), where she spent many years of devoted work among the natives, concentrating less on converting them to Christianity than on eradicating cruel tribal customs such as human sacrifice. Known among them as 'Great Mother', she was given legal authority in their territories by the British government.

SMALL, Leonard
(1905 –)

Church of Scotland minister, one of the most famed preachers of his generation. Educated at the universities of Edinburgh, Berlin and Zürich, he pursued ministries in Bathgate, Kilmarnock and finally at St Cuthberts, Edinburgh, where he distinguished himself as a preacher of international renown, becoming

a major figure in Scottish Church life. Moderator of the General Assembly in 1966, he was also appointed Chaplain to the Queen in 1967. A whole range of honours was heaped on him, including Doctor of Divinity, Edinburgh, and the CBE (1975). His small but significant body of writings was of a devotional and apologetic nature, and reflected his down-to-earth, colourful teaching and preaching style. Titles include *The Problem of Suffering* (1954) and *What I Believe* (1970). A man of boundless energy, he is a key figure in issues concerning the aged in Scotland.

SMELLIE, William
(1740–95)

Editor, printer and antiquary, born in Edinburgh, the son of an architect. Educated at the High School, he was apprenticed to a printer in 1752 but he gained permission to attend classes in botany at the university and was so well thought of that on his professor's absence he was once asked to continue his lectures. In 1765 he set up his own printing business, which in time became printer to the university, and, with Andrew Bell and Colin MacFarquhar, produced the first edition of the *Encyclopaedia Britannica* (1768–71), much of which was later ascribed to him. A founder member of the Society of Antiquaries in 1780, he helped prepare the ground for the first statistical account of Scotland (later undertaken by Sir **John Sinclair**). **Robert Burns** found his company congenial, and described him as 'that old Veteran in Genius, Wit and B[awd]ry'. Smellie printed the first edition of Burns's poems for the publisher **William Creech**.

SMILES, Samuel
(1812–1904)

Writer and social reformer, born in Haddington, East Lothian. He studied medicine at Edinburgh, and published *Physical Education* (1838). He practised in Haddington, and then settled as a surgeon in Leeds, but became Editor of the *Leeds Times* (1838–42), Secretary of the Leeds and Thirsk Railway (1845), and Secretary of the South Eastern Railway (1854–66). While at Leeds he met George Stephenson, and undertook a Life of him (1857). His most celebrated work was *Self-help* (1859), with its short biographies of great men and the admonition 'Do thou likewise', which made the ideal Victorian school-prize. He wrote many other improving works, including *Character* (1871), *Thrift* (1875), and *Duty* (1880), and also *Lives of the Engineers* (1861–2).

SMILLIE, Robert
(1857–1940)

Labour politician, born of Scottish parents in Belfast. Starting out as a miner in Lanarkshire, he was President of the Scottish Miners' Federation from 1894 to 1918 and again from 1921; from 1912 to 1921 he was President of the Miners' Federation of Great Britain. A friend of **Keir Hardie**, he was a founder member of the Independent Labour Party (ILP). He was Labour MP for Morpeth (1923–9).

SMITH, Adam
(1723–90)

Economist and philosopher, born in Kirkcaldy, whose *Wealth of Nations* is the first masterpiece in political economy. The posthumous son of the Comptroller of Customs, he studied at Glasgow and Oxford universities. From 1748 he became one of the brilliant circle in Edinburgh which included **David Hume**, **John Home**, **Hugh Blair**, Lord **Hailes** and **William Robertson**. In 1751 he became Professor of Logic at Glasgow, later becoming Professor of Moral Philosophy (1752–64). As a result of the suddenness of his appointment to Glasgow, he gave his Logic class the *Lectures on Rhetoric and Belles-Lettres* he had earlier delivered publicly in Edinburgh. This pioneered what was to become the teaching of English literature. In 1759 he published his *Theory of Moral Sentiments*, adapting a key doctrine of 'sympathy' from Frances Hutcheson. This involves comprehending others' feelings with the same feelings stirred in ourselves (as when I grieve when I see you in grief); and judging my own responses in relation to those of an imaginary 'impartial Spectator' within myself. In France as tutor to Henry, 3rd Duke of Buccleuch, he met in Paris Quesnay and Turgot, and worked on the masterpiece which he was to continue on his return to Kirkcaldy in 1766, enjoying access to Edinburgh's literary society once more. Before moving to London in 1776, he recognized the decline of his friend Hume's health, though Hume lived to applaud Smith's greatest success that year. Smith's moving account of Hume's end, written to the publisher Strahan and published with

Hume's autobiography, caused annoyance by depicting a non-religious man dying with such dignity. The masterpiece which brought Smith's success was a work in five sections, which he originally intended to be only the first part of a complete theory of society, which would cover natural theology, ethics, politics and law. This single volume, *Inquiry into the Nature and Causes of the Wealth of Nations* (1766), examined the consequences of economic freedom, such as the division of labour, the function of markets and mediums of exchange and the international implications. He attacked medieval mercantile monopolies and the theories of the French physiocrats, who saw land as the economic basis of wealth. His doctrine did not, however, support full 'laissez faire', for he sought to implement, through economics, his earlier work on moral influence. His powerful model of economic growth asserted that a desire for betterment leads to saving and investment, which makes possible the division of labour and increased productivity. At a public dinner, Pitt invited Smith to be seated first, as 'we are all your scholars'. Appointment as Commissioner of Customs took Smith back to Edinburgh in 1778; there he died and was buried in the Canongate churchyard. He was elected FRS in 1767 and Lord Rector of Glasgow University in 1787. His works (edited by **Dugald Stewart** in 1811–12) include essays on the formation of languages; the history of astronomy; classical physics and logic; and the arts. His Glasgow *Lectures on Justice, Police, Revenue, Arms* (1896) were edited from notes by a student.

SMITH, Alexander
(1830–67)

Poet and essayist, born in Kilmarnock, Ayrshire, the son of a lace-pattern designer. He himself became a pattern designer in Glasgow and Paisley, though he was not particularly gifted in this, and was more interested in his own poetry, sending occasional pieces to the *Glasgow Citizen*. His *Life Drama* (1851) was highly successful at first but was satirized by **Aytoun** in *Firmilian, a Spasmodic Tragedy* (1854), and the adjective 'spasmodic' has stuck to Smith's poetry ever since. In 1854 he was appointed Secretary to Edinburgh University, and the following year produced *Sonnets on the War* with Sydney Dobell, his brother poet of the 'Spasmodic' school. *City Poems* (1857) and *Edwin of Deira* (1861) were followed by essays, collected under the title *Dreamthorp* (1863), novels, and *A Summer in*

Skye (1865), an enthusiastic and vivid evocation of the island.

SMITH, Charles Stuart
(1936–91)

Naval architect, educated in Edinburgh and at Glasgow University. He joined the Admiralty Research Establishment at Dunfermline in 1962 and remained there until his untimely death. From the beginning he specialized in the theoretical analysis of ship structures and the application of the resulting data to practical and economic design procedures. When the navy decided to develop glass reinforced plastic (GRP) vessels for use against mines because of their non-magnetic properties, GRP was such a radically different material from steel that a whole new approach to structural design had to be evolved and tested. In this and many other aspects of naval architecture Smith's work was greatly respected, and his advice widely sought. He was awarded the **James Alfred Ewing** medal in 1989 for his contributions to structural engineering.

SMITH, Donald Alexander, Baron Strathcona
(1820–1914)

Financier, born in Forres, Morayshire. He joined the Hudson Bay Company in Canada as a clerk in 1838, and also carried on business as an independent financier. In 1862 he became a chief factor in the Company, and in 1868 was made head of its Montreal Department. In an astute move, he became the major shareholder, and by 1871 was controlling policy, in which capacity he negotiated new conditions with the traders whose ranks he had just left, to the benefit of the shareholders. Negotiating unsuccessfully with Louis Riel in the uprising which gave birth to Manitoba in 1871, he was held for a time by the rebels. He was a partner (with fellow-Scot **George Stephen**) in the company which rescued the Canadian Pacific Railway in 1880, and although not the prime mover, had the honour of driving the last spike in 1885. He became a director of the Hudson Bay Company in 1883, and Governor in 1889. Knighted in 1896, he was made Baronet the following year. A generous man, he made philanthropic donations to hospitals and schools, and served as High Commissioner to Canada in London from 1896, although lacking in sympathy with its Liberal administration.

SMITH, George
(1792–1871)

Distiller, born at the farm of Upper Drumin, on the Duke of Gordon's Glenlivet Estate, Banffshire. He was educated at the local school and by 1814 had become apprenticed to a carpenter. Taking advantage of the 1823 Act of Parliament he set himself up as a licensed distiller and was able to exploit the high reputation of Glenlivet whisky, hitherto built up by smugglers. A new distillery was built in 1825 with the support of the Duke of Gordon which, by the end of the 1830s, was producing 200 gallons a week of high quality malt. His son John Gordon was brought back from law studies in Edinburgh in order to assist expansion. In 1859 George Smith formed a new company with his son and built an additional distillery at Minmore to cope with demand. With the considerable assistance of the Edinburgh merchant, Andrew Usher, Smith ensured that Glenlivet became a household name.

SMITH, Sir George Adam
(1856–1942)

Biblical scholar, born in Calcutta. He was a minister in Aberdeen (1882–92), Professor of Hebrew at the Free Church College, Glasgow (1892–1909), and wrote studies on Isaiah and the minor prophets. From 1909 to 1935 he was Principal of Aberdeen University. His books include *Modern Criticism and the Preaching of the Old Testament* (1901), *Jerusalem* (1907–8), and *The Early Poetry of Israel* (1913).

SMITH, Iain Crichton, Gaelic Blain Mac A'Ghobhainn
(1928 –)

Poet and novelist, born on the Isle of Lewis. He was educated at the Nicolson Institute, Stornoway, and Aberdeen University. His career as a writer ran in tandem with that of a teacher in Clydebank, Dumbarton and Oban (retired 1977). Bilingual in Gaelic and English, he is an ambidextrous writer, rooted in the native culture but sensible to the wider audience that English admits. His first collection of poems, *The Long River*, appeared in 1955. Five years later came *Burn is Aran*, stories and poems in Gaelic which were highly praised. Since then he has been prolific and, while his output is of varied quality, at his best he is one of the modern masters of

Scottish literature. *Consider the Lilies* (1968) is undoubtedly his best-known work. Focusing on the plight of an old woman evicted from her croft and betrayed by the Church (Smith is no lover of the Free Church), it is a powerful indictment of the Clearances and the harsh reality of Highland life. *My Last Duchess* (1971) and *An End to Autumn* (1978) are similarly beautiful but bleak, although it would be wrong to imply that the sensibility behind them is humourless. Particularly since the publication of *Murdo and Other Stories* (1981) there is evidence of a writer hell-bent on mischief, the absurd side of his nature triumphing over a tendency towards introspection. In his poetry, however, Calvinism and the Isle of Lewis fuse to generate love and hate in almost equal measure, producing in the best poems a dramatic grandeur and awesome tension. His *Selected Poems* were published in 1982. He has been the recipient of many prizes.

SMITH, Ian McKenzie
(1935 –)

Painter, born in Montrose, Angus. He studied at Gray's School of Art, Aberdeen (1953–8) and, after teaching in Fife (1960–3), became an education officer for the Council of Industrial Design. He was appointed Director of Aberdeen Art Gallery and Museums in 1968. He was one of the first Scottish painters to adopt a style based on American minimal abstraction, whose intention is to evoke a meditative response, and his work is characterized by a restrained colour and tonal range.

SMITH, James
(c.1645–1731)

Architect, the son of the master mason of Tarbat, Ross-shire. He began studying for the priesthood in Rome, and thus received an architectural education in both Scotland and Italy. A pioneer of Scottish classicism, he was an instigator of British Palladianism. By 1677 he was working with Sir **William Bruce**, and by 1679 he was married to the eldest daughter of the Master Mason to the crown, Robert Mylne; in 1683 he became Surveyor of the Royal Works, responsible for Holyroodhouse. His fortunes fell, however, with the Union of the Parliaments in 1707. He was acquainted with **Colen Campbell**, author of *Vitruvius Britannicus*, and influenced the latter's work through unexecuted designs. He served as justice of the peace and member of parliament. A capable sculptor and experienced engineer, his major works include Drumlanrig Castle (c.1680–90, possibly inherited from Robert Mylne), Canongate Church, Edinburgh (1688), the regally proportioned Hamilton Palace (1693, demolished c.1920) and Dalkeith House (1702).

SMITH, James
(1789–1850)

Agricultural engineer, inventor and philanthropist, born in Glasgow but brought up in Deanston, Perthshire. After graduating from Glasgow University, he was appointed Manager of the Deanston cotton mills (1807). As well as reorganizing the mills, he spent much inventing, most notably the system of 'thorough drainage' by means of a subsoil plough. Subsequently the phrase to 'Deanstonize' land was coined to indicate this method. An inveterate inventor, he turned his hand to a vast range of innovations, from reaping machines and sheep-dips to a salmon-ladder for climbing a weir. In 1842 he left Deanston for London, where he set up successfully as an agricultural engineer, and became a commissioner on an inquiry into standards of public sanitation.

SMITH, James Moyr
(1839–1912)

Graphic artist and designer of furniture, wallpaper, fabrics, ceramics and book plates, and a proponent of the design reform movement in the second half of the 19th century. Born in Glasgow, he trained as an architect with James Salmon and was admitted to the Glasgow Architectural Society in 1864. After spending three years in Manchester working as an ecclesiastical architect, he moved to London in 1867 to work in the studios of **Christopher Dresser**. Between 1870 and 1897 he worked as an independent designer and is perhaps best known for the ceramic tile designs he produced for Mintons and Minton and Hollingsworth. As well as editing the magazine *Decoration*, from 1881 he became a prolific writer, his works including *Ancient Greek Female Costume* (1882), *Ornamental Interiors Ancient and Modern* (1887), *Studies for Pictures* (1868) and *Album of Decorative Figures* (1882). His work was exhibited at the Royal Academy in the 1870s and 1880s, and his designs formed part of the Minton exhibition at the Exposition Universelle held in Paris in 1878.

SMITH, John
(1724–1814)

Bookseller, born in Strathblane, Stirlingshire, the youngest son of the Laird of Craigend, Strathblane. He fought at the Battle of Laffeldt in Flanders (1747) and was wounded in action. In 1751 he founded the firm of John Smith and Son, having already set up three bookshops in Glasgow. He also established the first Circulating Library in Glasgow in 1753 (**Allan Ramsay** had initiated libraries in Scotland in 1725). Smith's Circulating Library was the largest collection in Glasgow for over 70 years and was a remarkably successful venture; it had several thousand volumes and a printed catalogue. He died at the age of 90, predeceased by his three spouses. The bookselling business he had founded was continued by his two sons, John Smith II and John Smith III.

SMITH, John
(1825–1910)

Dentist, and founder of Edinburgh Dental Hospital and School, the son of an Edinburgh dentist, whose practice he inherited in 1851. He published a *Handbook of Dental Anatomy and Surgery* in 1864. He was appointed surgeon dentist to the Royal Public Dispensary (1857–9), and founded the Edinburgh Dental Dispensary in 1860. Largely as a result of his efforts, the Edinburgh Dental Hospital and School was established in 1879, the Dispensary being merged with it. Smith left the running of the school to others, but remained a significant influence on its development. His practice was later shared and ultimately inherited by his son-in-law William Guy. He was also a theatre enthusiast, wrote the scripts of several Edinburgh Lyceum pantomimes and successfully adapted Sir **Walter Scott**'s *Waverley* for the stage.

SMITH, John
(1938 –)

Politician. Educated at Dunoon Grammar School and Glasgow University, where he studied law, he was called to the Bar in 1967 and made a QC in 1983. He distinguished himself as a public speaker at an early age, winning the 'Observer Mace' debating competition in 1962. In 1970 he entered the House of Commons, representing Lanarkshire North, and from 1983 Monklands East. He served in the administrations of Harold Wilson and James Callaghan, becoming Trade Secretary in 1978. Since 1979, in opposition, he has been front-bench spokesman on trade, energy, employment and economic affairs. His political career seemed threatened by a heart attack in 1988, but he made a complete recovery and returned in 1989 as one of Labour's most respected politicians.

SMITH, Joseph, 'General', known as 'Bowed Joseph'
(d.1780)

Cobbler and leader of the Edinburgh mobs. By beating a drum on the High Street of Edinburgh, he could have at his command a crowd of 10 000 within an hour. Resolutions of the City Magistrates could only be passed if consistent with his views. He generally acted to ensure fair play and for just causes, whether this involved attacking the home of an unscrupulous landlord or compelling traders to sell goods at reasonable prices. He was killed when he fell, drunk, from the top of a stagecoach.

SMITH, Madeleine Hamilton
(1835–1928)

Gentlewoman, born in Glasgow, the daughter of a Glasgow architect. She is notorious as the accused in a sensational murder trial. In 1857 she stood trial at the High Court in Edinburgh for the alleged murder by arsenic poisoning of her former lover Pierre Émile L'Angelier, a clerk and native of Jersey (Channel Islands) whom she had met in Glasgow in 1855. Her uninhibited love letters to him, published during the trial, stirred up considerable resentment against her. But although she had sufficient motive for ridding herself of L'Angelier, after her engagement to a more wealthy suitor, William Minnoch, and although she had purchased arsenic on three occasions, evidence was lacking of any meeting between them on the last days or nights prior to his last violent illness. She was brilliantly defended by **John Inglis**, Dean of the Faculty of Advocates, and the verdict was 'not proven'. Spurned by her family, she moved to London, where she became a popular social figure. In 1861 she married an artist-publisher George Wardle, an associate of William Morris, and after a normal family life in Bloomsbury, separated from her husband and eventually emigrated to the USA, where she married again, refusing all Hollywood offers to play herself in a silent film of her life.

SMITH, Norman Kemp
(1873–1958)

Philosopher, born in Dundee. He studied at St Andrews and on the continent. A lecturer in philosophy at Glasgow (1896–1906), he was a protégé of **Robert Adamson**. His *Studies in the Cartesian Philosophy* (1902) was a breakthrough in overcoming dualist confusions. From 1906 he was Professor of Philosophy at Princeton, where he remained until taking up wartime intelligence work in London. His pupils included Edmund Wilson and Scott Fitzgerald. Professor of Metaphysics at Edinburgh (1919–45), his *Commentary on Kant's Critique of Pure Reason* (1918) is perhaps the greatest such work. *Prolegomena to an Idealist Theory of Knowledge* (1924) restates Calvinist theory in modern psychological terms, suggesting that much we imagine we do for ourselves is done by nature's wise predestination. Finding a way forward by return to and revival of a classic, his *The Philosophy of David Hume* (1941) was another breakthrough, reviving **Hume** by freeing him from a lengthy period of misinterpretation.

SMITH, Robert Allan
(1909–80)

Physicist, born in Kelso, Roxburghshire, and educated at Kelso High School and Edinburgh University. He began research at the Cavendish Laboratory, Cambridge, and was a lecturer at the universities of St Andrews and Reading until 1939. He then worked successfully on the development of radar, mainly at the Telecommunications Research Establishment (TRE) in Malvern. After the war he was Head of Physics at TRE (which later became the Royal Radar Establishment), where he was engaged in fundamental work on the physics of semiconductors. He left Malvern in 1961 to become Professor of Physics at Sheffield, but resigned after a year to become Head of the Materials Science Centre at the Massachusetts Institute of Technology. In 1968 he returned to Scotland as Principal of Heriot-Watt University, Edinburgh. He was President of the Royal Society of Edinburgh from 1976 to 1979.

SMITH, Robert Archibald
(1780–1829)

Composer, born in Reading. His family were from Paisley, and he was apprenticed as a weaver to his father when they returned there in c.1800. Although self-taught, he was able to play flute and violin by the age of 10, and was a church chorister. He left weaving to teach music, especially church singing, and became Precentor at Paisley Abbey in 1807, where, against the prevailing Presbyterian sensibilities, he argued for more music in church. He was Choir Master and Precentor at St George's in Edinburgh from 1823, and is credited with opening a new era in Scottish church music. He composed religious and secular songs, the best known of which are the psalm tune 'Invocation' and 'Jessie, The Flow'r o' Dumlane', although 'St George's, Edinburgh', sometimes attributed to him, is not his. He made two important collections of songs, *The Scotish Minstrel* (sic) (1821–4) and *The Irish Minstrel* (1825), and published an *Introduction to Singing* (1826).

SMITH, Ronald Gregor
(1913–68)

Theologian, born in Edinburgh. Educated at Edinburgh University, he also studied at the universities of Munich, Marburg and Copenhagen. He was minister of Selkirk Memorial Church (1939–44), from where he went to serve as Chaplain to the Forces in 1944. There followed a spell as Associate Editor for SCM Press. He then went on to become Professor of Divinity at Glasgow University in 1956. Profoundly affected by his German experience, his brush with Nazism bred a desire to rework the ancient tenets of faith in response to the secular world he encountered, in such a way as to engage its interest. His translation of Martin Buber's *I and Thou* introduced to the English-speaking world a profoundly influential thinker. Among his most significant publications are *The Nature of Faith* (1961) and *Secular Christianity* (1965). One of the foremost theologians of his generation, his work is widely acknowledged as having made an original contribution to the sacred/secular dialogue.

SMITH, Stanley Desmond
(1931 –)

English physicist, educated at Cotham Grammar School and Bristol University. After research at the Royal Aircraft Establishment and in the Department of Meteorology at Imperial College he became a lecturer, and later Reader in Physics at Reading University. In 1970 he was appointed Professor of Physics at Heriot-Watt University, Edinburgh. He has been Chairman of Edinburgh Instruments Ltd since 1971. Distinguished for his research in semiconductor and laser physics, he has served on a number of committees of the Science and Engineering Research Council. He is a leading proponent of the use of optical techniques for very fast computation.

SMITH, Sydney Goodsir
(1915–75)

New Zealand-born poet, born in Wellington, son of Sir Sydney Alfred Smith. He moved to Edinburgh in 1928 when his father was appointed a professor there. He studied at Edinburgh University and Oriel College, Oxford, and with such works as *Skail Wind* (1941), *The Devil's Waltz* (1946), *Under the Eildon Tree* (1948, a great modern love poem), *Orpheus and Eurydice* (1955), *So Late into the Night* (1952), and *Figs and Thistles* (1959), established a reputation as the best modern Lallans poet after **Hugh MacDiarmid**. He published a loving description of Edinburgh in *Kynd Kittock's Land* in 1965. His first play, *The Wallace*, was commissioned for the Edinburgh Festival of 1960. He also wrote a comic novel, *Carotid Cornucopius* (1947).

SMITH, Sir Thomas Broun
(1915–88)

Jurist, probably born in Symington, Lanarkshire. Educated at Oxford, where he was Eldon Law Scholar, he was called to the English Bar in 1938 and, after distinguished war service, to the Scottish Bar in 1947. He was successively Professor of Scots Law at Aberdeen (1949–58), of Civil Law at Edinburgh (1958–68), and of Scots Law at Edinburgh (1968–72). Appointed to the Law Reform Committee for Scotland in 1954 he later served on the Scottish Law Commission (1965–80) and was instrumental in founding the Scottish Universities Law Institute in 1960, serving as its first director (1960–72). He received numerous honours, becoming QC in 1956 and knight in 1981. In retirement he served as General Editor of *The Laws of Scotland, Stair Memorial Encyclopaedia* until his death. He published a number of books and articles, but his main achievement was in making Scots Law much better known abroad, accomplishing this by his visiting professorships at Tulane, Cape Town and Harvard; by holding the Tagore Lectureship at Calcutta; and by extensive personal contacts abroad.

SMITH, Tommy (Thomas)
(1967 –)

Jazz musician, composer and bandleader. Born in Luton, Bedfordshire, to Scottish parents, he was brought up in Edinburgh and took up the saxophone at the age of 12. A teenage prodigy, he had made television and radio performances with internationally known musicians, as well as two records for Scottish labels, before he was 16. After studies in the USA at Berklee College, Boston, he brought his own quartet, Forward Motion, to play in Europe. In 1986 he became a member of vibraphone player Gary Burton's quintet, taking part in international tours and recording sessions. On his return to a Scottish base he was established as one of the brightest jazz stars of the new generation, playing wind synthesizer as well as saxophone, and leading a variety of groups in jazz and jazz-related settings.

SMITH, Sir William Alexander
(1854–1914)

Founder of the Boys' Brigade, born near Thurso, Caithness. An active worker in the Free College Church, Glasgow, and a member of the Lanarkshire Volunteers from 1874, he was well embarked on a successful career in commerce when he began his movement for 'the advancement of Christ's Kingdom among Boys' in 1883. Intended to meet a need at a vital stage in their lives, the organization instilled habits of discipline, provided recreation through camps and other pursuits, and was firmly based on Christian principles. By 1897, the year of Queen Victoria's Jubilee (in which a B B captain was Lord Mayor of London), the movement had spread to every continent.

SMITH, William Robertson
(1846–94)

Theologian and orientalist, born in Keig, Aberdeenshire. He studied at Aberdeen, Edinburgh, Bonn and Göttingen universities, and in 1870 became Professor of Hebrew and Old Testament Exegesis in the Free Church College, Aberdeen. His *Encyclopaedia Britannica* article 'Bible' (1875) was strongly attacked for heterodoxy, but he was acquitted of heresy (1880). He was deprived of his professorship (1881) for another article on 'Hebrew Language and Literature'. In 1883 he became Lord Almoner's Professor of Arabic at Cambridge, in 1886 University Librarian and Adams Professor of Arabic (1889). He became co-editor and chief editor (1887) of the *Encyclopaedia Britannica*. His chief works were *The Old Testament in the Jewish Church* (1881), *The Prophets of Israel* (1882), and *The Religion of the Semites* (1889).

SMITH, Sir William Wright
(1875–1956)

Botanist, born in Lochmaben, Dumfriesshire, and educated at Dumfries Academy and Edinburgh University, where he took an Arts degree, having determined on a teaching career. He also, however, devoted a considerable time to botany and zoology, such that Bayley Balfour, Professor of Botany at the University, asked him to become a lecturer there in 1902, where he stayed until his death, except for a four-year appointment in charge of the Government Herbarium in Calcutta (1907–11). This appointment enabled him not only to visit a number of tropical botanic gardens but also to explore the high Himalayas in Sikkim. He returned to Scotland in 1911 on the offer of the Deputy Keepership of the Royal Botanic Gardens. This was a time of considerable excitement, due to the recent arrival of the seeds from hundreds of different plant species. With Balfour the seeds were germinated and grown and over 550 new species were consequently described in the literature, producing a marked effect on horticulture around the world. Wright Smith succeeded to the Chair of Botany and the Keepership of the Botanic Gardens in 1922, was knighted in 1932, and elected FRS in 1945. Taking up his chair before the days of fixed retiral ages, he held both his principle appointments until his death, living in the magnificent house at the centre of the gardens.

SMOLLETT, Tobias George
(1721–71)

Novelist, born on the farm of Dalquharn in the Vale of Leven, Dunbartonshire, grandson of Sir James Smollett. He was educated at Dumbarton Grammar School and Glasgow University, where he took a degree in medicine. He moved to London in 1740 to find a producer for his tragedy, *The Regicide* (1749),

but, disappointed in his quest, sailed as surgeon's mate in the expedition to Carthagena against the Spanish in 1741. Three years later he settled in London, practising as a surgeon, but literature in the form of novel-writing was his real interest. His first efforts were successes — *Roderick Random* (1748) and *Peregrine Pickle* (1751). The former is modelled on Le Sage's *Gil Blas*, and as well as describing episodes in the life of the unprincipled hero, it made use of Smollett's experiences in the Carthagena expedition. *Peregrine Pickle* pursues the hero's adventures in love and war throughout Europe. *Ferdinand, Count Fathom* (1753) is the story of another heartless villain, whom an easy repentance saves from the gallows. Cervantes was now his model — he translated *Don Quixote* in 1755 — but his imitation of the master, *Sir Launcelote Greaves* (1762), is crude work. In 1753 he settled in Chelsea, editing the new *Critical Review*, which led to his imprisonment for libel in 1760, and writing his *History of England* (3 vols, 1757–8). Ordered abroad for his health, he visited France and Italy and saw little that pleased him. His caustic record, *Travels in France and Italy* (1766), earned for him Sterne's nickname of 'Smelfungus'. His next publication was a coarse satire on public affairs, *The Adventures of an Atom* (1769). In 1771 he wrote *Humphrey Clinker* (1771), which is much more kindly in tone and is still a favourite, in the form of a series of letters from and to members of a party touring round England and 'North Britain'. He spent the last years of his life abroad, and died in Livorno, Italy.

SMOUT, Thomas Christopher
(1933 –)

English-born economic and social historian of Scotland, born in Birmingham. Educated at Leys School, Cambridge, and Clare College, Cambridge, he was successively Assistant Lecturer, Lecturer, Reader and Professor in the Department of Economic and Social History at Edinburgh University (1959–79). He published *Scottish Trade On the Eve of the Union* (1963), the hugely popular *A History of the Scottish People 1560–1830* (1969), and *A Century of the Scottish People 1830–1950* (1986). He participated in Michael Flinn's *Scottish Population History from the Seventeenth Century to the 1930s* (1977), and co-operated with Ian Levitt to write *The State of the Scottish Working Class in 1843* (1979). He also set in motion a series of co-operative enterprises between Scottish social and economic historians and their counterparts in Ireland, Scandinavia, and the European continent. In this he was closely associated with **Rosalind Mitchison**. In 1990 he published, with Sydney Wood, an anthology of social history, *Scottish Voices*. He has also written many individual essays, including pioneer work on Scottish sexual history and conservation history. Chairman of the *Scottish International Review* in the early 1970s, he was at that time also an activist in Liberal Party politics. Professor of Scottish History at St Andrews University from 1980 to 1991, he has formed an important bridge between scholars who treat Scotland as an academic preserve and those more engaged with Scottish culture and opinion. Since 1986 he has been increasingly involved in the conservation movement with the Nature Conservancy Council, and in 1991 was appointed Deputy Chairman of Scottish Natural Heritage.

SMYTH, Charles Piazzi
(1819–1900)

Astronomer and photographic pioneer, born in Naples, the son of an English admiral. Coming to Scotland at the age of 27 he identified himself entirely with his adopted country as Astronomer Royal for Scotland and Professor of Astronomy at Edinburgh (1846–88). A pioneer of 'Mountain Astronomy', the advantages of which he demonstrated on a scientific expedition undertaken by himself and his wife Jessica to the Peak of Tenerife in 1856 (recorded in *Tenerife, an Astronomer's Experiment*, 1858), he also made significant contributions to solar and laboratory spectroscopy. In the field of photography he was an early and innovative worker: he illustrated his book on Tenerife with his own stereophotographs and designed cameras for special purposes, such as a miniature camera for a series of photographs taken in Egypt and a cloud-taking camera for meteorological work. A large collection of his photographs is preserved at the Royal Observatory Edinburgh. His undoubted talents did not preclude some bizarre research into the structure of the Great Pyramid of Giza, claimed by him to be a metrological monument built under divine guidance for the benefit of humankind. His popular book, *Our Inheritance in the Great Pyramid* (1864), ensured a wide following for his ideas.

SNEDDON, Ian Naismith
(1919 –)

Mathematician, born in Glasgow and educated at Glasgow University and Cambridge. After wartime scientific work, he lectured at Glasgow from 1946 to 1950, when he became the first Professor of Mathematics at the University College of North Staffordshire (now Keele University). In 1956 he returned to Glasgow as professor and retired in 1985. He became FRS in 1983. He has published copiously on differential equations, special functions, and applied mathematics, has held visiting professorships all over the world and has honorary degrees and distinctions from many countries. His public work includes service on many committees supporting music and theatre in Glasgow.

SNELL, John
(1629–79)

Philanthropist, born in Colmonell, Ayrshire. Educated at Glasgow University, he fought for the royalists and served in several battles, including Worcester (1651). Taken into the service of Sir Orlando Bridgeman, he acted first as his clerk, then, upon Bridgeman's appointment as Lord Keeper, as his sealbearer. Later he worked as secretary to the Duke of Monmouth. On his death he bequeathed money to found the Snell exhibitions at Balliol College, Oxford.

SOLE, David Michael Barclay
(1962–)

Rugby player, a grain buyer by profession, born in Aylesbury, Buckinghamshire. Educated at Glenalmond and Exeter University, he played club rugby for both before returning to Scotland to join Edinburgh Academicals. First selected for his country in 1986, he succeeded **Finlay Calder** as captain in 1990, leading the team to the Grand Slam that year, and to the semi-final of the World Cup in 1991. Relatively short for a prop forward, he compensates with a combination of strength and expert technique. He has played three times for the British Lions, all of them in 1989. With over 20 appearances as captain, he is the most capped player in that role.

SOMERSET, Earl of See **CARR, Robert**

SOMERVILLE, Jimmy
(1961 –)

Pop singer, born in Glasgow. With Larry Steinbachek and Steve Bronski he formed the group Bronski Beat in 1984. The band's electro pop sound was heavily dependent on Somerville's distinctive falsetto vocals. They built a strong following on the gay club scene in London and their first single 'Smalltown Boy' was a hit, despite the fact that it dealt overtly with gay problems. Other Bronski Beat hits included 'Why' as well as versions of George Gershwin's 'It Ain't Necessarily So' and Donna Summer's 'I Feel Love'. Somerville left the group in 1985, citing the pressures of being a pop star, but went on to further success as one half of The Communards with Richard Cole, and subsequently as a solo artist. His début solo album was *Read My Lips* (1989). Communards hits included 'Don't Leave Me This Way' (1986).

SOMERVILLE, Mary, née Fairfax
(1780–1872)

Scientific writer, born in Jedburgh, Roxburghshire. The daughter of Admiral Sir William Fairfax, she lived in London from 1816, where she moved in intellectual and scientific circles, and corresponded with foreign scientists. In 1831 she published *The mechanism of the heavens*, an account for the general reader of Pierre Simon Laplace's *Mécanique Céleste*. This had great success and she wrote several further expository works on science. She supported the emancipation and education of women, and Somerville College (1879) at Oxford is named after her. She was summed up as follows by the *Dictionary of National Biography*: 'the fair hair, delicate complexion, and small proportions which had obtained for her in her girlhood the sobriquet of "the rose of Jedburgh", formed a piquant contrast to her masculine breadth of intellect'.

SOMERVILLE, Mary
(1897–1963)

Educationist and broadcasting executive, born in New Zealand. She was brought up as a daughter of the manse in Gullane, East Lothian, and educated at Somerville College, Oxford, where she met **John** (later Lord) **Reith**. Seeing radio as a powerful educational tool, she asked Reith to employ her on a trial basis at the British Broadcasting Company (later Corporation) in 1925. A formidable lady, by 1929 she was responsible for all broadcasting to schools. In 1947 she was made Assistant Controller, Talks, with a wider remit, and rose to Controller, Talks in 1950, the first woman to hold the post of Controller in the BBC. On her retirement the BBC acknowledged that 'the service of broadcasting to schools is Miss Somerville's great monument'.

SORLEY, Charles Hamilton
(1895–1915)

Poet, born in Aberdeen, where his father was Professor of Moral Philosophy. Educated at King's College Choir School, in 1908 he won a scholarship to Marlborough College where, impressed by the rolling Wiltshire countryside, he started to write poetry. Just before the outbreak of World War I, and prior to taking his place at University College, Cambridge, he visited Germany, which coloured ambivalently his attitude to the events that followed. One of the first to enlist, he believed in the war as a necessary evil, as his poems show. In 1915 he went with his battalion to France, where he was killed by a sniper at the Battle of Loos. *Marlborough and Other Poems* was published in 1916, thanks to his family, and his best and probably unfinished work is unsentimental, direct and free from cant. *The Collected Poems of Charles Hamilton Sorley* were edited in 1985.

SORLEY, William Ritchie
(1855–1936)

Philosopher, born in Selkirk. He studied at Edinburgh University and began writing on Jewish culture and thought, on ethics, and on sociological and economic topics. Studying further at Cambridge he became Fellow of Trinity College (1883), Professor of Philosophy at Cardiff (1888–94), and of Moral Philosophy at Aberdeen (1894–1900), and Knightsbridge Professor of Moral Philosophy at Cambridge (1900–33). His major philosophic work is in the outstanding first nine chapters of his Gifford Lectures, *Moral Values and the Idea of God* (1921), in which he states that judgement of matters of 'fact' is derivative of judgements of value. He collated and edited the work of Robert Adamson, and did a similar melancholy duty to his son **Charles Hamilton Sorley**'s memory.

SOUNESS, Graeme James

(1953 –)

Footballer and manager, born in Edinburgh. Following spells with Tottenham Hotspur and Middlesbrough, he joined Liverpool in 1978, and grew to epitomize the combination of hard professionalism and consummate skill which brought the club league championships and European Cups. From 1984 to 1986 he played for Italian club Sampdoria, and then returned home to become player-manager of Rangers, transforming the Scottish game by buying leading English internationalists, and ending Rangers's unwritten policy of not signing Roman Catholics by recruiting **Maurice Johnston**. A magnificently arrogant midfielder for both club and country — 'If he was a chocolate drop he'd eat himself' said fellow Scotland player Archie Gemmill — he succeeded **Kenny Dalglish** as manager of Liverpool in 1991. In 1992 he underwent major heart surgery, a development which cast doubts on his long-term future in football. He published an autobiography, *No Half Measures*, in 1985.

SOUTAR, William

(1898–1943)

Poet, born in Perth, the son of a joiner. Educated at Perth Academy, he was conscripted into the Royal Navy (1916–19), where he contracted a form of spondylitis (ossification of the vertebrae), which was to confine him to bed for the last 13 years of his life. After demobilization he studied first medicine and then English at Edinburgh, returning to Perth in 1923. As an undergraduate he published his first volume of verse, anonymously, in *Gleanings by an Undergraduate* (1923), followed by *Conflict* (1931). In 1933 he published his first volume of verse in Scots, *Seeds in the Wind*, for children. This was followed by his *Poems in Scots* (1935) and *Riddles in Scots* (1937), which gave him a permanent place in the Scottish literary revival. The best examples of his work in English are *In the Time of Tyrants* (1939) and the collection *The Expectant Silence* (1944). His remarkable *Diaries of a Dying Man*, published in 1954, mark him out as an exceptional diarist.

SPALDING, John

(c.1609–1670)

Historian and antiquary. He was an ecclesiastical lawyer attached to the church of St Machar in Aberdeen. He wrote a valuable *History of the Troubles and Memorable Transactions of Scotland*, 1624–45 (posthumously published in 1792), an account of the events of King Charles I's reign in Scotland. The Spalding Club was founded in Aberdeen in 1839 in his memory to edit and print works of Scottish historical interest.

SPARK, Muriel Sarah, née Camberg

(1918 –)

Novelist, short-story writer, biographer and poet, born in Edinburgh. She was educated in Edinburgh at James Gillespie's School for Girls (the model for Marcia Blaine School in *The Prime of Miss Jean Brodie*) where she was 'the school's Poet and Dreamer', and Heriot-Watt College. After her marriage in 1938 she spent a few years in Central Africa. She came back to England in 1944 when her marriage broke down, and worked in the Political Intelligence Department of the Foreign Office, and stayed on in London after the war to become General Secretary of the Poetry Society and Editor of *Poetry Review* (1947–9). Since then she has devoted herself to writing, from the early 1960s living mainly in New York and Italy. She became a Catholic in 1954, an event of central importance to her life and work. Her early books include biographical studies of Wordsworth (1950) and Emily Brontë (1953), but she also published a collection of poems, *The Fanfarlo and Other Poems* (1952). She is pre-eminently a novelist and short-story writer. *The Comforters* (1957) was hailed by Evelyn Waugh as 'brilliantly original and fascinating' and her reputation grew steadily. She continued with *Memento Mori* (1959), *The Ballad of Peckham Rye* (1960) and *The Bachelors* (1961), but it was only with the publication of *The Prime of Miss Jean Brodie* (1961), an eerie portrait of a school-teacher with advanced ideas and her influence over her 'crème de la crème' pupils, that she achieved popular success. Her many novels, which are invariably slim, elegant and imbued with bizarre elements, include *The Girls of Slender Means* (1963), set in a Kensington hostel, *The Abbess of Crewe* (1974), an allegorical fantasy set in an abbey but with parallels to the Watergate scandal, and *A Far Cry from Kensington* (1988), an evocative, comic but sinister portrayal of London in the 1950s. Her stories were collected in 1967 and 1985, and the first volume of her autobiography, *Curriculum Vitae*, was published in 1992.

SPEAR, Walter Eric
(1921 –)

British physicist, educated at the Munsterschule, Frankfurt, and London University. He was a lecturer at Leicester University from 1953 to 1967, when he became Reader in Physics. He was appointed Harris Professor of Physics at Dundee University in 1968. He is distinguished for his research on the fundamental properties of amorphous semiconductors, and for the use of amorphous silicon as an economical means of generating electricity from sunlight (photodetection). He gave the Bakerian lecture to the Royal Society in 1988.

SPENCE, Sir Basil Urwin
(1907–76)

Architect, born in India. Educated at George Watson's College, Edinburgh, and London and Edinburgh Schools of Architecture, he assisted Lutyens with the drawings of the Viceregal Buildings in Delhi. He was twice mentioned in dispatches during World War II, and gradually emerged as the leading postwar British architect with his fresh approach to new university buildings and conversions at Queen's College, Cambridge, Southampton, Sussex, and other universities; his pavilions for the Festival of Britain (1951); the British Embassy in Rome; and his prize-winning designs for housing estates at Sunbury-on-Thames (1951). His best-known work is his prize design for the new Coventry Cathedral (1951), which boldly merged new and traditional structural methods. He was Professor of Architecture at Leeds (1955–6) and at the Royal Academy from 1961.

SPENCE, Catherine Helen
(1825–1910)

Scottish-born Australian writer and feminist, born near Melrose, Roxburghshire. She arrived in Adelaide in 1839 with her parents, with the ambition to be 'a teacher first and a great writer afterwards'. While a governess she worked on the first novel of Australian life written by a woman, published anonymously in London in 1854 as *Clare Morrison*. She wrote five more novels, the last one not published until after her death. Her early preoccupation with social problems, especially of the destitute and the young, led her into the public arena, and she made lecture tours in Britain and the USA. As well as taking part in reform work, she took several families of orphans into her care and became a member of the State Children's Council in 1886. She advocated proportional representation, her ideas outlined in *A Plea for Pure Democracy* (1861), and formed an Effective Voting League in South Australia. She stood as a candidate in the elections for the federal convention in 1897, going on to become Australia's first woman political candidate.

SPENCE, (James) Lewis Thomas Chalmers
(1874–1955)

Poet and anthropologist, born in Broughty Ferry, Dundee. He studied dentistry at Edinburgh, but turned to writing and in 1899 became a sub-editor on *The Scotsman*, and subsequently *The British Weekly* (1906–9). He became an authority on the folklore and mythology of Central and South America, and elsewhere, with numerous books, including *Mythologies of Mexico and Peru* (1907), *Dictionary of Mythology* (1913), *Encyclopaedia of Occultism* (1920), and *The Magic Arts in Celtic Britain* (1945). As a poet he was a pioneer of the use of archaic Scots language, in such collections as *The Phoenix* (1924) and *Weirds and Vanities* (1927). An ardent nationalist, he was one of the founder members of the National Party of Scotland in 1928, and the first nationalist to contest a parliamentary seat.

SPENCE, Peter
(1806–83)

Industrial chemist, born in Brechin. He worked in a grocery and a gasworks and then in 1845 patented and operated a novel process for making potash alum, then much used as a mordant in dyeing textiles. His works at Manchester used shale and sulphuric acid and produced much of the world's alum, and also such noxious fumes that he was forced to move from Manchester in 1857.

SPENS, Sir William (Will)
(1882–1962)

Educational administrator, born in Glasgow. Educated at Rugby and King's College,

Cambridge, where he studied both science and theology, he was Master of Corpus Christi College, Oxford, from 1927 to 1952. He was Chairman of the Consultative Committee on Education from 1934 and produced the report on *Secondary Education (Grammar Schools and Technical High Schools)* in 1938 which recommended the raising of the school leaving age to 15 and a widening of the provision of secondary education. It embodied the best thinking of the interwar period and paved the way for the *Norwood Report* (1943) and the Education Act of 1944.

SPOTTISWOOD, or SPOTISWOOD or SPOTSWOOD, Robert

(1596–1646)

Judge, son of Archbishop **Spottiswood** and grandfather of **John Spottiswood** (1666–1728). Educated at Glasgow, Oxford and in France, where he collected documents for his father's *History*, he was appointed to the Bench as Lord New Abbey in 1622 and promoted Lord President in 1633, but in 1641, having fallen foul of the Covenanters, he was replaced and took refuge in England. Returning to Scotland with **Montrose** he was taken prisoner at Philiphaugh and executed the following year. He compiled a *Practicks of the Law of Scotland* covering 1623–36 which was published by his grandson John in 1706.

SPOTTISWOOD, or SPOTISWOOD or SPOTSWOOD, John

(1565–1639)

Archbishop and historian, son of **John Spottiswood** (1510–85). Educated at Glasgow University, he was at first a Presbyterian, but later became Episcopalian. He became an assistant at Calder, and accompanied **James VI** to London on his accession as James I in 1603. He was Archbishop of Glasgow (1610) and of St Andrews (1615). He promoted Episcopal government, and forced the Perth Assembly (1618) to sanction the 'Five Articles of Perth'. He officiated at the coronation of Charles I at Holyrood in 1633, and in 1635 was appointed chancellor of Scotland. He reluctantly entered into the king's code of canons and prayer book, and so made himself hateful to the Covenanters. The king compelled him to resign the chancellorship in 1638, and he was deposed and excommunicated by the Glasgow General Assembly. His chief work is the *History of the Church of Scotland* (1655).

SPOTTISWOOD, or SPOTISWOOD or SPOTSWOOD, John

(1510–85)

Father of Archbishop **Spottiswood**. He graduated at Glasgow and, going to London, was ordained by Cranmer in c.1540. He became parson of Calder and, at the Reformation, superintendent of Lothian and Tweeddale. A supporter of **John Knox** and one of the leaders of the Reformed Church in Scotland, he was one of the authors of the *First Book of Discipline* in 1560. He crowned **James VI** in 1567 and was prominent in the Church for many years.

SPOTTISWOOD, or SPOTISWOOD or SPOTSWOOD, John

(1666–1728)

Jurist, great-grandson of Archbishop **Spottiswood** and grandson of Sir **Robert Spottiswood**. Educated at Edinburgh University, he passed advocate in 1696. In about 1703, to supply the lack of teaching of Scots Law in Edinburgh University, he established Spottiswood's College of Law in Edinburgh and made himself professor. The venture seems to have been a success for a considerable time. For his students he prepared several books, a *Compend or Abbreviate of the most important ordinary Securities* (1702, sometimes attributed to one Carruthers or to Sir Andrew Birnie), a *Stile of Writs* (1707), *Forms of Process* (1711), and several other small works. All went through several editions. He also published the *Decisions* of Lords President Gilmour and **Falconer** (1701), his grandfather's *Practicks* (1706) and an edition of **Hope**'s *Minor Practicks* (1734).

SPOTTISWOODE, Alicia Ann, Lady John Scott

(1810–1900)

Poet and songwriter, born in Westruther, Berwickshire. A friend of **Charles Kirkpatrick Sharpe**, she was a busy collector of traditional songs and wrote 69 of her own, often reworking original material, as with her most famous compositions, 'Annie Laurie' and 'Durrisdeer'. In 1836 she married Lord John Scott, a brother of the 5th Duke of Buccleuch.

STAFFORD-CLARK, Max

(1941 –)

English stage director, born in Cambridge. He began his career at the Edinburgh Traverse Theatre in 1966, becoming director there from 1968 to 1970. He subsequently became Director of the Traverse Theatre Workshop Company (1970–4), when he co-founded the Joint Stock Theatre Company. In 1981 he became Artistic Director of the English Stage Company at the Royal Court Theatre, London.

STAIR, James Dalrymple, 1st Viscount

(1619–95)

Judge and jurist. He studied at Glasgow University, served in the Covenanting army, as Regent in philosophy taught at Glasgow, joined the Bar (1648), and in 1659 was recommended by General George Monk to Cromwell for the office of a Lord of Session. He advised Monk to call a free parliament (1660). He was confirmed in office in 1661 and created a Nova Scotia baronet in 1664. The luckless marriage in 1669 of his daughter Janet inspired Sir **Walter Scott**'s *The Bride of Lammermoor* (1819). In 1671 he was made President of the Court of Session and member of the Privy Council; but when the Duke of York (later **James VII and II**) came to govern at Edinburgh in 1679 he retired to the country, and prepared for publication his famous *Institutions of the Law of Scotland* (1681), still the most authoritative work on Scots Law. His wife and his tenants were devoted to the Covenant, and he was soon involved in a fierce dispute with **Dundee**. He fled in 1682 to Holland, returned with William III, and, restored to the presidency, was created in 1690 Viscount Stair. He also published reports of court decisions and works on physics and religion.

STAIR, Sir John Dalrymple, 1st Earl of

(1648–1707)

Judge and politician, son of James Dalrymple, Viscount **Stair**. He studied law, and was knighted in 1667. He came into violent collision with **Dundee**, and was flung into prison in Edinburgh and heavily fined, but early in 1686 became King's Advocate, and in 1688 Lord Justice-Clerk. Under William III

he was Lord Advocate, and as Secretary of State from 1691 had the chief management of Scottish affairs. He was held responsible for the infamous massacre of Glencoe (1692), and resigned in 1695. In 1703 he was created an earl. He took an active part in the debates and intrigues that led to the Treaty of Union.

STAIR, John Dalrymple, 2nd Earl

(1673–1747)

Soldier, born in Edinburgh. At eight he shot his elder brother dead by accident, so was exiled by his parents to Holland, where he studied at Leiden, fought under William III at Steenkerk (1692), and by 1701 was Lieutenant-Colonel in the Scots Footguards, and in 1706 Colonel of the Cameronians. He was Aide-de-Camp to Marlborough in 1703, commanded an infantry brigade at Ramillies (1706), was made Colonel of the Scots Greys in 1706 and in 1708 secretly married Viscountess Primrose. He distinguished himself greatly at Oudenarde (1708) and Malplaquet. General in 1712, he retired to Edinburgh to intrigue for the Hanoverian succession. Under George I he was ambassador to Paris, and checkmated the Young Pretender (**Charles Edward Stuart**) and Alberoni. Recalled in 1720, he devoted himself to agriculture, growing turnips and cabbages. Made Field-Marshal (1742), he was Governor of Minorca and fought at Dettingen.

STALKER, James

(1848–1927)

Theologian, born in Crieff, Perthshire. A student at Edinburgh, Halle and Berlin, and a minister in Kirkcaldy and Glasgow, he was Professor of Church History at the United Free Church College, Aberdeen, from 1902 to 1924. He wrote more than a dozen books, including lives of Jesus (1879) and Paul (1884), *Imago Christi: the Example of Jesus Christ* (1889), and *The Preacher and his Models* (1891).

STARK, William

(1770–1813)

Architect. Like many contemporary architects, he visited St Petersburg (1798) and began practice in Glasgow. In about 1804 he moved to Edinburgh for health reasons, but died shortly after. His high reputation by the time of his death rested on a relatively small group of buildings. These included the Glasgow Court House (1807), with Greek Doric portico, St George's Church, Glasgow (1807), the upper Signet Library, Edinburgh, and his highly influential Glasgow Lunatic Asylum (1810, demolished), designed on a radial plan derived from Jeremy Bentham's panopticon. His posthumously published plans for laying out the ground between Edinburgh and Leith had an influence on his pupil **William Henry Playfair**.

ST CLAIR See SINCLAIR

STEAD, Tim
(1952 –)

English wood sculptor and furniture maker, born in Helsby, Cheshire. He trained as a sculptor in Cheshire, Nottingham and at Glasgow School of Art. One of his earliest projects was to furnish the interior of the Café Gandolfi in Glasgow, creating a distinctive wooden sculptured effect. He has also furnished a memorial chapel in Aberdeen. He successfully combines the role of a furniture maker working to public and private commissions with that of a sculptor, informing and enticing the viewer to appreciate the beauty of wood. He has exhibited regularly and has work in many public and private collections.

STEEL, Sir David Martin Scott
(1938 –)

Politician, last leader of the Liberal Party. A journalist and broadcaster, he was the youngest MP when first elected in 1965. He sponsored a controversial Bill to reform the laws on abortion (1966–7) and was active in the Anti-Apartheid Movement before succeeding Jeremy Thorpe as leader of the Liberal Party in 1976. He led his party into an electoral pact with Labour (1977–8) and subsequently an alliance with the Social Democratic Party (SDP) (1981–8). Despite Steel's undoubted popularity and the polling of a quarter of the total vote by the Alliance at the 1983 general election, they won only 23 seats. Steel is the author of several political publications. Immediately after the 1987 general election he called for a merger of the Liberals and SDP and announced that he did not intend to seek the leadership of the merged party.

STEEL, Flora Annie, née Webster
(1847–1929)

Social reformer and novelist, born in Harrow-on-the-Hill, London. The daughter of the Sheriff-Clerk of Forfarshire, she moved to Forfar at the age of nine. In 1867 she married Henry William Steel of the Indian Civil Service, with whom she travelled to the Punjab. Here she became an active member of the local community as a health worker and campaigner for the education of women. She became the first female Inspector of Schools in India (1884) and served on the Provincial Education Board (1885–8). In 1887 she published (with her friend Grace Gardiner) *The Complete Indian Housekeeper and Cook*, written in both English and Urdu. Her husband retired to England in 1889, but she returned to India in 1894 to research her most celebrated novel, *On the Face of the Waters* (1896), an account of the Indian Mutiny. Through this and her other novels she is remembered as a faithful contemporary chronicler of life in Northern India.

STEELL, Sir John
(1804–91)

Sculptor, born in Aberdeen. Educated as an artist in Edinburgh and Rome, most of his chief works are in Edinburgh, including the equestrian statue of the Duke of Wellington (1852), *Alexander taming Bucephalus* at the City Chambers, Sir **Walter Scott** and Prince Albert. His brother Gourlay (1819–94) was an animal painter and Curator of the National Gallery in Edinburgh.

STEIN, Jock (John)
(1922–85)

Footballer and manager, born in Burnbank, Lanarkshire. A player of only average ability, he became the greatest Scottish football manager of all time. His managerial career began with the unfashionable Fife club Dunfermline Athletic, which under his management won the Scottish Cup and became briefly a force in Europe. A short though highly successful spell followed with Hibernian and he then returned to his last senior club, Glasgow Celtic, as a player in 1965. In the next 13 years Celtic won nine championships in a row, the League Cup on five consecutive occasions and several Scottish Cups. Celtic also won the European Cup in 1967 and were finalists in 1970. Stein left

Celtic in 1978 for a brief period as Manager of Leeds United, but returned to Scotland to become National Manager. Under him the Scottish side qualified for the World Cup Finals in Spain in 1982. He died during an international against Wales at Cardiff as his side was about to qualify for a World Cup play-off.

STENHOUSE, Alexander Rennie
(1876–1952)

Insurance broker, born in Lenzie, Dunbartonshire. After a brief connection with the insurance business in Glasgow he worked in the USA with a firm specializing in fire insurance. He returned, determined to apply the experience he had gained in advanced methods of insurance, and established A R Stenhouse and Partners, a firm whose reputation for reliability was such that it became the leading Scottish insurance broking concern. After World War I he established the Scottish Western Trust as a vehicle for a variety of investments. His nadir followed the crash of 1929 and his arrest in 1931 on charges of fraud; these were subsequently dropped. Within a few years he had rebuilt his reputation and his business, and by the mid 1930s he was reputed to be worth 2 million. The business he had established continued to expand into England in the period after 1945.

STEPHEN, Sir Alexander Murray
(1892–1974)

Shipbuilder, born in Glasgow into a famous shipbuilding family. Educated at Kelvinside Academy, Glasgow, **Fettes** College in Edinburgh, and King's College, Cambridge, he joined the army and was awarded the MC for bravery in World War I. Taking over the family firm in the most difficult years of the depression, he nevertheless ensured the company's survival. Achieving prominence in the industry's organizations, he was President of the Shipbuilders' Employers Federation in 1938–9. In the postwar years he recognized the need for the industry to adapt if it were to survive, and thus innovated with welding and prefabrication techniques. He chaired the industry's research body, the BSRA (British Shipbuilders' Research Association) (1948–50), and was awarded an honorary LLD from Glasgow University in 1957. After retiral in 1965 he saw his shipyard merged into the Upper Clyde Shipbuilders. With the closure of the engineering side of the business in 1976, two years after his death, the family dynasty finally ended.

STEPHEN, David
(1910–89)

Self-taught naturalist and photographer, born in Airdrie, Lanarkshire. From 1946 onwards he wrote several classic animal stories, particularly for children, including *String Lug the Fox* (1976). A publicizer of nature conservation well before it became fashionable, in 1964 he was a founder member of the Scottish Wildlife Trust. He gained a worldwide reputation as a rigorous observer and recorder of the wildlife of Scotland, and at Palacerigg Country Park, Cumbernauld, he pioneered the display of native Scottish animals, including the wolf. His views became especially well known through his regular newspaper articles.

STEPHEN, George, Baron Mount Stephen
(1829–1921)

Financier and philanthropist, born in Dufftown, Banffshire. He was apprenticed to a draper in 1843, but a chance meeting in London led to his joining his cousin's cloth manufacturing firm in Montreal in 1850, which he inherited in 1860. Prospering in this, he became first a director (1873), then President (1876) of the Bank of Montreal. He was part of a group (which also included **Donald A Smith**) which rescued the ailing St Paul and Pacific (later Great Northern) Railway, a prelude to the completion of the partially built Canadian Pacific Railway (1880–8) by the same consortium. He was made a Baronet in 1886, and a Peer in 1891, taking the name Baron Mount Stephen after a peak named for him in the Canadian Rockies. He made his home in England from 1893, and gave large amounts of money to hospitals in London, Montreal and Aberdeen.

STEPHENS, Joseph Rayner
(1805–79)

Social reformer, born in Edinburgh, and educated at Manchester and Leeds. He spent several years as a Methodist preacher in Stockholm, and, after his return to Britain, accepted a post as Wesleyan minister in Cheltenham (1830). In 1834, however, he was expelled from his Methodist ministry for supporting Church disestablishment. He opened three independent chapels at Ashton-under-Lyne, and made himself a name as a factory reformer, being described by his brother as 'the tribune of the poor'. He took an active part in the anti poor-law demonstrations (1836–7) and the Chartist movement, of which, however, he refused actual membership. An impressive, persuasive orator, he was imprisoned for his struggle for the Ten Hours Act (1847).

STEPHENSON, Elsie
(1916–67)

English nurse educator, born in County Durham and trained as a nurse at the West Suffolk General Hospital. She qualified in midwifery at Queen Charlotte's Hospital, London, in 1938. After war service in the Red Cross in Egypt, Italy, Yugoslavia and later in Germany among refugees, in 1946 she was awarded a fellowship to study advanced public health administration at Toronto University. She then undertook missions to Germany, Singapore, North Borneo, Brunei and Sarawak on behalf of the British Red Cross Society. In 1948 she became the County Nursing Officer for East Suffolk where she developed the public health, district nursing and home-help services as well as infant welfare. In 1950 she became Nursing Officer for Newcastle-Upon-Tyne, where she created links between the hospital and the community and was one of the working party producing the influential Jameson Report, 'An Inquiry into Health Visiting' (1956). She was a member of the World Health Organization (WHO) Advisory Panel of the Expert Committee on Nursing. In 1956 she took up the post of Director of Nursing Studies Unit at Edinburgh University. This was the culmination of efforts by the Scottish Home and Health Department, the Scottish Board of the Royal College of Nursing, the Rockefeller Foundation and Edinburgh University to create the first academic nursing studies unit in Europe. In 1964 WHO established an International School of Nursing within the Nursing Studies Unit. With her broad background, drive and charismatic manner Elsie Stephenson was able to create a unit which had great influence on nursing throughout the world.

STERLING, John
(1806–44)

Man of letters, born at Kames Castle on the Island of Bute. Educated at Glasgow University and Trinity College, Cambridge, he turned to writing, and in 1828 bought the literary magazine, *The Athenaeum*, which he edited. He published numerous essays and long poems, and a novel, *Arthur Coningsby* (1833). He is best known as the subject of **Carlyle**'s *Life of John Sterling* (1851).

STEUART (later Denham), Sir James
(1712–80)

Political economist, born at Goodtrees, near Edinburgh and educated at North Berwick Parish School and Edinburgh University. He was called to the Scottish Bar in 1735, before travelling extensively in Europe (until 1740) where he became a fervent Jacobite. In 1745, he was a member of the Council of Prince **Charles Edward Stewart** during the Rebellion. In exile until 1763, he studied political economy and acquired an extensive knowledge of France and Germany. His *An Inquiry into the Principles of Political Oeconomy: being an Essay on the Science of Domestic Policy in Free Nations* (1767) anticipated Malthusian population theory, contained elements of Keynesian monetary theory and recommended many forms of state intervention in the economy, including public works, the subsidization of exports, state control of banks and taxation to redistribute wealth. As his mercantilist views opposed the spirit of the times, his *Principles* was soon eclipsed by **Adam Smith**'s *Wealth of Nations*.

STEUART, or STEWART, Sir James, of Gutters or Goodtrees
(1635–1713)

Jurist. He passed advocate in 1661 but had to take refuge in France and London for a while because of the publication of his *Jus Populi Vindicatum* (1669), an pseudonymous work in support of a book entitled *Napthali*, which recounted the grievances of the Covenanters. He returned to Scotland in 1679 but had again to take refuge in Holland in 1681. Outlawed in 1685 for his part in **Argyll**'s unsuccessful rebellion, he was later pardoned by William of Orange. He was reputed the ablest man at the Bar in his time and in 1692 he became Lord Advocate. Though ousted in 1709 he held the office again from 1711 to 1713. He was a member of the commission which investigated the Massacre of Glencoe. In 1702 he published an *Index or Abridgement of the Acts of Parliament and Convention from the reign of King James the First*, and *Dirle-*

ton's *Doubts and Questions in the Laws of Scotland Resolved and Answered* (1715), a book which came to be known as *Stewart's Answers*.

STEVENS, Thomas
(1900 –)

Organic chemist, born in Renfrew. After studying at Glasgow and Oxford universities, he taught at Glasgow (1921–7). He then moved to Sheffield and held the chair there from 1963 to 1966. He made extensive contributions to organic chemistry, and three reactions have been named after him. The best-known is the reaction he discovered in which the molecular structure of an organic zwitterion — an ion carrying both a positive and a negative electric charge — is rearranged to form a different compound with the same chemical formula (the Stevens rearrangement). He is the author of numerous papers and (with William Edward Watts) of *Selected Molecular Rearrangements* (1973).

STEVENSON, John James
(1831–1908)

Architect. Born in Glasgow, he abandoned a theological education to train with **David Bryce** in Edinburgh from 1856, moving to the London office of Sir George Gilbert Scott in 1858. He returned to Glasgow in 1860 to join Campbell Douglas in partnership until 1869, finally returning to London to be joined by E R Robson, architect to the School Board. He maintained strong links with Scotland, designing several exemplary Scots gothic revival churches, including South Church, Crieff (1881) and St Leonard's, Perth (1883), and provided a London training for several Scottish architects. A pioneer of the Queen Anne revival, he chose this style for his own residence, The Red House, in Bayswater (1872). His work in England was predominantly residential, focused on London, but included notable designs for Oxford University. The publication of his influential two-volume *House Architecture* (1880) revealed his practical, forward-looking study of the subject and his desire to correct errors in contemporary design. He was an active member of the Society for the Protection of Ancient Buildings.

STEVENSON, Robert
(1772–1850)

Engineer, born in Glasgow, grandfather of **Robert Louis Stevenson**. He lost his father in infancy, and his mother in 1786 married Thomas Smith, first engineer of the Northern Lighthouse Board. Stevenson then took to engineering, and in 1796 succeeded his stepfather. During his 47 years' tenure of office he planned or constructed 23 Scottish lighthouses, most notably that on the Bell Rock off Arbroath, employing the catoptric system of illumination, and his own invention of 'intermittent' or 'flashing' lights. He also acted as a consulting engineer for roads, bridges, harbours, canals and railways. One of his sons, Alan (1807–65), built the Skerryvore Lighthouse (1844). Two younger sons, David (1815–86) and Thomas (1818–87), his grandsons David A (1854–1938) and Charles (1855–1950), and his great-grandson D Alan (1891–1971), were all notable lighthouse engineers, the first four continuing the family position as engineers to the Northern Lighthouse Board until 1938. Several members of the family were also engineers to the Clyde Lighthouse Trustees.

STEVENSON, Robert Barron Kerr
(1913–92)

Archaeologist, born in Glasgow. After studying at Edinburgh, Bonn and London universities and excavating in Istanbul, he joined the staff of the National Museum of Antiquities of Scotland in 1938, later becoming Keeper (1946–78) with the task of developing the museum in preparation for a new building. Apprenticed on Byzantium and neolithic Italy, he concentrated on Scotland, publishing many papers, notably on early Christian sculpture and metalwork and on later coins. He became President of the Society of Antiquaries of Scotland (1975–8) and CBE in 1976. His extensive knowledge of Scottish archaeology, readily shared, continues to inspire the research of other scholars.

STEVENSON, Robert Louis Balfour
(1850–94)

Author, born in Edinburgh, grandson of **Robert Stevenson** and son of Thomas Stevenson, engineer to the Board of Northern Lighthouses. A constant invalid in childhood, he was educated at The Edinburgh Academy (1861–3) before his ill-health forced the family to travel abroad. He studied engineering at Edinburgh University for a session (1867) with a view to the family calling, but transferred to law, becoming an advocate in 1875.

His true inclination, however, was for writing. He collaborated in four mediocre plays, but for the next few years he travelled, mainly in France. His *Inland Voyage* (1878) describes a canoe tour in Belgium and northern France, and his *Travels with a Donkey in the Cevennes* describe a tour undertaken in the same year. In 1876 he was at Fontainebleau (which he made the subject of travel sketches), and it was at the neighbouring Barbizon that he met the divorcée, Fanny Osbourne, née Vandegrift (1840–1914), whom he followed to America and married in 1880. His return to Europe with his wife and stepson Lloyd Osbourne marked the beginning of a struggle against tuberculosis which his natural gaiety as a writer conceals. His wife and stepson have described their makeshift homes — Davox, Pitlochry and elsewhere — yet despite difficult circumstances he was 'making himself' as a writer not only of travel sketches but also of essays and short stories which found their way into magazines. *Thrawn Janet*, a story in the vernacular, appeared in *Cornhill Magazine* (1881), although an earlier tale, *An Old Song*, appeared in 1877 and was then lost until it was located and republished in 1982. *The Merry Men* was published serially in 1882, the same year as *The New Arabian Nights*. *Treasure Island*, the perfect romantic thriller, brought him fame in 1883 and his most successful adventure story, *Kidnapped*, appeared in 1886. *Catriona* (1893), introducing the love element, was also very popular. *The Master of Ballantrae* (1889) is a study in evil of a sort not uncommon in Scottish fiction, but here also are the wildest adventures. *The Strange Case of Dr Jekyll and Mr Hyde* (1886) is not a romance, but it further illustrates Stevenson's metaphysical interest in evil. *The Black Arrow* (1888) shows declining powers, but *Weir of Hermiston* (published posthumously in 1896), though unfinished, is acclaimed by some as his masterpiece, its scope larger, and the issues involved more serious. *St Ives*, which was also left unfinished, was completed by Sir Arthur Quiller Couch in 1897. Stevenson's work as an essayist is seen at its best in *Virginibus Puerisque* (1881) and *Familiar Studies of Men and Books* (1882). *A Child's Garden of Verses* (1885) is not poetry in the adult sense, but it is one of the best recollections of childhood in verse. *Underwoods* (1887) illustrates his predilection for preaching in prose or verse; here the poetry is of the good talker rather than the singer, and the tone is usually nostalgic. Only occasionally, as in *The Woodman*, does he touch on metaphysical problems, but vernacular poems such as *A London Sabbath Morn* subtly describe the Calvinism he had renounced but which intrigued him to the end. In 1889 Stevenson settled in Samoa and there with his devoted wife and stepson he spent the last five years of his life on his estate of Valima, which gives its name to the incomparable series of letters which he wrote, predominantly to friends in Britain.

STEVENSON, Ronald
(1928 –)

Composer, pianist and writer on music, born in Blackburn, Lancashire. He studied at the Royal Manchester College of Music. He champions music as world-language, seeking in his works to embrace a vast spectrum of international culture: notably the 80-minute *Passacaglia on DSCH* for piano, Piano Concerto No. 2 *The Continents* (1972), Violin Concerto (1979), choral settings, many songs ranging from settings of Scots to Japanese Haiku, and his transcriptions from the broadest range of music. His professed concern is an 'ethnic aesthetic'. He has composed for mentally-handicapped children and played in geriatric homes. An eminent contrapuntist, he is a master of keyboard technique and a distinguished melodist. His writings include *Western Music: An Introduction* (1971), many articles on music, and he is an authority on Busoni.

STEVENSON, (Ella) Savourna
(1961 –)

Composer, pianist and clarsach player, born in West Linton, Peebles-shire. A noted exponent of the Celtic harp, she has successfully embraced a highly varied repertoire, ranging through classical, jazz and international folk styles. Her most acclaimed work for her own instrument is the seven-movement suite, *Tweed Journey* (1989). She has also composed incidental music for theatre, radio and television.

STEWART, House of See STUART and ALBANIE

STEWART, Alexander
(1214–83)

Fourth hereditary Steward of Scotland. He was Regent of Scotland in **Alexander III**'s minority and commanded at the Battle of Largs (1263).

STEWART, Alexander, Earl of Buchan

(c.1343 – c.1405)

Son of King **Robert II**, and known as the 'Wolf of Badenoch'. He was overlord of Badenoch and received the earldom on his marriage (1382). He earned his nickname from his continued attacks on the bishopric of Moray.

STEWART, Allan Duncan

(1831–94)

Civil engineer. He graduated 9th Wrangler in the Mathematical Tripos at Cambridge in 1853. After gaining some engineering experience, in 1861 he began to practise as a consulting civil engineer in Edinburgh, preparing designs for railways, bridges, and water supply and drainage schemes. He was extensively employed by Sir Thomas Bouch on the design and supervision of bridges and other structures, including the ill-fated first Tay Bridge. In 1880 he gave important evidence to the Royal Commission on the Tay Bridge disaster, but his professional reputation, unlike that of Bouch, survived untarnished, and from 1881 to 1890 he acted as Chief Assistant Engineer for Fowler and Baker on the design and construction of the Forth Bridge.

STEWART, Andrew

(1907 –)

Broadcaster, born in Glasgow. He was educated at Glasgow University where, as a student, he took part as an actor in broadcasts from Scotland and (after the era of uncles and aunts) he appeared regularly in Children's Hour under the soubriquet of 'Longfellow', a name given because of his height. He joined the BBC in its infancy in Glasgow in 1926, remaining with them for five decades, broken only by his work in the Ministry of Information (1939–41). He became Scottish Programme Director in 1935, then became Controller, Northern Ireland in 1948. He was Controller, Home Service in London from 1953 to 1957, and Controller, Scotland in Glasgow from 1957 to 1968, at a time when the BBC was undergoing the critical change from being a radio-oriented organization to a

television-led one. He became a director of Scottish Television in 1968, a role he filled until 1977. Chairman of the Scottish Music Archive (1972–82), and a governor of the National Film School, he was Chairman of the Films of Scotland Committee (1971–6). He received an honorary LLD from Glasgow in 1970.

STEWART, Andy (Andrew)

(1933 –)

Comedian and singer, born in Glasgow and educated in Perth and Arbroath. He entered show business as an impressionist, appearing in revue on the Edinburgh Festival Fringe singing 'Ye Canna Shove Yer Granny Off a Bus'. He appeared with great success on the Scottish TV series *White Heather Club* (1960), and nationally in the annual Hogmanay TV special, singing his own composition, 'A Scottish Soldier'. His own series, *The Andy Stewart Show*, followed (1963). His radio shows include the series 17 *Sauchie Street* and *Scotch Corner* (1952).

STEWART, Balfour

(1828–87)

Physicist, born in Edinburgh. He studied at St Andrews and Edinburgh universities, and became assistant to **James David Forbes** at Edinburgh and afterwards Director of Kew Observatory (1859), and Professor of Physics at Owens College, Manchester (1870). He made his reputation by his work on radiant heat (1858), was one of the founders of spectrum analysis and wrote papers on terrestrial magnetism and sunspots.

STEWART, Belle

(1906 –)

Traditional singer and songwriter, born in a 'wee bow tent' by the River Tay near Caputh, Perthshire. The best known of the singing 'Stewarts of Blair' family, she came from travelling stock and married a traveller, Alec, in 1925. They had nine children, five of whom died in infancy. Her songs are rooted in the 'tinker' tradition, with emphasis on the ancient, classic ballads, but not to the exclusion of lighter material. Popular not only with folk-music audiences but also with academics (as an important folklore source), she is much in demand at folk festivals in Scotland and overseas. Her best-known composition is 'The Berryfields of Blair', which can be heard on her recording *Queen Amang the Heather* (1977).

STEWART, Daniel

(1740/1–1814)

Beneficiary and benefactor, born in Logierait, Strathtay, Perthshire. Probably a Gaelic speaker, he was the son of a crofter, whom he served as herd-boy. Following this he became a wig-maker's apprentice in Edinburgh, and was then taken to India as a valet by one of his master's clients. Stewart's fortune was described by the Edinburgh *Evening Courant* as 'acquired by industry and attention', beginning with the £11 000 left him by his employer. On his return to Edinburgh from India he engaged in house-property investment and dealing, becoming one of the macers of the Court of Exchequer. He was painted by **Raeburn** and complained because his portrait was not exhibited with those of prominent Edinburgh worthies. A life-long bachelor, he lived in Windmill Street from about 1786 (with a female housekeeper whom he seems to have hated). He left his fortune to a number of charitable institutions, which were only permitted to enjoy them after the decease of a retarded niece maintained by his estate. His main purpose, that of establishing an educational domicile or 'Hospital' for healthy but indigent boys, was realised in 1859, but with doubtful fidelity to his intentions the establishment became a fee-paying school in 1870.

STEWART, Sir David, of Garth

(1772–1829)

Soldier and historian, born in Perthshire. In his early career he served at various times with the 42nd, 77th and 78th Highlanders and with the 90th Perthshire Light Infantry. He saw operational service in the West Indies campaign of 1794 and later during the Napoleonic wars in Egypt and the Peninsula. In 1814 he retired on half-pay and wrote the first reliable history of the Scottish regiments and clan system, *Sketches of the Character, Manner and Present State of the Highlanders of Scotland* (1822). Although it was attacked for the author's Jacobite sympathies, the book was one of the first objective studies, treated in an unromantic way, of the history of the Scottish highlands. Stewart resumed his military career in 1825 when he was promoted major-general and in 1829 was appointed Governor-General of St Lucia. He died within a few months of his arrival.

STEWART, Dugald

(1753–1828)

Philosopher, born and educated in Edinburgh, where his father was Professor of Mathematics; he also studied at Glasgow University under **Thomas Reid**. He succeeded his father as professor in 1775, then from 1785 to 1810 was Professor of Moral Philosophy at Edinburgh in succession to **Adam Ferguson**. A follower of Reid's 'Common Sense' philosophy, he inherited Reid's mantle on becoming the leader of the Scottish School. He was not a highly original thinker and lacked philosophical curiosity, but he was a great teacher and lecturer, of whom a pupil said 'without derogation from his writings it may be said that his disciples were among his best works'. He was in fact a prolific author, his major work being *Elements of the Philosophy of the Human Mind* (3 vols, 1792, 1814, 1827). He also wrote *Outlines of Moral Philosophy* (1793) and *Philosophical Essays* (1810), the latter a witness to the breadth of his interests. He was the first person to give a lecture course on political economy in Britain (1800–1), discussing population, value, money, national wealth, the Poor Laws and education. A remarkably large monument on Calton Hill, Edinburgh, attests to his fame at the time of his death.

STEWART, Ena Lamont

(1912 –)

Dramatist, educated at the Woodside School in Glasgow and at Esdaile College in Edinburgh. She trained as a librarian at the Aberdeen Public Library and worked as a librarian and as a medical secretary while writing articles, short stories and plays for radio and stage. Her play *Distinguished Company* (1943) was produced by Rutherglen Theatre Company; thereafter her work was associated with the Glasgow Unity Theatre. Her best-known play, *Men Should Weep* (1947), which is related from a woman's point of view, is an unusual presentation of the Glasgow working class. Other plays include *Towards Evening* (produced 1975) and *High Places* (1987).

STEWART, Frances Teresa, Duchess of Richmond and Lennox

(1647–1702)

Noblewoman, the daughter of the 6th Duke of Lennox. A remarkable beauty, known as 'la belle Stewart', she was appointed maid of honour to Charles II's queen, Catherine of Braganza. She is thought to have become one of Charles's mistresses, and posed as the effigy of Britannia on the coinage. In 1667 she married the 3rd Duke of Richmond, and fled the court. In later years she was restored to the king's favour.

STEWART, Jackie (John Young)

(1939 –)

Racing driver and world champion, born in Dunbartonshire. In 1968 he won the Dutch, German and US Grands Prix in a Tyrell. He had been third in the world championships in 1965, his first season of Grand Prix racing, and he won the world title in 1969, 1971 and 1973. He retired at the end of the 1973 season. Gifted with exceptional reflexes, his second sport was clay-pigeon shooting, in which he reached Olympic standard.

STEWART, James

(1243–1309)

Fifth hereditary Steward of Scotland. He was one of the six Regents of Scotland after the death of **Alexander III**.

STEWART, James Stuart

(1896–1990)

Preacher and devotional writer, born in Dundee. A Church of Scotland parish minister before becoming Professor of New Testament at New College, Edinburgh (1947–66), he was Moderator of the General Assembly of the Church of Scotland (1963–4). He was joint-editor of the 1928 English translation of Schleiermacher's *The Christian Faith*, wrote popular books on Jesus, Paul, and the art of preaching, lectured widely in Britain and overseas, and published several volumes of sermons, including *The Gates of New Life* (1937), *River of Life* (1972), and *King for Ever* (1974).

STEWART, J I M (John Innes Mackintosh), pseudonym **Michael Innes**

(1906 –)

Novelist and critic, born in Edinburgh. Educated at The Edinburgh Academy and Oriel College, Oxford, he subsequently lectured at Leeds University, the University of Adelaide and Queen's University, Belfast. From 1969 to 1973 he was Reader in English Literature, Oxford University. The novels written under his own name are largely set in an academic and artistic milieu among the middle and upper classes. A prolific writer, he is best known in this vein for the so-called 'Pattullo' sequence, located in the sequestered world of the dons. *A Use of Riches* (1957) and *The Last Tresilians* (1963) are generally regarded as his most important works. As Michael Innes he has made an important contribution to the thriller genre. His range is remarkably wide, from intricate, locked-room type murders to large-sale crime intrigues. In his detectives, John Appleby, the gentleman turned policeman, and the formidable Inspector Cadover, he has created two memorable characters. Notable titles include *Hamlet, Revenge!* (1937), *Lament for a Makar* (1938) and *What Happened at Hazelwood?* (1946).

STEWART, John

(c.1381–1424)

Soldier, nephew of **Alexander Stewart**, Earl of Buchan. At the head of a Scottish force, he defeated the English at Baugé (1421). He became Constable of France but fell fighting at Verneuil.

STEWART, Matthew

(1717–85)

Mathematician, born in Rothesay, Bute, father of **Dugald Stewart**. He was a pupil of **Robert Simson** at Glasgow, and became professor at Edinburgh in 1747. He published books on geometry and astronomy, including a very inaccurate estimate of the distance of the earth from the sun. Failing health led him to hand over the chair to his son in 1775 and he retired to Catrine in Ayrshire where he died.

STEWART, Matthew John

(1885–1956)

Pathologist, born in Ayrshire. He graduated in medicine from Glasgow, came under the influence of Sir Robert Muir, and in 1910 became the clinical pathologist to the General Infirmary at Leeds and demonstrator in Clinical Pathology at the Medical School. After war service he returned (1918) to take the Chair of Pathology at the University of Leeds Medical School. Together with Professor **J K Jamieson** he soon established chairs of bacteriology and cancer research. A brilliant teacher and observer, his book (in collaboration with Sir Arthur Hurst), *Gastric and Duodenal Ulcers* (1929), was a major contribution to knowledge. He also wrote on cellular foreign-body reactions, myeloid tumours, asbestosis, siderosis and silicosis, and was a famous editor of the *Journal of Pathology* from 1934.

STEWART, Murdoch, 2nd Duke of Albany

(d.1425)

Regent of Scotland, the eldest son of **Robert Stewart**, 1st Duke of Albany and Regent of Scotland. He inherited the dukedom and regency on the death of his father in 1420. As next in line to the throne of Scotland to **James I**, who had been a prisoner in the Tower of London since 1406, Murdoch had high hopes of inheritance. Murdoch's sons, Sir Walter Stewart, Alexander and James, threw his attempts at diplomatic alliances with the Scottish nobility into disorder by their early reaching for their own inheritance and for returns from their position as regent's and heir-presumptive's children. The Exchequer audit of 1422 revealed years of fiscal mismanagement, corruption and extortion under Murdoch and his father. On the death of Henry V of England, the English began negotiations for the release of James I in the hope of raising much-needed revenue, and a treaty was concluded in 1423. James returned in 1424, suspicious of Murdoch and his father for having connived at his continued imprisonment and suspecting them of a part in the death of James's elder brother Rothesay; James was also opposed to Murdoch's being heir-presumptive. Murdoch's son Walter was arrested in 1424. Murdoch and his son Alexander were arrested at a parliament at Perth in 1425. Murdoch's third son James then burned Dumbarton, killing King James's bastard uncle John the Red. Walter was executed in 24 May 1425, after an assize of 21 nobles during the Stirling Parliament; Murdoch and Alexander were executed the next day, and James, their heir, fled to Ireland. Their estates, earldoms, etc, were declared confiscated by the king, to his considerable and necessary financial improvement. Murdoch was much less popular than his father but King James was very fortunate

in the speed and success with which he terminated his designs.

STEWART, Robert, 1st Duke of Albany

(?1340–1420)

Regent of Scotland, the third son of Robert Stewart, Earl of Strathearn, afterwards **Robert II**, and Elizabeth Mure before marriage legitimized; younger brother to John (afterwards **Robert III**), and elder brother to Alexander, the Wolf of Badenoch. He became Earl of Menteith on his marriage to its heiress in 1361, and Earl of Fife in 1371 by bargain with much-married and much-widowed Isabella, Countess of Fife. Hereditary governor of Stirling in 1373, he was appointed Chamberlain of Scotland (1382–1407). A participant in the raids on the English border (1385–6), he was declared guardian of the realm by the General Council because of his elder brother's disablement by horsekick in 1388. As a result he was virtual ruler of Scotland almost continuously for the rest of his life. He was created 1st Duke of Albany in 1398. Faced opposition from Robert III's heir David, Earl of Rothesay, who was ultimately imprisoned by him in 1402 after three years as royal lieutenant. Rothesay died in suspicious circumstances while in prison but his father, the disabled king, reinstated Albany and declared him innocent of Rothesay's death. Albany was now renewed from council to council as lieutenant-general until the sole other heir between himself and the crown, Prince James, was held to be of age. But James was captured on the way to France, was imprisoned by Henry IV of England, and Robert died within three weeks (1406). Albany now ruled as regent for the imprisoned King **James I**, clearly hoping for ultimate succession, and showing no great energy for his release. He crushed the rebellion of Donald Macdonald, Lord of the Isles in 1411, set up Inverness Castle, and supported the supposed 'Richard II' against Henry IV, until his death, when he buried him with royal honours at Stirling (1419).

STEWART, Walter

(d.1177)

Second son of William Fitzalan. He moved to Scotland and received from **David I** large possessions in Renfrewshire, Teviotdale, and Lauderdale, along with the hereditary dignity of Steward of Scotland, which gave his descendants the surname of Stewart, by some branches modified to 'Steuart' or the French form 'Stuart'.

STEWART, Walter
(1293–1326)

Sixth hereditary Steward of Scotland. He fought in the Scottish victory over the English at Bannockburn (1314), and defended Berwick against Edward II. His marriage in 1315 with Marjory, **Robert de Bruce**'s daughter, brought the crown of Scotland to his family; their son Robert came to the throne as **Robert II** in 1371.

STILES, Sir Harold Jalland
(1863–1946)

English-born surgeon, born in Spalding, Lincolnshire. He studied medicine in Edinburgh (1880–5), and graduated as most distinguished student of his year. He worked for 10 years in the dissecting room as preparation for a career in surgery, and was appointed to the surgical staff of the Royal Infirmary in 1895. He became surgeon at the Royal Hospital for Sick Children and Chalmers Hospital in 1898. While serving in the Army Medical Service (1914–18), he introduced improved methods of orthopaedic surgery. He was Regius Professor of Clinical Surgery at the Royal Infirmary from 1919 until his retirement in 1925. He brought many scientific advances to surgery in Scotland, including the sterilization of instruments by high-pressure steam. He was President of the Association of Surgeons of Great Britain and Ireland in 1921, and of the Royal College of Surgeons in Edinburgh in 1923, and received several honorary degrees in recognition of his achievements.

STILL, William
(1911 –)

Minister and influential 'guru' of the conservative Evangelical wing of the Church of Scotland, born in Aberdeen. After a career as a music teacher, he trained at the Salvation Army International Training College, and then at Aberdeen University (1939–44). Inducted to Gilcomston South Church, Aberdeen, in 1945, where he has spent his entire career, his ministry has served as a gathering point and driving force for that Biblicist right-of-centre opinion within the broad Church of Scotland. His expository preaching style has been much imitated by those who see him as their model for ministry. A significant proportion of those entering the ministry of the Church of Scotland since the 1960s have been 'disciples' of his theological stance and preaching method. The nature of his published work of commentaries and biblical interpretation is typical of the emphasis of his ministry.

STIRLING, Sir Archibald David
(1915–90)

Soldier and creator of the Special Air Service Regiment (SAS), educated at Ampleforth College, Yorkshire, and Cambridge. At the outbreak of World War II he was commissioned in the Scots Guards but later transferred to 3 Commando Group for service in the Middle East. While convalescing from a parachuting injury he formulated the idea of a small 'army within an army' to make swift and secret raids deep behind enemy lines. The result was the SAS, which quickly won a high reputation for its success in destroying aircraft and fuel dumps in German-held territory. In 1943 he was taken prisoner in Tunisia and was incarcerated in the notorious prison of Colditz in Germany. On his release he left the army to settle in East Africa, but continued to maintain links with the regiment he had founded. During his retirement from service life he was part of the syndicate which won the franchise for operating Hong Kong's television services. Throughout his life he was adamant that the SAS soldier should be motivated by self-discipline and should never appear a heroic figure.

STIRLING, James, known as 'the Venetian'
(1692–1770)

Mathematician, born in Garden, Stirlingshire. He studied at Glasgow and Oxford (1711–16), but left without graduating. His first book, on Newton's classification of cubic curves, was published in Oxford in 1717. He visited Venice at about this time, returned to Scotland in 1724, and went to London, where he taught mathematics. From 1735 he was superintendent of the lead mines at Leadhills, Lanarkshire, and corresponded with **Colin Maclaurin**. For his survey of the Clyde in 1752 he was presented with a silver tea-kettle by Glasgow Town Council. His principal mathematical work was *Methodus differentialis* (1730), in which he made important advances in the theory of infinite series and finite differences, and gave an approximate formula for the factorial function, still in use and named after him.

STIRLING, James Hutchison
(1820–1909)

Philosopher, born in Glasgow. Taking an MA at Glasgow University, he then studied medicine and practised in Wales until an inheritance allowed him the life of a private scholar. While he was touring France and Germany, it was suggested to him that in Hegel he might find a rational basis of Christianity. Becoming fascinated by Hegel's philosophy he published *The Secret of Hegel* (1865), an original but difficult work which prompted one reviewer to say that 'the secret had been well kept'. Despite this, wide interest ensued. He attacked Sir **William Hamilton**'s reform of **Thomas Reid**'s philosophy. Opposed to Darwinism, he held various misconceptions about biology which are, however, offset by acute criticism of misapplied evolutionist ideas. Though never given an academic post, he made important academic contacts with Germany and America, and had an interesting circle of friends, including **Simon Laurie, D G Ritchie** and **John Veitch**. Although the eccentricity of his writing style verged on mannerism, it allowed him to express German ideas which were not well translated in standard English. Other works include an introduction to Kant (1881), and critical studies of Sir William Hamilton (1865), Thomas Huxley (1869) and Darwin (1894), all of whom he regarded as misguided apostles of enlightenment. With characteristic spirit he (justly) claimed that his *Lectures on the Philosophy of Law* (1873) include an outstanding 15-page encapsulation of Hegel.

STIRLING, Patrick
(1820–95)

Mechanical engineer, born in Kilmarnock, Ayrshire, son of **Robert Stirling**. He became the most eminent of a remarkable family of locomotive engineers that included his brother James (1835–1917), his son Matthew (1856–1931) and his cousin Archibald Sturrock (1816–1909). He was apprenticed to his Uncle James (1800–76), who was manager of the Dundee Foundry which built steamers

and locomotives, then gained experience in several engineering works before being appointed in 1853 the locomotive superintendent of the Glasgow & South Western Railway. He moved to the Great Northern Railway in Doncaster in 1866 and succeeded his cousin as chief locomotive superintendent. It was there in 1870 that his famous 8-ft diameter driving wheel 4-2-2 'Stirling Single' first appeared, becoming a legend for its speed and power; one is preserved in the National Railway Museum in York.

STIRLING, Robert
(1790–1878)

Clergyman and inventor, born in Cloag, Perthshire. Educated for the ministry at the universities of Glasgow and Edinburgh, he was ordained in the Church of Scotland in 1816, and became minister of Galston, Ayrshire (1837–78). In the year of his appointment he patented a hot-air engine operating on what became known as the Stirling cycle, in which the working fluid (air) is heated at one end of the cylinder by an external source of heat. In drawing up the patent he was assisted by his brother James who was a mechanical engineer, and manager of a foundry in Dundee where in 1843 a steam engine was modified to work as a Stirling engine developing some 40 horse-power. It suffered, however, from the same problem as all the other hot-air engines built at that time: the hot end of the cylinder burnt out and had to be replaced after only one or two years' work. In spite of their greater efficiency, hot-air engines were superseded by the internal combustion engine and the electric motor, although some development work has been undertaken recently because of their non-polluting characteristics.

STIRLING, Ruth
(1957 –)

Photographer, trained at Edinburgh College of Art, where she took a post-graduate diploma in 1987. She came to photography through painting and established herself in residencies at the Marine Biological Station, Isle of Cumbrae, the Gatty Marine Laboratory at St Andrews University, and the Eastern Arctic Research Laboratories at Igloolik in Canada (resulting in the exhibition, *Igloolik; Towards the Night, the Light*). In 1989 she set up an independent studio on the Isle of Cumbrae, and in 1991 she began the first stage of a long-term project to establish a resource centre for cultural, artistic and scientific exchange, based in the Western Isles. Her work eludes traditional categories of art, science and technology to explore the relationship between outer appearance and inner structure, or meaning on different levels, from the biological to the spiritual. She has used electron and light microscopes to extend her research into a dimension of the visual world hitherto reserved for scientists. Her work challenges the inherited concepts of language.

STIRLING, William Alexander, 1st Earl of
(c.1567–1640)

Poet and courtier, born in Alva, Clackmannanshire. A tutor of young noblemen, in 1613 he was attached to the household of Prince Charles (Charles I). He had already published a collection of songs and madrigals in *Aurora* (1604); in 1614 he published part one of his huge poem *Doomesday*, (part two, 1637). He received in 1621 the grant of 'Nova Scotia' — a vast tract in North America soon rendered valueless by French expansion. In 1631 he was made sole printer of King **James VI and I**'s version of the Psalms. From 1626 until his death he was Secretary of State for Scotland. He was created Viscount (1630) and Earl of Stirling (1633), also Earl of Dovan (1639), but he died insolvent in London. His tragedies include *Darius* (1603), *Croesus* (1604), *The Alexandrean Tragedy* (1605) and *Julius Caesar* (1607).

STIRLING-MAXWELL, Sir William
(1818–78)

Historian and art critic, born in Kenmure, Stirlingshire. Educated at Trinity College, Cambridge, he travelled in Italy and Spain and became a connoisseur of Spanish art. He wrote *Annals of the Artists of Spain* (3 vols, 1848), *Cloister Life of Charles V* (1852) and *Velasquez* (1855). In 1866 he inherited property from his uncle and added the name Maxwell to his own. He was MP for Perthshire from 1852. In 1877, just before his death, he married the Irish social reformer Caroline Norton.

STONE, Norman
(1941 –)

Historian, journalist and broadcaster. Born in Glasgow, he was brought up by his widowed mother and was educated at Glasgow Academy, where he won a scholarship to Caius College, Cambridge. He followed this with a period as a research student in Austria and Hungary (1962–5). Appointed lecturer in Russian History at Cambridge in 1967, he first attracted popular attention with *The Eastern Front 1914–1917* (1975), which won the **Wolfson** Prize for History (1976). In 1983 he published *Europe Transformed 1878–1919*, a work which drew widespread praise and sealed his reputation as an outspoken, right-wing historian with an almost encyclopedic grasp of history. Professor of Modern History at Oxford from 1984, he has made various television documentaries on subjects as diverse as art and Hitler, and has established himself as a prolific journalist. Witty, eccentric and often consciously controversial, he has been dubbed 'the media face of modern history'.

STONEHAVEN, Sir John Lawrence Baird, 1st Viscount
(1874–1941)

Conservative politician, born in London and educated at Eton and Oxford University. After working in the diplomatic service (1896–1908), he was MP for Rugby (1910–22), and for Ayr Burghs (1922–5). Parliamentary Private Secretary to **Andrew Bonar Law** (1911–18), he was Minister for Transport (1922–4). A close confidant of Stanley Baldwin and an influential figure behind the scenes in the Conservative Party, he was Chairman of the party from 1931 to 1936. Made a peer in 1925, he was appointed Governor-General of Australia (1925–30). In Australia he helped to maintain good relations between the colony and Britain, and was well regarded for his achievements.

STOUT, George Frederick
(1860–1944)

English psychologist and philosopher, born in County Durham. He was educated at Cambridge. In 1893 he briefly took up the first separate psychology teaching post at Aberdeen, but settled in Scotland only when appointed Professor of Logic and Metaphysics at St Andrews (1903–36). A major thinker, dismissive of his pupil Bertrand Russell's pretence at philosophy, Stout was an important psychologist and, as a philosopher, was very influential in Scotland. His publications include *Analytic Psychology* (1896),

Studies in Philosophy and Psychology (1929), *Mind and Matter* (1931) and *God and Nature* (1952). Aged 80 he emigrated to Australia with his son. One of the greatest English eccentrics Scotland has had, he would hold up his umbrella, still furled, in the rain, and was liable to return home sooner than planned from any trip that involved changing trains.

STOUT, Sir Robert
(1844–1930)

Scottish-born New Zealand politician, born in Lerwick and educated at the local academy. He emigrated to New Zealand in 1864, where he was a teacher and then a lawyer. Elected to the House of Representatives in 1875, he was Attorney General in the first Liberal government of 1878–9, introducing trade union legislation. Prime Minister from 1884 to 1887, he passed major laws on land reform, and on improving education, hospital and welfare systems. In the 1890s he remained politically active, especially in the causes of women's suffrage and prohibition of alcohol; he also championed the Maoris' interests and advocated a greater British imperial presence in the Pacific. Knighted in 1886, he served as Chief Justice from 1899 to 1926.

STOW, David
(1793–1864)

Educationist and pioneer of coeducation, born in Paisley. After experience with Sabbath Schools and with the institution of Infant Schools in 1828, he became Secretary of the Glasgow Educational Society in 1834. This enabled him to play the leading part in founding the Glasgow Normal School in 1837. His book, *The Training System*, a manual for teachers and school managers, was reprinted ten times between 1834 and 1860. Stow's views were ahead of his time. Convinced of the need to humanize schools, he implemented coeducation and introduced women teachers in Infant Schools. He was opposed to corporal punishment and to the award of prizes and orders of merit. Believing that understanding should precede rote learning, he also considered that moral and personal development were more important than intellectual achievement, and he argued that some of the money spent on prisons and the police force would be better spent on education. In the 1830s the government made a direct approach to Stow to supply teachers

from Glasgow for Australia, Ceylon and the West Indies.

STRACHAN, Douglas
(1875–1950)

Artist, born in Aberdeen. After being political cartoonist for the *Manchester Chronicle* (1895–7) and a portrait painter in London, he found his true medium in stained-glass work. His first great opportunity was the window group which Britain contributed to the Palace of Peace at The Hague. He designed the windows for the shrine of the Scottish National War Memorial. Other examples of his work may be seen in King's College Chapel, Aberdeen, the University Chapel, Glasgow, and the church of St Thomas, Winchelsea. As an artist Strachan never wholly identified himself with any movement. His work glows with rich colour schemes and his subjects are treated with originality and imagination.

STRANG, William
(1859–1921)

Painter and etcher, born in Dumbarton, and studied in London from 1875 at the Slade School where he was taught and greatly influenced by Alphonse Legros. He was a prolific printmaker, and over 750 etchings, drypoints, mezzotints, aquatints and woodcuts have been recorded. He was an excellent draughtsman and many consider his portraits to be his greatest achievement. Among his many sitters were Rudyard Kipling and Thomas Hardy. He illustrated several books, among them *Paradise Lost*, *Don Quixote*, *The Pilgrim's Progress* and *The Ancient Mariner*. He won several awards at international exhibitions and in later years turned more to painting. He was an elected Royal Academician and was a member of the Royal Society of Painters, Etchers and Engravers.

STRANGE, Sir Robert, originally Strang
(1721–92)

Line-engraver, born in Kirkwall, Orkney. He fought on the Jacobite side at Prestonpans, Falkirk and Culloden, and in 1747 married a Jacobite, Isabella Lumisden. He studied in Paris and settled in London (1750). He had a European reputation as a historical line-engraver, in opposition to the stippling of his rival, Bartolozzi. His works include portraits of royalty and engravings of paintings by artists such as Titian and Van Dyck.

STRATHCONA, Donald Alexander Smith, 1st Baron See SMITH, Donald Alexander

STRUTH, William
(1875–1956)

Football manager and administrator, born in Glasgow. One of the most important figures in the history of Rangers Football Club, he joined the club as a trainer just prior to World War I, having held the same position at Clyde. He became manager in 1920, and stayed in the post until he retired in 1954; he also held a place on the club's board from 1947. The period was one in which Rangers dominated Scottish football, Struth's successes including five consecutive championships from the 1926–7 season, and three successive Scottish Cup victories, 1934–5–6. A far cry from today's tracksuited tacticians, he epitomized the old school of football manager, always impeccably dressed, and possessed of a stern demeanour more appropriate to a bank manager.

STUART, House of

Aristocratic family, from whom came the royal line of the (Stuart) sovereigns of Scotland and, later, of Great Britain and Ireland, from **Robert II** (1371) to Queen Anne (1714). The original family was descended from a Breton immigrant, Alan Fitzflaald (d.c.1114), who received the lands of Oswestry in Shropshire from Henry I. His elder son was William Fitzalan (c.1105–1160).

STUART, Arabella
(1575–1615)

Heiress and conspirator. She was the daughter of Charles Stuart, Earl of Lennox, younger brother of Lord **Darnley**, and thus the great-granddaughter of **Margaret Tudor**. Although she was in the line of royal succession immediately after **James VI and I**, her supporters argued that she had a superior claim, having been born in England. Since Elizabeth was jealous of any marriage that might transmit a claim to the throne,

Arabella was arrested shortly before the queen's death, on suspicion of planning to marry William Seymour, heir of the Suffolk line. James, on his accession, restored her to favour, but she was rumoured to have been involved in the plots of Cobham and Raleigh against him. She constantly complained of poverty and in 1609 was again arrested on a charge of planning an illicit marriage. James relented, released her and awarded her an annual pension of £1600. In 1610 she became engaged to Seymour, but he retracted the engagement before the Privy Council and Arabella received further financial support. In July, however, the couple secretly married, but were discovered and arrested. She was put in the custody of the Bishop of Durham in March 1611, but broke her journey north at Barnet, on the plea of ill health. In June she fled on board a French ship, but was captured at sea and brought to the Tower of London, where she died.

STUART, Prince Charles Edward Louis Philip Casimir
(1720–88)

Claimant to the throne of Great Britain, known variously as the 'Young Pretender', the 'Young Chevalier', and 'Bonnie Prince Charlie', elder son of **James Francis Edward Stuart**. Born in Rome, and educated there, he became the centre of Jacobite hopes. He first saw service at the siege of Gaeta (1734); fought bravely at Dettingen (1743); and the next year went to France to head Marshal Saxe's projected invasion of England. But the squadron which was to have convoyed the transports with 15 000 troops to Kent fled before the British fleet; the transports themselves were scattered by a storm; and for a year and a half Charles was kept hanging on in France, until at last, sailing from Nantes, he landed with seven followers at Eriskay in the Hebrides on 23 July 1745, and on 19 August raised his father's standard in Glenfinnan. The clansmen flocked in. On 17 September Edinburgh surrendered, though the castle held out, and Charles kept court at Holyrood, the palace of his ancestors. There followed the victory over Sir John Cope at Prestonpans (21 September), and on 1 November he left for London at the head of 6500 men. He took Carlisle and advanced as far as Derby. Londoners became alarmed, especially since the cream of the British army was engaged on the Continent. Eventually William, Duke of Cumberland, was dispatched against the insurgents. Charles meanwhile had been unwillingly argued into a withdrawal by his commanders and the Highlanders turned back, winning one last victory against the government forces at Falkirk, 17 January 1746, before suffering a crushing defeat by Cumberland's troops at Culloden Moor on 16 April. The rising was ruthlessly suppressed by the duke, who subsequently earned the name 'Butcher Cumberland'. Charles was hunted in the Highlands and islands for five months with a price of £30 000 on his head, but no one betrayed him. He was helped by **Flora Macdonald** when he crossed from Benbecula to Portree in June 1746, disguised as 'Betty Burke', her maid. He landed in Brittany on 29 September, and was given hospitality at the French court until the peace of Aix-la-Chapelle (1748) caused his forcible expulsion from France, although he spent a while at Avignon until the English found out and protested, and afterwards lived secretly in Paris with his mistress, Clementina Walkinshaw. He made two or three secret visits to London between 1750 and 1760, even declaring himself a protestant. On his father's death in 1766 he assumed the title of Charles III of Great Britain and retired to Florence, where in 1772 he married Louisa, Princess Louise of Stolberg, known after her marriage as Countess of Albany, but the marriage was later dissolved. His natural daughter, Charlotte (1753–89) by his mistress Clementina Walkinshaw, he had created Duchess of Albany. He died in Rome and was buried at Frascati, later at St Peter's.

STUART, Henry Benedict Maria Clement, Duke of York

(1725–1807)

Cardinal, brother of Prince **Charles Edward Stuart**, and the last of the Stuarts, born in Rome. After the failure of the 1745 rising he became in 1747 a cardinal and priest, and in 1761 Bishop of Frascati. Through the favour of the French court he enjoyed the revenues of two rich abbeys, as well as a Spanish pension. However, the French Revolution stripped him of his fortune, and he had to take refuge in Venice for three years. In 1800 George III granted him a pension of £4000. The crown jewels, taken away by **James VII and II**, were bequeathed by him to George IV, then Prince of Wales, who in 1819 gave 50 guineas towards Canova's monument in St Peter's to 'James III, Charles III, and Henry IX'. Next to the exiled Stuarts came the descendants of Henrietta,

Charles I's youngest daughter, who in 1661 was married to the Duke of Orléans. From this marriage sprang Anne Mary (1669–1728), who married Victor Amadeus, Duke of Savoy and King of Sardinia; their son Charles Emmanuel III (1701–73), King of Sardinia; his son, Victor Amadeus III (1726–96), King of Sardinia; his son, Victor Emmanuel I (1759–1824), King of Sardinia; his daughter Mary (1792–1840), who married Francis, Duke of Modena; their son, Ferdinand (1821–49), who married Elizabeth of Austria; and their daughter, Maria Teresa (1849–1919), who in 1868 married Prince (from 1913 to 1918 King) Ludvig III of Bavaria, and whom, as 'Mary III and IV', the 'Legitimist Jacobites' of 1891 put forward as the 'representative of the Royal House of these realms'. Rupert, her son, was ninth in descent from Charles I; he represented Bavaria at Queen Victoria's Diamond Jubilee, 1897, and early in World War I took command of a German army group in France. His son, Duke Albrecht of Bavaria, inherited the claim. The branch of the family which the Act of Settlement (1701) called to the throne on the death of Anne were the descendants of the electress Sophia of Hanover, granddaughter of **James VI and I** by her mother Princess Elizabeth, Electress Palatine and Queen of Bohemia. By that Act the abovementioned descendants of Henrietta of Orléans were excluded, and also the Roman Catholic descendants of the Princess Elizabeth's sons. Queen Elizabeth II is 26th in descent from Walter Fitzalan, 20th from **Robert II** and 12th from James VI and I. Lady **Arabella Stuart** was the daughter of the Earl of Lennox, Darnley's younger brother, and so a great-great-granddaughter of Henry VII, a third cousin to Queen Elizabeth, and a first cousin to James VI and I. At 27 she was suspected of having a lover in the boy William Seymour, who had Tudor blood in his veins; but on James's accession (1603) she was restored to favour, only, however, to contract a secret marriage in 1610 with him. Both were imprisoned, and both escaped — Seymour successfully to Ostend, but she was retaken, and died, insane, in the Tower. The cadets of the house of Stuart are: (1) descendants of Robert II; (2) descendants of natural sons of his descendants; (3) descendants of natural sons of Stuart kings; and (4) legitimate branches of the Stuarts before their accession to the throne. To the first belong the Stuarts of Castle-Stewart, descended from Robert, Duke of Albany, Robert II's third son, through the Lords Avondale and Ochiltree. They received the titles of Lord Stuart of Castle-Stewart in the peerage of Ireland (1619), Viscount Castle-Stewart (1793), and earl (1809). To the second class belong the Stuart Earls of Traquair (1633–1861), descended from a natural son of James Stewart, Earl of Buchan. To the third class belong the Regent **Moray**, the Marquis of Bute, and the Shaw-Stewarts; and to the fourth belong the Earls of Galloway (from a brother of the fifth High Steward), the Lords Blantyre, the Stewarts of Fort-Stewart, and the Stewarts of Grandtully (from the fourth High Steward; the last baronet died in 1890).

STUART, Prince James Francis Edward
(1688–1766)

Claimant to the throne of Great Britain, known as the 'Old Pretender', the only son of **James VII and II** and his second wife, Mary of Modena, born in St James's Palace, London. Six months later, he was conveyed by his fugitive mother to St Germain, where, on his father's death in 1701, he was proclaimed his successor as **James III**. On an attempt (1708) to make a descent upon Scotland, the young 'Chevalier de St George' was not allowed to land; after his return he served with the French in the Low Countries, distinguishing himself at Malplaquet. But in **Mar**'s ill-conducted rebellion, he landed at Peterhead (December 1715), only to leave six weeks afterwards from Montrose. France was then closed to him by the Treaty of Utrecht, and almost all the rest of his life was passed in Rome, where he died. In 1719 he had married Princess Clementina Sobieski (1702–35), who bore him two sons, **Charles** and **Henry Stuart**.

STUART, Gilbert
(1742–86)

Jurist and historian, a brilliant but rude, violent and dissipated man. He published in 1768 an *Historical Dissertation on the Antiquity of the English Constitution*, which he traced to a German source, and in 1778 *A View of Society in Europe in its Progress from Rudeness to Refinement*. In 1779 he published his most valuable work, *Observations on the Public Law and Constitutional History of Scotland*. Other works include *History of the Establishment of the Reformation in Scotland* (1780) and *The History of Scotland from the Establishment of the Reformation till the death of Queen Mary* (1782), in which he backed

William Robertson's view of the queen's guilt. He later bitterly attacked Robertson, believing himself insulted. One of the main contributors to *English Review* (1783), he was a good scholar but prejudiced and spiteful. About 1779 he was an unsuccessful candidate for the Chair of Public Law at Edinburgh.

STUART, John McDouall
(1815–66)

Scottish-born Australian explorer, born in Dysart, Fife, and educated at the Scottish Naval and Military Academy, Edinburgh. He accompanied Captain Charles Sturt's 17-month expedition to central Australia (1844–5), then returned to Adelaide to work as an estate agent. Between 1858 and 1862 he made six expeditions into the interior, one of which brought him a reward of 1000 square miles. In 1860 he crossed Australia from south to north, discovering the Finke River and the MacDonnell Ranges. In 1861, against great physical odds, he crossed the continent again, reaching the Indian Ocean and receiving a government grant of £2000. Mount Stuart is named after him.

STUART OF FINDHORN, James Gray Stuart, 1st Viscount
(1897–1971)

Conservative politician, born in Edinburgh, the third son of the Earl of Moray, and educated at Eton. In World War I he served as a captain in the Royal Scots, winning the Military Cross. Equerry to the Duke of York (later King George VI) in 1920–1, he was MP for Moray and Nairn from 1923 to 1959. He was Scottish Conservative Whip (1935–41), then Chief Conservative Whip (1941–7). As the latter, he was one of Winston Churchill's closest advisers and confidants. As Secretary of State for Scotland (1952–7) he was one of the longest occupants of the office. During this time he presided over a massive house-building programme in Scotland, and also initiated the construction of the Forth Road Bridge.

SUBAK-SHARPE, John Herbert
(1924–)

Austrian-born virologist, born in Vienna, and educated at the Humanistic Gymnasium there. He left school at 14 and moved to the UK in 1939. He served in the Parachute

Regiment from 1944 to 1947 before reading genetics in Birmingham, where he graduated in 1952, and took his PhD in 1956. He first went to Scotland in 1954 as an Assistant Lecturer in Genetics at Glasgow. After a period (1956–60) at the Agricultural Research Council Animal Virus Research Unit at Pirbright, he returned to Glasgow, joining the Medical Research Council Experimental Virus Research Unit. In 1968 he was appointed Professor of Virology at Glasgow University and Honorary Director of the Medical Research Council Virology Unit. His chief scientific interests have been in the genetics of viruses, but he has also contributed to our knowledge of the genetic material of higher organisms. He has served on many committees, both in Scotland and elsewhere, where his considerable knowledge of the molecular biology of viruses has been of great value in the fields of cancer and practical animal virus research.

SUTHERLAND, James
(1639–1719)

Horticulturalist, appointed head gardener to the Edinburgh Physic Garden by Sir **Robert Sibbald** in 1676, he was a self-made man who in just seven years wrote and published a catalogue in Latin, with English names, of all the plants in the garden. This catalogue is still of considerable interest to those studying the dates at which plants were introduced into the country. He supplemented his meagre stipend from the city by teaching medical students the names and uses of the various plants growing in the garden. He surmounted disaster in 1689 when the panic draining of the North Loch flooded the garden, destroying most of the plants, by obtaining money from the City and the Treasury which allowed him to re-collect the plants and extend the garden, building greenhouses and shelter so that oranges and lemons would grow.

SUTHERLAND, John Derg
(1905–91)

Psychoanalyst, born in Edinburgh. He studied chemistry, psychology and medicine at Edinburgh University and psychoanalysis in London. Early in his career he evolved model procedures for the selection of Army Officers and published important observations on the 'war neurosis'. As Medical Director of both the Tavistock Clinic, London (1947–68), and the Scottish Institute of Human Relations,

Edinburgh (1970–8), he played a central role in those institutions' development as leading centres of psychodynamic research and treatment. His chief publication was *Fairbairn's Journey into the Interior* (1989), a psychobiography of **Ronald Fairbairn**, his first teacher in psychoanalysis.

SUTHERLAND, Robert Garioch See GARIOCH, Robert

SWAN, Annie S (Shepherd).
(1859–1943)

Novelist, born near Coldingham, Berwickshire, and brought up in Edinburgh and at Gorebridge, Midlothian. In 1883 she married a schoolmaster (later doctor), James Burnett Smith, and from 1896 they lived in England; she returned to Scotland in 1927 after her husband's death. She published her first novel, *Ups and Downs*, in 1878, and made her name with a Border romance, *Aldersyde* (1883), followed by *Carlowie* (1884), *A Divided House* (1885) and *The Gates of Eden* (1887). From then on she published a large number of light romantic novels, and stories for women's magazines like *The Woman at Home*. She published her autobiography, *My Life*, in 1934.

SWEENEY, William
(1950–)

Composer and clarinettist, born in Glasgow. He studied at the Royal Scottish Academy of Music and at the Royal Academy of Music, his teachers including Frank Spedding and Harrison Birtwhistle (composition) and Alan Hacker (clarinet). His orchestral works include *Sunset Song* (1985), *Cumha* (1987), *An Rathad Ur* (1988, with tenor saxophone solo), and *Air, Strathspey and Reel* (1989). His chamber works make prominent use of his own instrument; he has also written a string quartet (1981), and many vocal pieces, including *The Heights of Macchu Picchu* (1978), *A Vision of Scotland* (1979, with orchestra), *Scenes from Old Stirling* (1987), and *El Pueblo* (1989).

SWINBURNE, Sir James, 9th Baronet
(1858–1958)

Electrical engineer, 'the father of British plastics'. Born in Inverness and brought up for much of his childhood on the island of

Eilean Shona in Loch Moidart, he started work as an apprentice in a locomotive factory in Manchester, quickly showing his talent. In 1885 he began work in R E B Crompton's electrical engineering firm, where he invented the 'hedgehog' transformer (used in early wireless sets), then in 1899 he set up as a consultant in London. A pioneer in the plastics industry, he carried out research on phenolic resins which resulted in a process for producing synthetic resin, but his patent application for this was anticipated by one day, by the Belgian chemist Leo Baekeland, working in the USA. Almost 20 years later he came to an agreement with Baekeland, and they merged their UK interests to form Bakelite Ltd in 1926. A man of wide interests, with more than 100 patents to his name, he was President of the Institution of Electrical Engineers (1902–3) and of the Plastics Institute (1937–8). He was elected a Fellow of the Royal Society in 1906.

SWINTON, Alan Archibald Campbell

(1863–1930)

Electrical engineer and inventor, born in Edinburgh. He was interested in all things mechanical and electrical from an early age, linking two houses some distance apart by telephone at the age of 15, only two years after its invention by **Alexander Graham Bell**. In 1882 he began an engineering apprenticeship in the Newcastle works of William George Armstrong, for whom he devised a new method of insulating electric cables on board ship by sheathing them in lead. While practising as a consulting engineer in London, he was one of the first to explore the medical applications of radiography (1896), and in a letter to *Nature* in 1908 he outlined the principles of an electronic system of television.

SWINTON, John

(1829–1901)

Scottish-born journalist, reform and labour crusader, born in Salton, East Lothian. He emigrated with his family to Montreal (1843), where he worked as an apprentice to the printers of the *Montreal Witness*. After a brief period in a seminary (1853), he travelled through the southern and mid-western states as a journeyman printer. He studied law and medicine in New York City in 1857. After ten years as head of the editorial staff on the New York *Times* he worked in various occupations (1870–4), identifying with the growing labour

movement and playing a major part in the labour demonstration at Tompkins Square (1874). In 1874 he stood as candidate for Mayor of New York for a small labour party, the Industrial Political Party. The following year he moved to a popular and less conservative newspaper, the New York *Sun*, run by Charles Anderson Dana, who made Swinton chief of editorial staff. He remained there until 1883, when he founded *John Swinton's Paper*, a four-page weekly journal devoted to labour affairs and intellectual theoretics, advocating reading for workers as a basis for self-education in the labour struggle. Characteristic of his approach was his advice that *Capital*, the important work by the late 'Dr Charles Marx', would prove a valuable addition to any student of labour's library shelf: he advocated such theory as stimulus, not as infallible doctrine. *John Swinton's Paper* ran until 1887 and remains the best single source of labour history in America of its day. Unfortunately, it beggared Swinton and he was obliged to discontinue it. Dana brought him back to the *Sun*, and subsequently he was American correspondent for several European newspapers. His *John Swinton's Travels* (1880) is a vigorous account of Europe as he saw it on a visit, and his *Striking for Life* (1894) is a valuable, personal account of the labour movement. His integrity was unquestioned, and acknowledged by Socialists and non-Socialists alike, however great their ideological differences. He influenced **Hugh MacDiarmid**, among many others.

SYME, James

(1799–1870)

Surgeon, born in Edinburgh, considered one of the finest surgeons of the age. He studied under **Robert Liston** at Edinburgh University and at Paris and in Germany. In 1818 he announced a method of waterproofing, afterwards patented by **Charles Macintosh**. From 1823 to 1833 he lectured on clinical surgery, and in 1829 established a private hospital in Edinburgh. In 1831 he published his treatise on *The Excision of Diseased Joints*, and in 1832 his *Principles of Surgery*. In 1833 he became Professor of Clinical Surgery. He also wrote on pathology, stricture, fistula, and incised wounds.

SYMINGTON, William

(1763–1831)

Engineer and inventor, born in Leadhills, Lanarkshire. He became a mechanic at the Wanlockhead mines. In 1787 he patented an engine for road locomotion and, in 1788, he constructed for **Patrick Miller** a similar engine on a boat 25 feet long, having twin hulls with paddle-wheels between, which was launched on Dalswinton Loch. In 1802 he completed at Grangemouth the *Charlotte Dundas*, one of the first practical steamboats ever built. It was intended as a tug, but vested interests prevented its use, asserting that the wash would injure the sides of the Forth and Clyde Canal. Symington died in London, in poverty.

T

TAIT, Archibald Campbell
(1811–82)

Anglican prelate, and Archbishop of Canterbury, born in Edinburgh. Reared as a Presbyterian, he was educated at the newly-founded Edinburgh Academy, Glasgow University and Balliol College, Oxford, where he became a fellow. He entered the Church of England in 1836, and became an opponent of the Oxford Movement, protesting in 1841 against John Newman's *Tract* 90. He succeeded Dr Thomas Arnold as headmaster of Rugby (1842), became Dean of Carlisle in 1849, and in 1856 Bishop of London. He showed firmness and broadmindedness, as well as tact, in dealing with controversies over church ritual; he condemned Bishop Colenso's critical views on the accuracy of the Bible, but intervened on his side against attempts to have him deposed. In 1869 he was appointed Archbishop of Canterbury (the first Scotsman to hold the post), and helped to lull the strife caused by Irish disestablishment, but was less successful in dealing with resentments over the Public Worship and Regulation Act (1874) and the Burials Act (1880). He did much to extend and improve the organization of the Church in the colonies, and presided over the 1878 Lambeth Conference. His books included *The Dangers and Safeguards of Modern Theology* (1861) and *Harmony of Revelation and the Sciences* (1864). His biography was published in 1891 by his son-in-law, **Randall Thomas Davidson**.

TAIT, Peter Guthrie
(1831–1901)

Mathematician and golf enthusiast, born in Dalkeith, Midlothian. He was educated at the universities of Edinburgh and Cambridge, where he graduated as senior wrangler in 1852. He became Professor of Mathematics at Belfast (1854) and of Natural Philosophy at Edinburgh (1860–1901). He wrote on quaternions, thermodynamics and the kinetic theory of gases, and collaborated with Lord **Kelvin** on a *Treatise on natural philosophy* (1867). His study of vortices and smoke rings led to early work on the topology of knots. He studied the dynamics of the flight of a golf-ball and discovered the importance of 'underspin'.

TAIT, Thomas Smith
(1882–1952)

Architect, born in Paisley, the son of a stonemason. He became the most prominent Scottish architect of the interwar period and a leading British exponent of the Modern Movement. He trained in Glasgow, becoming an assistant with Sir **John James Burnet** in 1903, studying simultaneously under Eugene Bourdon at the Glasgow School of Art, and imbibing Beaux Arts principles from both masters. After study travel on the Continent, he moved to the firm's London office in 1905. In 1914 he travelled to New York for a year's work with the modernist Donn Barber. In 1919 he joined Burnet in partnership. He was largely responsible for the steel-framed Kodak House, London (1910), and designed Adelaide House (1921–4), the *Daily Telegraph* office in London (1927) and St Andrews House, Edinburgh (1934). Assessor to several competitions, he won the competition for Hawkhead Infectious Diseases Hospital in Paisley (1938). He was controlling designer of the Glasgow Empire Exhibition of 1938. A large number of Modern Movement houses came from his hand. He drew from Egyptian and American sources, with Beaux Arts inspiration and an invaluable ability to interpret freely.

TAIT, William
(1792–1864)

Publisher. He was the founder of *Tait's Edinburgh Magazine* (1832–64), a literary and radical political monthly, among whose contributors were De Quincey, John Stuart Mill, Richard Cobden and John Bright.

TALBERT, Bruce James
(1838–81)

Designer. Educated at Dundee High School, he became a prolific and influential designer specializing in Gothic-style furniture. Originally apprenticed to a wood-carver, he was later trained as an architect. He moved from Glasgow to Manchester and Coventry, working for various firms before settling in London where he published his *Gothic Forms Applied to Furniture and Decoration for Domestic Purposes* in 1867. By 1873 he was working for Villons. Apart from furniture, he designed metalwork, wallpapers, tapestries and carpets.

TALIESIN
(late 6th century)

Court poet and subsequently mythical figure of supernatural powers. He is mentioned along with **Aneirin** by Nennius in his *Historia Britonum* (c.800) as a great poet of the Old North, but while his only certain association is with King Urien Rheged, which places him in what is now Cumbria, he would seem to have been a visitor, possibly from the p-Celtic kingdom of Strathclyde. The eight poems firmly ascribed to him, amidst many which are either doubtful or spurious in the much later *Book of Taliesin*, are poems in praise of Rheged and his son Owain. These, which seem authentic, describe battles against the Picts as well as the Angles from the east, which puts Taliesin firmly enough as a frontier bard of the Strathclyde as well as Cumbrian region. Although later Welsh opinion credited him with coming from Powys, he clearly thought of Urien as his patron. He also spoke warmly of the king and his son's courage in battle, and provided the basis for their place among leaders of the Brythonic resistance to the Anglo-Saxon invaders and Pictish predators. He aquired an extraordinary identity of his own in legend, which attributed to him a supernatural birth, vast odysseys of travel, and a collegiality with Myrddin (Merlin). This Welsh tradition may go back to the 9th or 10th century. If all of the work ascribed to him is authentic, he is not only the product of multiple successive births but is alive and will survive us all. Authenticity limits him to the western Scottish borders, and to a poet of dignity, fidelity, patriotism and human affection.

TANNAHILL, Robert
(1774–1810)

Poet and songwriter, born in Paisley, the son of a handloom weaver. He composed many of his best songs to the music of his shuttle.

He helped to found a Burns Club in 1803 for which he composed songs set on traditional airs. His *Poems and Songs* (1807) proved popular, the best known being 'Gloomy Winter's noo awa', 'Jessie the Flower o' Dunblane', 'The Braes o' Gleniffer', 'Loudon's Bonnie Woods and Braes' and 'The Wood o' Craigielea'. But after a publisher declined a revised edition he drowned himself in a canal near Paisley.

TASSIE, James
(1735–99)

Modeller and engraver, born in Pollokshaws, Glasgow. Apprenticed to a stonemason, he studied art at Foulis Academy in Glasgow. In 1763 he went to Dublin, where he developed a special 'white enamel composition' for making portrait medallions. In 1766 he moved to London where he used his paste to make reproductions of the most famous gems. He also executed many cameo portraits of his contemporaries, and the plaster reproductions of the Portland Vase.

TATE, Harry, originally Ronald Macdonald Hutchison
(1872–1940)

Comedian. He originally worked for the sugar firm of Henry Tate & Sons, taking their name when he turned professional comedian after spare-time appearances in smoking concerts. Starting as an impressionist, he made his London début at the Camberwell Empire (1875) in the sketch 'A Ward in Chancery', in which he mimicked Dan Leno, Eugene Stratton, George Robey and Cissie Loftus. He was filmed in his act as early as 1899. One of the first car owners, he developed the comedy sketch 'Motoring', and owned the first personalized number plate, 'T8'. His catchphrase 'Good-bye-ee' was turned into the first hit song of World War I. He appeared in the first Royal Command Performance (1912), and entered revue with *Hello Tango* (1913). His son, Harry Tate Jr, joined the act in 1917, and after his father's death continued the act in variety.

TAYLOR, C P (Cecil Philip)
(1929–81)

Playwright, born in Glasgow, but resident for most of his life in Northumberland. He came to prominence in the 1960s, when plays such as the political comedy *Allergy* (1966) were produced at the Edinburgh Traverse Theatre. He wrote over 50 plays for almost every kind of theatre, but his most famous, *Good* (1981), which was produced by the Royal Shakespeare Company, is a study of its protagonist's gradual but almost imperceptible drift into Nazism.

TAYLOR, Ernest Archibald
(1874–1951)

Furniture and stained-glass designer and painter, born in Greenock, Renfrewshire, the 15th of 17 children. He trained as a draughtsman in a shipyard before studying at Glasgow School of Art in the 1890s. Influenced by **Mackintosh**, in 1900 he joined the firm of Wylie and Lochhead, the Glasgow cabinet makers. He designed a drawing-room for their Pavilion at the 1901 Glasgow International Exhibition and also exhibited at Turin in 1902 alongside his fellow Glasgow School artists, winning a diploma and medal. He married the artist **Jessie Marion King** and moved to Manchester in 1908 after completing two important architectural commissions. He was very involved in stained-glass design. From 1911 to 1914 he taught, along with his wife, at the Shealing Atelier of Fine Art in Paris. He retired to Kirkcudbright after the outbreak of World War I and spent the rest of his life there.

TAYLOR, Sir George
(1904 –)

Botanist, born in Edinburgh. Winning a scholarship to George Heriot's School, he was educated there and at Edinburgh University, where he read botany and graduated in 1926. He then became a member and later leader of several botanical expeditions, including those to South Africa, East Africa and the Ruwenzori, Tibet and Sikkim. After serving in the Air Ministry during World War II, he became Deputy Keeper (1945), then Keeper (1950) of Botany at the British Museum (Natural History) before his appointment as Director of the Royal Botanic Gardens at Kew in 1956. Elected FRS in 1968 and knighted in 1962, he had a powerful influence, not only on the development of Kew Gardens, but on horticulture worldwide as an active member and often president of many horticultural societies. An expert on the Himalayan blue poppy, *Meconopsis*, he contributed learned papers on many other flowering plants.

TEACHER, William
(1811–76)

Whisky blender and wholesaler. He began his life in humble circumstances. At the age of seven he started work, helping his mother in a spinning mill at Bridge of Weir. After a brief spell apprenticed to a tailor he worked in a grocery shop in Anderston, Glasgow. In 1834 he married the owner's daughter and by 1840 he had taken charge of a business that sold only wines and spirits. Shortly afterwards he opened a number of small 'dram' shops, selling glasses of whisky, which became noted for their cleanliness and efficiency. Teacher was swift to adopt the new technique of blending, moving into new premises in St Enoch Square where he carefully supervised the process. By the year of his sudden death the firm had grown to such an extent that it employed a London agent. His sons maintained the company's expansion, launching the famous blend, Teacher's Highland Cream, in about 1880.

TEDDER, Arthur William, 1st Baron Tedder of Glenguin
(1890–1967)

Marshal of the RAF, born at Glenguin, Stirlingshire. He was in the Colonial Service when war broke out in 1914. By 1916 he had transferred to the RFC (Royal Flying Corps). Remaining in the service, at the outbreak of World War II he was Director-General of Research and Development, Air Ministry. From 1940 he organized the Middle East Air Force with great success, moving on to the Mediterranean theatre and later becoming Deputy Supreme Commander under Eisenhower. His services were recognized in his appointment as Marshal of the RAF (1945). Created a baron in 1946, in 1950 he became Chancellor of the University of Cambridge and also a governor of the BBC. He wrote *Air Power in the War* (1948) and an autobiography, *With Prejudice* (1966).

TELFORD, Thomas
(1757–1834)

Civil engineer, born in Westerkirk, Langholm, a shepherd's son. At the age of 14 he was apprenticed to a stonemason, in 1780 went to Edinburgh, and in 1782 to London. In 1784 he got work at Portsmouth dockyard; in 1787 he became surveyor of public works for Shropshire. His reputation was enhanced by his masonry arch bridge over the Severn at Montford (1790–2) and even more by the spectacular Pont Cysylte aqueduct and other works on the Ellesmere Canal (1793–1805). In 1801 he was commissioned by the government to report on the public works required for Scotland; and he constructed the Caledonian Canal (1803–23), more than 1000 miles of road, and 1200 bridges, besides churches, manses, harbours, etc. Other works by him included the road from London to Holyhead, with the remarkable 579-ft span wrought-iron Menai Suspension Bridge (1819–26), and the St Katherine's Docks (1824–8) in London; he was also responsible for draining large tracts of the Fen country.

TEMPERLEY, Joe (Joseph)
(1929 –)

Jazz musician, born in Lochgelly, Fife. He played tenor saxophone with local dance bands before moving to London in 1949 to work under a succession of leaders such as Harry Parry and Jack Parnell. He took up the baritone saxophone, playing this exclusively during seven years with the Humphrey Lyttelton Band. On emigrating to the USA in 1965, and living in New York, he worked in jazz big bands led by Woody Herman, Buddy Rich, Thad Jones-Mel Lewis, Clark Terry and (after the death of Duke Ellington) with the Ellington orchestra under the founder's son, Mercer Ellington. As a freelance musician he featured in many small-group recordings and in festival performances throughout the world, as well as doing much studio, television and film work, principally on baritone and soprano saxophones.

TENNANT, Charles
(1768–1838)

Chemical industrialist, born in Ochiltree, Ayrshire. Educated at the parish school there, he was apprenticed as a weaver. He studied bleaching and set up his own bleachfields near Paisley, becoming one of the first to make a fortune out of a heavy chemical industry. In 1799 he took out a patent for the manufacture of a dry bleaching powder made from chlorine and slaked lime (probably the invention of one of his partners, **Charles Macintosh**). Being easily transportable to the expanding textile industry (where chlorine could be regenerated by mixing with acid), demand for the bleaching powder grew until the factory at St Rollox near Glasgow became the largest chemical works in the world at that time.

TENNANT, William
(1784–1848)

Poet and scholar, born in Anstruther, Fife. He studied at St Andrews University, and in 1812 published a mock-heroic poem *Anster Fair*, which was the first attempt to naturalize the Italian *ottava rima*. He was a teacher from 1816 at Lasswade, from 1819 at Dollar Academy, and from 1835 Professor of Oriental Languages at St Andrews. His *Synopsis of Chaldaic and Syriac Grammar* (1840) became a standard authority. Other poems were the *Thane of Fife* (1822) and *Papistry Stormed* (1827); dramas were *Cardinal Beaton* (1823) and *John Baliol* (1825).

TENNENT, Hugh
(1863–90)

Brewer, born in Glasgow into a family who owned perhaps the largest brewing firm in the west of Scotland. Both his father and his grandfather died in 1864, leaving the business in the hands of trustees. At the age of 21 he assumed sole control of the company and proceeded to revolutionize the firm's activities. He innovated in lager brewing and marketing for both domestic and foreign consumption. So great was his success that he built a completely new and integrated lager brewery at Wellpark in the east end of Glasgow, utilizing the expertise of leading continental brewers. He died, aged 27, the last member of the family to have direct control of this vibrant company. Despite his short life his contribution to the drinking habits of millions of Scots over successive generations is incalculable.

TERRY, Charles Sanford
(1864–1936)

English-born historian, born in Newport Pagnell, Buckinghamshire. First destined for a musical career, he was educated at St Paul's Cathedral Choir School and King's College School, finishing at Lancing College, and afterwards at Clare College, Cambridge. Lecturer in History at Durham University College of Science, Newcastle-upon-Tyne (1890–8), he went to King's College, University of Aberdeen, as Lecturer in History in 1898, owing his appointment to his deep interest in Scottish history. In 1899 he published *The Life and Campaigns of Alexander Leslie, first Earl of Leven*, and followed this with *The Rising of* 1745 (1900), both showing what would prove a life-long enthusiasm for Scottish military history. Then came his tactfully entitled *The Chevalier de St George* (1901), thus neatly avoiding the twin pitfalls of allusion to the subject as 'James VIII and III' or the 'Old Pretender', although he firmly styled the life of his son Charles as *The Young Pretender* (1903). In 1902 he also produced two volumes of *The Albemarle Papers* and *The Cromwellian Union*. In 1903 he was named Burnett-Fletcher Professor of History at Aberdeen, and continued to pour out books: *John Graham of Claverhouse* (1905), *The Pentland Rising* (1905), *The Scottish Parliament* (1906), *An Index to the Papers relating to Scotland* (1908), and in a particularly important attempt to co-ordinate the mass of existing Scottish published historical sources, *A Catalogue of the Publications of Scottish Historical Clubs* (1909). He responded to the war with *A Short History of Europe* 1806–1914 (1915) and profited by its interruption of student enrolments by bringing out his three-volume *Bach's Chorale* (1915–21), followed by 10 more works on Bach, his family and their music, and by contributions to Grove's *Dictionary of Music and Musicians*. He returned to Scottish history with *The Army of the Solemn League and Covenant* (2 vols, 1917) and with two histories of Scotland (1920, 1921), *The Forty-Five* (1922) and *The Jacobites and the Union* (1922). The recipient of many honorary doctorates, he made a significant contribution to the study and professionalization of Scottish history, although he is remembered as something of a martinet.

THIN, James
(1823–1915)

Bookseller. Apprenticed in Edinburgh at the age of 11, he spent five years learning the trade. After a period in which he considered entering the Church, he was persuaded to remain in bookselling and went on to open his own shop on South Bridge, Edinburgh, in 1848. Although at first there was 'no embarrassing rush', he went on to expand the business until, some years later, it could claim to be 'the largest retail bookselling establishment' in the city. A keen Church official, he was also a well-known hymnologist, with a collection of more than 2500 hymnbooks. Since his death the firm has remained within the family.

THOM, Alexander
(1894–1985)

Engineer and archaeo-astronomer. Educated at Glasgow University, he worked in various engineering firms, then returned to Glasgow as lecturer from 1922 to 1939. On the outbreak of World War II he was seconded to the Royal Aircraft Establishment at Farnborough to lead the engineering work in the building of the High Speed Wind Tunnel. This was a major engineering achievement and played a vital role in testing the aerodynamics of many of Britain's advanced aircraft. Its work continued for several years after the war. Professor of Engineering Science at Oxford University (1945–61), from 1934 he was engaged on a detailed study of all the stone circles in the British Isles and Brittany, and after his retirement published two major works, *Megalithic Sites in Britain* (1967) and *Megalithic Lunar Observatories* (1971). He brought his engineering skills of mathematics and surveying to bear on the analysis of the data he had collected, and he claimed to have discovered two basic units, the 'megalithic yard' and the 'megalithic inch', which had been used in the setting out of most, if not all, of the circles. His conclusions have not been universally accepted, but his meticulous surveys are of lasting value in themselves.

THOM, Robert
(1774–1847)

Civil engineer, born in Tarbolton, Ayrshire. He studied at the Andersonian Institution in Glasgow. He had acquired an interest in cotton mills in West Lothian and at Rothesay, and he greatly increased the water power available to drive the mills by constructing dams and aqueducts, regulated by automatic sluices of his own design. His skill in the design of water supply and power schemes led to his being asked in 1824 to survey the high ground behind Greenock as a potential source for a domestic water supply. He went on to plan the famous Shaws Water Works, which not only provided domestic water but incorporated sites for up to 30 water mills along the courses of two artificial leats, each with a total fall of 500 feet. Inaugurated in 1827, parts of his scheme are still in use, modernized where necessary; the principal reservoir is now known as Loch Thom.

THOMAS THE RHYMER, or THOMAS RYMOUR OF ERCELDOUNE
(c.1220 – c.1297)

Seer and poet. He lived at Erceldoune (now Earlston, Berwickshire), and in 1286 is said to have predicted the death of **Alexander III** and the Battle of Bannockburn, thus becoming known as 'True Thomas'. **Boece** calls him Thomas Learmont. Legend relates that he was carried off to Elfland, and after three years allowed to revisit the earth, but ultimately returned to his mistress, the fairy queen. In a charter of Petrus de Haga of Bemersyde c.1260–1270 the Rhymer appears as a witness; and in another of 1294 Thomas of Erceldoune, 'son and heir of Thomas Rymour of Erceldoune', conveys lands to the hospice of Soutra. The Rhymer's 'prophecies' were collected and published in 1603. Sir **Walter Scott** believed him to be the author of the poem of *Sir Tristrem*, which was founded on a 12th-century French poem by another Thomas, a poet of genius, and almost certainly an Englishman.

THOMPSON, Sir Adam

(1926 –)

Aviator, educated at Rutherglen Academy, Coatbridge, and the Royal Technical College, Glasgow. A pilot in the Fleet Air Arm (1944–7), he became a flying instructor and charter pilot (1947–50). From 1951 to 1959 he was a transport pilot with British European Airways, West Africa Airways and Britavia. He was founder member and director of Airways Interests (Thompson) and Chairman and Chief Executive of the Caledonian Aviation Group (1970–88), building Caledonian Airways into the largest UK independent airline prior to its merging with British Airways.

THOMPSON, Sir D'Arcy Wentworth

(1860–1948)

Classical scholar, mathematician and zoologist, born in Edinburgh and educated at Edinburgh Academy. After three years studying medicine in Edinburgh, he went to Trinity College, Cambridge, to read zoology. He was appointed to his first chair at University College, Dundee, at the age of 24. His early interests were in fishery and whaling, and he made use of the few Dundee whalers then remaining, going in 1896 and 1897 to the Pribiloff Islands on a commission of inquiry into fur sealing. Thereafter he contributed many papers on whaling, fisheries and oceanography, while, at the same time, developing an interest into how the environment interacted with heredity to determine how an animal develops. He showed by simple mathematical transformations how different species could be related, this work culminating in his monumental study *On Growth and Form* (1917), which brought together his classical, mathematical and biological knowledge in a work of great literary and scientific merit. Also in 1917 he was appointed to the Chair of Zoology at St Andrews, where he remained for the rest of his life. His classical scholarship resulted in a *Glossary of Greek Fishes* (1945), which complemented his much earlier *Glossary of Greek Birds* (1895), as well as an annotated translation in 1910 of Aristotle's *Historia animalium*. Appointed CBE in 1898 and elected FRS in 1916, he was an inspired teacher and a commanding figure. His lecture without notes on his return from India a year before his death is still remembered.

THOMPSON, Derick (Ruaraidh MacThómais)

(1921 –)

Poet, born in Stornoway, Isle of Lewis. He was educated at the Nicolson Institute in Stornoway, and at the universities of Aberdeen, Cambridge and North Wales. He served in the Royal Air Force during World War II. He taught at the universities of Edinburgh, Aberdeen and Glasgow, where he became Professor of Celtic in 1963. In 1952 he founded, and remains the editor of, the Gaelic language quarterly *Gairm*, and helped set up the Gaelic Books Council in 1968. He has written important critical works on Gaelic poetry, notably *An Introduction to Gaelic Poetry* (1974, rev 1989), compiled a *New English-Gaelic Dictionary* (1981), and edited *The Companion to Gaelic Scotland* (1983). His own poetry constitutes one of the most significant bodies of modern Gaelic verse; much of it is collected, in both Gaelic and his own English versions, in *Creachadh na Clàrsaich* (Plundering the Harp, 1982). His poetry tends to focus on his ambivalent relationship with the Outer Hebrides, and on his sometimes impatient sense of nationalism, but, like that of **Sorley Maclean**, continually finds universal truths emerging from the particular.

THOMSON, Bryden

(1928–91)

Orchestral conductor, born in Ayr. He studied at the Royal Scottish Academy of Music and the Staatliche Hochschule für Musik, Hamburg, his teachers including Igor Markevich and Hans Schmidt-Isserstedt. After a period as Assistant Conductor to **Ian Whyte** at the BBC Scottish Orchestra, his principal conducting appointments were at the Royal Ballet (1962); Den Norske Opera, Oslo (1964); Royal Opera Stockholm (1966); BBC Northern Symphony Orchestra (1968–73); BBC Welsh Symphony Orchestra (1978–83); Artistic Director and Principal Conductor of the Ulster Orchestra (1977–85); Principal Conductor of the RTE (Radio Telefis Éireann) Symphony Orchestra since 1984, and Music Director of the Royal Scottish Orchestra (1988–91). He was a noted champion of contemporary Scottish music and made many international guest appearances.

THOMSON, Sir Charles Wyville
(1830–82)

Marine biologist and oceanographer, born in Bonsyde, Linlithgow, West Lothian. He studied at Edinburgh and held professorships in natural history at Cork (1853–4), Belfast (1854–68) and Edinburgh (1870–82). He was famous for his deep-sea researches, undertaken in Scotland, Ireland, the Bay of Biscay and the Mediterranean and described in *The Depths of the Oceans* (1872). In 1872 he was appointed scientific head of the *Challenger* round-the-word expedition (1872–6), and on his return wrote *The Voyage of the Challenger* (1877). A window was constructed in his memory in Linlithgow Cathedral.

THOMSON, David Couper
(1861–1954)

Newspaper proprietor, born in Dundee. At the age of 23 he left the family shipping firm to take charge of the newly-acquired Dundee newspaper concern, which he owned and managed until his death. Its principal publications were the *Dundee Courier and Advertiser*, the *Sunday Post*, the *Scots Magazine* (founded in 1739) and *The People's Friend*, but it was known outside Scotland particularly for its many popular children's comics, such as the *Beano* and *Dandy*. Well-known for his concern for local interests, he was a deputy lieutenant for the City of Dundee for 54 years, and a governor of the university college of Dundee for 62 years. He always resisted unionization in his company.

THOMSON, 'D P' (Donald Patrick)
(1896–1974)

Church of Scotland evangelist, born in Dundee. After war service (1914–17) he took an MA at Glasgow University and was ordained Secretary of the Missionary Society. Named Home Board Organiser for Evangelism in 1947, he concluded his ministry as Warden of St Ninian's Training Centre, Crieff, which was to become a hub of outreach activity within the church. During the 1950s and 60s he set the evangelistic agenda for the Church of Scotland. An important figure in the Tell Scotland Movement, he helped keep the Church's mission obligation within view, in a direct but unthreatening manner. Dedicating his whole life to this work, his gift lay in shaking the Church out of its smugness and inspiring a challenging vision for mission in new generations, such that St Ninian's became a Mecca for those in the Church of Scotland with a leaning to evangelism. His publications in the area of mission are extensive, works such as *Aspects of Evangelism* (1968) being typical of his interests and concerns.

THOMSON, George
(1757–1851)

Folksong collector and music publisher, born in Limekilns, Fife. He was chief clerk to the Board of Trustees for the Encouragement of Art and Manufacture in Scotland for 60 years, retiring in 1839. He collected melodies of folksongs and engaged **Robert Burns**, Sir **Walter Scott**, **James Hogg** and others, including Haydn and Beethoven, to contribute works, new words and settings, eventually compiling these into *A Select Collection of Original Scottish Airs* (6 vols, 1793–1841). An amateur musician, he was involved in the first Edinburgh Music Festival (1815), and often played the violin at city concerts.

THOMSON, Sir Godfrey Hilton
(1881–1955)

Educationist and psychologist, researcher in psychometrics and originator of the well-known Moray House tests, born in Carlisle. By winning scholarships he went on to study mathematics and physics at the universities of Durham and Strasbourg. These early studies soon gave way to preoccupation with psychology and mental testing, in which field his distinguished work began in Armstrong College, Newcastle (1906–25), where he began to apply his mathematical skills to tests that would open educational opportunities to children from poor economic backgrounds. This work reached its zenith in Edinburgh in the period 1925–51, when he was Professor of

Education at the university and, jointly, Head of the teachers' college at Moray House. His surveys of the intelligence of Scottish children attracted worldwide interest, as did his brilliant teaching, particularly in the field of factor analysis, but also in his exposition of Dewey's theory of education and its implications. He was knighted in 1949.

THOMSON, James
(1700–48)

Poet, born in Kelso, Roxburghshire. He was educated at Jedburgh School and studied at Edinburgh University for the ministry, but he abandoned his studies and went to seek his fortune as a writer in London. He published *Winter* (1726), a short poem in blank verse, *Summer* (1727), *Spring*, (1728), and *Autumn* which appeared with the other three under the collective title *The Seasons* (1730). It was substantially revised in 1744, and became a source-book for much later bird poetry. In 1729 his *Sophonisba* was produced. His other tragedies were *Agamemnon* (1738), *Edward and Eleonora* (1739), *Tancred and Sigismunda* (1745) and *Coriolanus* (1748). The poem *Liberty* (1735–6) was inspired by the Grand Tour which he undertook as tutor to Charles Talbot's son in 1731, and was dedicated to the Prince of Wales, who awarded him a pension. 'A Poem sacred to the Memory of Isaac Newton' (1727) and 'Britannia' (1729), which criticized Walpole's foreign policy, secured him further patronage and the sinecure of Surveyor-General of the Leeward Isles (1744). *Alfred, a Masque* (1740) contains the song 'Rule Britannia', also claimed by **David Mallet**. The Spenserian *The Castle of Indolence* (1748) is considered his masterpiece.

THOMSON, James
(1822–92)

Engineer, elder brother of Lord **Kelvin**, born in Belfast. He was Professor of Engineering at Belfast University (1851) and Glasgow University (1873–89). As an authority on hydraulics, he invented a turbine, discovered the effect of pressure upon the freezing-point of water, and wrote papers on elastic fatigue, under-currents and trade winds.

THOMSON, James, occasional pseudonym 'B V'
(1834–82)

Poet, born in Port Glasgow, the son of a merchant seaman. He was educated in the Royal Caledonian Asylum orphanage and trained as an army schoolmaster at the Royal Military Asylum, Chelsea, but was dismissed from army service for alcoholism in 1862. A friend of Charles Bradlaugh, editor and owner of the *National Reformer*, between 1862 and 1875 he contributed many of his sombre, sonorous poems to the paper, including *The City of Dreadful Night* (1874), his greatest work. He became a lawyer's clerk in 1862, went into business (1864–9), went to the USA as a mining agent (1872–3), was war correspondent in Spain with the Carlists (1873), and from 1875 onwards depended largely on contributions to a tobacconists' trade monthly. Ill-health and melancholia drove him to narcotics and stimulants. *The City of Dreadful Night and other Poems* (1880) was followed by *Vane's Story* (1881), *Essays and Phantasies* (1881), *A Voice from the Nile* (1884), *Shelley, a Poem* (1885), and *Biographical and Critical Studies* (1896). His pseudonym B V, Bysshe Vanolis, was partly from Shelley's second name, partly from an anagram of Novalis.

THOMSON, John
(1837–1921)

Photographer, traveller and writer, born and educated in Edinburgh. He was married with six children, two of whom worked with him. From 1862 to 1872 he travelled in the Far East, then settled in London, where he operated studios from 1881 to c.1910. A highly sensitive and subtle photographic artist, he was also a witty and readable writer, and produced many accounts of his journeys, one of the finest being *Foochow and the River Min* (1873). Described as one of the first great photojournalists, he is best known for *Illustrations of China and its People* (1873–4) and, with journalist and activist Adolph Smith Headingly, *Street Life in London* (1878). He was innovative both technically and in terms of his methods of integrating photographs and text for the purposes of social documentation. Although in some ways the 'quintessential Victorian traveller', he was unusual among his British contemporaries for the humility of his attitude to his work. In 1875 he wrote: 'The camera should be a power in this age of instruction for the instruction of the age'.

THOMSON, John, of Duddingston
(1778–1840)

Clergyman and painter, born in Dailly Manse, Ayrshire. Educated at Glasgow University, he became minister of Dailly in succession to his father from 1800, and from 1805 of Duddingston. He studied painting under **Alexander Nasmyth** and became one of the first and most successful landscape painters of Scotland.

THOMSON, Joseph
(1858–95)

Explorer, born near Thornhill, Dumfriesshire. He studied geology at Edinburgh University and joined the Royal Geographical Society east-central African Expedition (1878–9), taking charge on the death of the leader. He was the first European to reach Lake Nyasa (Malawi) from the north and went on to Lake Tanganyika, which he described in *To the Central African Lakes and Back* (1881). An unsuccessful attempt to search for coal in the Rovuma River valley for the Sultan of Zanzibar was followed in 1882 by an invitation from the Royal Geographical Society to find a route through hostile Masai country from the coast via Mount Kilimanjaro to Lake Victoria; this took him across the Nijiri Desert through the Great Rift Valley and led to his discovery of Lake Baringo and Mount Elgon. His careful notes throughout greatly added to the geographical knowledge of East Africa. For the British National African (later Royal Niger) Company he explored Sokoto in north-western Nigeria (1885), and for a South African company the Upper Congo (1890). He also travelled in the Atlas mountains of Morocco.

THOMSON, Robert William
(1822–73)

Engineer and inventor, born in Stonehaven, Kincardineshire. He was intended for the Church but, rebelling against classical studies, spent some time as a workshop apprentice while educating himself in mathematics and other practical subjects. He devised a method of detonating explosive charges by electricity, and for some time was employed as a civil engineer on the construction of railways. In 1845 he patented a vulcanized rubber pneumatic tyre which was successfully tested in London but was thought to be too expensive for general use; it had been quite forgotten by the time **John Boyd Dunlop** re-invented the pneumatic tyre in 1888. Thomson patented the principle of the fountain pen in 1849, and while working as a sugar-plantation engineer in Java he designed greatly improved production machinery and the first mobile steam crane. In 1867 he patented a steam traction engine with hinged segmental driving wheels supporting the weight of the vehicle on rubber pads; this was very successful in moving even the heaviest loads over poor or non-existent roads.

THOMSON, Thomas
(1768–1852)

Antiquary, educated at Dailly parish school in Ayrshire and Glasgow University. A friend of Sir **Walter Scott**, he became deputy clerk register and collaborated in founding the Bannatyne Club to publish historical records. He edited many vital Scottish historical records, particularly the great *Acts of the Parliaments of Scotland (1424–1707)*, and instituted systems for the orderly preservation of the public records of Scotland, work which still continues.

THOMSON, Thomas
(1773–1852)

Chemist, born in Crieff, Perthshire, and educated at the universities of St Andrews and Edinburgh, graduating as a doctor in 1799. He worked as a freelance editor, writer, teacher and historian before being appointed, in 1817, to the chair at Glasgow University, which he held until his death. He was a propagandist for the fledgling atomic theories of the day, endeavouring to prove Dalton's theories experimentally, and also to prove William Prout's hypothesis that the atomic weights of elements were whole-number multiples of the atomic weight of hydrogen. He was also the first university teacher to insist on systematic training in practical work.

THOMSON, Sir William Johnston
(1881–1949)

Engineer and transport manager, born in Muirend, Baillieston, near Glasgow. Leaving school at the age of 12, a few years later he began an engineering apprenticeship. On its completion he became a mechanic in the Arrol Johnston Motor Works at Paisley, where his ability was quickly recognized, and he became manager of a department before he was 21. By 1905 he had decided to start his own motor bus company, and on 14 June in Edinburgh he formed the Scottish Motor

Traction Company with a capital of £12 000. By 1949, when it was acquired by the British Transport Commission, the SMT was running a fleet of more than 3000 buses. From 1932 to 1935 Thomson was Lord Provost of Edinburgh; during his term of office he was knighted and received the honorary degree of LLD from Edinburgh University.

THOMSON, William Thomas
(1813–83)

Actuary, born in Edinburgh, a central figure in the development of the life assurance industry within Britain in the early and mid Victorian period. He became manager of the Edinburgh-based Standard Life Assurance Company at the age of 24, and remained in that position for the next 37 years. By the 1870s he had established an agency network across the country and had begun to develop a presence in the British Empire. Despite a tendency to conservatism his entrepreneurial skills were considerable, although his success came not just from personal talent but from the contribution of others at the top of Standard Life.

THOMSON OF MONIFEITH,
George Morgan Thomson
(1921 –)

Labour politician, born in Dundee, and educated at Grove Academy, Dundee. A journalist in Dundee, where he was Editor of *Forward* from 1948 to 1953, he was MP for Dundee East (1952–72). Chancellor of the Duchy of Lancaster (1966–7, 1969–70), he was Commonwealth Secretary (1967–8) and Minister without Portfolio (1968–9). He had the responsibility for trying to reach a settlement of the Southern Rhodesia (Zimbabwe) difficulty, and also for implementing sanctions against the illegal régime there. An ardent European, he was one of the first British Commissioners of the European Community (1973–7), where his portfolio was regional development. As Chairman of the Independent Broadcasting Authority (1981–8), he handled a controversial re-allocation of ITV network licences.

THORBURN, Archibald
(1860–1935)

Bird artist, born in Lasswade, near Edinburgh, the son of a painter. He studied at St John's Wood School of Art in London, and his first paintings were hung in the Royal Academy when he was only 20. He painted the majority of the plates of the monumental *Coloured Figures of the Birds of the British Isles* (1885–97). He also published *British Birds* (4 vols, 1915–16) and *British Mammals* (1920), and his paintings were used for T A Coward's *The Birds of the British Isles and their Eggs* (1920) and the immensely popular *Observer's Book of British Birds* (1937). More than 100 of his paintings have been reproduced as prints.

THORPE DAVIE, Cedric
(1913–83)

Composer, born in London. He studied in Glasgow at the Royal Scottish Academy, the Royal Academy, the Royal College, and with Kodály. He became Professor of Composition at the Scottish National Academy of Music in 1936. His early compositions include a string quartet, a sonatina for cello and piano and the *Dirge for Cuthullin* for chorus and orchestra (1935). His *Symphony in C* appeared in 1945, and he wrote the music for Tyrone Guthrie's acclaimed production of **David Lyndsay**'s *Satyre of the Thrie Estaitis* at the 1948 Edinburgh Festival; he also wrote many film scores and music for theatre productions and schools. In 1945 he became master of music at St Andrews University, founding its music department in 1947, and becoming Reader (1956) and then Professor (1973–8).

TIVY, Joy
(1924 –)

Irish-born geographer, educated at the universities of Dublin and Edinburgh. After periods in teaching and planning she started her lecturing career at Edinburgh University and was later appointed to Glasgow University, where she became Professor and Head of the geography department. She has held various posts, including editorship of the *Scottish Geographical Magazine* (1955–65) and was Chairman of the Scottish Field Studies Association (1984–7; 1990), and served on the Scottish Advisory Committee to the Nature Conservancy Council (Scotland) (1974–80) and the Geography Board of the Committee for National Academic Awards (1976–84). She has published widely; *Biogeography: The Role of Plants in the Ecosphere* (1982) is regarded as a pioneering text in the geography of organic resources.

TODD, Alexander Robertus, Baron of Trumpington
(1907 –)

Chemist, born in Glasgow. He became Professor at Manchester University (1938) and Cambridge University (1944), fellow and master (1963–78) of Christ's College, Cambridge, and, from 1978, he was first Chancellor of the new University of Strathclyde. He was awarded the Nobel Prize for Chemistry in 1957 for his researches on vitamins B_{12} and E, and was made a life peer in 1962.

TODD, Ruthven
(1914–78)

Poet, born in Edinburgh. Educated at **Fettes** College, Edinburgh, and the Edinburgh School of Art, he worked as a farm labourer on Mull for two years, and then as a journalist in Edinburgh. In 1935 he moved to London, then in 1947 moved to the USA (both his parents were American), where he remained for the rest of his life. He wrote a number of adventure novels under the pseudonym 'R T Campbell', but is best remembered for his own poetry, and for his edition of the *Poems* of William Blake. While not a major poet, his best work has a strong sense of place which is deeply-rooted in his Scottish upbringing, and shows a persistent concern with locating the particularities of personal experience within a wider historical context.

TORRANCE, Sam
(1953 –)

Golfer, born in Largs, Ayrshire. He turned professional in 1970, and has been Scottish professional champion four times. He was a regular tournament winner throughout the early 1980s, taking such titles as the Australian PGA (1980), the Spanish Open (1982) and the Benson and Hedges International (1984). The greatest moment of his career, however, came in 1985, when he sank the putt which won the Ryder Cup for Britain and Europe. Latterly, with his career suffering from the yips, he took to using an extraordinary 48-inch putter. His father Bob is a leading authority on golf.

TORRANCE, Thomas Forsyth
(1913 –)

Theologian, born of missionary parents in Chengtu, Szechwan, western China. He was Professor of Dogmatics at New College, Edinburgh (1952–79), Moderator of the General Assembly (1976–7), and winner of the Templeton Prize (1978). Drawing on the Greek Fathers and Karl Barth, he holds that while much recent theology mirrors an outdated model of detached and objective scientific investigation, post-Einsteinian science is open-ended, responding to the reality it encounters. Theology, therefore, should abandon its preconceptions and do the same, both in relation to science and in the quest for an acceptable ecumenical theology. His views have been expounded in many books, including *Theological Science* (1969), *Theology in Reconciliation* (1975), *Divine and Contingent Order* (1981), and *The Trinitarian Faith* (1988).

TRANTER, Nigel
(1909 –)

Novelist and historian, born in Glasgow. Educated at George Heriot's School in Edinburgh, he trained as an accountant before becoming a full-time writer in 1936. His output has been prodigious, numbering well over 100 books. His best known novels are those on historical themes, most notably the trilogy on the life of **Robert the Bruce**, *The Steps to the Empty Throne* (1969), *The Path of the Hero King* (1970), and *The Price of the King's Peace* (1971). His non-fiction works include significant studies of Scottish castles and fortified houses. A writer whose talent lies in careful historical research rather than stylistic graces, in *Nigel Tranter's Scotland* (1981) he gave an account of his life-long fascination with rural Scotland's history, heritage, and public affairs.

TRAQUAIR, Phoebe Anna
(1852–1936)

Irish embroiderer, illustrator and enameller, born in Dublin and educated at Dublin School of Art. In 1873 she married **Ramsay Traquair**, the head of the Natural History Museum in Edinburgh. She was one of the most renowned enamellers of her period and her work featured regularly in *Studio* magazine. Much of her later work was of a religious nature and throughout her career she carried out various commissions, mainly enamelled, bright, figurative triptychs, including work for Sir **Robert Lorimer**, St Mary's Cathedral, Edinburgh and many other churches and public buildings in Scotland. She was awarded medals at the International Exhibitions in Paris, St Louis and London. In 1887 she remarried, her full name becoming Phoebe Anna Traquair Reid.

TRAQUAIR, Ramsey Heatley
(1840–1912)

Palaeontologist, born at the Manse of Rhynd, Perthshire, and educated in Edinburgh, both at school and at the university, where he graduated MD in 1862. He then became Demonstrator in Anatomy there for three years, followed by brief appointments in Cirencester and Dublin. In 1873 he became Keeper of Natural History in the (then) Royal Scottish Museum in Edinburgh, from which post he retired in 1906 after 33 years. During this time he published extensively on fossil fishes, particularly those from the Palaeozoic era. Although his work covered the Silurian, Devonian and Carboniferous periods, he was especially known for his studies of the Old Red Sandstone fish faunas of Scotland. He was married to the enamellist **Phoebe Traquair**.

TRIDUANA, St
(4th century)

Christian religious. She is said to have come to Scotland with St **Regulus** and lived at Rescobie in Angus. Legend relates that, troubled by the attentions of the local king and learning of his admiration for her eyes, she plucked them out and sent them to him. She retired to Restalrig, where there is a well which was once famous as a cure for eye diseases.

TULLOCH, John
(1823–86)

Theologian, born in Bridge of Earn, Perthshire. He was a minister in Dundee (1844) and at Kettins (1849), and in 1854 was appointed Principal and Professor of Divinity at St Mary's College, St Andrews. He was a founder of the Scottish Liberal Church Party (1878) and wrote many religious and philosophical works, among them an address to young men entitled *Beginning Life* (1862).

TURNBULL, George
(1698–1748)

Philosopher, born in Alloa, Clackmannanshire. He graduated from Edinburgh in 1721. Radical in politics, liberal in theology, he was a member of the influential Rankenian discussion society, and taught at Aberdeen from 1721 to 1727, where **Thomas Reid** was a

pupil. Resigning in 1727, he toured Europe, was tutor to the Wauchopes of Niddry, and did various pieces of literary work. In 1739 he published *A Treatise on Ancient Painting*. Turning episcopalian, he became rector of a parish in Derry. Travelling to the continent to improve his health, he died at the Hague. A philosopher with important ideas on the interconnections in knowledge, his work is now being revived.

TURNBULL, William
(1922 –)

Artist, born in Dundee. He studied at the Slade School of Art (1946–8) and lived in Paris from 1948 to 1950. He held his first one-man show at the Hanover Gallery, London, in 1950, and taught at the Central School of Arts & Crafts in London from 1952 to 1972. He is married to the sculptor and printmaker Kim Lim. His sculptures are typically upright forms of roughly human height, standing directly on the floor. In the 1950s he liked organic forms and titles like *Totemic Figure*, but since the 1960s he has preferred purely abstract, geometrical shapes.

TURNER, Victor Witter
(1920–83)

Social anthropologist, born in Glasgow. He studied literature at London University, but after war service he studied anthropology under Max Gluckman at Manchester University. He taught at Manchester (1949–63) before moving to the USA where he was Professor of Anthropology at Cornell (1963–8), Professor of Social Thought at Chicago (1968–77) and at Virginia (1977–83). He carried out fieldwork among the Ndembu of Zambia (northern Rhodesia) from 1950 to 1954, which resulted in the classic monograph *Schism and Continuity in an African Society* (1957). In his later work he moved to the analysis of symbolism, as in *The Forest of Symbols* (1967), *The Drums of Affliction* (1968), *The Ritual Process* (1969) and *Dramas, Fields and Metaphors* (1972).

TURNER, Sir William
(1832–1916)

English-born anatomist and Principal of Edinburgh University, born in Lancaster, the son of an upholsterer and cabinet-maker, who died when Turner was five. Growing up in poverty, he was apprenticed to a local general practitioner, and completed his training at St Bartholomew's Hospital, London. He was invited to become Senior Demonstrator at Edinburgh in 1854, and successfully battled student ridicule for his English accent, then unique at Edinburgh. In 1857 he published *Atlas and Handbook on Human Anatomy and Physiology*, and was co-founder of *Journal of Anatomy and Physiology* (1867). He assisted Charles Darwin on rudimentary parts of human and animal structure. Appointed Professor of Anatomy in 1867, he was Dean of the Faculty of Medicine (1878–81), and opposed the admission of women students to medicine, being credited with encouragement of male students to rabble Sophia Jex-Blake and her supporters asserting their right. He helped to win financial support for new medical buildings, and organized an anatomy museum, in addition to persuading the brewer **William McEwan** to endow a new hall for graduation, and the brewer **John Usher** to endow an institute of public health and the establishment of a professorship. He represented Edinburgh and Aberdeen universities on the General Medical Council (1873–83), and Edinburgh alone on the reconstituted Council (1886–1905). Knighted in 1886, he was appointed Principal of Edinburgh University in 1903, the first English principal of a Scottish University. In this position he obtained new buildings at low cost to house Arts, Physics and Engineering; he helped to introduce tutorials, creating many lectureships and new chairs, and establishing a direct connection between the university and the Royal Infirmary's surgical and medical staff. Turner was not an innovator in either research or administration, somewhat ironically emerging more as a conserver of the Scottish medical and educational traditions than as forerunner of the future influx of English fashions and personel. However, he proved a forceful and resourceful principal, maximizing possibilities of co-operation with the town and business community.

TWEEDSMUIR See **BUCHAN, John**

TYTLER, Alexander Fraser
(1747–1813)

Jurist and historian, son of **William Tytler**.

In 1780 he became Professor of Universal History at Edinburgh University. He was Judge Advocate of Scotland (1790) and a judge of the Court of Session (1802) as Lord Woodhouselee. He published a memoir of Lord **Kames** (1807) and various legal works.

TYTLER, James 'Balloon'
(1745–1804)

Journalist, scientist and balloonist, born in Fearn, Angus, the son of a minister. He was a surgeon's apprentice in Forfar, a student at Edinburgh University and sailed to Greenland on a whaling ship, before embarking on the first of many ill-fated literary ventures, *The Gentleman and Lady's Magazine*, which lasted 13 issues. He was always ready to accept hack work to keep his creditors at bay, and took on the editorship of the second edition of the *Encyclopaedia Britannica*, on which he laboured for six or seven years for a modest wage of 16 shillings a week. In 1783 he constructed a balloon, and like others of his ventures it threatened never to take off. But it did, with him aboard, on 27 August 1784, and reached a height of 350 feet, thus earning him a footnote in aviation history as, according to the *Edinburgh Advertiser*, 'the first person in Great Britain to have navigated the air'. Following this he fell into debt, was divorced, arrested, outlawed, and fled to Ireland before journeying to America, where, in Salem, Massachusetts, he drowned while drunk.

TYTLER, Patrick Fraser
(1791–1849)

Historian, son of **Alexander Fraser Tytler**. He published a critical *History of Scotland* 1249–1603 (1828–43), which is still valuable.

TYTLER, William, of Woodhouselee
(1711–92)

Historian, father of **Alexander Tytler** and grandfather of **Patrick Tytler**. An Edinburgh lawyer, he published an exculpatory *Inquiry into the Evidence against Mary, Queen of Scots* (1759), and edited the *Poetical Remains of James I of Scotland* (1783).

U

UNNA, Percy
(1878–1950)

Environmental philanthropist, born in London. A civil engineer by profession, he became President of the Scottish Mountaineering Club in the mid 1930s. One of the first to appreciate the unique quality of Scottish mountain scenery, he compiled what are known as 'Unna's Rules'. These were guidelines for the conservation of the Scottish mountains, following the National Trust for Scotland's purchase of important mountain properties, such as Glencoe. His rules remain a touchstone for the management of access and the protection of 'wilderness quality' in the uplands. A generous anonymous donator to the National Trust, his bequests still provide for land management and purchase.

URE, Andrew
(1778–1857)

Chemist, born in Glasgow. He studied at Glasgow University, became Professor of Chemistry and Natural Philosophy in Anderson's College, astronomer in the City Observatory, and in 1834 analytical chemist to the Board of Customs in London. He produced a *Dictionary of Chemistry* (1821) and a *Dictionary of Arts, Manufactures and Mines* (1853).

URE, Midge, real name James Ure
(1953 –)

Pop singer and guitarist, born in Glasgow. He played in the bands The Rich Kids and Slik before joining the pop group Visage with Steve Strange in 1979 and then the new-wave group Ultravox with Warren Cann, Billy Currie and Chris Cross. Ultravox had their first hit with the title track from the album *Vienna* in 1980; subsequent albums have included *Rage In Eden* (1981) and *U-Vox* (1986). Ure also pursued a solo career, enjoying chart success with a version of the Walker Brothers' 'No Regrets' (1982) and his own 'If I Was' (1985). With Bob Geldof he co-wrote the song 'Do They Know It's Christmas' for the pop charity Bandaid in 1984. This became the world's fastest selling single and brought international fame. He was Musical Director of the Prince's Trust charity concerts (1987–8). He released the soul album *Pure* in 1991.

URQUHART, David
(1805–77)

Diplomatist, born in Cromarty. He served in the Greek navy during the Greek War of Independence and received his first diplomatic appointment in 1831, when he went to Constantinople with Sir Stratford de Canning. His anti-Russian policy caused his recall from Turkey in 1837 and he was Member of Parliament for Stafford from 1847 to 1852. A strong opponent of Palmerston's policy, he believed Turkey was capable of dealing with Russia without European intervention. He founded the *Free Press*, afterwards called the *Diplomatic Review*, in which these views were expressed. He retired in 1864. Among his many writings were *The Pillars of Hercules* (1850), in which he suggested the introduction of Turkish baths into Britain, and *The Lebanon* (1860).

URQUHART, Fred
(1912 –)

Short-story writer and novelist, born in Edinburgh, the son of a chauffeur. He grew up in Fife, Perth and Wigtown, leaving school at 15 and then working as bookseller's assistant and labourer. He published his first novel, *Time Will Knit*, in 1938. He has published 11 collections of his short stories, many initially broadcast by the BBC, and has edited nine anthologies of short stories. His other novels to date are *The Ferret Was Abraham's Daughter* (1949), *Jezebel's Dust* (1951) and *Palace of Green Days* (1979, the first of a projected series). He has been publisher's reader, and literary editor of *Tribune*. His outstanding achievement is his quite exceptional ability to convey narrative plots through the eyes of female characters, initially in the Scotland of his childhood and adolescence and more recently using ghost stories, historical fiction and other forms.

URQUHART, Sir Thomas
(c.1611–1660)

Author, born in Cromarty, the son of a landowner. He studied at King's College, Aberdeen, and travelled in France, Spain and Italy. On his return he took up arms against the Covenanting party in the north but was defeated and forced to flee to England. Becoming attached to the court, he was knighted in 1641. The same year he published his *Epigrams: Divine and Moral*. On succeeding his father in 1642 he returned north. In Cromarty, though much troubled by his creditors, he produced his *Trissotetras; or a most exquisite Table for Resolving Triangles, etc* (1645), a study of trigonometry based on Napier's invention of logarithms. In 1649 his library was seized and sold. He again took up arms in the royal cause, and was present at the battle at Worcester (1651), where he lost most of his MSS. In London, through Cromwell's influence, he was allowed considerable liberty, and in 1652 he published his *Pantochronochanon* (1652), an exact account of the Urquhart family, in which they are traced back to Adam. He also published *Ekskubalauron* (1652), better known as *The Discoverie of a most Exquisite Jewel*, an attack on the Scottish clergy which contains a ribald account of **James Crichton** (the 'Admirable Crichton'), but is chiefly a work praising the Scots nation. In 1653 he issued his *Introduction to the Universal Language* and the first two books of that English classic, his brilliant translation of *Rabelais*. The third was not issued till after his death. He is said to have died abroad, in a fit of mirth on hearing of the Restoration. His learning was vast, his scholarship defective.

V

VALENTINE, James
(1815–80)

Photographer/publisher, the son of a printer and lithographer. He originally trained as an engraver and designer of illustrated envelopes, and studied the Daguerreotype process in Paris in the late 1840s. In 1856 he opened a photographic portrait studio in Dundee and by the 1870s Valentine's of Dundee was one of the two largest photographic establishments in Scotland (the other being **George Washington Wilson**'s of Aberdeen). Like Wilson and Francis Frith, Valentine, alone or later with a team of employees, covered the whole of Britain, producing photographs of all the well-known views and buildings. 'Production-line' manufacturing methods were used, and most of the output of Valentine's was unremarkable, although James Valentine himself possessed considerable skill and judgement as a photographer.

VEITCH, John
(1829–94)

Poet and scholar, born in Peebles, the son of a Peninsular War veteran. He studied at Edinburgh University and, after the Disruption of the Church of Scotland (1843), studied theology at New College, Edinburgh. In 1856 he was appointed assistant to Sir **William Hamilton**, Professor of Logic and Metaphysics at Edinburgh, and in 1860 was appointed Professor of Logic at St Andrews University. He wrote biographies of **Dugald Stewart** (1857) and Hamilton (1869), and as a poet wrote of the Border country. His critical works included *History and Poetry of the Scottish Border* (1877) and *The Feeling for Nature in Scottish Poetry* (1877).

VEITCH, William
(1794–1885)

Classical scholar, born in Spittal near Jedburgh, Roxburghshire. He qualified for the Scottish ministry, but devoted himself to a life of scholarship at Edinburgh. His chief work was the invaluable *Greek Verbs Irregular and Defective* (1848). He revised Liddell and Scott's *Greek Lexicon*, and Smith's *Latin Dictionary*.

W

WADDELL, Willie
(1921 –)

Football player and manager, born in Forth, Lanarkshire. He played over 500 matches for Rangers from 1938 to his retirement in 1956. An outside-right, his main role on the field was to get the ball over for the prolific goalscorer Willie Thornton, but he did manage 143 goals himself. He became Kilmarnock Manager in 1957, taking them to the league championship in 1965. Appointed Rangers Manager in 1969 (he witnessed the Ibrox disaster of 1971), he guided the club to the European Cup Winners' Cup in 1972, the year he became General Manager. He was made a director in 1973.

WADDINGTON, Conrad Hal
(1906–75)

Geneticist, born in Coimbatore, South India, and educated at Clifton College and at Cambridge University, where in 1933 he became a lecturer in zoology and embryology. He was primarily a geneticist but his interests were wide-ranging and he published books on science, philosophy, poetry and art as well as works on theoretical and experimental biology. He was appointed Buchanan Professor of Animal Genetics at Edinburgh University in 1947, a post he held until his death. He experimented on the influences of genes on the development of Drosophila, the fruit fly, which led him to realize that the embryo was far from immutable and that its development was controlled by the interactions of genes coming into play at different and very specific times. He published numerous books, including *Organisms and Genes* (1940), *Epigenetics of Birds* (1952) and *New Patterns in Genetics and Development* (1962). As professor at Edinburgh he set up an international school in epigenetics, and the university's Institute for Animal Genetics became, under his direction, a Mecca for genetic research workers from all over the world.

WALKER, Sir Alexander
(1869–1950)

Distiller, born in Kilmarnock, Ayrshire, the son of the Chairman of John Walker and Sons. Educated at Ayr Academy, he joined the family firm at a time when it had become one of the largest whisky blending firms in Scotland. Knighted for his contribution to munitions procurement during World War I, he directed the company's progress to public status in 1923 and then to a merger with Distillers Company and Buchanan-Dewar Ltd two years later. As a director of DCL he was influential in diversifying the company's activities into the field of industrial alcohol and chemicals. As Chairman of the management committee after 1937 he enabled the firm to overcome many of the difficulties associated with entry into the chemicals industry. At the same time he maintained the prestige of the famous red- and black-labelled blended whiskies bearing the family name, with which the town of Kilmarnock is closely associated.

WALKER, David Morrison
(1933 –)

Architectural historian, born in Dundee. Educated at Dundee College of Art, he began his career working voluntarily when a student for the Scottish National Buildings Record in Edinburgh. In 1961 he became a senior investigator with the Historic Buildings Branch of the Department of Health (now Historic Scotland), where he currently serves as Chief Inspector of Historic Buildings. He worked with **Ian Gordon Lindsay** on the lists of buildings of special architectural or historic interest, and with **Catherine Cruft** and **Colin McWilliam** in research. Possessed of an exhaustive knowledge of architectural history, he has brought about the preservation of innumerable fine buildings and recorded a wide range of types. Among his many publications are *Dundee Nineteenth-Century Mansions* (1958) and the *Edinburgh* volume of the Buildings of Scotland series (1984, with John Gifford and Colin McWilliam). In 1970 he won the Alice Davis

Hitchcock Medallion. He received an honorary doctorate from Dundee University in 1989, and is an Honorary Fellow of the RIAS.

WALKER, Ernie (Ernest John Munro)

(1928 –)

Football administrator, born in Glasgow. Having served in the army immediately after the war, he then worked on the management side of the textiles industry for a decade from 1948, leaving to join the Scottish Football Association, where he was Assistant Secretary from 1958 to 1977. In the latter year he became SFA Secretary, a post he held until his retirement in 1990. He remains an active and influential figure in the sport through his membership of several FIFA and UEFA committees, among them the FIFA World Cup 1994 Inspection Group. The object of grudging admiration from the footballing fraternity, who gave him the sobriquet 'the Ayatollah', his level-headed, impassive approach to what is often a wildly irrational game has ensured a voice for Scotland in the sport's international governing bodies.

WALKER, Dame Ethel

(1861–1951)

Painter and sculptor, born in Edinburgh. From 1870 she lived in London, where she was educated privately. She attended Putney Art School, the School of Art at Westminster, and then the Slade School of Art (1892–4). Thereafter she divided her time between London, where she was a familiar figure in Chelsea, and Yorkshire, where she painted notable seascapes from her cottage in Robin Hood's Bay. Her early work is mannered in the style of the New English Art Club and Walter R Sickert, but she gradually developed a more individual style which owed something to her study of Impressionism, particularly in her work after World War I. She is best known for her portraits (often of young girls), flower paintings, and seascapes, and for more visionary canvases like *Nausicaa* (1920) or *The Zone of Love* (1931–3), which reflected her idealized vision of a golden age. She was made a DBE in 1943.

WALKER, Sir James

(1863–1935)

One of the pioneers of physical chemistry in the UK, born in Dundee. He studied at the universities of Edinburgh, Munich and Leipzig, and afterwards worked as assistant to **Alexander Crum Brown** in Edinburgh and to **William Ramsay** in London. He was appointed to the Chair of Chemistry at Dundee in 1894 and at Edinburgh in 1908. He is noted for his work on solution chemistry, particularly ionization constants, hydrolysis and amphoteric electrolytes (electrolytes with a dual nature which sometimes react as acids and sometimes as bases). Knighted in 1921, he retired in 1928. He was succeeded by **James Pickering Kendall**.

WALKER, Tommy

(1915 –)

Football player and manager, born in Livingston, Lothian. He joined Heart of Midlothian in 1932, winning the first of his 20 caps for Scotland two years later. He moved to Chelsea in 1946, but returned to Hearts in 1948, first as Assistant Manager, then (1951–66) as Manager. After administrative posts with Dunfermline and Raith Rovers, he returned to Hearts as a director in 1974, becoming vice-chairman five years later. An inside-forward, he was as popular as a player as he was respected as a manager. His tenure as Manager of Hearts, in which two league championships, a Scottish Cup and four League Cups were won, was the most successful in the club's history.

WALLACE, David James

(1945 –)

Physicist. He was educated at Hawick High School and Edinburgh University. After two years as a research fellow at Princeton, he was appointed Lecturer, later Reader, in physics, at Southampton University. In 1979 he was appointed Tait Professor of Mathematical Physics at Edinburgh. He is distinguished for contributions to theories of elementary particles and of solid state physics. More recently he has applied the techniques of parallel-process computing to solve problems in physics and applied physics.

WALLACE, also WALAYS or WALLENSIS ('Welshman'), Sir William

(c.1274–1305)

Patriot, chief champion of Scotland's independence, reputedly the second son of Sir

Malcolm Wallace of Elderslie, near Paisley. The poet **Blind Harry**, who wrote an epic about him, associates his early years with Dundee and Ayrshire; but it is uncertain whether he was present at the burning of the English garrison in Ayr, or if this marked the start of the War of Independence. In 1297, leading a small band of men, Wallace burnt Lanark and killed the English sheriff, Hazelrig. Later that year he met Edward I's army and won a decisive victory at Stirling Bridge, routing the English. Following this, the English were expelled from Scotland and a devastating raid was inflicted on the north of England. In retaliation Edward invaded Scotland in 1298, meeting Wallace at Falkirk, where the Scots were this time crushed. Wallace continued briefly to wage a guerrilla war before escaping to France in 1299, where he tried to enlist support for the Scottish cause. He returned in 1303, but in 1305 was arrested near Glasgow by Sir **John de Menteith**, Sheriff of Dumbarton. Taken to London he was condemned and hanged, drawn and quartered. His quarters were sent to Newcastle, Berwick, Stirling and Perth.

WALLACE, William
(d. 1631)

Master mason. He probably trained in Edinburgh while living in Musselburgh. Before beginning his term as Master Mason to the Scottish Crown, he worked at Edinburgh Castle, notably on the King's Lodging (1615). He supervised royal works at Linlithgow, where he restored the north range in Court Style classicism (1618–20), and at Stirling. The authorship of the design for Heriot's Hospital, Edinburgh, has not been confirmed, but certainly he supervised work there from 1628. The only major commission which can be verified as having fallen to him was the impressive enlargement and aggrandizement of Winton House, East Lothian (1620–7), which displays his command of the classical ornament employed on the royal works.

WALLACE, William
(1786–1843)

Self-taught mathematician, born in Dysart, Fife. Starting out as a bookbinder's apprentice, he became a teacher of mathematics at Perth in 1794, and at the Royal Military College, Marlow, in 1803, shortly before the arrival of Sir **James Ivory**. Professor of Mathematics at Edinburgh University

(1819–38) and Observer at the Astronomical Institution's observatory on Calton Hill, Edinburgh (1822–34), he was an outstanding teacher (he recommended to **Mary Somerville**, who approached him for advice, an ambitious list of books on the higher branches of mathematics and astronomy which she acquired and cherished all her life). Wallace was active in efforts to establish an astronomical observatory for Edinburgh University. Apart from many publications in scientific journals, he was a main contributor to both the *Edinburgh Encyclopaedia* and the *Encyclopaedia Britannica*.

WALLACE, William
(1844–97)

Philosopher, born in Cupar, Fife. A pupil of **J F Ferrier** at St Andrews, he studied under Thomas Green at Oxford and spent the rest of his life there. He deplored his lack of talent for sustained argumentation, but had great insight, seen, for example in his *Prolegomena* to his translation of Hegel's *Logic* (2nd ed 1892). A Fellow of Merton College from 1867, he succeeded Green as Whyte's Professor of Moral Philosophy in 1882. One of his major achievements was his translations of Hegel; his Hegelian reading of Marxism anticipated German developments by 70 years. He died as a result of a cycling accident. The incomplete text of his 1896 Gifford Lectures was published as *Lectures and Essays on Natural Theology and Ethics* (1898).

WALLACE, William
(1860–1940)

Composer, born in Greenock. He trained in medicine, but from 1889 devoted himself to music. He was the first British composer to experiment with symphonic poems, of which he wrote six. His other works include a symphony and songs.

WALLACE, Sir William
(1881–1963)

Marine engineer, born in Leicester of Scottish parents. He was educated in Paisley and at the Andersonian Institution in Glasgow, the latter during his apprenticeship in a Paisley shipyard. Following this he joined the British and Burmese Steam Navigation Company, rising to the rank of chief engineer before moving in 1910 to Brown Brothers in Edinburgh. A firm of ironfounders and engineers who already had a sound reputation in marine engineering, it provided an environment in which Wallace's inventive talents could flourish. He patented improvements in hydraulic steering gear and other ships' equipment, and by 1916 had been appointed managing director. In the 1930s he invented the steam catapult for aircraft carriers and, in association with Sir **Maurice Denny**, the very successful Denny-Brown stabilizer, for his part in which he was awarded the Churchill Gold Medal of the Society of Engineers (1954). He was elected a Fellow of the Royal Society of Edinburgh in 1946, and was given the honorary degree of LLD by Edinburgh University in 1956.

WALTON, Edward Arthur
(1860–1922)

Painter, born in Renfrewshire. He trained at the Glasgow School of Art and in Düsseldorf. His first success was with watercolour landscapes. He became a friend of Whistler when he led a campaign to have his portrait of **Thomas Carlyle** purchased by Glasgow Art Gallery, and he became Whistler's neighbour when he moved to London in 1894. He was persuaded to return to Scotland by **James Guthrie**, and settled in Edinburgh in 1904, where he specialized in portraiture.

WALTON, George
(1867–1933)

Designer, mainly of interiors, born in Glasgow. After studying at Glasgow School of Art, he set up in practice, obtaining the first of a number of commissions to design for the **Cranston** tea-rooms in conjunction with **Charles Rennie Mackintosh**. Their styles were similar, though later work by Walton was clearly influenced by C F A Voysey, who was a close friend. His work extended to architecture, furniture, glass and textiles.

WARD, David
(1922–83)

Operatic bass singer, born in Dumbarton. He studied at the Royal College of Music and with Hans Hotter in Munich, making his début with Sadler's Wells Opera in 1953, and joining the Royal Opera, Covent Garden, in 1960. He was successful in a variety of roles, from heroic to buffo, most notably as Wotan and Boris Godunov in productions with Scottish Opera. He was made CBE in 1972, and later emigrated to New Zealand.

WARDLAW, Henry
(d.1440)

Prelate. He studied and lived for some years in France, and later became tutor to King **James I** of Scotland. In 1403 he became Bishop of St Andrews, and played a prominent part in the foundation (1411) of St Andrews University, the first university in Scotland, of which he was the first chancellor. He also restored St Andrew's Cathedral.

WATERBOYS, THE See SCOTT, Mike

WATERS, Sir George Alexander
(1880–1967)

Journalist, born in Thurso, Caithness, and educated at Edinburgh University and the Sorbonne, Paris. After working as a teacher for a short time, he became a sub-editor on the *Weekly Scotsman* and joined *The Scotsman* at the age of 25. He remained with the paper for the rest of his journalistic career. As editor (1924–44) he developed the paper's use of pictures, expanded its financial and arts coverage, and vigorously promoted Scottish interests. A member of the first Royal Commission on the Press, he supported the establishment of a Press Council, but opposed the inclusion of lay members. He was knighted for his services to journalism in 1944.

WATERSTON, George
(1911–80)

Ornithologist. Born in Edinburgh, he became a noted ornithological writer, broadcaster and conservationist. A founding member of the Scottish Ornithologists Club in 1936, he was its first secretary. Elected FRSE in 1948, he received the RSPB Gold Medal in 1955. As the RSPB's first officer in Scotland (from 1959) he was largely responsible for the establishment of ospreys at Loch Garten. His memorial is the Reserve of Fair Isle, which he purchased in 1947, fulfilling a vow made while a prisoner-of-war in Germany. Six years later he sold it to the National Trust for Scotland at its original price.

WATERSTON, John James
(1811 – ?1883)

Physicist and engineer, born in Edinburgh, where he was educated at the High School. He studied science and medicine at Edinburgh, and practised as an engineer and teacher in London and Bombay, before returning home. He did some work in chemistry and then turned to physics, attracted by Joule's work on heat and gases. By 1845 he had developed the basis of the kinetic theory of gases and submitted a paper on it to the Royal Society, but their referee dismissed it. Lord Rayleigh found it in the Society's archives in 1892, saw its worth and had it published. It was then clear that Waterston had anticipated by more than ten years key ideas in kinetic theory and thermodynamics published by Clausius, *Clerk Maxwell* and Boltzmann. Waterston himself turned to studies in medicine, and particularly the physiology of mental processes, but became increasingly frustrated at the difficulties he encountered in getting his papers published. Finally, on 18 June 1883, he walked out of his Edinburgh home and was never heard of again.

WATKINS, Dudley Dexter
(1907–69)

English strip cartoonist and illustrator, born in Manchester, the creator of *Desperate Dan, Oor Wullie*, and many favourite comic characters. Acclaimed as a schoolboy genius for his painting of the Nottingham Historical Pageant at the age of 10, he studied at Nottingham School of Art, and joined the window display department of Boots the Chemist, contributing his first cartoon to the staff magazine in 1923. Joining Dundee publisher **D C Thomson**'s art department, he created *Oor Wullie* and *The Broons* strips for the *Sunday Post* (1936), then *Desperate Dan* for the *Dandy* (1937), *Lord Snooty* for the *Beano* (1938), and many more. He created classic picture serials, such as *Treasure Island*, later reprinted as books (1948). Highly religious, he contributed strips to *Young Warrior* (1960) without charge. He was the first D C Thomson artist allowed to sign his name.

WATSON, George
(1654–1723)

Merchant, born in Edinburgh into a merchant family and apprenticed to an Edin-

burgh merchant, James Cleland, in 1669. He studied book-keeping in Holland (1672–6), and on his return became a 'bound servant' to Sir James Dick in Edinburgh, in which capacity he attended to Dick's financial affairs; he also operated as a financier in his own right. He was briefly employed by the new Bank of Scotland in 1695, but ultimately made his fortune as a merchant banker. A religious man, he suffered from ill-health, and had a reputation for frugal living. From 1700 he was a governor of the Merchant Maiden Hospital inaugurated by **Mary Erskine**, and its treasurer from 1702 to 1704. Treasurer of the Society in Scotland for the Propagation of Christian Knowledge (1711–23), he left funds in his will to establish a hospital 'for the children of decayed merchants'. The hospital which bore his name became George Watson's College in 1870, under the provisions of the Educational Institutions (Scotland) Act of 1869.

WATSON, James Wreford
(1915–90)

Geographer and poet, born in Shensi, China, and educated at Edinburgh University. After a period at Sheffield University, he moved to Canada, where he embarked on a distinguished career. He was Professor and founder of the geography departments at both McMaster and Carleton universities, and was also Chief Geographer to the Canadian Government. In 1954 he became Professor and Head of the Department of Geography at Edinburgh University, and Convener and co-founder of the Centre of Canadian Studies there. His editorships included the *Atlas of Canada* (1949–54) and the *Scottish Geographical Magazine* (1975–8). Although primarily a regional geographer who received wide recognition for his work and publications, he was also a successful poet, and in 1954 was awarded the Governor General of Canada's Poetry Medal.

WATSON, Janet Vida
(1923–85)

Geologist, born in London, the daughter of David Watson, the vertebrate palaeontologist. Inspired first by Herbert Leader Hawkins at Reading University and then by Herbert Harold Read at Imperial College, London, she embarked on her life's work, the study of crystalline basement rocks, with her fellow student, John Sutton, whom she married in 1949, thus forming one of the most remarkable partnerships in geology. Their classic work, first published in 1951, on the Lewisian basement of North-West Scotland, led to the recognition of the older Scourian events, separated by some 1000 million years from the younger Laxfordian. Her gentle and unassuming manner belied great intellect and many honours were bestowed upon her, including a Personal Chair at Imperial College and fellowship of the Royal Society of London. She was the first and, to date, only Lady President of the Geological Society of London (1982–4).

WATSON, John See MACLAREN, Ian

WATSON, John
(1847–1939)

Philosopher, born in Glasgow. A student of **Edward Caird** at Glasgow, he was appointed Professor of Philosophy at Queen's University, Kingston, Ontario in 1872. (Caird's reference was so favourable it almost cost Watson the job.) Patient and moderate in expression, his writings cover the whole range of European thought, from a Cairdian Idealist point of view. A significant figure in the development of philosophy in Canada, his writings on religion and his practical efforts were crucial to the foundation of the United Church of Canada.

WATSON, Robert
(?1730–1781)

Historian, born in St Andrews, the son of an apothecary and brewer. Educated at St Andrews, Glasgow, and Edinburgh universities, and licensed as a preacher, he was rejected when presented to a church in St Andrews. Instead, he became Professor of Logic at St Salvator's College, St Andrews, and Principal of St Salvator's in 1777. In that year, he was presented by George III to the church and parish of St Leonard. His *History of Philip II of Spain* (1777) enjoyed a considerable vogue, being praised by Horace Walpole and translated into French, German and Dutch. It had a profound influence on Schiller, who drew on it for his *History* of the revolt of the Netherlands against Philip II, to the exclusion of most other works. Watson may therefore claim to have set Schiller on his

literary career. Watson's *Philip II* had reached a seventh edition by 1812, and held its own until the appearance of the American historian William Hickling Prescott's *Philip II*, 80 years after Watson's first publication. He thus forms a significant link between enlightenment and romanticism. Although he is a minor figure in the Scottish Enlightenment by comparison with his fellow-historians **William Robertson** and **David Hume**, his influence on the development of romantic history, however greatly strengthened by the absence of rivals, was immense. He is noteworthy less for his intellectual achievement than for his impact.

WATSON, Tom
(1932 –)

Actor, born in Glasgow. One of Scotland's most distinguished actors, he has appeared in many plays in Edinburgh and Glasgow, and has made many television appearances, as well as several films. His most notable stage performances include Sam Shepard's *Fool For Love* at the National Theatre in 1984, **Iain Heggie**'s *A Wholly Healthy Glasgow* at Manchester and the Royal Court Theatre, London, in 1987, and **Bill Bryden**'s *The Ship* at the Glasgow Dockyards in 1990. He has appeared at the Edinburgh Festival on several occasions.

WATSON, William, Lord
(1827–99)

Judge, born in Covington, Lanarkshire. Educated at Glasgow and Edinburgh universities, he initially had little legal practice, but by 1874 he was Solicitor-General for Scotland. He was appointed Dean of the Faculty of Advocates (1875–6) and Lord Advocate and MP (1876–80). At this point he was promoted direct from the Bar to be a Lord of Appeal in Ordinary (1880–99). As a judge he was greatly esteemed and the authority of his judgements is high, particularly in Scottish cases. His son William also became a Lord of Appeal, as Lord Thankerton (1929–48).

WATSON-WATT, Sir Robert Alexander
(1892–1973)

Physicist, born in Brechin, Angus. Educated at Dundee and St Andrews, he worked in the meteorological office, the DSIR (Department of Scientific and Industrial Research) and the National Physical Laboratory before becoming scientific adviser to the Air Ministry in 1940. He played a major role in the development and introduction of radar, for which he was knighted in 1942. In 1958 he published *Three Steps to Victory*. His wife, Katherine Jane (1899–1973), was Director of the Women's Auxiliary Air Force from 1939 to 1943.

WATT, Harry
(1906–87)

Film director, born in Edinburgh. Educated at Edinburgh University, he joined **John Grierson**'s film unit at the Empire Marketing Board, which was subsequently transferred to the GPO (General Post Office). A skilled and innovative documentarist, he brought elements of humour and fictional narrative to the form in such influential films as *Night Mail* (1934) and *Target for Tonight* (1941). Employed as a writer/director of feature films at Ealing Studios from 1942, his exotic adventure dramas include *The Overlanders* (1946), *West of Zanzibar* (1954) and *The Siege of Pinchgut* (1959). He also produced for Granada Television and wrote an autobiography, *Don't Look at the Camera* (1974).

WATT, James
(1736–1819)

Engineer and inventor, born in Greenock, Renfrewshire, the son of a merchant and town councillor. He went to Glasgow in 1754 to learn the trade of a mathematical-instrument maker, and there, after a year in London, he set up in business. The Hammermen's Guild put difficulties in his way, but the university made him its mathematical-instrument maker (1757–63). He was employed on surveys for the Forth and Clyde Canal (1767), the Caledonian and other canals, and was engaged in the improvement of harbours and in the deepening of the Forth, Clyde and other rivers. As early as 1759 his attention had been directed to steam as a motive force. In 1763–4 a working model of the Newcomen engine was sent for repair. He easily put it into order and, seeing the defects of the machine, hit upon the expedient of the separate condenser. Other progressive improvements included the air pump, steam jacket for cylinder, and double-acting engine. After an

abortive enterprise funded by **John Roebuck**, he entered into a partnership with Matthew Boulton of Soho, near Birmingham, in 1774, when (under a patent of 1769) the manufacture of the new engine was begun at the Soho Engineering Works. Watt's soon superseded Newcomen's machine as a pumping-engine; and between 1781 and 1785 he obtained patents for the sun and planet motion, the expansion principle, the double engine, the parallel motion, a smokeless furnace, and the governor. He described a steam locomotive in one of his patents (1784), but discouraged **William Murdock** from further experiments with steam locomotion. The watt, a unit of power, is named after him, and the term horsepower, another unit, was first used by him. He retired in 1800, and died at Heathfield Hall, his home near Birmingham. His son, James (1769–1848), a marine engineer, fitted the engine to the first English steamer to leave port in 1817, the *Caledonia*.

WATT, Jim
(1948 –)

Boxer, born in Glasgow. He won the WBC world lightweight title in April 1979, defeating Alfredo Pitalua in Glasgow, then went on to make four successful defences of his title, all in his home city. In June 1981, in a bout in London, he lost on points to Alexis Arguello. Since retiring from the ring he has become known as an articulate analyser of the sport on television.

WATT, Robert
(1774–1819)

Bibliographer and physician, born near Stewarton in Ayrshire. He began life as a ploughboy, went to university at Glasgow and Edinburgh, and became a schoolmaster in Symington, Ayrshire (1797). Turning to medicine he became a physician in Glasgow. He compiled a *Catalogue of Medical Books* (1812), and a monumental general catalogue of authors and subjects, *Bibliotheca Britannica*, published posthumously (1819–24).

WAUCHOPE, Sir Arthur Grenfell
(1874–1947)

Soldier and administrator, born in Edinburgh and commissioned into the 2nd Black Watch in 1896. He served in the Boer War and was badly wounded at the Battle of Magersfontein. During World War I he served in France and Mesopotamia. In 1923 he was promoted major-general and in that rank commanded the garrison in Northern Ireland. Between 1931 and 1938 he was a successful British High Commissioner in Palestine, and during the troubled years of the British mandate he managed to steer a reasonably neutral course between opposing Jewish and Arab interests. His health suffered during the Arab Revolt of 1936, and after his retirement he took no further part in public life, apart from his wartime service as titular colonel of the Black Watch.

WAVERLEY, John Anderson, 1st Viscount

(1882–1958)

Administrator and politician, born in Eskbank, Midlothian. Educated at Edinburgh and Leipzig, he entered the Colonial Office in 1905, was Chairman of the Board of Inland Revenue (1919–22), and Permanent Under-Secretary at the Home Office from 1922 until his appointment as Governor of Bengal in 1932. He was Home Secretary and Minister of Home Security from 1939 to 1940 (the Anderson air-raid shelter being named after him), became in 1940 Lord President of the Council, and Chancellor of the Exchequer in 1943, when he introduced the pay-as-you-earn system of income-tax collection devised by his predecessor Sir Kinglsey Wood. He was created viscount in 1952.

WEDDERBURN, Alexander See LOUGHBOROUGH, Alexander Wedderburn

WEDDERBURN, Joseph Henry Maclagan

(1882–1948)

Scottish-born American mathematician, born in Forfar, Angus. He graduated in mathematics at Edinburgh in 1903, visited Leipzig, Berlin and Chicago, and returned to Edinburgh as a lecturer (1905–9). In 1909 he went to Princeton but returned to fight in the British army during World War I. After the war he settled at Princeton until his retiral in 1945. His work on algebra includes two fundamental theorems known by his name, one on the classification of semi-simple algebras, and the other on finite division rings.

WEIPERS, Sir William

(1904–90)

Veterinary scientist. Educated at Whitehill School, Dennistoun, in Glasgow and at the University of Glasgow Veterinary School, he was in general practice from 1925 to 1949 while also serving on the staff of the Royal (Dick) Veterinary College in Edinburgh and later at Glasgow Veterinary School. He was largely instrumental in building up the present Glasgow Veterinary Faculty, becoming Dean (1981–4). He also made a considerable contribution to veterinary science in a wider sphere, culminating in his presidency of the Royal College of Veterinary Surgeons in 1963. He was knighted in 1966.

WEIR, Judith

(1954 –)

Composer and lecturer, born in Cambridge of an Aberdeenshire family. Her composition teachers were John Tavener, Robin Holloway and Olivier Messiaen. She was educated at King's College, Cambridge, and was Cramb Fellow, Glasgow University (1979–82), and Composer-in-Residence at the Royal Scottish Academy of Music (1988–91). She had notable success with her operas *The Black Spider* (1984), *A Night at the Chinese Opera* (Kent Opera, 1987), and *The Vanishing Bridegroom* (Scottish Opera, 1990). Other vocal works include *The Consolations of Scholarship* (1985), *Lovers, Learners and Libations* (1987), *Missa del Cid* (1988) and *HEAVEN ABLAZE* (1989, with two pianos and eight dancers). Her instrumental works include keyboard music, a string quartet (1990), *Sederunt Principes* (1987, for chamber orchestra), and many other works.

WEIR, Molly (Mary)

(1920 –)

Actress and writer, born in Glasgow, sister of **Tom Weir**. Determined to enter show-business, she nevertheless studied at commercial college, achieving a shorthand speed of 300 words a minute. Her boundless energy soon took her into the acting profession. Making her film début in 2000 *Women* (1944), she subsequently appeared in the likes of *Flesh and Blood* (1951) and *The Prime of Miss Jean Brodie* (1969), but achieved her greatest renown as the creator of such well-loved radio characters as Tattie Mackintosh in *ITMA* (1939–49) and the housekeeper Aggie in *Life With the Lyons*, which ran throughout the 1950s and also spawned the films *Life with the Lyons* (1954) and *The Lyons in Paris* (1955). She has appeared in numerous television series, acted on stage, served as a radio panellist and culinary expert, and also earned a place in the Guinness Book of Records for the longest piece of female autobiographical writing, which began with *Shoes Were for Sunday* (1970), and has continued with such volumes as *Best Foot Forward* (1972) and *Spinning Like a Peerie* (1983).

WEIR, Robert Hendry
(1912 –)

Engineer, educated at Allan Glen's School, Glasgow and later graduating in engineering at Glasgow University. First apprenticed to Wm Denny & Bros, Dumbarton (1929–33) he then moved to the Royal Aircraft Establishment at Farnborough as technical assistant. He was Technical Officer at the Air Ministry from 1939 to 1940, when he transferred to the Aircraft and Armament Experimental Establishment (A & AEE) at Boscombe Down as Senior Technical Officer. He returned to London to the Ministry of Aircraft Production (MAP) in 1942, becoming Principal Scientific Officer in 1947. By 1949 he was Assistant Director at the Ministry of Supply, then in 1950 became Director of Industrial Gas Turbines. This was followed in 1952 by his appointment as Director-General (Engine Research and Development) at the Ministry of Supply. From 1960 to 1970 he was Director of the National Gas Turbine Establishment at Pyestock, near Farnborough, thereafter becoming Director of the National Engineering Laboratory at East Kilbride (1970–4).

WEIR, Tom (Thomas)
(1914 –)

Hillwalker and broadcaster, born in Glasgow, brother of **Molly Weir**. Addicted to wildlife and the great outdoors from an early age, he worked in the Co-op, served with the Royal Artillery as a battery surveyor (1940–6) and was briefly employed as an ordnance surveyor before devoting himself to what had previously been a passionate hobby. His first book, *Highland Days*, was published in 1948 and he subsequently undertook numerous international climbing expeditions from the Himalayas to the remote peaks of northern Turkey and the Alps, recounting his adventures in several bestselling books and 30 years of his 'My Month' column for the *Scots Magazine*. A campaigner on environmental issues, he served on the executive committee of the Scottish Wildlife Trust, and gained wider public recognition through his television appearances, particularly in the many series of *Weir's Way* in the decade from its inception in 1976.

WEIR, William Douglas, Lord
(1877–1959)

Engineer, born in Glasgow. He was educated at Alan Glen's School and Glasgow High School. His father had founded the engineering firm of G & J Weir, and it was here that Weir was apprenticed. By 1902 he was Managing Director and thus he supervised the firm's growth in the years up to World War I, a period when it benefited from naval expansion through its supply of pumps and other components. He played a central role in the war effort, employed by the Ministry of Munitions to secure the supply of war materials from the west of Scotland. As a consequence he was knighted in 1917 and raised to the peerage a year later. A firm believer in work standardization and payment by results he encountered problems with the workforce during and after the war, but a greater threat was the downturn in trade after 1918. Perhaps his most significant achievement was to ensure the survival of the firm in the interwar years. An important figure in shaping public policy and in a range of industrial organizations, he was created a viscount in 1938. During World War II he was a director general at the Ministry of Supply.

WELLINS, Bobby (Robert Coull)
(1936 –)

Jazz musician and composer, born in Glasgow to parents of Russian and Polish roots. He took up the alto saxophone at age 12, taught by his father, later receiving formal tuition at Chichester College and at the RAF School of Music (on clarinet). From 1953 he worked with London-based dance bands and the tenor saxophone became his principal instrument. He progressed to full-time jazz playing, at first with drummer Tony Crombie's Jazz Inc., then as a member of the Stan Tracey Quartet. Returning to music in 1976 after a break, he led a succession of small modern jazz groups, toured the USA as

Musical Director of the British Charlie Watts Orchestra, and has been active in recording and teaching.

WELLS, Allan
(1952 –)

Athlete, born in Edinburgh. The most successful sprinter Scotland has produced since **Eric Liddell**, he was initially more noteworthy as a long-jumper, achieving his first Scottish title when he won the under-15 championship in that event. It was not until 1976 that he concentrated on sprinting. Two years later he won Commonwealth gold in the 100m, and silver in the 200m. In the Moscow Olympics of 1980 he became the oldest-ever winner of the 100m, but was beaten into second place in the 200m, despite setting a new British record of 20.21 seconds. He won both sprint titles in the 1982 Commonwealth Games, uniquely sharing the gold medal in the 200m with Mike McFarlane of England. A forthright, single-minded figure, he was much helped in his success by his wife Margot, a PE teacher and fitness coach.

WELSH, Alex
(1929–82)

Jazz cornettist and bandleader, born in Edinburgh. Gaining first musical experience with a silver band, he began to play locally with jazz bands led by **Sandy Brown** and Archie Semple, before moving to London in 1953 to join a band led by Scottish trombonist Dave Keir. Welsh formed his own band in 1954, playing a Chicago dixieland style which was outside the 'trad' revivalist repertoire of the period. The band, launched by a performance at the Royal Festival Hall, continued under his leadership for 28 years. Highly regarded by numerous American touring stars, the band was featured at the Antibes Jazz Festival in 1967 and at Newport (Rhode Island) in 1968, continuing to tour and record throughout Britain and Europe until Welsh's death.

WELSH, or WELCH, John
(c.1568–1622)

Presbyterian clergyman, born in Colliston, Dumfriesshire. An ancestor of **Jane Carlyle**, between 1590 and 1600 he was minister at Selkirk, Kirkcudbright and Ayr. After attending the prohibited General Assembly

of 1605, he was imprisoned and banished by **James VI and I**. Thereafter he preached in France, but in 1621 was banished by Louis XIII, and returned to London, unrepentant.

WELSH, Moray
(1947 –)

Cellist, born in Haddington, East Lothian. He studied at York University, where he was heard by Benjamin Britten, who arranged an introduction to Mstislav Rostropovich, with whom he studied for two years at the Moscow Conservatoire. As soloist and concerto player he has played throughout the UK, several times at the Proms, and has toured abroad with various orchestras, often as guest cellist with numerous groups, including the Amadeus Quartet. His repertoire and recordings range from the baroque to contemporary concertos, and he directs his own string sextet, the Arienski Ensemble.

WELWOD, or WELWOOD, William
(?1552–1622)

Jurist. He became professor, first of Mathematics (1578–87) and then of Law (1587) at St Salvator's College, St Andrews. In 1590 he published a small work on *The Sea Law of Scotland* and in 1597 was removed from office for engaging in religious controversy, King **James VI** ordering his replacement. In 1613 he published *An Abridgement of all Sea Lawes*, an important exposition, and in 1615 *De Dominio Maris* , supporting the English claim to supremacy in the Channel. This provoked a reply from the Dutch jurist Graswinckel. He wrote also a comparative study of Jewish and Roman law which, among other subjects, looked at ways of suppressing popular revolts.

WET WET WET See PELLOW, Marti

WHEATLEY, John
(1869–1930)

Labour politician. Born in Bonmahon, County Waterford, he moved to Scotland in his infancy. Educated at St Bridget's School, Baillieston, Lanarkshire, he began work at the age of 12 in coalmining, but subsequently ran a prosperous publishing and printing business. As a member of the Independent

Labour Party (ILP) from 1906 he clashed with the local Roman Catholic hierarchy for advocating Socialism. Instrumental in building up ILP support in Clydeside (1910–22), he was on Glasgow council in 1910 and was Labour MP for Shettleston (1922–30). A leading member of the 'Red Clydesiders' in Parliament, he was Housing Minister in 1924, scoring one of the few successes in the first Labour government by introducing generous state subsidies for municipal housebuilding. He declined to serve in the second Labour administration.

WHEATLEY, John, Lord of Shettleston

(1908–89)

Judge. Called to the Bar in 1932 he became an Advocate Depute in 1945, QC, Solicitor General and MP in 1947, and Lord Advocate 1947–51. Raised to the Bench in 1954 he was promoted Lord Justice Clerk in 1972, an office he held until 1985. He was a member, or chairman, of many inquiries, in particular Chairman of the Royal Commission on Local Government in Scotland 1966–9, which recommended the two-tier system of local authorities adopted in 1973. He was made a life peer in 1970. His autobiography, *One Man's Judgment*, was published in 1987.

WHITE, John

(1867–1951)

One of the most revered and influential Scottish churchman of the 20th century, the spirit behind Church reunion in 1929 and a major architect of the Church that was united. Born in Sandyford, Glasgow, and graduating from Glasgow University in 1891, he was ordained to Shettleston, Glasgow, in 1893, bringing such energy, skill and vision to the position that Cartyne and Tollcross Churches were built in his time, as was a new church at Shettleston. He moved to South Leith in 1911, and then to the Barony Church, Glasgow. During his ministry he held most of the key convenerships in the committees of the church — the Conference for Union with the United Free Church, Church and Nation, etc — and was first president of the Scottish Churches Council, and Convener of the Home Board, as well as holding chaplaincies to George V, Edward VII and George VI. Moderator of the Church of Scotland in 1925, he was appropriately also Moderator of the United Church in 1929. A prodigious worker for the Church, he made an enormous contribution to its life and work. Honours such as the Freedom of Edinburgh (1929) and Companion of Honour (1936) indicate the esteem in which he was held.

WHITE, Kenneth

(1936–)

Scottish-born poet, essayist and travel writer, born in Glasgow. He studied at Glasgow University, graduating with a double first in French and German. It could be said that he has made a career as an exile, first by spending many years travelling in Europe, America and elsewhere, and latterly as an academic in France, where he now holds the chair of 20th-century literature at the Sorbonne. For years his work remained out of print in Britain and he was largely unsung in Scotland. In France, however, he is highly acclaimed, both as a poet and as a thinker, his ruminative verse and Zen-influenced philosophy finding like minds. He has received some of France's most prestigious literary awards, including the Prix Medicis Etranger and the Grand Prix du Rayonnement. Early publications included *The Cold Wind of Dawn* (1966) and *The Most Difficult Area* (1968). Through the publisher Mainstream he has found a new generation of Scots more receptive to him, and recent publications, largely reprinting material unavailable in English, include *The Bird Path: Collected Longer Poems* (1989), *Travels in a Drifting Dawn* (1989), *Handbook for the Diamond Country: Collected Shorter Poems* 1960–1990 (1990) and *The Blue Road* (1990).

WHITELAW, Viscount William Stephen Ian

(1918–)

Politician, farmer and land-owner. Brought up in Nairn, he was educated at Winchester and Cambridge, and served in the Scots Guards during and after the war. From 1946 to 1955 he lived at the family estate in Gartmore, Perthshire, standing unsuccessfully as Conservative candidate for Dunbartonshire East in 1950 and 1951. He first became a Conservative MP (Penrith and the Border division of Cumberland) in 1955, retaining this seat until 1983. A former Secretary of State for Northern Ireland (1972–3) and for Employment (1973–4), he was Home Secretary for four years before being made a viscount in 1983. He was made a Companion of Honour in 1974. During the Conservative leadership contest of 1975 his loyalty to Edward Heath, which persuaded him not to stand directly against him in the first ballot, is thought to have allowed Margaret Thatcher to win in the second ballot. As her deputy, however, he displayed the same loyalty and was one of her firmest, although sometimes privately critical, allies.

WHITLEY, Harry
(1906–76)

Controversial Church of Scotland minister, born in Edinburgh. Graduating MA from Edinburgh (1930), BD from Glasgow (1935) and PhD from Edinburgh (1954), he held ministries in Port Glasgow, saw war service, and worked as a chaplain in the Forces (1943–5) in Western Europe. After a brief spell at Partick Old, Glasgow, he was appointed to St Giles' Cathedral in Edinburgh (1954). Never afraid to embrace controversy, he pursued a lively, very public and individualistic ministry, seeing St Giles' as a platform from which to extend Church frontiers in thinking and practice, challenge establishment assumptions, and take risks — ecumenical, ecclesiastical and political. Outspoken, courageous and abrasive, he made sure that the people of Edinburgh knew he was around; and while, because of his tendency to shoot from the hip, he did not always win friends among the traditionalists and the quietists, St Giles', Edinburgh, and the Church of Scotland were never dull, never safe and never asleep. Much loved as well as criticized, he tells it all in his autobiography, *Laughter in Heaven* (1962).

WHITTAKER, Sir Edmund Taylor
(1873–1956)

English mathematician, born in Birkdale, Lancashire, and educated at Manchester Grammar School and Trinity College, Cambridge, where he became a Fellow in 1896. Elected FRS in 1905, he became Professor of Astronomy in Dublin in 1907, and in 1912 Professor of Mathematics at Edinburgh, where he remained for the rest of his life, becoming the dominant figure in Scottish mathematics. He was knighted in 1945 and retired in 1946. In 1914 he established the first mathematical laboratory for numerical computation. His research ranged very widely, and included numerical analysis, automorphic functions, special functions, dynamics,

electromagnetic theory, quantum theory, and relativity. His textbooks *A course of modern analysis* (1902 and later editions with G N Watson), *Treatise on analytical dynamics* (1904), and *Calculus of observations* (1924 with G Robinson) were influential and remained standard works for many years. In 1910 he published *A history of the theories of aether and electricity*, greatly enlarged in 1951–3, the definitive account of the history of electromagnetism. A Roman Catholic from 1930, he was keenly interested in the philosophy of science and its relation with religion.

WHITTERIDGE, David
(1912 –)

English neurophysiologist, born in Croydon and educated at Whitgift School and Magdalen College, Oxford. He completed his clinical studies at King's College Hospital Medical School, London, obtaining a First in Physiology in 1934 and BM Bch in 1937. He became Demonstrator in Physiology in 1938, Best Memorial Fellow in 1940 and Fellow of Magdalen College in 1945. In 1950 he was appointed to the Chair of Physiology at Edinburgh where he remained until 1968. In 1968 he returned to Oxford as Professor of Physiology with a Fellowship of Magdalen College. He retired in 1979. He was elected FRS in 1953, FRCP London in 1966. During World War II he worked on blast injuries of the lungs and on phosgene poisoning. With Dr Ludwig Guttman he elucidated the failure of control systems for blood pressure and temperature in paraplegics. He also did stereotactic work on the brain pathways and studied the proprioceptive nerves of the extraocular muscles and the mapping of the visual cortex. He made many major contributions to neurophysiology. In Edinburgh he introduced the honours course in physiology which has since produced a steady stream of university teachers.

WHYTE, Ian
(1901–60)

Composer and conductor, born in Dunfermline. He studied composition with Stanford and Vaughan Williams at the Royal College of Music. He was Director of Music, BBC Scotland, 1931–45, and was founder and conductor of the BBC Scottish Orchestra, 1935–60. He composed prolifically and his works, many of which incorporate Scottish elements, include an opera, two operettas, ballets, symphonies, symphonic poems, concertos for piano, violin and viola, much chamber music, choral works, songs, vocal arrangements, piano music and incidental music.

WHYTE-MELVILLE, George John
(1821–78)

Novelist and authority on field sports, born in Mount-Melville, St Andrews. Educated at Eton, he became a captain in the Coldstream Guards and served in the Crimean War, commanding a regiment of Turkish cavalry irregulars. For the rest of his life he devoted himself to field-sports, and wrote numerous novels involving fox-hunting and steeple-chasing, including *Digby Dand* (1853) and *Tilbury Nego* (1861). He also wrote serious historical novels, including *The Gladiators* (1863) and *The Queen's Maries* (1862), on **Mary, Queen of Scots**.

WILKIE, Sir David
(1785–1841)

Painter, born in Cults Manse in Fife. In 1799 he was sent to study at the Trustees' Academy in Edinburgh, and returning home in 1804, painted his famous *Pitlessie Fair*. The great success of *The Village Politicians* (1806) caused him to settle in London. In 1817 he visited Sir **Walter Scott** at Abbotsford, and painted the family group now in the Scottish National Gallery. His fame mainly rests on his genre pictures in the Dutch style, such as the *Card Players* (1808), *Village Festival* (1810), *The Penny Wedding* (1818) and *Reading the Will* (1820). Later he changed his style, sought to emulate the depth and richness of colouring of the old masters, and chose more elevated historical subjects, for example *John Knox preaching before the Lords of Congregation*. He also painted portraits, and was successful as an etcher. In 1823 he was appointed King's Limner in Scotland, and in 1830 Painter-in-Ordinary to King William IV. In 1840, for his health, he visited Syria, Palestine and Egypt, but died on his voyage home.

WILKIE, Sir David
(1882–1938)

Surgeon, born in Kirriemuir, Angus. He was educated at Edinburgh Academy and Edinburgh University, graduating MB in 1904 and MD in 1908. He was elected FRCS (Edinburgh) in 1907, and served under F M Caird, a pioneer of abdominal surgery, the field in which Wilkie made his greatest con-tribution to medical research. He worked in a number of hospitals in Edinburgh, and served as a surgeon in World War I. He was appointed to the Chair of Systematic Surgery at Edinburgh University in 1924, where he was an influential teacher, and took a par-ticular interest in the research department. He served on many public and educational committees, and provided funds to set up Kirk O' Field College in response to male unemployment in the 1930s. On his death he bequeathed funds for the permanent endow-ment of the research department of the university, which was named the Wilkie Laboratory in his honour.

WILLIAM I
(1143–1214)

King of Scotland from 1165, the grandson of **David I**, and brother of **Malcolm IV**, whom he succeeded in 1165. His epithet, 'the Lion', was not used by contemporaries. His reign demonstrated both the continuing consoli-dation of Scotland as a feudal kingdom and increasing efforts to defend its integrity against the threats of Angevin kings of England. The homage paid by him to Henry II 'for Scotland and his other lands' after his capture at Alnwick in 1174, was more explicit than that paid by previous Scottish kings. This treaty (The Treaty of Falaise) was revoked by Richard I in 1189 with the Quitclaim of Canterbury in return for pay-ment of 10 000 marks. He enjoyed a repu-tation for personal piety and after his death was buried in the abbey church at Arbroath, which he had founded in 1178.

WILLIAMS, David
(1952 –)

Photographer, born in Edinburgh. He gradu-ated from Stirling University in 1973. With a background in music and composition, he first came to the fore as a photographer in the 1980s. His work as Artist in Residence at St Margaret's Girls' School, Edinburgh, exhibi-ted and published as *Pictures from No Man's Land* (1985), established him as a photogra-pher of wit, able to elicit a natural and telling response from self-conscious adolescence. In 1990 he was appointed Head of Photography at Edinburgh College of Art. His subsequent work is more clearly introspective and philos-ophical. The series, '*Is*': *Ecstasies*, exhibited by the Photographers' Gallery in 1989, is an internally-balanced set of 22 abstractions, visually rich and concentrated, and requiring a contemplative approach.

WILLIAMS, Gordon

(1934 –)

Novelist, born in Paisley, where he was educated at the Neilson Institution. He worked as a farm labourer and newspaper reporter, and served his National Service in the Royal Air Force. He based himself in Soho, for many years concentrating on his career as a novelist. His hallmark is gritty realism in which his own experience is palpable. *From Scenes Like These* (1968), the story of 15-year-old Duncan Logan, who leaves his tenement upbringing to work on a farm, is powerfully and memorably expressed and is perhaps his best-known work. It was short-listed for the Booker Prize. Filmed under the title *Straw Dogs, The Siege of Trencher's Farm* (1969) it gained him a certain notoriety. *The Upper Pleasure Garden* (1970) draws on his years in journalism, while *Walk Don't Walk* is a cautionary tale in which a poor unknown writer makes a book promotional tour of the USA. In 1972 he entered a highly successful literary partnership with the former football player Terry Venables, with whom he created the detective Hazel, the basis of a popular television series.

WILLIAMSON, Peter

(1730–99)

Adventurer and entrepreneur, born in Hirnlay, Aberdeenshire, and known as 'Indian Peter'. Kidnapped at the age of 13, he was shipped to America and indentured as a slave for seven years. In 1754 he was taken prisoner by Cherokee Indians and lived with them until he was able to make his escape. Enlisting in the army, he rose to the rank of Lieutenant. After being captured by the French he was shipped to Plymouth (1756) as an exchange prisoner, and some time afterwards published an account of his adventures entitled *French and Indian Cruelty* (1757). On his return to Aberdeen in 1758, copies of his book, which accused the Aberdeen Magistrates of being involved in the kidnapping business, were seized and burned, and Williamson was banished from the City as a vagrant. He moved to Edinburgh and established a Coffee Room in Parliament House, which became a favourite haunt of lawyers. He raised a successful action against the Aberdeen Magistrates and was awarded damages in 1763. Around 1770 he instituted a Penny Post in Edinburgh, which was taken over by the General Post Office in 1793. In 1773, he published Edinburgh's first street directory.

His Coffee Room and Penny Post are mentioned in poems by **Robert Fergusson**.

WILLIAMSON, Robin

(1943 –)

Songwriter, composer, instrumentalist, singer, storyteller and poet, born in Edinburgh. In 1965 he became a founder member of the Incredible String Band, whose highly unusual blending of various musical sources — Celtic, Asian, Arabic and rock — produced some of the most distinctive and colourful sounds of the 'flower power' era in the 1960s. His early musical interests as a teenager in Edinburgh were Scots and Irish traditional singers, fiddlers and pipers. Important later influences were North African and Arabic music. Out of his partnership in the Incredible String Band with Mike Heron, whose background was in rock music, came the musical fusion which made the band a major concert and recording attraction for almost 10 years. When it broke up in 1974 Williamson settled in the USA, where he formed the Merry Band. Later he became a solo performer and was also involved in several theatrical productions. His main instruments are harp, guitar and fiddle, but he plays many others and has produced his own recordings of traditional storytelling.

WILLIAMSON, Roy

(1937–90)

Folk singer and musician, born in Edinburgh. A partner in the Corries with **Ronnie Browne** from 1961, he was a talented singer and multi-instrumentalist. As well as playing guitar, concertina, Northumbrian pipes, mandolin and whistle, he also devised and built an entirely new instrument, the Combolin, which incorporated characteristics of bandurria, guitar and sitar. He also composed a number of songs, the best-known being 'Flower of Scotland', written in the 1960s, which has been widely adopted as an unofficial Scottish national anthem.

WILLIS, Dave, originally **David Williams**

(1894–1973)

Comedian, born in Glasgow. He made his stage début as half of a comedy double-act, Willis and Richards, at the Elm Row Cinema, Edinburgh, in 1920. His first London appearance was at the Pavilion (1932), and in 1936 he starred in the Scottish Royal Variety Performance at the Empire, Edinburgh. In 1938 he starred in two films for Charles Pathé, *Save a Little Sunshine* and *Me and My Pal*, both incorporating segments of his most popular variety acts. His strong Scottish accent prevailed against a film career, although he did make one further film, the burlesque on 'Dick Barton', *Slick Tartan* (1949). His longest run was as principal comedian in the summer shows, 'Half-past Eight'.

WILLIS, Roy Geoffrey

(1927 –)

English-born social anthropologist, born in London. After an early career as a journalist in East Africa he studied social anthropology at Oxford under Evans-Pritchard. Since 1967 his academic career has been almost entirely based at Edinburgh University, where he has been lecturer, reader and research fellow in social anthropology. He has also held visiting appointments in Canada, Sweden and the USA. He has carried out extensive research on the Ufipa of Tanzania, but he has also pioneered new approaches to the anthropology of healing and anthropological attitudes to the environment in Scotland. His best-known publications are *Man and Beast* (1974) and *A State in the Making* (1981).

WILSON, Alexander

(1714–86)

Astronomer and letter-founder, born in St Andrews. Graduating from St Andrews University in 1733, from 1737 to 1739 he worked as a surgeon's and apothecary's assistant in London. Returning to St Andrews in 1742 he set up a great letter-foundry which was transferred to Glasgow two years later. He won acclaim for the singular beauty of the Greek types which appeared in the books of the Foulis Press: in their 1756 edition of Homer he was described as 'egregius typorum artifex'. In 1760 he was appointed Glasgow University's first Professor of Astronomy, and became famous in this field through his discovery in 1769 of the 'Wilson effect', an apparent depression in the shape of sunspots near the edge of the Sun.

WILSON, Alexander

(1766–1813)

Scottish-born American ornithologist, born in Paisley, the son of a prosperous weaver,

and regarded as the 'father of American ornithology'. He worked as a weaver from the age of 13, and as a travelling pedlar. He also wrote nature poetry and verses about life in the weaving sheds, and published *Poems* (1790) and *Watty and Meg* (1792). He was prosecuted for a libellous poem against the mill-owners, which he denied writing, but was jailed for 18 months. In 1794 he emigrated to the USA, and became a schoolteacher in rural schools in New Jersey and Philadelphia. Encouraged by a neighbour, the naturalist William Bartram (son of botanist John Bartram), he decided to devote himself to ornithology. He made several journeys across America, collecting species and drawing them, and wrote a poetic account of his first journey, an excursion on foot to Niagara Falls, in *The Foresters, A Poem* (1805). In 1806 he was employed on the American edition of *Rees's Cyclopaedia*, and prevailed on the publisher to undertake an illustrated *American Ornithology* (7 vols, 1808–14); the 8th and 9th volumes were completed after his death. Wilson's Storm-Petrel and Wilson's Phalarope were named in his honour.

WILSON, Charles

(1810–63)

Architect, the son of a builder. He was apprenticed to **David** & John **Hamilton** in 1827, going on to become their chief draughtsman. In 1837 he set up in practice and in 1841 he visited Paris. One of his major early commissions was for the new Glasgow Royal Asylum (now Gartnavel Hospital) of 1842, which demonstrates his grasp of complex planning. He worked in a variety of styles which he used to great effect to produce some memorable buildings. These range from the Scottish Baronial Rutherglen Town Hall (1861–2) to the Italianate Free Church College, Lynedoch Street, Glasgow (1857) and the remarkable classical Queen's Rooms in La Belle Place, Glasgow (1857).

WILSON, Charles Martin

(1935 –)

Journalist. Educated at Eastbank Academy, Glasgow, he began his newspaper career as a 16-year-old copy boy on *The People*. After two years' service in the Royal Marines, he joined the *News Chronicle* as a reporter, progressing via the *Daily Mail* and *London Evening News* to the editorship of the *Glasgow Evening Times*. In 1981 he was the first editor of the short-lived but much-respected *Sunday Standard*. He was editor of *The Times* from 1985 to 1990, and is now Editorial Director of Mirror Group Newspapers. Pugnatious and volatile — he is popularly known as 'Gorbals Wilson' — he has won many admirers through his energy and love of newspapers.

WILSON, Charles Thomson Rees
(1869–1959)

Pioneer of atomic and nuclear physics, born in Glencorse, near Edinburgh. Educated at Manchester and Cambridge, where later he became Professor of Natural Philosophy (1925–34), he was noted for his study of atmospheric electricity, one by-product of which was the successful protection from lightning of Britain's wartime barrage balloons. His greatest achievement was to devise the cloud chamber method of marking the track of alpha-particles and electrons. The movement and interaction of atoms could thus be followed and photographed. In 1927 he shared with Arthur Compton the Nobel Prize for Physics, and in 1937 received the Copley Medal.

WILSON, Sir Daniel
(1816–92)

Archaeologist, born in Edinburgh. Educated at Edinburgh University, he had been Secretary to the Scottish Society of Antiquaries when in 1853 he became Professor of History and English Literature at Toronto. President of the university from 1881, he was knighted in 1888. One of the first writers to popularize the use of the term 'prehistory' for the preliterate past, his numerous works include *Edinburgh in the Olden Time* (1847; new ed 1892), *The Archaeology and Prehistoric Annals of Scotland* (1851; 2nd ed 1863), and *The Lost Atlantis* (1892).

WILSON, David
(1938 –)

Chef and restaurateur, born in Bishopbriggs, Strathclyde. Having developed his interest in eating and cooking while living in Glasgow, in 1970 he decided to leave his job as a marketing manager and take a new direction. He began work at 16 a week in a Huntingdonshire inn, following this with experience in France; French cuisine is the basis of his own individual style. In 1972 he and his wife, Patricia, took over the Peat Inn, then a pub in the tiny village of Peat Inn, Fife. Despite its rural location the restaurant gained national and then international (a Michelin rosette in 1986) recognition for its innovative cooking and remarkable wine list. David Wilson retains his chef's role, and renews his inspiration with annual trips to France.

WILSON, George Washington
(1823–93)

Photographer/publisher, born near Banff, the son of a farmer. He was originally apprenticed as a carpenter and later trained as a painter in Edinburgh and London, thereafter working as a miniaturist. He went to Aberdeen in 1850, where he first worked as a photographer in partnership with John Hay. He opened his own photographic portrait studio in 1855; by the 1880s he was probably the world's largest publisher of photographic views and lantern slides, operating a photographic 'factory', which utilized considerable division of labour in the production process. The firm's catalogue included material bought in from all over the world; views were produced in all the formats fashionable at the time, including lantern slides and postcards, and numerous illustrated topographical books were published between 1856 and 1871. Wilson's artistic training is evident in the composition of many of his picturesque landscapes, although much of his output and that of the firm was unexceptional.

WILSON, (Robert) Gordon
(1938 –)

Nationalist politician, born in Glasgow. Educated at Douglas High School, Lanarkshire, and Edinburgh University, he qualified as a solicitor. National Secretary of the Scottish National Party (1963–71), he initiated sweeping organizational reforms which modernized the party. He also masterminded important policy developments, in particular exploiting the benefits to the SNP of North Sea Oil. These laid the basis for the party's electoral gains in the 1970s. MP for Dundee West (1970–87), he was the party's leading parliamentary spokesman. As National Convenor of the SNP (1979–90) he represented the more traditional wing of the party in the conflict with left-wing elements, but eventually succeeded in reconciling the different factions.

WILSON, James
(1742–98)

Scottish-born American political ideologist and parent of the US Constitution, born in Carskerdo, near Ceres, Fife. He studied successively at St Andrews, Glasgow and Edinburgh (1757–65), subsequently moving to Philadelphia, where he became an active philosophico-legal publicist in the cause of American devolution. Elected to the Continental Congress in 1775 (serving 1775–6, 1782–3, 1785–6), he supported independence, advocated stronger US central government, and supported individual colonies' cession of their western land claims in common cause to result in the creation of new states. As delegate to the Constitutional Congress of 1787 he played such a major part in using Scottish precedents that modern scholars acknowledge his co-paternity of the final document with James Madison. His influence was outstanding in gaining almost immediate ratification of the constitution of Pennsylvania in 1790, the first major state to do so. He was Associate Justice of the US Supreme Court (1789–98), and was the first Professor of Law at Pennsylvania University (from 1790).

WILSON, James
(1805–60)

Economist, born in Hawick, Roxburghshire. A hatmaker until his self-education turned him into a first-rank economist, he was a leading authority on monetary economics and an originator of trade cycle theory. He founded *The Economist* in 1843 and was its editor until 1859. In 1847 he entered the House of Commons as MP for Westbury, Wiltshire, and later represented Devonport; from 1852 to 1859 he held a succession of ministerial appointments, as Secretary to the Board of Control, Financial Secretary to the Treasury, and Vice-President of the Board of Trade. He left Britain to become Financial Member of the Council of India, dying in Calcutta.

WILSON, Jocky (John Thomas)
(1951 –)

Darts player, born in Kirkcaldy. A miner at Fife's Seafield Colliery in his early years, he was unemployed when he won his first big prize — £500 in the Butlin's Grand Masters (1979), a sum which saw him declared ineligible for the dole. By the end of that year he was ranked among the top eight in the world. He became world champion in 1982, beating England's world No.2, John Lowe, in the final. He was the first Scot, and the first man not ranked world No.1, to win the title. Having been written off following a decline in his form, he bounced back with another world championship victory in 1989. A larger-than-life figure, he is one of Scotland's more unlikely sporting heroes.

WILSON, John, pseudonym Christopher North
(1785–1854)

Critic and essayist, born in Paisley. He studied at Glasgow University and Magdalen College, Oxford, where he won the Newdigate Prize for poetry and gained a reputation as an outstanding athlete. In 1807 he bought an estate at Elleray, Westmorland, and became acquainted with the Lake District circle of poets (Wordsworth, Coleridge, De Quincey, Southey). Here he wrote three long poems, *The Isle of Palms* (1812), *The Magic Mirror* (1812, addressed to Sir **Walter Scott**), and *The City of the Plague* (1816). Having lost his estate through an uncle's mismanagement, he settled in Edinburgh as an advocate in 1815. In 1817 he joined **John Gibson Lockhart** and **James Hogg** in launching *Blackwood's Magazine*. Despite lacking any qualification for the post, he was appointed Professor of Moral Philosophy at Edinburgh (1820–51) in succession to **Thomas Brown**. As contributing editor of *Blackwood's* he wrote several notable series under the pseudonym 'Christopher North', such as *Noctes Ambrosianae* (1822–35), and a series of rural short stories, *Lights and Shadows of Scottish Life* (1822). He also published two novels, *The Trials of Margaret Lyndsay* (1823) and *The Foresters* (1825). His *Works* (1855–8) were edited by his son-in-law, **James Frederick Ferrier**.

WILSON, John
(1804–75)

Missionary, born, a farmer's son, near Lauder, Berwickshire. Educated at Edinburgh University, he became a missionary with the Scottish Missionary Society and went to Bombay in 1829. Much consulted by government, especially during the crisis of 1857, he founded the *Oriental Christian Spectator* (1830), was twice president of the Bombay branch of the Asiatic Society, and was Vice-Chancellor of Bombay University. He founded the English School (later Wilson College) in Bombay in 1832. His chief writings were *The Parsi Religion* (1843) and *Lands of the Bible* (1847). His son, Andrew (1830–81), edited the *China Mail* and later the *Bombay Gazette*, but is best known for his account of **Gordon**'s *Ever-Victorious Army* (1868) and his book on the Himalayas, *The Abode of Snow* (1875).

WILSON, Robert
(1803–82)

Mechanical engineer, born in Dunbar, East Lothian, and apprenticed to a joiner at an early age. It is sometimes claimed that he invented the screw propeller for ships, but he was only one of many, and certainly not the first, to propose such a device. He carried out trials with a propeller-driven model boat in the 1820s, but could not interest the Admiralty in the idea at the time. After a few years in Edinburgh he moved to Manchester where, in 1838, he was appointed manager of **James Nasmyth**'s foundry at Patricroft. He made several important improvements to Nasmyth's steam hammer, and took out a total of 24 patents between 1842 and 1880 for locomotive and other steam engines, textile and hydraulic machinery, propellers and other mechanical devices. In 1856 he became a partner in the mechanical engineering firm of Nasmyth, Wilson and Company, where he built a double-acting steam hammer for Woolwich Arsenal, patented in 1861. He was later (1880) granted £500 by the War Department for the use of his contra-rotating screw propellers in torpedoes.

WILSON, Robert
(1909 –)

Tenor, born in Cambuslang, Lanarkshire. He made his stage début at Rothesay (1930), and his London début at the Royal Albert Hall eight years later. He toured with the D'Oyley Carte Opera Company throughout North America and Canada, and then went on the variety stage as a solo act (1939). He starred in several pantomimes in support of **Will Fyffe** (1943), **Harry Gordon** (1944) and Tessie O'Shea (1945), and a series of *Summer Show* at the Theatre Royal, Edinburgh. After *Gaiety Whirl* in Edinburgh (1947), he appeared at the Manhattan Central Auditorium, New York (1949). He was the star of many broadcasts and gramophone records.

WILSON, Scottie
(1888–1972)

Artist, born in Glasgow, who could not read or write. After working as a street vendor in Glasgow, London and Toronto, at the age of 40 he discovered his interest in drawing, and began producing highly imaginary paintings and drawings of, in particular, fishes, birds and trees. His unique naïve/surreal style caught the attention of many collectors, including Picasso. He exhibited widely in both joint and solo exhibitions and was commissioned in 1965 to design coffee, dinner and tea ware for Royal Worcester. His work work can be seen in many collections at home and abroad, including the Tate Gallery, the Scottish National Gallery of Modern Art, the Museum of Modern Art, New York, and the National Gallery of Canada, Ottawa.

WILSON, Simon
(1945 –)

Jewellery designer, born in Glasgow, the founding partner of Butler & Wilson jewellery. He started his career in 1968 by selling antique, art nouveau and art deco jewellery with his partner Nicky Butler, from a stand in the Antiquarius Antique Market in London. In 1979–80 he designed the Regent Street Christmas lights, and in the 1980s he began selling his own design pieces, establishing a new international trend for non-precious fantasy jewellery. This move was supported by a national bill-board advertising campaign featuring celebrities such as Jerry Hall, Catherine Deneuve, Ali McGraw and Faye Dunaway. He has shops within Jaeger's flagship store in London, and in Selfridges and Harrods, in addition to two Butler and Wilson shops in London, and other stores in Los Angeles and Glasgow.

WILSON, Thomas Brendan
(1927 –)

Composer, born in Trinidad, Colorado, and taken to Scotland at an early age. He studied with Ernest Bullock and Frederick Rimmer at Glasgow University, and later taught there, being given a chair in 1977. His works, which have won an international hearing, embrace all forms and almost every medium: opera (for example *The Confessions of a Justified Sinner*, 1976), orchestral (including symphonies and two BBC commissions, *Touchstone*, 1967, and *Introit*, 1982), choral-orchestral, a piano concerto (1985), ballet, a large range of chamber works (including four string quartets), brass-band pieces, piano and other solo instrumental works, and vocal music.

WILSON, William
(1905–72)

Artist and printmaker, born in Edinburgh. He began his training with James Ballantine, an Edinburgh stained-glass maker, prior to studying at Edinburgh College of Art, where he won numerous distinctions for his etching and engraving. He visited France, Germany, Spain and Italy on a travelling scholarship and completed his studies at the Royal College of Art, London. In 1937 he opened his own stained-glass studio and is regarded as one of the leading Scottish artist/printmakers of his period. He was elected RSW (Royal Scottish Society of Painters in Watercolours) in 1946 and RSA in 1949.

WINTERS, Larry
(1943–77)

Convicted murderer, born in Townhead, Glasgow, but brought up in the country. After time in an approved school and borstal, he joined the army. In 1964 he was convicted of the murder of a barman in London and sentenced to life imprisonment. He returned to his native Scotland to serve his sentence. While still in prison he was sentenced to a further 15 years for the attempted murder of two prison officers in 1968, and in 1973 he received a further six years for his part in the Inverness prison riot. He was eventually transferred to the Barlinnie Special Unit, where he settled down and took up poetry and philosophy. He died in the Special Unit from an overdose of Tuinal and his death led to considerable controversy over the liberal regime of the unit. His life story is told in the film *Silent Scream* (1990), his part being played by **Iain Glen**.

WINZET, Ninian
(1518–92)

Churchman, born in Renfrew. He was ordained priest in 1540, and in about 1552 became schoolmaster in the grammar school at Linlithgow, later becoming provost of the collegiate church there. At the Reformation (1561) he was deprived of his office for refusing to turn Protestant, moved to Edin-

burgh, and there wrote *Certane Tractatis for Reformation of Doctryne and Maneris* (1562). Forced to leave Scotland in 1563, he published his *Buik of Four Scoir Thre Questiouns*. He held office at the University of Paris, and in 1574 moved to the English College of Douai. In 1577 he became abbot at the Benedictine monastery at Ratisbon.

WISHART, George
(c.1513–1546)

Reformer and martyr, born in Angus; his eldest brother was a lawyer (king's advocate). In 1538 he was a schoolmaster at the grammar school in Montrose, where he incurred a charge of heresy for teaching the Greek New Testament. In 1539 he was in Bristol, and again had to abjure heresy. The next few years he spent on the Continent, during which time he translated the Swiss *Confession of Faith*. In 1543 he accompanied a commission sent to Scotland by Henry VIII to negotiate a marriage contract between his infant son, Prince Edward (the future Edward VI) and **Mary, Queen of Scots**; and he preached the Lutheran doctrine of justification by faith at Dundee and Montrose, in Ayrshire and East Lothian. At Cardinal **David Beaton**'s insistence he was arrested in 1546, and burned at St Andrews. **John Knox** was first inspired by Wishart.

WISZNIEWSKI, Adrian
(1958–)

Painter, born in Glasgow. He studied at the Mackintosh School of Architecture, Glasgow (1975–9), and then at Glasgow School of Art (1979–83). From 1986 to 1987 he was artist-in-residence at the Walker Art Gallery, Liverpool. He emerged as part of a revival of figurative painting in Glasgow in the 1980s and, in a similar manner to **Steven Campbell**, he developed a technique based on improvised drawing. The theme for which he is best known is the modern pastoral landscape, populated by introspective and langorous youths.

WITHERS, Moira and Bill
(both 1947–)

Fashion designers and manufacturers, born in Glasgow. Moira studied Printed Textiles and Bill studied Interior Design, both at Glasgow School of Art. In 1979 they established Pod & Jois, producing ladies' couture, cocktail and special occasion wear. Renowned for their luxury fabrics and extravagant use of embroidery and beading, they have a variety of outlets in Britain, including Harrods, Selfridges, Dickens and Jones in London, and Jenners in Edinburgh. Based in Glasgow, they show two collections each season, and have a showroom in Regent Street, London.

WITHERSPOON, John
(1723–94)

Scottish-born American clergyman and theologian, born in Gifford, East Lothian. He was minister at Beith, Ayrshire, and then Paisley, and in 1768 emigrated to America to become President of the College of New Jersey (now Princeton University) from 1768 to 1794. He taught many future leaders in American public life, including James Madison, whose co-authorship of *The Federalist* papers bore the influence of his teacher's calvinist social and political thought. He was a representative of New Jersey to the Continental Congress (1776–82), and helped to frame the American Declaration of Independence (1776). His writings include *Ecclesiastic Characteristics* (1753), against the Moderates; *Serious Enquiry into the Nature and Effects of the Stage* (1757); and two on *Justification* (1756) and *Regeneration* (1764).

WODROW, Robert
(1679–1734)

Ecclesiastical historian and hagiographer, born in Glasgow. He studied theology under his father, who was Professor of Divinity there. University Librarian at Glasgow from 1697 to 1701, in 1703 he became minister of Eastwood, holding this position until his death and refusing several more prestigious callings. In 1721–2 he published *History of the Sufferings of the Church of Scotland 1660–88*. Detailed, deeply researched and occasionally questionable in its evidence (as well as being highly partisan), it was dedicated to George I and was approved by the General Assembly. Posthumous works include *Lives of the Scottish Reformers* (1834–45), and *Analecta, or a History of Remarkable Providences, notably relating to Scotch Ministers and Christians* (1842–3). As a historian Wodrow is both emotive and informative.

WOLFE, Willie (William Cuthbertson)
(1924–)

Nationalist politician, born in West Lothian and educated at Bathgate Academy. After military service (1942–7) he qualified as a Chartered Accountant. He joined the Scottish National Party in 1958 and helped to make it an efficient and effective organization in the 1960s. He developed the party's interest in social and economic policies and fully exploited the political potential of North Sea Oil. An unsuccessful contestant for West Lothian in several elections, he was Chairman of the SNP (1968–79), leading the party through its most successful period. As President of the SNP (1980–2), he strove to reconcile the party's internal factions.

WOLFSON, Sir Isaac
(1897–1991)

Businessman and philanthropist, born in Glasgow. Educated at Queen's Park School in Glasgow, he left school early and became a travelling salesman. He joined Great Universal Stores in 1932, became managing director in 1934, and later honorary life president. In 1955 he set up the Wolfson Foundation, for the advancement of health, education and youth activities in the UK and the Commonwealth. He also founded Wolfson College, Oxford, in 1966. In 1973 University College, Cambridge, was renamed Wolfson College after a grant from the foundation. He was active in Jewish causes. His son, Leonard (1927–), is now a life peer.

WOMERSELY, (Charles) Peter
(1923–)

Architect, born in Newark, Aberdeenshire, and trained at the Architectural Association, London (1947–52). He worked in Scotland in independent practice from 1953 to 1978, and in 1962 he opened a further office in Hong Kong. He approaches each design as a creative challenge, and never delegates control of a project. He began designing in timber, moving to reinforced concrete, and demonstrated expressive mastery of both media. Among his commissions in the Scottish Borders, the Bernat Klein Studio near Galashiels (1972) encapsulates his design philosophy, and the consulting rooms, Kelso (1967), display the heights of his originality. The winner of various professional awards, his work has received international acclaim.

WOOD, Sir Andrew
(c.1455–1539)

Naval commander, a native of Largo, Fife. Associated with **James IV** in his efforts to build up a Scottish navy, he was particularly successful against English vessels raiding in the Firth of Forth.

WOOD, Sir Henry Peart
(1908 –)

English-born educationist and administrator, born in West Stanley, County Durham, and a graduate of Durham University. After experience of school and university teaching he joined the staff of Jordanhill College of Education, Glasgow, and from 1949 to 1971 was its principal. The College, the largest and most comprehensive teacher-training institution in Britain, caters for every category of Scottish teacher and had at that time around 3000 students. Under Wood's management it successfully negotiated the crises of the 1950s and 60s — teacher shortages, constitutional change, 'Robins' expansion, relations with universities and with the teaching profession. He has received doctorates from Glasgow and Strathclyde universities and is the author of a book on **David Stow**.

WOOD, Stanley Purdie
(1939 –)

Fossil collector and dealer, born in Edinburgh. After early education in Edinburgh, he spent some years in the Merchant Navy and with the Prudential insurance company. Attracted to fossil collecting, particularly vertebrates, by finding fossil fish on the Wardie shore in Edinburgh, he was encouraged by A L Panchen of Newcastle and went on to discover a complete fossil shark in the Carboniferous strata in a housing estate in Bearsden, Glasgow. More recently, by his work at East Kirkton on the edge of Bathgate, he has discovered the earliest known amphibian and, spectacularly, the earliest known reptile, now popularly known as Lizzie. He trades as Mr Wood's Fossils in the Grassmarket of Edinburgh, and is now a graduate of the Open University.

WOOD, Willie
(1938 –)

Bowler, born in Gifford, East Lothian. The outstanding figure in recent decades in Scottish bowls, he made his début for his country in 1966, and won the first of many Commonwealth Games medals — a bronze — in 1974. Partnered by Alex McIntosh, he won a silver in the pairs in 1978, then went one better in 1982, winning individual gold. He was a member of the Scotland team which won the world championship in 1984, as well as being runner-up in the singles. A dispute over professionalism saw him barred from competing in the Edinburgh Commonwealth Games of 1986, but four years later, having been reinstated, he again won a gold medal — this time in the fours — at the Auckland Games. A cheery, modest man, he still lives in his home village, where he works as a car mechanic.

WOODRUFF, Sir Michael Francis Addison
(1911 –)

Australian pioneer in transplant surgery, born in Melbourne and educated at Melbourne University where he graduated in medicine in 1937. He served in the Australian Army Medical Corps from 1940 to 1946. After completing the FRCS in 1946 he became tutor in surgery at Sheffield (1946–8), then senior lecturer in surgery at Aberdeen until 1952. He was then appointed Professor of Surgery at the University of Otago, New Zealand, and took the Chair of Surgery in Edinburgh from 1957 to 1976. He was a fellow of many foreign surgical academies. He published (jointly) the official report on *Deficiency Diseases in Japanese Prison Camps* (1951), but his main contributions to surgery have been work on renal transplantation and organ grafting. He published several books: *Transplantation of Tissues and Organs* (1960), *The Interaction of Cancer and Host* (1980) and *Cellular Variation and Adaptation in Cancer* (1990). He carried out the first renal transplant in Scotland.

WRIGHT, Frances, or Fanny, also known as Frances Darusmont
(1795–1852)

Scottish-born American reformer and abolitionist, born in Dundee, the heiress to a large fortune. She emigrated to the USA in 1818 and toured widely, publishing *Views of Society and Manners in America* in 1821. In the company of the reformer Marie Joseph Lafayette, she founded a short-lived community for freed slaves at Nashoba in western Tenessee. Settling in New York in 1829, she published with **Robert Dale Owen** a Socialist journal, *Free Enquirer*. One of the early suffragettes, whose courage and perseverance were a significant influence in the development of the women's movement, she campaigned vigorously against religion and for the emancipation of women. In 1838 she contracted an unhappy marriage with a Frenchman, William Philquepal d'Arusmont. They had one daughter and some time later divorced. After her marriage, the issues she championed grew increasingly controversial, such as birth control and the equal division of wealth.

WRIGHT, Ronald Selby
(1908 –)

Church of Scotland minister and broadcaster, born in Glasgow. As the familiar voice of the Radio Padre during the crucial war years, he became a well-known and appreciated figure within the life of Scotland. After study at Edinburgh University (1927–36) he was ordained and inducted to Canongate Kirk (1937). Following a period as an army chaplain, during which service he was mentioned in Despatches, he went on to become the reassuring voice of the BBC's Radio Padre, dealing with the troubling concerns of wartime with a measured good sense, realism and compassion. His mission and his gift was communication, and on his return to the Parish he pursued this in writing and preaching. His books, which deal with the lay person's pressing theological questions, remain helpful guides for searching minds. *Asking Them Questions* (1936), and *Let's Ask the Padre* (1942) might not be theological masterpieces, but as tools for dealing with people's religious perplexities, they serve well.

WYLIE, George
(1921 –)

Sculptor, born in Glasgow. After attending Bellahouston Academy and Allan Glen's School, Glasgow, he worked as an engineer until 1948 and then as a customs and excise officer until 1976, when he became a full-time artist. He has employed a wide variety of materials and techniques — from welded metal to mixed media — and, as a self-styled 'scul?tor', his reputation as an artist with a common touch has been built on work such as the full-scale 'Straw Locomotive' (1987). Suspended from the Finnieston crane on the Clyde, and eventually set alight, this made a dramatically visual comment on the decline of Glasgow's heavy industry. In 1990 he was awarded an honorary doctorate by Strathclyde University.

WYNTOUN, Andrew of
(?1350 – ?1420)

Chronicler. He was a canon regular of St Andrews, and in about 1395 became prior of the monastery of St **Serf** on Loch Leven. He wrote *The Orygynale Cronykil of Scotland*, written in rhyming couplets. Especially valuable as a specimen of old Scots, the work covers the period from the world's creation up until 1406; of its nine books, the first five give a valuable, though fragmentary, outline of the history and geography of the ancient and medieval Scottish world.

WYSE, Henry Taylor
(1870–1951)

Artist, potter, designer and author, born in Glasgow. He studied at both Dundee and Glasgow Schools of Art, and in Paris at the Académies Julian and Colarossi. Art Master at Arbroath, he later became a lecturer at Moray House Training College, Edinburgh. He established the Holyrood Pottery c.1918, producing a range of wares with coloured leadless glazes. He exhibited regularly at the Royal Scottish Academy and the Royal Glasgow Institute. He published many books, including *Modern Methods of Art Instruction* (1909) and *Memory and Imaginative Drawing* (1923). The Holyrood Pottery closed in 1927.

Y

YARROW, Alfred Fernandez
(1842–1932)

English-born shipbuilder, born in London. Educated in London, Reigate and at London University he was then apprenticed to a London firm of marine engine builders. Entering a partnership in 1864 he set up a small shipyard on the Isle of Dogs, building launches. Torpedo boats, however, secured his reputation since his were faster and technically superior to those of all his competitors, and he formed a close relationship with the Royal Navy. In 1906, for reasons of cost, space and supply of skilled workmen, he decided to move the firm to Scotstoun in Glasgow. By 1908, with a fully equipped shipyard, he was building destroyers, river vessels and naval boilers. Though he retired in 1913 he worked with Lord Fisher at the Admiralty during the war, supervising the building of destroyers. He was created a baronet in 1916 in recognition of his contribution to the war effort. His standing as a forward-looking warship builder and designer was in later life combined with a reputation as a generous philanthropist.

YATES, Edmund
(1831–94)

Journalist and novelist, born in Edinburgh, the son of the actor-manager Frederick Henry Yates (1797–1842). From 1854 he published over a score of novels and other works; was editor of *Temple Bar*, *Tinsley's* and other periodicals; and in 1874 founded, with Grenville Murray, a successful 'society' weekly, *The World*, which, for a libel on the 5th Earl of **Lonsdale**, involved him in 1884 in two months' imprisonment.

YONGE, Sir Maurice
(1899–1986)

Zoologist and marine biologist, educated at Edinburgh University, gaining his PhD there in 1924. In 1927 he became Balfour Student at Cambridge, where he organized and later led the expedition to the Great Barrier Reef in 1928–9, which largely determined how this great natural wonder was built up and maintained. Apart from the volumes of scientific reports on the expedition, he published a popular book, *A Year on the Great Barrier Reef* (1930). After appointments as physiologist at the Plymouth Marine Biological Laboratory and Professor of Botany at Bristol, he became Regius Professor of Zoology at Glasgow University in 1944. From Glasgow he had considerable influence on the teaching of zoology and marine biology in the whole of the UK, being elected FRS in 1946 and becoming a CBE in 1957, with a knighthood in 1967. His published work included *The Sea Shore* (1949) in Collins' New Naturalist series and their *Pocket Guide to the Sea Shore* (1958, with J Barrett), as well as over 140 scientific papers. One of the most distinguished marine biologists of his time, he continued active research and writing after retiring from Glasgow in 1964 as an Honorary Research Fellow in his old Edinburgh department.

YORK, Cardinal See STEWART, Henry Benedict

YOUNG, Andrew John
(1885–1971)

Poet and clergyman, born in Elgin, Moray. Educated at the Royal High School, Edinburgh, and at New College, Edinburgh, he became a United Free Church minister in Temple, Midlothian, in 1912. During World War I he was attached to the YMCA in France. After the war he left Scotland and took charge of the English Presbyterian Church at Hove in Sussex (1941–59). Later he joined the Anglican Church and became vicar of Stoneygate, Sussex (1941–59). His early verse — *Songs of Night* (1910), which was paid for by his father, *Boaz and Ruth* (1920) and *Thirty-One Poems* (1922) — revealed an almost mystical belief in the sanctity of nature and the part it plays in Christian belief, later confirmed by *Winter Harvest* (1933), and his *Collected Poems* (1936). He also wrote an account of the poetry, folklore and natural history of the British Isles in *The Poets and the Landscape* (4 vols, 1962).

YOUNG, Colin
(1927 –)

Film academic, born in Glasgow. A languages student at Glasgow University, he completed his National Service with the Intelligence Corps before taking a degree in philosophy and moral philosophy at St Andrews University, where he was one of the founders of the *Saltire* magazine. A brief spell as a film critic with the *Bon Accord and Northern Pictorial* in Aberdeen instilled in him a deep and abiding love of the cinema and he subsequently moved to America, working briefly as a filmmaker and teaching at the University of California at Los Angeles, where he became the professor in charge of the Theatre Arts Department in 1965. Among the many students who benefited from his influence were such major filmmakers as Francis Coppola and Paul Schrader. He returned to Britain to become the Director of the National Film and Television School in 1971, building its reputation as one of the finest establishments in the world for encouraging individuality and talent. A genial enthusiast, communicator and wily politician, he became Vice-Chairman of the Edinburgh Film Festival in 1972 and served as Chairman until 1991. In 1984 he received a BAFTA Award for services to the British film industry.

YOUNG, Douglas
(1913–73)

Poet, scholar and dramatist, born in Tayport, Fife. He spent his early childhood in India, and was educated at Merchiston Castle School, Edinburgh, and St Andrews University, where he read classics, and New College, Oxford. He was a lecturer in Greek at Aberdeen until 1941. Joining the Scottish National Party, he was jailed for refusing war service except in an independent Scotland's army; his attitude split the Scottish National Party, of which he was controversially elected chairman in 1942. Following the war, he became a Labour parliamentary candidate. After teaching at University College, Dundee, and St Andrews University, he was appointed Professor of Classics at McMaster University

in Canada, and Professor of Greek at the University of North Carolina in 1970. His three collections of verse were *Auntran Blads* (1943), *A Braird o' Thristles* (1947), and *Selected Poems* (1950). He is best known for *The Puddocks* (1957) and *The Burdies* (1959), translations into Lallans of Aristophanes' plays.

YOUNG, George
(1922 –)

Footballer and manager, born in Grangemouth, Stirlingshire. He played 678 games for Rangers, his only professional club, between 1941 and 1957, a period in which six league titles and four Scottish Cups were won. A formidably solid centre-half, he was an inspirational figure to younger players, and for much of his career was captain of both his club and Scotland, for whom he won a then record 53 caps, between 1946 and 1957. After retirement he concentrated for a while on various business interests, before being tempted back into the sport to manage the now-defunct Third Lanark for three years.

YOUNG, James
(1811–83)

Industrial chemist, born in Glasgow. Apprenticed to his carpenter father, he was educated at evening classes in Anderson's College, Glasgow, alongside **David Livingstone** and **Lyon Playfair**. In 1832 he was chosen by his professor, **Thomas Graham** as lecture assistant in chemistry. In 1837 he went with Graham to University College, London, and on Graham's recommendation was appointed chemist at James Muspratt's alkali works in Lancashire in 1839. There he proved that cast-iron could replace silver in the manufacture of caustic soda. He established the Scottish mineral-oil industry following his experiments on a petroleum spring at Ridding's Colliery, Alfreton in Derbyshire for burning and lubricating oils (1848–51). In 1850 he took out a patent for the distillation of bituminous substances, putting it into Scottish production with coal, shale and minerals, and successfully employing it in the making of naphtha and lubricating oils, and later illuminating oils and paraffin wax. On the expiry of the patent in 1866, he set up a limited company. Constantly experimenting, he advocated caustic lime to prevent corrosion of iron ships by bilge water (1872), and in 1878 began experiments to determine the velocity of white and coloured light by modification of the Fizeau method, in collaboration with Professor **George Forbes** at Pitlochry. Their final results obtained (1880–1) across the Firth of Clyde, produced higher values than Cornu-Michelson. He gave 10 000 guineas to endow a chair of technical chemistry at Anderson's College.

YOUNG, John
(?1750–1820)

Classicist, born in Glasgow, the son of a cooper, and educated at Glasgow University. Professor of Greek at Glasgow University (1774–1820), his pupils included the poet **Thomas Campbell**, novelist **Thomas Hamilton**, critic **John Wilson**, alias 'Christopher North', and the historian **George Robert Gleig**. Variously praised for humour, scholarship, oratory and sympathy, his genius was that of spoken, not written, scholarship. A teacher of immense influence, he was a vital force transmitting the ideas of the Scottish Enlightenment into the romantic age that gradually displaced it.

YOUNG, John
(1811–78)

Canadian economist and statesman, born in Ayr, where he was educated at the parish school. He emigrated to Canada in 1825. Entering Quebec trading office, he later became a partner, and in 1841 moved to Montreal, establishing Stephens, Young and Co, a finance company in which he won his fortune and stayed for life. He had raised a volunteer regiment during the rebellion of 1837. Active with the Free Trade Association of Montreal, he evangelized forthcoming free trade legislation in the *Economist*, exerting some influence on protectionist Canadian opinion (1842–6). Yet, despite his free trade principles he insisted on cheap and quick transport to enable Canada to compete with the USA, and is given credit for ensuring the decision to deepen Lake St Peter's (thus bringing ocean transport to Montreal), and build the railway line to Portland, Maine (giving winter port to Montreal). He was also involved in establishing the Montreal-Kingston railway and the Victoria Bridge of 1860 thereon, and campaigned with delayed but ultimate success for the enlargement of Welland, St Lawrence, and Lachine canals. He was brought into the Cabinet of Canada in the Hincks-Morin ministry, despite having no previous seat in Parliament, and brought steamship subsidies to Montreal-Liverpool shipping, as well as convening the intercolonial railway conference of 1851–2. He resigned in protest against differential tolls for American users of Canadian canals. He was a member of the Canadian parliament 1851–7 and 1872–4, Inspector of the Port at Montreal, and Chairman of the Harbour Commission 1874. Subsequently President of the Board of Trade, he published *Rival Routes from the West to the Ocean* (1859).

YOUNG, Sir Peter
(1544–1628)

Tutor and adviser to **James VI**, born in Dundee, with maternal descent from the Scrymgeours of Dudhope (later Earls of Dundee). Educated at Dundee Grammar School, he later styled himself *magister* implying either a university degree, or a brass neck. Through the influence of his uncle, Henry Scrymgeour, Professor of Civil Law at Geneva, he studied with Theodore Beza, returning to Scotland in 1568. The Regent Robert Stewart, Earl of **Moray**, appointed him joint tutor with **George Buchanan** to the infant **James VI** (1569/70), with Young probably doing most of the work. Zealous to retain James's affection, Young was less critical and thus more congenial than Buchanan and other counsellors. In 1577 he became master almoner, with consequent valuable emoluments. The success of his embassy to Frederick II of Denmark on Orkney won him privy councillorship in 1586. On further reconnaissances to Denmark, he was instrumental in choosing Anne for James's queen, and as an envoy (1594, 1596, 1598) he won Danish support for James's candidacy for the English throne. He accompanied James to England on his accession (1603). James wished to make him Dean of Lichfield, but found that the office was not in his gift. Tutor to Prince Charles in 1604, he was knighted in 1605. In 1616 he was made Master of St Cross Hospital, Winchester, by special licence. Pensioned, he retired to an estate in Forfarshire.

YOUNG, Thomas
(1587–1655)

Puritan theologian, born in Perthshire. He studied at St Andrews, was Milton's tutor until 1622, and afterwards held charges at Hamburg and in Essex. He was the chief author in 1641 of an anti-espiscopal pamphlet, an *Answer* to Bishop Joseph Hall by 'Smectymnuus', this name compounded of the initials of Stephen Marshall, Edmund Calamy, **Thomas Young**, Matthew Newcomen and William Spurstow.

YOUNGER, George Kenneth Hotson
(1931 –)

Conservative politician, born in Winchester into a family with deep roots in Scottish Conservatism. Educated at Oxford University, he became Manager and Director of the family brewing business. In 1963 he withdrew as candidate in the West Perth by-election to make way for the prime minister, Sir Alec Douglas-Home (**Home of the Hirsel**). He has been MP for Ayr Burghs since 1964. Scottish Conservative Whip (1965–7), and Chairman of the Scottish Conservative Party (1974–5), he was junior minister at the Scottish Office (1970–4), then Secretary of State for Scotland (1979–86, the longest holder of the office). In this post he built up the Scottish Development Agency and attracted high-technology industry to Scotland to balance the collapse of traditional manufacturing sectors. He was Defence Secretary from 1986 to 1989.

YOUNGER OF LECKIE, Sir George Younger, 1st Viscount
(1851–1929)

Conservative politician. Born in Alloa and educated at Edinburgh Academy and Edinburgh University, he left college at the age of 17 on his father's death to run the family brewery. Active in local government in Clackmannanshire, he was President of the Scottish Conservative and Unionist Association in 1904. MP for Ayr Burghs (1906–22), he was Chairman of the (British) Conservative Party organization from 1916 to 1923, and helped to run the 'Coupon' general election of 1918, ensuring the return of many Conservatives. In 1922 he was central in breaking up the Lloyd George coalition government and replacing it with the Conservative governments of **Bonar Law** and Baldwin. He was Treasurer of the Conservative Party (1923–9), and was created a peer in 1923. In the

tradition of his uncle, **William McEwan**, he combined a career as a politician with that of a successful brewer.

YOUNGSON, (formerly Brown) Alexander John
(1918 –)

Economist and historian, educated at Aberdeen Grammar School and Aberdeen University. After war service as a pilot in the Fleet Air Arm, he held lectureships at St Andrews (1948–50) and Cambridge (1950–8) universities. From 1958 to 1963 he was the first Professor of Economic History at Edinburgh University before succeeding Sir **Alan Peacock** as Professor of Political Economy (1963–74), as well as being Vice Principal of Edinburgh University (1971–4). He was Director of the Research School of Social Sciences, Australian National University (1974–80) and Professor of Economics, University of Hong Kong (1980–2). Returning to Scotland, he was Chairman of the Royal Fine Art Commission for Scotland (1983–90). He used an historical perspective to analyse economic growth and development in *Possibilities of Economic Progress* (1959), *The British Economy* (1920–57) (1960), *Overhead Capital: A Study in Development Economics* (1967) and *The Scientific Revolution in Victorian Medicine* (1979). His works on Scotland are the celebrated *The Making of Classical Edinburgh* 1750–1840 (1966), *After the Forty-five* (1973) and *The Prince and the Pretender. A Study in the Writing of History* (1985).

YULE, Sir David
(1858–1928)

Industrialist, born in Edinburgh. His great wealth stemmed from the jute, paper and tea industries which were established by his uncle in Calcutta and London. After the death of his uncle in 1902, he became sole director of the companies, and by 1903 employed more than 190 000 people in India alone. He was responsible for significant advances in the forestry and agricultural industries, as well as the establishment of roads, hospitals and schools. He was visited in India by King George V and awarded a knighthood. He received a Baronetcy in 1922, and in 1926 he bought the *Daily Chronicle* from Lloyd George. On his death, his widow was one of the wealthiest women in Britain.